PROFESSIONAL
MICROSOFT® SQL SERVER® 2012 A

PROFESSIONAL

Microsoft® SQL Server® 2012 Administration

PROFESSIONAL

Microsoft® SQL Server® 2012
Administration

Adam Jorgensen
Steven Wort
Ross LoForte
Brian Knight

WILEY

John Wiley & Sons, Inc.

Professional Microsoft® SQL Server® 2012 Administration

Published by
John Wiley & Sons, Inc.
10475 Crosspoint Boulevard
Indianapolis, IN 46256
www.wiley.com

Copyright © 2012 by John Wiley & Sons, Inc., Indianapolis, Indiana

Published simultaneously in Canada

ISBN: 978-1-118-10688-4
ISBN: 978-1-118-28684-5 (ebk)
ISBN: 978-1-118-28218-2 (ebk)
ISBN: 978-1-118-28388-2 (ebk)

Manufactured in the United States of America

10 9 8 7 6 5 4 3 2

For general information on our other products and services please contact our Customer Care Department within the United States at (877) 762-2974, outside the United States at (317) 572-3993 or fax (317) 572-4002.

Wiley publishes in a variety of print and electronic formats and by print-on-demand. Some material included with standard print versions of this book may not be included in e-books or in print-on-demand. If this book refers to media such as a CD or DVD that is not included in the version you purchased, you may download this material at http://booksupport.wiley.com. For more information about Wiley products, visit www.wiley.com.

Library of Congress Control Number: 2012933629

I'd like to dedicate this book to my Lord and Savior Jesus Christ, and my parents who always stressed the importance of the "All-important question." This time the answer is yes!

—ADAM JORGENSEN

To my wonderful team at Pragmatic Works, who inspire me to always take myself to the next level.

—BRIAN KNIGHT

To my parents, for being the pillars of the person that I am now, and to the three greatest loves of my life: my queen Madeline and my two princesses, Sofia and Stephanie, for filling my life with love, tenderness, and joy.

—JOSE CHINCHILLA

To my beautiful wife Jessica. I love you and thank you for all your patience, love, understanding, and support.

—JORGE SEGARRA

To my dad Chris A. R. Swanepoel. I owe everything I am to you. You are my hero.

—GARETH SWANEPOEL

ABOUT THE AUTHORS

 **ADAM JORGENSEN** (http://www.adamjorgensen.com) is the president of Pragmatic Works Consulting, a Director for the Professional Association of SQL Server (PASS), SQL Server MVP, and a well-known speaker, author, and executive mentor. His focus is on helping companies realize their full potential by using their data in ways they may not have previously imagined. Adam is involved in the community as the Director at large for the Professional Association of SQL Server (PASS) and delivers more than 75 community sessions per year. He is based in Jacksonville, FL, and has written and contributed to five previous books on SQL Server, analytics, and SharePoint.

 **STEVEN WORT** has been working with SQL Server since 1993, starting with version 4.2 running on OS2. He has more than 30 years of experience developing applications in the IT industry, working in a wide range of industries. Steven joined Microsoft in 2000 as an escalation engineer on the Systems Integration Engineering (SIE) team, where he co-authored multiple workshops on debugging Windows and .NET. In 2004, he moved to the SQL Server team to work on scalability for SQL Server 2005. After a short spell in the Windows group, spent working on scaling large database systems, he is now back in SQL Server where he is a Lead Engineer on the SQL Server Appliance Engineering Team, responsible for the Microsoft Database Consolidation Appliance. Steven has co-authored several books on SQL Server Administration, troubleshooting, and performance tuning.

 **ROSS LOFORTE** is a technology architect at the Microsoft Technology Center Chicago focused on Microsoft SQL Server solutions. Ross has more than 20 years of business development, project management, and SQL architecture solutions. For the past 11 years, Ross has been working with the Microsoft Technology Centers and has led architecture design and proof-of-concept engagements for Microsoft's largest and most strategic customers to design enterprise, mission-critical SQL Server solutions. Ross is a SQL Server instructor at DePaul University in Chicago, and regularly presents at TechEd, SQL PASS, Gartner, TDWI, and Microsoft internal conferences. Ross is a published author and has been active with the Professional Association for SQL Server, the Chicago SQL Server Users Group, and the SQL Server community for many years.

BRIAN KNIGHT, SQL Server MVP, MCITP, MCSE, MCDBA, is the owner and founder of Pragmatic Works. He is also the co-founder of BIDN.com, SQLServerCentral.com, and SQLShare.com. He runs the local SQL Server users group in Jacksonville (JSSUG). Brian is a contributing columnist at several technical magazines and does regular webcasts at Jumpstart TV. He is the author of a dozen SQL Server books. Brian has spoken at conferences such as PASS, SQL Connections and TechEd, SQL Saturdays, Code Camps, and many pyramid scheme motivational sessions. You can find his blog at http://www.bidn.com. Brian lives in Jacksonville, FL, where he has been baking at 350 degrees for the past 35 years.

ROBERT C. CAIN (http://arcanecode.com) is a Microsoft MVP in SQL Server, MCTS Certified in BI, and works as a Senior Consultant for Pragmatic Works. He is also a technical contributor to Plurasight Training and co-author of Volumes 1 and 2 of *SQL Server MVP Deep Dives* (Manning Publications, 2009). A popular speaker, Robert has presented at events such as TechEd, SQL Rally, and numerous SQL Saturdays. Robert has over 25 years of experience in the IT industry, working in a variety of fields ranging from manufacturing to telecommunications to nuclear power.

DENNY CHERRY is an independent consultant with more than a decade of experience working with platforms such as Microsoft SQL Server, Hyper-V, vSphere, and Enterprise Storage solutions. Denny's areas of technical expertise include system architecture, performance tuning, security, replication, and troubleshooting. Denny currently holds several of the Microsoft certifications related to SQL Server for versions 2000 through 2008 including the Microsoft Certified Master and has also been a Microsoft MVP for several years. Denny has written several books and dozens of technical articles on SQL Server management and on how SQL Server integrates with various other technologies.

JOSE CHINCHILLA (http://sqljoe.com) is a certified Microsoft SQL Server Database Administrator and Business Intelligence Professional with more than 12 years of experience in the Information Technology field. Jose has a proven record of success architecting and developing Data Warehouse and Business Intelligence solutions and incorporating Master Data Management and Data Quality frameworks for the retail, manufacturing, financial, health, not-for-profit, and local government sectors. Jose is president and CEO of Agile Bay, Inc. (http://agilebay.com), a full-service consulting firm based in Tampa, FL, and is a frequent speaker at SQL Saturday and Code Camp events around the country. He also serves as president of the Tampa Bay Business Intelligence user group and PASS Chapter. Jose is an avid networker and blogger active in social media and is known in Twitter under the @SQLJoe handle.

AUDREY HAMMONDS is a database developer, blogger, presenter, and thanks to this publication, writer. Fifteen years ago, she volunteered to join a newly formed database team so that she could stop writing COBOL. (And she never wrote COBOL again.) Audrey is convinced that the world would be a better place if people would stop, relax, enjoy the view, and normalize their data. She's the wife of Jeremy, mom of Chase and Gavin, and adoptive mother to her cats Bela, Elmindreda, and Aviendha. She blogs at http://datachix.com and is based in Atlanta, Georgia.

SCOTT KLEIN has taken his love and passion for SQL Server to Microsoft, recently joining the company as a SQL Azure technical evangelist. Prior to joining Microsoft, Scott was co-founder of Blue Syntax, an Azure consulting and services company. Scott's background is in SQL Server, having spent the last 20+ years working with SQL Server. He started with SQL Server 4.2, but after hearing about the Azure platform, he focused his efforts on SQL Azure and the Azure platform. He has presented at nearly two dozen Azure Boot Camps around the United States and Canada. Not forgetting his South Florida roots, Scott ran the South Florida SQL Saturday events as well as the South Florida SQL Server user group. Scott is the author of several other Wrox books, including *Professional SQL Server 2005 XML* (John Wiley & Sons, 2006), *Professional LINQ* (John Wiley & Sons, 2008), and the recently released *Pro SQL Azure* (Apress, 2010). He has also contributed chapters to a few other books and has written several articles for *MSDN Magazine*. Scott is the husband to a wonderful wife and the father to four wonderful children who won't stop growing up.

JORGE SEGARRA is a DBA-turned BI consultant for Pragmatic Works in Jacksonville, Florida. He's a SQL Server MVP, blogger (blogs at www.sqlchicken.com), PASS volunteer, and Regional Mentor, and is the founder of the online community blog project SQL University (www.sqluniversity.org).

GARETH SWANEPOEL (http://mygareth.com) is a systems administrator turned SQL Server DBA. He has been working in the IT industry doing support and administration for almost 20 years. He enjoys solving the complex problems that his clients encounter when deploying SQL Server in a data warehouse environment. He is originally from South Africa and currently lives in the quiet outskirts of Jacksonville, Florida, with his beautiful wife, 5-year-old-son, and soon-to-be baby daughter.

ABOUT THE TECHNICAL EDITORS

JASON STRATE, FROM DIGINEER INC., is a database consultant with more than 15 years of experience. His experience includes design and implementation of both OLTP and OLAP solutions as well as assessment and implementation of SQL Server environments for best practices, performance, and high availability solutions. He is a recipient of the Microsoft Most Valuable Professional (MVP) award for SQL Server since July 2009. Jason is a SQL Server MCITP and participated in the development of Certification exams for SQL Server 2008 and 2012.

DENNY CHERRY is an independent consultant with more than a decade of experience working with platforms such as Microsoft SQL Server, Hyper-V, vSphere, and Enterprise Storage solutions. Denny's areas of technical expertise include system architecture, performance tuning, security, replication, and troubleshooting. Denny currently holds several of the Microsoft certifications related to SQL Server for versions 2000 through 2008 including the Microsoft Certified Master as well as being a Microsoft MVP for several years. Denny has written several books and dozens of technical articles on SQL Server management and how SQL Server integrates with various other technologies.

CREDITS

EXECUTIVE EDITOR
Robert Elliott

PROJECT EDITOR
Victoria Swider

TECHNICAL EDITORS
Jason Strate
Denny Cherry

PRODUCTION EDITOR
Kathleen Wisor

COPY EDITOR
San Dee Phillips

EDITORIAL MANAGER
Mary Beth Wakefield

FREELANCER EDITORIAL MANAGER
Rosemarie Graham

ASSOCIATE DIRECTOR OF MARKETING
David Mayhew

MARKETING MANAGER
Ashley Zurcher

BUSINESS MANAGER
Amy Knies

PRODUCTION MANAGER
Tim Tate

VICE PRESIDENT AND EXECUTIVE GROUP PUBLISHER
Richard Swadley

VICE PRESIDENT AND EXECUTIVE PUBLISHER
Neil Edde

ASSOCIATE PUBLISHER
Jim Minatel

PROJECT COORDINATOR, COVER
Katie Crocker

PROOFREADER
Jen Larsen, Word One New York

INDEXER
Robert Swanson

COVER DESIGNER
Ryan Sneed

COVER IMAGE
© Christian Delbert

ACKNOWLEDGMENTS

I'D LIKE TO THANK my family and fiancée Cristina for their support while writing this book. I also want to applaud this incredible author and technical editing team! You'll see why this team is so exceptional in the introduction to this book. Special thanks go to Brad Schacht, whose help was critical in completing several of these chapters. My two pups, Ladybird and Mac, who kept my feet warm while writing on my patio in the winter (yes, I know it's FL winter) and a special thanks to Brian Knight and Bob Elliot for getting me started in this crazy writing game in the first place. Thank you to the Wrox team for keeping us on track and helping to make this title a reality. Your support of me and the team made all the difference!

—ADAM JORGENSEN

I'D LIKE TO THANK my wife Anna and my daughter Jennifer for the support and dedication while writing this book. I'd like to thank the Microsoft Technology Center's staff, including the director Adam Hecktman, for their support and for making the Microsoft Technology Center Chicago a great facility to learn and experience. In addition and foremost I'd like to thank the SQL Server development team for delivering another excellent release full of features in SQL Server 2012. Last but not least, thanks to the technical reviewer Jason Strate and several folks at Wiley, including Victoria Swider and Robert Elliott, for getting these words in print to enable our readers to share my passion for SQL Server.

—ROSS LOFORTE

THANKS TO EVERYONE who made this book possible. As always, I owe a huge debt to my wife Jenn, for putting up with my late nights and my children, Colton, Liam, Camille, and my newest son John for being so patient with their tired dad who has always overextended. Thanks also to the makers of Guinness and other hard liquors for sustaining my ability to keep on writing technical books. Thanks for all the user group leaders out there who work so hard to help others become proficient in technology. You make a huge difference! Finally, thanks to my vocal coach Mike Davis for getting me ready for my American Idol tryout this upcoming season. This time I won't disappoint.

—BRIAN KNIGHT

FIRST AND FOREMOST I NEED TO THANK my lovely wife Ammie. Without her patience and support none of this would be possible. I also need to thank my daughters, Raven and Anna, for putting up with Daddy's late nights and crazy schedule.

I would be remiss if I didn't acknowledge my coworkers at both Pragmatic Works and Pluralsight. Working with so many technical experts has both challenged and inspired me to continually strive for technical excellence.

Finally, I need to thank you, all of you in the SQL community. Thanks for reading my blog, my books, for listening to me when I present in person and on video. It's all of you wonderful folks in the community that infuse me with the passion to learn, teach, and share.

—Robert C. Cain

A LOT OF TIME AND EFFORT was dedicated to bring to you all the information contained in this book. My efforts would not have been possible without the support of my wife and my two daughters and their unconditional love and understanding of my professional commitments. I would also like to extend my eternal gratitude to Adam Jorgensen (`http://adamjorgensen.com`) for giving me the opportunity to contribute to this book and to my good friend Nicholas Cain (`http://sirsql.net`) for his expert contribution on the SQL Server Clustering Chapter.

—Jose Chinchilla

THANKS TO ADAM JORGENSEN for inviting me to participate on this book, Jason Strate for editing the crap out of my work (literally), and the good folks at Wiley Publishing for their patience and perseverance in keeping us all on the rails. A big thank you to my family: Jeremy, Chase, and Gavin, for fending for yourselves when I was buried in work. To Julie Smith, my fellow Datachix, thanks for broad meetings, pep talks, and wine. To the SQL Community, thanks for being so flippin' awesome, especially my Atlanta friends…you guys are the best. And finally, thanks to my grandfather, Bruce Bryant, who taught me that learning is a lifetime endeavor.

—Audrey Hammonds

FIRST I'D LIKE TO THANK my wife Jessica whose love, understanding, and support allow me to actually get stuff like this done. I'd like to especially thank Adam Jorgensen and Brian Knight for giving me the opportunity to propel my career in a direction I never thought possible and giving me the opportunity to write on titles like this. Thank you guys for your support and mentorship. Big thanks to Victoria Swider and Bob Elliot, professional cat herders/editors for this title. Sorry for all the stress guys! Finally, a HUGE thanks to the SQL Server Community as a whole. This Community truly is like a family, and without everyone supporting each other and freely sharing knowledge, I definitely would not be where I am today.

—Jorge Segarra

I WOULD LIKE TO THANK the Lord Jesus Christ who has provided me with the talents to embark on a project like this. I would like to thank my wonderful wife Jen who puts up with my stubbornness every day. Thank you, too, to my little guy who has had to go without "playing with daddy" at certain times due to deadlines. I would like to thank my family back home in South Africa for allowing me to seek my dreams in the Land of Opportunity. Mom, Dad, Bernie, Kirsty, and Tessie, this is for you.

—Gareth Swanepoel

CONTENTS

INTRODUCTION

SQL SERVER 2012 REPRESENTS A SIZABLE jump forward in scalability, performance, and usability for the DBA, developer, and business intelligence (BI) developer. It is no longer unheard of to have 40-terabyte databases running on a SQL Server. SQL Server administration used to just be the job of a database administrator (DBA), but as SQL Server proliferates throughout smaller companies, many developers have begun to act as administrators and BI developers as well. In addition, some of the new features in SQL Server are more developer-centric, and poor configuration of these features can result in poor performance. SQL Server now enables all roles through significantly improved data tools experiences, better security integration, and drastic improvements in data integration, administration, availability, and usability. *Professional Microsoft SQL Server2012 Administration* is a comprehensive, tutorial-based book to get you over the learning curve of how to configure and administer SQL Server 2012.

WHO THIS BOOK IS FOR

Whether you're an administrator or developer using SQL Server, you can't avoid wearing a DBA hat at some point. Developers often have SQL Server on their own workstations and must provide guidance to the administrator about how they'd like the production configured. Oftentimes, they're responsible for creating the database tables and indexes. Administrators or DBAs support the production servers and often inherit the database from the developer.

This book is intended for developers, DBAs, and casual users who hope to administer or may already be administering a SQL Server 2012 system and its business intelligence features, such as Integration Services. This book is a *professional* book, meaning the authors assume that you know the basics about how to query a SQL Server and have some rudimentary concepts of SQL Server. For example, this book does not show you how to create a database or walk you through the installation of SQL Server using the wizard. Instead, the author of the installation chapter provides insight into how to use some of the more advanced concepts of the installation. Although this book does not cover how to query a SQL Server database, it does cover how to tune the queries you've already written.

HOW THIS BOOK IS STRUCTURED

This book follows the same basic path of previous editions, with one major change. The author team has been selected specifically to focus on their areas of expertise. The authors are the same people seen at major conferences and delivering top-tier services for topics such as performance tuning, business intelligence, database design, high availability, PowerShell, and even SQL Azure! This approach has led to unprecedented focus on quality and content with even better access to folks at Microsoft to drive the content in this new release of SQL Server. Hundreds of Connect items were filed and resolved as a direct result of the work of this author team pushing for higher quality for you. Connect is the primary method for industry professionals and SQL Server MVPs to provide bug reports and vote on feature requests from Microsoft. It's a great outlet for improving the product.

This edition of the book covers all the same great information covered in the previous edition, but with loads of new content added for SQL Server 2012, which includes numerous new features to improve the DBA's life. In short, the new version of SQL Server focuses on improving your efficiency, the scale of your server, and the performance of your environment, so you can do more in much less time, and with fewer resources and people. The following is a brief description of each chapter.

Chapter 1: SQL Server 2012 Architecture — The book starts off with a review of the new architecture changes and focuses on the overall components that make up SQL Server 2012.

Chapter 2: Installing SQL Server 2012 Best Practices — This chapter reviews the different ways to install SQL Server 2012 and covers best practices for the process.

Chapter 3: Upgrading SQL Server 2012 Best Practices — This chapter covers upgrading to SQL Server 2012 and best practices to keep in mind while upgrading. Choosing the best upgrade method, requirements, and benefits of upgrading are also covered.

Chapter 4: Managing and Troubleshooting the Database Engine — This chapter focuses on the database engine and working through challenges as they arise. It also covers management and tools appropriate for the task.

Chapter 5: Automating SQL Server — This chapter focuses on automation throughout the SQL Server 2012 world including jobs, PowerShell, and other ways to automate.

Chapter 6: Service Broker in SQL Server 2012 — Service Broker is a great tool to handle messaging inside the database. This chapter covers setup, operations, and management of Service Broker.

Chapter 7: SQL Server CLR Integration — SQL Server and .NET work together inside the Common Language Runtime. This chapter focuses on integrating .NET and the CLR with SQL Server, including assemblies and other options.

Chapter 8: Securing the Database Instance — Security is critical in the database engine. This chapter helps you outline and implement your security plan.

Chapter 9: Change Management — Managing change is paramount to operational stability. This chapter focuses on features in SQL Server that support change management.

Chapter 10: Configuring the Server for Optimal Performance — Configuring and setting up your server properly is important for maximizing application and database performance. This chapter discusses storage, server options, and other settings critical to system performance.

Chapter 11: Optimizing SQL Server 2012 — This chapter covers topics that help the reader review and analyze performance. It also focuses on settings and configuration items that improve SQL Server performance.

Chapter 12: Monitoring Your SQL Server — SQL Server is critically important to make sure you keep performance where it needs to be. This chapter covers the important aspects and tools used to monitor SQL Server 2012.

Chapter 13: Performance Tuning T-SQL — Writing efficient and effective T-SQL is important to have good application performance and scalability. This chapter explains how to optimize your T-SQL to make it more efficient. It focuses on how SQL Server's engine and internals read and execute your queries. You then learn how to take advantage of areas where this process can be tweaked and best practices can be leveraged.

Chapter 14: Indexing Your Database — Indexing is critical to successful database performance. This chapter discusses considerations and strategies for effective indexing for your database.

Chapter 15: Replication — Replication is a key feature in SQL Server for keeping tables and databases in sync and supporting applications. This chapter will cover the types of replication, how to set them up, and the pros and cons of each.

Chapter 16: Clustering SQL Server 2012 — Clustering has been improved again in SQL 2012 and this chapter takes the reader through the setup, configuration, and testing of your clustered configuration.

Chapter 17: Backup and Recovery — Backup and recovery is critical to the success of a continuity plan and operational achievement. This chapter outlines the options in SQL Server for backups and recoveries, and provides recommendations to make the most of these features.

Chapter 18: SQL Server 2012 Log Shipping — This chapter goes through setup, configuration, and administration of log shipping.

Chapter 19: Database Mirroring — There is more functionality in this release for availability than ever before. This chapter covers new and existing features to help you keep your systems online for your organization.

Chapter 20: Integration Services Administration and Performance Tuning — Integration is the key to making sure systems stay in sync. This chapter focuses on administering and tuning this great feature in SQL Server.

Chapter 21: Analysis Services Administration and Performance Tuning — Analysis Services is the Online Analytical Processing (OLAP) product of choice and cannot be ignored by data administrators. This chapter helps you get prepared.

Chapter 22: SQL Server Reporting Services Administration — Reporting Services is often administered by the DBA and this book prepares you no matter what your role to handle those Reporting Services challenges.

Chapter 23: SQL Server 2012 SharePoint 2010 Integration — SharePoint is a bigger part of SQL Server than ever. This chapter covers what you need to know about how SharePoint 2010 integrates with SQL Server so you can be prepared to interact with that team or take on some SharePoint database administration responsibilities yourself.

Chapter 24: SQL Azure Administration and Configuration — This chapter introduces the reader to SQL Server Azure and gets you up and running on this exciting new cloud platform.

Chapter 25: AlwaysOn Availability Groups — This chapter focuses on the availability group feature in Always On. These groups allow you to control instances and servers as groups and assign prioritization and additional flexibility to how failover and high availability are handled in your environment.

WHAT YOU NEED TO USE THIS BOOK

To follow the examples in this book, you need to have SQL Server 2012 installed. If you want to learn how to administer the business intelligence features, you need to have Analysis Services and the Integration Services components installed. You need a machine that can support the minimum hardware requirements to run SQL Server 2012; and you also need the AdventureWorks and AdventureWorksDW databases installed. You can find instructions for accessing these databases in the ReadMe file on this book's website at www.wrox.com.

Some features in this book (especially in the high-availability part) require the Enterprise or Developer Edition of SQL Server. If you do not have this edition, you can still follow through some of the examples in the chapter with the Standard Edition.

CONVENTIONS

To help you get the most from the text and keep track of what's happening, you see a number of conventions throughout the book.

> *Boxes with a warning icon like this one hold important, not-to-be forgotten information that is directly relevant to the surrounding text.*

> *The pencil icon indicates notes, tips, hints, tricks, and asides to the current discussion.*

As for styles in the text:

➤ We *highlight* new terms and important words when we introduce them.

➤ We show keyboard strokes like this: Ctrl+A.

➤ We show file names, URLs, and code within the text like so: persistence.properties.

➤ We present code in two different ways:

```
We use a monofont type with no highlighting for most code examples.
```

```
We use bold to emphasize code that's particularly important in the context of
the chapter.
```

SOURCE CODE

As you work through the examples in this book, you may choose either to type in all the code manually or to use the source code files that accompany the book. All the source code used in this book is available for download at www.wrox.com. You will find the code snippets from the source code are accompanied by a download icon and note indicating the name of the program so you know it's available for download and can easily locate it in the download file. Once at the site, simply locate the book's title (either by using the Search box or by using one of the title lists) and click the Download Code link on the book's detail page to obtain all the source code for the book.

 Because many books have similar titles, you may find it easiest to search by ISBN; this book's ISBN is 978-1-118-10688-4.

After you download the code, just decompress it with your favorite compression tool. Alternatively, you can go to the main Wrox code download page at www.wrox.com/dynamic/books/download .aspx to see the code available for this book and all other Wrox books.

ERRATA

Every effort is made to ensure that there are no errors in the text or in the code. However, no one is perfect, and mistakes do occur. If you find an error in one of our books, such as a spelling mistake or a faulty piece of code, we would be grateful for your feedback. By sending in errata, you may save another reader hours of frustration, and at the same time you can help us provide even higher quality information.

To find the errata page for this book, go to www.wrox.com and locate the title using the Search box or one of the title lists. Then, on the book details page, click the Book Errata link. On this page you can view all errata that has been submitted for this book and posted by Wrox editors. A complete book list, including links to each book's errata, is also available at www.wrox.com/misc-pages/ booklist.shtml.

If you don't spot "your" error on the Book Errata page, go to www.wrox.com/contact/ techsupport.shtml and complete the form there to send us the error you have found. The information will be checked and, if appropriate, a message will be posted to the book's errata page and the problem will be fixed in subsequent editions of the book.

P2P.WROX.COM

For author and peer discussion, join the P2P forums at p2p.wrox.com. The forums are a Web-based system for you to post messages relating to Wrox books and related technologies and interact with other readers and technology users. The forums offer a subscription feature to e-mail you topics of interest of your choosing when new posts are made to the forums. Wrox authors, editors, other industry experts, and your fellow readers are present on these forums.

At http://p2p.wrox.com you can find a number of different forums to help you not only as you read this book, but also as you develop your own applications. To join the forums, follow these steps:

1. Go to p2p.wrox.com and click the Register link.

2. Read the terms of use and click Agree.

3. Complete the required information to join as well as any optional information you want to provide, and click Submit.

4. You will receive an e-mail with information describing how to verify your account and complete the joining process.

 You can read messages in the forums without joining P2P, but to post your own messages, you must join.

When you join, you can post new messages and respond to messages other users post. You can read messages at any time on the Web. If you want to have new messages from a particular forum e-mailed to you, click the Subscribe to this Forum icon by the forum name in the forum listing.

For more information about how to use the Wrox P2P, read the P2P FAQs for answers to questions about how the forum software works as well as many common questions specific to P2P and Wrox books. To read the FAQs, click the FAQ link on any P2P page.

1

SQL Server 2012 Architecture

WHAT'S IN THIS CHAPTER

➤ New Important Features in SQL Server 2012

➤ How New Features Relate to Data Professionals Based on Their Role

➤ SQL Server Architecture Overview

➤ Editions of SQL Server and How They Affect the Data Professional

SQL Server 2012 offers a fresh look at how organizations and their developers, information workers, and executives use and integrate data. A tremendous number of new features and improvements focus on extending SQL Server more into SharePoint, improving self-service options, and increasing data visualization, development, monitoring and exploration capabilities. This chapter is not a deep dive into the architecture but provides enough information to give you an understanding of how SQL Server operates.

SQL SERVER 2012 ECOSYSTEM

This thing called SQL Server has become quite large over the past few releases. This first section provides a review of the overall SQL Server ecosystem, which is now referred to as less of a product and more of an ecosystem, because there are so many interactions with other products and features that drive increased performance, scale, and usability. Following are three major areas of focus for the release of SQL Server 2012:

➤ **Performance:** Features such as improved core support, columnstore indexes, compression enhancements, and Always On make this the most powerful, available release of SQL Server.

➤ **Self Service:** With new data exploration tools such as Power View, improvements in SQL Azure Business Intelligence (BI,), data quality and master data offerings, and

PowerPivot for SharePoint enable users to be closer to the data at all times and to seek and deliver intelligence more rapidly than ever.

➤ **Integration and collaboration:** New integrations for reporting services, PowerPivot, and claims authentication in SharePoint 2010 provide a strong foundation for the significant focus on self-service in this release. The new BI semantic model approach extends into the cloud as well with reporting services now in SQL Azure and more features promised to come.

NEW IMPORTANT FEATURES IN 2012

There are a number of new things that you will be excited about, depending on your role and how you use SQL Server. This section touches on the features you should be checking out and getting your hands on. Many of these features are quick to get up and running, which is exciting for those readers who want to begin delivering impact right away.

Production DBA

Production DBAs are a company's insurance policy that the production database won't go down. If the database does go down, the company cashes in its insurance policy in exchange for a recovered database. The Production DBA also ensures that the server performs optimally and promotes database changes from development to quality assurance (QA) to production. New features include the following:

➤ **AlwaysOn:** Availability functionality including availability groups and the ability to file over databases in groups that mimic applications. This includes new readable secondary servers, a big enhancement.

➤ **FileTable:** Additional file-based data storage

➤ **Extended Events:** A new functionality built into SQL Server 2012 that provides lightweight and extensive tracing capability

➤ Improved functionality and stability in SQL Server Management Studio (now in Visual Studio 2010 shell)

➤ Distributed replay capabilities

➤ Improved debugging functionality including expression support and breakpoint validation.

➤ Columnstore indexes for optimizing large data volumes

➤ Improved statistics algorithm for very large databases

➤ Improved compression and partitioning capabilities

Development DBA

Since the release of SQL Server 2000, there has been a trend away from full-time Production DBAs, and the role has merged with that of the Development DBA. The trend may have slowed, though, with laws such as Sarbanes-Oxley, which require a separation of power between the person developing the change and the person implementing the change. In a large organization, a Production DBA may fall into the operations department, which consists of the network of administrators and Windows-support administrators. In other instances, a Production DBA may be placed in a development group. This removes the separation of power that is sometimes needed for regulatory reasons.

Development DBAs play a traditional role in an organization. They wear more of a developer's hat and are the development staff's database experts and representatives. This administrator ensures that all stored procedures are optimally written and that the database is modeled correctly, both physically and logically. The development DBA also may be the person who writes the migration processes to upgrade the database from one release to the next. The Development DBA typically does not receive calls at 2:00 A.M like the Production DBA might for failed backups or similar problems. Things development DBAs should be excited about in this new release include the following:

➤ New TSQL and spatial functionality

➤ SQL Server data tools: A new TSQL development environment integrated with Visual Studio

➤ New DAX expression language that provides Excel-like usability with the power of multidimensional capabilities

➤ New tabular model for Analysis Services: Provides in-memory OLAP capabilities in a quick time to value format

The Development DBA typically reports to the development group and receives requests from a business analyst or another developer. In a traditional sense, Development DBAs should never have modification access to a production database. They should, however, have read-only access to the production database to debug in a time of escalation.

Business Intelligence DBA and Developer

The Business Intelligence (BI) DBA is a new role that has evolved due to the increased capabilities of SQL Server. In SQL Server 2012, BI grew to be an incredibly important feature set that many businesses could not live without. The BI DBA or developer is an expert at these features. This release is a treasure trove of new BI functionality including new enhancements to Reporting Services Integration, data exploration tools such as Power View, and a dramatic set of enhancements that make PowerPivot easier and more accessible than ever. Additionally, the new Tabular model in SSAS delivers the ability to create new PowerPivot-like "in memory" BI projects to SharePoint for mass user consumption.

Development BI DBAs specialize in the best practices, optimization, and use of the BI toolset. In a small organization, a Development BI DBA may create your SSIS packages to perform Extract Transform and Load (ETL) processes or reports for users. In a large organization, developers create the SSIS packages and SSRS reports. The Development BI DBA is consulted regarding the physical implementation of the SSIS packages and Analysis Services (SSAS) cubes. Development BI DBAs may be responsible for the following types of functions:

➤ Model\consult regarding Analysis Services cubes and solutions

➤ Create reports using Reporting Services

➤ Create\consult around ETL using Integration Services

➤ Develop deployment packages to be sent to the Production DBA

These responsibilities, coupled with these following new features make for an exciting time for the BI-oriented folks:

➤ Rapid data discovery with Power View and PowerPivot

➤ Managed Self-Service BI with SharePoint and BI Semantic Model

➤ Credible, consistent data with Data Quality Services and Master Data Management capabilities

➤ Robust DW solutions with Parallel Data Warehouse and Reference Architectures

SQL SERVER ARCHITECTURE

Many people just use SQL Server for its classic use: to store data. This release of SQL Server focuses on expanding the capabilities that were introduced in SQL Server 2008 R2, which was largely a self-service business intelligence and SharePoint feature release. The additional functionality in SQL Server 2012 not only enables but encourages users to go beyond simply storing data in SQL Server; this release can now be the center of an entire data strategy. New tools such as Power View and PowerPivot quickly integrate on top of SQL Server and can provide an easy user interface (UI) for SQL Server and other systems' data. This section covers the primary file types in SQL Server 2012, file management, SQL Client, and system databases. It also covers an overview of schemas, synonyms, and Dynamic Management Objects. Finally, it also goes into the new SQL Server 2012 data types.

Database Files and Transaction Log

The architecture of database and transaction log files remains relatively unchanged from prior releases. Database files serve two primary purposes depending on their type. Data files hold the data, indexes, and other data support structure within the database. Log files hold the data from committed transactions to ensure consistency in the database.

Database Files

A database may consist of multiple filegroups. Each filegroup must contain one or more physical data files. Filegroups ease administrative tasks for a collection of files. Data files are divided into 8KB data pages, which are part of 64KB extents. You can specify how full each data page should be with the fill factor option of the `create/alter index` T-SQL command. In SQL Server 2012 Enterprise Edition, you continue to have the capability to bring your database partially online if a single file is corrupt. In this instance, the DBA can bring the remaining files online for reading and writing, and users receive an error if they try to access the other parts of the database that are offline.

In SQL 2000 and before, the largest row you could write was 8060 bytes. The exceptions to this limit are `text`, `ntext`, `image`, `varchar(max)`, `varbinary(max)`, and `nvarchar(max)` columns, which may each be up to 2 gigabytes and are managed separately. Beginning with SQL 2005, the 8KB limit applies only to those columns of fixed length. The sum of fixed-length columns and pointers for other column types must still be less than 8060 bytes per row. However, each variable-length column may be up to 8KB in size allowing for a total row size of well over 8060 bytes. If your actual row size exceeds 8060 bytes, you may experience some performance degradation because the logical row must now be split across multiple physical 8060-byte rows.

Transaction Log

The purpose of the transaction log is to ensure that all committed transactions are persisted in the database and can be recovered, either through rollback or point in time recovery. The transaction log is a *write-ahead log*. As you make changes to a database in SQL Server, the data is written to the log, and then the pages that need to be changed are loaded into memory (specifically into the write buffer portion of the buffer pool). The pages are then dirtied by having the changes written to them. Upon checkpoint, the dirty pages are written to disk, making then now clean pages which no longer need to be part of the write buffer. This is why you may see your transaction log grow significantly in the middle of a long-running transaction even if your recovery model is set to simple. (Chapter 17, "Backup and Recovery" covers this in much more detail.)

SQL Native Client

The SQL Native Client is a data-access method that shipped with SQL Server 2005 and was enhanced in 2012 and is used by both OLE DB and ODBC for accessing SQL Server. The SQL Native Client simplifies access to SQL Server by combining the OLE DB and ODBC libraries into a single access method. The access type exposes these features in SQL Server:

- ➤ Database mirroring
- ➤ Always On readable secondary routing
- ➤ Multiple Active Result Sets (MARS)
- ➤ Snapshot isolation
- ➤ Query notification
- ➤ XML data type support
- ➤ User-defined data types (UDTs)
- ➤ Encryption
- ➤ Performing asynchronous operations
- ➤ Using large value types
- ➤ Performing bulk copy operations
- ➤ Table-value parameters
- ➤ Large CLR user-defined types
- ➤ Password expiration

In these features, you can use the feature in other data layers such as Microsoft Data Access Components (MDAC), but it takes more work. MDAC still exists, and you can use it if you don't need some of the new functionality of SQL Server 2008\2012. If you develop a COM-based application, you should use SQL Native Client; and if you develop a managed code application like in C#, you should consider using the .NET Framework Data Provider for SQL Server, which is robust and includes the SQL Server 2008\2012 features as well.

Standard System Databases

The system databases in SQL Server are crucial, and you should leave them alone most of the time. The only exceptions to that rule is the `model` database, which enables you to deploy a change such as a stored procedure to any new database created, and `tempdb`, which may need to be altered to help with scaling your workload. The following sections go through the standard system databases in detail.

 If certain system databases are tampered with or corrupted, you run the risk that SQL Server will not start. The master database contains all the stored procedures and tables needed for SQL Server to remain online.

The Resource Database

SQL Server 2005 added the `Resource` database. This database contains all the read-only critical system tables, metadata, and stored procedures that SQL Server needs to run. It does not contain any information about your instance or your databases because it is written to only during an installation of a new service pack. The `Resource` database contains all the physical tables and stored procedures referenced logically by other databases. You can find the database by default in `C:\Program Files\Microsoft SQL Server\MSSQL11.MSSQLSERVER\MSSQL\Binn`, and there is only one `Resource` database per instance.

 The use of drive C: in the path assumes a standard setup. If your machine is set up differently, you may need to change the path to match your setup. In addition, the `.MSSQLSERVER` is the instance name. If your instance name is different, use your instance name in the path.

In SQL Server 2000, when you upgraded to a new service pack, you needed to run many long scripts to drop and re-create system objects. This process took a long time to run and created an environment that couldn't be rolled back to the previous release after the service pack. In SQL Server 2012, when you upgrade to a new service pack or hot fix, a copy of the `Resource` database overwrites the old database. This enables you to both quickly upgrade your SQL Server catalog and roll back a release.

The `Resource` database cannot be seen through Management Studio and should never be altered unless you're under instruction to do so by Microsoft Product Support Services (PSS). You can connect to the database under certain single-user mode conditions by typing the command **USE MSSQLSystemResource**. Typically, a DBA runs simple queries against it while connected to any database, instead of having to connect to the resource database directly. Microsoft provides some functions that enable this access. For example, if you were to run this query while connected to any database, it would return your Resource database's version and the last time it was upgraded:

```
SELECT serverproperty('resourceversion') ResourceDBVersion,
serverproperty('resourcelastupdatedatetime') LastUpdateDate
```

 Do not place the Resource *database on an encrypted or compressed drive. Doing this may cause upgrade or performance issues.*

The master Database

The master database contains the metadata about your databases (database configuration and file location), logins, and configuration information about the instance. You can see some of the metadata stored in master by running the following query, which returns information about the databases that exist on the server:

```
SELECT * FROM sys.databases
```

The main difference between the Resource and master databases is that the master database holds data specific to your instance, whereas the Resource database just holds the schema and stored procedures needed to run your instance but does not contain any data specific to your instance.

 You should rarely create objects in the master *database. If you create objects here, you may need to make frequent master db backups.*

tempdb Database

The tempdb database is similar to the operating system paging file. It's used to hold temporary objects created by users, temporary objects needed by the database engine, and row-version information. The tempdb database is created each time you restart SQL Server. The database will be re-created to its original database size when the SQL Server is started. Because the database is re-created each time, you cannot back it up. Data changes made to objects in the tempdb database benefit from reduced logging. You must have enough space allocated to your tempdb database because many operations that you use in your database applications use the tempdb. Generally speaking, you should set tempdb to autogrow as it needs space. Typically your tempdb size varies but you should understand how much temp space your application will use at peak and make sure there is enough space with 15–20 percent overhead for growth. If there is not enough space, the user may receive one of the following errors:

➤ **1101** or **1105:** The session connecting to SQL Server must allocate space in tempdb.

➤ **3959:** The version store is full.

➤ **3967:** The version store must shrink because tempdb is full.

model Database

`model` is a system database that serves as a template when SQL Server creates a new database. As each database is created, SQL Server copies the `model` database as the new database. The only time this does not apply is when you restore or attach a database from a different server.

If a table, stored procedure, or database option should be included in each new database that you create on a server, you may simplify the process by creating the object in `model`. When the new database is created, `model` is copied as the new database, including the special objects or database settings you have added to the `model` database. If you add your own objects to `model`, it should be included in your backups, or you should maintain a script that includes the changes.

msdb Database

`msdb` is a system database that contains information used by SQL Server agent, log shipping, SSIS, and the backup and restore system for the relational database engine. The database stores all the information about jobs, operators, alerts, and job history. Because it contains this important system-level data, you should back up this database regularly.

Schemas

Schemas enable you to group database objects together. You may want to do this for ease of administration because you can apply security to all objects within a schema. Another reason to use schemas is to organize objects so that the consumers may find the objects they need easily. For example, you may create a schema called `HumanResource` and place all your employee tables and stored procedures into it. You could then apply security policies on the schema to allow appropriate access to the objects contained within it.

When you refer to an object, you should always use the two-part name. The `dbo` schema is the default schema for a database. An `Employee` table in the `dbo` schema is referred to as `dbo.Employee`. Table names must be unique within a schema. You could create another table called `Employee` in the `HumanResources` schema. It would be referred to as `HumanResources.Employee`. This table actually exists in the AdventureWorks sample database for SQL Server 2012. (All SQL Server 2012 samples must be downloaded and installed separately from `wrox.com`.) A sample query using the two-part name follows:

```
SELECT BusinessEntityID, JobTitle
FROM HumanResources.Employee
```

Prior to SQL 2005, the first part of the two-part name was the user name of the object owner. The problem with that implementation was related to maintenance. If a user who owned objects were to leave the company, you could not remove that user login from SQL Server until you ensured that all the objects owned by the user were changed to a different owner. All the code that referred to the objects had to be changed to refer to the new owner. By separating ownership from the schema name, SQL 2005 through 2012 removes this maintenance problem.

Synonyms

A *synonym* is an alias, or alternative name, for an object. This creates an abstraction layer between the database object and the consumer. This abstraction layer enables you to change some of the physical implementation and isolate those changes from the consumer. The following example is related to the use of linked servers. You may have tables on a different server that need to be joined to tables on a local server. You refer to objects on another server using the four-part name, as shown in the following code:

```
SELECT Column1, Column2
FROM LinkedServerName.DatabaseName.SchemaName.TableName
```

For example, you might create a synonym for `LinkedServerName.DatabaseName.SchemaName.Tablename` called `SchemaName.SynonymName`. Data consumers would refer to the object using the following query:

```
SELECT Column1, Column2
FROM SchemaName.SynonymName
```

This abstraction layer now enables you to change the location of the table to another server, using a different linked server name, or even to replicate the data to the local server for better performance without requiring any changes to the code that refers to the table.

 A synonym cannot reference another synonym. The `object_id` *function returns the id of the synonym, not the id of the related base object. If you need column-level abstraction, use a view instead.*

Dynamic Management Objects

Dynamic Management Objects (DMOs) and functions return information about your SQL Server instance and the operating system. DMO's are grouped into two different classes: dynamic management views (DMVs) and dynamic management functions (DMFs). DMV's and DMF's simplify access to data and expose new information that was not available in versions of SQL Server prior to 2005. DMOs can provide you with various types of information, from data about the I/O subsystem and RAM to information about Service Broker.

Whenever you start an instance, SQL Server begins saving server-state and diagnostic information in memory which DMV's and DMF's can access. When you stop and start the instance, the information is flushed from the views and fresh data begins to be collected. You can query the views just like any other table in SQL Server with the two-part qualifier. For example, the following query uses the `sys.dm_exec_sessions` DMV to retrieve the number of sessions connected to the instance, grouped by login name:

```
SELECT login_name, COUNT(session_id) as NumberSessions
FROM sys.dm_exec_sessions GROUP BY login_name
```

Some DMFs are functions that accept parameters. For example, the following code uses the `sys.dm_io_virtual_file_stats` dynamic management function to retrieve the I/O statistics for the AdventureWorks data file:

```
USE AdventureWorks
GO
SELECT * FROM
```

```
sys.dm_io_virtual_file_stats(DB_ID('AdventureWorks'),
FILE_ID('AdventureWorks_Data'))
```

Many new DMV's and DMF's exist in SQL Server 2012. These views focus on improved insight into new and existing areas of functionality and include the following:

- AlwaysOn Availability Groups Dynamic Management Views and Functions
- Change Data Capture Related Dynamic Management Views
- Change Tracking Related Dynamic Management Views
- Common Language Runtime Related Dynamic Management Views
- Database Mirroring Related Dynamic Management Views
- Database-Related Dynamic Management Views
- Execution-Related Dynamic Management Views and Functions
- SQL Server Extended Events Dynamic Management Views
- FileStream and FileTable Dynamic Management Views
- Full-Text Search and Semantic Search Dynamic Management Views and Functions
- Index-Related Dynamic Management Views and Functions
- I/O-Related Dynamic Management Views and Functions
- Object-Related Dynamic Management Views and Functions
- Query Notifications Related Dynamic Management Views
- Replication-Related Dynamic Management Views
- Resource Governor Related Dynamic Management Views
- Security-Related Dynamic Management Views and Functions
- Server-Related Dynamic Management Views and Functions
- Service Broker Related Dynamic Management Views
- Spatial Data Related Dynamic Management Views and Functions
- SQL Server Operating System Related Dynamic Management Views
- Transaction-Related Dynamic Management Views and Functions

SQL Server 2012 Data Types

Data types are the foundation of table creation in SQL Server. As you create a table, you must assign a data type for each column. This section covers some of the more commonly used data types in SQL Server. Even if you create a custom data type, it must be based on a standard SQL Server data type. For example, you may create a custom data type (Address) by using the following syntax, but notice that it based on the SQL Server standard varchar data type:

```
CREATE TYPE Address
FROM varchar(35) NOT NULL
```

If you change the data type of a column in a large table in SQL Server Management Studio's table designer interface, the operation may take a long time. You can observe the reason for this by scripting the change from the Management Studio interface. Management Studio creates a secondary temporary table with a name such as tmpTableName and then copies the data into the table. Finally, the interface deletes the old table and renames the new table with the new data type. Other steps along the way, of course, handle indexes and any relationships in the table.

If you have a large table with millions of records, this process can take more than 10 minutes, and in some cases more than 1 hour. To avoid this, you can use a simple one-line T-SQL statement in the query window to change the column's data type. For example, to change the data type of the Job Title column in the Employees table to a varchar(70), you could use the following syntax:

```
ALTER TABLE HumanResources.Employee ALTER COLUMN JobTitle Varchar(70)
```

 When you convert to a data type that may be incompatible with your data, you may lose important data. For example, if you convert from a numeric data type that has data such as 15.415 to an integer, the number 15.415 would be rounded to a whole number.

You may want to write a report against your SQL Server tables that displays the data type of each column inside the table. You can do this dozens of ways, but a popular method shown in the following example joins the sys.objects table with the sys.columns table. There are two functions that you may not be familiar with in the following code. The TYPE_NAME() function translates the data type id into its proper name. To go the opposite direction, you could use the TYPE_ID() function. The other function of note is SCHEMA_ID(), which is used to return the identity value for the schema. This is useful primarily when you want to write reports against the SQL Server metadata.

```
USE AdventureWorks
GO
SELECT o.name AS ObjectName,
        c.name AS ColumnName,
        TYPE_NAME(c.user_type_id) as DataType
FROM sys.objects o
JOIN sys.columns c
ON o.object_id = c.object_id
WHERE   o.name ='Department'
and o.Schema_ID = SCHEMA_ID('HumanResources')
```

This code returns the following results (the **Name** data type is a user-defined type):

```
ObjectName           ColumnName      DataType
----------------------------------------------------

Department           DepartmentID    smallint
Department           Name            Name
Department           GroupName       Name
Department           ModifiedDate    datetime
```

Character Data Types

Character data types include `varchar`, `char`, `text`, and. This set of data types stores character data. The primary difference between the `varchar` and `char` types is data padding. If you have a column called `FirstName` that is a `varchar(20)` data type and you store the value of "Brian" in the column, only 5 bytes are physically stored plus a little overhead. If you store the same value in a `char(20)` data type, all 20 bytes would be used. SQL inserts trailing spaces to fill the 20 characters.

 You might ask yourself, if you want to conserve space, why would you ever use a `char` data type? There is a slight overhead to using a `varchar` data type. If you store a two-letter state abbreviation, for example, you're better off using a `char(2)` column. Although some DBAs have opinions about this that border on religious conviction, generally speaking it's good to find a threshold in your organization and specify that anything below this size becomes a `char` versus a `varchar`. A good guideline is that, in general, any column less than or equal to 5 bytes should be stored as a `char` data type instead of a `varchar` data type, depending on your application needs. Beyond that point, the benefit of using a `varchar` begins to outweigh the cost of the overhead.

The `nvarchar` and `nchar` data types operate the same way as their `varchar` and `char` counterparts, except these data types can handle international Unicode characters. This comes at a cost, though. Data stored as Unicode consumes 2 bytes per character. If you were to store the value of "Brian" in an `nvarchar` column, it would use 10 bytes, and storing it as an `nchar(20)` would use 40 bytes. Because of this overhead and added space, you should not use Unicode columns unless you have a business or language need for them. Think ahead to the future and consider instances in which you might need them. If there is no future business need, avoid them.

Table 1-1 shows the data types with short descriptions and the amount of storage required.

TABLE 1-1: SQL Server Data Types

DATA TYPE	DESCRIPTION	STORAGE SPACE
Char(n)	N between 1 and 8,000 characters	n bytes
Nchar(n)	N between 1 and 4,000 Unicode characters	(2 x n bytes)
Nvarchar(max)	Up to ((2 to the 30th power) – 1) (1,073,741,823) Unicode characters	2 x characters stored + 2 bytes overhead
Text	Up to ((2 to the 31st power) – 1) (2,147,483,647) characters	1 byte per character stored +2bytes overhead
Varchar(n)	N between 1 and 8,000 characters	1 byte per character stored + 2 bytes overhead
Varchar(max)	Up to ((2 to the 31st power) – 1) (2,147,483,647) characters	1 byte per character stored + 2 bytes overhead

Exact Numeric Data Types

Numeric data types consist of `bit`, `tinyint`, `smallint`, `int`, `bigint`, `numeric`, `decimal`, `money`, `float`, and `real`. Each of these data types stores different types of numeric values. The first data type, `bit`, stores only a null, 0 or a 1, which in most applications translates into true or false. Using the `bit` data type is perfect for on and off flags, and it occupies only a single byte of space. Table 1-2 shows other common numeric data types.

TABLE 1.2: Exact Numeric Data Types

DATA TYPE	DESCRIPTION	STORAGE SPACE
bit	0, 1, or Null	1 byte for each 8 columns of this data type
tinyint	Whole numbers from 0 to 255	1 bytes
smallint	Whole numbers from –32,768 to 32,767	2 bytes
int	Whole numbers from –2,147,483,648 to 2,147,483,647	4 bytes
bigint	Whole numbers from –9,223,372,036,854,775,808 to 9,223,372,036,854,775,807	8 bytes
numeric(p,s) or decimal(p,s)	Numbers from –1,038 + 1 through 1,038 –1	Up to 17 bytes
money	–922,337,203,685,477.5808 to 922,337,203,685,477.5807	8 bytes
smallmoney	–214,748.3648 to 214,748.3647	4 bytes

Numeric data types, such as `decimal` and `numeric` can store a variable number of digits to the right and left of the decimal place. *Scale* refers to the number of digits to the right of the decimal. *Precision* defines the total number of digits, including the digits to the right of the decimal place. For example, 14.88531 would be a `numeric(7,5)` or `decimal(7,5)`. If you were to insert 14.25 into a `numeric(5,1)` column, it would be rounded to 14.3.

Approximate Numeric Data Types

The data types `float` and `real` are included in this group. They should be used when floating-point data must be represented. However, because they are approximate, not all values can be represented exactly.

The `n` in the `float(n)` is the number of bits used to store the mantissa of the number. SQL Server uses only two values for this field. If you specify between 1 and 24, SQL uses 24. If you specify between 25 and 53, SQL uses 53. The default is 53 when you specify `float()`, with nothing in parenthesis.

Table 1-3 shows the approximate numeric data types with a short description and the amount of storage required.

TABLE 1-3: Approximate Numeric Data Types

DATA TYPE	DESCRIPTION	STORAGE SPACE
float[(n)]	–1.79E+308 to –2.23E-308,0, 2.23E-308 to 1.79E+308	N<=24 – 4 bytes N> 24– 8 bytes
real()	–3.40E+38 to –1.18E-38,0, 1.18E-38 to 3.40E+38	4 bytes

 The synonym for real *is* float(24).

Binary Data Types

Binary data types such as varbinary, binary, varbinary(maxstore binary data such as graphic files, Word documents, or MP3 files. The values are hexadecimal 0x0 to 0xf. The image data type stores up to 2GB outside the data page. The preferred alternative to an image data type is the varbinary(max), which can hold more than 8KB of binary data and generally performs slightly better than an image data type. New in SQL Server 2012 is the capability to store varbinary(max) objects in operating system files via FileStream storage options. This option stores the data as files and is not subject to the 2GB size limit of varbinary(max).

Table 1-4 shows the binary data types with a short description and the amount of storage required.

TABLE 1-4: Binary Data Types

DATA TYPE	DESCRIPTION	STORAGE SPACE
Binary(n)	N between 1 and 8,000 hex digits	n bytes
Varbinary(n)	N between 1 and 8,000 hex digits	1 byte per character stored + 2 bytes overhead
Varbinary(max)	Up to 231 – 1(2,147,483,647) characters	1 byte per character stored + 2 bytes overhead

Date and Time Data Types

The datetime and smalldatetime types both store date and time data. The smalldatetime is 4 bytes and stores from January 1, 1900, through June 6, 2079, and is accurate to the nearest minute.

The datetime data type is 8 bytes and stores from January 1, 1753, through December 31, 9999, to the nearest 3.33 millisecond.

SQL Server 2012 has four new date-related data types: datetime2, dateoffset, date, and time. You can find examples using these data types in SQL Server Books Online.

The datetime2 data type is an extension of the datetime data type, with a wider range of dates. Time is always stored with hours, minutes, and seconds. You can define the datetime2 data type with a variable parameter at the end — for example, datetime2(3). The 3 in the preceding expression means to store fractions of seconds to three digits of precision, or .999. Valid values are between 0 and 7, with a default of 3.

The datetimeoffset data type is just like the datetime2 data type, with the addition of the time offset. The time offset is + or − up to 14 hours, and contains the UTC offset so that you can rationalize times captured in different time zones.

The date data type stores the date only, a long-requested piece of functionality. Alternatively, the time data type stores the time only. The time data type also supports the time(n) declaration, so you can control granularity of the fractional seconds. As with datetime2 and datetimeoffset, n can be between 0 and 7.

Table 1-5 shows the date/time data types with a short description and the amount of storage required.

TABLE 1-5: Date and Time Data Types

DATA TYPE	DESCRIPTION	STORAGE SPACE
Date	January 1, 1 to December 31, 9999	3 bytes
Datetime	January 1, 1753 to December 31, 9999, Accurate to nearest 3.33 millisecond	8 bytes
Datetime2(n)	January 1, 1 to December 31, 9999 N between 0 and 7 specifies fractional seconds	6 to 8 bytes
Datetimeoffset(n)	January 1, 1 to December 31, 9999 N between 0 and 7 specifies fractional seconds +- offset	8 to 10 bytes
SmalldateTime	January 1, 1900 to June 6, 2079, Accurate to 1 minute	4 bytes
Time(n)	Hours:minutes:seconds.9999999 N between 0 and 7 specifies fractional seconds	3 to 5 bytes

Other System Data Types

Table 1-6 shows several other data types, which you have not yet seen.

TABLE 1-6: Other System Data Types

DATA TYPE	DESCRIPTION	STORAGE SPACE
Cursor	This contains a reference to a cursor and may be used only as a variable or stored procedure parameter.	Not applicable
Hierarchyid	Contains a reference to a location in a hierarchy	1 to 892 bytes + 2 bytes overhead
SQL_Variant	May contain the value of any system data type except `text`, `ntext`, `image`, `timestamp`, `xml`, `varchar(max)`, `nvarchar(max)`, `varbinary(max)`, and user-defined data types. The maximum size allowed is 8,000 bytes of data + 16 bytes of metadata.	8,016 bytes
Table	Used to store a data set for further processing. The definition is like a Create Table. Primarily used to return the result set of a table-valued function, they can also be used in stored procedures and batches.	Dependent on table definition and number of rows stored
Timestamp or Rowversion	Unique per table, automatically stored value. Generally used for version stamping, the value is automatically changed on insert and with each update.	8 bytes
Uniqueidentifier	Can contain Globally Unique Identifier (GUID). `guid` values may be obtained from the `Newse quentialid()` function. This function returns values that are unique across all computers. Although stored as a binary 16, it is displayed as a `char(36)`.	16 bytes
XML	is Unicode by definition	Up to 2GB

 A cursor *data type may not be used in a* Create Table *statement.*

The XML data type stores an XML document or fragment. It is stored like an `nvarchar(max)` in size depending on the use of UTF-16 or UTF-8 in the document. The XML data type enables the use of special constructs for searching and indexing. (This is covered in more detail in Chapter 15, "Replication".)

CLR Integration

In SQL Server 2012, you can also create your own data types, functions, and stored procedures using the portion of the Common Language Runtime referred to as (SQLCLR). This enables you to write more complex data types to meet your business needs in Visual Basic or C#, for example. These types are defined as a class structure in the base CLR language.

EDITIONS OF SQL SERVER

SQL Server 2012 is available in several editions, and the features available to you in each edition vary widely. The editions you can install on your workstation or server also vary based on the operating system. The editions of SQL Server range from SQL Express on the lowest end to Enterprise Edition on the highest.

Edition Overview

There are three major editions of SQL Server 2012. There are additional, smaller editions typically not recommended for production environments so they are not covered here. For more details on these, see www.microsoft.com/sqlserver. Figures 1-1 and 1-2 describe the new editions releasing with SQL Server 2012.

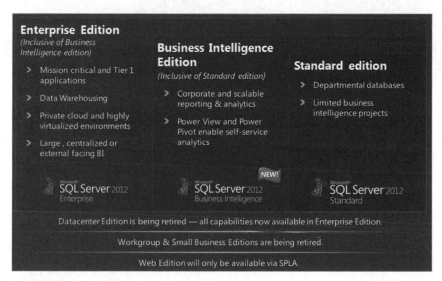

FIGURE 1-1

SQL Server 2012 offers three principal SKUs:

➤ **Enterprise Edition** contains all the new SQL Server 2012 capabilities, including high availability and performance updates that make this a mission critical-ready database. This edition contains all the BI functionality as well.

➤ **Business Intelligence Edition** is new in SQL Server 2012. The BI Server Edition offers the full suite of powerful BI capabilities in SQL Server 2012, including PowerPivot and Power View. One major focus of this edition is empowering end users with BI functionality. This is ideal for projects that need advanced BI capabilities but don't require the full OLTP performance and scalability of Enterprise Edition. The new BI Edition is inclusive of the standard edition and still contains the basic OLTP offerings.

➤ **Standard Edition** remains as it is today, designed for departmental use with limited scale. It has basic database functionality and basic BI functionality. New features are now included in Standard such as compression.

Figure 1-2 provides you with an at-a-glance view of some of the key features in SQL Server 2012 by edition.

SQL Server Capabilities	SQL Server Editions		
	Standard	Business Intelligence	Enterprise
Maximum Number of Cores	16 cores	16 cores – DB OS Max – BI	OS Max
Basic OLTP	•	•	•
Basic Reporting & Analytics	•	•	•
Programmability & Developer Tools	•	•	•
Manageability (Management studio, policy based management)	•	•	•
Enterprise Data Management (Data quality, master data services)		•	•
Self-service Business Intelligence (Power View, PowerPivot for SPS)		•	•
Corporate Business Intelligence (Semantic model, advanced analytics)		•	•
Advanced Security (Advanced auditing, transparent data encryption)			•
Data Warehousing (Column store index, compression, partitioning)			•
Maximum Scalability and Performance			•
High Availability	Limited	Basic	•
AlwaysOn			•
Virtualization Licensing	1 VM	1 VM	Unlimited w/ SA

FIGURE 1-2

The basic functionality is kept in the Standard Edition. Key enterprise BI features are included in the BI SKU. When you need to go to high end data warehousing and enterprise level high availability, the Enterprise Edition is the right edition for you.

Figure 1-2 provides a more detailed look at the SQL Server 2012 Editions and related capabilities. As you can see, for the Standard Edition, there is a 16 core maximum. For the Business Intelligence Edition, there is a 20 core maximum for database use and up to the OS Maximum for BI. The Enterprise Edition can be used up the maximum number of cores in the operating system.

Both the BI Edition and Enterprise Edition offer the full premium BI capabilities of SQL Server 2012, including Enterprise Data Management, Self-Server BI, and Corporate BI features. Enterprise Edition adds mission critical and Tier 1 database functionality with the maximum scalability, performance, and high availability. With the Enterprise Edition under Software Assurance, customers also get unlimited virtualization, with the ability to license unlimited virtual machines.

Licensing

SQL Server 2012 has significant licensing changes. This new licensing scheme can impact your environment if you do not run Software Assurance on those licenses. This section is an overview of the changes, not an exhaustive licensing discussion. See your Microsoft account manager for more details on these changes.

SQL Server 2012 pricing and licensing better aligns to the way customers purchase database and BI products. The new pricing and licensing offers a range of benefits for customers including the following:

➤ **SQL Server 2012 offers market leading Total Cost of Ownership (TCO):**

   ➤ SQL Server 2012 continues to be the clear high-value leader among major vendors. This is exemplified through the pricing model; features included in non-enterprise editions and world class support no matter the edition.

   ➤ Customers with Software Assurance get significant benefits and ways to help ease the transition to new licensing models. These benefits include access to upgrades and enhanced support options during your license term.

   ➤ Customers with Enterprise Agreements have the easiest transition to SQL Server 2012 and realize the greatest cost-savings.

➤ **SQL Server 2012 is cloud-optimized:**

   ➤ SQL Server 2012 is the most virtualization-friendly database with expanded virtualization licensing, the flexibility to license per VM, and excellent support for Hyper-V.

   ➤ Customers also have the ability to support hybrid scenarios that span on-premises, private cloud, and public clouds through better integration with SQL Azure.

➤ **SQL Server 2012 pricing and licensing is designed to enable customers to pay as they grow:**

   ➤ The new streamlined editions are aligned to database and BI needs.

   ➤ For datacenter scenarios, licensing is better aligned to hardware capacity.

   ➤ For BI, licensing is aligned to user-based access, which is the way most customers are accustomed to purchasing BI.

CPU Core (Not Processor) Licenses

With the release of SQL Server 2012, Microsoft switched to a per core processing model. Don't fret because for most of your servers the costs should stay the same. The CPU Core licenses (available only for the Standard and Enterprise Edition) are sold in two core "packs." So a quad core CPU needs two of these packs per socket. These license packs cost half of what a SQL Server 2008 R2 CPU license cost. The catch here is that you must purchase at least 4 cores per CPU.

For example:

   ➤ Two sockets with 2 cores each, you need 4 license "packs" (8 core licenses).

   ➤ Two sockets with 4 cores each, you need 4 license "packs" (8 core licenses).

   ➤ Two sockets with 6 cores each, you need 6 license "packs" (12 core licenses).

   ➤ Two sockets with 8 cores each, you need 8 license "packs" (16 core licenses).

Virtualized SQL Server and Host Based Licensing

When you run a virtualized SQL Server, you must license at least four cores for the VM. If you have more than four virtual CPUs on the VM, you must have a CPU Core license for each virtual CPU that you have assigned to the VM.

SQL Server 2012 still includes host-based licensing for those customers with Software Assurance and an Enterprise Agreement. The host-based licensing works just like it did before: you purchase enough Enterprise Edition CPU Core licenses for the host, and you can run as many virtual machines running SQL Server as you want. This will likely be the preferred way for many of you. For those customers not running with Software Assurance or an Enterprise Agreement, they will want to contact your Microsoft Representative or reseller since host based licensing is not available for those customers.

As you can see, this is a lot of change. The pricing has changed too but is not discussed here due to the wide variations depending on your individual agreements with Microsoft. Microsoft has tried hard to make sure the cost does not go up dramatically for many of you, so don't fret, but be judicious and check this out with your Microsoft Account teams.

SUMMARY

The architecture for SQL Server 2012 has advancements under the covers that will improve performance, increase developer efficiency and system availability, and decrease overall operating cost. It is important to focus on your current and future roles and understand the types of features and editions that will apply to your situation and organizational needs.

2

Installing SQL Server 2012 Best Practices

- ➤ How to Plan and Execute a Successful SQL Server 2012 Installation
- ➤ What Post-Installation Configurations are Necessary
- ➤ Troubleshoot Common Installation Issues

The installation process of SQL Server 2012 can be as easy as executing the Setup Wizard from the installation media and following the prompts in each of the setup screens. The Setup Wizard makes several important decisions for you during this process. Throughout this chapter you learn about those decisions and the appropriate configurations for a secure, stable, and scalable installation.

The core installation process follows these general steps:

1. Plan the system.
2. Prepare hardware and software.
3. Install the operating system and service packs.
4. Set up the I/O subsystem.
5. Install SQL Server and service packs.
6. Burn in the system.

7. Do post-install configurations if necessary.

8. Clean up for deployment and go!

This chapter focuses on the plan and the actual install.

PLANNING THE SYSTEM

The first step before initiating a SQL Server installation involves proper planning. A successful SQL Server installation starts with a good game plan. As the old proverb goes: "Failing to plan is planning to fail."

Some of the necessary planning includes the following tasks and considerations:

➤ Baseline of current workload

➤ Estimated growth in workload

➤ Minimum hardware and software requirements

➤ Proper storage system sizing and I/O requirements

➤ SQL Server Edition

➤ SQL Server collation, file locations, and `tempdb` sizing

➤ Service account selection

➤ Database maintenance and backup plans

➤ Minimum uptime and response time service levels

➤ Disaster recovery strategy

This list provides just a few of the things to keep in mind when deploying, upgrading, or migrating a SQL Server 2012 instance. The next sections cover some of these considerations and best practices in more detail.

Hardware Options

Choosing the right hardware configuration may not always be straightforward. Microsoft provides minimum hardware requirements to support a SQL Server 2012 installation, but as the word *minimum* implies, these are only the minimum requirements but not necessarily the most appropriate. Ideally, you want to provision hardware that exceeds the minimum requirements to meet current and future resource requirements.

This is the reason why you need to create a baseline of current resource requirements and also to estimate future needs. Having the necessary hardware to meet future requirements can not only save you money, but also avoid downtime required to carry out hardware upgrades.

To guarantee a smooth installation process and predictable performance, become familiar with the minimum hardware requirements provided by Microsoft, as listed in Table 2-1.

TABLE 2-1: SQL Server 2012 Minimum Hardware Requirements

COMPONENT	REQUIREMENT
Processor	64-bit installations: Speed: 1.4 Ghz or higher AMD Opteron, Athlon 64, Intel Pentium IV, Xeon with Intel EM64T support or 32-bit installations: Speed: 1.0 Ghz or higher Pentium III compatible
Memory	1GB (512MB Express Edition)
Storage	Database Engine and data files, Replication, Full-Text Search, and Data Quality Services: 811 MB Analysis Services and data files: 345 MB Reporting Services and Report Manager: 304 MB Integration Services: 591 MB Master Data Services: 243 MB Client Components (other than SQL Server Books Online components and Integration Services tools): 1,823 MB SQL Server Books Online Components to view and manage help content1: 375 KB

Processors

SQL Server 2012 instances that experience a high number of transactions and a high number of concurrent connections benefit from as much processing power as there is available. Processing power comes in the form of high clock-speed processors and a large number of available processors. Multiple slightly slower processors perform better than a single fast processor. For example, two 1.6 GHz processors perform faster than a single 3.2 GHz processor.

Newer processor models offer multiple cores in a single physical socket. These multicore processors have many advantages including space and power consumption savings. Multicore processors enable you to run more than one instance of SQL Server 2012 within the same physical server, either as named instances or as virtual machines. In other words, you can run as many SQL Server 2012 servers as your hardware and licensing allows with a single physical server. Space is drastically reduced in your data center as multiple physical servers can be consolidated into a single physical server. This consolidation enables you to reduce your power bill because you have fewer servers physically connected to the power grid.

Core-Based Licensing has changed for SQL Server 2012. In the new SQL Server 2012 Core-Based Licensing model, each core in a multicore processor is now required to be licensed. This change applies both to physical server and virtual machines. For more details on SQL Server 2012 Licensing, refer to the "Licensing" section of Chapter 1, "SQL Server 2012 Architecture."

Memory

Memory is an important resource for optimal performance of SQL Server 2012. Well-designed database systems make proper use of available memory by reading as much as possible from cached data pages in memory buffers.

Memory needs to be allocated both for the SQL Server instance and the operating system. As much as possible you should avoid installing memory-intensive applications in the same Windows server as your SQL Server instance.

A good starting point to decide how much memory you need is to factor the number of data pages of each of the databases hosted on the SQL Server instance along with query execution statistics such as minimum, maximum, and average memory utilization for a typical workload. The goal is to allow SQL Server to keep in cache as many data pages and execution plans in memory as possible to avoid costly data page reads from disk and execution plan compilations.

You also need to be aware of memory limitations imposed by specific SQL Server editions. For example, SQL Server 2012 Enterprise Edition supports up to 2 TB of RAM; Standard Edition supports up to 64 GB of RAM; and Express Edition supports up to 1 GB of RAM.

Storage

The storage system of a SQL Server 2012 instance requires special considerations because slow performing storage can bring database performance to a halt. When planning for storage for your SQL Server 2012 databases, consider your availability, reliability, throughput, and scalability requirements.

To test and validate your storage system's performance, you need to gather important metrics such as maximum number of I/O requests per second (IOPS), throughput (MBPS) and I/O latency. Table 2-2 lists these three key metrics along with a brief description.

TABLE 2-2: Key Storage Metrics

METRIC	DESCRIPTION
I/O requests per second (IOps)	Number of concurrent requests the storage system can handle in one second. You want this number to be high, usually between 150 to 250 IOPS for a single 15k rpm SAS drive and between 1,000 to 1,000,000 IOPS for enterprise SSDs and SANs depending on configuration and manufacturer.
Throughput (MBps)	Size of data the storage system can read or write in one second. You want this number to be high.
I/O latency (ms)	Time delay between I/O operations. You want this number to be zero or close to zero.

You can gather these key metrics by using free tools such as SQLIO, SQLIOSim, IOMeter, and CrystalDiskMark. The explanation on how to use these tools is beyond the scope of this chapter but you can find good documentation about them at `http://msdn.microsoft.com/en-us/library/cc966412.aspx`.

There are the two main types of storage used in SQL Server installations: DAS and SAN. The following sections explain these types in detail.

Direct-Attached Storage (DAS)

Direct Attached Storage (DAS) is the simplest storage option to understand. In this type of storage, the disk drives are located within the server box enclosure and attached directly to a disk controller. Alternatively, they can also be located in an external enclosure attached directly through a cable to a Host Bus Adapter (HBA). No additional equipment is required such as switches.

The main advantage of DAS is that they are easier to implement and maintain at a lower cost. The main disadvantage is limited scalability. Although, in recent years DAS storage systems have been catching up with features found only in higher-end SAN units, they are still bound by limitations such as the number of disk drives and volume size they can scale up to and manage, the number of servers they can be attached to, and the distance between the storage unit and a server.

Server connectivity and distance are in particular the biggest differentiators because DAS requires direct physical links between the storage unit and the servers, limiting the number of servers that can be attached simultaneously and the distance separating the storage unit and a server, usually just a couple feet long.

Storage Area Network (SAN)

Storage area networks (SAN) are specialized networks that interconnect storage devices made available to servers as directly attached storage volumes. This network of storage devices is interconnected through high-speed dedicated Fibre Channel (FC) devices known as fabric switches, or through the iSCSI protocol using regular Ethernet switches.

One of the great advantages of SANs is the ability to span over a large geographical area, typically through TCP/IP routing using dedicated wide area network (WAN) connections. This enables organizations to implement features such as storage replication between distant data centers in their Disaster Recovery efforts.

In addition, SANs offer the best reliability and scalability features for mission-critical database systems. Well- architected SANs offer much better throughput and reduced I/O latency then Direct Attached Storage (DAS). SANs can also scale up to handle many more disk arrays than DAS.

The main disadvantage of SANs is the higher cost and complexity to implement and maintain SANs.

Choosing the Right Type of Storage

The type of storage for your SQL Server installation depends on your specific needs. As you learned from the brief preceding comparison, DAS is a lot less expensive and easier to configure and maintain than a SAN; however, SANs offer many performance, availability, and scalability benefits.

A key element to take into consideration when choosing a storage system is the disk drive technology used in your storage system and how these disk drives are pooled together. Both DAS and SANs use an array of disk drives that are usually configured to create a storage pool that can then be presented to a server as a single entity.

In the next section, you learn about the different disk drive technologies and how they can be pooled together through RAID levels.

Disk Drives

As previously discussed, an important consideration involves the amount of throughput necessary to support your IO requirements. To satisfy large throughput requirements, you often need to spread reads and writes over a large number of fast-spinning disk drives.

Spreading these IO operations means storing small chunks of the data on each of the disk drives that are lumped together. In this type of distributed storage, no single disk drive contains the complete data. Therefore, a failure on one disk means total data loss. This is the reason you should always consider reliability with any decision for storage systems. To avoid data loss due to a disk failure, special arrangement of disks called *disk arrays* or RAID can be configured to satisfy both throughput and reliability. Choosing the right disk RAID level is a key decision that can impact overall server performance. Table 2-3 describes the most common disk RAID levels used for SQL Server environments.

TABLE 2-3: Commonly Used RAID Levels

RAID LEVEL	DESCRIPTION
RAID 0	Also known as a stripe set or striped volume. Two or more disks lumped together to form a larger volume. No fault tolerance. Fast read/writes.
RAID 1	Also known as mirrored drives. Data written identically to two drives. One drive can fail with no data loss. Slower writes. Only half of total raw storage available.
RAID 1+0	Also known as RAID 10. Mirrored sets in a striped set. Better write performance and fault tolerance. Only half of total raw storage available.
RAID 0+1	Striped sets in a mirrored set. Less fault tolerant than RAID 1+0. Good write performance.
RAID 5	Tolerates one drive failure. Writes are distributed among drives. Faster reads, slow writes. Some raw storage space lost.
RAID 6	Tolerates two drive failures. Faster reads, slower writes than RAID 5 due to added overhead of parity calculations. Similar raw storage loss as RAID 5.

In recent years, a faster type of disk drive technology has become more and more popular as it has become more affordable and reliable. This faster type of disk drive is called Solid State Drives (SSD) and involves drives that have no moving parts. SSD offer as much as 100x better read-and-write throughput than spinning disk drives. SQL Server can reap the benefits of faster read-and-write operations, especially for databases with high IO demand.

Adoption of SSD drives has grown in the last couple of years due in part to improved reliability and cost reduction. Several SAN storage system vendors also offer SSD drive arrays.

Even with the added reliability that SSD drives offer by eliminating spinning disks, SSDs should still be protected by RAID. SSD drives are still susceptible to electronic component failures and corruption.

Another key element to consider when selecting your storage system and in particular if you are leaning toward DAS, is the disk controller. In the following section you learn about specific features of disk controllers that improve DAS performance and reliability.

Disk Controllers

Disk controllers are a critical piece of hardware that you need to select with special care when using direct attached disk drives. Disk controllers can be the source of major IO bottlenecks because they have throughput limits as well.

Fast drives are not enough to ensure a fast storage system. Disk controllers can add an additional layer of overhead if not correctly configured. Most disk controllers provide settings that you can customize to your specific workloads. For example, you can configure a disk controller to be optimized for a higher percentage of write operations for high-transaction systems. You can optimize disk controllers dedicated to reporting database systems such as data warehouses and operational data stores for heavy read operations.

Another important consideration about disk controllers is write caching. Although this feature is handy to improve write operation performance, unexpected consequences can also occur, such as data loss and database corruption.

Disk controllers improve write operations by temporarily storing data in their cache and eventually flushing it to disk in batches. When the data is saved in the disk controller's cache, SQL Server acknowledges this as a committed transaction. In reality, the data has not been committed to disk and exists only in memory space. If a server is unexpectedly shut down without waiting for disk controllers to commit their cached data to disk, this data does not make it to the database transaction log, resulting in data loss.

Critical database environments should consider using enterprise-level disk controllers with redundant sources of power such as UPS and internal disk controller batteries to avoid potential data loss.

Software and Install Options

The next step is to ensure that several important configuration options are set up, correctly such as proper database file location and setting up the right service accounts.

Collation

SQL Server collation specifies a set of rules that store, sort, and compare characters. Collation is important because it specifies the code page used. Different code pages support different characters and behave differently when sorting or comparing strings. Setting the wrong collation may force you to reinstall your SQL Server instance as changing the collation of an instance can be complex.

You need to understand the locale requirements, sorting, case, and accent sensitivity of the data in your organization and your customers to determine which collation to use. The code page that a Windows Server uses can be found under `Control Panel ⇨ Regional Settings`. The code page selected for the Windows Server may not always be the code page required for you SQL Server instance.

Following are two types of collations: SQL Server and Windows.

SQL Server Collation

SQL Server collations affect the code page used to store data in `char`, `varchar`, and `text` columns. They affect how comparisons and sorting are done on these data types. For example, if you were to create a `SELECT` statement such as the following against a case-sensitive collation database, it would not return the employee named Jose stored in proper case as shown here.

```
 SELECT FROM Employees
WHERE EmployeeFirstName='JOSE'

Results: <none>

SELECT FROM Employees
WHERE EmployeeFirstName='Jose'

Results: Jose
```

Windows Collation

Windows collations use rules based on the chosen Windows locale for the operating system. The default behavior is that comparisons and sorting follow the rules used for a dictionary in the associated language. You may specify binary, case, accent, Kana, and width sensitivity. The key point is that Windows collations ensure that single-byte and double-byte character sets behave the same way in sorts and comparisons.

Case-Sensitivity

Your collation is either case-sensitive or not. Case-sensitive means that U is different from u. This is true for everything in the region to which the collation applies (in this case, master, model, resource, tempdb, and msdb). This is true for all the data in those databases. Here is the gotcha: Think about what the data in those databases actually is; it includes data in all the system tables, which means object names are also case-sensitive.

Sort Order

The collation you choose also affects sorting. Binary orders (Latinl_General_BIN, for instance) sort based on the bit value of the character; they are case-sensitive. Consider the following select statement for a table that contains employee names for Mary, Tom, mary, and tom, as seen in Figure 2-1. If you choose a dictionary sort order (Latinl_General_CS_AI, for instance), the previous statement would yield the following result set shown in Figure 2-2.

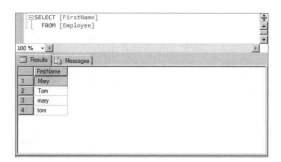

FIGURE 2-1

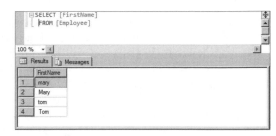

FIGURE 2-2

Service Accounts

Service accounts are an important part of your security model. When choosing service accounts, consider the principle of least privilege. Service accounts should only have the minimum required permissions to operate. Separate service accounts should be used for each service to track what each service is doing individually. Service accounts should always be assigned strong passwords. You can choose from several service account options:

➤ **Windows or Domain account:** This active directory or Windows account that you create is the preferred account type for SQL Server services needing network access.

➤ **Local System account:** This highly privileged account should not be used for services because it acts as the computer on the network and has no password. A compromised process using the Local System account can also compromise your database system.

➤ **Local Service account:** This special, preconfigured account has the same permissions as members of the Users group. Network access is done as a null session with no credentials. This account is unsupported.

➤ **Network Service account:** The same as the Local Service account, except that network access is allowed, credentialed as the computer account. Do not use this account for SQL Server or SQL Agent Service accounts.

➤ **Local Server account:** This local Windows account that you create is the most secure method you can use for services that do not need network access.

You should use dedicated Windows or domain accounts for production systems. Some organizations chose to create a single domain account for all their SQL Server instances, whereas others choose to create individual domain accounts for each service. Either one works as long as the service account passwords are strong and secured.

INSTALLING SQL SERVER

In this section you learn about the different types of installations: new installs, side-by-side installs, and upgrades. You also learn to perform unattended and attended installs using the graphical user interface (GUI), the Command Prompt, Configuration Files, and PowerShell scripts. More details about upgrades are covered in Chapter 3, "Upgrading SQL Server 2012 Best Practices."

New Installs

A new install occurs when you have a clean slate and no other SQL Server components are on the server. Check the directories and the Registry to ensure that you have a clean system and that you have no remnants of previous SQL installs.

Side-by-Side Installs

SQL Server also supports a side-by-side install. A side-by-side install occurs when you have multiple instances of SQL Server on a single server. SQL Server 2012 supports multiple instances of the Database Engine, Reporting Services, and Analysis Services on the same box. It also runs side by side with previous versions of SQL Server. If the existing instance is a default instance, your new install must be a named instance because only one default instance can exist on each server.

The biggest issue with side-by-side installs is memory contention. Make sure you set up your memory so that each instance does not try to acquire the entire physical memory. IO contention can also become an issue if database files from the different instances share the same storage resources.

Upgrades

If SQL Server components exist on the box, you can upgrade the existing instance. In this case, you install SQL Server on top of the existing instance, also known as in-place upgrade. To upgrade to SQL Server 2012 from a previous version of SQL Server, you launch the Upgrade Wizard from the SQL Server Installation Center using the Upgrade from SQL Server 2005, SQL Server 2008, or SQL Server 2008 R2 shortcut under the Installation tab.

Unattended Installs

SQL Server 2012 enables you to perform unattended installations via command-line parameters or a configuration file. Unattended installations enable you to install SQL Server with the exact same configuration on multiple servers with little or no user interaction during the setup process. All screen entries and dialog responses are made automatically using stored information in the configuration file or by passing them as command-line parameters.

Unattended Installation From the Command Line

To perform a new SQL Server 2012 installation from the command line, follow these steps.

1. Launch the Command Prompt window with elevated Administrator privileges by right-clicking on the Command Prompt executable and selecting Run as Administrator. The Command Prompt window opens.

2. In the Command line type the following command, and press Enter:

```
D:\setup.exe /ACTION=install /QS /INSTANCENAME="MSSQLSERVER" /
IACCEPTSQLSERVERLICENSETERMS=1
/FEATURES=SQLENGINE,SSMS
/SQLSYSADMINACCOUNTS="YourDomain\Administrators"
```

Your installation path may differ depending on your installation media. Parameters may vary depending on desired features to be installed. Also, you need to change the value for /SQLSYSADMINACCOUNTS *to a valid domain name and user account.*

This command line script performs an unattended installation of SQL Server Database Engine and SQL Server Management Tools - Basic. Table 2-4 describes each command-line parameter used in the preceding script.

TABLE 2-4: Command-Line Parameters

PARAMETER	DESCRIPTION
/ACTION	Specifies the action to be performed. In this case, a new installation.
/QS	Specifies that Setup runs and shows the installation progress but no input is accepted and no error messages are displayed.
/INSTANCENAME	Specifies required instance name.
/IACCEPTSQLSERVERLICENSETERMS	Required to acknowledge acceptance of the license terms when using /Q or /QS.
/FEATURES	Required parameter to specify features to install.
/SQLSYSADMINACCOUNTS	Required to provide members of the sysadmin role.

For a complete list of command-line parameters, visit http://msdn.microsoft.com/en-us/library/ms144259(v=sql.110).aspx.

Unattended Installation From a Configuration File

By default, SQL Server 2012 Setup creates a configuration file that logs the options and parameter values specified during an installation. This configuration file is useful for validation and auditing purposes. It is especially useful to deploy additional SQL Server installations using the same configurations.

To create a Configuration File, follow these steps:

1. Launch Setup.exe from your SQL Server 2012 installation media. SQL Server Setup launches.

2. Specify the options and parameters for your SQL Server 2012 installation. All options and values specified are recorded in the Configuration File as you go through the Setup Wizard.

3. Follow the Setup Wizard until the Ready to Install screen displays, as shown in Figure 2-1.

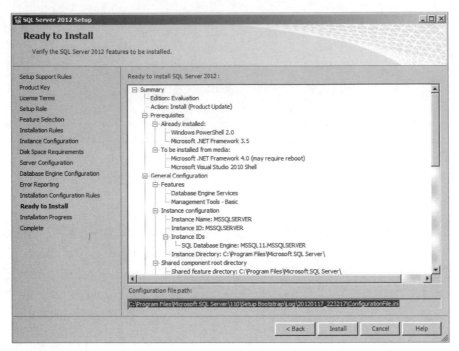

FIGURE 2-3

Notice in Figure 2-3 the path to `ConfigurationFile.ini`. At this point, the Configuration File has been created, and all options and parameter values specified in previous screens have been recorded.

4. Open Windows Explorer, and navigate to the folder where the Configuration File has been created. Click the Cancel button to stop the SQL Server 2012 Setup Wizard.

5. Locate `ConfigurationFile.ini` and copy it to a folder that can be referenced for unattended installs. For example, use a shared folder `\\fileserver\myshare`.

6. Open `ConfigurationFile.ini` to modify it. Make the following changes to prepare the file for unattended installs.

➤ Set `QUIET` = `"True"`

➤ Set `SQLSYSADMINACCOUNTS` = `"YourDomain\Administrators"`

➤ Set `IACCEPTSQLSERVERLICENSETERMS` = `"True"`

➤ Remove `ADDCURRENTUSERASSQLADMIN`

➤ Remove `UIMODE`

After you have customized the Configuration File for unattended installations, use the Command Prompt to execute `Setup.exe` and specify the path to the Configuration File. The following command line script exemplifies the syntax.

```
D:\Setup.exe /ConfigurationFile=\\fileserver\myshare\ConfigurationFile.ini
```

Scripted Installation with PowerShell

You can also use PowerShell to perform unattended installs. Simple PowerShell scripts can be written to execute SQL Server 2012 Setup through its command-line interface. For example, you can execute the command-line script used in the previous section from the command line as follows.

```
$cmd = "d:\setup.exe /ACTION=install /Q /INSTANCENAME="MSSQLSERVER" /
IACCEPTSQLSERVERLICENSETERMS=1
/FEATURES=SQLENGINE,SSMS
/SQLSYSADMINACCOUNTS="YourDomain\Administrators";
Invoke-Expression -command $cmd | out-null;
```

More complex PowerShell scripts can be written for larger SQL Server 2012 deployments. A common approach is the use of PowerShell functions that accept the setup parameters necessary to perform unattended installations. These PowerShell functions are then executed in batches or inside a process that loops through a list of server names with corresponding parameters.

For example, a PowerShell function can be saved in a PowerShell script file and called along with setup parameters to perform a large scale unattended deployment of SQL Server 2012. Listing 2-1 provides an example of a PowerShell function that can be used for SQL Server 2012 unattended installations.

LISTING 2-1: Install-Sql2012.ps1

Available for
download on
Wrox.com

```
Function Install-Sql2012
{
 param
 (
  [Parameter(Position=0,Mandatory=$false)][string] $Path,
  [Parameter(Position=1,Mandatory=$false)][string] $InstanceName =
   "MSSQLSERVER",
  [Parameter(Position=2,Mandatory=$false)][string] $ServiceAccount,
  [Parameter(Position=3,Mandatory=$false)][string] $ServicePassword,
  [Parameter(Position=4,Mandatory=$false)][string] $SaPassword,
  [Parameter(Position=5,Mandatory=$false)][string] $LicenseKey,
  [Parameter(Position=6,Mandatory=$false)][string] $SqlCollation =
  "SQL_Latin1_General_CP1_CI_AS",
  [Parameter(Position=7,Mandatory=$false)][switch] $NoTcp,
  [Parameter(Position=8,Mandatory=$false)][switch] $NoNamedPipes
 )
#Build the setup command using the install mode
if ($Path -eq $null -or $Path -eq "")
{
#No path means that the setup is in the same folder
$command = 'setup.exe /Action="Install"'
}
else
{
#Ensure that the path ends with a backslash
if(!$Path.EndsWith("\"))
{
 $Path += "\"
```

continues

LISTING 2-1 *(continued)*

```
}
$command = $path + 'setup.exe /Action="Install"'
}
#Accept the license agreement - required for command line installs
$command += ' /IACCEPTSQLSERVERLICENSETERMS'
#Use the QuietSimple mode (progress bar, but not interactive)
$command += ' /QS'
#Set the features to be installed
$command += ' /FEATURES=SQLENGINE,CONN,BC,SSMS,ADV_SSMS'
#Set the Instance Name
$command += (' /INSTANCENAME="{0}"' -f $InstanceName)
#Set License Key only if a value was provided,
#else install Evaluation edition
if ($LicenseKey -ne $null -and $LicenseKey -ne "")
{
 $command += (' /PID="{0}"' -f $LicenseKey)
}
#Check to see if a service account was specified
if ($ServiceAccount -ne $null -and $ServiceAccount -ne "")
{
#Set the database engine service account
$command += (' /SQLSVCACCOUNT="{0}" /SQLSVCPASSWORD="{1}"
/SQLSVCSTARTUPTYPE="Automatic"' -f
$ServiceAccount, $ServicePassword)
#Set the SQL Agent service account
$command += (' /AGTSVCACCOUNT="{0}" /AGTSVCPASSWORD="{1}"
 /AGTSVCSTARTUPTYPE="Automatic"' -f
$ServiceAccount, $ServicePassword)
}
else
{
#Set the database engine service account to Local System
$command += ' /SQLSVCACCOUNT="NT AUTHORITY\SYSTEM"
/SQLSVCSTARTUPTYPE="Automatic"'
#Set the SQL Agent service account to Local System
$command += ' /AGTSVCACCOUNT="NT AUTHORITY\SYSTEM"
 /AGTSVCSTARTUPTYPE="Automatic"'
}
#Set the server in SQL authentication mode if SA password was provided
if ($SaPassword -ne $null -and $SaPassword -ne "")
{
$command += (' /SECURITYMODE="SQL" /SAPWD="{0}"' -f $SaPassword)
}
#Add current user as SysAdmin
$command += (' /SQLSYSADMINACCOUNTS="{0}"' -f
 [Security.Principal.WindowsIdentity]::GetCurrent().Name)
#Set the database collation
$command += (' /SQLCOLLATION="{0}"' -f $SqlCollation)
#Enable/Disable the TCP Protocol
if ($NoTcp)
{
 $command += ' /TCPENABLED="0"'
}
```

```
else
{
 $command += ' /TCPENABLED="1"'
}
#Enable/Disable the Named Pipes Protocol
if ($NoNamedPipes)
{
 $command += ' /NPENABLED="0"'
}
else
{
 $command += ' /NPENABLED="1"'
}
if ($PSBoundParameters['Debug'])
{
 Write-Output $command
}
else
{
 Invoke-Expression $command
}
}
```

After you download Listing 2-1 from the Wrox companion website, save it to a folder, for example `c:\scripts`. Because this is a file that you download from the Internet, you may be required to right-click the file and unblock it. When downloaded, execute this function by following these steps.

1. Launch the PowerShell command line with elevated Administrator privileges by right-clicking the PowerShell executable and selecting Run as Administrator. The PowerShell command line opens.

2. Verify that you can run and load unsigned PowerShell scripts and files. In the PowerShell command line, type **get-executionpolicy** to verify the current execution policy. If it is not set to RemoteSigned you need to change it to this value by executing the following command:

```
Set-ExecutionPolicy RemoteSigned
```

3. Next, load the PowerShell function in the script file by executing the following command:

```
. c:\scripts\Install-Sql2012.ps1
```

Notice the . and blank space before the script file path. The . and blank space is a required character to dot-source the script file.

4. Verify that the function has been loaded by issuing the following command:

```
get-command Install-Sql2012
```

A single row is returned showing CommandType Function and Name Install-Sql2012.

5. At this point you are ready to invoke the PowerShell function you just loaded. Invoke the Install-Sql2012 as follows:

```
Install-Sql2012 -Param1 Param1Value -Param2 Param2Value ..
```

For example, the following command invokes the `Install-Sql2012` function and sets the SQL Server service account and password along with the Instance Name and initiates a SQL Server 2012 installation.

```
Install-Sql2012 -Path d:\ -ServiceAccount "winserver\Administrator" -
ServicePassword "P@ssword"
-SaPassword "P@ssword"
-InstanceName "MyInstanceName"
```

 The SQL Server 2012 installation path may differ depending on your installation media.

Figure 2-4 shows the PowerShell Command-line window with the steps necessary to invoke the `Install-Sql2012` function.

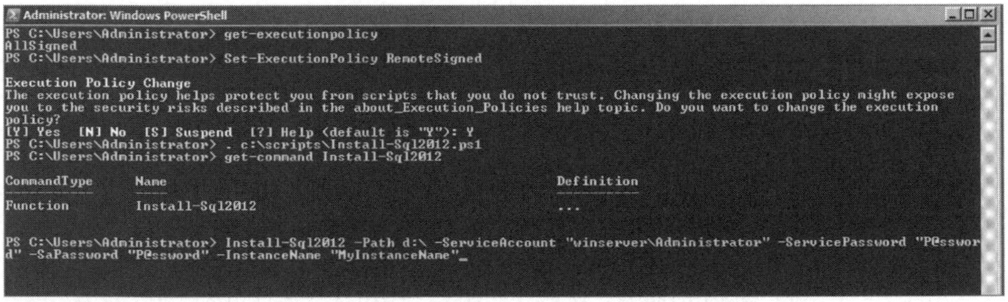

FIGURE 2-4

 A community-based project called SPADE that automates SQL Server installations using PowerShell is available for download at Codeplex.com. For more information about this project visit `http://sqlspade.codeplex.com/`.

Attended Installations

The simplest and most common way SQL Server is deployed is through attended installs using the GUI that the Setup Wizard provides. Attended installs require frequent user interaction to provide the information and parameter values required to complete a SQL Server 2012 installation.

To initiate an attended SQL Server 2012 install, follow these steps.

1. Launch `Setup.exe` from your SQL Server 2012 installation media. The Installation Center opens, as shown in Figure 2-5.

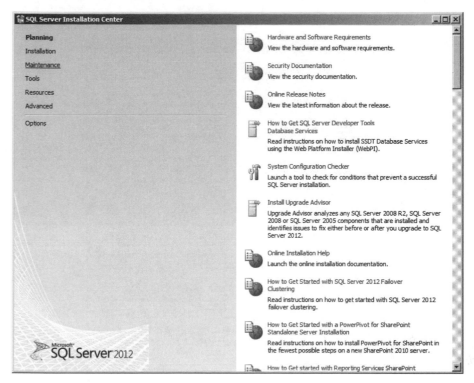

FIGURE 2-5

2. Click the Installation tab on the left, and then click the first option on the right titled New SQL Server Standard Installation or Add Feature to an Existing Installation The SQL Server 2012 Setup Wizard launches.

3. The Setup Support Rules runs to identify problems that may occur during the Setup Support Files installation. When this step finishes click OK. The Install Setup Files process initiates.

4. After the Install Setup Files completes, a second set of Setup Support Rules need to be checked. Click OK to continue.

5. Depending on the installation media and your license agreement, you may be prompted to select the SQL Server Edition and to enter a Product Key on the next screen. Click OK to continue.

6. The License Agreement screen opens. Accept the terms and click Next.

7. The Setup Role screen opens. Select the SQL Server Feature Installation option, and click Next.

8. The Feature Selection screen opens. Select Database Engine Services and Management Tools -Basic, and click Next. Figure 2-6 shows the list of features available to install in SQL Server 2012.

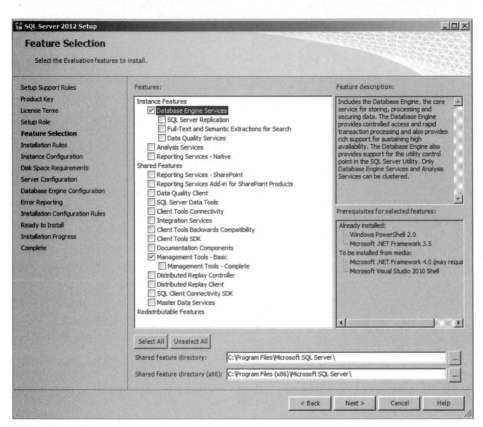

FIGURE 2-6

9. The Installation Rules screen opens to determine if anything can cause the installation process to lock. Click Next.

10. The Instance Configuration opens. In this screen you can decide to install the instance as a default instance or as a named instance. You can also provide an instance ID and change the default root directory. Click Next.

11. The Disk Space Requirements screen opens and displays a summary of space to be used by the features selected. Click Next.

12. The Server Configuration screen opens. Provide the service accounts under which SQL Server Database Engine, SQL Server Agent, and SQL Server Browser run under and the Collation to be used by SQL Server 2012. Click Next. Figure 2-7 shows the Server Configuration screen.

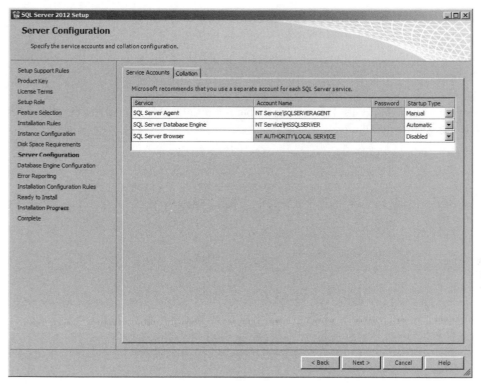

FIGURE 2-7

 As a Security best practice, always consider choosing Service Accounts following the principle of least privilege. Avoid whenever possible assigning Service Accounts that have elevated privileges in the domain or server.

13. The Database Engine Configuration screen opens. Specify the Authentication Mode, SQL Server Administrators, and default Data Directories, and enable FILESTREAM. It is important to assign at least one account that has SQL Server Administrator privileges on this screen. Also, the Authentication Mode needs to be defined on this screen either as Windows Authentication or Mixed mode. If Windows Authentication Mode is chosen, only authenticated windows accounts can log in. If Mixed Mode is chosen, both windows accounts and SQL Server accounts can log in. Click Next.

 Do not to leave the SA password blank. Always assign a strong password, and disable it after installation completes to avoid security attacks targeting this well-known account.

14. The Error Reporting opt-in screen opens. Choose to opt-in to send error reports to Microsoft by checking the opt-in check box. Click Next.

15. The Installation Configuration Rules screen opens. After the Installation Configuration Rules scan completes, click Next.

16. The Ready to Install screen opens. At this point all required information has been gathered by the Setup Wizard and displays for review before initiating the installation process. Click Install to start the installation.

This finalizes the attended installation process of SQL Server 2012.

 Microsoft makes available sample databases for download specifically for SQL Server 2012. You can download these sample databases along with sample project files for free from Codeplex.com at `http://msftdbprodsamples.codeplex.com/.`

INSTALLING ANALYSIS SERVICES

SQL Server Analysis Services is a straightforward installation. You can include it with other SQL Server 2012 features and services, or install it separately, as shown in Figure 2-8.

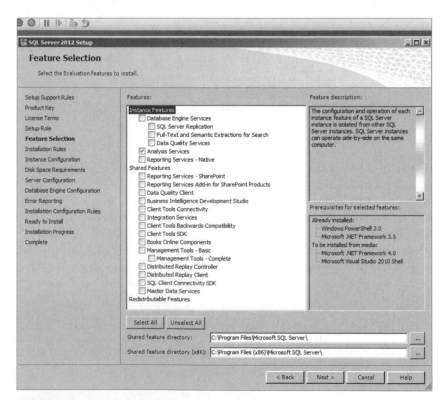

FIGURE 2-8

New in SQL Server 2012 is the option to install Analysis Services in either of two modes:

➤   Multidimensional and Data Mining Mode (UDM mode)

➤   Tabular Mode

The option to choose between these two modes is available in the Analysis Services Configuration screen in SQL Server 2012 Setup, as shown in Figure 2-9.

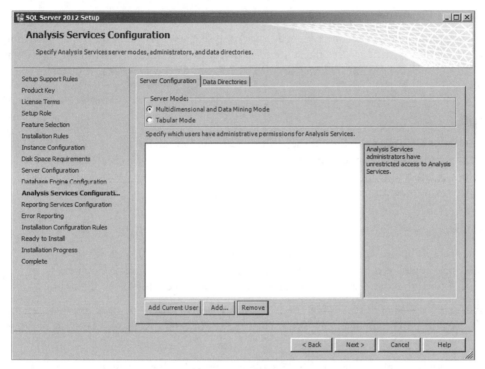

FIGURE 2-9

In the next sections, both Analysis Services modes are described briefly.

Multidimensional and Data Mining Mode (UDM Mode)

Analysis Services Multidimensional and Data Mining mode (UDM Mode), installs the traditional Analysis Services engine available since SQL Server 2005. This engine is based on the Unified Dimensional Model (UDM).

The UDM serves as an intermediate layer between one or more data sources and consolidates all the business rules. UDM acts as the hub of the multidimensional model, enabling users to query, aggregate, drill down, and slice and dice large Analysis Services databases with blink-of-an-eye response times.

The Analysis Services UDM mode supports MOLAP, ROLAP, and HOLAP storage and processing modes described in the next sections.

MOLAP (Multidimensional OLAP)

In MOLAP storage mode, data is stored and aggregated in one or more partitions of the multidimensional database. This storage mode is designed to maximize query performance. Data stored in MOLAP storage mode is current as of the last processing time.

ROLAP (Relational OLAP)

In ROLAP storage mode, data is not stored within the Analysis Services database. If queries cannot be satisfied from the query cache, it uses internal indexed views to retrieve data from the relational data source. Query times can be much slower than MOLAP, but data is more real time as its source transactional system.

HOLAP (Hybrid OLAP)

In HOLAP storage mode, some portions of the multidimensional database are stored in MOLAP, and some portions are retrieved directly from its relational source. Queries that access more aggregated data are satisfied from its multidimensional store as in MOLAP. Drill-down queries are retrieved directly from its relational data sources as in ROLAP.

Tabular Mode

The Analysis Services Tabular Mode is based on a new database engine called the VertiPaq engine. The Vertipaq engine is a column-based database that enables high levels of compression due to the reduced need to store discrete values along with advanced compression algorithms.

The ability to compress large amounts of data enables the Vertipaq engine to store, retrieve, and manipulate data from RAM memory much faster than the traditional disk-based Analysis Services engine.

Tabular Mode supports the new Semantic Model called Business Intelligence Semantic Model (BISM). The development environment is similar to that of the PowerPivot add-in for Excel. The PowerPivot add-in for Excel runs a scaled down version of the same Vertipaq engine that Analysis Services Tabular Mode uses.

Similar to the traditional Analysis UDM engine, Analysis Services Tabular Mode supports querying from its in-memory storage or directly from the relational data source or a hybrid of both. These query mode options are available in the BISM model properties. The four available query mode options include the following:

1. Vertipaq
2. Direct Query
3. InMemorywithDirectQuery
4. DirectQueryWithInMemory

These four query mode options are described in the next sections.

Vertipaq Query Mode

In Vertipaq Query Mode, data is stored and queried from in-memory stored datasets. Little or no latency is involved as disk IO latency costs are minimized or eliminated. Because of its in-memory dataset access, complex calculations and sorting operations are almost instantaneous.

Vertipaq Query Mode is similar to MOLAP storage in the traditional Analysis Services engine in that it holds point-in-time (PIT) data. If data changes in its relation data source, its in-memory storage needs to be refreshed with the new datasets.

Direct Query Mode

In Direct Query Mode, also known as pass-through mode, queries are processed by its data source, in most cases a relational database. The Direct Query Mode advantage over Vertipaq Query Mode resides on it is capability to provide real-time datasets over larger data volumes that cannot fit in-memory.

Similar to ROLAP in the traditional Analysis Services engine, Direct Query Mode is designed for real-time access requirements of the data source.

InMemoryWithDirectQueryMode

In this query mode, unless otherwise specified by the connection strings from the client, queries use the dataset stored in cache by default. It supports the ability for the client to switch to real-time data.

DirectQueryWithInMemoryMode

Opposite to InMemoryWithDirectQuery Mode, unless otherwise specified by the connection strings from the client, queries use the relational data source by default. It supports the ability for the client to switch to cached data.

INSTALLING POWERPIVOT FOR SHAREPOINT

PowerPivot for SharePoint Mode is a feature role option available since SQL Server 2008 R2. The PowerPivot for SharePoint option shown installs a version of the new Analysis Services Vertipaq engine to support server-side processing and management of PowerPivot workbooks that you publish to SharePoint 2010.

PowerPivot for SharePoint must be installed in a server joined to a domain, SharePoint 2010 Enterprise with Service Pack 1 and the instance name PowerPivot to be available on the server where it is installed.

To install PowerPivot for SharePoint follow these steps:

1. Launch Setup.exe from your SQL Server 2012 installation media. The Installation Center opens.

2. Click the Installation tab on the left, and then click the first option on the right titled New SQL Server Standard Installation or Add Feature to an Existing Installation. The SQL Server 2012 Setup Wizard launches.

3. The Setup Support Rules runs to identify problems that may occur during the setup support files installation. When this step finishes, click OK. The Install Setup Files process initiates.

4. When the Install Setup Files completes, a second set of Setup Support Rules need to be checked. Click OK to continue.

5. Depending on the installation media and your license agreement, you may be prompted to select the SQL Server Edition and to enter a Product Key on the next screen. Click OK to continue.

6. The License Agreement screen opens. Accept the terms and click Next.

7. The Setup Role screen opens. Select the PowerPivot for SharePoint option. You can also install an instance of SQL Server Database Services with this installation by checking the check box below, as shown in Figure 2-10.

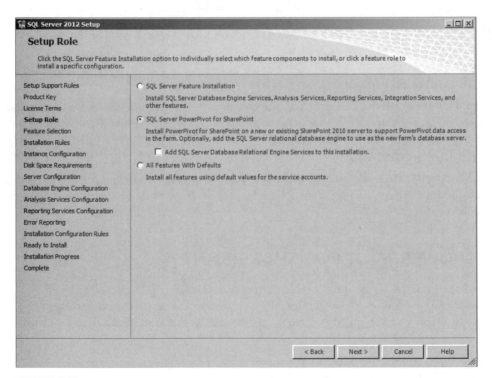

FIGURE 2-10

8. Click Next. The Feature Selection screen opens. The options are preselected and displayed for informational purposes.

9. Click Next. The Installation Rules screen opens to determine if anything can cause the installation process to fail. Click Next.

10. The Instance Configuration screen opens. You cannot change the instance name because it needs to be PowerPivot. Only the instance ID can be modified. Click Next.

11. The Disk Space Requirements screen opens and displays a summary of space to be used by the features selected. Click Next.

12. The Server Configuration screen opens. In this screen you provide the service account under which the Analysis Services Engine runs. A domain account is required. Click Next.

13. The Analysis Services Configuration screen opens. Add domain accounts that require administrative permissions of the Analysis Services instance.

14. Click next until you reach the Ready to Install screen. Review the installation summary page, and click Install.

This finalizes the installation steps of PowerPivot for SharePoint.

BURNING IN THE SYSTEM

Before you move a system into common use, you should "burn it in." This means that you should stress the server. It is not unusual for a server to work in production for months or years with a hardware problem that existed at the time the server was deployed. Many of these failures do not show up when the server is under a light load but become immediately evident when you push the server hard.

You can use several free tools to burn in and stress test a database server to ensure that the storage system is ready to handle required IO workloads, memory pressure, and CPU processing power demand. Some of these tools include the following:

➤ **SQLIOSim:** Free tool by Microsoft designed to generate similar SQL Server IO read and write patterns. This tool is great to test IO intensive operations such as DBCC CHECKDB and Bulk insert, delete, and update operations. SQLIOSim replaces SQLIOStress. You can download SQLIOSim at http://support.microsoft.com/kb/231619.

➤ **IOMeter:** Another free tool great for running a stress test with capability to simulate concurrent application workloads.

➤ **Prime95:** This free tool was designed to find Mersenne Prime numbers and is CPU and RAM memory-intensive. It can be customized to stress test CPU and memory workloads for sustained periods of time.

You can search online for several other free and paid applications that can perform an initial burn in and stress test. Some server and server component manufacturers also provide tools to benchmark and stress test your equipment.

POST-INSTALL CONFIGURATION

After you install SQL Server 2012, you need to configure additional settings and complete the tasks necessary to have a production-ready server. Some of these settings, including max server memory, parallelism threshold, and network packet size, are meant for fine-tuning the SQL Server instance for optimal performance. Other settings and tasks, typically changing default port, login auditing, and disabling SA account, are geared toward securing, auditing, and monitoring a SQL Server instance.

Configuring SQL Server Settings for Performance

SQL Server 2012 provides system settings that can be optimized to your particular environment and workload patterns. Some of the most important performance settings are discussed in the following sections.

Memory

Two important server property settings include maximum and minimum server memory. By default, SQL Server is configured with a minimum memory of 0MB and a maximum memory of 2,147,483647MB (2TB) as shown in Figure 2-11.

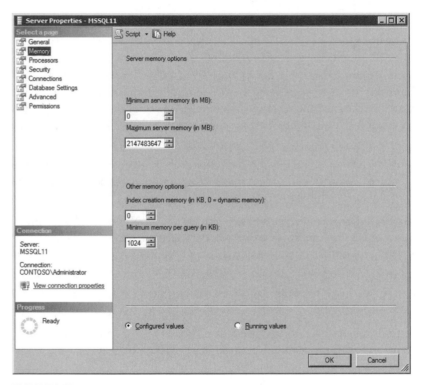

FIGURE 2-11

The consequences of leaving the default values for these two settings is sometimes misunderstood and often overlooked. The minimum server memory setting specifies the amount of memory that is not released back to the operating system by SQL Server when allocated. In other words, SQL Server holds on to this minimum amount of memory, even if it is no longer needed.

> *A common misconception is that SQL Server immediately allocates up to this minimum amount of memory upon startup. Actually, SQL Server allocates memory only as it is required and may or may not reach the minimum server memory value specified.*

The minimum server memory setting does not need to be changed unless the operating system constantly requests memory resources for other applications sharing the same memory space. You want to avoid releasing too much memory to the operating system because that could potentially starve a SQL Server instance from memory.

On the other hand, the maximum server memory sets limits for the maximum amount of memory a SQL Server instance can allocate. A value set too high can potentially starve an operating system from memory resources. The maximum server memory value should not equal or exceed the total amount of available server memory. This value should be at least 1GB less than the total server memory.

Network Packet Size

The default network packet size for SQL Server 2012 is 4,096 bytes. Setting a packet size larger than the default size can improve performance for SQL Server instances that experience a large number of bulk operations or that transfer large volumes of data.

If Jumbo Frames are supported and enabled by the server's hardware and the network infrastructure, increase the network packet size to 8,192 bytes.

Instant File Initialization

Each time a database file is created or needs to grow, it is first zero-filled by the operating system before the new space is made available for writing. This operation can be costly because all write operations are blocked until zero-fill completes. To avoid these types of blocks and waits, you can enable instant file initialization by adding the SQL Server service account to the list of users in the Perform Volume Maintenance Tasks policy under User Rights Assignment in the Local Policies of the server's Security Settings.

tempdb

One of the most important system databases that require special consideration and planning is tempdb. Over the years, tempdb has taken on more responsibility than it had in the past. Historically, tempdb has been used for internal processes such as some index builds and table variable storage, as well as temporary storage space by programmers. The following is a partial list of some of the uses for tempdb:

➤ Bulk load operations with triggers

➤ Common table expressions

➤ DBCC operations

➤ Event notifications

➤ Indexe rebuilds, including SORT_IN_TEMPDB, partitioned index sorts, and online index operations

➤ Large object type variables and parameters

➤ Multiple active result set operations

➤ Query notifications

➤ Row versioning

Creating additional `tempdb` files can dramatically improve performance in environments in which `tempdb` is used heavily. Depending on your workload, consider creating a number of `tempdb` files proportional to each logical CPU to enable SQL Server scheduler workers to loosely align to a file. Generally accepted ratios of `tempdb` files to logical CPUs vary between 1:2 and 1:4. In extreme cases, you may want to create one `tempdb` file per logical CPU (1:1 ratio). The only way to know how many `tempdb` files you should create is by testing.

An important consideration is the placement of `tempdb`. The `tempdb` file or files should be isolated from database and log files to avoid IO contention. If using multiple `tempdb` files, consider isolating each `tempdb` file in its own LUN and physical disks.

Properly sizing `tempdb` is crucial to optimize overall performance. Consider setting the initial size of `tempdb` something other than the default to avoid expensive file growths. The space to be preallocated depends on the expected workload and features enabled in your SQL Server instance.

A good methodology to estimate the initial size of `tempdb` is to analyze the query plan of the queries executed during a typical workload. In the query plan, query operators such as sort, hash match, and spool can provide important information to calculate size requirements. To estimate the space required by each operator, look at the number of rows and the row size reported by the operator. To calculate the space required, multiply the actual (or estimated) number of rows by the estimated row size. Although this method is not precise, it gives you a good reference point. Only experience and testing will guarantee more accurate sizing.

Model and User Databases

The model database is the most often overlooked system database. It serves as a template for all user databases. In other words, all database settings of the model database are inherited by each new database created in the SQL Server database instance.

Setting the model database's initial size, auto growth, and recovery model settings ensures that all user databases created are configured properly to optimize performance.

Set the initial database size to a size large enough to handle the expected volume of transactions in a large enough period of time. The key is to avoid constantly increasing the size of the database. When the database requires more space than originally allocated, you can allow it to automatically increase its size by enabling the *autogrowth* database setting. Even though you should enable autogrow, autogrow operations are expensive and time-consuming. Think of autogrow as an emergency growth operation. When you enable autogrow, choose a file-growth increment large enough so that autogrow operations do not frequently occur.

 You should never turn on the auto shrink database setting or schedule shrink operations on your database. Database shrinking operations can cause extensive waits and blocks, consume a lot of CPU, memory, and IO resources, and increase fragmentation.

Configuring SQL Server Settings for Security

SQL Server 2012 provides system settings that can be optimized for a more controlled and secure environment. Some of the most important security settings are discussed in the following sections.

SA Account

The SysAdmin (SA) account is a default system account with top level privileges in SQL Server. Because it is a well-known account, it is the target of a large number of exploit attacks. To eliminate exposure to these types of attacks, always assign a strong password that only you know and never gets used. Secure the password in a vault, and disable the SA account.

TCP/IP Ports

SQL Server uses the default TCP/IP port 1433 to communicate with clients. Named SQL Server instances on the other hand are dynamically assigned TCP/IP ports upon service startup. For hacking prevention and firewall configuration purposes, you may need to change default ports and control the port numbers over which named SQL Server instances communicate.

SQL Server 2012 includes a tool called SQL Server Configuration Manager (discussed in more detail later in this section) to manage SQL Server services and their related network configurations. You can find the SQL Server Configuration Manager under the `Microsoft SQL Server 2012\ Configuration Tools` folder in the Start menu. Figure 2-12 shows the TCP/IP Properties dialog box in SQL Server Configuration Manager where you can change the default 1433 port.

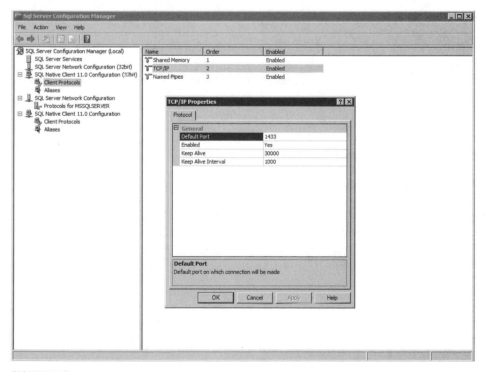

FIGURE 2-12

Service Packs and Updates

After a freshly installed SQL Server instance, you must review available updates. SQL Server updates may be available in the form of hotfixes, cumulative updates, and service packs. Carefully review all updates before applying them to avoid negatively impacting your applications. You absolutely want to install security fixes marked as critical to protect your database systems against known threats, worms, and vulnerabilities. Do not enable automatic updates on production SQL Server instances. Test all updates in a controlled testing environment before you apply them in production.

Additional SQL Server Settings

Additional SQL Server settings and properties are available through SQL Server Management Studio (SSMS) and the `sp_configure` System Stored Procedure.

For a complete list and description of all SQL Server configuration options available through the `sp_configure` System Stored Procedure, visit `http://msdn.microsoft.com/en-us/library/ms188787(v=sql.110).aspx`.

Chapter 4, "Managing and Troubleshooting the Database Engine," covers SQL Server configurations in more detail.

Best Practices Analyzer (BPA)

The Microsoft SQL Server 2012 Best Practices Analyzer (BPA) is a free diagnostic tool that gathers information about installed SQL Server 2012 instances, determines if the configurations align to recommended best practices, outlines settings that do not align to these recommendations, indicates potential problems, and recommends solutions.

BPA can help you identify potential issues for your SQL Server 2012 installation. It is always best to catch configuration issues before a server goes into production to avoid unplanned downtime.

You can download the Best Practices Analyzer for SQL Server 2012 at `http://technet.microsoft.com/en-us/sqlserver/bb671430`.

SQL Server Configuration Manager

The SQL Server Configuration Manager tool enables you to specify SQL Server Services options and whether these services are automatically or manually started after Windows starts. SQL Server Configuration Manager enables you to configure services settings such as service accounts, network protocols, and ports SQL Server listens on.

The SQL Server Configuration Manager can be accessed under Configuration Tools in the Microsoft SQL Server 2012 Program Menu folder. It is also available under Services and Applications in Computer Management Console.

Back It Up

Backup plans should be on your checklist after completing a SQL Server installation. You must define backup schedules and backup storage locations for system and user databases. In addition, if using encryption, you need to back up the encryption key.

Always create your backup files in a shared network drive or backup device and never on the same server being backed up. Consider keeping redundant copies of your backups and make sure that backups are secured and immediately available in case of a disaster.

Databases should be backed up in full or incrementally. Depending on the database recovery mode log, backups should also be part of your backup schedule to restore from the log if necessary. Refer to Chapter 17, "Backup and Recovery" for more details.

Define your backup retention policy to avoid storing unnecessary historical backups. Routinely restore backups to ensure they successfully restore at any given time to avoid surprises when facing a disaster. Remember, a good backup is as good as its last restore.

UNINSTALLING SQL SERVER

In some circumstances you need to uninstall a SQL Server instance completely due to problems such as incompatibility issues with a newer version or for licensing consolidation purposes. You can uninstall SQL Server using Programs and Features under Control Panel. During the uninstall process, you can choose to remove all or some of the features installed for a specific instance. If more than one instance is installed, the uninstall process prompts you to select the instance you want to remove.

Additional components and requirements installed during Setup may not be uninstalled and need to uninstalled separately.

Uninstalling Reporting Services

When you uninstall Reporting Services, you need to do manual cleanup on some items, as described in this section. Before the uninstall, though, you need to gather some information. Make sure you know which databases are used by this instance of Reporting Services. You can obtain this information using the Reporting Services Configuration tool. Discover which directory this instance of Reporting Services is installed in by running SQL Server Configuration Manager. You also need to discover which directory the Reporting Services usage and log files uses.

Uninstalling Reporting Services does not delete the ReportServer databases. You must manually delete these, or a new Reporting Services instance can reuse them.

Uninstalling Analysis Services

Uninstalling Analysis Services also requires some manual cleanup. You should always gather some information prior to the uninstall. Discover which directory this instance of Analysis Services is installed in by running SQL Server Configuration Manager.

Although the normal uninstall does not leave any databases behind, it does leave all the Analysis Services log files. The default location is the Analysis Services install directory or the alternative location you previously discovered. To delete them, simply delete the appropriate directories.

Uninstalling the SQL Server Database Engine

As with other services, log files are not deleted when you uninstall the SQL Server Database Engine. To delete them, simply delete the appropriate directories. You may need to separately remove the MS SQL Server Native Client, and you may find that some directories remain and must be manually removed as well.

If you have no other instances of SQL Server on your machine, instead of deleting only the 100 directory, under Program Files you can delete the entire MS SQL server directory. The .NET Framework is also left on the machine. If you want to remove it, do so from the Programs and Features in Control Panel, but make sure no other applications use it.

TROUBLESHOOTING A FAILED INSTALL

Failed installations may occur most commonly due to failed setup support and installation rules. During setup a series of rules are checked to identify issues that may prevent a successful SQL Server installation. When a rule failure is detected, it must be corrected before continuing. A rules error report link and description is always provided during attended installs, and error log files are generated for later review.

A detailed report is always available when a failure occurs. These reports provide valuable information to help you identify the root of the problem. In many cases, you can fix these failures by installing missing features or applications.

Error reports can be retrieved from the `%Program Files%\Microsoft SQL Server\110\Setup Bootstrap\Log` folder. Each installation attempt generates a time-stamped folder with detailed information stored in a log file that can help you troubleshoot any errors. For a complete list and description of the log files generated during Setup, visit `http://msdn.microsoft.com/en-us/library/ms143702(v=sql.110).aspx`.

SUMMARY

As you may conclude, installing SQL Server 2012 is generally quite simple and can be performed with little or no user interaction. Planning before you initiate an installation is key to a successful deployment. A successful SQL Server 2012 install starts with a good plan and a good definition of requirements. These requirements should define hardware and software requirements, prerequisites, authentication, collation, service accounts, file locations, and so on.

A successful SQL Server 2012 install does not conclude after the Setup Wizard completes. Several post-installation tasks require multiple default configuration settings to be modified such as max memory, parallelism thresholds, TCP/IP ports, patches, and more. You can use SQL Server Management Studio and SQL Server Configuration Manager to change these default configuration options. Database servers need to be burned in and stress tested to avoid unexpected behavior under heavy load.

If you plan to upgrade, Chapter 3 offers some good advice in that area.

3

Upgrading SQL Server 2012 Best Practices

Chapter 2, "Installing SQL Server 2012 Best Practices," covers performing a new installation of SQL Server 2012. This chapter discusses upgrading SQL Server from a previous version. The best strategy for a successful upgrade is planning and preparation. First, you cover reasons for upgrading to SQL Server 2012. You then consider the pros and cons of various upgrade strategies, and you learn about the various tools available to help mitigate risk during the upgrade process. Then you learn about SQL Server 2012 behavior changes and discontinued features that you need to know before upgrading. To wrap up, this chapter explores unexpected issues you might encounter after the upgrade. By the end of the chapter, you will have learned everything you need to know to perform a successful upgrade to SQL Server 2012.

WHY UPGRADE TO SQL SERVER 2012?

This book introduces significant enhancements throughout the product. During the development cycle, consider the three pillars of focus for the product: mission-critical confidence, breakthrough insight, and cloud on your terms. With the release of SQL Server 2012, Microsoft enhanced numerous features in the areas of scalability, reliability, availability, and security. Following are many benefits that these new features and capabilities provide:

- ➤ More efficient high availability and disaster recovery with AlwaysOn
- ➤ Support for column store indexes

- ➤ Built-in encryption capabilities

- ➤ Reduced operating system patching with support for Windows Server Core

- ➤ Accelerated I/O performance with new compression capabilities

- ➤ Default Schema for Groups

- ➤ SQL Server Audit for all editions

- ➤ Contained database authentication

- ➤ User-defined server roles

Risk Mitigation — the Microsoft Contribution

As with all previous versions of SQL Server, the SQL team took extraordinary steps to ensure that the quality of SQL Server 2012 is as high-grade as possible. The specific steps of the software engineering cycle are beyond the scope of this book, but a few points are highlighted here, considering public knowledge about the daily build process.

Today, a daily process produces x86, x64, and Itanium versions of SQL Server 2012 code (called *builds*) that have gone through a battery of tests. This process is utilized for both the development of new releases and the development of service packs for SQL Server 2012. These tests are a convergence of in-house build tests, customer-captured workloads, and Trustworthy Computing processes. Microsoft Research worked on bringing innovations to Microsoft's products. In the areas of software development, the Microsoft research team is an essential contributor to the software engineering and testing processes. It improves the test harness with enhancements in several areas, including threat modeling, testing efficiencies, and penetration analysis.

In addition, many customer-captured workloads are also part of the software testing harness. These workloads are acquired through an assortment of programs such as the Customer Playback program and various lab engagements, including SQL Server 2012 compatibility labs.

The daily builds are tested against this gathered information, and out of this process come performance metrics, security metrics, and bugs. Bugs are subsequently filed, assigned, prioritized, and tracked until resolution. After a bug is fixed, its code goes through security testing as part of the software engineering process. This happens before the code is checked back into the software tree for the next testing cycle. This rigorous development and quality assurance process helps ensure that the shipped product is reliable and ready for production environments. The bottom line is that the old adage, "Wait until the first service pack to upgrade," is no longer true for SQL Server 2012.

Independent Software Vendors and SQL Community Contributions

Starting with SQL Server 2005 and continuing with SQL Server 2012, the concept of community technology preview (CTP) was adopted. The November 2010 CTP was the first of several such releases, in addition to Release Candidate (RC) releases. The decision to adopt this snapshot in time of code (or build) resulted in hundreds of thousands of CTP and RC downloads, providing unprecedented access to updated code to both independent software vendor (ISV) and SQL community testing. At the time of this writing, Microsoft has published ten case studies detailing successful implementations of SQL Server 2012. This type of access to beta code was leveraged as a means to identify additional bugs, conducting additional testing of software fixes, and driving additional improvements based on community feedback.

UPGRADING TO SQL SERVER 2012

Chapter 2 covers the installation guidelines, so this section mainly focuses on upgrade strategies and considerations for the SQL Server 2012 database component. A smooth upgrade requires a good plan. When you devise an upgrade plan, you need to break down the upgrade process into individual tasks. This plan should have sections for pre-upgrade tasks, upgrade tasks, and post-upgrade tasks:

➤ Your *pre-upgrade tasks* consider SQL Server 2012 minimum hardware and software requirements. You should have an inventory of your applications that access the server, database-collation requirements, server dependencies, and legacy-systems requirements such as data-access methods. Your list should include database consistency checks and backup of all databases. Plans should be in place for testing the upgrade process and applications. You should have a thorough understanding of backward-compatibility issues and identify workarounds or fixes. You should also use the SQL Server 2012 Upgrade Advisor, as described later in this chapter, to assist in identifying and resolving these issues.

➤ The *upgrade execution process* is a smooth execution of your well-documented and rehearsed plan. To reiterate the importance of this step, ensure you make a backup of all the databases before you execute the upgrade process.

➤ *Post-upgrade tasks* consist of reviewing the upgrade process, bringing the systems back online, monitoring, and testing the system. You need to perform specific database maintenance before releasing the system to the user community. These and other recommended steps are outlined later in the chapter. Run your database in backward-compatibility mode after the upgrade to minimize the amount of change to your environment. Update the database-compatibility mode as part of a follow-up upgrade process and enable new SQL Server 2012 features.

As part of deciding your upgrade strategy, consider both in-place (upgrade) and side-by-side migration methods for upgrading.

In-Place Upgrading

The in-place server upgrade is the easier but riskier of the two options. This is an all-or-nothing approach to upgrading; meaning that after you initiate the upgrade there is no simple rollback procedure. This type of upgrade has the added requirement of greater upfront testing to avoid using a complex back-out plan. The benefit of this approach is that you don't need to worry about users and logins remaining in sync, and database connectivity changes are not be required for applications. In addition, SQL Server Agent jobs migrate during the upgrade process.

Following is a high-level scenario of an in-place upgrade based on Figure 3-1.

1. First, install the prerequisite files on your system. Before upgrading to SQL Server 2012, your server needs, at a minimum, the following:

   ➤ .NET Framework 4.0

   ➤ Windows PowerShell 2.0

   ➤ .NET 3.5 with Service Pack 1

   ➤ A current instance of SQL Server 2005, SQL Server 2008, or SQL Server 2008 R2

2. Next run the System Configuration Checker (SCC). The SCC examines the destination computer for conditions that would prevent an upgrade from completing, such as not meeting the minimum hardware or software requirements. If such a condition is found, setup aborts and the SQL Server 2012 components uninstall.

3. Once verified, the SQL Server setup program can lay the 2012 bits and backward-compatibility support files on a disk while SQL Server 2008 (or 2005) is still available to users. However, don't plan to upgrade a server while users are online. The setup program takes the server offline by stopping the existing SQL Server services. The 2012-based services assume control of the master database and the server identity. At this point, the SQL Server service takes over the databases and begins to update them while not allowing users back into the environment. When a request for data occurs in a database that has been only partially updated, the data associated with this request is updated, processed, and then returned to the user.

4. Finally, kick off the uninstall procedure for the old binaries. This step occurs only if no remaining SQL Server 2005 or 2008 instances are on the server. SQL Server Agent jobs are now migrated.

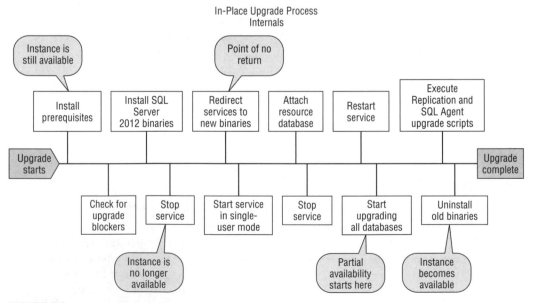

FIGURE 3-1

Following are the advantages of an in-place upgrade:

- ➤ Fast, easy, and automated (best for small systems).
- ➤ No additional hardware required.
- ➤ Applications retain same instance name.
- ➤ Preserves SQL Server 2008 (or 2005) functionality automatically.

The disadvantages of an in-place upgrade are as follows:

- ➤ Downtime incurred because the entire SQL Server instance is offline during upgrade.
- ➤ No support for component-level upgrades.
- ➤ Complex rollback strategy.
- ➤ Backward-compatibility issues must be addressed for that SQL instance.
- ➤ In-place upgrade is not supported for all SQL Server components.
- ➤ Large databases require substantial rollback time.

Additionally, if you would like to change editions as a part of your upgrade, you must be aware of some limitations. You can upgrade SQL Server 2005 and 2008 Enterprise, Developer, Standard, and Workgroup editions to different editions of SQL Server 2012. However, SQL Server 2005 and 2008 Express Editions may only be upgraded to SQL Server 2012 Express Edition. If this is of interest to you, see SQL Server 2012 Books Online (BOL), "Version and Edition Upgrades," under the section "Upgrading to SQL Server 2012."

Side-by-Side Upgrade

In a side-by-side upgrade, SQL Server 2012 installs either along with SQL Server 2008 (or 2005) as a separate instance or on a different server. This process is essentially a new installation followed by a database migration. You may want to select this option as part of a hardware refresh or migration to a new platform, such as Itanium or x64. Because of the backup and restore times involved in a back-out scenario, if you have a sizable database, this is definitely the option to use.

As part of this method, you can simply back up the databases from the original server and then restore them to the SQL Server 2012 instance. Other options are to manually detach your database from the old instance and reattach it to the new instance, use log shipping, or database mirroring. You can also leverage the Copy Database Wizard to migrate your databases to the new server. Although this approach provides for a good recovery scenario, it has additional requirements beyond those of the in-place upgrade, such as maintaining the original server name, caring for application connectivity, and keeping users and their logins in sync.

Following are the arguments in favor of a side-by-side upgrade:

- ➤ More granular control over upgrade component-level process (database, Analysis Services, and others)
- ➤ Ability to run SQL Servers side-by-side for testing and verification
- ➤ Ability to gather real matrix for upgrade (outage window)

➤ Rollback strategy because original server is still intact

➤ Best for large databases because restore time could be sizable

The arguments against a side-by-side upgrade are as follows:

➤ Does not preserve SQL Server 2008 (or 2005) functionality.

➤ Issue of instance name for connecting applications.

In-Place Upgrade versus Side-By-Side Upgrade Considerations

Consider numerous factors before selecting an upgrade strategy. Your strategy should include the need for a component-level upgrade, the ability to roll back in case of failure, the size of your databases, and the need for partial upgrade. Your top priorities might depend upon if you can upgrade to new hardware, facilitate a change of strategy such as a server consolidation, and manage a small server outage window for the upgrade. Table 3-1 shows a summary of the two upgrade methods.

TABLE 3-1: In-Place and Side-by-Side Upgrade Comparison

PROCESS	IN-PLACE UPGRADE	SIDE-BY-SIDE UPGRADE
Number of resulting instances	One	Two
Data file transfer	Automatic	Manual
SQL Server instance configuration	Automatic	Manual
Supporting upgrade utility	SQL Server setup	Various migration and data transfer methods

PRE-UPGRADE STEPS AND TOOLS

Now that you understand the reasons and options for upgrading to SQL Server 2012, you can move on to choosing your upgrade tools to assist in the upgrade process and performing pre-upgrade steps. Prior to the upgrade process, you can take preventative measures to avoid common upgrade issues, such as running out of disk space or executing startup stored procedures during the upgrade. There are also a number of tools that can help identify potential upgrade issues in your environment. The two most useful tools to aid in this process are the SQL Server Upgrade Advisor and the SQL Server Upgrade Assistant. These tools both provide pre-upgrade analysis and help you gain confidence that your upgrade will run successfully. Upgrade Assistant uses workload testing to test post-upgrade application behavior, while Upgrade Advisor performs in-place analysis of your databases for potential compatibility issues.

Pre-Upgrade Steps

There are a number of steps to take prior to performing the upgrade process. These precautions and preventative measures help eliminate nasty surprises during upgrade.

➤ Set your data and log files to autogrow during the upgrade process.

➤ Disable all startup stored procedures because the upgrade process stops and starts services on the SQL Server instance being upgraded.

➤ Before upgrading to SQL Server 2012, use the `sp_dropextendedproc` and `sp_addextendedproc` stored procedures to reregister any extended stored procedure not registered with the full pathname.

➤ Allocate additional space or have plenty of space for `tempdb` to grow during the upgrade process. Chapter 14, "Indexing Your Database," covers overall guidance for `tempdb` in greater detail.

`tempdb` *is responsible for managing temporary objects, row versioning, and online index rebuilds.*

➤ Disable all trace flags before upgrading to SQL Server 2012. The possibility exists that the trace-flag functionality is either different in SQL server 2012 or does not exist. After the upgrade process, you should work with Microsoft Support to determine which (if any) of your trace flags are still required.

➤ Migrate to database mail. SQL Mail has been discontinued.

Pre-Upgrade Tools

Performing an upgrade can be a daunting task. Mitigate the risk of a failed upgrade or unexpected post-upgrade behavior by examining your instances prior to performing the upgrade process. There are two tools to consider as you begin preparing for an upgrade: SQL Server Upgrade Advisor and Upgrade Assistant for SQL Server 2012.

SQL Server Upgrade Advisor

The rules checked by Upgrade Advisor represent conditions, situations, or known errors that might affect your upgrade to SQL Server 2012. If you want to take advantage of the lessons other SQL Server users have learned about upgrading, the SQL Server 2012 Upgrade Advisor is the tool for you. This tool is based on early adopters' feedback and internal lab-testing feedback. The SQL Server 2012 Upgrade Advisor is a free download available as part of the Microsoft SQL Server 2012 Feature Pack at `www.microsoft.com/download/en/details.aspx?id=26726` and is also available as part of the SQL Server 2012 installation media for all editions. The purpose of this tool is to identify known upgrade issues and provide guidance for workarounds or fixes for the identified issues on a per-server components' basis. Microsoft worked hard on this tool as a risk-mitigation effort to empower SQL Server 2005 and SQL Server 2008 users to upgrade to SQL Server 2012. So, whether you run Analysis Services, Integration Services, Reporting Services components, or a combination of components, the Upgrade Advisor tool can help.

Installing the SQL Server 2012 Upgrade Advisor

The Upgrade Advisor is a relatively simple tool to use. You can find it in the "Prepare" section of the default screen of the installation CD/DVD. It can also be found at `www.microsoft.com/download/`

en/details.aspx?id=26726. The Welcome screen for the Upgrade Advisor is shown in Figure 3-2. Be sure to select Check for Updates because upgraded versions of this tool are available online.

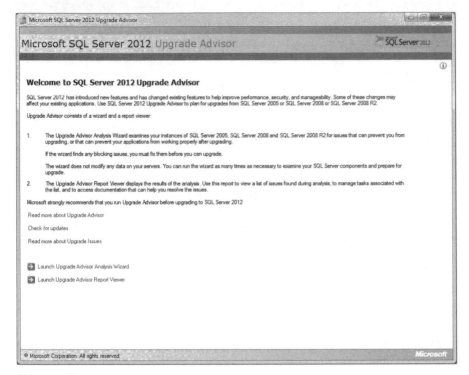

FIGURE 3-2

The tool is constantly updated to reflect the lessons learned by the DBAs who upgraded before you. The tool requires .NET 4.0, which you can download through the Windows Update service or from MSDN. In addition, you must install Microsoft SQL Server Transact-SQL ScriptDom before you install the Upgrade Advisor. It is available at www.microsoft.com/download/en/details .aspx?id=26726. Alternatively, you can choose to install a single instance and version of the tool to test servers across your enterprise. This option supports a zero-footprint interrogation with read-only access to servers.

 This tool is read-intensive and should be tested on a test server to evaluate the potential impact on your systems.

The installation process is straightforward; the only option is to select the location where you would like to install the tool. The default install path is C:\Program Files (x86)\Microsoft SQL Server Upgrade Advisor.

Using the Upgrade Advisor

When installed, the Upgrade Advisor presents you with two choices, Upgrade Advisor Analysis Wizard and Upgrade Advisor Report Viewer. Launch the Upgrade Advisor Analysis Wizard to run the tool. As shown in Figure 3-3, you simply select a server and the components to analyze for upgrade, or you can click the Detect button, which starts the inspection process that selects the components installed on your system.

After you select the components for testing, the next decision is to select the databases that you would like to have evaluated for upgrade, as shown in Figure 3-4. The best part of this process is that you have the option to analyze SQL Profiler trace and SQL batch files to help make this a comprehensive analysis. That is, by adding these files to the evaluation process, Upgrade Advisor evaluates not only the database but its trace workload and SQL scripts as well. By evaluating this additional information, Upgrade Advisor evaluates not only the database as it exists right now, but also information about past database usage and behavior contained in the trace and batch files. All you need to do is select the path to the directory where your trace files or your batch files are located.

FIGURE 3-3

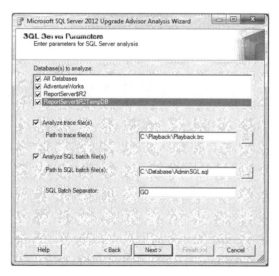

FIGURE 3-4

After you complete configuration of the components that you want to evaluate, you will be prompted to begin the analysis. If you have any questions during the configuration steps, the Help button brings up an Upgrade Advisor-specific Book Online (UABOL) that is rich in information and guides you through the options. As the component-level analysis completes, a green, yellow, or red dialog box indicates the outcome of the test.

When the test completes, you can view the discovered issues via the Upgrade Advisor Report Viewer. The reports, as shown in Figure 3-5, are presented in an interface similar to a Web browser. You can analyze the information by filtering the report presented by server, instance, or component, or issue type. How to interpret the results of this report is discussed later in this chapter.

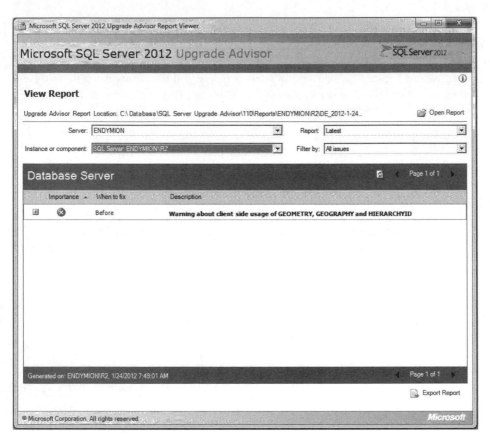

FIGURE 3-5

Scripting the Upgrade Advisor

If you have a server farm or just prefer scripting, a command-line capability is also available. With the UpgradeAdvisorWizardCmd utility, you can configure the tool via an XML configuration file and receive results as XML files. The following parameters can be passed to the UpgradeAdvisorWizardCmd utility:

➤ Command-line help

➤ The configuration path and filename

➤ The SQL Server login and password for SQL Server (if SQL Server authentication is used, rather than Windows authentication)

➤ An optional flag to indicate whether to output reports in a comma-separated value (CSV) format

The configuration file exposes all capabilities and parameters discussed in the wizard section. The results from a command-line execution can still be viewed in the Report Viewer, via XML documents or Excel if you use the CSV option. For example, the following XML document from Upgrade Advisor reflects the choices of analyzing all databases, Analysis Services, and SSIS packages on a server named SQL12Demo and an instance named SQL2012:

```
<Configuration>
   <Server>SQL12Demo</Server>
   <Instance>SQL2012</Instance>
  <Components>
     <SQLServer>
        <Databases>
           <Database>*</Database>
        </Databases>
     </SQLServer>
  </Components>
</Configuration>
```

You can modify the file in an XML editor, such as Visual Studio, and save the file with a new filename. Then, you can use the new file as input to the command line of Upgrade Advisor. For example, the following code snippet displays the command prompt entry required to run the command line of Upgrade Advisor using Windows authentication. The configuration file already contains names for a remote server named SQL2012 and an instance named SQL2012, and the PATH environment variable contains the path to the Upgrade Wizard:

```
C:\>UpgradeAdvisorWizardCmd -ConfigFile "SQL2012Config.xml"
```

From the command prompt, you can also install or remove the Upgrade Advisor application. From there you can control the install process with or without the UI. You can also configure the install path and process-logging options.

For more information on the Upgrade Advisor's configuration files, see the Upgrade Advisor Help section "UpgradeAdvisorWizardCmd Utility."

Resolving Upgrade Issues

The Upgrade Advisor's report contains a wealth of information. The key is to understand how this information appears, what you need to resolve, and when. As shown previously in Figure 3-5, the first column indicates the importance of a finding or a recommendation, the second column tells you when you need to address it, and the Description column tells you about the issue. Approach this analysis by first categorizing the information by Importance and When to Fix the items. Specifically, the sum of the indicators should dictate whether you need to address issues before or after the upgrade process. Table 3-2 provides recommendations of when to address these issues.

TABLE 3-2: When to Address Upgrade Issues

IMPORTANCE	WHEN TO FIX	OUR RECOMMENDATION
Red	Before	Resolve Before Upgrade
Red	Anytime	Resolve Before Upgrade
Red	After	Resolve After Upgrade
Yellow	Anytime	Resolve After Upgrade
Yellow	After	Resolve After Upgrade
Yellow	Advisory	Resolve After Upgrade

Issues that have been flagged with an Importance of Red, and a When to Fix of Before or Anytime should be addressed before starting an upgrade process. Typically, these issues require remediation because of SQL Server 2012 functionality changes, such as discontinued features. You can usually resolve the remaining issues after the upgrade process because they either have a workaround within the upgrade process or do not affect it at all. If you expand the error in question, additional information appears, as shown in Figure 3-6.

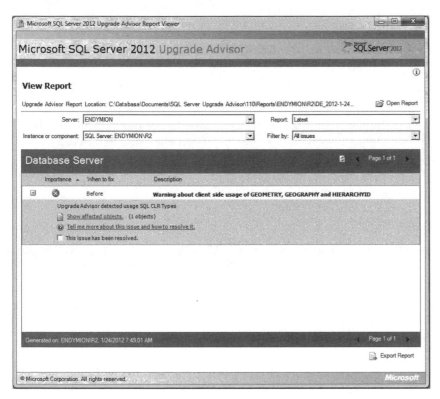

FIGURE 3-6

The Show Affected Objects link shows the exact objects flagged by the Upgrade Advisor process as affected, whereas the Tell Me More About This Issue and How to Resolve It link takes you to the corresponding section of the Upgrade Advisor Books Online (UABOL). The UABOL describes the conditions and provides guidance about corrective action to address the issue. The UABOL is a true gem because it provides guidance for problem resolution in areas beyond the scope of the tools (such as replication, SQL Server Agent, and Full-Text Search).

The This Issue Has Been Resolved check mark is for your personal tracking of resolved issues. This metadata check mark is in place to support remediation processes by enabling the report to be viewed by filtered status of resolved issues or pre-upgrade (unresolved) issues.

If you prefer command-line scripting, the viewer is nothing more than an XSLT transformation applied to the XML result file located in your My Documents\SQL Server 2012 Upgrade Advisor Reports\ directory. You can find individual component results and configuration files in each server's name-based directories. You can even export viewer-based reports to other output formats such as CSV or text.

Upgrade Assistant for SQL Server 2012 (UAFS)

UAFS was first developed for use in the SQL Server 2005 application-compatibility lab engagements run as part of the Microsoft Ascend (SQL 2005 customer training) and Touchdown (SQL 2005 partner training) programs. The purpose of these labs was to help customers analyze their SQL Server 2000 (or 7.0) applications to understand the impact of upgrading to SQL Server 2005 and to provide guidance on any changes that may be necessary to successfully migrate both their database and their application. The labs helped improve the quality of SQL Server 2005 by running upgrades and performing impact analysis on real customer workloads against SQL Server 2005. The labs were run by Microsoft personnel and staffed by partners such as Scalability Experts. Nearly 50 labs were run worldwide, and hundreds of SQL Server 2000 applications were tested using this tool. A new version of UAFS was developed specifically for SQL Server 2008 and has been updated for 2012; you can download it free from www.scalabilityexperts.com/tools/downloads.html.

From a conceptual standpoint, the difference between this tool and Upgrade Advisor is that UAFS naturally encompasses the essence of a true upgrade and testing methodology. By reviewing the results of a SQL Server 2008 (or 2005) workload against the results of the same workload run against SQL Server 2012, you can identify upgrade blockers and application-coding changes that may be required. For SQL Server 2012, the UAFS tool supports upgrading from SQL Server 2008 and 2005.

The following sections walk through an overview of this process to show details of the steps contained in the UAFS, as shown in Figure 3-7. By using the UAFS, you can back up all databases and users and capture a subset of production workload. You can then restore the databases and users you just backed up and process the captured workload. The goal is to develop a new output file, also known as a *baseline*. You then upgrade the test server to SQL Server 2012 and rerun the workload to capture a SQL Server 2012 reference output for comparison.

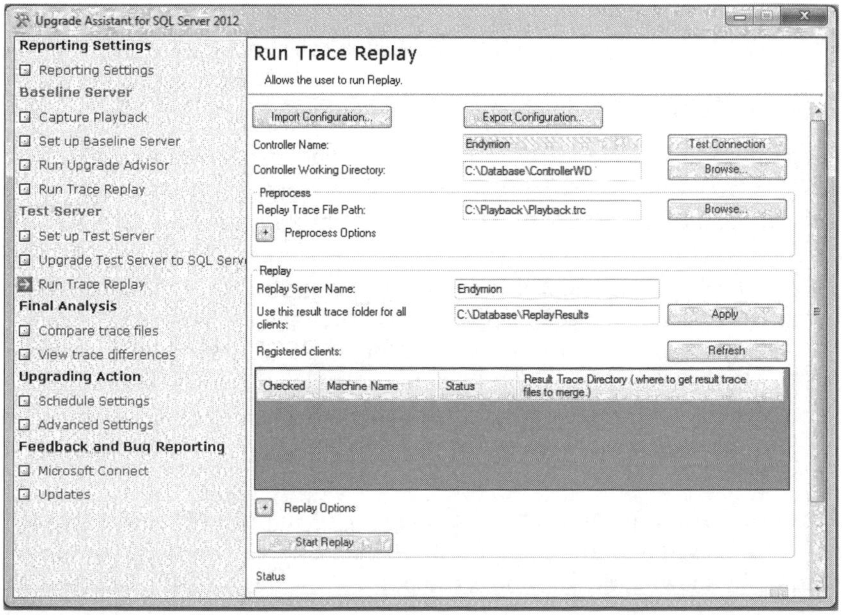

FIGURE 3-7

Capturing the Environment

You should establish your baseline by backing up all SQL Server 2008 (or 2005) systems and user databases from your server. Following this step, you need to start capturing your trace file to avoid gaps in the process. When you capture a trace file, it needs to be a good representation of the workloads that characterize your environment. To do this, you might need to create an artificial workload that better represents the workloads of the application over time. While capturing the trace file, it's a good idea to avoid multiserver operations such as linked server calls or bulk-copy operation dependencies. Be aware that there is a performance cost while tracing. The sum of the trace files and database backups represent a repeatable and reusable workload called a *playback*.

Setting Up the Baseline Server

Now that you have captured the playback, you can set up the baseline system to use for the remainder of the test. Load this server with SQL Server 2008 R2 SP1, 2008 SP2, or SQL Server 2005 SP2, with the minimum requirement for upgrading to 2012. In reality, it should be identical to the source system in collation and patching level. The tool then checks your server for this matching. If necessary, you are prompted to patch or rebuild the master database. It then restores your databases in the correct order so that your DB IDs match to production. (This also includes padding the DB creation process to accomplish this.) Finally, SSUA re-creates your logins and ensures that the IDs match production because all this is necessary to run the trace file. The next step in the process is to run the Upgrade Advisor as described earlier. When the environment has been remediated, you can then proceed to the next step to replay the trace.

Running the SQL Profiler Trace

When you run the trace, first the statistics update on all databases. The replay tool then uses the API and runs all the queries within the trace file in order. This tool is a single-threaded replay, but blocking can occur. If the trace appears to run slowly or stop, you may want to check SQL Server blocking; and if it does not clear up by itself, you need to kill the blocking processes. The output from this step generates a trace-output file for comparison in the final analysis.

Upgrading to SQL Server 2012

Now you are ready to upgrade to SQL Server 2012. You have two options. You can use SSUA to restore the state of the SQL Server 2008 (or 2005) to its baseline and then upgrade in-place to SQL Server 2012, or you can migrate the SQL 2008 (or 2005) databases to an existing SQL Server 2012 instance. As discussed earlier in this chapter, the decision to perform an in-place or side-by-side upgrade is based on a number of factors specific to your environment. You do not measure performance metrics, so these servers don't need to be identical. You measure workload behavior between two versions of SQL Server. After restoring the baseline on a SQL Server 2012 platform, go through the Running the SQL Profiler Trace step again, but this time on SQL Server 2012. The output from this step generates the other trace-output file for comparison in the final analysis.

Final Analysis

After completing all these processes, you will reach the final steps to compare the output files by filtering and comparing all batches in both trace files for discrepancies. The Report Viewer shows one error condition at a time by showing the last correct step, the error step, and the next correct sequences of the batch files. When a condition has been identified, it can be filtered from the error-reviewing process to enable the DBA to focus on identifying new error conditions. After the SQL Server 2012 upgrade completes, change the database compatibility mode to 110, and run your application to validate that it works in SQL Server 2012 compatibility mode. This ensures that no application behavior differences exist when your application runs on the database compatibility level of 110.

BACKWARD COMPATIBILITY

This section covers major product changes to SQL Server 2012 classified in one of three categories: unsupported, discontinued, or affecting the way SQL Server 2008 or 2005 behaves today. Although the Upgrade Advisor tool highlights these conditions if they are relevant to your environment, you should read this section to learn about these changes.

Unsupported and Discontinued Features in SQL Server 2012

From time to time, to move a technology forward, trade-offs must be made. From SQL 2008 to SQL Server 2012, the following lists some of the features no longer available:

➤ The system stored procedures `sp_ActiveDirectory_Obj`, `sp_ActiveDirectory_SCP`, and `sp_ActiveDirectory_Start`.

➤ `sp_configure` options `user instance timeout` and `user instances enabled`.

➤ Support for the VIA protocol.

➤ SQL Mail (Use Database Mail instead.)

➤ The creation of new remote servers using `sp_addserver` (Use Linked Servers instead.)

➤ Database compatibility level 80.

➤ `RESTORE {DATABASE | LOG}` ... `WITH DBO_ONLY` (Use the `WITH RESTRICTED USER` clause instead.)

This is a limited list of discontinued features. For a complete list of discontinued and deprecated features, go to `http://msdn.microsoft.com/en-us/library/cc280407(v=SQL.110).aspx`.

SQL Server 2012 Deprecated Database Features

These features are no longer available as of the SQL Server 2012 release or the next scheduled release of the product. Following are some of the features scheduled for deprecation; try to replace these features over time with the recommended items:

➤ SOAP/HTTP endpoints created with `CREATE ENDPOINT` and `ALTER ENDPOINT` (They have been replaced with Windows Communication Framework (WCF) or ASP.NET.)

➤ The compatibility level 90 will not be available after SQL Server 2012.

➤ Encryption using RC4 or RC4_128, is scheduled to be removed in the next version. Consider moving to another encryption algorithm such as AES.

➤ Not ending T-SQL statements with a semicolon will no longer be supported in a future version of SQL Server.

Other SQL Server 2012 Changes Affecting Behavior

The behavior changes in the following features could adversely affect migration to SQL Server 2012:

➤   If you create a new job by copying the script from an existing job, the new job might inadvertently affect the existing job. This is because the parameter @schedule_uid should not be duplicated. Manually delete it in the script for the new job.

➤   Deterministic scalar-valued CLR user-defined functions and deterministic methods of CLR user-defined types are now foldable. This seeks to enhance performance when these functions or methods are called more than once with the same arguments. However, if a nondeterministic function or method has been marked deterministic in error, it can create unexpected results.

➤   When a database with a partitioned index upgrades, there may be a difference in the histogram data for these indexes. This is because SQL Server 2012 uses the default sampling algorithm to generate statistics rather than a full scan.

➤   Using `sqlcmd.exe` with XML Mode behaves differently in SQL Server 2012.

For additional behavior changes, see SQL Server 2012 Books Online or go to `http://msdn` `.microsoft.com/en-us/library/cc707785(v=SQL.110).aspx`.

SQL SERVER COMPONENT CONSIDERATIONS

This section discusses individual components, along with any respective considerations that you need to evaluate during an upgrade process. Components not covered here are covered later in the book in their respective chapters.

Upgrading Full-Text Catalog

During the upgrade process, all databases with Full-Text Catalog are marked Full-Text disabled. This is because of the potential time involved in rebuilding the catalog. Before you upgrade your Full-Text Search environment, you should familiarize yourself with some of the enhancements. The database attach and detach processes also result in the Full-Text Catalog being marked as Full-Text Disabled. You can read SQL Server 2012 Books Online to learn about additional behavior.

Upgrading Reporting Services

Reporting Services 2008 and Reporting Services 2005 support upgrading to Reporting Services 2012. Reporting Services 2012 supports a Report database on SQL Server. Prior to upgrading, run the SQL Server 2012 Upgrade Advisor and follow its recommendations, guidance on possible mitigation options, and steps. Then, before executing the upgrade, back up the database, applications, configurations files, and the encryption key.

Following are two ways to upgrade Reporting Services:

➤   **In-place upgrade:** You can accomplish this by executing the SQL Server 2012 `setup.exe`; select the older Reporting Services to upgrade with Reporting Services 2012. This has the same advantages and disadvantages described earlier with the in-place upgrade. The risk with this is that it is an all-or-nothing approach, difficult to roll back except by reinstalling it again.

➤ **Side-by-side upgrade:** With this option, the Reporting Services 2012 instance installs in the same physical server along with the older version of Reporting Services or on a separate physical server. After the Reporting Services 2012 instance installs, the report content migrates either individually or in bulk, using one of the following options:

➤ Redeploy the reports using SQL Server 2012 Business Intelligence Development Studio

➤ Use rs.exe to extract and deploy the reports

➤ Use Report Manager.

Published reports and snapshot reports are upgraded. After upgrading Reporting Services 2012, redeploy any custom extensions and assemblies, test the applications on Reporting Services 2012 after it is fully operational, and then remove any unused applications and tools from the previous version.

 Chapter 19, "Database Mirroring," discusses upgrading your existing cluster in detail. Chapter 16, "Clustering SQL Server 2012," discusses upgrading database mirroring in detail.

Upgrading to 64-Bit

Upgrading from a SQL Server 2005 32-bit platform or SQL 2008 32-bit platform to SQL Server 2008 x64-bit platform is not supported. Although running a SQL Server 2005 32-bit platform with Service Pack 2 or SQL Server 2008 32-bit platform on a Windows x64-bit subsystem is supported, upgrading this configuration to a SQL Server 2012 x64-bit environment is not supported. Side-by-side migration is the only supported upgrade path for migrating databases from a 32-bit to x64-bit platform.

POST-UPGRADE CHECKS

The information in the following sections is about product behaviors that have surprised a lot of people after upgrading. There is nothing worse than successfully upgrading your environment and then having end users blame the upgrade for poor query performance. Proactive attention to post-upgrade issues lessens the risk that your careful planning and hard work will be tainted by post-upgrade problems.

Poor Query Performance After Upgrade

A possible reason for poor query performance after upgrading to SQL Server 2012 is that the old statistics are considered outdated and cannot be used by the query optimizer. For most situations, this should not be an issue as long as you have enabled the auto-update statistics and autocreate statistics options. This enables statistics to be automatically updated by default when needed for query compilation. The statistics built from these features are built only from data sampling. Therefore, they can be less accurate than statistics built from the entire dataset. In databases with large tables, or in tables where previous statistics were created with fullscan, the difference in quality may cause the SQL Server 2012 query optimizer to produce a suboptimal query plan.

 With SQL Server 2012, *when you create an index, the statistics use the query optimizer's default sampling algorithm.*

To mitigate this issue, you should immediately update the statistics after upgrading to SQL Server 2012. Using sp_updatestats with the resample argument rebuilds statistics based on an inherited sampling ratio for all existing statistics. Typically, that is a full sample for index-based statistics and sampled statistics for the rest of the columns. An additional benefit that you could gain from this process is that if the data is less than 8MB (the minimum sampling size), the statistics are also built with fullscan.

SUMMARY

There are many compelling reasons for upgrading to SQL Server 2012. Some strategies and tools for doing so include the Upgrade Assistant for SQL Server 2012 and the SQL Server 2012 Upgrade Advisor, which can be leveraged during the upgrade. The upgrade process includes the pre-upgrade, the actual upgrade, and the post-upgrade steps for a successful upgrade. There are several discontinued features to watch out for, including database compatibility level 80 and SQL Mail, along with features whose behavior changes could also affect your upgrade, such as partitioned index histograms post-upgrade and sqlcmd.exe with XML mode. Now that you have done the groundwork for a successful upgrade, jump into SQL Server 2012.

Managing and Troubleshooting the Database Engine

WHAT'S IN THIS CHAPTER

➤ Configure Your Instance Using Management Studio

➤ Use a Dedicated Administrator Connection to Access an Unresponsive Server

➤ Monitor Processes Using Dynamic Management Objects (DMOs)

In this chapter, you learn how to configure and monitor your SQL Server instance. This is the key to a smooth running, database — proper configuration and active monitoring. In addition, you learn some troubleshooting methods that help you identify what is happening when the instance is not performing as expected. This chapter assumes you already know the basics of Management Studio navigation and focuses on what you need to know as a database administrator (DBA). Many other chapters in this book cover various aspects of Management Studio, so those points are not duplicated here (backing up your database, for example, is covered in Chapter 17, "Backup and Recovery").

CONFIGURATION AND ADMINISTRATION TOOLS

After you install SQL Server or upgrade to SQL Server 2012, you will likely need to configure it for your needs. In SQL Server 2012, Microsoft maintained its policy to increase out-of-the-box security established with SQL Server 2008 by turning off features after installation, thereby reducing the software footprint. The features turned off vary based on the edition of SQL Server. For example, TCP/IP is disabled in Developer Edition by default, and every edition has CLR integration turned off. This makes the environment more usable for you as an administrator because features you don't care about are not crowding your administration screen. It also reduces the options that a hacker or, more likely, a malicious user can use to penetrate your system. As a result of these security measures, there is even more reason to invest time in configuring SQL Server 2012 towards your specific needs. In this section, you learn how to configure SQL Server for your specific environment and security needs in a few ways: by using SQL Server Configuration Manager, startup parameters, startup stored procedures, and partially contained databases. SQL Server Configuration Manager is the best place to start.

SQL Server Configuration Manager

The SQL Server Configuration Manager configures the SQL Server services much like the Services applet in the Control Panel, but it has much more functionality than the applet. For example, the program can also change what ports SQL Server listens on and what protocols each instance uses. You can open the program (see Figure 4-1) from Start ➪ All Programs ➪ Microsoft SQL Server 2012 ➪ Configuration Tools ➪ SQL Server Configuration Manager.

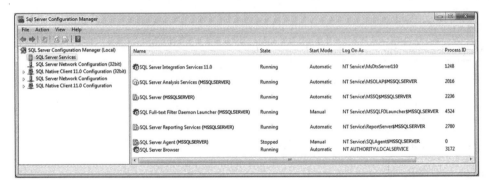

FIGURE 4-1

To start configuring SQL server to fit your environment's needs, follow these steps:

1. Select Start ➪ Microsoft SQL Server 2012 ➪ Configuration Tools ➪ SQL Server Configuration Manager ➪ SQL Server Services.

2. To configure an individual service such as SQL Server, double-click the service name to open the service Properties page. In the Log On tab, you can configure which account starts SQL Server. You should start SQL Server with a regular domain user account with minimal rights. The account should not have the privilege to Log on Locally, for example. There is no reason for the account to be a local or domain administrator in SQL Server 2012.

3. Next, create a non-expiring password so your SQL Server doesn't fail to start when the password expires. If the SQL Server services do not need to communicate outside the instance's machine, you could start the service with the Local System account, but the account may have more local rights than you want. (This is discussed more in Chapter 8, "Securing the Database Instance.")

Use Configuration Manager to change Services attributes instead of the Windows Services dialogs in the Administrative Tools area. Logins used as service accounts require minimum permission levels that are granted automatically when you use the Configuration Manager.

4. On the Service tab, specify whether you'd like the service to start automatically, manually, or be disabled.

The rest is optional, but highly recommended. For instance, if you go to the Advanced tab (shown in Figure 4-2) for each service, you can configure the more interesting options. Here you can turn off Customer Feedback Reporting. This feature enables Microsoft to receive utilization reports from your SQL Server. Even if you wanted to do this, in most production environments your SQL Server may not send the report because of a lack of Internet access from production servers.

You can also check the Error Reporting option in the Advanced tab to e-mail Microsoft whenever a critical error has occurred. The minimal and anonymous information is sent over a secure HTTPS protocol.

Additionally, on the SQL Server 2012 Network Configuration page in the Configuration Manager, you can see a list of network protocols that SQL Server is listening on by instance. If you want to turn a protocol on or off, you can do so by right-clicking the protocol and selecting Enable or Disable. By enabling only the Shared Memory protocol, only clients that run on the same computer can connect to your instance of SQL Server.

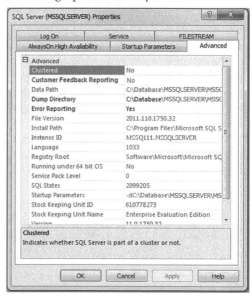

FIGURE 4-2

 The VIA protocol has been discontinued in SQL Server 2012.

Startup Parameters

SQL Server has an array of switches you can use to enable advanced settings for the Database Engine or help with troubleshooting. There are two ways to set these configuration options: from SQL Server Configuration Manager or via command prompt. You enable these switches via the SQL Server Configuration Manager by altering the SQL Server service's startup parameters. Configuring settings through Configuration Manager causes SQL Server to use the configured startup parameter every time it starts. Or, you can temporarily set the switches by running SQL Server from a command prompt. To enable a particular switch from a manual start-up, perform the following steps.

1. In the SQL Server 2012 Services page, double-click SQL Server (MSSQLServer by default but it may vary depending on your instance name).

2. Go to the Advanced tab and add any switches you want using the Startup Parameters option, separated by semicolons (see Figure 4-3).

To enable a particular switch from a command prompt start-up, perform the following steps.

1. Run `sqlservr.exe` from the command prompt. The file is located by default in the `C:\Program Files\Microsoft SQL Server\MSSQL11.MSSQLSERVER\MSSQL\Binn` directory.

2. Turn on any nondefault parameters you want by adding the switch after `sqlservr.exe`. This is generally the preferred way to start your SQL Server in a one-off debug mode because you won't leave any settings intact that you may not want. You can stop SQL Server by using the Ctrl+C combination or by closing the command prompt window.

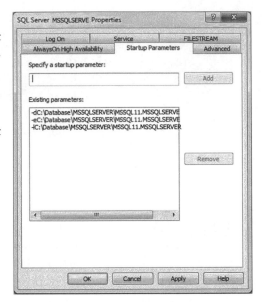

FIGURE 4-3

 Never start SQL Server with command prompt for normal use; after you log off the machine, your command prompt closes, stopping SQL Server.

The syntax for the `sqlserver` runtime is as follows:

```
SQLServr.exe [-dmaster_file_path] [-lmaster_log_path]
        -eerror_log_path] [-sinstance_name][-c] [-f]
        [-gmemory_to_reserve] [-h] [-kcheckpoint Speed in MB/sec]
        [-m] [-n] [-Ttrace#] [-ttrace#] [-x]
        [-ystack dump on this error] [-B] [-K]
```

The startup options are useful in troubleshooting a problem or for solving quick, one-off problems. Rather than describe every switch, only the ones you are likely to use most frequently are covered.

➤ `-d` **and** `-l` **switches:** You can change which master database SQL Server uses by using the `-d` and `-l` switches:

```
SQLServr.exe -d C:\temp\TempMasterDB.mdf -l C:\temp\TempMasterLog.ldf
```

The `-d` switch specifies the database file, and the `-l` switch specifies the log file. This may be useful if you want to use a temporary configuration of the master database that may not be corrupt.

➤ **−T switch:** Another useful switch is the −T, which enables you to start given trace flags for all the connections for a SQL Server instance. You can use this, for example, to turn on a trace flag to monitor deadlocks in your SQL Server instance (note that the "T" is uppercase):

```
SQLServr.exe -T1204
```

 SQL Server also includes a lowercase trace flag option: SQLServr.exe -t1204. *This should be used with caution because using this flag sets other internal trace flags.*

 If you try to start an instance of SQL Server while it is already running, you get errors. When SQL runs against a master file, it opens the file exclusively to prevent another instance from writing to the same file. One of the errors tells you that a file is in exclusive use or not available. No harm is done when this occurs.

➤ **−f switch:** This switch places SQL Server in minimal mode and only enables a single connection. By placing SQL Server in minimal mode, SQL Server starts with a minimum configuration and suspends the CHECKPOINT process, startup stored procedures, and remote connections. Use this to correct a configuration option that was inappropriately set, such as setting a memory option larger than the physical memory on the server. In such a case, SQL Server would fail to start. To fix this, start it from the command prompt with the −f option, correct the memory setting, and then restart SQL normally. Another use of this option is to repair startup stored procedures. An administrator may have defined a startup stored procedure that problematically prevents SQL Server from starting. To combat this, place SQL Server in minimal mode, remove or correct the startup stored procedure, and then start SQL Server again without the switch to repair the problem.

 Using SQL Server Configuration Manager, make sure you stop SQL Server Agent before placing SQL Server in single-user mode. Otherwise, SQL Server Agent takes the only available connection.

➤ **−g switch:** This switch reserves additional memory outside SQL Server's main memory pool for use by extended stored procedures, OLE DB providers used by distributed queries, and automation objects used by Transact-SQL queries. The general recommendation is to *not* use this flag unless you see either of the following error messages in your SQL Server error log:

```
"Failed Virtual Allocate Bytes: FAIL_VIRTUAL_RESERVE <size>"
"Failed Virtual Allocate Bytes: FAIL_VIRTUAL_COMMIT <size>"
```

These messages indicate that SQL Server is trying to free up memory pool space to allocate the memory in this virtual memory area. In this case, you may want to increase the amount of memory allocated to these objects by using the −g switch. If the −g switch is not used, the default of 256MB of memory is allocated to this area.

If you have a server that uses few extended stored procedures, distributed queries, or automation objects, you may want to use this switch with a value of less than 256 to reduce the amount of memory reserved for these objects. The memory would then be available for the general memory pool.

➤ −m **switch:** This switch puts SQL Server in single-user mode (sometimes called *master recovery mode*) and suspends the CHECKPOINT process, which writes data from disk to the database device. This switch is useful when you want to recover the master database from a backup or perform other emergency maintenance procedures.

➤ −k **switch:** This switch is used to influence the checkpoint frequency. It forces the regeneration of the system master key if one exists. Use this with extreme care, and only if directed by PSS.

➤ −s **switch:** This switch starts a named instance of SQL Server. When you start SQL Server from the command prompt, the default instance starts unless you switch to the appropriate BINN directory for the instance and provide the −s switch. For example, if your instance is named SQL2012, you should be in the C:\Program Files\Microsoft SQL Server\ MSSQL11.SQL2012\MSSQL\Binn directory and issue the following command:

```
sqlserver.exe -sSQL2012
```

➤ −c **switch:** This switch enables you to decrease startup time when starting SQL Server from a command prompt by taking advantage of the fact that the SQL Server Database Engine does not start as a service when starting from the command prompt. This switch bypasses the Service Control Manager, which is unnecessary in this situation.

You can obtain a complete list of switches by using the −? switch, as shown in Table 4-1 (complete details appear in the SQL Server documentation):

```
sqlservr.exe -?
```

TABLE 4-1: Startup Parameters

SWITCH	PURPOSE
−d	Defines the data file for the master database
−l	Defines the log file for the master database
−T	Enables you to start given trace flags for all connections of a SQL Server instance
−f	Places SQL Server in minimal mode an enables a single connection
−g	Reserves additional memory outside SQL Server's main memory pool for extended stored procedures
−m	Puts SQL Server in single-user mode (master recovery mode) and suspends the CHECKPOINT process
−k	Forces the regeneration of the system master key if one exists
−s	Specifies which named instance to start
−c	Bypasses the Service Control Manager, which is unnecessary when starting SQL Server from a command prompt
−?	Returns a complete list of switches

Startup Stored Procedures

Startup stored procedures work similarly to stored procedures except that they execute whenever the SQL Server instance starts. For example, you may have a startup stored procedure that e-mails you when the instance starts. You can also use startup stored procedures to create objects in `tempdb` and load them with data when SQL Server starts. These stored procedures run under the sysadmin server role, and only a sysadmin can create a startup stored procedure. Errors written from a startup stored procedure are written to the SQL Server error log.

In the following steps, startup stored procedures are enabled system-wide and an example startup stored procedure is created.

 Make sure that you do the examples in this section only against a development server until you're certain you want to do this in production.

1. The stored procedure `sp_configure` enables startup stored procedures, but to set it, the `show advanced options` setting must be turned on, as in the following code snippet:

```
sp_configure 'show advanced options', 1;
GO
RECONFIGURE;
GO
```

2. By default, SQL Server does not scan for startup stored procedures. To allow it to do so, you must use `sp_configure`, as follows:

```
sp_configure 'scan for startup procs', 1;
GO
RECONFIGURE;
GO
```

3. After you run this, you must restart the SQL Server instance to commit the setting. Try a simple example. Create a table called `SQLStartupLog` in the master database that logs the time a SQL Server instance starts:

```
CREATE TABLE master.dbo.SQLStartupLog
(StartTime datetime);
GO
```

4. Create a stored procedure to log to the table. Be sure to create this stored procedure in the master database. The following stored procedure can do the trick, logging the current date to the table:

```
USE master
GO
CREATE PROC dbo.InsertSQLStartupLog
 as
 INSERT INTO master.dbo.SQLStartupLog
 SELECT GETDATE();
GO
```

5. Use the `sp_procoption` stored procedure to make the stored procedure a startup stored procedure. The `sp_procoption` stored procedure sets only one parameter. You must first specify the stored procedure you want to set; the only available option name is `startup`, with a value of 1 (on) or 0 (off). Before running the following stored procedure, ensure that your SQL Server can scan for startup stored procedures, as shown here:

```
sp_procoption @ProcName = 'master.dbo.InsertSQLStartupLog',
  @OptionName= 'startup',
  @OptionValue = 1;
```

6. Stop and start your SQL Server instance, and query the `master.dbo.SQLStartupLog` to see if the record was written. Before you leave this section, make sure that you disable the setting by running the following query:

```
sp_procoption @ProcName = 'master.dbo.InsertSQLStartupLog',
  @OptionName= 'startup',
  @OptionValue = 0;

USE MASTER
GO
DROP TABLE master.dbo.SQLStartupLog;
DROP PROC dbo.InsertSQLStartupLog;
```

Partially Contained Databases

Partially contained databases are a new feature of SQL Server 2012 that provides an excellent configuration option for specific security scenarios. A full discussion of the security benefits is available in Chapter 8, "Securing the Database Instance." A contained database is a concept where all of the settings and metadata for that database have no configuration dependencies on the instance of SQL Server where the database resides. Users are able to connect to the database without authenticating a login at the instance level. This level of isolation makes a database with this configuration that is more portable from instance to instance, which can be quite beneficial when deploying a database to multiple instances, such as in a development environment.

In SQL Server 2012, fully contained databases are not implemented. Only partially contained databases are available for this release, meaning that objects or functions that cross the application boundary are allowed.

 An application boundary is the boundary between the application model (database) and the instance. For example, the system table `sys.endpoints` is outside the application boundary, because it references instance-level objects. The system table `sys.indexes` is within the application boundary.

By default, a 2012 instance does not have contained databases enabled. Use `sp_configure` (shown in the following code snippet) to enable contained databases prior to migrating an existing database to this model:

```
sp_configure 'contained database authentication', 1;
GO
RECONFIGURE;
GO
```

Before you migrate a database to a contained model, use the new DMO `sys.dm_db_uncontained_entities` to identify the containment level of your database. The output from the following query returns objects that can potentially cross the application boundary.

```
SELECT so.name, ue.*
FROM sys.dm_db_uncontained_entities ue
    LEFT JOIN sys.objects so
      ON ue.major_id = so.object_id;
```

 An additional option to identify uncontained events in an application is the extended event database_uncontained_usage_event. *This event fires whenever an uncontained event occurs in the application. See Chapter 12, "Monitoring Your SQL Server" for more information on extended events.*

If your database is a good candidate for partial containment and it is enabled, the CONTAINMENT option is used to convert a database to a partially contained database. Suitable candidates for partial containment include databases that do not use instance-level features, such as Service Broker. This is done by issuing an ALTER DATABASE command as shown in the following code snippet.

```
USE master
GO
ALTER DATABASE AdventureWorks SET CONTAINMENT = PARTIAL;
```

For more information on migrating to a partially contained database and the risks and limitations of this feature, go to `http://msdn.microsoft.com/en-us/library/ff929139(v=sql.110).aspx`.

TROUBLESHOOTING TOOLS

Imagine you get a call informing you that a server is not responding. You go to SSMS to connect to the server to see what is going on. Your connection request waits, and waits, and then times out. You cannot connect, you cannot debug, and you cannot see anything. In this situation, you need tools in your arsenal to help you troubleshoot and repair core issues with your instance. The Dedicated Administrator Connection (DAC) is a very reliable tool for this type of situation. An alternative troubleshooting method that this section also covers is the process of rebuilding system databases in the event of a corruption or lost database.

Dedicated Administrator Connection

The DAC is a specialized diagnostic connection that can be used when standard connections to the server are not possible. When you need to connect to the server to diagnose and troubleshoot problems, the DAC is an invaluable administration tool to have.

SQL Server attempts to make DAC connect in every situation and most of the time it does, but in very severe situations it cannot guarantee connection to an unresponsive server.

SQL Server listens for the DAC connection on a dynamically assigned port. A connection can be made on this port only by sysadmin role members from SSMS or the `sqlcmd` tool. To connect to the DAC using SSMS, add a prefix to the server name. For example, if the server name is `SQL2012`, connect to server `admin:Prod`. You merely add the prefix `admin:` to the server name.

To connect using `sqlcmd`, use the `-A` option as follows:

```
sqlcmd -sSQL2012 -E -A -d master
```

By default, DAC is only allowed on a client running on the local server. However, by using `sp_configure`, you can enable remote admin connections by executing the following:

```
sp_configure 'remote admin connection', 1;
GO
RECONFIGURE;
GO
```

On clustered instances, Microsoft recommends that you enable a remote admin connection. You may then need to connect using the TCP address and DAC port number found in the error log, as shown here:

```
Sqlcmd -S<serveraddress>,<DacPort>
```

If you connect locally using the IP address, use the Loopback Adapter address, as in the following example:

```
Sqlcmd -S127.0.0.1,1434
```

 The Loopback Adapter Address is the address of localhost (the local computer), and on most systems, this translates to the IPv4 address 127.0.0.1. Connecting to the Loopback Adapter Address is functionally the same as connecting to localhost.

When connecting remotely, you need to know the port that DAC has been assigned. Port 1434 is the default, but the instance might be assigned something different if the connection to the default port failed during startup. Additionally, if remote administration connections are enabled, the DAC must be started with an explicit port number. PowerShell is a good option for finding the port number, as it enables you to see assigned DAC ports across multiple instances at one time. The following PowerShell example enables you to see which port has been assigned for DAC on each instance listed in the `$instances` variable.

```
$instances = "PRODUCTION", "PRODUCTION\R2", "PRODUCTION\SQL2012"
foreach($instance in $instances)
{
get-SQLErrorlog -SQLServer $instance |
where {($_.Text -match "Dedicated admin connection")} |
format-table  $DisplayResults -AutoSize
}
```

Rebuilding the System Databases

If one of your system databases becomes corrupted and your backups cannot be found, your last resort may be to rebuild the system databases. This can essentially reinstall the system databases and rid your system of anything that may be causing it to act unpredictably. The repercussion of this is that you must reinstall any service packs; and all your user-defined databases, including the Reporting Services support database, will disappear. Additionally, any logins or server configurations must be redone.

 Rebuilding your system databases should not be taken lightly. It is a high-impact technical decision that you make when no other good option exists.

To rebuild your system databases, follow these steps:

1. Go to a command prompt.

2. From the command prompt, run setup.exe as if you were installing SQL Server, but pass in a few switches as shown here:

```
setup.exe /QUIET /ACTION=REBUILDDATABASE /INSTANCENAME=instance_name /SQLSYSADMI
NACCOUNTS=accounts /SAPWD=sa password
```

The switches indicate the following:

➤ /QUIET: suppresses the errors and warnings while the rebuild runs. You see a blank screen while the process completes. Errors will still be logged to the Error Log.

➤ /ACTION: indicates that the action is to rebuild the database, by providing the REBUILDDATABASE parameter.

➤ /INSTANCENAME: provides the name of the instance where system databases should be rebuilt. Use MSSQLSERVER for a default instance.

➤ /SQLSYSADMINACCOUNTS: provides windows groups or individual accounts that should be provisioned as sysadmin. Use this option when SQL Server is configured for Windows Authentication Mode.

➤ /SAPWD: specifies the SA password. Use this option when SQL Server is configured for Mixed Authentication Mode.

Prior to SQL Server 2008, the original installation media was required to rebuild system databases. Now, the system database and log files are copied to `C:\Program Files\Microsoft SQL Server\MSSQL11.MSSQLSERVER\MSSQL\Binn\Templates` *as part of installation. When you rebuild,* `setup.exe` *uses the files located here.*

3. After the databases are rebuilt, return to your default configuration and databases. You need to restore the master database (more on this in Chapter 17) or reattach each user-defined database and re-create the logins. The preferable option, of course, is to recover the master database from a backup rather than rebuilding. Then your logins and databases automatically appear.

When you rebuild the system databases, the databases may appear to have disappeared, but the files are still in the operating system and can be reattached or restored. Reattaching the databases is generally the lowest-impact action.

MANAGEMENT STUDIO

DBAs spend a lot of time in SQL Server Management Studio. This tool enables you to perform most of your management tasks and to run queries. SQL Server 2012 uses a version of Visual Studio 2010 as its shell. Because this is a professional-level book, it won't go into every aspect of Management Studio, but instead covers some of the more common and advanced features that you might like to use for administration.

Reports

One of the most impressive features of the SQL Server management environment is the integrated reports available in each area of administration. These standard reports are provided for the server instances, databases, logins, and Management tree item. Each runs as a Reporting Services report inside of SQL Server Management Studio. Server-level reports give you information about the instance of SQL Server and the operating system. Database-level reports drill into information about each database. You must have access to each database you want to report on, or your login must have enough rights to run the server-level report. You also have the capability to write custom reports and attach them to many other nodes in the Object Explorer window.

Server Reports

You can access server-level reports from the Object Explorer window in Management Studio by right-clicking an instance of SQL Server and selecting Reports from the menu. A report favorite at the server level is the Server Dashboard, which is shown in Figure 4-4. The Server Dashboard report gives you a wealth of information about your SQL Server 2012 instance, including:

➤ The edition and version of SQL Server you run

➤ Anything for that instance not configured to the default SQL Server settings

➤ The I/O and CPU statistics by type of activity (for example, ad hoc queries, Reporting Services, and so on)

➤ High-level configuration information such as whether the instance is clustered

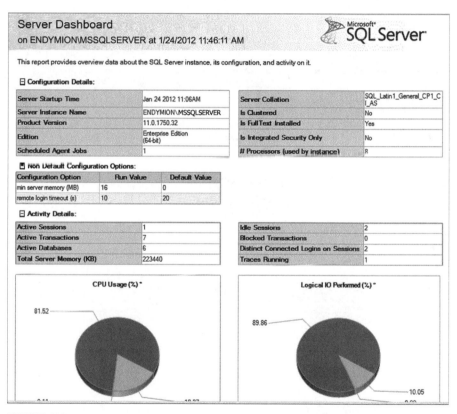

FIGURE 4-4

Most of the statistical information includes only data gathered since the last time you started SQL Server. For example, the Server Dashboard provides a few graphs that show CPU usage by type of query. This graph is not historical; it shows you the CPU usage only for the period of time that SQL Server has been online. Use caution when extrapolating information from this aspect of the Server Dashboard. Always keep in mind that what you see is a time-sensitive snapshot of server performance, not its entire history.

Database Reports

Database reports operate much like server-level reports. Select them by right-clicking the database name in the Object Explorer window in Management Studio. With these reports, you can see information that pertains to the database you selected. For example, you can see all the transactions currently running against a database, users being blocked, or disk utilization for a given database, as shown in Figure 4-5.

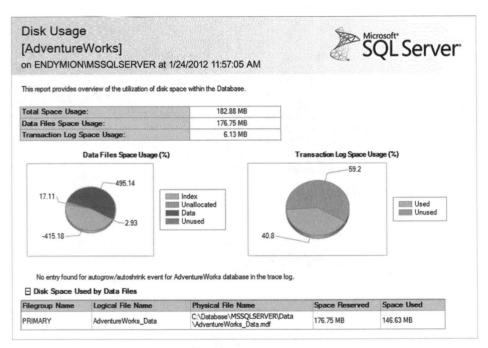

FIGURE 4-5

Object Explorer Details

The Object Explorer Details Pane provides a wealth of information in a consolidated GUI. You can access this feature in two ways. From the View menu, select Object Explorer Details. Alternatively, F7 opens the pane. If you have highlighted a node in Object Explorer, F7 opens the details for that object, as shown in Figure 4-6. The Synchronize button on the Object Explorer Pane synchronizes Object Explorer to Object Explorer Details.

The pane can be filtered and customized to your precise needs. Clicking on a column header sorts by that column, and right-clicking on the column header area gives you the opportunity to filter which details display.

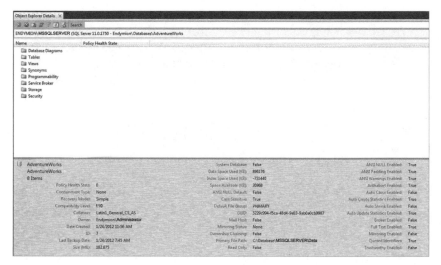

FIGURE 4-6

Configuring SQL Server in Management Studio

There are a few ways to configure your SQL Server. Earlier you used SQL Configuration Manager. This tool helps you turn on various features and services. Now look at other configuration options and take a more detailed look at `sp_configure`. For the Database Engine, you have two main methods to configure the instance: the `sp_configure` stored procedure or the Server Properties screen. To access the Server Properties screen, right-click the Database Engine you want to configure in Management Studio and select Properties. Be careful before altering the configuration of your instance. Adjusting some of these settings could affect your instance's performance or security. This section describes a few of the more important settings, but more are covered throughout the book.

 Another option for configuring database settings is through Policy-Based Management facets. This topic is covered in-depth in Chapter 9, "Change Management."

Using the Server Properties Screen

Using the Server Properties screen is much more user-friendly than `sp_configure`, but it doesn't provide all the options available to you through `sp_configure`. The following sections go through each screen in detail.

General

The General tab in the Server Properties screen shows you information about your SQL Server instance that cannot be altered, such as the version of SQL Server you currently have installed and whether your instance is clustered. It also provides server information, such as the number of processors and amount of memory on the machine, as shown in Figure 4-7.

Although your server may have 32GB of RAM available, that doesn't mean that all that RAM is available to SQL Server. Overhead from the operating system and other processes running on the server also use this available memory.

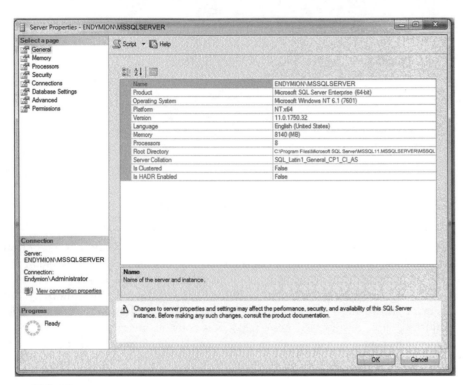

FIGURE 4-7

Memory

On the Memory page of the Server Properties screen, you can see how much memory SQL Server is configured to use. By default, SQL Server is configured to use as much memory as the operating system and the edition of SQL Server enable it to consume. Typically, it is a good idea to set the minimum and maximum amount of memory that your instances use in your environment.

Note the Configured Values and Running Values radio buttons at the bottom of the properties screens as shown in Figure 4-8. When you select Running Values, you see the values that SQL Server currently uses. When you select Configured Values, you see the values that SQL Server will use the next time it restarts. This is necessary because some values do not take effect until after a restart.

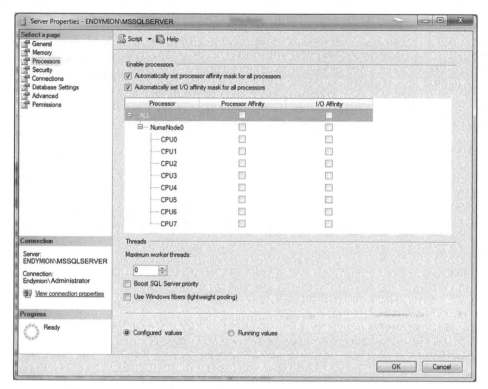

FIGURE 4-8

Processors

In the Processors page, you can restrict the SQL Server Engine to use named processors and assign some or all those processors to I/O or threading operations. This is useful typically if you have multiple CPUs and more than one instance of SQL Server. You may have one instance that uses four processors and the other instance use the other four processors. In some cases, when you have a large number of concurrent connections to your SQL Server, you may want to set the Maximum Worker Threads option. Configure this to 0 (the default) to enable SQL Server to automatically and dynamically find the best number of threads to enable on the processor. These threads can manage connections and other system functions, such as performing CHECKPOINTs. Generally, leaving this setting alone gives you optimal performance.

You can select the SQL Server Priority option to force Windows to assign a higher priority to the SQL Server process. Tweaking this setting may be tempting, but you should adjust it only after thorough testing because it may starve other system threads. Use of this option is not generally recommended unless directed by PSS.

Use the Lightweight Pooling option only on the rare occasion when the processor is highly utilized and context switching is extreme. Chapter 12, "Monitoring Your SQL Server," contains more information on lightweight pooling and how it works.

Security

On the Security page, you can adjust whether your SQL Server accepts connections through both SQL Server and Windows Authentication or Windows Authentication only. This same question is asked during setup of the instance, and this screen gives you another opportunity to change the setting. Under the Login Auditing section, you should always have at least Failed Logins Only selected. This enables SQL Server to audit when someone mistypes a password or is trying to force their way into the instance. (Chapter 8 talks much more about the other security settings on this page.)

Connections

On the Connections page, you can adjust the default connection properties. One possible option you may want to set here would be SET NOCOUNT. This setting can prevent the (8 Rows Affected) message from being sent to the client if they do not request it. There is a small performance enhancement by doing this because this message is an additional recordset sent from SQL Server and may be unneeded traffic.

Database Settings

You will not likely change many of the settings on the Database Settings page. The default index fillfactor of 0 is recommended. You may change fillfactors for specific indexes, but probably not the default. This page also includes settings for how long you wait on a tape for backup (specify how long SQL Server waits for a tape) and how long backups are kept before they expire (default backup media retention, in days). You may change them to suit your plan. Decide whether you plan to compress database backups and set the Compress Backup option accordingly, which is highly recommended. Details for these settings are covered in Chapter 17, "Backup and Recovery."

The last setting on this page enables you to choose the default database and log file locations. The installation default setting places the log and data files on the same drive under the %System Drive%\Program Files\Microsoft SQL Server\MSSQL11.MSSQLSERVER\Data and Log directories. Unless this SQL Server install is for playing around, do not put your data and log files on the C drive.

 A best practice is to separate data and logs on different drives. This enables you to get the most out of your RAID system and ensures proper recovery, as discussed in Chapter 11, "Optimizing SQL Server 2012."

Advanced

The Advanced page allows you to enable two features: Contained Databases and FILESTREAM. In addition, there is a catch-all area for Miscellaneous settings. In the vast majority of cases, these setting should remain at their defaults. The Network settings include the ability to set a Remote Login Timeout in seconds, which can be used to control how long remote logins can attempt to connect before they timeout. Finally, there is an area to configure Parallelism settings. A Max Degree of Parallelism of 0 means that all processors will be available for parallel queries.

Permissions

The Permissions page shows each of the logins and roles available on the instance. From here, you can explicitly grant or deny very granular permissions for each login or role from the Explicit tab. In addition, the Effective tab shows you which of these permissions are currently granted to the login or role.

Using sp_configure

`sp_configure` is a stored procedure that enables you to change many of the configuration options in SQL Server. Some of the more commonly adjusted settings include:

➤ **Cost threshold for parallelism:** Use to mitigate parallelism on lower costing transactions to reduce the need to modify the max degree of parallelism.

➤ **Max degree of parallelism:** For OLTP environments, this is usually set to the number of available sockets.

➤ **CLR enabled:** Enables CLR procedures to execute.

➤ **Blocked processes threshold:** Use to set time threshold before blocked process reports are generated.

When you run the stored procedure with no parameters, it shows you the options and their current settings. By default, only the basic, or commonly used, settings are returned, of which there are 15. To see additional options, you need to configure the instance to display advanced options. You can do so by running `sp_configure`, as shown here:

```
sp_configure 'show advanced options', 1;
RECONFIGURE;
```

The change does not take effect until the `RECONFIGURE` command is issued. SQL Server does a check for invalid or not recommended settings when you use `sp_configure`. If you have provided a value that fails any of these checks, SQL Server warns you with the following message:

```
Msg 5807, Level 16, State 1, Line 1
Recovery intervals above 60 minutes not recommended. Use the RECONFIGURE WITH
OVERRIDE statement to force this configuration.
```

 Issuing the RECONFIGURE *command results in a complete flush of the plan cache. This means that nothing remains in cache, and all batches are recompiled when submitted for the first time afterward. Be cautious of using* sp_configure *in a production environment and make sure that you understand the impact of the cache flush on your database.*

This gives you an opportunity to reconsider what may have been a bad choice, such as setting a memory option to more memory than exists on the box. The following code shows you how to issue the override for the setting:

```
EXEC sp_configure 'recovery interval', 90;
RECONFIGURE WITH OVERRIDE;
GO
```

Filtering Objects

You can also filter objects in Management Studio by following a few easy steps, which is useful when you begin to have dozens of objects:

1. Select the node of the tree that you want to filter, and click the Filter icon in the Object Explorer.

2. The Object Explorer Filter Settings dialog (shown in Figure 4-9) opens; here you can filter by name, schema, or when the object was created.

3. Use the Operator drop-down box to select how you want to filter, and then type the name in the Value column.

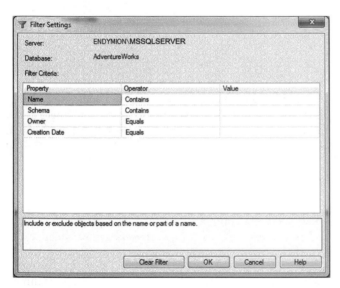

FIGURE 4-9

Error Logs

As you probably have already experienced, when something goes wrong with an application, one of the factors that you must consider is the database. It is up to the DBA to support the troubleshooting effort and to confirm that the database isn't the source of the problem. The first thing the DBA typically does is connect to the server and look at the SQL Server instance error logs and then the Windows event logs.

In SQL Server 2012, you can quickly look through the logs in a consolidated manner using Management Studio. To view the logs, right-click SQL Server Logs under the Management tree, and select View ⇨ SQL Server and Windows Log. This opens the Log File Viewer screen. From this screen, you can check and uncheck log files that you want to bring into the view. You can consolidate logs from SQL Server, Agent, and the Windows Event Files, as shown in Figure 4-10.

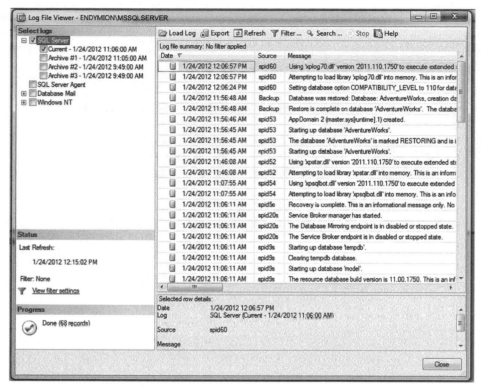

FIGURE 4-10

In some situations, you may want to merge the logs from several machines into a single view to determine what's causing an application problem. To do this, click the Load Log button, and browse to your .LOG file. That file could be a Windows error log that has been output to .LOG format or a SQL log from a different instance. For example, you can use this to consolidate all the SQL logs from every instance on a single server to give you a holistic view of all the physical machines' problems.

Activity Monitor

The Activity Monitor gives you a view of current connections on an instance. You can use the monitor to determine whether you have any processes blocking other processes. To open the Activity Monitor in Management Studio, right-click the Server in the Object Explorer, and then select Activity Monitor.

The tool is a comprehensive way to view who connects to your machine and what they do. The top section shows four graphs (Show Processor Time, Waiting Tasks, Database I/O, and Batch Requests/Sec) that are commonly used performance counters for the server. There are four lists under the graphs: Processes, Resource Waits, Data File I/O, and Recent Expensive Queries. In all these lists, you can also apply filters to show only certain hosts, logins, or connections using greater than a given number of resources. You can also sort by a given column by clicking the column header.

On the Process Info page (shown in Figure 4-11), you can see each login connecting to your machine (also called a Server Process ID, or SPID). It's easy to miss how much information is in this window. You can slide left to right to see loads of important data about each connection. When debugging, most of the following columns are useful:

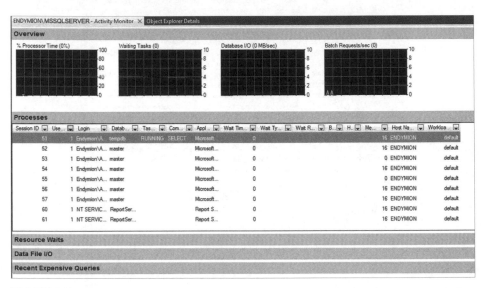

FIGURE 4-11

> **Session ID:** The unique number assigned to a process connected to SQL Server. This is also called a SPID. An icon next to the number represents what happens in the connection. If you see an hourglass, you can quickly tell that the process is waiting on or is being blocked by another connection.

> **User Process Flag:** Indicates whether internal SQL Server processes are connected. These processes are filtered out by default. You can change the value to see the SQL Server internal processes by clicking the drop-down and selecting the appropriate value.

> **Login:** The login to which the process is tied.

> **Database:** The current database context for the connection.

> **Task State:** Indicates whether the user is active or sleeping.

>> **Done:** Completed.

>> **Pending:** The process is waiting for a worker thread.

>> **Runnable:** The process has previously been active, has a connection, but has no work to do.

>> **Running:** The process is currently performing work.

>> **Suspended:** The process has work to do, but it has been stopped. You can find additional information about why the process is suspended in the Wait Type column.

➤ **Command:** Shows the type of command currently being executed. For example, you may see SELECT, DBCC, INSERT, or AWAITING COMMAND here, to name a few. This won't show you the actual query that the user executes, but it does highlight what type of activity is being run on your server. To see the actual command, select a row in this table, right-click, and choose Details.

➤ **Application:** The application that is connecting to your instance. This can be set by the developer in the connection string.

➤ **Wait Time (ms):** If the process is blocked or waiting for another process to complete, this indicates how long the process has been waiting, in milliseconds; it can have a value of 0 if the process is not waiting.

➤ **Wait Type:** Indicates the event you are waiting on.

➤ **Wait Resource:** The text representation of the resource you are waiting on.

➤ **Blocked By:** The Session ID (SPID) that is blocking this connection.

➤ **Head Blocker:** A value of 1 means the Blocked By Session ID is the head of the blocking chain; otherwise it's 0.

➤ **Memory Use (KB):** The current amount of memory used by this connection, represented by the number of kilobytes in the Procedure cache attributed to this connection. This was reported in pages prior to SQL Server 2008.

➤ **Host:** The login's workstation or server name. This is a useful item, but in some cases you may have a Web server connecting to your SQL Server, which may make this less important.

➤ **Workload Group:** The name of the Resource Governor workload group for this query.

By right-clicking any process, you can see the last query run with the connection, trace the process using Profiler, or kill the connection. You can also right-click over the graph area and select Refresh to manually refresh the data or click Refresh Interval to set how often Activity Monitor refreshes. The default refresh rate is 10 seconds. Don't set the refresh to anything too frequent because it can affect system performance, constantly running queries against the server.

Another important function you can perform with the help of Activity Monitor is identifying a locking condition. The following steps explain how to set up a blocked transaction and how to use activity monitor to resolve this issue.

1. Run the following query in one query window while connected to the AdventureWorks database, and ensure you back up the AdventureWorks database before performing these steps:

```
BEGIN TRAN
DELETE FROM Production.ProductCostHistory
WHERE ProductID = 707;
```

This query was intentionally not committed. In other words, there is a `BEGIN TRAN` command but no `ROLLBACK` or `COMMIT` command. This means that the rows deleted from Production.ProductCostHistory are still locked exclusively.

2. Next, without closing the first window, open a new query window, and run the following query:

```
SELECT * FROM Production.ProductCostHistory;
```

This query should hang up and wait on the `DELETE` from `Production.ProductCostHistory` because the first transaction locks row one. Do not close either window. At the top of each query window, your session ID displays in parentheses, and at the bottom your login displays. If you cannot see the SPID in the tab at the top, hover your mouse over the tab, and a small window pops up showing the entire tab title, which includes the SPID. While the query windows are open, go ahead and explore the Activity Monitor to see what these connections look like (Figure 4-12).

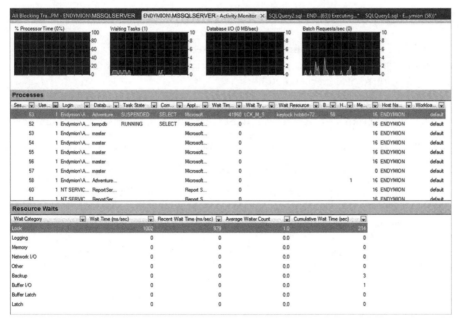

FIGURE 4-12

3. Open the Activity Monitor and note that one connection has a task state of `Suspended`. This is the query that is trying to do the `SELECT`. You can confirm this by comparing the session ID of the suspended session with the session ID of your query. Your wait type will be `LCK_M_S`, which means you are waiting on a shared lock for reading. If you hover the mouse over the Wait Resource column value, you can see more detailed information about the locks, including the object IDs of the resources. In the Blocked By column, you can also see the session ID of the process that blocks you, and it should match the SPID of your first query. You have the option to kill the blocking process; to do so, select the row for the blocking process, right-click, and choose Kill Process.

4. While the locks still exist, take a look at a standard blocking report that comes with SQL Server 2012. In Object Explorer, right-click on your server name, select Reports, Standard Reports, and choose Activity -All Blocking Transactions. You can see the report shown in Figure 4-13.

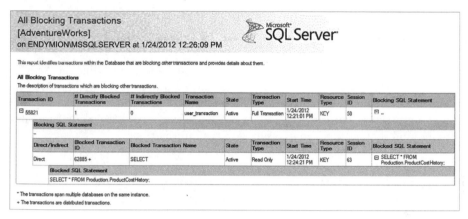

FIGURE 4-13

5. Now, back at the Activity Monitor, hover over the Wait Resource column to see the mode=X. This mode means that there is an exclusive lock on that resource. An exclusive lock means that no one else is allowed to read the data cleanly. If you see a request mode of S, then SQL Server has granted a shared lock, which in most situations is harmless, and others are allowed to see the same data. To request a dirty read of the uncommitted data, add a WITH (NOLOCK) clause like so:

```
SELECT *
FROM Production.ProductCostHistory
WITH (NOLOCK);
```

The (NOLOCK) query hint should rarely, if ever, be used in a production environment. If you find that (NOLOCK) is used regularly in your application, find out why dirty reads are necessary, and if they are, address that root issue first before resorting to query hints. One option to consider as an alternative to (NOLOCK) if dirty reads are absolutely necessary is to set the transaction isolation level to SNAPSHOT.

6. This query returns the data. Before you leave this section, execute the following SQL in the query window that contains the DELETE statement:

```
ROLLBACK TRAN;
```

MONITORING PROCESSES IN T-SQL

You can also monitor the activity of your server via T-SQL. Generally, DBAs prefer this as a quick way to troubleshoot long-running queries or users who complain about slow performance. DBAs typically prefer T-SQL because the information you can retrieve is more flexible than the Activity Monitor.

sp_who and sp_who2

The `sp who` stored procedure returns what is connecting to your instance, much like the Activity Monitor. You'll probably prefer the undocumented `sp_who2` stored procedure, though, which gives you more verbose information about each process. Whichever stored procedure you use, they both accept the same input parameters. For the purpose of this discussion, we go into more detail about `sp_who2`. Just keep in mind that `sp_who` shows a subset of the information.

Database administrators who are in the know have graduated from `sp_who2` to a tool called `sp_whoisactive`. This widely used procedure was developed by Adam Machanic, a SQL Server MVP and Boston-based independent consultant. If you're not familiar with it, download it, and read Adam's blog posts about what it can do to vastly improve your monitoring and troubleshooting efforts. A download file and installation instructions are available at `http://tinyurl.com/WhoIsActive`. While you're at it, check out Adam's blog series, "A Month of Activity Monitoring", that explains exactly why you should begin using `sp_whoisactive` straightaway at `http://tinyurl.com/WhoIsActiveDocs`.

For the most part, this tool is freely offered to the community, with a few exceptions: `http://bit.ly/WhoIsActiveLicensing`.

To see all the connections to your server, run `sp_who2` without any parameters. This displays the same type of information in the Activity Monitor. You can also pass in the parameter of `'active'` to see only the active connections to your server, like so:

```
sp_who2 'active';
```

Additionally, you can pass in the SPID, as shown here, to see the details about an individual process:

```
sp_who2 55;
```

Although the example uses SPID 55, your process IDs may be different and can be obtained from the Current Activity listing discussed earlier.

sys.dm_exec_connections

The sys.dm_exec_connections dynamic management view (DMV) gives you even more information to help you troubleshoot the Database Engine of SQL Server. This DMV returns a row per session in SQL Server. Because it's a DMV, it displays as a table and enables you to write sophisticated queries against the view to filter out what you don't care about, as shown in the following query, which shows only user connections that have performed a write operation:

```
SELECT * FROM
    sys.dm_exec_sessions
WHERE is_user_process = 1
AND writes > 0;
```

In addition to the information shown in the methods described earlier to view processes, this DMV indicates how many rows the user has retrieved since opening the connection, and the number of reads, writes, and logical reads. You can also see in this view the settings for each connection and what the last error was, if any.

sys.dm_exec_sql_text

You can use the sys.dm_exec_sql_text dynamic management function (DMF) to retrieve the text of a particular query. This can be used in conjunction with the sys.dm_exec_query_stats dynamic management view to retrieve the top 10 most poorly performing queries across all databases. Listing 4-1 retrieves the number of times a query has executed, the average runtime by CPU and duration, and the text for the query.

Available for
download on
Wrox.com

LISTING 4-1: Top10WorstPerformingQueries.sql

```
SELECT TOP 10 execution_count as [Number of Executions],
    total_worker_time/execution_count as [Average CPU Time],
     Total_Elapsed_Time/execution_count as [Average Elapsed Time],
    (
      SELECT SUBSTRING(text,statement_start_offset/2,
        (CASE WHEN statement_end_offset = -1
              THEN LEN(CONVERT(nvarchar(max), [text])) * 2
        ELSE statement_end_offset END - statement_start_offset) /2)
      FROM sys.dm_exec_sql_text(sql_handle)
    ) as query_text
FROM sys.dm_exec_query_stats
ORDER BY [Average CPU Time] DESC;
```

The sys.dm_exec_query_stats DMV, also, shows a great deal of other information that you can use. It shows you a line for each query plan that has been run. You can take the sql_handle column from this DMV and use it in the sys.dm_exec_sql_text function. Because this view is at a plan level, when someone changes some of the query's text, it shows the new query as a new line.

These are just a few examples of how processes can be monitored in T-SQL. With the introduction and widespread adoption of Dynamic Management Objects, you have more options than ever to pinpoint database issues using T-SQL.

MULTISERVER MANAGEMENT

In this age of expanding data, the number of databases that need to be managed is proliferating as well. SQL Server DBAs often have to administer a large number of instances and databases. Something as simple as adding a new login or setting a server option can become quite an endeavor if it must be done on dozens of servers. Luckily, Microsoft has provided a few tools to ease the DBA's life.

 If you are one of the growing number of database administrators who manages multiple servers, make some time to learn PowerShell. This language is a powerful tool that you can leverage to create reusable scripts that can consistently perform tasks across multiple servers, instances or databases.

Central Management Servers and Server Groups

SQL Server 2008 introduced a new feature intended to ease your life: central management servers and server groups. This feature enables you to run T-SQL scripts and apply policy-based management (PBM) policies to a group of servers at the same time. PBM is covered in Chapter 10, "Configuring the Server for Optimal Performance," but for now, take a look at executing T-SQL on multiple servers.

You may execute T-SQL on a group of servers and aggregate the results into a single result set or keep each result set separate. When you aggregate the result sets, you have the option to include an extra column that indicates from which server each row is returned. You can use this tool to do any multiserver administration and much more. If you have common error tables on each server, you can query them all in a single statement.

These capabilities are part of SQL Server Management Studio (SSMS), but before you start using them all, you must first register a central management server. In the Registered Servers dialog of SSMS, right-click and select Register Central Management Server. You can choose a configuration server from the resulting dialog. This server keeps metadata and does some of the background work for you.

After you create a central management server, you can create server groups and add server registrations to groups under the registration server. After you set up your servers, you may right-click anything — from the registration server to server groups or individual servers in groups — and select

New Query, Object Explorer, or Run Policy. Then choose New Query, add T-SQL, and run the query against all the servers in the group.

Create groups of servers based on common management needs. A couple of options are to organize them by environment, such as development, QA, and production or to organize them by subject area, such as Human Resources, Accounting, and Operations. Carefully consider what management tasks are generally performed together and use that as your grouping criteria.

Following are a few items about your registration server:

➤ It may not be a registered group under itself.

➤ All queries are executed using trusted connections.

➤ If your servers cross domains, you must have trusted relationships between them.

➤ Multiple central management servers can be configured.

To set options for multiserver result sets, select Tools ➪ Options ➪ Query Results ➪ SQL Server ➪ Multi-server results.

SQL Server Utility

In SQL Server 2008 R2, Microsoft continued to reinforce its commitment to creating tools to support consolidated server management by introducing SQL Server Utility. This tool enables you to set up a server as a Utility Control Point (UCP) to manage multiple instances of SQL Server from a single location.

The benefits of implementing SQL Server Utility include the following:

➤ Monitor CPU and disk usage of all instances.

➤ Monitor utilization to identify under- and over-utilized resources.

➤ Set up health policies for groups of instances or for single instances.

➤ Manage monitoring policies for one or more of the instances you manage.

More information about SQL Server Utility can be found online at `http://msdn.microsoft.com/en-us/library/ee210548(v=sql.110).aspx`.

TRACE FLAGS

Trace flags give you advanced mechanisms to tap into hidden SQL Server features and troubleshooting tactics. In some cases, they enable you to override the recommended behavior of SQL Server to turn on features such as network-drive support for database files. In other cases, you can use trace flags to turn on additional monitoring. There is a set of flags that help you diagnose deadlocks, including trace flag `1204`. To turn on a trace flag, use the DBCC TRACEON command, followed by the trace you'd like to turn on, as shown here:

```
DBCC TRACEON (1204)
```

To turn off the trace, use the DBCC TRACEOFF command. This command is followed by which traces you'd like to turn off (multiple traces can be separated by commas), as shown here:

```
DBCC TRACEOFF (1204, 3625)
```

 Trace flag 3625 used in the previous code snippet limits the amount of information returned to users who are not members of the sysadmin server role by masking the parameters of some error messages. This can be enabled as a security measure.

When you turn on a trace, you are turning it on for a single connection by default. For example, if you turn on trace flag 1224, which disables lock escalation based on the number of locks, lock escalation is disabled only in the scope of the connection that issued the DBCC TRACEON command. You can also turn on the trace at a server level by issuing the command followed by the -1 switch, as in the following:

```
DBCC TRACEON (1224, -1)
```

After you turn on the traces, you're probably going to want to determine whether the trace is actually running. To do this, you can issue the DBCC TRACESTATUS command. One method to issue the command is to interrogate whether a given trace is running, like so:

```
DBCC TRACESTATUS (3635)
```

This command would return the following results if the trace is not turned on:

```
TraceFlag Status Global Session
--------- ------ ------ -------
3625      0      0      0

(1 row(s) affected)
```

If you want to see all traces that apply to the connection, run the following command with the -1 parameter:

```
DBCC TRACESTATUS (-1)
```

As shown in the following results of this query, two traces are turned on. Trace flag 1224 is turned on globally for every connection into the SQL Server, and trace flag 3625 is turned on for this session:

```
TraceFlag Status Global Session
--------- ------ ------ -------
1224      1      1      0
```

```
3625      1      0      1

(2 row(s) affected)
```

If no traces are turned on, you would receive only the following message:

```
DBCC execution completed. If DBCC printed error messages, contact your system
administrator.
```

Your instance of SQL Server should not have trace flags turned on indefinitely, unless you have been instructed by Microsoft Product Support to do so. When left to run all the time, trace flags may cause your instance to behave abnormally. Moreover, the flag you use today may not be available in a future release or service pack of SQL Server. If you are in debug mode, you can turn on a trace flag from the command prompt when starting SQL Server. As mentioned earlier in this chapter, you can also start a trace when SQL Server starts at the command prompt by calling the sqlservr.exe program and passing the –T switch after it.

There is a lot to say about trace flags even though only a few are mentioned here, but as you proceed through this book, you see a number of other trace flags in practice.

 Some functionality provided by trace flags, such as deadlock monitoring, can be more efficiently implemented by using Extended Events. See Chapter 12, "Monitoring Your SQL Server" for a complete discussion of implementing Extended Events in your environment.

GETTING HELP FROM SUPPORT

Whenever you get stuck on a SQL Server issue, generally you call the next layer of support. Whether that next layer is Microsoft or a vendor, a number of new tools are available to communicate with that next layer of support. Use the SQLDumper.exe and SQLDiag.exe programs to better communicate with support to give them an excellent picture of your environment and problem while you reproduce the error.

SQLDumper.exe

Beginning in SQL Server 2000 SP3, SQLDumper.exe was included to help your SQL Server perform a dump of its environment after an exception occurs. A support organization, such as Microsoft's Product Support Services (PSS), may also request that you execute the program on demand while you have a problem such as a hung server.

If you want to create a dump file on demand, you need the Windows process ID for the SQL Server instance. You can obtain this ID in a few ways. You can either go to Task Manager and look in the SQL Server log, or go to SQL Server Configuration Manager, covered earlier in the chapter. On the SQL Server 2012 Services page of Configuration Manager, you can see each of the SQL Server services and the process ID.

By default, SQLDumper.exe can be found in the C:\Program Files\Microsoft SQL Server\ 110\Shared directory because it is shared across all the SQL Server instances installed on a server.

This directory may vary, though, based on where you installed the SQL Server tools. To create a dump file for support, go to a command prompt, and access the C:\Program Files\Microsoft SQL Server\110\Shared directory. As with many command-line utilities, you can see the options by running the following command, and get more details about them from the SQL Server documentation:

```
SQLdumper.exe -?
```

When you are at the command line, you can create a full dump or a minidump. If a minidump is less than a megabyte, a full dump may run 110MB on your system. To create a full dump, use the following command:

```
Sqldumper.exe <ProcessID> 0 0x1100
```

<ProcessID> is the Process ID of your SQL instance. This outputs the full dump to the same directory that you're in. The filename is called SQLDmpr0001.mdmp if this is the first time you've run the SQLDumper.exe program. Filenames are sequentially named after each execution. You cannot open the dump file in a text editor such as Notepad. Instead, you need advanced troubleshooting tools such as Visual Studio or one of the PSS tools. A more practical dump would be a minidump, which contains most of the essential information that product support needs. To create a minidump, use the following command:

```
Sqldumper.exe <ProcessID> 0 0x0120
```

You can view the SQLDUMPER_ERRORLOG.log file to determine whether there were any errors when you created the dump file or whether a dump occurred. You need to be a local Windows administrator to run SQLDumper.exe or be logged in with the same account that starts the SQL Server service.

SQLDiag.exe

A tool that's slightly less of a black box than SQLDumper.exe is SQLDiag.exe. This tool consolidates and collects information about your system from several sources:

➤ Windows System Monitor (sysmon)

➤ Windows event logs

➤ SQL Server Profile traces

➤ SQL Server error logs

➤ Information about SQL Server blocking

➤ SQL Server configuration information

Because SQLDiag.exe gathers so much diagnostic information, you should run it only when you're requested to or when you prepare for a call with support. The SQL Server Profiler trace files alone can quickly grow large, so prepare to output these files to a drive that has a lot of space. The process also uses a sizable amount of processing power as it runs. You can execute the tool from a command prompt or as a service; you can use the -? switch to see available switches.

The SQL Nexus Tool, available from Codeplex at `http://sqlnexus.codeplex.com` *can help you read and analyze SQLDiag output more efficiently.*

`SQLDiag.exe` can take a configuration file as input. By default, this file is called `SQLDiag.Xml`, but you can pass in a different filename. If a configuration XML file does not exist, one will be created called `##SQLDiag.XML`. This file can be altered to your liking and then later distributed as `SQLDiag.XML`.

Now that you know what `SQLDiag.exe` can do, follow this example to use the tool against a local development server. If you cannot get in front of the server, use a support tool such as Terminal Services to remote into a server because you can't point `SQLDiag.exe` at a remote instance.

1. To run the tool, go to a command prompt.

2. Because the SQL install adds the appropriate directory to the PATH environment variable, you don't need to go to the individual directory where the file is located. Instead, go to the `C:\Temp` directory or something similar to that on a drive that has more than 100MB available.

3. The default location for the executable file is `C:\Program Files\Microsoft SQL Server\110\Tools\Binn\SQLDIAG.EXE`, but you can alter that to a new location with the `/O` switch.

4. Type the following command (note the lack of spaces after the + sign):

```
sqldiag /B +00:03:00 /E +00:02:00 /OC:\temp /C1
```

This command instructs `SQLDiag.exe` to begin capturing trace information in 3 minutes from when you press Enter and run for 2 minutes. This is done with the `/B` and `/E` switches. You can also use these two switches to start and stop the diagnostic at a given 24-hour clock time. The command also tells `SQLDiag.exe` to output the results of the traces and logs to the `C:\Temp` directory, and the `/C` switch instructs the tool to compress the files using Windows compression. If you were running this in your environment, you would wait until you were instructed by `SQLDiag.exe` (in green text on your console) to attempt to reproduce the problem. In Figure 4-14, SQLDiag collects to the default directory. The results look something like what is shown in Figure 4-14. Enter CTRL+C, if you want to terminate the collection of data early.

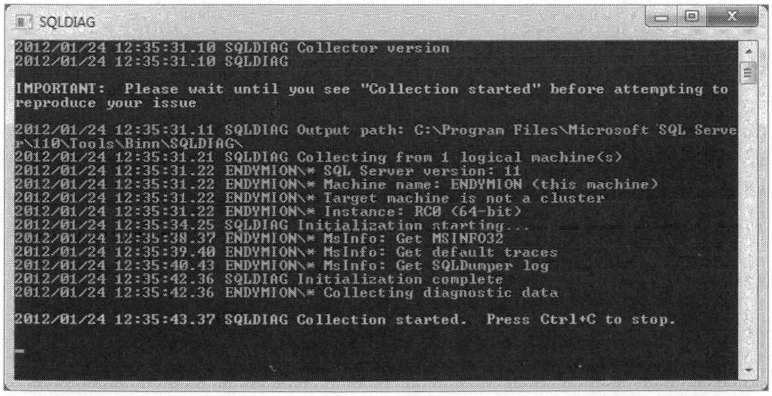

FIGURE 4-14

5. With the `SQLDiag.exe` now complete, go to the `C:\Temp` directory to zip the contents up and send them to Microsoft. In the directory, you can find a treasure chest of information for a support individual, including the following:

➤ `##files.txt:` A list of files in the `C:\Program Files\Microsoft SQL Server\110\Tools\binn` directory, with their creation date. Use this to determine whether you're running a patch that support has asked to be installed.

➤ `##envvars.txt:` A list of all the environment variables for the server.

➤ `SERVERNAME__sp_sqldiag_Shutdown.OUT:` A consolidation of the instance's SQL logs and the results from a number of queries.

➤ `log_XX.trc:` A series of Profiler trace files of granular SQL Server activities being performed.

➤ `SERVERNAME_MSINFO32.TXT:` A myriad details about the server system and hardware.

These files are not only useful to support individuals. You also may want to consider running this on a regular basis to establish a baseline of your server during key times (before patches, monthly, or whatever your metric is). If you decided to do this, you wouldn't want the Profiler part of `SQLDiag.exe` to run for more than a few seconds. You can gather useful baseline information if the tool periodically runs in snapshot mode. This mode performs the same functions just described but exits immediately after it gathers the necessary information. The following command uses the `/X` switch to run `SQLDiag.exe` in snapshot mode and the `/N` switch (with `2` as the option) to create a new directory for each run of `SQLDiag.exe`:

```
sqldiag /OC:\temp\baseline /X /N 2
```

The first directory created is called `baseline_0000`, and each new one is named sequentially after that. Many corporations choose to run this through SQL Agent or Task Manager on the first of the month or before key changes to have an automatic baseline of their server and instance.

SUMMARY

One of the most important things to remember when using SQL server is managing and troubleshooting your SQL Server. The key concepts for doing so are proper configuration, ongoing monitoring, and efficient troubleshooting. Methods for configuration include SQL Server Configuration Manager, startup parameters, and startup stored procedures. It is also important to use Management Studio and T-SQL to actively monitor your databases. The DAC provides an excellent way to connect to your instance and troubleshoot when issues arise. When you've exhausted your troubleshooting options, know how to provide the information that product support needs by using `SQLDumper.exe` and `SQLDiag.exe`. In the next chapter, you learn ways to automate SQL server.

5

Automating SQL Server

WHAT'S IN THIS CHAPTER

➤ Automate Common Maintenance Activities Using Maintenance Tasks

➤ Schedule Jobs to Perform Maintenance Activities Using SQL Server Agent

➤ Secure the Jobs You Create Using SQL Server Agent Security

➤ Configure SQL Server Agent to Meet Your Needs

➤ Set Up Database Mail to Enable the SQL Server Agent to Send Notifications

➤ Schedule Jobs Across Multiple Servers Using the Multi Server Admin Capabilities

Much of the work that a database administrator does is repetitive: backing up databases, rebuilding indexes, and checking for file sizes and disk-space availability. Responding to events such as a full transaction log being out of disk space may also be part of DBA daily life. The problems grow rapidly with the number of servers you must administer. Automating this work is more than a convenience; it is a requirement for enterprise systems.

Two features in SQL Server 2012 come to the rescue of the DBA: Maintenance Plans and SQL Server Agent. Maintenance Plans enable you to automate the routine maintenance activities for a database. Backups, database integrity checks, and index maintenance tasks can be automated with Maintenance Plans. The Maintenance Plan Wizard makes it easy to create Maintenance Plans. SQL Server Agent enables you to manually create a schedule of jobs to be run on a SQL Server, further enhancing the ability of the DBA to automate routine activities.

MAINTENANCE PLANS

Maintenance Plans are a quick-and-easy way to automate routine maintenance tasks in SQL Server. They are no more than a user interface on top of regular SQL Server Agent jobs. However, the tasks in a plan aren't equivalent to job steps because Maintenance Plans are built using SQL Server Integration Services (SSIS), and these are then run as a single SSIS job step in a job that maps to the Maintenance Plan name. For routine maintenance tasks, Maintenance Plans may be all that you need to automate on many SQL Servers.

There are two ways to create and maintain Maintenance Plans. The quick and easy way is to use the Maintenance Plan Wizard, and the manual way is to use the Maintenance Plan Designer.

Maintenance Plan Wizard

This section walks you through the steps to create a backup using the Maintenance Plan Wizard:

1. First, launch the wizard, which lives on the context menu on the Maintenance Plans node in the Object Explorer in SQL Server Management Studio. Select the Maintenance Plans Wizard menu item to launch the first page of the wizard. Figure 5-1 shows the menu selection to start the Maintenance Plan Wizard.

   You can opt to not show this page again and then select Next. This brings up the Select Plan Properties page, where you can set some of the Plan options.

2. On this page, as shown in Figure 5-2, specify a name and description for the plan and select the scheduling options.

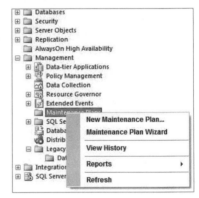

FIGURE 5-1

3. Select Next to move to the Select Maintenance Tasks screen where you can choose the tasks you want the plan to perform. For this example select the Back Up Database (Full) option, as shown in Figure 5-3.

FIGURE 5-2

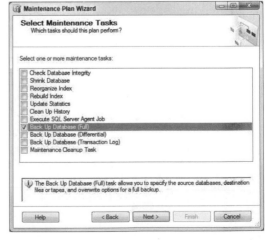

FIGURE 5-3

4. Select Next to move to the Select Maintenance Task Order screen, as shown in Figure 5-4. If you selected multiple tasks on the previous page, you can reorder them here to run in the order you want. In this example you have only a single task, so click Next.

5. The next page is the Define Back Up Database (Full) Task screen, as shown in Figure 5-5. On this page select the details for the backup task. If you selected a different task on the Select Maintenance Tasks screen, you need to supply the details for that task. In the case of multiple tasks, this step presents a separate page for each task you selected in your plan.

FIGURE 5-4

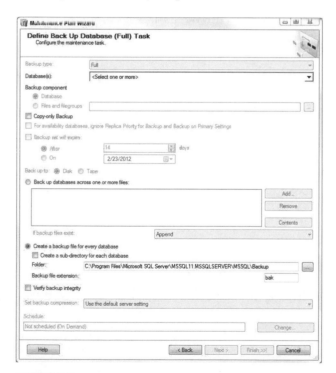

FIGURE 5-5

6. Figure 5-6 shows the dialog where you can select the databases you want to back up. This figure shows just one database to back up.

7. On the next page (shown in Figure 5-7), select the reporting options for the plan: write a log to a specific location, send an e-mail, or both.

FIGURE 5-6

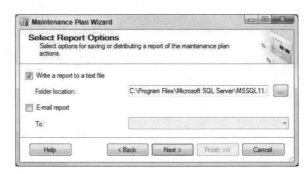

FIGURE 5-7

8. Select Next to go to the final page of the wizard, where you can confirm your selections (see Figure 5-8).

9. Click Finish to create your plan. While the plan is being created, a status page will show you the progress on each step of the plan's creation, as shown in Figure 5-9.

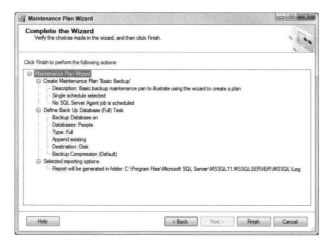

FIGURE 5-8

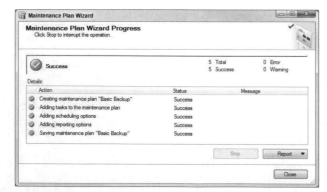

FIGURE 5-9

The new plan now displays in the Object Explorer under the Maintenance Plans node and can be manually run by using the menu from that node.

You should have noticed along the way that the Maintenance Plan Wizard can perform only a limited number of tasks, but these are some of the most important routine maintenance activities on the server. Using this wizard enables you to automate many of the essential tasks needed on a SQL Server.

To explore more details about the plan you just created, look at the job created for this plan in the SQL Server Agent node, under the Jobs node. The job will be named <Your plan name>. subplan_1, so in this example the job name is Basic Backup.Subplan_1.

Maintenance Plan Designer

Now that you've used the Wizard to create a basic backup job, it's time to learn how to use the Designer to achieve the same task:

1. Right-click on the Management Node in Object Explorer, and this time select the New Maintenance Plan item. This will open the New Maintenance Plan dialog, which you can see in Figure 5-10. Enter a new plan name, Basic Backup 2, so you don't conflict with the plan created using the Wizard. Click OK.

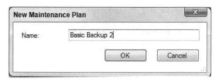

FIGURE 5-10

Figure 5-11 shows the Plan Designer dialog that appears. You see two new windows inside Management Studio. The Maintenance Plan Tasks toolbox appears as a pane below the Object Explorer. The Plan Designer window appears on the right side of the screen.

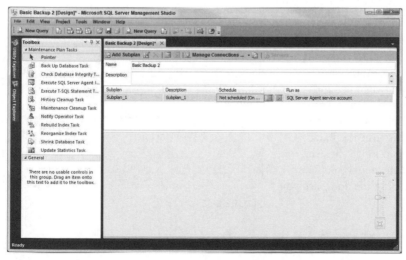

FIGURE 5-11

2. To create the basic backup task, click on the Back Up Database Task in the toolbox and drag it onto the designer's surface. After doing this, your designer will look like Figure 5-12.

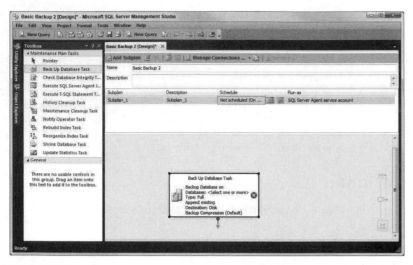

FIGURE 5-12

3. At this point you have created the basic Backup task, but haven't defined what the backup task needs to do. To specify the same parameters as you did when using the Wizard, edit the properties of the Back Up Database Task by double-clicking the task on the designer. This opens the task properties screen, shown in Figure 5-13.

4. This is the same dialog you completed using the Wizard, so select the same database to back up, and the same options you selected when using the Wizard. When you have finished making these changes, click OK to return to the designer. This time the Back Up Database Task no longer has the red warning sign, but now looks like Figure 5-14 (indicating the database you selected).

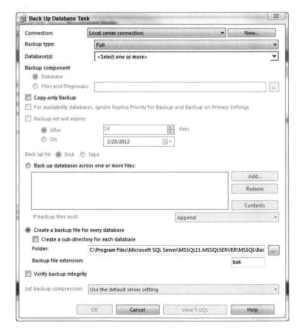

FIGURE 5-13

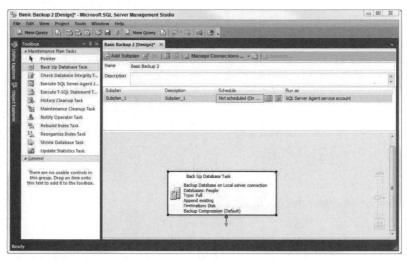

FIGURE 5-14

5. To create the plan you have just designed, merely save it. This creates the plan.

You can use the Plan Designer at any time to edit the plan's properties.

AUTOMATING SQL SERVER WITH SQL SERVER AGENT

When a Maintenance Plan does not cover all the automation you require on a SQL Server, or anytime you need to do more than you can with a Maintenance Plan, using SQL Server Agent directly is the way to go.

There are four basic components of SQL Server Agent, each of which the following sections discuss:

➤ **Jobs:** Defines the work to be done

➤ **Schedules:** Defines when the job will be executed.

➤ **Operators:** Lists the people who can be notified for job status and alerts

➤ **Alerts:** Enables you to set up an automatic response or notification when an event occurs

 By default, the SQL Server Agent service is not running, and the service is set to manual after the install of SQL Server. If you use SQL Server Agent service in production, be sure to use SQL Server Configuration Manager to set the Start Mode of this service to Automatic. You should never use the Services Console in the Administrative Tools folder to manage SQL Server Services. As indicated in SQL Server Books Online, using the Services Console to manage SQL Server services is unsupported.

Jobs

A great reason to use SQL Server Agent is to create tasks you can schedule to complete work automatically, such as backing up a database. A SQL Server Agent job contains the definition of the work to be done. The job itself doesn't do the work but is a container for the job steps, which is where the work is done. A job has a name, a description, an owner, a category, and a job can be enabled or disabled. Jobs can be run in several ways:

➤ By attaching the job to one or more schedules

➤ In response to one or more alerts

➤ By executing `sp_start_job`

➤ Manually via SQL Server Management Studio

Job Steps

A job consists of one or more job steps. The job steps are where the work is actually done. Each job step has a name and a type. Be sure to give your jobs and job steps good descriptive names that can be useful when they appear in error and logging messages. You can create a number of different types of job steps:

➤ **PowerShell Job:** Enables you to execute PowerShell scripts as part of a Job.

➤ **ActiveX Script:** Enables you to execute VBScript, JScript, or any other installable scripting language.

➤ **Operating System commands (CmdExec):** Enables you to execute command prompt items. You can execute `bat` files or any of the commands that would be contained in a `bat` or `cmd` file.

➤ **SQL Server Analysis Services command:** Enables you to execute an XML for Analysis (XMLA) command. This must use the `Execute` method, which enables you to select data and administer and process Analysis Services objects.

➤ **SQL Server Analysis Services Query:** Enables you to execute a Multidimensional Expression (MDX) against a cube. MDX queries enable you to select data from a cube.

➤ **SQL Server SSIS Package Execution:** Enables you to execute an SSIS package. You can assign variable values, configurations, and anything else you need to execute the package. This can save a great amount of time if you already have complex SSIS packages created, and want to execute them from a SQL Agent Job step.

➤ **Transact-SQL Script (T-SQL):** Enables you to execute T-SQL scripts. T-SQL scripts do not use SQL Server Agent Proxy accounts, described later in this chapter. If you are not a member of the sysadmin fixed-server role, the T-SQL step can run using your user credentials within the database. When members of the sysadm fixed-server role create T-SQL job steps, they may specify that the job step should run under the security context of a specific database user. If they specify a database user, the step executes as the specified user; otherwise, the step executes under the security context of the SQL Server Agent Service account.

The GUI for T-SQL security can be confusing. Although there is a Run As drop-down on the first page of the Job Step Properties dialog where you set up job steps, this is not where you set the security for T-SQL steps. The Run As drop-down here is used to specify security contexts for other types of steps. To set security for your T-SQL step, click the Advanced tab. At the bottom of the dialog is a Run as User drop-down. Set the T-SQL user security context here.

There are other job-step types that you do not usually create yourself, although it is possible to do so. These jobs, with their associated steps, are usually created by setting up replication. Each job step runs under a *security context*. The security contexts for other types of job steps are described later in this chapter. The process to set up replication defines jobs that use these step types:

➤ Replication Distributor

➤ Replication Merge

➤ Replication Queue Reader

➤ Replication Snapshot

➤ Replication Transaction Log Reader

There is some control of flow related to job steps as well. You may specify an action for when the step succeeds and when the step fails. These actions can be one of the following:

➤ Quit the job, indicating success.

➤ Quit the job, with failure.

➤ Go to another job step.

You may also require that the job step be retried before the job step fails. You may specify the number of retry attempts and the retry interval, in minutes. Once you set these guidelines, a job step will then be retried the number of times you specify in the Retry Attempts field before it executes the On Failure control of flow. If the Retry Interval in Minutes field has been set, the step waits for the specified time period before retrying. This can be useful when there are dependencies between jobs. For example, you may have a job step that does a bulk insert from a text file. The text file is placed into the proper directory by some other process, which may run late. You could create a VBScript job step that checks for the presence of the input file. To test for the file every 10 minutes for 30 minutes, you would set the retry attempts to 3 and the Retry Interval to 10.

When you create a job, you can place it into a job category. Each job can be in only one category. There are several predefined job categories, including [Uncategorized (Local)] and Database Engine Tuning Advisor. You can also create your own job categories.

1. From the Object Explorer Window of SQL Server Management Studio, open the SQL Server Agent item in the tree view and right-click the Jobs Node.

2. From the menu select Manage Job Categories. The dialog box shown in Figure 5-15 appears.

3. Select Add, and the dialog shown in Figure 5-16 appears.

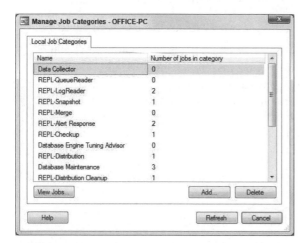

FIGURE 5-15

FIGURE 5-16

4. Enter the new Job Category name into the Name field, and select OK.

As trivial as it might seem, give some thought to organizing your jobs before creating your categories. You may be surprised how quickly the number of jobs on your server grows, making it difficult to find the correct job.

Job Step Logging

Each time a job is run, job history is created. Job history tells you when the job started, when it completed, and if it was successful. Each job step may be configured for logging and history as well. All the logging setup for a job step is on the Advanced Tab of the job step properties. The Advanced Tab of the Job Step Properties is shown in Figure 5-17 and the key options that affect logging are discussed in the following list.

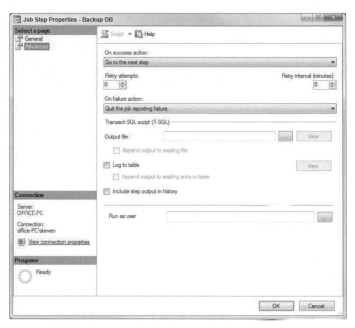

FIGURE 5-17

➤ **Output to File:** Job steps executed by `sysadmin` role members may also have the job step history written to a file. To do so, enter the filename in the Output File text box. Check the Append Output to Existing File check box if you do not want to overwrite the file. Job steps executed by others can log to only `dbo.sysjobstepslogs` in `msdb`.

➤ **Log to table:** You may also choose to have the information logged to `dbo.sysjobstepslogs` in `msdb`. To log to this table, check the Log to Table check box. To include step history from multiple job runs, also check the Append Output to Existing Entry in Table. Otherwise, you see only the most recent history.

➤ **Include step output in history:** To append the job step history to the job history, check the Include the step output in history check box.

 Anytime you refer to network resources such as operating system files, ensure that the appropriate proxy account has the correct permissions. In addition, always use the UNC name for files, so the job or its steps are not dependent on directory maps. This is an easy place to get into trouble between the test and production environments if you are not careful.

By default, SQL Server stores only 1,000 rows in its Job History Log and a maximum of 100 for any one job. The Job History Log is a rolling log, so the oldest records are deleted to make room for newer job history. If you have a lot of jobs, or jobs that run frequently, the Job History Log can soon become full and start deleting old records. If you need to change the size of the log, you can do so under the SQL Server Agent properties, as shown in Figure 5-18.

Job Notifications

You can configure SQL Server Agent to notify you when a job completes, succeeds, or fails. To do so, follow these steps:

1. In the Job Properties dialog, choose Notifications to see the dialog box shown in Figure 5-19.

2. A job can send a notification via e-mail, pager, and Net Send. A job can also write to the Windows Application Event Log. As Figure 5-19 shows, there is a line in the dialog box for each of these delivery methods. Place a check beside the delivery method you want; you may choose multiple methods.

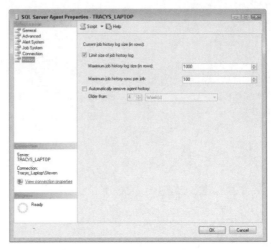

FIGURE 5-18

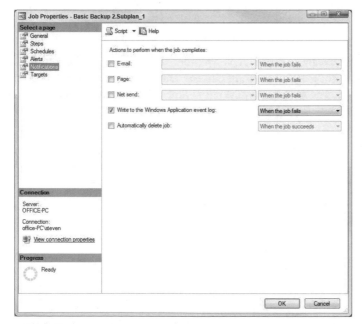

FIGURE 5-19

3. Click the drop-down menu for each option and choose an operator to notify. An operator enables you to define the e-mail address for the delivery. (Operator setup is described later in this chapter.)

4. Choose the event that should trigger the notification. It can be when the job completes, when the job fails, or when the job succeeds. You may not want to be notified at all for some jobs such as routine maintenance like Index Maintenance. However, for mission-critical

jobs, you might want to be e-mailed always when the job completes, and perhaps paged and notified through Net Send if the job fails, so you can know immediately. Examples of more critical jobs where you do want notification might be Backups and DBCC CHECKDB.

Windows Messenger Service must run on the server where SQL Server Agent runs to send notifications via Net Send. You can send a message to any workstation or user that can be seen from the SQL Server Agent server. The target workstation must also be running the Windows Messenger Service to enable it to receive the notification.

Schedules

One of the advantages of SQL Server Agent is that you can schedule your jobs. You can schedule a job to run at any of these times:

➤ When SQL Server Agent starts

➤ Once, at a specified date and time

➤ On a recurring basis

➤ When the CPU utilization of your server is idle

To create a schedule in Management Studio, select SQL Server Agent, right-click Jobs, and choose Manage Schedules. The scheduler is particularly easy to use. For instance, you can create a schedule that runs on the last weekday of every month. (It is convenient not to have to figure out which day is the last day of the month.) A schedule can be created when you create the job, or it can be created as an independent schedule, and later associated with jobs.

After your schedule is created, you can associate it with one or more jobs. A job can also have multiple schedules. You may want to create a schedule for nightly batching and another for end-of-month processing. A single job can be associated with both schedules. If a scheduled job is triggered when the job is already running, that schedule is simply skipped.

Care and planning should be taken when naming schedules, or confusion can occur. The most common difficulty is deciding if the schedule name should reflect *when* the schedule runs or *what* kind of work it includes. You actually can use both time and type indications on the same schedule. An example of this might be Daily Backup Schedule, or Daily Index Maintenance Schedule. For business-related schedules, you might create a schedule named End of Month Accounts Payable or Biweekly Payroll Cycle. Including business names can be convenient for quickly finding a schedule associated with a specific action or process. Including when the work occurs helps if you want to change the frequency of a schedule.

There are also times when the CPU utilization of your server is idle, and these jobs can be worthwhile. You can define when the CPU is idle by setting up the Idle CPU Condition in SQL Server Agent Properties on the Advanced tab. You can define a minimum CPU utilization and a duration here. When the CPU utilization is less than your definition for the duration you specify, CPU idle schedules are triggered. If the CPU is not otherwise busy, you can get some batch-related work done. Be careful, however; if you have many jobs scheduled for CPU idle; they can begin to run quickly and you can overpower your system. Be prudent with the number of jobs of this type that you schedule.

One item that is sorely lacking in SQL Server Agent's arsenal is the capability to link jobs together so that one begins as the other ends. You can still make this happen though by adding a final step in one job that executes the second job. You can do this using sp_start_job. However using this approach puts all the navigation inside job steps. Navigation between Jobs should not be happening at the Job Step level; it should be outside at the job level. Some third-party tools do a good job of this. However, if you want to do it on your own, it is likely to be difficult to maintain.

Operators

An operator is a SQL Server Agent object that contains a friendly name and some contact information. Operators can be notified on completion of SQL Server Agent jobs and when alerts occur. (Alerts are covered in the next section.) You may want to notify operators who can fix problems related to jobs and alerts, so they may go about their business to support the business. You may also want to automatically notify management when mission-critical events occur, such as failure of the payroll cycle.

You should define operators before you begin defining alerts. This enables you to choose the operators you want to notify as you are defining the alert, saving you some time. To create a new operator, follow these steps:

1. Expand the SQL Server Agent Node in the Object Explorer in SQL Server Management Studio.

2. From there, right-click Operators and select New Operator. The New Operator dialog shown in Figure 5-20 appears, and here you can create a new operator. The operator name must be unique and fewer than 128 characters.

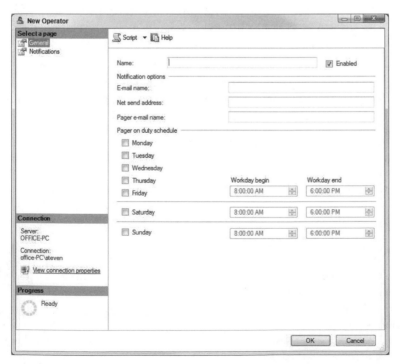

FIGURE 5-20

Operator Notifications

Jobs enable you to notify a single operator for three different send types:

➤ **E-mail**: To use e-mail or pager notifications, Database Mail must be set up and enabled, and SQL Server Agent must be configured. For e-mail notifications, you can provide an e-mail address. You may provide multiple e-mail addresses separated by semicolons. This could also be an e-mail group defined within your e-mail system. If you want to notify many people, it is better to define an e-mail group in your e-mail system. This enables you to change the list of people notified without having to change every job.

➤ **Pager**: For pager notifications, you also provide an e-mail address. SQL Server Agent does not come equipped with paging. You must purchase paging via e-mail capabilities from a third-party provider. SQL Server Agent merely sends the e-mail to the pager address. Your pager software does the rest. Some pager systems require additional configuration characters to be sent around the Subject, CC, or To line. This can be set up in SQL Server Agent Configuration, covered at the end of this chapter.

Notice that there is a Pager on Duty Schedule associated with the Pager E-mail Name. This applies only to pagers. You can set up an on-duty schedule for paging this operator and then set this operator to be notified regarding an alert or job completion. When the job completes or the alert occurs, the operator will be paged only during her pager on-duty schedule.

➤ **Net Send**: You can also use Net Send to notify an operator. To use Net Send, Windows Messaging Service must be running on the same server as SQL Agent. Additionally, you must provide the name of the workstation for this operator, and a Message dialog box pops up on her workstation. Out of these three, Net Send is the least reliable method of notification because the message is only available for a short period of time. If the operator is not at his desk at the time when the Net Send arrives, or the target server is offline or unavailable for any reason, the message will not be delivered.

Notifications from alerts can reach multiple operators. This provides you with several convenient options. For example, you can create an operator for each shift (First Shift Operators, Second Shift Operators, and Third Shift Operators), set up a group e-mail and a group page address for each of the shifts, set up the pager-duty schedule to match each shift's work schedule, and add all three operators to each alert. If an alert set up like this occurs at 2:00 a.m., then only the third-shift operators will be paged. If the alert occurs at 10:00 a.m., then only the first-shift operators will be paged.

There are several limitations of the schedule. Notice that the weekday schedule must be the same every day; although, you can specify a different schedule for Saturday and Sunday. Additionally, there is nothing to indicate company holidays or vacations. You can disable operators, perhaps because they are on vacation, but you cannot schedule the disablement in advance.

Failsafe Operator

What happens if an alert occurs and no operators are on duty, according to their pager on-duty schedule? Unless you specify a failsafe operator, no one would be notified. The failsafe operator is a security measure that enables an alert notification (not job notification) to be delivered for pager notifications (not e-mail or Net Send) that could not be sent. Failures to send pager notifications include the following:

➤ None of the specified operators are on duty.

➤ SQL Server Agent cannot access the appropriate tables in `msdb`.

To designate an operator as the Failsafe Operator, perform the following steps:

1. Select the properties of SQL Server Agent.

2. Select the Alert system tab as shown in Figure 5-21.

3. In the Fail-safe operator section select Enable fail-safe operator.

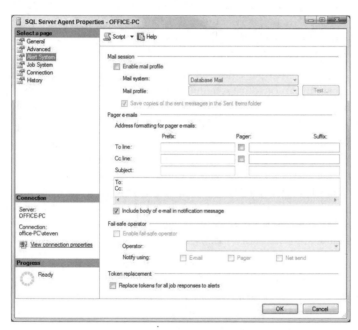

FIGURE 5-21

The failsafe operator is used only when *none* of the specified pager notifications could be made or `msdb` is not available. If you have three pager operators associated with a specific alert, and one of them is notified but two of them failed, the failsafe operator will *not* be notified.

You can indicate whether the failsafe operator will be notified using any or all of the three notification methods discussed in the previous section. However, a failsafe operator can be notified only if a pager notification cannot be successfully delivered, in which case the failsafe operator can be notified via e-mail, pager, Net Send, or a combination of these methods.

Because the failsafe operator is a security mechanism, you may not delete an operator identified as failsafe. First, you must either disable the failsafe setup for SQL Agent or choose a different failsafe operator. Then you can delete the operator. Disabling an operator defined as failsafe can prevent any normal alerts or job notifications from being sent but cannot restrict this operator's failsafe notifications.

Alerts

An *alert* is an automated response to an event. An *event* can be any of the following:

➤ SQL Server event

➤ SQL Server performance condition

➤ Windows Management Instrumentation (WMI) event

An alert can be created as a response to any of the events of these types. The following responses can be triggered as the result of an event alert:

➤ Start a SQL Server Agent job

➤ Notify one or more operators

 While you may notify only one operator of each notification type for job completion, you can notify multiple operators for alerts.

To create an alert, follow these steps:

1. Open the New Alert dialog (see Figure 5-22) by selecting New Alert from the context menu on the Alerts Node under the SQL Server Agent node in SQL Server Management Studio.

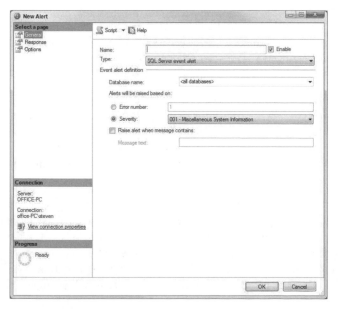

FIGURE 5-22

2. When you create an alert, you give it a name. Ensure that this name tells you something about what is going on; it will be included in all messages. Names such as Log Full Alert or Severity 18 Alert on Production might be useful.

3. Then choose the event type on which the alert is based (refer to Figure 5-22). SQL Server events and SQL Server performance condition events are covered in this section; WMI events are outside the scope of this book and not addressed here.

SQL Server Event Alerts

The SQL Server event alerts are based mainly on error messages. You can create an alert based on one of two things: a specific error number or on an error's severity level.

For an alert based on a specific error number, you might create an alert on error number 9002 (log file full) or error number 1105 (out of disk space). An alert can be fired for any particular database or all databases. You may for example care to get this alert only when the Production database transaction log is full, not when the other test and development databases run out of log space. In this case, choose the Production database in the Database name drop-down list. If you want to alert on two databases but not all of them, you have to create two separate alerts. SQL Server doesn't currently support multiple database alerts.

> *It is common to set up alerts on error 9002 for your important databases to notify you if the database is out of log space. This way, by the time your users call on the phone, you can tell them you are already aware of the problem and are working on it.*

Each error also has a severity level, and you can choose to create an alert based on this specific severity level. For instance, severity 19 and above are fatal server errors, and you may want to receive an alert when any fatal SQL error occurs. If so, you would create alerts for each severity level from 19 through 25.

When using various combinations of error number and severity level alerts, it is important to remember that error number alerts trump error severity level alerts. For example, if you create an alert on one specific error number that has a severity level of 16 and then also create another alert for all severity-16 errors, only the error number alert will fire. You can think of the severity-level alert as a backup. Alerts defined on specific error numbers fire when the error occurs. For all other errors of that severity, the severity-level alert fires as needed.

If you create two of the same error-level or severity-level alerts in the same database, then only one gets fired. For example, suppose you create an alert on message number 50001 in a database called Production and another alert on message number 50001 for <all databases>. In this case, when the error message occurs in Production, the alert for Production fires, not the <all databases> alert. The <all databases> alert fires for a message number 50001 that occurs in any database other than Production. The lesson here is that the most local handling of an event will trump a more general specification.

You may also create an alert that has an additional restriction on the text of the message. You can create an alert using the same process as previously stated at the beginning of the Alerts section, but check the box Raise Alert When Message Contains, and enter a text string in the text box. The alert then fires only on messages that include the specified text. For example, you could create an event that fires when the text `Page Bob` is included in the error message. Then applications could raise user errors that cause the alert to occur, paging Bob. The same principle as before applies here though: If a message with matching text is sent, the associated alert fires. The more general alert fires only if there is no text match.

> *SQL Server alerts work by watching the operating system application event log. If the event is not logged, the alert does not fire. However, you can use the* `sp_altermessage` *system stored procedure and specify* `@parameter = 'write_to_log'` *to change the behavior such that the event is now logged.*

You can create error messages with the `sp_addmessage` stored procedure. You may specify whether the message is logged. For example, you can create a simple message using the following SQL:

```
sp_addmessage 50001,16 ,'MESSAGE', @with_log =  'TRUE'
```

The preceding message has a message number of 50001 and a severity level of 16. You can then create alerts to test your system. Set these alerts to use e-mail as the response. To test the alert, use the following code:

```
Raiserror(50001,16,1)with log
Select * from msdb.dbo.sysmail_allitems
```

`Raiserror` sends the error message. You can log an error message using the `Raiserror` command if you have the appropriate permissions.

`Select` displays all the mail items. Scroll to the bottom of the list to check for the mail notification that has been attached as a response to the alert.

SQL Server Performance Condition Alerts

When you install SQL Server, a collection of Windows Performance Monitor counters is also installed. The Windows Performance Monitor tool enables the operations staff to monitor the performance of the server, including CPU utilization, memory utilization, and much more. When SQL Server is installed, an additional collection of monitor counters is added to enable DBAs to monitor the performance and status of SQL Server instances. You can create an alert on a condition based on any SQL Server counter. For more information on monitoring SQL Server using Performance Counters, refer to Chapter 12, "Monitoring Your SQL Server." A SQL Server performance condition alert is shown in Figure 5-23.

> *You cannot create multicounter alerts. For example, you cannot create an alert that fires when Percent Log Used is greater than 80 and Transactions/sec is greater than 100. You must choose to alert on a single counter.*

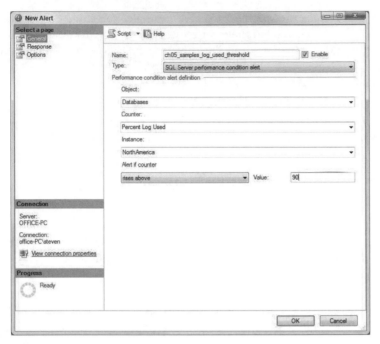

FIGURE 5-23

Performance counters are grouped according to their objects. For instance, the Databases object contains the counters associated with a specific database, such as Percent Log Used and Transactions/sec. The Buffer Manager object includes counters specific to buffer management. To begin creating an alert, follow these steps:

1. Choose the object and then the counter for which you want to create an alert.

 You cannot create SQL Server alerts on counters that are not specifically for SQL Server, such as CPU utilization. However, the Performance Monitor tool gives you the capability to set alerts for these other non-SQL Server counters.

2. The next choice you make is in the Instance text box. When you choose Databases objects, the Instance text box contains the list of databases. Select the database on which to create the alert.

3. Next is the Alert if Counter box. You can alert if the counter falls below, becomes equal to, or rises above a value you specify. Specify the value in the Value text box.

While you can still create an alert to notify you when the transaction log becomes full, this is not ideal because by then, it is a little too late. It would be better to know when it looks like the log may become full but before it actually does. You can do this by creating a performance condition alert on the Percent Log Used counter for the Databases object for the database you are interested in.

1. Choose when the counter rises above some safe limit, probably 80 to 95 percent. You can then be notified before the log is full.

2. Adjust this actual value so that you are not notified too quickly. If you have set up your log to be what you believe is large enough, you might instead want to notify on autogrowths.

WMI Event Alerts

Windows Management Instrumentation (WMI) is a tremendously powerful mechanism, but is also the least understood of all the alerting technologies.

SQL Server 2005 introduced the WMI Provider for Server Events which translates WMI Query Language (WQL) queries for events into event notifications in a specific database. For more information on using event notifications see Chapter 12, "Monitoring Your SQL Server."

To create a WMI event alert, select WMI event alert as the Type for the alert, validate the namespace is correct, and enter your WQL query.

Alert Responses

As was previously discussed, you can respond to an alert by starting a SQL Server Agent job or notifying one or more operators. You set this up on the Response tab of the Create Alert dialog box. To execute this job, simply check the check box and choose an existing job or create a new job. To notify an operator, check the appropriate box, and select the operators you want to notify by choosing one or more of the notification methods. For alerts, it is nice to have an operator for each shift you must cover, with the pager on duty set up appropriately, as discussed in the "Operators" section earlier in the chapter.

As you think about how you might best use this in your enterprise, imagine a scenario such as the transaction log getting full. You could set up a performance alert to notify operators when the log is actually full and run a job that grows the log. You could set up an alert that backs up the log when it becomes 80 percent full.

The scenario might play out as follows. You are having lunch and your pager goes off, notifying you that the log is 70 percent full. A job runs automatically that tries to back up the log to free space. In a couple of minutes you get a page telling you that the job completed successfully. After a few more potato chips, your pager goes off yet again — the log is now 80 percent full. The prior log backup did not free up any space. There might be a long-running transaction. The log backup job runs again, and you are notified upon its completion. You finish your lunch with no other pages. This means the last log backup freed up some space and you are now in good shape.

Your pager may have gone off again, telling you that the log is nearly full, and has either been extended with autogrow, or a job to extend the log has run and extended the transaction log onto an emergency log disk. It's probably time for you to get back to work, but the automation you have brought to the system has already been fighting this problem while you ate your lunch, notifying you of each step. With some thoughtful consideration, you might account for many planned responses such as this, making your life easier and operations tighter.

The Alert Options page in the Create Alert dialog box enables you to do several things:

➤ **Specify when to include more detailed information in the notification.** Sometimes the error text of the message might be long. Additionally, you may have a limit on the amount of data that can be presented on your devices. Some pagers limit you to as few as 32 characters. You should not include the error text for those message types that cannot handle the extra text, which are most commonly pagers.

➤ **Add information to the notification.** The dialog includes a large text box labeled Additional Notification Message to Send. You can type any text here, and it will be included in the notification message. Perhaps something such as Get Up, Come In, and Fix This Problem Immediately might be appropriate.

➤ **Delay the time between responses.** At the bottom of the dialog, you can set a delay between responses. The default value for this is 0. Imagine a scenario in which an alert goes off many times during a short period. Perhaps a program is repeatedly executing `raiserror` or a performance condition alert is going wild. The performance condition alerts that run to alert of limited resources are especially vulnerable to this problem. You run low on memory, which causes an alert or job to run, which uses more memory. This causes the alert to fire again, using more memory, repeatedly. You are paged repeatedly as well.

You can right-click any of the SQL Server Agent objects and create a script that can drop or create the object. If you want the same object to exist on many servers, you can script it out, change the server name, and load it onto a different server. This means you would have to keep operators, jobs, alerts, and proxies in sync between multiple servers, which could be painful and error prone. Event forwarding can also simplify your life when you administer many servers. Multiserver jobs and event forwarding are covered later in the section "Multiserver Administration."

SQL SERVER AGENT SECURITY

SQL Server Agent security is more fine-grained than ever. This section covers not only the service account, but also security issues such as who can create, see, and run SQL Server Agent jobs. SQL Server 2012 enables multiple, separate proxy accounts to be affiliated with each job step. These proxy accounts are associated with SQL logins, which provide excellent control for each type of job step.

Service Account

The SQL Server Agent service account should be a domain account if you plan to take advantage of Database Mail or require any network connectivity. The account should map to a login that is also a member of the sysadmin fixed-server role.

Access to SQL Agent

After the installation, only members of the sysadmin fixed-server role have access to SQL Server Agent objects. Others cannot even see the SQL Server Agent object in the Object Explorer of Management Studio. To give other users access to SQL Agent, you must add them to one of three fixed database roles in the `msdb` database:

➤ SQLAgentUserRole

➤ SQLAgentReaderRole

➤ SQLAgentOperatorRole

The roles are listed in order of increased capability, with `SQLAgentOperator` having the highest capability. Each higher role includes the permissions associated with the lower roles, so it is not necessary to assign a user to more than one role.

Members of the sysadmin fixed-server role have access to all the capabilities of SQL Server Agent and do not have to be added to any of these roles.

SQLAgentUserRole

Members of the user role have the most restricted access to SQL Server Agent. They can see only the Jobs node under SQL Server Agent and can access only local jobs and schedules that they own. They cannot use multi-server jobs, which are discussed later in this chapter. They can create, alter, delete, execute, start, and stop their own jobs and job schedules. They can view but not delete the job history for their own jobs. They can see and select operators to be notified on completion of their jobs and choose from the available proxies for their job steps.

SQLAgentReaderRole

The reader role includes all the permissions of the user role. It can create and run the same things as a user, but this role can see the list of multi-server jobs, including their properties and history. They can also see all the jobs and schedules on the local server, not just the ones they own. They can see only the Jobs node under SQL Server Agent as well.

SQLAgentOperatorRole

The operator role is the least restricted role and includes all the permissions of the reader role and the user role. This role has additional read capabilities and execute capabilities. Members of this role can view the properties of proxies and operators. They can list the available proxies and alerts on the server as well. Members of this role can also execute, start, or stop local jobs. They can enable or disable any job or operator; although, they must use the `sp_update_job` and `sp_update_schedule` procedures to do so. They can delete job history for any job. The Jobs, Alerts, Operators, and Proxies nodes under SQL Server Agent are visible to this role. Only the Error Log node is hidden.

SQL Server Agent Proxies

A SQL Server Agent Proxy defines the security context under which different job steps run. In the case where the user who creates a SQL Server Agent job does not have permissions to access the resources needed by the job, the job creator can specify a proxy. The proxy contains the credentials of a Windows user account that does have access to the resources needed by the job. For job steps that have a proxy specified, SQL Server Agent impersonates the proxy account and runs the job step while impersonating that user account.

SQL Server Agent Subsystems

SQL Server Agent subsystems are objects that group similar sets of functionality that can be used by SQL Server Agent proxies. These subsystems provide a security boundary that enables a more complex security model to SQL Agent Proxies.

SQL Server Agent has 11 subsystems on which security can be placed. When you add a job step, it appears in the following order:

➤ ActiveX Script

➤ Operating System (CmdExec)

➤ PowerShell

➤ Replication Distributor

➤ Replication Merge

➤ Replication Queue Reader

➤ Replication Snapshot

➤ Replication Transaction Log Reader

➤ Analysis Services Command

➤ Analysis Services Query

➤ SSIS Package Execution

➤ Transact SQL

The permissions for Transact SQL are not governed by proxy. All users execute T-SQL under their own account. If you are a member of the sysadmin group, you can choose any SQL login as the Run As Account. All the other subsystems use one or more proxies to determine permissions for the subsystem.

Subsystem Permissions

Each subsystem has its own permissions, but the proxy combines the permissions for the CmdExec step and the users who may run under this proxy. Figure 5-24 shows the basic relationship among the parts.

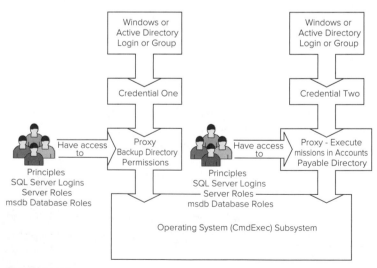

FIGURE 5-24

Because the proxy combines these permission, it is difficult to determine which operating-system permissions are used when someone executes a CmdExec job step. Issues may arise when setting permissions for proxies, so it is important to perform the set-up correctly the first time. The following steps show the setup for permissions for the operating system (CmdExec) subsystem.

1. First, you must create a credential. The easiest way to do this is in Management Studio: Expand Security, right-click on Credentials, and choose New Credential. A dialog box like the one shown in Figure 5-25 displays.

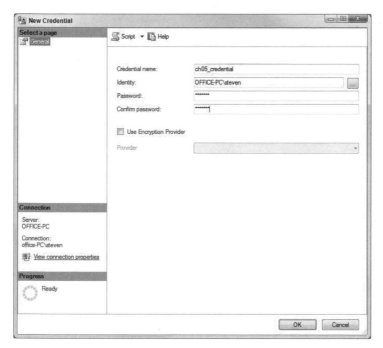

FIGURE 5-25

2. Give the credential a friendly name, and associate it with a Windows login or group. You must also provide the password to complete the creation. The permissions associated with this login or group will be the permissions applied to the CmdExec job step.

 If your SMTP Server requires a login, you may want to set up a specific local account with minimum permissions specifically for sending SMTP mail. The sole purpose of this account is to follow the principle of least privileges; it should be used for nothing else.

3. Now you can create your proxy. In Management Studio, expand SQL Server Agent, right-click Proxies, and choose New Proxy. You get a New Proxy Account dialog box, as shown in Figure 5-26.

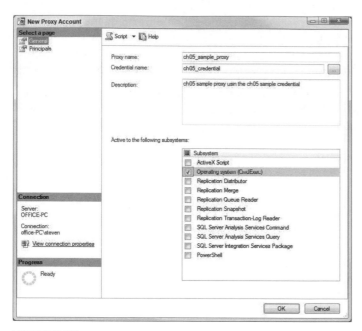

FIGURE 5-26

4. Give the proxy a name that provides information about its security level or its intended use. Then associate a credential with the proxy. The proxy provides the permissions associated with its credential when it is used. Provide a more detailed description of what the proxy enables and how it should be used and when.

5. Then select the subsystems that can use the proxy. A proxy can be associated with many subsystems.

6. Create a list of users (principles) who may use this proxy. This is done on the Principles page. A principle can be a Server Role, a SQL Login, or an `msdb` role.

7. Now assume you have created the two proxies for the `CmdExec` subsystem (refer to Figure 5-24). Your SQL login is associated with both proxies. You want to create a job that contains a CmdExec job step. When you add the job step, open the drop-down labeled Run As, which contains a list of all the proxies you are allowed to use for your job step. Each proxy has its own permissions. Choose the proxy that contains the permissions you need for your job step, and you should be ready to go.

CONFIGURING SQL SERVER AGENT

Now that you have learned how things work in SQL Agent, you can take on the configuration task. You already know about some of the configuration options, so now you can go through the different pages to configure the SQL Server Agent properties.

To start configuration, right-click the SQL Server Agent node in Management Studio, and choose Properties.

General Properties

The General page appears, as shown in Figure 5-27. Review each section on this page and consider the following:

➤ Check the two top check boxes: Auto Restart SQL Server If It Stops Unexpectedly and Auto Restart SQL Server Agent If It Stops Unexpectedly. The Service Control Manager watches both of these services and automatically restarts them if they fail.

➤ Usually you leave the error-log location at the default; however, you can change it if you want. If you need some additional logging, check Include Execution Trace Messages. Execution Trace Messages provide detailed information on SQL Agent operation which is written to the SQL Agent Error Log. Enabling this option increases the space used in the SQL Agent Log, so Agent log size is something to consider when enabling this option.

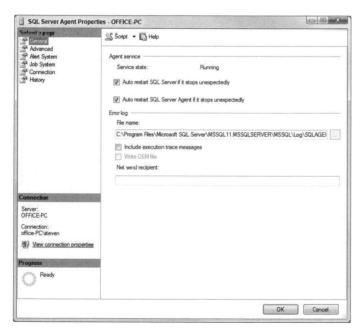

FIGURE 5-27

➤ To get a Net Send when errors are logged, enter a workstation name in the Net Send Recipient text box. Of course, Windows Messaging Service must be running on the server for Net Sends to occur.

Advanced Properties

Choose the Advanced Page on the top left, which brings up the dialog shown in Figure 5-28. There are several options from which to choose on this page:

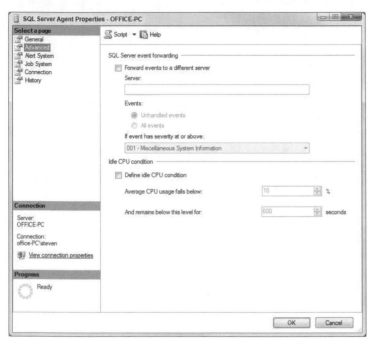

FIGURE 5-28

➤ The top section, SQL Server Event Forwarding, enables you to forward your events from one server to another. You can set up operators and alerts on a single server and then have the other servers forward their events to the single server. To use this capability, you also need to understand how to use SQL Server Agent tokens, which are covered in the section "Using Token Replacement" later in this chapter. If you want to employ this capability, check the box labeled Forward Events to a Different Server. Then select the server name. You can forward all events or only unhandled events. An unhandled event is one that does not have an alert defined for it. You also select how severe the error must be before it can be forwarded. For example, you may not want anything less than a severity 16 error (Miscellaneous User Error) to be forwarded. Whether you forward severity 16 errors depends on whether you have application-defined errors that specify notifications. If you plan to use this capability, you also need to understand how to use SQL Server Agent tokens, which are covered in the section "Using Token Replacement" later in this chapter.

➤ The second section is Idle CPU Condition. Recall that you can create a schedule that runs when the CPU becomes idle. This is where you define what *idle* means. The default is CPU utilization at less than 10 percent for 10 minutes.

Alert System Properties

The next page is for the Alert System, as shown in Figure 5-29.

FIGURE 5-29

➤ If you plan to use Database Mail, you do the setup here. Although you may have many mail profiles in Database Mail, SQL Server Agent uses only one profile. Choose the mail system and profile.

➤ The second section is for pager e-mails. If your pager system requires special control characters in the To, CC, or Subject line, you may add those characters here in front of the item (prefix) or after the item (suffix). As you make changes, you can see the effect in the small box below your data-entry section. You may also choose to include or exclude the body of the e-mail for pagers by indicating your selection in the appropriate check box.

➤ The third section enables you to provide failsafe operator information. Please use this if you are doing any notifications. It is too easy to change a schedule in such a way that results in no one being notified, so don't get caught. Enable this section, choose an operator, and indicate how the failsafe messages should be delivered (by e-mail, pager, Net Send, or some combination of these).

➤ The last check box enables you to specify whether you want to have tokens replaced in jobs run from alerts. Details of token replacement are covered in the section "Multiserver Administration" later in this chapter.

Job System Properties

The Job System page is next, as shown in Figure 5-30.

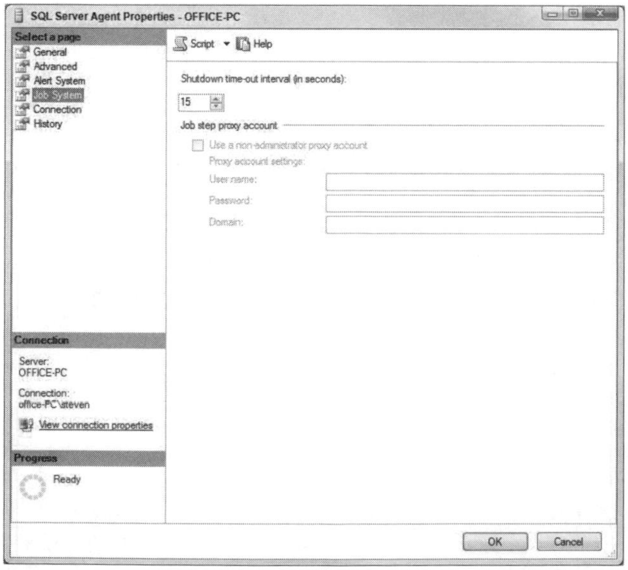

FIGURE 5-30

> ➤ In the first section, you can specify the shut-down period (in seconds) in the Shutdown time-out interval list. For instance, suppose you are trying to shut down SQL Agent, and jobs are running. You can specify how long SQL Server Agent should wait for jobs to complete before killing them and shutting down.

> ➤ The second section is only available if you administer a SQL Server 2000 Agent. This enables you to set the backward compatible nonadministrator proxy. SQL 2000 allowed only one proxy. SQL Server 2005, 2008, and 2012 allow many proxies, so this is not necessary when administering SQL Server 2005, 2008, and 2012 Agents.

Connection Properties

The Connection page is one that most users do not need. SQL Server Agent connects to SQL Server, by default, using the server name, the default port, the SQL Server Agent Service account, and the highest-matching protocol between the client configuration and the protocols enabled for SQL Server. There are several circumstances in which you may want to alter these defaults:

> ➤ Your server has multiple network cards, and you want to specify a particular IP or port.

> ➤ You want to connect using a specific protocol (IP, for instance).

> ➤ You want SQL Server Agent to connect to the server using a login different from the service account login.

To create an alias for SQL Server, follow these steps:

1. Open Configuration Manager.

2. Expand the SQL Native Client Configuration, right-click Aliases, and choose New Alias.

3. Set up the alias to suit your connectivity needs.

4. On the SQL Server Agent Connection page, enter the alias name and the connection information you want SQL Server Agent to use. Although SQL Server authentication is allowed, it is not recommended.

History Properties

The last page is the History page, shown previously in Figure 5-18. Here you can limit the size of the job history log to a fixed number of rows, and the Maximum Job History Rows per Job option is a lifesaver. Imagine a job that runs repeatedly. It could be a job scheduled by a user to run every second, or it could be a job that runs from an alert that occurs repeatedly. In any case, the log entries from this job could fill up your entire job history, and you would have no history information for any other jobs. That could leave you in a tough spot if any other job needed debugging. This is exactly the situation that Maximum Job History Rows per Job is intended to prevent. The default is 100 rows, but you can change it based on your needs.

DATABASE MAIL

Database Mail appeared with SQL Server 2005 and was a welcome replacement for SQLMail; Database Mail and SQLMail both enable you to notify operators via e-mail and to send e-mails via stored procedures, but Database Mail is more secure, more reliable, and does not rely on MAPI.

It uses Simple Mail Transfer Protocol (SMTP). It is cluster-aware, and enables automatic retry of failed e-mail messages and failover to another SMTP server should the first become unavailable. Database Mail also enables you to set up multiple accounts and provide secured or public access to the accounts.

 Database Mail is not available in the Express Edition of SQL Server.

Architecture

Database Mail is loosely coupled to SQL Server and it uses queuing provided by Service Broker technologies, as shown in Figure 5-31. When an e-mail is sent, either by calling `sp_send_dbmail` or from SQL Server Agent notifications, security is checked. The e-mail is stored in a table in `msdb`, and a message is placed in the Service Broker message queue in `msdb`. This activates an external program, `DatabaseMail.exe`, located in the `MSSQL\Binn` directory. `DatabaseMail.exe` reads the message and sends the e-mail with any attachments to one or more SMTP mail servers. It then places a message in the status queue, containing the results of the send process. The status queue insert activates a stored procedure in `msdb` to update the status of the e-mail in `msdb`.

Security

For security reasons, Database Mail is disabled by default. You can enable and configure it by running the Database Mail Configuration Wizard, or running the Database Mail XPs.

Additionally, to send notifications via Database Mail from SQL Agent, SQL Server Agent must be configured to use Database Mail, as covered in the "SQL Server Agent Configuration" section of this chapter.

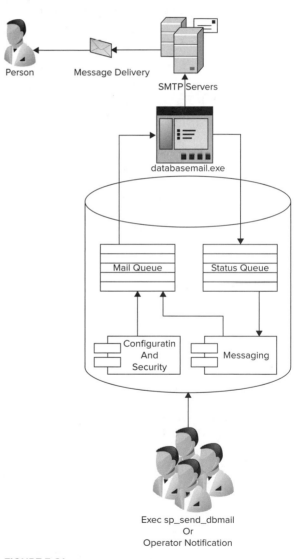

FIGURE 5-31

The external program, `DatabaseMail.exe`, must have network access to the SMTP servers. It runs using the security credentials for the SQL Server Service account. Therefore, the SQL Server Service account must have network access, and the SMTP servers must enable connections from the SQL Server computer. Database Mail supports Secure Sockets Layer (SSL) if it is required by the SMTP server.

 Local System and Local Service do not have network access and cannot be used as service accounts for SQL Server if you use Database Mail. Database Mail cannot connect to another computer (the SMTP server) when using either of these local accounts.

To send Database Mail, you must either be a member of the sysadmin fixed-server role or be a member of the `DatabaseMailUserRole` in `msdb`. You can place a size limit on mail attachments and prohibit attachments with certain file extensions.

Configuration

To use Database Mail, you need to do some configuration. Specifically, you need to set up the Database Mail account, configure the mail procedure itself, and set up archiving. This is achieved using the Database Mail configuration Wizard. The first page of the Database Mail configuration wizard is shown in Figure 5-32.

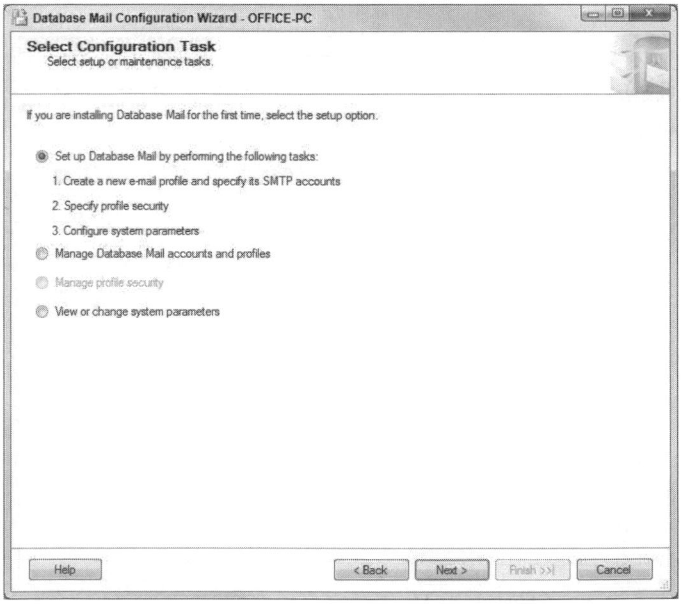

FIGURE 5-32

Database Mail Account

A Database Mail account is a basic unit of configuration for Database Mail. An account contains the following configuration information:

➤ **"From" information for the e-mail messages:** All outgoing e-mail messages indicate that they are from the account you provide here. This does not have to be a real e-mail account.

➤ **"Reply to" e-mail address:** If the recipient of one of these e-mails tries to reply, the reply is sent to the e-mail address provided for this account.

➤ **SMTP connection information:** The SMTP Server name and port number are included in the account configuration. Database Mail supports encrypted and unencrypted messages. Encryption is done via Secure Sockets Layer (SSL). Whether you want the messages from this account to be encrypted is included in the account configuration.

➤ **E-mail retry configuration:** You may specify how many times to retry sending an e-mail and a wait period between retries.

➤ **E-mail size limits:** You may set a maximum size limit allowed for e-mails from this account.

➤ **Excluded attachment extension list:** You may provide a list of file extensions. Any attachment that has a file extension in the prohibited list will not be allowed.

➤ **Logging level:** You may specify how much logging should be done for this account.

 If your passwords time out on a regular basis, your job steps begin to fail. You have to reset the passwords for each credential or increase or drop the password expiration for the special accounts. These accounts should be created specifically for this and have the minimum security necessary for the job step to complete successfully.

You should plan your implementation carefully. You may set up more than one Database Mail account. For example, you may want to have accounts for several different SMTP servers. This would enable you to automatically failover from one to another. This is done via profiles, which is covered in the next section. You may also want to set up a special account that allows dangerous extensions or large attachments to be sent, and restrict that account to special users.

Another reason to set up multiple accounts is to provide different From and Reply to addresses. You may want to do this for several departments in your company. For instance, you might set up an account named Accounts Payable that has a From address of `AccountsPayable@mycompany.com` and a Reply to address of `IncomingAPEmail@mycompany.com`. This reply address could be an e-mail group that sends to the accounts payable service reps at your company.

Setup

In this section, you set up Database Mail.

1. Use the wizard by expanding Management in SQL Server Management Studio. Right-click Database Mail and choose Configure Database Mail. This launches the Database Mail Configuration Wizard and shows the wizards welcome page.

2. Click Next on the Welcome page. The next page in the wizard is the Select Configuration page, and is shown previously in Figure 5-32. Check the top radio button to indicate you are setting up Database Mail for the first time. Click Next.

3. If you haven't previously enabled Database Mail, you receive a message box asking if you want to enable the Database Mail feature. Choose Yes and continue.

4. This brings you to the New Profile dialog box, as shown in Figure 5-33. To continue, you need to add at least one mail account. Click the Add button to display the New Database Mail Account dialog, as shown in Figure 5-34. Here you provide the information needed to communicate with an SMTP server. Choose a name and description for this account.

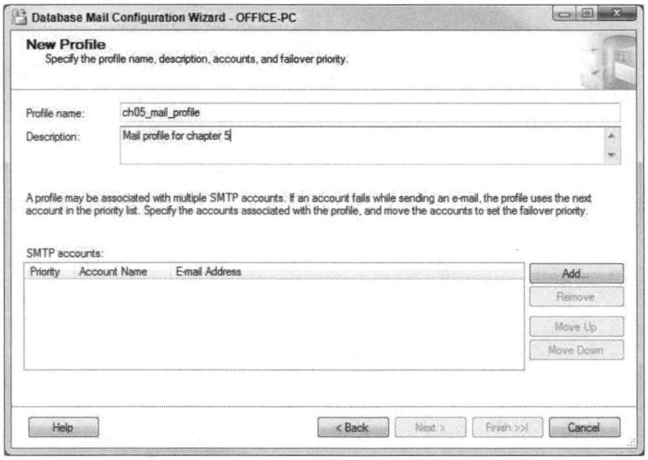

FIGURE 5-33

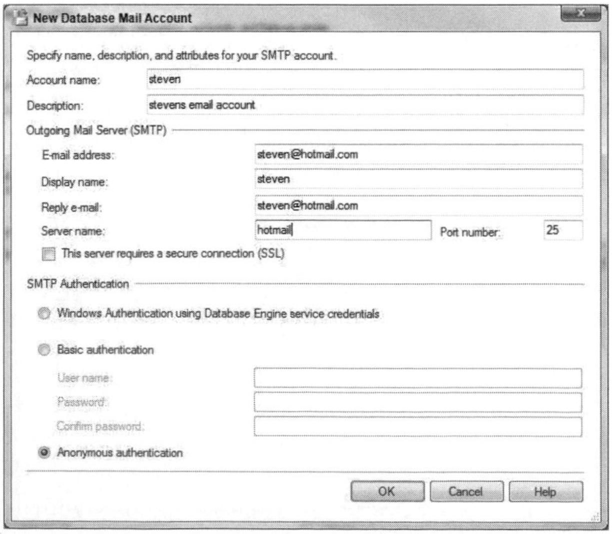

FIGURE 5-34

E-mails sent from this account will be tagged from the e-mail address and display name that you set in this section. If the recipients reply to the e-mail, the reply will be sent to the address you supply in the Reply e-mail text box.

5. In the Server name text box, provide the name of the SMTP server. This is usually in the form of smtp.*myserver*.com. Do not provide the complete URL, such as http://smtp .*myserver*.com. Database Mail does this for you. If you check the box labeled This Server Requires a Secure Connection (SSL), the URL created will be https://smtp.*myserver*.com. The default port number of 25 will suffice unless you have changed the SMTP port number.

6. Provide the SMTP login information in the SMTP authentication section. Not all SMTP servers require authentication; some require only a known sender e-mail, and others require nothing. After supplying the needed information, click OK to return to the New Profile dialog, and then click Next.

7. The next page is the Manage Profile Security dialog, as shown in Figure 5-35. Here you set up public and private profiles. Check the Public check box next to a profile to make it public. You may also want to set this as a default profile.

FIGURE 5-35

8. Click Next to move to the Configure System Parameters page. On this page you can change the values for system parameters such as retry attempts, maximum file size, prohibited extensions, and logging level. The default values work well in most cases.

9. Click Next to view the Complete the Wizard page, where you have a last chance to confirm the selections you made before they are applied.

10. Click Finish to apply the changes you made and view progress and a completion report as each set of changes is made.

11. To ensure things are working properly, you should send a test e-mail. In SQL Server Management Studio, expand Management, right-click Database Mail, and choose Send Test E-Mail. You are prompted to enter an e-mail address. Send the mail and wait for receipt.

Archiving

If you are using DBMail and sending mail and attachments, the mail you send and the attachments are stored in tables. These tables don't have any automatic maintenance, they just continue to grow. To prevent them from filling the database and causing errors, you will need to archive the data in them.

You can access mail information in the sysmail_allitems view. Attachments can be accessed via sysmail_mailattachments, and the mail log is in sysmail_eventlog. The tables under these views are not automatically maintained; they just get larger and larger. Therefore, to perform maintenance, Microsoft provides stored procedures to delete items from these tables: msdb.dbo. sysmail_delete_mailitems_sp and msdb.dbo.sysmail_delete_log_sp. Each of these has two parameters: @sent_before and @sent_status.

➤   @sent_before takes a datetime value and deletes all log or mail items with a time before the parameter time. When you do not specify a sent_status, all mail items that have a send_request_date prior to the parameter will be deleted, whether or not they have been sent; so be careful.

➤   @sent_status can have values of unsent, sent, failed, or retrying. When you specify a sent_status, only the mail items that have a sent_status equal to the parameter are deleted.

You may want to archive this information prior to its deletion.

MULTISERVER ADMINISTRATION

Several tactics within SQL Server 2012 enable you to easily administer multiple servers. The focus of these tactics is to centralize your administration. This can be done by forwarding events to a central event management server, which enables you to centralize alert handling. Another optimization is to use master and target servers to create jobs on a single master server and have the jobs run on multiple target servers.

Using Token Replacement

SQL Server 2012 has some nice capabilities related to SQL Server Agent job tokens. A *token* is a string literal that you use in your job steps (T-SQL scripts, CMDExec job steps, or Active Script). Before the job runs, SQL Server Agent does a string replacement of the token with its value. Tokens are usable only in SQL Server Agent jobs.

One of the tokens you can use is (STRTDT). For example, you might add the following in a T-SQL job step:

```
PRINT 'Job Start Date(YYYYMMDD):' + $ESCAPE_SQUOTE(STRTDT))
```

If you capture the output, it should look like this:

```
Job Start Date(YYYYMMDD):20120923
```

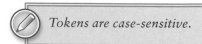

Tokens are case-sensitive.

The following is a list of tokens that you can use in any job:

➤ (DATE): Current Date (YYYYMMDD).

➤ (INST): Instance name of the SQL Server. This token is empty for the default instance.

➤ (JOBID): SQL Server Agent job ID.

➤ (MACH): Computer name where the job is run.

➤ (MSSA): Master SQLServerAgent service name.

➤ (OSCMD): Prefix for the program used to run CmdExec job steps.

➤ (SQLDIR): SQL Server's install directory. The default install directory is C:\Program Files\Microsoft SQL Server\MSSQL.

➤ (STEPCT): The number of times this step has executed. You could use this in looping code to terminate the step after a specific number of iterations. This count does not include retries on failure. This is updated on each step run during the job, such as a real-time counter.

➤ (STEPID): The job step ID.

➤ (SVR): The server name of the computer running SQL Server, including the instance name.

➤ (TIME): Current time (HHMMSS).

➤ (STRTTM): The job's start time (HHMMSS).

➤ (STRTDT): The job's start date (YYYYMMDD).

The following is a list of tokens that can be used only in a job that has been started from an alert. If these tokens are included in a job started any other way, the job throws an error:

➤ (A-DBN): Database name where the alert occurred

➤ (A-SVR): Server name where the alert occurred

➤ (A-ERR): Error number associated with the alert

➤ (A-SEV): Error severity associated with the alert

➤ (A-MSG): Message text associated with the alert

The following token is available for use only on jobs run as the result of a WMI alert (see the "Using WMI" section later in the chapter).

➤ (WMI(property)): Provides the value for the WMI property named property. $(WMI(DatabaseName)) returns the value of the DatabaseName property for the WMI alert that caused the job to run.

All these tokens must be used with escape macros. The purpose of this change is to increase the security related to the use of tokens from unknown sources. Consider the following token, which you might have included in a T-SQL job step:

```
Print 'Error message: $(A-MSG)'
```

The T-SQL job step runs as the result of a user error (`raiserror`). A malicious user could raise an error like this one:

```
Raiserror(''';Delete from dbo.Employee',16,1)
```

The error returned would be:

```
';Delete from dbo.Employee
```

The print message would be:

```
Print 'Error message:';Delete from dbo.Employee
```

If this happens, it means you have just been attacked with a SQL injection attack. The delete statement runs if the T-SQL job step has permission.

To combat an attack such as this, you must add an escape macro. Because the `print` statement uses single quotes, a SQL injection attack closes out the single quote and then insert its own SQL. To prevent this attack, you can double-quote any quote that comes in via the token. The escape macro `ESCAPE_SQUOTE` does exactly that. It is used like this:

```
Print 'Error message: $(ESCAPE_SQUOTE(A-MSG))'
```

Continuing the example, you end up with the following:

```
Print 'Error message:'';Delete from dbo.Employee
```

You then get an error due to the unmatched quote, and the step fails, keeping you safe.

The following is a list of escape macros:

➤ `$(ESCAPE_SQUOTE(token))`: Doubles single quotes (') in the replacement string.

➤ `$(ESCAPE_DQUOTE(token))`: Doubles double quotes (") in the replacement string.

➤ `$(ESCAPE_RBRACKET(token))`: Doubles right brackets (]) in the replacement string.

➤ `$(ESCAPE_NONE(token))`: The token replacement is made without changes. This is used for backward compatibility only.

You can also use these values directly if you ensure proper data types. The SQL script-looping job with tokens contains the following code that terminates a job step after it has executed five times. The top line converts the STEPCT token to an integer so it can be used in a comparison. Then the JOBID token for this job is converted to a binary 16 and passed to the `sp_stop_job` stored procedure, which can take the job ID of the job you want to stop:

```
IF Convert(int,$(ESCAPE_NONE(STEPCT))) >5
  BEGIN
  DECLARE @jobid binary(16)
  SELECT @jobid =Convert(Uniqueidentifier,$(ESCAPE_NONE(JOBID)))
  EXEC msdb.dbo.sp_stop_job @job_id = @jobid
  END
```

Imagine how you might use the alert-based tokens. You could create a SQL performance alert that fires when the `<any database>` transaction log becomes greater than 80 percent full. Create a job with a T-SQL step like this:

```
DECLARE @a varchar(100)
SELECT @a ='BACKUP LOG $(ESCAPE_SQUOTE(A-DBN))
  TO DISK = "\\UNCName\Share\$(ESCAPE_SQUOTE(A-DBN))\log.bak"'
SELECT @a
BACKUP LOG $(ESCAPE_SQUOTE(A-DBN))
  TO DISK = '\\UNCName\Share\\$(ESCAPE_SQUOTE(A-DBN))\log.bak'
```

Here UNCName is the name of the server where you want the backup to be stored and Share is the share on the server. Make sure the job runs when the alert occurs. If the alert fires for NorthAmerica, the backup command looks like this:

```
BACKUP LOG NorthAmerica TO DISK = \\UNCName\Share\\NorthAmerica\log.bak
```

You have to create the directory first and grant appropriate permissions to the proxy you use. You could create a CMDExec step, which creates the directory on-the-fly. Now, a single log backup job can back up any transaction log. You might improve the name of the directory you create in the CMDExec step by adding the date and time to the filename.

Event Forwarding

Where events and alerts are concerned, you can create operators and alerts on a single system and then have the other systems forward their events to your central alert-handling SQL Server, which responds to those alerts as necessary.

Designating a server to forward events to is done on the Advanced Page of the SQL Server Agent properties dialog (refer to Figure 5-28). Check Forward Events to a Different Server then you can specify the server to forward events to.

You can configure which events will be forwarded using by choosing from the options under Events. Here you can choose between Unhandled Events and All Events. If you choose All Events, you can then add a filter on the severity level If Event has Severity at or Above. You can set up operators on your master event management system. Create the jobs that respond to the alerts. Then create alerts on the single master event management system to handle the event. The jobs you create can take advantage of SQL Server Agent tokens and know on which server and database the original event occurred.

Using WMI

Windows Management Instrumentation (WMI) is a set of functions embedded into the kernel of Microsoft Operating Systems and Servers, including SQL Server. The purpose of WMI is to enable local and remote monitoring and management of servers. It is a standards-based implementation that incorporates the Distributed Management Task Force's (DMTF) Web-Based Enterprise Management (WBEM) and Common Information Model (CIM) specifications.

WMI is a big initiative and probably warrants an entire book of its own. What you need to know most is that WMI has many events for SQL Server. Search for WMI to start in Books Online, and you can discover the many, many events. You can create alerts on these events. Included are Data Definition Language (DDL) events that occur when databases are created or dropped and when tables are created or dropped, for example.

WMI has a specific language to query these events called Windows Management Instrumentation Query Language (WQL). It is similar to T-SQL, and you it is so easy that you should immediately feel comfortable with it.

Search Books Online for "WMI Provider for Server Events Classes and Properties." This material helps you navigate the many events available, and choose the specific event you want to monitor. Each event has a list of attributes, just like a table has a list of columns. Using WMI, you can select the attributes from the event in an alert.

To create an alert, use SQL Server Management Studio.

1. In Object Explorer, open the SQL Server Agent tree node, right-click Alerts, and choose New Alert. In the Alert Type drop-down box, choose WMI Event Alert. The namespace will be populated based on the server you connect to and should look like this:

    ```
    \\.\root\Microsoft\SqlServer\ServerEvents\SQL2012
    ```

    The period (.) represents the server name, which you can change, such as \\MYSQLSERVER\. The last node should be MSSQLSERVER for a default instance and the *<instance name>* for named instances. In the preceding example, the instance was called SQL2012.

2. In the text box, either enter your WQL query, as shown here:

    ```
    SELECT * FROM DDL_DATABASE_LEVEL_EVENTS
    ```

    Or to select only the TSQLCommand attribute, use this query:

    ```
    Select TSQLCommand from DDL_DATABASE_LEVEL_EVENTS
    ```

3. Click OK and there will be a pause. If your namespace is incorrect, or the syntax or event/attribute names are incorrect, you get a message immediately.

4. Then, in your job, you may use the WMI(attribute) event token — in this case:

    ```
    Print '$(ESCAPE_SQUOTE(WMI(TSQLCommand)))'
    ```

5. To get events from a database, Service Broker notifications must be turned on for that database. To turn on Service Broker notifications for NorthAmerica, use the following syntax:

    ```
    ALTER DATABASE NorthAmerica SET ENABLE_BROKER;
    ```

If your alerts occur but the text replacement for the WMI token is not being done, you probably need to turn on the Service Broker for your database.

The service account that SQL Server Agent uses must have permission on the namespace and ALTER ANY EVENT NOTIFICATION *permissions. This is done automatically if you use SQL Server Configuration Manager to set up accounts. However, to adjust these settings manually, from the Run prompt, type* **wmimgmt .msc.** *An administrative dialog appears, allowing you to set up permissions.*

If you want to try WMI, there is a test program for WMI on your server. To run it from the command line, type **WBEMTest**. It is installed in the WBEM directory of your Windows system directory. To find out more, Microsoft has an entire subsection of its website devoted to WMI. Just search for WMI on www.microsoft.com.

Multiserver Administration — Using Master and Target Servers

SQL Server enables you to set up a master server (MSX). The master server can send jobs to be run on one or more target servers (TSX), but the master server may not also be a target server that receives jobs from another master server. The target servers receive and run jobs from a single master server, in addition to their own local jobs. You may have multiple master servers in your environment, but a target server is associated with a single master server. This is a simple two-level hierarchy; a server is a master server, a target server, or neither. The language used to describe the process is military in character: You *enlist* target servers to add them, and they *defect* to go away.

Setting up servers is easy. Simply follow these steps:

1. In SSMS, right-click the SQL Server Agent node, select Multiserver Administration, and choose Make This a Master.

2. After the initial dialog box, you see a box where you can provide the e-mail address, pager address, and Net Send location to set up a *master server operator.* Fill in these fields appropriately. This operator will be set up on the master server and all target servers. This is the *only* operator who can be notified from multiserver jobs.

3. The next dialog box enables you to choose all the target servers. The list includes the servers that you have registered in SSMS. Choose the servers that you want to be targets of this master, and click Next. You may add additional registrations by clicking the Add Connection button.

4. Close this dialog box. SQL checks to ensure that the SQL versions of the master and targets are compatible. If the versions are not compatible, drop the target from the list and then continue. Later, you can upgrade the target or master, so the versions are the same.

5. Go to the next dialog box and use the wizard to create a login on the target, if necessary, and grant it login rights to the master server. Target servers must connect to the master server to share job status information. After you complete the setup, refresh your SQL Server Agent nodes and see the change. There will be a note on the master server (MSX) and a note on the target server.

Now you can create jobs to be used at multiple target servers. Notice on the MSX that the Jobs node is divided into two sections: local jobs and multiserver jobs. To create a job, follow these steps.

1. Right-click multiserver jobs, and select New Job to create a simple job.

2. Create a simple job on the MSX server and have it run at one or many TSX servers. While doing this, be sure to go to the notifications page. The only operator you can notify is MSXOperator.

Creating multiserver jobs is a nice way to manage a larger implementation without having to buy additional third-party products. No one on the TSX box can mess up your jobs. Use SSMS to connect to the target server as an administrator and look at the job properties for the job you just created and downloaded from the MSX. You can see the job, you can see the job history, and you can even run the job. You cannot delete the job, change the schedule, change the steps, or anything else. This job does not belong to you; it belongs to the MSX.

As you begin to think about how you might use this, be sure you consider the implications of a single job running on multiple servers. Any reference to directories, databases, and so on must be valid for all the TSXs where this job runs. You can create a single backup share that all the backups can use, for instance.

Because a job can start another job, you could also create a master job that has a single step that starts another job. This other job is created on each TSX and is specific to each TSX. This enables you to perform some customization, if necessary. To create a master job, perform the following steps:

1. Back in SSMS, right-click the SQL Server Agent node on the master server.

2. Choose Multi Server Administration. Here you can add target servers and manage target servers.

3. Choose Manage Target Servers. In this dialog box, you can monitor the status of everything. When you create a job for a target server, the job is automatically downloaded to the target server. If the unread instructions count does not go down to 0, poll the target server. This wakes it up to accept the instructions.

4. Click the relevant tab to see the details of downloaded instructions. This shows you details of when jobs are downloaded and updated.

5. Using the Post Instructions button in the Target Server Status dialog, you can synchronize clocks between the servers, defect target servers, set polling intervals, and start jobs. You can also start the job directly from the Jobs node on the MSX or the TSX.

6. Job histories can be viewed on the MSX for the job, just like any other job, but you cannot see job-step details. To get the step details, view the job history from the TSX.

7. You can defect TSXs from the TSX SQL Server Agent node or from the Manage Target Servers dialog on the MSX. When all the TSXs have been defected, the MSX is no longer an MSX.

SUMMARY

Automating SQL Server is one of the most important things you can learn to make your life and your business run smoothly and easily. Maintenance plans take away a lot of the work of automating routine maintenance activities, and are a great way to get started with automating common maintenance tasks. Additionally, SQL Server Agent provides many features and services to make your life easier. Just creating a few simple backup jobs that notify operators can automate many normal tasks. If you want to be fancy, go ahead, but do some planning first, especially when considering multiserver jobs.

Using Alerts is a great way to automate notifications about significant activities occurring on your database systems. You can use the pager notifications and the related on-duty schedules for regular e-mail or pagers. This is a good way to ensure that the correct people are notified. If you have many operators for alert notifications, consider creating e-mail groups and offloading some of the notification work to your e-mail server. Start small, and take your time. As you become more comfortable with Maintenance Plans and SQL Server Agent, you can spread your wings and fly.

Service Broker in SQL Server 2012

➤ Processing Data Asynchronously

➤ Configuring SQL Service Broker with TSQL

➤ Sending and Receiving Messages with SQL Service Broker

This chapter reviews the various objects that make up the SQL Server Service Broker. As you move through the chapter you look at the various object types and how to create the objects. Toward the end of the chapter you examine the T-SQL code to use the objects when sending and receiving messages within the SQL Server database, between databases on the same server, and on different servers.

ASYNCHRONOUS MESSAGING

Asynchronous data processing is a foreign concept to most data professionals. In traditional data processing everything is done synchronously. A command is run, and a result is stored or sent back to the end user, or whatever the command is supposed to do. With asynchronous messaging the command is sent and will be processed later when the SQL Server gets around to processing the command. This can't be done with traditional SQL commands, and you can't just flip a switch to put a database into some sort of asynchronous mode. Using asynchronous messaging with SQL Server Service Broker requires a specific setup and configuration.

There are a variety of scenarios where SQL Server Service Broker can fill the role. SQL Server Service Broker has been successfully deployed in applications where it handles Extract, Transform and Load (ETL) between an OLTP database and a data warehouse in real time, in banking applications where it handles nightly batch processing of transaction data, in social media handling friend requests on MySpace as well as a variety of other applications where the command needs to be completed, just not at the exact time that the command was issued.

SQL Service Broker Overview

SQL Server Service Broker provides an extremely flexible framework, which enables the creation of a variety of objects that can send messages within a database. The messages aren't limited to being sent within the database, though. Messages can also be sent from database to database. The databases that the messages are sent between can exist on the same database instance, different instances within a company's data center, or between two SQL Server instances across the Internet. Messages are sent within the context of a conversation, which this chapter discusses later.

When messages are sent, they can be received and processed on a schedule via the SQL Server Agent (or another job scheduler), on demand by a Windows application or service, or automatically when they are received by setting an activation stored procedure. Activation stored procedures are created on the queue and are triggered automatically when messages are received by the receiving queue. Activation procedures can be configured to run a single thread or multiple threads running in parallel with up to 62,767 parallel threads.

Messages can be sent in a single direction or bidirectionally as needed. Typically messages are sent in only one direction; however, there are situations in which after the initial message is processed you might want to send a confirmation message back to be processed on the sending side.

SQL Server Service Broker introduces three new commands that are used to send and receive messages, all of which are discussed in more detail later in this chapter. The first is the CREATE CONVERSATION DIALOG command that creates the conversation on which messages are then sent. The second is the SEND command that is used to send messages on the previously created conversation. The third is the RECEIVE command that is used to remove messages from the queue for processing.

The beauty of SQL Server Service Broker is that messages are processed once, and only once and in the order sent, provided the messages are sent within the same conversation. If messages are sent within different conversations, they may not be processed in the order they are sent.

You can use Service Broker to send messages of just about any size, from a blank message (not to be confused with a NULL message even though a blank message has a NULL value) to a message that fills the XML data type that caps at 1 billion bytes of Unicode data.

SQL Server Service Broker Versus Other Message Queues

A variety of message queuing technologies are available. Microsoft makes two: SQL Server Service Broker and Microsoft Message Queue (MSMQ). There are several third-party technologies that function similar to MSMQ that you can also use.

The big difference between SQL Server Service Broker and other queuing technologies is that SQL Server Service Broker stores the messages in queue within the database, and other queuing technologies store their data outside of the database. Because SQL Server Service Broker stores its messages within the database, this makes the queues transactionally consistent with the data that the queues back up and restore along with the database. The upside to this is that if the database is restored, the same messages will still be there when the database was backed up. When using a message queue such as MSMQ when the database is restored to an older point in time, any messages that were processed since the database was backed up are lost.

This doesn't necessarily mean that SQL Server Service Broker is a superior queuing technology over other message queuing technologies though. There are places in which SQL Server Service Broker makes more sense as the solution and places in which a message queue outside of the database makes more sense. For instance, if you have two Windows services (or applications) that need to send messages to each other and don't already have a need to access a database, then using SQL Server Service Broker would not be a good fit. This is true because it adds a dependency to SQL Server that doesn't already exist because the SQL Server would require the database to be online for the applications to send messages to each other. This occurs because for the application to send messages into a SQL Server Service Broker queue, the database must be online and available. There is no way to send a message to the SQL Server Service Broker without directly logging into the database. In the case of a situation like this, a message queue such as MSMQ would be a better solution because MSMQ allows you to send messages without being logged into the database.

On the other hand, if you have a situation in which you have a Windows service (or application) that needs to send messages to a database, and the database needs to process that message directly using T-SQL (or even SQLCLR code) then the SQL Server Service Broker might be a good choice. The reason SQL Server Service Broker is the better option is because the application needs to log into the database to get the message to the database and the SQL Server Service Broker can only be accessed via T-SQL. It makes sense to store the messages in a queue that can be accessed by T-SQL directly without any third-party, extended stored procedures.

CONFIGURING SQL SERVER SERVICE BROKER

There is actually no user interface to configure the bulk of SQL Server Service Broker, a fact that has greatly slowed the adoption of SQL Server Service Broker. Because there is no user interface for most of the object configuration, the majority of the setup must be completed using T-SQL as is shown through this section. The only part of SQL Server Service Broker that you can configure using the SQL Server Management Studio user interface is when you enable SQL Server Service Broker for the specific database. All the various objects, such as the message types, contracts, queues, services, and routes must be configured via T-SQL.

Configuring SQL Server Service Broker can be complex because it uses a lot of new terms, which can make the entire process confusing. If you are unsure of a term's definition initially, keep reading because the term will likely be defined in a few paragraphs.

Enabling

To enable or disable SQL Server Service Broker using SQL Server Management Studio, connect to the instance in question in the object explorer. Right-click the instance and select Properties, selecting the Options page; then under Other Options, scroll down to the Service Broker section, as shown in Figure 6-1. The Broker Enabled setting is the only setting that can be configured by selecting from either True or False.

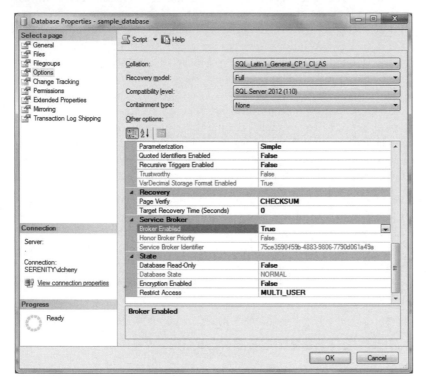

FIGURE 6-1

You can also enable SQL Server Service Broker using T-SQL by using the ALTER DATABASE statement. There are two important flags when using this method. The first is the NEW_BROKER flag that configures SQL Server Service Broker for the first time. The second is the ENABLE_BROKER flag that turns SQL Server Service Broker on if it is disabled, as shown in the following code. If SQL Server Service Broker has never been enabled and the ENABLE_BROKER flag is used, it has the same effect as if the NEW_BROKER flag was used.

```
ALTER DATABASE sample_database
SET ENABLE_BROKER
```

You see if SQL Server Service Broker is enabled by looking at the values of the is_broker_enabled and service_broker_guid columns of the sys.databases system catalog view. The is_broker_enabled column is a bit field with a value of either 0 or 1. The service_broker_guid column contains a unique guid value that represents the specific instance of SQL Server Service Broker within the specific database. When the guid within the service_broker_guid column is all zeros, this indicates that the SQL Server Service Broker has never been enabled for that database before.

After SQL Server Service Broker has been enabled for a specific database, the SQL Server Service Broker objects can be created, and messages can begin being sent.

Message Types

The first object type that you need to create when configuring SQL Server Service Broker is a message type. Message types validate that the data within a message is the correct, expected format. You can use four different validation options:

> **NONE:** Any data can be placed within the body of the message that is sent. When no value is specified for the VALIDATION option, the default value of NONE is used.

> **EMPTY:** Only messages that are empty can be sent.

> **WELL_FORMED_XML:** Only messages consisting of well-formed XML documents can be sent.

> **VALID_XML WITH SCHEMA COLLECTION:** Only XML documents that fit with the specified XML schema can be used. The XML schema to use with the VALID_XML WITH SCHEMA COLLECTION option requires that the XML schema already exists within the database by using the CREATE XML SCHEMA COLLECTION command.

Beyond the validation option, the CREATE MESSAGE TYPE command has only two other options. The first is the name of the message type, which must fit within the standard SQL Server object naming rules. The second option is the AUTHORIZATION option, which sets the owner of the message type when it is created. When the person creating the message type is a member of the sysadmin fixed server role or the db_owner fixed database role, then the value specified for AUTHORIZATION can be any valid database user or role. When the person creating the message type is not a member of the sysadmin fixed server role or the db_owner fixed database role, then the value specified for AUTHORIZATION must be that user, or another user that the user in question has the rights to impersonate. If no value is specified for the AUTHORIZATION parameter, the message type belongs to the current user. The following code snippet shows the creation of a message type.

```
CREATE MESSAGE TYPE YourMessageType
AUTHORIZATION dbo
VALIDATION = WELL_FORMED_XML
```

Contracts

The second object type to create is a contract. Contracts define the message types that are used within a single conversation. Contracts, similar to message types, have a couple of parameters that need to be specified when using the CREATE CONTRACT statement. These include the following:

> The name of the contract must follow the standard SQL Server object naming rules.

> The AUTHORIZATION value must be a user or role that exists within the database.

The CREATE CONTRACT requires a specific list of message types that are bound to the contract, and each message type can only be used by a specific member of the conversation. There are three options available for the user who can use each message type:

> **INITIATOR:** The SQL Server Service Broker SERVICE (SERVICEs are discussed later in this chapter) who initiated the conversation.

➤ **TARGET:** The SQL Server Service Broker SERVICE who received the conversation.

➤ **ANY:** Enables both the TARGET and the INITIATOR to use the message type. Although the following code example shows a single Message Type being specified, multiple message types can be specified with a comma-separated list, as shown in the next code example.

```
CREATE CONTRACT MyContract
AUTHORIZATION dbo
(YourMessageType SENT BY ANY)

CREATE CONTRACT MyContract
AUTHORIZATION dbo
(YourMessageType SENT BY INITIATOR,
AnotherMessageType SENT BY TARGET)
```

Queues

The third object types you can create are queues. Queues are where the messages within the SQL Server Service Broker are stored in the time period between when they are sent and when they are processed. Although the rest of the objects created are logical objects made up only of records in system tables, queues are physical objects that create physical tables under them that store the actual messages. Because queues are physical tables, one of the many options available to the person creating the queue is the file group that will contain the queue.

When creating the queue several other options can be specified. All these choices are optional with the exception of the name of the queue.

➤ The first option is the STATUS of the queue, which can be ON or OFF. When a queue is ON, it is available to receive messages, and messages can be received from the queue. When a queue has a STATUS of OFF and a stored procedure or other T-SQL code attempts to RECEIVE messages from the queue, the RECEIVE command returns an error message. The STATUS option defaults to ON.

➤ The second option is the RETENTION, which can be ON or OFF. When message retention is ON after messages are received, they are not removed from the queue; they are instead kept for auditing purposes. Although the messages cannot be received a second time, they can remain persisted on disk and can be viewed later by selecting them using the SELECT statement with the queue name in the FROM clause. When message retention is OFF, the messages will be removed from the queue as soon as they have been received.

Although the retention option on the queues is great for auditing purposes, there is one downside: there is no way to easily purge some of the data from the queue. You can use the ALTER QUEUE command to change the RETENTION from ON to OFF, which would then purge all the data in the queue. However if you wanted to only purge some data, for instance, all data except for the last 90 days, there is no built-in way to do it. You would instead need to export the last 90 days' worth of data into a table and then purge all the data.

➤ The third option is the POISON_MESSAGE_HANDLING, which can be ON or OFF. When poison message handling is enabled on a queue, which is the default, it causes the queue to automatically disable after five consecutive transaction rollbacks. When poison message handling is disabled, the message handling must be handled within the application.

➤ The fourth option is the activation stored procedure configuration, which is made up of four child settings:

➤ **STATUS:** Under the ACTIVATION setting, STATUS is used to enable or disable the activation procedure. When ACTIVATION is disabled, it stops only new threads of the activated stored procedure from being spawned; already running threads are left running.

➤ **PROCEDURE_NAME:** This parameter is the name of the stored procedure that should be activated.

➤ **MAX_QUEUE_READERS:** The number of threads that should be spawned, each of which calls the activated stored procedure.

➤ **EXECUTE AS:** This parameter specifies the username that the procedure should be run as. The values that can be specified are SELF, OWNER, or any valid user within the database.

The following code shows the various options that can be specified. Two queues should be used when sending messages within an application: one queue as the source queue, and one queue as the destination queue. This way, when conversations are closed, the acknowledgments that are sent automatically are not sent to the same queue that has the production work load in it. This becomes especially important for high load workloads because a large amount of time may be spent processing these acknowledgments instead of processing the production workload that needs to be done.

```
CREATE QUEUE YourQueue_Source
WITH STATUS=ON,
     RETENTION=OFF,
     ACTIVATION
         (STATUS=OFF,
          PROCEDURE_NAME=dbo.MySourceActivationProcedure,
          MAX_QUEUE_READERS=1,
          EXECUTE AS OWNER),
     POISON_MESSAGE_HANDLING=ON;
```

When creating a queue that has an activated stored procedure, you can configure the activated procedure when the queue is created, as shown in the previous code snippet. However, the stored procedure must exist before the queue can be created using this method. Because of this, the queue is often created without configuring the ACTIVATION settings. Instead, the stored procedure is created and the queue is altered using the ALTER QUEUE command to set the activation settings. The end result of creating a queue while enabling the activation settings would be the same if the queue was created without enabling the activation settings. In either case the queue would call the stored procedure when messages were received in the queue.

Services

Another object type you create is called a service. Although poorly named, SQL Server Service Broker Services play an important role. Service Broker Services are objects that are configured via the CREATE SERVICE statement in T-SQL. Services can specify which contracts (and therefore which message types) can be used when sending messages to a specific queue. When messages are sent, they are sent to a specific service that then delivers the message into a specific queue.

CREATE SERVICE has only a few parameters that can be set, which are shown in the following code.

- ➤ **Object name:** Like other objects, this setting follows the normal object-naming standards.

- ➤ **AUTHORIZATION:** this works just like the AUTHORIZATION parameter when creating a message type or contract.

- ➤ **Queue name:** The name of the queue to which the messages sent to the service will be delivered.

- ➤ **Comma-separated list of contracts:** This can be used when creating conversations sent to this service.

```
CREATE SERVICE YourService_Source
AUTHORIZATION dbo
ON QUEUE dbo.YourQueue_Source
(MyContract)
GO
```

When creating a queue for each side of the conversation, you must also create a service for each side of the conversation. These service names are then specified when using the BEGIN DIALOG CONVERSATION statement, which is explained in more detail later in this chapter.

 When selecting the name for your services, do not select the name ANY. Within SQL Server Service Broker the service name ANY is a reserved word that causes service broker priorities (found later in this chapter) to be applied to all services instead of to the specific service called ANY that is specified.

Routes

You can also create object types called routes. Routes control the database to which the messages should be routed. There is a default route created in every database called AutoCreatedLocal that can usually be left as-is. There are situations, however, where this default route needs to be removed. The primary reason why this default route needs to be removed is if multiple databases are on the same SQL Server instance that has services with the same name. If the default route is left in the database, the SQL Service Broker route will round robin the messages into the databases on the server that has the matching service name. For this reason you should either remove the default route or ensure unique service names across databases that may be unrelated to each other. When sending messages between databases, a route must exist in both databases referencing the remote database. Routes can be configured to redirect messages for a single service or for all services, depending on the needs.

Routes have a variety of parameters that you can configure via the CREATE ROUTE statement. These include the following:

➤ **Name of the route:** The name of the route follows the normal object naming rules.

➤ **Name of the service:** The name of the service to which the route should apply is another parameter. You can either specify the name of the specific service, or you can omit the service name from the CREATE ROUTE statement, which causes the route to apply to all services. When specifying the service name as part of the CREATE ROUTE statement, the service name is always case-sensitive, ignoring the databases collation setting. The reason for this is that the SQL Server does a binary compare of the route's service setting and the service name within the database. Because uppercase and lowercase characters have different binary values, if a single character does not match, the route will not apply.

➤ **BROKER_INSTANCE:** The BROKER_INSTANCE is an optional parameter that tells the route to which database on the server to send the messages. The BROKER_INSTANCE value can be queried from the sys.databases catalog view on the instance that hosts the database to which the route is pointing. If the BROKER_INSTANCE value is not specified, the SQL Service Broker attempts to identify the destination database on the instance based on matching the destination service name with the service names in the databases on the remote instance.

➤ **LIFETIME:** This is also an optional parameter. The LIFETIME parameter tells the SQL Service Broker for how many seconds the route should be active. When the lifetime of the route has expired, the route will be ignored. If the LIFETIME is omitted or a value of NULL is specified, the route will never expire.

➤ **ADDRESS:** The ADDRESS parameter is a required parameter that tells the SQL Service Broker how to contact the remote database. This parameter can specify an IP address, a network name, or a fully qualified domain name followed by the TCP port number of the service broker endpoint that must be created on the remote instance in the format of TCP://ServerName:PortNumber. If the destination database is located on the same instance as the source database, then the ADDRESS parameter can be specified as LOCAL. If the parameter is specified as TRANSPORT, then the SQL Service Broker attempts to identify which remote instance to connect to based on the name of the service.

➤ **MIRROR_ADDRESS:** This optional parameter configures the route to support database mirroring if the destination database is configured for database mirroring. If the destination database is configured for database mirroring and the MIRROR_ADDRESS is not specified and the database were to failover to the mirror instance, the messages would not be delivered until the database failed back to the instance specified in the ADDRESS parameter. The value of the MIRROR_ADDRESS parameter should be specified in the same format at the ADDRESS parameter.

The following code snippet shows the use of the various parameters when using the CREATE ROUTE statement.

```
CREATE ROUTE ExpenseRoute
    WITH SERVICE_NAME = 'MyService',
    BROKER_INSTANCE = '53FA2363-BF93-4EB6-A32D-F672339E08ED',
    ADDRESS = 'TCP://sql2:1234',
    MIRROR_ADDRESS = 'TCP://sql4:4567' ;
```

Priorities

SQL Server Service Broker priorities assign priorities to conversations to force specific conversations to always be processed before lower priority conversations. This can be important in high load environments in which some messages need to be processed before others. The conversation priority is assigned by matching the name of the contract, the source service name, and the destination service name to what was configured in the Service Broker Priority.

Because you don't specifically set a conversation's priority when the conversation is created, it is wise to create multiple contracts, all of which use the same message types and are configured to be used for the specified services. Using priorities to create a high priority conversation and a lower priority conversation could be done by creating a contract with the name "ContractLow" and a second contract named "ContractHigh." Then a priority could be named that triggers on the ContractHigh, which has a high priority level assigned.

Creating SQL Server Service Broker priorities is done via T-SQL using the CREATE BROKER PRIORITY statement. This statement accepts five different values, including the name of the priority. The next three values enable you to specify the name of a service, or you can specify the special value of ANY, which causes that priority to be applied to any conversation. The last parameter is the priority level that will be used for the conversations to which this priority will be applied. The priority can be any whole number inclusively between the numbers 1 and 10. Conversations that do not have a specific priority applied to them are assigned the priority of 5. The usage of the CREATE BROKER PRIORITY statement is shown in the following code snippet, in which a message sent to any service using the contract name MyHighPriority would be given the priority of 8 instead of the default of 5.

```
CREATE BROKER PRIORITY HighPriority
FOR CONVERSATION
SET ( CONTRACT_NAME = MyHighPriority ,
      LOCAL_SERVICE_NAME = ANY ,
      REMOTE_SERVICE_NAME = N'ANY' ,
      PRIORITY_LEVEL = 8
)
```

Conversation Groups

Conversation groups control the order that messages are processed when those messages are sent to different services. This is done by putting the conversations sent from the same service to different services into a single group. This in-order processing is done through a process called *conversation locks*, which ensures that messages within the conversations in the same conversation group are processed "exactly once in order" or EOIO. This conversation locking is done automatically whenever a message is sent or received on the conversation group.

By default each conversation is put into its own conversation group unless a conversation group is specified when the conversation is created. You can specify the conversation group into which the new conversation should be placed in two ways. You can do this by specifying the conversation group that should be used, or by specifying the handle of the conversation that the new conversation should be grouped with.

There is no specific command to create a new conversation group. When a new conversation is started, a new group is created automatically, and it is assigned a new GUID value as its identifier. To assign new conversations to a specific conversation group, a new GUID value simply needs to be assigned as the RELATED_CONVERSATION_GROUP parameter for the BEGIN DIALOG CONVERSATION statement, which is covered later in this chapter.

If you want to query the conversation group that the next message to be processed is a memory of, you can do this using the GET CONVERSATION GROUP statement. To use this statement, specify a variable that the next conversation group will be placed into, as well as the name of the queue to get the conversation group from, as shown in the following code.

```
DECLARE @conversation_group_id AS UNIQUEIDENTIFIER;

GET CONVERSATION GROUP @conversation_group_id
FROM YourQueue;
```

USING SQL SERVER SERVICE BROKER

Sending and receiving messages through SQL Server Service Broker is a basic task. Instead of using INSERT to put messages into the queue, like you would with a table, and SELECT to pull messages from the queue, you use the SEND statement to send messages and the RECEIVE statement to pull messages from the queue.

Sending Messages

You can send messages using the SEND command. The SEND command accepts only two parameters: the conversation ID and the body of the message, as shown in the following code snippet. You can get the conversation ID from the BEGIN DIALOG CONVERSATION command, as shown in the previous code snippet used to assign priorities.

```
DECLARE @message_body AS XML, @dialog_handle as UNIQUEIDENTIFIER

SET @message_body = (SELECT *
    FROM sys.all_objects as object
    FOR XML AUTO, root('root'))

BEGIN DIALOG CONVERSATION @dialog_handle
    FROM SERVICE [YourSourceService]
    TO SERVICE 'YourDestinationService'
    ON CONTRACT [YourContract];

SEND ON CONVERSATION @dialog_handle
MESSAGE TYPE YourMessageType
(@message_body)
GO
```

The BEGIN DIALOG CONVERSATION command accepts several parameters, some of which are required and some of which are optional. The first three parameters are required and are the source and destination services that you send the message and the contract from and to, respectively. Optionally, after the destination service name, you can specify the service broker GUID of the destination database or CURRENT DATABASE. The default value is CURRENT DATABASE which causes messages to be routed to the same database within which the user is running the code to send the message. The third parameter is the contract that defines the message types used to send the messages.

The rest of the parameters are all optional. The first two can be either the RELATED_CONVERSATION or the RELATED_CONVERSATION_GROUP that both specify a certain conversation group that relates the new conversation to another conversation. The RELATED_CONVERSATION accepts the conversation ID from another pre-existing conversation. The RELATED_CONVERSATION_GROUP accepts a specific conversation group ID that the new conversation would then be a member of.

The next parameter is the LIFETIME of the conversation, which specifies the amount of time that the conversation remains open. The LIFETIME is the number of seconds until the conversation closes automatically. The LIFETIME value is expressed as an integer data type with the default being the maximum value of the INT data type, which is $2^{31}-1$ (2,147,483,647).

The last parameter is the ENCRYPTION parameter, which specifies whether the messages within the conversation should be encrypted while in transmission to another instance of SQL Server. This parameter accepts only ON or OFF, and encryption is ON by default. When sending messages between database instances, it is highly recommended that encryption be ON. When ENCRYPTION is ON and messages are sent within the same instance while the data isn't actually encrypted, the database master key and the certificates needed for the encryption are required for the conversation to successfully begin and to send the message.

The code shown in the previous example is a great start, but it isn't good for high-performance SQL Server Service Broker workloads. This is because the cost of creating a conversation for each message is expensive. When working with high-load systems that send hundreds of thousands or millions of messages per day, you want to reuse conversations sending multiple messages per conversation to reduce the overhead of sending messages. You can easily do this by logging the conversation handle (the value of the @dialog_handle value that is set in the BEGIN DIALOG CONVERSATION command) to a table so that it can be retrieved by future sessions. A table like this is shown in following code snippet.

```
CREATE TABLE dbo.SSB_Settings
([Source] sysname NOT NULL,
[Destination] sysname NOT NULL,
[Contract] sysname NOT NULL,
[dialog_handle] uniqueidentifier
CONSTRAINT PK_SSB_Setting PRIMARY KEY ([Source], [Destination], [Contract])
```

One key requirement for using multiple messages per conversation is that there needs to be a way for the sending side of the conversation to tell the receiving side of the conversation that there will be no more messages sent over that conversation. An easy way to do this is to have an additional message type within the database that is specifically used as a trigger on the destination side so that it knows when to end the conversation. In the following code, you can notice that a message type named EndOfConversation is used to trigger the remote side to close the conversation.

In a high-load environment, a stored procedure could be used to decide if a new conversation should be created, as well as storing the value as needed. Listing 6-1 shows the send_sequence value from the `sys.conversation_endpoints` dynamic management view is used to decide if it is time to end the conversation.

LISTING 6-1: Creating A Reusable Conversation.sql

```sql
CREATE PROCEDURE dbo.CreateConversation
      @Destination sysname,
      @Source sysname,
      @Contract sysname,
      @MessageType sysname,
      @MessageBody XML,
      @dialog_handle uniqueidentifier
AS
/*Get the conversation id.*/
SELECT @dialog_handle = dialog_handle
FROM dbo.SSB_Settings
WHERE [Source] = @Source
      AND [Destination] = @Destination
      AND [Contract] = @Contract;

/*If there is no current handle, or the conversation has had 1000 messages
sent on it, create a new conversation.*/
IF @dialog_handle IS NULL OR
      (SELECT send_sequence
         FROM sys.conversation_endpoints
         WHERE conversation_id = @dialog_handle) >= 1000
BEGIN
    BEGIN TRANSACTION
    /*If there is a conversation dialog handle signal the destination
    code that the old conversation is dead.*/
    IF @dialog_handle IS NOT NULL
    BEGIN
        UPDATE dbo.SSB_Settings
        SET dialog_handle = NULL
        WHERE [Source] = @Source
              AND [Destination] = @Destination
              AND [Contract] = @Contract;

        SEND ON CONVERSATION @dialog_handle
        MESSAGE TYPE EndOfConversation;

    END

    /*Setup the new conversation*/
    BEGIN DIALOG CONVERSATION @dialog_handle
    FROM SERVICE @Source
    TO SERVICE @Destination
    ON CONTRACT @Contract;

    /*Log the new conversation ID*/
    UPDATE dbo.SSB_Settings
        SET dialog_handle = @dialog_handle
    WHERE [Source] = @Source
          AND [Destination] = @Destination
```

continues

LISTING 6-1 *(continued)*

```
                AND [Contract] = @Contract;

        IF @@ROWCOUNT = 0
            INSERT INTO dbo.SSB_Settings
              ([Source], [Destination], [Contract], [dialog_handle])
            VALUES
              (@Source, @Destination, @Contract, @dialog_handle);
    END;

    /*Send the message*/
    SEND ON CONVERSATION @dialog_handle
    MESSAGE TYPE @MessageType
    (@XML);

    /*Verify that the conversation handle is still the one logged in the table.
      If not then mark this conversation as done.*/
    IF (SELECT dialog_handle
        FROM dbo.SSB_Settings
        WHERE [Source] = @Source
            AND [Destination] = @Destination
            AND [Contract] = @Contract) <> @dialog_handle
        SEND ON CONVERSATION @dialog_handle
            MESSAGE TYPE EndOfConversation;
    GO
```

Receiving Messages

Receiving messages is done using the RECEIVE command. The RECEIVE command is written much like a SELECT statement where the person writing the statement can specify the columns that should be returned, and the queue is specified as the FROM statement, as shown in the following code snippet. After the data has been received into a variable, anything that needs to be done with it can be done.

```
DECLARE @dialog_handle UNIQUEIDENTIFIER, @message_body XML

RECEIVE TOP (1) @dialog_handle = conversation_handle,
    @message_body = CAST(message_body as XML)
FROM YourDestinationQueue

/*Do whatever needs to be done with your XML document*/

END CONVERSATION @dialog_handle
```

There should also be a second set of code, usually configured as an activated stored procedure on the source queue to read received all messages, and to then end the conversation of all messages that are received.

As with the code shown in the Sending Messages section, the basic code in this previous example is not the most efficient way to receive data. It is more efficient to receive multiple messages at once, and to receive the message body from the queue as the raw binary, and then convert it to XML (or whatever data type it was sent as) after it has been removed from the queue. The following code shows how to receive multiple messages in a single statement.

```
DECLARE @dialog_handle UNIQUEIDENTIFIER, @message_body XML

DECLARE @Messages TABLE
(conversation_handle uniqueidentifier,
message_type sysname,
message_body VARBINARY(MAX))

WAITFOR (
RECEIVE TOP (1000) conversation_handle, message_type_name, message_body
FROM YourDestinationQueue
INTO @Messages)

DECLARE cur CURSOR FOR select conversation_handle, CAST(message_body AS XML)
                       FROM @Messages
                       WHERE message_body IS NOT NULL
OPEN cur
FETCH NEXT FROM cur INTO @dialog_handle, @message_body
WHILE @@FETCH_STATUS = 0
BEGIN
    /*Do whatever needs to be done with your XML document*/
    FETCH NEXT FROM cur INTO @dialog_handle, @message_body
END
CLOSE cur
DEALLOCATE cur;


IF EXISTS (SELECT * FROM @Messages WHERE message_type = 'EndOfConversation')
    END CONVERSATION @dialog_handle
GO
```

Sending Messages Between Databases

Sending messages between databases that reside on the same instance of SQL Server is almost as easy as sending messages within a single database. Sending messages between databases requires creating the same objects on both the source and destination database and then creating routes between the two databases. The new routes within the sending databases should be created on the destination service and point to the second database. They should use an ADDRESS of LOCAL. The routes on the destination database should be created for the source service and point back to the source database, again using an ADDRESS of LOCAL.

> *You may notice that there is no code sample to show you for this section. The reason for this is that sending messages between databases when the databases are on the same instance doesn't require any changes to the code when sending or receiving the messages. You take the exact message types, contracts, queues, and services and use the same code that you use to send messages within a single database. The only thing that needs to be changed is that a route needs to be created within each database. In the source database a route is added referencing the destination service and in the destination database a route is added referencing the source service. Once the services are added the messages will now be sent from one database to another.*

Sending Messages Between Instances

One of the most powerful features of SQL Server's Service Broker is its capability to send messages between databases on different instances, which run on different physical (or virtual) servers. Configuring SQL Service Broker to send messages between instances is effectively the same as configuring SQL Service Broker to send messages between databases on the same SQL Server instance. The major difference is the steps needed to configure the authorization of communications between the instances. These steps are outlined in the following list; they should be done on both of the instances that will be exchanging SQL Service Broker Messages:

1. First, configure the Database Master Key in the master database.

2. Then, configure the Database Master Key in the application database.

3. Next, create a certificate in each database.

4. Exchange the certificates between the databases.

5. Now create SQL Service Broker Endpoints on each instance.

6. Finally, configure routes to connect to the remote instances SQL Service Broker Endpoint.

After you complete these steps, messages can route between the two databases.

Database Master Key

Before you begin using SQL Service Broker between instances, you must enable the database master key for both databases by using the CREATE MASTER KEY statement on both databases. If this has already been done, you do not need to do this again. Creating the master key is quite simple, as shown in the following code snippet, because the command accepts only a single parameter, which is the password used to secure the database master key.

The database master key is a symmetric key used to protect all the other keys within the database, including other symmetric keys, certificates, and asymmetric keys.

```
CREATE MASTER KEY ENCRYPTION BY PASSWORD = 'YourSecurePassword1!'
```

After you create the database master key, back it up using the BACKUP MASTER KEY statement so that the master key can be recovered if a database failure occurs. Securely store the backup of the database master key at an offsite location.

Creating Certificates

When using certificate authentication between the endpoints, you must create certificates in the master databases of the instances that exchange messages. You can create certificates using the CREATE CERTIFICATE statement within the master database, as shown in the following code snippet. When creating the certificates on each instance, assign a unique name to each one. The easiest way to do this is to include the server and instance name in the name of the certificate.

```
CREATE CERTIFICATE MyServiceBrokerCertificate
WITH SUBJECT = 'Service Broker Certificate',
    START_DATE = '1/1/2011',
    EXPIRY_DATE = '12/31/2099'
```

Exchanging Certificates

Once you create the certificates, you need to exchange them. You can exchange certificates between instances by backing up the certificate using the BACKUP CERTIFICATE statement, as shown in the following code, on the machine that has the certificate. You then need to restore the certificate to the remote instance using the CREATE CERTIFICATE statement, as shown in the second code snippet.

```
BACKUP CERTIFICATE MyServiceBrokerCertificate
    TO FILE='C:\MyServiceBrokerCertificate.cer'
CREATE CERTIFICATE MyServiceBrokerCertificate
FROM FILE='c:\MyServiceBrokerCertificate.cer'
```

SQL Service Broker Endpoints

Endpoints enable users or other SQL Servers to connect to the SQL Server instance that the endpoint is created on. For SQL Server instances to send messages to another instance, you must create endpoints on each SQL Server instance. You can create endpoints using the CREATE ENDPOINT statement, as shown in the following code. Each SQL Server Instance can have only one Service Broker endpoint; even if multiple instances send messages to a single server, all communication must be done through a single endpoint. Service Broker endpoints support a variety of authentication techniques including NTLM-, KERBEROS-, and CERTIFICATE-based authentication, as well as several combinations of those three authentication techniques. When doing cross-instance authentication for SQL Service Broker, messaging CERTIFICATE authentication is recommended because it removes the dependency on Active Directory.

```
USE master
GO
CREATE ENDPOINT ServiceBrokerEndpoint
STATE = STARTED
AS TCP (LISTENER_PORT = 1234, LISTENER_IP=ALL)
FOR SERVICE_BROKER
(AUTHENTICATION = CERTIFICATE MyServiceBrokerCertificate,
    ENCRYPTION = REQUIRED ALGORITHM RC4);
GO
```

You can also configure encryption on the endpoint with the encryption being either DISABLED, SUPPORTED, or REQUIRED. Encryption is supported using both the RC4 or AES algorithms as well as combinations of both algorithms specified as AES RC4 and RC4 AES.

When configuring the SQL Server Service Broker endpoint, a specific TCP port, separate from the default SQL Server TCP port that the instance is listening on, needs to be specified. You must also specify the IP address that the endpoint should be listening on. In the preceding code example, TCP port 1234 is used to listen on, and the endpoint can listen on all IP addresses that are configured on the server that the instance runs on. If the endpoint should listen only on a specific IP address, the IPv4 or IPv6 address should be specified where the LISTENER_IP setting is specified.

External Activation

External activation is different from the normal activated stored procedures, which are available via the CREATE QUEUE or the ALTER QUEUE statements. External Activation runs as a separate Windows service (ssbea.exe), which monitors the SQL Server queue waiting for new messages to arrive in the queue. Upon a new message arriving in the queue, the external activation service launches the Windows application that it is configured to run. The External Activation service monitors the SQL Server Service Broker queue by having you configure an event notification on your queue, which then sends a message to a second monitoring queue. When a message arrives in the application queue, the event notification sends a message to the notification queue, which causes the external activation service to launch the application. Sample code that can create the event notification is shown in the following code snippet. You can download the external activation service from http://bit.ly/SSB_EA.

WHY USE EXTERNAL ACTIVATION?

There are several cases in which people use external activation service. The most common involves something happening outside of the SQL Server after something has happened within the SQL Server. For example, imagine there are files stored on a file server and each file matches up to a row within a SQL Server table. You want to ensure that every time a row is deleted, the file is deleted as well and the external activation process is a good fit. To do so, you can set up a trigger on delete for the database table and have that trigger send a message to a queue with the file information to delete. Then the external activator would see that a message has arrived and launch the application that deletes the file from the file server. The application would then read the queue to which the trigger sent the message and delete the file based on the data within the message. You could use another technique to perform this same action without using external activation though: have the application that deletes the files run as a service looking into the queue every minute for messages to process. This, however, would be less efficient than using the external activation service, and therefore makes external activation the better option.

```
CREATE QUEUE dbo.MyDestinationQueueEA
GO
CREATE SERVICE MyDestinationServiceEA
ON QUEUE dbo.MyDestinationQueueEA
(
    [http://schemas.microsoft.com/SQL/Notifications/PostEventNotification]
)
GO
CREATE EVENT NOTIFICATION MyDestinationNotificationEA
ON QUEUE MyDestinationQueue
FOR QUEUE_ACTIVATION
TO SERVICE 'MyDestinationServiceEA', 'current database'
GO
```

The code in the previous code snippet assumes that the event notification and all the SQL Service Broker objects are created in the same database, which is why 'current database' has been specified. If you want to put the external activation queue and service in another database, then the service broker GUID for the destination database should be specified instead of the 'current database'.

SUMMARY

Although SQL Server Service Broker is quite complex to set up, it is an extremely powerful tool to use when you require asynchronous messaging. The SQL Server Service Broker is a flexible solution that can enable you to send messages within the database, from database to database within the same SQL Server instance, or from database to database between servers even if the servers are located next to each other or are half a world apart.

As you have seen through this chapter, you need to configure a variety of objects. Although SQL Server Service Broker may at first appear to be quite complex, after some time working with it, the system becomes quite easy to use, and all the pieces begin to make sense.

7

SQL Server CLR Integration

WHAT'S IN THIS CHAPTER

➤ How the CLR is Implemented in SQL Server

➤ SQLCLR Assembly Creation and Deployment

➤ Securing SQLCLR Assemblies

➤ Performance

SQL Server developers first saw the integration of the .NET Common Language Runtime (CLR) with the release of SQL Server 2005. Not a whole lot has changed with the release of SQL Server 2008 and 2012. Yet, SQLCLR provides great benefits to developers as well as database administrators, and is worth reviewing.

This chapter does not focus entirely on how to write SQLCLR .NET assemblies, (visit `http://technet.microsoft.com/en-us/library/ms131102(SQL.110).aspx` for a more in-depth discussion of that) but does provide a few examples on how to create and deploy an assembly. These serve as a nice foundation on which to focus the majority of the chapter, which covers SQLCLR Administration. This chapter focuses on the CLR as a hosted environment in SQL Server and discusses why you would use T-SQL over a SQLCLR solution. This chapter also discusses SQLCLR performance and security because these are critical concepts to consider when deciding to use SQLCLR.

INTRODUCTION TO THE CLR

With the integration of the .NET Framework CLR components in SQL Server, developers have the flexibility to write stored procedures, triggers, user-defined types and functions, and streaming table-valued functions using a variety of .NET Framework languages, the most common being C# and Visual Basic .NET. It's no secret that this addition and integration provides a powerful and much needed extension of the SQL Server database engine. The CLR supplies managed code capabilities with a plethora of services that the database engine simply cannot provide, such as object lifetime management, code access security, and cross-language integration. And that is just the tip of the iceberg. Taking a good look at what the CLR provides within the database engine can reveal a host of major benefits:

➤ **Improved performance and scalability:** It is not a given that the SQLCLR always performs better than T-SQL, but in many situations the .NET Framework model of language compilation and execution delivers improved performance over T-SQL through fast transactions between SQL Server and the CLR. T-SQL will always be faster in data access, but you will often see the CLR execute faster when executing functions such as advanced math or string parsing.

➤ **Efficient development via a standardized environment:** The last few years have brought both the .NET development environment and the database development environment more tightly integrated, and with the release of Visual Studio 2010 and SQL Server 2012 (and SQL Server Management Studio) this is even more apparent. Developers now can use the same tools and development environments to write their database objects and scripts that they would use to write their middle-tier and client components.

➤ **Enhanced security:** First and foremost, the Microsoft.SqlServer.Server API that enables managed procedures to send results back to the client performs better than the APIs used by extended stored procedures. In addition, the same Microsoft.SqlServer.Server API supports data types such as xml and varchar(max), which the extended stored procedures do not support.

However, most DBAs are leery about using extended stored procedures, and the CLR provides a safer and secure alternative by leveraging the CLR runtime environment in which to run managed code all hosted within the database engine. Conversely, SQL Server has no view or control over the resource usage of extended stored procedures and they can compromise the integrity of the SQL Server process. Managed code is safer and more secure because it runs in a CLR environment hosted by the database engine, enabling the code-access security of the .NET languages to be combined with the user-based permissions in SQL Server.

 Extended Stored Procedures will be removed in future versions of SQL Server.

➤ **Rich Programming Model:** The most powerful benefit is the tried-and-true programming model. To better understand this, you need to look at the differences between T-SQL and .NET. In many respects the .NET Framework languages offer a richer programming model over T-SQL simply because the T-SQL language is based fundamentally on its declarative query language (SELECT, INSERT, UPDATE/DELETE). This is where T-SQL shines, operating on set-based CRUD operations. By leveraging the .NET Framework libraries and their extensive set of classes, developers can now take advantage of many of the programming aspects that T-SQL does lend itself to easily.

Once you understand the benefits of CLR, the question then arises of how do you know when to use it, especially over T-SQL? The recommendation handed down by Microsoft is to use "CLR-based programming for logic that cannot be fully expressed declaratively in T-SQL, and to complement the expressive power of the T-SQL query language."

The key word in that sentence is "complement." The CLR should never be considered a replacement (except for extended stored procedures); rather the CLR should be used to quickly and efficiently solve the programming challenges that the T-SQL language cannot easily solve, such as string parsing, complex mathematics, CPU-centric workloads, and accessing external resources. You frequently see the CLR used when creating user-defined functions, such as scalar UDFs.

What makes this decision a little more difficult is that the T-SQL language continues to be improved, and many of the things that you couldn't easily do in T-SQL is now quite easy and efficient in T-SQL. So the answer to the question of which to use becomes, "it depends." Do some testing. Write the solution in both T-SQL and .NET to see which one performs better. The more you use it, the better feel you can get as to which method should be used for a given situation. It should be clear that the CLR rarely out-performs T-SQL when it comes to data access from within SQL Server.

With that introduction, now turn to how CLR is integrated into the database engine.

SQL Server as a .NET Runtime Host

A runtime host is defined as any process that loads the .NET runtime and runs code in a managed environment. In SQL Server 2008, the database programming model improved significantly by hosting the .NET Framework 3.5. With CLR integration, also called the SQLCLR, SQL Server enables .NET programmers to write stored procedures, user-defined functions, and triggers in any .NET-compatible language, especially C# and VB .NET.

With Visual Studio 2010, you can add user-defined types and aggregates to the list of CLR objects you can create with SQL Server 2008 and SQL Server 2008 R2. This functionality has been around for quite a while and has been the "go-to" method for deploying SQLCLR objects into SQL Server.

Alternatively, Microsoft created a set of tools for Visual Studio called SQL Server Data Tools (SSDT), which offers SQLCLR support. SSDT provides an integrated environment for database developers to easily create or edit database objects. SSDT is available as a free component targeted for SQL Server 2005, SQL Server 2008, SQL Server 2008R2, SQL Server 2012, and SQL Azure. SSDT will be updated every 4 to 6 months in coordination with SQL Azure releases. You need at least Visual Studio 2010 SP1 to work with SSDT.

To find out more, visit `http://msdn.microsoft.com/en-us/data/tools.aspx`.

One of the great benefits of the SQLCLR is that any .NET code that SQL Server runs is completely isolated from SQL Server itself. .NET code runs within the SQL Server process space, but SQL Server uses a construct in .NET called the Application Domain (AppDomain) to completely isolate and separate all resources that the .NET code uses from the resources that SQL Server uses. The AppDomain, which is discussed shortly, protects SQL Server from all malicious use of system resources. It should be noted that SQL Server manages its own thread scheduling, synchronization and locking, and memory management, which adds to the security and performance of the SQLCLR.

Application Domains

The primary design goal of placing assemblies in application domains is to achieve scalability, security, and the isolation goals needed. Application domains have existed for quite a while to provide a form of isolation between applications. This is necessary to ensure that code running in one application cannot and does not affect other unrelated applications. You can see this type of isolation between operating systems and runtime environments.

The isolation boundaries created by the application domains also help with the security and reliability needed for application development, especially for isolating applications running on the same computer. When multiple applications exist on the same computer, each application is loaded into separate processes, accomplishing the needed isolation because memory addresses are process-related.

Similarly, SQL Server isolates code between databases by using application domains. As such, Application Domains exist for each database that allows you to create, load, and register an assembly and call methods and functions within that database, independent of other assemblies registered in other databases.

You can have multiple assemblies per database and one assembly can discover other assemblies at execution time using the .NET Framework reflection application programming interfaces.

T-SQL versus CLR

With the integration of the CLR in SQL Server, the line that separates what is commonly known as the Business Logic Tier and the Data Tier just got a little fuzzier. That certainly is not meant to be taken in a negative tone; it just means that you need to do a little more homework when choosing where to do what.

Choosing where to put middle tier logic and database access logic was fairly easy. It is not so obvious now with the CLR integrated into SQL Server, but with that comes added functionality and flexibility that can enhance your applications.

Choosing between T-SQL and managed code is not a cut-and-dry decision. T-SQL does some things phenomenally well, and managed code does other things well. But that doesn't mean you should throw all data retrieval functionality into a T-SQL stored procedure.

Best practices state that when doing data retrieval, T-SQL is the way to go. Leave the data manipulation and CPU-intensive functions and procedures to the managed code side of things, especially if there is complex logic being processed on the returned data, such as complex mathematical calculations or string parsing. Obviously, you need to consider other things, but every situation is different, and more research is required to find the best plan.

The other thing to take into consideration is where the code will be executed. Is the client the best place to put certain logic, or will that same logic perform better on the server? Multi-tier applications typically have a data layer where much of the data logic is handled, adding the option of scalability at this layer. With SQL Server, however, both T-SQL and managed code can be run on the server. This brings the added benefit of server processing power and shortens the gap between data and code.

Don't discount the client because workstation computers are well powered and can handle a lot of the application processing without drastic performance degradation. This means that a lot of the application processing can be offloaded to the client, freeing up the server for other tasks.

From a performance viewpoint, the CLR is much faster at returning file information from the operating system than a T-SQL approach, simply because OLE Automation has more overhead than the different methods used in CLR. However, raw speed shouldn't be the only consideration. Important considerations include ease of development and ease of maintenance and might take precedence over speed, depending on the situation.

As you can see, there are many pros and cons of each method. Keep in mind that managed code can run on either the client or the server; T-SQL can run only on the server.

Enabling CLR Integration

By default, CLR is disabled. This means that you cannot execute any .NET code until you purposefully enable the CLR. Not everyone can enable the CLR; only members of the sysadmin and serveradmin server roles can do so, or any user granted the server-level permission ALTER SETTINGS.

Enabling CLR is as simple as running a query. There are a couple dozen "advanced" SQL Server settings that can be changed or modified only via T-SQL. They are not found in any Properties dialog; they are only accessible via the sp_configure option. The syntax for enabling CLR is the following:

```
EXEC sp_configure 'clr enabled', 1
GO
RECONFIGURE
GO
```

Don't enable the CLR yet though; there are still a few more things to consider.

There is another advanced setting called lightweight pooling that, when enabled, prevents the CLR execution. Per the MSDN documentation, CLR execution is not supported under lightweight pooling. The lightweight pooling option provides a means to reduce the system overhead associated with excessive context switching. Per Books Online (BOL):

> *When excessive context switching is present, lightweight pooling can provide better throughput by performing the context switching inline, thus helping to reduce user/kernel ring transitions.*

BOL recommends that you disable one or the other (setting the value to 0). You cannot have both options enabled (option set to 1). Features that rely on the CLR but do not work properly when lightweight pooling is enabled include the hierarchy data type, replication, and Policy-based management.

Finally, enabling the CLR is not an "enable it, leave it" option. When enabled, you should closely monitor the SQL Server for several error messages in the error log, including:

➤ Failed Virtual Allocate Bytes: FAIL_VIRTUAL_RESERVE <size>

➤ Failed Virtual Allocate Bytes: FAIL_VIRTUAL_COMMIT <size>

Either of these errors might indicate that SQL Server is trying to free parts of the SQL Server memory pool to find space for items such as extended stored procedures, .dll files, or automation objects.

If you consistently see these errors in your error logs, there is a SQL Server startup option that can help with this. Using the SQL Server Configuration Manager use the -g, startup option, which tells SQL Server to leave available memory for memory allocations within the SQL Server process, but outside of the SQL Server memory pool.

It is not a good idea to use the -g option and not monitor memory over a period of time though. However, using the -g option is a good way to help tune memory allocation, but only when physical memory exceeds the configured limit set by the operating system. Incorrect use of this option can lead to situations where SQL Server may not start or encounter run-time errors. If your CLR assemblies need a lot of memory, then you should go back and look at what your CLR is doing and make any necessary adjustments, such as breaking the assembly into smaller components.

CREATING CLR ASSEMBLIES

This section walks you through several examples to create, deploy, and register SQLCLR assemblies. These examples show you how to create and deploy the CLR assembly the "non-Visual Studio way"; without using Visual Studio, then the examples follow that up by showing how to use SQL Server Data Tools in Visual Studio to create and deploy CLR assemblies.

The Non-Visual Studio Way

Creating assemblies to deploy to SQL Server 2012 is not any different from previous versions. For this example, follow these steps:

1. First, fire up an instance of your favorite text editor and add the script in Listing 7-1:

Available for download on Wrox.com

LISTING 7-1: MyFirstSqlClr.cs

```
using System;
using System.Data;
using Microsoft.SqlServer.Server;
using System.Data.SqlTypes;

public class FirstSQLCLRProc
{
    [Microsoft.SqlServer.Server.SqlProcedure]
    public static void FirstSQLCLR(out string text)
    {
        SqlContext.Pipe.Send("Hello world!" + Environment.NewLine);
        text = "My First SQLCLR Assembly!";
    }
}
```

Listing 7-1 defines a public class that contains a single static method. The method uses the SqlContext and SqlPipe classes, which are used to create managed database objects to output a simple text message. The SqlContext object provides the environment in which the assembly code is activated and running. The managed code is executed from the server and thus running as part of the user connection, or within the user *context*. At this point, the SqlPipe is accessible. SQLPipe is the SQL Server component that enables managed stored procedures to return results back to the caller. Results from a query execution are sent back to the client via the caller's *pipe*. This is really no different for CLR database objects, in that results are sent back to the client via the methods associated with the SqlPipe object; send and ExecuteAndSend.

2. After you add the preceding code, save the file as MyFirstSqlClr.cs in a directory of your choice. (However, remember where you saved this file.) In this example, the syntax is C#.

3. Next, compile the assembly. By default, SQL Server installs the .NET Framework distribution files, which include csc.exe and vbc.exe, the command line compilers for C# and VB .NET. These exist in the following location (for .NET 4.0):

```
C:\Windows\Microsoft.NET\Framework\v4.0.30319
```

Open a command prompt and navigate to the directory where you previously saved your .cs file and type in the command, as shown in Figure 7-1.

FIGURE 7-1

4. Use the following syntax to compile your code into an assembly:

```
csc /target:library myfirstsqlclr.cs
```

The /target option is the parameter that specifies to compile the code into an assembly.

5. After the program has been compiled into a library, you should see a new file in the directory with the same name but with a .dll extension. This is the file that will be loaded into SQL Server.

6. Open up an instance of SQL Server Management Studio and open a new query window. Select the appropriate data in which you want to load the assembly, and type in the following T-SQL. (This example assumes that you have a Temp directory in the root of your C drive (c:\temp), if not you need to change the FROM location to where your assembly is located):

```
CREATE ASSEMBLY myfirstsqlclr
FROM 'c:\temp\myfirstsqlclr.dll'
WITH PERMISSION_SET = SAFE
```

The preceding code loads the assembly into SQL Server and creates a SQL Server assembly reference using the location of the compiled assembly created in the previous step. Notice also the `PERMISSION_SET` option. This option sets the security level of the assembly. We discuss these options in more details shortly.

7. Next, create a T-SQL stored procedure reference to the assembly previously created called `DoIt`. Type in the following T-SQL in the query windows and execute it:

```
CREATE PROCEDURE DoIt
@i nchar(50) OUTPUT
AS
EXTERNAL NAME myfirstsqlclr.FirstSQLCLRProc.FirstSQLCLR
```

After the procedure has been created, you can your newly created assembly and stored procedure by looking in Object Explorer, as shown in Figure 7-2.

8. With your stored procedure created, you can run it like any other stored procedure by using standard T-SQL. In the query window, type the following T-SQL and execute it:

```
DECLARE @var nchar(50)
EXEC DoIt @var out
PRINT @var
```

You should see the following results in the Results window:

```
Hello world!
My First SQLCLR Assembly!
```

This isn't the only way to add assemblies; take a look at another tool that enables you to easily add assemblies.

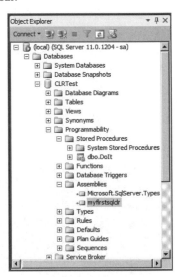

FIGURE 7-2

Using Microsoft SQL Server Data Tools

Creating and deploying SQLCLR objects using SQL Server Data Tools is an easy way to create and edit database objects. This section shows a quick example on how to use SSDT to create and deploy a SQLCLR stored procedure. This example assumes that CLR has been enabled.

1. First, add a new window to the Visual Studio IDE. From the view menu, select Other Windows ⇨ Data Tools Operations. This adds the Data Tools Operations windows to the bottom of the Visual Studio IDE. The Data Tools Operations shows the progress of many of the database operations done the SSDT, such as results from publishing objects to a database or deploying a database.

2. Now install the SQL Server Data Tools by going to the following URL: http://msdn .microsoft.com/en-us/data/tools.aspx

3. When you arrive at the SQL Server Data Tools page, click the Get It icon near the top of the page. This takes you to the download page for the Microsoft SQL Server Data Tools download page. As of this writing, SSDT is in CTP4, supporting SQL Server 2005, 2008, 2008R2, and 2012.

4. On the download page, click the Download SQL Server Data Tools link in the middle of the page, which launches the Web Platform Installer with the SSDT component selected. Click Install on the Web Platform Installer for SSDT. The install takes several minutes.

5. When installed, open Visual Studio, and from the View menu, select SQL Server Object Explorer (SSOE), which opens the SQL Server Object Explorer dockable window on the left of the Visual Studio IDE.

6. In SSOE, click the Add SQL Server button to register a new SQL Server instance in SSOE. In the Connect to Server dialog, enter the server name and login credentials, and then click Connect. This registers a new SQL Server in SSOE.

7. With a new server registered, expand the server node; then expand the databases node. Select the database you want to deploy the SQLCLR assembly to, and then right-click that database. From the context menu, select Create New Project, which opens the Create New Project dialog. In this dialog, type in a project name and location for the new project; then select the Create New Solution check box and the Create Directory for Solution check box. Click Start, which creates a new Database Project associated to the database selected in the SQL Server Object Explorer.

8. After you create the new project, right-click the new project, and from the context menu, select Properties, which opens the property pages for this project.

9. On the Project Settings tab, change the Target Platform to SQL Server 2012. Notice that you can also set the platform to several versions of SQL Server, including SQL Server 2008, 2008 R2, and SQL Azure. You can set the permission levels on this tab as well as the target framework (.NET 4.0, .NET 3.5, and earlier). Save the project and close the properties page.

10. Right-click the project again in Solution Explorer, and from the context menu, select Add ⇨ New Item. In the Add New Item dialog, select the SQLCLR C# from the list of installed templates; then select the SQLCLR C# Stored Procedure item. Keep the default name, and click OK. A new C# SQLCLR class will be added to the project and open ready for you to add code to.

   In the class, modify the method to return a string along with the code used in the Non-Visual Studio example:

   ```
   public static void SqlStoredProcedure1 (out string text)
   {
       SqlContext.Pipe.Send("Hello world!" + Environment.NewLine);
       text = "My First SQLCLR Assembly!";
   }
   ```

11. Save the class and then build the project to ensure no compile errors exist. With the project compiled, the next step is to deploy the new CLR stored procedure. Right-click the project in Solution Explorer, and from the context menu, select Publish, which opens the Publish Database dialog.

12. In the Publish Database dialog, click the Edit button to set the target server and database. When set, click the Publish button on the Publish Database dialog. This packages the

contents of the database project and deploys them to the selected database. In this case, all you have is a SQLCLR stored procedure so that will be the only thing deployed to your database.

The output of the publish displays in the Data Tools Operations window. Publish progress, messages, and errors display in this window. The publish of the CLR stored procedure should take only a minute, and when published, you should see it in the list of assemblies in SQL Server Object Explorer in Visual Studio.

When published, you can execute it just as you did in step 7 of the example in the section "The Non-Visual Studio Way" by calling the CREATE PROCEDURE statement and referencing the new assembly you published. At that point you can call the stored procedure the same as you did in step 8.

As you can see, it is easier to use the SQL Server Data Tools to create and publish SQLCLR assemblies because it provides a much easier and more efficient way to work with database objects, including CLR objects.

SECURING CLR

There is certainly a potential security risk by implementing the CLR in SQL Server. As such, Microsoft wanted to ensure that every measure was taken to ensure a secure hosting environment for the CLR, and includes the following goals:

➤ SQL Server should not be compromised by the running of managed code within SQL Server.

➤ No unauthorized access to user data or other user code by managed code should be permitted.

➤ Mechanisms should be in place to restrict user code from accessing any resources outside of SQL Server.

➤ Unauthorized access to system resources by managed code should be enforced.

To assist in upholding these goals, the CLR supports a security model called Control Access Security (CAS) for managed code. In this model, permissions are given to assemblies based on the identity of the code. The set of permissions that can be granted to the assemblies by the SQL Server host policy level are determined by the permission that is set and specified during the creation of the assembly in SQL Server. SQLCLR supports three permission sets:

➤ **SAFE:** Only local data access and internal computations are allowed. If no permission is specified during the assembly creation, SAFE permission is applied by default. No access to external system resources such as files or the registry exists.

➤ **EXTERNAL_ACCESS:** Same permission as SAFE but with the added ability to access external resources such as the file system, registry, networks, and environment variables.

➤ **UNSAFE:** Unrestricted access to all resources within SQL Server and outside SQL Server. This is the least secure and should rarely be used.

PERFORMANCE MONITORING

As stated earlier, using the CLR should not be considered an "enable it, leave it" option. When enabled, you need to make sure it performs as you expect and does what you need it to do. To help with this monitoring, several tools and options are available to you: Windows System Monitor, SQL Profiler, and Dynamic Management Views (DMVs).

Windows System Monitor

You can use Windows System Monitor (`PerfMon.exe`) to monitor CLR activities for SQL Server. Use the counter in the .NET CLR group in System Monitor but select the `sqlserver` instance when you monitor CLR counters for SQL Server, as shown in Figure 7-3. The following counters are extremely helpful in understanding the health and activity of the programs running in a SQL-hosted environment.

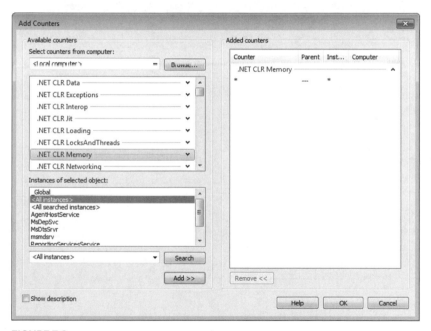

FIGURE 7-3

➤ **.NET CLR Memory:** Provides detailed information about the types of CLR heap memory, and garbage collection. These counters can be used to monitor CLR memory usage and to flag alerts if the memory used gets too large. If the code is copying a lot of data into memory, you may have to check the code and take a different approach to reduce memory consumption, or add more memory.

➤ **.NET CLR Loading:** SQL Server isolates code between databases by using `AppDomain`. This set of counters enables monitoring of the number of `AppDomains` and the number of assemblies loaded in the system. You can use this counter to determine loaded CLR assemblies. You can also use some of the DMVs for `AppDomain` monitoring.

➤ **.NET CLR Exceptions:** The Exceptions/Sec counter provides you with a good idea of how many exceptions the code generates. The values vary from application to application because sometimes developers use exceptions to test application functionality, so you should monitor over time to set the baseline and go from there. As this number increases, performance decreases.

Figure 7-4 shows the .NET CLR Memory:# Induced GC object, which displays the peak number of times garbage collection was performed due to an explicit call to `GC.Collect`. It is a good idea to let the garbage collection tune the frequency of its collection.

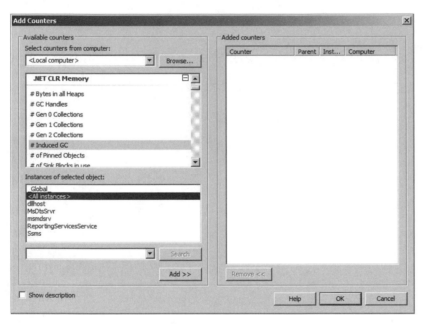

FIGURE 7-4

For more information on the different .NET counters, please see `http://msdn.microsoft.com/en-us/library/w8f5kw2e(v=VS.100).aspx`.

SQL Profiler

SQL Profiler has only a single event that you can use to monitor CLR assemblies. It is called `Assembly Load` and tells you via an Assembly Load Succeeded message when an assembly loads. If the load of the assembly fails, a message displays that indicates which assembly failed to load and provides error code information. Figure 7-5 shows the selection of the `Assembly Load` event. This event can be useful when troubleshooting a query that uses CLR such as a slow running server running CLR queries.

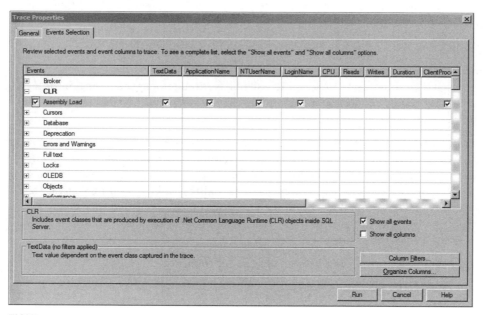

FIGURE 7-5

Dynamic Management Views (DMVs)

Dynamic management views (DMVs) return server state information that can be used to monitor the health of a server instance, diagnose problems, and tune performance. Following are four DMVs that pertain to the SQLCLR:

➤ `sys.dm_clr_appdomains`: Returns a row for each application domain in the server.

➤ `sys.dm_clr_loaded_assemblies`: Returns a row for each managed user assembly loaded into the server address space.

➤ `sys.dm_clr_properties`: Returns a row for each property related to SQL Server CLR integration, including the version and the state of the hosted CLR.

➤ `sys.dm_clr_tasks`: Returns a row for all CLR tasks currently running.

Although these four DMVs provide great information, they don't provide the performance tuning information you need. To provide more insight into the operation and execution of CLR assemblies, you can use the following DMVs to give you that information for CLR assemblies:

➤ `sys.dm_exec_query_stats`

➤ `sys.dm_exec_cached_plans`

Both of the preceding DMVs apply to the same executed query. The `sys.dm_exec_cached_plans` DMV can be used to view a cached query plan for a CLR query, whereas the `sys.dm_exec_query_stats` DMV contains a row per query statement within the cached plan. With these DMVs you can gather aggregate performance statistics for cached query plans. This information can help determine how any queries in your assemblies are performing.

CLR Integration Design Goals

When integrating the SQLCLR in your architecture, you should keep its design goals in mind:

➤ **Performance:** Best practice states that a CLR assembly should not be used to query data. This is what T-SQL is meant to do. CLR assemblies should not spend their time accessing data. Send the data you want worked on to the assembly instead of having the assembly pull it from the SQL Server.

➤ **Scalability:** SQL Server and the SQL handle memory management differently. SQL Server is more cooperative and supports a nonpreemptive threading model. The CLR supports a preemptive threading model and does not differentiate between physical and virtual memory. These differences present an interesting challenge when building systems that need to scale. Thus, as you design your database architecture, do so in such a way that the scalability and the integrity of the system are not compromised by user code calling unnecessary APIs for threading and memory directly.

➤ **Security:** Have a security plan and a set of rules for implementing SQLCLR, and stick to those rules. Ensure that any managed code follows the rules of SQL Server authentication and authorization. Not every piece of managed code needs access to external resources either.

➤ **Reliability:** The key with reliability is that any user code should not be allowed to execute any operations that compromise the integrity of the database and Database Engine, including not overwriting internal data structures or memory buffers.

SUMMARY

The SQLCLR integration opens up a new world of capabilities for data querying and processing. None of this is truly new though; it has been around for more than 6 years. Thus, the purpose of this chapter is to simply provide a look at why you should consider using the SQLCLR, what to expect, and some guidance for how to use it.

A great addition to working with the SQLCLR is the SQL Server Data Tools, which provide an easy way to work with database objects. You can work with different types of SQLCLR objects, including stored procedures and user-defined functions. Regardless of the type of CLR object you create, the key is to understand why you use SQLCLR over T-SQL.

The SQLCLR isn't a replacement for T-SQL, but complements the great functionality of T-SQL very well. It is up to you to decide how to use the SQLCLR.

Managed Code has its place within SQL Server. In fact, the SQL Server engine uses the CLR for some of its data types, such as the XML data type and the geographic data types. There are certainly some benefits for using the SQLCLR, and the more you work with it the more you will find places where you can use it to improve your applications.

Securing the Database Instance

WHAT'S IN THIS CHAPTER?

➤ SQL Server Authentication Types

➤ Windows Authentication Types

➤ Authorizing Object Level Security

➤ Maintaining Row Level Security

Security of a Microsoft SQL Server instance is probably one of the least sexy topics out there today. And unfortunately that will probably remain the case for many years to come, if not forever. However, properly securing the database instance is extremely important because without a properly secured instance, there is no way to guarantee that the data stored within the SQL Server instance is the data expected to be in the instance. Changes that an attacker could make to the data within an instance of SQL Server could be as small as simply changing names, to changing the prices that the customers are charged for products, to injecting Java script code or HTML, which is then served to customers or employees via their web browser and executes unexpected code on their machine. These changes could be minor; however more than likely they could install some sort of dangerous application on the user's computer such as a Trojan horse or key logger. So in reality, anything can happen, and it is best to be prepared for all scenarios.

AUTHENTICATION TYPES

There are two ways to connect to the Microsoft SQL Server instance: via SQL Server authentication and Windows authentication. When SQL Server is installed, there is an option to select if the SQL Server instance should support Windows authentication only or if it should support both Windows and SQL Server authentication.

SQL Authentication

SQL Server authentication was the original authentication method supported by SQL Server when it was based on the Sybase code base. With SQL Server authentication, the application or the user specifies the username and password to be used to authenticate against the SQL Server instance. When specified, the username and password are put into the connection string, which the application then uses when it connects to the SQL Server instance. With SQL Server authentication, the actual username and password are stored in the master database within the database instance.

When you use SQL Server authentication, the account and password are passed to the database instance, which then hashes the password and compares the username and password hash against the list of SQL accounts stored within the master database. If the passed-in username and password hash match an account stored within the master database, authentication succeeds, you can connect, and the rights associated with the SQL account are granted to you. If no match is found, an authentication error is returned.

SQL Server logins can be configured to force them to follow the Windows Active Directory security policies. For the domain policies to be enforced the Windows domain must be a Windows 2003 or higher and the SQL Server must be installed on a Windows 2003 or higher version of the Windows operating system. Care should be taken when planning your SQL Server installations as SQL Server 2012 is the first version of Microsoft SQL Server which requires that it be installed on Windows Server 2008 or higher. There are two domain policy settings which can be enabled. The first is to follow the domain password policies that control password complexity. The second is to enforce password expiration.

 Domain password policies are extremely complex and are outside the scope of this book.

Setting the password policies can be done via SQL Server Management Studio by editing the login and checking or unchecking the needed policies. The settings can also be enabled or disabled by using the ALTER LOGIN statement as shown in the following code snippet:

```
ALTER LOGIN chain_test
WITH CHECK_POLICY = ON, CHECK_EXPIRATION=ON
```

The domain policies are only verified when the account is created, or when the password is changed. This means that a SQL login could be created with a password that doesn't meet the domain policy requirements. Then after it is created the check policy setting could be enabled and it would be assumed that the account met the domain policy requirements when in fact it doesn't.

SQL Server 2012 introduces a new concept called the *contained user,* which is used within contained databases (for more information about contained databases see Chapter 4, "Managing and Troubleshooting the Database Engine"). A contained user exists only within a contained database and the password for the contained user exists within the database and not within the master database. As the contained user exists only within the database, no instance level rights can be granted to a contained user, and the contained user can only access objects within the database in which the contained user exists. Contained users are created by using the CREATE USER statement which is shown in the following code snippet by specifying the password parameter instead of the FROM LOGIN parameter.

```
CREATE USER MyContainedUser WITH PASSWORD='MySecurePassword'
GO
```

Within the context of the database in which the contained user is created, rights to objects and permission chains all work in exactly the same process as a traditional or non-contained user.

Contained users can be created based on local or domain Windows accounts, or they can be created as SQL Server users. A contained Windows user is simply a Windows account that doesn't have a corresponding login at the server level. Contained SQL users do not have the option of being configured to follow domain policies like traditional SQL logins.

Windows Authentication

Windows authentication was introduced to the SQL Server database engine in SQL Server 6.0. With Windows authentication, the username and password for the account are stored within the Active Directory database and not the SQL Server instance. This enables the Windows Active Directory infrastructure to handle the actual authentication of the account. Rights to connect to the SQL Server instance and to databases within the instance can be granted to individual Windows accounts or to groups which are created and managed within the Windows Active Directory domain.

When you connect to the SQL Server database using Windows authentication, the SQL Server isn't actually the one handling the Windows authentication. When you log into the Windows OS, an authentication token is generated by the domain controller, which is then passed to the client computer and stored within the computer's memory. When you attempt to connect to the SQL Server using Windows authentication, this token is then passed from the client computer's operating system to the SQL Server. The SQL Server then uses its operating system to verify with the domain controllers that the token is valid and verifies that your Security Identifier (SID) can access the SQL Server instance, and determines what level of permissions you should be granted.

 The full Windows authentication process is complex and has been documented in a couple of different places. You can dig through the Microsoft TechNet website to find the various articles that make up the documentation, or you can look at Chapter 3 of Securing SQL Server *by Denny Cherry (Syngress, 2010), in which the Windows authentication process is spelled out step by step.*

SQL Versus Windows Authentication

Because of the differences in SQL Server and Windows authentication, SQL Server authentication is considered to be a much less secure method of authentication and should be disabled whenever possible. When SQL Server authentication is enabled, those who want to attack the SQL Server instance can use brute force attacks to attempt to break in. This is because the username and password are simply sent to the SQL Server instead of the Windows authentication process that passes in the Windows token.

AUTHORIZING SECURABLES

Proper object level security within the database is key to keeping data within the SQL Server instance safe from intruders. This object level security extends from instance level objects, such as availability groups, and the ability to view the instances' server state objects to securing specific objects within the user databases.

Rights can be granted at both the server level, the database level, or to specific objects. Permissions can also be chained together, which simplifies the permissions both within the database, using permissions chains, as well as across databases by using the cross databases chaining.

Three statements are used when changing permissions in SQL Server.

➤ GRANT is used to assign rights.

➤ DENY is used to prevent access.

➤ REVOKE is used to remove either a GRANT or a DENY.

When granting permissions in SQL Server, you need to remember that DENY always overwrites a GRANT. If a user is a member of three different roles, and two of the roles have been granted rights to query from a table and the third role has been denied rights to query the table, then the user cannot query from the table.

Figuring out many of the object rights in this chapter can be hard to visualize when simply reading through descriptions of the rights. Microsoft has a visual diagram that can make this easier. You can download it from http://social .technet.microsoft.com/wiki/cfs-file.ashx/__key/communityserver- wikis-components-files/00-00-00-00-05/5710.Permissions_5F00_ Poster_5F00_2008_5F00_R2_5F00_Wiki.pdf.

The same applies if higher level sets of rights are granted. For example, if you have been granted rights to SELECT from a schema and denied the right to query a specific table, you cannot query from the table. The same applies if you have been granted rights to query from a table and denied rights to query at the schema level; you cannot query from any table within the schema, no matter what rights have been granted to the table.

You can use a second syntax when granting rights to users: WITH GRANT syntax. Adding WITH GRANT to the end of the GRANT statement, as shown in following code snippet, enables the user who has been granted the right the ability to grant the right to other users within the database.

```
GRANT SELECT, INSERT ON dbo.Users TO MyUser WITH GRANT
```

Server Securables

Dozens of instance-wide privileges can be granted at the instance level. These include connecting and managing the various endpoints within the SQL Server instance, managing the logins within the SQL Server instance, various instance-wide settings, the AlwaysOn Availability Groups, and the user-defined server roles that were introduced in SQL Server 2012.

The biggest difference between instance-wide privileges and database-wide privileges is that instance-wide privileges are granted directly to the login, whereas database-wide privileges are granted to users, and these users are then mapped to logins.

 The terms logins *and* users *get interchanged often, but within the scope of Microsoft SQL Server these are two very different things. Logins are used to log into the database instance, while users are mapped to a login from within the SQL Server databases.*

Now take a look at the different endpoint privileges available to the various objects within the scope of the SQL Server instance.

Endpoints

You can manage five privileges for each endpoint within the SQL Server instance:

➤ **Alter:** The Alter right enables the login that has the privilege to make configuration changes to the endpoint.

➤ **Connect:** The Connect privilege enables the user that has the privilege to connect to the endpoint; by default all logins are granted the privilege to connect to the default endpoints.

➤ **Control:** The Control privilege grants the other four privileges.

➤ **Take Ownership:** The Take Ownership privilege grants the login the ability to become the owner of the endpoint.

➤ **View Definition:** The View Definition privilege grants the login the ability to view the configuration of the endpoint without being able to make changes to the endpoint.

Logins

You can manage four privileges for each login within the SQL Server instance:

➤ **Alter:** The Alter privilege enables the login that has been given that right to make changes to the second login that the right was granted to. For example, if there were two logins named login1 and login2, login1 can be granted the ability to alter login2. Altering a login gives the granted login the ability to change the password, default database, default language, and so on of the grantee login.

➤ **Control:** The Control privilege grants the granted user the other three privileges to the grantee login. For example, if there were two logins named login1 and login2, login1 can be granted the ability to control login2.

➤ **Impersonate:** The Impersonate privilege grants the granted user the ability to use the EXECUTE AS syntax specifying the grantee login the ability to execute code as the grantee login.

➤ **View Definition:** The View Definition privilege grants the granted user the ability to view the configuration of the grantee login.

Instance-Wide Settings

Thirty-one privileges can be granted to a specific login. Table 8-1 shows these privileges and their meaning.

TABLE 8-1: Instance Privileges and Meanings

PRIVILEGE NAME	PRIVILEGE DEFINITION
Administrator bulk options	Enables the user to bulk insert data into the SQL Server instance using the BULK INSERT statement, the bcp command-line application, and the OPENROWSET(BULK) operation.
Alter any availability group	Grants the user the right to alter or failover any Always On availability group. By granting this privilege, the login is also granted to the Create Availability Group privilege.
Alter any connection	Grants the user the right to kill any user connection.
Alter any credential	Grants the user the right to alter any credential within the database instance.
Alter any database	Grants the user the right to change the database options for any database within the database instance. By having this right granted, the user is also granted the Create Any Database privilege.
Alter any endpoint	Grants the user the right to alter any endpoint that has been created on the SQL Server instance. By having this right granted, the user is also granted the Create Any Endpoint privilege.
Alter any event notification	Grants the user the right to alter any event notification that has been created within the SQL Server instance. By having this right granted, the login is also granted the Create Trace Event Notification privilege.
Alter any linked server	Grants the user the right to alter any linked server within the SQL Server instance.
Alter any login	Grants the user the right to alter any login within the instance.
Alter any server audit	Grants the user the right to change any server audit specification.
Alter any server role	Grants the user the right to change the user-defined server roles within the SQL Server instance.
Alter resources	Grants the user the right to change system resources.
Alter server state	Grants the user the right to change the server state. By having this right granted, the login is also granted the View Server State right.

PRIVILEGE NAME	PRIVILEGE DEFINITION
Alter settings	Grants the user the right to change instance-wide settings.
Alter trace	Grants the user the right to change other user's profiler and server side traces.
Authenticate server	Grants the user the right to authenticate against the SQL Server instance.
Connect SQL	Grants the user the right to connect to the SQL Server instance.
Control server	Grants a superset of instance level rights: Administrator bulk options, Alter Any Availability Group, Alter Any Connection, Alter Any Credential, Alter Any Database, Alter Any Endpoint, Alter Any Event Notification, Alter Any Linked Server, Alter Any Login, Alter Any Server Audit, Alter Any Server Role, Alter Resources, Alter Server State, Alter Settings, Alter Trace, Authenticate Server, Connect SQL, External Access Assembly, Shutdown, Unsafe Assembly, and View Any Definition.
Create any database	Enables the user to create a new database or to restore a database from backup.
Create availability group	Enables the user to create a new Always On availability group.
Create DDL event notification	Grants the user the privilege to create a DDL trigger.
Create endpoint	Grants the user the privilege to create a SQL Server endpoint.
Create server role	Grants the user the privilege to create a user defined server role.
Create trace event notification	Grants the user the privilege to create a trace event notification.
External access assembly	Grants the user the privilege to create an assembly that requires the external access setting.
Shutdown	Grants the user the privilege to shut down the SQL Server instance by using the SHUTDOWN T-SQL statement.
Unsafe assembly	Grants the user the privilege to create an assembly that requires the unsafe setting.
View any database	Grants the user the privilege to view the definition of any database within the SQL Server instance.
View any definition	Grants the user the privilege to view the definition of any object within the SQL Server instance. By granting this right, the login is also granted the View Any Database privilege.
View server state	Grants the user the privilege to view the server state objects. These server state objects include the SQL Servers dynamic management views and functions.

The "Control server" right can be granted to users who need a higher permission level without needing the full blown set of administrative rights which come with being a member of the sysadmin fixed server role. Heed the warning that a user with this right has elevated permissions to the SQL Server instance so this right should not be given out often.

Availability Groups

Availability Groups have four rights that can be granted to user-defined server roles:

➤ **Alter:** The Alter privilege enables the user that has been assigned the privilege to make changes to the AlwaysOn Availability Group.

➤ **Control:** The Control privilege grants the other three privileges to the user.

➤ **Take Ownership:** The Take Ownership privilege enables the user who has been assigned the privilege the ability to change the ownership of the availability group.

➤ **View Definition:** The View Definition privilege enables the user who has been granted the right the ability to view the definition of the availability group.

User Defined Server Roles

SQL Server 2012 introduces user defined server roles. User defined server roles are similar to fixed server roles except that they are created by the SQL Server administrator and not by Microsoft. The user defined server roles can be made members of any other server role, either fixed or user defined. Any server-wide right (shown earlier in this chapter) that can be granted to a login can be granted to a user defined server role.

Four privileges can be granted to a login for each user defined server role:

➤ **Alter:** The Alter privilege grants the login the privilege to alter the user-defined server role. This includes adding other logins as members of the fixed server roles.

➤ **Control:** The Control privilege grants the other three privileges.

➤ **Take Ownership:** The Take Ownership privilege grants the login the ability to set himself as the owner of the user-defined server role.

➤ **View Definition:** The View Definition privilege grants the login the ability to view the user-defined server role without having the ability to alter the user-defined server role.

Fixed Server Roles

SQL Server has nine fixed server roles that are pre-defined by Microsoft and cannot be changed. Eight of these fixed server roles have existed since at least SQL Server 7, and the ninth role was added in SQL Server 2005. The newer role is the *bulkadmin* fixed server role. This role gives the members of the role the right to bulk insert data into the database. In other previous versions of SQL Server, bulk loading data into the database required being a member of the most powerful fixed server role, the *sysadmin*, a role that provides the ability to perform any action against any database without restriction. Other fixed server roles grant various rights to the members of the roles and are discussed in the following list:

➤ The *dbcreator* fixed server role grants the user the right to create databases.

➤ The *diskadmin* fixed server role grants the user the rights to manage the physical database files.

➤ The *setupadmin* fixed server role grants the user the rights to add and remove linked servers.

➤ The *processadmin* grants the rights to kill other users' processes within the SQL Server instance.

➤ The *securityadmin* fixed server role enables the members of the role to GRANT, DENY, and REVOKE all server-level permissions as well as any database-level permissions for the databases which they have rights to.

➤ The *serveradmin* fixed server role enables the members to change any server-wide configuration option as well as use the SHUTDOWN command to shut down the SQL Server instance.

➤ The final fixed server role is the *public* role, which grants no rights; all logins on the instance are members of the public role.

Database Securables

Objects of various kinds exist within each SQL Server database, all of which have their own permissions. These permissions grant specific users rights to those objects so that the users can perform the functions needed to complete their tasks. It is a best practice to grant the users who will be using the database the minimum permissions needed to complete her job. This is done so that the users don't have rights to objects or data within the database that they don't need. An added benefit of this practice is to prevent someone who breaks into the database from gaining access to more secure data.

Database Permissions

Permissions can be granted against the database itself. Some of these rights are specific to the database level while some cascade down to objects within the database such as tables, views, and stored procedures.

Tables and Views

When dealing with tables and views, ten different rights can be granted to specific users or user-defined database roles. These are listed in Table 8-2.

TABLE 8-2: Rights for Tables and Views

RIGHT	DEFINITION
Alter	Grants the user the ability to change the schema of the object.
Control	Grants the user all other rights on the object.
Delete	Grants the user the ability to delete data from the object.
Insert	Grants the user the ability to insert data into the table.
References	Grants the user the ability to create a foreign key on the table. This right does not apply to views.
Select	Grants the user the ability to select the data from the object.
Take Ownership	Grants the user the ability to change the ownership of the object.
Update	Grants the user the ability to change data within the table.
View Change Tracking	Grants the user the ability to view the change tracking information for the object in question.
View Definition	Grants the user the ability to view the schema design of the object.

Stored Procedures and Functions

Stored procedures, functions, and most other database objects within SQL Server contain only five permissions that can be granted to users or roles, and are listed in Table 8-3.

TABLE 8-3: Rights for Stored Procedures, Functions, and Most Other Database Objects

PERMISSION	DEFINITION
Alter	Enables the user to change the schema of the database object the right was granted to
Control	Grants the user the other rights to the object
Execute	Enables the user to execute the object
Take Ownership	Enables the user to change the owner of the object
View Definition	Enables the user to view the schema of the object without having the ability to change the object

Permission Chains

Database permissions are chained from higher level code objects to lower level objects referenced within the object. If a table and stored procedure existed, as shown in the following code snippet, and a user were granted rights to execute the stored procedure, the permissions chain would enable the user the right to query the table, but only from within the context of the stored procedures. Any queries run from outside the stored procedure do not work unless the user has been granted specific rights to the table.

```
CREATE USER SampleUser WITHOUT LOGIN
GO
CREATE TABLE dbo.Users
(UserId INT IDENTITY (1,1) PRIMARY KEY,
UserName varchar(100),
Password varchar(100))
go
CREATE PROCEDURE dbo.SignIn
      @UserName varchar(100),
      @Password varchar(100)
AS
SELECT UserId
FROM Users
WHERE UserName = @UserName
      and Password = @Password
GO
GRANT EXEC ON dbo.SignIn to SampleUser
GO
```

Permissions chains work only within the context of the same execution of the parent object. This is a fancy way to say that the permission chain does not work with dynamic SQL. When using dynamic SQL, the user must be granted rights to the specific objects called within the dynamic SQL.

Permissions chaining works within all native SQL Server objects including stored procedures; scalar functions; table valued functions and views and chains down to other stored procedures; scalar functions, table valued functions, views, tables, and service broker objects. Permission chaining is enabled by default and cannot be disabled. Permission chaining is what enables the best practice of only granting the minimum set of permissions needed because it only requires execution rights on the stored procedures that are called and not the base objects.

Cross Database Permission Chains

Cross database permission chaining is a newer feature of SQL Server, introduced in SQL Server 2000 Service Pack 3a. Cross database permission chaining is an extension of traditional permission chaining, but it enables the permissions chaining to apply between databases. Without cross database permission chaining, accessing objects in a second database using the three-part name of the object would require that the user have the necessary rights on the object. Looking at the script shown in the following code snippet, for the stored procedure to work as written, the user would need to have the SELECT privilege.

```
USE master
GO
CREATE DATABASE Sample1
GO
CREATE DATABASE Sample2
```

```
GO
USE Sample1
GO
CREATE TABLE dbo.Users
(UserId INT IDENTITY (1,1) PRIMARY KEY,
UserName varchar(100),
Password varchar(100))
go
USE Sample2
GO
CREATE TABLE dbo.Users
(UserId INT IDENTITY (1,1) PRIMARY KEY,
UserName varchar(100),
Password varchar(100))
go
CREATE PROCEDURE dbo.VerifyUsers
AS
SELECT *
FROM dbo.Users b
WHERE NOT EXISTS (SELECT * FROM Sample1.dbo.Users a WHERE a.UserId = b.UserId)
GO
```

Cross database chaining is a database level setting which is disabled by default on all databases. To enable it, the cross database setting needs to be enabled on both the database that the procedure exists in and the database that the table exists in. You can see if cross database chaining is enabled in a couple ways. The easiest is to query the sys.databases catalog view, specifically looking at the is_db_chaining_on column that returns a 0 when cross database chaining is disabled and a 1 when cross database chaining is enabled, as shown in Figure 8-1.

FIGURE 8-1

The status of the database chaining can also be viewed by looking at the properties window of the database. This can be done by connecting to the database instance in the object explorer.

1. Navigate to Databases; then select the database in question.

2. Right-click the database and select Properties from the context menu that opens.

3. Select the options page, and scroll down in the Other Options section looking at the Miscellaneous section, as shown in Figure 8-2.

4. Within the Miscellaneous section, the Cross-Database Ownership Chaining Enabled field is visible, although grayed out. View the setting from the screen shown in Figure 8-2; although, you must use T-SQL to change this setting using the ALTER DATABASE statement.

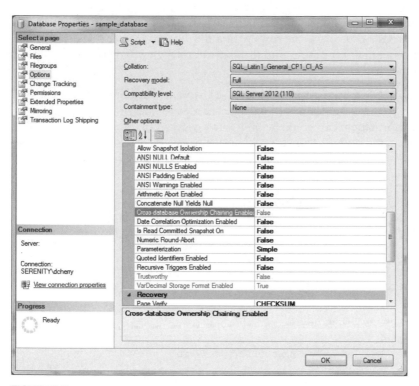

FIGURE 8-2

As stated, enabling cross database chaining requires using the T-SQL ALTER DATABASE statement so that the DB_CHAINING option is enabled, as shown in the following code snippet. The ALTER DATABASE statement must be used against both databases as shown in the following code snippet so that the stored procedure shown in the previous code snippet works as written.

```
ALTER DATABASE Sample1 SET DB_CHAINING ON
GO
ALTER DATABASE Sample2 SET DB_CHAINING ON
GO
```

One additional right must be granted for cross database chaining to correctly work. The user must be added as a user within the second database. The user does not need any additional rights within the database except to exist as a user within the second database either by creating a user that maps to the same login that the first database user is mapped to or by enabling the guest user within the second database. Enabling the guest user is not recommended because that would grant other users who may not need rights to the database rights that they do not need.

ROW LEVEL SECURITY

Row level security is something people are always asking about because Oracle has the concept for virtual private databases that enables the DBA to specify which rows the user can access.

The easiest way to do this is to create a view for each user who needs access, or a single view for each group of users that needs rights to specific rows within the database table. The user is then granted rights to the view and not to the table, and the user can then view only the rows that match the WHERE clause within the view.

Another technique that can be used is to design row-level security into the database schema. For example, if there were a department table and all managers needed to query the table and access only their direct reports information, this could be built into a view so that a single view could be used for all managers within the system. This can be done via some system functions such as the suser_sname() or current_user() functions. Listing 8-1 shows the suser_sname() function.

LISTING 8-1: Using the suser_sname() Function.sql

```
CREATE TABLE dbo.Employee
(EmployeeId INT IDENTITY(1,1) PRIMARY KEY,
LastName varchar(100),
FirstName varchar(100),
Emailaddress varchar(255),
ManagerId INT,
Username varchar(100))
GO
INSERT INTO dbo.Employee
(LastName, FirstName, EmailAddress, ManagerId, UserName)
VALUES
('Smith', 'John', 'jsmith@contonso.com', 0, 'CONTOSO\jsmith'),
    ('Gates', 'Fred', 'fgates@contonso.com', 1, 'CONTOSO\fgates'),
    ('Jones', 'Bob', 'bjones@contonso.com', 1, 'CONTOSO\bjones'),
    ('Erickson', 'Paula', 'perickson@contonso.com', 1, 'CONTOSO\perickson')
GO
CREATE VIEW dbo.EmployeeView
AS
SELECT *
FROM dbo.Employee
WHERE ManagerId = (SELECT EmployeeId FROM Employee WHERE UserName = suser_sname())
GO
```

Microsoft has released an excellent whitepaper that discusses row level security in more detail. More information about the whitepaper can be found on the Public Sector blog hosted on MSDN at http://blogs.msdn.com/b/publicsector/ archive/2011/08/23/row-level-security-for-sql-server-2008.aspx.

SUMMARY

Security must be done correctly because without database security all the information can be accessed by people who shouldn't have access to the data; this can leave the database susceptible to internal and external threats. Security shouldn't be limited to just the database and instance. A variety of levels of security need to be implemented both outside as well as inside the database.

This includes properly securing the network, the Windows operating system that hosts the database, the instance, the database permissions, and the application that needs to be secured to ensure that SQL Inject attacks are not be successful.

With each release of Microsoft SQL Server, the face of security within the platform changes and administrators must adapt. With the release of SQL Server 2012, a powerful new tool has been added in the user defined server roles that enables a much more flexible security model.

Change Management

WHAT'S IN THIS CHAPTER

➤ Organizing Code with Solutions and Projects

➤ Learning and Implementing Policy-Based Management

➤ Creating Custom Change Management Solutions Using DDL Triggers

➤ Standardizing Deployments Using Scripting Solutions

The challenges faced by database administrators have changed drastically since the early days of SQL Server. Laws such as Health Insurance Portability and Accountability Act (HIPAA) and Sarbanes-Oxley Act (SOX) have made a DBA's job much more structured because of their compliance requirements. These compliance laws require that administrators pass strict audits that require the administrator to answer questions such as "When was the last time a database was backed up?" or "Who has access to these tables in production?" The rise in popularity of quick development methodologies such as Agile and Rapid Application Development (RAD) bring their own challenges because now changes are occurring in your environments faster than ever before, making management of objects and versions a challenge to keep up with. With these challenges, Microsoft has evolved its products with features to help administrators ease these pains. Because of these new laws and methodologies, change management has become an issue that all DBAs need to pay close attention to.

In this chapter, you learn how to create projects for your SQL scripts and how to integrate those into Visual Source Safe, Microsoft's source control management system, to help manage object versioning. You also learn about Policy-Based Management and how it can help you monitor for unauthorized changes or help you enforce department/organizational IT policies for your systems. You also learn how to script database management actions using PowerShell. Finally, you learn about deploying changes using Data-Tier Applications to help easily encapsulate and deploy database applications.

CREATING SOLUTIONS AND PROJECTS

Visual Studio projects are generally a foreign concept to DBAs because the idea originated in the programming world. For SQL Server administrators, the Visual Studio concepts and tools are extended to SQL Server Data Tools and Management Studio as well. Solutions and projects enable you to separate your objects and resources into separate units to help in management and organization. Using the hierarchy of Visual Studio, first you create a *solution*, which can contain many *projects*, which can contain many *files* for the project. For example, you may have a solution called `LoanApplication` that contains two projects: one for your C# program and another for the DDL to create the database. In the business intelligence world, these solutions help you group all the related files, such as SSRS reports, SSAS cubes, and the SSIS packages to load the data. This separation of projects within solutions also aids in isolating changes using source control, especially when different teams or developers work on separate projects in the same solution. This is possible as each project and its related objects can be checked in and versioned individually using source control. You learn about source control later in this chapter.

Inside Management Studio, you can also create solutions and projects to hold your scripts and connections for easy access. When you double-click a script, it automatically implements the connection associated with the script. By placing script files in a project, you also can easily store files in Source Safe or another supported source control repository. This enables you to check code in and out, allowing for a collaborative development environment, wherein only one DBA or developer can be editing the code at one time. This requirement is discussed later in this chapter, but version controlling your scripts is often a requirement for change management. You could also check all your administrative scripts into Source Safe and share them with other administrators. The next few sections walk you through how to create the various pieces of a project that you can then check in to a version control system, but first, you'll need to learn how to create the project itself in Management Studio.

1. Select File ⇨ New ⇨ Project, and then select SQL Server Scripts as your project template.

2. Call the project `ProjectExampleScripts` and name the solution `AdminBookExamples` (see Figure 9-1).

3. To finish creating a new solution and project, click OK. Three folders are created in the project: Connections, Queries, and Miscellaneous. Your database connections reside in the Connections folder, and all the queries that you'd like to keep together in the project are in the Queries folder. The Miscellaneous folder holds files that don't have a `.SQL` extension but that you'd like to keep in the project, such as a `readme.txt` file that may describe instructions for using the project.

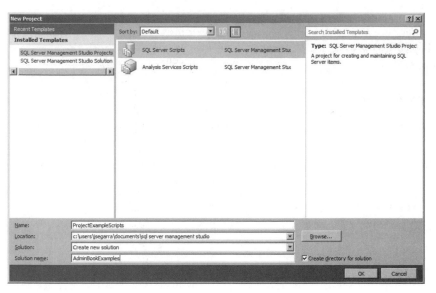

FIGURE 9-1

 If you have a tool such as Visual Source Safe installed, you can see a check box for automatically checking the solution into Source Safe upon creation. Any source management solution supported by Visual Studio can also work with SQL Server Management Studio.

Creating a Connection

Next you cover how to create a new database connection for your project. There are two methods to do this. The first method you work through has more steps than the second, but the first is covered so that you understand what the second method does and why. Follow these steps to create a new database connection for the project:

1. Right-click the Connections folder and select New Connection.

2. When the Connect to Server dialog opens, type your normal server connection information and how you want to authenticate.

3. On the Connection Properties tab (shown in Figure 9-2), select AdventureWorks for the Connect to Database option. You can also set the default protocol here if it differs from your preferred default.

4. Click OK and the connection is created in the Connections folder.

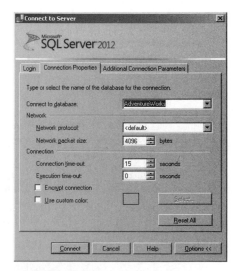

FIGURE 9-2

There are other ways to create this connection. If you create a query first, you'll be prompted for a connection prior to query creation. After you save this query, it also creates a connection in the Connections folder. Typically it is easier to create the connection as you create both the query and connection at same time.

Creating a Project Query

The Queries folder holds all the queries for your project. To create a query in the project, follow these steps:

1. Right-click the Queries folder, and select New Query. You are prompted to confirm the connection. The default query name is SQLQuery1.sql.

2. Type whatever you want in the Query window, and select File ➪ Save.

3. Rename the query SampleQuery1.sql by right-clicking it and selecting Rename. Click Save All to save the queries and the project.

4. With the query now saved, you're ready to begin using it. Close the Query window, and double-click the query file again. This time, the query opens automatically and does not prompt you for a connection. You can see what connection is associated with the query by right-clicking it and selecting Properties. You can then continue to add queries until your project is complete.

Again, generally the main point of creating an entire project and solution is to have integration with a source control system. If you use a source control system such as Source Safe, each time you add or delete a new script, the project control files are checked out. Individual files are checked out automatically as you open and edit them.

After you create your solution and projects within SQL Server Data Tools, if you have source control tools installed, you can then check in the solution or project to your repository. The details to use source control are beyond the scope of this book, but generally with a source control system such as Visual Source Safe, you can right-click on a project or solution and choose to link the item to source control from there. When the items are linked to source control, you can check items in and out for editing. When checking items in, you can specify version numbers and notes for other team members. This not only helps you properly manage changes, but you also have a built-in form of documentation to help support the code throughout its life.

POLICY-BASED MANAGEMENT

As mentioned in the opening paragraph to this chapter, many changes in government regulations have forced administrators everywhere to change the way they manage their environments. One of the major changes that DBAs have experienced is the need to implement and enforce policies departments have in writing regarding their database environments. The real challenge though is how do you enforce paper policies? Windows administrators have had the power of Active

Directory (AD) and policies for quite some time, but unfortunately those AD policies did not extend to the database world. Instead, database administrators have had to rely on either rolling their own solutions or spending money on third-party software to help monitor various parts of their environment, which even then was not necessarily equivalent to enforcing department data policies.

With the release of SQL Server 2008, database administrators finally had the power of policy enforcement bestowed upon them in the form of a new feature called Policy-Based Management. In SQL Server 2012 that story continues and is even a part of some major features such as AlwaysOn Availability Groups. Policy-Based Management gives administrators the ability to create policies that can do things such as prevent objects in the database from being created if they don't use a certain naming standard. You can also create a policy that quickly and easily checks to see (and change) the settings such as recovery model across multiple databases. Imagine switching hundreds of databases in a development environment to Simple recovery model with the single click of a button! In addition, you can use PowerShell to extend the power of Policy-Based Management for automation, which enables you to manage your environment in a predictable and scalable way.

Policy-Based Management Overview

The first questions most DBAs ask when the SQL development team rolls out a new feature are "What does it do?" and "Why should we care?" Policy-Based Management enables a DBA to declare her *intent* regarding how a specific server should act and then apply that intent to one or more target servers. The short answer to "What does it do?" is that it enables declarative, scalable, and repeatable SQL Server management.

Policy-Based Management begins with creating an overall policy that encapsulates several pieces: facets, targets, and conditions. First you start with an item called a *facet*. Facets expose individual elements of the SQL Server system so that they can be evaluated and compared to compliance criteria. The list of facets is loosely based on the objects in the SQL Server Management Object (SQL-SMO) hierarchy, which is the underlying object model for SQL Server Management Studio. Most facets are derived from combinations or subsets of SMO objects and other server state information. Facets present properties relevant to regular SQL Server management tasks.

For example, the Database Maintenance facet exposes several properties essential to the maintenance of individual databases, yet there is not a corresponding SMO object implementing this facet. Facets do not map directly to SMO objects, nor do they correspond to SQL Server Management Studio elements. Facets are a completely new representation of the SQL Server internal state.

Facets are listed in alphabetical order, making them easy to find. SQL Server Management Studio organizes the SMO objects in hierarchical order, which makes more sense as part of a GUI. Facet properties correspond to properties or combinations of properties of the underlying SMO objects. For example, a Stored Procedure object has facets for the 19 different properties, as shown in Figure 9-3.

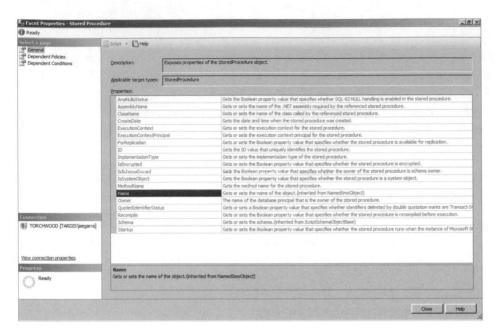

FIGURE 9-3

Properties can be compared using a combination of AND and OR logic to define a wanted state. This end state is referred to as a *condition*. Conditions, which are always expressed as a Boolean value, can detect and optionally enforce wanted configurations. One key limitation of a condition is that it can check the properties of only a single facet at a time. This is why the same property may appear in multiple facets. For example, Database Status appears in the Database Facet and the Database Maintenance Facet because it is necessary to completely evaluate conditions in both areas. Although you can evaluate only one facet at a time, you can choose multiple properties from a single facet to make a more flexible policy.

Policy-Based Management Step by Step

One of the first challenges DBAs face when inheriting a system is figuring out the backup and restore strategy. Because DBAs tend to inherit systems far more often than they develop them from scratch, rapidly learning about these systems is critical to the DBAs' ability to meet the fundamental requirements of their position. Looking at this situation from a change management perspective, Policy-Based Management can really help in this respect. Take a look at the following example and you can see how to create a policy that enforces naming conventions on stored procedures created in a database.

Example: Using Policy-Based Management to Enforce Stored Procedure Naming Conventions

One development best practice for stored procedures when creating a stored procedure is prefixing the name with usp_ to identify it as a user-created stored procedure. Some folks actually tend to name their stored procedures with sp_ to identify it as a stored procedure, but the problem with this is that there are system stored procedures that follow this naming convention. This can become an issue if you name your user stored procedure sp_Addusers, for instance, because the system would then try to look for the stored procedure inside the system databases first because it assumes it's a system stored procedure. On a busy system, this could cause a performance bottleneck. Also, by enforcing a naming convention for user stored procedures, management of those objects is easier, and you explicitly know what a user-created object is based on name.

In this example you want to ensure that when someone is attempting to create an object in your database, specifically a stored procedure, that it follows the required naming convention. To accomplish this you create a policy using a condition that uses the Stored Procedure facet to enforce this naming convention. If the object does not pass the policy, you set it so that the object won't get created at all in the database, and instead displays an error to the user. If it does pass, you can go ahead and allow the object to be created. You also see how to alternatively configure the policy to allow the change to occur but log it for documentation purposes.

1. In SQL Server Management Studio, under the Policy-Based Management node under Management, right-click the Conditions folder, and select Create New Policy. Name the new policy Stored Procedure Naming Policy.

2. From the Check Condition drop-down menu, click the down arrow, and select Create New Condition. This opens the Create New Condition box (see Figure 9-4). Name the condition Stored Procedure Naming Conventions.

3. From the Facet drop-down, select Stored Procedure.

4. After you select your facet, select the properties to create the condition from. The properties for each facet are located under the Field column. When you click the field, the drop-down automatically populates with all the properties for that particular facet. From the drop-down select the @Name option (see Figure 9-5).

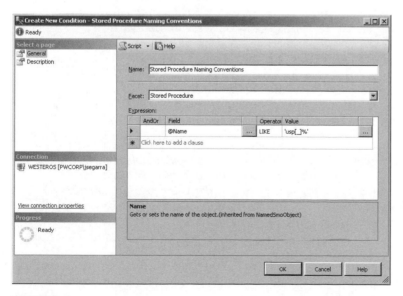

FIGURE 9-4

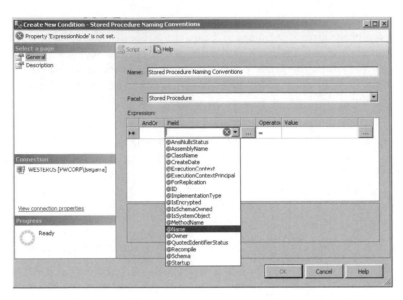

FIGURE 9-5

5. For a policy condition to be valid, create a Boolean condition. In other words, the result of the condition needs to be true or false. For this condition, set the conditional operator to LIKE because you compare the name using a wildcard operator for the comparison. Do this by clicking in the Operator column. From the drop-down, select LIKE.

> *You may notice sometimes that when you click the Operator column (as directed in Step 5), your options may change. This is because the values presented are based on the property you selected and what makes sense for that particular comparison. For instance, for the property of @Name, the options presented include options such as LIKE, NOT LIKE, and NOT IN. However, if you select a property such as @AnsiNullsStatus, the only options you're presented with are = or !=. The @Name property can (and does) include = and != along with the additional options because they're all valid. The latter property can't be anything but equal or not equal to a value, so those are the only options presented.*
>
> *This dynamic drop-down of values behavior also extends to the Value field. Using the preceding example, the @AnsiNullsStatus Value field, when clicked, populates with options of True or False because those are the only values for that property. However, with the @Name property, the Value field does not have prepopulated values because you can choose a number of custom options such as the one used in this stored procedure naming example.*

6. Set the value for the comparison value to `'usp[_]%'`. Include the single quotes as part of the value. The wildcard character of % should be familiar to SQL Server developers because that is same syntax used in T-SQL.

7. Click OK to finish creating your condition and return to the Create New Policy window.

Even though this example shows only a single property evaluated in a condition, a condition can uses multiple properties within a facet to create a more flexible condition. To add additional clauses to the condition, click the empty row underneath your initial property selection, and choose more properties. When you add additional clauses, you can select to make those additional clauses using AND or OR values.

Earlier this section mentioned Targets are one of the important aspects of Policy-Based Management. Now that you created a condition, you can configure a target to apply that condition to.

1. When you return to the Create New Policy menu, notice that the Against targets window has already been conveniently populated for you. Certain elements get prepopulated based on previously selected options. In this case because you created a condition using the Stored Procedure facet, the only logical targets for that are Stored Procedures. In addition, sometimes targets are nested in levels that result in multiple target options. In this case the targets show not only against all Stored Procedures, but all Databases as well because stored procedures are nested under the Database level. You can also further restrict targets by creating new conditions for target. Do this by clicking an arrow next to the word Every in the target's window and select the New Condition option from the menu. For this example, keep the defaults of Every as shown in Figure 9-6.

Each of the targets has a default condition of Every. For targets, "Every" means every user object. By default targets do not include system objects.

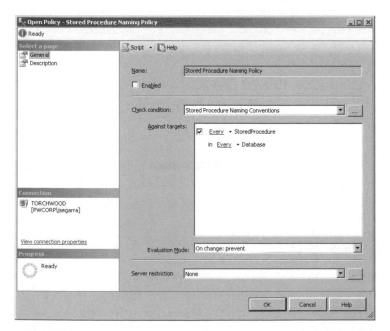

FIGURE 9-6

2. Next, select an Evaluation Mode for this policy. This selection determines the behavior for the policy. Listed here are the four possible options for modes:

   ➤ **On Demand:** Policy must be evaluated manually.

   ➤ **On Schedule:** Policy is evaluated on a schedule. This scheduled evaluation is done using SQL Server agent scheduler that uses PowerShell to evaluate the policy against the local instance.

   ➤ **On Change: Log Only:** Policy is actively enforced via a trigger. If an action violates the policy, the policy enables the change to occur but logs the event in the SQL Server event log.

   ➤ **On Change: Prevent:** Policy is actively enforced via trigger; however, if an action violates the policy, the default action is to rollback the offending transaction. In addition, this event is also logged to the event log.

   Be aware that not all evaluation modes will be listed for a policy because sometimes you get only a subset of the options. Again, these are options are presented based on previously chosen criteria. For this stored procedure naming example, you are presented with all four options. For another policy that is more static, for example a policy that checks the Recovery Model of a database, you are presented with only On Demand and On Schedule as evaluation options. For a detailed chart that shows which facets support the On Change evaluation modes, see `http://blogs.msdn.com/b/sqlpbm/archive/2008/05/24/facets.aspx`. Because you are using this example for change management purposes, you need to select the On Change: Prevent option. The On Change option is covered in more depth in the upcoming section "Policy-Based Management Implementation."

3. Finally, you can set Server restrictions with the policy. This restriction is yet another condition you can add to the policy that further restricts its evaluation. For example, you can create a condition that causes the policy to evaluate only against a server (default Facet used for this condition) if it is SQL Server 2005 and higher. For this example, leave it at the default of None. Click OK to complete creating your policy.

4. Because you chose to use the evaluation mode of On Change, you need to enable the policy for it to start taking effect. To do this, right-click the policy in SSMS, and select the Enable option. Visually you can see that the policy is now active because the red arrow on the icon disappears, as shown in Figure 9-7.

FIGURE 9-7

To test the policy you can run some code to trigger it. Run the code show in Listing 9-1.

Available for download on Wrox.com

LISTING 9-1: Create SampleNamingProc.sql

```
--Create procedure that fails policy evaluation
USE AdventureWorks
GO

CREATE PROCEDURE dbo.sp_SampleNamingProc
```

```
AS
     SELECT [Title],[FirstName],[LastName]
       FROM [Person].[Contact]
GO
```

The code in Listing 9-1 creates a new stored procedure in the AdventureWorks database called `sp_SimpleNamingProc`. Because the code attempts to create a stored procedure that does not follow your naming convention, you are greeted with the error message shown here.

```
Policy 'Stored Procedure Naming Policy' has been violated by
'SQLSERVER:\SQL\FL-WS-CON-JS2\WESTEROS\Databases\AdventureWorks\
StoredProcedures\dbo.sp_SampleProc'.
This transaction will be rolled back.
Policy condition: '@Name LIKE 'usp[_]%''
Policy description: ''
Additional help: '' : ''
Statement: '
CREATE PROCEDURE dbo.sp_SampleProc
AS
     SELECT [Title],[FirstName],[LastName]
       FROM [Person].[Contact]
'.
Msg 3609, Level 16, State 1, Procedure sp_syspolicy_dispatch_event, Line 65
The transaction ended in the trigger. The batch has been aborted.
```

As you can see, the error message gives you a lot of information as to why the stored procedure was not created. You can see that your policy was violated, and it shows you which object violated that policy. Next you see that the transaction itself was rolled back. You are also shown specifically the condition from the violated policy. The nice part about this is that it helps pinpoint, for the user, what part of your code specifically causes this policy to trigger, which in this case is the name portion of the stored procedure.

If you supplied a custom description and error message (not shown in this example), it's displayed in the Policy description and Additional help sections. The code statement that caused the policy failure to occur is also displayed in full. The last part shown is the error message thrown from SQL Server that tells you that the stored procedure you attempted to create caused a trigger to be fired, and the transaction did not complete successfully. The "DDL Trigger Syntax" section cover triggers more in depth later in this chapter.

Now that you know what part of your code isn't falling in line with your set policies, you can modify your code to come into compliance. Run the code in Listing 9-2 to do so.

LISTING 9-2: Create SampleProcCorrect.sql

Available for
download on
Wrox.com

```
--Create procedure that passes policy evaluation
USE AdventureWorks
GO

CREATE PROCEDURE dbo.usp_SampleProc
AS
     SELECT [Title],[FirstName],[LastName]
```

continues

LISTING 9-2 *(continued)*

```
        FROM [Person].[Contact]
GO
```

In this version of the script, you changed the name of the stored procedure from `sp_SampleProc` to `usp_SampleProc` to fall in line with your naming convention. This time when you run the code, you get a success message, and your stored procedure object is created in the database.

Although this particular policy is an active one, meaning when you enable it and it is actively triggered by an action, you also can evaluate it manually. To do this, simply right-click the policy in SSMS, and select Evaluate from the context menu. This evaluates the policy against the instance in which the policy is currently stored. This particular policy, evaluates against all *existing* stored procedures in all user databases. Because the objects already exist, the policy obviously can't prevent them from being created like it does for new code. The upside is that the results of the policy evaluation (see Figure 9-8) can give the administrator a comprehensive list of objects to investigate and follow up on for remediation. The results can be exported in XML format for reporting purposes by clicking the Export Results button.

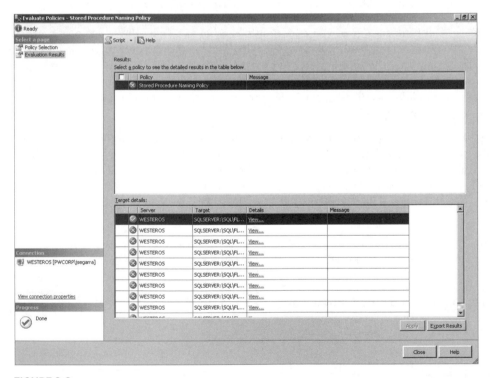

FIGURE 9-8

Scripting Policy-Based Management

After learning how to create a solution in SQL Server Management Studio for SQL administrative scripts and then implementing a management-based policy to enforce stored procedure naming conventions, the next natural question to arise is typically: Can you create source-managed scripts of your policies? As with almost any action since SQL 2005, the answer is yes; you can create a script. To do so simply right-click the object in Management Studio, and from the context menu, select Script [Object] As ⇨ Create To ⇨ New Query Editor Window. Listing 9-3 is the script for the condition from the earlier example:

LISTING 9-3: Create condition script.sql

```
Declare @condition_id int
EXEC msdb.dbo.sp_syspolicy_add_condition @name=N'Stored Procedure Naming
Conventions', @description=N'',
@facet=N'StoredProcedure', @expression=N'<Operator>
  <TypeClass>Bool</TypeClass>
  <OpType>LIKE</OpType>
  <Count>2</Count>
  <Attribute>
    <TypeClass>String</TypeClass>
    <Name>Name</Name>
  </Attribute>
  <Constant>
    <TypeClass>String</TypeClass>
    <ObjType>System.String</ObjType>
    <Value>usp[_]%</Value>
  </Constant>
</Operator>', @is_name_condition=2, @obj_name=N'usp[_]%'
, @condition_id=@condition_id OUTPUT
Select @condition_id

GO
```

Notice the large chunk of XML in the middle of the script. XML was introduced as a data type in SQL 2005. Now SQL Server manageability starts to embrace XML in server operations. Given that a condition is an arbitrary combination of facet comparisons, XML provides the perfect means to describe such an entity. Understanding XML and other rich data types is an essential DBA skill going forward, both for operations-oriented DBAs and development-focused DBAs. *Beginning XML Databases* by Gavin Powell (Wrox, 2006) is an excellent resource for the DBA who wants to learn XML.

Listing 9-4 provides the policy script:

LISTING 9-4: Create policy script.sql

```
Declare @object_set_id int
EXEC msdb.dbo.sp_syspolicy_add_object_set @object_set_name=N'Stored Procedure
Naming Policy_ObjectSet',
```

continues

LISTING 9-4 *(continued)*

```
@facet=N'StoredProcedure', @object_set_id=@object_set_id OUTPUT
Select @object_set_id

Declare @target_set_id int
EXEC msdb.dbo.sp_syspolicy_add_target_set @object_set_name=N'Stored Procedure
Naming Policy_ObjectSet', @type_skeleton=N'Server/Database/StoredProcedure'
, @type=N'PROCEDURE', @enabled=True, @target_set_id=@target_set_id OUTPUT
Select @target_set_id

EXEC msdb.dbo.sp_syspolicy_add_target_set_level @target_set_id=@target_set_id,
@type_skeleton=N'Server/Database/StoredProcedure',
@level_name=N'StoredProcedure', @condition_name=N''
, @target_set_level_id=0
EXEC msdb.dbo.sp_syspolicy_add_target_set_level @target_set_id=@target_set_id,
@type_skeleton=N'Server/Database'
, @level_name=N'Database', @condition_name=N'', @target_set_level_id=0
GO

Declare @policy_id int
EXEC msdb.dbo.sp_syspolicy_add_policy @name=N'Stored Procedure Naming Policy',
@condition_name=N'Stored Procedure Naming Conventions', @policy_category=N'',
@description=N'', @help_text=N''
, @help_link=N'', @schedule_uid=N'00000000-0000-0000-0000-000000000000',
@execution_mode=1, @is_enabled=True
, @policy_id=@policy_id OUTPUT, @root_condition_name=N'', @object_set=N'Stored
Procedure Naming Policy_ObjectSet'
Select @policy_id


GO
```

This script contains no XML. Because a policy contains only one condition, all its elements are deterministic and can be mapped to a well-defined set of parameters.

Policy-Based Management Implementation

Experienced DBAs often ask an extra question beyond just "What does it do?" They want to know "How can I apply this in my environment today?" It is important to know if the actual implementation of a feature is complete, secure, and scalable before you bet your systems (and your job) on it. This section covers how you can implement Policy-Based Management in your enterprise environment today.

You've already learned a bit about the On-Demand and Scheduled modes. These run directly from SQL Server Management Studio and from the SQL Agent, respectively. The other mode type is the On-Change event, which you used in the Stored Procedure Naming example. On-Change is precisely what the name implies: It captures a change event inside a target SQL Server and either logs the change event or prevents the change from occurring. SQL Server Policy-Based Management uses DDL triggers to either log or rollback a change event to implement On-Change policy evaluation.

On-Change works only for deterministic event-driven events in which something changes inside the SQL Server. The earlier example for Stored Procedure Naming used the On-Change mode because it specifically triggered a DDL event. In addition to raising a DDL event, all the properties within the chosen facet had to support the same set of events to use the On-Change:Prevent option. Refer to the previously mentioned blog post located here: http://blogs.msdn.com/b/sqlpbm/ archive/2008/05/24/facets.aspx.

The specific trigger used to evaluate a policy in On-Change mode can be either a DDL trigger or a server trigger, depending on the specific facet used to build the condition. Although Policy-Based Management greatly simplifies dynamic management for the DBA, it does have its limitations, such as certain facets not supporting certain modes. If you need to build a more customized solution that patterns Policy-Based Management's behavior, you can create your own DDL triggers. These steps are detailed later in the "DDL Trigger Syntax" section.

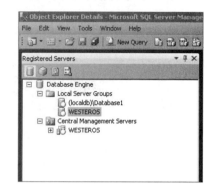

FIGURE 9-9

The next step in scalability is to use an item called a *Central Management Server* (CMS). A CMS is the mechanism a DBA uses to apply actions, including policies, from one server and have those actions repeated across a designated list of servers. Setting up a CMS is no more challenging than using the Registered Server list in SQL Server Management Studio. It even looks similar (see Figure 9-9).

Registering a Central Management Server is rather simple:

1. Open the Registered Servers by going to the View menu in SSMS and selecting Registered Servers. Alternatively, you can use the keyboard shortcut of Ctrl+Alt+G.

2. Expand the Database Engine node. You see a folder labeled Central Management Servers; right-click it and select Register Central Management Server from the context menu.

3. In the Server name box, supply the name of a SQL Server instance, which must be SQL Server 2008 or higher. Click Save to complete registration.

One difference between the two registration types is that when you save the credentials for member servers, you are telling the Central Management Server to save those registrations in its msdb database, rather than keeping that information stored on your local workstation. Another major difference between the two is that CMS supports only Windows authentication.

When you apply the policy to the Central Management Server, you are actually applying it across all the servers registered in the selected evaluation group, for example, say you create two server groups in your CMS: one called DEV and one called PROD. If you apply a policy on the PROD group, it evaluates only policies against servers under that group. However, if you try to evaluate policies against the CMS itself, it evaluates all the groups registered underneath it. You can also use the Central Management Server to execute T-SQL commands across multiple servers at the same time.

You may be asking yourself, "How do I automate this process?" Luckily there's already a great open-source project freely available on Codeplex called the Enterprise Policy Management

Framework (EPMF). The EPMF uses PowerShell with your CMS to evaluate polices against your enterprise on a scheduled basis. In addition to this, EPMF comes with built-in reports that display the policy health state of your environment. These reports enable you to see at a glance how far from compliance your enterprise is based on your policies. Setting up and configuring EPMF is beyond the scope of this chapter, but you can find the project and all its documentation at http:// epmframework.codeplex.com.

DDL TRIGGER SYNTAX

The syntax for a DDL (Data Definition Language) trigger is much like a DML (Data Manipulation) trigger, but with a DDL trigger, instead of monitoring an INSERT statement, you monitor a CREATE event such as a CREATE TABLE statement, for example. A DDL trigger is useful if you're monitoring for events such as objects being created. Going back to the previous PBM example that enforced naming conventions of new stored procedures being created, that policy is actually a DDL trigger in action! The generic syntax looks like this:

```
CREATE TRIGGER <trigger_name>
ON { ALL SERVER | DATABASE }
[ WITH <ddl_trigger_option> [ ,…n ] ]
{ FOR | AFTER } { event_type | event_group } [ ,…n ]
AS { sql_statement  [ ; ] [ …n ] | EXTERNAL NAME < method specifier >  [ ; ] }
```

Most of this syntax you probably recognize from DML triggers, so we'll focus mostly on the DDL-specific syntax. There are two scopes you can specify in a DDL trigger: ALL_SERVER or DATABASE. As the names imply, the ALL_SERVER scope monitors all server-level events, and the DATABASE option monitors database-level events.

The other important configurable part of the syntax is after the FOR clause. After the FOR clause, you specify what you'd like to monitor in the database or on the server with the DDL trigger option. This varies depending on what level of DDL trigger you have. The upcoming sections will break down these examples.

Database Triggers

Database DDL triggers are executed when you create, drop, or alter an object at a database level, such as a user, table, stored procedure, Service Broker queue, or view, to name a few. If you want to trap all database DDL events, you would use the trigger option in the earlier mentioned syntax of FOR DDL_DATABASE_LEVEL_EVENTS. The events are hierarchical, and the top-level database trigger types are shown in the following list.

➤ DDL_TRIGGER_EVENTS

➤ DDL_FUNCTION_EVENTS

➤ DDL_SYNONYM_EVENTS

➤ DDL_SSB_EVENTS

➤ DDL_DATABASE_SECURITY_EVENTS

- ➤ DDL_EVENT_NOTIFICATION_EVENTS

- ➤ DDL_PROCEDURE_EVENTS

- ➤ DDL_TABLE_VIEW_EVENTS

- ➤ DDL_TYPE_EVENTS

- ➤ DDL_XML_SCHEMA_COLLECTION_EVENTS

- ➤ DDL_PARTITION_EVENTS

- ➤ DDL_ASSEMBLY_EVENTS

To create a trigger that would audit for any stored procedure change, deletion, or creation, you could use a CREATE TRIGGER statement such as the following:

```
CREATE TRIGGER ChangeWindow
ON DATABASE
FOR DDL_PROCEDURE_EVENTS
AS
-- Trigger statement here
```

Under the trigger types mentioned in the list, you can get much more granular on certain events by using the event type after the FOR keyword. For example, rather than trap all events when any type of table event occurs, you can narrow it down to raise only the DDL event when a table is dropped by using the DROP_TABLE trigger option. To monitor for any DROP TABLE, CREATE TABLE, or ALTER TABLE statement issued, you could use the following code:

```
CREATE TRIGGER ChangeWindow
ON DATABASE
FOR CREATE_TABLE, DROP_TABLE, ALTER_TABLE
AS
-- Trigger statement here
```

Finally, you can monitor all changes by using the DDL_DATABASE_LEVEL_EVENTS event type:

```
CREATE TRIGGER ChangeWindow
ON DATABASE
FOR DDL_DATABASE_LEVEL_EVENTS
AS
-- Trigger statement here
```

Another important function in your DDL trigger toolbox is the EVENTDATA() system function. The EVENTDATA() system function is raised whenever a DDL trigger is fired at any level; it outputs the event type, the user who executed the query, and the exact syntax the user ran. The function outputs this data in XML format, as shown here:

```
<EVENT_INSTANCE>
  <EventType>CREATE_USER</EventType>
  <PostTime>2006-07-09T12:50:16.103</PostTime>
  <SPID>60</SPID>
  <ServerName>TORCHWOOD</ServerName>
```

```
    <LoginName>TARDIS\jsegarra</LoginName>
    <UserName>dbo</UserName>
    <DatabaseName>AdventureWorks</DatabaseName>
    <ObjectName>jorge</ObjectName>
    <ObjectType>SQL USER</ObjectType>
    <DefaultSchema>jorge</DefaultSchema>
    <SID>q7ZPUruGyU+nWuOrlc6Crg==</SID>
    <TSQLCommand>
      <SetOptions ANSI_NULLS="ON" ANSI_NULL_DEFAULT="ON" ANSI_PADDING="ON"
QUOTED_IDENTIFIER="ON" ENCRYPTED="FALSE" />
      <CommandText>CREATE USER [jorge] FOR LOGIN [jorge] WITH DEFAULT_SCHEMA
-
[dbo]</CommandText>
    </TSQLCommand>
</EVENT_INSTANCE>
```

You can then either pull all the data from the EVENTDATA() function and log it into a table as an XML data type, or pull selective data out using an XPath query. To do an XML XPath query in SQL Server, you would specify the path to the XML node. In DDL triggers, the key elements from the EVENTDATA() function are as follows:

➤ EventType: The type of event that caused the trigger.

➤ PostTime: The time the event occurred.

➤ SPID: The SPID of the user who caused the event.

➤ ServerName: The name of the instance on which the event occurred.

➤ LoginName: The login name that performed the action that triggered the event.

➤ UserName: The username that performed the action that triggered the event.

➤ DatabaseName: The name of the database in which the event occurred.

➤ ObjectType: The type of object that was modified, deleted, or created.

➤ ObjectName: The name of the object that was modified, deleted, or created.

➤ TSQLCommand: The T-SQL command that was executed to cause the trigger to be run.

To pull out selective data, you could use code like the following to do an XPath query. You would first pass in the fully qualified element name, such as /EVENT_INSTANCE/TSQLCommand, and the [1] in the following code means to pull out the first record. Because there is only one record in the EVENTDATA() function, you always pull only the first record. The EVENTDATA() function is only available to you in the scope of the trigger. If you were to run the following query outside the trigger, it would return NULL:

```
CREATE TRIGGER RestrictDDL
ON DATABASE
FOR DDL_DATABASE_LEVEL_EVENTS
AS

EXECUTE AS USER = 'DBO'

DECLARE @errordata XML
```

```
SET @errordata = EVENTDATA()

SELECT  @errordata
GO
```

You can use the ROLLBACK command in a DDL trigger to cancel the command that the user ran. You can also wrap this in a conditional IF statement to conditionally roll the statement back. Typically, though, you see that DDL triggers log that the event occurred and then potentially roll the command back if the user did not follow the correct change procedures.

Example: DDL Triggers Monitor Database Changes

Now walk through a complete example of how you could use DDL triggers to monitor for changes that occur in a database. The type of triggers that you try to monitor for are any database-level events, such as table or security changes. If a change occurs, you want to log that event into a table. If the user is not logged in as the proper account, you want to roll the change back. This way, you can prevent users in the sysadmin role from making changes. The table that you want to log the change events into is called DDLAudit. To create the table, use the following syntax in Listing 9-5:

LISTING 9-5: Create Audit Table.sql

Available for download on Wrox.com

```
CREATE TABLE DDLAudit
(
  AuditID       int            NOT NULL identity
                               CONSTRAINT DDLAuditPK
                               PRIMARY KEY CLUSTERED,
  LoginName     sysname        NOT NULL,
  UserName      sysname        NOT NULL,
  PostDateTime  datetime       NOT NULL,
  EventType     varchar(100)   NOT NULL,
  DDLOp         varchar(2500)  NOT NULL
)
```

You're now ready to create the trigger to log into the table. Most SQL Server environments allow changes to the database only between certain maintenance window hours. You can use the following DDL trigger in Listing 9-6 to prevent changes outside the 8:00 P.M. to 7:00 A.M. maintenance window. Changes made at any other time roll back. If you are inside the maintenance window, the change is logged to the DDLAudit table.

LISTING 9-6: Create ChangeWindow Trigger.sql

Available for download on Wrox.com

```
CREATE TRIGGER ChangeWindow
 ON DATABASE
 FOR DDL_DATABASE_LEVEL_EVENTS
 AS

DECLARE @errordata XML
```

continues

LISTING 9-6 *(continued)*

```
SET @errordata = EVENTDATA()

INSERT dbo.DDLAudit
       (LoginName,
        UserName,
        PostDateTime,
        EventType,
        DDLOp)
VALUES   (SYSTEM_USER, ORIGINAL_LOGIN(), GETDATE(),
    @errordata.value('(/EVENT_INSTANCE/EventType)[1]', 'varchar(100)'),
    @errordata.value('(/EVENT_INSTANCE/TSQLCommand)[1]', 'varchar(2500)') )

IF DATEPART(hh,GETDATE()) > 7 AND DATEPART(hh,GETDATE()) < 20
BEGIN

   RAISERROR ('You can only perform this change between 8PM and 7AM.
Please try this
change again or contact Production support for an override.', 16, -1)
   ROLLBACK
END
```

In this code, you trap the login used and the original login to check for context switching (`EXECUTE AS`). With the trigger now created, test it by running a simple DDL command such as the following:

```
CREATE table TriggerTest
(Column1 int)
```

If you executed this command after 7:00 A.M. and before 8:00 P.M., you would receive the following error, and the `CREATE` statement would roll back. If you looked at the tables in Management Studio, you should not see the `TriggerTest` table.

```
(1 row(s) affected)
Msg 50000, Level 16, State 1, Procedure ChangeWindow, Line 22
You can not perform this action on a production database. Please contact the
production DBA department for change procedures.
Msg 3609, Level 16, State 2, Line 2
The transaction ended in the trigger. The batch has been aborted.
```

If you were to run the statement before 7:00 A.M. or after 8:00 P.M., you see only (1 row(s) affected), meaning that the change was logged, but you successfully performed the action. You can test this by changing the server's time in Windows. After you try to create a few tables or make changes, select from the DDLAudit table to see the audited records.

There is little performance effect to this type of trigger because usually DDL events rarely happen. You can find the trigger in Management Studio by selecting the individual database, and then selecting Programmability ➪ Database Triggers. You can create a script of the trigger to modify an existing trigger, or you can delete the trigger by using Management Studio.

Of course, you still want to occasionally run a DDL statement in production by overriding the trigger. To allow access, you need to only temporarily turn off the trigger using the following syntax for database-level or server-level triggers:

```
DISABLE TRIGGER ChangeWindow ON DATABASE
GO
```

After the override, you can enable the triggers again by running the following syntax. (You should replace the keyword ALL with the specific trigger name to enable or disable the individual trigger.):

```
ENABLE TRIGGER ALL ON DATABASE
GO
ENABLE Trigger ALL ON ALL SERVER;
```

Server Triggers

Server-level triggers operate the same way as database-level triggers, but they are monitors for server configuration, security, and other server-level changes. The following list shows the top-level events, but these too are hierarchical. For example, you can monitor any login changes, as you'll see in an upcoming example.

- ➤ DDL_DATABASE_EVENTS
- ➤ DROP_DATABASE
- ➤ DDL_ENDPOINT_EVENTS
- ➤ CREATE_DATABASE
- ➤ DDL_SERVER_SECURITY_EVENTS
- ➤ ALTER_DATABASE

Now walk through another quick example. As mentioned in the last chapter, if you are in the sysadmin role, you can perform any function you want on the server. With this DDL trigger, you can ensure that only a single login can perform login-type events, such as creating logins. If anyone else tries to create, modify, or delete a login, it will be rolled back. Of course, you would need to implement additional security measures if this is your actual requirement, such as protecting the DDL trigger from change, but things are kept simple for this example in Listing 9-7:

Available for download on Wrox.com

LISTING 9-7: Create PreventChangeTrigger.sql

```
CREATE TRIGGER PreventChangeTrigger
 ON ALL SERVER
 FOR DDL_LOGIN_EVENTS

 AS

 IF SUSER_NAME() != 'TARDIS\JSEGARRA
```

continues

LISTING 9-7 *(continued)*

```
BEGIN
   RAISERROR ('This change can only be performed
by the server owner, Jorge Segarra.
 Please contact him at extension x4444 to follow the procedure.', 16, -1)
 ROLLBACK

 END
```

If users other than the TARDIS\JSEGARRA login attempted a login change, they would receive the following error. You can issue a permission context switch (EXECUTE AS LOGIN) to test out the trigger in your development environment.

```
Msg 50000, Level 16, State 1, Procedure PreventChangeTrigger, Line 9
This change can only be performed by the server owner, Jorge Segarra.
Please contact
him at extension x1701 to follow the procedure.
Msg 3609, Level 16, State 2, Line 1
```

The transaction ended in the trigger. The batch was aborted.

DDL server triggers can be found in Management Studio under Server Objects ➪ Triggers. Like the database triggers, you can script only the trigger for modifications, and delete the trigger, from Management Studio.

TRIGGER VIEWS

The Management Studio interface is still slightly lacking in what you can accomplish with DDL triggers, so a DBA must often use T-SQL as a management interface. One of the nice views available to show you all the database-level DDL triggers is sys.triggers; for server-level triggers, you can use sys.server_triggers. Between these two views, you can quickly see what triggers your server has installed on it with a query like this one:

```
SELECT type, name, parent_class_desc FROM sys.triggers
WHERE parent_class_desc = 'DATABASE'
UNION
SELECT type, name, parent_class_desc FROM sys.server_triggers
WHERE parent_class_desc = 'SERVER'
```

SCRIPTING OVERVIEW

Change management is all about creating a reproducible and auditable way to deploy and manage your changes. This is impossible to do properly when a DBA executes T-SQL scripts through a Management Studio environment. Most non-Windows system administrators use shell scripts to create a repeatable change management process for their OS and database server environments. This administrative practice has the broadest acceptance and the lowest risk. Scripting leverages both native OS and application capabilities, plus it works consistently regardless of the target system, at least outside the Windows environment. Just as experienced SQL DBAs have T-SQL script libraries, DBAs working with open-source and UNIX-variant systems have shell script libraries that just keep getting larger as they collect more and more useful scriptlets. Thanks to sqlcmd and PowerShell, you have the same scripting capabilities on the Windows platform, only better.

sqlcmd

The main way to create a repeatable change management system is by using sqlcmd files that encapsulate that T-SQL logic into a set of output logs. These logs provide an audit trail for your deployment activities. This way, you know that the change will deploy to each of your environments (test, QA, Production, etc.) and provide predictable results.

sqlcmd is a replacement for isql and osql. SQL 2005 launched sqlcmd as the first major attempt to create a scripting environment that could cross the boundary between T-SQL and the outside world, and it is still a great mechanism for mixing SQL and operating system scripts for database schema deployments. (PowerShell, covered next, takes this a step further, enabling you to script object behavior for scalable server configuration deployments.)

You can use either of two modes to execute a sqlcmd command: at a command line or in Management Studio. If you are a SQL Server 2000 DBA, the transition to sqlcmd will be an easy one; sqlcmd is similar to osql, with some additional switches to simplify your daily job. You probably won't be familiar with executing sqlcmd commands from Management Studio, though. Using Management Studio to execute these types of commands gives you a great deal of control and replaces many of the old extended stored procedures such as xp_cmdshell. This section covers both solutions.

Executing sqlcmd from the Command Prompt

Executing sqlcmd from the command prompt enables you to run any query from a command prompt. More important, it enables you to wrap these queries into a packaged install batch file for deployments, making it easy for anyone to install the database. You can use many switches in sqlcmd, most of which have only a specialized use. The following are some of the important switches (they are all case sensitive):

➤   -U: Username.

➤   -P: Password.

➤   -E: Use Windows authentication. If you use this switch, you do not need to pass in the -U and -P switches.

➤   -S: Instance name to connect to.

➤   -d: Database name to start in.

➤   -i: Input file that contains the query to run.

➤   -o: Output file to which you want to log the output of the query.

➤   -Q: Pass in the query with the -Q switch instead of an input file.

You need to change the actual file save locations to something appropriate for your particular system.

Try creating a sample sqlcmd by following these steps:

1. Create a new SQL file with Notepad or the text editor of your choice by typing the following query:

```
SELECT * FROM Purchasing.Vendor
```

2. Save the file as C:\users\demo\documents\TestQuery.sql.

3. Go to a command prompt and type the following command:

```
sqlcmd -i c:\testquery.sql -S localhost -d AdventureWorks
```

The −i switch represents the input file that contains the file; the −S switch represents the server name to connect to; and the −d switch represents the database name. The query retrieves all the records from the Vendor table and displays them in the console window. If you do not specify a username and password with the −U and −P switches, or the −E switch for Windows authentication, sqlcmd defaults to Windows authentication.

There are two variations of this command:

➤ Use the −Q switch to pass the query to sqlcmd and then quit sqlcmd after the query is complete. The −q switch can also be used if you don't want to exit.

➤ Use the −o switch. The −o switch passes the results of the query to an output file and does not display anything in the console:

```
sqlcmd -Q "select * from purchasing.vendor" -d adventureworks -S localhost
-o C:\testoutput.txt
```

Another way to execute sqlcmd from a command prompt is by typing sqlcmd if you'd like to connect to your local instance, or by specifying the instance with the −S switch. You are then presented with a 1> prompt, where you can type a query. If you want to execute an operating system command from the sqlcmd window, type !! in front of the command, like this:

```
1>!!dir
```

To execute a SQL command, type the command. After you press Enter, you see a 2> and 3> prompt until you finally issue a GO statement to execute the batch. After the GO statement, the batch runs and the prompt resets to 1>.

That covers the basic commands, but to simplify matters, you can create a set of commands that execute each time you run sqlcmd. An *initialization file* runs a series of commands after you execute sqlcmd but before control is handed off to the user.

To create an initialization file, follow these steps:

1. Create a T-SQL file called `C:\users\demo\documents\initexample.sql` with Notepad or another text editor.

This file is going to run a series of commands after you first run `sqlcmd`. The `:setvar` statement can be used to set user variables that can be employed later in the script with the `$` sign. This example initialization script creates three variables. One holds the database name, one holds the 60-second timeout, and the last one holds the server name. You use the variables later in the script by using `$(variablename)`.

```
:setvar  DBNAME AdventureWorks
:setvar sqlcmdlogintimeout 60
:setvar server "localhost"
:connect $(server) -l $(sqlcmdlogintimeout)
SELECT VersionofSQL = @@VERSION;
SELECT ServerName = @@SERVERNAME ;
```

2. At a command prompt, type the following command to set the `sqlcmdini` environment variable:

```
SET sqlcmdini=c:\users\demo\documents\initexample.sql
```

This sets the environment variable for the user's profile. After you execute this, each time the `sqlcmd` program is executed, the `initexample.sql` script executes before handing control to the user.

With the environment variable now set, just run `sqlcmd` from a command prompt (see Figure 9-10). After you run this, you see the version of SQL Server and the server name before you're given control to run any query against the database.

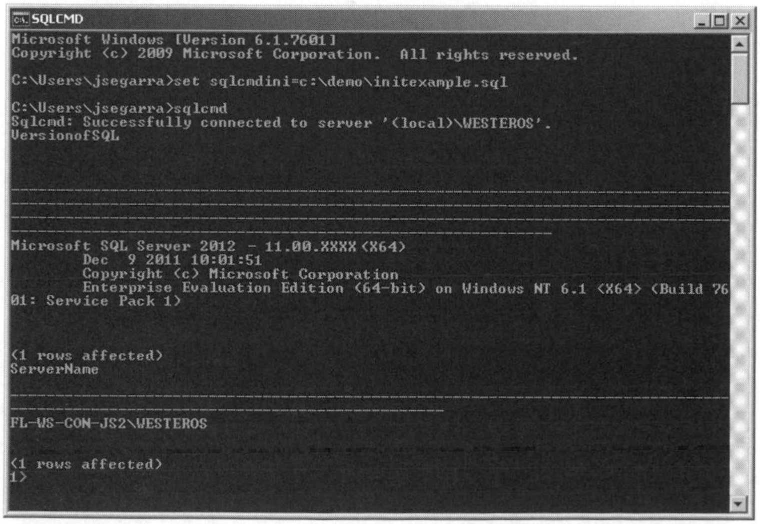

FIGURE 9-10

Executing sqlcmd from Management Studio

While doing your day-to-day job, eventually you're going to want to integrate `sqlcmd` scripts into your regular T-SQL scripts, or someone may pass you a script that has `sqlcmd` integrated into it. To use this script in Management Studio's query environment, simply click the SQLCMD Mode icon in the Query window. If you try to execute `sqlcmd` syntax from within the Query window without being in SQLCMD mode, you receive an error message like the following:

```
Msg 102, Level 15, State 1, Line 3
Incorrect syntax near '!'.
```

You can intermingle `sqlcmd` and T-SQL in the same script, and you can switch between script types easily as long as SQLCMD mode is enabled. When enabled, any `sqlcmd` syntax is highlighted in gray. You can also enable the mode each time a query is opened by going to Tools ➪ Options in Management Studio. In the SQL Server page of the Query Execution group (shown in Figure 9-11), enable the option By Default, Open New Queries in SQLCMD Mode. After you enable this option, any subsequent Query windows will open with the mode enabled.

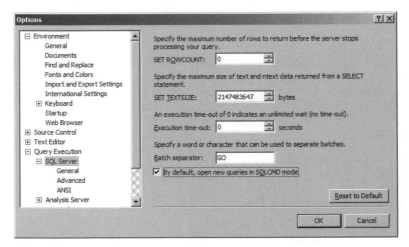

FIGURE 9-11

Using `sqlcmd` and T-SQL, you can connect to multiple servers from within the same script and run T-SQL statements. For example, the following script logs on to multiple servers and backs up the `master` database of each server. The `:CONNECT` command is followed by the name of the instance to which you want to connect. This is a simple example, but it can be strengthened in a disaster recovery situation to do massive repairing of your databases or SQL Server instances.

Again, you need to change the actual file save locations and server names to something appropriate for your particular system.

```
:CONNECT localhost
BACKUP DATABASE master TO  DISK = N'C:\MSSQL\Backup\test.bak'

:CONNECT localhost\sql2k5test
BACKUP DATABASE master TO  DISK = N'C:\MSSQL\Backup\test2.bak'
```

You can also use the :SETVAR command inside sqlcmd to create a script variable. This variable enables you to set the variable either from within the :SETVAR command, as shown in the following code, or by passing it through the command prompt. The following example shows you how to set a variable called SQLServer to the value of Localhost. You then use that variable by using the variable name prefixed with a dollar sign and wrapping it in parentheses. Another variable called DBNAME is also created and used in the T-SQL backup command. As you can see, in sqlcmd you can mix T-SQL and sqlcmd easily, and the variables can intermix.

```
:SETVAR SQLServer Localhost
:CONNECT $(SQLServer)
:SETVAR DBNAME Master

BACKUP DATABASE $(DBNAME) TO  DISK = N'C:\MSSQL\Backup\test.bak'
```

Now modify the script slightly to look like the following, and then save it to a file called C:\InputFile.sql. (Place the file wherever is appropriate on your machine.) This script can dynamically connect to a server and back up the master database:

```
:CONNECT $(SQLServer)
BACKUP DATABASE master TO  DISK = N'C:\MSSQL\Backup\test.bak'
```

With the script now saved, you can go to a command prompt and type the following command using the –v switch (again, all of these switches are case-sensitive) to pass in the variable. In this case, you pass in the name localhost to the SQLServer variable:

```
sqlcmd -i c:\users\demo\documents\inputfile.sql -v SQLServer="localhost"
```

PowerShell

Just as DBAs need to deploy database code changes reliably, they also need to deploy configuration changes in the same way. Although T-SQL scripts can take you a good way down this path, something more is needed. PowerShell is that something. PowerShell is a new and largely backward-compatible scripting environment for Windows. It is shipped as a native feature in Windows Server 2008 and can be downloaded and installed on Windows Server 2003, Windows XP, and Windows Vista. Although it is beyond the scope of this book to describe everything about PowerShell, the following introduces some of the features that highlight just how useful it can be.

 Professional Windows PowerShell Programming: Snap-Ins, Cmdlets, Hosts, and Providers, *by Arul Kumaravel et al. (Wrox, 2008), is an excellent in-depth guide to Windows PowerShell for readers who want a deeper look at the subject.*

PowerShell relies to a considerable degree on elements called *cmdlets* to do the heavy lifting. Cmdlets take an object model and present it like a disk drive. Natively, PowerShell can traverse and explore event logs, registry hives, file systems, and pretty much anything else built into the Windows operating system. For SQL Server, the SQL Development team wrote a custom cmdlet that presents the SQL-SMO object model as a drive. The cmdlet also has some extra smarts regarding how it presents data to the console, just to make your job a bit easier.

One neat trick of PowerShell is that it has a built-in set of aliases that map its native verb-noun syntax into legacy commands. `dir` works just as well as `get-childitem`; and for the folks who believe that `ls` is the proper command for enumerating a folder, that works, too. The arguments for all commands must still be in PowerShell format. Trying to match that level of compatibility would have been impossibly complex. Figure 9-12 provides a visual of the server object and a list of its members.

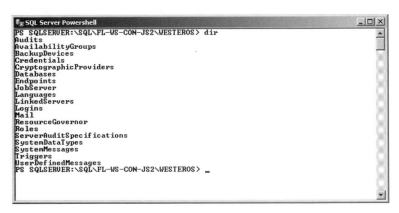

FIGURE 9-12

Because Server is an object, the cmdlet lists its properties and methods. If your current directory is a collection (folder), PowerShell instead lists all the members of the collection. You can `cd` to the database folder (collection) and list all the items in it (see Figure 9-13).

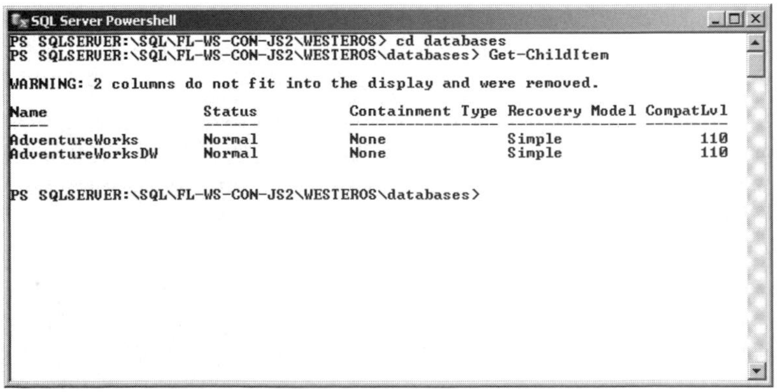

FIGURE 9-13

PowerShell is aware of the window size and accordingly adjusts the output format. In Figure 9-13, the SQL cmdlet stripped four columns from the output to fit the default PowerShell window size. A wider window shows more details, until the number of databases gets too large, at which point the cmdlet switches to listing names only.

> *Like nearly everything else in Windows, PowerShell is case-insensitive, at least regarding command and object names. If you execute code against a case-sensitive SQL instance or database, any comparisons executed by the server honor its collation rules.*

PowerShell supports all the legacy DOS/command shell commands and is mostly syntax-compatible with Windows Scripting Host. The largest difference between PowerShell and most UNIX-based shell environments is in how the pipe command (|) works. In UNIX-based shells, the pipe command connects the text output of one command to the input of the next command. This often requires creative use of `grep` to parse the list and create meaningful input for the next command in the sequence. PowerShell passes .NET objects to the next command. Collections are automatically iterated over, and hierarchies can usually be traversed with the `RECURSE` option, provided the cmdlet supports that functionality. As of this writing, PowerShell is at version 2.0 and getting better and better. It is the first truly universal Microsoft scripting environment.

CREATING CHANGE SCRIPTS

Creating change scripts is never a fun task for a DBA, but few things are more satisfying than a perfect deployment to four different environments. The only ways to achieve this "perfect" deployment is to either invest a lot of time in writing a good script, such as the one shown shortly, or invest in a tool.

Many tools are on the market to help a DBA package and deploy changes. For example, Red-Gate (www.red-gate.com) can compare two databases (test and production, for example) and package the change scripts to move production up to the same level. This same type of tool is available through many other vendors — ApexSQL, Idera, and Quest, to name a few. None of these tools entirely eliminates human intervention. You must have some interaction with the program to ensure that a change not meant to be deployed is not sent to production. The following sections address some specific tools for creating change scripts and deploying changes: Data-tier Applications, SQL Server Data Tools, and version tables.

DATA-TIER APPLICATIONS

SQL Server 2008 R2 introduced a feature called Data-tier Applications (DAC). A DAC defines all the objects related to a database application and instance such as tables, views, and logins.

The Data-tier Application feature enables developers to build their database projects for tier 2 and tier 3 databases and quickly and easily encapsulate objects and changes into a single DAC file. You then pass this DAC file along to your administrators to easily deploy the database application. This process not only makes deployments easy but it also simplifies database upgrades because you can use DACs to alter and upgrade existing registered Data-tier Applications.

Extracting a Data-Tier Application (DAC)

To begin extracting a DAC, the first thing you need to do is extract your database definitions (that is, objects and users) and save them into a Data-tier Application DAC file.

1. In Object Explorer, right-click the database you want to use for your database application. From the context menu, go to Tasks; then select the Extract Data-Tier Application option. The first screen that displays is an introduction screen; click Next to proceed.

2. At the next screen, set the properties for the DAC. Properties you can set include Application Name, Version Level, Application Description and Location of the resulting DAC package file (also referred to as a dacpac). Keep the default values and click Next. The wizard validates your selections and checks the databases to ensure the database contains all the supported elements for a DAC.

3. After the validation check is complete, a Validation Summary screen displays. Here you review any objects that may not be supported. You can also choose to save the results of the validation check by clicking the Save Report button. Click Next to initiate the extraction process and build the DAC package. When the package is built, click Finish.

Deploying a Data-tier Application

Now that you've built your DAC, you need to deploy it!

1. First, connect to a new instance in Management Studio. Right-click the instance, and from the context menu select Deploy Data-tier Application. Click Next to skip the Introduction screen.

2. At the Select Package screen, click the Browse button. Navigate to the area on the file system where you saved your DAC package, select your package, and click the Open button. After you select your DAC package, you notice that the metadata you provided in the Properties of the extraction process is loaded under the DAC details section. Click Next to proceed with the deployment.

3. The next screen is the Update Configuration screen. Here you can make modifications such as the database name and the location of the data and log files. The data and log file location defaults are the same configured ones set on the SQL Server instance. Click Next to proceed to the Summary screen.

4. At the Summary screen, review your selections and click Next to begin the deployment process. As the deployment occurs, you see the various action steps and their result. When

the deployment is complete, you can review the various results by clicking their link. You can choose to save the results by clicking the Save Report button.

5. After you review the results, click Finish. Now when you look at your instance in Object Explorer, you can notice your new database has been created in the Databases node and your new DAC has been added under Data-tier Applications under the Management node (see Figure 9-14).

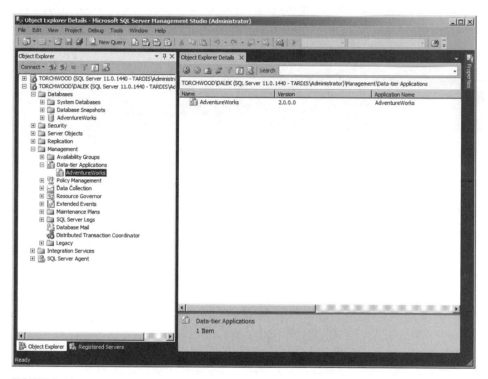

FIGURE 9-14

Upgrading a Data-tier Application

After your database application has been deployed, you can assume you've now gone through a new development life cycle and it is time to deploy new changes made to the database.

1. First, on the development database extract your DAC again, repeating the steps outlined in the previous section. However, this time make a few changes at the Set Properties screen. Leave the Application Name the same but now change the version level to 2.0.0.0.

2. In the Save to DAC package file section, a red exclamation point appears to the right of the Browse button. This is to let you know that there is already an existing DAC file with that

name. You can choose to create a new DAC with a new name or simply check the box for Overwrite Existing File. For this example, check the Overwrite Existing File box and then click Next.

3. Like before, it validates the database objects for the DAC, and after the validation checks are done, you are taken to the Validation and Summary screen. Review your validations, and click Next to build your DAC. After the DAC is built, click Finish.

4. Now in SSMS, connect to your second instance. Expand the management node, the Data-tier Application node, and right-click the DAC application you deployed previously. From the context menu, select Upgrade Data-tier Application, as shown in Figure 9-15.

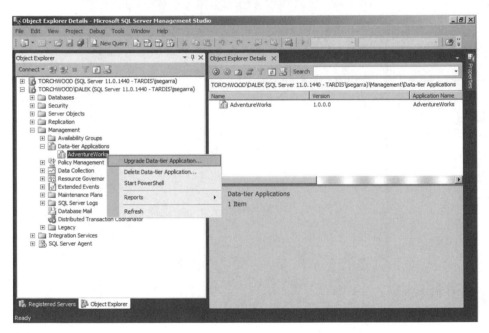

FIGURE 9-15

5. The first screen that displays is an Introduction screen; click Next to proceed.

6. At the Select Package screen, click the Browse button. Navigate to the location on the file system where you saved the DAC package; select the package, and click Open. After you select the DAC package, the metadata you supplied earlier is populated in the DAC details section. Click Next to proceed to the validation step.

7. In addition to the DAC validations, this step also performs a comparison of the existing DAC application to the new one. When the checks are done, the Detect Change screen displays what changes were detected between DAC versions. Click Next to proceed.

8. The Options screen gives you the option to gracefully rollback any changes caused by the DAC upgrade if something were to go wrong. To do so, check the box for Rollback on Failure, and click Next.

9. At the Review Upgrade Plan screen, a list displays with all the actions the DAC upgrade is about to perform. From here you can also save your change script. To save your change script, click the Save Script button. When you are ready to deploy the changes, click Next to proceed to the Summary screen. At the Summary screen, review your changes, and click Next to begin the upgrade process.

10. After the changes are applied, you see the results of all the individual upgrade steps. Click Finish to complete the process.

SQL Server Data Tools

Visual Studio Team System for Database Professionals, formerly known as "Data Dude," has now been replaced in SQL Server 2012 with SQL Server Data Tools (SSDT). One of the features of the tool is that it enables change detection and simple deployment to multiple environments. This is especially important in database deployment situations because developers rarely write comprehensive change scripts. Developers often "hand-tweak" a data type or add a column that never makes it into the schema creation script. SQL Server Data Tools compares the actual state of two databases and writes scripts to reconcile the two.

Think of your production system as version 1.0, and development as version 1.1. When you script the production schema (or back it up as a baseline) you can use it as the starting point. The scripts can then repeatedly and reliably take the database to version 1.1. You can use the scripts to deploy to your quality testing environment and then use the exact same scripts to deploy to production. Because the output is T-SQL scripts, you can use Visual Source Safe (or the version management software of your choice) to have controllable versions of your database. As a bonus, SQL Server Data Tools creates the reverse scripts that take a version 1.1 database back down to version 1.0. Rollback has typically been an "Oops, let's restore" operation at best. Now it can be a predictable part of your deployment repertoire.

Another useful feature of SQL Server Data Tools is its capability to refactor a database. Refactoring can be as simple as changing a column name or as complex as breaking off a column into its own table. Many applications start with a field for Address and later needing Billing Address, Shipping Address, and Mailing Address fields. SQL Server Data Tools not only enables such changes, but also updates every stored procedure and view that referenced the original column. You may have to make logic changes, but SQL Server Data Tools does the heavy lifting to find all the column references and updates where it can. Of course, that assumes all your data access code is in stored procedures and you don't do ad hoc SQL directly to the database tables. Following best design practices makes things easier in the long run in ways you cannot always predict.

Version Tables

An important practice when deploying changes is adding a version number to your changes, much as application developers do in their own version controlling. A table that the authors used for years is the db_version table, which holds what version of the database is currently installed and what versions have been installed over the history of the database.

By looking in the change history, you can use the table to determine whether the DBA who deployed the change skipped a build of the database. If you jump from 2.0 to 2.2, you know you may have an issue. You can also use a version table with the application's version number. For example, you may have a document specifying that version 2.1 of the application requires version 2.1.8 of the database. If the application did not match the db_version table, then it would throw an error. The table's schema looks like Listing 9-8.

LISTING 9-8: Db_version.sql

```
if not exists (select * from sys.objects where object_id =
object_id(N'[dbo].[DB_VERSION]') and OBJECTPROPERTY(object_id, N'IsUserTable')
= 1)
  BEGIN
CREATE TABLE [DB_VERSION] (
  [MajorVersion] [char] (5) NULL ,
  [MinorVersion] [char] (5) NULL ,
  [Build] [char] (5) NULL ,
  [Revision] [char] (5) NULL ,
  [OneOff] [char] (5) NULL,
  [DateInstalled] [datetime] NULL CONSTRAINT [DF__Version__DateIns__0876219E]
DEFAULT (getdate()),
  [InstalledBy] [varchar] (50) NULL ,
  [Description] [varchar] (255) NULL
) ON [PRIMARY]
END
```

For most environments, you won't use all the columns in this db_version table, but it was created as a catch-all, standard table. Every DBA who works at your company will know to go to the table, regardless of the application, to find the version. The version may match a document of known issues with the database. Typically, you may also find yourself creating views on top of the table to show you the last installed version. The following list describes a complete data dictionary for the table:

➤ MajorVersion: Major release of the application. In the application version it would be the following bolded number (**1**.0.5.1).

➤ MinorVersion: Minor release of the application. In the application version it would be the following bolded number (1.**0**.5.1).

➤ Build: Build number of the application. In the application version it would be the following bolded number (1.0.**5**.1).

➤ Revision: Also called the minor service pack (or patch) position. This number also refers to bug fixes found in QA. For example, you may have numerous iterations of Portal 2.5.3 as you fix bugs. You could increment this number (Application Build 2.5.3.**2**, for the second iteration). In the application version it would be the following bolded number (1.0.5.**1**).

➤ OneOff: In some cases, customization code may be required. For example, suppose Application A has a number of customized versions of Build 2.1.1. In those cases, you could have 2.1.1.0–**1** to indicate a customization (1 being for Client B, for example). This field is used only in specialized situations.

➤ DateInstalled: The date this application was installed in the environment. This is set to getdate() by default, which set it to the current date and time.

➤ InstalledBy: The name of the installer or creator of the service pack.

➤ Description: Description of the service pack. This can be used in an environment in which multiple clients share one database — for example, "Upgrade Application A 2.5.1.2 for Client B."

To insert a new change record into the table, use the following syntax:

```
INSERT INTO DB_VERSION  SELECT 1, 5, 0, 2, NULL, getdate(),'Jorge Segarra','Script
to promote zip code changes'
```

Ensure that the deploying DBA knows she must place the lines of code to create the table and insert the version information into it at the top of each command file you create. A standard template script file with fill-in-the-blank fields makes this task easier and more consistent. A last use for the table is to run a check before you perform a database upgrade. Before applying the database install for version 1.1, you can run an IF statement against the table to ensure that version 1.0 is installed. If it isn't installed, you can throw an error and stop the script from executing.

SUMMARY

SQL Server 2012 has many ways to help administrators deal with changes and management. One important feature, Policy-Based Management, helps bring your environment into compliance and enforce standardization. Using tools like Visual Studio to create database projects that integrate into Source Safe, and using the Data-tier Application feature to quickly and easily deploy database applications, enables you to manage changes and standardize deployment practices. The last key for creating a change management process is using sqlcmd and PowerShell for a smooth deployment by using scripts. In the next chapter, you learn how to properly configure a server for optimum performance before installing SQL Server 2012.

10

Configuring the Server for Optimal Performance

WHAT'S IN THIS CHAPTER

➤ Defining Good Performance

➤ What Every DBA Needs to Know about Performance

➤ Configuration of Server Hardware

➤ CPU Configuration Details

➤ Memory Configuration and Options

➤ I/O Design and Options

In the IT industry today, there are many different types of professionals that are responsible for databases and for the systems where those databases reside. The Developer DBA is primarily responsible for database design and for generating code (queries, stored procedures, etc.). The Production DBA is primarily responsible for database and database system configuration, maintenance, and availability. The Business Intelligence (BI) DBA is primarily responsible for the BI stack that is associated with SQL Server (SSIS, SSRS, SSAS and SharePoint, etc.) and relevant systems. One person may even be responsible for a combination of these tasks and is then referred to as a Hybrid DBA. Additionally, there are some DBAs who have never had formal training or may have taken over database servers out of necessity due to staff shortages. These are known as accidental DBAs. The accidental DBA will normally wear many hats and will need to get things right the first time due to resource constraints. (Refer to Chapter 1 for a more detailed description of each of these types of database professional.)

Developer database administrators need to know how to optimize performance to ensure that anything they design will perform up to its potential. The developer DBAs must ensure that, as inevitable changes are made to the system throughout its life cycle, they are made in a way that enables the application to continue to perform. As the system grows in terms of data, users, and functionality, it needs to grow in ways that keep the system operating optimally.

Similarly, Production DBAs need to understand performance so that the system they maintain starts out performing well and then continues to do so throughout the system's life cycle. Several different elements factor into this, from getting the server set up correctly, to monitoring the system as it starts working, to implementing a full monitoring strategy to keep the system operating optimally.

The three most important pillars to deliver high performance around scalability, response time, reliability, and usability are as follows:

➤ Knowing what your system can deliver in terms of CPU, memory, input/output (I/O)

➤ Finding the bottlenecks

➤ Knowing your target (how many, how fast)

This chapter discusses all these issues and addresses the most pressing questions about performance and configuring a server.

WHAT EVERY DBA NEEDS TO KNOW ABOUT PERFORMANCE

This chapter lays out a lot of specific hardware recommendations that can enable you to improve the performance of your system. However, shaving milliseconds off a transaction time isn't always worth the amount of time and hardware budget you spend to accomplish that goal. Frequently, good planning up front is worth more than clever optimization later. Always keep the following three things in mind regarding performance:

➤ The Performance Tuning Cycle

➤ Defining good performance

➤ Focusing on what is most important

The Performance Tuning Cycle

Too often performance and optimization are tacked on at the end. Performance tuning is an iterative process and ideally starts at the beginning of the design process. Obtaining favorable performance starts with configuring the server, and continues with designing an efficient schema and specifying tuned SQL statements, which leads to ideal index selection. The monitoring and analysis of performance can then feed back to changes to the server configuration, schema design, or any other point in this process. Figure 10-1 illustrates this design system.

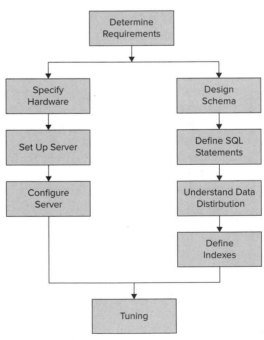

FIGURE 10-1

You start with your first best guess about how you think your application is going to work and what resources you think it's going to use and plan accordingly. Most often, it's only a best guess because you don't know yet exactly how the application is going to work.

In the case of a new application, you don't have an existing system to measure. In the best case, you have some metrics from either an existing user base or management predictions about who the users will be, what they do on a daily basis, and how that would impact the new application.

In the case of an existing system that you are either moving to a new server or to which you are adding functionality, you can measure specific metrics on system resource usage and use those as a starting point. Then you can add information about any new functionality including the answers to questions such as the following:

➤   Will this increase the user base?

➤   Will it increase the processing load on the server?

➤   Will it change the data volume?

All this information enables you to make a good estimate of the new system's impact on resources. Even before you implement the new system, while testing is taking place you have a great opportunity to start evaluating your estimates against the actual resource requirements and the performance you get from your test servers.

Defining Good Performance

The fundamental question that every DBA has to answer before refining a system is simple: Does the system in question have good performance now? Without either a specific target or some baseline to compare against, you will never know. Planning, sizing, testing, and monitoring can provide you with the information you need to start answering this question. You can break this process down into three steps:

1.   Start by identifying your critical targets for CPU, memory, and I/O.

2.   Then create a baseline.

3.   Finally, after deploying, monitor your critical measurements.

For example, consider how performance requirements can vary in the case of an online store. Here, response time to users is critical to keep them shopping. On a database such as this, there are likely to be clearly defined response times for the most important queries, and there may be a broad requirement that is defined by the management of the business that no query can take longer than 2 or 3 seconds. On a different database server that delivers management reports on warehouse inventory levels, there may be an expectation that these reporting queries take some time to gather the right information, so response times as long as a few minutes may be acceptable. Although, there may still be some queries that have much shorter response time requirements. In yet another database, the key performance criterion might be the time it takes to back up the database, or the time to load or unload data.

After the critical targets have been identified, the current system needs to be measured to create a baseline. This subject is extensive but is covered in more detail in the excellent Wrox publication

Professional SQL Server 2008 Internals and Troubleshooting (Wiley 2010). The references found in that book are valid for SQL Server 2012. SQL Server monitoring methodology is covered more in Chapter 12, "Monitoring Your SQL Server" of this book.

Focus on What's Most Important

The final essential aspect of performance is to focus on what's important — achieving the performance that users demand. You must know what you need to measure, how to measure it, and what the limitations of that measurement might be. Consider a typical system. The end users' experience is the net sum of all performance from their client machine through many layers to the database server and back again. Because the focus of this book is the DBA and SQL Server 2012, you can focus on measuring SQL Server 2012 performance, but it's worthwhile to have a basic understanding of the big picture, in which DBAs fit in, and some of the tools and metrics that may have an impact on your system.

Figure 10-2 shows a schematic diagram of a typical web-based architecture. This schematic is typical of any enterprise customer using the Microsoft Windows Server System Reference Architecture to implement an enterprise solution. This may be the first time that many DBAs have looked at something like this and understood where their puzzle piece (that is, the database) fits into the big picture.

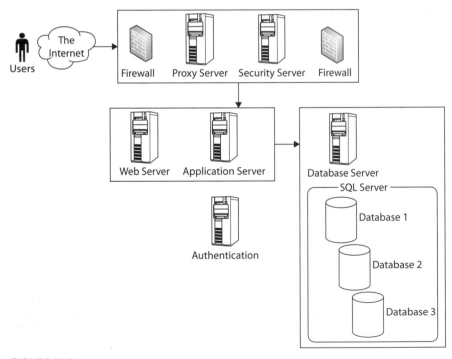

FIGURE 10-2

One of the first things you notice in the diagram is the number of elements in the bigger picture. When the user calls the help desk and complains of poor performance, finding the culprit involves a lot of possible candidates, so there may be a lot of time spent identifying which piece of the complex system architecture might be guilty. Unfortunately, a large, complex system needs multiple support personnel all focusing on their piece of the puzzle. For example, the Firewall and Security Server is supported by the network team, the Web Server and Application Server is supported by the application team, the Authentication is handled by the Windows team and the SQL Server is supported by the Database Administration team. The important thing to take away from this exercise is an understanding of both the big picture and how to zero in on what's important for you as a DBA.

WHAT THE DEVELOPER DBA NEEDS TO KNOW ABOUT PERFORMANCE

Good performance is built on a solid foundation upon which the rest of your application can be implemented; for a SQL database this foundation is a well-designed database schema. The performance tuning rules to follow are less simple than traditional concepts such as "normalize to the nth form." Instead, they require that you have a solid understanding of the use of the system, including the usage pattern, the SQL statements, and the data. The optimal schema for an online transaction processing (OLTP) system may be less preferable for a decision support system (DSS), or for a data warehousing (DW) system.

Users

You first need to know who is going to use the system: the number of users and their concurrency, peak usage level, and what they are going to do. The users usually fall into different groups based on either job function or feature usage. For an e-commerce-based system, for example, the user groups might be browsers, purchasers, order trackers, customers needing help, and others. For a sales analytics system, the user groups may be primarily analysts reading the data with report tools such as PerformancePoint Server, Power View, or Excel, and perhaps running reporting for the sales team. The e-commerce-based system example is an OLTP database workload optimized for fewer and faster reads, updates, and writes requests, whereas the sales analytics system example is a DSS database workload optimized for large queries to generate reports.

SQL Statements

After determining the different groups of users, you need to understand what they do, which SQL statements will be run, and how often each of these is run for a user action. In the e-commerce example, a browser might arrive at the site, which invokes the home page, for example, requiring 20 or 30 different stored procedures or SQL statements to be executed. When users click something on the home page, each action taken can require another set of stored procedures to be executed to return the data for the next page. So far it looks like everything has been read-only, but for ASP.NET pages, there may be the issue of session state, which may be kept in a SQL database. If that's the case, you may already have seen a lot of write activity just to get to this stage.

Data Usage Patterns

The final part of the picture is the data in the database. You need an understanding of the total data volume in each table, including how that data gets there and how it changes over time. For the e-commerce example, the main data elements of the site are the catalog of items available for sale. The catalog could come directly from the suppliers' websites through an Internet portal. After this data is initially loaded, it can be refreshed with updates as suppliers change their product line and as prices vary. The overall volume of data won't change much unless you add or remove items or suppliers.

What will change, hopefully quickly, is the number of registered users, any click-tracking you do based on site personalization, the number of orders placed, the number of line items sold, and the number of orders shipped. Of course, you hope that you can sell a lot of items, which results in a lot of new data growth every day.

A sound knowledge of the data, its distribution, and how it changes helps you find potential hot spots, which could be either frequently retrieved reference data, frequently inserted data, or frequently updated data. All these could result in bottlenecks that might limit performance.

Robust Schema

An understanding of all the preceding pieces — users, SQL statements, and data — needs to come together to help implement a well-designed and well-performing application. If the foundation stone of your database schema is not solid, anything you build on top of that foundation is going to be unstable. Although you may achieve something that's acceptable, you are unlikely to achieve an optimal solution.

How does all this information help you tune the server? You need to understand where the hot spots are in the data to enable the physical design to be implemented in the most efficient manner. If you are going through the process of designing a logical data model, you shouldn't care about performance issues. Only when you are ready to design the physical model do you take this information into account and modify the design to incorporate your knowledge of data access patterns.

WHAT THE PRODUCTION DBA NEEDS TO KNOW ABOUT PERFORMANCE

The production DBA's life is considerably different from that of the developer DBA in that a production DBA is dealing with a system that someone else may have designed, built, and handed over, either as a new or as an already-running system. The production DBA may also face challenges with performance on old systems running legacy applications on outdated hardware. In this case, the scenario changes from designing an efficient system to making the system you have been given work as well as possible on that limited hardware.

The starting point for this process must be an understanding of what the hardware can deliver; what hardware resources the system needs; and what the expectations of the users are in terms of user response time. The key elements to understand the hardware are processor speed, type, and cache size. Additionally you need to know how much memory there is and what the bus speed is. Finally it is important to determine how many I/O disks there are, how they are configured, and how many network interface cards (NICs) exist.

The next step is determining how each component of the system is required to perform. Are there any performance-related service-level agreements (SLAs) that have been implemented between the business and the DBA team? If any performance guidelines are specified anywhere, are you meeting them, exceeding them, or failing them? In all cases, you should also know the trend. Have you been maintaining the status quo, getting better, or, as is most often the case, slowly getting worse? The production DBA needs to understand all this, and then know how to identify bottlenecks and resolve them to get the system performing at the required level again.

The tools that the production DBA uses to perform these tasks may include the following:

➤ **Task Manager:** Gives a quick, high-level view of server performance and use of resources.

➤ **System Performance Monitor (or Reliability and Performance Monitor in Windows 2008 and Windows 7) (Perfmon):** Provides a more detailed view of Windows server performance and per-instance SQL Server specific counters.

➤ **SQL Server Management Data Warehouse (MDW):** The MDW is a relational database that collects and stores Perfmon and Data Collector outputs for retrieval when the DBA needs to troubleshoot a system issue.

➤ **SQL Server Management Studio (SSMS):** Enables long-running transactions to be analyzed and bottlenecks found and resolved. SSMS enables the DBA to run queries against DMV's and Extended Events to gather this data.

➤ **Dynamic Management Views (DMVs):** These are system objects that contain server state information that can be used to diagnose problems and monitor the health of a SQL Server.

➤ **Extended Events:** This is a light weight monitoring system that collects data about the performance of the SQL Server. This data can be viewed through the Session UI that is new for SQL Server 2012.

Chapter 13, "Performance Tuning T-SQL," covers these tools in more detail.

Optimizing the Server

The rest of this chapter covers optimizing the server. This includes the hardware and operating system configuration to provide SQL Server with the best environment in which to execute. You should consider three key resources any time you discuss optimization or performance:

➤ CPU

➤ Memory

➤ I/O

Starting with the CPU, there aren't a lot of options to play with here other than the number and type of processors. This part of the chapter focuses on understanding the different processor attributes so that you can make the right purchasing decisions.

Memory has more options, and it's a lot easier to add or remove system memory (Random Access Memory, or RAM) than it is to change the number or type of processors in a server. When you initially configure the server, you should have some idea of how much memory you might need and understand the available configuration options. These options can be discussed with the specific hardware vendor of your choice. Because SQL Server 2012 is (and will remain) available solely as a 64-bit server application, it should be installed on 64-bit hardware on top of Windows Server 2008 R2 64-bit, which is discussed in more detail later in this chapter.

In many ways I/O performance is perhaps the most important part of the server configuration to get right because everything you do lives on the disk. All the code you run in the operating system, SQL Server, and any other applications start off as files on the disk. All the data you touch in SQL Server also lives on the disk: it starts out there, is read into memory, and then has to be written back to disk before it becomes a permanent change. Every change that is made to a SQL Server database is written to the database transaction log file, which also lives on the disk. All these factors make a good I/O configuration an essential part of any SQL Server system.

The following sections cover these key resources in great detail but before you dig in, it will be helpful to put each of the three server resources back into perspective in terms of their relative performance to each other. As you refer to this book in the future, you can easily pencil in the current start of processor, memory, and I/O performance to see how the relative speeds of different elements have changed.

An example of typical speeds and throughput for system resources is as follows:

➤ A CPU speed of 3 GHz results in 12GB/sec.

➤ Memory speed of 800 MHz results in 12GB/sec.

➤ Disk speeds of 200MB/sec to 1GB/sec.

Use the preceding numbers to do the math for throughput for a 100GB table:

➤ A 3-GHz CPU with a throughput of 12GB/sec would access 100GB of data in 8.3 seconds.

➤ 800-MHz memory with a throughput of 12GB/sec would access 100GB of data in 8.3 seconds.

➤ Disks with a throughput of 200MB/sec would access 100GB in 500 seconds.

Graphically, this might look something like what is shown in Figure 10-3.

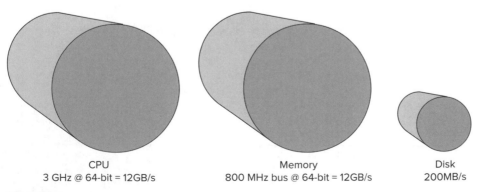

CPU
3 GHz @ 64-bit = 12GB/s

Memory
800 MHz bus @ 64-bit = 12GB/s

Disk
200MB/s

FIGURE 10-3

The conclusion here is that disk access is much slower than memory or CPU access. The key, therefore, is to design and build the server in such a way that there is a balance of resources.

Within SQL Server, you can't do much to alter how much data is processed by each cycle of the CPU; that's controlled by the developers at Microsoft who wrote SQL Server. What you can do, though, is obtain processors with larger caches, and at higher speeds. Add more memory, and design your storage subsystem to deliver the fastest performance possible within your requirements for speed, size, and cost.

Hardware Management

On most small- to medium-size database servers, a common configuration is to make a BIOS change to enable hyper-threading. Please see your server's documentation for details. In the "Hyper-threading" section later in this chapter, you can determine whether hyper-threading can provide a performance improvement for your scenario. Once the hyper-threading option has been decided, most of the remaining tasks are related to physically installing RAM, I/O adapters such as NICs, and disk adapters for SCSI or SATA. Review the vendors' documentation for any additional configuration options that they recommend.

On nearly all systems, you can find a variety of management software to help you configure, operate, and maintain the hardware. Most hardware vendors have their own version of this kind of software, offering a wide variety of capabilities and options. Examples of these are the iLO from Hewlett Packard (HP), the RSA from IBM, or the DRAC from Dell.

On large enterprise systems such as the HP Superdome 2, NEC Express5800, or SGI Altix UV, configuring the server hardware enters a whole new dimension. On these larger enterprise systems, you can find a *management processor (MP)* within the server. The management processor and its software interface control the hardware — from booting a hardware partition, to configuring a different hardware partition, to changing memory layout, and to managing the power to different hardware components. The management processor handles all these tasks.

The tasks that need to be achieved to manage all the large systems are similar, but the way each hardware vendor implements its interface is unique, from the Java/website approach on SGI to the Telnet-based command-line interface on HP and NEC systems.

 The Windows Server Catalog (www.windowsservercatalog.com) *should be your first stop when considering purchasing any new hardware. If the new hardware isn't in the catalog, it's not supported to run Windows Server 2008 and won't be supported when running SQL Server either.*

CPU

SQL Server 2012 operates in a different environment than previous versions of SQL Server. When SQL Server 2000 launched, a huge server used for SQL Server may have had four to eight processors. Now, SQL Server 2012 can run on the largest servers, with up to 64 processors and up to 256 cores. Additionally, SQL Server 2012 can run on machines with up to 2TB of RAM running Windows Server 2008 R2 Enterprise or Datacenter Edition. SQL Server 2012 is supported on one processor architecture only: 32-bit with 64-bit extensions (x64).

x64

x64 was originally introduced by AMD and implemented by Intel as EM64T. x64 requires Windows 2003 with SP1 or later. It is compatible with x86 machine code and can support 64-bit micro-code extensions. The x64 platform can run SQL Server 2012 (using Windows Server 2008 R2), delivering memory beyond 4GB and up to 2TB of natively addressable memory and up to 64 physical CPUs. Its processor clock speed is significantly faster than IA64 and it can natively run 32-bit applications.

> *The x64 platform is the only server platform for SQL Server 2012 database workloads. Itanium 64 (IA64) and x32 (x86-32) series' of processors are not supported by SQL Server 2012. Various editions and versions of SQL Server 2008 and 2008 R2 can be found that will be supported on these CPU families.*

Cache

The reason modern processors need onboard cache is because the processor runs at 2 to 3 GHz, and, while main memory is improving, it still cannot keep up with the processor's memory appetite. To try to alleviate this, processor designers added several layers of flash memory to keep recently used data in small, fast caches so that if you need to reuse that data it will already be available. In addition, because of the way cache works, it doesn't just load the byte requested; it loads the subsequent range of addresses as well. The amount of memory loaded on each request is determined by the cache line size and the processor's caching algorithm pre-fetch parameters.

Processor cache is implemented as a transparent look-through cache. This means that controlling functions on the chip manage the process of filling the cache and managing cache entries

The cache on modern processors is typically implemented as multiple layers: L1, L2, and L3. Each subsequent layer is physically farther from the processor core and is larger but slower until you are back at main memory. Some caches are general-purpose and hold copies of any memory such as L2 and L3. Other caches are specific and hold only address lookups (TLB), data (L1 data), or instructions (instruction cache). Typically, L1 is smaller and faster than L2, which is smaller and faster than L3. And L3 cache is often physically located on a separate chip or on the motherboard itself, and so is farther from the processor core than L1 or L2, but still closer and faster than the main memory.

When a processor executes instructions, the data that it needs to complete the execution must be available as quickly as possible. This is one reason why processor cache sizes have increased over the years — so that the cache can hold as much data as possible. For example, L1 cache has a latency of approximately 2 nanoseconds (ns) with a size of 32kB; L2 cache has a latency of approximately 4ns with a typical size of 256kB; and L3 cache has a latency of approximately 6ns and the size can vary from 2 to 32MB.

To put the cache performance into perspective, system memory has an average latency of 50ns and will range in size from 16 to 1024GB in total. Solid State Disks (SSDs) have latency and size figures of 30–100 microseconds (µs) and 50–1024GB respectively. Enterprise specification Hard Disk Drives will have latency figures in the range of 2–50 milliseconds (ms) and will range in size from 80–2048GB. The performance of your SQL Server, therefore, is extremely dependent on the size of the cache available. Processor manufacturers offer a large variety of models that have a range of L2 and L3 sizes. The high performance nature of the cache means that it is very costly. This is reflected in the cost of the processors that contain large amounts of cache. However, as SQL Server is commonly used in a mission- and business-critical manner, you should purchase the fastest processor with the biggest cache memory for your server. In addition, if a compromise needs to be made, it is always easier and cheaper to upgrade RAM than it is to upgrade a CPU.

Introducing cache to store small, frequently used pieces of data during the central processing process was a complex resolution to the memory issue. But, it has increased the performance of all systems.

Hyper-threading

Hyper-threading (officially Hyper-Threading Technology) is Intel proprietary technology that works by duplicating certain sections of the physical processor core to improve parallelization of computations. What this means is that, for each physical core present, two logical cores appear to the operating system. Although the system schedules multiple threads to be executed by the processor, the shared resources may cause certain threads to wait for other ones to complete prior to execution.

There is actually only one question about hyper-threading that you need to ask: Should you run with hyper-threading enabled or disabled? This is a difficult question to answer though, and a one-size-fits-all approach will not work. Any answer must involve customers testing their individual system. The items you need to consider to find this answer are outlined in this section.

One of the most important factors when considering hyper-threading is to understand the maximum theoretical performance benefit that you might get from hyper-threading. Intel's documentation on hyper-threading reveals that the maximum theoretical performance gain from hyper-threading is 30 percent. Many customers running with hyper-threading enabled for the first time expect to see double the performance because they see two processors. You should understand that hyper-threading can give you only a maximum performance increase of 1.3 times non-hyper-threading performance at best, and in practice it may be closer to 1.1 to 1.15 times. This knowledge helps put any decision about hyper-threading back into perspective.

In some cases, hyper-threading, at least theoretically, won't provide any benefit. For example, in any database workload where the code runs a tight loop entirely from cache, hyper-threading won't help because there is only a single execution engine. This scenario could result in degraded performance because the operating system tries to schedule activity on a processor that isn't physically there.

Another scenario in which hyper-threading can directly affect SQL Server performance is when a parallel plan might be chosen. One of the things a parallel plan does is split the work across the available processors with the assumption that each processor can complete the same amount of work in the given time. In a hyper-threading–enabled scenario, any thread that's not currently executing is stalled until the other thread on that processor completes.

No one can yet tell you whether hyper–threading can help or hurt your performance when running your workload. Plenty of theories abound about how it might impact different theoretical workloads exist, but no one has yet come up with prescriptive guidance that definitively says turn it on here and turn it off over there. Unfortunately, that leaves customers with the burden to figure it out for themselves. You can consider a few things that can help you make your decision:

➤ Hyper-threading itself has been evolving, and although there isn't any concrete evidence of changes in how it is implemented on different Intel processors, feedback from production deployments seems to indicate that it's getting better with each generation of processors. The point here is that hyper-threading on an older server may not perform as it would on a server with the latest generation of processors.

➤ The new Microsoft SQL Server 2012 licensing policy, which is done per core, should also be taken into consideration. Please see Chapter 1 for a breakdown of the new licensing changes. In this context it is important to note that having hyper-threading enabled does not change the number of cores that are licensed when SQL Server is installed on a physical machine. When a virtualization environment (VMWare or Hyper-V) is used, however, hyper-threaded processors could be presented to the guest machine as a full CPU core. In this case, those would need to be licensed for SQL Server 2012.

➤ The most important thing to consider about hyper-threading is the following: The maximum theoretical performance improvement with hyper-threading is only 30 percent compared to non-hyper-threaded systems. In practice, this can actually be a maximum of only just 10–15 percent. Moreover, for many customers this may be difficult to measure without performing a benchmark to compare it in their production environment and under consistent database workload.

To measure this benchmark, a comparative test needs to be performed that includes the following steps:

1. First, refer to your specific system's documentation to find out how to turn hyper-threading off and do so.

2. Now, run your benchmark test a number of times and get an average execution time.

3. Then, turn hyper-threading on again.

4. Run the benchmark test the same number of times again and compare results. What you will be looking for is the average run time of each test to be quicker with hyper-threading turned on. You should then calculate how much quicker it is, and use that information to make a decision on the value of hyper-threading.

Multicore

One of the biggest challenges facing multiprocessor system designers is how to reduce the latency caused by the physical limitations of the speed of light and the distance between processors and memory. One solution is to put multiple processors on a single chip. This is what a multicore system does, and it provides more potential for better performance than a single-core system because of this reduced latency between processors and memory. The big question is do you need it?

The answer to this depends on how many processors you need and how much you are willing to pay. If you need a 16-processor system, you can get a faster comparable system for less money by purchasing a dual-socket 8-core system, rather than a quad-socket quad-core system.

For the latest information on this issue, check out what the hardware vendors are doing with their Transaction Processing Council numbers (see www.tpc.org). The TPC results are a great way to compare hardware, although some hardware vendors may not publish results for the systems you want to compare.

Another factor to consider is scalability. Rather than purchase a straightforward dual-socket, 10-core system, you can purchase a dual-socket system with one quad-core processor capable of being upgraded to 10-core processors in the future. This way, you can defer the expense of adding 10-core processors when you need to add more processing power.

Before continuing, it's worth defining some clear terminology here to avoid confusion when discussing multicore systems:

➤ The *socket* is the physical socket into which you plug the processor. Before multicore systems arrived, there used to be a direct one-to-one relationship between sockets and execution units.

➤ A *core* is equivalent to an *execution unit*, or what you would previously have considered to be a processor. With a multicore processor there will be two or more of these per socket.

➤ A *thread* in this context is not the same as the thread you might create in your program, or the operating system threads; it is relevant only in the context of hyper-threading. A hyper-threading thread is not a new execution unit but a new pipeline on the front of an existing execution unit. Refer to the previous section "Hyper-threading" for more details about how this is implemented.

Now look at a specific example to see what this actually means. Figure 10-4 shows a single-socket, single-core processor with no hyper-threading, which results in one thread.

Figure 10-5 shows a single-socket, multicore processor with hyper-threading, which results in four threads This is licensed as 2 cores in the new licensing model (with a minimum of 4 cores per socket).

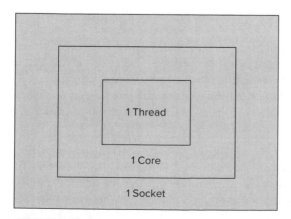

FIGURE 10-4

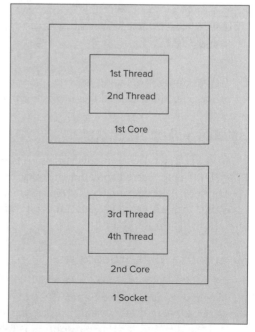

FIGURE 10-5

Figure 10-6 shows a dual-socket, dual-core processor with hyper-threading, which results in 8 threads, licensed as 4 cores in the new licensing model (with a minimum of 4 cores per socket) for a total of 8 core licenses.

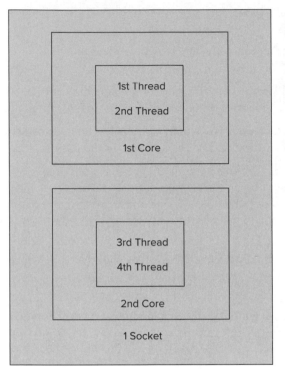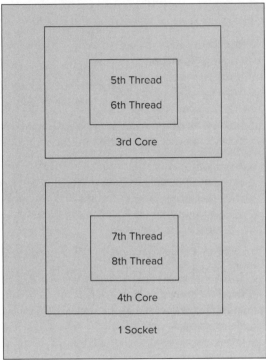

FIGURE 10-6

To summarize: A socket is a physical processor, a core is an execution unit within a physical processor, and a thread is a pipeline through the core.

System Architecture

Another key purchasing decision must be made about the machine architecture. For most modern systems you need to consider the options of Symmetric Multi-Processing (SMP) versus Non-Unified Memory Architecture (NUMA) systems. This isn't something you actually need to configure, but rather something you should understand as an option when considering the purchase of one type of system versus another.

Symmetric Multiprocessing

An SMP system is a system in which all the processors are connected to a common system bus in a symmetric manner (see Figure 10-7). For most cases, this architecture works very well for smaller systems where the physical distance between resources is short, the number of resources is small, and the demand for those resources is low.

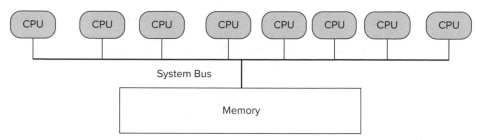

FIGURE 10-7

NUMA

NUMA stands for non-uniform memory access; this architecture is often also referred to as ccNUMA, meaning a cache-coherent version of NUMA. The main difference between an SMP system and a NUMA system is where the memory is connected to, and how processors are arranged on the system bus.

Whereas on an SMP system the memory is connected to all the processors symmetrically via a shared bus, on a NUMA system each group of processors has its own pool of "local" memory. The advantage of this is that each processor doesn't pay a cost of going to a bus past more than its local processors to access memory, provided the data it wants is in the local memory pool. If the data it wants is in the memory pool from another NUMA node, the cost of accessing it is a little higher than on an SMP system. Therefore, one of the objectives with a NUMA system is to try to maximize the amount of data you get from local memory, as opposed to accessing memory on another node.

NUMA systems typically have a four-sockets-per-node configuration (see Figure 10-8) and implement multiple nodes up to the system maximum.

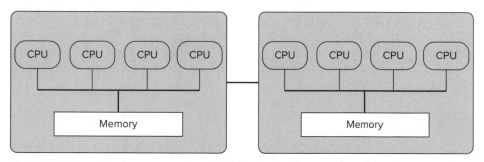

FIGURE 10-8

Smaller configurations that are any multiple of a 4-socket node can usually be accommodated, allowing for highly configurable servers and highly scalable servers. For example, a company could start with a single 4-socket node and scale up all the way to 16 4-socket nodes for 64 sockets.

One of the problems with NUMA systems is that as they grow, the issues of maintaining cache coherency also grow, introducing management overhead. Another problem is that as the number of nodes increases, the chance of the data you want being found in local memory is reduced.

The operating system must also be NUMA-aware to schedule threads and allocate memory local to the node, which is more efficient than allocating nonlocal memory or scheduling a thread to run on a different node. Either of these actions incurs an overhead of node memory access, either to fetch data or to fetch the thread's data from the old node and transfer it to the new node. Intel Xeon and AMD Opteron use different architecture implementations to access memory. Intel uses a Front Side Bus (FSB) whereby the sockets are connected through the bus to the external controller to the memory; as a result, all sockets are equal distance to the memory. AMD uses an integrated memory controller on each socket to connect to its local memory and the other sockets with their own memory by means of the HyperTransport link. This non-uniform memory arrangement is referred to as NUMA and the data latency depends on where the data requested by the CPU core is located in memory. For example, if the data is on a directly connected memory bank, access is fast; if it is on a remote memory bank that is on another socket, it can incur some latency. Although in the case of the Intel architecture, the FSB delivers equal-distance memory to each CPU core; the inefficiency with this approach is FSB contention, which Intel reduces by implementing larger caches.

MEMORY

The second hardware subsystem to consider is memory — specifically, memory on the server, including some of the issues associated with memory, the options you can use, and how they can impact the performance of the server. Following is a basic introduction to operating system memory. Then, you'll jump straight into the details of how to configure a server for different memory configurations.

Physical Memory

Physical memory is the RAM you install into the server. You are probably already familiar with memory in the form of Dynamic Inline Memory Modules (DIMM's) that go into desktop PCs and servers. This is *physical memory*, or RAM. This memory is measured in megabytes, gigabytes, or, if you are lucky, terabytes, as the latest editions of Windows Server 2008 R2 Datacenter and Enterprise Editions can now support systems with 2TB of RAM. Future editions of the operating system will increase this number as customers demand increasingly powerful systems to solve increasingly complex business problems.

Physical Address Space

The physical address space is the set of addresses that the processor uses to access anything on its bus. Much of this space is occupied by memory, but some parts of this address space are reserved for things such as mapping hardware buffers, and interface-specific memory areas such as video RAM. On a 32-bit processor, this was limited to a total of 4GB of memory addresses. On 32-bit Intel server processors with PAE, the address bus was 36 bits, which enabled the processor to handle 64GB of memory addresses. You might assume that on a 64-bit processor the address bus would be 64 bits, but because there isn't a need for systems that can address 18 exabytes (EB) of memory yet, or the capability to build a system that large, manufacturers have limited the address bus to 48 bits, which is enough to address 256TB of memory. The architecture enables an extension of this to 52 bits in the future, which would enable systems up to 4PB of memory.

Virtual Memory Manager

The Virtual Memory Manager (VMM) is the part of the operating system that manages all the physical memory and shares it between all the processes that need memory on the system. Its job is to provide each process with memory when it needs it, although the physical memory is actually shared between all the processes running on the system at the same time.

The VMM does this by managing the virtual memory for each process, and when necessary it takes back the physical memory behind virtual memory, and puts the data that resided in that memory into the page file so that it is not lost. When the process needs to use that memory again, the VMM retrieves the data from the page file, finds a free page of memory (either from its list of free pages or from another process), writes the data from the page file into memory, and maps the new page back into the processed virtual address space. The resulting delay or interruption is called a *page fault*. To determine whether SQL Server or another process is the cause of excessive paging, monitor the `Process: Page Faults/sec` counter for the SQL Server process instance. Please see the "Page Fault" section of this chapter for a more in-depth look at these.

On a system with enough RAM to give every process all the memory it needs, the VMM doesn't need to do much other than hand out memory and clean up after a process is done with it. On a system without enough RAM to go around, the job is a little more involved. The VMM must do some work to provide each process with the memory it needs when it needs it. It does this by using the page file to store data in pages that a process isn't using or that the VMM determines it can remove from the process.

The Page File

The page file is a disk file that the computer uses to increase the amount of physical storage for virtual memory. In other words, when the memory in use by all of the existing processes exceeds the amount of available RAM, the Windows operating system takes pages of one or more virtual address spaces and moves them to the page file that resides on physical disk. This frees up RAM for other uses. These "paged out" pages are stored in one or more page files that are located in the root of a disk partition. There can be one such page file on each partition.

On a server running SQL Server, the objective is to try to keep SQL Server running using just the available physical memory. SQL Server itself goes to great lengths to ensure that it doesn't over-allocate memory, and tries to remain within the limits of the physical memory available.

Given this basic objective of SQL Server, in most cases there is limited need for a page file. However, a frequently asked question is "Is there a recommended size for the page file?" The answer to this question, of course, is "it depends." It depends on the amount of RAM installed and what virtual memory will be required above and beyond SQL Server. A general guideline is to configure a page file total of 1.5 to 2 times the amount of RAM installed in the server.

However, in large systems with a large amount of RAM (more than 128GB), this may not be possible due to the lack of system drive space. Some good guidelines to adhere to in these cases are outlined in the following:

➤ Configure an 8GB page file on the system drive.

➤ Make sure that the Windows operating system startup parameters are configured to capture a kernel dump in the event of a failure. Please see this article from Microsoft Support on how to configure this setting: http://support.microsoft.com/kb/307973.

➤ Optional: Configure multiple page files (on disk volumes other than the system volume) that will be available for the OS to utilize if a larger page file is desired. It is recommended to use one additional page file of 200GB for each 256GB of RAM installed in the server.

In some cases, SQL Server and the OS might not cooperate well on sharing the available memory, and you may start to see system warnings about low virtual memory. If this occurs, you will ideally add more RAM to the server, reconfigure SQL to use less memory, or increase the size of the page file. It may be better to reconfigure SQL Server to remain within the available physical memory than it is to increase the size of the page file. Reducing paging always results in better performance. If paging occurs, for best performance, the page file should be on fast disks that have minimal disk usage activity, and the disks should be periodically defragmented to ensure that the page file is contiguous on the disks, reducing the disk head movement and increasing performance. The metric in the Windows System Monitor to measure page file usage is Paging file: %Usage, which should be less than 70 percent.

Page Faults

Page faults are generally problematic for SQL Server, but not all page faults are the same. Some are unavoidable, and some have limited impact on performance, whereas others can cause severe performance degradation and are the kind you want to avoid.

SQL Server is designed to work within the available physical memory to avoid the bad kind of page faults. Unfortunately, the System Performance Monitor page fault counter doesn't indicate whether you are experiencing the benign or bad kind of page fault, which means it doesn't tell you whether you are experiencing good or bad performance.

Soft Page Faults

The most common kind of page fault you will experience is the *soft page fault*. These occur when a new page of memory is required. Anytime SQL Server wants to use more memory, it asks the VMM for another page of memory. The VMM then issues a soft page fault to bring that memory into SQL Server's virtual address space. This actually happens the first time SQL Server tries to use the page and not when SQL Server first asks for it. For the programmers among you, this means that SQL Server is calling `VirtualAlloc` to commit a page of memory. The page fault occurs only when SQL Server tries to write to the page the first time.

Hard Page Faults

Hard page faults are the ones you want to try to avoid. A hard page fault occurs when SQL Server tries to access a page of its memory that has been paged out to the page file. When this happens, the VMM has to step in and take some action to get the needed page from the page file on disk, find an empty page of memory, read the page from disk, write it to the new empty page, and then map the new page into SQL Server's address space. All the while, the SQL Server thread has been waiting. Only when the VMM has replaced the missing page of memory can SQL Server continue with what it was doing.

Why Page Faults Are Problematic

If you look back to the section "Optimizing the Server," which discusses the relative difference in speed between the CPU, memory, and disks, you can see that disk speeds can be as slow as

200MB/sec, whereas memory speeds are likely to be approximately 5-12GB/sec. Whenever a hard page fault occurs, the thread on which it incurs remains waiting for a relatively long time before it can continue. If the thread running your query incurs a series of hard page faults, your query appears to run slowly.

The resolution to these hard page faults is to add more memory to the server, reduce the memory used by other applications on the server, or tune your SQL Server's SQL statements to reduce the amount of memory they consume.

System performance counters that identify page faults are Pages Input/sec (shows the rate of pages read), and Pages Output/sec (shows the rate of pages written). See Chapter 13 for a more detailed discussion of the performance counters.

I/O

I/O configuration is actually too big a subject to cover in one chapter; it requires a book of its own. This section introduces you to some of the I/O options available and then walks through several scenarios to provide some insight into how to make the right storage configuration decisions.

I/O encompasses both network I/O and hard disk I/O. In most cases with SQL Server, you are primarily concerned with disk I/O because that's where the data resides. However, you also need to understand the effect that poor network I/O can have as a bottleneck to performance.

Configuring I/O for a server storage system is perhaps the place where you have the most options, and it can have the largest impact on the performance of your SQL Server system. When you turn off your computer, the only thing that exists is the data stored on your hard drive. When you turn the power on, the processor starts running, the OS is loaded, and SQL Server is started; all this happens by reading data and code from the disk.

This basic concept is true for everything that happens on a computer. Everything starts its life on the disk and has to be read from the disk into memory and from there through the various processor caches before it reaches the processor and can be used as either code or data. Any results the processor arrives at must be written back to disk to persist any system event, for example, shutdown, failure, maintenance, and so on.

SQL Server is sensitive to disk performance, more so than many applications, because of the manner in which it manages large amounts of data in user databases. Many applications have the luxury of loading all their data from disk into memory and then running for long periods of time without having to access the disk again. SQL Server strives for that model because it is by far the fastest way to get anything done. Unfortunately, when the requested operation requires more data than can fit into memory, SQL Server must do some shuffling around to keep going as fast as it can, it starts to flush the write buffer and it must start writing that data back to disk, so it can use that memory to generate some new results.

At some point in the life of SQL Server data, every piece of data that SQL server uses must be read from disk and changed data must be written back to disk.

Network

Referring back to Figure 10-2, you can see that the network is a key component in any SQL Server system. The network is the link over which SQL Server receives all its requests to do something, and by which it sends all its results back to the client. In most cases, today's high-speed networks provide enough capacity to enable a SQL Server system to use all its other resources (CPU, memory, and disk) to their maximum before the network becomes a bottleneck.

In some systems the type of work done on the SQL Server is relatively small compared to the number of requests sent to the server, or to the amount of data returned to the client. In either of these cases, the network can be a bottleneck. Network bottlenecks can occur anywhere in the network. They can be on the NIC of the client, where the client is an application server that's serving the database server with hundreds of thousands of requests per second. Bottlenecks can occur on the fabric of the network between the server and the client (application server, web server, or the user's workstation). This network fabric can consist of many pieces of network infrastructure, from the simplest system in which two machines connect over a basic local area network (LAN) to the most complex network interconnected systems in either the Internet or a global corporate wide-area network (WAN). In these larger, more complex interconnected systems, much of the network can be beyond your control and may introduce bandwidth or latency issues outside of acceptable limits. In these cases you can do little more than investigate, document, and report your findings.

The parts of networking that you examine here are those over which you may have direct control, and all are on the SQL Server system. You can make the assumption that the remainder of the network fabric is up to the job of supporting the number of requests received, and of passing the results back to the client in a timely manner.

One thing, in particular, to be aware of is the speed and duplex settings for the network. It is, unfortunately, easy to cause a duplex mismatch. The result of which is that the network will work much slower than its normal rate. The standard setting is for the network to be set to full duplex. This means that communications are transmitted in both directions simultaneously. This requires the use of approved cabling. Current networks operate at a rate of 1GB/s but 10GB/s networks are becoming more and more prevalent.

Disks

The other area of I/O is disk I/O. With earlier versions of SQL Server, disks were quite simple, leaving you with limited options. In most cases you had only a couple of disks to deal with. Now, enterprise systems have the option to use Storage Area Network (SAN) or Network Attached Storage (NAS) storage, and some may use external disk subsystems using some form of Redundant Array of Independent Drives (RAID), and most likely using an SCSI interface that enables you to build disk subsystems with hundreds if not thousands of disks.

There are various interfaces that are used in disk storage systems:

➤ **Advanced Technology Attachment (ATA):** Also known as Integrated Drive Electronics (IDE) which refers not only to the connector and interface definition but also to the fact that the drive controller is integrated into the drive. Parallel ATA (PATA) interfaces allow the data to be transferred between the motherboard and the disk using a parallel stream up to a current maximum of 133MB/s. Serial ATA has been developed to overcome the architectural limitations of the parallel interface and can transmit data at speeds up to 3GB/s.

➤ **Small Computer Systems Interface (SCSI):** This is a set of standards that was developed to connect and transfer data between computers and a myriad of peripheral devices including disks. This was also using the parallel stream of data transfer with speeds up to a maximum of 640MB/s. Serial Attached SCSI (SAS) has been developed as an evolution of the SCSI standard and utilizes a serial data stream for speeds of up to 4800MB/s.

Now consider some of the basic physics involved in disk performance. You need to understand the fundamental differences between different types of disks, as they explain differences in performance. This in turn helps you make an informed decision about what kind of disks to use. Table 10-1 demonstrates example values, under ideal conditions, of the typical, fundamental disk latency information.

TABLE 10-1: Example Hard Disk Drive Latency

DISK ROTATIONAL SPEED	ROTATIONAL LATENCY	TRACK-TO-TRACK LATENCY	SEEK TIME	DATA TRANSFER RATE	TRANSFER TIME FOR 8KB	TOTAL LATENCY
5,400 RPM	5.5 ms	6.5 ms	12 ms	90MB/sec	88 µs	12.1 ms
7,200 RPM	4.1 ms	6.5 ms	10.7 ms	120MB/sec	66 µs	10.8 ms
10,000 RPM	3 ms	1.5 ms	4.5 ms	166MB/sec	48 µs	4.6 ms
15,000 RPM	2 ms	1.5 ms	3.5 ms	250MB/sec	32 µs	3.5 ms

Rotational latency is the time it takes the disk to make a half rotation. This figure is given for just half a rotation rather than a full rotation because on average the disk makes only a half rotation to find the sector you want to access. It is calculated quite simply as rotational speed in RPM divided by 60 (to give revolutions per second) and then divided by the number of rotations per second.

Track-to-track latency is the time it takes the disk head to move from one track to another. In the table, the number for 5,400 and 7,200 RPM disks is considerably slower than for the 10,000 and 15,000 RPM disks. This indicates that the slower disks are more likely to be ATA disks rather than SCSI disks. ATA disks have considerably slower internals than SCSI disks, which accounts for the considerable difference in price and performance between the two disk types.

Seek time is the magic number disk manufacturers publish, and it's their measure of rotational latency and track-to-track latency. This is calculated in the preceding table as the sum of rotational latency and track-to-track latency.

Data transfer rate is the average rate of throughput. This is usually calculated as the amount of data that can be read from a single track in one revolution. So for a modern disk with a data density of approximately 1MB/track, and for a 7,200 RPM disk, rotating at 120 revs per second, that equates to approximately 1MB per track at 120 revolutions per sec=120MB/sec of data that can be read from the disk.

Transfer time for 8KB is the time it takes to transfer a given amount of data at that transfer rate. To see how long it takes to transfer an 8KB block, you simply divide the amount of data you want to move by the transfer rate, so 8KB/120MB=66 micro seconds (or μs).

Total latency for a given amount of data is the sum of rotational latency, track-to-track latency, and disk transfer time.

Back in Table 10-1 you can see that for a single 8KB transfer, the largest amount of time is spent moving the head to the right position over the disk's surface. Once you are there, reading the data is a tiny percentage of the time.

Latency limits the disk's capability to service random read requests. Sequential read requests have an initial latency and are then limited by the disk's capability to read the data from the disk surface and get each I/O request back through the many layers, before reading the next sector from the disk's surface.

Disk write requests are often buffered to disk cache, which increases the SQL Server write performance but should be used only if the storage array implements a battery backup to protect that cache in case of a power failure. Otherwise, in a power failure, the database can become corrupted. Before using cache, check with your storage array vendor to verify that it has a battery backup and can guarantee writing the cache to disk if a power failure occurs. A typical storage array enables the cache to be configured as a range between read-and-write cache. As the database transaction log performs synchronous writes, it would benefit from having a greater amount of write cache assigned in the storage array.

Throughput in MB/sec is a measure of how many bytes the disk can transfer to or from its surface in a second. This is usually quoted as a theoretical number based on the disk's bus.

Throughput in IOs/sec or IOPS is a measure of how many I/Os the disk can service per second. This is also typically quoted as a theoretical number based on the disk's bus.

The database workload determines which will have a greater impact on SQL Server performance, MB/sec throughput or IOPS. From a disk I/O point of view, an OLTP database workload that does small, random reads and writes will be gated by the IOPS. Such data requests ask for few rows per request per user (`selects`, `deletes`, `inserts`, or `updates`), and the disk's capability to seek the request data in the disk and return it determines the user's response time. Conversely, an OLAP or a reporting database with large sequential reads will be gated by the MB/sec throughput and will benefit most from reducing data fragmentation, making the data physically contiguous on disk. These are reads where the disk finds the starting disk data request and pulls data sequentially, and the disk capability to return the data helps determines the user's response time. However, in an OLAP and reporting database, the database workload not only typically returns more data per request than the OLTP, but also the queries may be more complex and have more table joins, therefore requiring more system CPU work to deliver the final dataset to the users. As a result, the user response time must include that in addition to the MB/sec throughput.

Storage Considerations

After all that talk about the different pieces of a storage system, it's time to get serious about figuring out how best to configure *your* storage system. This is a challenging task because there is no single simple way to configure storage that's going to suit every purpose. SQL Server systems can be required to do dramatically different things, and each implementation could require a radically different storage configuration to suit its peculiar I/O requirements. The following sections offer a set of guidelines, and then provide the details showing how you can figure out what works best for you. These guidelines can also be used during discussions with the teams responsible for the storage.

Use the Vendors' Expertise

The vendors of each piece of hardware should be the people you turn to for expertise regarding how to configure their hardware. They may not necessarily know how to configure it best for SQL Server, however, so this is where you must convey SQL Server's requirements in a manner the hardware vendor can understand. This is best done by quoting specific figures for reads versus writes, sequential versus random I/O, block sizes, I/Os per second, MB/sec for throughput, and minimum and maximum latency figures. This information can help the vendor provide you with the optimal settings for their piece of the hardware, be it disks, an array controller, fiber, networking, or some other piece of the storage stack.

Every System Is Different

Each SQL Server system may have different I/O requirements. Understand this and don't try to use a cookie-cutter approach to I/O configuration (unless you have already done the work to determine that you do have SQL systems with the exact same IO requirements.)

Simple Is Better

It is an age-old engineering concept that simpler solutions are easier to design, easier to build, easier to understand, and hence easier to maintain. In most cases, this holds true for I/O design as well. The simpler solutions invariably work faster, are more robust and reliable, and require less maintenance than more complex designs. Unless you have a compelling, specific reason to use a complex storage design, keep it simple.

More Disks

More disks are invariably faster than fewer disks. For example, if you have to build a 4TB volume, it's going to deliver higher performance if it's built from a lot of small disks (ten 400GB disks) versus a few larger disks (two 2TB disks). This is true for various reasons. First, smaller disks are usually faster than larger disks. Second, you stand a better chance to use more spindles to spread read-and-write traffic over multiple disks when you have more disks in the array. This gives you throughput that in some cases is the sum of individual disk throughput. For example, if those 400GB disks and 2TB disks all delivered the same throughput, which was, say 20MB/sec, you would sum that for the two 2TB disks to achieve just 40MB/sec. However, with the ten smaller disks, you would sum that to arrive at 200MB/sec, or five times more.

Faster Disks

Not surprisingly, faster disks are better for performance than slower disks. However, this doesn't just mean rotational speed, which is but one factor of overall disk speed. What you are looking for is some indicator of the disk's capability to handle the I/O characteristics of the workload you are specifically interested in. Unfortunately, disk manufacturers rarely, if ever, provide any information other than rotational speed and theoretical disk bus speeds. For example, you often see a 10K or 15K RPM SCSI disk rated as delivering a maximum throughput of 300MB/sec because it's on an SCSI 320 bus. However, if you hook up that disk and start running some tests using a tool such as SQLIO, the chances are good that for small-block-size, non-queued random reads, you will be lucky to get much more than 2–4MB/sec from that disk. Even for the fastest I/O types, large-block sequential I/O, you will rarely get more than 60–70MB/sec. That's a long way from 300MB/sec. You can download the SQLIO Disk Subsystem Benchmark tool from `www.microsoft.com/download/en/details.aspx?id=20163`.

Here is a very good tutorial to follow when starting out with SQLIO: `http://sqlserverpedia.com/wiki/SAN_Performance_Tuning_with_SQLIO`.

Cache – Read and Write

Embedded on the controller board of every hard drive is a set of memory that is called the disk buffer or disk cache. This cache acts as a buffer between the disk and the attached system and is used to store the data that is being read from or written to the disk. The size of this cache ranges from 8 to 64MB. In the same way, disk controllers, whether they are internal to the server or external as part of a SAN, also have a cache that is used to store read and written data. The size of controller cache can vary from 512MB to 512GB. Following are the many uses for disk cache:

➤ **Read-ahead/read-behind**: When a read operation is sent to the disk, the disk may read unrequested data it deems SQL Server is going to need at a later date.

➤ **Write acceleration**: The disk controller may signal to SQL Server that the write operation has succeeded immediately after receiving the data, even though the data has not actually been written to the disk. The data is then stored in the write cache and written later. This does introduce the risk of data loss that could occur if the hard drive loses power before the data is physically written. To combat this very risk, most disk array controllers have a battery backup to ensure that all outstanding write operations complete even if the enclosure loses main power.

➤ **Input/Output speed balancing**: The rate of read and write operations sent to the disk may fluctuate during the normal course of operation. To ensure that the requests get serviced in a timely manner, the cache is used to store data waiting to be transferred in and out.

In most configurations, the read and write cache shares the same set of memory and the CPU of the disk (or array) controls the nuances of that arrangement. In some cases, certain OLTP database configurations can have their read cache disabled on the storage to free up more memory for the write cache.

Test

Testing is an absolutely essential part of any configuration, optimization, or performance tuning exercise. Too often you speak with customers who have been convinced that black is white based on absolutely nothing more than a gut feeling, or some half-truth overheard in a corridor conversation.

Until you have some test results in your hand, you don't truly know what the I/O subsystem is doing. Forget all that speculation, which is nothing more than poorly informed guesswork, and start testing your I/O systems to determine what's actually going on. IOMeter is a commonly used tool for I/O subsystem measurement and characterization to baseline an I/O subsystem. It is both a workload generator and a measurement tool that can emulate a disk or network I/O load. It can be found at www.iometer.org. Here is a good tutorial to follow when starting out with IOMeter: www.techrepublic.com/article/test-storage-system-performance-with-iometer/5735721.

A commonly used disk performance metric is disk latency, which is measured by Windows System Performance Monitor using the Avg Sec/Read, Avg Sec/Write, and Avg Sec/Transfer counters. Target disk latencies are as follows:

➤ Database Transaction Log: less than 5ms, ideally 0ms

➤ OLTP Data: less than 10ms

➤ Decision Support Systems (OLAP and Reporting) Data: less than 25ms

After you have set up the system and tested it, you need to keep monitoring it to ensure that you are aware of any changes to the workload or I/O subsystem performance as soon as it starts. If you have a policy of monitoring, you can also build a history of system performance that can be invaluable for future performance investigations. Trying to track down the origins of a slow-moving trend can be hard without a solid history of monitoring data. See Chapter 13, "Performance Tuning T-SQL" for more specifics on what and how to monitor.

Designing a Storage System

There are important steps you need to take when designing a storage system. The following sections introduce each of the different parts of a storage system, providing some guidance on key factors, and offering recommendations where they are appropriate.

The first questions you must to answer when designing a new storage system are about the disks:

➤ How many disks do you need?

➤ What size should they be?

➤ How fast should they be?

A Word About Space

The first thing you need to determine is how much space you need. After you have sized the data, you need to factor in index space, growth, room for backups, and recovery. All these factors can increase the amount of space required.

How Many Disks

After the total space requirement has been set, you need to decide on the total throughput (what level of IOPS performance) that is required. From there, consider the redundancy desired and, therefore, what RAID level is needed to satisfy the space and I/O pattern requirement. Use those details to determine the disk layout and spindle count.

Cost

Much as everyone would like to have an unlimited budget, that's unlikely to be the case in most environments, so the ideal design must be modified to bring it in line with the available budget. This often results in less than optimal designs, but it's a necessary factor when designing any system.

Desired I/O Characteristics

The first thing you need to consider here are the I/O characteristics of the operations you are going to perform in SQL Server. This can be a complex issue to resolve, and in many cases the easiest way to determine this is through testing and monitoring an existing system so that you can identify the exact types and volume of I/O that each major feature or function requires.

If you don't have an existing system, you might use the information in Table 10-2 as a guideline to get you started.

TABLE 10-2: I/O Characteristics

OPERATION	RANDOM/SEQUENTIAL	READ/WRITE	SIZE RANGE
Create Database	Sequential	Write	512KB (Only the log file is initialized in SQL Server 2012 — see featured note.)
Backup Database	Sequential	Read/Write	Multiple of 64KB (up to 4MB).
Restore Database	Sequential	Read/Write	Multiple of 64KB (up to 4MB).
DBCC - CHECKDB	Sequential	Read	8KB–64KB.
Alter Index - on - rebuild (Read Phase)	Sequential	Read	See "Read Ahead" in Books Online.
Alter Index - on - rebuild (Write Phase)	Random or Sequential	Write	Any multiple of 8KB up to 128KB.
Sys.dm_db_index_physical_stats	Sequential	Read	8KB–64KB.
Insert / Update / Delete	Random or Sequential	Write	64KB–512KB
SELECT	Random or Sequential	Read	64KB–512KB
TempDB	Random or Sequential	Read/Write	8KB–64KB
Transaction Log	Sequential	Write	60KB

The data files in Table 10-2 are created without being zeroed out when instant file initialization is enabled.

To reduce storage cost, it is not necessary for all the disk space you need to have the same storage characteristics. The SQL `tempdb` file should be deployed onto the fastest, most robust storage you can afford. The SQL data and log files should be on a disk that is fairly fast and robust. Space for backup, recovery, and other repeatable tasks can be on slower and less robust storage.

 Remember that if the backups are on such slow and less robust storage, and the storage fails, and there's a corruption problem with the production database, then the database has been lost.

In some cases in which your database is a copy of some other source system, you might decide to build the whole system on inexpensive, nonrobust storage. If a failure occurs, you could then rebuild the whole system from the source system. However, if your copy has an SLA that requires minimal downtime and doesn't allow for a full rebuild, even though the data is only a copy, you must implement some form of robust storage so that you never need to take unacceptable time to rebuild from the source system.

RAID

As part of the "how many disks do you need?" question, you must consider the RAID level you require because this can influence the total number of disks required to build a storage system of a certain size and with the I/O characteristics you require:

➤ **Availability:** The first factor when thinking about RAID is the level of availability you need from the storage.

➤ **Cost:** An important part of any system is meeting the cost requirements. There's no point in specifying the latest, greatest high-performance system if it costs 10, 100, or 1,000 times your budget.

➤ **Space:** Another major factor in combination with cost is how much physical space you need to provide.

➤ **Performance:** The performance of the storage is another major factor that should help you determine what level of RAID you should choose.

RAID 0 — Striping without Parity or Mirroring

A RAID 0 set contains two or more disks and the data is striped across all the disks. This RAID level provides no redundancy or fault tolerance as a disk failure destroys the array. During a write operation, the data is broken up into blocks and the blocks are written onto the disks simultaneously.

This increases bandwidth during read operations because multiple sections of the entire chunk of data are able to be read in parallel. However, RAID 0 does not implement any error checking and there is a higher risk of corruption. This is not recommended for any SQL Server volume.

RAID 1 — Mirroring without Striping or Parity (2 disks)

With RAID 1, one disk is mirrored onto another — meaning a two disks are needed to be configured in the RAID set. This is fast because reads can (but not always) occur from both disks and writes incur minimal performance reduction. It provides redundancy from a disk failure but increases storage costs because usage capacity is 50 percent of the available disk drives. For storage cost reasons, backups, data loads, and read-only database operations may not require this level of protection.

RAID 10 — Striping with Mirroring (minimum 4 disks)

RAID 10 (also known as RAID 1+0) is a mirrored set in a stripped set with a minimum of four disks. There will always be an even number of disks in the set. This is normally the fastest arrangement available. RAID 5 (discussed next) is faster during read operations when the same number of disks is used in the set. Reads can occur from multiple disks, and writes incur minimal performance reduction. It also provides redundancy — it can survive more than one disk failure provided that the disk failures are not in the same mirrored set — but increases storage costs, as usage capacity is 50 percent of the available disk drives. Database systems that require the most I/O read/write performance and redundancy should be deployed on RAID 10. For storage cost reasons, backups, data loads, and read-only database operations may not require this level of protection. RAID 0+1 is an alternative to RAID 1+0 in that it creates a second striped set to mirror the first striped set as opposed to RAID 1+0 which creates a striped set from a series of mirrored drives.

RAID 5 — Striping with Parity (minimum 3 disks)

Raid 5 is striping with parity with a minimum of three disks. During writes it must calculate the data parity — for example, for each write operation in a three disk array, it writes data across two disks and parity across the third disk. The RAID firmware distributes the parity blocks across all the disks in the RAID set to avoid a write hotspot. There is a performance penalty to calculating the parity and therefore RAID 5 is not a good choice for databases that must handle a significant amount of writes. Another downside of RAID 5 is that, in the event of a disk failure, performance can be seriously degraded while rebuilding the array with the new disk. If running with a failed disk, performance can also suffer because parity needs to be calculated per each read to return the data. During read operations, RAID 5 may perform faster than some other RAID type as multiple disks are able to serve the data in parallel. As a result, RAID 5 is efficient for predominantly read databases such as decision support systems (DSS). In addition, RAID 5 is more cost-effective than RAID 1 or RAID 10 because the disk space of one single drive is required for parity storage for each RAID 5 set, whereas for RAID 1 or RAID 10 it requires 50 percent of the disk space for redundancy.

RAID 6 — Striping with Double Parity (minimum 4 disks)

A RAID 6 set contains a minimum of four disks and distributes two copies of the parity across the disks. This provides enhanced fault tolerance as two drive failures could occur without destroying the data on the array. This RAID implementation makes large RAID groups more practical as larger capacity drives extend the time needed to recover from a drive failure.

RAID-Level Recommendations

You should use fast, robust storage for SQL data files and SQL log files. In general, for most SQL Server implementations, the recommendation for both is to use striping with mirroring (RAID 10). There are, of course, exceptions. If the nature of the database implementation is to service an application that has a high number of reads operations compared to writes, or the database is configured to be read-only, then RAID 5 (or 6) with a large number of disks per RAID set is acceptable.

Additionally, if you know your application is going to make extensive use of tempdb, use the fastest, most robust storage available. This might seem a little strange because the data in tempdb is always transitory, but the requirement for robustness comes from the need to keep the system running, not from a concern about losing data. If the rest of the system uses robust storage but tempdb doesn't, a single disk failure can prevent that SQL Server instance from running. The requirement for speed comes from the fact that tempdb is highly random I/O utilization data file.

The operating system and SQL binary files can live on a simple mirror although, in many cases the time it takes to rebuild the OS and SQL may be within acceptable downtime, in which case a single disk can suffice.

 Remember that, even if the time taken to rebuild and patch the OS, install and patch SQL, and attach the databases is less than the outage window, the cost of staff time to rebuild everything will be much higher than the cost of a second disk with the two disks setup in a RAID 1 array.

For critical systems, the OS and SQL binary files should be on a mirrored disk array, but it needs to be only a single mirrored pair. OS and SQL binary files don't have high I/O requirements; they are typically read once when the application is loaded, and then not touched until new code paths need to be used, and then a few more 4KB random reads are issued. Therefore, these files don't require high-performance storage.

Isolation

Isolation is needed at several levels. You want to isolate the different types of I/O SQL Server generates to optimize each storage system. You don't want to mix the heavy random I/O generated by a high-volume OLTP system with the highly sequential write access to the log file.

At the same time, on a shared storage system such as a SAN, you want to ensure that your storage is isolated from the I/O generated by other systems using the same shared storage. Isolation is primarily concerned with the sharing of disks that results from virtualization on a SAN system, but the principle can also apply to other parts of the storage subsystem, specifically the ports, fiber, and switches that make up the SAN fabric.

Separating SQL Data from the Transaction Log

I/O to SQL data files is different in nature from I/O to the SQL log file. SQL data traffic is random in nature with relatively larger block sizes, occasionally becoming large sequential I/O for large table scans. SQL log traffic is sequential in nature and consists predominantly of write operations.

Because of this, it's important to separate SQL data files and log files onto separate physical disks. Doing this enables the heads on the log disks to track sequentially, matching the log write activity. The heads on the SQL data traffic have a lot of seeks because they need to get the next random disk block, but this won't impact log performance, nor will it be further randomized by having to intersperse random data reads and writes with sequential log writes.

Using tempdb

SQL Server 2012 makes extensive use of `tempdb`, so you must know how often you need to use this database. See Chapter 13 for more details on monitoring. You should always consider placing `tempdb` on separate physical disks.

Another option considered by some users is placing `tempdb` on a RAM disk or other high-performance solid state disks (SSDs). SSDs may not be a good solution though if the workload on `tempdb` is predominately sequential because the SSDs don't respond well to sequential writes. Because of the lightning-fast response times of these kinds of disks, this can provide a considerable performance boost for systems that make extensive use of `tempdb`. Additionally, the RAM disks or SSDs could be used in a mirrored configuration for redundancy.

`tempdb` is discussed in more detail in Chapter 2, "Installing SQL Server 2012 Best Practices," and Chapter 12, "Monitoring Your SQL Server."

 Although it's okay to place `tempdb` on volatile disks such as RAM disks, it's not okay to put any other SQL files on these kinds of volatile storage. SQL Server has specific requirements for its storage to ensure the integrity of data.

Large Storage System Considerations: SAN Systems

More and more SQL Server systems use storage provided by an external storage array of some kind. Frequently, these large external systems are called *SAN systems*, but they could be NAS or some other storage array technology. This terminology doesn't refer to the storage but to the technology used to connect your SQL Server to the box of disks on a network of some kind. Typically, a SAN or a NAS contains large numbers of high performance disks and has a disk controller configured with cache memory to speed disk transfer times.

In the case of a SAN system, the network is a dedicated storage network, frequently built using fiber-optic cables and is called a fiber channel attached SAN. An iSCSI connected system is one where the storage network is an IP network (the IP part of TCP/IP) built with compatible network cards but using a private network dedicated to storage traffic. iSCSI can be, and frequently is, configured to use the existing network. Another way to connect the storage to the system is fiber-channel over Ethernet (FCoE) which uses an Ethernet network to transmit fiber channel data to and from the disk subsystem.

The benefits of using SAN storage over local storage include the following:

➤ **Availability:** SAN storage is generally more reliable than local storage and can reduce the costs associated with downtime due to hardware failure.

➤ **Management:** A central SAN can reduce the time spent on managing multiple individual servers' storage. Increasing the storage within a server requires new drives to be installed manually (a process which requires downtime) whereas assigning additional space from a SAN can be done remotely and may not require a reboot.

➤ **Improved disaster recovery:** Centralizing data backup can improve recovery time while reducing overall costs. Using snapshots and data replication ensures that copies of the data are available if disaster strikes.

➤ **Space utilization:** In general, local storage is underutilized because much more disk is purchased than is required.

Any discussion on SQL Server storage configuration must include information on the concepts involved in configuring an external storage array.

Disk Virtualization

SAN systems present many challenges when you place large numbers of fast, high-capacity disks in a single unit. One of these challenges is how to provide the fastest storage to the largest number of people. You know that to increase disk performance, you need to stripe across as many spindles as possible, but many users of the SAN may require as little as 500GB or less of storage. If your SAN system is filled with 300GB disks, you could deliver that 500GB using three or four disks. Unfortunately, delivering 500GB from just four disks isn't going to the performance required. Step back and consider that the SAN itself may have thousands of disks. If you could take a small piece of a larger number of disks, you could build the same 500GB chunk of storage, but it would be much faster.

Now consider the theoretical situation in which you can take a 5GB chunk from each of 100 disks that are 300GB each. When you combine all those 5GB chunks together, you end up with 500GB of raw disk space. Sure, you wasted a little bit of space for the overhead of managing 100 disks, but now you have a 500GB chunk of storage that has the potential to deliver I/O at the rate of the sum of 100 disks; or if each disk were capable of 80MB/sec for sequential 64K reads, you would have a combined I/O throughput that runs at approximately 8000MB/sec. In practice, you won't get anywhere near that theoretical I/O rate, but you can see considerably higher I/O rates than you would if you just combined three or four disks.

Disk virtualization is the technique that some SAN vendors use to present chunks of storage to a system. SAN vendors that offer storage virtualization have their own unique method, but they are all based on the same basic concept: Slice each disk up into slices, or chunklets, recombine these small slices into larger chunks of storage, and present these virtualized chunks to each application. This process can be performed by following these steps:

1. Start with a single disk and create multiple slices on the disk.

2. Do the same thing across multiple disks.

3. Group a collection of these disk-slices together using some level of RAID and present it to the server as a LUN.

Logical Unit Numbers

A *logical unit number* (LUN) is, technically, the number used to define a physical device addressed by the SCSI or Fiber Channel protocol. The term is also used to refer to the logical disk that is created on a SAN.

When considering the LUNs that the storage is going to present to the OS, you have to answer two questions: How big should each LUN be, and how many should you have? The starting point for answering these questions is determining how much storage you need. If you have differing storage requirements, you also need to know how much of each different type you require. Different types of storage might range from high speed, high reliability for data and log; low speed, high reliability for archive data; high speed, low reliability for backup staging (before writing to tape), and low speed, low reliability for "other" storage that doesn't have tight performance criteria or present reliability concerns.

LUN Size

The next factor to be considered is LUN size. For a SAN-based system, or large local storage array, this equates to how big you make each chunk of storage to be presented to the operating system. These LUN-sized chunks of storage are how the OS sees the storage. By now, you may know from virtualization that the OS has no way to know how many disks, or how much from each disk, each LUN represents.

A number of factors can influence your decision about LUN size. For instance, you need to consider how the storage is to be mounted in the OS. If you mount each LUN as its own volume, you can make them a little larger. You want to stay well below this limit due to backup, restore, and startup times. On startup, the OS runs a basic check of each volume. If an error is found on the volume, the OS runs a Check Disk (CHKDSK). If the volume is large, the time taken to run CHKDSK can become long — in some cases, extremely long — which can start to have a large impact on system startup time. For large enterprise servers with less than one server restart scheduled per year, this isn't a major problem, except when it's time to set up everything — installing the OS and drivers and configuring the server. Many reboots may be required. If each reboot takes 30–45 minutes, restarting the server eight or more times becomes a two day labor, rather than something you do while getting another coffee refill.

On Windows 2008, the maximum size of Master Boot Record (MBR) volume is 2TB. GBT volumes have a maximum size of 9+ zettabytes. One ZB is equivalent to 1 million petabytes.

Number of LUNs

If there are no clear criteria that set an ideal size for each LUN, there may be factors that dictate a specific number of LUNs. The simplest way to determine the number of LUNs you need is to decide how you want the data laid out on the physical disks in the storage array. As a starting point, you need one LUN for tempdb, one LUN for data files and one LUN for database log files. This is in addition to the system volume as no data, log, or tempdb files should reside on the system volume.

Server Configuration

After spending a lot of time configuring the storage, you still must configure the server. The main configuration options on the server are related to the number, placement, and configuration of the *host bus adapter (HBA)*, and then you're into the details of the operating system — specifically, the device manager and the file system. The HBA is the I/O interface that connects a host system to the SCSI bus or SAN. Moreover, HBA cards are available in a variety of different throughputs (such as 4, 8 or 16GB/s), and some servers may have a limited number of faster PCI slots among all their available PCI slots. You want to put the HBA in a PCI slot that can enable it to run at its maximum throughput. Check the server documentation.

Disk Adapters

The disk adapter is the interface card that you plug into the PCI bus inside your server to enable the PCI bus to connect to the ATA, SCSI, iSCSI, or fiber channel cabling required to connect to the disks. Several factors should be considered with disk adapters.

Number of Adapters

When determining the number of disk adapters, you first must consider how many disks you need to support. On some interfaces, such as ATA and SCSI, there are physical limits to the number of disks allowed per bus: two disks per ATA bus (one master, one slave) and either 4, 8, or 16 per SCSI bus (depending on which version of SCSI is in use and length of cable). If you need an ATA-based system with eight disks, you need to have enough disk adapters to provide four ATA buses. If you need an SCSI-based system with 32 disks, and you use a version of SCSI that supports 16 disks per bus, you would need two, or possibly, four buses.

One adapter can provide more than one bus. You might find an ATA adapter that implements two or maybe four ATA buses, so your eight-disk system might need only a single adapter. In the case of SCSI adapters, many are multi-bus, so you should deliver two SCSI buses from a single adapter card.

At a minimum, one dual-port adapter or two single port adapters should be used to connect the server to the SAN switch.

Multipath I/O

Multipath I/O (MPIO) solutions use redundant physical path components — adapters, cables, and switches — to create logical "paths" between the server and the storage device. If one or more of these components fails, causing the path to fail, multipathing logic uses an alternative path for I/O so that applications can still access their data.

Keeping a highly available solution requires redundancy in each of the following components:

➤ Application availability through server clustering such as Microsoft Clustering Service provides redundancy among computers so that if a computer has a system failure, the running services — for example, SQL Server 2012 — can failover to another computer in that failover cluster. Microsoft Clustering Services is included with Windows 2008 Enterprise and Datacenter Editions. Moreover, multiple NIC card teaming can be implemented if a network card failure occurs.

➤ Storage redundancy through RAID enables you to configure drives for performance and fault-tolerance to provide protection from a disk failure.

➤ Storage availability through multipathing enables multiple interfaces to the same storage unit (LUN) to deliver on the storage network components' redundancy. Multipathing

manages the redundant I/O connections so that read/write requests are instantaneously rerouted in case of an I/O path failure. Microsoft MPIO with the Microsoft Device-Specific Module (DSM) provides a tightly integrated Windows System multipathing solution that can be deployed in failover mode, whereby one I/O path is implemented as a failover partner to another, or it can be deployed in a dynamic load balancing mode whereby the I/O workload is balanced across all the available I/O paths based on an algorithm — for example, round-robin. Within either mode, if one path — for example, the fiber cable or the Host Bus Adapter (HBA) — were to fail, the I/O would continue through the surviving I/O paths. Other MPIO workload routing algorithms include: round robin with subset, least queue depth, weighted paths, and least blocks. For a detailed description of these algorithms, please see the MPIO Policies article that can be found here: `http://technet`
`.microsoft.com/en-us/library/dd851699.aspx`.

Moreover, MPIO in dynamic load balancing mode enables you to performance scale the I/O across many HBAs, enabling more total throughput I/O to flow to the I/O subsystem. This is not supported by Microsoft MPIO. An additional, third party driver is required to do this.

Furthermore, if the I/O subsystem is connected through the server by way of a fabric switch, redundant fabric switches should be deployed to prevent it from becoming a single point of failure.

Figure 10-9 shows an example HP MPIO implementation. Following is a description of each of the common MPIO parameters that can be found in this package:

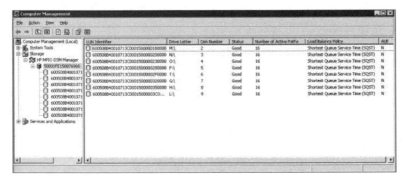

FIGURE 10-9

➤ **LUN Identifier:** A value used by the storage array to identify a particular LUN.

➤ **Drive Letter:** Assigned by the user.

➤ **Disk Number:** Assigned by Windows. Disk 0 is normally the C: drive, for example.

➤ **Status:** Can be good or degraded, failed, and so on. The terminology depends on the vendor.

➤ **Number of Active Paths:** Number of active paths to the LUN.

➤ **Load Balancing Policy:** Indicates the load balancing policy for the LUN, which can be as follows:

- ➤ **Round Robin:** The I/O requests are distributed across all active paths to the device in a round-robin manner.

- ➤ **Shortest Queue Requests:** Each I/O request is routed to the active path with the least number of outstanding requests.

- ➤ **Shortest Queue Bytes:** Each I/O request is routed to the active path with the least number of outstanding data bytes.

- ➤ **Shortest Queue Service Time:** Each I/O request is routed to the active path where the total outstanding time for pending I/O requests is the least.

- ➤ **No Load Balance:** All I/O requests are routed through a chosen active path.

➤ **ALB:** Indicates whether the adaptive load balance is enabled or disabled for the LUN. (This is an HP–specific feature.)

Placement

In larger servers, the physical placement of the adapter card in the PCI slots can have an impact on performance. Placement can affect performance in two ways. On a large system, the physical distance between the furthest PCI slot and the CPU can increase latency and reduce overall bandwidth.

On some systems, the PCI slots are not all of the same type. It is increasingly common for systems to have a few PCI-X or fast 64-bit PCI slots, with the remainder being slower slots. Placing a high-speed 64-bit, PCI-X, or PCI-Express disk adapter into a slow-speed PCI slot (some won't physically fit, but some will) can force the whole bus to run at a considerably slower speed than expected. Check the server documentation or ask the vendor to identify the faster PCI slots.

Firmware

All disk adapters have firmware that can be upgraded. Even when you first purchase a new disk adapter, you should check the vendor's website to make sure you have the highest firmware version which is supported on your storage array, which may not be the highest available firmware version. Vendors change their firmware to fix bugs, improve performance and match specific drivers, so you must always confirm that you have the latest firmware to ensure optimal performance.

Drivers

Even though the disk adapter probably comes with drivers, there is a good chance that they are outdated by the time you purchase the adapter, so even before installing anything you should check the vendor's website for the highest driver version which is supported in your configuration. This may not be the newest driver version.

Configuration

Many disk adapters have options that can be set to change the way they work in different environments, or for different types of disks to which they may be attached. For ATA and SCSI adapters, this configuration is usually minimal, unless the adapter includes RAID. In most cases the configuration involves fiber channel options on HBA's. One configuration that should be considered is the HBA queue depth. This setting specifies the maximum number of I/O operations that can be in the HBA queue before it no longer accepts more I/O commands. If this setting is misconfigured,

SQL Server performance is not optimal. The queue depth setting varies by HBA card vendor. Please refer to the documentation for configuration options.

iSCSI adapters that are NICs also have configuration options. Some of these are the same settings you may have used to configure any IP-based network adapter and were covered earlier in the material on NICs. One setting that needs to be evaluated is the option of using Jumbo Frames to enable the transmission of 9000 bytes of information per frame as opposed to 1500 bytes of information, which is the default Ethernet behavior. This improves performance considerably by reducing the packet processing overhead which provides CPU relief. However, this change needs to be applied to all devices on the network path. A single network device set to the default frame size can cause the entire network to transmit at that (smaller), frame size.

Partitioning

After installing the disks, you need to configure the disks themselves, and the first step with a new disk is to consider the disk partitions. What kind of partition do you want to create on the disk? There are two main options: a MBR partition or a GUID Partition Table (GPT) partition. The MBR partition is older and has partition size (up to 2TB) and number of partitions (4 partitions) limitations. It is the type most commonly deployed. A GPT partition can be used for large partitions (up to 9.4 zettabytes) and large number of partitions (up to 128 partitions).

Start Sector Alignment

Sector alignment (also known as partition alignment, disk alignment, and volume alignment) is a topic that frequently comes up for discussion. A hard drive consists of a platter that is covered in a magnetic media that stores the information and a head that moves across the platter to read the information. The media is arranged on the surface of the platter in a number of tracks, which are arranged in concentric circles. Those tracks are divided into a number of sectors. A sector is the minimum chunk of data that can be written to a disk. Sector size can be 512 bytes or 4 KB (on newer disks). The first track on the disk is taken up by the MBR and data can be written starting at Track 2, Sector 1. This default start sector alignment (or start partition offset) is 1024KB (1MB).

Windows Server 2008 R2 correctly aligns new partitions as they are created. However, disks that have been retained in the server after an operating system upgrade may have a sector alignment that differs from the standard default. In fact, the default alignment in Windows 2003 was 31.5KB and leaving it set to this can have enormous performance implications for your SQL Server.

 It has been reported that certain disk subsystem vendors interfere with the default alignment setting, even on Windows 2008 servers. So, in the words of Ronald Reagan, "Trust, but verify!"

To determine the start sector alignment of your basic disks, use the following WMic.exe command at a Command prompt:

```
wmic partition get BlockSize, StartingOffset, Name, Index
```

The StartingOffset number of 1048576 confirms a 1MB alignment.

To determine the start sector alignment on dynamic disks, the process is a little different. Execute the following command at a Commend prompt:

```
dmdiag.exe -v
```

 To download dmdiag.exe, *visit this web page: www.microsoft.com/download/ en/details.aspx?displaylang=en&id=17044.*

If your partitions are not aligned correctly, the only way to fix this is to copy all the data to a volume that has the alignment set correctly; alternatively, you could reformat the disk with the correct configuration.

Volume Types

After you have partitioned the disks, you must decide what kind of volumes you want. The choice here is between using a *basic volume* or a *dynamic volume*. Basic volumes are recommended unless you need specific features that only a dynamic volume can provide, which include the ability to create volumes that span multiple disks or the ability to create fault-tolerant volumes (mirrored and RAID-5 volumes). If you run in a clustered environment, dynamic volumes are not supported at all.

File Systems — NTFS Versus FAT

New Technology File System (NTFS) and File Allocation Table (FAT) are standard file systems that enable data to be organized on disk. The choice between these two shouldn't be an issue anymore though: Always use NTFS. Microsoft has recommended that NTFS be the only option when using Windows Server 2008 R2. The reliability and security offered by NTFS and the speed and functional improvements of NTFS over FAT make it the only choice for your file system.

NTFS Allocation Unit Size

Another topic that frequently comes up is the NTFS allocation unit size, also known as NTFS cluster size. SQL Server stores rows of data in 8KB pages. In general, eight of these 8KB pages are read and written to the disk at one time, and this is known as an *extent*. Doing simple math, you can find that an extent is 64KB in size. Therefore, each read or write performed by SQL Server is 64KB in size. Best practices state that you should make sure that the volume used for SQL Server has been formatted with a minimum block size of 64KB. These blocks are known as the file allocation units. In some cases, a file allocation unit size of 512KB (8 x 8 extents) is used. Examples of where this might be appropriate include large data warehouse servers and Fast Track systems.

Fragmentation

Any discussion on disks would not be complete without considering fragmentation. Fragmentation can occur in several forms with SQL Server:

> Internal SQL fragmentation occurs when pages are split due to many inserts, updates, and deletes. This is covered in Chapter 14, "Indexing Your Database."

➤ External fragmentation, which you are interested in here, can take two forms:

  ➤ Classic file fragmentation occurs when a file is created and the file system doesn't have enough contiguous disk space to create the file in a single fragment. You end up with a single file spread across multiple file fragments.

  ➤ Autogrow fragmentation is the fragmentation that occurs when you enable autogrow and the database size continuously grows with the addition of more file fragments. These fragments may or may not have classic file fragmentation as well.

One important point to consider here is that SQL database files don't become more fragmented after they have been created. If files are created when there isn't enough contiguous free space, they are created in multiple fragments. If the disk is defragmented (and the OS has enough space to fully defragment all files) right after the files are created, the files are no longer fragmented and won't ever become fragmented.

In the ideal scenario, you have dedicated disks for your SQL database files, and you can correctly size each file, create the files, and disable autogrow. In this situation, you start with clean disks, create one or two files that aren't fragmented, and they stay that way forever. That way, you need to deal only with internal fragmentation.

However, back in the real world, you start from the previous situation but enable autogrow at some tiny size or percentage, so you end up adding hundreds or thousands of small files. In this case, those files may or may not be fragmented, depending on how much free space is available on the disk when each autogrow operation occurs. Your only solution here to remove the fragmentation is to schedule server downtime to rebuild each database using a few large files, sized correctly for the expected database growth, and then disable autogrow. This way, you resolve any disk fragmentation that occurs. The ideal way to prevent external, filesystem fragmentation from ever occurring is to disable autogrow on the database files. This is, however, in the majority of cases, not practical.

 When a defragmentation operation is run on a volume that contains a SQL Server database, that database file is not able to be defragmented until the SQL Server service has been stopped. What this means is that to defragment the SQL Server volumes, SQL Server needs to be offline to make sure there are no open files.

In the worst-case scenario, you don't have dedicated disks; you used the default database sizes and enabled autogrow. Now you may have several problems to resolve. Your SQL database files are competing for I/O capacity with the OS, and anything else running on the server. Until you add dedicated disks for SQL Server, this won't be resolved. In addition, you may also end up with a lot of file fragments because each autogrow operation adds another data or log file fragment. As each new file fragment is created by autogrow, it might be fragmented over the disk surface. As more fragments are added and the disk fills up, the chance of creating fragmentation increases.

The best way to avoid problems is to follow these steps:

1. Install the OS.

2. Defragment the disk.

3. Install any applications (SQL Server).

4. Defragment the disk.

5. Create data and log files at maximum size.

6. Check for fragmentation and defragment if necessary.

7. Disable autogrow.

8. Routinely defragment the disk to clean up fragmentation caused by other applications. This preserves the free space should you ever need to add more SQL data or log files.

In most cases, the operating system's disk defragmenter does a great job and is all you need. In some situations, however, you may need to consider purchasing a third-party disk defragmentation utility. Some benefits of using a third-party tool include increased speed of operation, background processing, multiple simultaneous volume defragmentation, and the ability to schedule defragmentation operations.

SUMMARY

Performance tuning can be tricky when a system has been operating sub-optimally for an extended period of time. The performance issues can be multiplied when the underlying system has not been designed in an optimal way from the outset.

Before starting to make decisions about a system's hardware layout, there are multiple areas of the system that need to be discussed: user interaction with the system; data usage patterns; number and type of SQL statements that will be run against the system; schema design; and more.

There are a number of hardware decisions that need to be made when configuring a server for optimal performance. The central processing unit of the server plays a large role in determining if the system will perform acceptably under the expected workload. CPU components such as cache, hyper-threading, multi-core and system architecture need to be investigated and the available options need to be weighed. You should also consider the memory and the various technologies that are at work within the memory. These technologies include physical and virtual address spaces, the virtual memory manager, and the page file.

The slowest part of a system is I/O. Care should be taken to choose between the myriad of options when designing network and storage subsystems. Some of the questions that need to be answered include: How fast should the network be? How much storage space do I need? How many disks? What type of disks? How fast do the disks need to be? SAN or NAS? What RAID should I use? Storage adapter cards? Allocation unit size? and so on.

You should now have many tools to choose from when configuring a SQL Server for optimal performance.

11

Optimizing SQL Server 2012

WHAT'S IN THIS CHAPTER

- ➤ Benefits to Optimizing Application Performance
- ➤ Using Partitioning and Compression to Improve Performance
- ➤ Tuning I/O, CPU, and Memory to Increase the Speed of Query Results

Since the inception of SQL Server 7.0, the database engine has been enabled for self-tuning and managing. With the advent of SQL Server 2012, these concepts have reached new heights. When implemented on an optimized platform (as described in Chapter 10, "Configuring the Server for Optimal Performance") with a properly configured SQL Server instance that has also been well maintained, SQL Server 2012 remains largely self-tuning and healing. This chapter introduces and discusses the SQL Server 2012 technologies needed to accomplish this feat.

APPLICATION OPTIMIZATION

There are many ways to squeeze more performance out of your SQL Server, and it is a good idea to make sure the application is running optimally. Therefore, the first order of business for scaling SQL Server 2012 on the Windows Server platform is optimizing the application. The *Pareto Principle*, which states that only a few vital factors are responsible for producing most of the problems in scaling such an application, is reflected in this optimization. If the application is not well written, getting a bigger hammer only postpones your scalability issues, rather than resolving them. Tuning an application for performance is beyond the scope of this chapter.

The goal of performance tuning SQL Server 2012 is to minimize the response time for each SQL statement and increase system throughput. This can maximize the scalability of the entire database server by reducing network-traffic latency, and optimizing disk I/O throughput and CPU processing time.

Defining a Workload

A prerequisite to tuning any database environment is a thorough understanding of basic database principles. Two critical principles are the logical and physical structure of the data and the inherent differences in the application of the database. For example, different demands are made by an online transaction processing (OLTP) environment than are made by a decision support (DSS) environment. A DSS environment often needs a heavily optimized I/O subsystem to keep up with the massive amounts of data retrieval (or reads) it performs. An OLTP transactional environment needs an I/O subsystem optimized for more of a balance between read-and-write operations.

In most cases, SQL Server testing to scale with the actual demands on the application while in production is not possible. As a preferred practice, you need to set up a test environment that best matches the production system and then use a load generator such as Quest Benchmark Factory or Idera SQLscaler to simulate the database workload of the targeted production data-tier environment. This technique enables offline measuring and tuning the database system before you deploy it into the production environment.

Further, the use of this technique in a test environment enables you to compartmentalize specific pieces of the overall solution to be tested individually. As an example, using the load-generator approach enables you to reduce unknowns or variables from a performance-tuning equation by addressing each component on an individual basis (hardware, database, and application).

System Harmony Is the Goal

Scaling an application and its database is dependent on the harmony of the memory, disk I/O, network, and processors, as shown in Figure 11-1. A well-designed system balances these components and should enable the system (the application and data tiers) to sustain a run rate of greater than 80 percent processor usage. Run rate refers to the optimal CPU utilization when the entire system is performing under heavy load. When a system is balanced properly, this can be achieved as all sub-systems are performing efficiently.

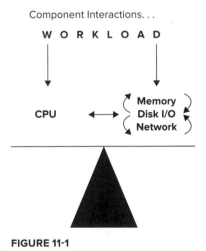

FIGURE 11-1

Of these resource components, a processor bottleneck on a well-tuned system (application\database) is the least problematic to diagnose because it has the simplest resolution: add more processors or upgrade the processor speed/technology. There are, however, increased licensing costs associated with adding more processors and CPU cores.

THE SILENT KILLER: I/O PROBLEMS

Customers often complain about their SQL Server performance and point to the database because the processors aren't that busy. After a discussion and a little elbow grease, frequently the culprit is an I/O bottleneck. The confusion comes from the fact that disk I/O is inversely proportional to

CPU. In other words, over time, the processors wait for outstanding data requests queued on an overburdened disk subsystem. This section is about laying out the SQL Server shell or container on disk and configuring it properly to maximize the exploitation of the hardware resources. Scaling any database is a balancing act based on moving the bottleneck to the least affected resource.

SQL Server I/O Process Model

Windows Server 2008 with the SQL Server 2012 storage engine work together to mask the high cost of a disk I/O request. The Windows Server I/O Manager handles all I/O operations and fulfills all I/O (read or write) requests by means of *scatter-gather* or asynchronous methods. Scatter-gather refers to the process of gathering data from, or scattering data into, the disk or the buffer. For examples of scatter-gather or asynchronous methods, refer to SQL 2012 Books Online (BOL) under "I/O Architecture."

The SQL Server storage engine manages when disk I/O operations are performed, how they are performed, and the number of operations that are performed. However, the Windows operating system (I/O Manager Subsystem) performs the underlying I/O operations and provides the interface to the physical media. SQL Server 2012 is only supported on Windows Server 2008 R2. For Windows 2008 R2 details, see www.microsoft.com/en-us/server-cloud/windows-server/default.aspx and select Editions under the Overview heading for edition specifics.

The job of the database storage engine is to manage or mitigate as much of the cost of these I/O operations as possible. For instance, the database storage engine allocates much of its virtual memory space to a data buffer cache. This cache is managed via cost-based analysis to ensure that memory is optimized to efficiently use its memory space for data content — that is, data frequently updated or requested is maintained in memory. This benefits the user's request by performing a logical I/O and avoiding expensive physical I/O requests.

Database File Placement

SQL Server stores its database on the operating system files — that is, physical disks or Logical Unit Numbers (LUNs) surfaced from a disk array. The database is made up of three file types: a primary data file (MDF), one or more secondary data files (NDF), and transaction log files (LDF).

 In SQL Server 2012, as in some previous versions, the use of MDF, NDF, and LDF file extensions is optional.

Database file location is critical to the I/O performance of the Database Management System (DBMS). Using a fast and dedicated I/O subsystem for database files enables it to perform most efficiently. As described in Chapter 10 "Configuring the Server for Optimal Performance," available disk space does not equate to better performance. Rather, the more, faster physical drives there are, (or LUNs), the better your database I/O subsystem can perform. You can store data according to usage across data files and filegroups that span many physical disks. A *filegroup* is a collection of data files used in managing database data-file placement.

> *To maximize the performance gain, make sure you place the individual data files and the log files all on separate physical LUNs. You can place reference archived data or data that is rarely updated in a read-only filegroup. This read-only file group can then be placed on slower disk drives (LUNs) because it is not used very often. This frees up disk space and resources so that the rest of the database may perform better.*

tempdb Considerations

Since database file location is so important to I/O performance, you need to consider functional changes to tempdb when you create your primary data-file placement strategy. The reason for this is that tempdb performance has a rather large impact on system performance because it is the most dynamic database on the system and needs to be the quickest.

Like all other databases, tempdb typically consists of a primary data and log files. tempdb is used to store user objects and internal objects. It also has two version stores. A *version store* is a collection of data pages that hold data rows required to support particular features that use row versioning. These two version stores are as follows:

➤ Row versions generated by data modification transactions in tempdb that use snapshot or read committed row versioning isolation levels

➤ Row versions in tempdb generated by data modification transactions for features such as online index operations, Multiple Active Result Sets (MARS), and AFTER triggers

Beginning with SQL Server 2005 and continuing in SQL Server 2012, tempdb has added support for the following large set of features that create user and internal objects or version stores:

➤ Query

➤ Triggers

➤ Snapshot isolation and read committed snapshots

➤ Multiple Active Result Sets (MARS)

➤ Online index creation

➤ Temporary tables, table variables, and table-valued functions

➤ DBCC Check

➤ Large Object (LOB) parameters

➤ Cursors

➤ Service Broker and event notification

➤ XML and Large Object (LOB) variable

➤ Query notifications

➤ Database mail

➤ Index creation

➤ User-defined functions

As a result, placing the `tempdb` database on a dedicated and extremely fast I/O subsystem can ensure good performance. A great deal of work has been performed on `tempdb` internals to improve scalability.

 Consider reading BOL under "Capacity Planning for tempdb" for additional information and functionality details regarding `tempdb` usage. This can be found at: `http://msdn.microsoft.com/en-us/library/ms345368.aspx`.

When you restart SQL Server, `tempdb` is the only database that returns to the original default size of 8MB or to the predefined size set by the administrator. It can then grow from there based on usage requirements. During the autogrow operation, threads can lock database resources during the database-growth operation, affecting server concurrency. To avoid timeouts, the autogrow operation should be set to a growth rate that is appropriate for your environment. In general, the growth rate should be set to a number that will allow the file to grow in less than 2 minutes.

You should do at least some type of capacity planning for `tempdb` to ensure that it's properly sized and can handle the needs of your enterprise system. At a minimum, perform the following:

1. Take into consideration the size of your existing `tempdb`.

2. Monitor `tempdb` while running the processes known to affect `tempdb` the most. The following query outputs the five executing tasks that make the most use of `tempdb`:

```
SELECT top 5 * FROM sys.dm_db_session_space_usage
ORDER BY (user_objects_alloc_page_count + internal_objects_alloc_page_count) DESC
```

3. Rebuild the index of your largest table online while monitoring `tempdb`. Don't be surprised if this number turns out to be two times the table size because this process now takes place in `tempdb`.

Following is a recommended query that needs be run at regular intervals to monitor `tempdb` size. It is recommended that this is run every week, at a minimum. This query identifies and expresses `tempdb` space used, (in kilobytes) by internal objects, free space, version store, and user objects:

```
select sum(user_object_reserved_page_count)*8 as user_objects_kb,
    sum(internal_object_reserved_page_count)*8 as internal_objects_kb,
    sum(version_store_reserved_page_count)*8 as version_store_kb,
    sum(unallocated_extent_page_count)*8 as freespace_kb
from sys.dm_db_file_space_usage
where database_id = 2
```

The output on your system depends on your database setup and usage. The output of this query might appear as follows:

```
user_objects_kb      internal_objects_kb  version_store_kb     freespace_kb
-------------------- -------------------- -------------------- ----------------
256                  640                  0                    6208
```

 If any of these internal SQL Server objects or data stores run out of space, tempdb will run out of space and SQL Server will stop. For more information, please read the BOL article on tempdb disk space that can be found here: http://msdn.microsoft.com/en-us/library/ms176029.aspx.

Taking into consideration the preceding results, when configuring tempdb, the following actions need to be performed:

➤ Pre-allocate space for tempdb files based on the results of your testing, but leave autogrow enabled in case tempdb runs out of space to prevent SQL Server from stopping.

➤ Per SQL Server instance, as a rule of thumb, create one tempdb data file per CPU or processor core, all equal in size up to a maximum of eight data files.

➤ Make sure tempdb is in simple recovery model, which enables space recovery.

➤ Set autogrow to a fixed size of approximately 10 percent of the initial size of tempdb.

➤ Place tempdb on a fast and dedicated I/O subsystem.

➤ Create alerts that monitor the environment by using SQL Server Agent or Microsoft System Center Operations Manager with SQL Knowledge Pack to ensure that you track for error 1101 or 1105 (tempdb is full). This is crucial because the server stops processing if it receives those errors. Right-click SQL Server Agent in SQL Server Management Studio and fill in the dialog, as shown in Figure 11-2. Moreover, you can monitor the following counters using Windows System Performance Monitor:

    ➤ **SQLServer:Databases: Log File(s) Size(KB):** Returns the cumulative size of all the log files in the database.

    ➤ **SQLServer:Databases: Data File(s) Size(KB):** Returns the cumulative size of all the data files in the database.

    ➤ **SQLServer:Databases: Log File(s) Used (KB):** Returns the cumulative used size of all log files in the database. A large active portion of the log in tempdb can be a warning sign that a long transaction is preventing log cleanup.

➤ Use instant database file initialization. If you are not running the SQL Server (MSSQLSERVER) Service account with admin privileges, make sure that the SE_MANAGE_ VOLUME_NAME permission has been assigned to the service account. This feature can reduce a 15-minute file-initialization process to approximately 1 second for the same process.

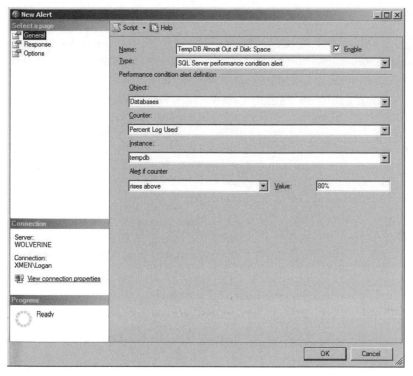

FIGURE 11-2

Another great tool is the `sys.dm_db_task_space_usage` DMV, which provides insight into `tempdb`'s space consumption on a per-task basis. Keep in mind that once the task is complete, the counters reset to zero. In addition, you should monitor the per disk Avg. Sec/Read and Avg. Sec/Write as follows:

> ➤ Less than 10 milliseconds (ms) = Very good

> ➤ Between 10–20 ms = Borderline

> ➤ Between 20–50 ms = Slow, needs attention

> ➤ Greater than 50 ms = Serious IO bottleneck

If you have large `tempdb` usage requirements, read the Q917047, "Microsoft SQL Server I/O subsystem requirements for tempdb database" at `http://support.microsoft.com/kb/917047` or look in SQL Server 2012 Books Online (BOL) for "Optimizing tempdb Performance."

Hopefully this section has impressed upon you that in SQL Server 2012, more capacity planning is required to optimize `tempdb` for performance.

TABLE AND INDEX PARTITIONING

Simply stated, *partitioning* is the breaking up of a large object, such as a table, into smaller, manageable pieces. A *row* is the unit on which partitioning is based. Unlike DPVs, all partitions must reside within a single database.

Partitioning has been around for a while. This technology was introduced as a distributed partitioned view (DPV) during the SQL 7.0 launch. This feature received a lot of attention because it supported the ability to use constraints with views. This provided the capability for the optimizer to eliminate partitions (or tables) joined by a union of all statements on a view. These partitions could also be distributed across servers using linked servers.

However, running queries against a DPV on multiple linked servers could be slower than running the same query against tables on the same server due to the network overhead. As systems have become increasingly faster and more powerful, the preferred method has become to use the SQL Server capability to partition database tables and their indexes over filegroups within a single database. This type of partitioning has many benefits over DPV, such as being transparent to the application (meaning no application code changes are necessary). Other benefits include database recoverability, simplified maintenance, and manageability.

Although this section discusses partitioning as part of performance-tuning and as a way to present a path to resolve I/O problems, partitioning is first and foremost a manageability and scalability tool. In most situations, implementing partitioning also offers performance improvements as a byproduct of scalability.

You can perform several operations only on a partitioned table including the following:

➤   Switch partition data into or out of a table

➤   Merge partition range

➤   Split partition range

These benefits are highlighted throughout this section.

 Partitioning is supported only in SQL Server 2012 Enterprise and Developer Editions.

Why Consider Partitioning?

There are a variety of reasons that you may have large tables. When these tables (or databases) reach a certain size, it becomes difficult to perform activities such as database maintenance, backup, or restore operations that consume a lot of time. Environmental issues such as poor concurrency due to a large number of users on a sizable table result in lock escalations, which translates into further challenges. If archiving the data is not possible because of regulatory compliance needs, independent software vendor (ISV) requirements, or cultural requirements, partitioning is most likely the tool for you. If you are still unsure whether to implement partitioning, run your workload through the Database Tuning Advisor (DTA), which makes recommendations for partitioning and generates the code for you. Chapter 15 "Replication," covers the DTA, which you can find under the "Performance Tools" section of the Microsoft SQL Server 2012 program menu.

Various chapters in this book cover partitioning to ensure you learn details in their appropriate contexts.

Following is a high-level process for partitioning:

1. Create a partition function to define a data-placement strategy.
2. Create filegroups to support the partition function.
3. Create a partition scheme to define the physical data distribution strategy (map the function data to filegroups).
4. Create a table or index on the partition function.
5. Enjoy redirected queries to appropriate resources.

After implementation, partitioning can positively affect your environment and most of your processes. Make sure you understand this technology to ensure that every process benefits from it. The following list presents a few processes that may be affected by partitioning your environment:

➤ Database backup and restore strategy (support for partial database availability)

➤ Index maintenance strategy (rebuild), including index views

➤ Data management strategy (large insert or table truncates)

➤ End-user database workload

➤ Concurrency:

   ➤ **Parallel partition query processing:** In SQL Server 2005, if the query accessed only one table partition, then all available processor threads could access and operate on it in parallel. If more than one table partition were accessed by the query, then only one processor thread was allowed per partition, even when more processors were available. For example, if you have an eight-processor server and the query accessed two table partitions, six processors would not be used by that query. In SQL Server 2012, parallel partition processing has been implemented whereby all available processors are used in parallel to satisfy the query for a partition table. The parallel feature can be enabled or disabled based on the usage requirements of your database workload.

   ➤ **Table partition lock:** escalation strategy.

➤ Enhanced distribution or isolated database workloads using filegroups

Creating a Partition Function

A *partition function* is your primary data-partitioning strategy. When creating a partition function, the first order of business is to determine your partitioning strategy. Identifying and prioritizing challenges is the best way to decide on a partitioning strategy. Whether it's to move old data within a table to a slower, inexpensive I/O subsystem, enhance database workload concurrency, or simply maintain a large database, identifying and prioritizing is essential. After you select your strategy, you need to create a partitioning function that matches that strategy.

Remember to evaluate a table for partitioning because the partition function is based on the distribution of data (selectivity of a column and the range or breadth of that column). The range supports the number of partitions by which the table can be partitioned. There is a product limit of 15,000 partitions per table. This range should also match up with the desired strategy — for example, spreading out (or partitioning) a huge customer table by customer last name or by geographical location for better workload management may be a sound strategy. Another example of a sound strategy may be to partition a table by date for the purpose of archiving data based on date range for a more efficient environment.

> *You cannot implement user-defined data types, alias data types, timestamps, images, XML, varchar(max), nvarchar(max), or varbinary(max) as partitioning columns.*

Take for example a partition of a trouble-ticketing system for a telephone company. When a trouble ticket is generated based on an outage, it is submitted to the database. At this point, many activities are initiated: Technicians are dispatched, parts are replaced or reordered, and service can be rerouted within the network. Service-level agreements (SLAs) are monitored and escalations are initiated. All these activities take place because of the trouble ticket. In this system, the activities table and ticketing table have hot spots, as shown in Figure 11-3.

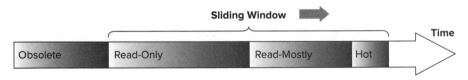

FIGURE 11-3

In Figure 11-3, the information marked as Hot is the new or recent data, which is only relevant or of interest during the outage. The information marked as Read-Only and Read-Mostly is usually used for minor analysis during postmortem processes and then for application reporting. Eventually, the data becomes obsolete and should be moved to a warehouse. Unfortunately, because of internal regulatory requirements, this database must be online for 7 years. Partitioning this environment can provide sizable benefits. Under a *sliding-window* scenario (explained in the "Creating a Partition Scheme" section later in this chapter), every month (or quarter) a new partition would be introduced to the environment as a retainer for the current (Hot) data for the tickets and activities tables. As part of this process, a partition with data from these tables that is older than 7 years would also be retired.

As described earlier, there is a one-to-many relationship between tickets and activities. Although obvious size differences exist between these tables, you need to put them through identical processes. This enables you to run processes that affect resources shared by and limited to these objects. To mitigate the impact of doing daily activities such as backups and index maintenance on all this data, these tables will be partitioned based on date ranges. You can create a right partition function based on the `ticketdate` column, as outlined in Listing 11-1 (if you execute the following statement, remove the line breaks):

LISTING 11-1: CreatePartitionFunction

```
CREATE PARTITION FUNCTION
PFL_Years (datetime)
AS RANGE RIGHT
FOR VALUES (
'20050101 00:00:00.000', '20070101 00:00:00.000',
'20090101 00:00:00.000', '20110101 00:00:00.000',
'20120101 00:00:00.000')
```

SQL Server rounds time to .003 seconds, meaning that a time of .997 would be rounded up to 1.0 second.

➤ The leftmost partition is the first partition and includes all values less than `'20050101 00:00:00.000'`.

➤ The boundary value `'20050101 00:00:00.000'` is the start of the second partition, and this partition includes all values greater than or equal to `'20050101 00:00:00.000'` but less than `'20070101 00:00:00.000'`.

➤ The boundary value `'20070101 00:00:00.000'` is the start of the third partition, and this partition includes all values greater than or equal to `'20070101 00:00:00.000'` but less than `'20090101 00:00:00.000'`.

➤ The boundary value `'20090101 00:00:00.000'` is the start of the fourth partition and this partition includes all values greater than or equal to `'20090101 00:00:00.000'` but less than `'20110101 00:00:00.000'`.

➤ The boundary value `'20110101 00:00:00.000'` is the start of the fifth partition and includes all values greater than or equal to `'20110101 00:00:00.000'` but less than `'20120101 00:00:00.000'`.

➤ Finally, the boundary value '`20120101 00:00:00.000`' is the start of the sixth partition, and this partition consists of all values greater than `'20120101 00:00:00.000'`.

The range partition function specifies the boundaries of the range. The `left` or `right` keyword specifies to which side of each boundary value interval, left or right, the `boundary_value` belongs, when interval values are sorted by the Database Engine in ascending order from left to right. If this keyword is not specified, `left` is the default. There can be no holes in the partition domain; all values must be obtainable. In this code sample, all transactions must fall within a date specified by the sample value range.

Creating Filegroups

You should create filegroups to support the strategy set by the partition function. As a best practice, user objects should be created and mapped to a filegroup outside of the primary filegroup, leaving the primary filegroup for system objects. This ensures database availability if an outage occurs that affects the availability of any filegroup outside of the primary filegroup.

 To continue with this example exercise, you need to create filegroups CY04, CY06, CY08, CY10, CY11, and CY12 in the database before creating the partition scheme.

Creating a Partition Scheme

A partition scheme is what maps database objects such as a table to a physical entity such as a filegroup, and then to a file. There are definitely backup, restore, and data-archival considerations when making this decision. (These are discussed in Chapter 17, "Backup and Recovery.") Listing 11-2 maps the partition functions or dates to individual filegroups. The partition scheme depends on the PFL_Years partition function to be available from the earlier example.

LISTING 11-2: **CreatePartitionScheme1**

Available for
download on
Wrox.com

```
CREATE PARTITION SCHEME CYScheme
AS
PARTITION PFL_Years
TO ([CY04], [CY06], [CY08], [CY10], [CY11], [CY12])
```

This supports the placement of filegroups on individual physical disk subsystems. Such an option also supports the capability to move old data to an older, inexpensive I/O subsystem and to reassign the new, faster I/O subsystem to support Hot data (CY12). When the older data has been moved to the inexpensive I/O subsystem, filegroups can be marked as read-only. When this data has been backed up, it no longer needs to be part of the backup process. SQL Server automatically ignores these filegroups as part of index maintenance.

The other option for a partition-function scheme enables the mapping of the partition scheme to map the partition function to a single filegroup. Listing 11-3 maps the partition function to the default filegroup.

 This code will fail if you have not created the PFL_Years partition function.

LISTING 11-3: CreatePartitionScheme2

```
CREATE PARTITION SCHEME CYScheme2
AS
PARTITION PFL_Years
TO ([Default], [Default], [Default], [Default], [Default], [Default])
```

Partitioning enables the ability to delete or insert gigabytes of data on a 500+ GB partitioned table with a simple metadata switch (in seconds) provided that the delete or insert is based on the partitioned column. The process used to accomplish this is called *sliding window*. On a non-partitioned table, this process would take hours because of lock escalation and index resynchronization. However, using a partitioned table with the sliding-window process consists of the following three steps:

1. An empty target table or partitioned table is created outside of the source data partitioned table.

2. The source data partitioned table is switched with the empty target.

3. At the conclusion of this process, the data is now in the target table and can be dropped.

This process could be repeated in reverse to insert a new partition with data into this source partitioned table as the repository for the Hot data. Again, the only impact to the source partitioned table is a brief pause while a schema-lock is placed during the partition swaps, which can take a few seconds. This switch process can be performed only on partitions within the same filegroup. Implementation details and best practices are covered later in this chapter and in upcoming chapters.

Creating Tables and Indexes

As Listing 11-4 shows, the syntax for creating a table is accomplished as it has always been. The only exception is that it is created on a partition schema instead of a specific or default filegroup. SQL Server 2012 provides the capability to create tables, indexes, and indexed views on partition schemes. This supports the distribution of database objects across several filegroups. This is different from the existing capability to create an entire object within a filegroup (which is still available in SQL Server 2012).

LISTING 11-4: CreateTables

```
CREATE TABLE [dbo].[Tickets]
(     [TicketID] [int] NOT NULL,
      [CustomerID] [int] NULL,
      [State] [int] NULL,
      [Status] [tinyint] NOT NULL,
      [TicketDate] [datetime] NOT NULL
      CONSTRAINT TicketYear
      CHECK ([TicketDate] >= '20050101 00:00:00.000'
AND [TicketDate] < '20120101 00:00:00.000'))
```

continues

LISTING 11-4 *(continued)*

```
 ON CYScheme (TicketDate)
GO

CREATE TABLE [dbo].[Activities]
(      [TicketID] [int] NOT NULL,
        [ActivityDetail] [varchar] (255) NULL,
        [TicketDate] [datetime] NOT NULL,
        [ActivityDate] [datetime] NOT NULL
        CONSTRAINT ActivityYear
        CHECK ([ActivityDate] >= '20050101 00:00:00.000'
AND [ActivityDate] < '20120101 00:00:00.000'))
ON CYScheme (TicketDate)
GO
```

The following sections cover two areas of best practices when creating indexes: index alignment and storage alignment.

Index Alignment

An aligned index uses an equivalent partition function and includes the same partitioning columns as its table (as shown in Figure 11-4). These indexes actually don't need to use the identical partition function or scheme, but there must be a one-to-one correlation of data-to-index entries within a partition.

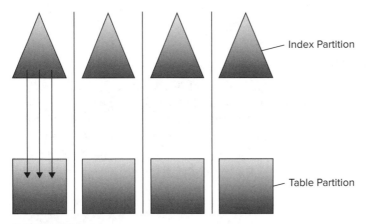

FIGURE 11-4

A benefit derived from index alignment is the ability to switch partitions in or out of a table with a simple metadata operation. In Listing 11-4, you can programmatically add a new partition for the new month (or current month) and delete the outgoing month from the table as part of the 7-year cycle.

Storage Alignment

Index alignment is the first requirement of a storage-aligned solution. There are two options for storage alignment. The big differentiator is the ability to use the same partition scheme, or a different one, as long as both tables and indexes have an equal number of partitions. The first option, as shown in Figure 11-5, demonstrates a storage-aligned solution with the index and relevant data in distinct and dedicated filegroups. If a query to compare data in CY08 and CY06 is executed on an aligned index and data, the query is localized to the aligned environment. This benefits users working in other table partitions isolated from the ongoing work within these two partitions.

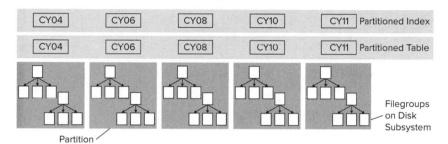

FIGURE 11-5

Figure 11-6 shows the same query executed on a different architecture. Because of the alignment of index and data, the query is still localized but runs in parallel on both the relevant index and data partitions. This would still benefit users working in other partitions isolated from the ongoing work within these four partitions.

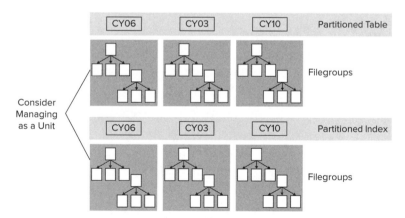

FIGURE 11-6

Additional benefits derived from storage alignment are partial database availability and piecemeal database restores. For instance, in Listing 11-2, the CY08 partition could be offline, and the application would still be processing trouble tickets. This would occur regardless of which partition went down, as long as the primary filegroup that contains the system-tables information (as is the best practice) and the partition that contains the current month's data are online. Considerations that affect query parallelism of this environment are discussed later in the CPU Considerations section of this chapter.

Listing 11-5 is an example of a SQL script for partitioning operations on a table using the AdventureWorks database. For simplicity in this example, all the partitions are placed on the primary file group, but in a real-life scenario, to achieve I/O performance benefits, partitions may be placed on different filegroups, which are then placed on different physical disk drives.

1. First, create the partition function:

LISTING 11-5: StorageAlignment

```
USE AdventureWorks;
CREATE PARTITION FUNCTION [OrderDateRangePFN](datetime)
AS RANGE RIGHT
FOR VALUES (N'2009-01-01 00:00:00', N'2010-01-01 00:00:00',
N'2011-01-01 00:00:00', N'2012-01-01 00:00:00');
```

2. Then create the partition scheme:

```
CREATE PARTITION SCHEME [OrderDatePScheme]
AS PARTITION [OrderDateRangePFN]
TO ([Primary], [Primary], [Primary], [Primary], [Primary]);
```

3. Now, create two tables: SalesOrderHeader is the partitioned table and SalesOrderHeaderOLD is the nonpartitioned table.

4. Load data into the SalesOrderHeader table and then create clustered indexes on both tables.

5. Finally, apply a check constraint to the SalesOrderHeaderOLD table to allow the data to switch into the SalesOrderHeader partitioned table:

```
CREATE TABLE [dbo].[SalesOrderHeader](
   [SalesOrderID] [int] NULL,
   [RevisionNumber] [tinyint] NOT NULL,
   [OrderDate] [datetime] NOT NULL,
   [DueDate] [datetime] NOT NULL,
   [ShipDate] [datetime] NULL,
   [Status] [tinyint] NOT NULL
) ON [OrderDatePScheme]([OrderDate]);

CREATE TABLE [dbo].[SalesOrderHeaderOLD](
   [SalesOrderID] [int] NULL,
   [RevisionNumber] [tinyint] NOT NULL,
   [OrderDate] [datetime] NOT NULL   ,
   [DueDate] [datetime] NOT NULL,
   [ShipDate] [datetime] NULL,
   [Status] [tinyint] NOT NULL);

INSERT INTO SalesOrderHeader SELECT [SalesOrderID],[RevisionNumber],
[OrderDate],[DueDate],[ShipDate],[Status] FROM SALES.[SalesOrderHeader];

CREATE CLUSTERED INDEX SalesOrderHeaderCLInd
ON SalesOrderHeader(OrderDate) ON OrderDatePScheme(OrderDate);

 CREATE CLUSTERED INDEX SalesOrderHeaderOLDCLInd ON
SalesOrderHeaderOLD(OrderDate);

ALTER  TABLE [DBO].[SalesOrderHeaderOLD]  WITH CHECK  ADD CONSTRAINT
```

```
[CK_SalesOrderHeaderOLD_ORDERDATE] CHECK   ([ORDERDATE]>=('2011-01-01
00:00:00') AND [ORDERDATE]<('2012-01-01 00:00:00'));
```

Before you start to do table partition operations, you should verify that you have data in the partitioned table and no data in the nonpartitioned table. The following query returns which partitions have data and how many rows:

```
SELECT $partition.OrderDateRangePFN(OrderDate) AS 'Partition Number',
min(OrderDate) AS 'Min Order Date',
max(OrderDate) AS 'Max Order Date',
count(*) AS 'Rows In Partition'
FROM SalesOrderHeader
GROUP BY $partition.OrderDateRangePFN(OrderDate);
```

You should also verify that no data has been inserted into the SalesOrderHeaderOLD nonpartitioned table; this query should return no data:

```
SELECT * FROM [SalesOrderHeaderOLD]
```

To simply switch the data from partition 4 into the SalesOrderHeaderOLD table, execute the following command:

```
ALTER TABLE SalesOrderHeader
SWITCH PARTITION 4 TO SalesOrderHeaderOLD;
```

To switch the data from SalesOrderHeaderOLD back to partition 4, execute the following command:

```
ALTER TABLE SalesOrderHeaderOLD
SWITCH TO SalesOrderHeader PARTITION 4;
```

To merge a partition range, execute the following command:

```
ALTER PARTITION FUNCTION OrderDateRangePFN()
MERGE RANGE ('2011-01-01 00:00:00');
```

You may want to split a partition range. The split range area should be empty of data because if data were available, SQL Server would need to physically (I/O) move the data across the range. For a large table, the data movement can take time and resources. Therefore, if the range is not empty, the split is not instantaneous. To split a range, you must add a new filegroup for the range before splitting it, like so:

```
ALTER PARTITION SCHEME OrderDatePScheme NEXT USED [Primary];
ALTER PARTITION FUNCTION OrderDateRangePFN()
SPLIT RANGE ('2013-01-01 00:00:00');
```

This section discussed what partitioning is and why it should be considered as a performance option or as a manageability and scalability feature. You ran through the steps to create the partition function and the partition scheme. Remember that filegroup creation needs to be performed prior to these steps. The section ended with an outline of the various options used when creating tables and indexes that use the partition scheme. Next you will learn about Data Compression and how it pertains to increasing efficiency in a database.

DATA COMPRESSION

SQL Server 2012 data compression brings enhancements in storage and performance benefits. Reducing the amount of disk space that a database occupies reduces the overall data files storage footprint and offers increase in throughput with the following improvements:

➤ Better I/O utilization, as more data is read and written per page

➤ Better memory utilization, as more data will fit in the buffer cache

➤ Reduction in page latching, as more data will fit in each page

It is true that disk space is becoming less expensive. However, implementation of a high-performance database system requires a high-performing disk system or Storage Area Network (SAN) or Network Attached Storage (NAS), which is not inexpensive. In addition, this may require additional storage for high availability, backups, QA, and test environments. Overall, it lowers SQL Server 2012's total cost of ownership, making it more competitive.

Before implementing data compression, you must consider the trade-off between I/O and CPU. To compress and uncompress data requires CPU processing utilization, so it would not be recommended for a system that is CPU-bound. However, it would benefit a system that is more I/O-bound. Additionally, keep in mind that accessing the compressed data requires CPU processing work, and if this data is highly selected, there is a CPU performance penalty. Data compression makes most sense on data that is older and less queried. As a simple example, with a large partitioned table, the older partitions that are less queried may be compressed, whereas the highly volatile partitions are not. You can compress volatile data, but you must consider the costs versus benefits for your database workload, and the capacity of your hardware to support it with the goal to achieve the highest throughput.

 Data compression is only available in SQL Server 2012 Enterprise and Developer Editions.

You can use data compression on the following database objects:

➤ Tables (but not system tables)

➤ Clustered indexes

➤ Non-clustered indexes

➤ Index views

➤ Partitioned tables and indexes where each partition can have a different compression setting

Row Compression

SQL Server 2012 implements *row* and *page* data compression. The data compression ratio depends on the schema and data distribution, where compression stores fixed-value data types in a variable format — that is, a 4-byte column with a 1-byte value can be compressed to a size of 1 byte.

A 1-byte column with a 1-byte value has no compression, but NULL or 0 values take no bytes. Compression does take a few bits of metadata overhead to store per value. For example, an `Integer` data type column storing a 1-byte value can have a 75 percent compression ratio. To create a new compressed table with row compression, use the `CREATE TABLE` command, as follows:

```
USE AdventureWorks
GO
CREATE TABLE [Person].[AddressType_Compressed_Row](
  [AddressTypeID] [int] IDENTITY(1,1) NOT NULL,
  [Name] [dbo].[Name] NOT NULL,
  [rowguid] [uniqueidentifier] ROWGUIDCOL  NOT NULL,
  [ModifiedDate] [datetime] NOT NULL,
)
WITH (DATA_COMPRESSION=ROW)
GO
```

To change the compression setting of a table, use the `ALTER TABLE` command:

```
USE AdventureWorks
GO
ALTER TABLE Person.AddressType_Compressed_Row REBUILD
WITH (DATA_COMPRESSION=ROW)
GO
```

Page Compression

Page compression includes row compression and then implements two other compression operations:

➤ **Prefix compression:** For each page and each column, a prefix value is identified that can be used to reduce the storage requirements. This value is stored in the Compression Information (CI) structure for each page. Then, repeated prefix values are replaced by a reference to the prefix stored in the CI.

➤ **Dictionary compression:** Searches for repeated values anywhere in the page, which are replaced by a reference to the CI.

When page compression is enabled for a new table, new inserted rows are row compressed until the page is full, and then page compression is applied. If afterward there is space in the page for additional new inserted rows, they are inserted and compressed; if not, the new inserted rows go onto another page. When a populated table is compressed, the indexes are rebuilt. Using page compression, nonleaf pages of the indexes are compressed using row compression. To create a new compressed table with page compression, use the following commands:

```
USE AdventureWorks
GO
CREATE TABLE [Person].[AddressType_Compressed_Page](
  [AddressTypeID] [int] IDENTITY(1,1) NOT NULL,
  [Name] [dbo].[Name] NOT NULL,
  [rowguid] [uniqueidentifier] ROWGUIDCOL  NOT NULL,
  [ModifiedDate] [datetime] NOT NULL,
)
WITH (DATA_COMPRESSION=PAGE)
GO
```

To change the compression setting of a table, use the ALTER TABLE command:

```
USE AdventureWorks
GO
ALTER TABLE Person.AddressType_Compressed_Page REBUILD
WITH (DATA_COMPRESSION=PAGE)
GO
```

Moreover, on a partitioned table or index, compression can be applied or altered on individual partitions. The following code shows an example of applying compression to a partitioned table and index:

```
USE AdventureWorks
GO

CREATE PARTITION FUNCTION [TableCompression](Int)
AS RANGE RIGHT
FOR VALUES (1, 10001, 12001, 16001);
GO

CREATE PARTITION SCHEME KeyRangePS
AS
PARTITION [TableCompression]
TO ([Default], [Default], [Default], [Default], [Default])
GO

CREATE TABLE PartitionTable
(KeyID int,
Description varchar(30))
ON KeyRangePS (KeyID)
WITH
(
DATA_COMPRESSION = ROW ON PARTITIONS (1),
DATA_COMPRESSION = PAGE ON PARTITIONS (2 TO 4)
)
GO

CREATE INDEX IX_PartTabKeyID
 ON PartitionTable (KeyID)
WITH (DATA_COMPRESSION = ROW ON PARTITIONS(1),
DATA_COMPRESSION = PAGE ON PARTITIONS (2 TO 4 ) )
GO
```

Table partition operations on a compression partition table have the following behaviors:

➤ **Splitting a partition:** Both partitions inherit the original partition setting.

➤ **Merging partitions:** The resultant partition inherits the compression setting of the destination partition.

➤ **Switching partitions:** The compression setting of the partition and the table to switch must match.

➤ **Dropping a partitioned clustered index:** The table retains the compression setting.

In addition, data compression can be managed from SQL Server 2012 Management Studio in Object Explorer by choosing the table or index to data compress. For example, to compress a table, follow these steps:

1. Choose the table and then right-click. From the pop-up menu, choose Storage ➪ Manage Compression.

2. On the Data Compression Wizard that opens, click Next, and in the Select Compression Type dialog of the Data Compression Wizard, select the Compression Type drop-down to change the compression (None, Row, or Page). Figure 11-7 shows the Select Compression Type dialog.

3. After making a Compression Type change, to see the estimated space savings, click the Calculate button. Then, click Next to complete the wizard.

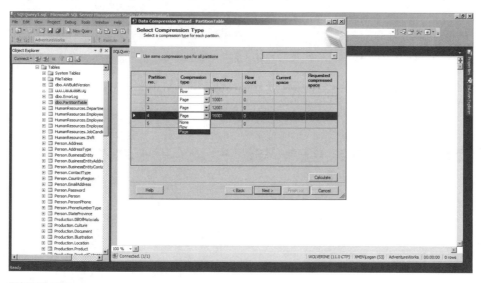

FIGURE 11-7

Estimating Space Savings

Prior to enabling data compression, you can evaluate the estimated compression cost-savings. For example, if a row is more than 4KB and the whole value precision is always used for the data type, there may not be much compression savings. The sp_estimate_data_compression_ savings stored procedure creates a sample data set in tempdb and evaluates the compression space savings, returning the estimated table and sample savings. It can evaluate tables, clustered indexes, nonclustered indexes, index views, and table and index partitions for either page or row compression. Moreover, this stored procedure can estimate the size of a compressed table, index, or partition in the uncompressed state. This stored procedure performs the same cost-saving calculation that was performed by the Data Compression Wizard shown in Figure 11-7 when clicking the Calculate button.

The syntax of the `sp_estimate_data_compression_savings` stored procedure follows:

```
sp_estimate_data_compression_savings
[ @schema_name = ] 'schema_name'
, [ @object_name = ] 'object_name'
, [@index_id = ] index_id
, [@partition_number = ] partition_number
, [@data_compression = ] 'data_compression'
[;]
```

In this code:

➤ `@schema_name` is the name of the schema that contains the object.

➤ `@object_name` is the name of the table or index view that the index is on.

➤ `@index_id` is the ID number of the index. Specify NULL for all indexes in a table or view.

➤ `@partition_number` is the partition number of the object; it can be NULL or 1 for nonpartitioned objects.

➤ `@data_compression` is the type of compression to evaluate; it can be NONE, ROW, or PAGE.

Figure 11-8 shows an example of estimating the space savings for the `SalesOrderDetail` table in the AdventureWorks database using page compression.

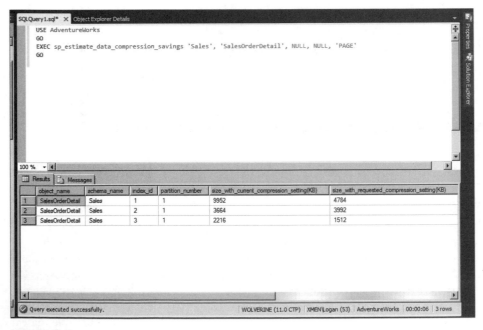

FIGURE 11-8

As shown in the result information in Figure 11-8:

➤ `index_id` identifies the object. In this case, 1 = clustered index (includes table); 2 and 3 are nonclustered indexes.

➤ `Size_with_current_compression_setting` is the current size of the object.

➤ `Size_with_requested_compression_setting` is the compressed size of the object

In this example, the clustered index, including the table, is 9952KB but when page-compressed, it is 4784KB, saving a space of 5168KB.

Monitoring Data Compression

For monitoring data compression at the SQL Server 2012 instance level, two counters are available in the `SQL Server:Access Method` object that is found in Windows Performance Monitor:

➤ Page compression attempts/sec counts the number of page compression attempts per second.

➤ Pages compressed/sec counts the number of pages compressed per second.

The `sys.dm_db_index_operational_stats` dynamic management function includes the `page_compression_attempt_count` and `page_compression_success_count` columns which are used to obtain page compression statistics for individual partitions. It is important to take note of these metrics because failures of attempted compression operations waste system resources. If the ratio of attempts to successes gets too high then there may be performance impacts that could be avoided by removing compression. In addition, the `sys.dm_db_index_physical_stats` dynamic management function includes the `compressed_page_count` column, which displays the number of pages compressed per object and per partition.

To identify compressed objects in the database, you can view the `data_compression` column (0=None, 1=Row, 2=Page) of the `sys.partitions` catalog view. From SQL Server 2012 Management Studio in Object Explorer, choose the table and right-click; then, from the pop-up menu choose Storage ➪ Manage Compression for the Data Compression Wizard. For detailed information on data compression, refer to "Data Compression" in SQL Server 2012 Books Online, which can be found here: `http://msdn.microsoft.com/en-us/library/cc280449(v=SQL.110).aspx`.

Data Compression Considerations

When deciding whether to use data compression, keep the following items in mind:

➤ Data compression is available with SQL Server 2008 Enterprise and Developer Editions only.

➤ Enabling and disabling table or clustered index compression can rebuild all non-clustered indexes.

➤ Data compression cannot be used with sparse columns.

➤ Large objects (LOB) that are out-of-row are not compressed.

➤ Non-leaf pages in indexes are compressed using only row compression.

➤ Non-clustered indexes do not inherit the compression setting of the table.

➤ When you drop a clustered index, the table retains those compression settings.

➤ Unless specified, creating a clustered index inherits the compression setting of the table.

 A word of caution for high-availability systems: Changing the compression setting may generate extra transaction log operations.

CPU CONSIDERATIONS

The challenge in building a large Symmetric Multiprocessing (SMP) system is that, because processors have increased performance through technology enhancements and the use of increasingly larger caches, the performance gains achieved through leveraging these caches are significant. Consequently, you need to cache relevant data whenever possible to enable processors to have relevant data available and resident in their caches. Chip and hardware vendors have attempted to capitalize on this phenomenon through expansion of the processor and system cache.

As a result, new system architectures such as cellular multiprocessing (CMP), CC-NUMA (see Figure 11-9), and NUMA (noncache coherent) are now available in the market. Although this has been successful, it has produced two challenges: the need to manage data locally and cache coherency.

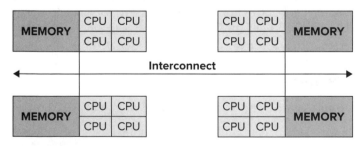

FIGURE 11-9

With Windows 2008 and SQL Server 2012, SQL Server supports hot-add CPU, whereby CPUs can be dynamically added while the server is online. The system requirements to support hot-add CPU are as follows:

➤ Hardware support for hot-add CPU.

➤ Supported by the 64-bit edition of Windows Server 2008 Datacenter or the Windows Server 2008 Enterprise Edition for Itanium-Based Systems operating system.

➤ Supported by SQL Server 2012 Enterprise Edition.

➤ SQL Server 2012 must not be configured for soft NUMA. For more information about soft NUMA, search for the following topics online: "Understanding Non-Uniform Memory Access" and "How to Configure SQL Server to Use Soft-NUMA."

Once you have met these requirements, execute the RECONFIGURE command to have SQL Server 2012 recognize the new dynamically added CPU.

Cache Coherency

For reasons of data integrity, only one processor can update any piece of data at a time; other processors that have copies in their caches can have their local copy "invalidated" and thus must be reloaded. This mechanism is referred to as *cache coherency*, which requires that all the caches are in agreement regarding the location of all copies of the data and which processor currently has permission to perform the update. Supporting coherency protocols is one of the major scaling problems in designing big SMPs, particularly if there is a lot of update traffic. Cache coherency protocols were better supported with the introduction of NUMA and CMP architectures.

SQL Server 2012 has been optimized to take advantage of NUMA advancements exposed by both Windows and the hardware itself. As discussed in the "Memory Considerations and Enhancements" section, SQLOS is the technology that the SQL Server leverages to exploit these advances.

Affinity Mask

The affinity mask configuration option restricts a SQL Server instance to running on a subset of the processors. If SQL Server 2012 runs on a dedicated server, allowing SQL Server to use all processors can ensure best performance. In a server consolidation or multiple-instance environment, for more predictable performance, SQL Server may be configured on dedicated hardware resources that affinitize processors by SQL Server instance.

SQL Server Processor Affinity Mask

SQL Server's mechanism for scheduling work requests is handled through a data structure concept called a *scheduler*. The scheduler is created for each processor assigned to SQL Server through the affinity mask configuration setting at startup. *Worker threads* (a subset of the max worker threads configuration setting) are dynamically created during a batch request and are evenly distributed between each CPU node and load-balanced across its schedulers (see Figure 11-10).

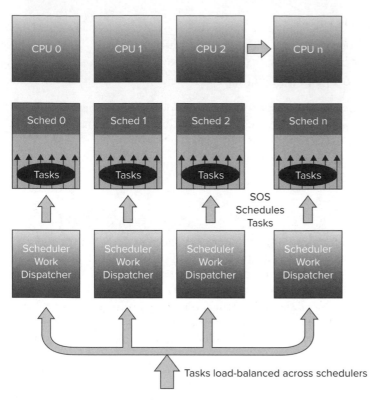

FIGURE 11-10

Incoming connections are assigned to the CPU node. SQL Server assigns the batch request to a task or tasks, and the tasks are managed across schedulers. At any given time, only one task can be scheduled for execution by a scheduler on a processor. A task is a unit of work scheduled by the SQL Server. This architecture guarantees an even distribution of the hundreds, or in many cases, thousands of connections that can result from a large deployment.

Default SQL Server Work Scheduling

The default setting for affinity mask is 0, which enables the Windows scheduler to schedule and move schedulers across any available processor within a CPU node to execute its worker threads. SQL Server 2012 in this configuration has its processes controlled and scheduled by the Windows scheduler. For example, suppose a client requests a connection and the connection is accepted. If no threads are available, then one is dynamically created and associated with a task. The work assignments from the scheduler to the processors are managed through the Windows scheduler, which has its work distributed among all processors within a CPU node. This is the preferred method of execution, as Windows load-balances the schedulers evenly on all processors.

SQL Server Work Scheduling Using Affinity Mask

You can use the affinity mask configuration setting to assign a subset of the available processors to the SQL Server process. SQL Server worker threads are scheduled preemptively by the scheduler.

A worker thread continues to execute on its processor until it is forced to wait for a resource, such as locks or I/O, to become available. If the time slice expires, the thread voluntarily yields, at which time the scheduler selects another worker thread to begin execution. If it cannot proceed without access to a resource such as disk I/O, it sleeps until the resource is available. When access to that resource is available, the process is placed on the run queue before being put back on the processor. When the Windows kernel transfers control of the processor from an executing process to another that is ready to run, this is referred to as a *context switch*.

Context Switching

Context switching is expensive because of the associated housekeeping required to move from one running thread to another. Housekeeping refers to the maintenance of keeping the context or the set of processor register values and other data that describes the process state. The Windows kernel loads the context of the new process, which then starts to execute. When the process taken off the processor next runs, it resumes from the point at which it was taken off the processor. This is possible because the saved context includes the instruction pointer. In addition to this *user mode* time, context switching can take place in the Windows operating system (OS) for *privileged mode* time.

The total processor time is equal to the privileged mode time plus the user mode time.

Privileged Mode

Privileged mode is a processing mode designed for operating system components and hardware-manipulating drivers. It enables direct access to hardware and all memory. Privileged time includes time-servicing interrupts and deferred process calls (DPCs).

User Mode

User mode is a restricted processing mode designed for applications such as SQL Server, Exchange, and other application and integral subsystems. The goal of performance tuning is to maximize user mode processing by reducing privileged mode processing. This can be monitored with the *Processor: % Privileged Time* counter, which displays the average busy time as a percentage of the sample time. A value above 15 percent may indicate that a disk array is being heavily used or that there is a high volume of network traffic requests. In some rare cases, a high rate of privileged time might even be attributed to a large number of interrupts generated by a failing device.

Priority Boost

The Priority Boost option is an advanced option under SQL Server. If you are using the `sp_configure` system stored procedure to change the setting, you can change Priority Boost only when Show Advanced Options is set to 1. The setting takes effect after the server is restarted. By enabling the Priority Boost option, SQL Server runs at a priority base of 13 in the Windows System scheduler, rather than its default of 7. On a dedicated server, this might improve performance, although it can also cause priority imbalances between SQL Server functions and operating system functions, leading to instability. Improvements in SQL Server 2012 and Windows make the use of this option unnecessary.

Priority boost should not be used when implementing failover clustering.

SQL Server Lightweight Pooling

Context switching can often become problematic. In most environments, context switching should be less than 1,000 per second per processor. The SQL Server lightweight pooling option provides relief for this by enabling tasks to use NT "fibers," rather than threads, as workers.

A *fiber* is an executable unit that is lighter than a thread and operates in the context of user mode. When lightweight pooling is selected, each scheduler uses a single thread to control the scheduling of work requests by multiple fibers. A fiber can be viewed as a "lightweight thread," which under certain circumstances takes less overhead than standard worker threads to context switch. The number of fibers is controlled by the Max Worker Threads configuration setting.

Common Language Runtime (CLR) execution is not supported when lightweight pooling is enabled. Make sure to disable the option: "clr enabled" when lightweight pooling is desired.

Max Degree of Parallelism (MAXDOP)

By default, the MAXDOP value is set to 0, which enables SQL Server to consider all processors when creating an execution plan. In most systems, a MAXDOP setting equivalent to the number of cores (to a maximum of 8) is recommended. This limits the overhead introduced by parallelization. In some systems, based on application-workload profiles, it is even recommended that you set this value to 1 (including for SAP and Siebel). This can prevent the query optimizer from choosing parallel query plans. Using multiple processors to run a single query is not always desirable in an OLTP environment, although it is desirable in a data warehousing environment.

In SQL Server 2012, you should assign query hints to individual queries to control the degree of parallelism. If, however, a third party application is generating the query, consider using resource pools to control this.

Partitioned table parallelism is also affected by the MAXDOP setting. Returning to Listing 11-5, a thread can be leveraged across each partition. Had the query been limited to a single partition, multiple threads would be spawned up to the MAXDOP setting.

Affinity I/O Mask

The affinity I/O mask feature, as shown in Figure 11-11, was introduced with SP1 of SQL Server 2000. This option defines the specific processors on which SQL Server I/O threads can execute. The affinity I/O mask option has a default setting of 0, indicating that SQL Server threads are allowed to execute on all processors. The performance gains associated with enabling the affinity I/O mask feature are achieved by grouping the SQL threads that perform all I/O tasks (no-data cache retrievals — specifically, physical I/O requests) on dedicated resources. This keeps I/O processing and related data in the same cache systems, maximizing data locality and minimizing unnecessary bus traffic.

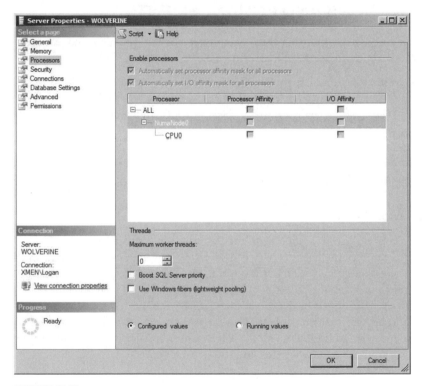

FIGURE 11-11

When using affinity masks to assign processor resources to the operating system, either SQL Server processes (non-I/O) or SQL Server I/O processes, you must be careful not to assign multiple functions to any individual processor.

You should consider SQL I/O affinity when there is high privileged time on the processors that is not affinitized to SQL Server. For example, consider a 32-processor system running under load with 30 of the 32 processors affinitized to SQL Server, leaving two processors to the Windows OS and other non-SQL activities. If the `Processor: % Privileged` time is high (greater than 15 percent), SQL I/O affinity can be configured to help reduce the privileged-time overhead in the processors assigned to SQL Server.

The following steps outline the SQL I/O affinity procedure for determining what values to set:

1. Add I/O capability until there is no I/O bottleneck (disk queue length has been eliminated) and all unnecessary processes have been stopped.

2. Add a processor designated to SQL I/O affinity.

3. Measure the CPU utilization of these processors under heavy load.

4. Increase the number of processors until the designated processors are no longer peaked. For a non-SMP system, select processors that are in the same cell node.

MEMORY CONSIDERATIONS AND ENHANCEMENTS

Because memory is fast relative to disk I/O, using this system resource effectively can have a large impact on the system's overall ability to scale and perform well.

SQL Server 2012 memory architecture and capabilities vary greatly from those of previous versions of SQL Servers. Changes include the ability to consume and release memory-based, internal-server conditions dynamically using the AWE mechanism. In SQL Server 2000, all memory allocations above 4GB were static. Additional memory enhancements include the introduction of hierarchical memory architecture to maximize data locality and improve scalability by removing a centralized memory manager. SQL Server 2012 has resource monitoring, dynamic management views (DMVs), and a common caching framework. All these concepts are discussed throughout this section.

Tuning SQL Server Memory

The following performance counters are available from the System Performance Monitor. The *SQL Server Cache Hit Ratio* signifies the balance between servicing user requests from data in the data cache and having to request data from the I/O subsystem. Accessing data in RAM (or data cache) is exponentially faster than accessing the same information from the I/O subsystem; thus, the wanted state is to load all active data in RAM. Unfortunately, RAM is a limited resource. A wanted cache hit ratio average should be well over 90 percent. This does not mean that the SQL Server environment would not benefit from additional memory. A lower number signifies that the system memory or data cache allocation is below the wanted size.

Another reliable indicator of instance memory pressure is the *SQL Server:Buffer Manager:Page-life-expectancy (PLE)* counter. This counter indicates the amount of time that a buffer page remains in memory, in seconds. The ideal number for PLE varies with the size of the RAM installed in your particular server and how much of that memory is used by the plan cache, Windows OS, and so on. The rule of thumb nowadays is to calculate the ideal PLE number for a specific server using the following formula: `MaxSQLServerMemory(GB) x 75`. So, for a system that has 128GB of RAM and has a MaxServerMemory SQL setting of 120GB, the "minimum PLE before there is an issue" value is 9000. This can give you a more realistic value to monitor PLE against than the previous yardstick of 300. Be careful not to under-allocate total system memory because it forces the operating system to start moving page faults to a physical disk. A page fault is a phenomenon that occurs when the operating system goes to a physical disk to resolve memory references. The operating system may incur some paging, but when excessive paging takes places, it uses disk I/O and CPU resources, which can introduce latency in the overall server, resulting in slower database performance. You can identify a lack of adequate system memory by monitoring the *Memory: Pages/sec performance* counter. It should be as close to zero as possible because a higher value indicates that more hard-paging is taking place, as can happen when backups are taking place.

SQL Server 2012 has several features that should help with this issue. With Windows Server 2008, SQL Server 2012 has support for hot-add memory, a manager framework, and other enhancements. The SQL Server operating system (SQLOS) layer is the improved version of the User Mode Scheduler (UMS), now simply called *scheduler.* Consistent with its predecessor, SQLOS is a user-mode cooperative and on-demand thread-management system. An example of a cooperative workload is one that yields the processor during a periodic interval or while in a wait state, meaning that if a batch request does not have access to all the required data for its execution, it requests its data and then yields its position to a process that needs processing time.

SQLOS is a thin layer that sits between SQL Server and Windows to manage the interaction between these environments. It enables SQL Server to scale on any hardware. This was accomplished by moving to a distributed model and creating an architecture that would foster locality of resources to aid in getting rid of global resource management bottlenecks. The challenge with global resource management is that in large hardware design, global resources cannot keep up with the demands of the system, slowing overall performance. Figure 11-12 highlights the SQLOS components that perform thread scheduling and synchronization, perform SQL Server memory management, provide exception handling, and host the Common Language Runtime (CLR).

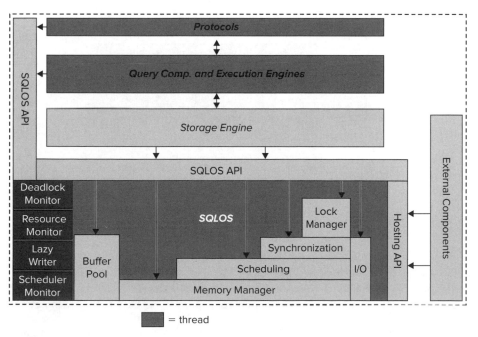

FIGURE 11-12

The goal of this environment is to empower the SQL Server platform to exploit all of today's hardware innovation across the X86, X64, and IA64 platforms. SQLOS was built to bring together the concepts of data locality, support for dynamic configuration, and hardware workload exploitation. This architecture also enables SQL Server 2012 to better support both Cache Coherent Non-Uniform Memory Access (CC-NUMA), Interleave NUMA (NUMA hardware with memory that behaves like an SMP system), Soft-NUMA architecture (registry-activated, software-based emulated NUMA architecture used to partition a large SMP system), and large SMP systems, by affinitizing memory to a few CPUs.

The architecture introduces the concept of a *memory node*, which is one hierarchy between memory and CPUs. There is a memory node for each set of CPUs to localize memory and its content to these CPUs. On an SMP architecture, a memory node shares memory across all CPUs, whereas on a NUMA architecture, a memory node per NUMA node exists. As shown in Figure 11-13, the goal of this design is to support SQL Server scalability across all hardware architectures by enabling the software to adapt to or emulate various hardware architectures.

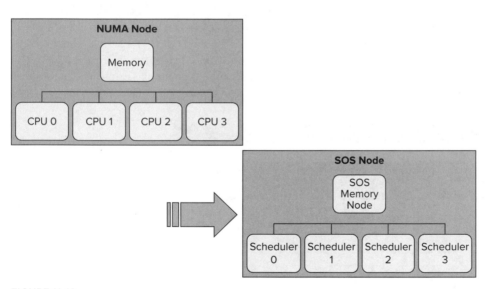

FIGURE 11-13

Schedulers are discussed later in this chapter, but for the purposes of this discussion, they manage the work executed on a CPU.

Memory nodes share the memory allocated by Max Server Memory, setting evenly across a single memory node for SMP system and across one or more memory nodes for NUMA architectures. Each memory node has its own lazy writer thread that manages its workload based on its memory node.

As shown in Figure 11-14, the CPU node is a subset of memory nodes and provides for logical grouping for CPUs.

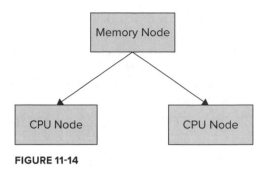

FIGURE 11-14

A CPU node is also a hierarchical structure designed to provide logical grouping for CPUs. The purpose is to localize and load-balance related workloads to a CPU node. On an SMP system, all CPUs would be grouped under a single CPU node, whereas on a NUMA-based system, there would be as many CPU nodes as the system supported. The relationship between a CPU node and a memory node is explicit. There can be many CPU nodes to a memory node, but there can never be more than one memory node to a CPU node. Each level of this hierarchy provides localized services to the components that it manages, resulting in the capability to process and manage workloads in such a way as to exploit the scalability of whatever hardware architecture SQL Server runs on. SQLOS also enables services such as dynamic affinity, load-balancing workloads, dynamic memory capabilities, Dedicated Admin Connection (DAC), and support for partitioned resource management capabilities.

SQL Server 2012 leverages the common caching framework (also part of SQLOS) to achieve fine-grain control over managing the increasing number of cache mechanisms (Cache Store, User Store, and Object Store). This framework improves the behavior of these mechanisms by providing a common policy that can be applied to internal caches to manage them in a wide range of operating conditions. For additional information about these caches, refer to SQL Server 2012 Books Online.

SQL Server 2012 also features a memory-tracking enhancement called the Memory Broker, which enables the tracking of OS-wide memory events. Memory Broker manages and tracks the dynamic consumption of internal SQL Server memory. Based on internal consumption and pressures, it automatically calculates the optimal memory configuration for components such as buffer pool, optimizer, query execution, and caches. It propagates the memory configuration information back to these components for implementation. SQL Server 2012 also supports dynamic management of conventional, locked, and large-page memory, as well as the hot-add memory feature mentioned earlier.

The Windows policy Lock Pages in Memory is granted by default to the local administrative accounts but can be explicitly granted to other user accounts. To ensure that memory runs as expected, it needs this privilege to enable SQL Server to manage which pages are flushed out of memory and which pages are kept in memory.

Hot-add memory provides the ability to introduce additional memory in an operational server without taking it offline. In addition to OEM vendor support, Windows Server 2008 and SQL Server 2012 Enterprise Edition are required to support this feature. Although a sample implementation script is provided in the following section, refer to BOL for additional implementation details.

64-bit Versions of SQL Server 2012

As SQL Server 2012 is only found in an x64 variety, you are in luck. SQL Server 2012 64-bit supports 1TB of RAM, and all of it is native addressable memory so there's no need for /3GB or

/PAE switches in your boot.ini file. The mechanism used to manage AWE memory in 32-bit systems can be used to manage memory on 64-bit systems. Specifically, this mechanism ensures that SQL Server manages what is flushed out of its memory. To enable this feature, the SQL Server service account requires the Lock Pages in Memory privilege. To grant this access to the SQL Service account, use the Windows Group Policy tool (gpedit.msc) and perform the following steps:

1. On the **Start** menu, click **Run**. In the **Open** box, type gpedit.msc. The **Group Policy** dialog box opens.

2. On the **Group Policy** console, expand **Computer Configuration,** and then expand **Windows Settings.**

3. Expand **Security Settings,** and then expand **Local Policies.**

4. Select the **User Rights Assignment** folder.

5. The policies will be displayed in the details pane. In this pane, double-click **Lock pages in memory.**

6. In the **Local Security Policy Setting** dialog box, click **Add.**

7. In the **Select Users or Groups** dialog box, add the account that will be used to run sqlservr.exe.

You need to identify the type of application driving the database and verify that it can benefit from a large SQL Server data-cache allocation. In other words, is it memory-friendly? Simply stated, a database that does not need to keep its data in memory for an extended length of time cannot benefit from a larger memory allocation. For example, a call-center application in which no two operators handle the same customer's information and where no relationship exists between customer records has no need to keep data in memory because data won't be reused. In this case, the application is not deemed memory-friendly; thus, keeping customers' data in memory longer than required would not benefit performance. Another type of inefficient memory use occurs when an application stores excessive amounts of data, beyond what is required by an operation — for example, a table scan. This type of operation suffers from the high cost of data invalidation. Larger amounts of data than are necessary are read into memory and thus must be flushed out.

Data Locality

Data locality is the concept of having all relevant data available to the processor on its local NUMA node while it's processing a request. All memory within a system is available to any processor on any NUMA node. This introduces the concepts of *near memory* and *far memory*. Near memory is the preferred method because it is accessed by a processor on the same NUMA node. As shown in Figure 11-15, accessing far memory is expensive because the request must leave the NUMA node and traverse the system interconnect crossbar to get the NUMA node that holds the required information in its memory.

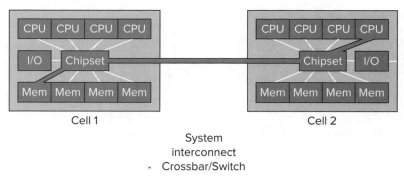

FIGURE 11-15

The cost of accessing objects in far memory versus near memory is often threefold or more. Data locality is managed by the system itself and the way to mitigate issues with it is to install additional memory per NUMA node.

Max Server Memory

When max server memory is kept at the default dynamic setting, SQL Server acquires and frees memory in response to internal and external pressure. SQL Server uses all available memory if left unchecked, so the max server memory setting is strongly recommended. The Windows OS needs some memory to function, so a value of 8GB to 16GB less than the total system memory should be configured. Please refer to the following table for configuration guidelines:

TOTAL SYSTEM MEMORY (GB)	OS RESERVED MEMORY (GB)	MAX SQL SERVER MEMORY (GB)
16	4	12
32	6	26
64	8	56
128	16	112
256	16	240

Index Creation Memory Option

The index creation memory setting, as shown in Figure 11-16, determines how much memory can be used by SQL Server for sort operations during the index-creation process. The default value of 0 enables SQL Server to automatically determine the ideal value. In conditions in which index creation is performed on large tables, pre-allocating space in memory enables a faster index-creation process.

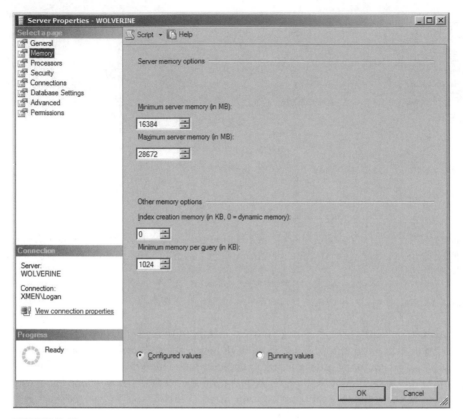

FIGURE 11-16

 After memory is allocated, it is reserved exclusively for the index-creation process, and values are set in KB of memory. The index creation setting should only be changed when issues are observed.

Minimum Memory per Query

You can use the Minimum Memory per Query option to improve the performance of queries that use hashing or sorting operations. SQL Server automatically allocates the minimum amount of memory set in this configuration setting. The default Minimum Memory per Query option setting is equal to 1024KB (refer to Figure 11-16). It is important to ensure that the SQL Server environment has the minimum amount of query memory available. However, in an environment with high query-execution concurrency, if this setting is configured too high, SQL Server waits for a memory allocation to meet the minimum memory level before executing a query.

RESOURCE GOVERNOR

Resource Governor is a SQL Server technology that limits the amount of resources that can be allocated to each database workload from the total resources available to SQL Server 2012. When enabled, Resource Governor classifies each incoming session and determines to which workload group the session belongs. Each workload group is then associated to a resource pool that limits those groups of workloads. Moreover, Resource Governor protects against runaway queries on the SQL Server and unpredictable workload execution, and sets workload priority. For Resource Governor to limit resources, it must differentiate workloads as follows:

➤ Classifies incoming connections to route them to a specific workload group

➤ Monitors resource usage for each workload group

➤ Pools resources to set limits on CPU and memory to each specific resource pool

➤ Identifies workloads and groups them together to a specific pool of resources

➤ Sets workload priority within a workload group

The constraints on Resource Governor are as follows:

➤ It applies only to the SQL Server Relational Engine and not to Analysis Services, Report Services, or Integration Services.

➤ It cannot monitor resources between SQL Server instances. However, you can use Windows Resource Manager (part of Windows) to monitor resources across Windows processes, including SQL Server.

➤ It can limit CPU bandwidth and memory.

➤ A typical OLTP workload consists of small and fast database operations that individually take a fraction of CPU time and may be too miniscule to enable Resource Governor to apply bandwidth limits.

The Basic Elements of Resource Governor

The main elements of Resource Governor include resource pools, workload groups, and classification support, explained in the following sections.

Resource Pools

The resource pools are the physical resources of the SQL Server. During SQL Server installation, two pools are created: *internal* and *default*. The resources that can be managed are min and max CPU and min and max memory. By default, the Resource Governor is disabled; to enable it, use the `ALTER RESOURCE GOVERNOR RECONFIGURE` command. You can disable it again with the command `ALTER RESOURCE GOVERNOR DISABLE`.

The internal pool is used for SQL Server's own internal functions. It contains only the internal workload group; it cannot be altered, and it is not restricted.

The default pool is the predefined user resource pool. It contains the default workload group and can contain user-defined workload groups. It can be altered but cannot be created or dropped.

You can create user-defined pools using the CREATE RESOURCE POOL DDL statement or by using SQL Server Management Studio. Moreover, you can modify a pool by using the ALTER RESOURCE POOL command, and delete it by using the DROP RESOURCE POOL command. You may define any number of resource pools as you want, up to a maximum of 20. This includes the *internal* and *default* pools.

The following syntax creates a resource pool for Resource Governor:

```
CREATE RESOURCE POOL pool_name
[ WITH
        ( [ MIN_CPU_PERCENT = value ]
    [ [ , ] MAX_CPU_PERCENT = value ]
    [ [ , ] CAP_CPU_PERCENT = value ]
    [ [ , ] AFFINITY {SCHEDULER = AUTO | (Scheduler_range_spec) | NUMANODE = (NUMA_
node_range_spec)}]       [ [ , ] MIN_MEMORY_PERCENT = value ]
    [ [ , ] MAX_MEMORY_PERCENT = value ] )
]   [;]
```

Please note that CAP_CPU_PERCENT and AFFINITY are new options available in SQL Server 2012. Please see the Books Online topic for more information which can be found here: http://msdn .microsoft.com/en-us/library/bb934024(v=SQL.110).aspx.

Workload Groups

A workload group is a container for similar sessions according to the defined classification rules and applies the policy to each session of the group. It also contains two predefined workload groups: *internal* and *default*. The internal workload group relates to the internal resource pool and cannot be changed. The default workload group is associated with the default resource pool and is the group used when no session classification user-defined function exists, when a classification failure occurs, or when a classification user-defined function returns NULL.

You can create the user-defined workload group by using the CREATE WORKLOAD GROUP command, modify it by using the ALTER WORKLOAD GROUP command, and drop it by using the DROP WORKLOAD GROUP command.

The following syntax creates a workload group for Resource Governor:

```
CREATE WORKLOAD GROUP group_name
[ WITH
    ( [ IMPORTANCE = { LOW | MEDIUM | HIGH } ]
            [ [ , ] REQUEST_MAX_MEMORY_GRANT_PERCENT = value ]
            [ [ , ] REQUEST_MAX_CPU_TIME_SEC = value ]
            [ [ , ] REQUEST_MEMORY_GRANT_TIMEOUT_SEC = value ]
            [ [ , ] MAX_DOP = value ]
            [ [ , ] GROUP_MAX_REQUESTS = value ] )
  ]
[ USING { pool_name | "default" } ] [ ; ]
```

You can apply seven configuration settings to a workload group:

➤ Maximum memory allocation per request

➤ Maximum CPU time per request

➤ Resource time-out per request

➤ Relative importance setting per request

➤ Workgroup limit per number of requests

➤ Maximum degree of parallelism

➤ Specific resource pool

Classification

Resource Governor supports classifying incoming connections into existing workload groups. It supports system-wide provided rules and user-defined rules using connection-specific attributes. In the absence of a user-defined classification function, it can use the default workload group. After the user-defined classification function is registered with Resource Governor, the function is executed for every new connection, and the connection is routed to one of the existing workload groups to be limited by the resource pool. Only one user-defined classification function can be designated as a classifier, and after registering it, it takes effect after an ALTER RESOURCE GOVERNOR RECONFIGURE command is executed.

Resource Governor uses connection-specific functions such as HOST_NAME(), APP_NAME(), SUSER_NAME(), SUSER_SNAME(), IS_SRVROLEMEMBER() and IS_MEMBER() to identify each connection.

Figure 11-17 shows the components of Resource Governor and their relationships.

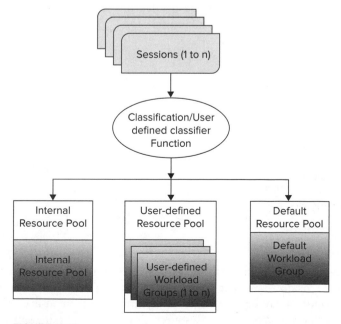

FIGURE 11-17

Following is a Resource Governor Implementation example that creates three resource pools to support the resource requirements for three different workload groups.

1. First, create three resource pools: adhoc, reports, and admin requests:

Available for
download on
Wrox.com

LISTING 11-6: ResourcePools

```
USE Master;
BEGIN TRAN;
CREATE RESOURCE POOL poolAdhoc with
( MIN_CPU_PERCENT = 10, MAX_CPU_PERCENT = 30,
MIN_MEMORY_PERCENT= 15, MAX_MEMORY_PERCENT= 25);

CREATE RESOURCE POOL poolReports with
( MIN_CPU_PERCENT = 20, MAX_CPU_PERCENT = 35,
MIN_MEMORY_PERCENT= 15,  MAX_MEMORY_PERCENT= 45);

CREATE RESOURCE POOL poolAdmin with
( MIN_CPU_PERCENT = 15, MAX_CPU_PERCENT = 25,
MIN_MEMORY_PERCENT= 15,  MAX_MEMORY_PERCENT= 30);
```

2. Next, create three workload groups and associate them with the three resource pools:

```
CREATE WORKLOAD GROUP groupAdhoc using poolAdhoc;
CREATE WORKLOAD GROUP groupReports with (MAX_DOP = 8) using poolReports;
CREATE WORKLOAD GROUP groupAdmin using poolAdmin;
GO
```

3. Create a user-defined classification function that identifies each new session and routes it to one of the three workload groups. Any request that cannot be identified by the user-defined classification function is directed to the default workload group:

```
CREATE FUNCTION rgclassifier_v1() RETURNS SYSNAME
WITH SCHEMABINDING
AS
BEGIN
    DECLARE @grp_name AS SYSNAME
      IF (SUSER_NAME() = 'sa')
          SET @grp_name = 'groupAdmin'
      IF (APP_NAME() LIKE '%MANAGEMENT STUDIO%')
          OR (APP_NAME() LIKE '%QUERY ANALYZER%')
          SET @grp_name = 'groupAdhoc'
      IF (APP_NAME() LIKE '%REPORT SERVER%')
          SET @grp_name = 'groupReports'
    RETURN @grp_name
END;
GO
```

4. Next, the user-defined classification function needs to be registered to Resource Governor. All these operations are contained inside an explicit transaction. That's a preventive measure so that if a user error occurs, it can be rolled back. In addition, only one user-defined classification function can be registered to the Resource Governor at any one time:

```
ALTER RESOURCE GOVERNOR WITH (CLASSIFIER_FUNCTION= dbo.rgclassifier_v1);
COMMIT TRAN;
```

5. Finally, to have these new changes take effect or to enable Resource Governor, run the following command:

```
ALTER RESOURCE GOVERNOR RECONFIGURE;
```

Using Resource Governor from SQL Server 2012 Management Studio

From inside SQL Server 2012 Management Studio in Object Explorer, Resource Governor is in the Management node. By default, Resource Governor is disabled. To enable it, right-click Resource Governor and then click Enable. Moreover, from Object Explorer inside the Management node, right-click Resource Governor, and then click Properties to add, delete, or modify properties of the resource pools and workload groups or to add or remove a user-defined classification function and enable Resource Governor. From the Resource Governor Properties dialog, you can see that two resource pools, Internal and Default, with two corresponding workload groups, are visible. These are created by SQL Server 2012 during installation. No classification function is available until one is created. If Resource Governor is enabled, it uses the default system-defined rules and the default pool, as configured in Figure 11-18.

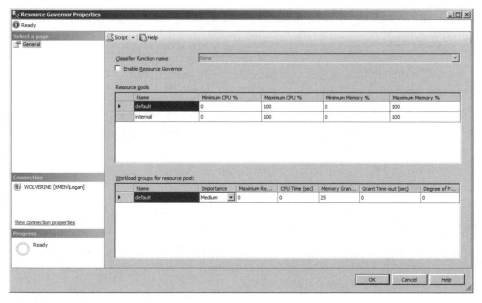

FIGURE 11-18

After running the script in Listing 11-6 to create the three user-defined resource pools, workload groups, and the user-defined classification function, and after enabling the Resource Governor, the properties should match what is shown in Figure 11-19.

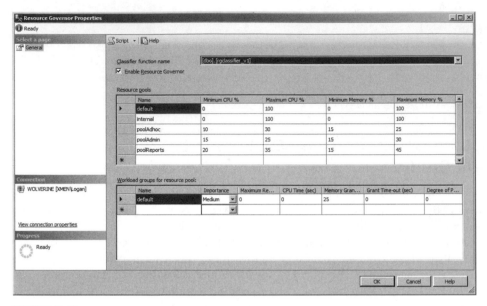

FIGURE 11-19

Monitoring Resource Governor

SQL Server 2012 includes two performance objects to collect workload group and pool statistics for each SQL Server instance:

> ➤ **SQLServer: Resource Pool Stats for resource-specific statistics:** Please see this article for more information: `http://msdn.microsoft.com/en-us/library/cc645958(v=SQL.110).aspx`

> ➤ **SQLServer: Workload Group Stats for workload-specific statistics:** Please see this article for more information: `http://msdn.microsoft.com/en-us/library/cc627354(v=SQL.110).aspx`

Moreover, there are Resource Governor Dynamic Management Views (DMVs) that return information specific to resource statistics, as indicated in the following table.

RESOURCE GOVERNOR DYNAMIC MANAGEMENT VIEWS	DESCRIPTION
`sys.dm_resource_governor_configuration`	For current in-memory configuration state
`sys.dm_resource_governor_resource_pools`	For resource pool state, configuration, and statistics
`sys.dm_resource_governor_workload_groups`	For workload group statisticvs and in-memory configuration

For more detailed information on Resource Governor, refer to SQL 2012 Books Online under "Resource Governor." This can be found at: `http://msdn .microsoft.com/en-us/library/bb933866(v=SQL.110).aspx.`

SUMMARY

There are many important points to consider when setting up and configuring SQL Server 2012. Database files (data and log files) should be placed on separate LUNs, which are made up of fast disks. tempdb should be placed on its own set of disks which should be the fastest possible. Partitioning can be used to increase performance and offers manageability advantages. Compression can be used to increase I/O performance but care needs to be taken not to overtax the CPU. CPU and memory can be tweaked from within SQL Server, but care must also be taken here not to use settings that are detrimental. Remember: test, test, test!

If you apply these lessons correctly, SQL Server 2012 is more than capable of tuning itself automatically to predictably provide the availability and performance to support the requirements of your enterprise.

12

Monitoring Your SQL Server

WHAT'S IN THIS CHAPTER

- ➤ Monitor SQL Server Behavior with Dynamic Management

- ➤ Monitor SQL Server Error Log, and the Windows Event Logs

- ➤ A Quick Look at the Management Data Warehouse, UMDW, and Utility Control Point

- ➤ Monitoring SQL with the SCOM Management Pack, SQL Server Best Practices Analyzer, and System Center Advisor

Implementing good monitoring enables you to move from reactively dealing with events to proactively diagnosing problems and fixing them before your users are even aware there is a problem. This chapter teaches you how to proactively monitor your SQL Server system so that you can prevent or react to events before the server gets to the point where users begin calling.

Here's a quick example. Say you recently took over an existing system after the DBA moved to a different team. This system's applications ran well, but there was something that needed fixing every other day — transaction logs filling, tempdb out of space, not enough locks, and filegroups filling up; Nothing major, just a slow steady trickle of problems that needed fixing. This is the DBA's death of 1,000 cuts. Your time is sucked away doing these essential maintenance tasks until you get to the point where you don't have time to do anything else.

After a few weeks of this, you manage to put some new monitoring in place and make several proactive changes to resolve issues before anything breaks. These changes aren't rocket science; they are simple things such as moving data to a new filegroup, turning on autogrow for several files and extending them to allow a known amount of growth, and rebuilding badly fragmented indexes that were reserving unneeded space. All this takes considerably less time than dealing with the steady stream of failures and provided a greatly improved experience for the users of this system.

So what does it take to monitor this system? Nothing dramatic — just a few simple steps, mostly some T-SQL monitoring of tables, database and filegroup free space, index usage, and fragmentation. I did a few things to monitor resource usage and help find the key pain points. After you understood the pain points, you can take a few steps to get ahead of the curve on fixing things.

Now that you've seen the value in monitoring SQL Server, you can learn how to do this for yourself.

THE GOAL OF MONITORING

The goal when monitoring databases is to see what's going on inside SQL Server — namely, how effectively SQL Server uses the server resources (CPU, Memory, and I/O). You want this information so that you can see how well the system performs. The data needs to be captured over time to enable you to build a profile of what the system normally looks like: How much of what resource do you use for each part of the system's working cycle? From the data collected over time you can start to build a baseline of "normal" activity. That baseline enables you to identify abnormal activities that might lead to issues if left unchecked.

Abnormal activity could be an increase in a specific table's growth rate, a change in replication throughput, or a query or job taking longer than usual or using more of a scarce server resource than you expected. Identifying these anomalies before they become an issue that causes your users to call and complain makes for a much easier life. Using this data, you can identify what might be about to break, or where changes need to be made to rectify the root cause before the problem becomes entrenched.

Sometimes this monitoring is related to performance issues such as slow-running queries or deadlocks, but in many cases the data points to something that you can change to avoid problems in the future.

This philosophy is about the equivalent of "an apple a day keeps the doctor away" — preventative medicine for your SQL Server.

Determining Your Monitoring Objectives

Before you start monitoring you must first clearly identify your reasons for monitoring. These reasons may include the following:

➤ Establish a baseline.

➤ Identify new trends before they become problems.

➤ Monitor database growth.

➤ Identify daily, weekly, and monthly maintenance tasks.

➤ Identify performance changes over time.

➤ Audit user activity.

➤ Diagnose a specific performance problem.

Establishing a Baseline

Monitoring is extremely important to help ensure the smooth running of your SQL Server systems. However, just monitoring by itself, and determining the value of a key performance metric at any point in time, is not of great value unless you have a sound baseline to compare the metric against. Are 50 transactions per second good, mediocre, or bad? If the server runs at 75 percent CPU, is that normal?

Is it normal for this time of day, on this day of the week, during this month of the year? With a baseline of the system's performance, you immediately have something to compare the current metrics against.

If your baseline shows that you normally get 30 transactions per second, then 50 transactions per second might be good; the system can process more transactions. However, it may also be an indication that something else is going on, which has caused an increase in the transactions. What your baseline looks like depends on your system, of course. In some cases it might be a set of Performance Monitor logs with key server resource and SQL counters captured during several periods of significant system activity, or stress tests. In another case, it might be the results of analysis of a SQL Profiler trace captured during a period of high activity. The analysis might be as simple as a list of the stored procedure calls made by a particular application, with the call frequency.

To determine whether your SQL Server system performs optimally, take performance measurements at a regular interval over time, even when no problem occurs, to establish a server performance baseline. How many samples and how long each needs to be are determined by the nature of the workload on your servers. If your servers have a cyclical workload, the samples should aim to query at multiple points in several cycles to allow a good estimation of min, max, and average rates. If the workload is uniform, then fewer samples over shorter periods can provide a good indication of min, max, and average rates. At a minimum, use baseline performance to determine the following:

➤ Peak and off-peak hours of operation

➤ Query or batch response time

Another consideration is how often the baseline should be recaptured. In a system that is rapidly growing, you may need to recapture a baseline frequently. When current performance has changed by 15 to 25 percent compared to the old baseline, it is a good point to consider recapturing the baseline.

Comparing Current Metrics to the Baseline

A key part of comparing current metrics to those in the baseline is determining an acceptable limit from the baseline outside of which the current metric is not acceptable and which flags an issue that needs investigating.

What is acceptable here depends on the application and the specific metric. For example, a metric looking at free space in a database filegroup for a system with massive data growth and an aggressive archiving strategy might set a limit of 20 percent free space before triggering some kind of alert. On a different system with little database growth, that same metric might be set to just 5 percent.

You must make your own judgment of what is an acceptable limit for deviation from the baseline based on your knowledge of how your system is growing and changing.

CHOOSING THE APPROPRIATE MONITORING TOOLS

After you define your monitoring goals, you should select the appropriate tools for monitoring. The following list describes the basic monitoring tools:

➤ **Performance Monitor:** Performance Monitor is a useful tool that tracks resource use on Microsoft operating systems. It can monitor resource usage for the server and provide information specific to SQL Server either locally or for a remote server. You can use it to capture a baseline of server resource usage, or it can monitor over longer periods of time to help identify trends. It can also be useful for ad hoc monitoring to help identify any resource bottlenecks responsible for performance issues. You can configure it to generate alerts when predetermined thresholds are exceeded.

➤ **Extended Events:** Extended Events provide a highly scalable and configurable architecture to enable you to collect information to troubleshoot issues with SQL Server. It is a lightweight system with a graphical UI that enables new sessions to be easily created.

Extended Events provides the `system_health` session. This is a default health session that runs with minimal overhead, and continuously collects system data that may help you troubleshoot your performance problem without having to create your own custom Extended Events session.

While exploring the Extended Events node in SSMS, you may notice an additional default session, the `AlwaysOn_health` session. This is an undocumented session created to provide health monitoring for Availability Groups.

➤ **SQL Profiler:** This tool is a graphical application that enables you to capture a trace of events that occurred in SQL Server. All SQL Server events can be captured by this tool into the trace. The trace can be stored in a file or written to a SQL Server table.

SQL Profiler also enables the captured events to be replayed. This makes it a valuable tool for workload analysis, testing, and performance tuning. It can monitor a SQL Server instance locally or remotely. You can also use the features of SQL Profiler within a custom application, by using the Profiler system stored procedures.

SQL Profiler has been deprecated in SQL Server 2012, so you should plan on moving away from using this tool, and instead use Extended events for trace capture activities, and Distributed Replay for replaying events.

➤ **SQL Trace:** SQL Trace is the T-SQL stored procedure way to invoke a SQL Server trace without needing to start up the SQL Profiler application. It requires a little more work to set up, but it's a lightweight way to capture a trace; and because it's scriptable, it enables the automation of trace capture, making it easy to repeatedly capture the same events.

With the announcement of the deprecation of SQL Server profiler, you should start moving all your trace based monitoring to Extended Events.

➤ **Default trace:** Introduced with SQL Server 2005, the default trace is a lightweight trace that runs in a continuous loop and captures a small set of key database and server events. This is useful in diagnosing events that may have occurred when no other monitoring was in place.

➤ **Activity Monitor in SQL Server Management Studio:** This tool graphically displays the following information:

  ➤ Processes running on an instance of SQL Server

  ➤ Resource Waits

  ➤ Data File IO activity

  ➤ Recent Expensive Queries

➤ **Dynamic management views and functions:** Dynamic management views and functions return server state information that you can use to monitor the health of a server instance, diagnose problems, and tune performance. These are one of the best tools added to SQL Server 2005 for ad hoc monitoring. These views provide a snapshot of the exact state of SQL Server at the point they are queried. This is extremely valuable, but you may need to do a lot of work to interpret the meaning of some of the data returned, because they often provide just a running total of some internal counter. You need to add quite a bit of additional code to provide useful trend information. There are numerous examples in the "Monitoring with Dynamic Management Views and Functions" section later in this chapter that show how to do this.

➤ **System Stored procedures:** Some system-stored procedures provide useful information for SQL Server monitoring, such as sp_who, sp_who2, sp_lock, and several others. These stored procedures are best for ad hoc monitoring, not trend analysis.

➤ **Utility Control Point (UCP):** The Utility Control Point is a management construct introduced in SQL Server 2008 R2. It adds to the Data Collection sets of the Management Data Warehouse and includes reports on activity within a SQL Server Utility. The SQL Server Utility is another addition for SQL Server 2008 R2, and is a management container for server resources that can be monitored using the UCP.

➤ **Standard Reports:** The standard reports that ship with SQL Server are a great way to get a look into what's happening inside SQL Server without needing to dive into DMVs, Extended Events, and the default Trace.

➤ **SQL Server Best Practice Analyzer:** A set of rules implemented in Microsoft Baseline Configuration Analyzer (MBCA) that implement checks for SQL Server best practices. The tool is available as a download, and has a fixed set of rules. Also see System Center Advisor.

➤ **System Center Advisor:** An extension of the SQL Server Best Practice Analyzer, this is a cloud-based utility to analyze your SQL Servers and provide feedback on their configuration and operation against the set of accepted best practices for configuring and operating SQL Server.

➤ **System Center Management Pack:** SQL Server has had a management pack for some time now, but it's not well known, or used by DBAs. The Management Pack enables you to create exception-driven events that drive operator interaction with SQL Server to resolve specific issues. The rest of the chapter discusses these tools in detail.

PERFORMANCE MONITOR

Performance Monitor, also known as Perfmon, or System Monitor, is the User Interface that most readers will become familiar with as their interface with Performance Monitoring. Performance Monitor is a Windows tool that's found in the Administrative Tools folder on any Windows PC, or Server. It has the ability to graphically show performance counter data as a graph (the default setting) or as a histogram, or in a textual report format.

Performance Monitor is an important tool because not only does it inform you about how SQL Server performs, it is also the tool that indicates how Windows performs. Performance Monitor provides a huge set of counters, but don't be daunted. This section covers a few of them, but there is likely no one who understands all of them.

This section is not an introduction to using Performance Monitor. (Although later in this section you learn about two valuable tools, Logman, and Relog, that make using Performance Monitor a lot easier in a production environment.) This section instead focuses on how you can use the capabilities of this tool to diagnose performance problems in your system. For general information about using Performance Monitor, look at the Windows 7 or Windows Server 2008 R2 documentation.

As mentioned in the previous section "The Goal of Monitoring," you need to monitor three server resources:

➤ CPU

➤ Memory

➤ I/O (primarily disk I/O)

Monitor these key counters over a "typical" interesting business usage period. Depending on your business usage cycles, this could be a particular day, or couple of days when the system experiences peaks of usage. You would not gather data over a weekend or holiday. You want to get an accurate picture of what's happening during typical business usage, and not when the system is idle. You should also take into account any specific knowledge of your business and monitor for peaks of activity such as end of week, end of month, or other special activities.

> **DETERMINING SAMPLE TIME**
>
> The question of what sample period to use often comes up. (Sample period is displayed as the "Sample Every" value on the general tab of a Performance Monitor chart's property page.) A general rule of thumb is that the shorter the overall monitoring period, then the shorter the sample period. If you are capturing data for 5-10 minutes you might use a one second sample interval. If you are capturing data for multiple days, then 15 seconds, 30 seconds, or even 1-5 minutes might be better sample periods. The real decision points are around managing the overall capture file size, and ensuring that the data you capture has fine enough resolution to let you discern interesting events. If you are looking for something that happens over a short period of time, then you need an even shorter sample time to be able to see it. So for an event that you think might last 10-15 seconds, you should aim for a sample rate that gives you at least 3-5 samples during that period; for the 15 second event, you might choose a 3 second sample period, which would give you 5 samples during the 15 second event. One last point to consider is that if you're interested in maintenance activity performance, such as for backups, index maintenance, data archival, and so on, then that actually is a case where you might want to monitor at night and on weekends, and during normal business down time, as that's when the maintenance activities are typically scheduled to run.

CPU Resource Counters

Several counters show the state of the available CPU resources. Bottlenecks due to CPU resource shortages are frequently caused by problems such as more users than expected, one or more users running expensive queries, or routine operational activities such as index rebuilding.

The first step to find the cause of the bottleneck is to identify that the bottleneck is a CPU resource issue. The following counters can help you do this:

➤ **Object: Processor - Counter: % Processor Time:** This counter determines the percentage of time each processor is busy. There is a `_Total` instance of the counter that for multiprocessor systems measures the total processor utilization across all processors in the system. On multiprocessor machines, the `_Total` instance might not show a processor bottleneck when one exists. This can happen when queries execute that run on either a single thread or fewer threads than there are processors. This is often the case on OLTP systems, or where MAXDOP has been set to less than the number of processors available.

In this case, a query can be bottlenecked on the CPU as it's using 100 percent of the single CPU it's scheduled to run on, or in the case of a parallel query as it's using 100 percent of multiple CPUs, but in both cases other idle CPUs are available that this query is not using.

If the `_Total` instance of this counter is regularly at more than 80 percent, that's a good indication that the server is reaching the limits of the current hardware. Your options here are to buy more or faster processors, or optimize the queries to use less CPU. See Chapter 11, "Optimizing SQL Server 2012," for a detailed discussion on hardware.

➤ **Object: System - Counter: Processor Queue Length:** The processor queue length is a measure of how many threads sit in a ready state waiting on a processor to become available to run them. Interpreting and using this counter is an advanced operating system performance-tuning option needed only when investigating complex multithreaded code problems. For SQL Server systems, processor utilization can identify CPU bottlenecks much more easily than trying to interpret this counter.

➤ **Object: Processor - Counter: % Privileged Time:** This counter indicates the percentage of the sample interval when the processor was executing in kernel mode. On a SQL Server system, kernel mode time is time spent executing system services such as the memory manager, or more likely, the I/O manager. In most cases, privileged time equates to time spent reading and writing from disk or the network.

It is useful to monitor this counter when you find an indication of high CPU usage. If this counter indicates that more than 15 percent to 20 percent of processor time is spent executing privileged code, you may have a problem, possibly with one of the I/O drivers, or possibly with a filter driver installed by antivirus software scanning the SQL data or log files.

➤ **Object: Process - Counter: % Processor Time - Instance: sqlservr:** This counter measures the percentage of the sample interval during which the SQL Server Process uses the available processors. When the Processor % Processor Time counter is high, or you suspect a CPU bottleneck, look at this counter to confirm that it is SQL Server using the CPU, and not some other process.

➤ **Object: Process - Counter: % Privileged Time - Instance: sqlservr:** This counter measures the percentage of the sample that the SQL Server Process runs in kernel mode. This will be the kernel mode portion of the total %ProcessorTime shown in the previous counter. As with the previous counter, this counter is useful when investigating high CPU usage on the server to confirm that it is SQL Server using the processor resource, and not some other process.

➤ **Object: Process - Counter: % User Time - Instance: sqlservr:** This counter measures the percentage of the sample that the SQL Server Process runs in User mode. This is the User mode portion of the total %ProcessorTime shown in the previous counter. Combined with %Privileged, time should add up to %ProcessorTime.

After determining that you have a processor bottleneck, the next step is to track down its root cause. This might lead you to a single query, a set of queries, a set of users, an application, or an operational task causing the bottleneck. To further isolate the root cause, you need to dig deeper into what runs inside SQL Server. See the Performance Monitoring Tools section later in this chapter to help you do this. After you identify a processor bottleneck, consult the relevant chapter for details on how to resolve it. See Chapter 10 for information on "Configuring the Server for Optimal Performance," Chapter 11 for "Optimizing SQL Server 2012," Chapter 13 for "Performance Tuning T-SQL," and Chapter 14 for information on "Indexing Your Database."

Disk Activity

SQL Server relies on the Windows operating system to perform I/O operations. The disk system handles the storage and movement of data on your system, giving it a powerful influence on your system's overall responsiveness. Disk I/O is frequently the cause of bottlenecks in a system. You need to observe many factors in determining the performance of the disk system, including the level of usage, the rate of throughput, the amount of disk space available, and whether a queue is developing for the disk systems. Unless your database fits into physical memory, SQL Server constantly brings database pages into and out of the buffer pool. This generates substantial I/O traffic. Similarly, log records need to be flushed to the disk before a transaction can be declared committed. SQL Server 2005 started to make considerably more use of `tempdb` and this hasn't changed with SQL Server 2012, so beginning with SQL Server 2005, `tempdb` I/O activity can also cause a performance bottleneck.

Many of the disk I/O factors are interrelated. For example, if disk utilization is high, disk throughput might peak, latency for each I/O starts to increase, and eventually a queue might begin to form. These conditions can result in increased response time, causing performance to slow.

Several other factors can impact I/O performance, such as fragmentation or low disk space. Make sure you monitor for free disk space and take action when it falls below a given threshold. In general, the level of free space to raise an alert is when free disk space falls below 15 percent to 20 percent. Above this level of free space, many disk systems start to slow down because they need to spend more time searching for increasingly fragmented free space.

You should look at several key metrics when monitoring I/O performance:

➤ **Throughput, IOPS:** How many I/Os per second (IOPS) can the storage subsystem deliver?

➤ **Throughput, MB/sec:** How many MB/sec can the I/O subsystem deliver?

➤ **Latency:** How long does each I/O request take?

➤ **Queue depth:** How many I/O requests are waiting in the queue?

For each of these metrics you should also distinguish between read-and-write activity.

Physical Versus Logical Disk Counters

There is often confusion around the difference between Physical and Logical Disk Counters. This section explains the similarities and differences, provides specific examples of different disk configurations, and explains how to interpret the results seen on the different disk configurations.

One way to think about the difference between the logical and the physical disk counters is that the logical disk counters monitor I/O where the I/O request leaves the application layer (or as the requests enter kernel mode), whereas the physical disk counters monitor I/O as it leaves the bottom of the kernel storage driver stack. Figure 12-1 shows the I/O software stack and illustrates where the logical disk and physical disk counters monitor I/O.

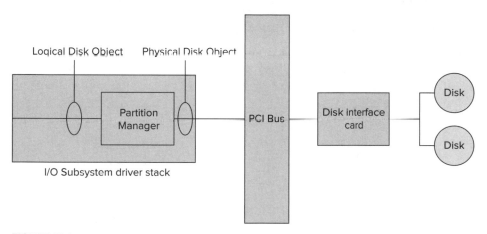

FIGURE 12-1

In some scenarios the logical and physical counters provide the same results; in others they provide different results.

The different I\O subsystem configurations that affect the values displayed by the logical and physical disk counters are discussed in the following sections.

Single Disk, Single Partition

Figure 12-2 shows a single disk with a single partition. In this case there will be a single set of logical disk counters and a single set of physical disk counters. This configuration works well in a small SQL Server configuration with a few disks, where the SQL data and log files are already spread over multiple Single Disk, Single Partition disks.

FIGURE 12-2

Single Disk, Multiple Partitions

Figure 12-3 shows a single disk split into multiple partitions. In this case, there are multiple instances of the logical disk counters, one per partition, and just a single set of physical disk counters. This kind of configuration doesn't provide any performance advantages, but it does allow more accurate monitoring of I/O to the different partitions. If you place different sets of data onto different partitions, you can see how much I/O goes to each set by monitoring the logical disk counters.

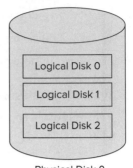

Physical Disk 0

FIGURE 12-3

One danger with this configuration is that you may be mislead into thinking you actually have different physical disks, and so you think you are isolating data IO from Log IO from `tempdb` IO because they are on different "drives," when in fact, all the IO is going to the same physical disk.

An example of this might be to put SQL log files on one partition, `tempdb` data files on another partition, a filegroup for data on another partition, a filegroup for indexes on another partition, and backups on another partition.

Multiple Disks, Single Volume — Software RAID

Figure 12-4 shows multiple disks configured in a software RAID array and mounted as a single volume. In this configuration there is a single set of logical disk counters and multiple sets of physical disk counters.

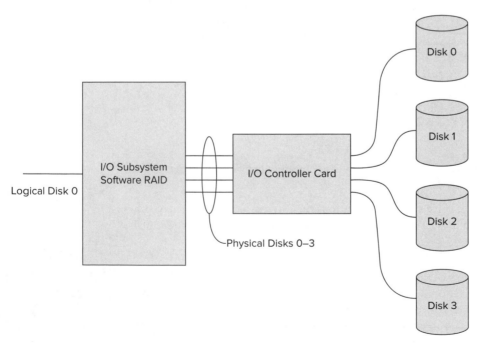

FIGURE 12-4

This configuration works well in a small SQL Server configuration where the hardware budget won't stretch to a RAID array controller, but multiple disks are available and you want to create a RAID volume spanning them. For more information on RAID, refer to Chapter 10, "Configuring the Server for Optimal Performance."

Multiple Disks, Single Volume — Hardware RAID

Figure 12-5 shows a hardware RAID array. In this configuration, multiple disks are managed by the hardware RAID controller. The operating system sees only a single physical disk presented to it by the array controller card. The disk counters appear to be the same as the single disk, single partition configuration — that is, a single set of physical disk counters and a corresponding single set of logical disk counters.

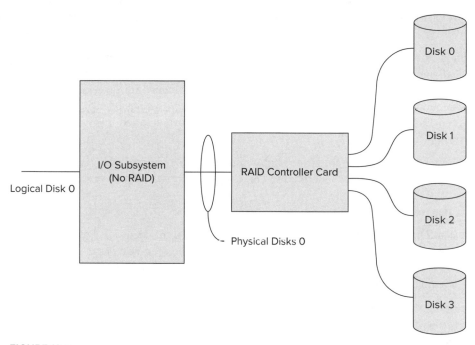

FIGURE 12-5

The Object: Physical Disk - *Counter*: Disk Writes/Sec and Object: Physical Disk - *Counter*: Disk Reads/Sec provide information about how many I/O operations are performed per second over the sample interval. This information is useful to determine whether the I/O subsystem is approaching capacity. It can be used in isolation to compare against the theoretical ideal for the I/O subsystem based upon the number and type of disks in the I/O subsystem. It is also useful when compared against the I/O subsystem baseline to determine how close you are to maximum capacity.

Monitoring I/O Throughput - MB/Sec

The Object: Physical Disk - *Counter*: Disk Write Bytes/Sec and Object: Physical Disk - *Counter*: Disk Read Bytes/Sec provide information about how many MB/Sec are read and written to and from the disk over the sample interval. This is an average over the sample period, so with long sample periods it may average out to big peaks and troughs in throughput. Over a short sample period, this may fluctuate dramatically, as it sees the results of one or two larger I/Os flooding the I/O subsystem. This information is useful to determine whether the I/O subsystem is approaching its capacity.

As with the other Disk IO counters, Disk Read Bytes/Sec and Disk Write Bytes/Sec can be used in isolation to compare against the theoretical throughput for the number and type of disks in the I/O subsystem, but it is more useful when it can be compared against a baseline of the maximum throughput available from the I/O subsystem.

Monitoring I/O Latency

The Object: Physical Disk - *Counter*: Avg. Disk Sec/Write and Object: Physical Disk - *Counter*: Avg. Disk Sec/Read provide information on how long each read-and-write operation is taking. These two counters show average latency. It is an average taken over every I/O issued during the sample period.

This information is extremely useful and can be used independently to determine how well the I/O subsystem deals with the current I/O load. Ideally, these counters should be below 5–10 milliseconds (ms). On larger data warehouse or decision support systems, it is acceptable for the values of these counters to be in the range of 10–20 ms. Sustained values over 50 ms are an indication that the I/O subsystem is heavily stressed, and that a more detailed investigation of I/O should be undertaken.

These counters show performance degradations before queuing starts. These counters should also be used with the following disk queue length counters to help diagnose I/O subsystem bottlenecks.

Monitoring I/O Queue Depth

The Object: Physical Disk - *Counter*: Avg. Disk Write Queue Length and Object: Physical Disk - *Counter*: Avg. Disk Read Queue Length provide information on the read-and-write queue depth. These two counters show the average queue depth over the sample period. Disk queue lengths greater than 2 for a single physical disk indicate that there may be an I/O subsystem bottleneck.

Correctly interpreting these counters is more challenging when the I/O subsystem is a RAID array, or when the disk controller has built-in caching and intelligence. In these cases, the controller will have its own queue, which is designed to absorb and buffer, and effectively hide from this counter, any queuing going on at the disk level. For these reasons, monitoring these counters is less useful than monitoring the latency counters. If these counters do show queue lengths consistently greater than 2, it's a good indication of a potential I/O subsystem bottleneck.

Monitoring Individual Instances Versus Total

In multidisk systems with several disks, monitoring all the preceding counters for all available disks provides a mass of fluctuating counters to monitor. In some cases, monitoring the _Total instance, which combines the values for all instances, can be a useful way to detect I/O problems. The scenario in which this doesn't work is when I/O to different disks has different characteristics. In this case, the _Total instance shows a reasonably good average number, although some disks may sit idle and others melt from all the I/O requests they service.

Monitoring Transfers Versus Read and Write

One thing you may have noticed in the list of counters is that the transfer counters are missing. This is because the transfer counters average out the read-and-write activity. For a system that is heavy on one kind of I/O at the expense of the other (reads versus writes), the transfer counters do not show an accurate picture of what happens.

In addition, read I/O and write I/O usually have different characteristics, and different performance than the underlying storage. Monitoring a combination of two potentially disparate values doesn't provide a meaningful metric.

Monitoring %Disk Counters

Another set of disk counters missing from this list are all the %Disk counters. Although these counters can provide interesting information, there are enough problems with the results (that is, the total percentage can often exceed 100) that these counters don't provide a useful detailed metric.

If you can afford to monitor all the counters detailed in the preceding sections, you can have a much more complete view of what's going on with your system.

If you want a few simple metrics that provide a good approximate indication of overall I/O subsystem activity, then the %Disk Time, %Disk Read Time, and %Disk Write time counters can provide that.

Isolating Disk Activity Created by SQL Server

All the counters you should monitor to find disk bottlenecks have been discussed. However, you may have multiple applications running on your servers, and one of those other applications could cause a lot of disk I/O. To confirm that the disk bottleneck is being caused by SQL Server, you should isolate the disk activities created by SQL Server. Monitor the following counters to determine whether the disk activity is caused by SQL server:

➤ SQL Server: Buffer Manager: Page reads/sec

➤ SQL Server: Buffer Manager: Page writes/sec

Sometimes your application is too big for the hardware you have, and a problem that appears to be related to disk I/O may be resolved by adding more RAM. Make sure you do a proper analysis before making a decision. That's where trend analysis is helpful because you can see how the performance problem evolved.

Is Disk Performance the Bottleneck?

With the help of the disk counters, you can determine whether you have disk bottlenecks in your system. Several conditions must exist for you to make that determination, including a sustained rate of disk activity well above your baseline, persistent disk queue length longer than two per disk, and the absence of a significant amount of paging. Without this combination of factors, it is unlikely that you have a disk bottleneck in your system.

Sometimes your disk hardware may be faulty, and that could cause a lot of interrupts to the CPU. Another possibility could be that a processor bottleneck is caused by a disk subsystem, which can have a systemwide performance impact. Make sure you consider this when you analyze the performance data.

If, after monitoring your system, you come to the conclusion that you have a disk bottleneck, you need to resolve the problem. See Chapter 10, for more details on configuring SQL Server for optimal performance, Chapter 11 for optimizing SQL Server, and Chapter 13, "Performance Tuning T-SQL" for SQL query tuning.

Memory Usage

Memory is perhaps the most critical resource affecting SQL Server performance. Without enough memory, SQL Server is forced to keep reading and writing data to disk to complete a query. Disk access is anywhere from 1,000 to 100,000 times slower than memory access, depending on exactly how fast your memory is.

Because of this, ensuring SQL Server has enough memory is one of the most important steps you can take to keep SQL Server running as fast as possible. Monitoring memory usage, how much is available, and how well SQL Server uses the available memory is therefore a vitally important step.

In an ideal environment, SQL Server runs on a dedicated machine and shares memory only with the operating system and other essential applications. However, in many environments, budget or other constraints mean that SQL shares a server with other applications. In this case you need to monitor how much memory each application uses and verify that everyone plays well together.

Low memory conditions can slow the operation of the applications and services on your system. Monitor an instance of SQL Server periodically to confirm that the memory usage is within typical ranges. When your server is low on memory, *paging* — the process of moving virtual memory back and forth between physical memory and the disk — can be prolonged, resulting in more work for your disks. The paging activity might need to compete with other transactions performed, intensifying disk bottleneck.

Since SQL Server is one of the best behaved server applications available, when the operating system triggers the low memory notification event, SQL releases memory for other applications to use; it actually starves itself of memory if another memory-greedy application runs on the machine. The good news is that SQL releases only a small amount of memory at a time, so it may take hours, and even days, before SQL starts to suffer. Unfortunately, if the other application desperately needs more memory, it can take hours before SQL frees up enough memory for the other application to run without excessive paging. Since issues such as those mentioned can cause significant problems, monitor the counters described in the following sections to identify memory bottlenecks.

Solid State Drives (SSD) are starting to appear at lower cost points that make them attractive for use in more database configurations. Although the I/O throughput of SSDs is 100s to 1000s of times larger and faster than even the fastest spinning disks, their throughput is still considerably lower, and their latency higher than direct memory access. However, it is still too soon to determine how the slow march of solid state devices can alter how you think about memory usage in SQL Server.

Monitoring Available Memory

The Object: Memory - *Counter*: Available Mbytes reports how many megabytes of memory are currently available for programs to use. It is the best single indication that there may be a memory bottleneck on the server.

Determining the appropriate value for this counter depends on the size of the system you monitor. If this counter routinely shows values less than 128MB, you may have a serious memory shortage.

On a server with 4GB or more of physical memory (RAM), the operating system can send a low memory notification when available memory reaches 128MB. At this point, SQL releases some of its memory for other processes to use.

Ideally, aim to have at least 256MB to 500MB of Available MBytes. On larger systems with more than 16GB of RAM, this number should be increased to 500MB–1GB. If you have more than 64GB of RAM on your server, increase this to 1–2GB.

Monitoring SQL Server Process Memory Usage

Having used the Memory – *Counter*: Available Mbytes to determine that a potential memory shortage exists; the next step is to determine which processes use the available memory. As your focus is on SQL Server, you hope that it is SQL Server that uses the memory. However, you should always confirm that this is the case.

The usual place to look for a process's memory usage is in the Process object under the instance for the process. For SQL Server, these counters are detailed in the following list:

➤ **Object: Process – Instance: sqlserver - Counter: Virtual Bytes:** This counter indicates the size of the virtual address space allocated by the process. Virtual address space (VAS) is used by a lot of processes that aren't related to memory performance. This counter is of value when looking for the root cause of SQL Server out-of-memory errors. If running on a 32-bit system, virtual address space is limited to 2GB (except when the /3GB switch is enabled). In this environment, if virtual bytes approach 1.5GB to 1.7GB, that is about as much space as can be allocated. At this point the root cause of the problem is a VAS limitation issue, and the resolution is to reduce SQL Server's memory usage, enable AWE, boot using /3GB, or move to a 64-bit environment. On a 64-bit system this counter is of less interest because VAS pressure is not going to occur. To learn more about AWE, refer to Chapter 11.

This counter includes the AWE window, but it does not show how much physical memory is reserved though AWE.

➤ **Object: Process – Instance: sqlservr – Counter: Working Set:** This counter indicates the size of the working set for the SQL Server process. The working set is the total set of pages currently resident in memory, as opposed to being paged to disk. It can provide an indication of memory pressure when this is significantly lower than the Private Bytes for the process.

This counter does not include AWE memory allocations.

➤ **Object: Process – Instance: sqlservr – Counter: Private Bytes:** The Private Bytes counter tells you how much memory this process has allocated that cannot be shared with other processes — that is, it's private to this process. To understand the difference between this counter and virtual bytes, you just need to know that certain files loaded into a process's memory space — the EXE, any DLLs, and memory mapped files — will automatically be shared by the operating system. Therefore, Private Bytes indicates the amount of memory used by the process for its stacks, heaps, and any other virtually allocated memory in use. You could compare this to the total memory used by the system. When this value is a significant portion of the total system memory, it is a good indication that SQL Server memory usage is the root of the overall server memory shortage.

It does not show anything about AWE memory.

Monitoring SQL Server AWE Memory

 In SQL Server 2012, support for using AWE on 32-bit systems has been removed, so this section is only relevant to 64-bit systems.

If your SQL Server is configured to use AWE memory, the regular process memory counters do not show how much memory SQL Server actually uses. In this scenario, you may see "AvailableMB," indicating that 15GB of the available 16GB of memory is in use, but when you add up the memory actually in use (the working set) for all running processes, it falls a long way short of the 15GB used. This is because SQL Server has taken 12GB of memory and uses it through AWE.

In this case, the only way to see this AWE memory is to look at the SQL Server–specific counters that indicate how much memory SQL uses:

➤ **Object: SQL Server:Buffer Manager – Counter: Database Pages:** Shows the number of pages used by the buffer pool for database content

➤ **Object: SQL Server:Buffer Manager – Counter; Target Pages:** Shows how many pages SQL Server wants to allocate for the buffer pool

➤ **Object: SQL Server:Buffer Manager – Counter: Total Pages:** Shows how many pages SQL Server currently uses for the buffer pool

➤ **Object: SQL Server:Memory Manager – Counter: Target Server Memory (KB):** Shows how much memory SQL Server would like to use for all its memory requirements

➤ **Object: SQL Server:Memory Manager – Counter: Total Server Memory (KB):** Shows how much memory SQL Server currently uses

Other SQL Server Memory Counters

The following is a list of some additional SQL Server memory counters. When looking at memory issues, these counters can provide more detailed information than the counters already described:

➤ **Buffer Cache Hit Ratio:** This counter indicates how many page requests were found in the buffer pool. It tends to be a little coarse in that 98 percent and above is good, but 97.9 percent might indicate a memory issue.

➤ **Free Pages:** This counter indicates how many free pages SQL Server has for new page requests. Acceptable values for this counter depend on how much memory you have available and the memory usage profile for your applications. Having a good baseline is useful, as the values for this counter can be compared to the baseline to determine whether there is a current memory issue, or whether the value is part of the expected behavior of the system.

This counter should be read with the Page Life Expectancy counter.

➤ **Page Life Expectancy:** This counter provides an indication of the time, in seconds, that a page is expected to remain in the buffer pool before being flushed to disk. The current Best Practices from Microsoft state that values above 300 are generally considered okay. Values approaching 300 are a cause for concern. Values below 300 are a good indication of a memory shortage. These Best Practices are now getting a bit dated however. They were written when a large system might have 4 dual or quad core processors, and 16GB of RAM. Today's commodity hardware comes with a 2P system with 10, 12, 16+ cores, and the ability to have 256GB or more of memory. Therefore, those best practice numbers are less relevant. Because of this, you should interpret this counter in conjunction with other counters to understand if there really is memory pressure.

Read this counter with the Free Pages counter. You should expect to see Free Pages drop dramatically as the page life expectancy drops below 300. When considered together, Free Pages and Page Life expectancy provide an indication of memory pressure that may result in a bottleneck.

Scripting Memory Counters with Logman

Following is a Logman script that can create a counter log of the memory counters discussed in this section (see the "Logman" section later in the chapter for more information):

```
Logman create counter "Memory Counters" -si 05 -v nnnnnn -o
"c:\perflogs\Memory Counters" -c "\Memory\Available MBytes"
"\Process(sqlservr)\Virtual Bytes" "\Process(sqlservr)\Working Set"
"\Process(sqlservr)\Private Bytes" "\SQLServer:Buffer Manager\Database
pages" "\SQLServer:Buffer Manager\Target pages" "\SQLServer:Buffer
Manager\Total pages" "\SQLServer:Memory Manager\Target Server Memory (KB)"
"\SQLServer:Memory Manager\Total Server Memory (KB)"
```

Resolving Memory Bottlenecks

The easy solution to memory bottlenecks is to add more memory; but previously stated, tuning your application always comes first. Try to find queries that are memory-intensive, for instance queries with large worktables — such as hashes for joins and sorts — to see if you can tune them. You can learn more about tuning T-SQL queries in Chapter 13 "Performance Tuning T-SQL."

In addition, refer to Chapter 10 to ensure that you have configured your server properly. If you are running a 32-bit machine and after adding more memory you are still running into memory bottlenecks, then look into a 64-bit system.

Performance Monitoring Tools

A few tools are well hidden in the command-line utilities that have shipped with Windows operating systems for some time. Two of these that are extremely valuable when using Performance Monitor are Logman and Relog.

Logman

Logman is a command-line way to script performance monitoring counter logs. You can create, alter, start, and stop counter logs using Logman.

You have seen several examples earlier in this chapter of using Logman to create different counter logs. Following is a short command-line script file to start and stop a counter collection:

```
REM start counter collection
logman start "Memory Counters"
timeout /t 5
REM add a timeout for some short period
REM to allow the collection to start
REM do something interesting here

REM stop the counter collection
logman stop "Memory Counters"
timeout /t 5
REM make sure to wait 5 to ensure its stopped
```

Complete documentation for Logman is available through the Windows help system.

Logman Script for I/O Counters

The following script can create a new counter log called IO Counters and collect samples for every counter previously detailed, for all instances and with a 5-second sample interval, and write the log to `c:\perflogs\IO Counters`, appending a six-digit incrementing sequence number to each log:

```
Logman create counter "IO Counters" -si 05 -v nnnnnn -o "c:\perflogs\IO
Counters" -c "\PhysicalDisk(*)\Avg. Disk Bytes/Read" " \PhysicalDisk(*)\Avg.
Disk Bytes/Write" "\PhysicalDisk(*)\Avg. Disk Read Queue Length"
"\PhysicalDisk(*)\Avg. Disk sec/Read" "\PhysicalDisk(*)\Avg. Disk sec/Write"
"\PhysicalDisk(*)\Avg. Disk Write Queue Length" "\PhysicalDisk(*)\Disk Read
Bytes/sec" "\PhysicalDisk(*)\Disk Reads/sec" "\PhysicalDisk(*)\Disk Write
Bytes/sec" "\PhysicalDisk(*)\Disk Writes/sec"
```

After running this script, run the following command to confirm that the settings are as expected:

```
logman query "IO Counters"
```

Relog

Relog is a command-line utility that enables you to read a log file and write selected parts of it to a new log file.

You can use it to change the file format from `blg` to `csv`. You can use it to resample data and turn a large file with a short sample period into a smaller file with a longer sample period. You can also use it to extract a short period of data for a subset of counters from a much larger file.

Complete documentation for Relog is available through the Windows help system.

MONITORING EVENTS

Events are fired at the time of some significant occurrence within SQL Server. Using events enables you to react to the behavior at the time it occurs, and not have to wait until some later time. SQL Server generates many different events and has several tools available to monitor some of these events.

The following list describes the different features you can use to monitor events that happened in the Database Engine:

➤ **system_health Session:** The system_health session is included by default with SQL Server, starts automatically when SQL Starts, and runs with no noticeable performance impact. It collects a minimal set of system information that can help resolve performance issues.

➤ **Default Trace:** Initially added in SQL Server 2005, this is perhaps one of the best kept secrets in SQL Server. It's virtually impossible to find any documentation on this feature. The default trace is basically a flight data recorder for SQL Server. It records the last 5MB of key events. The events it records were selected to be lightweight, yet valuable when troubleshooting a critical SQL event.

➤ **SQL Trace:** This records specified events and stores them in a file (or files) that you can use later to analyze the data. You have to specify which Database Engine events you want to trace when you define the trace. Following are two ways to access the trace data:

    ➤ Using SQL Server Profiler, a graphical user interface

    ➤ Through T-SQL system stored procedures

➤ **SQL Server Profiler:** This exploits all the event-capturing functionality of SQL Trace and adds the capability to trace information to or from a table, save the trace definitions as templates, extract query plans and deadlock events as separate XML files, and replay trace results for diagnosis and optimization. Another option, and perhaps least understood, is using a database table to store the trace. Storing the trace file in a database table enables the use of T-SQL queries to perform complex analysis of the events in the trace.

➤ **Event notifications:** These send information to a Service Broker service about many of the events generated by SQL Server. Unlike traces, event notifications can be used to perform an action inside SQL Server in response to events. Because event notifications execute asynchronously, these actions do not consume any resources defined by the immediate transaction, meaning, for example, that if you want to be notified when a table is altered in a database, then the ALTER TABLE statement would not consume more resources or be delayed because you have defined event notification.

➤ **Extended Events:** These were new with SQL Server 2008 and extend the Event Notification mechanism. They are built on the Event Tracing for Windows (ETW) framework. Extended Events are a different set of events from those used by Event Notifications and can be used to diagnose issues such as low memory conditions, high CPU use, and deadlocks. The logs created when using SQL Server Extended Events can also be correlated with other ETW logs using `tracerpt.exe`. See the topic on Extended Events in SQL Server Books Online for more references to information on using ETW and `tracerpt.exe`. For more details, see the section "SQL Server Extended Event Notification" later in this chapter.

Following are a number of reasons why you should monitor events that occur inside your SQL Server:

➤ **Find the worst-performing queries or stored procedures:** You can do this using either Extended Events or through SQL Profiler / SQL Trace. To use SQL Profiler, you can find a trace template on this book's website at www.wrox.com, which you can import into your SQL Server Profiler to capture this scenario. This includes the Showplan Statistics Profile, Showplan XML, and Showplan XML Statistics Profile under Performance event groups. These events are included because after you determine the worst-performing queries, you need to see what query plan was generated by them. Just looking at the duration of the T-SQL batch or stored procedure does not get you anywhere. Consider filtering the trace data by setting some value in the Duration column to retrieve only those events that are longer than a specific duration so that you minimize your dataset for analysis.

➤ **Audit user activities:** You can either use the new SQL Audit capabilities in Extended Events to create a SQL Audit, or create a trace with Audit Login events. If you choose the latter, select the EventClass (the default), EventSubClass, LoginSID, and LoginName data columns; this way you can audit user activities in SQL Server. You may add more events from the Security Audit event group or data columns based on your need. You may someday need this type of information for legal purposes in addition to your technical purposes.

➤ **Identify the cause of a deadlock:** You can do this using Extended Events. Much of the information needed is available in the system_health session that runs by default on every instance of SQL Server. You look into how to do that in more detail later in this chapter.

You can also do this the "old way" by setting the startup trace flags for tracing deadlocks. SQL Trace doesn't persist between server cycles unless you use SQL Job to achieve this. You can use startup trace flag 1204 or 1222 (1222 returns more verbose information than 1204 and resembles an XML document) to trace a deadlock anytime it happens on your SQL Server. Refer to Chapter 4, "Managing and Troubleshooting the Database Engine," to learn more about these trace flags and how to set them. To capture deadlock information using SQL Trace, you need to capture these events in your trace: Start with Standard trace template and add the Lock event classes (Lock: Deadlock graph, Lock: Deadlock, or Lock: Deadlock Chain). If you specify the Deadlock graph event class, SQL Server Profiler produces a graphical representation of the deadlock.

➤ **Collect a representative set of events for stress testing:** For some benchmarking, you want to reply to the trace generated. SQL Server provides the standard template TSQL_Replay to capture a trace that can be replayed later. If you want to use a trace to replay later, make sure that you use this standard template because to replay the trace, SQL Server needs some specific events captured, and this template does just that. Later in this chapter you see how to replay the trace.

➤ **Create a workload to use for the Database Engine Tuning Adviser:** SQL Server Profiler provides a predefined Tuning template that gathers the appropriate Transact-SQL events in the trace output, so it can be used as a workload for the Database Engine Tuning Advisor.

➤ **Take a performance baseline:** Earlier you learned that you should take a baseline and update it at regular intervals to compare with previous baselines to determine how your application performs. For example, suppose you have a batch process that loads some data once a day and validates it, does some transformation, and so on, and puts it into your warehouse after deleting the existing set of data. After some time there is an increase in data volume and suddenly your process starts slowing down. You would guess that an increase in data volume is slowing the process down, but is that the only reason? In fact, there could be more than one reason. The query plan generated may be different — because the stats may be incorrect, because your data volume increased, and so on. If you have a statistic profile for the query plan taken during the regular baseline, with other data (such as performance logs) you can quickly identify the root cause.

The following sections provide details on each of the event monitoring tools.

The Default Trace

The default trace was introduced in SQL Server 2005. This trace is always on and captures a minimal set of lightweight events. If after learning more about the default trace you decide you actually do not want it running, you can turn it off using the following T-SQL code:

```
-- Turn ON advanced options
exec sp_configure 'show advanced options', '1'
reconfigure with override
go
-- Turn OFF default trace
exec sp_configure 'default trace enabled', '0'
reconfigure with override
go
-- Turn OFF advanced options
exec sp_configure 'show advanced options', '0'
reconfigure with override
go
```

 If you do turn the default trace off, and then you realize how valuable it is and want to turn it back on again, you can do that by using the same code you used to turn it on, just set the sp_configure value for 'default trace enabled' to 1 and not 0.

The default trace logs 30 events to five trace files that work as a First-In, First-Out buffer, with the oldest file being deleted to make room for new events in the next `trc` file.

The default trace files live in the SQL Server log folder. Among the SQL Server Error log files you can find five trace files. These are just regular SQL Server trace files, so you can open them in SQL Profiler.

The key thing is to have some idea of what events are recorded in the default trace, and remember to look at it when something happens to SQL Server. The events captured in the default trace fall into six categories,

➤ **Database:** These events are for examining data and log file growth events, as well as database mirroring state changes.

➤ **Errors and warnings:** These events capture information about the error log and query execution based warnings around missing column stats, join predicates, sorts, and hashes.

➤ **Full-Text:** These events show information about full text crawling, when a crawl starts, stops, or is aborted.

➤ **Objects:** These events capture information around User object activity, specifically Create, Delete, and Alter on any user object. If you need to know when a particular object was created, altered, or deleted, this could be the place to go look.

➤ **Security Audit:** This captures events for the major security events occurring in SQL Server. There is quite a comprehensive list of sub events (not listed here). If you're looking for security based information, then this should be the first place you go looking.

➤ **Server:** The server category contains just one event, Server Memory Change. This event indicates when SQL Server memory usage increases or decreases by 1MB, or 5% of max server memory, whichever is larger.

You can see these categories by opening one of the default trace files in SQL Server Profiler and examining the trace file properties. By default, you don't have permission to open the trace files while they live in the Logs folder, so either copy the file to another location, or alter the permissions on the file that you want to open in profiler.

When you open the trace file properties, you see that for each category all event columns are selected for all the events in the default trace.

system_health Session

The system_health session is a default extended events session that is created for you by SQL Server. It is very lightweight and has minimal impact on performance. With previous technologies like SQL Server Profiler and the default trace, customers have worried about the performance impact of running these monitoring tools. Extended Events and the system_health session mitigate those concerns.

The system_health session contains a wealth of information that can help diagnose issues with SQL Server. The following is a list of some of the information collected by this session.

➤ SQL text and Session ID for sessions that:

➤ Have a severity ≥ 20

➤ Encounter a memory related error

➤ Have waited on latches for ≥ 15 seconds

➤ Have waited on Locks for ≥ 30 seconds

➤ Deadlocks

➤ Nonyielding scheduler problems

SQL Trace

As mentioned earlier, you have two ways to define the SQL Trace: using T-SQL system stored procedures and SQL Server Profiler. This section first explains the SQL Trace architecture; then you study an example to create the server-side trace using the T-SQL system stored procedure.

Before you start, you need to know some basic trace terminology:

➤ **Event:** The occurrence of an action within an instance of the Microsoft SQL Server Database Engine or the SQL Server Database Engine, such as the Audit: Logout event, which happens when a user logs out of SQL Server.

➤ **Data column:** An attribute of an event, such as the `SPID` column for the Audit:Logout event, which indicates the SQL SPID of the user who logged off. Another example is the `ApplicationName` column, which gives you an application name for the event.

 In SQL Server, trace column values greater than 1GB return an error and are truncated in the trace output.

➤ **Filter:** Criteria that limit the events collected in a trace. For example, if you are interested only in the events generated by the SQL Server Management Studio – Query application, you can set the filter on the `ApplicationName` column to SQL Server Management Studio – Query and you see only events generated by this application in your trace.

➤ **Template:** In SQL Server Profiler, a file that defines the event classes and data columns to be collected in a trace. Many default templates are provided with SQL Server, and these files are located in the directory `\Program Files\Microsoft SQL Server\110\Tools\Profiler\Templates\Microsoft SQL Server\110`.

For even more terminology related to trace, refer to the Books Online section "SQL Trace Terminology."

SQL Trace Architecture

You should understand how SQL Trace works before looking at an example. Figure 12-6 shows the basic form of the architecture. Events are the main unit of activity for tracing. When you define the trace, you specify which events you want to trace. For example, if you want to trace the SP: Starting event, SQL Server traces only this event (with some other default events that SQL Server always captures). The event source can be any source that produces the trace event, such as a T-SQL statement, deadlocks, other events, and more.

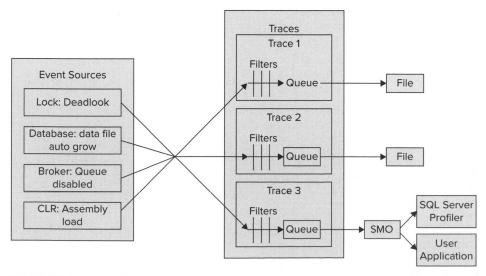

FIGURE 12-6

After an event occurs, if the event class has been included in a trace definition, the event information is gathered by the trace. If filters have been defined for the event class (for example, if you are interested only in the events for LoginName= 'foo') in the trace definition, the filters are applied and the trace event information is passed to a queue. From the queue, the trace information is written to a file, or it can be used by Server Management Objects (SMO) in applications, such as SQL Server Profiler.

Creating a Server-Side Trace Using T-SQL Stored Procedures

If you have used SQL Profiler before, you know that creating a trace using it is easy. Creating a trace using T-SQL system stored procedures requires some extra effort because it uses internal IDs for events and data column definitions. Fortunately, the sp_trace_setevent article in SQL Server Books Online (BOL) documents the internal ID number for each event and each data column. You need four stored procedures to create and start a server-side trace:

1. Use sp_trace_create to create a trace definition. The new trace will be in a stopped state.

2. After you define a trace using sp_trace_create, use sp_trace_setevent to add or remove an event or event column to a trace. sp_trace_setevent may be executed only on existing traces that are stopped (whose status is 0). An error is returned if this stored procedure is executed on a trace that does not exist or whose status is not 0.

3. Apply a filter to a trace using. sp_trace_setfilter. This stored procedure may be executed only on existing traces that are stopped. SQL Server returns an error if this stored procedure is executed on a trace that does not exist or whose status is not 0.

4. Use sp_trace_setstatus to modify the current state of the specified trace.

5. Now you can create a server-side trace. This trace can capture the events Audit Login and SQL: StmtStarting. It can capture the data columns SPID, DatabaseName, TextData, and HostName for the Audit Login event; and it can capture the data columns ApplicationName, SPID, TextData, and DatabaseName for the SQL: StmtStarting event.

6. Capture the trace data for the application SQL Server Management Studio–Query only. Save the trace data in a file located on some remote share. The maximum file size should be 6MB, and you need to enable file rollover so that another file is created when the current file becomes larger than 6MB.

7. Finally, you want the server to process the trace data, and to stop the trace at a certain time.

 Server-side traces are much more efficient than client-side tracing with SQL Server Profiler. Defining server-side traces using stored procedures is a bit hard, but there is an easy way to do it, discussed soon.

An example of the code to create a server side trace is shown in Listing 12-1.

LISTING 12-1: CreateTrace.sql

```sql
-- Create a Queue
declare @rc int
declare @TraceID int
declare @maxfilesize bigint
declare @DateTime datetime

set @maxfilesize = 10
set @DateTime = '2012-06-28 14:00:00.000'
---------------------
-- The .trc extension will be appended to the filename automatically.
-- If you are writing from remote server to local drive,
-- please use UNC path and make sure server has write access to your network
share
exec @rc = sp_trace_create @traceid = @TraceID output
,@options = 2
,@tracefile = N'<SQL Server Drive>:\temp\trace\ServerSideTrace'
,@maxfilesize  = @maxfilesize
,@stoptime  = @Datetime
,@filecount = NULL
if (@rc != 0) goto error

-- Set the events
declare @on bit
set @on = 1
exec sp_trace_setevent
 @traceid = @TraceID
,@eventid  = 14
,@columnid = 8
,@on - @on

exec sp_trace_setevent @TraceID, 14, 1, @on
exec sp_trace_setevent @TraceID, 14, 35, @on
exec sp_trace_setevent @TraceID, 14, 12, @on
exec sp_trace_setevent @TraceID, 40, 1, @on
exec sp_trace_setevent @TraceID, 40, 10, @on
exec sp_trace_setevent @TraceID, 40, 35, @on
exec sp_trace_setevent @TraceID, 40, 12, @on


-- Set the Filters
declare @intfilter int
declare @bigintfilter bigint

exec sp_trace_setfilter
 @traceid = @TraceID
,@columnid = 10
,@logical_operator = 1
,@comparison_operator = 6
,@value = N'SQL Server Management Studio - Query'

-- Set the trace status to start
```

continues

LISTING 12-1 *(continued)*

```
exec sp_trace_setstatus @traceid = @TraceID, @status = 1

-- display trace id for future references
select TraceID=@TraceID
goto finish

error:
select ErrorCode=@rc

finish:
go
```

Let's take a look at this stored procedure. The `@traceid` parameter returns an integer that you must use if you want to modify the trace, stop or restart it, or look at its properties.

The second parameter, `@options`, enables you to specify one or more trace options. A value of 1 tells the trace to produce a rowset and send it to Profiler. You can't use this option value if you capture to a server-side file. Typically, only Profiler-created traces have this option value. Traces that use the `sp_trace_create` stored procedure should never have an option value of 1 because this value is reserved for Profiler-defined traces. Because the value for the `@options` parameter is a bitmap, you can combine values by adding them together. For example, if you want a trace that enables file rollover and shuts down SQL Server if SQL Server can't write to the trace file, the option value is 6 (4+2). In this case, the option value 2 means that when the trace file reaches the size specified by the value in the parameter `@maxfilesize`, the current trace file is closed, and a new file is created. All new records will be written to the new file; and the new file will have the same name as the previous file, but an integer will be appended to indicate its sequence. For details about other `@option` values, refer to the `sp_trace_setevent` article in SQL Server Books Online at http:// technet.microsoft.com/en-us/library/ms186265(SQL.110).aspx.

Not all option values can be combined. For example, option value 8, by definition, doesn't combine with any other option value.

In the `@tracefile` parameter, you can specify where you want to store the trace results: either a local directory (such as `N 'C:\MSSQL\Trace\trace.trc'`) or a UNC to a share or path (`N'\Servername\Sharename\Directory\trace.trc'`). The extension `.trc` is added automatically, so you don't need to specify that.

You cannot specify the `@tracefile` if you set the `@option` value to 8; in that case, the server stores the last 5MB of trace information.

You can specify the maximum size of the trace file before it creates another file to add the trace data using the @maxfilesize parameter, in MB. In this case you have specified 10MB, which means that when the trace file size exceeds 10MB, SQL Trace creates another file and starts adding data there. Use this option because if you create one big file, it's not easy to move it around; and if you have multiple files, then you can start looking at the older files while trace is writing to the new file. In addition, if disk space issues arise while gathering the trace data, you can move files to different drives or servers.

You can optionally specify the trace stop time using the @stoptime parameter, which is of the datetime type.

The @filecount parameter specifies the maximum number of trace files to be maintained with the same base filename. Refer to Books Online for a detailed description of this parameter.

Now look at how to set up the events and choose the data columns for those events. The stored procedure sp_trace_setevent can do that job with the following steps:

1. The first parameter you use is the traceid, which you got from the sp_trace_create stored procedure.

2. The second parameter you use, @eventid, is the internal ID of the event you want to trace. The first call of the stored procedure specifies 14, which is the Audit Login event.

3. In the third parameter, specify which data column you want to capture for the event indicated. In this case, you have set @columnid to 8, which is the data column HostName. Call this stored procedure for each data column you want for a particular event. Call this stored procedure multiple times for @eventid 14 because you want multiple data columns.

4. The last parameter you use is @ON, which is a bit parameter that specifies whether you want to turn the event on or off. As mentioned earlier, the sp_trace_setevent article in SQL Server Books Online documents the internal ID number for each event and each data column.

5. Once the event is established, set the filter on it. Use the stored procedure sp_trace_setfilter to set the filter on a particular event and the data column. The article sp_trace_setfilter in BOL documents the internal ID number for the @comparison_operator and @logical_operator parameters. In this case, you want only the trace generated by the application name SQL Server Management Studio – Query.

6. To start the trace use the stored procedure sp_trace_setstatus. You can specify the trace ID you want to take action on with the option 0, 1, or 2. Because you want to start the trace, you have specified 1. If you want to stop it, specify 0. If you specify 2, it closes the specified trace and deletes its definition from the server.

7. You're all set to run the server-side trace. You specified the @datetime option to stop the trace. You need to change the datetime value as your needs dictate. Make sure that if you specify the UNC path for the trace file, the SQL Server service account has write access to the share. Run the script now.

It seems like plenty of work to get these internal IDs right when you create the server-side trace. Fortunately, there is an easy way to create the server-side trace using SQL Server Profiler, as you see in a moment.

> *You can define all the events, data columns, filters, filenames (you need to select the option to save to the file because you cannot store to a table when you create a server-side trace) and size using SQL Server Profiler and then click Run. After that, select File ⇨ Export ⇨ Script Trace Definition ⇨ For SQL Server, and save the script. Now you have the script to create the server-side trace. You may need to check the @maxfilesize option to ensure that it has the correct value if you have changed something other than the default, which is 5MB.*

When you define the server-side trace, you cannot store the trace result directly into the table. You must store it into the file; later you can use a function, discussed next, to put the trace data into a table.

Retrieving the Trace Metadata

Now that you have defined the trace, you also need to understand how to get the information about the trace. There are built-in functions you can use to do that. The function fn_trace_getinfo (trace_id) can get the information about a particular trace. If you do not know the trace_id, specify DEFAULT as the function argument, and it lists all the traces.

Run the following T-SQL. Be sure to change the trace_id parameter value to whatever trace_id you got when you ran the script in Listing 12-1:

```
SELECT
* FROM fn_trace_getinfo (2)
```

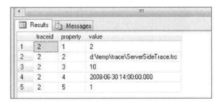

FIGURE 12-7

Figure 12-7 shows the output. Notice, the Property 1 row contains the @options parameter value. A trace with a Property 1 value of 1 is most likely a trace started from Profiler. The Property 2 row contains the trace filename, if any. The Property 3 row contains the maximum file size, which is 10MB in this case; and the Property 4 row contains the stop time, which has some value for this trace. The Property 5 row shows the trace's status — in this case 1, which means that Trace is running.

The function fn_trace_geteventinfo()shows you the events and data columns that a particular trace captures, but the function returns the data with the event and data column IDs, instead of a name or explanation, so you must track down their meaning.

The function fn_trace_getfilterinfo() returns information about a particular trace's filters like so:

```
SELECT
* FROM fn_trace_geteventinfo (2)
```

Retrieving Data from the Trace File

You can retrieve the trace data from the file in two ways: using the function `fn_trace_gettable` or with SQL Server Profiler. Both are valuable in different situations.

The function `fn_trace_gettable` is a table-valued function, so you can read directly from the file using this function and insert the data into a table to analyze like so:

```
SELECT * FROM fn_trace_gettable
( '<SQL Server Drive>:\temp\trace\ServerSideTrace .trc' , DEFAULT)
```

You can also use `SELECT INTO` in this query to store the result in a table. Put the trace data into a table because then you can write a T-SQL statement to query the data. For example, the `TextData` column is created with the `ntext` data type. You can alter the data type to `nvarchar` (`max`) so that you can use the string functions. You should not use the `ntext` or `text` data types anyway, because they will be deprecated in a future SQL Server release; use `nvarchar(max)` or `varchar(max)` instead. Even though the trace is running, you can still read the data from the file to which Trace is writing. You don't need to stop the trace for that. The only gotcha in storing the trace data into a table is that the `EventClass` value is stored as an `int` value and not as a friendly name. Listing 12-2 creates a table and inserts the `eventclassid` and its name into that table. You can then use this table to get the event class name when you analyze the trace result stored there. You can write a query like the following to do that, assuming that you have stored the trace result in the table `TraceResult`:

LISTING 12-2: EventClassID_Name.sql

```
SELECT ECN.EventClassName, TR.
* FROM TraceResult TR
 LEFT JOIN EventClassIdToName ECN
    ON ECN.EventClassID = TR.EventClass
```

SQL Server Profiler

SQL Server Profiler is a rich interface used to create and manage traces and analyze and replay trace results. SQL Server Profiler shows how SQL Server resolves queries internally. This enables you to see exactly what Transact-SQL statements or multidimensional expressions are submitted to the server and how the server accesses the database or cube to return result sets.

In SQL Server 2012, SQL Server profiler has been marked as being deprecated. Because of this, you should move any monitoring capabilities using this tool to the newer tools based on extended events.

You can read the trace file created using a T-SQL stored procedure with SQL Profiler. To use SQL Profiler to read the trace file, just go to the File menu and open the trace file you are interested in.

> *In SQL Server 2008, the server reports both the duration of an event and CPU time used by the event, in milliseconds. In SQL Server 2005, the server reports the duration of an event in microseconds (one millionth of a second) and the amount of CPU time used by the event in milliseconds (one thousandth of a second). In SQL Server 2000, the server reported both duration and CPU time in milliseconds. In SQL Server 2005, the SQL Server Profiler graphical user interface displays the* Duration *column in milliseconds by default, but when a trace is saved to either a file or a database table, the* Duration *column value is written in microseconds. If you want to display the duration column in microseconds in SQL Profiler, go to Tools ⇨ Options and select the option Show Values in Duration Column in Microseconds (SQL Server 2005 Only).*

Being able to capture and examine the XML plan for a particular query is very valuable when trying to troubleshoot issues with a particular query. SQL Server Profiler makes this possible using the XML Showplan option. Additionally, being able to correlate a Profiler trace with a Performance Monitor chart can help to diagnose performance problems by enabling you to correlate which queries are executing in a Profiler trace against performance counters captured in Performance Monitor. With this capability you can see exactly what was executing when a particular behavior was observed in the perfmon graph. The following sections discuss these options in more detail.

Showplan XML

You can get the query plan in an XML document and use this document later to generate the graphical query plan. Showplan output in XML format can be moved from one computer to another and thus rendered on any computer, even on computers where SQL Server is not installed. Showplan output in XML format can also be programmatically processed using XML technologies, such as XPath, XQuery, and so on. XML Showplan processing is supported in SQL Server 2005, which contains a built-in query evaluation engine for XPath and XQuery.

You can generate XML Showplan output using the following means:

- ➤ From the query editor toolbar in SQL Server Management Studio, select Display Estimated Execution Plan or Include Actual Execution Plan.
- ➤ Use the Transact-SQL Showplan SET statement options SHOWPLAN_XML and STATISTICS XML.
- ➤ Select the SQL Server Profiler event classes Showplan XML, Showplan XML for Query Compile, and Showplan XML Statistics Profile for tracing.
- ➤ Use the sys.dm_exec_query_plan dynamic management view.

XML Showplans are returned in the nvarchar (max) data type for all these methods except the last. XML Showplans are returned in the xml data type when you use this dynamic management view.

You can visit http://schemas.microsoft.com/sqlserver/2004/07/showplan/showplanxml.xsd for the XML Showplan schema, or you can look in the directory where SQL Server is installed:

```
C:\Program Files (x86)\Microsoft SQL Server\110\Tools\Binn\schemas\sqlserver\
2004\07\showplan.
```

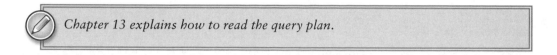

Chapter 13 explains how to read the query plan.

Figure 12-8 shows what a query plan looks like in SQL Profiler when you choose the Showplan XML event. This event is under the Performance object. To see these additional events, you need to click the Events Selection tab and select the Show All Events option.

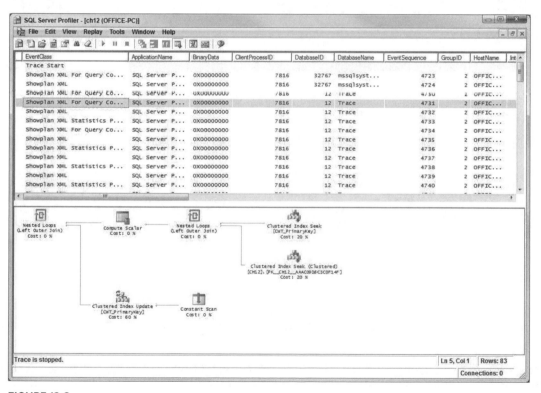

FIGURE 12-8

If you right-click the Showplan XML event, you see a menu item Extract Event Data. This saves the query plan with a `.sqlplan` extension. You can later open that file with SQL Server Management Studio or Profiler, and it displays the graphical plan exactly, as shown in Figure 12-8. You can also use File ➪ Export ➪ Extract SQL Server Event in SQL Profiler to achieve the same results.

When you set up the trace using Profiler, if you choose Showplan XML or Showplan Statistics Profile or Showplan XML for Query Compile, a tab shows up in the Trace Properties dialog, as shown in Figure 12-9.

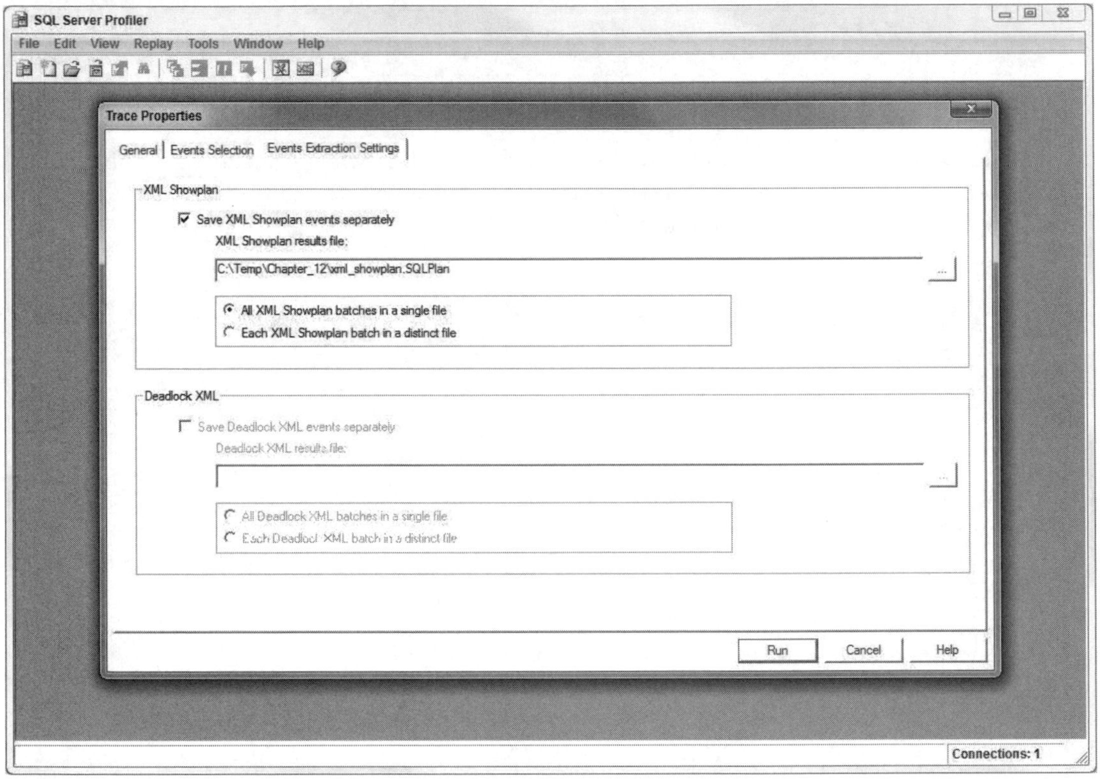

FIGURE 12-9

Also shown in Figure 12-9 is a Deadlock XML option to store the deadlock graph in an XML document, which you can view later in SQL Management Studio or Profiler. This option is enabled only if you choose the Deadlock Graph event.

You can also use SET SHOWPLAN_XML ON before you execute the query, which can give you an estimated execution plan in XML without executing it. You can also use SET STATISTICS XML ON, which can give you an execution plan in XML format, as shown in Figure 12-10. Click the link in the XML Showplan to open an XML editor within SQL Server Management Studio.

If you want to see the graphical execution plan from this XML document, you can save the document with a .sqlplan extension. Open that file in SQL Server Management Studio, and you get the graphical execution plan. Figure 12-11 shows the graphical execution plan generated from the XML document.

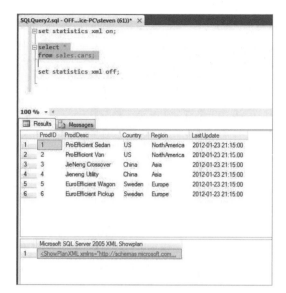

FIGURE 12-10

FIGURE 12-11

 When the Showplan XML event class is included in a trace, the amount of overhead significantly impedes performance. Showplan XML stores a query plan that is created when the query is optimized. To minimize the overhead incurred, limit the use of this event class to traces that monitor specific problems for brief periods of time, and be sure to use the data column filter based on specifics you are going to trace.

Correlating a Trace with Windows Performance Log Data

In SQL Server 2005, a new feature was added to correlate the trace data with Performance Monitor log data based on the StartTime and EndTime data columns in the SQL trace file. If you have taken Trace and Performance Monitor data at the same time, you can relate the events that happened in SQL Server with the server activities such as processor time, disk activity, and memory usage. Figures 12-12 and 12-13 show an example of correlating trace and Performance Monitor log data.

To bring up the performance data after you open a trace file, click File ➪ Import Performance Data. That brings up the dialog shown in Figure 12-12. This option is not enabled unless you open a saved trace file. The trace file must also contain the starting and completed events for the types of activity you are interested in, including SPStarting, SPComplete, StmtStarting, StmtComplete, and so on. Without these events, the Import Performance Data option remains disabled. You can select the performance counters you are interested in and then click OK. That brings the performance counters inside the Profiler to correlate the SQL Server activity during a specific time, as shown in Figure 12-13. Move the red vertical bar to select a particular time you are interested in to see what was happening at that time in SQL Server.

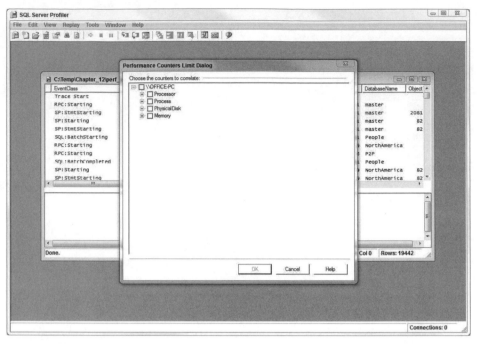

FIGURE 12-12

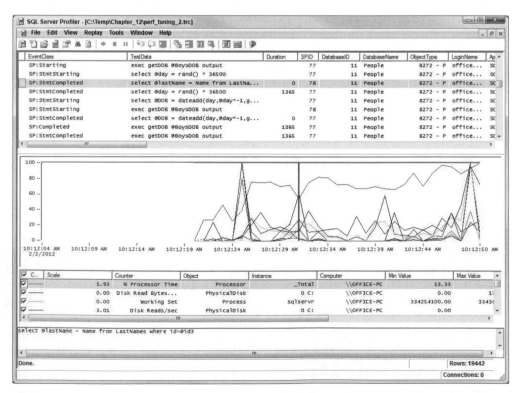

FIGURE 12-13

If you look at the peak value for a performance counter — for example, average disk queue length — that brings up whatever query SQL Server was executing at the time. However, that doesn't mean the query caused the disk queue length to increase exactly at that time. The query might have started a little earlier and now requests a lot of data from disk, which may cause the average disk queue length to shoot up. In short, be careful before you jump to conclusions; make sure you look at the whole picture.

Replaying a Trace

Replay is the capability to save a trace and replay it later. This functionality enables you to reproduce the activity captured in a trace. When you create or edit a trace, you can save the trace to replay it later. Be sure to choose the predefined template called TSQL_Replay when you create the trace using SQL Profiler. SQL Server needs specific events and data columns to be captured to replay the trace later. If you miss those events and data columns, SQL Server does not replay the trace. Trace replay supports debugging by using the Toggle Breakpoint and the Run to Cursor options on the SQL Server Profiler Replay menu. These options especially improve the analysis of long scripts because they can break the replay of the trace into short segments so they can be analyzed incrementally.

The following types of events are ignored when you replay the trace:

➤ Traces that contain transactional replication and other transaction log activity. These events are skipped. Other types of replication do not mark the transaction log, so they are not affected.

➤ Traces that contain operations involving globally unique identifiers (GUID). These events are skipped.

➤ Traces that contain operations on text, ntext, and image columns involving the bcp utility, the BULK INSERT, READTEXT, WRITETEXT, and UPDATETEXT statements, and full-text operations. These events are skipped.

➤ Traces that contain session binding: sp_getbindtoken and sp_bindsession system stored procedures. These events are skipped.

➤ SQL Server Profiler does not support replaying traces collected by Microsoft SQL Server version 7.0 or earlier.

In addition, some requirements must be met to replay the trace on the target server:

➤ All logins and users contained in the trace must be created already on the target and in the same database as the source.

➤ All logins and users in the target must have the same permissions they had in the source.

➤ All login passwords must be the same as those of the user who executes the replay. You can use the Transfer Login task in SSIS to transfer the logins to the target server on which you want to replay the trace.

> ➤ The database IDs on the target ideally should be the same as those on the source. However, if they are not the same, matching can be performed based on the database name if it is present in the trace, so make sure that you have the `DatabaseName` data column selected in the trace.

> ➤ The default database on the target server for a login should be the same as on the source when the trace was taken.

> ➤ Replaying events associated with missing or incorrect logins results in replay errors, but the replay operation continues.

Distributed Replay

New for SQL Server 2012 is Distributed Replay, a tool for replaying traces from multiple machines. While SQL profiler can replay a trace, it can only do so from a single machine. Distributed replay can also replay traces, but can do so from a pool of machines. Because of this, distributed replay provides a more scalable solution than SQL profiler, and is better at simulating mission critical workloads.

Now that there are two tools for replaying traces, the question becomes when to use which tool. As a general rule, you should use SQL profiler for all trace replays, and always for replaying traces against Analysis Services. You only need to resort to distributed replay *if* the concurrency in the captured trace is so high that a single server cannot sufficiently simulate the load you want to put onto the target server.

A Distributed Replay system known as a *Distributed Replay Utility* consists of a number of different servers, the Admin tool, the controller, a number of clients, and the target SQL Server.

Because Distributed Replay can replay a trace from multiple servers, you need to do a little additional work on the Trace file before it can be used in a distributed replay. Specifically you have to pre-process the trace file and spilt it into multiple streams of commands that are replayed from the different client servers in the distributed replay utility.

Performance Considerations When Using Trace

SQL Server tracing incurs no overhead unless it captures an event, and most events need few resources. Profiler can become expensive as you add events, and increase the amount of event data captured for each event. Normally, you see a maximum of from 10-20 percent overhead. If you see more than this, or even if this level of overhead is impacting the production system, either reduce the number of events, reduce the amount of data, or use an alternate approach. Most of the performance hit results from a longer code path; the actual resources that the trace needs to capture event data aren't particularly CPU-intensive. In addition, to minimize the performance hit, you can define all your traces as server-side traces, avoiding the overhead of producing rowsets to send to the Profiler client.

Event Notifications

Event notifications are special database objects that send messages to the Service Broker service (see Chapter 7, "SQL Server CLR Integration," for details on the Service Broker) with information regarding server or database events. Event notifications can be programmed against many of the same events captured by SQL Trace, but not all. Event Notifications can also be programmed against many DDL events. Unlike creating traces, event notifications can be used to perform an action inside an instance of SQL Server in response to events. Later in this chapter you see an example that shows how to create an event notification for specific events, and take actions if needed.

To subscribe to an event, you must create the Service Broker queue that receives the details regarding the event. In addition, a queue requires the Service Broker service to receive the message. Then you need to create an event notification. You can create a stored procedure and activate it when the event message is in the queue to take a certain action. This example assumes you know how the Service Broker works, so be sure to read Chapter 8, "Securing the Database Instance," if you don't already know about the Server Broker.

You can also be notified for grouped events. For example, if you want to be notified when a table is created, altered, or dropped, you don't need to create three separate event notifications. You can use the group event called `DDL_TABLE_EVENTS` and just create one event notification to achieve the same thing. Another example is related to monitoring all the locking events using the event group `TRC_LOCKS`. When you create an event notification with this group, you can be notified about the following events: `LOCK_DEADLOCK`, `LOCK_DEADLOCK_CHAIN`, `LOCK_ESCALATION`, and `DEADLOCK_GRAPH`.

Refer to the BOL topic "DDL Event Groups for Use with Event Notifications" for all the event groups.

Event notifications can be used to do the following:

➤ Log and review changes or activity occurring on the database or server.

➤ Perform an action in response to an event in an asynchronous, rather than synchronous, manner.

Event notifications can offer a programming alternative to DDL triggers and SQL Trace.

 Event notifications are created at the server or database level.

You can create an event notification in a database whereby you will be notified when a new table is created. To do so, perform the following steps:

1. Open the project `EventNotification` using SQL Server Management Studio, and then open the `CreateDatabase.sql` script. This script creates a database called `StoreEvent` for the example. Run this script.

2. Next, open the `CreateQueue.sql` script, shown in Listing 12-3:

LISTING 12-3: CreateQueue.sql

```
USE StoreEvent
GO

--CREATE QUEUE to receive the event details.
IF OBJECT_ID('dbo.NotifyQueue') IS NULL
CREATE QUEUE dbo.NotifyQueue
WITH STATUS = ON
    ,RETENTION = OFF
GO

--create the service so that when event happens
--server can send the message to this service.
--we are using the pre-defined contract here.
IF NOT EXISTS(SELECT * FROM sys.services WHERE name =
'EventNotificationService')
CREATE SERVICE EventNotificationService
ON QUEUE NotifyQueue
([http://schemas.microsoft.com/SQL/Notifications/PostEventNotification])

IF NOT EXISTS(SELECT * FROM sys.routes WHERE name = 'NotifyRoute')

CREATE ROUTE NotifyRoute
WITH SERVICE_NAME = 'EventNotificationService',
ADDRESS = 'LOCAL';
GO
```

3. This script creates a queue in the StoreEvent database to store the event data when a table is created in the StoreEvent database. It creates a Service Broker service EventNotificationService such that SQL Server can send the message when a subscribed event happens. The route NotifyRoute helps route the message to a local SQL server instance. Run this script.

4. Now you need to create the event notification. Open the script CreateEventNotification. sql, shown in the following code snippet:

```
USE StoreEvent
GO
CREATE EVENT NOTIFICATION CreateTableNotification
ON DATABASE
FOR CREATE_TABLE
TO SERVICE 'EventNotificationService', 'current database' ;
```

CreateEventNotification.sql

This script creates an event notification called CreateTableNotification that notifies you when a table is created in the StoreEvent database.

Messages are sent from one service to another, as discussed in Chapter 6. In this case, you have created the target end of the service, which is EventNotificationServer; the initiator end of the service is SQL Server itself.

5. When a table is created in the StoreEvent database, you get the message in the queue NotifyQueue, so create a table and run the following script to see what's in the queue:

```
SELECT CAST(message_body AS xml)
FROM NotifyQueue
```

6. Following is what the final XML message in the queue looks like:

```
<EVENT_INSTANCE>
  <EventType>CREATE_TABLE</EventType>
  <PostTime>2012-09-23T21:53:14.463</PostTime>
  <SPID>56</SPID>
  <ServerName>CIPHER</ServerName>
  <LoginName>REDMOND\ketanp</LoginName>
  <UserName>dbo</UserName>
  <DatabaseName>StoreEvent</DatabaseName>
  <SchemaName>dbo</SchemaName>
  <ObjectName>TestTable1</ObjectName>
  <ObjectType>TABLE</ObjectType>
  <TSQLCommand>
    <SetOptions ANSI_NULLS="ON" ANSI_NULL_DEFAULT="ON" ANSI_PADDING="ON"
QUOTED_IDENTIFIER="ON" ENCRYPTED="FALSE" />
    <CommandText>CREATE TABLE TestTable1 (col1 int, col2 varchar(100), col3
xml)
</CommandText>
  </TSQLCommand>
</EVENT_INSTANCE>
```

You can take some action with this event if you create a stored procedure and have it activated when a message arrives in the queue. You create the serverwide event in the same way. For a full list of the events for which you can be notified, you can query the sys.event_notification_event_types view. Refer to the script Metadata_EventNotification.sql to get the catalog view list that stores the metadata about event notifications.

SQL Server Extended Events

SQL Server Extended Events (XEvents) was a completely new feature for SQL Server 2008. Extended Events have been enhanced in SQL Server 2012 with increased event coverage and a new GUI interface in SSMS. Extended Events provide a deep insight into SQL Server internals and are designed to enable faster diagnosis of issues with SQL Server. They provide the capability to act either synchronously or asynchronously to SQL Events and are designed to be extremely lightweight and highly scalable. The system_health session is a lighter weight and more powerful version of the default_trace. Extended events are also lighter weight and more flexible and scalable than SQL Server Trace and SQL Profiler.

Extended events are designed to replace some of the older monitoring technologies such as SQL Server Profiler. All the events and columns available in SQL Server Profiler are available through Extended Events.

XEvent Objects

This section introduces the new objects in XEvents. The object hierarchy for XEvent objects is shown in Figure 12-14.

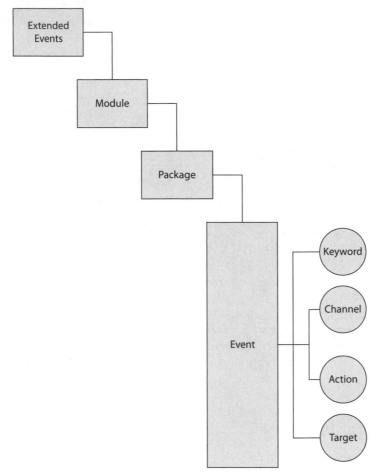

FIGURE 12-14

Module

The `Module` object is equivalent to the binary that contains the events. `Module` is equivalent to `SQLServr.exe`, or `MyDll.dll` if you were to write your own code and load it into SQL Server. The only place you see the module is as an attribute of the package in the DMV `sys.dm_xe_packages`.

Package

A package is a container object within the module. The packages that come with SQL Server can be seen in the DMV `sys.dm_xe_packages`. The following code lists the contents of this DMV, the results of which are shown in Table 12-1.

```
select name, description
from sys.dm_xe_packages
```

TABLE 12-1: sys.dm_xe_packages

NAME	DESCRIPTION
package0	Default package; contains all standard types, maps, compare operators, actions, and targets
sqlos	Extended events for SQL operating system
XeDkPkg	Extended events for SQLDK binary
sqlserver	Extended events for Microsoft SQL Server
SecAudit	Security Audit Events
Ucs	Extended events for Unified Communications Stack
Sqlclr	Extended events for SQL CLR
Filestream	Extended events for SQL Server FILESTREAM and FileTable
sqlserver	Extended events for Microsoft SQL Server

As with modules, you won't be creating any packages unless you write your own code and create your own new events.

Event

Events are the first "real" objects in the hierarchy. An event represents an occurrence of a significant activity within SQL Server. To get a better understanding of events, take a look at some of the events available. You can find these in the DMV sys.dm_xe_objects and they have a type of 'event'. The following code outputs a list of event types:

```
select name
from sys.dm_xe_objects
where object_type ='event'
order by name
```

This returns a list of 618 different events. This is quite an increase from the 254 event types that were originally available in SQL Server 2008. A select few are listed here:

```
checkpoint_begin
checkpoint_end
lock_acquired
lock_deadlock
lock_released
locks_lock_waits
sp_statement_completed
```

```
sp_statement_starting
sql_statement_completed
sql_statement_starting
wait_info
wait_info_external
```

All events have two additional attributes: `Keyword` and `Channel`. The `Keyword` for an event is a way to group events based on who fires the event, so keywords are memory, broker, server, and so on. The `Channel` for an event reflects who might be interested in the event. Following are four channels in SQL Server 2012:

➤ debug

➤ analytical

➤ operational

➤ administration

To see the `Channel` and `Keyword` for the events requires that you join several of the XEvent DMVs, as in the following code:

```
select p.name as package_name
, k.event
, k.keyword
, c.channel
, k.description
from (
select c.object_package_guid as event_package
, c.object_name as event
, v.map_value as keyword
, o.description
from sys.dm_xe_object_columns as c inner join sys.dm_xe_map_values as v
  on c.type_name = v.name
  and c.column_value = v.map_key
  and c.type_package_guid = v.object_package_guid
inner join sys.dm_xe_objects as o
  on o.name = c.object_name
  and o.package_guid = c.object_package_guid
where c.name = 'keyword'
) as k inner join (
select c.object_package_guid as event_package
, c.object_name as event
, v.map_value as channel
, o.description
from sys.dm_xe_object_columns as c inner join sys.dm_xe_map_values as v
  on c.type_name = v.name
  and c.column_value = v.map_key
  and c.type_package_guid = v.object_package_guid
inner join sys.dm_xe_objects as o
  on o.name = c.object_name
  and o.package_guid = c.object_package_guid
where c.name = 'channel'
) as c
```

```
on
k.event_package = c.event_package and k.event = c.event
inner join sys.dm_xe_packages as p on p.guid = k.event_package
order by keyword
, channel
, event
```

Table 12-2 shows a few of the events, including their keywords and channels.

TABLE 12-2: Select Extended Events

PACKAGE NAME	EVENT	KEYWORD	CHANNEL	DESCRIPTION
sqlserver	broker_activation_task_aborted	broker	Admin	Broker activation task aborted
sqlserver	broker_activation_task_started	broker	Analytic	Broker activation task started
sqlserver	change_tracking_cleanup	change_tracking	Debug	Change Tracking Cleanup
sqlserver	app_domain_ring_buffer_recorded	clr	Debug	AppDomain ring buffer recorded
sqlserver	cursor_manager_cursor_end	cursor	Analytic	Cursor manager cursor end
sqlserver	checkpoint_begin	database	Analytic	Checkpoint has begun
sqlserver	database_started	database	Operational	Database started
sqlserver	deadlock_monitor_state_transition	deadlock_monitor	Debug	Deadlock Monitor state transition
sqlserver	error_reported	errors	Admin	Error has been reported
sqlserver	trace_print	errors	Debug	Trace message published
sqlserver	assert_fired	exception	Debug	Assert fired
sqlos	dump_exception_routine_executed	exception	Debug	Dump exception routine executed

continues

TABLE 12-2 *(continued)*

PACKAGE NAME	EVENT	KEYWORD	CHANNEL	DESCRIPTION
sqlserver	sql_statement_starting	execution	Analytic	SQL statement starting
sqlserver	databases_log_file_size_changed	io	Analytic	Database log file size changed
sqlserver	file_read	io	Analytic	File read
sqlserver	flush_file_buffers	io	Debug	FlushFileBuffers called

Action

Actions are what you want to happen when an event fires. They are invoked synchronously on the thread that fired the event. The available actions are stored in the DMV `sys.dm_xe_objects` with an `object_type = 'action'`. The action enables you to do things such as correlate a `plan_handle`, and T-SQL stack with a specific event. This kind of flexibility creates an incredibly powerful framework that exceeds anything that SQL Trace and SQL Profiler could do.

The following query returns all the actions available.

```
select name
from sys.dm_xe_objects
where object_type = 'action'
order by name
```

This query returns 50 actions, some of which are listed here:

```
attach_activity_id
attach_activity_id_xfer
callstack
collect_cpu_cycle_time
collect_system_time
create_dump_all_thread
create_dump_single_thread
database_context
database_id
debug_break
plan_handle
session_id
sos_context
sql_text
transaction_id
tsql_stack
```

Predicate

A predicate is a filter that is applied to the event right before the event is published. A Boolean expression, it can be either local or global and can store state.

Predicates are stored in the DMV `sys.dm_xe_objects` and can be seen using the following T-SQL:

```
select name, description
from sys.dm_xe_objects
where object_type = 'pred_compare'
order by name
-- 77 rows

select name, description
from sys.dm_xe_objects
where object_type = 'pred_source'
order by name
-- 44rows
```

Table 12-3 shows a few of the `pred_compare` objects.

TABLE 12-3: Selected pred_compare objects

NAME	DESCRIPTION
divides_by_uint64	Whether a uint64 divides another with no remainder
equal_ansi_string	Equality operator between two ANSI string values
greater_than_equal_float64	Greater than or equal operator between two 64-bit double values
greater_than_i_sql_ansi_string	Greater than operator between two SQL ANSI string values
less_than_ansi_string	Less than operator between two ANSI string values
less_than_equal_i_unicode_string_ptr	Less than or equal operator between two UNICODE string pointer values
less_than_int64	Less than operator between two 64-bit signed int values
not_equal_ptr	Inequality operator between two generic pointer values

Table 12-4 lists some of the `pred_source` objects.

TABLE 12-4: Selected pred_source objects

NAME	DESCRIPTION
Counter	Counts the number of times evaluated.
cpu_id	Gets the current CPU ID.
current_thread_id	Gets the current Windows thread ID.
database_id	Gets the current database ID.
node_affinity	Gets the current NUMA node affinity.

continues

TABLE 12-4 *(continued)*

NAME	DESCRIPTION
`partitioned_counter`	Per-CPU partitioned counter. The value is aggregated and approximate.
`scheduler_address`	Gets the current scheduler address.
`scheduler_id`	Gets the current scheduler ID.
`session_id`	Gets the current session ID.
`system_thread_id`	Gets the current system thread ID.
`task_address`	Gets the current task address.
`task_elapsed_quantum`	Gets the time elapsed since quantum started.
`task_execution_time`	Gets the current task execution time.
`transaction_id`	Gets the current transaction ID.
`worker_address`	Gets the current worker address.

Target

A target is a way to define what you want to happen to the events you monitor. The fifteen targets defined for SQL Server 2012 are shown in the following table. Like the other XEvent objects, they can be found in the DMV `sys.dm_xe_objects` with an `object_ type = 'target'`.

The following T-SQL code returns the list of targets from `sys.dm_xe_objects`:

```
select name, description
from sys.dm_xe_objects
where object_type = 'target'
order by name
```

The fifteen different targets can be seen in Table 12-5.

TABLE 12-5: Targets

NAME	DESCRIPTION
`asynchronous_router`	Route events to asynchronous listeners.
`asynchronous_security_audit_event _log _target`	Asynchronous security audit NT event log target.
`asynchronous_security_audit_file _target`	Asynchronous security audit file target.
`asynchronous_security_audit _security _log_target`	Asynchronous security audit NT security log target.

NAME	DESCRIPTION
etw_classic_sync_target	Event Tracing for Windows (ETW) Synchronous Target.
Event_counter	Counts the number of occurrences of each event in the event session.
Event_file	Saves the event data to an XEL file, which can be archived and used for later analysis and review. You can merge multiple XEL files to view the combined data from separate event sessions.
Event_stream	Asynchronous live stream target.
histogram	Aggregates event data based on a specific event data field or action associated with the event. The histogram enables you to analyze distribution of the event data over the period of the event session.
pair_matching	Pairing target.
ring_buffer	Asynchronous ring buffer target.
router	Route events to listeners.
synchronous_security_audit_event _log _target	Synchronous security audit NT event log target.
synchronous_security_audit_file _target	Synchronous security audit file target.
synchronous_security_audit _security _log_target	Synchronous security audit NT security log target.

Event Session

The event session is where all the objects detailed earlier are brought together to actually do something. You create the event session to define which of those objects you want to use to perform your event capture.

Event sessions are created using the DDL CREATE EVENT SESSION syntax. This one statement enables you to define all the objects you need to create a new event session. The only thing you cannot do is start the session. For transaction consistency, the session must be created first. When it has been created, it can be started using the ALTER EVENT SESSION syntax:

```
ALTER EVENT SESSION <session name>  STATE = START
```

Listing 12-4 shows an example of code to create a new event session that gathers sql_text, and the tsql_stack for any SQL statement that has a duration > 30 ms. It then writes the output to the xml file specified in the target specification, and flushes results from memory to the file every second.

LISTING 12-4: XE_long_running_queries.sql

```
-- Create a new event session
create event session long_running_queries on server
-- Add the sql_statement_complete event
add event sqlserver.sql_statement_completed
(
    -- for this event get the sql_text, and tsql_stack
    action(sqlserver.sql_text, sqlserver.tsql_stack)
    -- Predicate on duration > 30 ms ( milli seconds )
    where sqlserver.sql_statement_completed.duration > 30
)

-- Send the output to the specified XML file
add target package0.asynchronous_file_target
(
    set filename=N'c:\chapter_12_samples\XEvents\long_running_queries.xel'
    , metadatafile = N'c:\chapter_12_samples\XEvents\long_running_queries.xem'
)
-- Specify session options,
-- max_dispatch_latency specifies how long we buffer in memory before pushing
 to the target
with (max_dispatch_latency = 1 seconds)
```

ALTER SESSION is probably most frequently used to start and stop sessions, but it can also be used to add or remove events from an existing session. The following code snippet shows how to start the session you created in Listing 12-4.

```
-- Which event session do we want to alter
alter event session long_running_queries on server
-- Now make any changes
-- change the state to start
state = start
```

The code shown in Listing 12-5 below shows how to use ALTER SESSION to add an additional event to the existing event session.

LISTING 12-5: XE_alter_long_running_queries.sql

```
-- Which event session do we want to alter
alter event session long_running_queries on server
-- Now make any changes
-- add another event, this time the long_io_detected event
add event sqlserver.long_io_detected
(
-- for this event get the sql_text, and tsql_stack
    action(sqlserver.sql_text, sqlserver.tsql_stack)
    -- No predicate, we want all of these to see if there is any correlation
)
```

To see which sessions are currently active, use the following queries:

```
select
* from sys.dm_xe_sessions

select
* from sys.dm_xe_session_events
```

Catalog Views

Following are several of the catalog views that expose information about XEvents:

➤ `server_event_sessions`

➤ `server_event_session_targets`

➤ `server_event_session_fields`

➤ `server_event_session_events`

➤ `server_event_session_actions`

DMVs

You have already seen some of the Extended Event DMVs in action. For completeness, here is the full list:

➤ `sys.dm_xe_map_values`: Returns a mapping of internal numeric keys to human-readable text.

➤ `sys.dm_xe_object_columns`: Returns the schema information for all the objects.

➤ `sys.dm_xe_objects`: Returns a row for each object exposed by an event package. Objects can be one of the following:

  ➤ **Events:** Indicate points of interest in an execution path. All events contain information about a point of interest.

  ➤ **Actions:** Run synchronously when events fire. An action can append run-time data to an event.

  ➤ **Targets:** Consume events, either synchronously on the thread that fires the event or asynchronously on a system-provided thread.

  ➤ **Predicate sources:** Retrieve values from event sources for use in comparison operations. Predicate comparisons compare specific data types and return a Boolean value.

  ➤ **Types:** Encapsulate the length and characteristics of the byte collection, which is required to interpret the data.

➤ `sys.dm_xe_packages`: Lists all the packages registered with the extended events engine.

➤ `sys.dm_xe_session_event_actions`: Returns information about event session actions. Actions are executed when events are fired. This management view aggregates statistics about the number of times an action has run and the total run time of the action.

➤ `sys.dm_xe_session_events`: Returns information about session events. Events are discrete execution points. Predicates can be applied to events to stop them from firing if the event does not contain the required information.

> ➤ `sys.dm_xe_session_object_columns`: Shows the configuration values for objects that are bound to a session.

> ➤ `sys.dm_xe_session_targets`: Returns information about session targets.

> ➤ `sys.dm_xe_sessions`: Returns information about an active extended events session. This session is a collection of events, actions, and targets.

Working with Extended Event Sessions

There are several ways that you can create, modify, display, and analyze sessions and session data.

You can manipulate extended events using DDL in T-SQL as you saw in some of the previous examples. There are additional T-SQL examples on creating Extended Event Sessions later in this section.

There are two graphical user interfaces that you can use with Extended Events: The New Session Wizard and the New Session UI.

New Session Wizard

The new session wizard guides you through the creation of a new session with the following steps:

1. Launch it from SQL Server Management Studio. Open the Management node, then the Extended Events Node, and then the Session Node. Right click on Sessions, and choose New Session Wizard. This launches the New Session Wizard and displays the Introduction page as shown in Figure 12-15.

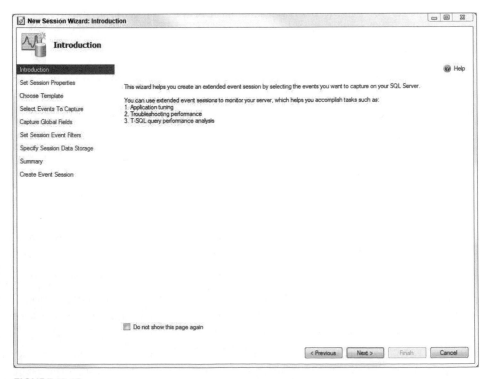

FIGURE 12-15

2. Select Next to move onto the set session properties page. Here you provide a session name, and select if you want the session to start up each time the server starts (see Figure 12-16). For this example, enter the name **chapter_12_test**.

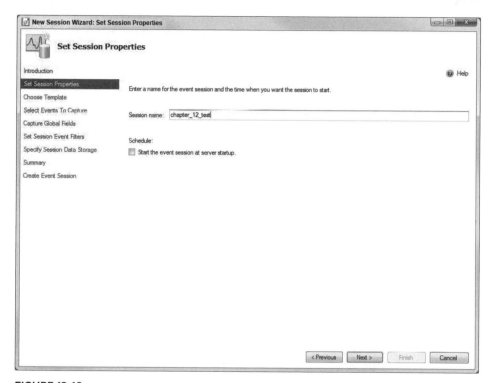

FIGURE 12-16

3. Select Next to move onto the Choose template page. Here you choose a predefined template for the events in the template, or you can select to not use a template, and manually select events. In this example, select "Use this event session template" which populates the list of event session templates shown in Figure 12-17. For this example select the "Query Wait Statistics" template and select Next.

4. The Next page in the Wizard is the Select Events To Capture page (see Figure 12-18). Because you chose to use a template, this is already populated with the events from the template. You can see the event selected in the template in the selected events box. Because you used a template, you don't need to do anything here.

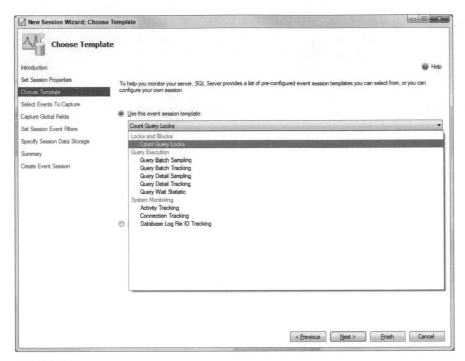

FIGURE 12-17

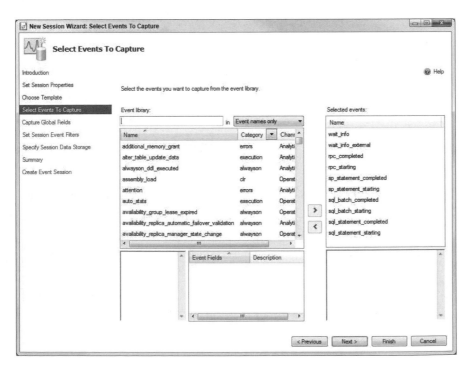

FIGURE 12-18

5. Select Next to move onto the Capture Global Fields page. This page is shown in Figure 12-19. Again, because you selected a template, a number of global fields are already preselected. The preselected fields are those with a checkbox next to them. In Figure 12-19 you can see client_app_name, and database_id are checked. Scrolling down shows the other fields that are selected from the template.

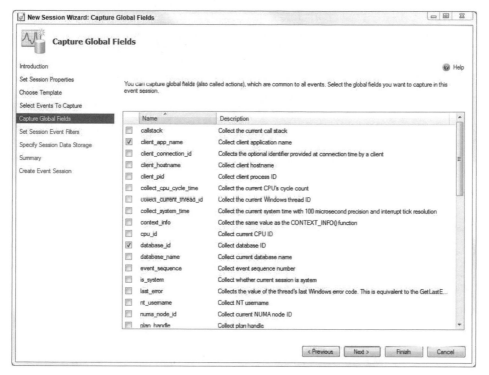

FIGURE 12-19

6. Select Next to move onto the Set Session Event Filters page (see Figure 12-20). Here you can select any filters (also known as predicates) that would restrict the amount of data to be captured. For this example you are not going to apply any filters.

7. Select Next to move onto the Specify Session Data Storage page (see Figure 12-21). Here you can specify where you want the data to be collected. The two options are to save data to a file for alter analysis, or to put it into a ring buffer. For this example, select Save data to a file for later analysis (event_file target), and leave the default values for filename, max file size, enable file rollover, and max number of file.

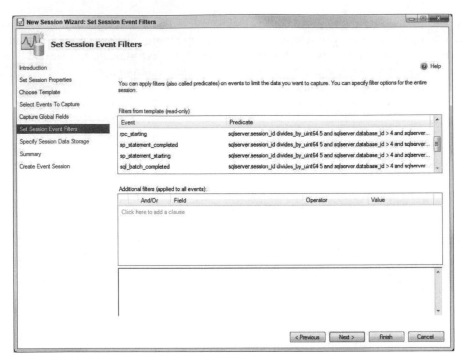

FIGURE 12-20

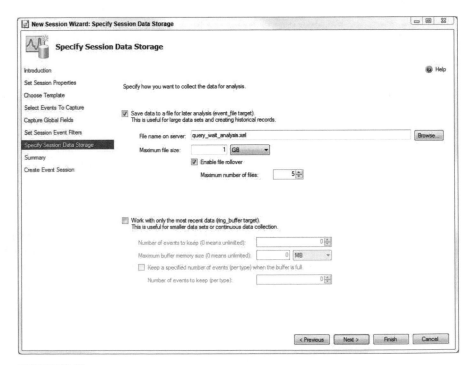

FIGURE 12-21

8. Select Next to move onto the Summary page. This page shown in Figure 12-22 provides a summary of the selections made throughout the wizard. This provides one last opportunity to confirm the values selected before the wizard applies these settings and creates the new event session.

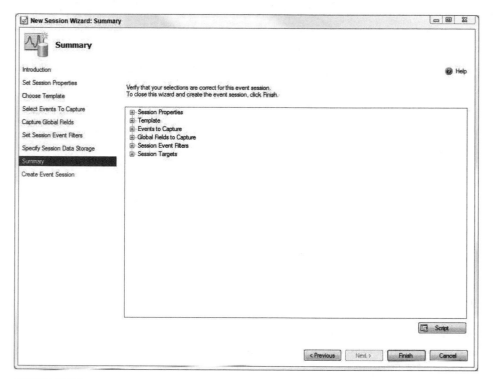

FIGURE 12-22

9. Select Finish and the wizard creates the new event session. If it creates the event session successfully, you see the success page and have the option to start the event session immediately and watch live data as it is captured. The Create Event Session success screen is shown in Figure 12-23. Select both options: start the event session immediately, and watch live data on screen as shown in Figure 12-23.

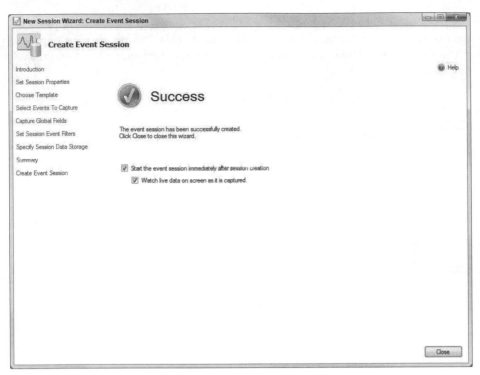

FIGURE 12-23

10. Select Close to close the wizard, start the event session, and watch live data being captured. The wizard closes, and SSMS displays a new tab showing the Live Data for the new session.

New Session UI

The New Session UI is launched from SQL Server Management Studio. To start using this interface, perform the following steps:

1. Open the Management node, then the Extended Events Node, and then the Session Node. Right click on Sessions, and choose New Session. This opens the New Session UI on the General Page. Enter a session name of chapter_12_test2, and select the Connection Tracking template. Select to start the event session at server startup. You see a page similar to that shown in Figure 12-24.

2. Select the Events Page to see which events have been pre selected with this template (see Figure 12-25). Because you selected a template, there is no need to change anything here.

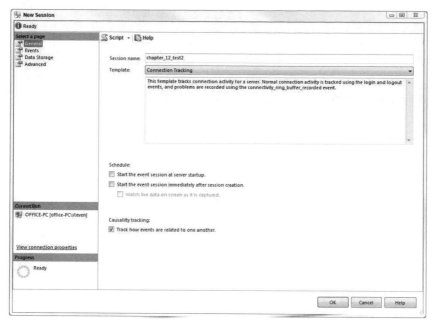

FIGURE 12-24

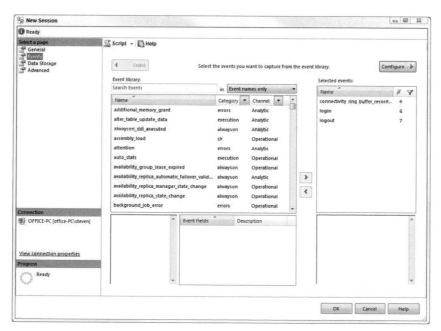

FIGURE 12-25

3. Select the Data Storage page to define how the data is going to be stored. The default here is to store data into a ring_buffer target. To change this, select Add which adds a new line to the list of targets, with a drop down for "Please choose a target type." Expand this drop down and you see the full set of targets, as shown in Figure 12-26.

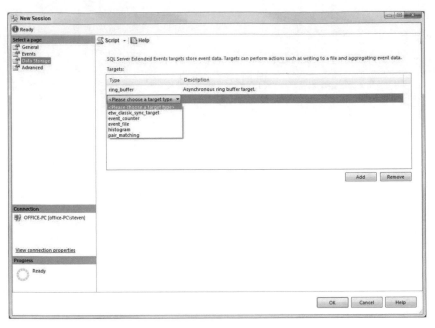

FIGURE 12-26

4. Select event_file. This adds a set of target specific properties below the list of targets. For this example, the default values are acceptable, so there is no need to change them.

5. Select the Advanced page to specify advanced settings for the New Session. The Advanced page is shown in Figure 12-27. These settings are acceptable for this example.

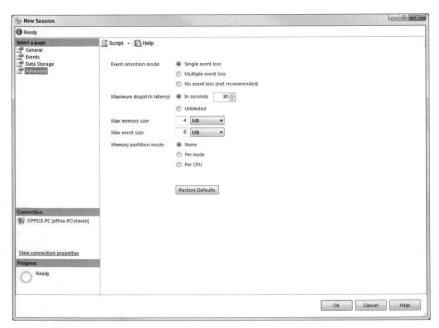

FIGURE 12-27

6. At this point you have examined all the options for creating the new session. To create the new session, select OK. The UI disappears, and if you go look in SSMS under Management ➪ Extended Events ➪ Sessions, you see that a new session called chapter_12_test2 has been created. Because of the options you selected, it is not currently running.

7. To start the new session, right click it, and select Start Session. To view live data for the session, right click it and select Watch Live Data.

Editing a Session

To edit a session, select it in SSMS right click its node, and select Properties. This brings up the same set of pages seen in the New Session UI, but this time preloaded with the session info, and with some options disabled. Select properties on the chapter_12_test2 session to display the dialog seen in Figure 12-28.

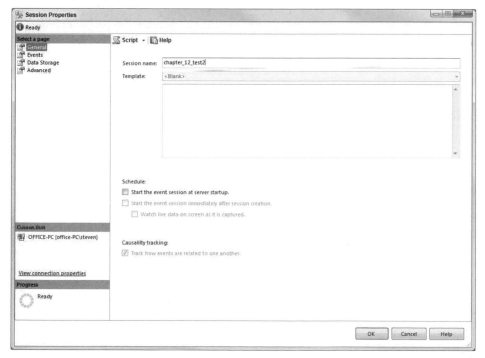

FIGURE 12-28

Using this dialog, you can edit many of the session properties. There are additional options throughout the session UI that have not been discussed here. Most of these options are self explanatory, but it is recommended to explore these in conjunction with the available documentation in Books Online.

MONITORING WITH DYNAMIC MANAGEMENT VIEWS AND FUNCTIONS

Dynamic management views (DMVs) and dynamic management functions (DMFs) are a godsend to the DBA. They provide plenty of information about server and database state. DMVs, and DMF's are designed to give you a window into what's going on inside SQL Server. They return server state information that you can use to monitor the health of a server instance, diagnose problems, and tune performance. Following are two types of DMVs and DMFs:

➤ Server-scoped dynamic management views and functions

➤ Database-scoped dynamic management views and functions

All DMVs and functions exist in the sys schema and follow the naming convention dm_* respectively. To view the information from a server-scoped DMV, you have to grant the SERVER VIEW STATE permission to the user. For database-scoped DMVs and functions, you have to grant the VIEW DATABASE STATE permission to the user. After you grant the VIEW STATE permission, that user can see all the views; to restrict the user, deny the SELECT permission on the dynamic management views or functions that you do not want the user to access. The following example grants the VIEW SERVER STATE permission to the user Aish:

```
GRANT VIEW SERVER STATE TO [MyDom\Aish]
```

If you want the user [MyDom\Aish] to be restricted from viewing information in the view sys.dm_os_wait_stats, you need to DENY SELECT as follows:

```
DENY SELECT ON sys.dm_os_wait_stats TO [MyDom\Aish]
```

DMVs and DMFs are generally divided into the following categories:

➤ Always On Availability Group

➤ Change Data Capture–related

➤ Change Tracking–related

➤ CLR-related

➤ Database mirroring–related

➤ Database-related

➤ Execution-related

➤ Filestream and FileTable

➤ Full-Text-Search and Semantic Search

➤ Index-related

➤ I/O-related

➤ Object related

➤ Query notifications related

➤ Replication–related

➤ Resource Governor

➤ Security–related

➤ Service Broker–related

➤ SQL Server OS–related

➤ Transaction-related

Rather than describe all the views here, this section looks at examples for the common tasks a DBA would perform to monitor a SQL Server. For details about all the DMVs and functions, please refer to the Books Online topic "Dynamic Management Views and Functions."

Following are some of the scenarios in which you can use DMVs and functions. You can also open a sample DMV to get all the scripts. Following are just a few examples, but in the sample DMV solution you can find many examples for monitoring your SQL Server.

What's Going on Inside SQL Server?

The following sections illustrate querying the DMVs to determine what is currently going on inside SQL Server.

Currently Running Queries

Listing 12-6 shows the SQL text for currently running queries. It helps you find which queries are currently running and displays the SQL text for each currently running query. This is useful when you try to determine what is currently running in terms of T-SQL code, and not just SPIDs / session_ids.

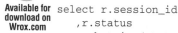

LISTING 12-6: Current running queries.sql

```
select r.session_id
     ,r.status
     ,substring(qt.text,r.statement_start_offset/2,
     (case when r.statement_end_offset = -1
     then len(convert(nvarchar(max), qt.text)) * 2
     else r.statement_end_offset end - r.statement_start_offset)/2)
     as query_text
     ,qt.dbid
     ,qt.objectid
     ,r.cpu_time
     ,r.total_elapsed_time
     ,r.reads
     ,r.writes
     ,r.logical_reads
     ,r.scheduler_id
from sys.dm_exec_requests as r
cross apply sys.dm_exec_sql_text(sql_handle) as qt
inner join sys.dm_exec_sessions as es on r.session_id = es.session_id
where es.is_user_process = 1
order by r.cpu_time desc
```

Who Is Using Which Resources?

Listing 12-7 samples the system tables which are now deprecated. It samples `sysprocesses` over a 10-second interval and reports on the delta between the first and second sample. While `sysprocesses` is deprecated, it has all the information nicely formatted in one place, whereas the corresponding DMVs require joins to multiple DMVs. Because `sysprocesses` is so easy to use, you are better off continuing to use `sysprocesses` for as long as it is available:

LISTING 12-7: Resource Usage.sql

```
-- Who is using all the resources?
select spid, kpid, cpu, physical_io, memusage, sql_handle, 1 as sample,
getdate() as sampleTime, hostname, program_name, nt_username
into #Resources
from master..sysprocesses

waitfor delay '00:00:10'

Insert #Resources
select spid, kpid, cpu, physical_io, memusage, sql_handle, 2 as sample,
getdate() as sampleTime, hostname, program_name, nt_username
from master..sysprocesses

-- Find the deltas
select r1.spid
, r1.kpid
, r2.cpu - r1.cpu as d_cpu_total
, r2.physical_io - r1.physical_io as d_physical_io_total
, r2.memusage - r1.memusage as d_memusage_total
, r1.hostname, r1.program_name, r1.nt_username
, r1.sql_handle
, r2.sql_handle
from #resources as r1 inner join #resources as r2 on r1.spid = r2.spid
    and r1.kpid = r2.kpid
where r1.sample = 1
and r2.sample = 2
and (r2.cpu - r1.cpu) > 0
order by (r2.cpu - r1.cpu) desc

select r1.spid
, r1.kpid
, r2.cpu - r1.cpu as d_cpu_total
, r2.physical_io - r1.physical_io as d_physical_io_total
, r2.memusage - r1.memusage as d_memusage_total
, r1.hostname, r1.program_name, r1.nt_username
into #Usage
from #resources as r1 inner join #resources as r2 on r1.spid = r2.spid
    and r1.kpid = r2.kpid
where r1.sample = 1
and r2.sample = 2
and (r2.cpu - r1.cpu) > 0
```

```
order by (r2.cpu - r1.cpu) desc

select spid, hostname, program_name, nt_username
, sum(d_cpu_total) as sum_cpu
, sum(d_physical_io_total) as sum_io
from #Usage
group by spid, hostname, program_name, nt_username
order by 6 desc

drop table #resources
drop table #Usage
```

Who Is Waiting?

Listing 12-8, which shows the tasks that are currently waiting, uses the same sampling principle as the preceding query:

LISTING 12-8: Who is waiting.sql

```
select
* , 1 as sample
, getdate() as sample_time
into #waiting_tasks
from sys.dm_os_waiting_tasks

waitfor delay '00:00:10'

insert #waiting_tasks
select
* , 2
, getdate()
from sys.dm_os_waiting_tasks

-- figure out the deltas
select w1.session_id
, w1.exec_context_id
,w2.wait_duration_ms - w1.wait_duration_ms as d_wait_duration
, w1.wait_type
, w2.wait_type
, datediff(ms, w1.sample_time, w2.sample_time) as interval_ms
from #waiting_tasks as w1 inner join #waiting_tasks as w2 on w1.session_id =
w2.session_id
and w1.exec_context_id = w2.exec_context_id
where w1.sample = 1
and w2.sample = 2
order by 3 desc

-- select * from #waiting_tasks

drop table #waiting_tasks
```

Wait Stats

Listing 12-9 samples the wait stats to see what has changed over the sample period:

LISTING 12-9: Wait Stats.sql

```
select *, 1 as sample, getdate() as sample_time
into #wait_stats
from sys.dm_os_wait_stats

waitfor delay '00:00:30'
insert #wait_stats
select *, 2, getdate()
from sys.dm_os_wait_stats

-- figure out the deltas

select w2.wait_type
,w2.waiting_tasks_count - w1.waiting_tasks_count as d_wtc
, w2.wait_time_ms - w1.wait_time_ms as d_wtm
, cast((w2.wait_time_ms - w1.wait_time_ms) as float) /
cast((w2.waiting_tasks_count - w1.waiting_tasks_count) as float) as avg_wtm
, datediff(ms, w1.sample_time, w2.sample_time) as interval
from #wait_stats as w1 inner join #wait_stats as w2 on w1.wait_type =
w2.wait_type
where w1.sample = 1
and w2.sample = 2
and w2.wait_time_ms - w1.wait_time_ms > 0
and w2.waiting_tasks_count - w1.waiting_tasks_count > 0
order by 3 desc

drop table #wait_stats
```

Viewing the Locking Information

Listing 12-10 can help you get the locking information in a particular database:

LISTING 12-10: Locks.sql

```
SELECT l.resource_type, l.resource_associated_entity_id
,OBJECT_NAME(sp.OBJECT_ID) AS ObjectName
,l.request_status, l.request_mode,request_session_id
,l.resource_description
FROM sys.dm_tran_locks l
LEFT JOIN sys.partitions sp
 ON sp.hobt_id = l.resource_associated_entity_id
WHERE l.resource_database_id = DB_ID()
```

Viewing Blocking Information

Listing 12-11 returns blocking information on your server:

LISTING 12-11: Blocking.sql

```
SELECT
 t1.resource_type
,t1.resource_database_id
,t1.resource_associated_entity_id
,OBJECT_NAME(sp.OBJECT_ID) AS ObjectName
,t1.request_mode
,t1.request_session_id
,t2.blocking_session_id
FROM sys.dm_tran_locks as t1
JOIN sys.dm_os_waiting_tasks as t2
  ON t1.lock_owner_address = t2.resource_address
LEFT JOIN sys.partitions sp
  ON sp.hobt_id = t1.resource_associated_entity_id
```

Index Usage in a Database

Listing 12-12 can give you index usage for the database in which you run the query. It creates a table and stores the results in that table so that you can analyze it later. This query can be helpful to determine which indexes are truly useful in your application. Make sure you run these queries for several days because this can give you a better idea of the overall picture than looking at data for just one day. Keep in mind that dynamic management views are volatile, and whenever SQL Server is restarted, these views are initialized again.

LISTING 12-12: Index Usage Stats.sql

```
---------------------------------------------------------------------
IF OBJECT_ID('dbo.IndexUsageStats') IS NULL
CREATE TABLE dbo.IndexUsageStats
(
 IndexName sysname NULL
,ObjectName sysname NOT NULL
,user_seeks bigint NOT NULL
,user_scans bigint NOT NULL
,user_lookups bigint NOT NULL
,user_updates bigint NOT NULL
,last_user_seek datetime NULL
,last_user_scan datetime NULL
,last_user_lookup datetime NULL
,last_user_update datetime NULL
,StatusDate datetime NOT NULL
,DatabaseName sysname NOT NULL
)

GO
----Below query will give you index USED per table in a database.
INSERT INTO dbo.IndexUsageStats
(
 IndexName
,ObjectName
```

continues

LISTING 12-12 *(continued)*

```
        ,user_seeks
        ,user_scans
        ,user_lookups
        ,user_updates
        ,last_user_seek
        ,last_user_scan
        ,last_user_lookup
        ,last_user_update
        ,StatusDate
        ,DatabaseName
        )
    SELECT
     si.name AS IndexName
    ,so.name AS ObjectName
    ,diu.user_seeks
    ,diu.user_scans
    ,diu.user_lookups
    ,diu.user_updates
    ,diu.last_user_seek
    ,diu.last_user_scan
    ,diu.last_user_lookup
    ,diu.last_user_update
    ,GETDATE() AS StatusDate
    ,sd.name AS DatabaseName
    FROM sys.dm_db_index_usage_stats  diu
    JOIN sys.indexes si
      ON diu.object_id = si.object_id
     AND diu.index_id = si.index_id
    JOIN sys.all_objects so
      ON so.object_id = si.object_id
    JOIN sys.databases sd
      ON sd.database_id = diu.database_id
    WHERE is_ms_shipped <> 1
      AND diu.database_id = DB_ID()
```

Indexes Not Used in a Database

Listing 12-13 can give you information about which indexes are not being used. If certain indexes are not used, then you should consider dropping them because they take unnecessary time to create or maintain. The results stored in the table, NotUsedIndexes, indicate which indexes are not used. Make sure you run this query for several days because this can give you a better idea of the overall picture than looking at data for just one day. Keep in mind that dynamic management views are volatile, and whenever SQL Server is restarted, these views are initialized again.

LISTING 12-13: Indexes not being used.sql

```
-----------------------------------------------------------------------
--This will store the indexes which are not used.
IF OBJECT_ID('dbo.NotUsedIndexes') IS NULL
CREATE TABLE dbo.NotUsedIndexes
```

```
(
 IndexName sysname NULL
,ObjectName sysname NOT NULL
,StatusDate datetime NOT NULL
,DatabaseName sysname NOT NULL
)

----Below query will give you indexes which are NOT used per table in a database.
INSERT dbo.NotUsedIndexes
(
 IndexName
,ObjectName
,StatusDate
,DatabaseName
)
SELECT
 si.name AS IndexName
,so.name AS ObjectName
,GETDATE() AS  StatusDate
,DB_NAME()
FROM sys.indexes si
JOIN sys.all_objects so
  ON so.object_id = si.object_id
WHERE si.index_id NOT IN (SELECT index_id
                          FROM sys.dm_db_index_usage_stats diu
                          WHERE si.object_id = diu.object_id
                            AND si.index_id = diu.index_id
                          )
  AND so.is_ms_shipped <> 1
```

View Queries Waiting for Memory Grants

Listing 12-14 indicates the queries waiting for memory grants. SQL Server analyzes a query and determines how much memory it needs based on the estimated plan. If memory is not available at that time, the query is suspended until the memory required is available. If a query is waiting for a memory grant, an entry shows up in the DMV sys.dm_exec_query_memory_grants:

LISTING 12-14: waiting for memory grants.sql

Available for
download on
Wrox.com

```
SELECT
 es.session_id AS SPID
,es.login_name
,es.host_name
,es.program_name, es.status AS Session_Status
,mg.requested_memory_kb
,DATEDIFF(mi, mg.request_time
, GETDATE()) AS [WaitingSince-InMins]
FROM sys.dm_exec_query_memory_grants mg
JOIN sys.dm_exec_sessions es
  ON es.session_id = mg.session_id
WHERE mg.grant_time IS NULL
ORDER BY mg.request_time
```

Connected User Information

Listing 12-15 can tell you which users are connected, and how many sessions each of them has open:

LISTING 12-15: Connected Users.sql

```sql
SELECT login_name
    , count(session_id) as session_count
FROM sys.dm_exec_sessions
GROUP BY login_name
```

Filegroup Free Space

Listing 12-16 indicates how much free space remains in each filegroup. This is valuable when your database uses multiple filegroups. Please note that this query uses catalog views rather than DMVs.

LISTING 12-16: filegroup free space.sql

```sql
-- Find the total size of each Filegroup
select data_space_id, (sum(size)*8)/1000 as total_size_MB
into #filegroups
from sys.database_files
group by data_space_id
order by data_space_id

-- Find how much we have allocated in each FG
select ds.name, au.data_space_id
, (sum(au.total_pages) * 8)/1000 as Allocated_MB
, (sum(au.used_pages) * 8)/1000 as used_MB
, (sum(au.data_pages) * 8)/1000 as Data_MB
, ((sum(au.total_pages) -  sum(au.used_pages) ) * 8 )/1000 as Free_MB
into #Allocations
from sys.allocation_units as au inner join sys.data_spaces as ds
    on au.data_space_id = ds.data_space_id
group by ds.name, au.data_space_id
order by au.data_space_id
-- Bring it all together
select f.data_space_id
, a.name
, f.total_size_MB
, a.allocated_MB
, f.total_size_MB - a.allocated_MB as free_in_fg_MB
, a.used_MB
, a.data_MB
, a.Free_MB
from #filegroups as f inner join #allocations as a
on f.data_space_id = a.data_space_id
order by f.data_space_id

drop table #allocations

drop table #filegroups
```

Query Plan and Query Text for Currently Running Queries

Use the following query to find out the query plan in XML and the query text for the currently running batch for a particular session. Make sure that you use a grid to output the result in SQL Server Management Studio. When you get the result, you can click the link for the XML plan, which opens an XML editor inside Management Studio. If you want to look at the graphical query plan from this XML plan, click on the link to the XML plan, and it opens in anew window in SSMS. Listing 12-17 provides the query:

LISTING 12-17: query plan for running queries.sql

Available for
download on
Wrox.com

```
SELECT
  er.session_id
 ,es.login_name
 ,er.request_id
 ,er.start_time
 ,QueryPlan_XML = (SELECT query_plan FROM
sys.dm_exec_query_plan(er.plan_handle))
 ,SQLText = (SELECT Text FROM sys.dm_exec_sql_text(er.sql_handle))
FROM sys.dm_exec_requests er
JOIN sys.dm_exec_sessions es
  ON er.session_id = es.session_id
WHERE es.is_user_process = 1
ORDER BY er.start_time ASC
```

Memory Usage

Listing 12-18 indicates the memory used, in KB, by each internal SQL Server component:

LISTING 12-18: memory usage.sql

Available for
download on
Wrox.com

```
SELECT
  name
 ,type
 ,SUM(single_pages_kb + multi_pages_kb) AS MemoryUsedInKB
FROM sys.dm_os_memory_clerks
GROUP BY name, type
ORDER BY SUM(single_pages_kb + multi_pages_kb) DESC
```

Buffer Pool Memory Usage

Listing 12-19 lists out all the objects within the buffer pool, along with the amount of space used by each. This is a great way to see who uses the Buffer Pool:

LISTING 12-19: Buffer Pool Memory Usage.sql

Available for
download on
Wrox.com

```
SELECT count(*)AS cached_pages_count
     ,name ,index_id
FROM sys.dm_os_buffer_descriptors AS bd
```

continues

LISTING 12-19 *(continued)*

```
    INNER JOIN
    (
        SELECT object_name(object_id) AS name
            ,index_id ,allocation_unit_id
        FROM sys.allocation_units AS au
            INNER JOIN sys.partitions AS p
                ON au.container_id = p.hobt_id
                    AND (au.type = 1 OR au.type = 3)
        UNION ALL
        SELECT object_name(object_id) AS name
            ,index_id, allocation_unit_id
        FROM sys.allocation_units AS au
            INNER JOIN sys.partitions AS p
                ON au.container_id = p.partition_id
                    AND au.type = 2
    ) AS obj
        ON bd.allocation_unit_id = obj.allocation_unit_id
WHERE database_id = db_id()
GROUP BY name, index_id
ORDER BY cached_pages_count DESC;
```

MONITORING LOGS

Another aspect of monitoring that is frequently overlooked is monitoring the various log files available. SQL Server writes its own error log, and then there are the Windows Event logs, and you may find events logged in the Application, Security, or System Event logs.

Traditionally, the SQL Server and Windows Event logs have been viewed through separate applications: Windows Logs through the Windows Event Viewer, and SQL Logs through a text editor. The SQL Server Management Studio Log File viewer enables you to combine both sets of logs into a combined view. There are root level nodes for SQL Server, SQL Server Agent, Database Mail, and Windows NT that enable you to do this.

Monitoring the SQL Server Error Log

The SQL Server Error log is the location where SQL Server writes all its error information, and also a lot of additional informational messages about how it is working and what it is doing.

The error log is a text file written to the `C:\Program Files\Microsoft SQL Server\MSSQL11 .MSSQLSERVER\MSSQL\Log folder`. A new log file is opened each time the SQL Server process starts. SQL Server keeps seven log files: the current one is called simply `errorlog`, and the oldest one is called `errorlog.6`.

The error log contains a lot of useful information. It is definitely the place to go looking for deadlock information after the relevant deadlock trace flags have been enabled.

Anytime a significant issue occurs, the first place to search for additional information should be the SQL Server Error Log. Additionally, both Event Notifications and Extended Events can be used if additional data is required to help troubleshoot a particular issue.

Monitoring the Windows Event Logs

Three Windows event logs may hold entries of relevance to a SQL Server event:

➤   Application event log

➤   Security event log

➤   System event log

These event logs contain additional event information about the server environment, other processes/ applications operating on the server, and also additional information about the SQL Server process that may not be logged into the SQL Server Error log. These logs should be another place that you go to look for additional information about any issues that arise with SQL Server.

MANAGEMENT DATA WAREHOUSE

New to SQL Server 2008 was the Management Data Warehouse (MDW) and Data Collection. This was a new framework for data collection, storage, and reporting.

SQL Server 2008 R2 added the SQL Utility, the Utility Control Point (UCP), and the Utility Management Data Warehouse (UMDW) as a new location for data storage. The SQL Utility is a container for "managed instances" of SQL Server. The UMDW is a destination for data collection. The UCP data collector sets differ from the MDW in the granularity of data being collected. The MDW data collector is focused on troubleshooting individual queries. The UCP data collector set focuses on higher level system resource usage and is there to help the DBA determine when a SQL instance is under- or over-utilized. The UCP also provides additional reporting capabilities that were not available in SQL Server 2008 RTM.

For SQL Server 2012, you get the basics of Data Collection, a few Data Collection sets, the Management Data Warehouse, and some reports.

Following is a list of the basic concepts:

➤   **Data provider:** A data provider is a source of data to be captured. SQL Server 2012 has four data providers:

  ➤   SQL Trace

  ➤   Performance Monitor Counters

  ➤   T-SQL

  ➤   Query Activity

➤   **Collection item:** A collection item is a specific item of data to be collected. This might be a single performance monitor counter, a SQL Trace event, or a T-SQL query of a DMV.

➤ **Collection set:** A collection set is a logical grouping of collection items that are collected together. This might be all the performance counters monitoring disk I/O, or all the SQL trace events to look for long-running queries.

➤ **Management Data Warehouse (MDW):** The Management Data Warehouse is where the items in each collection set are stored. It is the repository of historical data that you have collected. This can be either an MDW, or a UMDW. MDW data collections can be written to a UMDW, but UMDW data collections cannot be written to an MDW.

➤ **Target servers:** The target servers are the systems that you want to monitor. Ideally, the MDW should be on a separate server. If it's on one of the target servers, you run the risk of recording activity about the data collection, rather than the target server you are actually interested in.

➤ **Data collection process:** Data collection is performed by a series of SQL Agent jobs running SSIS packages that perform the data collection. Data is then captured based on the schedule defined for each collection set. It is then cached and written only to the MDW when the current buffer is full. This helps optimize I/O to the MDW.

You should expect to consume between 200–400MB/day for each server being monitored. These figures come from using the basic set of data collection sets, with 200MB per day for an idle server, and 400MB per day for a busy server.

System Data Collection Sets

Three system data collection sets ship with SQL Server 2012:

➤ **Disk Usage:** The Disk Usage system collector set collects disk usage performance counters. It is helpful for monitoring disk usage. The collected data is cached and then uploaded to the warehouse every 6 hours, where it is retained for 90 days.

➤ **Query Activity:** The Query Activity system collection set captures query activity on the target server. It collects data from the server every 15 minutes and helps you identify the most interesting queries running on a server without having to run a Profiler trace. It captures the top three queries from several different resource usage categories.

➤ **Server Activity:** The Server Activity system collection set collects a set of performance counters. Wait Statistics, Scheduler, Performance Counters, and Memory Counters are collected every 60 seconds. The active sessions and requests are collected every 10 seconds. The data is uploaded to the warehouse every 5 minutes and is deleted from the warehouse after 14 days.

Viewing Data Collected by the System Data Collection Sets

Along with the system data collection sets is a set of reports that displays the history collected in the Management Data Warehouse for each of these data collection sets. To access these reports in SQL Server Management Studio, follow these steps:

1. Open Object Explorer and select Management ➪ Data Collection ➪ System Data Collection Sets. Under the System Data Collection Sets node, you see the three system data collection sets listed.

2. To see the reports, right-click on a data collection set node (for example, Disk Usage) and select the reports item from the menu.

3. Then select Reports ➪ Historical ➪ Disk Usage Summary. Figure 12-29 shows this navigation path. The Disk Usage report displays, showing the history of disk usage data stored in the Management Data Warehouse. It look something like the report shown in Figure 12-30.

4. Click a database name to see the detailed report for that database, as shown in Figure 12-31.

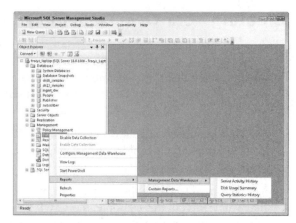

FIGURE 12-29

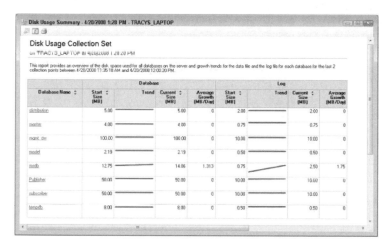

FIGURE 12-30

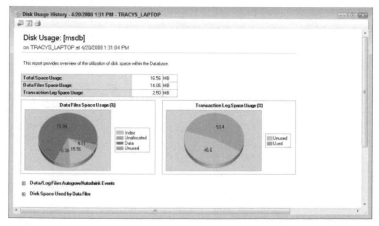

FIGURE 12-31

Creating Your Own Data Collection Set

After seeing the system data collection sets, the next step is to set up your own custom data collection sets. Currently, there is no wizard or easy user interface to handle this process, so you need to write T-SQL to execute the steps required. Fortunately, there are only a couple of simple steps. The hardest part is determining what data you want to collect, where it needs to come from, and what schedule you want to capture the data on.

For this example you create a custom collection set to execute a T-SQL query that queries the max ID from an example table that has a high insertion rate. This information enables you to report on insertion rates over a period of time.

You first need to create the sample table, which can live in either an existing database or a new database that you create. In this example, the T-SQL to create a 50MB database in the default location is included with the table-creation code. The steps needed to complete this are described along with the code.

1. Create the sample database and table:

```
CREATE DATABASE [ch12_samples] ON  PRIMARY
( NAME = N'ch12_samples'
, FILENAME = N'C:\Program Files\Microsoft SQL
 Server\MSSQL11.MSSQLSERVER\MSSQL\DATA\ch12_samples.mdf'
, SIZE = 51200KB
, MAXSIZE = UNLIMITED
, FILEGROWTH = 1024KB )
 LOG ON
( NAME = N'ch12_samples_log'
, FILENAME = N'C:\Program Files\Microsoft SQL
Server\MSSQL11.MSSQLSERVER\MSSQL\DATA\ch12_samples_log.ldf'
, SIZE = 10240KB
, MAXSIZE = 2048GB
, FILEGROWTH = 10%)
GO


create table Sales (
ID int identity (1,1) not null,
sku int not null,
quantity int not null
)
go


-- insert some sales
insert sales (sku, quantity) values (1,1)
```

2. Create the collection set to get the max (id) every hour, and keep this for 45 days in the Management Data Warehouse:

```
-- Create the collection set
-- Make sure this runs in msdb as that's where the DC SPs live.
use msdb
GO


-- Find the uid for the schedule you want to use which is every 60 minutes
declare @schedule_uid uniqueidentifier
```

```
select @schedule_uid = (select schedule_uid
  from sysschedules_localserver_view
    where name=N'CollectorSchedule_Every_60min')

-- Create a new custom collection set
declare @collection_set_id int
exec dbo.sp_syscollector_create_collection_set
    @name = N'Sample insertion rate',
    @schedule_uid = @schedule_uid,  -- 60 minutes
    @collection_mode = 1, -- Set collection mode to non cached,
ie collection and upload are on the same schedule
    @days_until_expiration = 45, -- Keep data for 45 days
    @description = N'Sample max(id) so we can
determine hourly insertion rates',
    @collection_set_id = @collection_set_id output

select @collection_set_id as collection_set_id

declare @paramters xml
declare @collection_item_id int
declare @collection_type_uid uniqueidentifier

-- Create the XML parameters for the collection item
select @paramters = convert(xml,
    N'<TSQLQueryCollector>
        <Query>
          <Value>select max(id) as max_id from sales</Value>
          <OutputTable>max_sales_id</OutputTable>
        </Query>
        <Databases>
            <Database>Ch13_samples</Database>
        </Databases>
      </TSQLQueryCollector>')

-- Find the Collector type you want to use which is TSQL
select @collection_type_uid  = collector_type_uid
from syscollector_collector_types
where name = 'Generic T-SQL Query Collector Type'

-- Create the new collection item
exec dbo.sp_syscollector_create_collection_item
    @collection_set_id = @collection_set_id,
    @collector_type_uid = @Collection_type_uid,
    @name = 'Sales max ID',
    @frequency = 60,
    @parameters = @paramters,
    @collection_item_id = @collection_item_id output;

-- report the ID that just got created
select @collection_item_id as collection_item_id

-- start the collection set
exec dbo.sp_syscollector_start_collection_set
    @Collection_set_id = @collection_set_id
```

Now you have created a new custom snapshot that contains the max ID from the sales table, sampled over time. This enables you to report on the growth of records in the sales table.

Examining the Data You Collected

The data collected is stored in the Management Data Warehouse. From the preceding example, there is now a new custom snapshot table created, called `custom_snapshots.max_sales_id`, as shown in Figure 12-32.

The table you created has some additional columns, not defined in the data you selected for the snapshot. These are `database_name`, `collection_time`, and `snapshot_id`. In addition, the collection time is stored in a `datimeoffset` column. This was a new data type in SQL Server 2008 and when queried, returns the date/time as a UTC time.

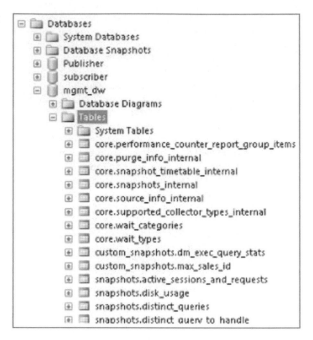

FIGURE 12-32

Following is the T-SQL to retrieve the data stored by the collection set you just created:

```
-- Find the data you recorded
-- Switch to the MDW
use mgmt_dw
go

-- Query the custom snapshot
select
* from custom_snapshots.max_sales_id
```

Table 12-6 shows the results of this query after the collector has been running for a few minutes with no inserts to the table.

TABLE 12-6: Custom Snapshots

MAX_ID	DATABASE_NAME	COLLECTION_TIME	SNAPSHOT_ID
1	Ch12_samples	9/23/2012 1:59:44 AM +00:00	93
1	Ch12_samples	9/23/2012 2:00:21 AM +00:00	97

To fully leverage the data stored in the Management Data Warehouse, consider creating SQL Server Reporting Services reports to display the data.

SQL SERVER STANDARD REPORTS

One of the best kept secrets in SQL Server is the standard reports that started shipping with the SQL Server 2005 Performance dashboard reports. Since then, each edition of SQL Server has added to the standard reporting capabilities, until today whence a comprehensive set of reports that provide a great deal of detailed information on what's going on inside SQL Server has come about.

The standard reports are accessible through SQL Server Management Studio. Starting with the Server Node in SSMS, right-click the server node, then Reports, and then Standard Reports to see the list of reports for the SQL Server Instance. The list of standard reports for the server node is shown in Figure 12-33.

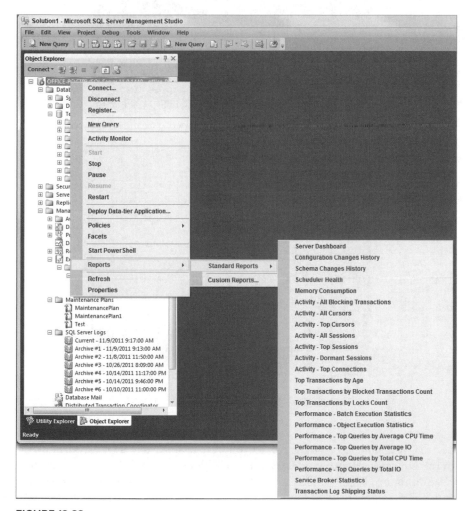

FIGURE 12-33

As you navigate through the various nodes in the Object Explorer, different reports are available at different key nodes. In some cases, no standard reports exist and just a custom report node that's empty can be found. In other cases, such as when you select a specific database, a long list of standard reports is available. Figure 12-34 shows the standard reports for a database.

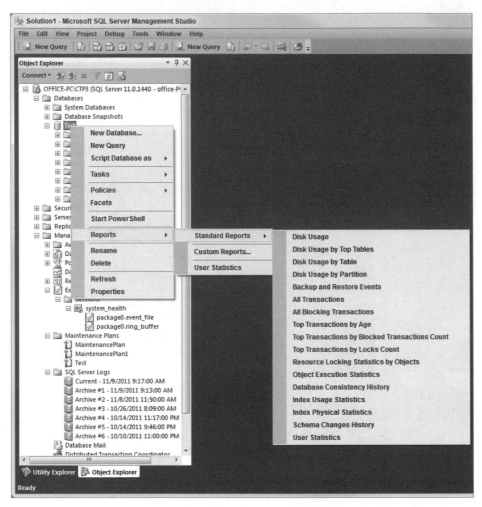

FIGURE 12-34

Unfortunately, these are not documented anywhere, so you have to find your own way around the various nodes in the Object Explorer by clicking nodes and looking in the Reports menu to see where there are any Standard Reports. Figure 12-35 shows one more location where there are standard reports, which is under Security ⇨ Logins.

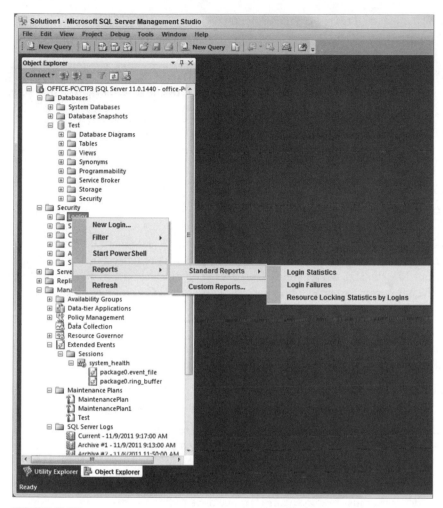

FIGURE 12-35

SYSTEM CENTER MANAGEMENT PACK

All the monitoring discussed so far has been interactive in nature and has been based around activities that a single DBA executes against a small number of SQL Servers.

As DBAs must cover more and more databases, they need to change from an interactive monitoring mode to an exception-driven monitoring model. This is where the System Center suite, and specifically System Center Operations Manager comes in. System Center Operations Manager (SCOM) provides a product that delivers exception and performance monitoring that can gather a broad set of performance, health, and exception data from a large number of servers. SCOM then consolidates the data and presents a high-level rollup of your entire datacenter health.

This approach lets a relatively small team manage or operate a large number of servers, knowing that any time something needs to happen, an alert or exception will be raised that lets them react to the relevant activity.

SQL Server 2012 has a new management pack that integrates both with the current shipping version of System Center Operations Manager 2007, and also with the next version, System Center Operations Manager 2012.

SCOM 2012 provides some considerable enhancements to SCOM functionality that make the upgrade worthwhile. These are primarily the new dashboards that provide a consolidated view of SQL Server health.

SQL SERVER BEST PRACTICE ANALYZER

The SQL Server Best Practice Analyzer is a tool introduced around the SQL Server 2005 time frame to help you know if your SQL Server instance meets currently accepted best practices. It was originally a stand-alone tool developed by the SQL Server Release Services team but has since evolved into a set of rules implemented in the Microsoft Baseline Configuration Analyzer (MBCA) framework.

SQL Server Best Practice Analyzer (BPA) is a stand-alone tool installed to each instance on which you want to run it. Once you install it, you then run the BPA and point it at a given SQL instance, provide credentials for it to connect, and it scans the SQL Instance and compares its configuration with the set of rules included in that version of the SQL BPA.

Any exceptions to the rules are reported in the output, and each exception will include some basic text, and a link to an online resource providing more information about the rule that was infringed.

Something important to remember about SQL BPA is that these are general purpose best practices, and in some cases it's perfectly acceptable that your SQL Server instance doesn't meet the relevant best practice. However every exception should be considered, and you should ensure that you understand why your instance doesn't meet the relevant rule.

Something else to consider is that just because your instance doesn't fire any exceptions does not mean that everything is fine. There are plenty of specific best practices that are not incorporated into the SQL BPA, so a clean report doesn't necessarily mean you're optimally configured. However it is a great place to start.

SYSTEM CENTER ADVISOR

System Center Advisor (SCA) is the natural evolution of SQL Server Best Practice Analyzer. One of the challenges with SQL BPA is that the set of rules are encoded into each version for BPA that's released, and knowledge about best practices can change more quickly than new versions can be released. SQL BPA is also a tool that needs to be manually executed on each server.

System Center Advisor is the result of a lot of effort by folks who work with SQL Server and the SQL teams within PSS to deliver a more effective tool for validating SQL Server configurations.

System Center Advisor is a cloud-based configuration monitoring tool that can continuously monitor a large number of servers and provide online analysis of the results. One of the benefits of being cloud-based is that new best practices can be incorporated into the validation checks quickly, and with no activity on you, the end user's part. The System Center Advisor team can introduce a new rule with minimal effort, and every server being monitored by SCA can immediately gain the benefit of being checked against the new rule.

SUMMARY

Monitoring SQL Server regularly and gathering performance data is key to helping identify performance problems. Increasingly, today's DBAs need to cover more systems than ever before and must spread their net widely. The tools and techniques introduced in this chapter help the DBAs do that to move from a hands-on approach to an event-driven approach.

Performance Monitor enables the DBA to monitor resource usage for a server, and helps troubleshoot performance issues with server and SQL resource usage.

The SQL Server Dynamic Management Views and Functions provide a deep insight into what's going on inside SQL Server, and the samples provided help illustrate how to use some of the DMVs and DMFs to troubleshoot specific issues.

The SQL Trace architecture with SQL Profiler, SQL Trace, and now Distributed Replay provide tools for capturing, analyzing, and replaying SQL Server events.

Event Notifications provides a framework to execute actions outside SQL Server asynchronously in response to events occurring inside the server.

Extended Events provides a scalable framework for capturing data when specific events occur within SQL Server. This is a powerful framework that enables complex data collection to assist with troubleshooting SQL Server issues.

Data Collection sets, the Management Data Warehouse, and Utility MDW are a mechanism to collect performance related data and store it in a data warehouse. The Data Collector framework is a powerful way to store large amounts of performance data in a data warehouse for analysis should a performance issue occur, or just for trend analysis to see how load and performance is changing over time.

The System Center Operations Manager and the SQL Server 2012 Management Pack provide a central management interface for a data center operations team to monitor the health of hundreds of SQL Servers, and react to critical events when they occur.

SQL Server Best Practice Analyzer tells you when your SQL Server instance is in compliance with the established Best Practices.

System Center Advisor provides a cloud based service for best practices and for patch and update checking to help you keep your SQL Servers current with the very latest knowledge around SQL Server Best Practices.

In the next chapter you learn how to performance tune T-SQL.

13

Performance Tuning T-SQL

➤ Query Processing Including Tools Usage and Optimization

➤ The Query Tuning Process Including Joins, Query Plans, and Indexes

Performance tuning T-SQL is interesting but also quite frequently frustrating. It is interesting because there is so much involved in tuning that knowledge of SQL Server's architecture and internals plays a large role in doing it well. It can be frustrating when you do not have access to change the source query as it resides inside a vendor application, or when it seems that whatever optimization technique is tried, the performance issue does not seem to be resolved. Of course, knowledge alone is not sufficient without the right tools, which you learn about in this chapter. If you have tuned a query and reduced its runtime, you may have jumped up and down with excitement, but sometimes you cannot achieve that result even after losing sleep for many nights.

In this chapter, you learn how to gather the data for query tuning, the tools for query tuning, the stages a query goes through before execution, and a little bit on how to analyze the execution plan. You must understand which stages a query passes through before actually being executed by the execution engine, so start with physical query processing.

PHYSICAL QUERY PROCESSING PART ONE: COMPILATION AND RECOMPILATION

SQL Server performs two main steps to produce the desired result when a query fires. As you would guess, the first step is query compilation, which generates the query plan; the second step is the execution of the query plan (this will be discussed later in the chapter). The compilation phase in SQL Server 2012 goes through three steps: parsing, algebrization, and optimization. In SQL Server 2000, there was a *normalization* phase, which was replaced with the algebrization piece in SQL Server 2005. The SQL Server team has spent much effort to re-architect and rewrite several parts of SQL Server. Of course, the goal is to redesign logic to serve current and future expansions of SQL Server functionality. Having said that, after the three steps just mentioned are completed, the compiler stores the optimized query plan in the plan cache.

Now you are going to investigate compilation and recompilation of queries, with a detailed look at parsing, algebrization and optimization in detail.

Compilation

Before a query, batch, stored procedure, trigger, or dynamic SQL statement begins execution on SQL Server 2012, the batch is compiled into a plan. The plan is then executed for its effects or to produce results. The flowchart in Figure 13-1 displays the steps in the compilation process in SQL Server 2012.

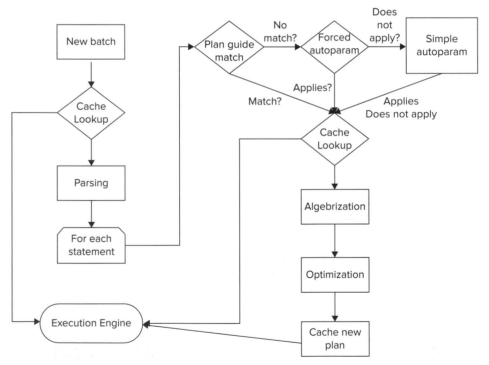

FIGURE 13-1

When a batch starts, the compilation process tries to find the cached plan in the plan cache. If it finds a match, the execution engine takes over. If a match is not found, the parser starts parsing (explained later in this section). The plan guide match feature (introduced with SQL Server 2005) determines whether an existing plan guide for a particular statement exists. (You learn how to create the plan guide later.) If it exists, it uses the plan guide for that statement for execution. (The concepts of *forced autoparam* and *simple autoparam* are described later in the chapter.) If a match is found, the plan is sent to the algebrizer (explained later in this section), which creates a logical, or parse, tree for input to the optimizer (also explained later in this section). The logical tree or parse tree is generated by the process that checks whether the T-SQL is written correctly. The parse tree represents the logical steps necessary to execute the query. The plan is then cached in the plan cache. Of course, not all the plans are cached; for example, when you create a stored procedure with WITH RECOMPILE, the plan is not cached.

Recompilation

Sometimes a cached plan needs to be recompiled because it is not valid for some reason. Suppose that a batch has been compiled into a collection of one or more query plans. SQL Server 2012 checks for validity (correctness) and optimality of that query plan before it begins executing any of the individual query plans. If one of the checks fails, the statement corresponding to the query plan or the entire batch is compiled again, and a possibly different query plan is produced. Such compilations are known as *recompilations*.

From SQL Server 2005 onward, if a statement in a batch causes the recompilation, then only that statement recompiles, not the whole batch. This *statement-level recompilation* has some advantages. In particular, it results in less CPU time and memory use during batch recompilations and obtains fewer compile locks. Prior to this change, if you had a long stored procedure, it was sometimes necessary to break it into small chunks just to reduce compile time.

The reasons for recompilation can be broadly classified in two categories:

➤ Correctness

➤ Plan optimality

Correctness

If the query processor decides that the cache plan would produce incorrect results, it recompiles that statement or batch. There are multiple reasons why the plan would produce incorrect results — changes to the table or view referenced by the query, changes to the indexes used by the execution plan, updates to the statistics, an explicit call to sp_recompile, or executing a stored procedure using the WITH RECOMPILE option. The following sections investigate how the changes that can occur to the schemas of objects cause recompilation as well as how SET options can cause recompilation.

Schemas of Objects

Your query batch could be referencing many objects such as tables, views, user-defined functions (UDFs), or indexes; and if the schemas of any of the objects referenced in the query have changed since your batch was last compiled, your batch must be recompiled for statement-correctness reasons. Schema changes could include many things, such as adding an index on a table or in an indexed view, or adding or dropping a column in a table or view.

Since the release of SQL Server 2005, manually dropping or creating statistics on a table causes recompilation. Recompilation is triggered when the statistics are updated automatically, too.

Manually updating statistics does not change the schema version. This means that queries that reference the table but do not use the updated statistics are not recompiled. Only queries that use the updated statistics are recompiled.

> *Using two-part object names (*`schema.objectname`*) is recommended as a best practice. Including the server and database name can cause issues when moving code between servers, for example, from Dev to QA.*

Batches with unqualified object names may result in the generation of multiple query plans. For example, in `"SELECT * FROM MyTable,"` `MyTable` may legitimately resolve to `Fred.MyTable` if Fred issues this query and he owns a table with that name. Similarly, `MyTable` may resolve to `Joe.MyTable` if Joe issues the query. In such cases, SQL Server 2012 does not reuse query plans. If, however, Fred issues `"SELECT * FROM dbo.MyTable,"` and Joe issues the SAME query, there is no ambiguity because the object is uniquely identified, and query plan reuse can happen. However, if Fred runs the query `"SELECT * FROM MyTable"` a second time, the cached plan will be reused.

SET Options

Some of the `SET` options affect query results. If the setting of a `SET` option affecting plan reuse is changed inside of a batch, a compilation happens. The `SET` options that affect plan reusability are `ANSI_NULLS`, `ANSI_NULL_DFLT_ON`, `ANSI_PADDING`, `ANSI_WARNINGS`, `CURSOR_CLOSE_ON_COMMIT`, `IMPLICIT_TRANSACTIONS`, and `QUOTED_IDENTIFIER`.

> *A number of SET options have been marked for deprecation in a future version of SQL Server. The SET options* `ANSI_NULLS`*,* `ANSI_PADDING`*, and* `CONCAT_NULLS_YIELDS_NULL` *will always be set to ON.* `SET OFFSETS` *will be unavailable.*

These `SET` options affect plan reuse because SQL Server performs *constant folding*, evaluating a constant expression at compile time to enable some optimizations, and because the settings of these options affect the results of such expressions.

Listing 13-1 demonstrates how `SET` options cause recompilation:

LISTING 13-1: RecompileSetOption.sql

```
USE AdventureWorks
GO

IF OBJECT_ID('dbo.RecompileSetOption') IS NOT NULL
    DROP PROC dbo.RecompileSetOption
GO

CREATE PROC dbo.RecompileSetOption
```

```
AS
SET ANSI_NULLS OFF

SELECT s.CustomerID, COUNT(s.SalesOrderID)
FROM Sales.SalesOrderHeader s
GROUP BY s.CustomerID
HAVING COUNT(s.SalesOrderID) > 8
GO


EXEC dbo.RecompileSetOption      -- Causes a recompilation
GO
EXEC dbo.RecompileSetOption      -- does not cause a recompilation
GO
```

By default, the SET ANSI_NULLS option is ON, so when you compile this stored procedure, it compiles with this option ON. Inside the stored procedure, you have set ANSI_NULLS to OFF, so when you begin executing this stored procedure, the compiled plan is not valid and recompiles with SET ANSI_NULLS OFF. The second execution does not cause a recompilation because the cached plan compiles with "ansi_nulls" set to OFF.

 To avoid SET *option–related recompilations, establish* SET *options at connection time, and ensure that they do not change for the duration of the connection. You can do this by not changing set options at any point within a query statement.*

Plan Optimality

SQL Server is designed to generate the optimal query execution plan as data changes in your database. As you know, data distributions are tracked with statistics (histograms) for use in the SQL Server query processor. The table content changes because of INSERT, UPDATE, and DELETE operations. Table contents are tracked *directly* using the number of rows in the table and *indirectly* using statistics on table columns (explained in detail later in the chapter). The query processor checks the threshold to determine whether it should recompile the query plan, using the following formula:

```
[ Colmodctr (snapshot) - Colmodctr (current) ] >= RT
```

Since SQL Server 2005, the table modifications are tracked using Colmodctr. The Colmodctr is stored for each column, so changes to a table can be tracked with finer granularity in SQL Server 2005 and later. Rowmodctr is available in SQL Server 2005 and later, but it is only there for backward compatibility.

In this formula, `colmodctr (snapshot)` is the value stored at the time the query plan was generated, and `colmodctr (current)` is the current value. If the difference between these counters as shown in the formula is greater or equal to recompilation threshold (RT), then recompilation happens for that statement. RT is calculated as follows for permanent and temporary tables. The *n* refers to a table's cardinality (the number of rows in the table) when a query plan is compiled.

For a permanent table, the formula is as follows:

```
If n <= 500, RT = 500
If n > 500, RT = 500 + 0.20 * n
```

For a temporary table, the formula is as follows:

```
If n < 6, RT = 6
If 6 <= n <= 500, RT = 500
If n > 500, RT = 500 + 0.20 * n
```

For a table variable, RT does not exist. Therefore, recompilations do not happen because of changes in cardinality to table variables. Table 13-1 shows how the `colmodctr` is modified in SQL Server 2005 and later through different data manipulation language (DML) statements.

TABLE 13-1: colmodctr Modification

STATEMENT	COLMODCTR
INSERT	All `colmodctr += 1` (`colmodctr` is incremented by 1 for each column in the table for each insert).
DELETE	All `colmodctr += 1`
UPDATE	If the update is to non-key columns, `colmodctr+= 1` for all of the updated columns. If the update is to key columns, `colmodctr+= 2` for all the columns.
BULK INSERT	Like n INSERTs. All `colmodctr += n` (n is the number of rows bulk inserted).
TABLE TRUNCATION	Like n DELETEs. All `colmodctr += n` (n is the table's cardinal).

You can see the physical query process in action by following the code in Listing 13-2 and performing the steps associated with it. The goal is to determine whether the stored procedure plan is reused. Listing 13-2 also uses SQL Profiler and the dynamic management view (DMV) `sys .dm_exec_cached_plans` to examine some interesting details. To determine whether a compiled plan is reused, you must monitor the events `SP:CacheMiss`, `SP:CacheHit`, and `SP:CacheInsert` under the Stored Procedures event class. Figure 13-2 shows these stored procedure plan compilation events in SQL Profiler.

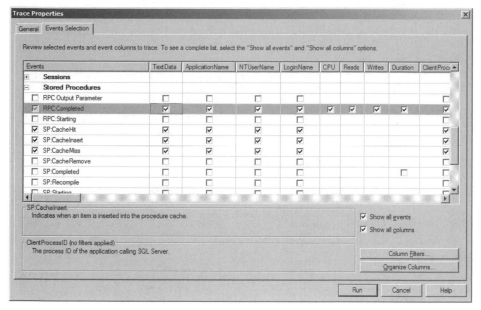

FIGURE 13-2

The following steps and code provide a working example of physical query processing.

1. Connect to the SQL Server on which you have the AdventureWorks database.

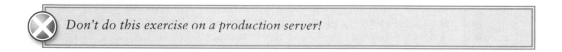

Don't do this exercise on a production server!

2. Compile the stored procedure TestCacheReUse in AdventureWorks. The code is as follows in Listing 13-2.

LISTING 13-2: ExecuteSP.sql

```
USE AdventureWorks
GO
IF OBJECT_ID('dbo.TestCacheReUse') IS NOT NULL
    DROP PROC dbo.TestCacheReUse
GO
CREATE PROC dbo.TestCacheReUse
AS

SELECT BusinessEntityID, LoginID, JobTitle
FROM HumanResources.Employee
WHERE BusinessEntityID = 109
GO
```

3. Connect the SQL Profiler to your designated machine, and start it after selecting the events (refer to Figure 13-2). Now execute the stored procedure `TestCacheReUse` as follows:

```
USE AdventureWorks
GO
EXEC dbo.TestCacheReUse
```

In SQL Server Profiler you can find the `SP:CacheMiss` and `SP:CacheInsert` events, as shown in Figure 13-3.

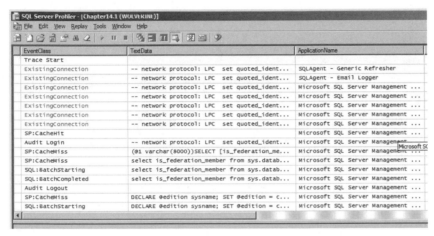

FIGURE 13-3

The `SP:CacheMiss` event indicates that the compiled plan is not found in the plan cache (refer to Figure 13-3). The stored procedure plan is compiled and inserted into the plan cache indicated by `SP:CacheInsert`, and then the procedure `TestCacheReUse` is executed.

4. Execute the same procedure again. This time SQL Server 2012 finds the query plan in the plan cache, as shown in Figure 13-4.

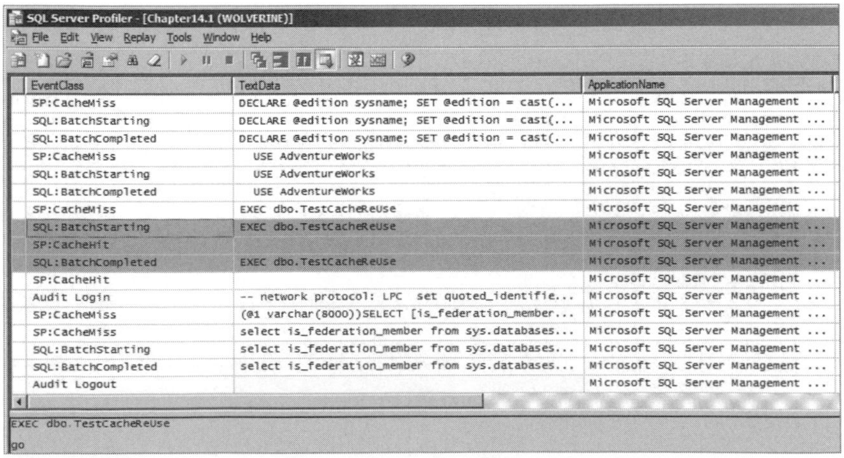

FIGURE 13-4

The plan for the stored procedure `TestCacheReUse` was found in the plan cache, which is why you see the event `SP:CacheHit` (refer to Figure 13-4).

5. The DMV `sys.dm_exec_cached_plans` also provides information about the plans that are currently cached, along with some other information. Open the script `DMV_CachePlanInfo.sql` from the solution `QueryPlanReUse`, shown here; the syntax in the following query is valid only when the database is in level 90 compatibility mode or higher:

```
SELECT  bucketid, (SELECT Text FROM sys.dm_exec_sql_text(plan_handle)) AS
SQLStatement, usecounts,size_in_bytes, refcounts
FROM sys.dm_exec_cached_plans
WHERE cacheobjtype = 'Compiled Plan'
  AND objtype = 'proc'
```

6. Run this script; you should see output similar to what is shown in Figure 13-5.

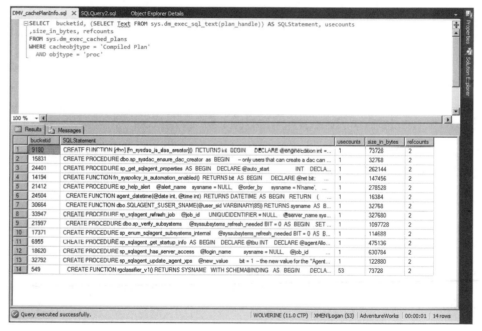

FIGURE 13-5

This script uses the dynamic management function (DMF) `sys.dm_exec_sql_text` to get the SQL text for the `plan_handle`. Refer to Figure 13-5 to see that the compiled plan for the stored procedure `TestCacheReUse` that you executed earlier is cached. The column `UseCounts` in the output shows how many times this plan has been used since its inception. The first inception of the plan for this stored procedure was created when the `SP:CacheInsert` event happened (refer to Figure 13-3). You can also see the number of bytes consumed by the cache object (refer to Figure 13-5). In this case, the cache plan for the stored procedure `TestCacheReUse` has consumed 32KB in the plan cache. If you run `DBCC FREEPROCCACHE` now, and then run the query in the `DMV_cachePlanInfo.sql` script, you notice that the rows returned are 0 because `DBCC FREEPROCCACHE` cleared the procedure cache.

If you use WITH RECOMPILE in the stored procedure TestCacheReUse (as shown in the Listing 13-3) and run the stored procedure, the plan will not be cached in the procedure cache because you tell SQL Server 2012 (with the WITH RECOMPILE option) not to cache a plan for the stored procedure, and to recompile the stored procedure every time you execute it. Use this option wisely because compiling a stored procedure every time it executes can be costly, and compilation eats many CPU cycles.

LISTING 13-3: RecompileSP.sql

```
USE AdventureWorks
GO
IF OBJECT_ID('dbo.TestCacheReUse') IS NOT NULL
    DROP PROC dbo.TestCacheReUse
GO
CREATE PROC dbo.TestCacheReUse
WITH RECOMPILE
AS

SELECT BusinessEntityID, LoginID, JobTitle
FROM HumanResources.Employee
WHERE BusinessEntityID = 109
GO
```

Tools and Commands for Recompilation Scenarios

You can use the following tools to observe or debug the recompilation-related events if you feel that recompilations are a source of bottlenecks on your system. One way to quickly assess that is to have a look at the Windows Performance Monitor counter SQL Server: SQL Statistics: SQL Re-Compilations/sec. This doesn't provide specific details, but if this number is high compared to previously observed measurements, then it may indicate that there is an issue.

SQL Profiler

Capture the following events under the event classes Stored Procedure and TSQL to see the recompilation events. Be sure to select the column EventSubClass to view what caused the recompilation:

➤ SP:Starting

➤ SP:StmtCompleted

➤ SP:Recompile

➤ SP:Completed

➤ SP:CacheInsert

➤ SP:CacheHit

➤ SP:CacheMiss

You can also select the AutoStats event under the Performance event class to detect recompilations related to statistics updates.

Sys.syscacheobjects Virtual Table

Although this virtual table exists in the `resource` database, you can access it from any database.

 The `resource` *database was first introduced in SQL Server 2005. The* `resource` *database is a read-only database that contains all the system objects included with SQL Server 2012. SQL Server 2012 system objects, such as* `sys.objects`, *are physically persisted in the* `resource` *database, but they logically appear in the* `sys` *schema of every database. The* `resource` *database does not contain user data or user metadata.*

The `cacheobjtype` column of this virtual table is particularly interesting. When `cacheobjtype =` `"Compiled Plan"`, the row refers to a query plan. When `cacheobjtype = "Executable Plan"`, the row refers to an execution context. Each execution context must have its associated query plan, but not vice versa. The `objtype` column indicates the type of object whose plan is cached (for example, `"proc"` or `"Adhoc"`). The `setopts` column encodes a bitmap indicating the `SET` options that were in effect when the plan was compiled. Sometimes multiple copies of the same compiled plan (that differ in only their `setopts` columns) are cached in a plan cache. This indicates that different connections use different sets of `SET` options (an undesirable situation). The `usecounts` column stores the number of times a cached object has been reused since the time the object was cached.

System Dynamic Management Views (DMV's)

There are system DMV's that can be used to investigate query plan recompilation issues. The most important one is `sys.dm_exec_cached_plans`. The view presents one row for every cached plan and can be used in conjunction with the `sys.dm_exec_sql_text` view to retrieve the SQL text of the query contained in the plan cache. Following is an example of this:

```
SELECT st.text, cp.plan_handle, cp.usecounts, cp.size_in_bytes,
   cp.cacheobjtype, cp.objtype
FROM sys.dm_exec_cached_plans cp
   CROSS APPLY sys.dm_exec_sql_text(cp.plan_handle) st
ORDER BY cp.usecounts DESC
```

The information to gather here can be found in the following columns:

➤ `text`: SQL Text of the query that generated the query plan.

➤ `usecounts`: Number of times a query plan has been reused. This number should be high and, if large amounts of low numbers are found, then the system is dealing with a large number of re-compilations.

➤ `size_in_bytes`: Number of bytes consumed by the plan.

➤ `cacheobjtype`: Type of the cache object. That is, if it's a compiled plan or something similar.

Another system DMV to investigate is `sys.dm_exec_query_stats`. This view can be used to return performance statistics for all queries, aggregated across all executions of those queries. The following query will return the top 50 CPU consuming queries for a specific database (for example, AdventureWorks):

```
-- Top 50 CPU Consuming queries
USE AdventureWorks
GO
SELECT TOP 50
  DB_NAME(DB_ID()) AS [Database Name],
  qs.total_worker_time / execution_count AS avg_worker_time,
  SUBSTRING(st.TEXT, (qs.statement_start_offset / 2) + 1,
    ((CASE qs.statement_end_offset
      WHEN -1 THEN DATALENGTH(st.TEXT)
      ELSE qs.statement_end_offset
    END - qs.statement_start_offset) / 2) + 1)
  AS statement_text, *
FROM
  sys.dm_exec_query_stats AS qs
  CROSS APPLY sys.dm_exec_sql_text(qs.sql_handle) AS st
ORDER BY avg_worker_time DESC;
```

DBCC FREEPROCCACHE

The DBCC FREEPROCCACHE command clears the cached query plan and execution context. Use the full command *only* in a development or test environment. Avoid running it in a production environment because this could clear ALL the procedure caches on the entire server and cause all subsequent queries to be recompiled. This could lead to severe performance problems. This command can be run with parameters to target a specific SQL handle, plan handle, or resource pool as shown here:

```
DBCC FREEPROCCACHE [ ( { plan_handle | sql_handle | pool_name } ) ]
[ WITH NO_INFOMSGS ]
```

See the article in BOL for more information at `http://msdn.microsoft.com/en-us/library/ms174283(v=sql.110).aspx`.

DBCC FLUSHPROCINDB (db_id)

The DBCC FLUSHPROCINDB (db_id) command is the same as DBCC FREEPROCCACHE except it clears only the cached plan for a given database. The recommendation for use is the same as DBCC FREEPROCCACHE.

Parser and Algebrizer

Parsing is the process to check the syntax and transform the SQL batch into a parse tree. Parsing includes, for example, whether a non-delimited column name starts with a digit.

Parsing does not check whether the columns you have listed in a WHERE clause actually exist in any of the tables you have listed in the FROM clause. That is taken care of by the *binding* process (algebrizer). Parsing turns the SQL text into logical trees. One logical tree is created per query.

The *algebrizer* component was added in SQL Server 2005. This component replaced the *normalizer* in SQL Server 2000. The output of the parser — a parse tree — is the input to the algebrizer. The major function of the algebrizer is *binding*, so sometimes the entire algebrizer process is referred as binding. The binding process checks whether the semantics are correct. For example, if you try to JOIN table A with trigger T, then the binding process errors this out even though it may be parsed successfully. The following sections cover other tasks performed by the algebrizer.

Name Resolution

The algebrizer performs the tasks to check whether every object name in the query (the parse tree) actually refers to a valid table or column that exists in the system catalog, and whether it is visible in the query scope.

Type Derivation

The algebrizer determines the type for each node in the parse tree. For example, if you issue a UNION query, the algebrizer figures out the type derivation for the final data type. (The columns' data types could be different when you union the results of queries.)

Aggregate Binding

The algebrizer binds the aggregate to the host query and makes its decisions based on query syntax. Consider the following query in the AdventureWorks database:

```
SELECT s.CustomerID
FROM Sales.SalesOrderHeader s
GROUP BY s.CustomerID
HAVING EXISTS(SELECT * FROM Sales.Customer c
WHERE c.TerritoryID > COUNT(s.SalesPersonID))
```

In this query, although the aggregation is done in the inner query that counts the ContactID, the actual operation of this aggregation is performed in the outer query. For example, in the query plan shown in Figure 13-6, you can see that the aggregation is done on the result from the SalesOrderHeader table although the aggregation is performed in the inner query. The outer query is converted to something like this:

```
SELECT COUNT(s.SalesPersonID)
  FROM Sales.SalesOrderHeader s
  GROUP BY s.SalesPersonID
```

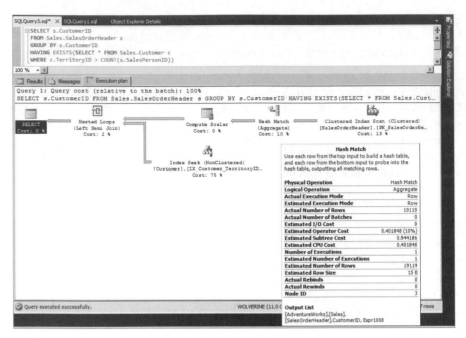

FIGURE 13-6

Grouping Binding

Consider the following query:

```
SELECT s.CustomerID, SalesPersonID, COUNT(s.SalesOrderID)
FROM Sales.SalesOrderHeader s
GROUP BY s.CustomerID, s.SalesPersonID
```

If you do not add the CustomerID and SalesPersonID columns in the GROUP BY list, the query does error out. The grouped queries have different semantics than the nongrouped queries. All nonaggregated columns or expressions in the SELECT list of a query with GROUP BY must have a direct match in the GROUP BY list. The process to verify this via the algebrizer is known as *grouping binding*.

Optimization

Optimization is probably the most complex and important piece to processing your queries. The logical tree created by the parser and algebrizer is the input to the optimizer. The optimizer needs the logical tree, metadata about objects involved in the query, such as columns, indexes, statistics, and constraints, and hardware information. The optimizer uses this information to create the compiled plan, which is made of physical operators. The logical tree includes logical operators that describe *what to do*, such as "read table," "join," and so on. The physical operators produced by the optimizer specify algorithms that describe *how to do*, such as "index seek," "index scan," "hash join," and so on. The optimizer tells SQL Server how to exactly carry out the steps to get the results efficiently. Its job is to produce an efficient execution plan for each query in the batch or stored procedure. Figure 13-7 shows this process graphically.

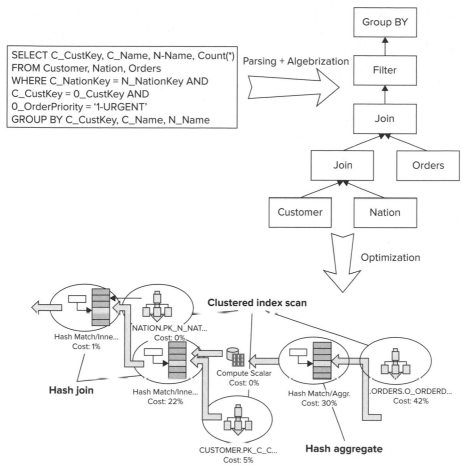

```
SELECT C_CustKey, C_Name, N-Name, Count(*)
FROM Customer, Nation, Orders
WHERE C_NationKey = N_NationKey AND
C_CustKey = 0_CustKey AND
0_OrderPriority = '1-URGENT'
GROUP BY C_CustKey, C_Name, N_Name
```

FIGURE 13-7

The parser and the algebrizer describe "what to do," and the optimizer describes "how to do it" (refer to Figure 13-7). SQL Server's query optimizer is a cost-based optimizer, which means it can create a plan with the least cost. Prior to embarking on a full-blown, cost-based optimization, the query optimizer checks to see if a trivial plan can suffice. A trivial plan is used when the query optimizer knows that there is only one viable plan to satisfy the query. SELECT * FROM <tablename> is one example of this. Complex queries may have millions of possible execution plans. The optimizer does not explore them all though; instead it tries to find a plan that has a cost reasonably close to the theoretical minimum. This is done to come up with a good plan in a reasonable amount of time. Sometimes the query optimization stage ends with a Good Enough Plan Found message or a Time Out. The Good Enough Plan Found message is raised when the query optimizer decides that the current lowest cost plan is so cheap that additional optimization is not worth the cost of doing additional optimization. The Time Out is generated when the optimizer has explored all allowed optimization rules and the optimization stage ends. At that point, the optimizer returns the best complete query plan. The lowest estimated cost doesn't mean the lowest resource cost. The optimizer chooses the plan to get the results quickly to the users. Suppose the optimizer chooses a parallel plan for your queries that uses multiple CPUs, which typically uses more resources than the serial plan but offers faster results. Of course, the optimizer cannot always come up with the best plan, which is why you have a job — for query tuning.

Optimization Flow

The flowchart in Figure 13-8 explains the steps involved in optimizing a query. These steps are simplified for explanation purposes. (The state-of-the-art optimization engine written by the SQL Server development team isn't oversimplified.)

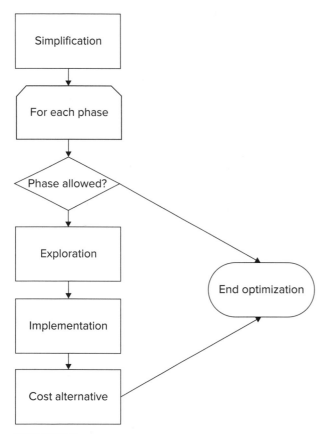

FIGURE 13-8

The input to the optimizer is a logical tree produced by the algebrizer (refer to Figure 13-8). The query optimizer is a transformation-based engine. These transformations are applied to fragments of the query tree. Three kinds of transformation rules are applied: simplification, exploration, and implementation. The following sections discuss each of these transformations.

Simplification

The simplification process creates an output tree that is more optimized and returns results faster than the input tree. For example, it might push the filter down in the tree, reduce the group by columns, reduce redundant or excessive items in the tree, or perform other transformations. Figure 13-9 shows an example of simplification transformation (filter pushing).

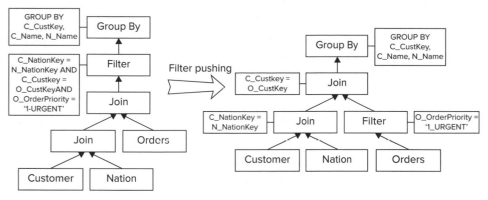

FIGURE 13-9

You can see that the logical tree on the left has the filter after the join (refer to Figure 13-9). The optimizer pushes the filter further down in the tree to filter the data out of the Orders table with a predicate on O_OrderPriority. This optimizes the query by performing the filtering early in the execution.

Figure 13-10 is another example of the simplification transformation (aggregate reduction). It differs from Figure 13-9 because it includes reducing the number of Group By columns in the execution plan.

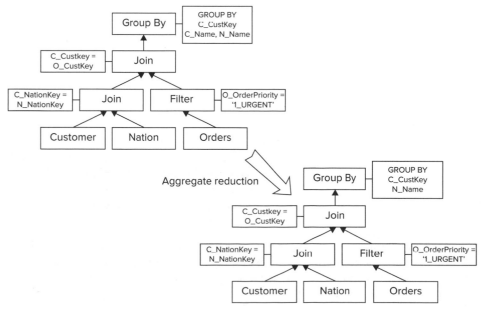

FIGURE 13-10

The C_Name column is removed from the Group By clause because it contains the column C_Custkey (refer to Figure 13-7 for the T-SQL statement), which is unique on the Customer table, so there is no need to include the C_Name column in the Group By clause.

Exploration

As mentioned previously, SQL Server uses a cost-based optimizer implementation. Therefore, during the exploration process, the optimizer looks at alternative options to come up with the cheapest plan (see Figure 13-11). It makes a global choice using the estimated cost.

FIGURE 13-11

The optimizer explores the options related to which table should be used for inner versus outer joins. This is not a simple determination because it depends on many things, such as the size of the table, the available indexes, statistics, and operators higher in the tree. It is not a clear choice like the examples you saw in the simplification transformation.

Implementation

The third transformation is implementation. Figure 13-12 shows an example.

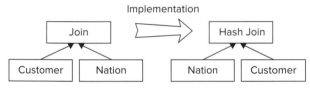

FIGURE 13-12

As explained earlier, the implantation transforms the "what to do" part into the "how to do" part. In this example, the JOIN logical operation transforms into a HASH JOIN physical operation. The query cost is derived from physical operators based on model-of-execution algorithms (I/O and CPU) and estimations of data distribution, data properties, and size. Needless to say, the cost also depends on hardware such as the number of CPUs and the amount of memory available at the time of optimization.

Refer back to Figure 13-8. If the optimizer compared the cost of every valid plan and chose the least costly one, the optimization process could take a long time, and the number of valid plans could be huge. Therefore, the optimization process is divided into three *search phases*. As discussed earlier, a set of transformation rules is associated with each phase. After each phase, SQL Server 2012 evaluates the cost of the cheapest query plan to that point. If the plan is cheap enough, then the optimizer stops there and chooses that query plan. If the plan is not cheap enough, the optimizer runs through the next phase, which has an additional set of rules that are more complex.

The first phase of the cost-based optimization, Phase 0, contains a limited set of rules. These rules are applied to queries with at least four tables. Because JOIN reordering alone generates many valid plans, the optimizer uses a limited number of join orders in Phase 0 and considers only hash and loop joins in this phase. In other words, if this phase finds a plan with an estimated cost below 0.2 (internal cost unit), the optimization ends there.

The second phase, Phase 1, uses more transformation rules and different join orders. The best plan that costs less than 1.0 would cause optimization to stop in this phase. Until Phase 1, the plans are nonparallel (serial query plans).

Consider this: What if you have more than one CPU in your system? In that case, if the cost of the plan produced in Phase 1 is more than the *cost threshold for parallelism* (see sp_configure for this parameter; the default value is 5), then Phase 1 is repeated to find the best parallel plan. Then the cost of the serial plan produced earlier is compared with the new parallel plan, and the next phase, Phase 2 (the full optimization phase), is executed for the cheaper of the two plans.

PHYSICAL QUERY PROCESSING PART TWO: EXECUTION

After compilation, the execution engine takes over; it generates the execution plan, it copies the plan into its executable form and executes the steps in the query plan to produce the wanted result. If the same query or stored procedure is executed again, the compilation phase is skipped, and the execution engine uses the same cached plan to start the execution. Once that is complete, the data needs to be accessed and there are a myriad of ways to perform that index access. There is always room for tuning, but you must have enough data to start with. Therefore, you need to take a baseline of the system's performance and compare against that baseline so that you know where to start. Chapter 12, "Monitoring Your SQL Server," has details on getting the baseline. Just because a process is slow doesn't mean that you have to start tuning SQL statements. First you need to do many basic things, such as configure the SQL Server 2012 database, and make sure tempdb and the log files are on their own drives. It is important to get the server configuration correct. See Chapter 10, "Configuring the Server for Optimal Performance," and Chapter 11, "Optimizing SQL Server 2012," for details about configuring your server and database for optimal performance. There is also a white paper on tempdb that you should read. This document is for SQL Server 2005, but it's useful for SQL Server 2012 as well and can be found at: www.microsoft.com/technet/prodtechnol/sql/2005/workingwithtempdb.mspx.

Don't overlook the obvious. For example, suppose you notice that performance is suddenly quite bad on your server. If you have done a baseline and that doesn't show much change in performance, then it is unlikely that the sudden performance change was caused by an application in most cases, unless a new patch for your application caused some performance changes. In that case, look at your server configuration to see if that changed recently. Sometimes you merely run out of disk space, especially on drives where your page files reside, and that can bring the server to its knees.

Database I/O Information

Normally, an enterprise application has one or two databases residing on the server, in which case you would know that you need to look into queries against those databases. Each query may require a high level of I/O and, ideally, would like to take the maximum level of I/O available to entire server. However, if you have many databases on the server and you are not sure which database is causing a lot of I/O and may be responsible for a performance issue, you must look at the I/O activities against the database to find out which causes the most I/O and stalls on the I/O and how that can affect the execution time of your specific query. The DMF called sys.dm_io_virtual_file_stats comes in handy for this purpose.

Listing 13-4 provides this information.

LISTING 13-4: DatabseIO.sql

```
-- Database IO analysis.
WITH IOFORDATABASE AS
(
SELECT
 DB_NAME(VFS.database_id) AS DatabaseName
,CASE WHEN smf.type = 1 THEN 'LOG_FILE' ELSE 'DATA_FILE' END AS DatabaseFile_Type
,SUM(VFS.num_of_bytes_written) AS IO_Write
,SUM(VFS.num_of_bytes_read) AS IO_Read
,SUM(VFS.num_of_bytes_read + VFS.num_of_bytes_written) AS Total_IO
,SUM(VFS.io_stall) AS IO_STALL
FROM sys.dm_io_virtual_file_stats(NULL, NULL) AS VFS
JOIN sys.master_files AS smf
  ON VFS.database_id = smf.database_id
  AND VFS.file_id = smf.file_id
GROUP BY
 DB_NAME(VFS.database_id)
,smf.type
)
SELECT
 ROW_NUMBER() OVER(ORDER BY io_stall DESC) AS RowNumber
,DatabaseName
,DatabaseFile_Type
,CAST(1.0 * IO_Read/ (1024 * 1024) AS DECIMAL(12, 2)) AS IO_Read_MB
,CAST(1.0 * IO_Write/ (1024 * 1024) AS DECIMAL(12, 2)) AS IO_Write_MB
,CAST(1. * Total_IO / (1024 * 1024) AS DECIMAL(12, 2)) AS IO_TOTAL_MB
,CAST(IO_STALL / 1000. AS DECIMAL(12, 2)) AS IO_STALL_Seconds
,CAST(100. * IO_STALL / SUM(IO_STALL) OVER() AS DECIMAL(10, 2)) AS IO_STALL_Pct
FROM IOFORDATABASE
ORDER BY IO_STALL_Seconds DESC
```

Figure 13-13 shows sample output from this script.

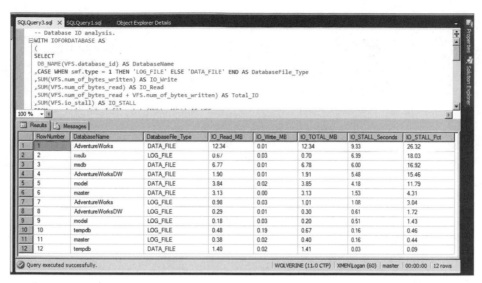

FIGURE 13-13

The counters can be explained as such:

➤ `DatabaseName`: Name of the database

➤ `DatabaseFile_Type`: Data file or Log file for the associated database name

➤ `IO_Read_MB`: Number of bytes read from the database file

➤ `IO_Write_MB`: Number of bytes written to the database file

➤ `IO_TOTAL_MB`: Total number of bytes transferred to/from the database file

➤ `IO_STALL_Seconds`: Time, in seconds, that users waited for I/O to be completed on the file

➤ `IO_STALL_Pct`: IO stall percentage relative to the entire query

The counters show the value from the time the instance of SQL Server starts, but it gives you a good idea of which database is hammered. This query gives you a good starting point to further investigate the process level (stored procedures, ad-hoc T-SQL statements, and so on) for the database in question.

Next, look at how to gather the query plan and analyze it. You also learn about the different tools you need in this process.

Working with the Query Plan

Looking at the query plan is the first step to take in the process of query tuning. The SQL Server query plan comes in different flavors: textual, graphical, and, with SQL Server 2012, XML format. *Showplan* describes any of these query plan flavors. Different types of Showplans have different information. SQL Server 2012 can produce a plan with operators only, with cost information, and with XML format, which can provide some additional runtime details. Table 13-2 summarizes the various Showplan formats.

TABLE 13-2: Showplan Formats

PLAN CONTENTS	TEXT FORMAT	GRAPHICAL FORMAT	XML FORMAT
Operators	SET SHOWPLAN_TEXT ON	N/A	N/A
Operators and estimated costs	SET SHOWPLAN_ALL ON	Displays the estimated execution plan in SQL Server Management Studio	SET SHOWPLAN_XML ON
Operators + estimated cardinalities and costs + runtime information	SET STATISTICS PROFILE ON	Displays the actual execution plan in SQL Server Management Studio	SET STATISTICS XML ON

Estimated Execution Plan

This section describes how to get the *estimated* execution plan. In a later section you learn how to get the *actual* execution plan. There are five ways you can get the estimated execution plan:

➤   SET SHOWPLAN_TEXT

➤   SET SHOWPLAN_ALL

➤   SET SHOWPLAN_XML

➤   Graphical estimated execution plan using SQL Server Management Studio (SSMS)

➤   SQL Trace

The SQL Trace option is covered in a separate section at the end of the chapter; the other options are described in the following sections.

SET SHOWPLAN_TEXT and SET SHOWPLAN_ALL

Start with a simple query to demonstrate how to read the query plan. The code for the query is shown in Listing 13-5:

LISTING 13-5: SimpleQueryPlan.sql

Available for
download on
Wrox.com

```
USE AdventureWorks
GO
SET SHOWPLAN_TEXT ON
GO
SELECT sh.CustomerID, st.Name, SUM(sh.SubTotal) AS SubTotal
FROM Sales.SalesOrderHeader sh
JOIN Sales.Customer c
  ON c.CustomerID = sh.CustomerID
JOIN Sales.SalesTerritory st
  ON st.TerritoryID = c.TerritoryID
```

```
GROUP BY sh.CustomerID, st.Name
HAVING SUM(sh.SubTotal) > 2000.00
GO
SET SHOWPLAN_TEXT OFF
GO
```

When you SET the SHOWPLAN_TEXT ON, the query does not execute; it just produces the estimated plan. The textual plan is shown next.

The output tells you that there are seven operators: Filter, Hash Match (Inner Join), Hash Match (Aggregate), Clustered Index Scan, Merge Join, Clustered Index Scan, and Index Scan, which are shown in bold in the query plan here.

```
SELECT sh.CustomerID, st.Name, SUM(sh.SubTotal) AS SubTotal
FROM Sales.SalesOrderHeader sh
   JOIN Sales.Customer c
     ON c.CustomerID = sh.CustomerID
   JOIN Sales.SalesTerritory st
     ON st.TerritoryID = c.TerritoryID
   GROUP BY sh.CustomerID, st.Name   HAVING SUM(sh.SubTotal) > 2000.00
```

StmtText
  |--**Filter**(WHERE:([Expr1006]>(2000.00)))
       |--**Hash Match(Inner Join**, HASH:([st].[TerritoryID])=([c].[TerritoryID]),
RESIDUAL:([AdventureWorks].[Sales].[SalesTerritory].[TerritoryID]
as [st].[TerritoryID]=[AdventureWorks].[Sales].[Customer].[TerritoryID]
as [c].[TerritoryID]))
            |--**Clustered Index
Scan**(OBJECT:([AdventureWorks].[Sales].[SalesTerritory].
[PK_SalesTerritory_TerritoryID] AS [st]))
            |--**Hash Match(Inner Join**, HASH:([sh].[CustomerID])=([c].[CustomerID]))
                 |--**Hash Match(Aggregate**, HASH:([sh].[CustomerID]) DEFINE:
([Expr1006]=SUM([AdventureWorks].[Sales].[SalesOrderHeader].[SubTotal]
as [sh].[SubTotal])))
                 | |--**Clustered Index Scan**(OBJECT:
([AdventureWorks].[Sales].[SalesOrderHeader].
[PK_SalesOrderHeader_SalesOrderID] AS [sh]))
                 |--**Index Scan**(OBJECT:
([AdventureWorks].[Sales].[Customer].[IX_Customer_TerritoryID]
AS [c]))

It may be easier to view the plan output in SSMS since the formatting here doesn't look that good. You can run this query in the AdventureWorks database. In this plan all you have are the operators' names and their basic arguments. For more details on the query plan, other options are available, which you explore soon.

To analyze the plan you read branches in *inner levels* before outer ones (bottom to top), and branches that appear in the *same level* from top to bottom. You can tell which branches are inner and which are outer based on the position of the pipe (|) character. When the plan executes, the general flow of the rows is from the top down and from right to left. An operator with more indentation produces rows consumed by an operator with less indentation and produces rows for the next operator above, and so forth. For the JOIN operators, two input operators exist at the same level to the right of the JOIN operator, denoting the two row sets. The higher of the two (in this case, Clustered Index Scan on the object Sales.SalesTerritory) is the *outer table* (so Sales. SalesTerritory is the outer table) and the lower (Index Scan on the object Sales.Customer) is the *inner table*. The operation on the outer table is initiated first, and the one on the inner table is repeatedly executed for each row of the outer table that arrives to the join operator. The join algorithms are explained in detail later.

Now you can analyze the plan for the query. As shown in the plan, the hash match (inner join) operation has two levels: hash match (aggregate) and merge join. Now look at the merge join. The merge join has two levels: The first is the clustered index scan on Sales.Territory, and the index scanned on this object is PK_SalesTerritory_TerritoryID. You explore index access methods in more detail a little later in the chapter. That is the outer table for the merge join. The inner table Sales.Customer is scanned only once because of the merge join, and that physical operation is done using an index scan on index IX_Customer_TerritoryID on the sales.Customer table. The merge join is on the TerritoryID, as per the plan Merge Join(Inner Join, MERGE:([st].[Terr itoryID]) = ([c].[TerritoryID]). Because the RESIDUAL predicate is present in the merge join, all rows that satisfy the merge predicate evaluate the residual predicate, and only those rows that satisfy it are returned.

Now the result of this merge join becomes the inner table for hash match (inner join): Hash Match (Inner Join, HASH:([sh].[CustomerID]) = ([c].[CustomerID])). The outer table is the result of Hash Match (Aggregate). You can see that the CustomerID is the hash key (HASH:([sh]. [CustomerID]) in the hash aggregate operation. Therefore, the aggregation is performed and, as per the query, the SUM operation is done on the column SubTotal from the Sales.SalesOrderHeader table (defined by the DEFINE:([Expr1006]). Now the Hash Match (Inner join) operation is performed on CustomerID (the result of the merge join) repeatedly for each row from the outer table (the result of hash match [aggregate]). Finally, the filter is applied on column SubTotal using the filter physical operator with the predicate (WHERE:([Expr1006]>(2000.00))) to get only rows with SubTotal > 2000.00.

 The merge join itself is fast, but it can be an expensive choice if sort operations are required. However, if the data volume is large and the wanted data can be obtained presorted from existing B-tree indexes, Merge Join *is often the fastest available join algorithm. In addition,* Merge Join *performance can vary a lot based on one-to-many or many-to-many joins.*

In the query file, you set the SET SHOWPLAN_TEXT OFF following the query. This is because SET SHOWPLAN_TEXT ON is not only causing the query plan to show up, but it is also turning off the query execution for the connection. The query execution is turned off for this connection until you execute SET SHOWPLAN_TEXT OFF on the same connection. The SET SHOWPLAN_ALL command is similar to SET SHOWPLAN_TEXT. The only difference is the additional information about the query plan produced by SET SHOWPLAN_ALL. It adds the *estimated* number of rows produced by each operator in the query plan, the estimated CPU time, the estimated I/O time, and the total cost estimate that was used internally when comparing this plan to other possible plans.

SET SHOWPLAN_XML

The SET SHOWPLAN_XML feature was added in SQL Server 2005 to retrieve the Showplan in XML form. The output of the SHOWPLAN_XML is generated by a compilation of a batch, so it produces a single XML document for the whole batch. See Listing 13-6 to see how you can get the estimated plan in XML.

LISTING 13-6: ShowPlan_XML.sql

```
USE AdventureWorks
GO
SET SHOWPLAN_XML ON
GO
SELECT sh.CustomerID, st.Name, SUM(sh.SubTotal) AS SubTotal
FROM Sales.SalesOrderHeader sh
JOIN Sales.Customer c
  ON c.CustomerID = sh.CustomerID
JOIN Sales.SalesTerritory st
  ON st.TerritoryID = c.TerritoryID
GROUP BY sh.CustomerID, st.Name
HAVING SUM(sh.SubTotal) > 2000.00
GO
SET SHOWPLAN_XML OFF
GO
```

When you run this query in Management Studio, you can see a link in the result tab. Click the link to open the XML document inside Management Studio and save that document with the extension .sqlplan. When you open that file using Management Studio, you get a graphical query plan. Figure 13-14 shows the graphical plan from the XML document generated by this query.

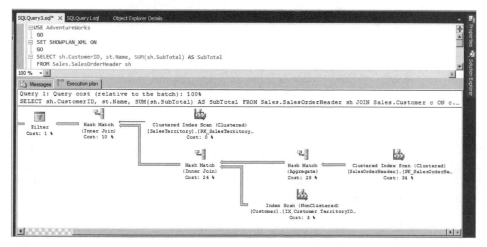

FIGURE 13-14

XML is the richest format of the Showplan. It contains some unique information not available in other Showplan formats. The XML Showplan contains the size of the plan in cache (the CachedPlanSize attributes) and parameter values for which the plan has been optimized (the Parameter sniffing element). When a stored procedure compiles for the first time, the values of the parameters supplied with the execution call optimize the statements within that stored procedure. This process is known as *parameter sniffing*. Also available is some runtime information, which is unique to the XML plan and described further in the section, "Actual Execution Plan" later in this chapter.

You can write code to parse and analyze the XML Showplan. This is probably the greatest advantage it offers because this task is hard to achieve with other forms of the Showplan.

Refer to the white paper at http://msdn.microsoft.com/en-us/library/ms345130.aspx for information on how you can extract the estimated execution cost of a query from its XML Showplan using CLR functions. This document is for SQL Server 2005 but still applies. You can use this technique to ensure that users can submit only those queries costing less than a predetermined threshold to a server running SQL Server, thereby ensuring it is not overloaded with costly, long-running queries.

Graphical Estimated Showplan

You can view a graphical estimated plan in Management Studio. To access the plan, either use the shortcut key Ctrl+L or select Query ⇨ Display Estimated Execution plan. You can also select the button indicated in Figure 13-15.

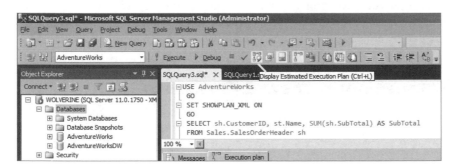

FIGURE 13-15

If you use any of these options to display the graphical estimated query plan, it displays the plan as soon as compilation is completed because compilation complexity can vary according to the number and size of the tables. Right-clicking the graphical plan area in the Execution Plan tab reveals different zoom options and properties for the graphical plan.

Actual Execution Plan

This section describes the options you can use to get the actual execution plan (SET STATISTICS XML ON|OFF and SET STATISTICS PROFILE ON|OFF) using the graphical actual execution plan option in Management Studio. You can get the actual execution plan using SQL Trace as well; see the section, "Gathering Query Plans for Analysis with SQL Trace" later in this chapter.

SET STATISTICS XML ON|OFF

Two kinds of runtime information are in the XML Showplan: *per SQL statement* and *per thread*. If a statement has a parameter, the plan contains the `parameterRuntimeValue` attribute, which shows the value of each parameter when the statement was executed. The `degreeOfParallelism` attribute shows the actual degree of parallelism. The degree of parallelism shows the number of concurrent threads working on the single query. The compile time value for degree of parallelism is always half the number of CPUs available to SQL Server unless two CPUs are in the system. In that case, the value will be 2 as well.

The XML plan may also contain warnings. These are events generated during compilation or execution time. For example, missing statistics are a compiler-generated event. One important feature in SQL Server 2012 (originally added in SQL Server 2005) is the USE PLAN hint. This feature requires the plan hint in XML format, so you can use the XML Showplan. Using the USE PLAN hint, you can force the query to be executed using a certain plan. For example, suppose you find that a query runs slowly in the production environment but faster in the preproduction environment. You also find that the plan generated in the production environment is not optimal for some reason. In that case, you can use the better plan generated in the preproduction environment and force that plan in the production environment using the USE PLAN hint. For more details on how to implement it, refer to the Books Online (BOL) topic, "Using the USE PLAN Query Hint."

There are new warnings that have been included in SQL Server 2012 execution plan. These two messages specifically warn against implicit (or, sometimes, explicit) type conversions that cause the available index not to be used. The first warning message is:

```
Type conversion in expression ColumnExpression may affect
"CardinalityEstimate" in query plan choice
```

This means that there is a type conversion on a certain column that will affect the `CardinalityEstimate`. The other warning message is:

```
Type conversion in expression ColumnExpression may affect
"SeekPlan" in query plan choice.
```

This means that the type conversion that is happening on a certain column will cause the index not to be used.

SET STATISTICS PROFILE ON|OFF

The SET STATISTICS PROFILE ON|OFF option is better than the previous option, which you should use it for query analysis and tuning. Run the following query using the code shown in Listing 13-7. If you don't want to mess with your AdventureWorks database, you can back up and restore the AdventureWorks database with a different name. If you do that, be sure to change the USE DatabaseName line in the script.

LISTING 13-7: Statistics_Profile.sql

```
USE AdventureWorks
GO
SET STATISTICS PROFILE ON
GO
SELECT p.Name AS ProdName, c.TerritoryID, SUM(od.OrderQty)
FROM Sales.SalesOrderDetail od
JOIN Production.Product p
  ON p.ProductID = od.ProductID
JOIN Sales.SalesOrderHeader oh
  ON oh.SalesOrderID = od.SalesOrderID
JOIN Sales.Customer c
  ON c.CustomerID = oh.CustomerID
WHERE OrderDate >= '2006-06-09'
  AND OrderDate <= '2006-06-11'
GROUP BY p.Name, c.TerritoryID
GO
SET STATISTICS PROFILE OFF
```

After you run the query, you get output similar to what is shown in Figure 13-16.

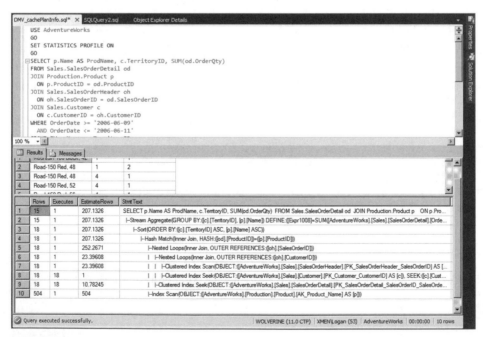

FIGURE 13-16

The four most important columns in the output of SET STATISTICS PROFILE are Rows,
EstimateRows, Executes, and, of course, the StmtText. The Rows column contains the number of
rows actually returned by each operator.

Graphical Actual Execution Plan

You can use Management Studio to view the graphical actual execution plan. Again, either use the shortcut Ctrl+M, select Query ⇨ Include Actual Execution plan, or select the button indicated in Figure 13-17.

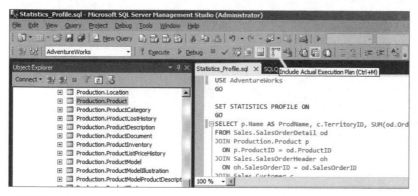

FIGURE 13-17

If you use any of these options to display the graphical actual query plan, nothing happens. After query execution, the actual plan displays in a separate tab.

Index Access Methods

There are a number of index access methods that SQL Server uses to retrieve data needed to build execution plans. In this section you get to explore the ways that these methods are different from each other and how the index access methods may affect the performance of the query. You can use this knowledge when you tune the query and decide whether it uses the correct index access method and take the appropriate action.

In addition, you should make a copy (Backup and Restore, or take a snapshot) of the AdventureWorks database on your machine so that if you drop or create indexes on it, the original AdventureWorks database remains intact. When you restore the database, call it AW_2 for these examples.

Table Scan

A table scan involves a sequential scan of all data pages belonging to the table. Run the following script in the AW_2 database:

```
SELECT * INTO dbo.New_SalesOrderHeader
FROM Sales.SalesOrderHeader
```

After you run this script to make a copy of the SalesOrderHeader table, run the following script:

```
SELECT SalesOrderID, OrderDate, CustomerID
FROM dbo.New_SalesOrderHeader
```

Because this is a heap, this statement causes a table scan. If you want, you can always get the actual textual plan using SET STATISTICS PROFILE ON. Figure 13-18 displays the graphical plan.

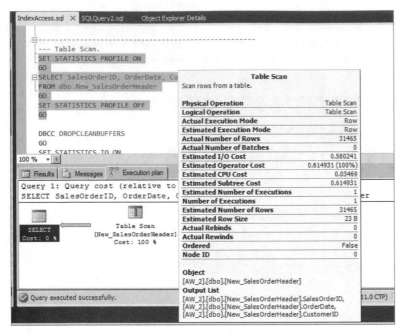

FIGURE 13-18

In a table scan, SQL Server uses Index Allocation Map (IAM) pages to direct the disk arm to scan the extents belonging to the table according to their physical order on disk. As you might guess, the number of physical reads would be the same as the number of pages for this table.

Now look at the STATISTICS IO output for the example query in Listing 13-8. This is a session-level setting. STATISTICS IO provides you with I/O-related statistics for the query statement that caused a table scan which was run.

> SET STATISTICS IO *is set at runtime and not at parse time. This is an important tool in your query-tuning arsenal because disk I/O is normally a bottleneck on your system, so you must to identify how many I/O's your query generates and whether they are necessary.*

LISTING 13-8: IndexAccess1.sql

```
DBCC DROPCLEANBUFFERS
GO
SET STATISTICS IO ON
GO
SELECT SalesOrderID, OrderDate, CustomerID
FROM dbo.New_SalesOrderHeader
GO
SET STATISTICS IO OFF
```

The statistics I/O information is as follows:

```
Table 'New_SalesOrderHeader'. Scan count 1, logical reads 794,
physical reads 0, read-ahead reads 276, lob logical reads 0,
lob physical reads 0, lob read-ahead reads 0.
```

The scan count tells you how many times the table was accessed for this query. If you have multiple tables in your query, you see statistics showing I/O information for each table. In this case, the New_SalesOrderHeader table was accessed once.

The logical reads counter indicates how many pages were read from the data cache. In this case, 794 reads were done from cache. The logical reads number may be a little different on your machine. As mentioned earlier, because of the whole table scan, the number of logical reads equals the number of pages allocated to this table.

You can also run the following query to verify the number of pages allocated to the table.

```
select in_row_reserved_page_count
from sys.dm_db_partition_stats
 WHERE OBJECT_ID = OBJECT_ID('New_SalesOrderHeader')
```

The physical reads counter indicates the number of pages read from the disk. It shows 0 for the preceding code. This doesn't mean that there were no physical reads from disk though.

The read-ahead reads counter indicates the number of pages from the physical disk that are placed into the internal data cache when SQL Server guesses that you will need them later in the query. In this case, this counter shows 276, which is the total number of physical reads that occurred. Both the physical reads and read-ahead reads counters indicate the amount of physical disk activity. These numbers may, too, be different on your machine.

The lob logical reads, lob physical reads, and lob read-ahead reads are the same as the other reads, but these counters indicate reads for the large objects — for example, if you read a column with the data types varchar(max), nvarchar(max), xml, or varbinary(max). When T-SQL statements retrieve lob columns, some lob retrieval operations might require traversing the lob tree multiple times. This may cause SET STATISTICS IO to report higher than expected logical reads.

Clustered Index Scan (Unordered)

Try creating a clustered index on the New_SalesOrderHeader table. A clustered index is structured as a balanced tree. (Most indexes in SQL Server are traditionally structured as balanced trees. New indexes found in SQL Server 2012, such as ColumnStore, full-text, and spatial indexes are not.) A *balanced tree* is one in which "no leaf is much farther away from the root than any other leaf" (adopted from www.nist.gov/dads/HTML/balancedtree.html). Different balancing schemes allow different definitions of "much farther" and different amounts of work to keep them balanced. A clustered index maintains the entire table's data at its leaf level.

 A clustered index is not a copy of the table's data; it is the data.

Now run the script in Listing 13-9 and query to see the effect of adding a clustered index.

LISTING 13-9: IndexAccess2.sql

```
CREATE CLUSTERED INDEX IXCU_SalesOrderID ON New_SalesOrderHeader(SalesOrderID)
GO
DBCC DROPCLEANBUFFERS
GO
SET STATISTICS IO ON
GO
SELECT SalesOrderID, RevisionNumber, OrderDate, DueDate
FROM New_SalesOrderHeader
GO
SET STATISTICS IO OFF
```

The results of `Statistics IO` are shown here, and the query plan is shown in Figure 13-19:

```
Table 'New_SalesOrderHeader'. Scan count 1, logical reads 794,
physical reads 0, read-ahead reads 276, lob logical reads 0,
lob physical reads 0, lob read-ahead reads 0.
```

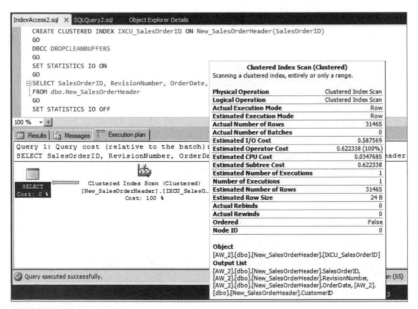

FIGURE 13-19

As shown in the `Statistics IO` output, the number of pages read was 794 (logical reads), which is the same as the table scan (a little more actually because the leaf level in a clustered index also contains unique row information plus a link to the previous and next page in a doubly linked list, so more space is required to hold that information). Even though the execution plan shows a clustered index scan, the activities are the same as the table scan, so unless you have a predicate on a clustered index key, the whole clustered index will be scanned to get the data, which is the same as a table scan. You can also see in Figure 13-19, in the information box of the clustered index scan operators, that the scan was not ordered (Ordered = False), which means that the access method did not rely on the linked list between the data pages and the leaf-level that maintains the logical order of the index.

Clustered Index Scan (Ordered)

An ordered clustered index scan is also a full scan of the clustered index, but the data is returned in order by the clustering key. This time, run the query found in Listing 13-10. This query can access the same table but is ordered by the SalesOrderID column:

LISTING 13-10: IndexAccess3.sql

```
DBCC DROPCLEANBUFFERS
GO
SET STATISTICS IO ON
GO
SELECT SalesOrderID,RevisionNumber, OrderDate, DueDate
FROM New_SalesOrderHeader
ORDER BY SalesOrderID
GO
SET STATISTICS IO OFF
```

The statistics I/O information is as follows:

```
Table 'New_SalesOrderHeader'. Scan count 1, logical reads 794,
physical reads 0, read-ahead reads 276, lob logical reads 0,
lob physical reads 0, lob read-ahead reads 0.
```

The query plan is shown in Figure 13-20.

FIGURE 13-20

As you can see, the query plan is the same in Figure 13-20 as the one in Figure 13-19, but here you have Ordered = True. The statistics IO information is also the same as the unordered clustered index scan. Unlike the unordered clustered index scan, the performance of the ordered clustered index scan depends on the fragmentation level of the index. *Fragmentation* is out-of-order pages, which means that although Page 1 appears after Page 2 according to the linked list, *physically* Page 2 comes before Page 1 on the disk, or there is a gap in sequential pages. It is more expensive to swing back but gaps going forward can affect the size of the reads. The percentage of fragmentation is greater if more pages in the leaf level of the index are out of order with respect to the total number of pages. Moving the disk arm sequentially is always faster than random arm movement, so if the fragmentation is higher than for ordered data, there will be more random arm movement, resulting in slower performance.

> *If you do not need the data sorted, do not include the* ORDER BY *clause.*

Even though you have a covering non-clustered index, the optimizer in Figure 13-19 did not choose it this time because you asked that the data be sorted on the SalesOrderID column (which is obviously not sorted on the leaf level of the non-clustered index).

Covering Non-Clustered Index Scan (Unordered)

A covering index means that a non-clustered index contains all the columns specified in a query. Look at this using the query used in Listing 13-11:

LISTING 13-11: IndexAccess4.sql

```
CREATE NONCLUSTERED INDEX IXNC_SalesOrderID ON New_SalesOrderHeader(OrderDate)
INCLUDE(RevisionNumber, DueDate)
GO
DBCC DROPCLEANBUFFERS
GO
SET STATISTICS IO ON
GO
SELECT SalesOrderID, RevisionNumber, OrderDate, DueDate
FROM New_SalesOrderHeader
GO
SET STATISTICS IO OFF
```

This script creates a non-clustered index on the OrderDate column. Notice the INCLUDE clause with the column names RevisionName and DueDate. The INCLUDE feature, introduced in SQL Server 2005, enables you to specify the non-key columns to be added to the leaf level of the non-clustered index. The RevisionName and DueDate columns are included because your query needs these columns. The non-clustered index is chosen for this operation so that the data can be served directly from the leaf level of the non-clustered index (because the non-clustered index has the data for these included columns). See the CREATE INDEX topic in BOL for details on the INCLUDE clause. The statistics I/O information for the query is shown here:

```
Table 'New_SalesOrderHeader'. Scan count 1, logical reads 108,
physical reads 0, read-ahead reads 0, lob logical reads 0,
lob physical reads 0, lob read-ahead reads 0.
```

The query plan is shown in Figure 13-21.

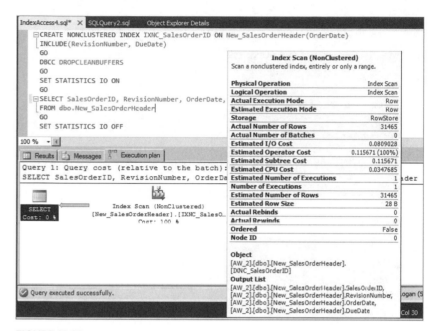

FIGURE 13-21

As you can see from the statistics I/O result, only 108 logical reads were done to fulfill this query. The results returned by the clustered index query and the covering non-clustered index query are identical (number of columns and number of rows), but there were 794 logical reads in the clustered index and only 108 logical reads in the non-clustered scan because the non-clustered index has covered the query and served the data from its leaf level.

The clustered index leaf level contains the full data rows (all columns), whereas the non-clustered index has only one key column and two included columns. That means the row size is smaller for a non-clustered index, and the smaller row size can hold more data and requires less I/O.

Covering Non-Clustered Index Scan (Ordered)

If you run the query found in Listing 13-11 with OrderDate in the ORDER BY clause, the optimizer chooses the covering non-clustered index. The query plan would be exactly the same as shown in Figure 13-21, except that you see Ordered = True in the information box. The statistics IO information is also the same as for the non-ordered covering non-clustered index scan. Of course, an ordered index scan is not only used when you explicitly request the data sorted; the optimizer can also choose to sort the data if the plan uses an operator that can benefit from sorted data.

Non-Clustered Index Seek with Ordered Partial Scan and Lookups

To demonstrate the non-clustered index seek with ordered partial scan and lookups access method, you first need to drop the clustered index on the `New_SalesOrderHeader` table. Run the script in Listing 13-12:

LISTING 13-12: IndexAccess5.sql

```
DROP INDEX New_SalesOrderHeader.IXCU_SalesOrderID
GO
DBCC DROPCLEANBUFFERS
GO
SET STATISTICS IO ON
GO
SELECT SalesOrderID,RevisionNumber, OrderDate, DueDate
FROM New_SalesOrderHeader
WHERE OrderDate BETWEEN '2007-10-08 00:00:00.000' AND '2007-10-10 00:00:00.000'
GO
SET STATISTICS IO OFF
```

The `statistics IO` looks like this:

```
(186 row(s) affected)
Table 'New_SalesOrderHeader'. Scan count 1, logical reads 188,
physical reads 0, read-ahead reads 0, lob logical reads 0,
lob physical reads 0, lob read-ahead reads 0.
```

The query execution plan is shown in Figure 13-22.

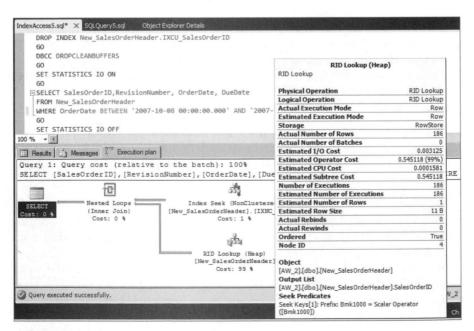

FIGURE 13-22

Remember that you don't have a clustered index on this table. This is called a *heap*. In the query, you have requested the SalesOrderID, RevisionNumber, OrderDate, DueDate, and SalesOrderNumber columns, and added a predicate on the OrderDate column. Because of the predicate on the key column in the IXNC_SalesOrderID index, the optimizer chooses this index and looks for all the rows that have the OrderDate specified in the WHERE clause. This index also has all the columns at its leaf level except for SalesOrderID. To find the SalesOrderID column value, SQL Server performs RID lookups of the corresponding data row for each key. As each key is found, SQL Server can apply the lookup. In addition, because this is a heap table, each lookup translates to a single page read. Because there are 186 rows qualified by the WHERE clause, there will be 186 reads for data row lookup. If you look at the statistics IO information, there are 188 logical reads, which means that out of those 188 logical reads, 186 are the result of the RID lookup. You can probably guess that most of the cost in this query is in the RID lookup, which is also evident in the query plan, which shows that the cost of the RID lookup operation is 99 percent. Lookups are always random I/Os (as opposed to sequential), which are more costly. When seeking many times, however, SQL Server often sorts to make I/Os more sequential.

This query plan demonstrated an RID lookup on a heap. Run the script in Listing 13-13 to create a clustered index and run the same query again:

LISTING 13-13: IndexAccess6.sql

```
CREATE CLUSTERED INDEX IXCU_SalesOrderID ON New_SalesOrderHeader(SalesOrderID)
GO
DBCC DROPCLEANBUFFERS
GO
SET STATISTICS IO ON
GO
SELECT SalesOrderID,RevisionNumber, OrderDate, DueDate, SalesOrderNumber
FROM New_SalesOrderHeader
WHERE OrderDate BETWEEN '2007-10-08 00:00:00.000' AND '2007-10-10 00:00:00.000'
GO
SET STATISTICS IO OFF
The following code shows the statistics IO output for this query:
(186 row(s) affected)
Table 'New_SalesOrderHeader'. Scan count 1, logical reads 581,
physical reads 0, read-ahead reads 5, lob logical reads 0,
lob physical reads 0, lob read-ahead reads 0.
```

Figure 13-23 shows the query plan for this query.

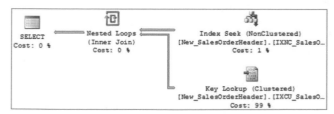

FIGURE 13-23

The query plans in Figure 13-22 and Figure 13-23 are almost identical except that in Figure 13-23 a clustered index is sought for each row found in the outer reference (the non-clustered index). Again, you can see in Figure 13-23 that the clustered index seek incurs most of the cost (99 percent) for this query, but note the `statistics IO` information for the two queries. The logical reads in the clustered index seek query plan are a lot higher than those in the RID lookup plan. This doesn't mean that a clustered index on the table is bad, though. This index access method is efficient only when the predicate is highly selective, or a point query. *Selectivity* is defined as the percentage of the number of rows returned by the query out of the total number of rows in the table. A *point query* is one that has an equals (=) operator in the predicate. Because the cost of the lookup operation is greater, the optimizer decided to just do the clustered index scan. For example, if you change the `WHERE` clause in the query to `WHERE OrderDate BETWEEN '2007-10-08 00:00:00.000' AND '2007-12-10 00:00:00.000'`, then the optimizer would just do the clustered index scan to return the result for that query. Remember that the *non-leaf* levels of the clustered index typically reside in cache because of all the lookup operations going through it, so you shouldn't concern yourself too much about the higher cost of the query in the clustered index seek scenario shown in Figure 13-23.

Clustered Index Seek with Ordered Partial Scan

The optimizer normally uses the clustered index seek with an ordered partial scan technique for range queries, in which you filter based on the first key column of the clustered index. To observe this technique, run the query in Listing 13-13:

LISTING 13-14: IndexAccess7.sql

```
DBCC DROPCLEANBUFFERS
GO
SET STATISTICS IO ON
GO
SELECT SalesOrderID, RevisionNumber, OrderDate, DueDate, SalesOrderNumber
FROM New_SalesOrderHeader
WHERE SalesOrderID BETWEEN 43696 AND 45734
GO
SET STATISTICS IO OFF
```

The `statistics IO` output is as follows:

```
(2039 row(s) affected)
Table 'New_SalesOrderHeader'. Scan count 1, logical reads 56,
physical reads 0, read-ahead reads 0, lob logical reads 0,
lob physical reads 0, lob read-ahead reads 0.
```

The query plan is shown in Figure 13-24.

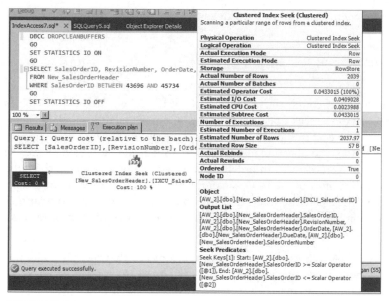

FIGURE 13-24

This index access method first performs a seek operation on the first key (43696 in this case) and then performs an ordered partial scan at the leaf level, starting from the first key in the range and continuing until the last key (45734). Because the leaf level of the clustered index is actually the data rows, no lookup is required in this access method.

Look at Figure 13-25 to understand the I/O cost for this index access method. To read at least a single leaf page, the number of seek operations required is equal to the number of levels in the index.

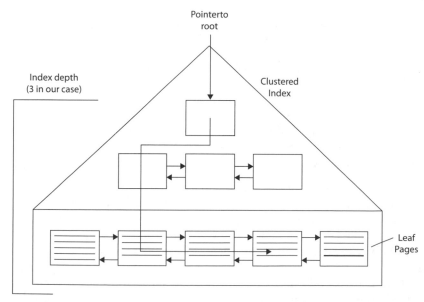

FIGURE 13-25

How do you find the level in the index? Run the INDEXPROPERTY function with the IndexDepth property:

```
SELECT INDEXPROPERTY (OBJECT_ID('New_SalesOrderHeader'), 'IXCU_SalesOrderID',
'IndexDepth')
```

In this case, the index depth is 3, and of course the last level is the leaf level where the data resides. As shown in Figure 13-25, the cost of the seek operation (three random reads in this case because that is the depth of the index) and the cost of the ordered partial scan within the leaf level to get the data (in this case 53, according to the read-ahead reads) add up to 56 logical reads, as indicated in the statistics IO information. As you can see, an ordered partial scan typically incurs the bulk of the query's cost because it involves most of the I/O to scan the range (53 in this case). As mentioned earlier, index fragmentation plays an important role in ordered partial scan operations, so when there is high fragmentation in the index, the disk arm needs to move a lot, which results in degraded performance.

The query plan shown in Figure 13-24 is called a *trivial plan*, which means that there is no better plan than this and the plan does not depend on the selectivity of the query. As long as you have a predicate on the SalesOrderID columns, no matter how many rows are sought, the plan is always the same *unless* you have a better index that the query optimizer can choose from.

Fragmentation

Throughout this chapter, there have been a number of places in which fragmentation was mentioned. Most specifically, in the difference between ordered and unordered index scans, you looked at how fragmentation can affect the performance of the query due to the order of pages and extents in a table. The following section elaborates on this. The two types of fragmentation are *logical scan fragmentation* and *average page density*. Logical scan fragmentation is the percentage of out-of-order pages in the index in regard to their physical order, rather than their logical order, in the linked list. This fragmentation has a substantial impact on ordered scan operations like the one shown in Figure 13-24. This type of fragmentation has no impact on operations that do not rely on an ordered scan, such as seek operations, unordered scans, or lookup operations.

The average page density is the percentage of pages that are full. A low percentage (fewer pages full) has a negative impact on the queries that read the data because these queries end up reading more pages than they could, were the pages better populated. The upside of having free space in pages is that insert operations in these pages do not cause page splits, which are expensive and lead to fragmentation. In short, free space in pages is bad for a data warehouse type of system (more read queries), whereas it is good for an OLTP system that involves many data modification operations. However, you need to remember that this is a balancing act between free space and page splits.

Rebuilding the indexes and specifying the proper fill factor based on your application reduces or removes the fragmentation. Using appropriate data types, that is, char(2) for state, can also be the difference between good performance and page splits when they are updated from empty to populated. You can use the following DMF to find out both types of fragmentation in your index. Be aware that querying this DMF can affect performance because it reads data from both the leaf and nonleaf levels depending on the value (LIMITED, SAMPLED or DETAILED) that is specified for the final parameter of the DMF. For example, to find out the fragmentation for indexes on the New_SalesOrderHeader table, run the following query:

```
SELECT
* FROM sys.dm_db_index_physical_stats (DB_ID(),
  OBJECT_ID('dbo.New_SalesOrderHeader'), NULL, NULL, NULL)
```

Look for the `avg_fragmentation_in_percent` column for logical fragmentation. Ideally, it should be 0, which indicates no logical fragmentation. For average page density, look at the `avg_page_space_used_in_percent` column. It shows the average percentage of available data storage space used in all pages.

SQL Server 2005 added a feature to build the indexes online — an `ONLINE` option is added to the `CREATE` and `ALTER INDEX` statements. This Enterprise Edition feature enables you to create, drop, and rebuild the index online. See Chapter 14, "Indexing Your Database," for more details. Following is an example of rebuilding the index `IXNC_SalesOrderID` on the `New_SalesOrderHeader` table:

```
ALTER INDEX IXNC_SalesOrderID ON dbo.New_SalesOrderHeader
REBUILD WITH (ONLINE = ON)
```

Statistics

SQL Server 2012 collects statistical information about the distribution of values in one or more columns of a table or indexed view. The uniqueness of data found in a particular column is known as *cardinality*. High-cardinality refers to a column with values that are unique, whereas low-cardinality refers to a column that has many values that are the same. The two main types of statistics are single-column or multicolumn. . Each statistical object includes a histogram that displays the distribution of values in the first column of the list of columns contained in that statistical object.

The query optimizer uses these statistics to estimate the cardinality and thus the selectivity of expressions. When those are calculated, the sizes of intermediate and final query results are estimated. Good statistics enable the optimizer to accurately assess the cost of different query plans and choose a high-quality plan. All information about a single statistics object is stored in several columns of a single row in the `sysindexes` table and in a statistics binary large object (`statblob`) kept in an *internal-only* table.

If your execution plan has a large difference between the estimated row count and the actual row count, the first things you should check are the statistics on the join columns and the column in the `WHERE` clause for that table. (Be careful with the inner side of loop joins; the row count should match the estimated rows multiplied by the estimated executions.) Make sure that the statistics are current. One way to verify this is to check the `UpdateDate`, `Rows`, and `Rows Sampled` columns returned by `DBCC SHOW_STATISTICS`. You must keep up-to-date statistics. Up-to-date statistics are a reflection of the data, not the age of the statistics. With no data changes, statistics can be valid indefinitely. You can use the following views and command to get details about statistics:

> To see how many statistics exist in your table, you can use the `sys.stats` view.

> To view which columns are part of the statistics, you can use the `sys.stats_columns` view.

> To view the histogram and density information, you can use `DBCC SHOW_STATISTICS`. For example, to view the histogram information for the `IXNC_SalesOrderID` index on the `New_SalesOrderHeader` table, run the following command:

```
DBCC SHOW_STATISTICS ('dbo.New_SalesOrderHeader', 'IXNC_SalesOrderID')
```

Join Algorithms

You saw earlier the different types of joins in the query plans. Now consider how you can use the physical strategies in SQL Server 2012 to process joins. Before SQL Server 7.0, there was only one join algorithm, called *nested loops*. Since version 7.0, SQL Server also supports *hash* and *merge* *join* algorithms. This section describes each of them and explains the conditions under which each provides better performance.

Nested Loop or Loop Join

The nested loop join, also called *nested iteration*, uses one join input as the outer input table (shown as the top input in the graphical execution plan; see Figure 13-26) and the other input as the inner (bottom) input table. The outer loop consumes the outer input table row by row. The inner loop, executed for each outer row, searches for matching rows in the inner input table. Listing 13-15 is an example that produces a nested loop join.

LISTING 13-15: Join.sql

Available for
download on
Wrox.com

```
--Nested Loop Join

SELECT C.CustomerID, c.TerritoryID
FROM Sales.SalesOrderHeader oh
JOIN Sales.Customer c
  ON c.CustomerID = oh.CustomerID
WHERE c.CustomerID IN (10,12)
GROUP BY C.CustomerID, c.TerritoryID
```

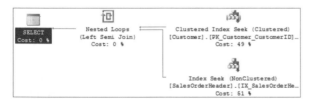

FIGURE 13-26

A nested loop join is particularly effective if the outer input is small and the inner input is sorted and large. In many small transactions, such as those affecting only a small set of rows, indexed nested loop joins are superior to both merge joins and hash joins. In large queries, however, nested loop joins are often not the optimal choice. Of course, the presence of a nested loop join operator in the execution plan doesn't indicate whether it's an efficient plan. A nested loop join is the default algorithm. This does not mean that it is the first algorithm used (that would be the in-memory hash join), but that it can always be applied if another algorithm does match the specific criteria. For example, the "requires join" algorithm must be *equijoin*. (The join condition is based on the equality operator.)

In the example query, a clustered index seek is performed on the outer table Customer where CustomerID is 10 or 12, and for each CustomerID, an index seek is performed on the inner table SalesOrderHeader. Therefore, Index IX_SalesOrderHeader_CustomerID is sought two times (one time for CustomerID 10 and one time for CustomerID 12) on the SalesOrderHeader table.

Hash Join

The hash join has two inputs like every other join: the *build input* (outer table) and the *probe input* (inner table). The query optimizer assigns these roles so that the smaller of the two inputs is the build input. A variant of the hash join (hash aggregate physical operator) can do duplicate removal and grouping, such as SUM (OrderQty) GROUP BY TerritoryID. These modifications use only one input for both the build and probe roles.

The following query is an example of a hash join, and the graphical execution plan is shown in Figure 13-27:

```
--Hash Match

SELECT p.Name As ProductName, ps.Name As ProductSubcategoryName
FROM Production.Product p
JOIN Production.ProductSubcategory ps
   ON p.ProductSubcategoryID = ps.ProductSubcategoryID
ORDER BY p.Name,  ps.Name
```

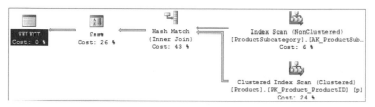

FIGURE 13-27

As discussed earlier, the hash join first scans or computes the entire build input and then builds a hash table in memory if it fits the memory grant. (In Figure 14-27, it is the Production .ProductSubCategory table.) Each row is inserted into a hash bucket according to the hash value computed for the hash key, so building the hash table needs memory. If the entire build input is smaller than the available memory, all rows can be inserted into the hash table. (You see what happens if there is not enough memory shortly.) This build phase is followed by the probe phase. The entire probe input (refer to Figure 14-27; it is the Production.Product table) is scanned or computed one row at a time, and for each probe row (from the Production.Product table), the hash key's value is computed, the corresponding hash bucket (the one created from the Production .ProductSubCategory table) is scanned, and the matches are produced. This strategy is called an *in-memory hash join.*

If you're talking about the AdventureWorks database running on your laptop with 1GB of RAM, you won't have the problem of not fitting the hash table in memory. In the real world, however, with millions of rows in a table, there might not be enough memory to fit the hash table. If the build input does not fit in memory, a hash join proceeds in several steps. This is known as a *grace hash join.* In this hash join strategy, each step has a build phase and a probe phase. Initially, the entire build and probe inputs are consumed and partitioned (using a hash function on the hash keys) into multiple files. Using the hash function on the hash keys guarantees that any two joining records must be in the same pair of files. Therefore, the task of joining two large inputs has been reduced to multiple, but smaller, instances of the same tasks. The hash join is then applied to each pair of partitioned files. If the input is so large that the preceding steps need to be performed many times, multiple partitioning steps and multiple partitioning levels are required. This hash strategy is called a *recursive hash join*.

> *SQL Server always starts with an in-memory hash join and changes to other strategies if necessary.*

Recursive hash joins (or *hash bailouts*) cause reduced performance in your server. If you see many Hash Warning events in a trace (the Hash Warning event is under the Errors and Warnings event class), update statistics on the columns that are being joined. You should capture this event if you see that you have many hash joins in your query. This ensures that hash bailouts are not causing performance problems on your server. When appropriate indexes on join columns are missing, the optimizer normally chooses the hash join.

Merge Join

The merge join, exemplified in the following code, relies on sorted input and is an efficient algorithm if both inputs are available sorted (see Figure 14-28).

With a *one-to-many merge join*, a merge join operator scans each input only once, which is why it is superior to other operators if the predicate is not selective. For sorted input, the optimizer can use a clustered index. If a non-clustered index covers the join and select columns, the optimizer can choose that option because it has fewer pages to fetch.

A *many-to-many merge join* is a little more complicated. A many-to-many merge join uses a temporary table to store rows. If duplicate values exist from each input, one of the inputs must rewind to the start of the duplicates as each duplicate from the other input is processed.

In this query, both tables have a clustered index on the `SalesOrderID` column, so the optimizer chooses a merge join. Sometimes the optimizer chooses the merge join, even if one of the inputs is not presorted by an index, by adding a sort to the plan. The optimizer would do that if the input were small. If the optimizer chooses to sort before the merge, check whether the input has many rows and is not presorted by an index. To prevent the sort, you must add the required indexes to avoid a costly operation.

```
SELECT oh.SalesOrderID, oh.OrderDate,od.ProductID
  FROM Sales.SalesOrderDetail od
  JOIN Sales.SalesOrderHeader oh
    ON oh.SalesOrderID = od.SalesOrderID
```

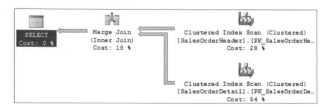

FIGURE 13-28

Data Modification Query Plan

When you execute data modifications, the generated plan has two stages. The first stage is read-only, which determines which rows need to be inserted, updated, or deleted.

During the first stage, the execution plan generates a data stream that describes the changes. For INSERT statements you have column values, so the data stream contains the column values. DELETE statements have key column(s), and UPDATE statements have both data streams, the changed columns' values and the table key. If you have foreign keys, the plan includes performing constraint validation. It also maintains indexes; and if any triggers exist, it fires these triggers as well.

The two maintenance strategies for INSERT, UPDATE, and DELETE statements are per-row and per-index. Consider the following DELETE query, which has a per-row query plan:

```
DELETE FROM New_SalesOrderHeader
WHERE OrderDate = '2007-07-01 00:00:00.000'
```

The query plan is shown in Figure 13-29.

With a per-row plan, SQL Server 2012 maintains the indexes and the base table together for each row affected by the query. The updates to all non-clustered indexes are performed with each row update on the base table. The base table could be a heap or a clustered index. If you look at the Clustered Index Delete information box in Figure 13-29, in the Object information you can notice that both the clustered index and the non-clustered index are listed, which indicates that the indexes are maintained with a per-row operation.

FIGURE 13-29

 Because of the short code path and update to all indexes and tables together, the per-row update strategy is more efficient in terms of CPU cycles.

Now consider another query plan with the following query. The change in this query is to the WHERE clause (changed to <). Use the Sales.SalesOrderHeader table to produce the plan for this example:

```
DELETE FROM Sales.SalesOrderHeader
WHERE OrderDate < '2006-07-01 00:00:00.000'
```

The query plan is shown in Figure 13-30. This figure shows only part of the plan because so many indexes are on this table in the AdventureWorks database. Run the statement in SSMS to see the full query plan.

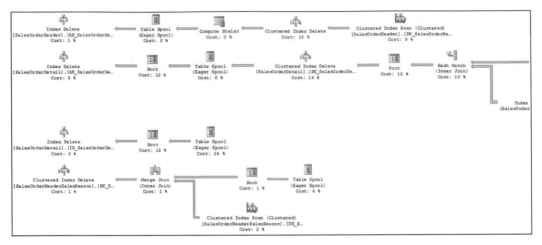

FIGURE 13-30

This query plan performs per-index maintenance. The plan first deletes qualifying rows from the clustered index, and at the same time it builds the temporary spool table containing the clustering key values for the other non-clustered indexes that must be maintained. SQL Server 2012 reads the spool data as many times as the number of non-clustered indexes on the table. The `sort` operator between the index `delete` operator and the `spool` operator indicates that SQL Server 2012 sorts the data according to the key column of the index it is about to delete so that the index pages can be accessed optimally. The `sequence` operator enforces the execution order of each branch. SQL Server 2012 updates the indexes one after another from the top of the plan to the bottom.

As shown in the query plan, per-index maintenance is more complicated; but because it maintains individual indexes after sorting the key (`Sort` operator), it never visits the same page again, saving in I/O. Therefore, when you update many rows, the optimizer usually chooses the per-index plan.

Query Processing Enhancements on Partitioned Tables and Indexes

Before you look further into this topic, you may want to refer to the section "Partition Tables and Indexes" in Chapter 15 for a better understanding of partitioned tables.

SQL Server 2012 improves query processing performance on partitioned tables for many parallel plans, changing the way parallel and serial plans are represented. It also enhances the partitioning information provided in both compile-time and run-time execution plans to help you better understand what's going on in the query plan.

 Partitioned tables and indexes are supported only in SQL Server Enterprise and Developer editions.

Partition-Aware Seek Operation

The partition-aware SEEK operation is best understood through an example. Suppose you have a table called Sales with columns WeekID, GeographyID, ProductID, and SalesAmount. This table is partitioned on WeekID, which means each partition contains sales for a week. Suppose also that this table has a clustered index on GeographyID. Now say you want to perform a query like the following:

```
SELECT * FROM Sales WHERE GeographyID = 4 AND WeekID < 10
```

The partition boundaries for table Sales are defined by the following partition function:

```
CREATE PARTITION FUNCTION myRangePF1 (int) AS RANGE LEFT FOR VALUES (3, 7, 10);
```

In SQL Server 2012, when the query optimizer starts processing this query, it inserts PartitionID (which is hidden to represent the partition number in a partitioned table) as a leading column in the SEEK or SCAN operation. The query optimizer looks at the clustered index on GeographyID with composite columns, with PartitionID as the leading column (PartitionID, GeographyID). First, SQL Server 2012 determines which partitions it needs to look at during the first-level SEEK operation. In this case, because this table is partitioned on WeekID, and the predicate in the query is WeekID < 10, SQL Server 2012 can find all the partitions that have WeekID less than 10 first (see Figure 13-31). Here SQL Server 2012 finds three partitions that have WeekID less than 10, so it performs a second-level SEEK operation within those three partitions to find the records that have GeographyID = 4.

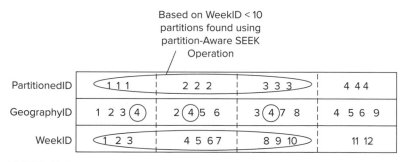

FIGURE 13-31

Parallel Query Execution Strategy for Partitioned Objects

SQL Server 2012 has implemented a new way to use parallelism to improve query performance when you access the partitioned table. If the number of threads is less than the number of partitions, the query processor assigns each thread to a different partition, initially leaving one or more partitions without an assigned thread. When a thread finishes executing on a partition, the query processor assigns it to the next partition until each partition has been assigned a single thread. This is the only case in which the query processor reallocates threads to other partitions.

If the number of threads is equal to the number of partitions, the query processor assigns one thread to each partition. When a thread finishes, it is *not* reallocated to another partition.

What if SQL Server 2012 has more threads than the number of partitions it actually needs to access to get the data? Refer to Figure 13-31. You have data in three partitions, and SQL Server has 10 threads to access the partitions. SQL Server uses all the available threads to access those partitions, but how can it assign those threads to each partition? It assigns three threads to each partition, and the remaining thread is assigned to one partition. Therefore, out of three partitions, two have six threads working on them (three threads each), and one partition has four threads working on it. If you have only one partition to access, then all the available threads are assigned to that partition — in this case, 10. When a thread finishes its execution, it is not reassigned to another partition.

Remember the following key points to achieve better query performance on partitioned tables when you access large amounts of data:

➤   Use more memory to reduce I/O cost if your performance data proves that your system is I/O bound.

➤   Take advantage that multicore processors are on a commodity server because SQL Server 2012 can also use it for parallel query processing capabilities.

➤   Make sure you have a clustered index on partitioned tables so that the query processor can take advantage of index scanning optimizations done in SQL Server 2012.

➤   If you aggregate a large amount of data from a partitioned table, make sure you have enough `tempdb` space on your server. See the article "Capacity Planning for tempdb" in BOL for more information on how to monitor `tempdb` space usage.

Execution Plans for Partitioned Heaps

As mentioned earlier, `PartitionID` is always a leading column to seek for a particular partition or range of partitions, even if the partitioned table is a heap. In SQL Server 2012, a partitioned heap is treated as a logical index on the partition ID. Partition elimination on a partitioned heap is represented in an execution plan as a `Table Scan` operator with a `SEEK` predicate on partition ID. The following example shows the Showplan information provided:

```
|-- Table Scan (OBJECT: ([db].[dbo].[Sales]),
    SEEK: ([PtnId1001]=[Expr1011]) ORDERED FORWARD)
```

As you can see, even if it looks like a table scan, it still seeks on `PartitionID`.

Gathering Query Plans for Analysis with SQL Trace

Earlier you examined the query plans with different option such as `SET STATISTICS PROFILE ON` and `SET STATISTICS XML ON`. This technique does not work when you want to gather the query plans in your production environment. You have to use SQL Trace to get the query plan for analysis. See Chapter 12 for details about how to create server-side traces and import the trace data into a database table. You should create a server-side trace to capture events. In addition, import the data into a database table for analysis, rather than in SQL Profiler because SQL Profiler doesn't offer as many options to play with data.

Please make sure that you set filters for your criteria when you gather the data with a server-side trace because the file size can grow quickly. In addition, depending on whether you prefer a textual execution plan or XML, you can check one of the events Showplan Statistics Profile or Showplan XML Statistics Profile.

SUMMARY

In this chapter you learned how to do Query parsing, compiling, and optimization are all key performance tuning strategies in SQL Server 2012. Additionally, knowing how to read the query plan is imperative. When you read the query plan (using STATISTICS PROFILE, for example) the most important columns you want to look at are Rows, Executes, and EstimatedRows. If you see a big discrepancy between Rows (the actual row count) and EstimatedRows, remove that small query from your main query and start your analysis there. Not every performance problem with a query stems from bad statistics or cardinality estimations. In the real world, where users are less experienced, most performance problems result from user errors (lack of indexes and such). Check the statistics on the columns in the JOIN and WHERE clauses.

Another important part of Performance tuning includes the various index access methods and join algorithms. Normally, I/O is the slowest process, so your goal in query tuning is to reduce the number of I/Os and balance the data modification operation (in an OLTP system), and for that knowledge of the index, access methods and join algorithms are vital. Tuning is not easy, but with patience and attention to details, you can get to the root of the problem. Of course, make sure that your server and disk configuration are done properly. New features starting in SQL Server 2008 help facilitate the performance tuning you will perform, such as the MERGE and the query-processing enhancements on partitioned tables and indexes. Now that you know about configuring your server, optimizing SQL Server, and tuning queries, you can move on to learn about indexing your database in the next chapter.

14

Indexing Your Database

WHAT'S IN THIS CHAPTER

➤ Index-Related Features Available in SQL Server 2012 and Previous Versions

➤ How Partitioned Tables and Indexes Enable your Databases to be More Manageable and Scalable

➤ Implementing Partitioned Tables and Indexes

➤ Maintaining and Tuning Indexes

One of the most important functions of production database administrators is to ensure that query times are consistent with service-level agreements (SLAs) or within user expectations. One of the most effective techniques to improve query performance is to create indexes.

Query performance is generally measured in the amount of time the query takes to run and the amount of work and resources it consumes. Long-running and expensive queries consume resources over an extended period of time and may slow down or cause applications, reports, and other database operations to time-out.

For this reason understanding what indexing features are available in SQL Server 2012 and how to implement them is essential to any production DBA.

This chapter offers an overview of the indexing-related features available in SQL Server 2012, including the newest feature known as *column-store indexes*, which can greatly increase query performance over traditional row-based indexes.

NOTEWORTHY INDEX-RELATED FEATURES IN SQL SERVER

This section highlights the new indexing features introduced in SQL Server 2012 and overviews the index-related features introduced in previous versions of SQL Server.

What's New for Indexes in SQL Server 2012

SQL Server 2012 introduces a new type of index called columnstore index based on the Vertipaq engine acquisition. Additionally, online index operations such as index build and rebuild containing LOB columns are now supported. The next two sections describe these two new enhancements in detail.

Columnstore Index

Columnstore index is the new type of index introduced in SQL Server 2012. It is a column-based non-clustered index geared toward increasing query performance for workloads that involve large amounts of data, typically found in data warehouse fact tables.

This new type of index stores data column-wise instead of row-wise, as indexes currently do. For example, consider an Employee table containing employee data, as shown in Table 14-1.

TABLE 14-1: Sample Employee Table

FIRSTNAME	LASTNAME	HIREDATE	GENDER
Adam	Jorgensen	5/9/2008	Male
Sherri	McDonald	7/1/2009	Female
Brian	McDonald	09/15/2009	Male
Jose	Chinchilla	1/10/2010	Male
Tim	Murphy	7/1/2009	Male
Tim	Moolic	6/1/2008	Male

In a row-based index, the data in the Employee table is stored in one or more data pages, as shown in Figure 14-1.

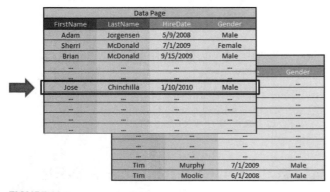

FIGURE 14-1

In a column-based index, the data in the Employee table is stored in separate pages for each of the columns, as shown in Figure 14-2.

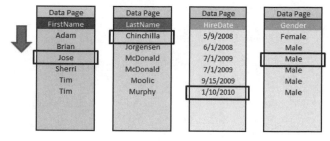

FIGURE 14-2

Performance advantages in columnstore indexes are possible by leveraging the VertiPaq compression technology, which enables large amounts of data to be compressed in-memory. This in-memory compressed store reduces the number of disk reads and increases buffer cache hit ratios because only the smaller column-based data pages that need to satisfy a query are moved into memory.

For wide tables, such as those commonly found in data warehouses, columnstore indexes come in handy as you essentially reduce the amount and size of data needed to be accessed for any given query. For example, consider the following query:

```
SELECT
FirstName,
LastName,
FROM EmployeeTable
WHERE HireDate >= '1/1/2010'
```

A column-store index is more efficient for this example because only one smaller-sized (compressed) data page is needed to satisfy the query. In this case, the columnstore index for the HireDate column satisfies the WHERE clause. A row-based index is not as efficient because it may need to load one or more larger-sized data pages into memory and read the entire rows, including columns not needed to satisfy the query. A larger-sized data page and additional unnecessary columns increases data size, memory usage, disk reads, and overall query time. Imagine if this table had 20 or more columns!

Columnstore indexes have some requirements and limitations, as shown in Table 14-2.

TABLE 14-2: Requirements and Limitations of Columnstore Index

DESCRIPTION	REQUIREMENT/LIMITATION
No. of columnstore indexes per table	1
Index record size limit of 900 bytes	No limit/Not applicable.
Index limit of 16 key columns	No limit/Not applicable.
Table partitioning support	Yes, as a partition aligned index.

continues

TABLE 14-2 *(continued)*

DESCRIPTION	REQUIREMENT/LIMITATION
Can be combined with row-based indexes?	Yes, if clustered index, all columns must be present in columnstore index.
Update, Delete, Insert, Merge supported?	No, columnstore indexes are read-only but workarounds exist. Refer to Books Online: Best Practices: Updating Data in a Columnstore Index.
Data types that can be included in a columnstore index	Char, varchar except varchar(max), nchar, nvarchar except nvarchar(max), decimal and numeric except with precision greater than 18 digits, int, bigint, smallint, tinyint, float, real, bit, money, smallmoney, all date and time data types except datetimeoffset with scale greater than 2.
Data types that cannot be included in a columnstore index.	Binary, varbinary, ntext, text, image, varchar(max), nvarchar(max), uniqueidentifier, rowversion, timestamp, sql_variant, decimal and numeric with precision greater than 18 digits, datetimeoffset with scale greater than 2, CLR types including hierarchyid and spatial types, xml.

Following is the basic syntax to create a columnstore index:

```
CREATE COLUMNSTORE INDEX idx_cs1
ON EmployeeTable (FirstName, LastName, HireDate, Gender)
```

You can also create columnstore indexes using SQL Server Management Studio. Simply navigate to the Indexes section of the table, and select New Index ⇨ Non-Clustered Columnstore Index.

Online Index Operations with LOB Columns

In previous versions of SQL Server, online index operations were not possible on indexes with columns defined as large object data types. LOB datatypes include image, text, ntext, varchar(max), nvarchar(max), varbinary(max), and xml datatypes.

SQL Server 2012 supports building and rebuilding indexes that contain LOB columns while keeping the index available for read and write operations. A new reference consistency and sharing mechanism is employed during the online rebuild process to keep track of the data referenced by the old index and the new index.

Index Features from SQL Server 2008R2, SQL Server 2008, and SQL Server 2005

While the core functionality of index hasn't changed, there have been a number of enhancements in the last few releases of SQL Server. This section highlights all the index-related features introduced in previous versions of SQL Server that are now part of SQL Server 2012.

SQL Server 2008 introduced index-related features:

➤ **Support for up to 15K partitions:** In SQL Server 2008 Service Pack 2 and SQL Server 2008 R2 Service Pack 1 (SP1), the limit of 999 table partitions increased to 15,000.

➤ **Filtered indexes and statistics:** You can use a predicate to create filtered indexes and statistics on a subset of rows in the table. Prior to SQL Server 2008, indexes and statistics were created on all the rows in the table. Now you can include a WHERE predicate in the index or statistics you create to limit the number of rows to be included in the indexes or stats. Filtered indexes and statistics are especially suitable for queries that select from well-defined subsets of data; columns with heterogeneous categories of values; and columns with distinct ranges of values.

➤ **Compressed storage of tables and indexes:** SQL Server 2008 added support for on-disk storage compression in both row and page format for tables, indexes, and indexed views. Compression of partitioned tables and indexes can be configured independently for each partition. Chapter 12, "Monitoring Your SQL Server," covers this topic in detail.

➤ **Spatial indexes:** SQL Server 2008 introduced support for spatial data and spatial indexes. Spatial data in this context represents geometric objects or physical location. SQL Server supports two spatial data types: geography and geometry. A spatial column is a table column that contains data of a spatial data type, such as geometry or geography. A spatial index is a type of extended index that enables you to index a spatial column. SQL Server uses the NET CLR (Common Language Runtime) to implement this data type. Refer to the topic "Working with Spatial Indexes (Database Engine)" in Books Online (BOL) for details.

SQL Server 2005 introduced these index-related features:

➤ **Partitioned tables and indexes:** Beginning with SQL Server 2005, you can create tables on multiple partitions and indexes on each partition. This enables you to manage operations on large datasets, such as loading and unloading a new set of data, more efficiently by indexing just the new partition, rather than having to re-index the whole table. You can find a lot more information about partitioned tables and indexes later in this chapter.

➤ **Online index operations:** Online index operations were added as an availability feature in SQL Server 2005. They enable users to continue to query against a table while indexes are built or rebuilt. The main scenario for using this new feature is when you need to make index changes during normal operating hours. The new syntax for using online index operations is the addition of the ONLINE = ON option with the CREATE INDEX, ALTER INDEX, DROP INDEX, and ALTER TABLE operations.

➤ **Parallel index operations:** Parallel index operations are another useful feature from SQL Server 2005. They are available only in Enterprise Edition and only apply to systems running on multiprocessor machines. The key scenario for using this feature is when you need to restrict the amount of CPU resources that index operations consume. This might be either for multiple index operations to coexist, or more likely when you need to allow other tasks to complete while performing index operations. They enable a DBA to specify the MAXDOP for an index operation. This is useful on large systems, enabling you to limit the maximum number of processors used in index operations. It's effectively a MAXDOP specifically for index operations, and it works with the server-configured MAXDOP setting. The new syntax for parallel index operations is the MAXDOP = n option, which can be specified on CREATE INDEX, ALTER INDEX, DROP INDEX (for clustered indexes only), ALTER TABLE ADD (constraint), ALTER TABLE DROP (clustered index), and CONSTRAINT operations.

➤ **Asynchronous statistics update:** This is a performance SET option -AUTO UPDATE STATISTICS_ASYNC. When this option is set, outdated statistics are placed on a queue and are automatically updated by a worker thread later. The query that generated the autoupdate request continues before the stats are updated. Asynchronous statistics updates cannot occur if any data definition language (DDL) statements such as CREATE, ALTER, or DROP occur in the same transaction.

➤ **Full-text indexes:** Beginning with SQL Server 2005, Full-Text Search supports the creation of indexes on XML columns. It was also upgraded to use MSSearch 3.0, which includes additional performance improvements for full-text index population. It also means that there is now one instance of MSSearch for each SQL Server instance.

➤ **Nonkey columns in non-clustered indexes:** With SQL Server 2005 and SQL Server 2008, nonkey columns can be added to a non-clustered index. This has several advantages. It enables queries to retrieve data faster because the query can now retrieve everything it needs from the index pages without having to do a bookmark lookup into the table to read the data row. The nonkey columns are not counted in the limits for the non-clustered index number of columns (16 columns) or key length (900 bytes). The new syntax for this option is INCLUDE (column Name, ...), which is used with the CREATE INDEX statement.

➤ **Index lock granularity changes:** In SQL Server 2005, the CREATE INDEX and ALTER INDEX T-SQL statements were enhanced by the addition of new options to control the locking that occurs during the index operation. ALLOW _ROW_LOCKS and ALLOW_PAGE_LOCKS specify the granularity of the lock to be taken during the index operation.

➤ **Indexes on XML columns:** This type of index on the XML data in a column enables the Database Engine to find elements within the XML data without having to shred the XML each time.

➤ **Dropping and rebuilding large indexes:** The Database Engine was modified in SQL Server 2005 to treat indexes occupying more than 128 extents in a new, more scalable way. If a drop or rebuild is required on an index larger than 128 extents, the process is broken down into logical and physical stages. In the logical phase, the pages are simply marked as deallocated. After the transaction commits, the physical phase of deallocating the pages occurs. The deallocation takes place in batches, occurring in the background, thereby avoiding taking locks for a long period of time.

➤ **Indexed view enhancements:** Indexed views have been enhanced in several ways. They can now contain scalar aggregates and some user-defined functions (with restrictions). In addition, the query optimizer can now match more queries to indexed views if the query uses scalar expressions, scalar aggregates, user-defined functions, interval expressions, and equivalency conditions.

➤ **Version Store:** Version Store provides the basis for the row-versioning framework used by Online Indexing, Multiple Active Result Sets (MARS), triggers, and the new row-versioning-based isolation levels.

> **Database Tuning Advisor:** The Database Tuning Advisor (DTA) replaced SQL Server 2000's Index Tuning Wizard (ITW). DTA offers the following new features:

> ➤ Time-bound tuning

> ➤ Tune across multiple databases

> ➤ Tune a broader class of events and triggers

> ➤ Tuning log

> ➤ What-if analysis

> ➤ More control over tuning options XML file support

> ➤ Partitioning support

> ➤ Offloading tuning load to lower-spec hardware

> ➤ Execution by Database_owners

 This chapter uses the sample database AdventureWorks available to download from Codeplex.com at http://msftdbprodsamples.codeplex.com/.

PARTITIONED TABLES AND INDEXES

This section offers an overview of the process that goes into creating indexes and partitioning tables and how they can be combined to manage large tables and to scale.

Understanding Indexes

Good index design starts with a good understanding of the benefits indexes provide. In books, table of contents help readers locate a section, chapter, or page of interest. SQL Server indexes serve the same function as a table of contents in a book. It enables SQL Server to locate and retrieve the data requested in a query as fast as possible.

Consider a 500-page book with dozens of sections and chapters and no table of contents. To locate a section of a book, readers would need to flip and read through every page until they locate the section of interest. Imagine if you have to do this for multiple sections of the book. It would be a time-consuming task.

This analogy also applies to SQL Server database tables. Without proper indexes, SQL Server has to scan through all the data pages that contain the data in a table. For tables with large amounts of data, this becomes time-consuming and resource-intensive. This is the reason why indexes are so important.

Indexes can be classified in several ways depending on the way they store data, their internal structure, their purpose, and the way they are defined. The following sections briefly describe these types of indexes.

Row-based Indexes

A row-based index is a traditional index in which data is stored as rows in data pages. These indexes include the following:

Clustered Indexes

Clustered indexes store and sort data based on the key column(s). There can only be one clustered index per table because data can be sorted in only one order. A clustered index is created by default when a table definition includes a primary key constraint.

Non-clustered Indexes

Non-clustered indexes contain index key values and row locators that point to the actual data row. If there is no clustered index, the row locator is a pointer to the row. When there is a clustered index present, the row locator is the clustered index key for the row.

Non-clustered indexes can be optimized to satisfy more queries, improve query response times, and reduce index size. The two most important of these optimized non-clustered indexes are described in the next two sections.

Covering Indexes

Covering indexes are non-clustered indexes that include nonkey columns in the leaf level. These types of indexes improve query performance, cover more queries, and reduce IO operations as the columns necessary to satisfy a query are included in the index itself either as key or nonkey columns. Covering indexes can greatly reduce bookmark lookups.

The ability to include nonkey columns enables indexes to be more flexible by including columns with data types not supported as index key columns Nonkey columns also enable indexes to extend beyond the 16 key column limitation. Nonkey columns do not count towards the 900 byte index key size limit.

Filtered Indexes

Filtered indexes can take a WHERE clause to indicate which rows are to be indexed. Since you index only a portion of rows in a table, you can create only a non-clustered filtered index. If you try to create a filtered clustered index, SQL Server returns a syntax error.

Why do you need a non-clustered index with a subset of data in a table? A well-designed filtered index can offer the following advantages over full-table indexes:

> ➤ **Improved query performance and plan quality:** If the index is deep (more pages because of more data), traversing an index takes more I/O and results in slow query performance. If you have a large table and you know that there are more user queries on a well-defined subset of data, creating a filtered index makes queries run faster because less I/O will be performed since the number of pages is less for the smaller amount of data in that filtered index. Moreover, stats on the full table may be less accurate compared to filtered stats with less data, which also helps improve query performance.

> ➤ **Reduced index maintenance costs:** Maintaining a filtered index is less costly than maintaining a full index because of smaller data size. Obviously, it also reduces the cost of updating statistics because of the smaller size of the filtered index. As mentioned earlier, you must know your user queries and what kind of data they query often to create a well-defined filtered index with a subset of that data. If the data outside of the filtered index is modified frequently, it won't cost anything to maintain the filtered index. That enables you to create many filtered indexes when the data in those indexes is not modified frequently.

> ➤ **Reduced index storage costs:** Less data, less space. If you don't need a full-table non-clustered index, creating a smaller dataset for a non-clustered filtered index takes less disk space.

Column-based Indexes

Column-based indexes are a new type of index introduced in SQL Server 2012 in which only column data is stored in the data pages. These indexes are based on the Vertipaq engine implementation, which is capable of high compression ratios and handles large data sets in memory.

How Indexes are Used by SQL Server?

A good understanding of how indexes are used by SQL Server is also important in a good index design. In SQL Server, the Query Optimizer component determines the most cost-effective option to execute a query. The Query Optimizer evaluates a number of query execution plans and selects the execution plan with the lowest cost.

The execution plan selected by the Query Optimizer may or may not make efficient use of indexes, or it may not use indexes at all. The following sections describe how execution plans can use indexes.

Table Scan

Indexes are not required by SQL Server to retrieve data requested by a query. In the absence of indexes or if determined to be least cost effective, SQL server scans every row of a table until the query is satisfied. This is known as a *table scan*. As you may suspect, table scans can bring forth expensive IO operations for large tables. SQL Server has to read every single data page until it finds the data that satisfies the query. A table scan can take from a couple of seconds to several minutes. Some users may even experience time-outs by applications with short response-time thresholds.

Table scans generally occur when there is no clustered indexed available; in other words, when the table is a heap.

Index Scan and Index Seek

An *index scan* is similar to a table scan in that SQL Server has to read every single data page in the index until it finds the data that satisfies the query. Index scans can be both IO and memory intensive operations.

An *index seek* on the other hand, is a more efficient way of retrieving data because only data pages and rows that satisfy the query are read. Index seeks result in less data pages read, hence reducing IO and memory consumption.

Depending on how selective a query is, meaning what percentage of the total number of rows in a table is requested, SQL Server Query Optimizer can choose to do an index scan rather than an index seek. The tipping point at which an index scan is preferred by the SQL Server Query Optimizer is not always a definitive percentage. There are many factors such as parallelism settings, memory availability, and number of rows that contribute in the decision for the more cost-effective option.

Bookmark Lookup

It is quite common to see queries that require additional columns than the ones included in a non-clustered index. To retrieve these additional columns, SQL Server needs to retrieve additional data pages to cover all requested columns. Bookmark lookups can become expensive operations when dealing with a large number of rows because more data pages need to be retrieved from disk and loaded into memory.

To avoid excessive bookmark lookup operations, the required columns that need to be covered by the query can be included in the index definition. These types of indexes are known as *covering indexes*.

Creating Indexes

At this point you should be familiar with the different types of indexes and how they are used in execution plans. This understanding is crucial to design and fine tune indexes to improve query performance.

Indexes are created manually using T-SQL commands or by using a graphical user interface such as SQL Server Management Studio. SQL Server 2012 also includes a tool called the Database Engine Tuning Advisor (DTA) that suggests and generates missing indexes for you. This tool is discussed later in this chapter.

To create an index using T-SQL commands, perform the following steps:

1. Open SQL Server Management Studio and connect to the SQL server instance.

2. Open a new query window and follow one of the sample syntaxes provided in the following list:

   ➤ To create a clustered index you use the CREATE CLUSTERED INDEX T-SQL command as follows:

   ```
   CREATE CLUSTERED INDEX idx_EmployeeID
   ON EmployeeTable (EmployeeID)
   ```

   ➤ To create a non-clustered index you use the CREATE NONCLUSTERED INDEX T-SQL command. NONCLUSTERED is the default index type and can be omitted:

   ```
   CREATE NONCLUSTERED INDEX idx_LastName
   ON EmployeeTable (LastName)

   Or

   CREATE INDEX idx_LastName
   ON EmployeeTable (LastName)
   ```

   ➤ To create a covering index you use the CREATE NONCLUSTERED INDEX T-SQL command along with the INCLUDE keyword as follows:

```
CREATE NONCLUSTERED INDEX idx_LastName
ON EmployeeTable (LastName)
INCLUDE (FirstName, HireDate)
```

➤ To create a filtered index you use the CREATE NONCLUSTERED INDEX T-SQL command along with the WHERE keyword as follows:

```
CREATE NONCLUSTERED INDEX idx_GenderFemale
ON EmployeeTable (Gender)
WHERE Gender = 'Female'
```

Why Use Both Partitioned Tables and Indexes?

Partitioned tables are a way to spread a single table over multiple partitions, and while doing so each partition can be on a separate filegroup. Following are several reasons for doing this:

➤ **Faster and easier data loading:** If your database has a large amount of data to load, you might want to consider using a partitioned table. "A large amount of data," doesn't mean a specific amount of data, but any case in which the load operation takes longer than is acceptable in the production cycle. A partitioned table enables you to load the data to an empty table that's not in use by the "live" data, so it has less impact on concurrent live operations. Clearly, there will be an impact on the I/O subsystem, but if you also have separate filegroups on different physical disks, even this has a minimal impact on overall system performance. After the data is loaded to the new table, you can perform a switch to add the new table to the live data. This switch is a simple metadata change that quickly executes, which is why partitioned tables are a great way to load large amounts of data with limited impact to users who touch the rest of the data in the table.

➤ **Faster and easier data deletion or archival:** For the same reasons, partitioned tables also help you to delete or archive data. If your data is partitioned on boundaries that are also the natural boundaries on which you add or remove data, the data is considered to be aligned. When your data is aligned, deleting or archiving data is as simple as switching a table out of the current partition, after which you can unload or archive it at your leisure. There is a bit of a catch to this part: With archiving, you often want to move the old data to slower or different storage. The switch operation is so fast because all it does is change metadata. It doesn't move any data around, so to actually move the data from the filegroup where it lived to the old, slow disk archival filegroup, you need to move the data, but you move it when the partition isn't attached to the existing partitioned table. Therefore, although this may take quite some time, it can have a minimal impact on any queries executing against the live data.

➤ **Faster queries:** You are probably interested in an opportunity to get faster queries. When querying a partitioned table, the query optimizer can eliminate searching through partitions that it knows won't hold any results. This is referred to as *partition elimination*. This works only if the data in the partitioned table or index is aligned with the query. That is, the data must be distributed among the partitions in a way that matches the search clause on the query. You learn more details about this as you consider how to create a partitioned table. SQL Server 2008 offers some improvements for parallel query processing enhancements on partitioned tables and indexes. Refer to the section "Query Processing Enhancements on Partitioned Tables and Indexes" in Chapter 13 for details on this topic.

➤ **Sliding windows:** A sliding window is basically what was referred to earlier in the discussion about adding new data and then deleting or archiving old data. What you did was fill a new table, switch it into the live table, and then switch an existing partition out of the live table for archival or deletion. It's kind of like sliding a window of new data into the current partitioned table, and then sliding an old window of data out of the partitioned table.

Creating Partitioned Tables

Table partitioning requires SQL Server 2012 Enterprise Edition. There are also some expectations about the hardware in use, in particular the storage system; although these are implicit expectations, and you can store the data anywhere you want. You just won't get the same performance benefits you would get if you had a larger enterprise storage system with multiple disk groups dedicated to different partitions.

SQL Server 2012 supports up to 15,000 partitions by default and is fully supported in 64-bit systems. In 32-bit systems, it is possible to create more than 1,000 table or index partitions, but it is not fully supported.

To create a partitioned table or index, perform the following steps:

1. Specify how the table or index is partitioned by the partitioning column, and the range of values included for each partition. Only one partitioning column can be specified. For example, to create four partitions based on a DateKey column, you execute the following command:

```
CREATE PARTITION FUNCTION DateKeyRange_PF (int)
AS RANGE LEFT FOR VALUES (20021231, 20031231, 20041231);
```

Either LEFT or RIGHT boundaries can be specified in the partition function. If no partition boundary is specified LEFT is used as default. Table 14-3 describes the partitions created by the preceding partition function.

TABLE 14-3: Partition Results for DateKeyRange Function.

PARTITION NO.	DESCRIPTION
1	All records with DateKey <= 20021231
2	Records between Datekey>20021231 and Datekey<=20031231
3	Records between Datekey>20031231 and Datekey<=20041231
4	All records with DateKey > 20041231

2. To determine the partition number where a record will be placed based on the DateKey column value, use the $PARTITION function as follows:

```
SELECT '20010601' DateKey, $PARTITION.DateKeyRange_PF(20010601)
PartitionNumber
UNION
SELECT '20030601' DateKey, $PARTITION.DateKeyeRange_PF(20030601)
PartitionNumber
UNION
```

```
SELECT '20040601' DateKey, $PARTITION.DateKeyRange_PF(20040601)
PartitionNumber
UNION
SELECT '20050601' DateKey, $PARTITION.DateKeyeRange_PF(20050601)
```

The results of the $PARTITION function are shown in Figure 14-3.

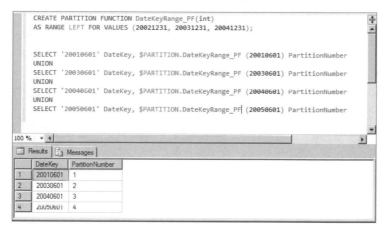

FIGURE 14-3

3. Now create a partition scheme. For example, create a partition scheme with four filegroups that can be used to hold the four partitions defined in the DateKeyRange_PF partition function as follows:

```
CREATE PARTITION SCHEME DateKeyRange_ps
AS PARTITION DateKeyRange_PF
TO (FileGroup1, FileGroup2, FileGroup3, FileGroup4, FileGroup5)
```

INDEX MAINTENANCE

Another important task of database administrators is to monitor existing index health and identify where new indexes are needed. Every time data is inserted, updated, or deleted in SQL Server tables, indexes are accordingly updated.

Over time, the distribution of data in data pages can become unbalanced. Some data pages become loosely filled, whereas others are filled to the maximum. Too many loosely filled data pages create performance issues as more data pages need to be read to retrieve the requested data.

On the other hand, pages filled close to their maximum may create page splits when new data is inserted or updated. When page splits occur, about half of the data is moved to a newly created data page. This constant reorganization consumes resources and creates data page fragmentation.

The goal is to store as much data into the smallest number of data pages with room for growth to prevent excessive page splits. This delicate balance can be achieved by fine-tuning the index fill factor. For more information on fine-tuning the index fill factor, refer to Books Online at http://msdn.microsoft.com/en-us/library/ms177459(v=SQL.110).aspx.

Monitoring Index Fragmentation

You can monitor index fragmentation through the provided Data Management Views (DMVs) available in SQL Server 2012. One of the most useful DMVs is `sys.dm_db_index_physical_stats`, which provides average fragmentation information for each index.

For example, you can query the `sys.dm_db_index_physical_stats` DMV as follows:

```
SELECT index_id,avg_fragmentation_in_percent
FROM sys.dm_db_index_physical_stats
(
DB_ID('AdventureWorks'),
OBJECT_ID('AdventureWorks'),
NULL, NULL, 'DETAILED'
)
```

Figure 14-4 shows the results of this query.

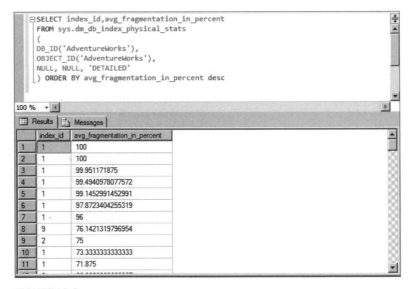

FIGURE 14-4

From execution results of this DMV, you can observe indexes with high fragmentation. Indexes with high defragmentation percentages need to be defragmented to avoid performance issues. Heavily fragmented indexes are stored and accessed inefficiently by SQL Server depending on the type of fragmentation, internal or external. External fragmentation means that data pages are not stored in logical order. Internal fragmentation means that pages store much less data then they can hold. Both types of fragmentation cause query execution to take longer.

Cleaning Up Indexes

Index cleanup should always be part of all database maintenance operations. You need to perform these index cleanup tasks on a regular basis, depending on how fragmented indexes become due to changes to the data. If your indexes become highly fragmented, you can defragment it through one of the operations described here:

➤ Reorganize an index:

    ➤ Reorders and compacts leaf level pages

    ➤ Performs index reordering online, no long-term locks

    ➤ Good for indexes with low fragmentation percentages

➤ Rebuild an index:

    ➤ Drops and re-creates the index

    ➤ Reclaims disk space

    ➤ Reorders and compacts rows in contiguous pages

    ➤ Online index rebuilt option available in Enterprise Edition

    ➤ Better for highly fragmented indexes

Table 14-2 lists the general syntax for index operations for the DimCustomer table.

TABLE 14-2: Index /operations Syntax for DimCustomer Table

OPERATION	SYNTAX
Create Index	`CREATE INDEX IX_CustomerAlternateKey ON DimCustomer_CustomerAlternateKey`
Reorganize Index	`ALTER INDEX IX_DimCustomer_CustomerAlternateKey ON DimCustomer REORGANIZE`
Rebuild Index	`ALTER INDEX IX_DimCustomer_CustomerAlternateKey ON DimCustomer REBUILD`
Drop Index	`DROP INDEX IX_DimCustomer_CustomerAlternateKey FROM DIMCustomer`

Indexes may become heavily fragmented over time. Deciding whether to reorganize or rebuild indexes depends in part on their level of fragmentation and your maintenance window. Generally accepted fragmentation thresholds to perform an index rebuild range between 20 percent and 30 percent. If your index fragmentation level is below this threshold, performing a reorganize index operation may be good enough.

But, why not just rebuild indexes every time? You can, if your maintenance window enables you to do so. Keep in mind that index rebuild operations take longer to complete, time during which locks are placed and all inserts, updates, and deletions have to wait. If you are running SQL Server 2012 Enterprise Edition, you can take advantage of online index rebuild operations. Unlike standard rebuild operations, online index operations allow for inserts, updates, and deletions during the time the index is being rebuilt.

IMPROVING QUERY PERFORMANCE WITH INDEXES

SQL Server 2012 includes several Dynamic Management Views (DMVs) that enable you to fine-tune queries. DMVs are useful to surface execution statistics for a particular query such as the number of times it has been executed, number of reads and writes performed, amount of CPU time consumed, index query usage statistics, and so on.

You can use the execution statistics obtained through DMVs to fine-tune a query by refactoring the T-SQL code to take advantage of parallelism and existing indexes, for example. You can also use them to identify missing indexes, indexes not utilized, and identify indexes that require defragmentation.

For example, explore the existing indexes in the FactInternetSales table from the AdventureWorks database. As shown in Figure 14-5, the FactInternetSales table has been indexed fairly well.

FIGURE 14-5

To illustrate the query tuning process, run through a series of steps to generate execution statistics that can surface through DMVS:

1. Drop the existing ProductKey and OrderDateKey indexes from the FactInternet Sales table as follows:

```
USE [AdventureWorks]
GO
-- Drop ProductKey index
IF  EXISTS (SELECT * FROM sys.indexes
WHERE object_id = OBJECT_ID(N'[dbo].[FactInternetSales]') AND
name = N'IX_FactInternetSales_ProductKey')
DROP INDEX [IX_FactInternetSales_ProductKey] ON [dbo].[FactInternetSales]
GO

-- Drop OrderDateKeyIndex
IF  EXISTS (SELECT * FROM sys.indexes WHERE object_id = OBJECT_ID(N'[dbo].[FactInter
netSales]')
AND name = N'IX_FactInternetSales_OrderDateKey')
DROP INDEX [IX_FactInternetSales_OrderDateKey] ON [dbo].[FactInternetSales]
GO
```

2. Execute the following script three times, like so:

```
/*** Internet_ResellerProductSales ***/
SELECT
 D.[ProductKey],
 D.EnglishProductName,
 Color,
 Size,
 Style,
```

```
ProductAlternateKey,
sum(FI.[OrderQuantity]) InternetOrderQuantity,
sum(FR.[OrderQuantity]) ResellerOrderQuantity,
sum(FI.[SalesAmount]) InternetSalesAmount,
sum(FR.[SalesAmount]) ResellerSalesAmount
FROM [FactInternetSales] FI
INNER JOIN DimProduct D
 ON FI.ProductKey = D.ProductKey
INNER JOIN FactResellerSales FR
 ON FR.ProductKey = D.ProductKey
WHERE
FI.OrderDateKey BETWEEN 20000101 AND 20041231
AND FR.OrderDateKey BETWEEN 20000101 AND 20041231
GROUP BY
D.[ProductKey],
D.EnglishProductName,
Color,
Size,
Style,
ProductAlternateKey
```

Figure 14-6 displays T-SQL script executed along with results and an execution time of 11 seconds. Your execution results may vary depending on the resources available to your machine.

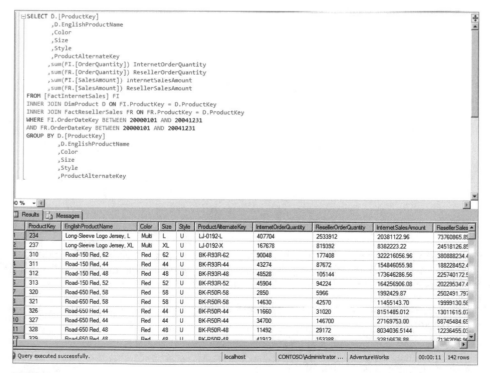

FIGURE 14-6

3. Run the following script to analyze the execution statistics of the previous query.

```
SELECT TOP 10
 SUBSTRING(qt.TEXT, (qs.statement_start_offset/2)+1,
 ((CASE qs.statement_end_offset WHEN -1 THEN DATALENGTH(qt.TEXT)
 ELSE qs.statement_end_offset
 END - qs.statement_start_offset)/2)+1) QueryText,
 qs.last_execution_time,
 qs.execution_count ,
 qs.last_logical_reads,
 qs.last_logical_writes,
 qs.last_worker_time,
 qs.total_logical_reads,
 qs.total_logical_writes,
 qs.total_worker_time,
 qs.last_elapsed_time/1000000 last_elapsed_time_in_S,
 qs.total_elapsed_time/1000000 total_elapsed_time_in_S,
 qp.query_plan
FROM
 sys.dm_exec_query_stats qs
 CROSS APPLY sys.dm_exec_sql_text(qs.sql_handle) qt
 CROSS APPLY sys.dm_exec_query_plan(qs.plan_handle) qp
ORDER BY
 qs.last_execution_time DESC,
 qs.total_logical_reads DESC
```

Figure 14-7 shows the execution statistics reported mainly by the sys.dm_exec_query_stats DMV.

	QueryText	last_execution_time	execution_count	last_logical_reads	last_logical_writes
1	SELECT F.[ProductKey] ,D.EnglishProductName ...	2011-09-15 05:21:29.477	1	4372	0
2	select table_id, item_guid, oplsn_fseqno, oplsn_bOffset, o...	2011-09-15 05:21:25.440	268	0	0
3	SELECT TOP 10 SUBSTRING(qt.TEXT, (qs.statement_s...	2011-09-15 05:21:14.633	1	0	0
4	SELECT dtb.name AS [Name], dtb.database_id AS [ID], ...	2011-09-15 05:21:13.137	37	14	0
5	SELECT dtb.collation_name AS [Collation], dtb.name AS [...	2011-09-15 05:21:13.130	41	2	0
6	SELECT SUBSTRING(qt.TEXT, (qs.statement_start_offs...	2011-09-15 05:21:05.043	6	12700	66
7	SELECT D.[ProductKey] ,D.EnglishProductName ...	2011-09-15 05:20:48.120	2	523129	20
8	SELECT SUBSTRING(qt.TEXT, (qs.statement_start_offs...	2011-09-15 05:18:44.563	1	12700	66
9	SELECT SUBSTRING(qt.TEXT, (qs.statement_start_offs...	2011-09-15 05:17:59.957	1	12698	64
10	SELECT TOP 10 SUBSTRING(qt.TEXT, (qs.statement_s...	2011-09-15 05:17:28.930	1	0	0

FIGURE 14-7

From this DMV you can observe that there was a large number of reads and long period of time the processor was busy executing the query. Keep these baseline numbers in mind. At the end of this example, you can reduce these numbers.

4. Query the sys.dm_db_missing_index_details DMV to check if missing indexes are reported like so:

```
SELECT
 DatabaseName = DB_NAME(database_id,)
 [Number Indexes Missing] = count(*)
```

```
FROM
 sys.dm_db_missing_index_details
GROUP BY
 DB_NAME(database_id)
ORDER BY 2 DESC;
```

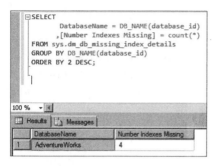

Figure 14-8 shows the results of the `sys.dm_db_missing_index_details` DMV. The `sys.dm_db_missing_index_details` DMV is a great way to quickly identify if you need indexes. If you have a substantial number of missing indexes, you may want to run the Database Tuning Advisor to let the Query Optimizer recommend which indexes to implement.

FIGURE 14-8

  You could also try to identify which indexes are needed by analyzing the query text captured by the sys.dm_exec_sql_text *(refer to Figure 14-7).*

5. Continuing with your query tuning endeavor, create the `ProductKey` and `OrderDateKey` indexes on the `FactInternetSales` table as follows:

```
USE [AdventureWorks]
GO
IF EXISTS
 (SELECT * FROM sys.indexes
  WHERE object_id = OBJECT_ID(N'FactInternetSales')
  AND name = N'IX_FactInternetSales_OrderDateKey')

  DROP INDEX IX_FactInternetSales_OrderDateKey ON
  FactInternetSales
GO

IF NOT EXISTS
 (SELECT * FROM sys.indexes
  WHERE object_id = OBJECT_ID(N'[dbo].[FactInternetSales]') AND
  name = N'IX_FactInternetSales_ProductKey')

  CREATE NON-CLUSTERED INDEX IX_FactInternetSales_ProductKey ON
  FactInternetSales
(ProductKey ASC)
  WITH
  (PAD_INDEX = OFF,
   STATISTICS_NORECOMPUTE = OFF,
   SORT_IN_TEMPDB =  OFF,
   DROP_EXISTING = OFF,
   ONLINE = OFF,
```

```
      ALLOW_ROW_LOCKS = ON,
      ALLOW_PAGE_LOCKS = ON
   ) ON [PRIMARY]
GO
```

6.   Execute the `Internet_ResellerProductSales` query defined in step 2 three more times. Figure 14-9 shows that execution time went down to 8 seconds! That is a 28% improvement in query execution simply by adding the appropriate index.

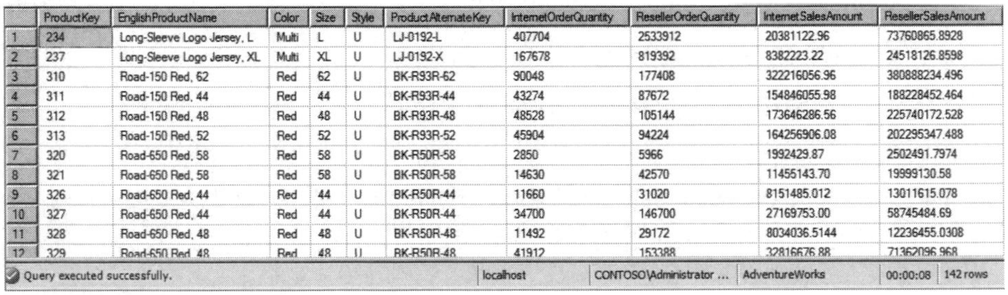

	ProductKey	EnglishProductName	Color	Size	Style	ProductAlternateKey	InternetOrderQuantity	ResellerOrderQuantity	InternetSalesAmount	ResellerSalesAmount
1	234	Long-Sleeve Logo Jersey, L	Multi	L	U	LJ-0192-L	407704	2533912	20381122.96	73760865.8928
2	237	Long-Sleeve Logo Jersey, XL	Multi	XL	U	LJ-0192-X	167678	819392	8382223.22	24518126.8598
3	310	Road-150 Red, 62	Red	62	U	BK-R93R-62	90048	177408	322216056.96	380888234.496
4	311	Road-150 Red, 44	Red	44	U	BK-R93R-44	43274	87672	154846055.98	188228452.464
5	312	Road-150 Red, 48	Red	48	U	BK-R93R-48	48528	105144	173646286.56	225740172.528
6	313	Road-150 Red, 52	Red	52	U	BK-R93R-52	45904	94224	164256906.08	202295347.488
7	320	Road-650 Red, 58	Red	58	U	BK-R50R-58	2850	5966	1992429.87	2502491.7974
8	321	Road-650 Red, 58	Red	58	U	BK-R50R-58	14630	42570	11455143.70	19999130.58
9	326	Road-650 Red, 44	Red	44	U	BK-R50R-44	11660	31020	8151485.012	13011615.078
10	327	Road-650 Red, 44	Red	44	U	BK-R50R-44	34700	146700	27169753.00	58745484.69
11	328	Road-650 Red, 48	Red	48	U	BK-R50R-48	11492	29172	8034036.5144	12236455.0308
12	329	Road-650 Red, 48	Red	48	U	BK-R50R-48	41912	153388	32816676.88	71362096.968

| Query executed successfully. | | localhost | CONTOSO\Administrator ... | AdventureWorks | 00:00:08 | 142 rows |

FIGURE 14-9

DATABASE TUNING ADVISOR

One of the more useful tools available for database administrators since SQL Server 2005 is the Microsoft Database Engine Tuning Advisor (DTA). DTA enables you to analyze a database for missing indexes and other performance-tuning recommendations such as partitions and indexed views. DTA accepts the following types of workloads:

➤   SQL script files (*.sql)

➤   Trace files (*.trc)

➤   XML files (*.xml)

➤   Trace table

➤   Plan Cache (new)

Figure 14-10 displays the Database Engine Tuning Advisor's workload selection screen, including the new Plan Cache option. One of the great benefits of the Database Tuning Advisor to database administrators and SQL Server developers is the ability to rapidly generate database performance improvement recommendations without knowing the underlying database schema, data structure, usage patterns, or even the inner workings of the SQL Server Optimizer.

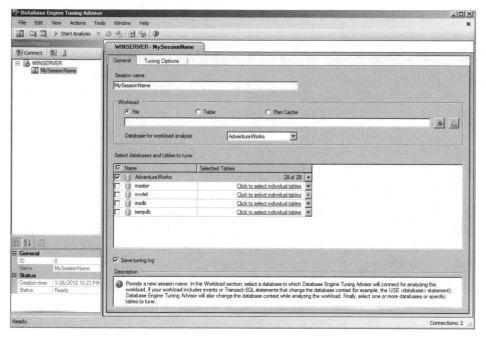

FIGURE 14-10

In addition, new in SQL Server 2012, the plan cache can also be used as part of a DTA workload. This new workload option eliminates the need to manually generate a workload for analysis, such as trace files.

TOO MANY INDEXES?

The saying "Too much of a good thing is not always good" holds true when discussing indexes. Too many indexes create additional overhead associated with the extra amount of data pages that the Query Optimizer needs to go through. Also, too many indexes require too much space and add to the time it takes to accomplish maintenance tasks.

Still, the Data Tuning Wizard typically recommends a large number of indexes, especially when analyzing a workload with many queries. The reason behind this is because queries are analyzed on an individual basis. It is a good practice to incrementally apply indexes as needed, always keeping a baseline to compare if the new index improves query performance.

SQL Server 2012 provides several Dynamic Management Views (DMV) to obtain index usage information. Some of these DMVs include:

- ➤ `sys.dm_db_missing_index_details`: Returns detailed information about a missing index.

- ➤ `sys.dm_db_missing_index_columns`: Returns information about the table columns that are missing an index.

➤ `sys.dm_db_missing_index_groups`: Returns information about a specific group of missing indexes.

➤ `sys.dm_db_missing_index_group_stats`: Returns summary information about missing index groups.

➤ `sys.dm_db_index_usage_stats`: Returns counts of different types of index operations and the time each type of operation was last performed.

➤ `sys.dm_db_index_operational_stats`: Returns current low-level I/O, locking, latching, and access method activity for each partition of a table or index in the database.

➤ `sys.dm_db_index_physical_stats`: Returns size and fragmentation information for the data and indexes of the specified table or view.

For example, to obtain a list of indexes that have been used and those that have not been used by user queries, query the `sys.dm_db_index_usage_stats` DMV. From the list of indexes that have been used you can obtain important statistics that help you fine tune your indexes. Some of this information includes index access patterns such index scans, index seeks, and index bookmark lookups.

To obtain a list of indexes that have been used by user queries, execute the following script:

```
SELECT
 SO.name Object_Name,
 SCHEMA_NAME(SO.schema_id) Schema_name,
 SI.name Index_name,
 SI.Type_Desc,
 US.user_seeks,
 US.user_scans,
 US.user_lookups,
 US.user_updates
FROM sys.objects AS SO
 JOIN sys.indexes AS SI
  ON SO.object_id = SI.object_id
 INNER JOIN sys.dm_db_index_usage_stats AS US
  ON SI.object_id = SI.object_id
  AND SI.index_id = SI.index_id
WHERE
 database_id=DB_ID('AdventureWorks')
 SO.type = 'u'
 AND SI.type IN (1, 2)
 AND (US.user_seeks > 0 OR US.user_scans > 0 OR US.user_lookups > 0 );
```

To obtain a list of indexes that have not been used by user queries, execute the following script:

```
SELECT
 SO.Name TableName,
 SI.name IndexName,
 SI.Type_Desc IndexType
 US.user_updates
FROM sys.objects AS SO
 INNER JOIN sys.indexes AS SI
  ON SO.object_id = SI.object_id
 LEFT OUTER JOIN sys.dm_db_index_usage_stats AS US
```

```
  ON SI.object_id = US.object_id
  AND SI.index_id = US.index_id
WHERE
 database_id=DB_ID('AdventureWorks')
 SO.type = 'u'
AND SI.type IN (1, 2)
AND (US.index_id IS NULL)
OR  (US.user_seeks = 0 AND US.user_scans = 0 AND US.user_lookups = 0 );
```

Indexes that are not used by user queries should be dropped, unless they have been added to support mission critical work that occurs at specific points in time, such as monthly or quarterly data extracts and reports. Unused indexes add overhead to insert, delete, and update operations as well as index maintenance operations. Index usage statistics are initialized to empty when the SQL Server service restarts. The database is detached or shutdown when the AUTO_CLOSE property is turned on.

SUMMARY

The newest index type introduced in SQL Server 2012 is the columnstore index. Columnstore indexes are column-based, non-clustered indexes that store data based on discrete values found in a column. This new type of index has greater advantages over regular row-based indexes. These advantages include smaller-sized indexes and faster retrieval of data.

An important part of indexing your database includes creating partitions and indexes, along with advanced indexing techniques such as filtered indexes using the WHERE keyword and covering indexes using the INCLUDED keyword. Reorganizing and rebuilding indexes is an important maintenance operation to reduce and eliminate index fragmentation. SQL Server 2012 Database Tuning Advisor has been enhanced and can now help you tune your databases based on the plan cache.

You can put the finishing touches on your indexed database by tuning a query, which you can accomplish by utilizing the data from Data Management Views (DMVs). It is also important to remember the benefits of finding indexes that are not used by user queries and removing them.

15

Replication

WHAT'S IN THIS CHAPTER

➤ The Different Types of Replication

➤ Replication Models

➤ Setting up Snapshot Replication

➤ Setting up the Distributor

➤ How Snapshot Differs from Transactional, and Merge Replication

➤ Peer to Peer Replication

➤ How to Monitor Replication

Today's enterprise needs to distribute its data across many departments and geographically dispersed offices. SQL Server replication provides ways to distribute data and database objects among its SQL Server databases, databases from other vendors such as Oracle, mobile devices such as Windows Phone 7, and point-of-sale terminals. Along with log shipping, database mirroring, and clustering, replication provides functionalities that satisfy customers' needs for load balancing, high availability, and scaling.

This chapter introduces you to the concept of replication, explaining how to implement basic snapshot replication, and noting things to pay attention to when setting up transactional and merge replication.

REPLICATION OVERVIEW

SQL Server replication closely resembles the magazine publishing process, so we use that analogy to explain its overall architecture. Consider a popular magazine. The starting point is the large pool of journalists writing *articles*. From all the available articles, the editor picks which ones to include in the current month's magazine. The selected set of articles is then published in a *publication*. After a monthly publication is printed, it is shipped out via various distribution channels to *subscribers* all over the world.

SQL Server replication uses similar terminology. The pool from which a publication is formed can be considered a database. Each piece selected for publication is an *article*; it can be a table, a stored procedure, or another database object. Like a magazine publisher, replication also needs a *distributor* to deliver publications, keep track of delivery status, and track a history of synchronization to maintain data consistency. Depending on the kind of replication model you choose, articles from a publication can either be stored as files in a folder to which both publisher and subscriber(s) have access, or as records in tables in a distribution database synchronously or asynchronously. Regardless of how publications are delivered, replication always needs a distributor database to keep track of delivery status. Depending on the capacity of the publication server, the distributor database can be located on the Publisher, the Subscriber, or on another server that might be dedicated purely to serving as the distribution database.

Conceptually, however, there are differences between SQL Server replication and a magazine publishing company, the biggest being the contributor-like role the subscriber can sometimes take on. For example, in some replication models, a subscriber or subscribers can update articles and have them propagated back to the publisher or other subscribers. In the peer-to-peer replication model, each participant of replication acts both as publisher and subscriber so that changes made in different databases replicate back and forth between multiple servers.

Replication Components

Now that you have an idea of how replication works in comparison to magazine publishing, it is time to examine what these terms and functions mean in direct relation to the SQL Server. SQL Server replication is comprised of several key components which are grouped into the following areas: replication roles, replication data, replication agents, and replication internal components.

Replication Roles

Following are three key roles in replication:

➤ **Publisher:** The publisher is the server, or database instance, that is the source, or master, for the articles being published.

➤ **Distributor:** The distributor is the intermediary in the act of publishing and subscribing, and in some types of replication is the medium whereby the data gets from the publisher to the subscriber. The distributor stores the data to be replicated from the Publisher, and also stores the location of snapshots. The distributor is a database that can live on the publishing server, its own dedicated server, or the subscriber.

➤ **Subscriber:** The subscriber is the server, or database instance, that is the destination, for the articles being published. In some replication models the subscriber can also be a publisher. The subscriber can republish articles when they need to be sent onto another subscriber in the Updating Subscriber model. The subscriber can also republish articles in a peer-to-peer model (explained in the "Replication Types" section).

Subscriptions can be setup as either Push or Pull subscriptions. The difference is where the agent executes. For a Push subscription, the agent executes on the Publisher, and so when it executes, it pushes changes down to the Subscriber. For a Pull subscription, the agent runs on the publisher, and pulls changes down from the Publisher.

Replication Data

There are three key components to replication data: articles, publications, and subscriptions:

➤ **Article:** An article is the smallest set of data that can be configured for replication. It can consist of a table, a view, or a stored procedure and can have additional restrictions on the rows and columns included in each article.

➤ **Publication:** A publication is a grouping of articles published together. Using a publication enables the replication of logically grouped articles to be managed together, rather than having to manage each article individually.

➤ Subscription: A subscription is a request to receive data from one or more publications. It can add additional constraints to the publication regarding how and when the data is distributed.

Replication Agents

Replication Agents are executable programs that perform much of the work of replication. They are commonly executed through SQL Server Agent jobs, but can also be run manually. A number of SQL Agent jobs are created by replication:

➤ **Snapshot Agent:** The Snapshot agent is a SQL Agent job that takes and applies a snapshot for the three types of replication: transactional, merge or snapshot replication. These types are explained in greater detail in the "Replication Types" section. For transactional and merge replication, the snapshot is only needed when replication is being setup, or when an article is added, or changed significantly. For snapshot replication, the snapshot agent is run on every synchronization.

➤ **Log Reader Agent:** The Log Reader agent is a SQL Agent job that reads the transaction log on the publisher and records the transactions for each article being published into the distribution database.

➤ **Distribution Agent:** The Distribution agent is a SQL Agent job that reads the transactions written to the distribution database and applies them to the subscribing databases.

➤ **Merge Agent:** The Merge agent is a SQL Agent job that moves changes at the publisher to the subscriber, moves changes from the subscriber to the publisher, and initiates the conflict resolution process if necessary.

> ➤ **Queue Reader Agent:** The Queue Reader Agent is used to read messages stored in a SQL Server queue, or a Microsoft Message Queue. It then applies those messages to the Publisher. The Queue Reader Agent is used in either snapshot or transactional replication publications, which allow queued updating (see the section on "Replication Types" for details on snapshot and transactional replication).

Replication Maintenance Jobs

Replication uses a number of additional SQL Agent Jobs to perform maintenance.

> ➤ **Agent History Cleanup**: This job removes replication agent history that is stored in the distribution database. This job is scheduled to run every ten minutes.
>
> ➤ **Distribution Cleanup:** This job removes transactions from the distribution database after they are no longer needed. This job is scheduled to run every ten minutes.
>
> ➤ **Expired Subscription Cleanup:** This job determines when a snapshot has expired, and will remove it. This job is scheduled to run once a day at 1 A.M.
>
> ➤ **Reinitialize Failed Subscriptions:** This job looks for subscriptions that have failed, and marks them for re-initialization. This job is not enabled by default, so it can either be run manually when required, or you can create a custom schedule to suite your needs.
>
> ➤ **Replication Agent Monitor:** This job monitors the execution of the SQL Agents and writes to the Windows event log when a job step fails. This job is scheduled to run every 10 minutes.

Replication Types

SQL Server 2012 provides three types of replication. The three types are as follows:

➤ Snapshot replication

➤ Transactional replication

➤ Merge replication

Peer-to-Peer replication and Oracle Publishing replication are variations of the three types of replication previously listed and are also discussed in this section.

Snapshot Replication

As its name implies, snapshot replication takes a snapshot of a publication and makes it available to subscribers. When the snapshot is applied on the subscribing database, the articles at the subscriber, such as tables, views, and stored procedures, are dropped and re-created. Snapshot replication is a one-shot deal; there is no continuous stream of data from the publisher to the subscriber. The data at the publisher at the time the snapshot is taken is applied to the subscriber.

Snapshot replication is best suited for fairly static data, at times when it is acceptable to have copies of data that are out of date between replication intervals, or when article size is small. For example, suppose you have to look up tables that maintain ZIP codes. Those tables can be good snapshot replication candidates in most cases because they are typically static.

 During the period when a snapshot refresh is being applied, the article is unavailable for use.

Transactional Replication

Transactional replication replicates changes to an article as they occur. To set up transactional replication, a snapshot of the publication is taken and applied to the subscriber once to create the same set of data. After the snapshot is taken, the Log Reader agent reads all the transactions that occur against the articles being published and records them in the distribution database. The transactions are then applied to each subscriber according to the subscription's configuration.

Transactional replication enables faster data synchronization with less latency. Depending on how it is set up, this data synchronization can occur in nearly real time, so it is useful for cases in which you want incremental changes to quickly happen on the subscriber.

Merge Replication

Merge replication is usually used whenever there is a slow, or intermittent network connection between the publisher and subscriber. It enables sites to work fairly autonomously and synchronize the changes to the data when they are next online. It needs a snapshot to initialize the replication, after which subsequent changes are tracked with triggers.

One side effect of merge replication is the possibility of conflicts when offline changes are synchronized in. Merge replication automatically resolves these issues though in the Merge agent using the conflict resolver model chosen when the publication was created. If you don't want to use automatic conflict resolution, you can configure the publication for interactive conflict resolution. When the publication is configured for interactive conflict resolution, each conflict must be manually resolved. You can do this using the Interactive Resolver user interface.

Other "Types" of Replication

The following two options are often considered additional types of replication, but they are not actually separate replication types. Instead, these are just variations of the ones listed previously:

> **Peer-to-peer replication:** Peer-to-peer replication is a subtype of transactional replication. In peer-to-peer replication, each publisher owns a subset of the total set of rows in an article. Each Peer publishes its own rows, to which each of its peers subscribes, and it subscribes to the other rows from each of its peers. More details about peer-to-peer transactional replication appear later in this chapter.

➤ **Oracle Publishing:** SQL Server 2000 enabled the capability to subscribe to data published from an Oracle database. Using Oracle Publishing, you can subscribe using either snapshot or transactional replication, but not merge replication.

 This chapter does not cover programming replication using Replication Management Objects (RMO). RMO is a managed code-programming model for SQL Server replication. All of the steps and processes discussed in the chapter can be programmed using RMO. For more information on RMO see the sample applications and code samples from Books Online.

Replication Enhancements in SQL Server 2012

There are only two new additions to SQL Server 2012 from SQL Server 2008 R2 pertaining to Replication, and they are the following:

➤ Peer-to-peer transactional replication is now shown as a new replication type in the wizard page to create a new publication. This is a change from SQL 2008, in which peer-to-peer replication was created first as a transactional replication type and then switched to a property of the publication.

➤ Replication Monitor has a new view to monitor a distributor. This new view can be helpful when monitoring a distributor that serves multiple publishers.

REPLICATION MODELS

Replication can be set up in quite a few different ways. This section covers some of the most common replication topologies. These are the basic building blocks, and from these, considerably more complex topologies can be constructed.

Single Publisher, One or More Subscribers

A Single Publisher Model is perhaps the simplest topology to use with a single publishing database that has one or more subscription databases. This topology might be used where you need to keep a hot standby system or distribute data from a central office to multiple field offices. Figure 15-1 shows the basic structure of this topology with the distributor on the publishing server.

Figure 15-2 shows a more advanced option with a separate server for the distribution database. Use this option when you need more performance at the distributor than you can get from a single server acting as the publisher and distributor.

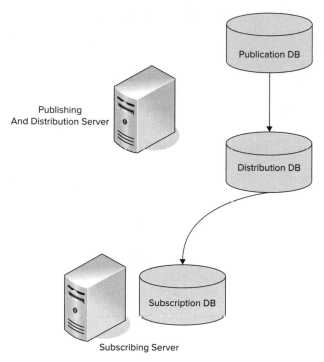

FIGURE 15-1

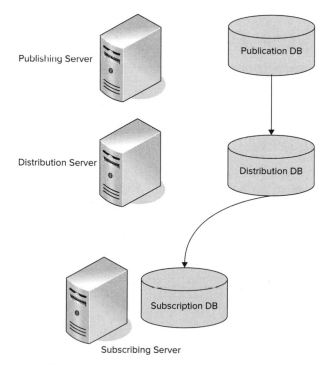

FIGURE 15-2

Figure 15-3 shows the next variant of the single Publisher model, with multiple subscription databases.

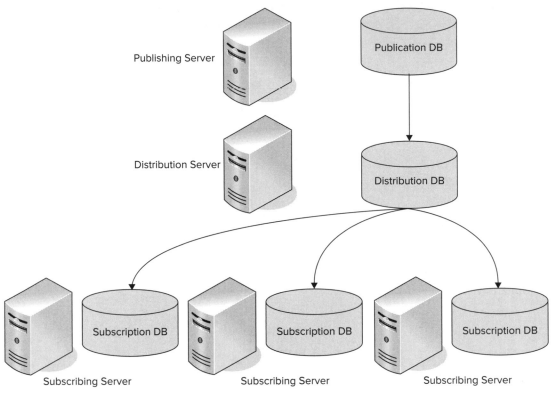

FIGURE 15-3

Multiple Publishers, Single Subscriber

A Point of Service (POS) application is a good example of a Multiple Publisher model. A POS application has multiple publishers but only one subscriber. In a POS, it is often necessary to send data from the many POS terminals in a store to a central system either in the store or at the head office where the individual transactions can be consolidated. The replication topology to use for this is a multiple publisher, single subscriber model. Figure 15-4 shows this topology.

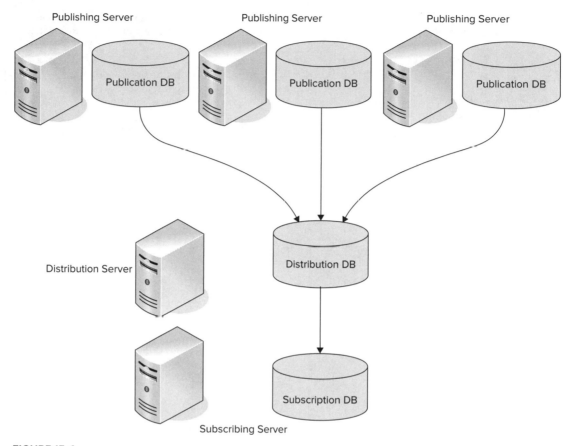

FIGURE 15-4

Multiple Publishers Also Subscribing

A Customer Resource Management (CRM) application is a good example of the Multiple Publishers also Subscribing model. In the CRM application it might be necessary to have an address book that contains all contacts that is updated locally, yet is synchronized across all sites. One way to do this is to have each branch office publish the updates made at that office, and also subscribe to the updates made by all other branch offices. Figure 15-5 shows how to achieve this.

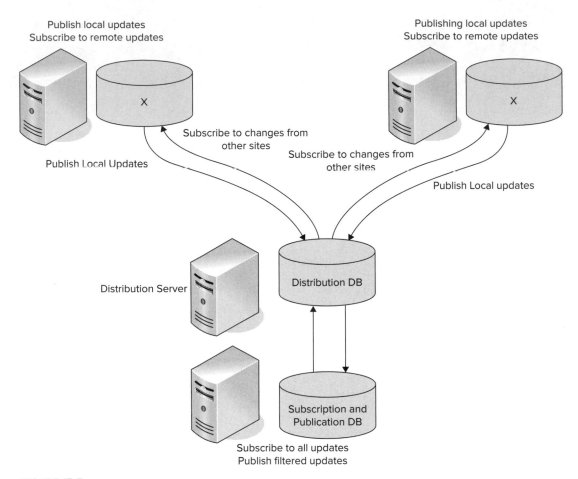

Publish local updates
Subscribe to remote updates

Publishing local updates
Subscribe to remote updates

Subscribe to changes from
other sites

Subscribe to changes from
other sites

Publish Local Updates

Publish Local updates

Distribution Server

Distribution DB

Subscription and
Publication DB

Subscribe to all updates
Publish filtered updates

FIGURE 15-5

Updating Subscriber

The CRM application can also be implemented when using an Updating Subscriber model. In this topology, the master copy of the contacts is held at a central location. This would be published to all branch offices. Any changes at the branch offices are then updated back to the publisher using the Updating Subscriber feature built into replication. Figure 15-6 shows the updating subscriber topology.

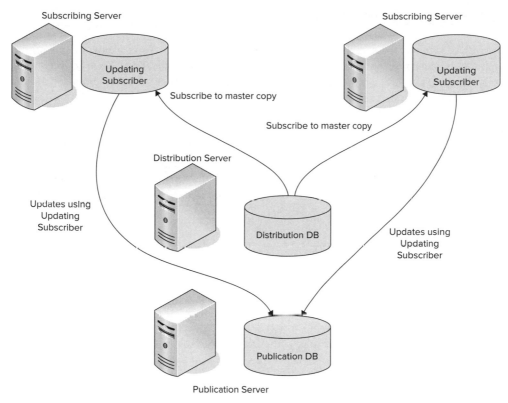

FIGURE 15-6

Peer-to-peer

Finally, a Peer-to-peer topology is also exemplified by implementing the CRM application. The Peer-to-peer model doesn't have the concept of a master copy of the data; instead, each instance owns its own set of rows and receives any updates made at the other instances. Figure 15-7 shows a peer-to-peer topology.

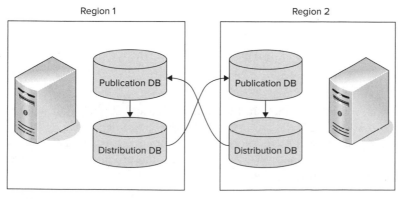

FIGURE 15-7

IMPLEMENTING REPLICATION

Now that you've learned the terminology, types, and models, it is time to implement replication. To start with, this section provides an exercise to set up snapshot replication. Transactional and merge replication are similar, but they each have a few differences that are reviewed after the snapshot replication setup discussion.

> *It's always worth reminding yourself that after a fresh install of SQL Server, all the external protocols are disabled. To talk to a remote SQL Server, you have to run the SQL Server Configuration Manager, enable one of the external protocols, either Named Pipes, or TCP-IP, and then remember to restart the SQL Service.*

Setting Up Snapshot Replication

To keep things simple, you only create two new databases in this replication example: a new database called Publisher that is the publisher, and a new database called Subscriber that is the subscriber. For the purposes of this example, you create a sales schema, and in that schema create a single table, Cars. You then insert a small set of rows into that table. The scenario is based on a car company that sells fuel-efficient hybrid cars in the United States, China, and Sweden. You set up snapshot replication between database servers in the United States and China to refresh data. Furthermore, you can set up transactional replication between database servers in the United States and Sweden. The data can also be used to set up merge replication.

Replication can be implemented through both GUI wizard pages and scripting. If you are new to replication, we recommend that you first go through the GUI and property pages through SQL Server Management Studio. As you work through the GUI, you are able to generate SQL scripts at the end of processes, which you can save to a file and edit for other deployments.

You must implement a distributor before you can create publications and subscribe to publications, so first create the distributor which you need for all types of replications.

Setting Up Distribution

As mentioned earlier, a distributor consists of a distribution database (where replication history, status, and other important information are stored) and a shared folder (where data and articles can be stored, retrieved, and refreshed).

To begin setting up distribution, you need to find out the domain name and account that will be used during the process to run various replication agents, such as the Snapshot agent, Log Reader agent, and Queue Reader agent. For the purpose of this example right now, you can just choose to impersonate the SQL Server Agent account, but when you put things into production, a dedicated domain account is recommended for security reasons.

Following is a step-by-step process of how to set up distribution:

1. Using SQL Server Management Studio, connect to the distributor server. Expand the server in Object Explorer.

2. Right-click Replication and select Configure Distribution.

> *If you use a fresh default install of SQL Server 2012, by default the Agent XPs are disabled. This prevents you from starting the SQL Agent Service. If SQL Agent is not running, you see an error when you try to complete Step 2. To prevent this error, enable the Agent XPs using the following script, and then start the SQL Agent service, either from SSMS, or SQL Server Configuration Manager.*
>
> ```
> sp_configure 'show advanced options', 1;
> GO
> RECONFIGURE;
> GO
> sp_configure 'Agent XPs', 1;
> GO
> RECONFIGURE
> GO
> ```
>
> *After executing this script the SQL Server Agent node in SSMS will no longer have the "Agent XPs disabled" tag appended.*

3. At the Welcome screen, click Next. You see the Distributor screen, where you pick which server to use as the distributor. This example uses the current machine. For a more complex topology, you can choose a separate server.

4. Click Next. The SQL Server Agent Start page appears. This enables you to configure the SQL Server Agent to start automatically or manually. Select the option to start the agent automatically.

5. Click Next. The Snapshot Folder screen appears. Here you can enter the snapshot folder. If you want to use a pull subscription, the path entered here should be a network path. This example sets up a local replication topology, so a network path is not necessary.

6. After you pick the snapshot folder, move to the Distribution Database screen shown in Figure 15-8, where you configure the name of the distribution database (distribution, in this example), and the folder locations for the database and log files. Click Next to continue.

7. Next you see the Publishers screen, shown in Figure 15-9, where you set the list of servers that can use this distribution database.

FIGURE 15-8

FIGURE 15-9

8. Next, define what the wizard should do from the Wizard Actions screen, shown in Figure 15-10. Choose to either configure the distribution database or create scripts. If you want to create scripts, select both options.

9. The next page of the wizard displays a list of actions the SQL Server can perform. Confirm that the list of actions is what you expect and select Finish. If it's not correct, go back and fix the incorrect settings. You then see a screen indicating the progress the wizard has made at executing the actions you selected.

10. Figure 15-11 shows the wizard actions completed successfully. If any errors are reported, investigate and resolve each one before attempting to rerun the wizard.

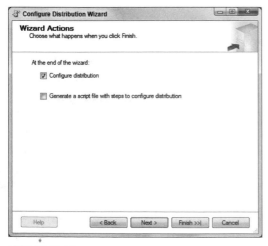

FIGURE 15-10

FIGURE 15-11

After executing the wizard you can browse to the new distribution database using the Server Explorer in Management Studio. The new distribution database appears under System Databases, as shown in Figure 15-12. Additionally, you can expand the SQL Server Agent in Object Explorer, and open the Jobs folder; you see that a number of new jobs were created for the replication, as shown in Figure 15-13.

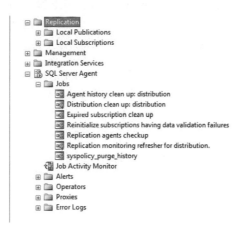

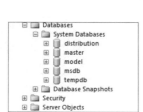

FIGURE 15-12   **FIGURE 15-13**

Implementing Snapshot Replication

Now that you've set up the distributor, you can use that for the replication exercise later in this chapter. Before you set up snapshot replication though, you need to create the databases to use as the Publisher and Subscriber.

Available for download on Wrox.com

In this example, you create these databases on a single server. You can find a script to create these databases in the code samples, `01 Create Databases.sql`, or you can create them manually using Management Studio. To create them manually, follow these steps:

1. Right-click on the Databases Node and select the New Database option.

2. Make sure the publication database is called Publisher, and the subscription database is called Subscriber. All other settings can be left at default for now.

3. After creating the Publisher, you also need to create some tables, and load some data. To do this, download and run the script in the samples called `02 Create and load sales.sql`.

After you complete these initial steps, you can move onto the steps involved in setting up Snapshot Publication which is covered in the next section.

Setting Up Snapshot Publication

The best way to set up Snapshot Publication is to use Management Studio and elect to have everything scripted at the end of the process:

1. Within Management Studio, while connected to the server where the publication database resides, expand the Replication folder. Right-click Local Publications and select New Publication.

2.   You see the Publication Wizard welcome screen; click Next. On the Publication Database screen, pick a database for publication. Select Publisher as your database to create a publication, and click Next.

3.   Figure 15-14 shows the Publication Type screen where you select the type of replication. In this case, select Snapshot Publication and click Next to continue.

4.   Next is the Articles screen where you select the tables in this article. By default, nothing is selected, so you have to expand the Tables node and pick the tables you want to publish. Once you expand, select the Cars table you created earlier for publication and its children, as shown in Figure 15-15. You can see that the Cars table under the sales schema is selected. In other scenarios if necessary, you can pick and choose columns of the table for publication by unchecking the box next to the column name.

FIGURE 15-14   **FIGURE 15-15**

You can also set properties of articles that you choose to publish. These properties affect how the article is published and some behaviors when it is synchronized with the subscriber. Don't change the default properties here; however, they can be useful in other situations. Click Next to continue.

5.   On the Filter Table Rows page, the wizard gives you an option to filter out rows. Click the Add button to display the Add Filter page.

6.   As mentioned earlier, because you want to replicate data to the Chinese market, you need to filter the cars by country. To do this add a WHERE clause to the filter statement to match the following SQL text as shown in Figure 15-16.

```
SELECT <published_columns>
FROM [Sales].[Cars]
WHERE [Country] = 'China'
```

After you click OK, the filter is applied. This returns you to the previous screen, which now has a filter defined, as shown in Figure 15-17.

FIGURE 15-16

FIGURE 15-17

7. Figure 15-18 shows the Snapshot Agent screen, where you define how the snapshot should be created, and when it should be scheduled to run. In this case, don't schedule it or create one immediately; instead, in the example, you will invoke it manually by running a SQL Server Agent job yourself. Click Next to continue.

8. The next screen is the Snapshot Agent Security screen, where you can specify the accounts used to run the snapshot agent job and to connect to the Publisher. As mentioned earlier, different replication models call for different agents to be run. Click the Security Settings button to configure the accounts needed for your replication model.

FIGURE 15-18

It is convenient to have a dedicated domain account with a secure password that doesn't need to be changed often for this purpose. However, if you don't have that access, you can choose to impersonate the SQL Server Agent account, as mentioned previously. Even though you will do so for this exercise, it is a best practice to always use a dedicated account. Enter the account details on the Snapshot Agent Security screen, shown in Figure 15-19. After the account is set, click OK.

9. Figure 15-20 shows the Wizard Actions screen, where you can specify whether you want the wizard to create the publication or script the creation. For now leave these settings on the default, and just create the publication.

FIGURE 15-19

FIGURE 15-20

10. The next screen is the wizard action confirmation screen. Here you can assign a name to this publication. Enter the name `Pub_Cars_China` in the Publication Name text box. Review the actions specified here, and if anything is incorrect go back and fix it. When everything is correct, click Finish.

11. The next screen (see Figure 15-21) confirms your actions, which in this case are to Create the Publication and then add the articles, (of which we have just one). The status should indicate success showing that you have now successfully created a new publication. If any errors are reported, investigate and resolve them before attempting to execute the actions again.

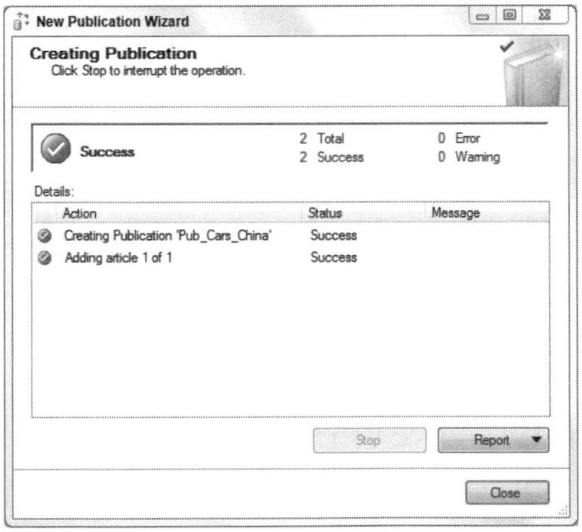

FIGURE 15-21

The rest of the process is quite similar to the distributor creation documented earlier. After you click Finish, the snapshot publication is created. Again, you can use Object Explorer to see the publication and SQL Server jobs created during this process.

At this point no files or folders have been created, and the snapshot has not been created because no one is subscribed to the snapshot. To get SQL Server to do anything further, you have to subscribe to the new publication. When there is a subscriber, SQL Server creates all the necessary files. You can find these in the shared folder defined when the distributor was set up earlier. The default location is `C:\Program Files\Microsoft SQL Server\MSSQL11.MSSQLSERVER\MSSQL\ReplData`. If you specified a different location during setup, you can always retrieve the current location by expanding the Replication node in SQL Server management Studio Object Explorer, expanding Local Publications, and selecting the relevant publication. Right-click and select properties. On the Snapshot page (see Figure 15-22) you see a section titled Location of Snapshot Files that shows you the current location.

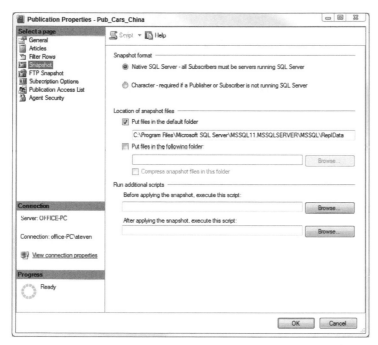

FIGURE 15-22

Setting Up a Subscription to the Snapshot Publication

Now that a snapshot publication is created, you can subscribe to it from a different server:

1. If you are not already connected to it, connect to the subscription server using SQL Server Management Studio, and expand the Replication node in Object Explorer. Right-click Local Subscription and select New Subscriptions (see Figure 15-23).

2. You see the welcome screen of the New Subscription Wizard. Click Next to choose the publication you want to subscribe to.

FIGURE 15-23

This example has the Publisher and Subscriber on the same server, so the page should already be populated with the available publications. In a real scenario in which the Publisher and Subscribers are on different servers, you need to find the Publishing server. Do this by selecting <Find SQL Server Publisher...> from the drop-down list (see Figure 15-24). You see the typical Connect to Server window that is common in SQL Server Management Studio. To connect to the server where you set up the snapshot publication earlier, select the Publishing server, and click Connect. You then see the Publication screen, as shown in Figure 15-25. Expand the database (Publisher) and select the publication you just created by the name you gave it: Pub_Cars_China. Click Next to continue.

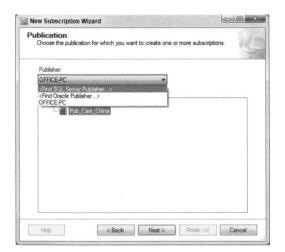

FIGURE 15-24

FIGURE 15-25

3. The next screen is the Distribution Agent Location screen, shown in Figure 15-26. Here, select the location for the distribution agents to execute. This can be either at the distributor for a *push subscription* or at the subscriber for a *pull subscription*. Make your subscription a push subscription by selecting the first option, Run All Agents at the Distributor, and click Next.

4. The next screen is the Subscribers screen, (see Figure 15-27) where you can set the subscriber properties. Select the Server where the subscriber will be; in this case it is the current server. Then select the subscription database. If you want to add additional subscribers, you can do so on this page as well, by using the Add Subscriber button. Select Next to move to the next screen.

FIGURE 15-26

FIGURE 15-27

5. Figure 15-28 shows the Distribution Agent Security screen, where you see the familiar screen used for setting agent security settings. Click the ellipsis (...) to set up the security options. If you want to specify a different domain account for Distribution Agent Security, fill out account information here. For this example, select the options shown in Figure 15-29.

FIGURE 15-28

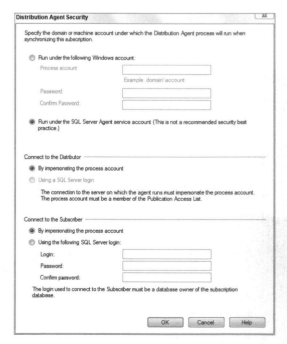

FIGURE 15-29

6. Specify the synchronization schedule. Because this is just your first test example, make it simple and set it to run on demand. Click the drop-down and select Run on Demand Only. As shown in Figure 15-30. Click Next to continue.

7. Figure 15-31 shows the Initialize Subscriptions screen where you specify when the snapshot is initialized. Check the box to select initialization; and in the drop-down, choose to initialize immediately.

FIGURE 15-30   **FIGURE 15-31**

8. Next is the Wizard Actions screen shown earlier (refer to Figure 15-21), where you can choose to create the subscription and script the creation. Make your selection and click Next to continue.

9. From the confirmation screen that appears, confirm that the actions are as you expect. If not, then go back and fix anything before executing the wizard actions you selected. When you are satisfied, click Finish.

10. The next screen shows the actions and their status. You should see three actions, with the last of these indicating a warning. Clicking the message for this action should reveal a message indicating the snapshot is not available. Although you marked the subscription to initialize immediately, it has to wait until you manually run the snapshot agent to create a snapshot that is available to be applied. You can see this in Figure 15-32. If this step shows any errors, investigate and resolve before attempting to rerun the wizard.

FIGURE 15-32

Verifying Snapshot Replication

So far, the setup is simple, but how do you know it actually works? Following are some tests you can conduct to make sure it does indeed work properly:

1. Connect to the publication server and verify the records there using the following SQL code:

Available for download on Wrox.com

```
use publisher;
 select * from Sales.Cars;

ProdID       ProdDesc                            Country LastUpdate
-----------  ----------------------------------- ------- ----------------------
1            ProEfficient Sedan                  US      2011-05-07 12:43:00
2            ProEfficient Van                    US      2011-05-07 12:43:00
3            JieNeng Crossover                   China   2011-05-07 12:43:00
4            Jieneng Utility                     China   2011-05-07 12:43:00
5            EuroEfficient Wagon                 Sweden  2011-05-07 12:43:00
6            EuroEfficient Pickup                Sweden  2011-05-07 12:43:00

(6 row(s) affected)
```

Code snippet 03 verify publisher.sql

2. Now connect to the subscription server using the following SQL code. You've already initialized the subscription, so you see only cars for the Chinese market.

Available for download on Wrox.com

```
use subscriber;
 select * from Sales.Cars;


    ProdID       ProdDesc                            Country LastUpdate
```

```
----------  ---------------------------------  -------  ----------------------
3           JieNeng Crossover                   China    2011-05-07 12:43:00
4           Jieneng Utility                    China    2011-05-07 12:43:00

(2 row(s) affected)
```

Code snippet 04 verify subscriber.sql

3. Now suppose you made some changes to cars for the Chinese market and upgraded JieNeng Crossover to JieNeng Crossover LE at the publication server. To make these changes, use the following code.

```
use publisher;

update Sales.Cars set proddesc = 'JieNeng Crossover LE' where prodid = 3;
```

Code snippet 05 Update Publication.sql

4. You've updated records at the publisher, so you need to take a new snapshot by running the SQL Server Agent jobs. You can do this using either of the following methods:

➤ In Object Explorer, expand the SQL Server Agent Jobs folder, right-click the `OFFICE-PC-Publisher-Pub_Cars_Chine-1` job, and select Start Job from the context menu.

➤ In Object Explorer right-click the replication node, and select Launch Replication Monitor. Using Replication Monitor is covered in the "Monitoring Replication" section later in this chapter. In the example, this should open up, and because you're connected to the current server, it already knows about the local Publications, so under the My Publications Node, you see the local server, in this case called `OFFICE-PC`. Open that node and you see the publication you set up on the Publisher database called `[Publisher]: Pub_Cars_China`. Right-click and select Generate Snapshot. This creates the new snapshot but has not yet applied it to the subscriber.

5. Because you implemented a pull subscription, go to the subscriber and run the job to refresh this snapshot. Again, this can be done by either running the specified job or through the replication monitor.

➤ To run the specified job, open Object Explorer on the subscriber and expand the SQL Server Agent Jobs folder. Locate the job with a name of `OFFICE-PC-Publisher-Pub_Cars_Chine-OFFICE-PC-1`, right-click the job, and select Start Job from the context menu.

➤ In the Replication Monitor, select the node for your publication. In the right pane, select the Agent Tab. Right-click the line for the Snapshot Agent job, and select Start Agent.

6. Now ensure that the data is indeed refreshed by running the same SQL code from step 2:

```
use subscriber;

select * from Sales.Cars;


    ProdID      ProdDesc                            Country LastUpdate
    ----------- ----------------------------------- ------- ----------------------
    3           JieNeng Crossover LE                China   2011-05-07 12:43:00
    4           Jieneng Utility                     China   2011-05-07 12:43:00


    (2 rows affected)
```

Code snippet file 04 verify subscriber.sql

Implementing Transactional and Merge Replication

Procedurally, setting up transactional and merge replication is similar to the snapshot replication discussed earlier; refer back to that section for step-by-step instructions. This section notes the additions, exceptions, and a few other noteworthy highlights.

Transactional Replication

The typical transactional replication is not too different from snapshot replication, but with one major component added: the Log Reader agent. This agent tracks all changes made to the article so that it can be propagated to the subscriber. As a result, the load on the distribution database is higher than with snapshot replication, which means you need to keep a closer eye on it, especially the log file of the distribution database.

One variation of transactional replication you may encounter is having updateable subscriptions. If you implement a transactional publication with an updateable subscription, changes at the subscriber are applied back to the publisher. To enable this, SQL Server adds one additional column in tables included in the publication to track changes. This column is called MSrepl_tran_version and is a unique identifier column. Therefore, code such as the following fails because it does not have a column list.

```
insert into Sales.Cars values (9,'English Car','UK', getdate());
```

As a result, the application of that code needs to be updated. To fix that, the column list that corresponds to the values in parentheses must be provided right after the table name, as shown next.

```
insert into Sales.Cars (prodid, proddesc, country, lastupdate)
values (9,'English Car','UK', getdate());
```

For transactional replication with updatable subscription, a linked server is used among SQL Server publishing and subscribing databases. The linked server uses the MS Distributed Transaction Coordinator (MS DTC) to coordinate transactions; therefore, MS DTC on the publisher must be enabled to accept remote connections.

Merge Replication

For merge replication, all articles must have a unique identifier column with a unique index and the ROWGUIDCOL property. If they don't have it, SQL Server adds one for you. Just like the transactional replication with an updateable subscription, an INSERT statement without the column list will fail.

Additional agents are used for transactional and merge replication, such as the Log Reader agent and Queue Reader agent. The agents require a domain account to run under. The domain account can be their own or shared with other agents. How you choose to implement that depends on your company's security policy.

PEER-TO-PEER REPLICATION

In peer-to-peer replication, every participant is both a publisher and a subscriber. It is suitable for cases in which user applications need to read or modify data at any of the databases participating in the setup. It provides an interesting alternative for load-balancing and high-availability scenarios. This feature is available only in the Enterprise Edition of SQL Server. Oracle calls this kind of replication *multimaster*, whereas DB2 calls it *update anywhere*.

Consider the following when evaluating and setting up peer-to-peer replication:

➤ It is designed for a small number of participating databases. A good rule-of-thumb number is less than 10. If you use more than that, you are likely to encounter performance issues.

➤ Peer-to-peer replication handles conflict resolution but in a different way from Merge replication. Starting with SQL Server 2008, peer-to-peer replication causes a critical error to occur when it detects a conflict. This critical error causes the Distribution Agent to fail. Because of this, you should design your application so that you do not have conflicts.

➤ Peer-to-peer does not support data filtering. That would defeat its purpose because everybody is an equal partner here for high availability and load balancing.

➤ Applications can scale out read operations across multiple databases, and databases are always online. Participating nodes can be added or removed for maintenance.

➤ As mentioned previously, peer-to-peer replication is available only in the Enterprise Edition; however, for your testing purposes, it is available in Developer Edition of SQL Server 2012.

Setting Up Peer-to-Peer Replication

From an implementation standpoint, the process to setup peer to-peer replication is similar to setting up snapshot, transactional, or merge replication. However, there are some differences, as you will see in the following sections as you walk through an example to set up peer-to-peer replication.

1. To start out, begin with one database, back it up, and restore it on all other participating databases. This way, you start from a clean and consistent slate.

2. All nodes in the topology need a distributor, so set one here. Although you can use a single distribution database for all publications, this is not recommended for a production system, but for the purpose of these examples it is fine. The examples here use a local distribution database, one on each Publishing server.

3. After the distributor is set, create a publication just like a regular transactional replication publication, except that there is now a new replication type to choose from: peer-to-peer publication. Choose this new option, as the Publication Type on the Publication Type page which was previously shown in Figure 15-14.

4. After selecting the replication type of Peer-to-Peer Publication, complete the new Publication wizard, which is similar to the steps used to create the snapshot publication previously.

5. After the new peer-to-peer Publication is created, you must create additional peer-to-peer publications to act as peers in the topology. This example has two separate servers, one with a peer-to-peer publication called NorthAmerica publication, the other with a peer-to-peer publication called Europe. You can use the same sample code from the previous snapshot replication example to create a single table to be replicated in each of these systems.

6. Proceed with the rest of the setup by right-clicking the publication and selecting Configure Peer-to-Peer Topology. The resulting dialog box is shown in Figure 15-33. This option is only available for a peer-to-peer publication. This feature is only available in SQL Server 2012 Enterprise Edition. Click Next to continue.

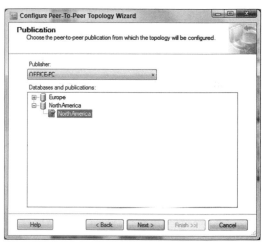

FIGURE 15-33

Configuring Peer-to-Peer Replication

After setting up peer to peer replication a welcome screen appears. From here you can begin configuring the peer-to-peer topology:

1. Select which peer-to-peer publication will configure the topology. For this example, choose to configure the topology from the local publication, which is NorthAmerica.

2. After choosing NorthAmerica, click Next, and you see the Configure Topology page, which presents you with a designer surface that looks like the screen shown in Figure 15-34. To add nodes to the topology, right-click the designer surface, and select Add a New Peer Node.

3. You now see the standard SQL Server Management Studio server connection

FIGURE 15-34

dialog, where you can specify which server the peer is on. In this example everything is on the same server, so specify "." as a reference to the local server.

4. Next you see the Add a New Peer Node dialog, as shown in Figure 15-35. Select the `Europe` database, as shown in the figure.

5. Select OK, and the node is added to the topology designer, as shown in Figure 15-36. It is hard to know which node is which from just looking at the display surface. Fortunately, extensive tips are available when you hover your mouse over each node.

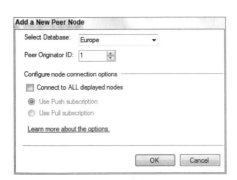

FIGURE 15-35

FIGURE 15-36

6. The next step is to connect the nodes in the topology. To connect the two nodes, right click on either node on the designer and select either Connect to ALL displayed nodes, or Add a new peer connection. For this example, select Connect to ALL displayed nodes because you have only two nodes displayed. This adds a two-way arrow between the two nodes.

Since there are only two nodes in this particular example, you could have done this previously by selecting Connect to ALL displayed nodes (refer to Figure 15-35), but you can perform this step earlier (and should) only when you have only two nodes.

7. Select Next and the wizard moves onto the Log reader Agent Security page. Set the security information by clicking the ellipsis ("…") button, and choose Run under the SQL Server Agent service account option. Click Next and the Distribution Agent Security page appears.

8. On the Distribution Agent Security page, you need to provide security information for the distribution agents on all nodes in the topology. For this example, select the same options for both servers: Run Under the SQL Server Agent Service Account, and choose By Impersonating the Process Account for how you connect to the distributor and subscriber, as shown in Figure 15-37. Select Next to move onto the next page.

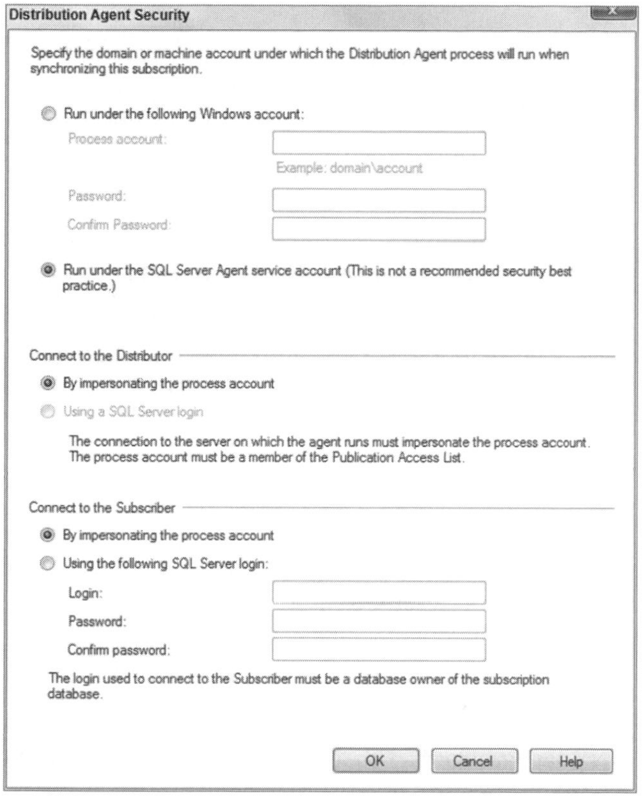

FIGURE 15-37

9. The next page in the wizard is the New Peer Initialization page, where you can specify how the new peer should be initialized. In this case, the DBs were created manually, and the same data was loaded into each database, so you can select the first option. Select Next to move onto the next page.

10. The Complete the Wizard page displays; here you see all the choices made in the wizard. If these all appear to be correct, then select Finish to start applying the actions selected in the wizard.

11. The final page in the wizard shows the actions as they are executed and reports any warnings or errors with the process. If there are any actions that report other than success, you need to investigate each and resolve the reported issue before attempting to rerun the topology wizard.

You have just completed the build out of a peer-to-peer topology. You can alter the topology at any time by re-running the Configure topology wizard and adding additional nodes, removing existing nodes, and changing connections.

SCRIPTING REPLICATION

For many the preferred interface for managing replication is the graphical interface provided in SQL Server Management Studio in the various replication wizards. However, DBAs want to create a script that can be checked into a source code control system such as Visual Source Safe or Visual Studio Team Foundation Server.

To script replication, you have two options. You can use either the various replication wizards, which provide a scripting option, or use SQL Server Management Studio and script individual objects.

You can save the scripts into your source code control system, where you can version-control them and use them to deploy a replication configuration to development, test, QA, preproduction, and production systems. See Chapter 9, "Change Management" for more information on using Visual Studio Team Server Database Edition (VSTS DB Pro) and Team Server Source Control (TSSC).

MONITORING REPLICATION

You can use three tools for monitoring replication: Replication Monitor, Performance Monitor, and the replication-related DMVs. This section discusses these three tools in detail.

Replication Monitor

Replication Monitor is built into SQL Server Management Studio. It shows the status of replication and can be used to make configuration changes. It can also show the current latency and the number of outstanding commands. It does not show the transaction or command rates; nor does it show any history of what happened at any time before the current snapshot of data was read.

You can invoke the Replication Monitor from Management Studio.

1. First, navigate to either the context menu of the top level replication node, or the context menu of any server listed under Publications or Subscriptions.

2. From here choose the Launch Replication Monitor option. Figure 15-38 shows the Replication Monitor after it has been started when running on a server with a local replication configuration. If you start Replication Monitor from a computer without a local replication configuration, you need to specify the servers with the replication topology to see any information.

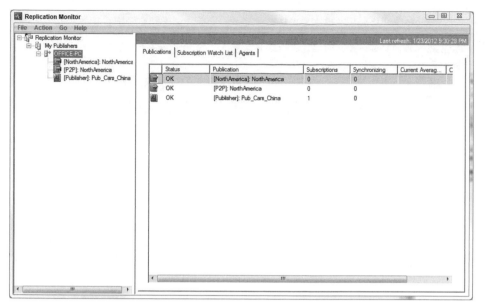

FIGURE 15-38

Following are a few of the key options in the Replication Monitor that you can choose from once invoked:

➤ You can see the new SQL Server 2012 Distributor view by selecting the root node Replication Monitor. Doing this displays in the right pane the options to add a publisher or to Switch to Distributor View. Selecting this second option changes the display to present nodes based on their distributor. This example uses a local distributor, so this doesn't change the display. In a more complex configuration with multiple replication streams using multiple distributors, this would change the ownership of publications and subscriptions to live under their parent distributor. To switch back, select the root node again, and select Switch to Publisher Group View.

➤ To look at subscription status (see Figure 15-39), double-click any entry of the All Subscriptions tab to bring up a window where you can easily view reports and the status of publication to distribution, distribution to subscription, and undistributed commands. It is a user-friendly tool that provides a good overview of all your replication status information.

➤ Tracer tokens are a way to measure the current performance of replication. The Tracer Tokens tab is shown in Figure 15-40. Think of a tracer token as a dummy record that the Replication Monitor uses to gauge the performance of your replication model. It can give you a good idea of latency between your publisher, distributor, and subscriber.

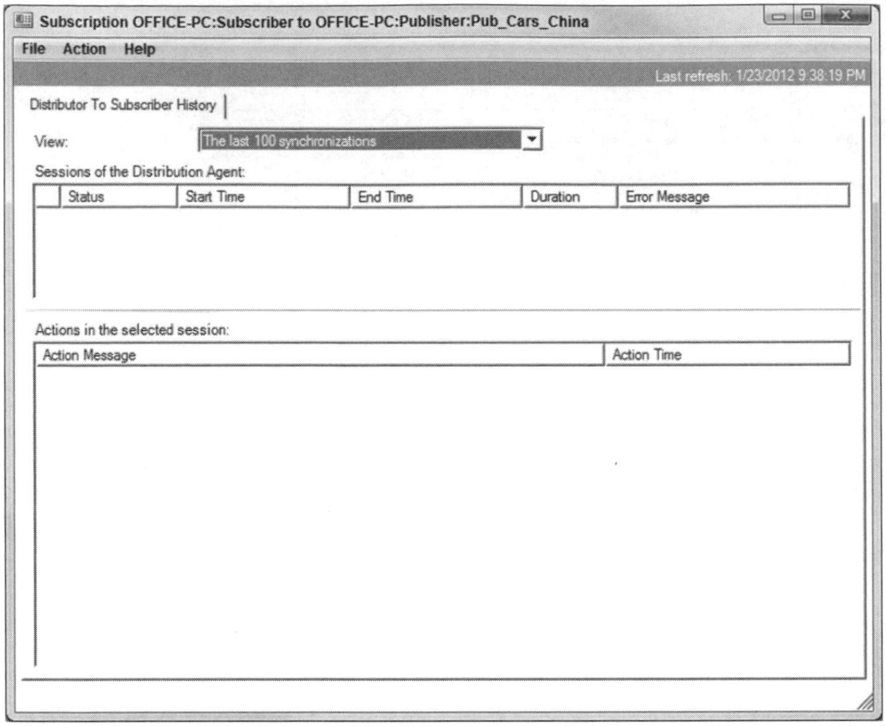

FIGURE 15-39

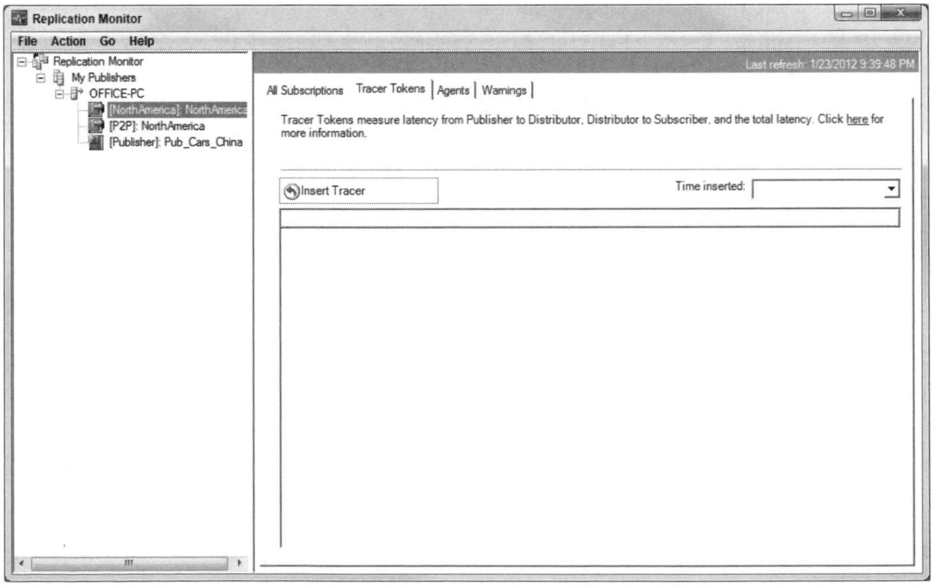

FIGURE 15-40

Performance Monitor

You can monitor several replication-related Performance Monitor objects and counters in SQL Server:

➤ **SQLServer: Replication Agent:** Has a single counter called Running that shows the number of replication agents running on the server

➤ **SQL Server: Replication Log Reader:** Shows the statistics for the Log Reader, with counters for Commands per second, Transactions per second, and Latency

➤ **SQL Server: Replication Dist:** Shows the statistics for the distributor with the same counters as for the Log Reader

➤ **SQL Server: Replication Merge:** Shows the statistics for the Merge agent, with counters for Conflicts per second, Downloaded changes per second, and Updates per second

➤ **SQL Server: Replication Snapshot:** Shows the statistics for the Snapshot agent, with counters for Delivered commands per second and Delivered transactions per second

When considering which performance counters to use, your replication type is the key factor to consider. For snapshot replication, look at the Replication Snapshot counters. For merge replication, look at the Replication Merge counters. For transactional replication, look at the Replication Log Reader and Replication Dist counters.

Here is some more information on the counters you should monitor for transactional replication:

➤ **Object: SQL Server:Replication Log Reader - Counter: LogReader: Delivered Cmds/Sec and Tx/Sec:** These two counters are repeated for each publication; they display the commands or transactions read per second and indicate how many commands or transactions are read by the Log Reader per second. If this counter increases, it indicates that the Tx rate at the publisher has increased.

➤ **Object: SQL Server: Replication Dist. - Counter: Dist:Delivered Cmds/Sec and Tx/Sec:** These two counters are repeated for each subscription and display the commands or transactions per second delivered to the subscriber. If this number is lower than the Log Reader delivered number, it is an indication that commands may be backing up on the distribution database. If it is higher than the Log Reader rate and there is already a backlog of commands, it might indicate that replication is catching up.

Replication DMVs

Following are four replication-related DMVs in every SQL Server database:

➤ `sys.dm_repl_articles`: Contains information about each article being published. It returns data from the database being published and returns one row for each object being published in each article. The syntax is as follows:

```
select
* from sys.dm_repl_articles
```

➤ sys.dm_repl_schemas: Contains information about each table and column being published. It returns data from the database being published and returns one row for each column in each object being published. The syntax is as follows:

```
select
* from sys.dm_repl_schemas
```

➤ sys.dm_repl_tranhash: Contains information about the hashing of transactions. The syntax is as follows:

```
select
* from sys.dm_repl_tranhash
```

➤ sys.dm_repl_traninfo: Contains information about each transaction in a transactional replication. The syntax is as follows:

```
select
* from sys.dm_repl_traninfo
```

These DMVs show information about what is being published from a specific database. They cannot help you monitor what's going on with replication. For that, you have to either run the sp_replcounters system stored procedure (discussed in the next section) or go digging into the distribution database. It's much easier to just execute the sp_replcounters stored procedure than dig into the inner workings of replication in the MSDB or distribution databases; although, it may not have all the information you want to monitor. If you do need more information, you will need to search the distribution database. This is currently undocumented territory, but a good place to start is the source code for the replication stored procedures. Use these to begin determining where the data you want is located, and take it from there.

sp_replcounters

The sp_replcounters replication system stored procedure returns information about the transaction rate, latency, and first and last log sequence number (LSN) for each publication on a server. Run it on the publishing server. Calling this stored procedure on a server that is acting as the distributor or subscribing to publications from another server does not return any data.

Table 15-1 is an example of the output of this stored procedure. The results have been split over two lines for clarity.

TABLE 15-1: Example Output From sp_replcounters

DATABASE	REPLICATED TRANSACTIONS	REPLICATION RATE TRANS/SEC	REPLICATION LATENCY (SEC)
Publisher	178	129.0323	0.016

REPLBEGINLSN	REPLNEXTLSN		
0x0002FACC003458780001	0x0002FACC003459A1003D		

SUMMARY

Replication is an important technology within SQL Server for moving data between servers. The various types of replication include snapshot, transactional, and merge — and the different topologies that can be used with replication include Single Publishers, Multiple Publishers, Updating Subscribers, and Peer to Peer. You can monitor replication using Replication Monitor, Performance Monitor, and relevant performance counters. Additionally, some of the replication DMVs and system stored procedures help to identify the root cause of issues when they occur.

Along with log shipping, database mirroring, and clustering, SQL Server 2012 provides many features to satisfy customers needs for load balancing, high availability, disaster recovery, and scaling.

16

Clustering SQL Server 2012

WHAT'S IN THIS CHAPTER

➤ Identifying Clustering and Mastering its Intricacies

➤ Researching Hardware and Software Configurations to Identify What Works Best for your Organization

➤ Configuring Hardware

➤ Configuring and then Clustering the Operating System

➤ Configuring SQL Server 2012 on the Cluster

➤ Testing

➤ Documenting

➤ Administering and Troubleshooting the Production SQL Server 2012 Cluster

Unlike most aspects of the DBA's job, the task of installing, configuring, and administering a clustered SQL Server can be an adventure, complete with excitement, danger, and an uncertain outcome. But with this chapter's tried-and-true information, you can successfully install, configure, and administer a clustered instance of SQL Server 2012. In this chapter, you learn how a Windows Failover Cluster works and whether it's the right solution for your organization. You learn how to choose between upgrading a previous version of a Windows Failover cluster and building a new cluster; how to plan for clustering, including hardware and the operating system; and how to install a SQL Server 2012 on a Windows Failover Cluster. Finally, you learn how to maintain and troubleshoot an operational instance of SQL Server on a cluster. Although you can deploy a geographically dispersed cluster in Windows 2008, this chapter primarily focuses on co-located clustering as well as the most commonly deployed Windows Failover Cluster configuration.

If you don't have Storage Area Network (SAN) or the hardware to create these examples on physical hardware, consider using a Hyper-V VM solution. You can download Internet Small Computer Systems Interface (ISCSI) target software such as StarWind by Rocket Division (www.rocketdivision.com) to simulate shared disk arrays for the cluster. Regardless of the Windows Failover Cluster, disk configuration is one of the most challenging pieces of the puzzle, and ISCSI makes this slightly less challenging, but you may pay a performance penalty if your network is not correctly optimized.

CLUSTERING AND YOUR ORGANIZATION

Many DBAs seem to have difficulty understanding exactly what clustering is. Following is a good working definition:

Microsoft Windows Failover Clustering is a high-availability option designed to increase the uptime of SQL Server instances. A cluster includes two or more physical servers, called *nodes*; identical configuration is recommended. One is identified as the *active node*, on which a SQL Server instance is running the production workload, and the other is a *passive node*, on which SQL Server is installed but not running. If the SQL Server instance on the *active node* fails, the *passive node* becomes the *active node* and begins to run the SQL Server production workload with some minimal failover downtime. Additionally, you can deploy a Windows Failover Cluster to have both nodes active, which means running different SQL Server instances where any SQL Server instances can failover to the other node.

This definition is straightforward, but it has a lot of unclear implications, which is where many clustering misunderstandings arise. One of the best ways to more fully understand what clustering can and cannot do is to drill down into the details.

What Clustering Can Do

Clustering is designed to improve the availability of the physical server hardware, operating system, and SQL Server instances but excluding the shared storage. Should any of these aspects fail, the SQL Server instance fails over. The other node in a cluster automatically takes over the failed SQL Server instance to reduce downtime to a minimum.

Additionally, the use of a Windows Failover Cluster can help reduce downtime when you perform maintenance on cluster nodes. For example, if you need to update hardware on a physical server or install a new service pack on the operating system, you can do so one node at a time. To do so, follow these steps:

1. First, you upgrade the passive node that is not running a SQL Server instance.

2. Next, manually failover from the active node to the now upgraded node, which becomes the active node.

3. Then upgrade the currently passive node.

4. After it is upgraded, if you choose, you can fail back to the original node. This cluster feature helps to reduce the overall downtime caused by upgrades.

When running an upgrade, you need to ensure that you do not manually failover to a node that has not been upgraded because that would cause instability since the binary would not have been updated.

 A Windows 2003 Failover Cluster cannot be upgraded to a Windows 2008 Failover Cluster because architecturally the two versions are different. Instead, create a Windows 2008 Failover Cluster and migrate the databases.

What Clustering Cannot Do

The list of what clustering cannot do is much longer than the list of what it can do, and this is where the misunderstandings start for many people. Clustering is just one part of many important and required pieces in a puzzle to ensure high availability. Other aspects of high availability, such as ensuring redundancy in all hardware components, are just as important. Without hardware redundancy, the most sophisticated cluster solution in the world can fail. If all the pieces of that puzzle are not in place, spending a lot of money on clustering may not be a good investment. The section "Getting Prepared for Clustering" discusses this in further detail.

Some DBAs believe that clustering can reduce downtime to zero. This is not the case; clustering can mitigate downtime, but it can't eliminate it. For example, the failover itself causes an outage lasting from seconds to a few minutes while the SQL Server services are stopped on one node then started on the other node and database recovery is performed.

Nor is clustering designed to intrinsically protect data as the shared storage is a single point of failover in clustering. This is a great surprise to many DBAs. Data must be protected using other options, such as backups, log shipping, or disk mirroring. In actuality, the same database drives are shared, albeit without being seen at the same time, by all servers in the cluster, so corruption in one would carry over to the others.

Clustering is not a solution for load balancing either. Load balancing is when many servers act as one, spreading your load across several servers simultaneously. Many DBAs, especially those who work for large commercial websites, may think that clustering provides load balancing between the cluster nodes. This is not the case; clustering helps improve only uptime of SQL Server instances. If you need load balancing, then you must look for a different solution. A possibility might be Peer-to-Peer Transactional Replication, discussed in Chapter 15, "Replication."

Clustering purchases require Enterprise or Datacenter versions of the Windows operating system and SQL Server Standard, Enterprise, or BI editions. These can get expensive and many organizations may not cost-justify this expense. Clustering is usually deployed within the confines of a data center, but can be used over geographic distances (*geoclusters*). To implement a geocluster, work with your storage vendor to enable the storage across the geographic distances to synchronize the disk arrays. SQL Server 2012 also supports another option: multi-site clustering across subnet. The same subnet restriction was eliminated with the release of SQL Server 2012.

Clustering requires experienced DBAs to be highly trained in hardware and software, and DBAs with clustering experience command higher salaries.

Although SQL Server is cluster-aware, not all client applications that use SQL Server are cluster-aware. For example, even if the failover of a SQL Server instance is relatively seamless, a client application may not have the reconnect logic. Applications without reconnect logic require that users exit and then restart the client application after the SQL Server instance has failed over, then users may lose any data displayed on their current screen.

Choosing SQL Server 2012 Clustering for the Right Reasons

When it comes right down to it, the reason for a clustered SQL Server is to improve the high availability of the whole SQL Server instances which includes all user/system databases, logins, SQL Jobs but this justification makes sense only if the following are true:

➤ You have experienced DBA staff to install, configure, and administer a clustered SQL Server.

➤ The cost (and pain) resulting from downtime is more than the cost of purchasing the cluster hardware and software and maintaining it over time.

➤ You have in place the capability to protect your storage redundancy. Remember that clusters don't protect data.

➤ For a geographically dispersed cluster across remote data centers, you have a Microsoft certified third-party hardware and software solution.

➤ You have in place all the necessary peripherals required to support a highly available server environment (for example, backup power and so on).

If all these things are true, your organization is a good candidate for installing a clustered SQL Server, and you should proceed; but if your organization doesn't meet these criteria, and you are not willing to implement them, you would probably be better with an alternative, high-availability option, such as one of those discussed next.

Alternatives to Clustering

SQL Server clustering is just one of many options available to help provide high availability within your SQL Server 2012 instances, and high-availability solutions consist of multiple layers of solutions to ensure uptime. This section takes a brief look at alternatives to clustering, starting with the least expensive and easy-to-implement options and working along to the more expensive and more difficult-to-implement options.

Cold Backup Server

A *cold backup* refers to having a spare physical server available that you can use as your SQL Server 2012 server should your production server fail. Generally speaking, this server does not have SQL

Server 2012 or any database backups installed on it. This means that it can take time to install SQL Server 2012, restoring the databases and redirecting applications to the new server, before you are up and running again. It also means that you may lose some of your data if you cannot recover the last transaction logs from the failed production server and you have only your most recent database backups to restore from.

If being down a while or possibly losing data is not a major concern, having a cold backup server is the least expensive way to ensure that your organization stays in business should your production SQL Server 2012 server go down.

Warm Backup Server

The major difference between a cold backup server and a warm backup server is that your spare server (the "warm" one) has SQL Server 2012 preinstalled, may be used as a development server where it has some less recent production databases installed. This means that you save a lot of installation and configuration time, getting back into production sooner than you would with the use of a cold backup server. You still need to redirect your database applications, refresh the data to the most current, and you may lose some of your data should you not recover the last transaction logs from the failed server.

Log Shipping

In a log-shipping scenario, you have two SQL Servers, includes the primary (production) server and a secondary. The secondary server also has SQL Server 2012 installed and configured. The major difference between a warm backup server and log shipping is that log shipping adds the capability not only to restore database backups from the production server to the spare server automatically, but also to ship database transaction logs and automatically restore them. This means there is less manual work than with a warm backup server, and less chance for data loss, as the most data you might lose would be the equivalent of one transaction log. For example, if you create transaction logs every 15 minutes, in the worst case you would lose only 15 minutes of data.

 Log shipping is covered in detail in Chapter 18, "SQL Server 2012 Log Shipping."

Replication

Many experts include SQL Server replication as a means to increase high availability, but the authors are not among them. Although replication is great for moving data from one SQL Server to others, it's not a good high-availability option. It is much too complex and limited in its capability to easily replicate entire databases to be worth the effort of spending any time trying to make it work in failover scenarios unless you already have the replication expertise.

 Replication is covered in detail in Chapter 15, "Replication."

Database Mirroring

Database mirroring in many ways is a good alternative to clustering SQL Server. Like clustering, you can use database mirroring to automatically failover a failed SQL Server instance to the mirror server, on a database-by-database basis. The biggest difference between clustering and database mirroring is that data is actually protected when there are two different copies of the data stored in mirroring. In clustering, the shared disk can be a single point of failure. In addition, database mirroring can operate over long distances, is less expensive than clustering, requires less knowledge to set up and manage, and the failover can be fully automated in some circumstances, like clustering is. In some cases, database mirroring may be a better choice instead of clustering for high availability.

AlwaysOn Availability Groups

AlwaysOn is a high-availability and disaster recovery solution new to SQL Server 2012 that enables you to maximize availability for one to many user databases as a group. Deploying AlwaysOn involves configuring one or more *availability groups*. Each availability group defines a set of user databases that can failover as a single unit by leveraging a Windows Failover Cluster and its clustered SQL Server name and IP address. The availability group involves a set of five failover partners, known as *availability replicas*. Each availability replica possesses a non-shared copy of each of the databases in the availability group where the data can be maintained either synchronously or asynchronously. One of these replicas, known as primary replica, maintains the primary copy of each database. The primary replica makes these databases, known as primary databases, available to users for read-write access. For each primary database, other availability replicas, known as secondary replicas, maintain failover copy for each database that can also be configured for read-only access.

 See Chapter 25, "AlwaysOn Availability Groups," for more information on this subject.

Third-Party Clustering Solutions

In addition to Microsoft, there are third-party partners that also offer high availability solutions for SQL Server. In general, these options may be more expensive than and as complex as Microsoft's clustering option, but some offer additional features and benefits beyond what Microsoft offers.

What to Do?

Although this brief introduction clarifies your options, it may not be enough information for you to make a good decision. If the best solution is not self-evident, then you need to spend time researching the preceding options before you can determine what is best for your organization.

CLUSTERING: THE BIG PICTURE

If you're going to deploy and manage clustering, you need to know how it works, including clustering configuration options.

How Clustering Works

In this section, you consider active and passive nodes, the shared disk array, the quorum, public and private networks, and the cluster server. Then, you learn how a failover works.

Active Nodes Versus Passive Nodes

A Windows Failover Cluster can support up to sixteen nodes; however, most clustering deployment is only two nodes. A single SQL Server 2012 instance can run on only a single node at a time; and should a failover occur, the failed instance can failover to another node. Clusters of three or more physical nodes should be considered when you need to cluster many SQL Server instances. Larger clusters are discussed later in this chapter.

In a two-node Windows Failover Cluster with SQL Server, one of the physical nodes is considered the *active* node, and the second one is the *passive* node for that single SQL Server instance. It doesn't matter which of the physical servers in the cluster is designated as active or passive, but you should specifically assign one node as the active and the other as the passive. This way, there is no confusion about which physical server is performing which role at the current time.

When referring to an active node, this particular node is currently running a SQL Server instance accessing that instance's databases, which are located on a shared disk array.

When referring to a passive node, this particular node is not currently running the SQL Server. When a node is passive, it is not running the production databases, but it is in a state of readiness. If the active node fails and a failover occurs, the passive node automatically runs production databases and begins serving user requests. In this case, the passive node has become active, and the formerly active node becomes the passive node (or the failed node, if a failure occurs that prevents it from operating).

Shared Disk Array

Standalone SQL Server instances usually store their databases on local disk storage or nonshared disk storage; clustered SQL Server instances store data on a shared disk array. *Shared* means that all nodes of the Windows Failover Cluster are physically connected to the shared disk array, but only the active node can access that instance's databases. To ensure the integrity of the databases, both nodes of a cluster never access the shared disk at the same time.

Generally speaking, a shared disk array can be an iSCSI, a fiber-channel, SAS connected, a RAID 1, a RAID 5, or a RAID 10 disk array housed in a standalone unit, or a SAN. This shared disk array must have at least two logical disk partitions. One partition is used for storing the clustered instance's SQL Server databases, and the other is used for the quorum drive, if a quorum drive is used. Additionally, you need a third logical partition if you choose to cluster MSDTC.

The Quorum

When both cluster nodes are up and running and participating in their respective active and passive roles, they communicate with each other over the network. For example, if you change a configuration setting on the active node, this configuration is propagated automatically, and quickly, to the passive node, thereby ensuring synchronization.

As you might imagine, though, you can make a change on the active node and have it fail before the change is sent over the network and made on the passive node. In this scenario, the change is never applied to the passive node. Depending on the nature of the change, this could cause problems, even causing both nodes of the cluster to fail.

To prevent this change from happening, a Windows Failover Cluster employs a *quorum*. A quorum is essentially a log file, similar in concept to database logs. Its purpose is to record any change made on the active node. This way, should any recorded change not get to the passive node because the active node has failed and cannot send the change to the passive node over the network, the passive node, when it becomes the active node, can read the quorum log file to find out what the change was. The passive node can then make the change before it becomes the new active node. If the state of this drive is compromised, your cluster may become inoperable.

In effect, each cluster quorum can cast one "vote," where the majority of total votes (based on the number of these cluster quorums that are online) determine whether the cluster continues running on the cluster node. This prevents more than one cluster node attempting to take ownership of the same SQL Server instance. The voting quorums are cluster nodes or, in some cases, a disk witness or file share witness. Each voting cluster quorum (with the exception of a file share witness) contains a copy of the cluster configuration. The cluster service works to keep all copies synchronized at all times.

Following are the four supported Windows Failover Cluster quorum modes:

> **Node Majority:** Each node that is available and in communication can vote. The cluster functions only with a majority of the votes.

> **Node and Disk Majority:** Each node plus a designated disk in the cluster storage (the "disk witness") can vote, whenever they are available and in communication. The cluster functions only with a majority of the votes.

> **Node and File Share Majority:** Each node plus a designated file share created by the administrator (the "file share witness") can vote, whenever they are available and in communication. The cluster functions only with a majority of the votes.

> **No Majority: Disk Only:** The cluster has a quorum if one node is available and in communication with a specific disk in the cluster storage. Only the nodes that are also in communication with that disk can join the cluster. The disk is the single point of failure, so use highly reliable storage. A *quorum drive* is a logical drive on the shared disk array dedicated to storing the quorum and as a best practice should be around 1GB of fault tolerant disk storage.

With two-node clusters Disk only is the most often used quorum configuration, commonly known as the *quorum disk*. The quorum configuration can be switched after the cluster has been deployed based on the number of clustered nodes and user requirements. While in clusters with greater than two nodes, the other three quorum modes are more commonly used.

Public and Private Networks

Each node of a cluster must have at least two network cards to be a fully supported installation. One network card is connected to the public network, and the other network card will be connected to a private cluster network.

➤ The public network is the network to which the client applications connect. This is how they communicate to a clustered SQL Server instance using the clustered IP address and clustered SQL Server name. It is recommended to have two teamed network cards for the public network for redundancy and to improve availability.

➤ The private network is used solely for communications between the clustered nodes. It is used mainly for the *heartbeat communication*. Two forms of communications are executed:

➤ **LooksAlive:** Verifies that the SQL Server service runs on the online node every 5 seconds by default

➤ **IsAlive:** Verifies that SQL Server accepts connections by executing `sp_server_diagnostics`.

This health detection logic determines if a node is down and the passive node then takes over the production workload.

The SQL Server Instance

Surprisingly, SQL Server client applications don't need to know how to switch communicating from a failed cluster node to the new active node or anything else about specific cluster nodes (such as the NETBIOS name or IP address of individual cluster nodes). This is because each clustered SQL Server instance is assigned a Network name and IP address, which client applications use to connect to the clustered SQL Server. In other words, client applications don't connect to a node's specific name or IP address but instead to the cluster SQL network name or cluster SQL IP address that stays consistent and fails over. Each clustered SQL Server will belong to a Failover Cluster Resource Group that contains the following resources that will fail together:

➤ SQL Server Network Name

➤ IP Address

➤ One or more shared disks

➤ SQL Server Database Engine service

➤ SQL Server Agent

➤ SQL Server Analysis Services, if installed in the same group

➤ One file share resource, if the FILESTREAM feature is installed

How a Failover Works

Assume that a single SQL Server 2012 instance runs on the active node of a cluster and that a passive node is available to take over when needed. At this time, the active node communicates with both the database and the quorum on the shared disk array. Because only a single node at a time can access the shared disk array, the passive node does not access the database or the quorum. In addition, the active node sends out heartbeat signals over the private network, and the passive node monitors them, so it can take over if a failover occurs. Clients are also interacting with the active node via the clustered SQL Server name and IP address while running production workloads.

Now assume that the active node stops working because of a power failure. The passive node, which is monitoring the heartbeats from the active node, notices that the heartbeats stopped. After a predetermined delay, the passive node assumes that the active node has failed and initiates a failover. As part of the failover process, the passive node (now the active node) takes over control of the shared disk array and reads the quorum, looking for any unsynchronized configuration changes. It also takes over control of the clustered SQL Server name and IP address. In addition, as the node takes over the databases, it has to perform a SQL Server startup and recover the databases.

The time this takes depends on many factors, including the performance of the hardware and the number of transactions that might have to be rolled forward or back during the database recovery process. When the recovery process is complete, the new active node announces itself on the network with the clustered SQL Server name and IP address, which enables the client applications to reconnect and begin using the SQL Server 2012 instance after this minimal interruption.

Clustering Options

Up to this point, simple two-node, active/passive clusters running a single SQL Server instance have been discussed. However, this is only one of many options you have when clustering SQL Server. Two other popular options include active/active clustering and multi-node clustering. Additionally, it is available to cluster multiple instances of SQL Server on the same server. The following sections discuss these alternatives in detail.

Active/Active Cluster

The examples so far have described what is called an *active/passive cluster*. This is a two-node cluster in which there is only one active instance of SQL Server 2011. Should the active node fail, the passive node takes over the single instance of SQL Server 2011, becoming the active node.

To save hardware costs, some organizations like to configure an *active/active cluster*. Like active/passive, this is also a two-node cluster, but instead of only a single SQL Server instance running, there are two instances, one on each physical node of the cluster.

The advantage of an active/active cluster is that you make better use of the available hardware. Both nodes of the cluster are in use instead of just one, as in an active/passive cluster. The disadvantage is that when a failover occurs, both SQL Server instances are running on a single physical server, which can reduce performance of both instances where memory may need to be readjusted to ensure that each has adequate memory. To help overcome this problem, both of the physical servers can be oversized to better meet the needs of both instances should a failover occur. Chances are good, however, that the perfect balance will not be met and there will be some performance slowdown when failing over to the other node. In addition, if you have an active/active cluster running two SQL Server instances, each instance needs its own logical disk on the shared disk array. Logical disks cannot be shared among SQL Server instances.

In the end, if you want to save hardware costs and don't mind potential application slowdowns, use an active/active two-node cluster.

Multi-node Clusters

If you think you will be adding even more clustered SQL Server 2012 instances in the future you may want to consider a third option: multi-node clusters. For the more conservative, a three-node cluster, or *active/active/passive*, is a good option that provides more redundancy and it won't cause any application slowdown should a failover occur with the passive node. For those that don't mind the complexity of large clusters, you can add even more nodes.

The number of physical nodes supported for SQL Server clustering depends on which version of the software you purchase, along with which version of the operating system you intend to use.

Purchasing the Right Software

One of the reasons it is important to research your clustering needs is that they directly affect what software you need, along with licensing costs. Following are your options:

➤ SQL Server 2012 Standard Edition (32-bit or 64-bit): Supports up to two-node clustering.

➤ SQL Server 2012 BI Edition (32-bit or 64-bit): Supports up to two-node clustering.

➤ SQL Server 2012 Enterprise Edition (32-bit or 64-bit): Supports up to sixteen-node clustering.

If you need only a two-node cluster, you can save by licensing Windows Server 2008 Enterprise Edition and SQL Server 2012 Standard Edition. If you want more than a two- node cluster, your licensing costs will escalate quickly because you will need SQL Server 2012 Enterprise Edition.

 SQL Server 2012 is not supported on Windows 2003.

Number of Nodes to Use

As covered earlier, in a two-node cluster, a SQL Server instance runs on the active node, while the passive node is currently not running SQL Server but is ready to do so when a failover occurs. This same principle applies to multi-node clusters.

As an example, say that you have a three-node cluster. In this case, there are two active nodes running their own individual SQL Server instances, and the third physical node acts as a passive node for the other two active nodes. If either of the two active nodes fails, the passive node can take over. You can set up a failover preferred node to predetermine the failover sequence from node to node.

Now look at an eight-node cluster. In this case, you have seven active nodes and one passive. Should any of the seven active nodes fail, then the passive node takes over after a failover. In this case, with a large number of nodes, it is more preferable to have a passive node to avoid multiple node failures that cause the surviving nodes to carry all that additional workload.

In an active/passive configuration, the advantage of many nodes is that less hardware is used for failover needs. For example, in a two-node cluster, 50 percent of your hardware is used for redundancy; but in an eight-node cluster, only 12.5 percent of your cluster hardware is used for redundancy.

Ultimately, deciding how many nodes your cluster has should depend on your business restrictions like your budget, your in-house expertise, and your level of aversion, if any, to complexity. Some organizations have many different SQL Server instances that they need to cluster, but choose to use multiple two-node active/passive clusters instead of a single multi-node cluster, working under the impression that it is best to keep things as simple as possible.

Clustering Multiple Instances of SQL Server on the Same Server

As indicated in the types of clustering discussed previously, a single SQL Server instance can run on a single physical server, however, this is not a requirement. SQL Server Enterprise Edition can actually support up to 25 SQL instances on a single clustered configuration. This is a restriction of drive letter limitations though so you need mount points to achieve this. The effectiveness of this depends on the business requirements, the capacity of the hardware, SLAs, and the expertise of the IT organization managing it.

The purpose of clustering is to boost high availability. Adding many SQL Server instances to a cluster adds complexity, and complexity can increases risk and failover points in the solution. But complexity can also be managed depending on the IT expertise to support it; speak to your IT support when considering this option.

UPGRADING SQL SERVER CLUSTERING

If your organization is like many, it probably already has some older versions of SQL Server clusters in production. If so, it is time to decide how to upgrade them to SQL Server 2012. Your available options include the following:

➤ Don't upgrade.

➤ Perform an in-place SQL Server 2012 upgrade.

➤ Rebuild your cluster from scratch, and then install SQL Server 2012 clustering. Or leave the Windows Failover Cluster intact, if it is a Windows 2008 R2, but install a new SQL Server 2012 on it and migrate the databases.

This section considers each of these three options.

Don't Upgrade

This is an easy decision. Not upgrading is simple and doesn't cost anything. Just because a new version of SQL Server comes out doesn't mean you have to upgrade. If your current SQL Server cluster is running satisfactory, it may not be worth the costs and upgrade work. A properly configured Windows 2008 cluster is stable running SQL Server 2005, 2008, and 2008 R2.

On the other hand, SQL Server 2012 offers scalability, ease of use, capabilities and reliability, and new functionality of which you may want to take advantage. Before you upgrade, do the research to determine whether the new features of SQL Server 2012 are what you need. Otherwise, you can choose to stay on the current SQL Server version, provided that it is still supported by Microsoft.

Upgrading Your SQL Server 2012 Cluster In Place

Before talking about how to upgrade a Windows Failover Cluster to SQL Server 2012, first consider what operating system you currently run. If you are on Windows Server 2008 with the latest service pack or R2, you are in good shape and an in-place upgrade to SQL Server 2012 should not be a problem.

If, however, you still run Windows Server 2003, you should deploy Windows 2008 (or R2). Upgrading from Windows 2003 to Windows 2008 Failover Cluster is not supported; a total rebuild is required.

If you run a Windows 2008 Failover Cluster where SQL Server needs to be upgraded to SQL Server 2012, you can perform a rolling upgrade with minimum downtime by performing the following steps:

1. Identify the cluster node that you want to upgrade first.

2. Failover all the SQL instances from that node. As a result, no SQL instances will run on that node, therefore, that node becomes passive.

3. Install prerequisites on each passive node, and upgrade the shared SQL Server components.

4. Restart passive nodes as prompted.

5. Run the SQL Server 2012 setup to perform an in-place upgrade. Prior to doing any upgrades, SQL upgrade validation procedures should be completely followed. Set up a test environment, run the SQL Server 2012 Upgrade Advisor, upgrade the test environment to SQL 2012, replay a production SQL Profiler trace, and test the application connectivity and performance test. Not following upgrade procedures can result in a failed upgrade that results in a need to back out, which is more challenging in a Windows Cluster than in standalone SQL Server environment.

6. After more than half of the passive nodes have been upgraded, the upgrade process automatically initiates a failover to the upgraded nodes and maintains a list of possible owners to which the resources can fail while the remaining nodes are upgraded.

> *Not all SQL instances need to be upgraded; Windows Failover Cluster supports a mix of SQL Server 2005, 2008 (and R2), and 2011 on a single Windows 2008 Failover Cluster.*

Rebuilding Your Cluster

Rebuilding your cluster from scratch is a good idea if any one of the following conditions exists:

➤ You need to upgrade your current hardware. (It is either old or underpowered.)

➤ The server is using the Windows 2003 operating system.

➤ The current cluster installation is unstable.

➤ You have disdain for upgrading software in place and prefer a fresh install.

If you do decide to upgrade from scratch, you also have to decide whether to install on new hardware or use your old hardware. If you install on new hardware, you have the convenience of building the cluster, and testing it, at your own pace, while the current cluster is still in production. This helps to ensure that you have done an outstanding job and at the same time relieves some of the stress that you might experience if you have to reuse your old hardware and then rebuild the cluster during a brief and intense time period.

If you don't have the luxury of acquiring new hardware, you have to identify a down time when your system can be shut down while the rebuild occurs. This could range from a 4-hour period to a 12-hour period, depending on the size of the cluster and complexity. Besides the time your cluster will be down, there is also the added risk of unexpected problems. For example, you might make an installation mistake halfway through the upgrade and have to start over. Because of the uncertainty involved, you should first estimate how much time you think the upgrade will take under good circumstances, and then double that estimate as the size of your requested downtime window. This way, your users are prepared.

Whether you upgrade using new hardware or old hardware, you have to consider two additional issues:

➤ Will you reuse your current clustered SQL Server name and IP address or select new ones?

➤ How will you move your data from the previous cluster to the new cluster?

The clients that access your current SQL Server cluster do so using the cluster's SQL Server name and IP address. If you want the clients to continue using the same clustered SQL Server name and IP address, you need to reuse the old clustered SQL Server name and IP address in the new cluster. This is the most common approach because it is generally easier to change a single clustered SQL Server name and IP address than to reconfigure dozens, if not hundreds, of clients that access the SQL Servers on the Windows Failover cluster.

If you upgrade using old hardware, reusing the former clustered SQL Server name and IP address is not an issue because the old cluster is brought down and then the new one is brought up, so there is never a time when the clustered SQL Server name and IP address are on two clusters at the same time (which won't work).

If you upgrade by using new hardware, you need to assign a clustered SQL Server name and IP address for testing, but you won't use the old ones because they are currently in use. In this case, you need to use a temporary clustered SQL Server name and IP address for testing; when you are ready for the actual changeover from the old cluster to the new cluster, you need to follow these general steps:

1. Back up the data.

2. Remove SQL Server clustering from the old cluster or turn off the old cluster.

3. On the new cluster, change the clustered SQL Server name and IP address from the old cluster.

4. Restore the data.

How you move the data from the old cluster to the new cluster depends on both the size of the databases and somewhat on whether you use old hardware or new hardware.

Regardless of the option you choose, before you proceed, back up all the databases. Remember, identify any objects in the System databases such as SQL jobs, SSIS packages and logins, and re-create them in the new Windows Failover cluster. If you use old hardware, all you have to do is backup or detach the user databases. When the cluster rebuild is complete, restore or reattach the user databases.

If you move to new hardware or change the database file locations, you should first backup or detach user databases. Next, move these to the new cluster or new database location. Then when the cluster rebuild completes, restore or reattach the user databases.

There isn't space here to include detailed steps for every possible scenario, such as what happens if the drive letter changes, and so on. The key to success is to plan all these steps and, if possible, perform a trial run before you do an actual cutover.

Back-Out Plan

No matter how you decide to upgrade to SQL Server 2012 clustering, you need to have a back-out plan. Essentially, a back-out plan is what you do if your upgrade fails. Typically, a back-out plan consists of reinstalling SQL Server, restoring the system and user databases, and incurring at least a few hours of outage, but because each particular circumstance can vary, it is impossible to create one set of steps to follow for all back-out plans. Therefore, as you plan your upgrade, consider how the plan could fail, and come up with options to get you back in business should things not go well. Your job could depend on how good your back-out plan is.

Which Upgrade Option Is Best?

Speaking from experience, the authors always prefer to upgrade by rebuilding clusters from scratch on new hardware. This is the easiest, fastest, least risky, and least stressful way. Unfortunately, you may not have this option for whatever reasons based on your circumstances. In this case, you have to work with what you have been given. The key to a successful upgrade is a lot of detailed planning, as much testing as possible, and, of course, having a complete back-out plan.

GETTING PREPARED FOR CLUSTERING

For SQL Server 2012 clustering, the devil is in the details. If you take the time to ensure that every step is done correctly and in the right order, your cluster installation will be smooth and relatively quick and painless; but if you don't like to read instructions, and instead prefer the trial-and-error approach to computer administration, then expect to face a lot of frustration and a lot of time installing and reinstalling your SQL Server 2012 cluster.

The best way to ensure a smooth cluster installation is to create a detailed, step-by-step plan for the installation, down to the screen level. Yes, this is boring and tedious, but it forces you to think through every option and how it can affect your installation and your organization (after it is in production). In addition, such a plan can come in handy the next time you build a cluster and can be great documentation for your disaster recovery plan.

Preparing the Infrastructure

Before you begin building a SQL Server 2012 cluster, you must ensure that your network infrastructure is in place. Following is a checklist of everything required before you begin installing a SQL Server 2012 cluster. In many cases, these items are the responsibility of others on your IT staff, but it is your responsibility to ensure that all these are in place before you begin building your SQL Server 2012 cluster:

➤ Your network must have at least one Active Directory server and ideally two for redundancy.

➤ Your network must have at least one DNS server and ideally two for redundancy.

➤ Your network must have available switch ports for the public network cards used by the nodes of the cluster. Be sure to set them to match the manually set network card settings used in the nodes of the cluster. SQL Server 2012 supports nodes in different subnets, but for SQL Server versions prior to SQL Server 2012 all the nodes of a cluster must be on the same subnet.

➤ You must secure IP addresses for all the public network cards. Windows 2008 does support DHCP but you should use static IPs.

➤ You must decide how you will configure the private heartbeat network. Choose between using a direct network card-to-network card connection using a cross over cable (only possible with a two-node cluster), or use a hub or switch. The hub or switch should be different than the one supporting the public network for redundancy.

➤ You need to secure IP addresses for the private network cards. Generally you should use a private network subnet such as 10.0.0.0–10.255.255.255, 172.16.0.0–172.31.255.255, or 192.168.0.0–192.168.255.255. Remember, this is a private network seen only by the nodes of the cluster. Again, Windows 2008 enables DHCP to claim these IP addresses.

➤ Ensure that you have proper electrical power for the new cluster nodes and shared disk array.

➤ Ensure that battery backup power is available to all the nodes in your cluster and your shared disk array.

➤ If you don't already have one, create a SQL Server service account to be used by the SQL Server services running on the cluster. This must be a domain account with the password set to never expire.

➤ If you don't already have one, create a cluster service account to be used by the Windows Clustering service. This must be a domain account with the password set to never expire.

➤ Determine a name for your Windows Failover Cluster and secure an IP address for it. This name will be used for management of the cluster after it is created.

➤ Determine a name for your SQL Server 2012 cluster and secure an IP address for it. This will be the name that clients will connect to.

These preparations will come back into play during the installation process.

Preparing the Hardware

Hardware typically presents certain issues, often taking the most time to research and configure. Part of the reason for this is that there are many hardware options, some of which work, some of which don't. Unfortunately, there is no complete resource you can use to help you sort through this. Each vendor offers different hardware, and the available hardware is always changing, along with new and updated hardware drivers, making this entire subject a moving target with no easy answers. In spite of all this, here is what you need to know to start selecting the proper hardware for your SQL Server 2012 cluster.

Finding Your Way Through the Hardware Jungle

This section describes the basic hardware you need for a SQL Server cluster. To keep things simple, only a two-node active/passive cluster is referred to; although, these same recommendations apply to multinode clusters. Additionally, most Windows Failover clusters are configured with a quorum drive so assume a quorum drive configuration. The following are the author's minimum hardware recommendations. If you check out Microsoft's minimum hardware requirements for a SQL Server 2012 cluster, they will be somewhat less.

 Each node in your cluster should be identical. This will avoid installation and administrative headaches.

The minimum specifications for the server nodes should be the following:

- Dual CPUs, 2GHz or higher, 2MB L2 Cache (32-bit or 64-bit)
- 2GB or more RAM
- Local mirrored SCSI drive for the application drive (RAID 10, 5 or 1) (c:), 9GB or larger
- SCSI DVD drive
- SCSI connection for local SCSI drive and DVD drive
- SCSI or fiber connection to shared disk array or SAN or shared ISCSI drives
- Redundant power supplies
- Private network card
- Public network card
- Mouse, keyboard, and monitor (can be shared)

The shared disk array should have a SCSI-attached RAID 10, 5, or 1 array with an appropriate high-speed SCSI connection. With Microsoft Windows Failover clustering, SCSI is supported only if you have a two-node cluster. If you want to cluster more than two nodes, you must use a fiber-attached disk array or SAN; or you may have a fiber-attached RAID 10, 5, or 1 array with an appropriate high-speed connection. You could also use a fiber-attached SAN storage array with an appropriate high-speed connection (generally a fiber switch).

There is much more to learn about hardware specifics that is beyond the scope of this chapter. If you are new to clustering, contact your hardware vendor for specific hardware recommendations. Keep in mind that you will be running SQL Server 2012 on this cluster, so ensure that whatever hardware you select meets the needs of your predicted production workload.

Preparing the Hardware

As a DBA, you may not be the one who installs the hardware. In any case, here are the general steps most people follow when building cluster hardware:

1. Install and configure the hardware for each node in the cluster as if it will be running as a standalone server. This includes installing the latest approved drivers and firmware.

2. After the hardware is installed, install the operating system and the latest service pack, along with any additional required drivers. Then run Windows Update.

3. Configure the nodes to the public network. To make things easy to identify, name the network used for public connections **public network.**

4. Configure the private heartbeat network. To make things easy to identify, name the private heartbeat network **private network.**

5. Set up and configure the shared disk array, iSCSI targets, or SAN.

6. Install and configure the iSCSI or fiber cards in each of the nodes, and install the latest drivers. In Windows 2008, you can also use iSCSI. In this case, you need to set up the iSCSI initiators to connect to the drives.

7. One at a time, connect each node to the shared disk array, iSCSI drive, or SAN, following the instructions for your specific hardware. It is critical that you do this one node at a time. In other words, only one node at a time should be physically on and connected to the shared disk array or SAN and configured. After that node is configured, turn it off and turn the next node on and configure it, and so on, one node at a time. If you do not follow this procedure, you risk corrupting the disk configuration on your nodes, requiring you to start the process over.

8. Use Disk Administrator to configure and format the drives on the shared disk array. You need at minimum two logical drives on the shared disk array: one for storing your SQL Server databases, and the other for the quorum drive. The data drive must be big enough to store all the required data and the quorum drive must be at least 500MB (which is the smallest size that an NTFS volume can efficiently operate). When configuring the shared drives using Disk Administrator, each node of the cluster is required to use the same drive letter when referring to the drives on the shared disk array or SAN. For example, you might want to assign your data drive as drive "F:" on all the nodes, and assign the quorum drive letter "Q:" on all the nodes.

9. When all the hardware is put together, ensure that there are no problems before you begin installing clustering services by checking the Windows Event Viewer. Although you may do some diagnostic hardware testing before you install the operating system, you need to wait until after installing the operating system before you can fully test the hardware.

10. Ensure that you can ping the cluster nodes over the public and then the private networks. Likewise, ensure that you can ping the domain controller and DNS server to verify that they are available.

11. Write a file in the shared disks by one node, which should be visible by the other node.

12. Additionally, verify that the drive letters correspond between nodes and that there is not a mismatch in drive letters from the shared disks between nodes.

After all the hardware has been configured and tested, you are ready to install Windows Failover clustering.

CLUSTERING WINDOWS SERVER 2008

Before you can install SQL Server 2012 on the cluster, you must first install Windows Server 2008 Failover Cluster services. After it is successfully installed and tested, you can cluster SQL Server. This section takes a high-level, step-by-step approach to installing and configuring a Windows Failover Cluster.

Before Installing Windows 2011 Clustering

To install Windows Failover clustering, you need to perform a series of important steps. This is especially important if you didn't build the cluster nodes because you want to ensure everything is working correctly before you begin the actual cluster installation. When they are completed, you can install Windows 2008 Failover clustering. Following are the steps you must perform:

1. Ensure that all the physical nodes are working properly and are configured identically (hardware, software, and drivers).

2. Verify that none of the physical nodes have been configured as a domain controller or for any other critical services such as Exchange. Also, ensure that you have multiple domain controllers in your environment.

3. Verify that all drives are NTFS and are not compressed.

4. Ensure that the public and private networks are properly installed and configured.

5. SQL Server failover cluster installation supports Local Disk only for installing the `tempdb` files. Ensure that the path specified for the `tempdb` data and log files is valid on all the cluster nodes. During failover, if the `tempdb` directories are not available on the failover target node, the SQL Server resource will fail to come online.

6. Verify that you have disabled NetBIOS for all private network cards.

7. Verify that there are no network shares on any of the shared drives.

8. If you intend to use SQL Server encryption, install the server certificate with the fully qualified DNS name of the clustered SQL Server on all cluster nodes.

9. Check all the error logs to ensure that there are no problems. If there are, resolve them before proceeding with the cluster installation.

10. Add the SQL Server and clustering service accounts to the Local Administrators group of all the cluster nodes.

11. Verify that no antivirus software has been installed on the cluster nodes. Antivirus software can reduce the availability of a cluster. If you want to check for possible viruses on a Windows Failover Cluster, run scans on the cluster nodes remotely from another computer.

These are many things to check, but each is important. If skipped, any one of these steps could prevent your cluster from installing or working properly.

Installing Windows Server 2008 Failover Clustering

Now that all your physical nodes and shared disk array, iSCSI device, or SAN is ready, you are ready to install a Windows 2008 Failover Cluster. This section describes the process from beginning to end.

To begin, you must enable the clustering feature for each of the Windows 2008 node candidates. In Windows 2008 the decision was made to reduce the Windows surface area by disabling the feature by default. To enable the failover clustering feature, from the Server Manager, open the Add Features Wizard. Check Failover Clustering, and the wizard completes the installation for you (shown in Figure 16-1). This doesn't actually cluster your machines but installs the necessary components on your server to manage the cluster and perform the failover. This step needs to be repeated on each physical node participating on the Windows Failover Cluster.

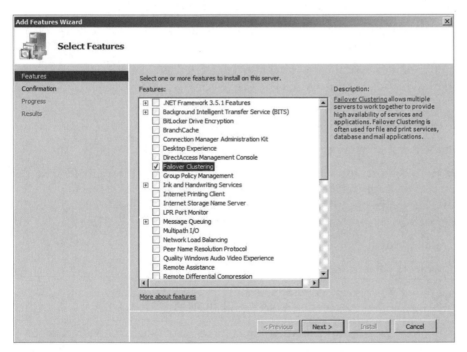

FIGURE 16-1

Validating the Windows Failover Cluster

Before you create the cluster, you want to validate that the cluster physical nodes run on supported hardware. You can tell if this is true if the nodes by pass the cluster validation. To do this, open the Failover Cluster Management tool, and click Validate a Configuration. This opens the Validate a Cluster Configuration Wizard, which runs a full diagnosis of your cluster prior to the installation.

Additionally, this wizard can also be used after installation of the cluster to ensure that you still meet the cluster hardware requirements and that all the hardware is in proper working condition.

 Microsoft supports a Windows Failover Cluster if it passes the cluster validation. Gone are the days of looking over a long compatibility matrix list to determine whether your Windows Failover Cluster was supported on a given hardware platform!

When you're in the Validate a Configuration Wizard, you will be asked which physical nodes or potential nodes you want to validate. Enter each of them into the list, and click Next. You are then asked what types of tests you want to run. The tests begin to run, and you get a visual confirmation as the validation tests move from step to step, as shown in Figure 16-2. If you fail a test, do not install the cluster, even though you can override the test and still cluster the nodes. Review the report; you see a component-by-component evaluation of your configuration to determine whether your hardware is suitable.

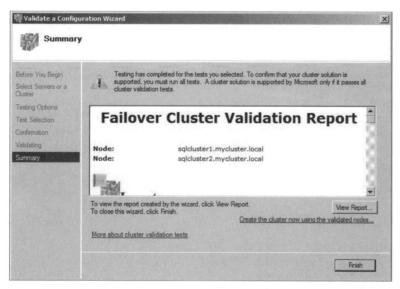

FIGURE 16-2

Viewing the report is as easy as clicking the View Report button. Doing so takes you to an HTML report, a granular report about each of your hardware components, and whether they're cluster approved.

Installing the Clustered Nodes

Windows 2008 Failover Cluster has simplified substantially from Windows 2003. This is mainly because you can now cluster all nodes at once in a wizard that asks you two questions. If you've deployed a Windows 2003 Failover Cluster, you will be amazed when you see how easy these steps are to cluster Windows 2008:

1. From within the Failover Cluster Management, click Create a Cluster. This opens the Create Cluster Wizard. The first screen after the welcome screen asks you which physical nodes will participate in the cluster. Type in each physical node and click Add, as shown in Figure 16-3. More physical nodes can be added later if need be.

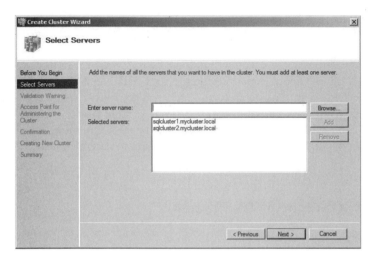

FIGURE 16-3

2. Assign the Windows cluster an IP address, and specify which network you want the cluster to use, as shown in Figure 16-4. In the figure, you can see that "SQL2012Cluster" was the Windows cluster name used for management. That name is too long for NetBIOS though so it is shortened for customers using the NetBIOS network protocol.

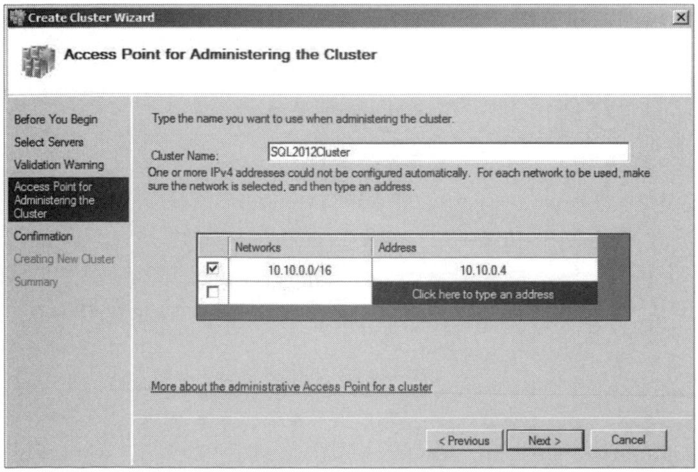

FIGURE 16-4

The cluster then begins to be created and configured (see Figure 16-5) and you will be notified when the build process is done. This is a much shorter process than it was in Windows 2003; it takes no more than 2 minutes in a test environment.

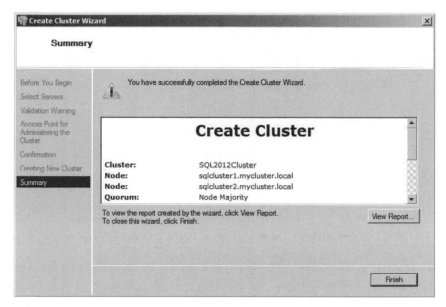

FIGURE 16-5

Preparing Windows Server 2008 for Clustering

Before you can install SQL Server, there is one small step you need to perform, and that is to prepare the cluster for SQL Server. In the previous section, you clustered Windows but didn't tell Windows which are the shared disks. This is because Microsoft now deploys a minimalist approach to clustering during the installation, doing the absolute minimum it needs to get it clustered and then enabling you to add the necessary components later.

To prepare the cluster for SQL Server, perform the following steps from the Failover Cluster Management tool:

1. Under Navigate, click the Storage shortcut.

2. From the Actions pane, click Add Disk.

3. Add any disks that you want to be visible to the Windows Failover Cluster.

4. Click OK (see Figure 16-6).

If you cannot see the shared disks, they are either already added as a disk resource or the disks are not visible to all nodes in the cluster. This might indicate that the masking is incorrect or there's a communication problem of some sort.

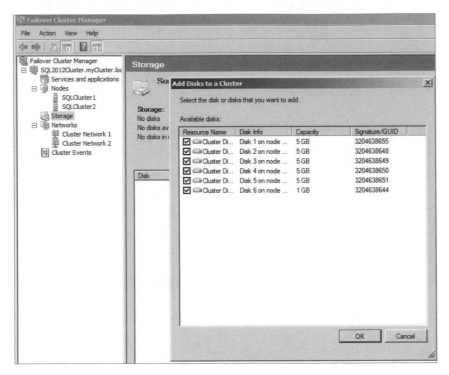

FIGURE 16-6

CLUSTERING MICROSOFT DISTRIBUTED TRANSACTION COORDINATOR

To coordinate transactions across SQL Servers in a clustered environment, you will need to leverage Microsoft Distributed Transaction Coordinator (MSDTC) to make it highly available.

Windows 2003 supported only one cluster MSDTC resource; as a result, all applications across the cluster needed to use the single MSDTC instance. However, when a MSTDC is highly utilized, it can become a bottleneck. On Windows 2008 and later, for better performance, you can install multiple MSDTC instances on a single Windows Failover Cluster as shown in the following steps. The first MSDTC instance installed becomes the default instance but can be changed from the Component Services Management Console (dcomcnfg).

1. Launch the Component Services Management Console from the Administration folder or by executing dcomcnfg from a command prompt.

2. Expand Computers and then right-click My Computer.

3. Click Properties, click the MSDTC tab, and select the default coordinator.

If multiple MSDTC instances exist, SQL Server uses the following rules to identify the MSDTC instance to be chosen in priority order:

1. Use the MSDTC instance installed to the local SQL Server group.

2. Use the mapped MSDTC instance. To create a mapping, execute the following at the command prompt:

```
msdtc -tmMappingSet -name <MappingName>
-service <SQLServerServiceName> -clusterResource <MSDTCResourceName>
```

> ➤ `<MappingName>` is any chosen name to identify the mapping.

> ➤ `<SQLServerServiceName>` is the service name from the SQL Server instance such as `MSSQLServer` or `MSSQL$<InstanceName>`.

> ➤ `<MSDTCResourceName>` is the MSDTC resource name to map.

3. Use the cluster's default MSDTC instance.

4. Use the local node MSDTC instance.

SQL Server automatically uses its local group MSDTC instance if it exists; otherwise, it uses the default instance. If the local group MSDTC instance fails, you need to tell SQL Server to use another MSDTC instance; it does not automatically use the default instance. To create a cluster MSDTC instance, use the Failover Cluster Management tool.

1. Identify a small shared disk to store the MSDTC log file. It is best to put the log file on its own shared disk or mount point to protect it from any other service that may corrupt the disk.

2. If the MSDTC resource is installed within a SQL Server Resource Group, it can share the IP and clustered SQL Server name of that group.

3. The default MSDTC should be installed on its own Cluster Resource Group to avoid a failover of MSDTC, which in turn fails other services contained in that own resource group. When installed on its own resource group, it needs its own IP and network name in addition to a shared disk.

After creating the MSDTC resource(s), you need to enable MSDTC network access to allow MSDTC to access network resources and for applications to access it. To do so perform these steps:

1. Launch the Component Services Management Console from the Administration folder or by executing `dcomcnfg` from a command prompt.

2. Expand Computers, and then right-click My Computer. Expand Distributed Transaction Coordinator and then expand `<Your instance of MSDTC>`.

3. Right-click the Properties of your MSDTC instance.

4. Under Security Settings, select the Network DTC Access tab and Allow Inbound and Allow Outbound check boxes, and click OK.

CLUSTERING SQL SERVER 2012

The procedure to install a SQL Server instance onto a Windows Failover Cluster is one of the easiest parts of getting your SQL Server cluster up and running. The SQL Server 2012 setup program is used for the install and does the heavy lifting for you. All you have to do is make a few (but critically important) decisions, and then sit back and watch the installation complete. The setup program even goes to the trouble to verify that your nodes are all properly configured; and if not, it suggests how to fix any problems before the installation begins.

When the installation process does begin, the setup program identifies the physical node, and after you give it the go-ahead to install on each one, it does so, all automatically. SQL Server 2012 binaries are installed on the local drive of each node, and the system databases are stored on the shared disk array you designate.

The next section shows the step-by-step instructions for installing a SQL Server 2012 instance in a Windows Failover Cluster. The assumption for this example is that you will install this instance in a two-node active/passive cluster. Even if you install in a two-node active/active or a multi-node cluster, the steps in this section are applicable. The only difference is that you have to run SQL Server 2012 setup on every node you want to install SQL Server, and you have to specify a different logical drive on the shared disk array for each SQL Server instance.

Step by Step to Cluster SQL Server

To begin installing your SQL Server on the cluster, you need the installation media (DVD or ISO). You can either install it directly from the media or copy the install files from the media to the current active node of the cluster, and run the setup program from there. The general process for SQL Server installation is the same as a normal, non-clustered installation; this is covered in Chapter 2. Therefore, the following steps outline the differences from a normal non-clustered installation.

1. To begin installation, run `Setup.exe`. The prerequisite components (which you learned about in Chapter 2, "SQL Server 2012 Installation Best Practices") install first. It is a good idea to run these prerequisites on each of the nodes prior to clustering because doing so can save time and enable you to debug visually if something goes wrong during the installation.

2. When you get to the SQL Server Installation Center, click New SQL Server Failover Cluster Installation. In this screen you can also add new nodes to the cluster after the installation, as shown in Figure 16-7.

    For the most part, the cluster installation is exactly the same as the standalone SQL Server installation with the exception of just a few screens. When you get to the Setup Support Rules page, you notice a number of new rules that are checked (see Figure 16-8). For example, a check is made to determine whether MSDTC is clustered. Although SQL Server can work without MSDTC clustered, some features such as distributed transactions for linked servers or SSIS will not work without it.

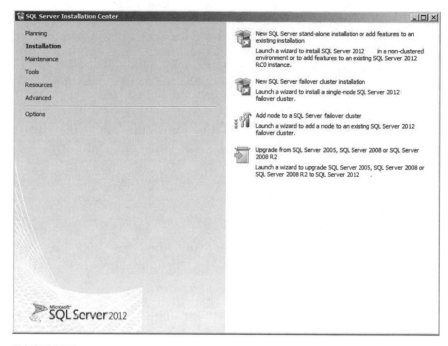

FIGURE 16-7

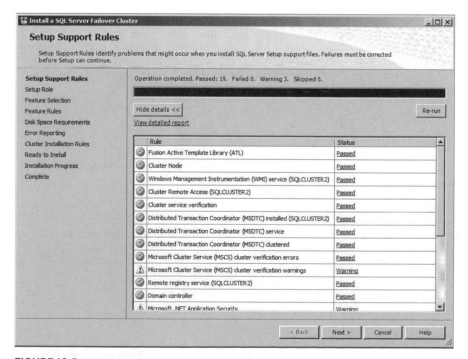

FIGURE 16-8

3. In the Instance Configuration dialog, specify the clustered SQL Server Network Name for your SQL Server instance, as shown in Figure 16-9. This is the name that all the client applications use to connect in their connection strings. The name of the directory where your program files will be copied is also based on this name by default.

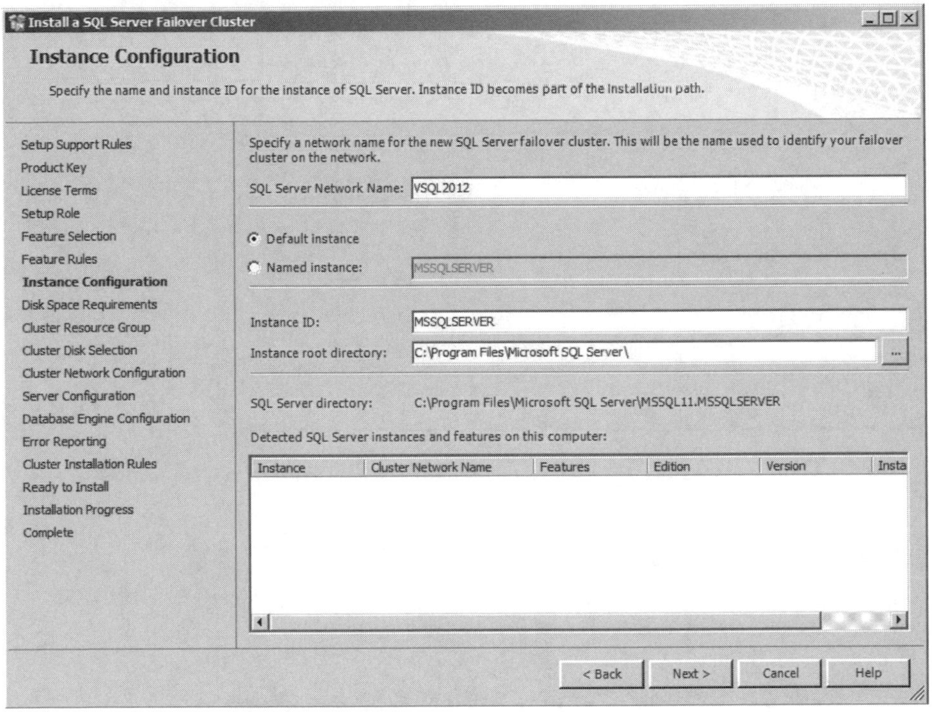

FIGURE 16-9

4. Specify the cluster resource group that will group all your SQL Server resources, such as your network name, IP, and SQL Server services, as shown in Figure 16-10.

A nice improvement since SQL Server 2008 is that you can have SQL Server use multiple drives in a cluster during the installation. In SQL Server 2005, you had to configure this behavior afterward, and you weren't able to back up to another disk other than the main SQL Server disk until you fixed the dependencies. In SQL Server 2012, simply check which clustered drive resources you want SQL Server to access, as shown in Figure 16-11.

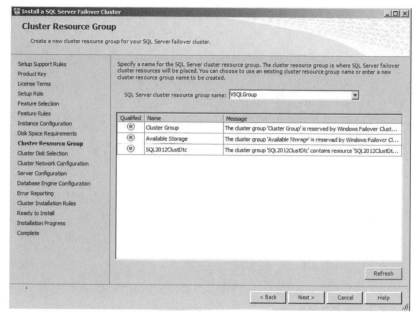

FIGURE 16-10

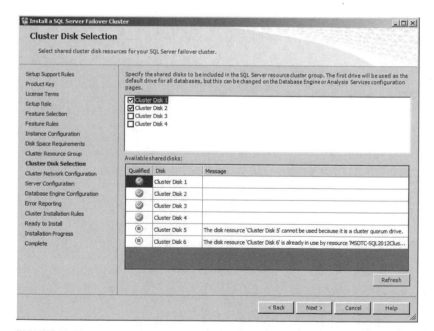

FIGURE 16-11

5. With the drive configuration complete, specify the network that SQL Server will use to communicate with client applications, and choose an IP address for each of the networks. This IP address should have been obtained earlier from a network administrator. Notice in Figure 16-12 that Windows 2008 can also use DHCP.

6. Then for Server Configuration, specify the service accounts and collation configuration as shown in Figure 16-13.

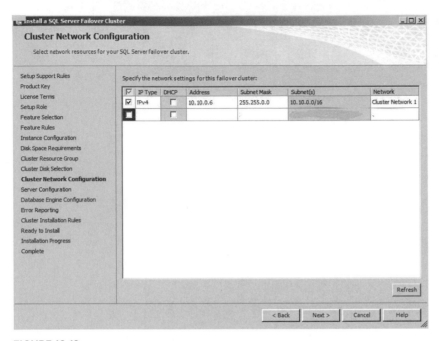

FIGURE 16-12

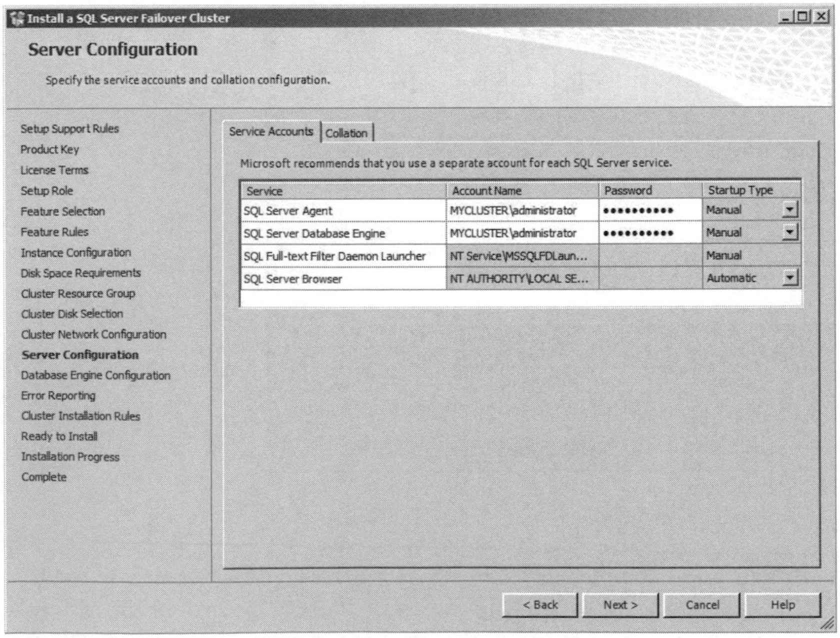

FIGURE 16-13

Then continue with the installation to proceed to copy the files to the cluster node and run the setup. Additionally, all the SQL cluster resources will be created and configured. When finished with that cluster node, you can go to the other cluster node to Add Node to join each other node a part of the SQL Server cluster instance. Unlike clustering SQL Server 2005 where the SQL setup program copied the SQL binary to all clustered nodes, starting in SQL Server 2008 the SQL setup program clusters the current node onto where the setup is executing. To add another node for SQL Server 2008 or later perform the following steps:

1.   Log in to the node that you want to join to the cluster.

2.   Run the SQL Setup on the node.

3.   Choose Add Node to a SQL Server Failover Cluster.

4.   As the setup proceeds, you will be asked for the name of the SQL Cluster to join to. Provide the appropriate name.

5.   Then the setup will proceed to join that node. If you want to add more nodes to the cluster, follow above steps for each node.

When the cluster installation is complete, from within the Windows Failover Cluster Manager, your two-node Cluster installation should look similar to Figure 16 14.

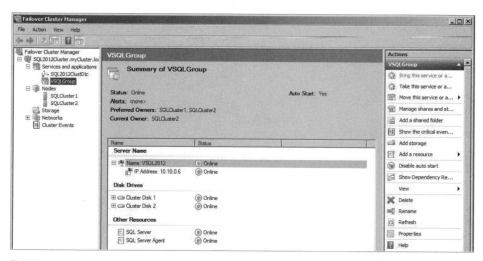

FIGURE 16-14

 Like clustering the SQL Server relational engine that is fully integrated with the Windows Failover Cluster, Analysis Services is fully clustered. Moreover, Integration Services can only be clustered as a generic resource, whereas Reporting Services cannot be clustered.

After each SQL Server instance that has been clustered, the resource group should contain the following resources:

➤ Network name

➤ IP address

➤ One or more shared disks

➤ SQL Server Database Engine service

➤ SQL Server Agent service

➤ SQL Server Analysis Services service, if installed. As a best practice, install it on its own resource group to avoid a failure in one resource to affect the other.

➤ One file share resource, if the FILESTREAM feature is installed.

After the clustered SQL Server installation completes, evaluate the resources' dependencies to identify what other resources in the group must be online before a particular resource can be brought online for. For example, SQL Server Agent depends on SQL Server being online, and SQL Server depends on the shared disks and clustered SQL Server name and IP address. The complete Windows Failover Cluster installation should look like Figure 16-14.

Installing the Service Pack and Cumulative Updates

After you install and cluster SQL Server, your next step is to install any available SQL Server service pack and cumulative updates, which you can download from *Windows Update* .You can perform a rolling upgrade as described in the "Upgrading Your SQL Server 2012 Cluster In-Place" section. Installing a service pack and/or a cumulative update is fairly straightforward because they are cluster-aware.

Test, Test, and Test Again

After you cluster SQL Server on the nodes, you need to thoroughly test the installation, just as you did after first installing Windows 2008 Failover Cluster. For example, check the Windows Event Viewer for any error messages, and validate that you can failover the SQL Server across nodes and fails back. However, not only do you want to test the SQL Server cluster, but you also want to test how your client applications "react" to failovers. Because of this, the following testing section is similar to the one you previously read but has been modified to meet the more complex needs of the additional client applications testing you need to perform.

The following is a series of tests you can perform to verify that your SQL Server 2012 cluster and its client applications work properly during failover situations. After you perform each test, verify whether you get the expected results (a successful failover), and be sure you check the Windows log files for any possible problems. If you find a problem during one test, resolve it before proceeding to the next test.

Preparing for the Testing

As with your previous cluster testing, identify a workstation with the Failover Cluster Management tool to interact with your cluster during testing.

To be prepared, you need to test each client application that will be accessing your clustered SQL Server to see what happens should a failover occur. Some client applications deal with clustering failovers by reconnecting, whereas others that are not designed with reconnect logic just fail to reconnect. You must determine beforehand how each client application responds.

To do this, first identify all the client applications; there may be dozens. Each of these has to be reconfigured to use the clustered SQL Server name (and IP address) for the new clustered SQL Server instance. In addition, for the client applications to work, you need to have the appropriate databases restored or installed on the new cluster. This is necessary if you want a highly available cluster solution.

After you have each of your client applications connected to the SQL Server instance, you are ready for testing. Keep in mind that you are testing multiple things, including the Windows 2008 Cluster, the clustered SQL Server, and the client applications.

Moving Resource Groups Between Nodes

The easiest test to perform is to use the Failover Cluster Management tool to manually move the SQL Server resource group from the active node to a passive node, and then back again. To do this, follow these steps:

1. Go to the resource group that contains SQL Server, right click to select Move This Service, and specify where you'd like to move the resource group. This initiates the resource group move from your active node to the designated passive node.

2. After this happens, check the Failover Cluster Management tool and each of the client applications. Each should continue to operate as if no failover had occurred. The Failover Cluster Management tool should pass this test easily. The clients are another story; you must check each client application to see if it reconnected. If not, you need to determine why not, which is not always easy. Most client applications that stop working after a failover do so because of no reconnect logic for. For example, they reconnect if you exit and restart the client application.

3. When the resource group has been successfully moved from the active node to a passive node, use the same procedure to move the group back to the original node; and as before, check the Failover Cluster Management tool, the client applications, and the event logs to see if there were any problems. If you noticed any Windows Failover Cluster or SQL Server problems because of the failover test, you need to resolve them before proceeding. If you have a client applications problem, you can continue with your testing and try to resolve it later. In most cases, if a client application fails this first test, it will fail all the other tests.

Manually Failing Over Nodes by Turning Them Off

To validate that the failover from node to node is taking place and that each node can take over the SQL Server, you can perform a failover test by manually turning nodes off.

1. Turn off the active node. When this happens, watch the failover in the Failover Cluster Management tool and the client applications. As before, check for any problems.

2. Next, turn on the node and wait until it boots back up successfully. Then turn off the now current active node. Again, watch the failover in the Failover Cluster Management tool and the client applications, and check for problems.

3. Turn the node back on when done.

Manually Failing Over Nodes by Disconnecting the Public Network Connections

You can also manually failover nodes by turning off public network connections.

1. Unplug the public network connection from the active node. This causes a failover to a passive node, which you can watch in the Failover Cluster Management tool and the client applications. Check for any problems.

2. Now plug the public network connection back into the server and unplug the public network connection from the now active node. This causes a failover to the current passive node, which you can watch in the Failover Cluster Management tool. Watch the failover in the Failover Cluster Management tool and the client applications, and check for problems.

3. When the testing is complete, plug the network connection back into the node.

Manually Failing Over Nodes by Breaking the Shared Array Connection

You can perform a third manual failover test by breaking a shared array connection.

1. From the active node, remove the shared disk array connection. This can cause a failover that you can watch in the Failover Cluster Management tool and client applications. Check for any problems.

2. Next, reconnect the connection from the now active node, and remove the shared disk array connection. Watch the failover in the Failover Cluster Management tool and the client applications, and check for problems.

3. When done, reconnect the connection. If you run into problems in any of these tests, resolve them before continuing.

MANAGING AND MONITORING THE CLUSTER

After you have your clustered SQL Server up, running, and tested, you are ready to deploy it into production. This may involve creating new databases, moving databases from older servers to this one, setting up SQL jobs, and so on. In most cases, managing SQL Server on a cluster is the same as managing it as a standalone SQL Server instance. The key thing to keep in mind is that whenever you access your cluster with any of your SQL Server 2012 administrative tools, such as Management Studio, you access it using its SQL cluster network name and IP address; but if you use any of the operating system tools, such as System Monitor, you need to use the SQL cluster network or IP address of the node to monitor (which is usually the active node).

In most cases, as a DBA, you probably will administer SQL Server 2012 using Management Studio, but sometimes you need to access the individual nodes of the cluster. If you have easy access to the cluster, you can always log on locally; if you prefer remote administration, you can use Remote Desktop (Terminal Services) to access the individual nodes.

When DBAs begin to administer their first Windows Failover cluster, they get a little confused as to where SQL Server actually runs. Keep in mind that a clustered SQL Server instance consists of an active node which is running a SQL Server and the passive node which is not running a SQL Server. At any one time, a SQL Server instance runs on the active node only, so when you need to look at the nodes directly, generally you want to look at the active node. If you don't know which node is currently active, you can find out by using the Failover Cluster Management tool.

When you log into the active node (or connect to it remotely using Remote Desktop) and then bring up Windows Explorer (a routine task), you can access the SQL Server shared data disks; but if you log on to the passive node, you cannot access the SQL Server shared data disks. This is because drives can be accessed from only a single SQL Server node at a time.

If you access your cluster through Remote Desktop (Terminal Services), be aware of a couple of odd behaviors. For example, if you use Remote Desktop to connect to the cluster using the SQL cluster network name or IP address, you will connect to the active node, just as if you used Remote Desktop to connect to the active node directly (using its network name and IP address); but if a failover should occur and you use Remote Desktop to access the cluster using the SQL cluster network name and IP address, Remote Desktop gets a little confused, especially if you use Windows Explorer. For example, you may discover that your data drives no longer appear to be accessible, even though they actually are. To resolve this problem, you may need to log out of Remote Desktop and reconnect after the failover.

TROUBLESHOOTING CLUSTER PROBLEMS

Troubleshooting cluster-related issues require a lot of fortitude, persistence, and experience, and a support contract with Microsoft Technical Support. The problem is that clustering is somewhat complex and requires that you know hardware, shared disk array, hardware drivers, operating systems, clustering services, and SQL Server. Any problem you have could be caused by any one of them, and identifying the exact cause of a problem is often difficult.

Another reason cluster troubleshooting is difficult is that the feedback you get, in the form of messages or logs, is not easy to understand, assuming you get any feedback at all. And when you do get feedback, the resources for identifying and remedying problems are minimal.

Because of all this, if you have a Windows Failover Cluster, you should plan to purchase Microsoft Technical Support. This is a good investment, and one that will pay for itself. The authors have used Microsoft Technical Support many times, and in most cases it assisted adequately. You don't need to automatically call support as soon as you have a problem; always try to identify and resolve problems on your own if you can. But at some point, especially if your cluster is down and you need assistance getting it back up, you need to recognize when you can't resolve the problem by yourself and when you need outside help.

The next section includes some general advice to get you started when you need to identify and resolve cluster-related problems.

How to Approach Windows Failover Clustering Troubleshooting

The discussion about how to install clustering in this chapter emphasized the importance of testing each task after it is performed and only proceeding to the next step if everything works. This methodical approach helps you more easily identify causes the problem as soon as possible after it happens. For example, if things work correctly but you perform a task and the test fails, you can fairly assume that what you just did is directly or indirectly responsible for the problem, making problem identification easier. If you don't perform regular testing and don't notice a problem until after many tasks have been performed, identifying the cause of a problem or problems is much more difficult. Therefore, the best way to troubleshoot problems is to perform incremental testing. This also makes it much easier if you have a detailed installation plan that you can follow, helping to ensure that you perform all the necessary steps (including testing at appropriate places).

Doing It Right the First Time

You can save a lot of troubleshooting problems by preventing them. Here's how:

➤ Be sure that all the hardware for the physical nodes and shared disk array passes the Cluster Validation.

➤ Ensure that you use the latest hardware and software drivers and service packs.

➤ Create a detailed installation plan that you can use as your guide for the installation and for disaster recovery should the need arise.

➤ Learn as much as you can about Windows Failover Cluster before you begin your installation. Many cluster problems are user-created because the people responsible guessed instead of knowing for sure what they needed to do.

➤ Develop a Windows Failover Cluster runbook identifying the state, configuration, and instructions on running each cluster to establish a consistent and stable system.

Gathering Information

To help identify the cause of a problem, you often need a lot of information. Unfortunately, the information you need may not exist, or it may be scattered about in many different locations, or it may be downright misleading. In any event, to troubleshoot problems, you need to find as much information as you can. To try to combat these issues, use the following guidelines and resources when gathering information to troubleshoot a cluster problem:

➤ **Know what is supposed to happen.** If you expect a specific result, and you are not getting it, be sure that you fully understand what is supposed to happen, and exactly what is happening. In other words, know the difference between the two.

➤ **Know what happened directly before the problem occurred.** This is much easier if you test incrementally, as described earlier.

➤ **Know whether the problem is repeatable.** Not all problems can be easily repeated, but if they can, the repetition can provide useful information.

➤ **Take note of any onscreen error messages.** Be sure that you take screen captures of any messages for reference. Some DBAs have the habit of clicking OK after an error message without recording its exact content. Often, the exact content of a message is helpful if you need to search the Internet to learn more about it.

➤ **View logs.** There are a variety of logs you can view, depending on how far along you are in the cluster setup process. These include the three operating system logs: the cluster log (located at `c:\windows\cluster\cluster.log`); the SQL Server 2012 Setup log files (located at `%ProgramFiles%\Microsoft SQL Server\110\Setup Bootstrap\LOG\ Summary.txt`); and the SQL Server 2012 log files. There can be a variety of error messages in the log; once you identify the error, you can perform a web search to see if anyone else has had this error and if there are any suggestions around on how to resolve.

➤ **Perform an Internet search for the error message.** If the error messages you identify aren't obvious (are they ever?), search on the Internet, including newsgroups.

The more information you can gather about a problem, the better position you are to resolve the problem.

Resolving Problems

Many cluster problems are due to the complexity of the software involved, and it is sometimes faster to just rebuild the cluster from scratch, including the operating system. This is especially true if you have tried to install Windows Failover Cluster or clustered SQL Server and the setup process aborted during setup and did not setup itself cleanly.

When you build a new Windows Failover cluster, rebuilding it to resolve problems is usually an option because time is not an issue. However, suppose you have a clustered SQL Server in production and it fails where neither node works. Since time now becomes an issue, you should bring in Microsoft.

Working with Microsoft

Operating a clustered SQL Server without having a Microsoft Technical Support contract is like operating a car without insurance. You can do it, but if you have any unexpected problems, you will be sorry you went without.

Generally, there are two main reasons to call Microsoft Technical Support for clustering issues. The first situation would be when it's a noncritical issue that you just can't figure out for yourself. In this case, you will be assigned an engineer, and over a period of several days, you work with that engineer to resolve that problem. This may involve running diagnostics to gather information about your cluster so the Microsoft support engineer can diagnose it.

The second reason to call is because your production cluster is down, and there are no obvious solutions that you know of to get it quickly back up. Generally, in this case, call Microsoft Technical Support as soon as you can to get the problem ticket started. In addition, you should emphasize to the technical call screener (the first person who answers the phone) and the support engineer you is assigned to that you are facing a production down situation and that you want to declare a *critical situation (critsit)*. This tells Microsoft that your problem is top priority, and you will get special attention. When you declare a critsit, the person on the phone will validate that it is a critsit because it causes a chain of events to happen within Microsoft Technical Support; but if your production cluster is down, you need to emphasize the serious nature of your problem. If it is, you can get immediate help with your problem until your Windows Failover Cluster is resolved.

SUMMARY

This chapter represents only the tip of the iceberg when it comes to covering everything the DBA should know about clustering SQL Server 2012. It is important to understand the basics around installing, configuring, testing monitoring, troubleshooting and maintaining a Windows 2008 Failover Cluster running SQL Server 2012. To successfully install a Windows Failover Cluster, start with identifying the hardware and verify that it meets the cluster prerequisites. Follow step-by-step to configure the hardware to be clustered. All of these steps must be configured as described; any variation will likely prevent the cluster to install successfully. You should run the Cluster Validation to verify that the cluster configuration can be clustered; if any errors are identified, address them before proceeding. Then, you may go ahead and create the cluster. Determine the need for MSDTC(s) and install them. Using the SQL Server 2012 setup, install the SQL Server instance on the cluster. You can have more than one SQL Server instance on a node, or have many nodes each running SQL Server instances supported by a passive node or even without a passive node. Run the SQL Server 2012 setup to install additional SQL Server cluster instances. Clustering can be combined to offer high availability and disaster recovery by deploying a geographically dispersed cluster where a cluster is established with nodes that live across two data centers which may even be on different subnets. There are different Windows Failover Cluster deployed configurations possible that you can learn more about by reading clustering articles, the SQL Server 2012 Books Online, and any additional information from the Microsoft's website and elsewhere on the Internet.

17

Backup and Recovery

Data is a critical asset for an organization to maintain information about its customers, inventory, purchases, financials, and products. Over the course of many years, organizations amass information to improve the daily customer experience, as well as to leverage this information to support strategic decisions. Downtime is unacceptable and can be costly for the organization; for example, without their databases, a stock brokerage house cannot take stock orders and an airline cannot sell tickets. Every hour the database is down can add up to millions of dollars of business opportunities lost. To keep their business activities going, organizations deploy high-availability solutions, such as failover clustering, database mirroring, replication, and log shipping so that when a database server fails, they can continue to run their business on a standby database server. All these topics are covered in other chapters in this book.

In addition, the underlying storage for the database may be protected by the use of fault tolerant or highly available storage technologies such as Redundant Array of Inexpensive Disks (RAID). Even with these fault-tolerant technologies, businesses still need to have database backups to allow recovery from a data-corrupting event, from data loss, or as part of a disaster recovery plan to cover the complete failure of the primary data center.

Although a high-availability solution tries to keep the business data online, a database backup plan is crucial to protect the business data asset. If a data-error problem exists and the database is unrecoverable, the DBA can use the database backup to recover the database to a consistent state. Moreover, a good database backup strategy can reduce the amount of data loss for certain kinds of errors encountered during the course of the daily database activities. This chapter first presents an overview of backup and restore. Then you walk through planning and developing a backup plan, managing backups, and performing restores. You also explore data archiving and disaster recovery planning.

TYPES OF FAILURE

A variety of failures can bring down your database — anything from a user error to a natural disaster could take your database offline. Your backup and recovery plan needs to account for the possibility of these failures and more.

Hardware Failure

Hardware is more reliable than it has been in the past. However, components can still fail, including the CPU, memory, bus, network card, disk drives, and controllers. A database system on a high-availability solution can mitigate a hardware failure such that if one database server fails, SQL Server can failover to the standby database server. All this helps keep the database online. However, high-availability solutions cannot protect against a faulty controller or a disk that causes I/O failures and corrupts the data.

> *Use SQLIOSim to help identify the optimal disk configuration or troubleshoot I/O faults. SQLIOSim replaces SQLIOStress in prior releases. You can get more information or download SQLIOSism from* http://support.microsoft.com/ default.aspx?scid=kb;en-us;231619. *You can read more about running SQLIOSim in the Wiley Wrox book* Professional SQL Server 2005 Performance Tuning, *in Chapter 12, "How Fast and Robust Is Your Storage."*

Data Modification Failure

Data Modification failures are another way that your system can "fail." Data Modification Failures occur when the data is intentionally changed, but the change has unintentional side effects. This can happen when a user executes a poorly constructed query, or when an application has a bug that executes a query that deletes, updates, or inserts erroneous data. It can also occur when a user has too much privilege and has access to data that they should not.

User Error

A common user error is incorrectly restricting the scope of a TSQL query and modifying more rows than expected during an update or delete operation. As a preventive measure, users should test all data modification queries using a SELECT statement to test the action of their query, and the scope in the WHERE clause. After testing with a SELECT, you can achieve additional peace of mind by wrapping the whole data modification into an explicit transaction, starting the batch with a BEGIN TRANSACTION. Then users can verify that the correct number of rows was updated before executing a COMMIT TRANSACTION. If the data modifications were not performed inside a transaction, the data will be permanently changed. In some cases a bad update can be reversed when it is an UPDATE, but in the case of a DELETE, the data must be reentered, which makes recovery a lot harder, and requires the use of a data recovery operation, either to reload an affected table completely, or to recover the data from a restored database backup.

 In large data update operations, it is common practice to take a copy of the affected tables using BCP so that you have an additional option to recover data in the event of an undetected bug in your TSQL code. This is not always an option, especially if the table is large or there is not adequate space on disk to store the bcp data. Another reason for not using BCP is if the database has complex foreign key relationships. This can make it much harder to reconstruct "damaged" data other than to restore a complete database backup.

Application Failure

The user application may contain a bug that causes unwanted data modifications. To prevent this possibility, the application should go through a strict QA process to uncover any such bugs. However, there is no guarantee that an undetected bug may not cause unwanted data modifications in the future. When the bug is detected and corrected, the DBA may need to recover the database from backup or possibly use a log explorer utility. The process needs to identify the time that the problem occurred and to recover to that point in time.

Too Much Privilege

Sometimes applications use SQL Server logins that have more privilege than necessary. That is, instead of restricting security to just what the application needs, it is faster and easier to just grant DBO or sysadmin security. As a result, the application with this privilege may delete data from the wrong table because of either a bug or a user accidentally using a free-form query window. To reduce this risk, give application users only the database permissions required to do their work, and restrict sysadmin and DBO permissions only to users who need them and have the experience to know how to use them.

 DBA, this also applies to you. It is fairly common for DBAs to type in a quick update to fix some problem. Just as you press the key to execute the query, you realize that you have made a huge mistake but are powerless to stop the execution. That sinking feeling that you have messed things up happens quickly. This is another reason to have a Test or QA system available to run all queries on first before running them in production. Make your mistakes on the test or QA system, not in production. If you don't have the ability to test on a Test or QA system first, then try using a low-privileged account as well as your high-privilege account. Use the low-privilege account for routine activity, switching to your high-privilege account only when necessary. This also raises your awareness, enabling you to avoid mistakes.

Software Failure

The operating system can fail, as can the relational database system. A software driver may be faulty and cause data corruption; for example, the I/O hardware controller may function correctly, but the software driver may not. One preventive measure is to keep the system current with service packs and patches, including security patches. The DBA may choose any of the following patch-management solutions:

➤ Automatic updates from Windows Update

➤ Microsoft Update

➤ Corporate Windows Server Update Services (WSUS)

➤ SMS

➤ System Center Configuration Manager

➤ A partner solution to keep the servers updated

Unfortunately, some of these updates may require you to restart the SQL Server process or reboot the Windows OS that causes some planned downtime. However, planned downtime can be mitigated by a high-availability solution, such as a Failover Cluster, that enables you to fail over to a standby database server. Choose a maintenance time frame when there is lowest user activity; identify the patches that require a reboot ahead of time, and apply them at one time whenever possible to enable only a single reboot. Record each software driver version, and check the vendor website for the most current updates. In addition, the driver must be approved for the computer hardware and the Windows version. Having a supported and updated driver version can make a significant difference to the reliability and performance of the hardware device.

 You should never do anything for the first time on a production database; test your patches on a Test or QA system before applying them to production. Then you can apply them all at once. You will know from your testing if a reboot is required. This should occur during a "planned" maintenance period. If you use clusters, you may failover, apply patches, and reboot one server while the other still provides access. That way, users see only a minimum interruption in service.

Local Disasters

An unexpected disaster can devastate an area, resulting in an inoperable or completely destroyed data center. In such cases, you need to relocate the data center, and that is where disaster planning comes into play: to quickly bring up the new data center and reopen for business. Depending on the disaster, data loss may occur because the location is inaccessible, and you may be unable to extract the last few data records. To reduce the exposure from a local disaster, a company can set up a disaster recovery site by means of data mirroring, a geographically dispersed failover cluster, log shipping, or replication.

MAKING PLANS

You (or your company) should have a plan for high availability, backup/recovery, and disaster recovery. There may be a plan for each, or they may all be included in a single document. In a small company, by default this task may fall directly on your shoulders. For larger companies, you may be part of a team that plans for these events. In all cases, a risk/benefit analysis must be done. You must consider the likelihood of the event occurring, the cost of the downtime and other potential costs associated with the event, and the cost of the solution. Your first job will be the research and documentation regarding the risks, costs, and benefits. Management will then decide which events to plan for and make the risk decision. The DBA is *not* the risk decision-maker — that's management's job. However, it *is* your job to ensure that management understands the issues and that a decision is made. It is then your job to implement whatever plan is necessary and to test the plan on a regular basis.

In this section you learn the basics of a backup/recovery plan and a disaster recovery plan. There is enough information about recovery plans to fill up entire books, so consider this a basic introduction. High availability is not covered here but you can find information on it in Chapters 15, 16, 18, and 19.

Backup/Recovery Plan

You or your team has the primary responsibility for the backup/recovery plan, including the following:

➤ Analyze business requirements.

➤ Categorize databases by recovery criteria.

➤ Document the plan.

➤ Validate, implement, and test the plan.

➤ Establish a failed backup notification policy.

➤ Maintain the plan.

Analyze Business Requirements

First, you must gather some requirements for your plan. You need to have answers to the following questions:

➤ **Who are the stakeholders/owners for each application or database?** You need to determine the people from whom you should ask questions. You must also identify the decision-makers who can approve your final plan.

➤ **What is the purpose for this database?** Knowing a database's purpose, such as whether it is for a data mart, a data warehouse, or the general ledger accounting database, gives you great insight into what might be necessary for your plan.

➤ **What is the acceptable downtime for the application/database in the case of an error, such as a disk drive error?** This is also known as the Recovery Time Objective (RTO).

You ask this question because it takes time to restore the database when a problem has occurred. Knowing the answer helps you design a backup/restore plan that works within the downtime constraints.

Often the first answer to this last question is, "There is no acceptable downtime." And this is a common answer from the business. A standard response to that is to let the company know that although that is potentially possible, they now added at least one, and possibly two, '0's to the end of the check they need to write to pay for the solution. This then leads into a more meaningful conversation around the costs associated with their answers. Now that there is a cost associated with the various options, you begin to get closer to the real need. This is an iterative process as you communicate with management and business users.

You may also need to get several answers, depending on business cycles. For instance, while finance is closing the monthly books, the cost of any downtime is extremely high. During the rest of the month, the cost of downtime is much less. You may choose to implement a different plan during month-end close than you do during the rest of the month. This might include more frequent log backups, or you may choose to implement a single plan that meets the strictest requirements. In either case, document everything.

It may be that this question should be broken down into two questions: What is the cost of downtime? How much cost is reasonable for the business to absorb?

➤ **What data changes and how often?** You ask this question to determine what types of backups are necessary. Maybe data changes during the nightly batch only and is read during the rest of the day. Maybe some tables change frequently, but others are historical. Maybe there are numerous updates but they occur on a small number of rows, while the rest of the database is read-only.

If the database is already in production, looking at the transaction log growth can also provide useful information.

➤ **How much data loss is acceptable?** This is another tricky question, and is also known as the Recovery Point Objective (RPO). What is the value of the data? What harm would befall the company if this data or part of it became lost? When thinking about this subject, you must also consider any regulatory requirements, as well. Some data must be kept available for a certain period of time. Some businesses may have a low tolerance for data loss, whereas others may tolerate a great deal of data loss. It depends not only on the value of the data, but also how much risk the business is willing to accept. You must also consider non-SQL Server options. For example, maybe the business cannot accept any loss of customer orders, but customer orders are entered manually and a paper copy is kept. If yesterday's orders were lost, someone could reenter the data. This might be a preferable solution — or not. The point is to consider all your business options, not just SQL Server backup/restore.

 The answer to these questions may change over time. As business processes change or as the business grows, the business requirements change. Therefore, your backup/restore plan may need to change. Review the requirements with the business on a regular basis that you deem reasonable. Document each review.

➤ **What is the size and growth of the database?** If this database has not been implemented, you are not likely to get great information, but get the best you can. For all implemented databases, your normal monitoring procedures can provide this information. You should also work in concert with any project teams that develop new projects around this database, which may change the answers to this and any of the other questions. For more information on estimating the size of your database, read the "Estimating the size of a database" topic in Books Online at `http://msdn.microsoft.com/en-us/library/ms187445.aspx`.

➤ **What is the maintenance window for this database?** Certain maintenance tasks that must be done on the database affect the online response. Items such as Database Console Commands (DBCCs), index maintenance, and potentially backups are among these items. Your plan must ensure that your work stays within the maintenance window.

➤ **What are the budget constraints for this database?** Often, there is no specific answer to this question. Instead, evaluating the risks and the costs is a negotiation process with the business. However, a specific budget exists; you certainly need to know what it is.

➤ **What is the notification plan for this database?** When errors occur for which you must restore, who should be notified? How should you notify them? In addition, how can you know when a database error occurs?

Categorize Databases by Recovery Criteria

If you have many databases, you can do yourself a favor by categorizing the databases into groups. Then you can have a plan for each group. You might categorize by the following criteria:

➤ **Criticality:** Is this database mission-critical?

➤ **Size:** Large databases need more time for backup/restore than small databases. However, you can mitigate the time with filegroup backups or other interim measures. Filegroup backups are covered later in this chapter.

➤ **Volatility:** Databases with a larger volume of data change need a different plan than inactive databases.

Once you categorize, you can name the groups something useful, like the following:

➤ Mission-Critical Large

➤ Mission-Critical Small

➤ Business-Critical

➤ Moderate Impact

➤ Low / No Impact / Noncritical

For each category, choose the following:

➤ **Recovery model:**

➤ **Full:** Used when no data loss is acceptable.

➤ **Bulk Logged:** Used when your database is using the Bulk Logged recovery model.

➤ **Simple:** Used when we can afford to lose data between full backups.

➤ **Backup plan:** All groups need a periodic full database backup. Depending on the category and recovery model, choose between differential backups, file/filegroup backups, and log backups. Also choose whether to use compression and which backup media to use.

➤ **Backup frequency:** How often should each of the backups be executed?

➤ **Backup security policy:** The Backup security policy will detail how long backups are retained, as well as how they are electronically and/or physically secured. For tape media, what is the rotation policy? How can you implement offsite storage? If you use disk-to-disk backups (using an external D2D device), or on-disk backups (writing backups to a separate set of local disks), how can you secure access to the backup file store?

Disaster Recovery Planning

Disaster recovery requires considerable planning. A local disaster can cause severe financial loss to the organization. To reduce this, the organization must quickly execute the disaster recovery (DR) plan to bring its systems online. It requires a robust disaster recovery plan and periodic DR drills to ensure that everything works as planned. Often, organizations have well-intended disaster recovery plans, but they have never tested them for readiness; then, in a real disaster, the plan does not go smoothly. DR planning is based on the specific organization's business requirements, but some general areas need to be addressed to put any plan into action.

➤ Use project management software, such as Microsoft Project, whereby people, resources, hardware, software, and tasks and their completion can be input to provide a systematic approach to managing the tasks, resources, and critical paths.

➤ Develop a checklist of detailed steps for recovery. More information on what should be on this checklist is covered in the next section.

Disaster recovery solutions with Windows failover clusters are commonly used to provide hardware redundancy within the data center site and can be configured across data centers by using a geographically dispersed Windows Server Failover Cluster. Prior to Windows Server 2008, this required expensive SAN based solutions. Windows Server 2008 eased the restrictions around subnets, and heartbeat latency, which now makes it easier to implement a geographically dispersed cluster. However, this is still an extremely complicated, expensive option. Moreover, AlwaysOn Availability groups, database mirroring, replication, and log shipping can all be inexpensively deployed as alternate disaster recovery solutions.

Some organizations have a standby disaster recovery site available to take over all operations or, at the least, the mission-critical operations. A few of these organizations failover to the disaster recovery site periodically to validate that their plan can work in a real disaster. Others may not have a disaster recovery plan but an agreement with another organization that offers disaster recovery capabilities.

If you are going to implement a Disaster Recovery Site, then you need compatible hardware at the DR Site. If this hardware is not already available, you need a plan to acquire the hardware required to bring the organization online quickly. Document the current necessary hardware. For computers, consider the number and type of CPUs and speed, Intel versus AMD, hyper-threading, number of cores, disk drive capacity, RAID level, and the amount of physical memory required. Preferably, try to acquire the exact hardware to minimize surprises. For the storage subsystem, consider the disk space requirements, the number of LUNs required, and the RAID level. For the network, acquire a similar network infrastructure to maintain the same performance. Some questions to ask include the following:

➤ How quickly can these computers be made available? Who will deliver or pick up the hardware?

➤ Will the computers be preconfigured, or will the DR team need to configure them? Who will provide the expertise, and what is the availability for that staff resource?

➤ Will the storage be preconfigured with the LUNs and RAID levels, or will the DR team need to configure it? Who will provide the expertise, and what is the availability for that staff resource?

➤ Who will acquire the network equipment, and who will have the expertise to set it up and configure it?

➤ Will the DR site have Internet access — to download service packs, for hotfixes, and for e-mail?

Make a detailed list of all software required, any hotfixes, and service packs. Take an inventory of how each is going to be available to the DR team. Make sure that the software is at the required version level and that licensing keys are available and valid. Determine who is responsible to make available the software and the contact information for that staff member. If the software is in a certain location, know who has the physical keys and what access they have. In this scenario, 24/7 access is required. In the event of a disaster, you need a list of staff resources to be contacted, which must be current and therefore periodically updated. Know who is responsible to maintain this list and where it will be found during a disaster. You also need to know the chain of command and who is onsite and offsite.

Additionally, you should create a detailed plan of the onsite roles required to execute the plan and who will fill those roles. Ensure that there is a backup resource in case a staff resource is missing. Determine how many staff are needed in each role, how they will arrive at the site, and who will be the overall project manager or lead to escalate any issues. Assign and record who has the passwords and what logins are required to make the systems available for business.

As mentioned previously, the DR site must be accessible 24/7 and conveniently located. As larger DR deployment can take days to execute, the site should have beds for staff to take naps and easy access to food and transportation. Identify who has the key to access the remote site; if that person is not available, who is the designated replacement? Can resources remotely access the site if they must work from a remote location, and what is required to have remote access turned on? Are the backups for all the databases available at the DR site, or who is responsible to bring them there? If that staff resource is unavailable, who is the designated replacement?

To ensure that the DR plan will work during a real disaster and to reduce loss, as a best practice, periodically simulate a disaster drill and put the DR planning in action to identify any steps that were not taken into account, how quickly the organization can be expected to be online again, and areas that can be streamlined to speed the process. Most importantly, ensure that the plan will execute as expected, smoothly and quickly. To get the most effect from this simulated scenario, everyone should approach it as if it were a real disaster and take all actions exactly as planned.

Creating the Disaster Recovery Plan

To create your Disaster Recovery plan, start by collecting some important information. First, interview the business owners of any applications that use databases under your control. You need to find out from them what their requirements are in the event of a disaster. This information enables you to start categorizing the databases under your control into different classes of disaster recovery options. This categorization might be as simple as Databases That Need Disaster Recovery, and Databases That Don't Need Disaster Recovery. Or, if everyone needs disaster recovery, but some need to be able to continue running while other systems are okay with hours, days, or weeks of down time before they are online at the disaster recovery site, this could be another way to categorize the databases.

You will also need to document the following information:

> ➤ Contact list

> ➤ Decision tree

> ➤ Recovery success criteria

> ➤ Location of keys, backups, software, and hardware

> ➤ Infrastructure documentation

You should have a *contact list* of management people who can declare and activate the emergency callout. All necessary contact information must be available. Make sure that you know how to contact people in the event of an emergency and that relevant staff are potentially waiting for a call, email, text, page, and so on. You also need to document alternate contact points in the event that people are out of phone coverage, on a flight somewhere, with a dead phone battery, or otherwise un-contactable. Having that alternate contact point could make the difference between finding someone to help, and not being able to get your Disaster recovery plan started. The procedures for responding must also be documented (such as who makes calls).

You should also have a contact list for everything else. This list should include vendors, technicians, off-site storage people, service people, parts suppliers, transportation companies, and so on — everyone! The list should also include backups when primaries cannot be contacted.

Departments should have fallback operational procedures; although, this might not be in your documents. It is more likely this would be in departmental documentation. However, both plans should sync and make sense when put together.

The *decision tree* specifies what you need to do based on the circumstances. You may have a separate decision tree for disaster recovery than the one you use for normal recovery. When a disaster strikes and mission-critical processes are down, things can get stressful. The decision tree prompts you, so you mostly just follow the plan, instead of making on-the-fly mistakes. The decision tree must be logical, clear, and easy to understand and follow because you will be using it under duress. Keep it simple to the point where it can be completed while still encompassing enough to cover most scenarios.

The decision tree should classify database loss scenarios, such as natural disasters — for example, hurricane, earthquake, and so on — that can affect a wide area. You may not rely on locally held backups, software, or hardware. The tree must cover single-location loss — power loss, fire, explosion; you might recover to a site close to the affected location.

The specific decision tree for your purposes should include normal recovery scenarios, such as single server/data corruption or single database loss, disk drive, controller, memory failure, user error, and application failure. You should work to recover the missing data quickly, while not affecting other systems.

Another item you might include in your decision tree is loss of performance or service. In these cases, the database is not damaged but inaccessible or slow. You should debug and correct this quickly. Refer to Chapter 13 for guidance on performance tuning T-SQL.

The decision tree should also prioritize recovery steps. Thinking about these steps can enable you to make a plan that minimizes downtime and maximizes parallel work between all the players who need to be involved.

The decision tree should identify the most critical databases so that recovery can be completed in the best order for the business. Don't forget about dependencies between databases.

Critical processes should be identified in the decision tree: SQL Server Integration Services (SSIS), SQL Server Analysis Services (SSAS), SQL Agent, Extract, Transform, Load (ETL) processes, and so on. What should be done for each of these processes? For instance, you might need to stop a process scheduler until the restore is complete.

You may also include security failures, whereby the database health is okay, but security is compromised due to malicious software, individual access, virus attack, and so on. You should discover security breaches and protect data. Refer to Chapter 8 for guidance on securing the database instance.

The *recovery success criteria* can be layered and may include service-level agreements (SLAs). When talking about SLAs, two terms come up very frequently and are discussed in the following list:

➤ **Recovery Time Objective (RTO)**: Recovery Time Objective is the amount of time that you have to restore a particular system to operation in the event of a disaster. An RTO of 8 hours means that the affected system must be operational after a disaster within 8 hours from the disaster occurring.

➤ **Recovery Point Objective (RPO)**: Recovery Point Objective is a measure of the amount of data that can be lost from a system in the event of a disaster. An RPO of 8 hours means that it is acceptable to lose any data entered in the 8 hour period before a disaster.

The first measure of success could be that you have met the SLA on RTO, such that the system is online again within the RTO period. The second level of success is that the RPO has been met, and that no more than the acceptable amount of data as defined by the RPO has been lost. Be sure you understand and document these criteria; you are likely to be measured by them.

Your documentation should include everything you need to get the job done. The location of keys or keyholders and the ability to contact and arrange for offsite storage people to deliver backups is important. Hardware, or access to and a prompt response from hardware people, as well as software support and availability of the software disks is also necessary. You should also have easy access to the levels of software, service packs, and driver levels for your server.

Any other *infrastructure documentation* you might need should also be included, such as naming conventions, DNS, or network information — anything you need to get the job done.

List recovery steps in the correct order based on business needs. Don't assume you will think calmly and make the best decisions on-the-fly when bad things happen. Make all the basic decisions in advance, and when the bad thing happens, engage your brain, but follow the documented process.

Validating, Implementing, and Testing the Plan

This is often not nearly as difficult as getting the proper information from the business — so don't worry. If you can get the true needs of the business, then you can usually implement your backup/restore plan. Of course, no plan is good if it doesn't work, and you won't know whether it works until you test it.

The people who need to implement this plan should practice it regularly through testing. You should plan for regular testing. Test at some well known period, maybe every 6 months. Also test anytime changes are made to the systems that require changes to plans. Make sure that any new staff understands the plans. Ideally, have new staff training that includes at least a discussion of these plans, and preferably include a practice run through for code Disaster scenarios. Anytime there is a significant percentage change in staff since the last planned test, run another test.

Make sure that testing includes setting up secondary servers, completing the restores, and making the applications/data available. You should simulate failures as well, and practice the responses to them. Simulated failures might be loss of the most recent full backup or a transaction log. You should consider that the restore sight might be in a different time zone, or a database might be much, much larger than it used to be. What happens if key people do not respond or your contact list is inaccurate? What if access cards no longer work or keys are not available?

Failed Backup Notification Policy

Because the success of your plan depends on successful backups, you need a plan to receive notification when backups fail. Remember you don't have a backup until it's copied to a separate server, restored, and checked to be valid, so routinely restoring backups and validating should be an integral part of your planning.

You should also use DBCC commands to ensure that you back up a healthy database. In addition, the database backups should occur after other normal maintenance tasks, such as database shrinking and index maintenance. This is because when you have to restore from a database backup, you are restoring a database ready to go and not a database in need of additional maintenance.

Maintaining the Plan

Following are four steps to successfully maintain the plan:

> **Communicate the plan:** For effective communication, the documentation should be publicly available within your company; and IT, the business users, and management should be informed of its content and location.

> **Establish a policy to periodically rehearse the plan:** Some companies carry out a drill every other year; others do this annually. You might have a complete companywide call out once

a year and an IT test more frequently. In any case, you must test the plan on a schedule. Infrastructure changes and software and hardware updates can all conspire to make your plan unusable. You may have worked hard to do all the steps up to this point, and you may have done them all perfectly, but when disaster strikes, you will be measured solely by your ability to actually recover, not by how fine a plan you may have. Rehearsal is the only way to guarantee success.

➤ **Establish a policy to periodically validate the plan:** The policy to periodically validate the plan centers around the changing business environment. The business may have changed processes, or the ability or willingness to absorb risk, or some other factor that may have invalidated your plan. You should revalidate the information you gathered from the business and reassess your plan on a scheduled basis. In addition, be aware of new projects and how they may affect your planning.

➤ **Revise the plan as needed:** The last requirement is to keep the plan up to date. Revisit the plan, and revise whenever needed. It is fairly common to come up with a plan and then let it grow stale on the shelf. This often renders the plan useless or, even worse, dangerous to use.

OVERVIEW OF BACKUP AND RESTORE

Before you can effectively formulate a backup and restore plan, you need to know how backup and recovery work on a mechanical level. SQL Server has several different backup and restore processes that you can use, depending on the needs of your organization. This section examines how backup and restore work and helps you choose the best plan for your needs.

How Backup Works

Database backup is a procedure that safeguards your organization's investment to reduce the amount of data loss. A database backup is the process of making a point-in-time copy of the data and transaction log into an image on either disks or tapes. SQL Server implements versatile backup processes that can be used separately or together to produce the optimal backup strategy required by an organization. Moreover, SQL Server can perform the database backup while it is online and available to users. In addition, it supports up to 64 concurrent backup devices. The following types of backup are available:

➤ **Full backup:** This is a copy of all data in the database, including the transaction log. Using this backup type, you can restore the database to the point in time when the backup was taken. It is the most basic of the backups and is often required prior to any of the other backup types. When restoring from a full database backup, all the database files are restored without any other dependencies, the database is available, and it is transactionally consistent.

➤ **Partial backup:** This is a way to back up only those parts of the database that change. This reduces the size of the backup and the time it takes to backup and restore. It is a copy of the primary filegroup and read/write filegroups. To take advantage of this type of backup, you need to group together the tables that change into a set of filegroups and the tables that are static or history in a different set of filegroups. The filegroups containing historical data will be marked read/write or read-only. A partial backup normally includes the primary filegroup and read-write filegroups, but read-only filegroups can optionally be included. A partial backup can speed up the backup process for databases with large read-only areas. For example, a large database may have archival data that does not change, so there is no need to back it up every time, which reduces the amount of data to back up.

➤ **File/filegroup backup:** This is a copy of selected files or filegroups of a database. This method is typically used for large databases for which it is not feasible to do a full database backup. A transaction-log backup is needed with this backup type if the backup includes read/write files or filegroups. The challenge is maintaining the files, filegroups, and transaction-log backups because larger databases have many files and filegroups. It also requires more steps to restore the database.

 During a file or filegroup backup, a table and all its indexes must be backed up in the same backup. SQL Server checks for this and sends an error when this rule is violated. To take advantage of file/filegroup backups, you may need to plan the location of your indexes with the backup plan in mind.

➤ **Differential backup:** This is a copy of all the data that has changed since the last full backup. The SQL Server 2012 backup process identifies each changed extent and backs it up. Differentials are cumulative: If you do a full backup on Sunday night, the differential taken on Monday night includes all the changes since Sunday night. If you take another differential on Tuesday night, it includes all the changes since Sunday night. When restoring, you would restore the last full database backup and the most recent differential backup. Then you would restore any transaction-log backups since the last differential. This can mean quicker recovery. Whether differentials are good for you depends on what percentage of rows change between full database backups. As the percentage of rows changed approaches the number of rows in the database, the differential backup gets closer to the size of an entire database backup. When this occurs, it is often better to get another full database backup and start a new differential.

Another benefit to use differentials is realized when a group of rows is repeatedly changed. Remember that a transaction log backup includes each change that is made. The differential backup includes only the last change for a row. Imagine a database that keeps track of 100 stock values. The stock value is updated every minute. Each row is updated 1,440 times per day. Consider a full database backup on Sunday night and transaction-log backups during the week. At the end of the day Friday, restoring from all the transaction logs would mean that you have to replay each change to each row. In this case, each row would be updated 7,200 times (1,440 times/day times 5 days). When you include 100 stocks, the restore would have to replay 720,000 transactions. If you had done a differential backup at the end of each day, you would have to replace only the 100 rows. The differential keeps the most recent version only; and in some situations, it can be a great solution.

➤ **Partial differential backup:** This works the same as a differential backup but is matched to data from a partial backup. It is a copy of all extents modified since the last partial backup. To restore requires the partial backup.

➤ **File differential backup:** This is a copy of the file or filegroup of all extents modified since the last file or filegroup backup. A transaction-log backup is required after this backup for read/write files or filegroups. Moreover, after the restore, you need to restore the transaction log as well. Using the file backup and file differential backup methods increases the complexity of the restore procedures. Furthermore, it may take longer to restore the complete database.

➤ **Copy-only backup:** This can be made for the database or transaction log. The copy-only backup does not interfere with the normal backup restore procedures. A normal full database backup resets the differential backups made afterward, whereas a copy-only backup does not affect the next differential backup; it still contains the changes since the last full backup. A copy-only backup of the transaction log does not truncate the log or affect the next normal transaction log backup. Copy-only backups are useful when you want to make a copy of the database for testing or development purposes without affecting the restore process. Copy-only backups are not supported in SSMS and must be done via T-SQL.

The transaction log in SQL Server is a main component for a relational database system that maintains the ACID properties for transactions: atomicity, consistency, isolation, and durability. SQL Server implements the write ahead logging (WAL) protocol, which means that the transaction-log records are written to a stable media prior to the data being written to disk and before SQL Server sends an acknowledgment that the data has been permanently committed. Stable media is usually a directly attached disk drive, but it can be any device that guarantees that on power loss, no data will be lost. Even on direct attached systems, this can be a challenge; as disk drives implement write caches, RAID controllers, even at the simplest level, also implement caches, which either need to be write-disabled, or battery-backed. Any external storage system such as a SAN system must also be checked to confirm that the cache is battery-backed and will guarantee the consistency of any written log records during a power failure. There is a new trend for using solid state storage devices, which can take many forms. If you leverage these devices, you need to ensure that they either deliver guarantees around writes if a power failure occurs, or that they are used in places where write cache performance is not an issue, such as if used for tempdb, where all data is deleted in the event of a system restart. An increasingly common trend on high-performance systems that need the highest levels of Transaction Log write performance is to place the Transaction Log on solid state storage. Although this is great from a performance perspective, you must also guarantee that the log records can survive a power outage.

The SQL Server database engine expects the Transaction Log to be consistent on restart; if it is not, it will identify the database as corrupted because the data consistency of the database cannot be determined.

In addition, when a data modification occurs, SQL Server generates a new log sequence number (LSN) used on restart to identify the consistency of the data while performing database recovery. The LSN is used when restoring the transaction log; SQL Server uses it to determine the sequences of each transaction log restored. If, for example, a transaction-log backup from a backup log chain is not available, that is known as a *broken log chain*, which prevents a transaction-log recovery past that point. Backing up the transaction log to point-in-time recovery is a critical part of a backup strategy. A DBA can perform three types of transaction-log backup:

➤ **Pure transaction-log backup:** This is when there have not been any bulk-logged operations performed on the database. That is, every data modification performed is represented in the transaction log. The database recovery model can be in Full or Bulk-Logged mode, provided that no bulk-logged operation has been performed. This is the most common transaction-log backup type because it best protects the data and provides the capability to recover to a point in time.

➤ **Bulk transaction-log backup:** This is when bulk-logged operations have been performed in the database, so point-in-time recovery is not allowed. To improve performance on bulk operations — that is, to reduce transaction logging — the database can be set in the bulk-logged recovery model whereby only the allocation pages are logged, not the actual data modifications in the transaction log. During a transaction-log backup, SQL Server extracts and includes the bulk-logged data inside the transaction-log backup to allow recoverability.

There is no syntax difference between the pure transaction log backup and the bulk transaction log backup. SQL Server works automatically to back up whatever is available and necessary. The descriptions of the three transaction-log backups can help you understand the difference between the recovery models.

➤ **Tail transaction-log backup:** This is a transaction-log backup that you make after the database has been damaged. Imagine you take a full database backup every night and do transaction-log backups on the hour. Your data files are corrupted at 1:30 P.M. Your last log backup occurred at 1:00 P.M., so you can recover until that time. What about the transactions that occurred between 1:00 P.M. and 1:30 P.M.? The transaction log disk is still good, but you cannot do a normal transaction log backup now because the database is not accessible. The tail transaction-log backup enables you to do a final transaction log backup, even when the database is unavailable to capture the transactions between 1:00 P.M. and 1:30 P.M. That way, you can restore up to 1:30 P.M. Whew — what a save! The biggest risk here is forgetting to do the backup. When you have confirmed that you must go through a restore, do this backup first.

A tail transaction-log backup cannot be performed if the database is in the bulk-logged recovery model and bulk operations have been performed because the transaction-log backup would need to retrieve the data modifications for the bulk operations from the data files, which are not accessible.

Copying Databases

There are times when you don't need a backup of the database, but might want a copy of the data instead. This section covers several ways that you can copy a database.

Detach/Attach

Detach/Attach is a great way to move a database to a new server. However it can also be used to create a copy. The Detach/Attach feature detaches the database or shuts down SQL Server. After the files are detached, you can use the OS to copy the database files to a backup device. To back up the database files using this method, you detach the database like this:

```
EXEC MASTER.dbo.sp_detach_db @dbname = N'AdventureWorks2012',
@keepfulltextindexfile=N'TRUE'
```

To restore, you attach the database files like this:

```
EXEC MASTER.dbo.sp_attach_db @dbname = N'AdventureWorks2012',
@filename1=N'C:\ProgramFiles\Microsoft SQL Server\MSSQL11.MSSQLSERVER
\MSSQL\Data\AdventureWorks2012_Data .mdf'
,@filename2=N'C:\ProgramFiles\Microsoft SQL Server\MSSQL11.MSSQLSERVER
\MSSQL\Data\AdventureWorks2012_log.ldf' ;
```

The drive letter "C" as well as the rest of the file location should be changed to reflect the directory where your data files are stored. The example uses the default location for data files.

> *If you attach an encrypted database, the database owner must open the master key of the database by using the following command:*
>
> ```
> OPEN MASTER KEY DECRYPTION BY PASSWORD = '<password>'
> ```
>
> *Microsoft recommends you enable automatic decryption of the master key by using the following command:*
>
> ```
> ALTER MASTER KEY ADD ENCRYPTION BY SERVICE MASTER KEY
> ```

BCP

The second backup option is done through BCP. You can run it via a simple batch script and export all the data from a database. This doesn't capture everything in the database, but it can be a useful way to get a copy of specific data within the database.

If you need to export more than 2 billion rows from a table, you MUST use BCP from SQL Server 2008 onward. There was a bug in older versions of BCP (SQL Server 2005, and older) that prevented it from exporting or importing more than 2 billion rows, and it also failed to report any error.

Following are two example BCP command lines that show how to export (OUT) and import (IN) a table called People from the Seattle_SQL server to the London_SQL server.

```
BCP address OUT address.dat -SSeattle_SQL -T -c -dPeople
BCP address IN address.dat -SLondon_SQL -T -c -dPeople
```

Scripting Wizard

SSMS provides a scripting wizard that enables you to generate scripts for selected objects within the database. This is a great way to keep a record of the scripts needed to regenerate a database and can be a good way to get a version check on any recent changes to the DB.

Use this with a source code control system to determine the delta between previously generated scripts and scripts currently generated to find changes to objects in the database.

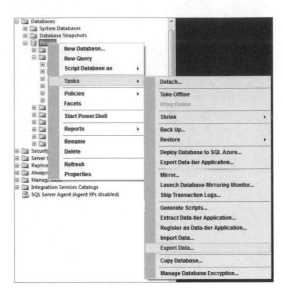

FIGURE 17-1

Import/Export Wizard

SSMS provides Import/Export capabilities which are accessed from the Tasks item on the database context menu (see Figure 17-1).

As you can see, you can drive this from either end.
In the following example you walk through an export driven from the source database.

1. Select Export Data to start the wizard. The wizard welcome screen appears as shown in Figure 17-2.

2. Select Next in the welcome screen and you are taken to the Choose a Data Source page, shown in Figure 17-3. Enter the server name and authentication method for this server, and then you can select the database you wish to export data from.

FIGURE 17-2

FIGURE 17-3

3. The next page in the wizard enables you to choose a Destination (see Figure 17-4). Again, choose a server, authentication method, and then database name. The wizard defaults to using the default database for the login used to authenticate against this server.

4. On this page choose Table Copy to use a table copy, or Query to write a query to select data. In this example, choose the first option to copy data from one or more tables or views (see Figure 17-5).

FIGURE 17-4

FIGURE 17-5

5. The wizard now presents you with a list of all the tables and views that are available. In the example database, there are only a small number of tables that you can see in Figure 17-6. Select the tables and views to be exported.

6. You now have the option to run the package immediately, or to save the SSIS package. If you choose to save the package, you can specify if you want to save it to SQL Server, or the file system. You can also define a package protection level to secure the package contents. You can see these options

FIGURE 17-6

in Figure 17-7. The penultimate stage of the wizard (shown in Figure 17-8) shows you the selections you have made.

FIGURE 17-7

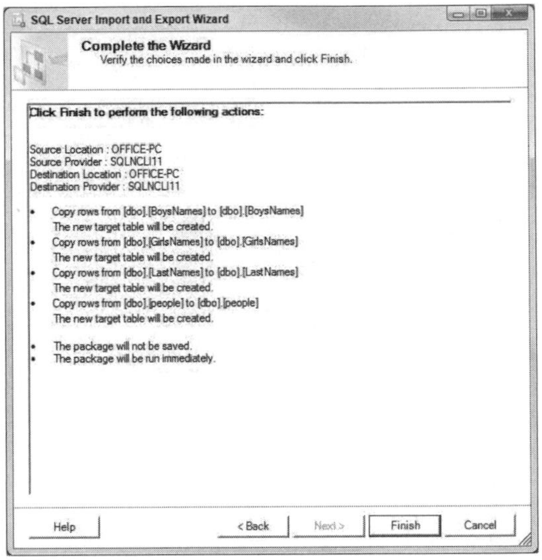

FIGURE 17-8

7. Select Finish to execute the selections made during the wizard. In this case it executes one SSIS package to export the selected tables from the Source Server, creates the new tables in the destination server, and imports the data to the newly created tables. The wizard then reports on the status of the package execution. Figure 17-9 shows everything completed successfully.

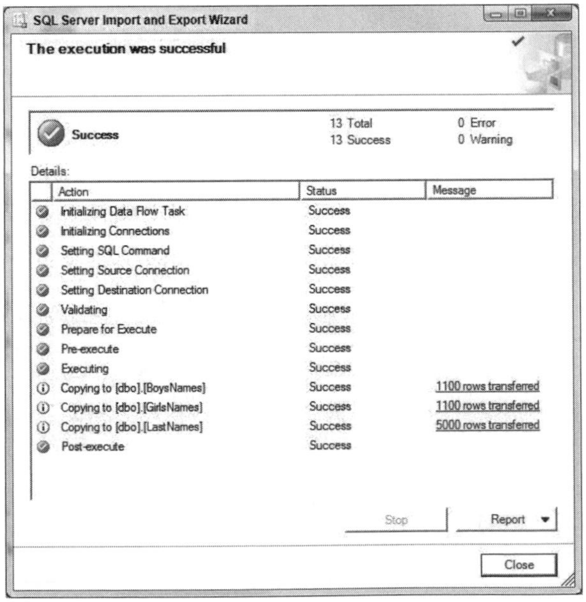

One thing to note is that if you get errors here and you go back to make changes and re-run the package, you may encounter additional errors caused because the wizard doesn't attempt any cleanup if it fails part way through.

The most obvious errors you might encounter are when tables are created, but the data

FIGURE 17-9

import fails, possibly due to transaction log being full. In this case you can resolve the issue by either manually deleting any tables or viewing the created tables in the destination database and rerunning the package again.

 When you run the package, the SQL Agent service does not need to be running.

Extract Data Tier Application (DAC)

If your database uses the set of features that are compatible with Data Tier Applications, then you have the added option to create a Data Tier Application (DAC) using this wizard in SSMS. The DAC contains just the DB schema, without data, but this can be useful for transferring schema from development to test to QA and onto production. See the DAC documentation in BOL for complete details on using DACs.

Copy Database Wizard

SSMS provides a Copy Database Wizard. This can either utilize attach/detach or SMO to make a copy of a database and move it to another server. Using Attach/Detach requires the database to be taken offline. Using the SMO method enables the copy to be made while the database remains online. The Copy Database Wizard is found on the database context menu under the Tasks menu item as shown in Figure 17-10. See the following steps on how to use this wizard.

1. Open the Copy database wizard and you will see the welcome page shown in Figure 17-11.

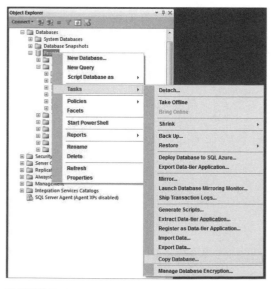

FIGURE 17-10

FIGURE 17-11

2. On the next page select your source server, as shown in Figure 17-12.

3. Select the destination server as shown in Figure 17-13.

FIGURE 17-12

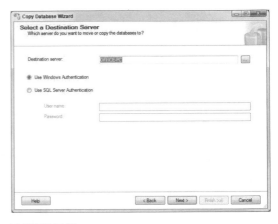

FIGURE 17-13

4. On the next page choose how you would like the wizard to make the transfer. You can choose between Detach/Attach, or using SMO. Figure 17-14 exemplifies choosing the SMO method.

5. Select which databases to copy. You can choose to either copy or move the selected databases, and this choice is on a per database basis, so you can move some databases, and copy others if that's what you want to do. Figure 17-15 shows the People database being selected to be copied.

FIGURE 17-14

FIGURE 17-15

6. Now specify what the new database will be called, and which files will be created. By default these options are pre-populated with the information from the source database. There are other options available on this page (see Figure 17-16) that determine what action to take if the destination database exists.

7. Next specify which objects outside the selected databases you want to include with the copy, as shown in Figure 17-17.

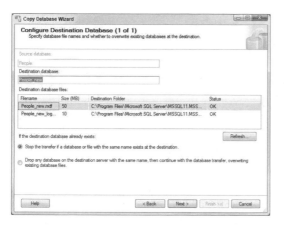

FIGURE 17-16

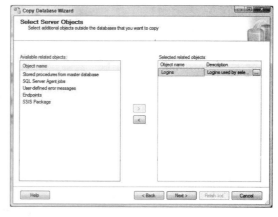

FIGURE 17-17

8. Configure the SSIS package that will perform the database copy, as shown in Figure 17-18.

9. Now schedule the package. At this point you can choose to run the package immediately, or schedule it for execution later. In Figure 17-19 runs the package immediately. Be sure to confirm all the choices made before running the package (see Figure 17-20).

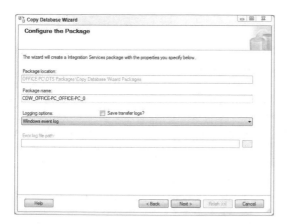

FIGURE 17-18

FIGURE 17-19

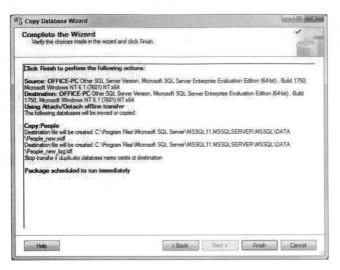

FIGURE 17-20

10. Select Finish to run the package and copy the selected databases and objects from the source to the destination server. While the package is executing, the wizard reports the status of each step. Upon completion, the Wizard displays the results of executing the package.

Make sure you have SQL Agent running on the Destination server. This is where the package is scheduled to execute, through a SQL Agent Job, even if the package is specified to execute immediately. This behavior is different from the import export wizard that does not need SQL Agent to immediately run the packages it creates.

Backup Compression

SQL 2008 Enterprise edition introduced backup compression. With SQL Server 2012, backup compression is now available in Standard Edition. This feature enables the backup files to be stored in compressed form. This can lead to both shorter backup times and smaller files containing the backup. The trade-off you make is increased CPU usage to do the compression, in exchange for less I/O due to the smaller files. Generally, the result of backup compression is greatly reduced backup times. Whether you can benefit from using compression is relative to the availability or scarcity of CPU and I/O resources, as well as the degree of compression obtained. You can determine the state of your system by looking at the following performance counters in Performance Monitor. For more information on monitoring Performance Counters, see Chapters 12, "Monitoring Your SQL Server" and 13, "Performance Tuning T-SQL."

➤ Windows performance monitor counters for your disks.

➤ SQL Server performance counters:

➤ `SQLServer:Backup Device/Device Throughput Bytes/sec.`

➤ `SQLServer:Databases/Backup/Restore Throughput/sec.`

Backup media beginning with SQL Server 7 used a media format called Microsoft Tape Format (MTF). This is the same format that Windows operating system backups used, enabling SQL Server backups to coexist on the same media with Windows backups. This was especially convenient for users with a single tape drive. Beginning with SQL 2008 however, compressed backups use a different media format, which is incompatible with Windows backups. This leads to some restrictions regarding the use of backup compression:

➤ Compressed and uncompressed backups cannot coexist in the same media set.

➤ Prior versions of SQL Server cannot read compressed backups.

➤ NT backups and compressed backups cannot coexist in the same media set.

If you violate one of these restrictions, SQL Server returns an error.

A new server level configuration option, backup compression default, enables your default backups to be either compressed or uncompressed. You can set this option via `sp_configure` and from SSMS. Backup compression is turned off by default. You may override the default using the `with compression` or `with no_compression` option in the `backup` T-SQL command or using the Backup dialogs in SSMS or the Database Maintenance Plan Wizard.

> *Log backup compression for the primary database in log shipping is always dependent on the default backup compression value.*

How much compression you achieve depends on several factors:

➤ Databases that are compressed do not see additional compression in backups.

➤ Encrypted data does not compress as well as unencrypted data.

➤ Character data types compress better than other data types.

➤ Greater levels of compression are achieved when a page has multiple rows in which a column contains the same value.

Comparing Recovery Models

Understanding the recovery models is essential to developing an effective backup strategy. The recovery model determines how the transaction log is managed by SQL Server. The model you choose depends on the backup/restore plan you have for a database. In the *full recovery model*, the transaction log records all data modifications, makes available all database recovery options, and implements the highest data protection while using the most transaction-log space. This recovery model can be used with all database backup operations, it is capable of point-in-time recovery, and it enables backing up the transaction log. Most OLTP production systems and mission-critical applications that require minimal data loss should use the full recovery model.

 The first transaction log backup cannot be completed until after a full database backup has been done.

The *bulk-logged recovery model* performs minimal logging for certain database operations, including bulk import operations, such as the following:

➤   BCP

➤   BULK INSERT

➤   SELECT INTO

➤   CREATE INDEX

➤   ALTER INDEX REBUILD

➤   DBCC DBREINDEX

Instead of logging every modification for these database operations, the bulk-logged recovery model logs the extent allocations and flags the changed extents. As a result, these operations execute faster, as they are minimally logged, but it presents possible data-loss risks for recovery. A transaction-log backup copies everything in the transaction log, checks the extents flagged as changed, and copies them from the data files into the log backup. In addition, after a bulk-logged operation, point-in-time recovery using transaction-log backup is disallowed.

Consider the same scenario presented earlier. The database uses the bulk-logged recovery model. The full database backup occurred at 1:00 P.M. A transaction log backup occurs at 1:30 P.M. Then a bulk-logged database operation is performed. Next, the physical drives containing the data files fail at 2:00 P.M. You cannot recover up to 2:00 P.M. because the transaction-log backup would need to access the data files to retrieve the data modifications performed during the bulk-logged operations. You cannot perform a tail-log backup. As a result, data will be lost and you can only recover up to 1:30 P.M.

When you do bulk operations in this mode, you are at risk of losing data until you complete a log backup after the bulk operations. You can minimize the data loss in this scenario with some bulk-logged database operations by implementing shorter transactions that perform transaction-log backups during and immediately after the bulk-logged operations. Oftentimes, this recovery model is used when the DBA performs bulk-logged operations and then switches back to full after the bulk-logged operation completes, to improve the performance for bulk operations. In addition, this model is commonly used in an OLAP or Report database for which there are nightly bulk data loads. A backup is taken, and afterward no data is modified during the day, so if the data is lost because of a failure, it can be restored from backup.

The *simple recovery model* implements minimal logging, just like the bulk-logged recovery model, except that it keeps the transaction-log records only until the next checkpoint process occurs, writing the dirty changes to the data files. Then the checkpoint process truncates the transaction log. Transaction-log backups are not allowed; therefore, point-in-time recovery is not available. Typically, this recovery model is used for development or test servers, where data loss is acceptable and data can be reloaded. Moreover, this model may be used by an OLAP and Reporting database for which there may be only a nightly data load and then a full or differential backup is performed. With this model, if the database were to fail during the data load, you would have to start from the beginning, unless a full or differential backup was taken during the process. In addition, if a DBA switches from one of the other recovery models to this one, the transaction-log continuity is broken, as it truncates the transaction log. In addition, during the time that the database is in this recovery mode, the database is more exposed to potential data loss.

 Transactional replication, log shipping, or data mirroring is not allowed in the simple recovery model, as there is no persistent storage of transactions in the transaction log.

Choosing a Model

Choosing the best recovery model depends on the amount of acceptable data loss, the database's read-and-write daily activities, and how critical that database is to the daily business of your organization. Following are recommendations for choosing between the full, bulk-logged, and simple recovery models.

Full Recovery Model

Choose the full recovery model for a mission-critical database to keep data loss to a minimum because it is fully logged; and in case of damaged data files, the tail transaction log can be backed up and used to restore the database to a given point in time. Therefore, OLTP production systems usually use the full recovery model, except when the database is modified nightly, as is sometimes the case with OLAP or Reporting databases.

Bulk-Logged Recovery Model

You can use the bulk-logged recovery model to increase bulk operations' performance because it does minimal logging. For example, you could do a nightly bulk operation and then switch back to full recovery. The bulk-logged model will fully log, as is the case with the full recovery model, except for the bulk operations. Therefore, you could use bulk-logged recovery as a permanent recovery model, except it poses a risk of data loss. As long as there are no bulk-data operations, the DBA can back up the transaction log; but oftentimes, unknown to the DBA, the tail transaction-log backup recovery may no longer be available if a bulk operation has been performed. To guard against someone doing bulk operations without a database backup and to reduce that data risk, you should switch to bulk-logged only when a bulk operation needs to be performed. Bulk-logged can be a permanent recovery model in an OLAP or Report database where there is no daily modification activity, as there is limited data loss risk if the databases are backed up right after any nightly data load. There is no chance of data loss throughout the day, as nothing would have changed. In addition, some data loss may be acceptable, as the OLAP and Reporting databases can be reloaded from the OLTP data source whenever needed.

Simple Recovery Model

The simple recovery model does not save the transaction log; instead, the checkpoint process truncates it. Therefore, no one has to maintain the transaction log. This recovery model is commonly used for development, read-only, and test systems for which transaction-log backups are not required. If there is data loss, a new copy of the data can be reloaded from the OLTP data source. If the DBA switches to this recovery model from one of the others, the transaction- log continuity is broken because there is no way to back up the transaction log. In this recovery model, there is no point-in-time recovery because the DBA cannot back up the transaction log. Therefore, any restore would be from the previous full, and any differential, backups.

Switching Recovery Models

SQL Server provides complete flexibility to switch among the recovery models. However, be aware of the limitations when switching among them, as switching can result in data loss during recovery. The following list outlines the limitations of switching recovery models:

➤ **Switching from full to bulk-logged:** Because bulk-logged database operations may be performed, a transaction-log backup is recommended at a minimum so that the DBA can recover to this last transaction log if the tail transaction log is not available. To change to this recovery model, use this command:

```
ALTER DATABASE < db_name> SET RECOVERY BULK_LOGGED
```

➤ **Switching from full to simple:** Because the transaction-log continuity is broken by this recovery model, a transaction-log backup is recommended, at minimum, before the switch. After the recovery model switch, transaction-log backups and point-in-time recovery are disallowed. To change to this recovery model, use the following command:

```
ALTER DATABASE < db_name> SET RECOVERY SIMPLE
```

➤ **Switching from bulk-logged to full:** Because bulk-logged database operations may have been performed and to minimize potential data loss if the tail transaction log is not accessible, a transaction-log backup is recommended after the switch. To change to this recovery model, use the following command:

```
ALTER DATABASE < db_name> SET RECOVERY FULL
```

➤ **Switching from bulk-logged to simple:** In this recovery model there is a greater chance of data loss in case of a database failure, so at a minimum, a transaction-log backup is highly recommended before the switch. To change to this recovery model, use the following command:

```
ALTER DATABASE < db_name> SET RECOVERY SIMPLE
```

➤ **Switching from simple to full:** To enable the full recovery model to start to apply transaction-log backups, a full, differential, file, or filegroup backup is required after the switch. To change to this recovery model, use the following command:

```
ALTER DATABASE < db_name> SET RECOVERY FULL
```

➤ **Switching from simple to bulk-logged:** To enable the bulk-logged recovery model to start to apply transaction-log backups, a full, differential, file, or filegroup backup is required after the switch. To change to this recovery model, use the following command:

```
ALTER DATABASE < db_name> SET RECOVERY BULK_LOGGED
```

The recovery model is configured for each database. You can also switch the recovery model from SQL Server Management Studio by opening the Database Properties and choosing Options, as shown in Figure 17-21.

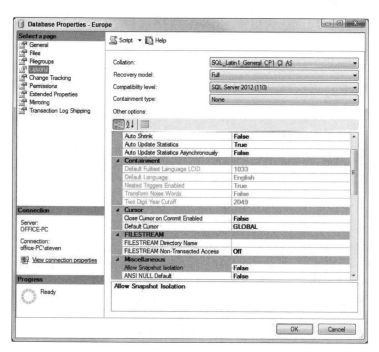

FIGURE 17-21

Backing Up History Tables

SQL Server maintains the backup history for the server in the MSDB database in a group of tables from which it can identify the backup available for a database. In the Restore dialog, SQL Server presents the restores available for the database. The tables are as follows:

➤ `Backupfile`: A row for each data or log file backed up

➤ `Backupfilegroup`: A row for each filegroup in a backup set

➤ `Backupmediafamily`: A row for each media family

➤ `Backupmediaset`: A row for each backup media set

➤ `Backupset`: A row for each backup set

> *A media set is an ordered collection of all tapes or disks from all devices that took part in the backup. A media family is a collection of all backup media on a single device that took part in the backup. A media backup is a tape or disk device used for backup.*

The following three backup information statements return information from the history backup tables:

➤ `RESTORE FILELISTONLY`: Returns a list of database and log files in a backup set from the backup file table:

```
RESTORE FILELISTONLY FROM NorthAmerica_Backup
```

➤ `RESTORE HEADERONLY`: Returns all the backup header information for all the backup sets in a device from the `backupset` table:

```
RESTORE HEADERONLY FROM NorthAmerica_Backup
```

➤ `RESTORE LABELONLY`: Returns information about the backup media of a backup device from the `backupmediaset` table:

```
RESTORE LABELONLY FROM NorthAmerica_Backup
```

> `RESTORE HEADERONLY`, `RESTORE FILELISTONLY`, `RESTORE VERIFYONLY` *and* `RESTORE LABLELONLY` *do not actually restore anything and therefore are completely safe to run. They provide only information. It may be a bit confusing though; just remember to look for the contextual use of* `RESTORE`.

Permissions Required for Backup and Restore

SQL Server provides granular permission for both backup and restoring a database. A Windows or SQL Server authenticated user or group can be given permission to perform the backup and restore operations. To have permission to back up a database, a user must have at minimum the following permissions:

➤ Server role: `none`

➤ DB role: `db_backupoperator`

To restore a database, a user must have at minimum the following permissions:

➤ Server role: `dbcreater`

➤ DB role: `db_owner`

Backing Up System Databases

SQL Server system databases are critical to the operation of each SQL Server instance. These databases are not often modified, but they contain important information that needs to be backed up. After creating a new SQL Server instance, develop a backup plan to perform a full backup of all the system databases, except for `tempdb`. SQL Server re-creates `tempdb` every time it is restarted because it does not contain any data to recover. Backing up these system databases takes only minutes, so there is no excuse for not having a proper backup. You could often schedule these backups nightly and do extra backups to your local hard drive before and after any changes you make. That keeps you safe until the current night's normal backup.

Master

The master database contains the login information: metadata about each database for the SQL instance. Moreover, it contains SQL Server configuration information. For example, the database is altered every time you do the following:

➤ Add, remove, or modify a database level setting.

➤ Add or delete a user database.

➤ Add or remove a file or filegroup in a user database.

➤ Add, remove, or modify a login's security.

➤ Modify a SQL Server serverwide configuration.

➤ Add or remove a logical backup device.

➤ Configure distributed queries or remote procedure calls (RPC).

➤ Add, modify, or remove a linked server or remote login.

Although these modifications occur infrequently, when they do, consider doing a full database backup. If a backup is not performed, you stand to lose the modifications if a previous backup of the master is restored. Moreover, as a precautionary measure, before and after adding any service pack or hotfix, perform a new backup of the master database.

MSDB

The `msdb` database contains SQL jobs, backup jobs, schedules, operators, and backup and restore histories and can contain Integration Services packages and other items. If you create a new job or add a new Integration Services package and `msdb` were to fail, the previous backup would not contain these new jobs and would need to be recreated.

tempdb

tempdb cannot be backed up. Because it is re-created every time SQL Server is restarted, no data in it needs to be recovered.

Model

Typically, the model database changes even less frequently than the other system databases. Model is the template database used when a new database is created. If you want a certain database object to be present in every new database, such as a stored procedure or table, place it in Model. In these cases, it should be backed up; otherwise, any Model modifications will be lost and need to be re-created. In addition, keep scripts of any changes you make to the model, just to add another layer of safety.

Full-Text Backup

Full-text search performs fast querying of unstructured data using keywords based on the words in a particular language. It is primarily used to search char, varchar, and nvarchar fields. Prior to querying, the full-text index must be created by a population or crawl process, during which full-text search performs a breakdown of the keywords and stores them in the full-text index. Each full-text index is then stored in a full-text catalog. Then a catalog is stored in a filegroup. Unlike previous versions of SQL Server, in SQL Server 2012 a full backup includes the full-text indexes. In SQL 2005, full-text indexes were part of a catalog that existed in a filegroup with a physical path and was simply treated as a database file. SQL Server 2012 treats all the catalog as a virtual object–simply a collection of full-text indexes. Full-text indexes are now stored and treated like other indexes for the purpose of backups. To backup all the full-text indexes, you must discover the files that contain any full-text index and then backup the file or filegroup.

The end result is that backups for full-text indexes are completely incorporated into the standard backup architecture. You can place full text indexes on separate filegroups and the Primary filegroup, or allow them to live in the same filegroup as the base table. This improvement makes administration easier than in prior releases.

Verifying the Backup Images

With any backup solution, a critical operation is verifying the backup images that they will restore. Often, a DBA may be meticulously doing backups, but along the way the database becomes corrupted, and every backup from that point on is not usable. Plan on doing periodic restores to verify recoverability. In addition, perform database consistency checks to validate the database structures. Use the RESTORE VERIFYONLY T-SQL command to perform validation checks on the backup image. It does not restore the backup, but it performs validation checks, including the following:

- ➤ Confirms the backup set is readable.
- ➤ Page ID.
- ➤ If the backup were created WITH CHECKSUMS, then it will validate it.
- ➤ Checks destination devices for sufficient space.

However, the RESTORE VERIFYONLY command does not completely guarantee that the backup is restorable. That is why you need a policy to randomly restore a backup to a test server. RESTORE VERIFYONLY simply provides another level of validation. Here's the syntax:

```
RESTORE VERIFYONLY FROM <backup_device_name>
```

Following is an example resulting message:

```
The backup set on file 1 is valid.
```

 RESTORE VERIFYONLY *does not work on database snapshots. If you plan to revert (restore) from a database snapshot, then use* DBCC CHECKDB *to ensure that the database is healthy.*

For higher reliability, to guard against a malfunctioning backup device that may render the entire backup unrecoverable, use mirroring of backup sets for redundancy. They can be either disk or tape and have the following restrictions:

➤   Backup devices must be identical.

➤   To create a new, or extend an existing, backup, the mirror backup set must be intact. If one is not present, the media backup set cannot be used.

➤   To restore from a media backup set, only one of the mirror devices must be present.

➤   If one mirror of the media backup set is damaged, no additional mirroring can be performed on that media backup set.

For example, use the following command to use a backup device mirroring on the AdventureWorks2012 database:

```
BACKUP DATABASE NorthAmerica

TO TAPE = '\\.\tape0', TAPE = '\\.\tape1'

MIRROR TO TAPE = '\\.\tape2', TAPE = '\\.\tape3'

WITH FORMAT, MEDIANAME = 'NorthAmericaSet1'
```

How Restore Works

Restore brings back the database in case of a failure and is a major function of a transactional relational database system. When a DBA restores a database, three restore phases must happen:

➤   Copy Phase

➤   Redo Phase

➤   Undo Phase

RESTORE VERSUS RECOVERY

The terms *restore* and *recovery* are often confused and misused. Restore is what occurs when you use the RESTORE T-SQL command to get a database back.

Recovery is a process that brings a database into a consistent state. This means that committed transactions are applied to disk (redo phase) and transactions that are begun but not yet committed are rolled off (undo phase). The result is a database that contains only committed transactions — a consistent state.

Each time the server starts, an automatic recovery process runs. At startup, you do not know how SQL Server last stopped. It could have been a clean shutdown, or a power outage could have brought the server down. In the case of the power outage, there may have been transactions that were begun but not yet completed. Recovery does the work necessary to ensure that committed transactions are included and not yet committed transactions are removed.

The last step in a restore process that you begin is also recovery. The RESTORE command enables you to specify when recovery runs. If recovery has not yet run, you may restore a differential or continue to restore transaction logs. After recovery has run, no more log restores may occur, and the database is brought online.

In the *copy phase*, the database image is created and initialized on disk, and then the full backup is copied. That can be followed by any differential and transaction-log backups. These are done via the RESTORE T-SQL command.

After the full backup has been applied and any differential and transaction logs have been restored, the DBA allows recovery to run. During the recovery process, SQL Server performs both a *redo phase* and an *undo phase*. During the *redo phase*, all committed transaction records that were in the transaction log but not in the data files are written to the data files. The WAL protocol guarantees that the transaction records that were committed have been written to the transaction-log stable media. Then, during the redo, SQL Server evaluates the transaction-log records and applies the data modifications to the data files in the database.

The duration of the redo phase depends on how many data modifications SQL Server performed, which depends on what SQL Server was doing at the time of the failure and the recovery interval setting. For example, if SQL Server just finished updating 10 million rows from a table and committed the transaction but was unexpectedly shut down right after, during recovery it would have to redo those data modifications to the data. The SQL Server recovery interval setting influences recovery time according to how many dirty pages are kept in memory before the checkpoint process must write them to stable media. By default, the recovery interval is set to 0, which means that SQL Server keeps less than a minute of work that is not yet written to the data files. With that setting, during recovery, there is minimal redo work before the database becomes available for users. The higher the recovery interval value, the longer the recovery may take.

After the redo phase is the *undo phase*, where any transactions that did not complete are rolled back. Depending on the amount of work and the length of the transactions at the time before shutdown, this phase can take some time. For example, if the DBA was in the middle of deleting 10 million rows, SQL Server is required to roll back all those rows during recovery. SQL Server does make the database available to users while in the undo phase, but users should expect some performance impact while in the redo phase.

PREPARING FOR RECOVERY

To mitigate the risk and extent of data loss, one of the DBA's most important tasks is database backup and planning for recovery. You need to develop a backup plan that minimizes data loss and can be implemented within the maintenance window of time allowed. Choose the best SQL Server backup capabilities to achieve the preferred backup plan — one that meets the continuity and data loss requirements for the business. You must also set up the backup procedure and monitor it every day to ensure that it works successfully. That includes validating that the database backup restores properly.

An organization may be current with its backups and assume that it has the necessary backups to restore the database, only to find that the database was corrupted and some of the recent database backups will not restore. Cases like these can go undiscovered for months until someone needs to restore a database and finds out that it is not recoverable. To reduce this risk, run the database-consistency checks against each database and design a process to test the recoverability of the database backup. In addition, send database backups offsite to protect them in case of a local disaster, but keep local copies of recent backups in case you need to perform a quick restore.

Another critical task is disaster recovery planning. If the organization data center were to be completely destroyed, you should quickly deploy a new data center with minimum data loss and minimum business disruption. Disaster recovery planning is not complete until a team periodically simulates a data center failure and proceeds through the test drill to deploy a new data center.

Recoverability Requirements

Any backup planning should start with the end goal in mind: the recoverability requirements. You have already covered the planning in the previous section, "Making Plans," but following are a few more things you might also consider:

➤ Perhaps only part of the database must be online. You can consider a piecemeal restore to reduce your restore time, especially on larger databases for which a restore can take a long time. Determine what parts of the database must be available, and arrange the data into filegroups so that you can recover the most critical filegroups first. Archived data or reporting data is less critical and can be recovered last.

➤ The organization may allocate newer, redundant hardware and RAID array with a high-availability solution to mitigate downtime. A company might also consider faster and more backup devices to quickly restore the database.

➤ Determine how easy or difficult it would be to re-create lost data for each database. For some databases, data can be easily re-created by extracting data from another system or from flat-file data loads. Typically, decision-support databases use ETL tools to extract data; for example, if some unrecoverable data loss occurred, the ETL tool can be executed to reload the data.

➤ What is the acceptable downtime in a media failure, such as a failed disk drive? As disk technology continues to become less expensive, most organizations deploy databases on a fault-tolerant disk array that reduces the exposure of one of the disk drives failing, causing the database to become unavailable. For example, on a RAID 5 set, loss of a single drive can cause a noticeable performance slowdown. If a second drive in the same RAID 5 were to fail, the data would be lost. To mitigate this risk, have spare drives in the disk array system and get a service-level agreement from the hardware provider to deliver and install the drives. Another common scenario is a department inside the organization deploying a database in a less than ideal hardware environment. With time, the database becomes mission critical to that department, but it lives under the DBA's radar with no accountability. The DBA should attempt to identify all database sources within the organization and develop a recovery plan.

➤ Determine which databases have any external dependencies on other databases, requiring both databases to be restored for users to perform their daily activity. Determine whether there is any linked server(s), external application(s), or mainframe connectivity on which a database has dependencies.

➤ Identify the available hardware that can be allocated for redeployment and where it is located.

➤ Identify the staff required for backup, restore, and disaster recovery. They need to understand the disaster recovery procedures and where they fit in these procedures. Record when all staff members are available, their contact numbers, the chain of communication, and the responsibility of each member. Determine the chain of command and find out, if the lead is unavailable, whether backup members have the expertise to carry out the duties for backup, restore, and disaster recovery. Find out the expertise of the staff and what additional training they might need to support the environment. Identify any training classes that may be beneficial.

➤ Finally, document any information about stored SQL jobs, linked servers, and logins that may be needed when the database is restored onto another database server.

Data Usage Patterns

Part of your recovery plan should include analyzing how your data is used in a typical scenario. Determine for each database how often the data is modified. You ll require different backup strategies for a database that may have a data load once a day than for others that may be read-only or some that change every minute. Separate the tables that are modified from read-only tables. Each type can be placed on different filegroups and a backup plan developed around it.

Identify the usage pattern of the databases during the day to determine the backup strategy to use. For example, during high activity, a DBA may schedule more frequent differential or transaction-log backups, whereas full backups may be performed during off-peak hours.

Determine the disk space used by the transaction log during peak times and the log's performance. For example, during peak times, the transaction log may fill the available disk drive allocated to it. Moreover, during peak times, the number of disks allocated for the transaction log may not be adequate to sustain the database's performance. The database recovery model setting affects both disk space and performance.

For a database in the full recovery model, consider switching to bulk-logged mode during bulk operations to improve performance, as that will incur minimal transaction logging. Prior to the start of the bulk operations, you should at minimum perform a transactional or differential backup to guard against the risk of a data-drive failure when the tail transaction log may not be accessible.

Also consider how the database is to be used. If the database is mission critical, apply redundancy around the hardware. Start with a highly redundant storage system, using RAID10, and then add on additional hardware capabilities as you can afford them, up to and including a completely duplicate hot standby system using a failover cluster. Identify what level of data loss the company can afford, and plan to back up the transaction log to meet the time requirement. Also use the full recovery model so that you can get recovery to the point of failure.

Maintenance Time Window

Sometimes, the backup strategy is dictated by the maintenance time window available to perform database defragmentation, backups, statistics updates, and other maintenance activities. To keep enhancing the customer experience, organizations demand more timely information and give customers greater access to information, and customers are therefore more dependent on having this information. This presents a challenge to create the best customer experience, mitigate the risk of data loss, and enable quick restores if the database system fails.

The task of the DBA is to find the best backup strategy to meet the organization's business requirements. Usually, the maintenance time window is limited. SQL Server implements various backup options that can be used in combination to meet these requirements. The following are some of the challenges you face when designing a backup strategy:

➤ Available backup time may be limited in a mission-critical, highly available database. Organizations often have SLAs and must finish their maintenance by a certain time when users are back on the system. If the backup takes longer, it may delay other database activities, which might not finish by the time users log in to the system, costing a company opportunity loss.

➤ There may be a large number of databases to back up during the maintenance time window. You can try to optimize your time for all available backup media by performing concurrent backups within the capacity of the database server.

➤ A growing database puts pressure on the maintenance window. Additional backup devices, higher-performance database servers, and faster I/O may be needed to relieve the pressure. Sometimes the maintenance time window can be increased, but oftentimes it cannot. You may need to consider a SAN copy solution to speed the backup process.

➤ Other database activities are likely performed on all the databases in the database server (for example, database-consistency checking, defragmentation, update statistics, and perhaps data loads). As the database grows, these other activities may take longer to perform, too.

➤ Software updates, security patches, service packs, and database structure updates may need to fit within this maintenance time window.

➤ Full-text catalogs may need to be processed.

➤ As more organizations see the benefit of decision-support systems such as SQL Server Analysis Services, the analysis services database may need to be processed during this time.

To meet these requirements, a small database can use a full database backup every night. However, as the database becomes larger, that may not be possible. A good next step is to perform a full database backup on the weekend and nightly full differential backups. As the database becomes larger, consider moving read-only and read/write data to different filegroups, and then use full partial backups during the weekend and partial differential backups at night. As the database continues to grow, consider nightly backup of individual files.

Other High-Availability Solutions

When your database has been deployed in a high-availability solution, such as AlwaysOn, failover clustering, log shipping, or data mirroring, it may require additional backup considerations:

➤ If you use the AlwaysOn technology new in SQL Server 2012, you can modify your backup plans. For example, one reason to create a secondary replica might be to offload the IO load from backups from the Primary Replica to the Secondary. In this model, you would not take backups from the Primary Replica, or other Secondary Replicas, but have a dedicated Secondary Replica specifically for taking backups from. You can specify a Replica to be the preferred location to run backups using the BACKUP_PRIORITY configuration setting for the availability group. For more information on the new AlwaysOn technologies see Chapter 25, "AlwaysOn Availability Groups."

➤ In log shipping, the transaction log is backed up by the log-shipping process. No other transaction-log backup should be permitted, as that will break the log chain and prevent any additional transaction log restores on the standby server. If that occurred, you would need to reconfigure log shipping.

➤ In data mirroring, if the mirror server is down, the principal server transaction log queues all modifications to be sent to the mirror in the transaction log. The transaction log cannot be truncated past the point where it has not sent data modifications to the mirror server.

➤ A failover cluster is a single database, so there are no special considerations. However, if the failover cluster is integrated with log shipping or data mirroring, the transaction-log limitations already mentioned apply.

➤ Any use of replication requires you to make a detailed backup recovery plan that includes the synchronization of the source database, the distribution database, and the subscribers. Replication can introduce a new level of complexity to the backup/recovery plan. Although you can recover a replicated database from a backup, additional criteria must be met to make this successful. You should consider if using backups is a reasonable solution for recovering the subscriber databases. In the case of small databases, it may be easier and more reliable to simply regenerate and apply a new snapshot from the publisher.

In transaction replication, if the subscriber is down, the transaction log cannot be truncated past the point in which it has not replicated those data modifications to the subscriber server.

DEVELOPING AND EXECUTING A BACKUP PLAN

SQL Server provides three methods for planning and executing backups. You can use the graphical interface of Management Studio, Database Maintenance Plans, or the T-SQL backup commands. This section covers all of these methods.

Using SQL Server Management Studio

SQL Server Management Studio (SSMS) exposes backup management capabilities for a DBA to either develop a scheduled maintenance plan or directly perform a backup. Before you start, decide the destination for the backup image. It can be a backup location such as a directory path with a filename or a separate backup device.

If you use a backup device, first you need to create a logical device that defines where SQL Server will copy the backup image. From SQL Server Management Studio, select Server Objects ⇨ Backup Devices ⇨ New Backup Device. You see the dialog shown in Figure 17-22. There are two destination options:

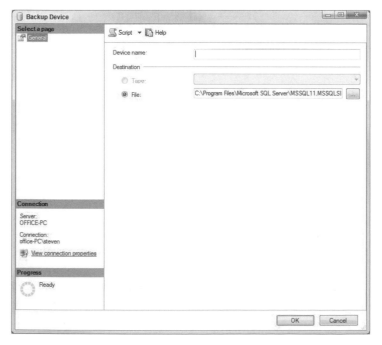

FIGURE 17-22

➤ **Tape:** Requires that a local tape drive be present on the database server

➤ **File:** Requires a valid disk destination

You do not need to use backup devices when backing up to disk because the location is hard-coded. Instead, create unique backup filenames that include the database name, the backup type, and some date/time information to make the name unique. This is much more flexible than using a backup device. To perform a database backup from SQL Server Management Studio, follow these steps:

1. Select the database you want to back up, right-click, and choose Tasks ➪ Backup. The Back Up Database dialog appears, as shown in Figure 17-23.

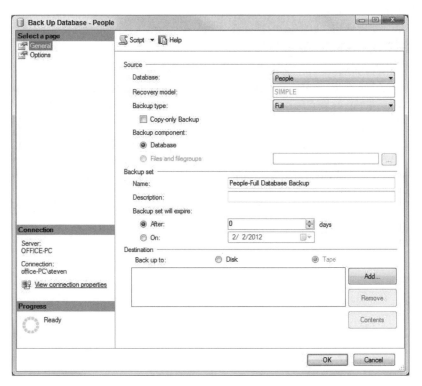

FIGURE 17-23

2. In the Source area of this dialog, configure the following:

➤ **Database:** Choose the database to back up.

➤ **Recovery model:** This value is grayed out because it cannot be changed. This is in full recovery model. If it were simple recovery model, the transaction log could not be backed up because the transaction log is truncated by the checkpoint process and files, and filegroup backups would not be available, except for read-only files or filegroups.

➤ **Backup type:** Choose among Full, Differential, or Transaction Log.

➤ **Copy Only Backup:** Enables you to do a backup that does not affect the transaction chain or truncate the log.

➤ **Backup component:** Choose from the following options:

➤ **Database:** Backs up the database.

➤ **Files and filegroups:** Backs up files or filegroups. This option presents a dialog from which you can choose one or more files or filegroups.

3. In the Backup Set area of this dialog, configure the following:

➤ **Name:** Give the backup set a name for easier identification. This name distinguishes the backup from others in the backup device.

➤ **Description:** Provide an optional description for this media set.

➤ **Backup set will expire:** Configure these options based on your business's retention policy; this guards against SQL Server's backup process overwriting the backup set.

➤ **After:** This determines the number of days, from 0 to 99,999, after which the set can be overwritten. Zero is the default, which means the set never expires. You can change the serverwide default by choosing SQL Server Properties ⇨ Database Settings. Change the default backup media retention (in days).

➤ **On:** Specify a date on which the backup set will expire.

4. SQL Server supports up to 64 backup devices. In the Destination area of this dialog, configure the following:

➤ **Disk:** Specify a full valid destination path with a filename or a disk backup device.

➤ **Tape:** Specify a tape drive or a tape backup device. The tape drive must be local to the database server.

 Clicking the Contents button shows the media set or media family of the device selected.

5. While in the Back Up Database dialog, select the Options page to see the dialog shown in Figure 17-24.

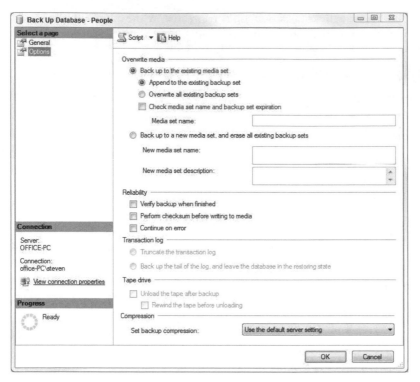

FIGURE 17-24

6. In the Overwrite Media section, you can choose to back up to the existing media set, in which case you have to configure these options:

   ➤ **Append to the existing backup set:** Preserves the existing backups by appending to that media set. This is the default.

   ➤ **Overwrite all existing backup sets:** Erases all the existing backups and replaces them with the current backup. This overwrites all existing backup sets unless the Check Media Set Name and Backup Set Expiration box is checked.

   Alternatively, you can choose to back up to a new media set and erase all existing backup sets, which erases all backups in the media and begins a media set, according to your specifications.

7. The Reliability section of this dialog has three check boxes that are all good recommended practices because a backup is of no value if it is not recoverable. Check these boxes:

   ➤ **Verify Backup When Finished:** After the backup finishes, SQL Server confirms that all volumes are readable.

   ➤ **Perform Checksum Before Writing to Media:** SQL Server does a checksum prior to writing to media, which can be used during recovery to verify that the backup was not tampered with. There is a performance penalty with this operation.

➤ **Continue on Error:** Backup should continue to run after encountering an error such as a page checksum error or torn page.

8. The Transaction Log section of this dialog contains options that only apply during transaction-log backups. If you are performing a transaction log backup, select whichever of these is appropriate to the log backup you are trying to accomplish:

➤ **Truncate the Transaction Log:** During normal transaction-log backups, it is common practice to manage the size of the transaction log and to truncate it after it has been backed up to a backup media.

➤ **Back Up the Tail of the Log and Leave the Database in the Restoring State:** This option is useful when the data files of the database are not accessible. (For example, the physical drives have failed but the transaction log in separate physical drives is still accessible.) As a result, during database recovery, apply this as the last transaction-log backup to recover right to the point of failure.

9. The Tape Drive section of the dialog contains check boxes to let you specify how to handle the tape. The two options include:

➤ Unload the tape after backup

➤ Rewind the tape before unloading

10. In the Compression section of this dialog, specify one of three compression options for the backup:

➤ Use the Default Server Setting

➤ Compress Backup

➤ Do Not Compress Backup

11. Click OK and the backup process executes.

Database Maintenance Plans

Another approach to executing the backup plan is to develop database maintenance plans for each database, schedule them, and have SQL Server e-mail you a backup history report.

The purpose of the database maintenance plan is ease of use and reuse. A database maintenance plan is beneficial because it includes many of the normal maintenance actions you must do for a database, but grouped all together, executed on a schedule, with history and reporting. You can create a plan manually or use the wizard, which walks you through a series of dialogs.

To create maintenance plans for one or more databases from SQL Server Management Studio, choose the folder Management ➪ Maintenance Plans, and then right-click and choose New Maintenance Plan. After naming the maintenance plan, you go to the maintenance plan design screen and perform the following steps:

Note that you may need to display the Maintenance Plan Tasks toolbox, as this does not show up by default anymore. To do this press CTRL+ALT+X, or use the View ➪ Toolbox menu option. Now perform the following steps:

1. Choose the Back Up Database Task, and drag it to the Designer.

2. Right-click the Back Up Database Task, and choose Edit to open the Backup Database Task dialog, as shown in Figure 17-25.

3. In the Connection field, choose Local Server Connection, or if this maintenance plan is to back up databases on another server, choose New Connection and provide the connection information.

4. In the Database(s) field, choose one or more databases. You can choose more than one database if they have identical backup requirements.

5. In the Backup Component field, choose either Database or Files and Filegroups. If you choose Files and Filegroups, you need to specify which files or filegroups to back up.

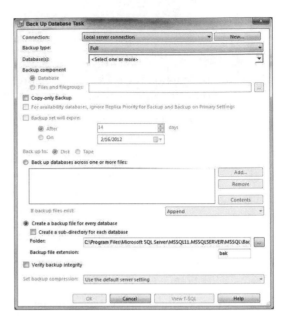

FIGURE 17-25

6. You may optionally choose an expiration date for the backup set. This prevents accidental overwrites.

7. In the Back Up To field, choose either Disk or Tape.

8. You can choose a list of hard-coded files to backup your databases to or have the maintenance plan create an automatically named backup file for each database.

    a. If you choose Back Up Databases Across one or More Files:

        1. Click the Add button to configure the backup location. For disk, provide the full path to the filename or the disk backup device. For tape, provide the tape location or the tape backup device. You can use more than one file or backup device. If more than one is chosen, all the databases will be backed up across them, up to the 64 backup devices that SQL Server supports.

        2. On the If Backup Files Exist field, select whether to append to the existing backup file or to overwrite; the default is Append.

    b. If you choose Create a Backup File for Every Database:

        1. Choose the Create a Backup File for Every Database option.

        2. Select the root directory for the backups.

        3. Choose a backup file extension.

9. Click the Verify Backup Integrity check box as a recommended practice.

10. For transaction log backups, you can optionally choose to back up the tail of the log.

11. In the Set Backup Compression field, specify whether the backup should be compressed.

12. Click OK.

13. Click the Reporting and Logging button on the Maintenance Plan [Design] Menu tab, and choose how to receive the backup history report. If you choose e-mail, Database Mail must be configured. Moreover, a SQL Server Agent Operator must be configured to e-mail the report. Then click OK.

14. Click the Schedule button, and set up the schedule for this maintenance plan.

When you allow a maintenance plan to create a backup file for each database, it creates a file formatted as NorthAmerica_backup_2012_09_01_090243_2394128 *for the* NorthAmerica *database. This includes the backup type and date and time of the backup, which is good because it means all the backup file names indicate when the backup was taken, and what type of backup is contained within the file. The down side of using this option is that you get a single backup file and cannot get the performance benefits of a multi-file backup.*

You can include additional backup database tasks for other database backups with various backup requirements. For example, one Back Up Database Task may be performing full database backups on several databases; another may be performing differential backups; whereas a third may be performing filegroup backups. They share the same schedule.

Earlier in this chapter you organized your databases into categories based on the backup/restore needs. You could create maintenance plans that satisfy the needs of each category. Then, when a new database is created on that server, you simply categorize it, adding it to the appropriate maintenance plan.

When the maintenance plan is complete, it is automatically scheduled as a SQL job in SQL Agent.

Using Transact-SQL Backup Commands

All the backup commands using SQL Server Management Studio and all functionality are available directly using T-SQL. For a full list of BACKUP syntax refer to Books Online at http://msdn .microsoft.com/en-us/library/ms186865(v=sql.110).aspx. Following are some examples of the syntax:

➤ Create a logical backup device for the NorthAmerica database backup:

```
EXEC sp_addumpdevice 'disk', 'NorthAmericaBackup',
'C:\BACKUP\NorthAmerica.bak';
```

Your drive letters may be different, so you may have to change the filename reference. If you use a file share, you should use the UNC name instead of a shared drive letter, as shown here: \myserver\myshare\Backup\NorthAmerica.bak.

➤ Create a full NorthAmerica database backup:

```
BACKUP DATABASE NorthAmerica TO NorthAmericaBackup;
```

➤ Create a full differential backup:

```
BACKUP DATABASE NorthAmerica TO NorthAmericaBackup  WITH DIFFERENTIAL;
```

➤ Create a tail transaction-log backup. This type of backup is used only after a database failure when the transaction logs are still available:

```
BACKUP LOG NorthAmerica TO tailLogBackup WITH NORECOVERY;
```

The prior tail log backup assumes you have created a new backup device called tailLogBackup.

➤ Create a backup filename for the NorthAmerica database backup:

```
DECLARE @devname varchar(256)
SELECT @devname = 'C:\BACKUP\ NorthAmerica_Full_'+ REPLACE
(REPLACE(CONVERT(Varchar(40), GETDATE(), 120),'-','_'),':','_') + '.bak';
```

➤ Create a full NorthAmerica database backup:

```
BACKUP DATABASE NorthAmerica TO DISK = @devname;
```

➤ Create a backup filename for the NorthAmerica differential backup:

```
DECLARE @devname varchar(256)
SELECT @devname = 'C:\BACKUP\NorthAmerica_Differential_' + REPLACE
(REPLACE(CONVERT(Varchar(40), GETDATE(), 120),'-','_'),':','_') + '.bak';
```

➤ Create a full differential backup:

```
BACKUP DATABASE NorthAmerica TO DISK = @devname    WITH DIFFERENTIAL;
```

➤ Create a backup filename for the NorthAmerica database backup:

```
DECLARE @devname varchar(256)

SELECT @devname = 'C:\BACKUP\NorthAmerica_Log_' + REPLACE
(REPLACE(CONVERT(Varchar(40), GETDATE(), 120),'-','_'),':','_') + '.bak';
```

➤ Create a normal transaction log backup:

```
BACKUP LOG NorthAmerica TO DISK = @devname;
```

When using disk files, place each backup in its own backup file, and name the file appropriately. The name should include the unique database name (which might include some server part, if you have databases named the same in several servers), backup type, and date information. The preceding examples use yyyy_mm_dd hh_mm_ss as the date part. It is not unusual to create a stored procedure or user-defined function (UDF) that accepts parameters and returns the name of the backup file.

 Do not use mapped drive letters in your backup filenames. If backing up to files on file shares, use the UNC name. Mapped drive letters may vary depending on who is logged in to the physical server. You can create permanent mapped drive letters, but UNC names are preferred.

MANAGING BACKUPS

Managing your backups is another important DBA task. The better your maintenance procedure, the faster and more accurately the backups will be identified and quickly restored. Meticulously running backups does little good if the backups cannot be identified or, worse, were lost or overwritten. The following tips should help your backup management program:

➤ Descriptively label all the backups to prevent overwriting or misplacing a backup. You can use a naming scheme similar to the one previously mentioned using something like the following: *<Server_Name>_<database_name>_<year>><month>_<day>*.bck

➤ Set up a retention policy to prevent a tape or disk backup from being overwritten. These may be dictated by corporate policy, government regulations, cost, space, or logistics.

➤ Tapes can go bad, so set up a reuse policy. Define how many times a tape may be reused before throwing it away. This adds a tape cost, but a worn tape can stop a successful restore.

➤ Set up a storage location where the backups can easily be organized, found, and accessed. For example, if you're not available and someone else needs to perform the restore, that person must be able to get to the location and correctly identify the backups. You should also keep a copy of the backups stored offsite in a location where they will be protected from a local disaster. This offsite location should allow 24-hour access in case you need a backup. Moreover, keep a copy of the more recent backups locally in case they are quickly needed for a restore.

➤ The backup storage location should be secured such that unauthorized individuals do not have access to sensitive data. Furthermore, for the most sensitive data, use SQL Server column-level encryption.

➤ You must backup and maintain any encryption keys used with databases that are encrypted. These keys must be backed up again when the accounts (commonly the service account or machine account) change. These certificates *must* be maintained or the database will not be restorable or the data will not be accessible.

➤ Set up a logistical procedure to promptly move a copy of each backup to the offsite location to prevent it from being destroyed in a disaster.

BACKUP AND RESTORE PERFORMANCE

SQL Server supports 64 backup devices and uses multiple backup devices in parallel to back up and restore for faster throughput. The backup devices should be on a different controller from the database for better throughput. For disk devices, consider the RAID level used for fault tolerance and performance. Using RAID 5 on drives used to store backups is a bad idea because the additional overhead of calculating parity can reduce IO throughput, and therefore slow down backups. RAID 10 is the preferred choice for write performance, especially if your RAID controller has the intelligence to split writes across both sides of the mirror. This can dramatically increase write throughput. Work with your storage vendor to get recommendations for your storage hardware.

In many cases, disk based backups are written to large slow disks because of the cost savings from using cheaper, large capacity disks. This immediately has a performance impact on the ability of backup to write to these disks. This is just something that backups have to live with, as very few companies are willing to spend large amounts of money on a high performance disk subsystem to store backups.

A combination of full, differential, and transaction-log backups can improve performance by reducing the amount of data that needs to be read from the database and written to the backup device. If you take a full backup of a 5 TB database every day, that's a lot of data to be backing up so often. If only a small percentage of the DB changes every day, then taking a full backup once a week (on the weekend, or other slack period perhaps), with daily differential backups can dramatically reduce the amount of data being read and written during the week.

Network bandwidth can become an issue when backing up to a network device or other server. Ideally backups should use a dedicated network with enough bandwidth to satisfy all of the backup, and restore throughput needs.

PERFORMING RECOVERY

Recovery is the action of restoring a database, and bringing it back to a consistent state. This section explains the various methods of recovery, through both Management Studio and T-SQL. You also learn how to restore the system databases.

Restore Process

It is a DBA's task to ensure that backups are consistently taken and validated to restore. Each backup sequence is labeled and stored to enable quick identification to restore a database. These restore procedures include the following:

➤ Full Database Restore

➤ Transaction-Log Restore

> ➤ Partial Database Restore
>
> ➤ File/File Group Restore
>
> ➤ Database Snapshot Restore
>
> ➤ History Tables Restore

> *Versions prior to SQL Server 2005 required file initialization by filling the files with zeros to overwrite any existing data inside the file for the following SQL Server operations: creating a database; adding files, logs, or data to an existing database; increasing the size of an existing file; and restoring a database or filegroup. As a result, for a large database, file initialization would take significant time. Beginning with SQL Server 2005, however, data files can use instant file initialization, provided that the SQL Server service account is assigned to the Windows SE_MANAGE_VOLUME_NAME permission, which can be done by assigning the account to the Perform Volume Maintenance Tasks security policy. Instant file initialization reduces the time required to create a database or perform other tasks by initializing the new file areas with zeros. Instant file initialization works only on data files and not on Transaction Log files.*

Full Database Restore

A full restore contains the complete backup image of all the data in all the files and enough of the transaction log to enable a consistent restore of committed transactions and uncommitted transactions. A full restore can be the base restore for differential and transaction-log restores to bring the database to a certain point in time. During the full restore, choose whether you want to overwrite the current database, whether the database should be left in operation mode, or whether to allow additional restores, such as differential backups or transaction logs. You also need to choose with move if the database files are to be moved to a different directory location or filename. Then perform the full database restore, followed by all differential and transaction-log backups. The advantage of this process is that it recovers the database in fewer steps. However, it is slow; you need a maintenance window to perform it.

A full differential restore image contains all extents that have been modified since the last full backup. Typically, it is smaller and faster than a full backup image, provided there is not a high turnover of modification activity. A differential restore is commonly used to augment the full restore. During the restore, the full backup is restored, the database is left in NORECOVERY mode, and the differential restore is performed.

Transaction-Log Restore

As mentioned previously, a mission-critical database reduces data-loss exposure by performing periodic transaction log backups. The transaction-log restore requires a full database backup, a file backup, or a filegroup backup as its base. Then you apply the differential restores and next apply all transaction-log backups in sequence, with the oldest first, to bring the database to a point in time — either by completing all the transaction-log restores or by stopping at a specific point. For example, you can restore the database to a point before a certain error by using one of the following transaction-log restore options:

➤ With `Stopat`: Stop the transaction restore at the specified time.

➤ With `Stopatmark`: Stop the transaction-log restore at the marked transaction.

➤ With `Stopbeforemark`: Stop the transaction-log restore before the marked transaction.

You can insert a transaction-log mark in the transaction log by using the `WITH MARK` option with the `BEGIN TRANSACTION` command. During each mark, a row is inserted into the `logmarkhistory` table in `msdb` after the commit completes. Normally, restoring to a point in time requires that you specify the exact time for the restore point. Perhaps a batch process went awry and you want to restore the database to the point immediately prior to the beginning of the batch process. What time did the batch process begin? That is hard to determine unless you have some sort of log-reading utility. This is where logmarks are helpful. For the first transaction in the batch process, add a logmark with a unique name for the batch. That way, if you need to restore to the beginning of the batch, you can restore to the logmark — easy.

An example of a transaction-log restore sequence might be as follows:

1. Restore the full database with `NORECOVERY`.

2. Restore any differential backups with `NORECOVERY`.

3. Restore each transaction log with `NORECOVERY`. You can use the `STOP` clause to restore the database to a point in time.

4. If you have the tail transaction log, restore it. Then set the database to `RECOVERY`.

 After the database is recovered, no additional restores can be performed without starting over.

Partial Database Restore

A partial backup contains the primary filegroup, all the read/write filegroups, and any read-only filegroups specified. A filegroup is read-only if it were changed to read-only prior to its last backup. A partial restore of a read-only database contains only the primary filegroup. This kind of backup is typically used when a database has read-only filegroups and, more important, large read-only filegroups that can be backed up to save disk space.

A partial differential backup image contains changes in the primary filegroup and any changes to read/write filegroups. Restoring a partial differential requires a partial backup image.

File/Filegroup Restore

This is also called a piecemeal restore. You first restore the primary filegroup using the `PARTIAL` keyword. Then, the remaining filegroups can be restored. Each filegroup, when consistent, can be brought online while the other filesgroups are being restored. This allows the DBA to make parts of the database available more quickly, without having to wait on the entire database restore. The following is an example of restoring a database in piecemeal by filegroup, starting with the `Primary` filegroup:

```
RESTORE DATABASE NorthAmerica FILEGROUP='PRIMARY' FROM NorthAmerica_
Backup WITH PARTIAL, NORECOVERY;
RESTORE DATABASE NorthAmerica FILEGROUP='NorthAmerica' FROM
AdventureWorks_Backup  WITH NORECOVERY;
RESTORE LOG NorthAmerica FROM NorthAmerica_Backup WITH NORECOVERY;
RESTORE LOG NorthAmerica FROM NorthAmerica_Backup WITH NORECOVERY;
RESTORE LOG NorthAmerica FROM NorthAmerica_Backup WITH NORECOVERY;
RESTORE LOG NorthAmerica FROM TailLogBackup WITH RECOVERY;
```

The Filegroup `NorthAmerica`, which is read/write, is recovered next:

```
RESTORE DATABASE NorthAmerica FILEGROUP='NorthAmerica' FROM
NorthAmerica_Backup WITH NORECOVERY;
RESTORE LOG NorthAmerica FROM NorthAmerica_Backup WITH NORECOVERY;
RESTORE LOG NorthAmerica FROM NorthAmerica_Backup WITH NORECOVERY;
RESTORE LOG NorthAmerica FROM TailLogBackup2 WITH RECOVERY;
```

The Filegroup `NorthAmerica4`, which is read-only, is restored last and does not require transaction logs, as it is read-only:

```
RESTORE DATABASE NorthAmerica FILEGROUP='NorthAmerica' FROM
NorthAmerica_Backup WITH RECOVERY;
```

> *File and filegroup backups require that the recovery model is either full or bulk-logged to enable transaction-log backups, unless the database is read-only.*

The previous code example is appropriate when you place many backups in a single device. If you put each backup in its own file, then you must use the filenames in the RESTORE commands.

Database Snapshot Restore

SQL Server supports database snapshots whereby a read-only, point-in-time copy of the database can be taken. The snapshot file, when taken, contains no data because it uses the "copy on first write" technology. As the database is modified, the first time a value is modified, the old value is placed in the snapshot file. This type of restore is not intended for restore of media failures. It is generally used when you want to make a series of changes to the database and then revert back to the original version prior to the changes. If the changes are minimal, this can occur quickly. A common use for this is when testing—make changes during the test; then revert to the original version. A restore from snapshot returns the database to the point in time when the snapshot was taken. There are limitations to snapshots, as well. Blobs, read-only or compressed filegroups, offline files, and multiple snapshots prevent you from reverting using a snapshot. Reverting a database by restoring a snapshot backup also breaks any backup chain that may have existed before the restore. This means that after a snapshot restore, you must take a full backup (or file backup) before attempting to take any log backups

To create a database snapshot, use the following syntax:

```
CREATE DATABASE NorthAmerica_dbss9AM ON ( NAME = NorthAmerica_Data
, FILENAME =ÐC:\Program Files\Microsoft SQL Server
\MSSQL11.MSSQLSERVER\MSSQL\Data\NorthAmerica_data
```

To restore from a snapshot, use this syntax:

```
USE MASTER
RESTORE DATABASE NorthAmerica
FROM DATABASE_SNAPSHOT=ÐNorthAmerica_dbss9AMÐ
```

Beginning with SQL 2005, there has been a much-improved page-level reporting structure available. Page errors are now logged in the suspect_pages table in MSDB. Along with the ability to log page errors, the SQL team has provided the DBA with the ability to restore suspect pages. SQL Server can restore pages while the database remains online and available, even the filegroup and file that contains the suspect pages. Other versions of SQL Server allow only offline restore of suspect pages.

Only data pages can be restored, which excludes allocation pages, full-text indexes, the transaction log, and the database and file boot pages. Page restore also does not work with the simple recovery model.

The restoration process for page restore is just like that of a file restore, except you provide the page numbers you want to restore. The syntax follows:

```
RESTORE DATABASE <dbname>
PAGE = '<file:page>,…'
FROM <backup file or device>
WITH NORECOVERY
```

You then restore any differential backup and then log backups with NORECOVERY. Then you create a normal log backup and restore it:

```
BACKUP LOG <dbname> TO <filename>
RESTORE LOG <dbname> FROM <filename> WITH RECOVERY
```

You can identify suspect pages from the suspect_pages table in msdb, the SQL error log, SQL event traces, some DBCC commands, and Windows Management Instrumentation (WMI) provider for server events. Page restores can be a great thing–the ability to restore pages quickly without having to restore the whole database. This is especially useful when you have hardware failures like controller or disk drive intermittent failures.

History Tables Restore

The msdb database maintains restore metadata tables, which are restored as part of msdb database restore. The following list details the meta data tables, and what each contains:

➤   dbo.restorefile: Contains one row for each restored file, including files restored indirectly by filegroup name

➤ `dbo.restorefilegroup`: Contains one row for each restored filegroup

➤ `dbo.restorehistory`: Contains one row for each restore operation

SQL Server Management Studio Restore

To restore a database from SQL Server Management Studio, perform the following steps:

1. Choose the Database folder, right-click the database of your choice, and choose Tasks ➪ Restore ➪ Database. The Restore Database dialog, as shown in Figure 17-26, exposes the restore capability.

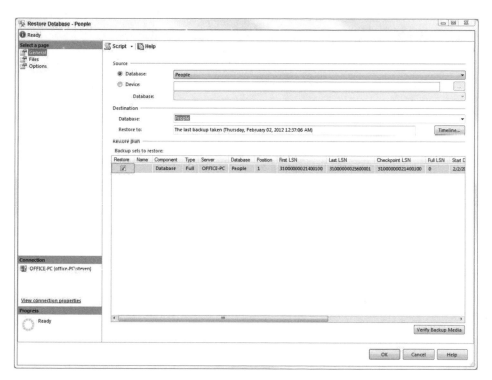

FIGURE 17-26

2. In the Restore Database dialog, in the Destination for Restore area, select from the following options:

➤ **To Database:** Choose the name of an existing database or type the database name.

➤ **To a Point in Time:** For a transaction log restore, choosing a stop time for the restoration is equivalent to STOPAT in the Restore Log command. A point in time is commonly used when a database is being restored because of a user or application data modification error and you have identified the time when the error occurred. Therefore, you want to stop the restoration before the error. This option is not possible for the Simple recovery model because the transaction log is truncated.

3. In the Source for Restore area of this dialog, choose between the following options:

➤ **From Database:** The name of the database to restore; this information is retrieved from the backup history tables in `msdb`.

➤ **From Device:** Choose either the backup device or the backup file name to restore from. This may be used when restoring a database onto another SQL Server 2012 instance and there is no restore data in the backup tables in `msdb`.

4. Next, select the backup sets to restore from the list at the bottom of the dialog. When selecting the restore source, it populates this field with the backup sets available for the database. It also provides an option to choose which backup sets to restore.

5. From the Restore Database dialog, select the Options page, and you'll be taken to the dialog shown in Figure 17-27.

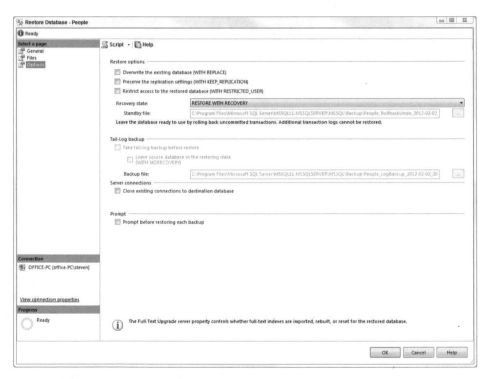

FIGURE 17-27

6. Choose from the following options in the Restore Options section of this dialog:

➤ **Overwrite the Existing Database:** Use this check box when the database you want to restore already exists in the SQL Server instance. Checking this box overwrites the existing database; this is equivalent to the `REPLACE` option in the Restore Database command.

➤ **Preserve the Replication Settings:** Use this check box when you restore a publisher database; it is equivalent to the PRESERVE_REPLICATION option in the Restore Database command.

➤ **Prompt Before Restoring Each Backup:** Use this check box when you swap tapes that contain backup sets.

➤ **Restrict Access to the Restored Database:** Use this check box when you need to perform additional database operations or validation before allowing users to access the database. This option limits database access to members of db_owner, dbcreator, or sysadmin and is equivalent to the RESTRICTED_USER option in the Restore Database command.

➤ **Restore the Database Files As:** Here you can choose to restore the database in another directory and with a different filename. For example, if a new database copy has been created in the same directory, you need to change the filename of the restored database. This is equivalent to the MOVE option in the Restore Database command. If the filenames are not changed, SQL Server generates the following error:

```
Restore failed for Server 'Server1'.
(Microsoft.SqlServer.SmoExtended)System.Data.SqlClient.SqlError:
Exclusive access could not be obtained because the database is in
use.(Microsoft.SqlServer.Smo)
```

7. In the Recovery State section of this dialog, select one of these options:

➤ **Restore with RECOVERY:** The default setting recovers the database, which means that no more backup images can be restored and the database becomes available to users. If additional backup images need to be restored, such as a full database restore followed by several transaction logs, the recovery should be performed after the last step because after recovery, no additional backup images can be restored without starting the restore over. This is equivalent to the WITH RECOVERY option in the Restore Database command.

➤ **Restore with NORECOVERY:** After a backup image is restored, the database is not recovered to enable additional backup images to be applied, such as a database differential or a transaction log backup. Moreover, the database is not user accessible while in NORECOVERY. This state is used on the mirror server in data mirroring and is one of the states available on the secondary server in log shipping. This is equivalent to the WITH NORECOVERY option in the Restore Database command.

➤ **Restore with STANDBY:** After a backup image has been restored, the database is left in a state in which it allows additional backup images to be restored while allowing read-only user access. In this state for the database to maintain data consistency, the undo and uncommitted transactions are saved in the standby file to allow preceding backup images to commit them. Perhaps you plan to apply additional backup images and want to validate the data before each restore. Oftentimes, this option is used on the secondary server in log shipping to allow users access for reporting. This is equivalent to the WITH STANDBY option in the Restore Database command.

T-SQL Restore Command

All the restore commands using SQL Server 2012 Management Studio and all functionality are available directly from T-SQL. For example, to conduct a simple restore of a full database backup, use this syntax:

```
RESTORE DATABASE [NorthAmerica] FROM  DISK ='
C:\Program
Files\Microsoft SQL Server\MSSQL11.MSSQLSERVER\MSSQL\Backup\NorthAmerica.bak'
```

The following is a more complex example of a database restore using a full database, differential, and then transaction-log restore, including the STOPAT option. This option enables the DBA to stop the restore at a point in time before a data modification that caused an error. As a good practice, the STOPAT option has been placed in all the transaction-log backups. If the stop date is in the previous transaction-log backup, it stops there. Otherwise, if the stop date has been passed over, the restore process must be started again.

```
--Restore the full database backup
RESTORE DATABASE NorthAmerica FROM NorthAmericaBackup
   WITH NORECOVERY;
--Restore the differential database backup
RESTORE DATABASE NorthAmerica FROM NorthAmericaBackup
   WITH NORECOVERY;
-- Restore the transaction logs with a STOPAT to restore to a point in time.
RESTORE LOG NorthAmerica
   FROM NorthAmericaLog1
   WITH NORECOVERY, STOPAT = 'Nov 1, 12:00 AM';
RESTORE LOG NorthAmerica
   FROM NorthAmericaLog2
   WITH RECOVERY, STOPAT = 'Nov 1, 2012 12:00 AM';
```

 Databases that use transparent encryption automatically have their backups encrypted with the same key. When you restore these backups, the server encryption key must also be available. No key — no access to the data. The encryption keys must be saved for as long as the backups.

Restoring System Databases

The cause of the master database failure determines the procedure to follow to recover it. For a failure that necessitates the installation of a new SQL Server instance, if you have a copy of the most recent master full database backup, follow these steps:

1. Install the new SQL Server instance.
2. Start the SQL Server instance.
3. Install service packs and hotfixes.

4. Stop the SQL Server agent; if you don't, it may take the only single-user connection. In addition, shut down any other services that may be accessing the SQL Server instance because that may take the only connection.

5. Start the SQL Server instance in single-user mode. There are several ways to set SQL Server to single user mode: by using SQL Server Configuration Manager, executing the SQL Server binary from the command line, or from Windows Services, locating the SQL Server service.

In all cases, add the –m startup parameter to set SQL Server to single user mode, and then restart. The recommended approach is to go to SQL Server Configuration Manager, under SQL Server Services, and locate the SQL Server instance. Stop that SQL service. Then, on the Startup Parameters tab of the Service properties dialog, add the –m startup parameter to the service, and restart the SQL service, as shown in Figure 17-28.

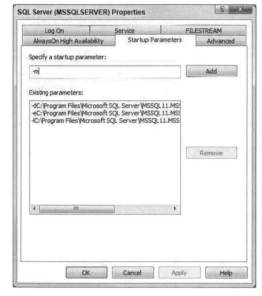

6. Use SQLCMD or an administration tool to log on to the SQL Server instance with a system administrator account. Restore the master database by executing the following command:

```
RESTORE DATABASE [MASTER] FROM  DISK =
N'C:\Program
Files\Microsoft SQL Server\MSSQL11.
MSSQLSERVER\MSSQL\Backup\master.bak'
```

FIGURE 17-28

7. If SQL Server does not start because the master database is corrupted and a current master backup is not available, the master database must be rebuilt. Execute the SQL Server `Setup.exe` to repair the system databases.

 The `rebuildm.exe` *application, available in SQL Server 2000, has been discontinued.*

8. After the rebuild and SQL Server starts, if a current copy of the master database backup is available, set the SQL Server instance in single-user mode and restore it, according to the previous instructions. If a current master database backup is not available, any modifications to the master database (for example, login security, endpoints, or linked server) will be lost and need to be redeployed.

9. Additionally, `setup.exe` creates a new `msdb` and model during the system database rebuild. If a current copy of the model and `msdb` are available, restore them. If not, all modifications performed to the model and msdb need to be redeployed. The syntax to rebuild the master database is as follows:

```
start /wait setup.exe /qn INSTANCENAME=<InstanceName> REINSTALL=SQL_Engine
```

10. Then attach the user databases.

If only the model or msdb databases are damaged, you can restore them from a current backup. If a backup is not available, then you have to execute Setup.exe, which re-creates all the system databases. Typically, model and msdb reside in the same disk system with the master, and if a disk-array failure occurred, most likely all three would be lost. To mitigate disk failure, consider using a RAID array where master, model, and msdb reside. tempdb does not need to be restored because it is automatically re-created by SQL Server at startup. tempdb is a critical database and is a single point of failure for the SQL Server instance; as such, it should be deployed on a fault-tolerant disk array.

ARCHIVING DATA

Archiving a large amount of data from large tables can be challenging. For example, selecting millions of rows from a billon-row table, copying them, and then deleting them is a long-running delete process that may escalate to a table lock and reduce concurrency, which is not acceptable, unless no one will be using the table. A commonly used procedure is to periodically delete a small number of rows to improve table concurrency because the smaller number of rows may take page locks and use an index for faster access, completing faster.

An efficient procedure to archive large amounts of data is to use a sliding time window table partitioning scheme. There are two approaches to this solution: using SQL Server table partitioning or using a partitioned view.

SQL Server Table Partitioning

SQL Server supports table partitioning, whereby a table can be carved into as many as 15,000 pieces, with each residing on its own filegroup. Each filegroup can be independently backed up. Different filegroups can also be located on different storage; for example, current data can be held on fast disks, possibly even on solid state disks. Older/archive data can then be moved to larger, slower disks and more easily deleted when the data is no longer needed. The deletion of a partition can be achieved extremely quickly, and with virtually no impact to queries against the current data.

Look at a partitioning example in which each partition contains one month's data. With table partitioning, a new empty partition is created when the next monthly data becomes available. Then the oldest partition can be switched out into a table and moved to an archive table monthly. The basic steps to create a table partition are as follows:

1. Create a partition function that describes how you want the data partitioned.

2. Create a partition schema that maps the pieces to the filegroups.

3. Create one or more tables using the partition scheme.

Following is an example of creating a partition table using a monthly sliding window:

```
--Create partition function
CREATE PARTITION FUNCTION [OrderDateRangePFN](datetime)
AS RANGE RIGHT
FOR VALUES (N'2009-01-01 00:00:00'
, N'2009-02-01 00:00:00'
, N'2009-03-01 00:00:00'
,N'2009-04-01 00:00:00');
--Create partition scheme
CREATE PARTITION SCHEME [OrderDatePScheme]
AS PARTITION [OrderDateRangePFN]
TO ([filegroup1], [filegroup2], [filegroup3], [filegroup4], [filegroup5]);
--Create partitioned table SalesOrderHeader
CREATE TABLE [dbo].[SalesOrderHeader](
  [SalesOrderID] [int] NULL,
  [RevisionNumber] [tinyint] NOT NULL,
  [OrderDate] [datetime] NOT NULL,
  [DueDate] [datetime] NOT NULL,
  [ShipDate] [datetime] NULL,
  [Status] [tinyint] NOT NULL
) ON [OrderDatePScheme]([OrderDate]);
```

This example places each partition on a different filegroup. Splitting and merging partitions requires data movement. You can achieve high-speed splits and merges without table locking or reducing concurrency if you place the partitions on the same filegroup. When partitions are on the same filegroup, switching out a partition or merging is only a schema change and occurs quickly. There are several other smaller restrictions for high-speed partitioning, but the filegroup restriction is more important.

Partitioned View

This technique has been available since earlier versions of SQL Server. It uses a partition view to group independent, identical tables together (for example, a new table for each month). Following is the procedure:

1. Create individual, identical tables with a check constraint to limit the data that can reside in each.

2. Create a view to unite all these tables together.

3. Load the data through the partition view. SQL Server evaluates the table constraint to insert the data in the correct table.

4. Before the next date period, create a new table with the date period constraint and include it as part of the view definition. Then load the current data through the view.

5. To archive, remove the oldest table from the view definition and then archive it. Each table can be placed in its own filegroup and backed up individually.

This technique does not have the 15,000-partition limitation, but it requires more management because each table is independent and managed.

SUMMARY

Backup and recovery are the last defenses to recover an organization data asset when everything else fails. The backup and restore functionality must guarantee that many years of customer information, buying patterns, financial data, and inventory can be recovered. SQL Server 2012 is a scalable and highly available RDBMS solution supporting some of the largest databases with the highest number of concurrent users running mission-critical applications. These key backup and restore functionalities ensure that it can support a larger database with less management. If you followed along throughout this chapter, you should now both understand the details needed to create a robust plan for backing up your company's data and possess one or more documents that constitute your recovery plan.

18

SQL Server 2012 Log Shipping

WHAT'S IN THIS CHAPTER

➤ Overview of Log Shipping

➤ Practical Usage Scenarios

➤ Log Shipping Architecture

➤ Log Shipping Deployment

➤ Role Changing within Log Shipping

➤ Monitoring and Troubleshooting

Log shipping is a low-cost, efficient, and simple SQL Server technique that became available many releases ago and has been vital to organizations for their business continuity. In log shipping, the database transaction log from one SQL Server is backed up and restored onto a secondary SQL Server, where it is often deployed for high-availability, reporting, and disaster-recovery scenarios. Beginning with SQL Server 2005, log shipping delivers business continuity and is one of the high-availability solutions to maintain a warm standby and, with a secondary server, used for failover.

This chapter covers log-shipping architecture and deployment scenarios and discusses how to configure log shipping and the various scenarios for switching roles between the primary and secondary servers. You also learn how to troubleshoot your log-shipping setup and how to integrate log shipping with other high-availability solutions.

 SQL Server 2008 Enterprise Edition only supports backup compression. Since SQL Server 2008 R2 both Standard Edition and Enterprise Edition support backup compression.

LOG SHIPPING DEPLOYMENT SCENARIOS

Log shipping takes advantage of the transaction-log backup and restores functionalities of SQL Server. The two log-shipping SQL Server partners can be located next to each other for high availability or across a distance for disaster recovery. The only distance restriction for the two SQL Servers is that they share connectivity that enables the secondary SQL Server to copy the transaction log and restore it. There are three different scenarios in which log shipping can be deployed:

➤ **Warm standby server:** Maintains a backup database copy in the same physical location to protect from a primary server failure

➤ **Disaster recovery solution:** Two servers are geographically separated in case the local area where the primary server resides suffers from a disaster

➤ **Reporting solution:** The secondary server is used to satisfy the reporting needs

Log Shipping to Create a Warm Standby Server

A warm standby server involves creating a full backup and periodic transaction log backups at the primary server, and then applying those backups, in sequence, to the standby server. The standby server is left in a read-only state between restores. When the standby server needs to be made available for use, any outstanding transaction log backups, including the backup of the active transaction log from the primary server, are applied to the standby server and the database is recovered. A common log-shipping scenario is creating a warm standby server whereby the log-shipping secondary server is located close to the primary server. If the primary server goes down for planned or unplanned downtime, the secondary server takes over and maintains business continuity. Then, the DBA may choose to failback to the primary server when the primary server becomes available.

It is simple to configure a warm standby server with log shipping because it uses the dependable transaction log backup, operating system copy file, and transaction log restore. In most warm standby scenarios, you should configure the log-shipping jobs to execute at a shorter interval to maintain the secondary server closely in sync with the primary server, to reduce the amount of time to switch roles, and to reduce data loss. Additionally, to further limit data loss, if the active portion of the primary server's transaction log is available, the secondary server would be restored to the point in time of the failed primary server.

However, in some situations, the active portion of the transaction log may not be available when the storage where the transaction log resided on is not accessible, or some transaction log files that were in transit may not have made it to the secondary server, causing some data loss. In a typical role-switch scenario, you would recover all in-transit transaction logs and the active portion of the transaction log before recovering the secondary server. Users would also need to be redirected because log shipping, unlike Windows failover clustering, has no automatic user redirect.

Sometimes, when performing a failback, log shipping is used in place of Windows failover clustering because it is a less expensive solution; for example, clustering requires a shared disk system that an organization may not own. Log shipping does not have such hardware requirements, so an organization may already own hardware that is not failover — cluster-compatible that can be used for log shipping. Moreover, in log shipping, the primary and secondary databases exist on separate servers. This is a shared-nothing environment. Windows failover clustering uses one shared disk system with a single copy of your database on the shared disk, which could become corrupted.

Unlike clustering, log shipping failover is always a manual process. This means you must initiate and monitor the status of the failover process and update the client application's connection strings to the new primary. When you use Windows Clustering for SQL Server, the monitoring and failover is done automatically. When you determine that you must failover to the secondary log shipping server, the execution of the steps can be manual or automated. If you choose automation, then you must create scripts that do work on your behalf. Examples of these scripts are covered later.

Another difference between log shipping and clustering is that clustering protects the whole SQL Server instance. In failover clustering, all databases on the instance are included in the solution. Log shipping is done per database. You can even log ship from one database to another on the same server. If you need high availability for all the databases on a server, you can achieve it using either clustering or log shipping. If you choose log shipping, you have to set it up for each database on the server. If you want some, but not all, of the databases on a server to be highly available, log shipping is the best choice.

Log Shipping as a Disaster Recovery Solution

Even if an organization already has a local high-availability solution, regardless if it is based around Windows failover clustering or log shipping, an alternative, site-to-site solution is a vital tool to employ. If you deploy log shipping to a secondary server at a remote location, you can protect your organization from a power grid failure or local disaster.

If the transaction log files in the backup folder or the active transaction log are not accessible, such as in a disaster where the primary server cannot be restarted because of a power grid failure, you may stitch the primary server's active transaction log and transaction log files together by using a third-party transaction log analyzer to identify transactions that did not make it across and manually apply them. However, your availability or recovery plan should not depend on these log analyzers. The transaction log files backed up by the backup job should be archived to provide point-in-time recovery of the primary server if, for example, a user error modifies some data that needs to be recovered.

Moreover, archiving the transaction logs along with a full database backup offers another disaster recovery option when needed. To control when the transaction log files are deleted so that the OS backup program can back up these files on its own schedule, set the Delete Files Older Than option to a time period great than that of the OS backup program schedule. You can find this option in the Transaction Log Backup Settings. For example, if the OS backup is scheduled to run every night, set the Delete Files Older Than option to at least keep the files there until the OS backup completes.

The challenges with this scenario are that the network bandwidth must have the capacity to support log shipping large log files to the remote location. Moreover, in the event of a disaster, there is a potential that some of the files may be in transit and may not make it to the secondary server. Even if the bandwidth supports log shipping comfortably, during a disaster the bandwidth may be constrained by other activity that can slow down the file transfers. That means the possibility of data loss. The databases are kept in sync using the transaction logs. The amount of data that might be at risk during a disaster is the data included in the transaction log. For mission-critical applications for which you want to minimize any data loss, you may need to choose another solution. For instance, database mirroring can send transactions to be synchronized as soon as the transaction commits, without waiting for a transaction log backup. Using log shipping, you may need to accept a greater amount of data loss because of a missing log file, or an inaccessible backup log folder.

Log Shipping as a Report Database Solution

Out of the three deployment solutions for which you can use log shipping, using it as a report database solution is the least effective. However, it does have its advantages. Log shipping is a low cost solution, leverages inexpensive hardware and it is a simple solution to implement and manage. Therefore, in certain scenarios, it may be feasible to use the secondary server's database for production reporting, provided that the database recovery mode is STANDBY. However, there are several inherent disadvantages to using this server for reporting.

The restore process needs exclusive access to the database while restoring; if users run reports, the restore process fails to restore and the job waits for the next restore interval to try again. Log shipping alerts may trigger, sending an alert that the secondary server has fallen behind. Moreover, at the time of role-switching, there may be transaction logs that have not been applied because reporting prevented it, which increases the role-switching time because these transaction logs are applied. However, log shipping can be configured to disconnect users who are in the database to restore the transaction logs, but longer-running reports may be kept from completing in that case. As an example, if you have the restore run every 10 minutes, but you have a report that takes 30 minutes to complete, the report would never run to completion because log shipping would kill the connection every 10 minutes. To improve the chances that the report will run to completion, the restore job interval would have to be longer, which makes the secondary server fall further behind. Additionally, the data for the reports will not be current; and the secondary server's database schema cannot be optimized for reporting because it is read-only. For example, if particular indices are beneficial to the report database, the indices need to be created in the primary server's database, which may suffer from having the additional indices.

For these reasons, using log shipping for reporting has several challenges and does not make a good reporting solution for some environments. For occasional reporting, provided the organization can live with these challenges, it is possible to use log shipping for reporting; however, a better report solution may be transactional replication, which provides concurrency, granularity, and near real-time synchronization, with the added flexibility to allow modification of the database schema. See Chapter 15 for more on transactional replication.

 The fact that log shipping must have exclusive access to the database can be a big disadvantage. If you apply logs every hour, then any current running report must be killed before the log can be applied. This kind of partial access inconveniences users and might cause them to bypass the use of log shipping for reporting purposes many times. However, if you can live with this issue, then log shipping is a viable solution.

LOG-SHIPPING ARCHITECTURE

Figure 18-1 shows the basic log-shipping architecture. The architecture requires three servers:

- ➤ Primary server
- ➤ Secondary server (also known as the standby server)
- ➤ Monitor server (optional)

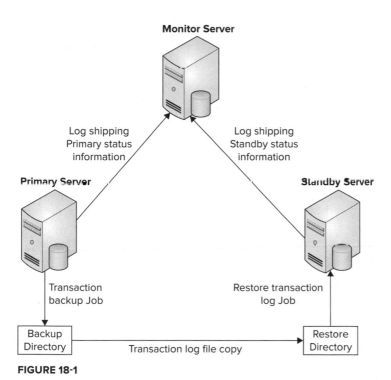

FIGURE 18-1

Primary Server

The primary server is the production server to which users connect and do work. It holds the SQL Server 2012 instance that needs to be protected in case of hardware failure, software error, natural disaster, or user-induced errors for example accidentally deleting data. You can consider configuring the secondary server to restore the log at a delay interval to react to these user-induced errors. In log shipping, the primary server is configured to execute a SQL Agent job to back up the transaction log to a file. For log shipping to function, the server must use the database recovery models of either *Bulk Logged* or *Full*. (Open the Database Properties Using SQL Server 2012 Management Studio.)

Secondary Server

The secondary server is the backup SQL Server 2012 instance that maintains a copy of the primary server database. The secondary server uses the SQL Agent to copy the transaction log file from the backup folder, where it was placed by the primary server, and to restore the transaction log backup. The secondary server is configured with two SQL Agent jobs: one to copy the transaction-log file from the shared backup folder and the other to restore the transaction log. This server should have similar performance specifications to those of the primary server to maintain a consistent user experience during failover. Log shipping can also support multiple secondary servers at a time. For instance, one can be setup for warm-standby and another for reporting and another may even have a transaction-log with a time delay.

The secondary database can be configured using either the NORECOVERY or STANDBY recovery option:

➤ STANDBY: This provides users read-only access to the log shipped database between transaction log restores. This means you can offload read-only access to a secondary server. However, for a transaction log restore to succeed, no read-only access is allowed.

➤ NORECOVERY: The database will not be available for users for read-only access.

Monitor Server

Having a monitor server as part of log shipping is optional, but recommended. The monitor server should be a different physical server to prevent it from becoming a single point of failure from the primary or secondary server. Any SQL Server version including SQL Server Express can be configured as a monitor server. When the monitor server participates in log shipping, it manages the jobs that produce monitoring information, such as the last time the transaction log was backed up on the primary server, the last transaction log that was restored on the secondary server, and the time deltas between the processes. The monitor server can also send alerts to page or e-mail the operator when log-shipping thresholds are crossed. A single monitor server can monitor multiple log-shipping environments.

Having a separate physical monitor server is recommended. Deploying a monitor server on the primary or secondary server has the risk that if that server were to fail, you would lose monitoring server capabilities as well. Without the monitor server, log shipping will continue to operate and monitoring can be performed using DMVs.

LOG SHIPPING PROCESS

SQL Agent is used on the participating servers to execute the processes that implement log shipping. There are three main processes:

➤ **Back up the transaction log on the primary server:** A SQL Agent job on the primary server backs up the transaction log at a user-configurable time interval to a file in a backup folder. By default, the filename is time-stamped to provide uniqueness — for example, databasename_yyyymmddhhmmss.trn. By default, the backup job is named LSBackup_databasename, and it executes an operating system command to back up the transaction log:

```
"C:\Program Files\Microsoft SQL Server\110\Tools\Binn\sqllogship.exe"
 -Backup 0E5D9AA6-D054-45C9-9C6B-33301DD934E2 -server SQLServer1
```

➤ **Copy the transaction log to the secondary server:** A SQL Agent job on the secondary server uses UNC or a shared drive to access the backup folder on the primary server to copy the transaction-log file to a local folder on the secondary server. By default, the copy job is

named `LSCopy_servername_databasename`, and it executes an operating system command
to copy the transaction-log file:

```
"C:\Program Files\Microsoft SQL Server\110\Tools\Binn\sqllogship.exe"
-Copy F2305BFA-B9E3-4B1C-885D-3069D0D11998 -server SQLServer1\SQLServer2
```

➤ **Restore the transaction log on the secondary server:** A SQL Agent job on the secondary
server restores the transaction log on the secondary server. To restore the transaction log,
the database must be in either Standby or NORECOVERY mode. The default restore job
name is `LSRestore_servername_databasename`, and it executes an operating system
command to copy the transaction-log file:

```
"C:\Program Files\Microsoft SQL Server\110\Tools\Binn\sqllogship.exe"
-Restore F2305BFA-B9E3-4B1C-885D-3069D0D11998 -server SQLServer1\SQLServer2
```

 You can find most of the log-shipping objects in MSDB. *For more information, see
Microsoft SQL Server 2012 Books Online.*

SYSTEM REQUIREMENTS

The servers that participate in log shipping must meet the minimum SQL Server 2012 hardware
requirements; see Microsoft SQL Server 2012 Books Online. Additionally, certain hardware
infrastructure requirements are necessary to deploy log shipping. The following sections outline
what the system requirements are and discuss what you can do to ensure you follow them accurately.

Network

The log-shipping SQL Servers are required to be networked such that the primary server has access
to the backup folder, and the secondary server has access to copy the transaction-log files from the
backup folder and into its local folder. In addition, the monitor server must connect to both the
primary and secondary servers. To improve copying the transaction-log file in an active log-shipping
environment, place the participating servers on their own network segment and use an additional
network card dedicated to log shipping. Log shipping can function with any feasible network speed,
but on a slow network the transaction-log file transfer can take longer, and the secondary server can
likely be further behind the primary server.

Identical Capacity Servers

The primary and secondary servers are recommended to have identical performance capacity so
that in a failover the secondary server can take over and provide the same level of performance and
user experience. Additionally, some organizations have service-level agreements (SLA) to meet. The
SLA may require that you provide the same performance during failover as you would normally,
requiring your secondary server to have the same capacity as the primary. Some businesses allow the
secondary server to be of smaller capacity. You should understand the specific requirements of your
business and configure the secondary server appropriately.

Storage

Unlike a Windows failover cluster that requires a shared-disk infrastructure, log shipping has no such requirements. On the contrary, to mitigate the risk of storage failure becoming a single point of failure, the primary and secondary servers should not share the same disk system. In a disaster recovery scenario configuration, the primary and secondary servers would be located at a distance from each other and would be unlikely to share the same disk system. Plan the disk space requirements for the backup share that holds the transaction-log backups to avoid running out of disk space. Moreover, when identifying the performance specification for the disk systems, consider the log-shipping I/O activities.

When deploying log shipping with Management Studio, the SQL Server service and the SQL Agent account (or its proxy running the backup job) must have read-and-write permission to the backup folder. If possible, this folder should reside on a fault-tolerant disk system so that if a drive is lost, all the transaction log files are not lost.

Software

Three SQL Server editions are supported for log shipping:

➤ SQL Server 2012 Enterprise Edition

➤ SQL Server 2012 Standard Edition

➤ SQL Server 2012 Business Intelligence Edition

➤ Monitor server can be any edition including SQL Express

The log-shipping servers are required to have identical case-sensitivity settings, and the log-shipping databases must use either the full or bulk-logged recovery model.

DEPLOYING LOG SHIPPING

Before you can begin the log-shipping deployment process, you need to do some initial configuration. Then you have a choice regarding how you want to deploy: using the SQL Server 2012 Management Studio or using T-SQL scripts. Typically, a DBA uses SQL Server 2012 Management Studio to configure log shipping and then generates SQL scripts for future redeployment. Both procedures are covered here.

Initial Configuration

Prior to deploying Log Shipping, some specific directories are needed for log shipping to copy the transaction log files and SQL configuration to prepare the Log Shipping process to execute. To configure your shared directories for log shipping, perform the following steps:

1. First create a backup folder that the primary server can access; share it, and ensure that it is accessible by the secondary server. For example, you could use the folder `c:\primaryBackupLog`, which is also shared as a UNC path: `\\primaryserver\primaryBackupLog`. Use the UNC when you are accessing to the share from a remote server; when the share is local, you can access either by UNC or by the directory letter. The primary server's SQL Agent account must have read-and-write permission to the folder, and the secondary server's SQL Agent account or the proxy account executing the job should have read permission to this folder. Additionally, the SQL Agent account must have permission to execute the log shipping extended stored procedure.

2. Next, create a destination folder on the secondary server, such as `c:\secondaryBackupDest`. The secondary server's SQL Agent account, or the proxy account executing the job, must have read-and-write permission to this folder. Additionally, the account must have permission to execute the log shipping extended stored procedures.

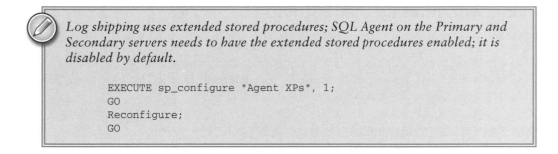

Log shipping uses extended stored procedures; SQL Agent on the Primary and Secondary servers needs to have the extended stored procedures enabled; it is disabled by default.

```
EXECUTE sp_configure "Agent XPs", 1;
GO
Reconfigure;
GO
```

3. Set the recovery model for the log-shipped database to either `Full` or `Bulk_logged`. There are two ways to do this, depending on how you want to deploy: with Management Studio or with a T-SQL command. To use Management Studio, open the Database Properties window and select Options. From the Recovery Model drop-down, choose the recovery model, as shown in Figure 18-2.

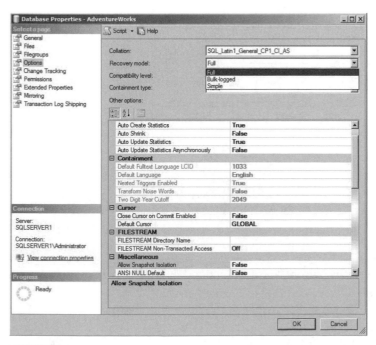

FIGURE 18-2

To use T-SQL, open a SQL query window and use the ALTER DATABASE command to change the recovery model. For example, to change the AdventureWorks database to Full, use this T-SQL:

```
USE master;
GO
ALTER DATABASE AdventureWorks
SET RECOVERY FULL;
GO
```

Deploying with Management Studio

To deploy log shipping with SQL Server Management Studio, perform the following steps:

1. Start by opening the database to be configured and select the database properties; then select Transaction Log Shipping. Click the check box that reads Enable This as a Primary Database in a Log Shipping Configuration, as shown in Figure 18-3.

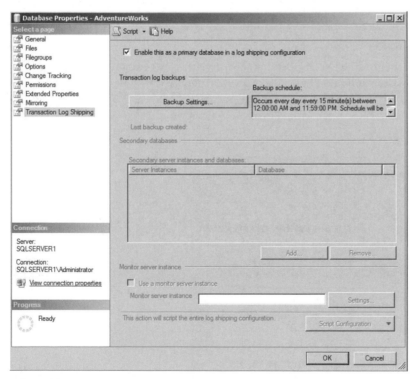

FIGURE 18-3

2. Next, click the Backup Settings button. The Transaction Log Backup Settings dialog appears, as shown in Figure 18-4.

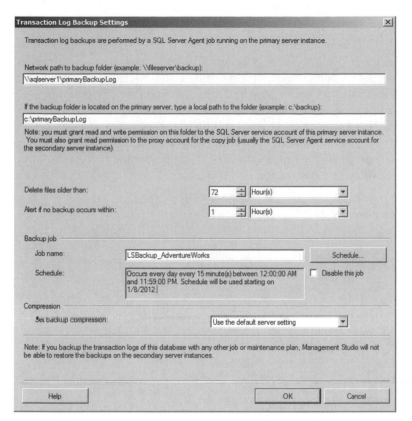

FIGURE 18-4

3. Here, you need to provide the network path to the backup folder and the local path if the folder is local to the primary server. If the folder is local to the primary server, log shipping uses the local path. Remember that the SQL Server service and the SQL Agent account or its proxy running the backup job must have read read-and and-write permission to this folder. If possible, this folder should reside on a fault-tolerant disk system so that if a drive is lost, all the transaction log files are not lost.

Typically you can delete transaction-log backup files that have been applied and are older than the value in the Delete Files Older Than field to control the folder size containing older transaction backup log files. However, for an additional level of protection, if the business requires point-in-time recovery, leave the files there until the OS backup program backs them up to another storage device, provided that a full database backup is also available to apply these transaction logs. The default setting is 72 hours.

4. In the Alert if No Backup Occurs Within field, choose a value based on the business requirements. The amount of data your organization can stand to lose determines the transaction backup interval setting or how critical the data is. The alert time also depends on the transaction backup interval setting. For example, if the business requires a highly available secondary server, where the transaction log is backed up every couple of minutes, this setting should be configured to send an alert if the job fails to run within that interval. The default setting is 1 hour.

5. Click the Schedule button to display the Job Schedule Properties page, and set up a schedule for the transaction-log backup job. The important setting is the "Occurs Every Field," which defaults to 15 minutes. This setting can be configured to once every minute for higher availability. However, the time interval should be appropriately set to allow the previous transaction-log backup job to complete. This value is the degree to which the primary and secondary servers are in sync. When you're done here, click OK on the Job Schedule Properties page; then click OK in the Transaction Log Backup Settings dialog to return to the Database Properties page for Transaction Log Shipping.

6. Click Add to display the Secondary Database Settings dialog to set up a secondary (standby) server, as shown in Figure 18-5.

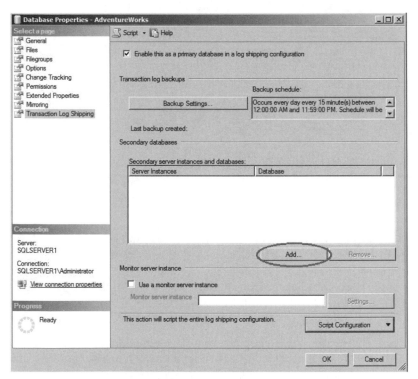

FIGURE 18-5

Then click Connect and choose the Secondary Server instance. Then choose an existing database or a new database name. On the Initialize Secondary Database tab as shown in Figure 18-6, there are three options to choose (described in the following list).

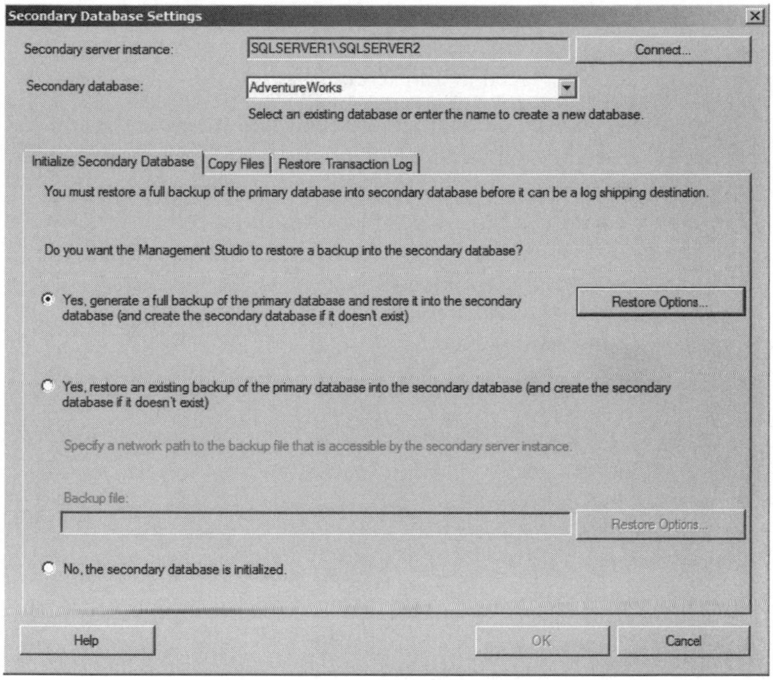

FIGURE 18-6

These options answer the question, "Do you want the Management Studio to restore a backup into the secondary database?

➤ **Yes, generate a full backup of the primary database and restore it into the secondary database (and create the secondary database if it does not exist):** The Restore Options setting enables you to set the database folder locations for the data and the log files. If this is not set, the default database locations are used.

➤ **Yes, restore an existing backup of the primary database into the secondary database (and create the secondary database if it does not exist):** The Restore Options setting enables you to set database folder locations for the data and the log files. You also specify the network location of the backup file you want to restore.

➤ **No, the secondary database is initialized:** The option means that the database has already been created. The transaction logs preceding the database restore must be available to enable log shipping to work. For example, the log sequence number (LSN) of the primary server and the secondary server databases must match. Also, the secondary database must be in either NORECOVERY or STANDBY mode to allow additional transaction-log files to be applied.

7. Next, restore the secondary database from the primary backup; the new database file path and name created will be the same as the primary database. You cannot alter the filename, but you can change the path and specify path names in the dialog box by clicking the Restore Options button. For the examples in this section, the primary and secondary databases are on the same Windows server but different SQL Server 2012 instances. The secondary database AdventureWorks was created with the same filenames as those for the primary database AdventureWorks but placed in a different directory.

8. On the Copy Files tab as shown in Figure 18-7, in the "Destination folder for the copied files directory" textbox, type the destination folder (e.g., `c:\secondaryBackupDest`). The Delete Copied Files After option controls the folder size after the transaction log is restored on the secondary server's database. Any files older than the specified time are deleted. The default is 72 hours.

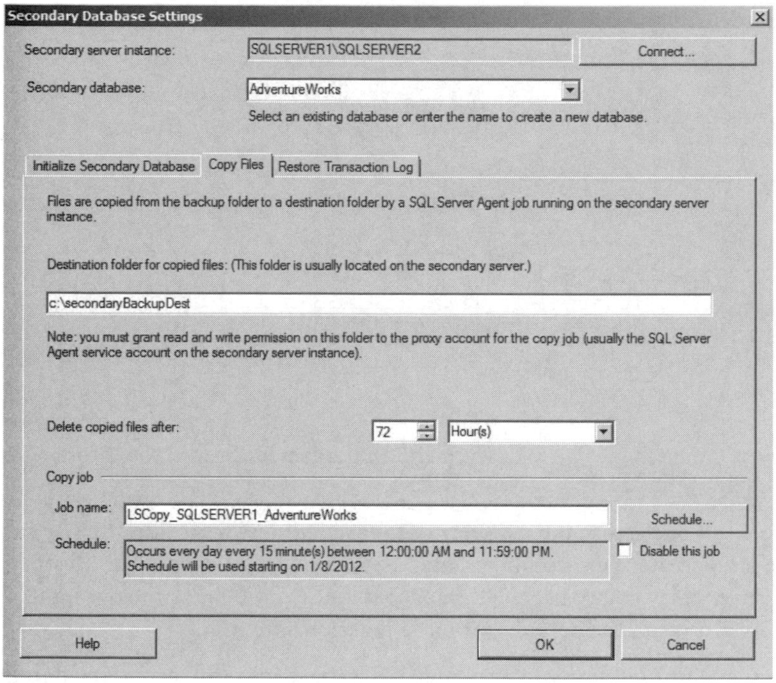

FIGURE 18-7

9. Click the Schedule button to set up a schedule for the transaction-log-file copy job. The important setting is the Occurs Every field, which defaults to 15 minutes. You can reduce this time to have the secondary closer in data sync with the primary. Click OK when you finish to return to the Secondary Database Settings page.

10. Click the Restore Transaction Log tab as shown in Figure 18-8.

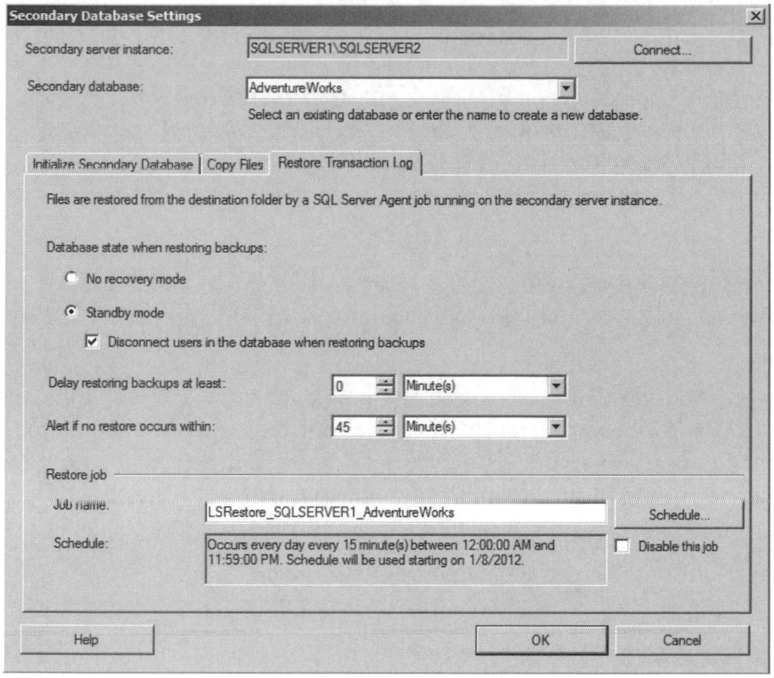

FIGURE 18-8

You have two options for the On Database State When Restoring Backups field:

➤ **No Recovery mode:** The secondary database is left in NORECOVERY mode, which enables the server to restore additional transactional-log backups but doesn't enable user access.

➤ **Standby mode:** The secondary database enables read-only operations to be performed in the database, such as reporting. However, as mentioned previously, the restore process needs exclusive access to the secondary database; if users are accessing the database, the restore process cannot complete.

For the Delay Restoring Backups at Least setting, the default is 0 minutes. Typically, you would change this setting if your organization wants to keep the secondary database around in case of a primary database's data corruption or unintended data deletions. This delay may prevent the secondary database from restoring the corrupted transaction-log file.

The Alert if No Restore Occurs Within setting defaults to 45 minutes and should be set to the tolerance level of the business.

An alert can be a symptom of a serious error on the secondary database that prevents it from accepting additional transaction-log restores. When this occurs, look in the history of the restore job; the default name is `LSRestore_ServerName_PrimaryDatabaseName` *and is found under SQL Agent jobs on the secondary server. Additionally, look in the Windows Event Viewer for any additional information. You can also copy and paste the restore job command into a SQL command window, which may provide additional error information to help diagnose the problem.*

11. Click OK on the Secondary Database Settings page when you finish. To add another secondary server instance, click Add and follow the same steps to add another secondary server.

12. To add a monitor server, from the Transaction Log Shipping page of the primary database properties, click Use a Monitor Server Instance. Then click Settings. A separate monitor instance from either the primary or secondary server is recommended so that a failure of the primary or secondary server won't bring down the monitor server.

13. On the Log Shipping Monitor Settings page shown in Figure 18-9, click Connect and then choose a monitor server instance for this log-shipping environment.

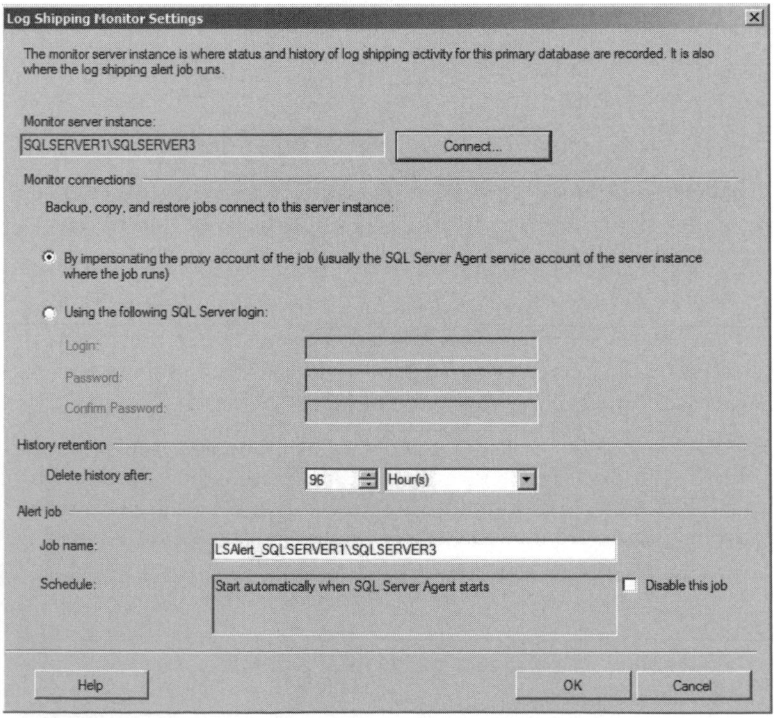

Log Shipping Monitor Settings

The monitor server instance is where status and history of log shipping activity for this primary database are recorded. It is also where the log shipping alert job runs.

Monitor server instance:
SQLSERVER1\SQLSERVER3   [Connect...]

Monitor connections

Backup, copy, and restore jobs connect to this server instance:

⦿ By impersonating the proxy account of the job (usually the SQL Server Agent service account of the server instance where the job runs)

○ Using the following SQL Server login:

Login:
Password:
Confirm Password:

History retention

Delete history after: 96 ⇕ Hour(s) ▾

Alert job

Job name: LSAlert_SQLSERVER1\SQLSERVER3

Schedule: Start automatically when SQL Server Agent starts   ☐ Disable this job

[Help]   [OK] [Cancel]

FIGURE 18-9

14. The account must have system administrator permissions on the secondary server. In the By Impersonating the Proxy Account of the Job or Using the Following SQL Server Login field, choose how the backup, copy, and restore jobs connect to this server instance to update MSDB job history information. For integrated security, the jobs should connect by impersonating the proxy account of the SQL Server Agent running the jobs or by SQL Server login.

The "Delete History After" field controls the amount of history data held in MSDB; the default is 96 hours. How long you hold history depends on your business-retention requirements and your available disk space. The default value is fine for most deployments unless you plan to perform data analysis over time; then you should change the default.

15. When you finish, the complete log shipping setup should look like Figure 18-10. Click OK on the Log Shipping Monitor Settings page. Then click OK on the Database Properties to finish setting up the Log Shipping Configuration.

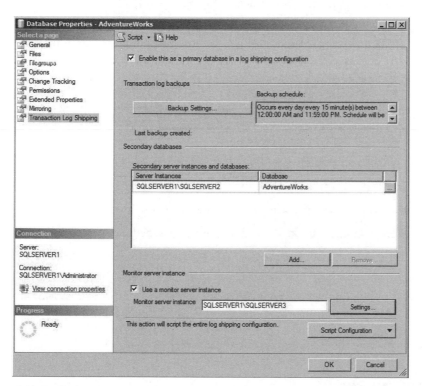

FIGURE 18-10

Deploying with T-SQL Commands

Another deployment option is to use the actual T-SQL commands to configure log shipping. Even if you choose to use the SQL Server Management Studio to configure log shipping, saving the generated command script enables you to quickly reconfigure the server to expedite a disaster recovery scenario while avoiding any user-induced errors. The following T-SQL commands are equivalent to the steps you took in SQL Server Management Studio.

On the primary server, execute the following stored procedures in the MSDB:

➤ `master.dbo.sp_add_log_shipping_primary_database`: Configures the primary database for a log-shipping configuration; this configures the log-shipping backup job.

➤ `msdb.dbo.sp_add_schedule`: Creates a schedule for the log-shipping configuration.

➤ `msdb.dbo.sp_attach_schedule`: Links the log-shipping job to the schedule.

➤ `msdb.dbo.sp_update_job`: Enables the transaction-log backup job.

➤ `master.dbo.sp_add_log_shipping_alert_job`: Creates the alert job and adds the job ID in the `log_shipping_monitor_alert` table. This stored procedure enables the alert notifications.

On the secondary server, execute the following stored procedures:

➤ `master.dbo.sp_add_log_shipping_secondary_primary`: Sets up the primary information, adds local and remote monitor links, and creates copy and restore jobs on the secondary server for the specified primary database

➤ `msdb.dbo.sp_add_schedule`: Sets the schedule for the copy job

➤ `msdb.dbo.sp_attach_schedule`: Links the copy job to the schedule

➤ `msdb.dbo.sp_add_schedule`: Sets the schedule for the restore job

➤ `msdb.dbo.sp_attach_schedule`: Links the restore job to the schedule

➤ `master.dbo.sp_add_log_shipping_secondary_database`: Sets up secondary databases for log shipping

➤ `msdb.dbo.sp_update_job`: Enables the copy job

➤ `msdb.dbo.sp_update_job`: Enables the transaction-log restore job

Back on the primary server, execute this stored procedure in the MSDB:

➤ `master.dbo.sp_add_log_shipping_primary_secondary`: Adds an entry for a secondary database on the primary server

MONITORING AND TROUBLESHOOTING

Log shipping has monitoring capabilities to identify the progress of the backup, copy, and restore jobs. Additionally, monitoring helps to determine whether the backup, copy, or restore jobs are out of sync with the secondary server. A few indicators that something has gone wrong include a job that has not made any progress or a job that has failed, both of which will be discussed later in this section.

There are two approaches to monitor the progress of the log-shipping operation: using the Transaction Log Shipping Status report, performed through Management Studio or executing the `master.dbo.sp_help_log_shipping_monitor` stored procedure. Either method can help you determine whether the secondary server is out of sync with the primary server, and the time delta between the two. Using Management Studio, you can visually see the operation; but using the stored procedure enables setup of a recurring batch SQL Agent job command to monitor the log shipping operation to send alerts. With both of these methods, you can also determine which jobs are not making any progress and the last transaction-log backup, copy, and restore filename processed on the secondary server.

To inform you of any errors found, log shipping also performs alerts jobs that periodically check if a preset threshold has been exceeded by executing the `sys.sp_check_log_shipping_monitor_alert` stored procedure. If the threshold has been exceeded, the stored procedure raises an alert that is returned to the log shipping monitoring status. You can choose to modify the log-shipping alert jobs to capture the alert and notify you using SQL Agent.

In log shipping, if a monitor server is deployed, these alerts reside on the monitor server that reports on the transaction-log backup, copy file, and restore transaction log. If not, the primary server manages the alert job for the transaction-log backup, and the secondary server manages the alert job for the copy file and restore transaction log. If the monitoring server is present, the primary and secondary servers will not deploy alert jobs.

The following is an example error that results if the transaction-log backup process has exceeded the preset threshold of 30 minutes:

```
Executed as user: NT AUTHORITY\SYSTEM. The log shipping primary database
SQLServer1.AdventureWorks has backup threshold of 30 minutes and has not
performed a backup log operation for 60 minutes. Check agent log and log shipping
monitor information. [SQLSTATE 42000](Error 14420). This step failed.
```

The next example shows an error that results if the restore transaction-log process has exceeded the preset threshold of 30 minutes:

```
Executed as user: NT AUTHORITY\SYSTEM. The log shipping secondary database
SQLServer2.AdventureWorks has restore threshold of 30 minutes and is out of
sync. No restore was performed for 60 minutes. Restored latency is 15 minutes. Check
agent log and log shipping monitor information. [SQLSTATE 42000](Error 14421).
The step failed.
```

As an alternative, you can set up an alert for when errors 14420 or 14221 are raised; SQL Agent sends an alert to the operator.

Monitoring with Management Studio

The Transaction Log Shipping Status report displays monitoring information from Management Studio. This report executes the `sp_help_log_shipping_monitor` stored procedure. When executed on the primary server, it reports on the transaction-log backup details; when executed on the secondary server, it reports on the copy and transaction-log restore details. When the monitor server is configured, the report executed from the monitor server produces a consolidated report of the transaction-log backup, copy, and transaction-log restore details in one report. To access the Transaction Log Shipping Status report:

1. Connect to the primary, secondary, or monitor server. The monitor server is the most useful option because it has the consolidated log-shipping detail data.

2. If the Object Explorer is not visible, select View ➪ Object Explorer.

3. Right-click the server node in the Object Explorer and select Reports ➪ Standard Reports ➪ Transaction Log Shipping Status.

Figure 18-11 shows an example of a Transaction Log Shipping Status report executed from the monitor server, showing the details for all log-shipping activities with alerts.

FIGURE 18-11

Monitoring with Stored Procedures

Executing the `sp_help_log_shipping_monitor` stored procedure in the `master` database from a SQL query window produces log-shipping status details, similar to the Transaction Log Shipping Status report. If you execute it from the primary server, it returns detailed information on the transaction-log backup job. If you execute it from the secondary server, it returns information on the copy and transaction-log restore jobs. If it is executed from the monitor server, it returns a consolidated detail result of the transaction-log backup, copy, and transaction-log restore, as the monitor server is visible to all log-shipping processes.

For additional log-shipping operational and troubleshooting detail information, the log-shipping tables can be queried using the log-shipping stored procedures found in the `msdb` database. For more information, see SQL Server 2012 Books Online.

Troubleshooting Approach

As mentioned previously, log shipping consists of three basic operations: backing up the transaction log, copying the file, and restoring the transaction log. Troubleshooting this process is simply a matter of identifying which operation is not functioning. You can use both of the log-shipping monitoring capabilities to identify the problem.

For example, say the restore transaction-log file shows that no new files have been restored in the last 60 minutes. You need to look at the log-shipping job history on the secondary server first under the SQL Agent and the Windows Event Viewer to determine the actual error message. If, for instance, the copy file job is failing, it may be because the network is down. If the restore transaction-log job is failing, it may be because the server is unavailable or that users are using the database if the database is in standby mode.

 Be aware that changing the database recovery model to Simple *will break log shipping because the transaction log is truncated instead of backed up. If this occurs, you need to reconfigure log shipping. If you saved the log-shipping configuration scripts, the reconfiguration should be fairly simple. Additionally, there should not be any other transaction-log backup operation outside of log shipping because that will also break log shipping since the log chain will not match on the secondary server. Finally, note that large transaction-log files will take longer to copy and restore increasing latency.*

MANAGING CHANGING ROLES

For business continuity, a high availability solution must allow smooth role-switching between the current primary and secondary servers. To accomplish this goal, log shipping requires that certain dependencies are available on the secondary server because the scope of log shipping is at the database level. Any object outside of the log-shipped database will not be maintained by log shipping. For example, SQL Server logins are contained in the master database, and SQL jobs are contained in msdb. Therefore, these dependencies and others need to be systematically maintained by other procedures to enable users to connect to the secondary server after it becomes the new primary server. Furthermore, you need to develop an approach to redirect the client applications to the new primary server. For examples see the section, "Redirecting Clients to Connect to the Secondary Server" later in this chapter.

Synchronizing Dependencies

Log shipping applies changes that occur inside the log-shipping database, but it does not maintain any outside dependencies. Moreover, log shipping cannot be used to ship system databases. Newly added logins, new database users, jobs, and other dependencies that live in other databases are not synchronized by log shipping.

SQL Server 2012 resolves the login dependency by using the new Contained Database property in the database property where user authentication can then be stored directly in the database and authentication can be made directly to the database removing the login dependency. For new deployments, you should consider using the Contained Database property and removing the login dependency.

In a failover scenario, when users attempt to log in to the secondary server's database, they will not have a login there. Moreover, any jobs configured on the primary server will not be present either; and if the primary server uses linked servers to access a remote SQL Server, then the database operations would fail because they would not find the linked server. Therefore, you need to identify the outside dependencies that the log-shipping database uses and develop a plan to make these resources available during the failover. The following sections describe common log-shipping dependencies and their solutions.

Login and Database Users

When developing a process to synchronize SQL Server logins with the secondary server and database you should begin by setting it up as a recurring SQL job that runs at certain scheduled intervals. In a planned failover, you should run these SQL jobs before failover to update the secondary server with the most current access information. Following are the steps:

1. Develop an Integration Services (SSIS) package to Transfer logins. Open SQL Server Business Intelligence Development Studio, and start a new Integration Services project.

2. In the Solution Explorer, name the SSIS project `Transfer Logins`, and rename the SSIS Package to `Transfer Logins`.

3. Click the Toolbox, and drag the Transfer Logins Task into the package.

4. Right-click the Transfer Logins Task, and choose Edit.

5. Click Logins. You see the dialog shown in Figure 18-12.

6. For `SourceConnection`, enter a new connection to the primary server.

7. For `DestinationConnection`, enter a new connection for the secondary server.

8. For `LoginsToTransfer`, choose `AllLoginsFromSelectedDatabases`.

9. For `DatabasesList`, choose the log-shipping database.

10. In the Options section, in the `IfObjectExists` entry, choose what to do if the login exists, such as `FailTask`, `Override`, or `Skip`. If the secondary server is hosting other databases, you may encounter duplicate logins.

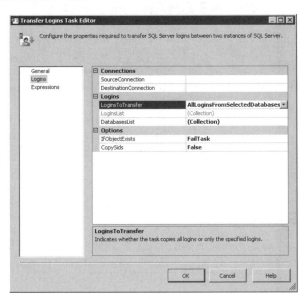

FIGURE 18-12

11. Save the package, and choose Build ⇨ Build SSIS Transfer Logins to compile the package.

12. From Microsoft SQL Server 2012 Management Studio, connect to the Integration Services of the primary server.

13. Under Stored Packages, choose MSDB; right-click, and choose Import Package.

This next job resolves the logins on the secondary server after the secondary database has been recovered. The SQL Server Agent service account or a proxy account must have the system administrator role to run this job. Steps to synchronize logins between primary and secondary servers are the following:

1. Create a new SQL Agent job on the primary server and rename it Sync Secondary Server Access Information.

2. Create a step named `BCP Syslogins` with these characteristics:

➤ **Type:** Operating system.

➤ **Run As:** SQL Agent Service. (This is the account that needs system administrator permission to execute this command and needs read/write permission on the folder from which it copies the file.)

➤ **Command:** `BCP Master.sys.syslogins out c:\login1\syslogins.dat /N /S <Server_Name> -T`

3. Create a step named `Copy Syslogins` with these characteristics:

➤ **Type:** Operating system.

➤ **Run As:** SQL Agent Service. (This account needs read access to the source folder and read/write access to the destination folder.)

➤ **Command:** `COPY c:\login1\syslogins.dat \\SecondaryServer\login2`

4. Create a step named `Transfer Logins` Task with these characteristics:

➤ **Type:** Operating system.

➤ **Run As:** SQL Agent Service. (The account needs sysadmin permission to execute this command.)

➤ **Command:** `DTEXEC /sq` *Transfer Logins* `/Ser <Server_Name>`

5. Create a step named Resolve Logins with these characteristics:

➤ **Type:** Transact-SQL script (T-SQL)

➤ **Command:** `EXEC sp_resolve_logins @dest_db = '<Database_Name>', @dest_path = 'c:\login2\', @filename = 'syslogins.dat'`

When using the method of synchronizing logins as described in this section, you should run this SQL job on a regular schedule to avoid inconsistent logins, in case of a primary server failure.

SQL Agent Jobs

You can use the Integration Services Transfer Jobs Task to synchronize jobs from the primary server to the secondary server.

1. Create a package using SQL Server Business Intelligence Studio, and choose the Transfer Jobs Task.

2. Provide the connection information and the jobs to transfer.

3. Then compile and import the package into SQL Server 2012 or as an SSIS file system.

4. Finally, schedule and execute it as a SQL Agent job to periodically synchronize changes with the secondary server. The frequency depends on how frequent jobs are changed that then need to be synchronized.

Other Database Dependencies

Make a list of all dependencies on which the log-shipping database relies. These can be distributed queries/linked servers, encrypted data, certificates, user-defined error messages, event notifications and WMI events, extended stored procedures, server configuration, full-text engine, permissions on objects, replication settings, Service Broker applications, startup procedures, triggers, CLR procedures, and database mail. Develop a plan to synchronize these to the secondary server.

Switching Roles from the Primary to Secondary Servers

If the primary server were to fail, the secondary server needs to assume the role of the primary server. This is called *role switching*. There are two potential types of role switches: planned failover and unplanned failover. A planned failover is most likely when the DBA needs to perform some type of maintenance, usually scheduled at a time of low business activity or during a maintenance window — for example, switching roles to apply a service pack on the primary server. An unplanned failover is when the DBA switches roles for business continuity because the primary server becomes unavailable.

Planned Failover

For a planned failover, identify a time when the primary server has little or no activity. During a time like this, it is likely that the secondary server will not have restored all the transaction logs from the primary server, and transaction logs will be in the process of being copied across by the SQL Agent job that the restore SQL Agent job has not completed. Additionally, the active transaction log may contain records that have not been backed up. Before you start your planned failover, you must completely synchronize the secondary server and the active transaction log must be restored on the secondary server. The steps to do that are as follows:

1. Stop and disable the primary server transaction log backup job.

2. Execute the log-shipping copy, and restore jobs to reinstate the remainder of the transaction logs. Use the log-shipping monitoring tool or report to verify that the entire set of transaction-log backups has been copied and restored on the secondary server. A manual option is to copy all transaction-log backups that have not been copied from the primary server backup folder to the secondary server folder. Then restore each transaction log in sequence to the secondary server.

3. Stop and disable the secondary server's copy and restore jobs.

4. Execute the Sync Secondary Server Access Information job to synchronize database dependencies and then disable it.

5. Back up the active transaction log from the primary to the secondary server with NORECOVERY:

```
USE MASTER;
BACKUP LOG <Database_Name> TO DISK =
'C:\primaryBackupLog\<Database_Name>.trn'
WITH NORECOVERY;
```

This accomplishes two goals:

➤ It backs up the active transaction log from the primary server so that it can be restored to the secondary server to synchronize the secondary database.

➤ It changes the old primary server database to NORECOVERY mode to enable transaction logs from the new primary server to be applied without initializing the database by a restore, as the log chain would not have been broken.

6. Copy the backup log files to the secondary server. On the secondary server, restore the tail of the transaction log and then recover the database:

```
RESTORE LOG <Database_Name>
FROM DISK ='c:\secondaryBackupDest\Database_name.trn'WITH RECOVERY;
```

7. If the active transaction log is not accessible, the database can be recovered without it:

```
RESTORE DATABASE <Database_Name>  WITH RECOVERY;
```

8. On the new primary server, execute the Resolve Logins job to synchronize the logins. The secondary server's database becomes the primary server's database and starts to accept data modifications.

9. Redirect all applications to the new primary server.

10. Configure log shipping from the new primary server to the secondary server. The secondary server (the former primary server) is already in NORECOVERY mode. During log-shipping configuration, in the Secondary Database Settings dialog box, choose No, The Secondary Database Is Initialized.

11. When you finish configuring log shipping, the new primary server executes the transaction-log backup job, and the secondary server copies and restores the transaction-log files. Set up and enable all SQL jobs that were synchronizing from the old primary server (e.g., to synchronize the logins and database users to the old primary server).

Unplanned Failover

If the primary server becomes unavailable in an unplanned situation, some data loss is probable. This could be because the active transaction log cannot be backed up or some of the transaction-log backup may not be reachable. Therefore, in an unplanned failover, you have to verify that the last copy and restore transaction logs have been restored by using the log-shipping monitoring and reporting functions. If the active transaction-log backup is accessible, it should be restored to bring the secondary server in synchronization with the primary server up to the point of failure. Then restore the secondary database with RECOVERY.

After assessing the damage and fixing the old primary server, you will most likely need to reconfigure log-shipping configuration because the active transaction log may not have been accessible, or the log chain may have been broken. When you configure log shipping, in the Secondary Database Settings dialog, choose either to restore from a previous database backup or to generate a new database backup to restore. You may choose to switch roles to promote the original primary server, which is discussed next.

Switching Between Primary and Secondary Servers

In a planned failover, after performing the steps to switch the primary and secondary server in a server change whereby the Log Shipping jobs have been deployed to both primary and secondary servers, you can switch between primary and secondary servers by following these steps:

1. Stop and disable the primary server's transaction-log backup job.

2. Verify that all the transaction-log backups have been copied and restored, either manually or by executing the SQL jobs.

3. Execute the Sync Logins job.

4. Stop and disable the transaction-log copy and restore jobs on the secondary server.

5. Back up the active Transaction log on the primary server with NORECOVERY.

6. Restore the active transaction-log backup on the secondary server.

7. Restore the secondary server's database with RECOVERY.

8. Execute the Resolve Logins job.

9. Enable the transaction-log backup on the new primary server to log-ship to the secondary server.

10. Enable the secondary server transaction-log copy and restore jobs.

11. Enable synchronization of the logins and database users.

12. Enable any other SQL jobs.

Redirecting Clients to Connect to the Secondary Server

After switching roles, the client connections need to be redirected to the secondary server with minimal disruptions to users. Log shipping does not provide any client-redirect capability, so you need to choose another approach. The approach you choose may depend on the infrastructure and who controls it as well as the number of clients that need to be redirected, the required availability of the application (such as a service-level agreement [SLA]), and the application activity. At minimum, users will experience a brief interruption as the client applications are redirected. The following sections discuss a few common approaches to redirecting client connections to the secondary server.

Application Coding

The application can be developed as failover-aware with the capability to connect to the secondary server either with automatic retry or by manually changing the server name. The application logic would connect to the primary server first, but if it is unavailable, and after the retry logic has run unsuccessfully, the application can attempt to connect to the secondary server if it has been promoted to a primary server.

After the secondary database has been recovered however, it may not necessarily be ready to serve user requests. For example, you may need to run several tasks or jobs first, such as running the Resolve Logins task. To overcome this circumstance, the database may need to be put into single-user mode to prevent other users from connecting while you perform tasks or jobs. Therefore, the application logic must handle this situation in which the primary server is no longer available and the secondary server is not yet accessible.

Network Load Balancing

Use a network load balancing solution, either Windows Network Load Balancing (NLB) or a hardware solution. With this solution, the application connects using the load balancing network name or IP address, and the load balancing solution directs the application to the database server. Therefore, in a failover scenario, the application continues to connect to the network load balancer's network name or IP address, while the load balancer is updated manually or by script with the new primary server network name and IP address. Then clients are redirected. NLB is included with certain versions of Microsoft Windows. Configuration is straightforward and can act as the cross-reference to direct applications to the current primary server.

Domain Name Service (DNS)

DNS provides name-to-IP address resolution and can be used to redirect clients to the new primary server. If you have access to the DNS server, you can modify the IP address to redirect client applications after a failover, either by script or by using the Windows DNS management tool. DNS acts as a cross-reference for the client applications because they continue to connect to the same name, but the DNS modification redirects the database request to the new primary server.

SQL Client Aliasing

SQL Aliasing is another method that can be used to redirect clients to the new primary server. To configure aliasing, go to the SQL Server Configuration Manager, under the SQL Native Client Configuration. This method may be less favorable if many client applications connect directly to the database server because the alias would have to be created at each client computer, which may not be feasible. It is more feasible if the client applications connect to a Web or application server that then connects to the database server. Then the SQL client alias can be applied on the Web or application server, and all the clients would be redirected to the new primary server.

DATABASE BACKUP PLAN

Regardless of the high-availability solution, a database backup plan is strongly recommended to protect data from corruption or user error. A secondary database is not enough since a corruption in the primary database can cause corruption on the secondary database as well. There are two routes you can take when choosing a backup plan: a full database back up and a differential database backup.

A full database backup copies all the data and the transaction log to a backup device, which is usually a tape or disk drive. It is used in case of an unrecoverable failure so that the database can be restored to that point in time at which it was last backed up. A full database restore is also required as a starting point for differential or transaction-log restores. The backup should be stored offsite so that the database is not lost in the event of a disaster.

A differential database backup copies all modified extents in the database since the last full database backup. An *extent* is a unit of space allocation that consists of eight database pages that SQL Server uses to allocate space for database objects. Differential database backups are smaller than the full database backup, except in certain scenarios where the database is active and every extent is modified since the last full backup. To restore from a differential database backup, a full database backup is required prior to the differential backup.

Full or differential database backup operations will not break log shipping, provided no transaction-log operations are performed that change it. However, the inverse is possible in that log shipping can impact some backup and recovery plans in the following ways:

➤ Another transaction-log backup cannot be performed in addition to log shipping because that breaks the log chain for the log-shipping process. SQL Server will not prevent an operator from creating additional transaction-log backup jobs on a log-shipping database.

➤ A transaction-log backup that truncates the transaction log will break the log chain, and log shipping will stop functioning.

➤ If you change the database to the simple recovery model, the transaction log will truncate by the SQL Server and log shipping will stop functioning.

INTEGRATING LOG SHIPPING WITH OTHER HIGH-AVAILABILITY SOLUTIONS

Log shipping can be deployed along with other Microsoft high-availability solutions because log shipping provides disaster recovery while the other solution provides high availability. There are three main solutions with which you can integrate log shipping:

➤ **Data mirroring:** Maintains a remote site if the data-mirroring pair becomes unavailable.

➤ **Windows failover clustering:** Maintains a remote disaster recovery site if the local Windows failover cluster becomes unavailable.

➤ **Replication:** Maintains a highly available replication publisher.

SQL Server 2012 Data Mirroring

A scenario in which log shipping can be best integrated with a SQL Server 2012 data mirroring solution would be if an organization deployed local data mirroring and log shipping from the principal server to a remote location. However, during a data-mirroring role switch, log shipping does not automatically switch roles. Therefore manual steps must be taken to enable the former mirror, which would now be the principal, to start to log ship its transaction log to the secondary server by deploying log shipping from the new principal server.

Windows Failover Clustering

The best scenario in which log shipping can be deployed to ship a database from inside a Windows failover SQL cluster to a remote location is in a local disaster. During disaster recovery, when the Windows failover cluster is not available, log shipping can offer business continuity at the remote location. Unless an organization deploys a geographically dispersed cluster, the cluster nodes are located near each other and can both be down during a disaster.

When deploying log shipping in a cluster environment, the backup folder and BCP folder should be set up as a cluster resource and should be in the same cluster group with the SQL Server that contains the log-shipping database. That way, in a cluster-failover scenario, the backup folder will failover while the log-shipping SQL Server remains accessible by the other Windows failover cluster node. Any configuration and data files in that Windows failover cluster that the other cluster node needs to access should also be set up as a cluster resource included in the log-shipping SQL Server cluster group. For example, if you choose to execute the SSIS Transfer Logins Task package from a file instead of storing it in the SQL Server, that folder should be included as a cluster resource to make it available to all cluster nodes. To set up a folder as a cluster resource, follow these steps:

1. First create the folder.

2. Then, using the cluster administrator, create a new resource and choose Shared Folder. Be sure to place it in the same group with the SQL Server that contains the log-shipping database.

3. Now, inside the Windows failover cluster, you can set SQL Server to depend on the folder. For example, if the folder is not yet online, SQL Server waits for that resource.

 The decision to make something a dependency is based on whether the resource must be available before SQL Server starts. For example, if the backup folder for the transaction-log files is not available, then SQL Server doesn't need to wait to come online because a database that is up and serving users is more important than the transaction-log backup.

SQL Server 2012 Replication

A replication topology where the SQL Server 2012 publisher is the data consolidator can quickly become a single point of failure. All the subscribers connect to the distributor who then connects to the publisher to receive data updates, and if the publisher fails, replication stops until the publisher can be brought online again. Log shipping can be used as a high-availability solution to protect the publisher from becoming a single point of failure. Log Shipping is supported by transactional and merge replication.

In this configuration log shipping is protecting the publisher. The primary server, which is also the replication's publisher, log ships its transaction log to a secondary server.

Then, in a role switch, follow the steps in the previous sections, "Switching Between Primary and Secondary Servers" and "Redirecting Clients to Connect to the Secondary Server" in this chapter.

Additionally, the following should be taken into consideration when using transactional replication with log shipping.

➤ For replication to continue to work after the role switch, the primary and secondary server configurations must be identical after the switch.

➤ For transactional replication, to prevent the subscribers from having data that has to be shipped to the secondary server, the primary server should be configured to use the *sync with backup* parameter in the transaction log backup command of log shipping, whereby a transaction is not replicated to the subscribers until a transaction log backup has been performed. This does introduce a latency penalty whereby the subscribers are not quite in real time because replication needs to wait for log shipping. This latency can be reduced by decreasing the interval to perform the transaction log backup. Without *sync with backup*, there is a possibility that the subscriber's data may not match with the publisher during a log-shipping role switch, and data loss may occur.

➤ In merge replication, after the role switch, the merge publisher may synchronize any changes lost during the role switch by merge replicating with each subscriber. A more common high-availability solution to prevent a single point of failure for the publisher is to configure a Windows failover cluster so that in case of a failure, replication fails over to the other cluster node.

REMOVING LOG SHIPPING

Before deleting the log-shipping database, you need to remove log shipping from it. When you remove log shipping, all schedules, jobs, history, and error information are deleted. Recall that there are two ways to remove log shipping: with Management Studio and with T-SQL. You may want to script the log-shipping configuration before deleting to quickly redeploy log shipping in the future.

Removing Log Shipping with Management Studio

To use Management Studio to remove log shipping, follow these steps:

1. Choose the primary server's database properties.

2. Under Select a Page, choose Transaction Log Shipping.

3. Clear the Enable This as a Primary Database in a Log Shipping Configuration check box, and click OK.

4. If necessary, choose to remove a secondary server from the primary server's database properties. Under Secondary Databases, choose the secondary server instance, and click Remove.

5. To remove a monitor server instance, uncheck the Use a Monitor Server Instance check box.

Removing Log Shipping with T-SQL Commands

To remove log shipping with T-SQL, issue this command on the primary server:

```
Use Master;
sp_delete_log_shipping_primary_secondary  @primary_database, @secondary_server,
@secondary_database;
```

This command deletes secondary information on the primary server from the `msdb.dbo.log_shipping_primary_secondaries` table.

On the secondary server, issue this command:

```
Use Master;
sp_delete_log_shipping_secondary_database @secondary_database;
```

This command deletes the secondary information on the secondary server and its jobs by executing the `sys.sp_delete_log_shipping_secondary_database_internal` stored procedure.

Back on the primary server, issue this command:

```
Use Master;
sp_delete_log_shipping_primary_database @database;
```

This command deletes the log-shipping information from the primary server and its jobs, removes monitor info and the monitor, and deletes the `msdb.dbo.log_shipping_primary_databases` table.

Then, if desirable, you can delete the secondary database.

LOG-SHIPPING PERFORMANCE

A performing log shipping solution is critical to provide faster failover to support the warm standby requirements, such as service level agreements (SLA). To perform, the following key areas must be tuned and optimized to handle the additional capacity of log shipping:

➤ Networking is required for copying the transaction log files from the primary to the secondary server.

➤ IO on both the file share on the primary server (where the transaction log files are getting backed up) and on the secondary server (that is receiving the transaction log files) and then applying them needs to have the read/write throughput. Consider placing the log-shipping backup directory on a separate disk drive from the database files. Additionally, backup compression improves IO performance. As part of ongoing administration, monitor the I/O performance counters for any bottlenecks (for example, the average second/read and average second/write should preferably be less than 10ms).

➤ To keep the secondary server more closely in sync with the primary server, maintain shorter database transactions, when possible. A database transaction is log shipped only after it has been committed on the primary database.

➤ Perform database administration activities, such as index defragmentation, during a period of lower activity. Depending on the level of fragmentation, the transaction-log file will be larger and take longer to back up, copy, and restore increasing latency.

➤ To maintain performance after failover, both the primary and secondary servers should be of identical hardware and server configurations.

Log shipping uses the default settings for backup compression on the server. Whether a log is compressed depends on the Backup Compression default setting.

This enables it to stay in sync with the primary server. Also, in a role switch, the secondary server can provide the same performance experience that users expect. Similarly, separate the file copy directory from the database; and as part of ongoing administration, monitor I/O performance counters. Furthermore, monitor network bandwidth to ensure that there is capacity to move the transaction-log file in a timely manner.

UPGRADING TO SQL SERVER 2012 LOG SHIPPING

Certain procedures must be followed to upgrade an existing log shipping deployment from an earlier SQL Server version to SQL Server 2012 to prevent disruption to the log shipping configuration between the primary and secondary server. These are three common approaches to upgrading log shipping: minimum downtime approach, with downtime approach, and deploy log shipping approach. These are discussed in the following sections.

Minimum Downtime Approach

The minimum downtime approach requires that the secondary server be upgraded in place using the setup program to SQL Server 2012 first. This does not break log shipping because SQL Server 2005/2008 transaction logs can be applied to SQL Server 2012. Afterward, a planned failover takes place where the role-switch procedures are followed and users are redirected to the secondary server. After the role switch and users are redirected, perform the following steps:

1. Stop and disable the log shipping jobs. The newly upgraded SQL Server 2012 primary server cannot log-ship to the old primary server running SQL Server 2005/2008/2008R2.

2. Complete an in-place upgrade on the old primary server using the SQL Server 2012 setup program and leave it as the secondary server.

3. Configure SQL Server 2012 log shipping from the new primary server to the secondary server using the same log-shipping shared folders used by SQL Server 2005/2008/2008R2. Additionally, in the Secondary Database Settings, on the Initialize Secondary Database page, choose No, the Secondary Database Is Initialized. SQL Server 2012 log shipping then starts shipping the transaction log. If you prefer, switch the roles back to the original primary server.

With Downtime Approach

With the downtime approach, the primary and secondary servers are not available during the upgrade because both are upgraded in place using the setup program. Use this method if you have allocated downtime to upgrade the SQL Server 2005/2008 servers. This is the simpler approach because it does not involve going through the failover process.

1. Verify that the secondary server is in sync with the primary server by applying all the transaction-log backups and the active transaction log from the primary server.

2. Stop and disable the log-shipping jobs; then do an in-place upgrade on the secondary server, followed by an upgrade to the primary server.

3. Reconfigure SQL Server 2012 log shipping using the same shared folders. Additionally, in the Secondary Database Settings, on the Initialize Secondary Database page, choose No, the Secondary Database Is Initialized. SQL Server 2012 log shipping starts shipping the transaction log without having to take a database backup and restore on the secondary server.

Deploy Log Shipping Approach

The deploy log shipping approach is more feasible when the log-shipping databases are small and can quickly be backed up, copied, and restored on the secondary server which has already been upgraded to SQL Server 2012. It is similar to the downtime approach, but instead of verifying and waiting for synchronization of the secondary database, after the upgrade and during the SQL Server 2012 log-shipping configuration, on the Initialize Secondary Database page, choose Yes, Generate a Full Backup of the Primary Database. The log-shipping process performs a database backup on the primary server and restores the backup onto the secondary server to start the log shipping.

SUMMARY

Log shipping is a simple, inexpensive, dependable SQL Server high-availability solution with a long track record. As a disaster recovery solution, it has been deployed to maintain a secondary server over a distance for business continuity to protect from a local disaster, power-grid failure, and network outages. Log shipping can ship the log anywhere in the world. Its only limitation is the network bandwidth capacity to transfer the transaction log file in a timely manner. It can be combined with a reporting solution when an organization requires point-in-time reporting, rather than real time. Moreover, it has been deployed as an alternative to Windows failover clustering to provide a local, high-availability solution, where it is less expensive to implement because it does not require a shared disk system.

The main challenge in deploying log shipping is that it does not provide any automatic client redirect; therefore, an operator needs to have an approach for it. In addition, the role switch requires some user intervention to ensure that all the transaction logs have been restored to the secondary server. Switching the roles back also requires some manual intervention. Another challenge is that log shipping is at the user database level that does not copy new logins, SQL jobs, Integration Services, and linked servers from the primary server. However, using Integration Services' Tasks and SQL Agent jobs, it can be accomplished.

Regardless of the risks and challenges, many organizations have successfully used log shipping by scripting all the processes, such as role switching, login synchronization, and client's redirects, and can quickly failover with minimal manual downtime.

Furthermore, as log shipping involves two or more physical separate servers that do not have any shared components (like a Windows failover cluster does), you can achieve patch-management independence whereby one server is patched, the roles are switched, and then the other server is patched.

AlwaysOn Availability Groups is the newest high-availability technology that may eventually replace log shipping. However, log shipping is a time-tested, high-availability solution that many large, strategic customers with mission-critical applications depend on every day to provide local disaster recovery.

19

Database Mirroring

Database mirroring is a reliable, high-availability solution in SQL Server 2012. Maximizing database availability is a top priority for most DBAs. It is hard to explain the pain a DBA goes through when a database goes down; you cannot get it right back online, and at the same time, you're answering pointed questions from your manager. Database mirroring can come to the rescue in certain scenarios, which this chapter explains. It can help you get the database back online with automatic or manual failover to your mirror database, adding another high availability alternative to the SQL Server 2012 arsenal. This chapter explains database mirroring concepts, shows you how to administer the mirrored database, and provides an example demonstrating how to implement database mirroring. The database snapshot is also discussed, which you can use with database mirroring to read the mirrored databases.

OVERVIEW OF DATABASE MIRRORING

Database mirroring is a high-availability solution at the database level, implemented on a per-database basis. To maximize database availability, you need to minimize planned as well as unplanned downtime. Planned downtime is common, such as changes you have to apply to your production system, hardware upgrades, software upgrades (security patches and service packs), database configuration changes, or database storage upgrades. These all require your database or server to be unavailable for short periods of time if everything goes as planned. Unplanned downtime can be caused by hardware failures such as storage failure, by power outages, by human error, or by natural disasters, all of which can cause the production server or datacenter to be unavailable.

Figure 19-1 illustrates a number of mirroring concepts, which are discussed in detail.

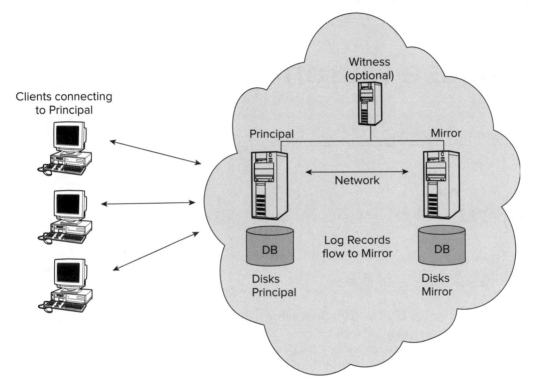

FIGURE 19-1

Database mirroring involves two copies of a single database, residing on separate instances of SQL Server, usually on different computers. You can have separate instances of SQL Server 2012 on the same computer, but that would most likely not fit your high-availability requirements other than for testing purposes. At any given time, only one copy of the database is available to clients. This copy of the database is the *principal database*. The SQL Server that hosts this principal database is the *principal server*. Database mirroring works by transferring and applying the stream of database log records to the copy of the database. The copy of the database is the *mirror database*. The SQL Server that hosts this mirror database is the *mirror server*. The principal and mirror servers are each considered a *partner* in a database mirroring *session*. Database mirroring applies every database modification (DML, DDL, and so on) made to the principal database to the mirror database, including physical and logical database changes such as database files and indexes. As you would guess, a given server may assume the role of principal for one database and the role of mirror for another database. For automatic failover, a third server called the *witness* is required. The witness server is discussed in the "High-Safety Operating Mode with Automatic Failover" section of this chapter.

Database mirroring helps minimize both planned and unplanned downtime in the following manners:

➤ It provides ways to perform automatic or manual failover for mirrored databases.

➤ It keeps the mirrored database up-to-date with the principal database, either synchronously or asynchronously. You can set these operating modes for database mirroring, which are discussed in the "Operating Modes of Database Mirroring" section in this chapter.

➤ It enables the mirrored database to be in a remote data center, to provide a foundation for disaster recovery.

 You cannot mirror the `master`, `msdb`, `tempdb`, *or* `model` *databases. You can mirror multiple databases from a SQL Server instance, though. You cannot re-mirror the mirror database. Mirroring does not support a principal database having more than one mirrored partner.*

OPERATING MODES OF DATABASE MIRRORING

To keep the mirror database up-to-date, database mirroring transfers and applies the stream of database log records on the mirror database. For this reason, you need to understand which *operating mode* database mirroring is configured in. There are three possible operating modes for a database mirroring session. The exact mode of the operation is based on the transaction safety setting and whether the witness server is part of the mirroring session. Table 19-1 outlines the three operating modes of database mirroring.

TABLE 19-1: Operating Modes of Database Mirroring

OPERATING MODE	TRANSACTION SAFETY	TRANSFER MECHANISM	QUORUM REQUIRED	WITNESS SERVER	FAILOVER TYPE
High Performance	OFF	Asynchronous	No	N/A	Forced failover only (with possible data loss). This is a manual step.
High Safety **without** automatic failover	FULL	Synchronous	Yes	No	Manual or forced.
High Safety **with** automatic failover	FULL	Synchronous	Yes	Yes	Automatic or manual.

When you set up database mirroring, you have two options: SAFETY FULL or SAFETY OFF. When weighing these options, you have to decide whether you want the principal database and mirror database to be in sync at all times (SAFETY FULL) or whether you can live with some data loss in case of principal failure (SAFETY OFF). These options are part of the ALTER DATABASE statement when you set up database mirroring.

If you choose SAFETY FULL, you are setting up database mirroring in *high-safety mode* (also known as *synchronous mirroring mode*). As the principal server hardens log records of the principal database to disk (aka flushes the log buffer to disk), it also sends log buffers to the mirror. The principal then waits for a response from the mirror server. The mirror responds to a commit when it has hardened those same log records to the mirror's transaction log. The commit is then reported to the client. Synchronous transfer guarantees that all transactions in the mirror database's transaction log will be synchronized with the principal database's transaction log so that the transactions are considered safely transferred. Figure 19-2 shows the sequence of events when SAFETY is set to FULL.

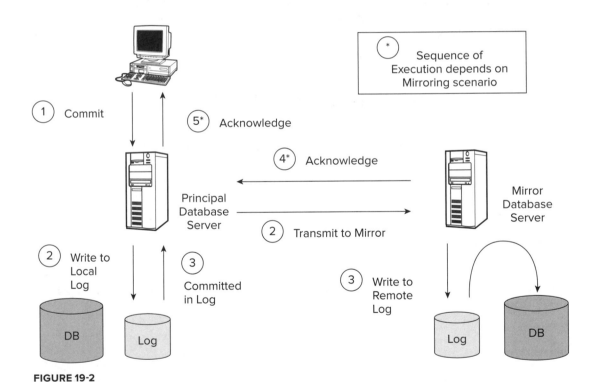

FIGURE 19-2

Keep in mind that with SAFETY FULL it is guaranteed that you won't lose data and that both the principal and mirror will be in sync as long as the transaction is committed successfully. There is some performance impact here because the transaction is not committed until it is hardened to the transaction log on the mirror server. There will be a slight, noticeable increase in perceived user response time and a reduction in transaction throughput because the principal server has to wait for an acknowledgment from the mirror that the transaction is hardened to the mirror transaction log.

How long that delay might be depends on many factors, such as server capacity, database workload, network latency, application architecture, disk throughput, and more. An application with a lot of small transactions has more impact on response time than one with long transactions because transactions wait for acknowledgment from the mirror, and the wait time adds proportionately more to the response time of short transactions.

If you choose the SAFETY OFF option, you are setting up database mirroring in high performance mode, or asynchronous mirroring mode. In this mode, the log transfer process is the same as in synchronous mode, but the principal does not wait for acknowledgment from the mirror that the log buffer is hardened to the disk on a commit. As soon as step 3 in Figure 19-2 occurs, the transaction is committed on the principal. The database is synchronized after the mirror server catches up to the principal server. Because the mirror server is busy keeping up with the principal server, if the principal suddenly fails, you may lose data, however it will only be that which hasn't been sent to the mirror. In this operating mode, there is minimal impact on response time or transaction throughput because it does not wait for the mirror to commit. Note three important terms in database mirroring which are:

➤ **Send queue:** While sending the log records from the principal to the mirror, if the log records can't be sent at the rate at which they are generated, a queue builds up at the principal, in the database transaction log which is known as the *send queue*. The send queue does not use extra storage or memory. It exists entirely in the transaction log of the principal. It refers to the part of the log that has not yet been sent to the mirror.

➤ **Redo queue:** While applying log records on the mirror, if the log records can't be applied at the rate at which they are received, a queue builds up at the mirror in the database transaction log which is known as the *redo queue*. Like the *send queue*, the *redo queue* does not use extra storage or memory. It exists entirely in the transaction log of the mirror. It refers to the part of the hardened log that remains to be applied to the mirror database to roll it forward. Mostly, a single thread is used for redo, but SQL Server Enterprise Edition implements *parallel redo* — that is, a thread for every four processing units (equivalent to four cores).

➤ **Stream compression:** When transferring data across the partners, data mirroring uses stream data compression, which reduces network utilization and can achieve at least a 12.5 percent compression ratio. In the data mirror scenario, the principal compresses the data before sending it to the mirror, and the mirror uncompresses the data before applying it. This slightly increases the CPU utilization on both the principal and the mirror to compress and uncompress the data, while reducing network utilization. It is especially useful for database workloads that incur a great deal of data modification throughout the day, reducing the amount of network resources that data mirroring uses.

DATABASE MIRRORING IN ACTION

Now that you understand transaction safety, you can look at an example to better understand the operating modes and other mirroring concepts. You need to designate three SQL Server instances for this example: one principal server, one mirror server, and one witness server. In this example, as shown in Figure 19-3, you set up high-safety mode with automatic failover. This example assumes that all three SQL server instances are on the network and run under the same domain account, which is Administrator on the SQL Server instance and has access to the other SQL Server instances.

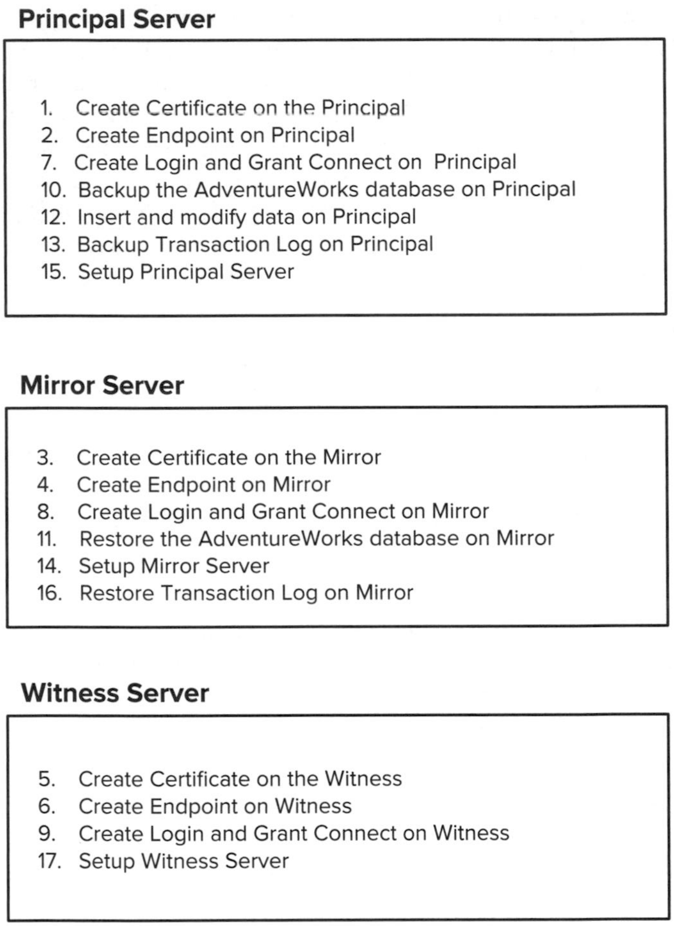

Principal Server

1. Create Certificate on the Principal
2. Create Endpoint on Principal
7. Create Login and Grant Connect on Principal
10. Backup the AdventureWorks database on Principal
12. Insert and modify data on Principal
13. Backup Transaction Log on Principal
15. Setup Principal Server

Mirror Server

3. Create Certificate on the Mirror
4. Create Endpoint on Mirror
8. Create Login and Grant Connect on Mirror
11. Restore the AdventureWorks database on Mirror
14. Setup Mirror Server
16. Restore Transaction Log on Mirror

Witness Server

5. Create Certificate on the Witness
6. Create Endpoint on Witness
9. Create Login and Grant Connect on Witness
17. Setup Witness Server

FIGURE 19-3

Preparing the Endpoints

For database-mirroring partners to connect to each other, they must trust each other. This trust is established by means of Transmission Control Protocol (TCP) endpoints. Therefore, on each partner you have to create the endpoint using the T-SQL statement CREATE ENDPOINT and grant the connect permission on these endpoints using the GRANT CONNECT ON ENDPOINT statement. The endpoint concept is exactly the same as discussed in Chapter 8, "Securing the Database Instance" so the rules are the same. The only difference is that instead of creating an endpoint for Service Broker, here you are creating an endpoint for database mirroring. The security rules are the same; you can use either Windows authentication or certificates for authentication. This example uses certificates so that you can learn how to use them for transport authentication. Windows authentication is easy to establish, so that is a separate exercise.

> *You can find all the example scripts for this chapter on this book's website at* www.wrox.com, *but you need to make a few modifications before running the scripts.*

1. First, for data mirroring to work, the TPC/IP protocol has to be enabled. Use the SQL Server Configuration Manager to verify that the TCP/IP protocol is enabled.

2. Second, in the principal, mirror, and witness, create a new folder at a location of your choosing to store the data mirror example.

> Your folder *refers to the created folder in the scripts in this chapter. You need to change this to match your folder name.*

3. Next, create the certificates on each partner server. Connect to the principal server, and execute the CreateCertOnPrincipal.sql script:

LISTING 20-1: CreateCertOnPrincipal.sql

Available for
download on
Wrox.com

```
USE MASTER
 GO
 IF NOT EXISTS(SELECT 1 FROM sys.symmetric_keys where name =
 '##MS_DatabaseMasterKey##')
 CREATE MASTER KEY ENCRYPTION BY PASSWORD = '23%&weq⁵yzYu3000!'
 GO

 IF NOT EXISTS (SELECT 1 FROM sys.databases where
 [is_master_key_encrypted_by_server] = 1)
 ALTER MASTER KEY ADD ENCRYPTION BY SERVICE MASTER KEY
 GO

 IF NOT EXISTS (SELECT 1 FROM sys.certificates WHERE name = 'PrincipalServerCert')
 CREATE  CERTIFICATE PrincipalServerCert
 WITH SUBJECT = 'Principal Server Certificate'
 GO
```

For simplicity, the example uses certificates created by SQL Server, but there are other ways to create and distribute certificates as well.

```
BACKUP CERTIFICATE PrincipalServerCert TO FILE = '<your folder>
 \PrincipalServerCert.cer'
```

The BACKUP CERTIFICATE statement backs up the public key certificate for this private key.

4. Now create the endpoint on the principal server. Connect to the principal server, and execute the CreateEndPointOnPrincipal.sql script:

```
--Check If Mirroring endpoint exists
IF NOT EXISTS(SELECT * FROM sys.endpoints WHERE type = [type_desc]
CREATE ENDPOINT DBMirrorEndPoint
STATE = STARTED AS TCP (LISTENER_PORT = port_num)
FOR DATABASE_MIRRORING ( AUTHENTICATION = CERTIFICATE PrincipalServerCert,
                         ENCRYPTION - REQUIRED
                        ,ROLE = ALL
                        )
```

code snippet CreateEndPointOnPrincipal.sql

This code creates the endpoint DBMirrorEndPoint, and you have specified the PrincipalServerCert certificate to use for authentication. You also specified ROLE=ALL, which indicates that this server can act as either the principal, mirror, or witness server. If you want this server to act only as the witness, you can specify WITNESS as a parameter. You can also specify the PARTNER option, which indicates that the server can act as either the principal or the mirror, but not the witness.

5. Now create the certificates on both the mirror and the witness servers. Connect to the mirror server and execute the CreateCertOnMirror.sql script:

```
USE MASTER
 GO
 IF NOT EXISTS(SELECT 1 FROM sys.symmetric_keys where name =
 '##MS_DatabaseMasterKey##')
 CREATE MASTER KEY ENCRYPTION BY PASSWORD = '23%&weqᴮyzYu3000!'GO

 IF NOT EXISTS (select 1 from sys.databases where
 [is_master_key_encrypted_by_server] = 1)
 ALTER MASTER KEY ADD ENCRYPTION BY SERVICE MASTER KEY
 GO

 IF NOT EXISTS (SELECT 1 FROM sys.certificates WHERE name = 'MirrorServerCert')
 CREATE  CERTIFICATE MirrorServerCert
 WITH SUBJECT = 'Mirror Server Certificate'
 GO

 BACKUP CERTIFICATE MirrorServerCert TO FILE = '<your folder>\MirrorServerCert.cer'
```

code snippet CreateCertOnMirror.sql

6. Next, while connected to the mirror server, execute the CreateEndPointOnMirror.sql script:

```
--Check If Mirroring endpoint exists
IF NOT EXISTS(SELECT * FROM sys.endpoints WHERE type = 4)
CREATE ENDPOINT DBMirrorEndPoint
STATE=STARTED AS TCP (LISTENER_PORT = port_num)
```

```
FOR DATABASE_MIRRORING ( AUTHENTICATION = CERTIFICATE MirrorServerCert,
                         ENCRYPTION = REQUIRED
                    ,ROLE = ALL
                    )
```

code snippet CreateEndPointOnMirror.sql

7. Connect to the witness server, and execute the `CreateCertOnWitness.sql` script:

```
USE MASTER
GO
IF NOT EXISTS(SELECT 1 FROM sys.symmetric_keys where name =
'##MS_DatabaseMasterKey##')
CREATE MASTER KEY ENCRYPTION BY PASSWORD = '23%&weqᴾyzYu3000!'GO

IF NOT EXISTS (select 1 from sys.databases where
[is_master_key_encrypted_by_server] = 1)
ALTER MASTER KEY ADD ENCRYPTION BY SERVICE MASTER KEY
GO

IF NOT EXISTS (SELECT 1 FROM sys.certificates WHERE name = 'WitnessServerCert')
CREATE  CERTIFICATE WitnessServerCert
WITH SUBJECT = 'Witness Server Certificate'
GO

BACKUP CERTIFICATE WitnessServerCert
TO FILE = '<your folder>\WitnessServerCert.cer'
```

code snippet CreateCertOnWitness.sql

8. Finally, while connected to the witness server, execute the `CreateEndPointOnWitness.sql` script:

```
--Check If Mirroring endpoint exists
IF NOT EXISTS(SELECT * FROM sys.endpoints WHERE type = 4)
CREATE ENDPOINT DBMirrorEndPoint
STATE=STARTED AS TCP (LISTENER_PORT = port_num)
FOR DATABASE_MIRRORING
( AUTHENTICATION = CERTIFICATE WitnessServerCert, ENCRYPTION
= REQUIRED
                    ,ROLE = ALL
                    )
```

code snippet CreateEndPointOnWitness.sql

Because all the partners can talk to each other, each partner needs permission to connect to the others. To do that, you have to create logins on each server and associate the logins with certificates from the other two servers and grant connect permission to that user on the endpoint.

1. First, copy the certificates created in the previous scripts with the BACKUP CERTIFICATE command to the other two servers. For example, copy the certificate

PrincipalServerCert.cer on the principal from the new folder you created earlier to the similar folders on both the witness and mirror servers.

2. Connect to the principal server and execute the Principal_CreateLoginAndGrant.sql script:

```
USE MASTER
GO

--For Mirror server to connect
IF NOT EXISTS(SELECT 1 FROM sys.syslogins WHERE name = 'MirrorServerUser')
CREATE LOGIN MirrorServerUser WITH PASSWORD = '32sdgsgyᵇ%$!'
IF NOT EXISTS(SELECT 1 FROM sys.sysusers WHERE name = 'MirrorServerUser')
CREATE USER MirrorServerUser;

IF NOT EXISTS(SELECT 1 FROM sys.certificates WHERE name = 'MirrorDBCertPub')
CREATE CERTIFICATE MirrorDBCertPub  AUTHORIZATION MirrorServerUser
FROM FILE = '<your folder>\MirrorServerCert.cer'

GRANT CONNECT ON ENDPOINT::DBMirrorEndPoint TO MirrorServerUser
GO

--For Witness server to connect
IF NOT EXISTS(SELECT 1 FROM sys.syslogins WHERE name = 'WitnessServerUser')
CREATE LOGIN WitnessServerUser WITH PASSWORD = '32sdgsgyᵇ%$!'
IF NOT EXISTS(SELECT 1 FROM sys.sysusers WHERE name = 'WitnessServerUser')
CREATE USER WitnessServerUser;

IF NOT EXISTS(SELECT 1 FROM sys.certificates WHERE name = 'WitnessDBCertPub')
CREATE CERTIFICATE WitnessDBCertPub  AUTHORIZATION WitnessServerUser
FROM FILE = '<your folder>\WitnessServerCert.cer'

GRANT CONNECT ON ENDPOINT::DBMirrorEndPoint TO WitnessServerUser
GO
```

code snippet Principal_CreateLoginAndGrant.sql

This script creates two users on the principal server: MirrorServerUser and WitnessServerUser. These users are mapped to the certificates from the mirror and the witness. After that, you granted connect permission on the endpoint, so now the mirror and the witness server have permission to connect to the endpoint on the principal server. Perform the same steps on the mirror server and witness server.

3. Next, connect to the mirror server, and execute the Mirror_CreateLoginAndGrant .sql script. Finally, connect to the witness server, and execute the Witness_ CreateLoginAndGrant.sql script.

Now you have configured the endpoints on each server, using certificates. If you want to use the Windows authentication, the steps to configure the endpoints are a bit easier than using certificates. Simply do the following on each server (this example is for the principal):

```
IF NOT EXISTS(SELECT * FROM sys.endpoints WHERE type = 4)
CREATE ENDPOINT DBMirrorEndPoint
```

```
STATE = STARTED AS TCP (LISTENER_PORT = 5022)
FOR DATABASE_MIRRORING ( AUTHENTICATION = WINDOWS, ROLE = ALL)

GRANT CONNECT ON ENDPOINT::DBMirrorEndPoint TO
[MyDomain\MirrorServerServiceAccount]
GO

GRANT CONNECT ON ENDPOINT::DBMirrorEndPoint TO
[MyDomain\WitnessServerServiceAccount]
GO
```

code snippet Mirror_CreateLoginAndGrant.sql
code snippet Witness_CreateLoginAndGrant.sql

Of course, you have to change the logins appropriately. In Windows authentication mode, each server uses the service account under which it is running to connect to the other partners, so you have to grant connect permission on the endpoint to the service account of SQL Server 2012. Additionally, you can use SQL Server 2012 Management Studio to configure data mirroring with Windows authentication. Right-click the database you want to mirror, and choose Tasks, then ⇨ Mirror. A wizard starts, as shown in Figure 19-4. Click the Configure Security button, which takes you through the steps to configure database mirroring. The wizard tries to use 5022 as the default TCP port for database mirroring, but you can change it if you want.

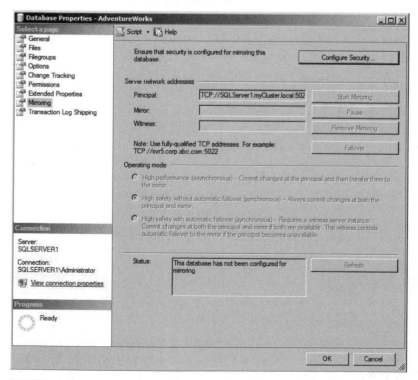

FIGURE 19-4

You need only one mirroring endpoint per server; it doesn't matter how many databases you mirror. Be sure to use a port that is not used by other endpoints. You can specify any available port number between 1024 and 32767.

Do not reconfigure an in-use database mirroring endpoint (using ALTER ENDPOINT). The server instances use each other's endpoints to learn the state of the other systems. If the endpoint is reconfigured, it might restart, which can appear to be an error to the other server instances. This is particularly important in high-safety mode with automatic failover, where reconfiguring the endpoint on a partner can cause a failover to occur.

Preparing the Database for Mirroring

Before you can set up the data mirroring, you need a database to work with.

1. Use the AdventureWorks database for this example, which must use the recovery model of FULL:

```
-- As a reminder you will need to set the database Recovery model to FULL
-- recovery in order to establish mirroring.
ALTER DATABASE AdventureWorks SET RECOVERY FULL
```

2. Connect to the principal server and execute the BackupDatabase.sql script:

```
--Take a full database backup.
BACKUP DATABASE [AdventureWorks] TO DISK = N'<your folder>
\AdventureWorks.bak'
WITH FORMAT, INIT,
NAME = N'AdventureWorks-Full Database Backup',STATS = 10
GO
```

3. Using this script, back up AdventureWorks using a full database backup.

4. Next, restore this database on your designated mirror server with the NORECOVERY option for the RESTORE DATABASE statement. Connect to the designated mirror server, and execute the RestoreDatabase.sql script: The following script assumes that the backup of the principal database exists in the folder you created earlier on the mirror server.

```
--If the path of the mirror database differs from the
--path of the principal database (for instance, their drive letters differ),
--creating the mirror database requires that the restore operation
--include a MOVE clause. See BOL for details on MOVE option.

RESTORE DATABASE [AdventureWorks]
FROM DISK = '<your folder>\AdventureWorks.bak'
WITH   NORECOVERY
,MOVE N'AdventureWorks_Data' TO N'<your folder>\AdventureWorks_Data.mdf'
,MOVE N'AdventureWorks_Log' TO N'<your folder>\AdventureWorks_Log.LDF'
```

This code restores the database AdventureWorks in NORECOVERY mode on your mirror server; the NORECOVERY option is required. Now that you have a database ready to be mirrored, you should understand what it takes to do initial synchronization between the principal and mirror servers.

To establish the mirroring session, the database name must be the same on both principal and mirror. Before you back up the principal database, make sure that the database is in FULL recovery model.

Initial Synchronization Between Principal and Mirror

You have just backed up and restored the AdventureWorks database for mirroring. Of course, mirroring a database the size of AdventureWorks does not simulate a real-life scenario. In real life, you might mirror a production database with hundreds of thousands of MB. Therefore, depending on the database's size and the distance between the servers, it may take a long time to copy and restore the database on the mirror. During this time, the principal database may have produced many transaction logs. Before you set up mirroring, you must copy and restore all these transaction logs with the NORECOVERY option on the mirror server. If you don't want to bother copying and restoring these transaction logs on the mirror, you can suspend the transaction log backups (if you have a SQL job to do backup transaction logs, you can disable that job) until the database on the mirror is restored and the database mirroring session is established in the "Establishing the Mirroring" section. (You learn that soon.) After the database mirroring session is established, you can resume the transaction log backup on the principal server again. It is important to understand that in this approach, because you have stopped the transaction log backups, the transaction log file will grow, so make sure you have enough disk space for transaction log-file growth.

For the database mirroring session to be established, both databases (principal and mirror) must be in sync, so at some point you have to stop the transaction log backup on your principal. Decide when you want to do it: before backing up the full database and restoring on the mirror server or after backing up the full database. In the first case, you have to plan for transaction-file growth; and in the second case, you have to copy and restore all the transactions logs on the mirror before you establish the mirroring session.

If you are mirroring a large database, it is going to take a longer time to back up and then restore it on the mirror server. To minimize the performance impact on the principal server, try to plan mirroring setup during low-activity periods on your system. On a highly active system, you may want to increase the time between each transaction log backup so that you have a smaller number of logs to copy and restore on the mirror; although, this increases the database's data loss exposure in case of a principal failure. If you have minimal database activities, you can stop taking transaction log backups on the principal, back up the database on the principal, restore on the mirror, establish the mirroring session, and then restart the transaction log backup job on the principal.

Establishing the Mirroring Session

With the servers prepared for database mirroring, you next need to create some database activities in the AdventureWorks database before you establish the mirroring session so that you can better understand the previous section. Perform the following steps to do so:

   1. Connect to the principal server, and execute the ModifyData.sql script. This script updates data in the AdventureWorks.person.address table.

2. Connect to the principal server and execute `BackupLogPrincipal.sql`:

```
USE MASTER
GO
BACKUP LOG AdventureWorks TO DISK = '<your folder>\AdventureWorks.trn'
```

code Snippet BackupLogPrincipal.sql

That backs up the transaction log of `AdventureWorks`. Now the `AdventureWorks` databases on the principal and the mirror are *not* in sync. See what happens if you try to establish the mirroring session between these two databases.

3. Connect to the mirror server, and execute the `SetupMirrorServer.sql` script (this runs successfully):

```
USE MASTER
GO
ALTER DATABASE AdventureWorks
SET PARTNER = 'TCP://YourPrincipalServer:5022'
```

code Snippet SetupMirrorServer.sql

4. Now connect to the principal server, and execute `SetupPrincipalServer.sql` script which will fail with Msg 1412:

```
USE MASTER
GO
ALTER DATABASE AdventureWorks
SET PARTNER = 'TCP://YourMirrorServer:5023'
```

code Snippet SetupPrincipalServer.sql

This script fails on the principal with the following message:

```
Msg 1412, Level 16, State 0, Line 1
The remote copy of database "AdventureWorks" has not been rolled forward to
a point
in time that is encompassed in the local copy of the database log.
```

5. This shows that the database on the mirror server is not rolled forward enough to establish the mirroring session, so now you have to restore the transaction log that you backed up on the principal server to the mirror server with NORECOVERY mode to synchronize the mirror with the principal. Connect to the mirror server, and execute the `RestoreLogOnMirror.sql` script:

```
USE MASTER
GO
RESTORE LOG AdventureWorks
FROM DISK = '<your folder>\AdventureWorks.trn'
WITH NORECOVERY
```

code Snippet RestoreLogOnMirror.sql

This script assumes that you have copied the transaction log in the `c:\` drive on the mirror server. If you put the transaction log somewhere else, substitute that folder location, and then run the script. Now the principal and mirror databases are in sync.

6. Connect to the mirror server and execute the `SetupMirrorServer.sql` script again.

7. Then connect to the principal server, and execute the `SetupPrincipalServer.sql` script. It should succeed now because the transaction log has been restored, and you have just established the mirroring session.

code Snippet SetupMirrorServer.sql
code Snippet SetupPrincipalServer.sql

When you execute the `SetupPrincipalServer.sql` or `SetupMirrorServer.sql` scripts, you may get the following type of error:

```
Database mirroring connection error 4 'An error occurred
  while receiving data: '64(The specified network name
  is no longer available.)'.' for TCP://YourMirrorServer:5022'.
  Error: 1443, Severity: 16, State: 2.
```

It's possible that the firewall on the mirror or principal server is blocking the connection on the port specified. Go to Windows Firewall and Advanced Security to verify that the port numbers chosen for database mirroring are not blocked.

High-Safety Operating Mode Without Automatic Failover

When you establish the mirroring session, the transaction safety is set to FULL by default, so the mirroring session is always established in high-safety operating mode *without* automatic failover. In this operating mode, a witness is not set up, so automatic failover is not possible. Because the witness server is not present in this operating mode, the principal doesn't need to form a quorum to serve the database. If the principal loses its quorum with the mirror, it still keeps serving the principal database and the mirror transactions are queued on the principal and send once the mirror becomes available.

Next you will learn how to change it to *automatic failover*.

High-Safety Operating Mode with Automatic Failover

Automatic failover means that if the principal database (or the server hosting it) fails, the database mirroring will failover to the mirror server, and the mirror server will assume the principal role and serve the database. However, you need a third server, the witness, for automatic failover to the mirror. The witness just sits there as a third party and is used by the mirror to verify that the principal is really down, providing a "2 out of 3" condition for automatic failover. No user action is necessary to failover to the mirror if a witness server is present.

Witness Server

If you choose the SAFETY FULL option, you have an option to set up a witness server (refer to Figure 19-1). The presence of the witness server in high-safety mode determines whether you can perform automatic failover or not when the principal database fails. Automatic failover happens when the following conditions are met:

➤ Witness and mirror are both connected to the principal when the principal is failing (going away).

➤ Safety is set to FULL.

➤ Mirroring state is synchronized.

You must have a separate instance of SQL Server other than the principal and mirror servers to fully take advantage of database mirroring with automatic failover. You can use the same witness server to participate in multiple, concurrent database mirroring sessions.

Returning to the example, you establish the witness server in your example.

1. Connect to either the principal or mirror server, and execute the SetupWitnessServer.sql script:

Available for download on Wrox.com

```
USE MASTER
GO
ALTER DATABASE AdventureWorks
SET WITNESS = 'TCP://YourWitnessServer:5024'
```

code Snippet SetupWitnessServer.sql

You must connect to either the principal or the mirror to execute this script. When you execute the script, both the principal and the mirror servers must be up and running. You have now established a witness server, which provides automatic failover support. Any SQL Server edition from SQL Express to Enterprise Edition can act as a witness. A witness can be a SQL Server instance that is used by other database operations; it does not have to be exclusively a Witness server.

 The witness server is optional in database mirroring, though it is required if you want automatic failover.

The Quorum

When you set up the witness server, it becomes the *quorum* in the database mirroring session for automatic failover. A quorum is a relationship between two or more connected server instances in a database mirroring session, which acts as a tiebreaker to determine which server instance should be the principal.

Quorums can be in three modes types during database mirroring:

➤ **Full:** Both partners and witness are connected.

➤ **Partner-to-partner:** Both partners are connected but not the witness.

➤ **Witness-to-partner:** A witness and one of the partners are connected.

A database in its data mirroring session must be in one of these three quorum event types to serve as the principal database.

High-Performance Operating Mode

By default, the SAFETY is ON when you establish the mirroring session, so to activate the high-performance operating mode, you have to turn the safety OFF, like so:

```
USE Master
ALTER DATABASE AdventureWorks SET PARTNER SAFETY OFF
```

There is minimal impact on transaction throughput and response time in this mode. The log transfer to the mirror works the same way as in high-safety mode, but because the principal doesn't wait for hardening the log to disk on the mirror, it's possible that if the principal goes down unexpectedly, you may lose data.

You can configure the witness server in high-performance mode, but because you cannot do automatic failover in this mode, the witness will not provide any benefits. Therefore, don't define a witness when you configure database mirroring in high-performance mode. You can remove the witness server by running the following command if you want to change the operating mode to high performance with no witness:

```
USE Master
ALTER DATABASE AdventureWorks SET WITNESS OFF
```

If you configure the witness server in a high-performance mode session, the enforcement of quorum means the following:

➤   If the mirror server is lost, then the principal must be connected to the witness. Otherwise, the principal server takes its database offline until either the witness server or the mirror server rejoins the session.

➤   If the principal server is lost, then forcing failover to the mirror requires that the mirror server be connected to the witness.

The only way you can failover to the mirror in this mode is by running the following command on the mirror when the principal server is disconnected from the mirroring session. This is called *forced failover*. Refer to Table 19-1 for the different failover types.

```
USE MASTER
ALTER DATABASE AdventureWorks SET PARTNER FORCE_SERVICE_ALLOW_DATA_LOSS
```

The forced failover causes an immediate recovery of the mirror database, which may cause data loss. This mode is best used for transferring data over long distances (for disaster recovery to a remote site) or for mirroring an active database for which some potential data loss is acceptable. For example, you can use high-performance mode for mirroring your warehouse. Then, you can use a database snapshot as discussed in the "Database Snapshot" section of this chapter to create a snapshot on the mirror server to enable a reporting environment from the mirrored warehouse.

DATABASE MIRRORING AND SQL SERVER 2012 EDITIONS

Now that you understand the operating modes of database mirroring, it is a good idea to keep in mind which of these operating modes is available on your edition of SQL Server. Table 19-2 summarizes which features of database mirroring are available in which SQL Server 2012 editions.

TABLE 19-2: SQL Server 2012 Features Supported by Edition

DATABASE MIRRORING FEATURE	ENTERPRISE EDITION	DEVELOPER EDITION	STANDARD EDITION	BUSINESS INTELLIGENCE EDITION	SQL EXPRESS EDITION
Partner (principal or mirror)	√	√	√	√	
Witness	√	√	√	√	√
Safety = FULL	√	√	√	√	
Safety = OFF	√	√			
Available during UNDO after failover	√	√	√	√	
Parallel REDO	√	√			

The SQL Express edition can be used only as a witness server in a mirroring session. Some other features such as high-performance operating mode, you need the Enterprise or Developer edition.

SQL Server 2012 may use multiple threads to roll forward the log in the *redo queue* on the mirror database. This is called *parallel redo*. If the mirror server has fewer than five CPUs, SQL Server uses only a single thread for redo. Parallel redo is optimized by using one thread per four CPUs. This feature is available only in the Enterprise or Developer editions.

DATABASE MIRRORING CATALOG VIEWS

In the example so far, you have set up the mirroring session but you still haven't learned how to get information about the mirroring configuration. Therefore, before continuing with failover scenarios and other topics, you need to learn how you can get that information. The following sections describe the catalog views you can use to get information about database mirroring. SQL Server 2012 Books Online describes every column in database mirroring catalog views.

The following shows you when and how you should use these views.

sys.database_mirroring

The most important view to monitor mirroring state, safety level, and witness status (when present) is sys.database_mirroring. See the following query, which you can execute on either partner (principal or mirror), and you will get the same results:

```
SELECT
 DB_NAME(database_id) AS DatabaseName
,mirroring_role_desc
,mirroring_safety_level_desc
,mirroring_state_desc
,mirroring_safety_sequence
,mirroring_role_sequence
,mirroring_partner_instance
,mirroring_witness_name
,mirroring_witness_state_desc
,mirroring_failover_lsn
,mirroring_connection_timeout
,mirroring_redo_queue
FROM sys.database_mirroring
WHERE mirroring_guid IS NOT NULL
```

You use this query often when you establish the mirroring session. If you run this query after you establish the mirroring session in the example scenario, you see output similar to the result in Table 19-3. Of course, some values will be different based on your server names, and so on.

TABLE 19-3: sys.database_mirroring view

METADATA COLUMN IN SELECT LIST	PRINCIPAL VALUES: YOURPRINCIPALSERVER	MIRROR VALUES: YOURMIRRORSERVER
DatabaseName	AdventureWorks	AdventureWorks
mirroring_role_desc	PRINCIPAL	MIRROR
mirroring_safety_level_desc	FULL	FULL
mirroring_state_desc	SYNCHRONIZED	SYNCHRONIZED
mirroring_safety_sequence	1	1
mirroring_role_sequence	3	3
mirroring_partner_instance	SQLServer1\SQLServer2	SQLServer1
mirroring_witness_name	TCP://SQLServer1. myCluster.local:5024	TCP://SQLServer1. myCluster.local:5024
mirroring_witness_state_desc	CONNECTED	CONNECTED
mirroring_failover_lsn	1157000000027300001	1157000000027300001
mirroring_connection_timeout	10	10
mirroring_redo_queue	NULL	NULL

Some values in Table 19-3 are self-explanatory, but others require some additional explanation:

➤ mirroring_safety_sequence gives a count of how many times the safety has changed (from FULL to OFF and back) since the mirroring session was established.

➤ mirroring_role_sequence gives a count of how many times failover has happened since the mirroring session was established.

➤ `mirroring_failover_lsn` gives the log sequence number of the latest transaction that is guaranteed to be hardened to permanent storage on both partners. In this case, because there is little database activity, both of these numbers are the same if you use the `ModifyData.sql` script in a `WHILE` loop. (If you change the script, be sure not to use an infinite loop!)

➤ `mirroring_connection_timeout` gives the mirroring connection timeout, in seconds. This is the number of seconds to wait for a reply from a partner or witness before considering them unavailable. The default timeout value is 10 seconds. If it is null, then the database is inaccessible or not mirrored. It can be set by using this command:

```
ALTER DATABASE [database] SET PARTNER TIMEOUT [seconds]
```

➤ `mirroring_redo_queue` displays the maximum amount of the transaction log to be redone at the mirror in megabytes when the `mirroring_redo_queue_type` is not set to `unlimited`. When the maximum is reached, the principal transaction log temporarily stalls to enable the mirror to catch up; therefore, it can limit the failover time. When the `mirroring_redo_queue_type` is set to `unlimited` which is the default, data mirroring does not inhibit the redo_queue. It can be set by using this command:

```
ALTER DATABASE <database> SET PARTNER REDO_QUEUE <UNLIMITED or MB>
```

sys.database_mirroring_witnesses

If you have a witness established for your mirroring session, then `sys.database_mirroring_witnesses` returns data mirroring information with the following query:

```
SELECT * FROM sys.database_mirroring_witnesses
```

You can execute this query on the witness server to list:

➤ principal and mirror server names

➤ the database name

➤ safety level for all the mirroring sessions

You get the following multiple rows from this query if the same witness server acts as a witness for more than one mirroring session.

➤ `role_sequence_number` column displays how many times failover has happened between mirroring partners since the mirroring session was established.

➤ `is_suspended` column displays whether database mirroring is suspended. If this column value is 1, then mirroring is currently suspended.

sys.database_mirroring_endpoints

The following query returns information about database mirroring endpoints such as port number, whether encryption is enabled, authentication type, and endpoint state:

```
SELECT
 dme.name AS EndPointName
,dme.protocol_desc
```

```
,dme.type_desc AS EndPointType
,dme.role_desc AS MirroringRole
,dme.state_desc AS EndPointStatus
,te.port AS PortUsed
,CASE dme.is_encryption_enabled
      WHEN  1 THEN 'Yes'
      ELSE 'No'
 END AS Is_Encryption_Enabled
,dme.encryption_algorithm_desc
,dme.connection_auth_desc
FROM sys.database_mirroring_endpoints dme
JOIN sys.tcp_endpoints te
  ON dme.endpoint_id = te.endpoint_id
```

This query uses the `sys.tcp_endpoints` view because the port information is not available in the `sys.database_mirroring_endpoints` catalog view.

DATABASE MIRRORING ROLE CHANGE

In the example so far, you have learned how to establish and monitor a database mirroring session. You have likely noticed that if you try to query the `AdventureWorks` database on your mirror server, you get an error like the following:

```
Msg 954, Level 14, State 1, Line 1
The database "AdventureWorks" cannot be opened. It is acting as a mirror database.
```

You cannot access the mirrored database, so how do you switch the roles of the mirroring partners? You can failover to the mirror server in three ways (also described earlier):

➤ Automatic failover

➤ Manual failover

➤ Forced Failover

The failover types depend on which transaction safety is used (FULL or OFF) and whether a witness server is present.

Automatic Failover

Automatic failover is a database mirroring feature in high-availability mode (SAFETY FULL when a witness server is present). When a failure occurs on the principal, automatic failover is initiated. Because you have set up database mirroring in high-availability mode with a witness server, you are ready to do automatic failover. The following events occur in an automatic failover scenario:

1. **The failure occurs:** The principal database becomes unavailable. This could be the result of a power failure, a hardware failure, a storage failure, or some other reason.

2. **The failure is detected:** The failure is detected by the mirror and the witness. Both partners and witness continually ping each other to identify their presence. Of course, it is more than just a simple ping, detecting things such as whether the SQL Server is available, whether the principal database is available, and so on. A timeout is specified for the ping, which is set to

10 seconds by default when you set up the database mirroring session. You can change the timeout using the ALTER DATABASE as described earlier.

If the principal does not respond to the ping message within the timeout period, it is considered to be down, and failure is detected. You should leave the default setting for timeout at 10 seconds, or at least do not change it to less than 10 seconds because under heavy load and sporadic network conditions, false failures may occur, and your database will start failing over back and forth.

3. **A complete redo is performed on the mirror:** The mirror database has been in the restoring state until now, continuously redoing the log (rolling it forward onto the database). When failure is detected, the mirror needs to recover the database. In order to do that, the mirror needs to redo the remaining log entries in the redo queue.

4. **The failover decision is made:** The mirror now contacts the witness server to form a quorum and determines whether the database should failover to the mirror. In the high-safety mode with automatic failover, the witness must be present for automatic failover. The decision takes about 1 second, so if the principal comes back up before step 3 is complete, that failover is terminated.

5. **The mirror becomes the principal:** The redo continues while the failover decision is being made. After both the witness and the mirror have formed a quorum on the failover decision, the database is recovered completely. The mirror's role is switched to principal; recovery is run (this involves setting up various database states and rolling back any in-flight system transactions and starting up rollback of user transactions); then the database is available to the clients; and normal operations can be performed.

6. **Undo:** There may be uncommitted transactions, the transactions sent to the mirror while the principal was available but not committed before the principal went down in the transaction log of the new principal, which are rolled back.

Normally, the time taken to failover in this operating mode is short, usually seconds, but that mostly depends on the redo phase. If the mirror is already caught up with the principal before the principal has gone down, the redo phase will not introduce time lag. The time to apply the redo records depends on the redo queue length and the redo rate on the mirror. The failover will not happen if the mirroring_state is not synchronized. There are some performance counters available, which are examined in the "Performance Monitoring Database Mirroring" section. From these counters, you can estimate the time it will take to apply the transaction log for the redo queue on the mirror server.

To measure the actual time, you can use the SQL Profiler to trace the event. See Chapter 13, "Performance Tuning T-SQL," to learn more about running traces with SQL Profiler, which you use here to measure the actual time it takes to failover:

1. Open SQL Profiler.

2. Connect to the mirror server.

3. Choose the Database Mirroring State Change event under the Database events group.

4. Choose the TextData and StartTime columns.

5. Start the trace.

6. Stop the SQL Server service on the principal server. Soon, automatic failover happens.

Two columns in the trace are of interest: TextData provides the description of the database mirroring state change event. StartTime represents the timestamp at which time the event took place. Figure 19-5 shows the SQL Profiler trace of the events.

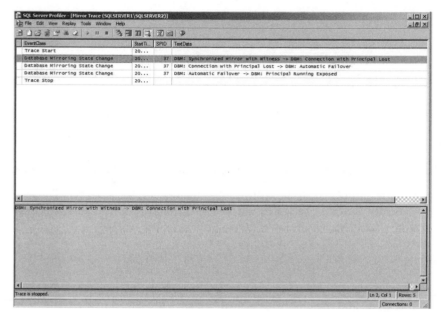

FIGURE 19-5

In the event Synchronized Mirror with Witness, the mirror informs the witness server that the connection to the principal is lost, as shown in the step 4 event in Figure 19-2. Then the mirror fails over to become the principal; this means that the principal will be running without a partner and if it were to fail, the database will be offline. You also see a message similar to the following in the mirror server SQL error log:

```
The mirrored database "AdventureWorks" is changing roles from "MIRROR" to
"PRINCIPAL" due to Auto Failover.
```

In the StartTime column, the actual failover time for this automatic failover was approximately 7 seconds.

The duration of the failover depends upon the type of failure and the load on the database. Under load, it takes longer to failover than in a no-load situation. You see messages similar to the following in the SQL error log:

```
The mirrored database "AdventureWorks" is changing roles from "MIRROR" to
"PRINCIPAL" due to Failover from partner.
Starting up database 'AdventureWorks'.
Analysis of database 'AdventureWorks' (9) is 81% complete (approximately 0
seconds
remain).
```

```
Analysis of database 'AdventureWorks' (9) is 100% complete (approximately 0
seconds
remain).
Recovery of database 'AdventureWorks' (9) is 0% complete (approximately 30
seconds
remain). Phase 2 of 3.
Recovery of database 'AdventureWorks' (9) is 16% complete (approximately 17
seconds
remain). Phase 2 of 3.
13 transactions rolled forward in database 'AdventureWorks' (9).
Recovery of database 'AdventureWorks' (9) is 16% complete (approximately 17
seconds
remain). Phase 3 of 3.
Recovery of database 'AdventureWorks' (9) is 100% complete (approximately 0
seconds
remain). Phase 3 of 3.
```

The additional steps during analysis and recovery of the database cause the manual failover to take longer.

When the failover happens, the clients need to be redirected to the new principal server. The "Preparing the Mirror Server for Failover" section discusses that, along with other tasks you have to do on the mirror server to prepare it for failover and take on the database workload.

Manual Failover

In a manual failover, you make a decision to switch the roles of the partners. The current mirror server becomes the new principal, and the current principal becomes the new mirror. You can use the following command for manual failover:

```
ALTER DATABASE AdventureWorks SET PARTNER FAILOVER
```

 For manual failover, the SAFETY *must be set to* FULL. *It doesn't matter whether you have a witness server set up.*

You have to run this command on the principal server to successfully failover. In addition, the `mirroring_state` must be synchronized for failover to succeed. If it is not synchronized, you get the following message when you try to execute the failover command on the principal:

```
Msg 1422, Level 16, State 2, Line 1
The mirror server instance is not caught up to the recent changes to database
"AdventureWorks". Unable to fail over.
```

Now you can do a manual failover using your database mirroring servers.

1. Open the `DatabaseMirroringCommands.sql` script. When you performed automatic failover earlier, you stopped the original principal SQL Server service. Make sure you start that service back up before the manual failover, because both the mirror and principal must be up and running for this step.

2. To see what's happening behind the scenes, start SQL Profiler, connect it to the mirror server, and select the event Database Mirroring State Change under the Database event group.

3. Then run the trace. Two columns in the trace are of interest: `TextData` and `StartTime`.

4. To see activities on the principal, start another instance of SQL Profiler and connect it to the principal.

5. Now connect to your principal server and execute the following command:

```
ALTER DATABASE AdventureWorks SET PARTNER FAILOVER
```

You have just forced a manual failover from the principal to the mirror. You can also use SQL Server 2012 Management Studio to execute a manual failover as follows:

1. Right-click the principal database, and select Tasks ⇨ Mirror to access the dialog shown in Figure 19-6.

2. Click the Failover button to get a failover confirmation dialog.

3. Click OK again.

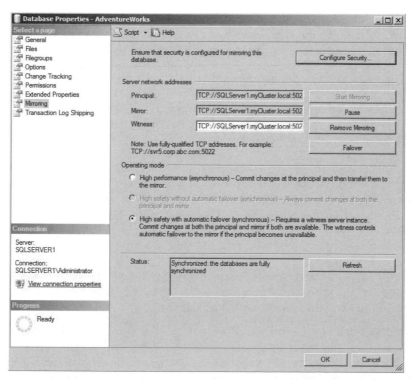

FIGURE 19-6

You can use manual failover for planned downtime, migrations and upgrading, as discussed in the section "Preparing the Mirror Server for Failover."

Forced Failover

For forced failover, you need to execute the following command on the mirror server.

```
ALTER DATABASE AdventureWorks SET PARTNER FORCE_SERVICE_ALLOW_DATA_LOSS
```

 Be cautious about using this command because you risk data loss by running it.

When you run this command, the mirror should not be able to connect to the principal; otherwise, you cannot failover. If your principal is up and running and the mirror can connect to it when you try to run the command, you get the following error message:

```
Msg 1455, Level 16, State 2, Line 1
The database mirroring service cannot be forced for database "AdventureWorks"
because the database is not in the correct state to become the principal database.
```

Now try this exercise using your data mirroring servers.

1. Because you have set up the database mirroring in full-safety mode with automatic failover, you first need to remove it. Open the DatabaseMirroringCommands.sql script, and execute the following command on either the principal server or the mirror server:

```
ALTER DATABASE AdventureWorks SET WITNESS OFF
```

2. Then execute the following command on the principal server:

```
ALTER DATABASE AdventureWorks SET SAFETY OFF
```

3. Now the database AdventureWorks is set with SAFETY OFF with no witness, and you can force a failover. You have to simulate the scenario whereby the mirror server cannot form a quorum (cannot connect) with the principal server. To achieve that, stop the SQL Server service on the principal, and execute the following command on the mirror server:

```
ALTER DATABASE AdventureWorks SET PARTNER FORCE_SERVICE_ALLOW_DATA_LOSS
```

This command now forces the AdventureWorks database on the mirror server to recover and come online. The mirroring_state (sys.database_mirroring) doesn't matter (synchronized or not) in this case because it is a forced failover, which is why you may lose data.

Now notice that if you bring the original principal server (the one on which you stopped the SQL Server service) back online, the mirroring session will be suspended. You can execute the sys.database_mirroring catalog view in the MirroringCatalogView.sql script to view the mirroring state by connecting to either the principal server or the mirror server. To resume the mirroring session, execute the following command from the DatabaseMirroringCommands.sql script on either the principal or the mirror:

```
ALTER DATABASE AdventureWorks SET PARTNER RESUME
```

DATABASE AVAILABILITY SCENARIOS

So far you have learned about database mirroring operating modes and how to failover in different operating modes. This section describes what happens to the database availability of clients when the server is lost. The server might be lost not only because the power is off but also because of a communication link failure or some other reason; the point is that the other server in the mirroring session cannot communicate. Several different scenarios exist. To keep matters clear, you use three server names in this section: ServerA (principal), ServerB (mirror) and ServerC (witness).

Principal Is Lost

If the principal server is lost, the failover scenario depends on the transaction safety (FULL or OFF) and whether a witness is present.

Scenario 1: Safety FULL with a Witness

In this scenario (covered in further detail in the automatic failover section), the mirror forms a quorum with the witness because the principal is lost. Automatic failover will happen (of course, certain conditions must be met, as mentioned earlier), the mirror becomes the new principal server, and the database will be available on the new principal.

In this situation, before the failure, ServerA was the principal, ServerB was the mirror, and ServerC was the witness. ServerA now fails. After failover, ServerB becomes the principal and serves the database. However, because there is no mirror server after failover (because ServerA is down), ServerB runs exposed, and the mirroring state is DISCONNECTED. If ServerA becomes operational, then it automatically assumes the mirror role, except that the session is suspended until a RESUME is issued.

If SAFETY is FULL and you have configured a witness, to serve the database, at least two servers need be available to form a quorum. In this scenario, if ServerA fails, then ServerB becomes the principal and serves the database; but now if ServerC (witness) goes down, ServerB cannot serve the database.

Scenario 2: Safety FULL Without a Witness

In this operating mode, SAFETY is FULL, but automatic failover is not possible. Therefore, if ServerA (principal) fails, the database is unavailable to the clients. You need to manually perform several steps to force the database to become available again.

In this situation, before the failure, ServerA was the principal, ServerB was the mirror, and there was no witness. ServerA is now lost, so the database is unavailable to clients. To make the database available, you need to execute the following commands on the mirror:

```
ALTER DATABASE <database_name> SET PARTNER OFF
RESTORE DATABASE <database_name> WITH RECOVERY
```

These commands bring the database on ServerB online, making it available again. When ServerA comes online, you have to reestablish the mirroring session. However, an alternative in which you do not have to reestablish the mirroring session does exist. Execute the following command on ServerB (which is still the mirror after ServerA becomes unavailable):

```
ALTER DATABASE <database_name> SET PARTNER FORCE_SERVICE_ALLOW_DATA_LOSS
```

That brings the database online on ServerB, which becomes the principal server. When ServerA comes online, it automatically assumes the mirror role. However, the mirroring session is suspended, meaning no transaction logs will be sent from ServerB to ServerA. You'll need to resume the mirroring session by starting to send the transaction logs from ServerB to ServerA. To do so, execute the following command:

```
ALTER DATABASE <database_name> SET PARTNER RESUME
```

Whether you choose to break the mirroring session or force failover, you lose any transactions that were not sent to the mirror at the time of failure.

Scenario 3: SAFETY OFF

When SAFETY is OFF, the witness doesn't add any value, you do not need to configure a witness in that case. If ServerA (principal) is lost in this scenario, the database becomes unavailable. Then you have to force failover for the database to become available again.

In this scenario, before the failure, ServerA was the principal and ServerB was the mirror. ServerA now fails and the database is not available to clients. You can manually failover to ServerB by using the following command:

```
ALTER DATABASE <database_name> SET PARTNER FORCE_SERVICE_ALLOW_DATA_LOSS
```

However, the SAFETY is OFF, so any transactions that were not received by the mirror at the time of the principal failure will be lost. Therefore, manual failover with SAFETY is OFF involves acknowledging the possibility of data loss. When ServerA becomes operational again, it automatically assumes the mirror role, but the mirroring session is suspended. You can resume the mirroring session again by executing the following command:

```
ALTER DATABASE <database_name> SET PARTNER RESUME
```

Mirror Is Lost

If the mirror fails, then the principal continues functioning, so the database continues to be available to the clients. The mirroring state is DISCONNECTED, and the principal runs exposed which means without a failover partner. You can use the sys.database_mirroring catalog view to see the mirroring state on the principal server.

When the mirror goes down, you have to be a little careful and take steps to ensure that the principal continues to serve the database without any issue. The mirroring state changes to DISCONNECTED, and as long as the state is DISCONNECTED the transaction log space cannot be reused, even if you back up the transaction log. If your transaction log files keep growing and reach their maximum size limit, or your disk runs out of space, the database can no longer process transactions. Then you may want to do the following:

➤ Make sure you have plenty of disk space for the transaction log to grow on the principal, and be sure to bring the mirror server online before you run out of disk space.

➤ Break the database mirroring session using the following command: ALTER DATABASE <database_name> SET PARTNER OFF.

The issue here is that when your mirror server becomes operational, you have to reestablish the mirroring session by a backup and restore of the principal database and then by reestablishing the mirror partnership.

For a large database, the backup and restore operations can take some time; consider the following best practices:

➤ Break the database mirroring session using the following command: ALTER DATABASE <database_name> SET PARTNER OFF.

➤ Make a note of the time when the mirror went down, and make sure the job that backs up the transaction log is running on the principal.

➤ When the mirror comes back online, apply all the transaction logs on the mirror database.

➤ The first transaction log you should apply is the one you backed up after the mirror went down. Be sure to apply the transaction log on the mirror database with the NORECOVERY option. That way, you don't have to back up the entire database and restore it on the mirror. Of course, you have to perform other steps to reestablish the mirroring session because the session was broken.

Witness Is Lost

If the witness is lost, the database mirroring session continues functioning without interruption, and the database will be available. Automatic failover will not happen. When the witness comes back online, it automatically joins the mirroring session, of course, as a witness. With SAFETY FULL, if the witness is lost and then the mirror or the principal is lost, the database becomes unavailable to the clients.

Mirror and Witness Are Lost

Assuming that you have configured the mirroring session with a witness, if the mirror server is unavailable, the principal continues and the database is available, but it is running exposed. If the witness is also lost, then the principal becomes isolated and cannot serve the clients. Even though the principal database is running, it is not available to the clients because it cannot form a quorum. You want to consider locating the witness in a third datacenter to prevent a datacenter failover bringing down both the partner and the witness. If you try to access the database, you get the following message:

```
Msg 955, Level 14, State 1, Line 1
Database <database_name> is enabled for Database Mirroring,
but neither the partner
nor witness server instances are available: the database cannot be opened.
```

With both the mirror and the witness lost, the only way you can bring the database online to serve clients is by breaking the mirroring session with the following command on the principal:

```
ALTER DATABASE <database_name> SET PARTNER OFF
```

When the mirror becomes available, you can reestablish the mirroring session. To do so, you may have to back up and restore the database on the mirror, but if you want to avoid that step, refer to the third option in the "Mirror Is Lost" section. When the witness becomes available, it can join in again as a witness, but you must reestablish the mirroring session for the mirror first, then reestablishing the witness partnership.

MONITORING DATABASE MIRRORING

You can monitor database mirroring in different ways, based on what information you want to track. For basic information about the database mirroring state, safety level, and witness status, you can use catalog views. Refer to the "Database Mirroring Catalog Views" section earlier in this chapter for more details about catalog views. To monitor the performance of database mirroring, SQL Server 2012 provides a set of System Monitor performance objects. There is also a Database Mirroring Monitor GUI available with SQL Server 2012 Management Studio, which you can access if your database is mirrored. This section discusses both the key System Monitor counters and the GUI.

Monitoring Using System Monitor

The object `SQL Server: Database Mirroring` has plenty of counters to monitor database mirroring performance. You can use these counters to monitor the database mirroring activities on each partner, and the traffic between them, as shown in Figure 19-7. You can do this for each database instance, so if you mirror more than one database on a server, select the database you want to monitor from the list box. The key counters are described in the following sections.

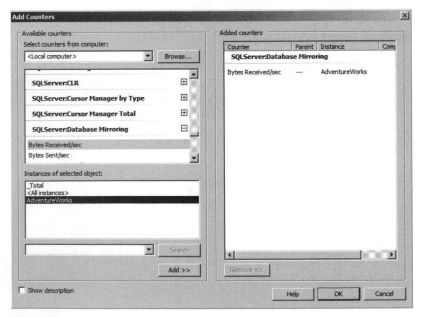

FIGURE 19-7

Counters for the Principal

The following System Monitor counters are used on the principal server:

➤ **Log Bytes Sent/Sec:** The rate at which the principal sends transaction log data to the mirror.

➤ **Log Send Queue KB:** The total kilobytes of the log that have not been sent to the mirror server yet. As the transaction log data is sent from the principal to the mirror, the Log Send Queue is depleted, growing again as new transactions are recorded into the log buffer on the principal.

➤ **Transaction Delay:** The delay (in milliseconds) spent waiting for commit acknowledgment from the mirror. This counter reports the total delay for all the transactions in process at the time. You can determine the average delay per transaction by dividing this counter by the Transactions/Sec counter. For high-performance mode, this counter is zero because the principal doesn't wait for the mirror to harden the transaction log to disk.

You can do a simple exercise using the `ModifyData.sql` script to get a feel for how this counter reports on the transaction delay:

1. Start the System Monitor, and add this counter on your principal.

2. On the principal, execute the `ModifyData.sql` script, and note the average for this counter. It should show a value greater than 0.

3. On the principal, execute this command:

```
ALTER DATABASE AdventureWorks SET SAFETY OFF
```

This puts database mirroring in high performance mode.

4. Execute the `ModifyData.sql` script again. You should now notice that this counter is 0.

➤ **Transaction/Sec:** You can find this counter in the `SQL Server: Databases` object, which measures database throughput and shows how many transactions are processed in a second. This counter gives you an idea of how fast the log file will grow if your mirror is down, the mirror state is `DISCONNECTED`, and you need to expand the log file. Be sure to choose the database instance you are interested in for this counter.

➤ **Log Bytes Flushed/Sec:** This counter is under the `SQL Server: Databases` object, which indicates how many bytes are written to disk (log hardening) per second on the principal. This is the log-generation rate of your application. These are also the bytes sent to the mirror when it is flushed to the disk on the principal. In normal operating conditions, the Log Bytes Flushed/Sec and Log Bytes Sent/Sec counters should show the same value. If you refer to Figure 19-2, the activity labeled 2 happens at the same time, which is exactly what the System Monitor indicates.

Counters for the Mirror

The following System Monitor counters are on the mirror server under the object `SQL Server: Database Mirroring`:

➤ **Redo Bytes/Sec:** The rate at which log bytes are rolled forward (replayed) to the data pages, per second, from the redo queue.

➤ **Redo Queue KB:** This counter shows the total KB of the transaction log still to be applied to the mirror database (rolled forward). You learn later how to calculate the estimated time the mirror takes to redo the logs using this counter and the Redo Bytes/Sec counter. The failover time depends on how big this queue is and how fast the mirror can empty this queue.

➤ **Log Bytes Received/Sec:** The rate at which log bytes are received from the principal. If the mirror can keep up with the principal to minimize the failover time, then ideally the Log Bytes Received/Sec and Redo Bytes/Sec counter shows the same *average* value, which means that the Redo Queue KB is zero. Whatever bytes the principal sends are immediately rolled forward to the data pages on the mirror, and there is no redo left, so the mirror is ready to failover right away.

Counters for the Principal and the Mirror

From a DBA standpoint, you want to know approximately how far the mirror is behind the principal; and after the mirror catches up, how long would it take to redo the transaction log so that it can failover. To do this, a calculation is required.

To calculate the estimated time for the mirror to catch up (in seconds) with the principal, you can use the Log Send Queue counter from the principal and the Log Bytes Received/Sec counter on the mirror. Moreover, you can use the Log Bytes Send/Sec counter on the principal instead of Log Bytes Received/Sec on the mirror. Use their average values and calculate as follows:

```
Estimated time to catch up (in seconds) = (Log Send Queue)/(Log Bytes Received
/sec)
```

To calculate the estimated time for the mirror to replay the transaction log (redo) to get ready for failover, you can use the Redo Queue KB counter (this counter gives you KB value, so convert it to bytes) and the Redo Bytes/Sec counter on the mirror. Use their average values and calculate as follows:

```
Estimated time to redo (in seconds) = (Redo Queue)/(Redo Bytes/sec)
```

In addition to the calculation, you can also use the Database Mirroring Monitor that ships with SQL Server 2012. This option provides all the same information that a calculation does.

Monitoring Using Database Mirroring Monitor

The SQL Server 2012 Database Mirroring Monitor will monitor the database mirroring activities. This makes the DBA's life easier. You can access this tool by right-click any user database in Object Explorer in SQL Management Studio on any registered SQL Server 2012 server and select Tasks ➪ Launch Database Mirroring Monitor. You can monitor all your mirroring sessions from it.

You have to register the mirrored database in the Database Mirroring Monitor before you can use it. To do so, click Action ➪ Register Mirrored Database, and follow the wizard. You can give the wizard either the principal server name or the mirror server name; it will figure out the other partner. Figure 19-8 shows the Database Mirroring Monitor with a registered mirrored database.

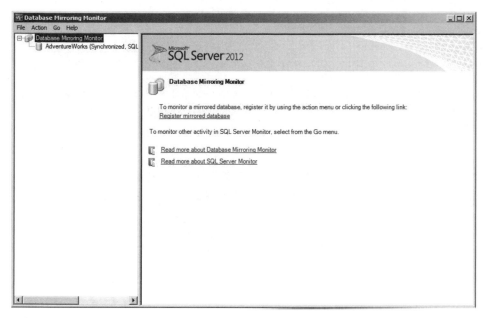

FIGURE 19-8

You can monitor the key counters mentioned in the previous section using this GUI. You can also set alerts for these counters to receive an e-mail or take an action if any counter exceeds a set threshold, as covered later.

If you set up mirroring using the SQL Server 2012 Management Studio, it creates the SQL job called Database Mirroring Monitor Job, which runs every 1 minute by default to refresh these counters. This data is stored in the `msdb.dbo.dbm_monitor_data` table. You can change the job schedule if wanted. If you set up database mirroring using the scripts provided here, you can create the SQL job using the following command to refresh the counters:

```
sp_dbmmonitoraddmonitoring [ update_period ]
```

By default, the [update_period] is 1 minute. You can specify a value between 1 and 120, in minutes. If you don't create this job, just press F5 when you are at the Database Mirroring Monitor screen. It calls the `sp_dbmmonitorresults` stored procedure to refresh the data (adding a row for new readings) in the `msdb.dbo.dbm_monitor_data` table. Actually, `sp_dbmmonitorresults` calls another stored procedure in the `msdb` database called `sp_dbmmonitorupdate` to update the status table and calculate the performance matrix displayed in the UI. If you press F5 more than once in 15 seconds, it won't refresh the data again in the table.

Look at the Status tab details in Figure 19-9. The Status area is where the server instance names, their current role, mirroring state, and witness connection status (if there is a witness) comes from the `sys.database_mirroring` catalog view. If you click the History button, you get a history of the mirroring status and other performance counters. The mirroring status and performance history is kept for 7 days (168 hours) by default in the `msdb.dbo.dbm_monitor_data` table. If you want to change the retention period, you can use the `sp_dbmmonitorchangealert` stored procedure, like this:

```
EXEC sp_dbmmonitorchangealert AdventureWorks, 5, 8, 1
```

This example changes the retention period to 8 hours for the `AdventureWorks` database where 5 is the `alter_id` and 1 is enabled. You can refer to SQL 2012 Books Online for a description of this stored procedure.

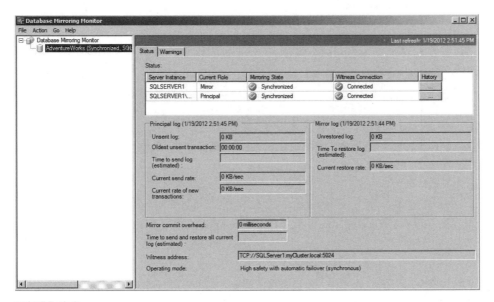

FIGURE 19-9

Following are detailed explanations of the different counters that are available in the Status tab.

➤ **Principal Log: Unsent Log:** This counter provides the same value as the Log Send Queue KB counter on the principal. Unsent Log reads the last value, so if you want to compare the Performance Monitor and this counter, look at its last value. You can run the script `ModifyData.sql` from earlier in the chapter after suspending the mirroring session using the following command:

```
ALTER DATABASE AdventureWorks SET PARTNER SUSPEND
```

You can see this counter value start to go up.

➤ **Principal Log: Oldest Unsent Transaction:** This counter gives you the age, in hh:mm:ss format, of the oldest unsent transaction waiting in the Send Queue. It indicates that the mirror is behind the principal by that amount of time.

➤ **Principal Log: Time to Send Log (Estimated):** The estimated time the principal instance requires to send the log currently in the Send Queue to the mirror server. Because the rate of the incoming transaction can change, this counter can provide an estimate only. This counter also provides a rough estimate of the time required to manually failover. If you suspend the mirroring, you notice that this counter shows a value of "Infinite," which means that because you are not sending any transaction logs to the mirror, the mirror never catches up.

➤ **Principal Log: Current Send Rate:** This counter provides the rate at which the transaction log is sent to the mirror, in KB/Sec. This is the same as the Performance Monitor counter Log Bytes Sent/Sec. The counter Current Send Rate provides the value in KB, whereas the counter Log Bytes Sent/Sec provides the value in bytes. When Time to Send Log is infinite, this counter shows a value of 0 KB/Sec because no log is being sent to the mirror server.

➤ **Principal Log: Current Rate of New Transaction:** The rate at which new transactions are coming in per second. This is the same as the Transaction/sec counter in the `Database` object.

➤ **Mirror Log: Unrestored Log:** This counter is for the mirror server. It provides the amount of log in KB waiting in the Redo Queue yet to be restored. This is the same as the Redo Queue KB counter for the mirror server. If this counter is 0, the mirror is keeping up with the principal and can failover immediately if required.

➤ **Mirror Log: Time to Restore Log:** This counter provides an estimate, in minutes, of how long the mirror will take to replay the transactions waiting in the Redo Queue. You saw this calculation earlier; this is the estimated time that the mirror requires before failover can occur.

➤ **Mirror Log: Current Restore Rate:** The rate at which the transaction log is restored into the mirror database, in KB/Sec.

➤ **Mirror Committed Overhead:** This counter measures the delay (in milliseconds) spent waiting for a commit acknowledgment from the mirror. This counter is the same as the Transaction Delay on the principal. It is relevant only in high-safety mode. For high-performance mode, this counter is zero because the principal does not wait for the mirror to harden the transaction log to disk.

➤ **Time to Send and Restore All Current Log (Estimated):** This counter measures the time needed to send and restore all of the log that has been committed at the principal at the current time. This time may be less than the sum of the values of the Time to Send Log (Estimated) and Time to Restore Log (Estimated) fields, because sending and restoring can operate in parallel. This estimate does predict the time required to send and restore new transactions committed at the principal while working through backlogs in the Send Queue.

➤ **Witness Address:** The fully qualified domain name of the witness, with the port number assigned for that endpoint.

➤ **Operating Mode:** The operating mode of the database mirroring session. It can be one of the following:

  ➤ High performance (asynchronous)

  ➤ High safety without automatic failover (synchronous)

  ➤ High safety with automatic failover (synchronous)

Setting Thresholds on Counters and Sending Alerts

You can set warnings for different mirroring thresholds so that you receive alerts based on the threshold you have set. Figure 19-10 shows the Warnings tab of the Database Mirroring Monitor.

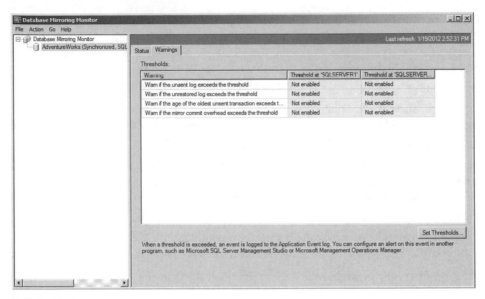

FIGURE 19-10

Following are instructions on how to set thresholds for the different warnings.

1. Start by clicking the Set Thresholds button on the Warnings tab, which opens the dialog shown in Figure 19-11. Here, you can set the threshold for counters on both the principal and mirror servers individually so that you can either keep the thresholds the same or vary them based on your requirements.

2. For this example, select the check box for the first warning, Warn if the Unsent Log Exceeds the Threshold, and set the threshold value to 100KB, just for the principal server.

3. Next, under the Alert folder in SQL Server Agent in SQL Server 2012 Management Studio, add a new alert. You see a dialog similar to the one shown in Figure 19-12. Type the alert name, and select the database name for which you need this alert — in this case, AdventureWorks.

4. SQL Server raises the error when the threshold you set is exceeded. Enter **32042** for the error number. Refer to the section "Using Warning Thresholds and Alerts on Mirroring Performance Metrics" in SQL 2012 Books Online to get the error numbers for other events.

5. Now click Response on the left pane and fill out the operator information to specify who will receive the alert when the threshold is exceeded.

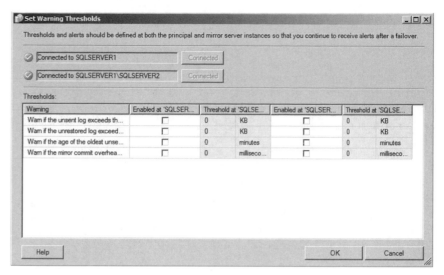

FIGURE 19-11

FIGURE 19-12

On the principal, you can test this alert by suspending database mirroring using the following command:

```
ALTER DATABASE AdventureWorks SET PARTNER SUSPEND
```

The log will not be sent to the mirror, and the Unsent Log counter will start increasing. When it reaches the threshold of 100KB, you should get the alert. You'll look at "Mirroring Event Listener Setup" section to set up the database mirroring event change (suspended, synchronizing, and synchronized) and send a notification.

 You can monitor database mirroring with SQL Profiler using the Database Mirroring State Change event under the Database event class of SQL Profiler in SQL Server. This event records all the database mirroring state changes (suspended, synchronizing, synchronized, and so on) that occur on the server.

TROUBLESHOOTING DATABASE MIRRORING

Database mirroring errors typically occur between two error categories: during setup and at runtime. This section covers each.

Troubleshooting Setup Errors

Errors typically occur most often during setup because of setup configurations; it is important to verify the following to ensure that data mirroring is configured.

➤ Make sure that the SQL Server service accounts on each server are trusted and that the user account under which the SQL Server instance is running has the necessary connect permissions. If the servers are on non-trusted domains, make sure the certificates are correct. Refer to the "Preparing the Endpoints" section earlier in this chapter for details regarding how to configure the certificates.

➤ Ensure that the endpoint status is started on all partners and the witness. You can use the MirroringCatalogView.sql script, which is included in the download for this chapter. Check the EndPointStatus column, and ensure that the value is STARTED.

➤ Make sure you aren't using a port used by another process. The port number must be unique per server, not per SQL Server instance. You can use any port number between 1024 and 32767. Use the MirroringCatalogView.sql script to view the port information under the PortUsed column.

➤ Verify that the encryption settings for the endpoints are compatible on the principal, mirror, and witness. You can check the encryption setting using MirroringCatalogView.sql. Look for the script that selects from the sys.database_mirroring_endpoints catalog view, and check the IS_ENCRYPTION_ENABLED column. This column has a value of either 0 or 1. A value of 0 means encryption is DISABLED for the endpoint, and a value of 1 means encryption is either REQUIRED or SUPPORTED.

➤ Make sure you have identified the correct fully qualified names of the partners and witness (if any) in the ALTER DATABASE command.

The most common types of set up errors have to do with the data mirroring partners not being able to network with each other or the mirror database not being ready to accept transactions. For example, you may get the following error while setting up database mirroring:

```
Database mirroring connection error 4
  'An error occurred while receiving data: '64
The specified network name is no longer available.)'.'
  for 'TCP://yourMirrorServer:5023'.
Error: 1443, Severity: 16, State: 2.
```

This error could indicate that the firewall on the mirror server or the principal server is blocking the connection on the specified port. Check whether the firewall is blocking that communication port.

Finally, a mirror database that is not in the correct state to accept transactions can also produce an error while setting up database mirroring on the principal server:

```
Msg 1412, Level 16, State 0, Line 1 The remote copy of database "AdventureWorks" has
not been rolled forward
  to a point in time that is encompassed in the local copy
of the database log.
```

This indicates that the database on the mirror server is not rolled forward enough to establish the mirroring session. You may have backed up some transaction logs while backing up and restoring the database, so you have to restore these transaction logs to the mirror server with the NORECOVERY option to synchronize the mirror with the principal. See the RestoreLogOnMirror.sql script for an example.

Troubleshooting Runtime Errors

If your database mirroring setup is done correctly but you get errors afterward, the first thing you want to look at is the sys.database_mirroring catalog view. Check the status of the mirroring state. If it is SUSPENDED, check the SQL error log for more details. You may have added a data file or log file on the principal for which you do not have the exact same path on the mirror, which will cause a Redo error to occur on the mirror, causing the database session to be suspended. You see an error similar to the following in the mirror server error log:

```
Error: 5123, Severity: 16, State: 1.
CREATE FILE encountered operating system error 3(The system cannot find the path
specified.) while attempting to open or create the physical file
'<your folder>\AdventureWorks_1.ndf'.
```

If you get this error, perform the following steps:

1. Create the folder on the mirror and then resume the mirroring session using the following command:

```
ALTER DATABASE AdventureWorks SET PARTNER RESUME
```

2. If you have added a data file and you do not have that drive on the mirror, delete the data file from the principal. If pages are allocated on the file, empty the data file before you can delete it. Then resume the mirroring session again.

If you cannot connect to the principal database even though your server is online, it is most likely because safety is set to FULL, and the principal server cannot form a quorum because both the witness and mirror are lost. This can happen, for example, if your system is in high-safety mode with the witness, and the mirror and witness have become disconnected from the principal. You can force the mirror server to recover, using the following command on the mirror:

```
ALTER DATABASE AdventureWorks SET PARTNER FORCE_SERVICE_ALLOW_DATA_LOSS
```

After that, because both the old principal and the witness are not available, the new principal cannot serve the database, so turn the SAFETY to OFF using the following command:

```
ALTER DATABASE AdventureWorks SET PARTNER SAFETY OFF
```

Ensure that there is sufficient disk space on the mirror for both redo (free space on the data drives) and log hardening (free space on the log drive).

Automatic Page Repair

On SQL Server Enterprise and Developer Editions, database mirroring can automatically correct error numbers 823 and 824, which are caused by data *cyclic redundancy check (CRC)* errors raised while the server is attempting to read a page. When a mirror partner cannot read a page, it asynchronously requests a copy from its partner; if the page requested is successfully applied, the page is repaired and the error is resolved. During the repair, the actual data is preserved. It does not repair control type pages, such as allocation pages. The page repair operation varies depending on whether the principal or mirror is requesting the page.

Principal Request Page

The principal identifies a page read error, marks the page with an 829 error (restore pending), inserts a row into the suspect_pages table in MSDB with the error status, and requests the page from the mirror. If the mirror is successful in reading the page, it returns the page to the principal who applies it. After the page is repaired, the principal marks the page as restored — that is, event_type = 5 in the suspect_pages table. Then any deferred transactions are resolved.

Mirror Request Page

The mirror identifies a page read error, marks the page with an 829 error (restore pending), and inserts a row into the suspect_pages table in MSDB with the error status. It requests the page from the principal and sets the mirror session in a SUSPENDED state. If the principal is successful in reading the page, it returns the page to the mirror. After the page is applied at the mirror, the mirror resumes the data mirroring session and marks the page as restored in the suspect_pages table — that is, event_type = 5.

The `sys.dm_db_mirroring_auto_page_repair` DMV view displays corrupted pages in the data mirroring environment. This catalog view returns a maximum of 100 rows per database of every automatic page repair attempt; as it reaches this maximum, the next entry replaces the oldest entry. Use the following command to execute the catalog view:

```
SELECT * FROM sys.dm_db_mirroring_auto_page_repair
```

This will return six columns. One column in particular, `error_type` column, indicates errors encountered that are to be corrected. Additionally, the `page_status` column indicates where the program is in the process of repairing that page. The rest of the columns are self-explanatory.

PREPARING THE MIRROR SERVER FOR FAILOVER

When you set up mirroring, your intentions are clear that in the event of failover, the mirror takes on the full load. For the mirror to be fully functional as a principal, you have to do some configurations on the mirror server. Database mirroring is a database-to-database failover solution only; the entire SQL Server instance is not mirrored. If you want to implement full SQL Server instance failover, then you should consider Windows failover clustering, discussed in Chapter 16, "Clustering SQL Server 2012."

When preparing your mirror server for failover, the first place to start is with your hardware and software.

Hardware, Software, and Server Configuration

Your mirror server hardware should be identical (CPU, memory, storage, and network capacity) to that of the principal if you want your mirror server to handle the same load as your principal. You may argue that if your principal is a 16-core, 64-bit server with 32GB of RAM, having identical mirror hardware is a costly solution if your principal is not going down often and such expensive hardware is sitting idle. If your application is not critical, then you may want to have a smaller server just for failover and taking the load for some time, but it is arguable that if the application is not that critical, you do not need to have such extensive hardware on the primary either.

Moreover, with such huge hardware, the process on the server must be heavy, so if you failover, your mirror should handle that load even if it is for a short time. In addition, you have to consider the business cost versus the hardware cost and then make the decision. You can also use your mirror server for noncritical work so that even though it is a mirror, it can be used for some other work. Of course, you have to plan that out properly to make good use of your mirror server. Provided that your database server performance characteristics can be supported within the virtual server maximum performance capacity, data mirroring can be deployed on virtual servers.

Make sure that you have the same operating system version, service packs, and patches on both servers. During a rolling upgrade (as discussed in the "Database Availability During Planned Downtime" section), service packs and patch levels can be temporarily different.

You need to have the same edition of SQL Server on both partners. If you use a witness, then you don't need the same edition on it. You can use a smaller server for the witness because it doesn't carry any actual load — it is used only to form a quorum. Of course, the availability of the witness server is critical for automatic failover. Refer to the table in the section "Database Mirroring and SQL Server 2012 Editions" for more details on which editions support which database mirroring features.

Make sure you have an identical directory structure for the SQL Server install and database files on both the partners. If you add a database file to a volume/directory and that volume/directory does not exist on the mirror, the mirroring session will be suspended immediately.

On both principal and mirror, make sure that all the SQL Server configurations are identical (for example, tempdb size, trace flags, startup parameters, memory settings, and degree of parallelism).

All SQL Server logins on the principal must also be present on the mirror server; otherwise, your application cannot connect if a failover occurs. You can use SQL Server 2012 Integration Services, with the "Transfer Logins task, to copy logins and passwords from one server to another. (Refer to the section "Managing Changing Roles" in Chapter 18, "SQL Server 2012 Log Shipping," for more information.) Moreover, you still need to set the database permission for these logins. If you transfer these logins to a different domain, then you have to match the security identifier (SID) — that is, the unique name that Windows uses to identify a specific user name or group.

On the principal, many other objects may exist and be needed for that application(for example, SQL jobs, SQL Server Integration Services packages, linked server definitions, maintenance plans, supported databases, SQL Mail or Database Mail settings, and DTC settings). You also have to transfer all these objects to the mirror server.

If you use SQL Server authentication, you have to resolve the logins on the new principal server after failover. You can use the sp_change_users_login stored procedure to resolve these logins.

Be sure to have a process in place so that when you make any changes to any configuration on the principal server, you repeat or transfer the changes on the mirror server.

After you set up your mirror, failover the database and let your application run for some time on the new principal because that is the best way to ensure that all the settings are correct. Try to schedule this task during a slow time of the day, and deliver the proper communication procedures prior to testing failover.

Database Availability During Planned Downtime

This section describes the steps required to do a *rolling upgrade* technique to perform a software and hardware upgrade while keeping the database online for applications. The steps to perform a rolling upgrade vary based on database mirroring session transaction safety configuration which is: SAFETY FULL or SAFETY OFF.

Safety Full Rolling upgrade

Assuming that you have configured the mirroring session with SAFETY FULL, if you have to perform software and hardware upgrades, perform the following steps in order:

1. Perform the hardware and software changes on the mirror server first. If you have to restart the SQL Server 2012 or the server itself, you can do so. As soon as the server comes back

up again, the mirroring session will be established automatically and the mirror will start synchronizing with the principal. The principal is exposed while the mirror database is down, so if you have a witness configured, make sure that it is available during this time; otherwise, the principal will be running in isolation and cannot serve the database because it cannot form a quorum.

2. After the mirror is synchronized with the principal, you can failover using the following command:

```
ALTER DATABASE <database_name> SET PARTNER FAILOVER
```

The application now connects to the new principal. The "Client Redirection to the Mirror" section covers application redirection when the database is mirrored. Open and in-flight transactions during failover will be rolled back at this point. If that is not tolerable for your application, you can stop the application for the brief failover moment and restart the application after failover completes.

3. Now perform the hardware or software upgrade on your old principal server. When you finish with upgrades and the database becomes available on the old principal, it assumes the mirror role, the database mirroring session is automatically established, and it starts synchronizing.

4. If you have a witness set up, perform the hardware or software upgrade on that server.

5. At this point, your old principal acts as a mirror. You can fail back to your old principal now that all your upgrades are done. If you have identical hardware on the new principal, you may leave it as is so that you don't have to stop the application momentarily; but if your hardware is not identical, consider switching back to your original principal.

Safety Off Rolling Upgrade

If you have configured the database mirroring with SAFETY OFF, you can still use the rolling upgrade technique by following these steps:

1. Perform the hardware and software changes on the mirror first. See the preceding section for more details.

2. On the principal server, change the SAFETY to FULL using this command:

```
ALTER DATABASE <database_name> SET SAFETY FULL
```

Plan this activity during off-peak hours to reduce the mirror server synchronization time.

3. After the mirror is synchronized, you can perform the failover to the mirror.

4. Perform the hardware and software upgrade on the old principal. After the old principal comes back up, it assumes the mirror role and starts synchronizing with the new principal.

5. When synchronized, you can fail back to your original principal.

If you use mirroring just to make a redundant copy of your database, you may not want to failover for planned downtime because you may not have properly configured all the other settings on the mirror, as described in the section "Hardware, Software, and Server Configuration." In that case, you have to take the principal down for upgrade, and the database will not be available.

SQL Job Configuration on the Mirror

For identical configuration on both the principal server and the mirror server, you also have to synchronize SQL jobs on your mirror server as mentioned earlier. When the database is the mirror, you do not want these SQL jobs to run. Following are the recommended options regarding how to do that:

➤ Have some logic in the SQL job steps that checks for the database mirroring state and runs the next step only if the database mirroring state is the principal.

➤ Listen for the database mirroring change event when the database becomes the principal, and execute a SQL job that enables all the SQL jobs you want to run. Stop or disable these jobs again when the event is fired, indicating that the database state has changed to mirror. You learn how to listen to these database mirroring state change events in the section "Mirroring Event Listener Setup," later in the chapter.

 Technically, you could also disable the jobs and enable them manually when the database becomes the principal. However, as a DBA, you do not want to manually manage these jobs, so this is not a good option.

Database TRUSTWORTHY Bit on the Mirror

The TRUSTWORTHY database property is used to indicate whether the instance of SQL Server trusts the database and the contents within it. If you restore the database, the TRUSTWORTHY bit is automatically set to 0, so when you set up database mirroring, this bit is set to 0 as soon as you restore your database on your mirror server. If your application requires this bit to be 1, in case of failover, your application will not work because this bit is set to 0 on the mirror, which is now the new principal. To avoid this, when you set up database mirroring, after it is set up correctly, failover to the mirror and set this bit to 1 using the following command:

```
ALTER DATABASE <database_name> SET TRUSTWORTHY ON
```

Then optionally fail back to your original principal.

Client Redirection to the Mirror

In SQL Server 2012, if you connect to a database that is being mirrored with ADO.NET or the SQL Native Client, your application can take advantage of the drivers' capability to automatically redirect connections when a database mirroring failover occurs. You must specify the initial principal server and database in the connection string and optionally the failover partner server.

You can write the connection string in several ways, but here is one example, specifying ServerA as the principal, ServerB as the mirror, and `AdventureWorks` as the database name:

```
"Data Source=ServerA;Failover Partner=ServerB;Initial Catalog=AdventureWorks;
Integrated Security=True;"
```

The failover partner in the connection string is used as an alternative server name if the connection to the initial principal server fails. If the connection to the initial principal server succeeds, the failover partner name is not used, but the driver stores the failover partner name that it retrieves from the principal server in the client-side cache.

Assume a client is successfully connected to the principal, and a database mirroring failover (automatic, manual, or forced) occurs. The next time the application attempts to use the connection, the `ADO.NET` or SQL Native Client driver detects that the connection to the old principal has failed and automatically retries connecting to the new principal as specified in the failover partner name. If successful, and a new mirror server is specified for the database mirroring session by the new principal, the driver retrieves the new partner failover server name and places it in its client cache. If the client cannot connect to the alternative server, the driver tries each server alternatively until the login timeout period is reached.

The advantage of using the database mirroring client support built into `ADO.NET` and the SQL Native Client driver is that you do not need to recode the application, or place special codes in the application, to handle a database mirroring failover.

If you do not use the `ADO.NET` or SQL Native Client automatic redirection, you can use other techniques that enable your application to failover. For example, you could use network load balancing (NLB) to redirect connections from one server to another while remaining transparent to the client application that is using the NLB virtual server name. On failover, you can reconfigure NLB to divert all client applications using the database to the new principal by tracking the mirroring state change event to; then change the NLB configuration to divert the client applications to the new principal server. Additionally, you could consider writing your own redirection code and retry logic. Moreover, the Domain Name System (DNS) service provides a name-to-IP resolution that can be used to redirect clients to the new principal server. Provided that the administrator has access to the DNS server either by script or by using the Windows DNS management tool to modify the IP address to redirect client applications during a failover, DNS acts as the cross-reference for the client applications, as they will continue to connect to the same name; after the DNS modification, it redirects the database request to the new principal server.

MIRRORING MULTIPLE DATABASES

As discussed previously, it is possible to mirror multiple databases on the same server. You can either use the same server for a mirror partner or use a different mirror server for each database. I recommend using the same mirror server for mirroring multiple databases from a principal server. That way, maintenance is reduced, and the system is less complex; otherwise, you have to perform all the steps mentioned in "Hardware, Software, and Server Configuration" on each mirror server.

If you want to use the database mirroring feature with database dependencies, especially with high-safety and automatic failover, you have to be careful when you design your application. Consider a scenario in which your application is using two databases, DB1 and DB2, on a server called ServerA. Now you have set up database mirroring for both of these databases to your mirror server, ServerB, with automatic failover. Suppose a failover occurs with only DB1 (perhaps because of a disk failure on the disk where DB1 resides or a sporadic network issue that could cause the mirroring session of one database to time out); and because of the automatic failover, the database fails over to the mirror ServerB. Therefore, ServerB will be the principal for database DB1, and ServerA the principal for database DB2. Where would your application connect? Even though both databases are available, your application may not function correctly. This could also happen if you manually failover one database and not the other.

> An application that relies on multiple databases is not a good candidate for a high-safety with automatic failover scenario. You can probably have high-safety mode without *automatic failover and specify an alert when mirroring state changes so that you can manually failover all the databases or have a SQL job that does that for you. A better option is to use Availability Groups, new in SQL Server 2012, (see Chapter 25, "AlwaysOn Availability Groups" for more information).*

Additionally, remember that you cannot mirror a system database. Moreover, make sure that you do not mirror too many databases on a single server, or it may affect server and application performance. Because of resource constraints, on a 32-bit server you do not want to mirror more than 10 databases per SQL Server instance. Use System Monitor counters and the Database Mirroring Monitor to understand how your servers are performing.

DATABASE MIRRORING AND OTHER HIGH-AVAILABILITY SOLUTIONS

Database mirroring is another weapon in the arsenal of SQL Server high-availability solutions. SQL Server 2012 provides at least five high-availability solutions. Of course, each solution has some overlap with the others, and each has some advantages and disadvantages:

- ➤ **Database mirroring:** For this discussion, consider the high-safety mode with a witness.

- ➤ **Failover clustering:** This is a typical solution for high availability with a two or more nodes Windows failover cluster running SQL Server instances. Clustering is discussed in more detail in Chapter 16, "Clustering SQL Server 2012."

- ➤ **Transactional replication:** For comparison purposes, consider a separate distribution server with a single subscriber server as a standby if the publisher fails.

- ➤ **Log shipping:** SQL Server 2012 has built-in log shipping. Log shipping is discussed in detail in Chapter 18, "SQL Server 2012 Log Shipping."

➤ **AlwaysOn:** Server 2012 has Availability Groups in SQL Server 2012. Availability Groups is discussed in detail in Chapter 25, "AlwaysOn Availability Groups."

Now see how database mirroring compares with these other technologies.

Database Mirroring versus Clustering

Obviously, the biggest difference between database mirroring and a Window failover cluster solution is the level at which each provides redundancy. Database mirroring provides protection at the database level, as you have seen, whereas a cluster solution provides protection at the SQL Server instance level.

As discussed in the section "Mirroring Multiple Databases," if your application requires multiple database dependencies, clustering is probably a better solution than mirroring. If you need to provide availability for one database at a time, mirroring is a good solution and has many advantages compared to clustering — for example: ease of configuration.

Unlike clustering, database mirroring does not require shared storage hardware and does not have a single failure point with the shared storage. Database mirroring brings the standby database online faster than any other SQL Server high-availability technology and works well in ADO.NET and SQL Native Access Client for client-side redirect.

Another important difference is that in database mirroring, the principal and mirror servers are separate SQL Server instances with distinct names, whereas a SQL Server instance on a cluster gets one virtual server name and IP address that remains the same no matter which node of the cluster hosts that SQL Server instance.

You can use database mirroring within a cluster to create a hot standby for a cluster SQL Server 2012 database. If you do, be aware that because a cluster failover is longer than the timeout value on database mirroring, a high-availability mode mirroring session will react to a cluster failover as a failure of the principal server. It would then put the cluster node into a mirroring state. You can increase the database mirroring timeout value by using following command:

```
ALTER DATABASE <database_name> SET PARTNER TIMEOUT <integer_value_in_seconds>
```

Database Mirroring versus Transactional Replication

The common process between database mirroring and transactional replication is reading the transaction log on the originating server. Although the synchronization mechanism is different, database mirroring directly initiates I/O to the transaction log file to transfer the log records.

Transactional replication can be used with more than one subscriber, whereas database mirroring is a one-database-to-one-database solution. You can read nearly real-time data on the subscriber database, whereas you cannot read data on the mirrored database unless you create a database snapshot, which is a static, point-in-time snapshot of the database.

Database Mirroring versus Log Shipping

Database mirroring and log shipping both rely on moving the transaction log and restoring it. In database mirroring, the mirror database is constantly in a recovering state, which is why you cannot query the mirrored database. In log shipping, the database is in standby mode, so you can query the database if the log is not being restored at the same time. In addition, log shipping supports the bulk-logged recovery model, whereas mirroring supports only the full recovery model.

If your application relies on multiple databases for its operation, you may want to consider log shipping for failover. Sometimes it is a bit tedious to set up log shipping going the other way once a failover has occurred, whereas mirroring is easy in that aspect.

In the high-performance mode, there is a potential for data loss if the principal fails and the mirror is recovered using a forced failover recovery. If you are log shipping the old principal, and the transaction log file of the old principal is undamaged, you can make a "tail of the log" backup from the principal to get the last set of log records from the transaction log. If the standby log-shipping database has had every other transaction log backup applied to it, you can then apply the "tail of the log" backup to the standby server and not lose any of the old principal's data. You can then compare the data in the log-shipping standby server with the remote database and potentially copy missing data to the remote server.

You can use log shipping and mirroring together if you like. You can use log shipping to ship the log to a remote site for disaster recovery and have a database-mirroring, high-availability configuration locally.

Database Mirroring Versus Availability Groups

Database mirroring and AlwaysOn both rely on moving the transaction log records and restoring it. AlwaysOn is a new high-availability feature of SQL Server 2012 with similar functionality to data mirroring but has the following additional capabilities:

➤ AlwaysOn relies on Windows Failover clustering for a virtual IP/virtual name for client connection. But unlike Windows Failover clustering, it doesn't require a shared disk resource but instead uses nonshared disks such as data mirroring.

➤ AlwaysOn implements Availability Groups that can contain one or more databases to failover as a single failover group; data mirroring failover is a single database.

➤ AlwaysOn can support up to five failover partners in a combination of synchronous or asynchronous modes; instead data mirroring supports two partners.

➤ AlwaysOn supports read-only replica databases kept in sync that can be used for reporting or database backup while in data mirroring; the mirrored database is only accessible using a database snapshot.

MIRRORING EVENT LISTENER SETUP

This section provides steps you can use to take some action when the database mirroring session changes state (for example, from disconnected to synchronizing or from synchronized to suspended). You can perform the following steps to configure an alert for mirroring state change events and take some action on these events.

1. Right-click the Alert folder under SQL Server Agent in SQL Server 2012 Management Studio and select New Alert. The dialog shown in Figure 19-13 appears.

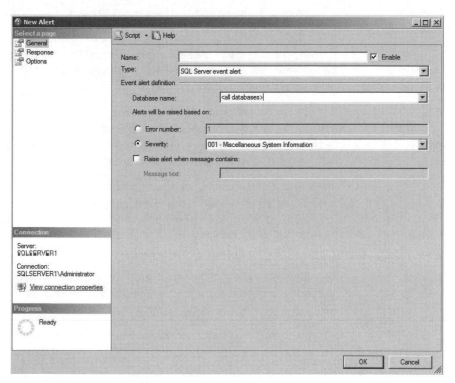

FIGURE 19-13

2. Type the name of the event, and select the event type WMI Event Alert from the drop-down menu. The namespace is automatically filled out for you. In the query field, type the following query:

```
SELECT * FROM DATABASE_MIRRORING_STATE_CHANGE
```

3. In this example, the alert is fired for all database mirroring state change events for all the databases mirrored on this server. If you want to be alerted about a specific database mirroring state change event for a specific database, add a WHERE clause to the SELECT statement:

```
SELECT * FROM DATABASE_MIRRORING_STATE_CHANGE WHERE State = 8 AND
DatabaseName = 'AdventureWorks'
```

This statement listens only for the "automatic failover" state change (state = 8) for the AdventureWorks database. Table 19-4 lists all the database mirroring state change events, so that you can use it to build the WHERE clause to listen to specific events.

TABLE 19.4: DATABASE_MIRRORING_STATE_CHANGE State

STATE	NAME	DESCRIPTION
0	Null Notification	Occurs briefly when a mirroring session is started.
1	Synchronized Principal with Witness	Occurs on the principal when the principal and mirror are connected and synchronized and the principal and witness are connected. For a mirroring configuration with a witness, this is the normal operating state.
2	Synchronized Principal without Witness	Occurs on the principal when the principal and mirror are connected and synchronized but the principal does not have a connection to the witness. For a mirroring configuration without a witness, this is the normal operating state.
3	Synchronized Mirror with Witness	Occurs on the mirror when the principal and mirror are connected and synchronized and the mirror and witness are connected. For a mirroring configuration with a witness, this is the normal operating state.
4	Synchronized Mirror without Witness	This state occurs on the mirror when the principal and mirror are connected and synchronized but the mirror does not have a connection to the witness. For a mirroring configuration without a witness, this is the normal operating state.
5	Connection with Principal Lost	Occurs on the mirror server instance when it cannot connect to the principal.
6	Connection with Mirror Lost	Occurs on the principal server instance when it cannot connect to the mirror.
7	Manual Failover	Occurs on the principal server instance when the user fails over manually from the principal, or on the mirror server instance when a forced service is executed at the mirror.
8	Automatic Failover	Occurs on the mirror server instance when the operating mode is high safety with automatic failover (synchronous) and the mirror and witness server instances cannot connect to the principal server instance.
9	Mirroring Suspended	Occurs on either partner instance when the user suspends (pauses) the mirroring session, or when the mirror server instance encounters an error. It also occurs on the mirror server instance following a forced service command. When the mirror comes online as the principal, mirroring is automatically suspended.

STATE	NAME	DESCRIPTION
10	No Quorum	If a witness is configured, this state occurs on the principal or mirror server instance when it cannot connect to its partner or to the witness server instance.
11	Synchronizing Mirror	Occurs on the mirror server instance when there is a backlog of unsent log. The status of the session is Synchronizing.
12	Principal Running Exposed	Occurs on the principal server instance when the operating mode is high safety (synchronous) and the principal cannot connect to the mirror server instance.
13	Synchronizing Principal	Occurs on the principal server instance when there is a backlog of unsent log. The status of the session is Synchronizing.

4. Now select the Response page, as shown in Figure 19-14. This dialog enables you to specify what you want SQL Server 2012 to do if the event occurs. In Figure 19-14, you want to execute the SQL job.

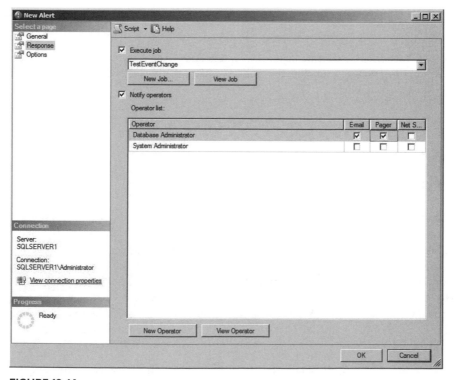

FIGURE 19-14

5. In the `TestEventChange` SQL job, you can actually add the following script to store the history of database mirroring state change events in a table. Create this table first in some other database, such as `msdb`:

```
CREATE TABLE dbo.MirroringStateChanges
(
 EventTime varchar(max) NULL
,EventDescription varchar(max) NULL
,NewState int NULL
,DatabaseName varchar(max) NULL
)
```

6. Add the following script as a job step to insert into this table:

```
INSERT INTO dbo.MirroringStateChanges
(
 [EventTime]
,[EventDescription]
,[NewState]
,[DatabaseName]
)
VALUES
(
 $(ESCAPE_NONE(WMI(StartTime)))
,$(ESCAPE_NONE(WMI(TextData)))
,$(ESCAPE_NONE(WMI(State)))
,$(ESCAPE_NONE(WMI(DatabaseName)))
 )
```

You can change the database mirroring state using the ALTER DATABASE command to test this alert. Additionally, the database mirroring state change is logged to Event Viewer under the Application events as something like the following:

```
The mirrored database "AdventureWorks" is changing roles from "MIRROR" to
"PRINCIPAL" due to Failover from partner
```

DATABASE SNAPSHOTS

As you have probably figured out by now, the mirror database is in NORECOVERY mode, so you cannot query the mirror database. If you want to read data from the mirror database to be used for reporting, SQL Server 2012 (Enterprise Edition and Developer Edition) has a feature called Database Snapshots, first introduced in SQL Server 2005. A database snapshot is a point-in-time, read-only, static view of a database (the source database). This feature comes in handy for reading the mirror database. Multiple database snapshots can exist but they always reside on the same SQL Server instance as the database. Each database snapshot is transactionally consistent with the source database at the point in time of the snapshot's creation. A snapshot persists until it is explicitly dropped by the database owner.

Using this feature, you can create a snapshot on the mirror database. Then, you can read the database snapshot as you would read any other database. The database snapshot operates at a data-page level. Before a page of the source database is modified for the first time after the database snapshot, the original page is copied from the source database to the snapshot file. This process is called a *copy-on-write* operation. The snapshot stores the original page, preserving the data records as they existed when the snapshot was created. Subsequent updates to records in a modified page on the source database do not affect the data contents of the snapshot. In this way, the snapshot preserves the original pages for all data records that have ever been modified since the snapshot was taken. Even if you modify the source data, the snapshot will still have the same data from the time when it was created. (See the topic "Database Mirroring and Database Snapshots" in SQL Server 2012 Books Online for more information.)

The following example shows how to create a snapshot on the AdventureWorks database:

```
CREATE DATABASE AdventureWorks_Snapshot ON
(NAME = AdventureWorks, FILENAME = '<your folder>\ADW_Mirroring_
snapshot_Data1.SS')
AS SNAPSHOT OF AdventureWorks
```

Because new data changes will be continuous on the mirrored database, if you want to read more recent data not in the database snapshot after you have created it, you need to drop the database snapshot and re-create it. You can drop the snapshot in the same manner as you would drop a database:

```
DROP DATABASE AdventureWorks_Snapshot
```

Generating a database snapshot has some performance impact on the mirror server, so evaluate the impact if you want to create many snapshots on multiple databases on a server. Most important, from a database mirroring perspective, having too many snapshots on a mirror database can slow down the redo and cause the database to fall more and more behind the principal, potentially resulting in huge failover times.

In addition, prepare an area of disk space as big as the size of the source database because as data changes on the source database, the snapshot will start copying the original pages to the snapshot file, and it will start growing. Additionally, you may want to evaluate SQL Server replication as an alternative reporting solution.

SUMMARY

Database mirroring provides a database redundancy solution using the log-transfer mechanism. The transaction log records are sent to the mirror transaction log as soon as the log buffer is written to the disk on the principal. Mirroring can be configured in either high-performance mode or high-safety mode. In high-safety mode, if the principal fails, the mirror server automatically becomes a new principal and recovers its database. Understanding application behavior in terms of log-generation rate, number of concurrent connections, and size of transactions is important to achieve the best performance. Network bandwidth plays an important role in a database mirroring environment. When used with a high-bandwidth and low-latency network, database mirroring can provide a reliable, high-availability solution against planned and unplanned downtime.

20

Integration Services Administration and Performance Tuning

WHAT'S IN THIS CHAPTER

➤ Overview of SSIS

➤ Deploy and Configure SSIS Packages

➤ Secure and Administer SSIS

➤ Common Pitfalls with SSIS Performance

In keeping with the theme of focusing on how SQL Server 2012 changes the role of the DBA, in this chapter you learn how you can be better equipped as a DBA to maintain SQL Server's Business Intelligence components. The SQL Server 2012 Business Intelligence stack includes Integration Services (SSIS), Analysis Services (SSAS), and Reporting Services (SSRS).

This chapter looks at the many and varied administrative tasks required for managing Integration Services. First, an overview of the Integration Services service is provided so that you will have a better understanding of the moveable parts that require the attention of an administrator. After becoming comfortable with the architecture of Integration Services, you can focus on the administration of Integration Services, including configuration, event logs, and monitoring activity. Next, you gain an understanding of the various administrative tasks required of Integration Services packages, the functional component within SSIS, including creation, management, execution, and deployment. Last, you learn how to secure all the Integration Services components.

For more in-depth information about Integration Services, see Professional Microsoft SQL Server 2012 Integration Services, *by Brian Knight et al. (Wrox, 2012).*

A TOUR OF INTEGRATION SERVICES

Certainly the most important Business Intelligence (BI) component to Microsoft's arsenal is SSIS. Its core responsibility is the movement and cleansing of data. Without this cleansing and movement, every other component would not exist or, at a minimum, would report bad data.

Integration Services is a solution that provides enterprise-level data integration and workflow solutions that have as their goal the extraction, transformation, and loading (ETL) of data from various sources to various destinations. SSIS includes a wide range of tools and wizards to assist in the creation of the workflow and data flow activities that you need to manage in these complex data-movement solutions.

Integration Services Uses

Before diving into the detailed components within Integration Services, you should understand some of the more common business scenarios that involve creating SSIS solutions. Some common uses for SSIS include:

➤ Archival of data (export)

➤ Loading of new data (import)

➤ Transferring data from one data source to another

➤ Data cleansing or transformation of dirty data

➤ DBA tasks like purging old files or indexing a database

One of the first scenarios is combining data from different sources stored in different storage systems. In this scenario, SSIS is responsible for connecting to each data source, extracting the data, and merging it into a single dataset. For example, in today's information systems topology, this is becoming increasingly common because businesses archive information that is not needed for regular operations but is invaluable to analyze business trends or meet compliance requirements. You can also find this scenario when different parts of a business use different storage technologies or different schemas to represent the same data. In these cases, SSIS performs the homogenization of the information. SSIS seamlessly handles multiple divergent data sources and the transformations that can alter data types, split or merge columns, and look up descriptive information that becomes a powerful asset for these situations.

Another common scenario is the population and maintenance of data warehouses and data marts. In these business uses, the data volumes tend to be exceptionally large, and the window of time in which to perform the extraction, transformation, and loading of the data tends to be rather short. SSIS includes the capability to bulk-load data directly from flat files in SQL Server and has a destination component that can perform a bulk load into SQL Server. A key feature for large data volume and complex enrichment and transformation situations such as these is restartability. SSIS includes checkpoints to handle rerunning a package from a task or container within the control flow so that you can elegantly handle various types of errors that may occur during these complex data-loading scenarios.

Also important in data warehouse loads is the ability to source a particular destination from many different tables or files. In the database world, this is referred to as *denormalization*, and SSIS packages can easily merge data into a single dataset and load the destination table in a single process without the need to stage or land the data at each step of the process.

You often require the management or partitioning of history within your data warehouses to review the state of activity at a certain point in time. This history management creates complex updating scenarios, and SSIS handles this with the assistance of the Slowly Changing Dimension Wizard. This wizard dynamically creates and configures a set of data transformation tasks used to manage inserting and updating records, updating related records, and adding new columns to tables to support this history management.

Often, businesses receive data from outside of their systems and need to perform data-quality routines to standardize and clean the data before loading it into their systems. SSIS can handle most data situations from heterogeneous databases or flat files. This is commonly the case when different areas of the business use different standards and formats for the information or when the data is being purchased, such as with address data. Sometimes the data formats are different because the platforms from which they originate differ from the intended destination. In these cases, SSIS includes a rich set of data-transformation tasks to perform a wide range of data-cleaning, converting, and enriching functions. You can replace values or get descriptions from code values by using exact or fuzzy lookups within SSIS. Identifying records that may be duplicates by using SSIS grouping transformations helps to successfully remove them before loading the destination.

The ability to dynamically adjust the data transformations being performed is a common scenario within businesses. Often, data needs to be handled differently based on certain values it may contain or even based upon the summary or count of values in a given set of records. SSIS includes a rich set of transformations that are useful for splitting or merging data based upon data values, applying different aggregations or calculations based on different parts of a dataset, and loading different parts of the data into different locations. SSIS containers specifically support evaluating expressions, enumerating across a set of information, and performing workflow tasks based on results of the data values.

Lastly, you commonly have operational administrative functions that require automation. SSIS includes an entire set of tasks devoted to these administrative functions. You can use tasks specifically designed to copy SQL Server objects or facilitate the bulk loading of data. You also have access in SSIS to a SQL Management Objects (SMO) enumerator to perform looping across your servers to perform administrative operations on each server in your environment. When complete, you can also schedule all your SSIS packages and solutions using SQL Server Agent jobs.

The Main Parts of Integration Services

In SQL Server 2012, Integration Services has introduced two models that can impact your team's development and you as an administrator: package deployment model and project deployment model. The decision on which model to use is made when you first create the project and can always be changed later but should not be changed lightly. While you can use both models in your environment interchangeably, you should try to guide your development towards the project deployment model since it turns on all the new features of 2012.

Package deployment model was the only model a DBA and developer had prior to SQL Server 2012. This model has you deploy a package by itself, and the package's project is just an arbitrary container that doesn't do a lot. Packages run in this model can be deployed to the MSDB database or the server's file system. There is also an SSIS service in this model that monitors the execution of packages. Packages can be configured externally at runtime with configuration files or entries in a configuration table.

Project deployment model is a new model to SQL Server 2012 in which the project that contains the packages is more important in previous SQL Server editions. In this model, parameters can be passed into the project or package to reconfigure the package at runtime. Projects take a more vital role in this model because you deploy the entire project at a time, and you cannot deploy individual packages. When you deploy packages, they are added to the SSIS catalog database and can be executed in T-SQL or through PowerShell.

Moving forward in SQL Server 2012, you should use the new project deployment model because it offers a more robust configuration, logging, and management infrastructure. The package deployment model remains available for backward compatibility but should not be used as your first choice.

The package deployment model contains many important components including the service, runtime engine and components, object model, and dataflow engine and components. The following sections cover each of these components. In the package deployment model, the components have not changed in SQL Server 2012.

Integration Services Service

The component of architecture within Integration Services, responsible for monitoring packages as they execute and managing the storage of packages, is the SSIS service. Its primary job is to cache the data providers, monitor which packages are being executed, and monitor which packages are stored in the package store. This service is used only in the package deployment model.

Integration Services Runtime Engine and Runtime Components

The SSIS runtime engine works across both deployment models and is responsible for saving the layout and design of the packages, running the packages, and providing support for all additional package functionality such as transactions, breakpoints, configuration, connections, event handling, and logging. The specific executables that make up this engine include packages, containers, and tasks. You can find three default constraints within SSIS: success, completion, and failure.

Integration Services Object Model

The managed application programming interface (API) used to access SSIS tools, command-line utilities, and custom applications in the SSIS object model. Although this object model isn't discussed in detail, it is a major component of Integration Services.

Integration Services Data Flow Engine and Data Flow Components

Within an SSIS package's control flow, a Data Flow Task creates instances of the data flow engine. This engine is responsible for providing the in-memory data movement from sources to destinations. In addition, this engine performs the requested transformations to enrich the data for the purposes you specify. Three primary components make up the data flow engine: sources, transformations, and destinations. The *sources* provide connectivity to, and extract data from, a wide range of sources such as database tables or views, files, spreadsheets, and even XML files. The *destinations* permit the insert, update, and deletion of information on a similar wide range of destinations. Lastly, the *transformations* enable you to modify the source data before loading it into a destination using capabilities such as lookups, merging, pivoting, splitting, converting, and deriving information.

Project Management and Change Control

One of the areas needing an entirely different mindset from the previous version of SQL Server involves how DBAs interact with the development team. In BI, the line between development and DBA has blurred and the two must now work closer together. The shared view of development by administrators and developers alike is enacted through the SQL Server Data Tools (SSDT), previously named Business Intelligence Development Studio (BIDS). SSDT is a Visual Studio shell that optionally installs when you install SQL Server. For Integration Services, SSIS solutions and projects are created in the SSDT environment. Generally, the configuration of the SSDT solutions and projects is handled by the developers; however, administrators are called upon to help configure various aspects of these solutions. The administration and management of Integration Services is primarily performed within SQL Server Management Studio. Often, moving the Integration Services solutions from environment to environment means changing dynamic information within the package and setting up any information referenced by the packages. Examples of these elements include Package Configuration settings, referenced XML or configuration files, and solution data sources, which are all covered later in this chapter.

When a developer clicks Save or executes the package in SSDT, the old version of the package is immediately overwritten in the file system. To remedy this, you should integrate the SSIS development environment into a source control system — such as Visual SourceSafe, for example. After such integration, when a package is saved you can always roll back to an earlier release of the package. You can use any type of source control system that integrates with Visual Studio.

ADMINISTRATION OF THE INTEGRATION SERVICES SERVICE

Now that you have a better understanding of the parts of Integration Services, you can take a look at the various administrative aspects of Integration Services, including the details needed to become comfortable working with the components. You start with a review of the Integration Services service and then look at various configuration elements of the service. Next, you look at how you can adjust properties of the SSIS service using either the Windows Services Snap-In or the SQL Server Configuration Manager. Understanding how you can modify Windows Firewall follows, and then you look at the management and configuration of event logs and performance monitoring.

An Overview of the Integration Services Service

The Integration Services service is a Windows service used to manage SSIS packages deployed in the package deployment model. Accessed through SQL Server Management Studio, it provides the following management capabilities:

➤ Starting and stopping local and remote packages

➤ Monitoring local and remote packages

➤ Importing and exporting packages from different sources

➤ Managing the package store

➤ Customizing storage folders

➤ Stopping running packages when service stops

➤ Viewing the Windows Event Log

➤ Connecting to multiple SSIS server instances

To be clear, you don't need this service for designing or executing packages. The primary purpose of this service is to manage packages within Management Studio. One side benefit to having the service running is that the SSIS Designer in SSDT can use the service to cache the objects used in the designer, thus enhancing the designer's performance.

Configuration

The configuration of the Integration Services service includes viewing and possibly modifying the XML file responsible for the runtime configuration of the service, setting service properties using either the Windows Services Snap-In or SQL Server Configuration Manager, and, potentially, configuring Windows Firewall to permit access by Integration Services.

XML Configuration File

The `MsDtsSrvr.ini.xml` file responsible for the configuration of the Integration Services service is located in `<SQL Server Drive>\Program Files\Microsoft SQL Server\110\DTS\Binn` by default. You can also move this file to a new location by changing the `HKEY_LOCAL_MACHINE\SOFTWARE\Microsoft\ Microsoft SQL Server\100\SSIS\ServiceConfigFile` Registry key. This file includes settings for specifying whether running packages stop when the service stops, a listing of root folders to display in the Object Explorer of Management Studio, and settings for specifying which folders in the file system are managed by the service.

You can change the configuration filename and location. You can obtain this information by Management Studio from the Windows registry key `HKEY_LOCAL_MACHINE\SOFTWARE\Microsoft\MSDTS\ServiceConfigFile`. As with most Registry key changes, you should back up the Registry before making any changes, and you need to restart the service after making changes for them to take effect.

One example of a configuration change that must be made is when you connect to a named instance of SQL Server. The following example shows the modification for handling a named instance

(MyServerName\MyInstanceName). This is because the default configuration for the SSIS service always points to "." and must be configured for a clustered or named instance.

```xml
<?xml version="1.0" encoding="utf-8"?>
<DtsServiceConfiguration xmlns:xsd="http://www.w3.org/2001/XMLSchema"
xmlns:xsi="http://www.w3.org/2001/XMLSchema-instance">
  <StopExecutingPackagesOnShutdown>true</StopExecutingPackagesOnShutdown>
  <TopLevelFolders>
    <Folder xsi:type="SqlServerFolder">
      <Name>MSDB</Name>
      <ServerName>MyServerName\MyInstanceName</ServerName>
    </Folder>
    <Folder xsi:type="File systemFolder">
      <Name>File System</Name>
      <StorePath>..\Packages</StorePath>
    </Folder>
  </TopLevelFolders>
</DtsServiceConfiguration>
```

There isn't a lot to configure in this file but it has some interesting uses. The first configuration line tells the packages how to react if the service stops. By default, packages that the service runs stop upon the service stopping or being failed over. You could also configure the packages to continue to run until they complete after the service stops by changing the StopExecutingPackagesOnShutDown property to False:

```xml
<StopExecutingPackagesOnShutdown>false</StopExecutingPackagesOnShutdown>
```

Other common configuration file change scenarios include adding additional paths from which to display packages other than the default SSIS package store path of C:\Program Files\SQL Server\110\Packages and creating a centralized folder structure for multiple servers by storing the service configuration file in a central file share.

Creating a Central SSIS Server

Many enterprise companies have so many packages that they decide to separate the service from SQL Server and place it on its own server. When you do this, you must still license the server just as if it were running SQL Server. The advantages of this are that your SSIS packages do not suffocate the SQL Server's memory during a large load, and you have a central spot to manage. The disadvantages are that now you must license the server separately, and you add another layer of complexity when you debug packages. When you create a dedicated server, you create a fantastic way to easily scale packages by adding more memory to your central server, but you also create an added performance hit, as all remote data must be copied over the network before entering the data flow buffer.

To create a centralized SSIS hub, you need to modify only the MsDtsSrvr.ini.xml file and restart the service. The service can read a UNC path such as \\ServerName\Share and can point to multiple remote servers. Mapped drives are not recommended because the account that starts the SSIS service would need to be aware of the drive and could create an unnecessary dependency on that account. In the following example, the service enumerates packages from three servers, one of which is local and another that is a named instance. After restarting the service, you see a total of six folders to expand in Management Studio. The Management Studio aspect of SSIS is covered in detail later in this chapter.

```xml
<?xml version="1.0" encoding="utf-8" ?>
<DtsServiceConfiguration xmlns:xsd="http://www.w3.org/2001/XMLSchema"
xmlns:xsi="http://www.w3.org/2001/XMLSchema-instance">
  <StopExecutingPackagesOnShutdown>true</StopExecutingPackagesOnShutdown>
 <TopLevelFolders>
<Folder xsi:type="SqlServerFolder">
  <Name>Server A MSDB</Name>
  <ServerName>localhost</ServerName>
  </Folder>
  <Name>Server B MSDB</Name>
  <ServerName>SQLServerB</ServerName>
  </Folder>
<Folder xsi:type="File systemFolder">
  <Name>Server A File System</Name>
  <StorePath>P:\Packages</StorePath>
  </Folder>
<Folder xsi:type="File systemFolder">
  <Name>Server B File System</Name>
  <StorePath>\\SQLServerB\Packages</StorePath>
  </Folder>
  </TopLevelFolders>
  </DtsServiceConfiguration>
```

Your next issue is how to schedule packages when using a centralized SSIS hub. You can schedule your packages through SQL Server Agent or through a scheduling system such as Task Scheduler from Windows. You already pay for a license of SQL Server, so it's better to install SQL Server on your server and use Agent because it gives you much more flexibility. You can also store configuration tables and logging tables on this SQL Server to centralize its processing as well. Both scheduling mechanisms are covered later in this chapter.

Each time you make a change to the configuration file, you need to stop and start the SSIS service, as described in the following sections. Now that you know how to configure the MsDtsSrvr.ini .xml file responsible for the configuration of the Integration Services service, you need to know how to set the service's properties.

Setting Service Properties Using the Windows Services Snap-In

As with any other Windows service, the Integration Services service has properties that dictate how it is to be started. Specifically, you can manage the following from the Windows Services Snap-In:

➤ Configure the startup type as Manual, Automatic, or Disabled.

➤ Request that the service is started, stopped, or restarted.

➤ Establish how the computer reacts to service failures.

➤ View or modify a listing of dependent services (none are set up by default).

To view and modify SSIS services properties using the Windows Services Snap-in, follow these steps:

1. Open the Services Snap-In from Control Panel ⇨ Administrative Tools (or using the Category view from Performance and Maintenance ⇨ Administrative Tools).

2. Locate and right-click SQL Server Integration Services in the list of services.

3. Select Properties to view the currently applied settings.

4. On the General tab, you can view or change the Startup type (Automatic, Manual, or Disabled). When set to either Manual or Automatic, you can change the Service status to Start, Stop, or Resume.

5. On the Log On tab (see Figure 20-1), you can view or alter the account used to start and run the service. By default, this runs under the NT Service\MsDtsServer110 account but most people use a domain service account.

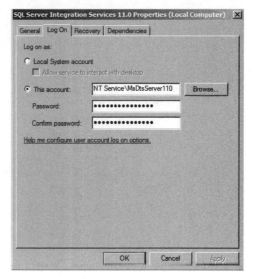

FIGURE 20-1

6. On the Recovery tab, you can configure how the server responds to failures of the service by setting the First, Second, and Subsequent failures options to either Take No Action (the default), Restart the Service, Run a Program, or Restart the Computer. You can also instruct the service to reset the failure count after a certain number of days.

7. You can modify the list of services on which the SSIS service depends (none by default) and view the list of services dependent on the SSIS service (none by default) on the Dependencies tab.

Setting Service Properties Using SQL Server Configuration Manager

As with using the Windows Services Snap-In, you can also configure a limited set of Integration Services service properties using the SQL Server Configuration Manager. Specifically, you can both configure the logon information used by the service and establish the startup model of the service.

Follow these steps to view and modify SSIS Services properties using the SQL Server Configuration Manager:

1. Open the SQL Server Configuration Manager from All Programs ⇨ Microsoft SQL Server 2012 ⇨ Configuration Tools.

2. On the list of services on the right side, right-click SQL Server Integration Services and select Properties.

3. On the Log On tab, you can view or alter the account used to start and run the service. By default, this runs under the NT Service\MsDtsServer110account. This resembles Figure 20-1.

4. On the Service tab, you can view or change the Startup type (Automatic, Manual, or Disabled).

Now that you are comfortable setting up the service properties for the Integration Services service using either the Windows Services Snap-In or the SQL Server Configuration Manager, you next learn how you can modify Windows Firewall to permit access to Integration Services.

Configuring Windows Firewall for Access

You'll probably find that your service requires modifications to be made to the Windows Firewall system to provide consistent access to Integration Services. The Windows Firewall system controls access to specific computer resources primarily by limiting access to preconfigured ports. You cannot modify the port number used by Integration Services because it works using only port 135.

In addition to using the user interface mentioned in this section, you can also script out this process from the command line by running the following (the line is wrapped here but everything should be on a single command when you type it):

```
netsh firewall add portopening protocol=TCP port=135 name="RPC (TCP/135)"
model=ENABLE scope=SUBNET

netsh firewall add allowedprogram program="%ProgramFiles%\Microsoft SQL
Server\100\DTS\Binn\MsDtsSrvr.exe" name="SSIS Service" scope=SUBNET
```

To configure the Windows Firewall to permit Integration Services access, follow these steps:

1. From the Control Panel, open the Windows Firewall.

2. Select the Exceptions tab and click Add Program.

3. In the Add Program dialog, click Browse and select `C:\Program Files\Microsoft SQL Server\100\DTS\Binn\MsDtsSrvr.exe`. You should also use the Change Scope option to detail the computers that have access to the program by specifying a custom list of IP addresses, subnets, or both. The resulting exception is shown in the Windows Firewall dialog.

4. Alternatively, you can open the port instead of allowing the executable to have full reign of your network. To do this, click Add Port.

5. In the Add Port dialog, type a meaningful description such as **RPC(TCP/135) Integration Services**, type **135** in the Port Number box, and select TCP as the protocol. You should also use the Change Scope option to indicate which computers have access to the port by specifying a custom list of IP addresses, subnets, or both.

That covers a substantial amount of the configuration required for the Integration Services service. The next focus is event logging.

Event Logs

Integration Services records events raised by packages during their execution in logs. The SSIS log providers can write log entries to text files, SQL Server Profiler, SQL Server, Windows Event Log, or XML files. To perform logging, SSIS packages and tasks must have logging enabled. Logging can occur at the package, container, and task level, and you can specify different logs for packages, containers, and tasks.

To record the events raised, a log provider must be selected and a log added for the package. You can create these logs only at the package level, and a task or container must use one of the logs created for the package. After you configure the logs within packages, you can view them either using Windows Event Viewer or within SQL Server Management Studio.

To view SSIS event logs using the Windows Event Viewer, follow these steps:

1. Open the Event Viewer from Control Panel ⇨ Administrative Tools (or use the Category view from Performance and Maintenance ⇨ Administrative Tools).

2. Within the Event Viewer dialog, click Application.

3. After the Application snap-in displays, locate an entry in the Source column valued at `SQLISService110` or `SQLISPackage110`. The `SQLISPackage110` source logs would be generated from the package logs, and the `SQLISService110` source logs would be simple messages from the SSIS service.

4. Right-click the entry, and select Event Properties to display descriptive information about the entry.

To view these events in SQL Server Management Studio, follow these steps:

1. Open Management Studio, and connect to the target Integration Services server.

2. In Object Explorer, right-click Integration Services (the topmost node) and click View Logs.

3. Select SQL Server Integration Services from the Select Logs section.

4. You can see the details for an event displayed in the lower pane by clicking an event in the upper pane.

Monitoring Activity

Part of the performance monitoring of the Integration Services service includes configuring the logging of performance counters. These counters enable you to view and understand the use of resources consumed during the execution of SSIS packages. Specifically, the logging encompasses event-resource usage, whereas packages perform the Data Flow Tasks.

Begin by focusing on some of the more insightful counters, including the following (at a server-level):

➤ **Rows Read:** Provides the number of rows read from all data sources during package execution

➤ **Buffers in Use:** Details the number of pipeline buffers (memory pools) in use throughout the package pipeline

➤ **Buffers Spooled:** Specifies the number of buffers used to handle the data flow processes

The Buffers Spooled counter is important because it is a good indicator of when your machine runs out of physical memory or runs out of virtual memory during data flow processing. The importance of using buffers rather than spooling to disk is the difference between a package with 20 minutes execution time versus 20 hours in some cases. Each time you see a buffer spooled, a 10MB buffer has been written to disk.

One example of how these performance counters can be used includes ensuring that your server running the SSIS packages has enough memory. One of the bottlenecks in any transformation process includes input/output operations, whereby data is staged to disk during the transformations. Integration Services was designed to optimize system resources when transforming data between a source and destination, including attempting to perform these transformations in memory, rather than having to stage data to disk and incur I/O performance penalties. You should expect to see the value of the Buffers Spooled counter remain at zero (0) when only memory is being used during the transformation processes being performed by the SSIS packages. When you observe that the Buffers Spooled counter is normally valued higher than zero (0), it's a good indication that more memory is needed on the server processing the SSIS packages.

SQL Server Profiler enables you to analyze the data operations and query plans generated for various data flow pipeline activities. You can use this information to refine indexes or apply other optimization techniques to the data sources your SSIS solution uses.

ADMINISTRATION OF INTEGRATION SERVICES PACKAGES IN PACKAGE DEPLOYMENT MODEL

Now that you've learned about the various aspects of Integration Services service administration, this section provides an overview of SSIS package elements and administration, and then you look at various ways to create packages. Next, you look at the management of the developed SSIS packages. When you understand how to create and manage packages, you can move on to the deployment, execution, and scheduling of SSIS packages and solutions.

Using Management Studio for Package Management

As discussed earlier in the "Integration Services Service" section, packages are managed primarily via Management Studio and its connection to the Integration Services service. Upon connecting to the service, you see two main folders: Running Packages and Stored Packages. The packages displayed are stored in either the `msdb` database `sysssispackages` table or the file system folders specified in the Integration Services service configuration file.

The main uses of Management Studio include monitoring running packages and managing the packages stored within the Integration Services environment.

You can see information regarding currently executing packages within the Running Packages folder. Information about these packages displays on the Summary page, whereas you can obtain information about a particular executing package by clicking the package under the Running Packages folder and viewing the Summary page. You can stop the execution of a package listed within this folder by right-clicking the package and selecting Stop.

You can make changes to the storage of packages by adding custom folders and by copying packages from one type of storage to another using the Import and Export utilities. You can configure the logical folders displayed within the MSDB folder in Management Studio by right-clicking on a given folder or by altering the syssisspackagefolders table within the msdb database. The root folders in this table are those in which the parentfolderid column contains null values. You can add values to this table to add logical folders, bearing in mind that the folderid and parentfolderid columns are the key values used to specify the folder hierarchy. In addition, you can configure the default folders in the file system that Management Studio displays. This is discussed in the "XML Configuration File" section earlier in this chapter. Importing and exporting packages are discussed in the "Deployment" section of this chapter.

The main management tasks you can perform on packages within Management Studio include the following:

➤ Creating new Object Explorer folders to display packages saved in either the file system or SQL Server (msdb database syssspackages table)

➤ Importing and exporting packages

➤ Running packages

➤ Deleting packages

➤ Renaming packages

Using the DTUtil Package Management Utility

Other than using Management Studio to manage packages, you also have the assistance of a command prompt utility named DTUtil. The primary reason you need to understand DTUtil is that this utility permits you to manage packages using schedulers or batch files. As with using Management Studio, DTUtil enables you to copy, delete, move, sign, and even verify whether the server contains specified packages.

Using this utility, you include either the /SQL, /FILE, or /DTS options to specify where the packages that you want to manage are located. You use options (parameters) to specify particular behavior you want to use when running the utility. The options start with either a slash (/) or a minus sign (-) and can be added to the command line in any sequence.

You receive exit codes that let you know when something is wrong with your syntax or arguments, or you simply have an invalid combination of options. When everything is correct, DTUtil returns exit code 0 and displays the message The Operation Completed Successfully. The following other exit codes may be returned:

➤ 1 — Failed

➤ 4 — Cannot locate package

➤ 5 — Cannot load package

➤ 6 — Cannot resolve the command

You must observe the following syntactical rules when you create the commands:

➤ Values for options must be strings and must be enclosed in quotation marks or contain no whitespace.

➤ Escaping single quotation marks in strings is done by enclosing the double-quoted string inside single quotation marks.

➤ Other than passwords, there is no case-sensitivity.

One way you can use DTUtil is to regenerate package IDs for packages copied from other packages. Recall that when a copy of an existing package is made, the name and ID of the new package matches that of the copied package. You can use DTUtil along with the /I [D Regenerate] switch to regenerate the package IDs, and in some cases to correct corruption issues within your package.

> To *update multiple packages with just a single execution of* DTUtil, *you can create a batch file that can iterate through a given folder looking for all* .dtsx *(package) files and have* DTUtil *regenerate the package IDs.) If you want to execute this command from within a batch file, use the following syntax from the directory containing the SSIS project:*
>
> ```
> for %%f in (<FilePath>\*.dtsx) do dtutil.exe /i /File %%f
> ```

By understanding the DTUtil utility, you have a powerful weapon to add to your package management arsenal.

Importing and Exporting Packages

Another common activity you need to understand as an administrator involves the ways in which you can move packages among the various storage locations and formats. The import and export functionality enables you to add or copy packages from one storage location and format to another storage location and format. Thus, not only can you add or copy the packages, but also change storage formats (for example, from file system folders to the SQL Server msdb database).

To import a package using Integration Services from within Management Studio, follow these steps:

1. Open Management Studio, and connect to an Integration Services server.

2. In Object Explorer, expand the Stored Packages folder and any subfolders to locate the folder into which you want to import a package.

3. Right-click the target folder, and select Import Package.

4. On the Import Package dialog, select the package location from SQL Server, File System, or SSIS Package Store.

5. On the Import Package dialog, when the package location is SQL Server, specify the server, authentication type, username, and password. When the package location is SSIS Package Store, specify the server.

6. Also on the Import Package dialog, click the Browse button next to Package path, and select the package to import. From this screen, you can also change the package name to how it should appear in the new location and specify the protection level of the package.

Using similar steps, you can export packages. The one notable difference is that you right-click the package to be exported and select Export, rather than right-click the target folder and select Import. You can also perform these import and export operations using the DTUtil command-line utility.

Deployment

When Integration Services packages and solutions have been developed either on local computers or on development servers, they need to be deployed to test on production servers. Usually, you start the deployment process after you ensure that the packages run successfully within SSDT.

You deploy your packages or solutions via one of the following methods:

➤ Creating a package deployment utility and using the Package Installer Wizard

➤ Using import or export package utilities in Management Studio

➤ Saving or moving copies of packages in the file system

➤ Executing the DTUtil Package Management Utility

Often, the modifications made to your Integration Services solution dictate which deployment method and tools to use. For example, if you modify only a single package out of a 30-package solution, using the import package utility within Management Studio or saving or moving copies of packages in the file system might be simpler than deploying the entire solution using the Package deployment utility and Package Installer Wizard.

You can further categorize these four options for deployment into automated and manual. Using a Package deployment utility with the Package Installer Wizard would be best categorized as an automated deployment method, whereas the other options represent manual deployment methods. The following sections take a detailed look at each of these deployment methods.

Automated Package Deployment

A common way to deploy packages involves using the Package deployment utility. This utility builds your SSIS packages, package configurations, and any supporting files into a special deployment folder located within the bin directory for the Integration Services project. In addition, this utility creates a special executable file named ProjectName.SSISDeploymentManifest and places it within this deployment folder. After creating the deployment utility, you then execute the manifest file to install the packages.

This deployment method relies upon two separate steps. First, you create a deployment utility that contains all the files needed for deployment. Second, you use the Package Installer Wizard to perform the deployment of these files to a target deployment server.

Using the Package Deployment Utility

The following steps walk you through using the Package deployment utility to deploy your Integration Services solution:

1. Open SQL Server Data Tools and an Integration Services solution.

2. Right-click your solution or project (the topmost node) in Solution Explorer, and select Properties.

3. On the [*Solution/Project Name*] Property Pages dialog, select the Deployment Utility section.

4. Within the Deployment Utility section of the Property Pages dialog, set the value of the `CreateDeploymentUtility` to True (see Figure 20-2).

5. Optionally, you can configure the deployment to enable configuration changes by setting the `AllowConfigurationChanges` value to True. This option enables updating the configuration of key elements of your packages that would be machine or environment dependent, such as server names or database initial catalogs that are both properties of database connection managers.

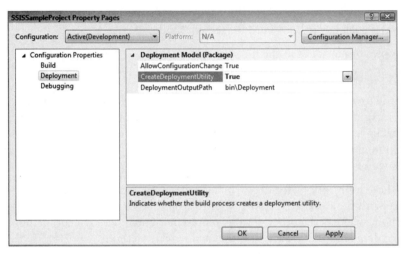

FIGURE 20-2

6. Build your project as normal. The build process creates the `ProjectName` `.SSISDeploymentManifest` file and copies the packages to the `bin/Deployment` folder or whatever folder was specified for the `DeploymentOutputPath` on the project's Property Page in the Deployment Utility section.

Because this utility copies all solution files as part of the process, you can deploy additional files, such as a `Readme` file, with the project by simply placing these files in the Miscellaneous folder of the Integration Services project.

Using the Package Installer Wizard

After you create an `SSISDeploymentManifest` file using the Package deployment utility, you can install the packages by using the Package Installer Wizard, which can be started by clicking the `SSISDeploymentMainfest` file. This wizard runs the `DTSInstall.exe` program and copies the packages and any configuration to a designated location.

Using the Package Installer Wizard provides you with some useful functionality that you either can't find or is hard to achieve using the manual deployment methods. For example, you may choose either a file-based or SQL-based deployment. Your file-based dependencies will always be installed to the file system. Another important, as well as useful, capability of this deployment process includes the ability to modify configurations for use on the target deployment server. This enables you to update the values of the configuration properties, such as server name, as part of the wizard.

Following are the steps you need to take to ensure a successful deployment of your packages using the Package Installer Wizard:

1. Use Windows Explorer to browse to the file path location in which the SSISDeploymentManifest file was created (usually the solution or project location /bin/Deployment).

2. After creating the files within the Deployment folder, copy the Deployment folder and all its files to a target deployment server.

3. On the target deployment server, open the Deployment folder, and double-click the SSISDeploymentManifest file to launch the Package Installer Wizard (DTSInstall.exe).

4. On the Deploy SSIS Packages page, select whether you want to deploy your packages to the file system or to SQL Server (see Figure 20-3). Optionally, you can also have the packages validated after they have been installed.

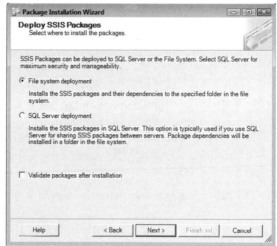

FIGURE 20-3

5. On the Select Installation Folder page, either provide a folder path for a file system deployment or provide a server name and the appropriate server credentials for a SQL Server deployment.

6. For a SQL Server deployment, on the Select Installation Folder page, provide a folder path for the package dependencies that require storing within the file system. If you accept the default property here, you could be moving the location of your package configuration files.

7. Optionally, if the package includes configurations and you set the AllowConfigurationChanges value to true when the deployment manifest was created, the Configure Packages page displays so that you can update the values for the configurations.

8. Optionally, if you requested validation of the packages, the Packages Validation page displays so that you can review the validation results.

Import or Export Package Deployment

Earlier in the chapter, you looked at using the import and export functionality, which enables you to add or copy packages from one storage location and format to another storage location and format. One obvious use of this functionality is to deploy packages after development and testing have been completed.

An interesting benefit this approach may yield involves the capability of the import or export to change storage formats (for example, from file system folders to the SQL server msdb database). This alteration of storage formats may be useful for disaster recovery, as a further safeguard for your Integration Services solutions, by saving them in various storage formats and locations.

File Save/Move Package Deployment

Probably the simplest way to get packages deployed involves copying them out of the Visual Studio project bin directory and copying it to the target server. This method does not have any of the more useful capabilities, but it can work quite well for smaller-scale Integration Services solutions. One distinct capability missing from this deployment method is the ability to deploy to SQL Server.

DTUtil Package Deployment

As with using Management Studio, DTUtil enables you to copy or move packages. As previously stressed in this chapter, the benefit of using DTUtil is that the commands created can be scheduled or run later. Therefore, using these capabilities, you could schedule the deployment of your packages to another server simply by using DTUtil copy or move commands to move the modified packages to a target server.

The following example demonstrates how you can use a DTUtil copy command for deployment:

```
dtutil /DTS srcPackage.dtsx /COPY SQL;destPackage
```

ADMINISTRATION OF INTEGRATION SERVICES PACKAGES IN PROJECT DEPLOYMENT MODEL

Much of this chapter to this point has focused on the package deployment model, which was the only way to operate in SQL Server 2005 and 2008. In SQL Server 2012, you can now administer and deploy packages as a project, which is a group of packages and how most developers operate. This section shows how to configure the SSIS catalog and then deploy packages to it.

Configuring the SSIS Catalog

In the package deployment model, you can deploy to the MSDB database or the file system of the server. With the project deployment model, you can deploy only to the SSIS catalog, which exists inside the database instance. This means that you also no longer need the Integration Services Windows service. The packages execute in the context of the database instance, and if the database engine were to fail, SSIS also fails or fails over in a cluster.

Before you can deploy your project, you need an SSIS catalog to deploy to. To do this, open Management Studio and follow these steps:

1. Connect to the database engine in Management Studio.

2. Right-click on Integration Services Catalogs, and select Create Catalog. This opens the Create Catalog dialog box (shown in Figure 20-4). In the dialog box, you must type a password that generates a key for encryption. Common Language Runtime (CLR) is also turned on here to execute packages via T-SQL. Click OK to create the catalog.

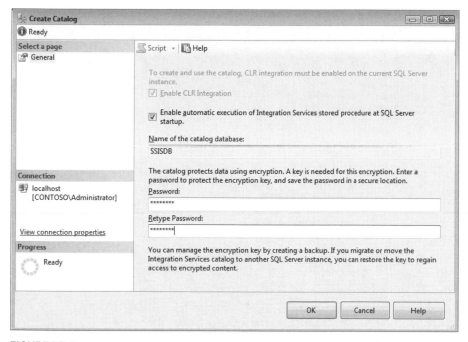

FIGURE 20-4

Creating the catalog also creates a database called SSISDB. There is only one catalog per database instance, and you can use this database to query to find some metadata about your packages. You can also read some of the tables in this database to gather operational data about which packages have failed recently from some of the logs.

With the catalog now created, it is time to configure it. To do so, right-click on the previously created catalog and select Properties. This opens the catalog Properties dialog box (shown in Figure 20-5). In this dialog box, you can choose the level of logging and the amount of days you're retaining the logs. You can set the level of logging to be basic (default), verbose, performance or none. If you choose verbose or performance, you will see SSIS performance issues with SSIS packages. Those two options are only for temporary debugging of the package.

You can also select how many versions of the project will be kept as you deploy. This enables you to rollback to a previous release of the project. By default, 10 versions of packages are kept.

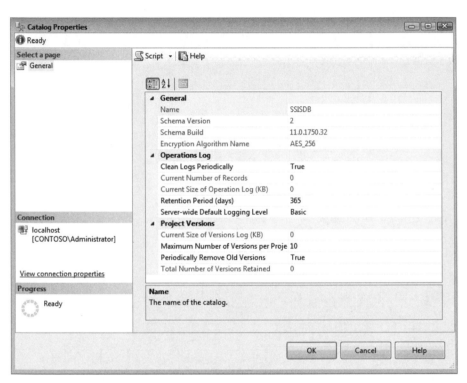

FIGURE 20-5

Deploying Packages

The simplest way to deploy packages is with the project deployment model with the Integration Services Deployment Wizard. You can launch it from SSDT by right-clicking the project and selecting Deploy or by selecting the wizard in the SQL Server 2012 ➪ Integration Services program group. The wizard asks you a few questions to complete the deployment. The first screen asks which server you want to deploy to and which path (shown in Figure 20-6).

If the folder does not exist on the server you want to deploy, click Browse and you can create it. To deploy, you must have a folder. The folder acts as a container for one or more projects and helps control the configuration of your environment later.

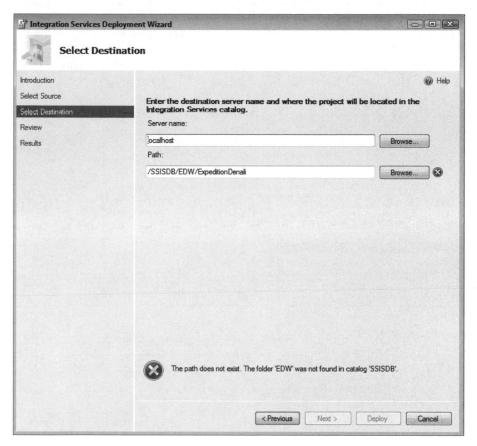

FIGURE 20-6

After you select a valid path, select Next to deploy the package. You can also now find an `.ispac` file in your project's Deployment folder in Windows Explorer. If you send this one file to the administrator, he can double-click it to reopen this same wizard. The file contains all package and configuration information necessary for the entire project.

ROLLING PROJECT CHANGES

Imagine the developer accidentally sends the DBA the wrong project file to deploy, and at 3 A.M. the DBA can't seem to get the environment rolled back. In SQL Server 2012, you can easily roll the project back by right-clicking the project in Management Studio and selecting Versions. In the Project Versions dialog box (shown in Figure 20-7), simply select the older version and click Restore to Selected Version to roll back to entire project to an earlier release. Do not use this as your core source control system. This is only a mechanism to roll back changes on your server and does not fix developer errors during development prior to the deployment.

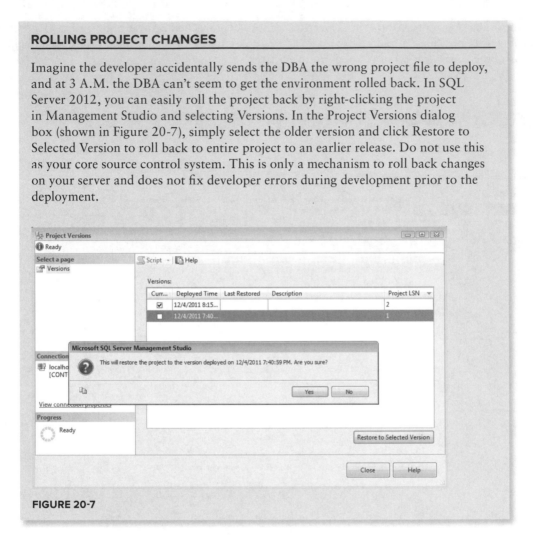

FIGURE 20-7

Configuring Packages

The next step after deployment is to configure the package to run in your environment. For example, the developer may have left the packages using the development server's name and passwords. In the package deployment model, you would use configuration files, but SQL Server 2012 introduced parameters in the project deployment model. The developer's responsibility is to create parameters and configure the packages to use those parameters. When the developer creates those, the DBA can then change those parameters' values to reconfigure the package.

Environments

Environments are ways to do a large reconfiguration of packages to point to new variables for different clients on the same server or perhaps reconfigure the packages to use development variables versus production variables. Environments contain a collection of variables that you can create that hold the configuration for the project or package. To do so, perform the following steps:

1. Open Management Studio, and expand the Integration Services Catalogs node.

2. Under the node expand your folder, right-click the Environments node, and select Create Environment.

3. For this example, create one environment called Client A and another called Client B. After each environment is created, right-click the environment and select Properties, which opens the Environment Properties dialog box (Figure 20-8).

4. Go to the Variables tab and create a new string variable called ServerName with the value of ServerA. Repeat this step for the Client B environment but use ServerB for its value. You can also click Sensitive if you want to encrypt the value.

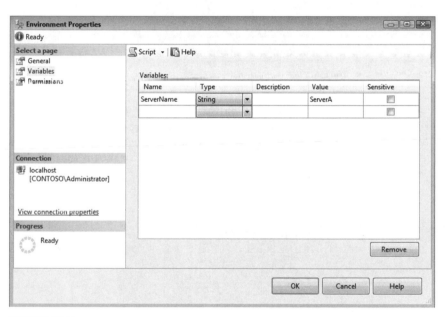

FIGURE 20-8

Using Environments

To use the environments, you must first allow the project to see the environments and then follow these steps:

1. Right-click the project in the folder and select Configure.

2. Then, go to the References tab, and add a reference to any environment you want to be used by this project by clicking the Add button (shown in Figure 20-9).

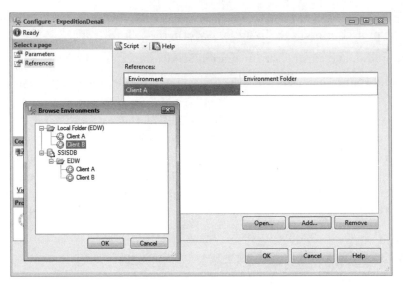

FIGURE 20-9

3. With the references now created, you can reconfigure the package to use them. In the Configure Project screen go to the Parameters tab (shown in Figure 20-10). Here, you see a list of parameters and connection managers and can configure them outside the package easily. In Figure 20-10 the ServerName parameter is underlined. This means that it actually references the environment variable you created in the last section.

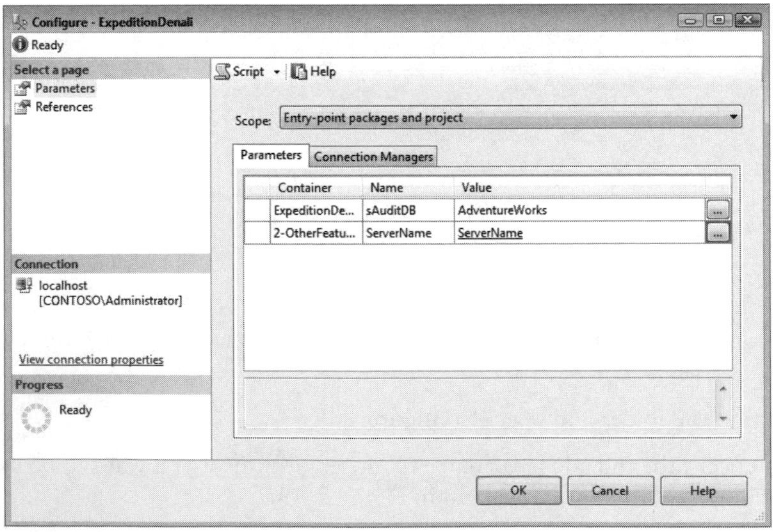

FIGURE 20-10

4. To change the value of any parameter, select the ellipsis button next to the parameter. This opens the Set Parameter Value dialog box (shown in Figure 20-11). In this screen you can change the parameter's value to any value you want by selecting the Edit Value radio box or change it to an environment's value by selecting the environment's variable in the drop-down box.

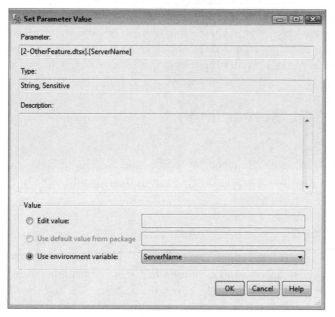

FIGURE 20-11

EXECUTION AND SCHEDULING

Thus far, you have looked at ways to create, manage, and deploy Integration Services solutions. This section focuses on the ways in which you can execute and schedule execution of these solutions. As you have seen with other package and solution administrative tasks, the execution of packages can be performed using different tools. Specifically, you can execute packages from the following:

➤ SQL Server Data Tools

➤ SQL Server Import and Export Wizard (when run from Management Studio)

➤ DTExec package execution command-line utility

➤ DTExecUI package execution utility

➤ Execute Package Tool

➤ SQL Server Agent jobs

➤ T-SQL (for project deployment model packages)

Which tool you should use often depends on factors such as in which stage of the package life cycle you are presently working. For example, the SSIS Designer within SSDT is a logical choice for package execution during development due to the features designed to assist in development (such as visually displaying package execution progress by changing the background color of tasks).

Running Packages in SQL Server Data Tools

Probably the first executions of packages will occur within SSDT because this is the development environment used to create your Integration Services solutions. Within SSDT, you simply either right-click the package and then select Execute Package or press the F5 function key (or the Start button on the menu bar). The best way to execute packages from SSDT is by right-clicking the package and selecting Execute Package. Executing this way can prevent other packages from executing in case of misconfiguration.

Running Packages with the SQL Server Import and Export Wizard

When you use the Import and Export Wizard from Management Studio, you have an option to execute the package immediately. This provides an opportunity to both relocate and execute packages in one administrative step.

Running Packages with DTExec

The primary use of DTExec is to enable you to run packages either from the command line, from a script, or using a scheduling utility. All configuration and execution features are available using this command. You can also load and run packages from SQL Server, the SSIS service, and the file system.

The following additional syntactical rules must be followed when you create these commands:

➤ All command options start with a slash (/) or a minus sign (–).

➤ Arguments are enclosed in quotation marks when they contain any whitespace.

➤ Values that contain single quotation marks are escaped by using double quotation marks within quoted strings.

The general syntax for the DTExec commands is as follows:

```
Dtexec /option value
```

Following is an example that shows running a sample package called CaptureDataLineage.dtsx. The /FILE is pointing to a package stored on the file system in package deployment model. The /CONNECTION switch is changing a connection manager at runtime.

```
Dtexec /FILE "C:\Program Files\Microsoft SQL Server\110\Samples\Integration
Services\Package Samples\CaptureDataLineage
Sample\CaptureDataLineage\CaptureDataLineage.dtsx " /CONNECTION
" (local).AdventureWorks "; "\ "Data Source=(local);Initial
```

```
Catalog=AdventureWorks;Provider=SQLNCLI.1;Integrated Security=SSPI;Auto
Translate=False;\ " "  /REPORTING
E
```

Whenever you execute a package using DTExec, one of the following exit codes may be returned:

- ➤ 0 — Successful execution
- ➤ 1 — Failed
- ➤ 3 — Canceled by User
- ➤ 4 — Unable to Find Package
- ➤ 5 — Unable to Load Package
- ➤ 6 — Syntax Not Correct

There are numerous options you can use to alter how the package execution is run. Some examples include /Decrypt, which sets the package password used to secure information within the package, and /Set, which you use to assign values to SSIS variables at runtime. The options are processed in the order in which they are specified. When using the /Set and /ConfigFile commands, the values are also processed in the order in which they are specified. Neither options nor arguments (except passwords) are case-sensitive.

Running Packages with DTExecUI (Package Deployment Model)

You can configure the various options you need to run packages using the graphical equivalent to the DTExec utility: the DTExecUI utility. With the wizard that this utility uses to gather details regarding the package execution, you can better understand many of the options and see the syntax required to run the package execution. To use this wizard, complete the following steps:

1. Launch the DTExecUI utility by double-clicking a file with a .dtsx extension or from inside Management Studio by right-clicking a package and selecting Run.

2. Then select the options that you need to run the package along the left side of the utility pages and configure the options in the main part of the page. When you finish, you can view the last page, which shows you the command line needed to execute the package with the options you selected.

3. After you complete the various pages and review the command line that will be submitted, click the Execute button. This submits the command line to the Integration Services engine by using the DTExecUI utility. Be careful when you use this utility in a 64-bit environment because this utility runs in Windows on Win32, not on Win64. Thus, for 64-bit environments, you should use the 64-bit version of the DTExec utility at the command prompt or use SQL Server Agent.

The main reason you should become more familiar with both the DTExec and DTExecUI utilities is that they are useful for testing your packages and ultimately validating the proper command line that you may schedule using the SQL Server Agent.

Running Packages with the Execute Package Tool (Project Deployment Model)

In the project deployment model, package execution and configuration are even easier. To execute packages in this model, complete the following steps:

1. Right-click the package in Management Studio, and select Execute. This opens the Execute Package dialog box (shown in Figure 20-12).

2. If your package requires an environment variable, check the box, and select your environment that you want to execute under. Doing this reconfigures the package to run under the collection of environment variables you created earlier.

3. If you need to change the connection managers, use the Connection Manager tab. This changes only the connection for one execution. In the Advanced tab, you can configure the package to run in 32-bit mode and the logging levels.

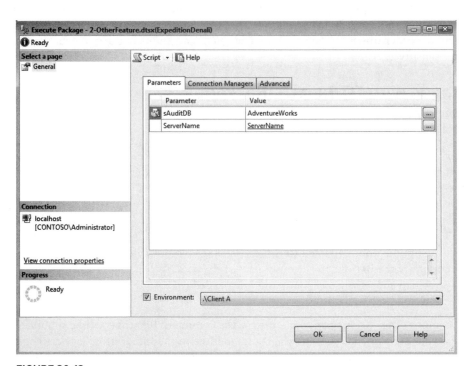

FIGURE 20-12

4. Click OK and the package executes asynchronously, meaning that the package execution runs in T-SQL in the background.

5. To view the status of the package execution, open the operational reports by right-clicking the SSIS catalog and selecting Reports ⇨ Standard Reports ⇨ Integration Services

Dashboard. When opened, you can drill into the package execution by viewing the Overview report. This report (shown in Figure 20-13) enables you to see what parameters were passed to the package and performance-related information.

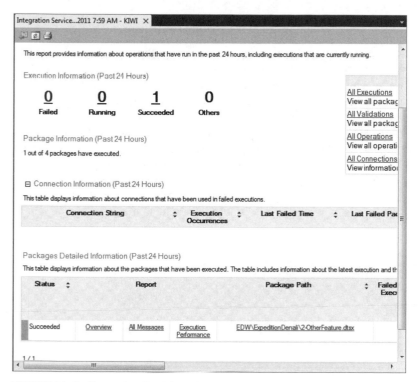

FIGURE 20-13: Execution Dashboard

Scheduling Execution with SQL Server Agent

You need the ability to automate the execution of your Integration Services packages. Although many popular scheduling tools are available to accomplish this automation, here you look at how SQL Server Agent can assist in automating execution.

You start by creating a job and then including at least one step of the SQL Server Integration Services Packages type. You can also configure other job options. One option you may configure includes job notifications to send e-mail messages when the job completes, succeeds, or fails. Another job option you may configure includes job alerts to send notifications for SQL Server event alerts, performance condition alerts, or WMI event alerts. Much of this configuration can be done through environments setup by the DBA.

To set up SQL Server Agent to execute a package, follow these steps:

1. Open Management Studio, and connect to a SQL Server.

2. In Object Explorer, expand the SQL Server Agent.

3. Within the SQL Server Agent section of Object Explorer, right-click the Jobs folder, and select New Job.

4. On the General page of the New Job dialog, provide a name, owner, category, and description for the job.

5. On the Steps page of the New Job dialog, click the New button along the bottom.

6. On the New Job Step dialog, provide a step name, and select SQL Server Integration Services Packages type. In addition, configure the SSIS-specific tabbed sections with the information required to run your package. This SSIS section is almost identical to the options you provided when using the DTExecUI utility or the Package Execution dialog box. You have a package source that you set to SSIS Catalog for the project deployment model (shown in Figure 20-14) or for the package deployment model you have SQL Server, file system, or SSIS package store. Next, you provide the package you want to schedule. When you select the Command Line tab, you can review the detailed command line that will be submitted by the SQL Server Agent to execute the package. You may want to compare this to the command-line values generated by the DTExecUI utility while you were testing package execution.

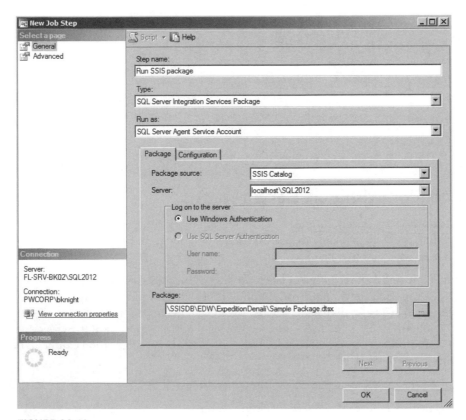

FIGURE 20-14

7. On the Advanced page of the New Job Step dialog, you can specify actions to perform when the step completes successfully, the number of retry attempts, the retry interval, and actions to perform should the step fail. After accepting the step configuration by pressing OK, the Step page of the New Job dialog shows your new step. After adding multiple steps, you can reorder the steps on this page.

8. After accepting the step configuration, from the New Job dialog you can optionally configure execution schedules, alerts, notifications, and target servers.

Running Packages with T-SQL

To execute a package in T-SQL, you can use the stored procedures in the catalog schema. First, you must create an execution using the `catalog.create_execution` stored procedure. This creates a unique identifier, (GUID), that you then call and execute using the `catalog.start_execution` stored procedure. You can also set parameters of the package using the `catalog.set_execution_parameter_value` stored procedure. A complete execution can be seen in the following code snippet:

```
Declare @execution_id bigint
EXEC [SSISDB].[catalog].[create_execution] @package_name=N'2-OtherFeature.dtsx', @
execution_id=@execution_id OUTPUT,
@folder_name=N'EDW', @project_name=N'ExpeditionDenali',
@use32bitruntime=False, @reference_id=Null

Select @execution_id
DECLARE @var0 sql_variant = N'localhost'

EXEC [SSISDB].[catalog].[set_execution_parameter_value] @execution_id,  @object_
type=30, @parameter_name=N'ServerName',
@parameter_value=@var0

DECLARE @var1 smallint = 1

EXEC [SSISDB].[catalog].[set_execution_parameter_value] @execution_id,  @object_
type=50, @parameter_name=N'LOGGING_LEVEL',
@parameter_value=@var1
EXEC [SSISDB].[catalog].[start_execution] @execution_id
GO
```

APPLYING SECURITY TO INTEGRATION SERVICES

You have now looked at most of the important package administrative tasks, including creating, managing, deploying, and executing Integration Services solutions. In addition, you have reviewed the major Integration Services service administrative tasks. This section describes the detailed security options available within Integration Services.

An Overview of Integration Services Security

Integration Services, like all of SQL Server, uses layers of security that rely on different mechanisms to ensure the integrity of both the design of packages and the administration and execution of packages. For the package deployment model, SSIS security is found on both the client and the server, implemented with features such as the following:

➤ Package-protection levels to encrypt or remove sensitive information from the package

➤ Package-protection levels with passwords to protect all or just sensitive information

➤ Restricting access to packages with roles

➤ Locking down file locations where packages may be stored

➤ Signing packages with certificates

Within packages, Integration Services generally defines sensitive data as information such as passwords and connection strings. You cannot define what should and should not be considered sensitive by SSIS unless you do so within a custom-developed task.

Integration Services defines sensitive information as the following:

➤ Connection string password (Sensitive) or Whole connection string (All)

➤ Task-generated XML nodes tagged as sensitive by SSIS

➤ Variables marked as sensitive by SSIS

For the project deployment model, much of this complexity goes away. As you deploy the package to the catalog database, the database handles the encryption and then you secure the package with roles.

Securing Packages in Package Deployment Model

The two primary ways in which you secure packages within Integration Services include setting package-protection levels and configuring appropriate database SSIS roles. The following sections look at these two security implementations.

Package Protection Levels

Many organizations have sensitive information in the SSIS package and want to control where that information resides within the organization. Your packages may contain passwords from your environment that if executed by the wrong individual may produce data files that could be sensitive.

These security concerns are addressed in Integration Services through the use of package protection levels. First, you can ensure that sensitive information that would provide details about where your information resides, such as connection strings, can be controlled by using EncryptSensitive package protection levels. Second, you can control who can open or execute a package by using EncryptAll package passwords.

The following package protection levels are at your disposal within Integration Services:

➤ Do not save sensitive.

➤ Encrypt (all/sensitive) with User Key.

➤ Encrypt (all/sensitive) with Password.

➤ Rely on server storage for encryption (SQL storage only).

The package protection levels are first assigned using SSDT. You can update these levels after deployment or during import or export of the package using Management Studio. In addition, you can alter the package protection levels when packages are copied from SSDT to any other location in which packages are stored. This is a nice compromise between development and administration because developers can configure these levels to suit their rapid development requirements, and administrators can follow up and revise these levels to meet production security standards.

Database Integration Services Roles for Package Deployment Model

If you deploy your packages to SQL Server (msdb database), you need to protect these packages within the database. Like traditional databases, this security is handled by using database roles. Three fixed database-level roles can be applied to the msdb database to control access to packages: db_dtsadmin, db_dtsltduser, and db_dtsoperator.

You apply these roles to packages within Management Studio, and these assignments are saved within the msdb database, in the sysssispackages table within the readerrole, writerrole, and ownersid columns. As the column names imply, you can view the roles that have read access to a particular package by looking at the value of the readerrole column, the roles that have write access to a particular package by looking at the value of the writterrole column, and the role that created the package by looking at the value of the ownersid column.

Follow these steps to assign a reader and writer role to packages for packages in the package deployment model:

1. Open Management Studio, and connect to an Integration Services server.

2. In Object Explorer, expand the Stored Packages folder, and expand the subfolder to assign roles.

3. Right-click the subfolder to assign roles.

4. In the Packages Roles dialog, select a reader role in the Reader Role list and a writer role in the Writer Role list.

For packages in the project deployment model, the configuration steps are almost identical. The only difference is you configure the project, not the packages. You can right-click the project and select Properties and then go to the Permissions tab. Because packages in this model are all stored in the database instance, you can also run them with SQL authenticated logins.

You may also create user-defined roles if the default execute and update actions for existing roles do not meet your security needs. To define these roles, you connect to a SQL Server instance and open the Roles node within the msdb database. In the Roles node, right-click the database roles, and select New Database Role. After a new role has been added to the msdb database, you must restart the SSIS service before you can use the role.

These database Integration Services roles help to configure your msdb database sysssispackages table with package security options for reading and writing to specific packages. By applying this level of security, you provide security at the server, database, and table levels. Again, the security discussed within this section applies only when you save your packages within SQL Server (msdb database).

Database Integration Services Roles for Project Deployment Model

If you deploy packages using the project deployment model to the SSIS catalog, you can secure the packages at a project-level. To do so, perform the following steps:

1. To configure permissions, right-click on the project in Management Studio and select Properties.

2. Go to the Permissions tab (shown in Figure 20-15) and click Browse to grant rights to a new role or SQL Server user that's in the catalog database called SSISDB. One important note is that by default any user in the DBO role of the SSISDB database will automatically have full rights to your project (see Figure 20-14) unless you revoke those rights.

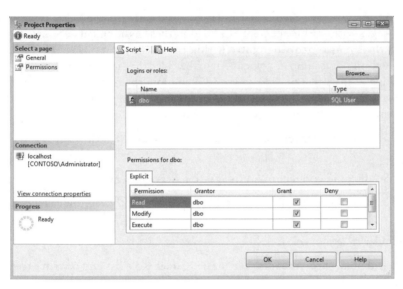

FIGURE 20-15

You can grant a user read rights if you just want them to be able to see the package and perhaps scan the metadata from the packages in the project. Execute rights enables the user or role to run a package in the project and Modify rights enables the user to overwrite the project or configure it.

SUMMARY

You are now familiar with many of the various administrative functions related to Integration Services. There are now two modes for deployment in SSIS: the package and project deployment models. The project deployment model only enables you to deploy the entire project and has most of the new 2012 features associated with it. The package deployment model is similar to what you've had in SQL Server 2005 and 2008. Packages in the project deployment model can be configured with environments easily so you can run the package with a set of variables for a give customer. In Chapter 21, "Analysis Services Administration and Performance Tuning," you learn about similar administrative functions related to Reporting Services.

21

Analysis Services Administration and Performance Tuning

WHAT'S IN THIS CHAPTER

➤ Overview of the Two Types of Analysis Services Instances

➤ Administer the SSAS Server Properties

➤ Performance Tune SSAS

➤ Secure an SSAS Instance

Now that you've learned how to administer SSAS, you will now continue your exploration of business intelligence administration and performance tuning by looking at how the DBA can perform Analysis Services administrative and performance tuning tasks. The focus is on the regular activities that a DBA may be called upon to perform, rather than the various details that developers might perform. First, take a quick tour of Analysis Services so that you have some common frame of reference for both the covered administrative and optimization aspects. Next, you look at the administration of the Analysis Server, including reviewing server settings and required services. You also learn how to script various administrative activities such as moving an Analysis Services database from development to production and backing up an Analysis Services database. With that covered, you can review the management of the Analysis Services databases, including deployment, backup, restore, and synchronization, and then look at how you can monitor the performance of Analysis Services. Next is a look at administration of storage, including storage modes and configuring partitions, as well as the design of aggregations. With storage concepts in mind, you turn next to the administration of processing tasks used to connect your designs with the data. Last, of course, you learn how to configure security for Analysis Services.

A discussion of how to use Analysis Services from a developer's perspective is beyond the scope of this book, so you do not examine that issue here. If you want to learn more, read Professional Microsoft SQL Server Analysis Services 2012 with MDX *(Harinath et al., 2012).*

TOUR OF ANALYSIS SERVICES

To better understand the various touch points that you must manage as a DBA, begin with a quick tour of Analysis Services. The primary value that Analysis Services brings to businesses is useful, important, and timely information that can be difficult or even impossible to obtain from other sources (enterprise resource planning systems, accounting systems, customer relationship management systems, supply chain management systems, and so on). If you hear the term *self-service reporting*, the person is likely using an Online Analytical Processing (OLAP) system, which is the type of server that SSAS provides its users.

Analysis Services has two modes: Multidimensional (MOLAP) and the Tabular model (new for 2012). When you install the instance of Analysis Services and when you start a project from the development side, you must decide the type of model to use. Each has its strengths and weaknesses, which are covered in this section.

The MOLAP model starts with a full star-schema data model (see the Data Warehousing Toolkit by Ralph Kimball for more information about this type of modeling) that has data in it and then builds a cube from this. The MOLAP model also gives you access to data mining and the highest possible scalability. Refreshing the data is much more flexible in this model, giving you options such as incremental loads.

The Tabular model has a lower learning curve and development cost by starting with data (with or without a data warehouse) and then building the cube from that data. It's extremely simple to build, enabling users to build the cube from within Excel or Visual Studio. The Tabular model's other strength is its front-end clients such as Power View, which supports only the Tabular model at the first release of SQL Server 2012.

Whichever model you go with, you produce a cube behind the scenes with the Analysis Services engine. The decision for most depends on data refresh. With the Tabular model, the entire cube or partition is wiped and loaded when you refresh the cube. With the MOLAP model, you can refresh individual partitions through a full or incremental refresh of the data.

In both models it is important to note that the OLAP engine must be optimized for lightning-quick data retrieval, but it also offers the following strategic benefits:

➤ Consolidated shared data access across multiple data sources that includes security at the most granular level and the ability to write back data

➤ Rapid, unencumbered storage and aggregation of vast amounts of data

➤ Multidimensional views of data that go beyond the traditional row and column two-dimensional views

➤ Advanced calculations that offer better support and performance than RDBMS engine capabilities

➤ Advanced data mining techniques to predict future activities based on the historical data in your database

So what is the DBA role within SSAS? If you take a look at a traditional DBA, Table 22-1 shows some of what a DBA does in SSAS:

TABLE 22-1: Mapping your DBA to SSAS

SQL SERVER DBA SKILL	SSAS SKILL COMPARISON
Creating logins	Creating roles
Creating indexes	Configuring aggregations
Partitioning tables	Partitioning measure groups
Backing up a database	Backing up an SSAS database

Now that you have an overview of the MOLAP and tabular models, the next section focuses on a deeper dive into each of the models.

MOLAP Components

In the 2012 release of Analysis Services, the Multidimensional OLAP model (MOLAP model) is the cube. The MOLAP model cube combines dimensions and fact tables into a single navigable view for users to do self-service analytics against. Following is a look at the composition of the MOLAP model:

➤ **Data source view:** At the heart of the MOLAP model is the logical data schema that represents the data from the source in a familiar and standard manner. This schema is known as the data source view (DSV), and it isolates the cube from changes made to the underlying sources of data.

➤ **Dimensional model:** This model provides the framework from which the cube is designed. Included are the measures (facts) that users need to gain measurable insight into their business and the dimensions that users employ to constrain or limit the measurements to useful combinations of factors.

➤ **Calculations (expressions):** Often, a cube needs to be enhanced with additional calculations to add the necessary business value that it is expected to achieve. The calculations within the MOLAP model are implemented by writing Multi Dimensional Expression (MDX) language code snippets. MDX is to the cube what SQL is to the database. In other words, MDX is what you use to get information from a cube to respond to various user requests.

➤ **Familiar and abstracted model:** Many additional features enhance the end-users' analysis experience by making their reporting and navigation through the cube more natural. Again, like calculations, the model is often enhanced to include features not found in the data sources from which the cube was sourced. Features such as language translations, aliasing of database names, perspectives to reduce information overload, or Key Performance Indicators (KPIs) to quickly summarize data into meaningful measurements are all part of the MOLAP model.

➤ **Administrative configuration:** With the cube designed and developed, the administrative aspects of the MOLAP model come to the forefront. Often, administrative tasks such as configuring the security to be applied to the cube or devising a partitioning scheme to enhance both query and processing performance are applied to the MOLAP model.

Tabular Model Components

A Tabular model has very similar components to the MOLAP model except simplified. Instead of starting with a model and working backwards, the user creates a Tabular model by first importing data. Then, the user creates the model with the data she imported. The data can be imported from a variety of sources like Excel, flat files, or nearly any OLE DB or ODBC compliant data source. Following are some of the elements you'll find in a Tabular model:

➤ **Connections:** A list of data connections required to make the cube

➤ **Tables:** Contains the actual data that the cube is built on

➤ **Roles:** The DBA mechanism to secure the cube or data in the cube

Analysis Services Architectural Components

Now that you understand the basics about the MOLAP and the Tabular models, it's time to turn to the components that make up Analysis Services. The Analysis Services server (`msmdsvr.exe` application) is implemented as a Microsoft Windows service and consists of a query processor (for MDX queries and DMX data-mining queries), an XMLA listener, and XML for Analysis. The following list describes these components in greater detail:

➤ **Query processor:** The query processor parses and processes statements similarly to the query processing engine within SQL Server. This processor is also responsible for the caching of objects, storage of MOLAP model objects and their data, processing calculations, handling server resources, and managing transactions.

➤ **XMLA listener:** This listener component facilitates and manages communications between various clients and the Analysis Services server. The port configuration for this listener is located in the `msmdsrv.ini` file, which is located in the `C:\Program Files\Microsoft SQL Server\MSAS11.MSSQLSERVER\OLAP\Config` folder by default. A value of 0 in this file under the `<Port>` tag simply indicates that SSAS is configured to listen on the default TCP/IP port of 2383 for the default instance of SSAS and 2382 for other instances of SSAS.

SSAS named instances can use a non-default port. The SQL Server Browser keeps track of the ports on which each named instance listens and performs any redirection required when a client does not specify the port number along with the named instance. You should use a firewall to restrict user access to Analysis Services ports from the Internet.

➤ **XML for Analysis:** XML for Analysis (XML/A) is a SOAP-based protocol used as the native protocol for communicating with SSAS. All client application interactions use XML/A to communicate with SSAS. This protocol is significant in that clients who need to communicate with SSAS do not need to install a client component, as past versions of Analysis Services required (such as Pivot Table Services). As a SOAP-based protocol, XML/A is optimized for disconnected and stateless environments that require time- and resource-efficient access. In addition to the defined protocol, Analysis Services also added extensions to support metadata management, session management, and locking capabilities. You have two different methods to send XML/A messages to Analysis Services: The default method uses TCP/IP, and an alternative is HTTP.

Analysis Services can be quite RAM and IO hungry and can suffocate your other resources, such as SQL Server, if not configured correctly. As your implementation crosses over into a larger implementation, for instance a hundred gigabytes of data, consider creating an isolated instance of Analysis Services on its own physical machine. Watch memory pressure to determine if you've reached this threshold.

ADMINISTERING ANALYSIS SERVICES SERVER

This section looks at some of the important administrative activities for the server instance of SSAS. The SSAS usage is divided into two tools: SQL Server Data Tools (SSDT) for development and Management Studio (SSMS) for administration. First you look at a review the configuration settings for the server in Management Studio, followed by details of the services needed for SSAS to run. Finally you end with an introduction to the Analysis Services Scripting Language (ASSL) and its use in performing administrative tasks.

Notice that when you connect to SSAS inside of Management Studio, the icons for SSAS appear different based on the type of instance. You must connect to SSAS using Windows Authentication only. The dialog shown in Figure 21-1 shows you three instances of SSAS. The first (localhost) is a Tabular model instance. The second is an instance of SSAS configured for SharePoint PowerPivot. This SharePoint model supports PowerPivot spreadsheets stored in SharePoint and is essentially the same thing as a Tabular model. The final instance is configured to run in traditional MOLAP model mode (localhost\MOLAP).

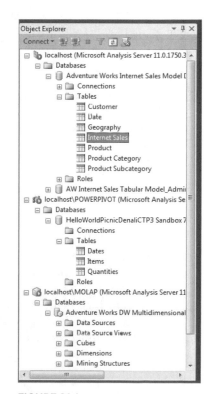

FIGURE 21-1

One thing you might notice in Figure 21-1 is the two similar databases in the localhost Tabular instance. This is because as you open the development tools a temporary workspace is created while you modify the cube in the SSDT. The database name for this temporary workspace ends with the user's name and a GUID. This applies only to the Tabular models because the MOLAP model is developed offline and then deployed to the server.

Server Properties

The server properties covered in this section are important for configuring the behavior of the SSAS server instance. To review and adjust the server properties, perform the following steps:

1. Open SQL Server Management Studio.

2. Connect to the Analysis Services server using the Object Explorer.

3. Right-click the server (the topmost node) and choose Properties.

By going to the Properties window, you can see dozens of properties that can help you tune your SSAS instance. You can see more properties by checking Show Advanced Properties. This section covers some of the important properties to SSAS.

Log Properties

If you're trying to diagnose why a query is taking longer than anticipated, this set of properties will help you troubleshoot performance. The log properties control how and where logging takes place. This property group includes details related to error logging, exception logging, the flight recorder, query logging, and tracing. Some examples include the `QueryLog\QueryLogConnectionString` and `QueryLog\QueryLogTableName` properties, which direct the server to where the query logging is persisted (database and table). The `QueryLog\QueryLogConnectionString` property specifies the SQL Server instance and database that hold the Analysis Services query log. By default, after you specify this and set the `CreateQueryLog Table` property to True, SQL Server begins to log every tenth query to the table. If you have an active Analysis Services instance, you may want to decrease this setting to every hundredth query.

This query log can later be used to tune your SQL Server by using a Usage Based Optimization tool, whereby you tune the Analysis Services cube based on queries used in the past.

Memory Properties

The memory properties dictate how the server utilizes system memory resources. The `LowMemoryLimit` represents a threshold percentage of total physical memory, at which point the server attempts to perform garbage collection for unused resources to free more resources. The default value is configured at 65 percent of total physical memory. The `TotalMemoryLimit` tells the server how much of the total physical memory of the server hardware should be made available for use by Analysis Services. This limit is configured to 80 percent of all server memory by default.

Essentially, this means that Analysis Services can take between 65 to 80 percent of your server's memory resource and not give it back after it crosses 65 percent.

In the Tabular model, the `VertipaqMemoryLimit` property identifies at what point the SSAS will start allowing paging. This paging occurs only if the `VertipaqPagingPolicy` property is set to 1 (advanced property only available if you check the Show Advanced Properties checkbox). Paging is turned on by default.

Network Properties

The network properties are a group of properties to control the network communication resources used by the server. Most notable are the settings that dictate whether the listener uses IPv4 or IPv6 protocols and whether the server permits the use of Binary XML for requests or responses. In Windows 2008 R2 and Windows 7, IPv6 is enabled by default.

OLAP Properties

The OLAP properties control how the server performs processing of the server objects (cubes, dimensions, and aggregations). Along with the processing properties, this section includes configuration properties for the way the server processes queries. Some of these query-processing properties are useful for simulating many testing scenarios. For example, you could adjust the `IndexUseEnabled`, `UseDataSlice`, and `AggregationUseEnabled` properties to benchmark different query-handling scenarios to determine whether some of these optimizations can provide the wanted performance enhancement.

Security Properties

The security properties are responsible for controlling how the server handles permissions. Examples of these properties include `RequireClientAuthentication`, which configures whether clients connecting to the server require authentication. By setting `BuiltInAdminsAreServerAdmins` to False, local server administrators are not implicitly given administrator rights to your SSAS instance. Both the local administrators and the service account are given escalated rights to Analysis Services by default because of this property.

Required Services

The Windows services required by Analysis Services include SQL Server Analysis Services, SQL Server Agent (only if you want to schedule processing of jobs), and SQL Server Browser. The SQL Server Browser service supports the Analysis Services redirector used when clients connect to named instances.

Commonly, the logon account used by any service should be one that has the least number of privileges required to function properly. More often than not, an account that has network rights is required, and this account would need to be granted access rights on the remote resources in addition to configuring the account to be used by the service.

Analysis Services Scripting Language

Now consider how many of your administrative tasks can be automated by using the built-in scripting language as a DBA. The Analysis Services Scripting Language, or ASSL, is a language that will automate administrative tasks for Analysis Services. This language is based on XML and is what client applications use to get information from Analysis Services.

The scripting language has two distinct parts. The first part defines the objects and server properties that are part of the server, including the objects used to develop solutions (measures and dimensions). The other part requests the server to perform actions, such as processing objects or performing batch operations.

It is important to focus on the scripting language components that help you manage the Analysis Services server. Start by looking at some examples of how you can use the language to process objects. Processing enables you to fill objects with data so that they may be used by end users for business analyses. Some of the objects you can process include cubes, databases, dimensions, and partitions. To perform this processing using the scripting language, you use the language's `Process` command.

An example of a script that would process the AdventureWorks `Employee` dimension follows:

```
<Batch xmlns="http://schemas.microsoft.com/analysisservices/2003/engine">
<Parallel>
<Process xmlns:xsd="http://www.w3.org/2001/XMLSchema"
xmlns:xsi="http://www.w3.org/2001/XMLSchema-instance"
xmlns:ddl2="http://schemas.microsoft.com/analysisservices/2003/engine/2"
xmlns:ddl2_2="http://schemas.microsoft.com/analysisservices/2003/engine/2/2"
xmlns:ddl100_100="http://schemas.microsoft.com/analysisservices/2012/engine/10
0/100">
<Object>
<DatabaseID>Adventureworks DW</DatabaseID>
<DimensionID>Dim Employee</DimensionID>
</Object>
<Type>ProcessUpdate</Type>
<WriteBackTableCreation>UseExisting</WriteBackTableCreation>
    </Process>
  </Parallel>
</Batch>
```

You can script many of the actions that you can configure in SQL Management Studio. For example, you can generate the example script shown here by right-clicking the AdventureWorks cube and selecting the Process Menu option. This displays the Process Cube dialog (see Figure 21-2). From this dialog, click the Script button located along the top under the title bar, and then select the location in which you want to generate the script.

Don't worry about the options in this screen yet; the "Processing Analysis Services Objects" section discusses them.

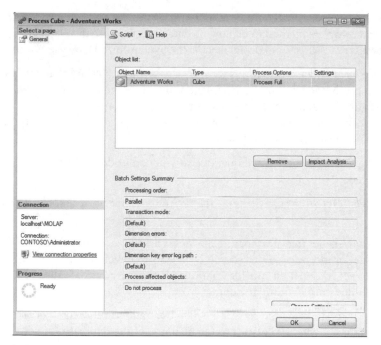

FIGURE 21-2

ADMINISTERING ANALYSIS SERVICES DATABASES

Now that you understand more about the Analysis Services server, look at the administrative tasks needed for the databases that are ultimately deployed and run on the Analysis Services server. The primary tasks associated with managing the Analysis Services databases include deployment to the server, processing Analysis Services objects, performing disaster recovery activities such as backup and restore operations, and synchronizing databases to copy entire databases.

Deploying Analysis Services Databases

Obviously, without deploying databases, there is no value to running an Analysis Services. Through deployment of Analysis Services databases to the server, changes to the design of the database are applied to the server.

When performing administrative tasks, you can either use Management Studio to affect changes directly in a database in what is commonly referred to as *online mode*, or you can work within SSDT to affect changes via a Build and Deploy process commonly referred to as *offline mode*. More specific to database deployment, you have the following options:

➤ Deploy changes directly from SSDT.

➤ Script changes and deploy from within Management Studio.

➤ Make incremental deployments using the Deployment Wizard.

➤ Process changes using the Synchronize Database Wizard.

Many of these options are useful only in specific circumstances and as such are not given much attention in this chapter. The most useful and complete method to deploy the databases is to use the Deployment Wizard. Alternatively, the next best tool to assist with deployment is the Synchronize Database Wizard.

The main advantage of the Deployment Wizard is that it is the only deployment method that applies the database project definition to production or any environment and enables you to keep many of the production database configuration settings, such as security and partitioning. This is important because neither direct deployment from SSDT nor scripting from Management Studio permits the deployment to maintain existing configuration settings.

The following steps show how the Deployment Wizard operates so you can understand how valuable it is for handling deployment:

1. From the Start menu under Microsoft SQL Server 2012 ⇨ Analysis Services, launch the Deployment Wizard.

2. On the Specify Source Analysis Services Database page, enter a full path to an Analysis Services database. This file should be provided to you by the SSAS developer, or you can find it under the SSAS project folder. This one file contains all the metadata for the cube, security, and partitions. It does not contain any data.

3. On the Installation Target page, indicate the server to which the database should be deployed, along with the wanted database name. (It defaults to the filename of the database.) If you don't like the default database name, you can type over it, as shown in Figure 21-3.

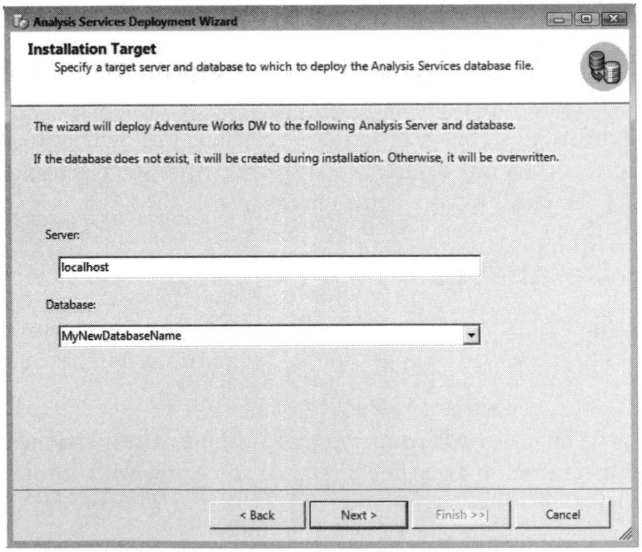

FIGURE 21-3

4. On the Specify Options for Partitions and Roles page, indicate which configuration options (Partitions and Roles) should be maintained on the deployment target database and thus not overwritten by this deployment (see Figure 21-4). This screen is especially useful if you

make changes in Management Studio to roles or partitions and do not want the developer's files to overwrite your own configuration.

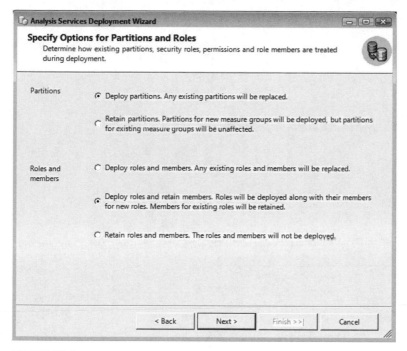

FIGURE 21-4

5. On the Specify Configuration Properties page, select which configuration settings from the current configuration file (.configsettings) should be applied to the target database. These settings provide a useful way to redirect items such as data source connection strings to point to production sources, rather than those used for development and testing. The Retain check boxes at the top provide an elegant way to manage updates of previous deployments because they disable overwriting of both the configuration and the optimization setting (see Figure 21-5). On this screen, you can also change the source for your data and the target of where your physical files will be stored.

6. On the Select Processing Options page, enter the desired processing method and change any writeback table options that the developer may have set. To support a robust deployment, you may also select the option to include all processing in a single transaction that can roll back all changes should any part of the deployment fail. The Default processing method enables Analysis Services to review the modifications to be applied and determine the optimal processing needed (see Figure 21-6).

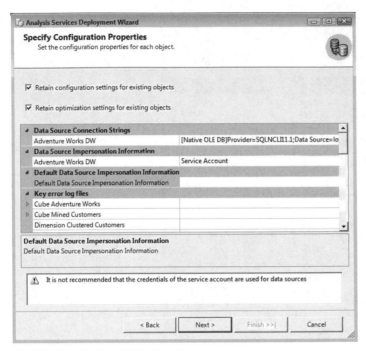

FIGURE 21-5

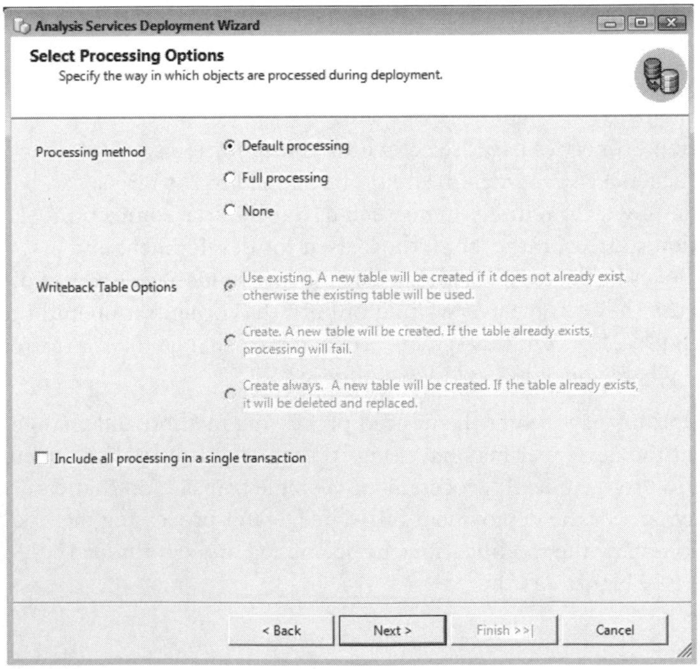

FIGURE 21-6

7. On the Confirm Deployment page is an option to script the entire deployment. This option is useful when either the person running the Deployment Wizard is not authorized to perform the actual deployment or the deployment needs to be scheduled so as not to interfere with other activities.

Processing Analysis Services Objects

Now that you understand how to deploy Analysis Services databases, you must add data to these objects by processing them. In addition, if the cubes need to be updated to reflect development changes made after the initial deployment, you need to reprocess them. Last, when data sources have changes made to their information, you need to perform, minimally, an incremental reprocessing of the cube to ensure that you have up-to-date data within the Analysis Services solution. Developers often build and test designs locally; the local schema from SSDT must first be deployed to the server before performing any processing.

Processing a MOLAP Model

The Analysis Services MOLAP model objects that require processing include measure groups, partitions, dimensions, cubes, mining models, mining structures, and databases. The processing is hierarchical — that is, processing an object that contains any other objects also processes those objects. For example, take a database that includes one or more cubes, and these cubes contain one or more dimensions, so processing the database would also process all the cubes contained within that database and all the dimensions contained in or referenced by each of the cubes. For the Tabular model, you simply reprocess the tables fully (not incrementally). The following sections cover how to process individual objects. If your SSAS database is smaller (roughly less than 20 gigabytes), then you could potentially process the entire database and still be online prior to your users needing the data. This could then be done with fully processing the database (essentially a wipe and load) with much less complexity to you.

Processing Dimensions

Analysis Services processes dimensions by simply running queries that return data from the data source tables for the dimensions. This data is then organized into the hierarchies and ultimately into map files that list all the unique hierarchical paths for each dimension. Processing dimensions can be optimized primarily through strategic indexes on the primary key and other key attributes. Prior to processing your cube or partition, you must first process the dimension if you are processing items selectively.

Processing Cubes

The cube contains both measure groups and partitions and is combined with dimensions to give the cube a data definition. You can process a cube by issuing queries to get fact-table members and the related measure values such that each path of dimensional hierarchies includes a value.

Processing Partitions

Just as in database partitioning, the goal of Analysis Services partitioning is to improve query response times and administrator processing durations by breaking large data sets into smaller files — typically, by some sort of time slice. This processing is special in that you must evaluate your hardware space and Analysis Services data structure constraints. Partitioning is the key to ensuring that your query response times are fast and your processing activities are efficient.

Reprocessing

After deploying an Analysis Services database, many events create the need to reprocess some or all the objects within the database. Examples of when reprocessing is required include object structural/schema changes, aggregation design changes, or refreshing object data.

Performing Processing

To perform processing of Analysis Services objects, you can either use SQL Server Management Studio or Business Intelligence Development Studio or run an XML for Analysis (XMLA) script. An alternative approach is to use Analysis Management Objects (AMO) to start processing jobs via programming tools.

> *When using these methods to process manually, as Analysis Services objects are being committed, the object is not available to process user requests. That's because the processing commit phase requires an exclusive lock on the Analysis Services objects being committed. User requests are not denied during this commit process, but rather are queued until the commit successfully completes. One alternative to processing your cube manually is called* proactive caching. *This is a more advanced option that incrementally gathers new data and loads the data into a new cached cube while queries are still happening in the original cube. As soon as the processing finishes, the new cube is opened to users and the old one is disposed. Once configured, your cube remains online during processing and changes automatically move online and become available to your users a few moments after being inserted into the warehouse.*

To perform processing for an Analysis Services database from within SQL Server Management Studio, follow these steps:

1. Open Management Studio, and connect to an Analysis Services server.

2. Right-click an Analysis Services database, and select Process. The Process Database dialog appears, where you can configure the details of the processing (refer to Figure 21-2).

3. Click the Impact Analysis button to get an idea of the effect that performing the specified process can have on related objects. For example, by fully processing a dimension, all measure groups pointing to that dimension also need to be processed.

4. Configure processing options such as the processing order by clicking Change Settings. Available options for the order include processing in parallel within a single transaction or processing sequentially within one or separate transactions. An important option is Process Affected Objects. This option controls whether all the other objects that have dependencies

on the database can also be processed (see Figure 21-7). A common architectural design employed in data warehousing involves the use of shared dimensions. These dimensions can be shared across the organization and allow for low maintenance and uniformity. The Process Affected Objects setting can therefore have a profound impact when you use an architecture involving shared dimensions because it may force reprocessing of many other databases in which the shared dimensions are used.

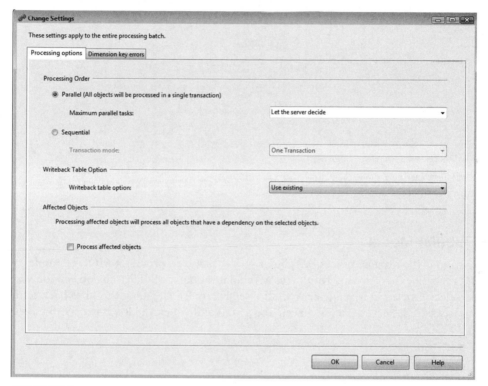

FIGURE 21-7

5. You can also configure sophisticated dimension key error handling (see Figure 21-8). For example, you can configure the options to use a custom error configuration, which converts key errors to an unknown record, rather than terminating the processing. In addition, you can specify error limits and what action to take when those limits have been exceeded. Last, you can choose to handle specific error conditions such as "key not found" or duplicate keys by reporting and continuing to process, by ignoring the error and continuing to process, and by reporting and stopping the processing. Using these settings typically means you have data issues and you should go back to the ETL to fix such issues because you're simply masking issues.

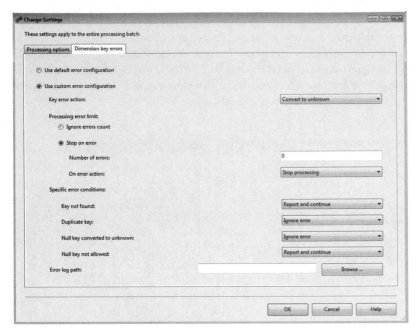

FIGURE 21-8

Processing a Tabular Model

Although the action is the same to process a Tabular model as it is to process a MOLAP model, what happens behind the scenes is different. To process a Tabular model, right-click the object you want to process, and select Process in Management Studio (see Figure 21-9). Doing this goes back to the original data sources (SQL Server, Access, Excel, and so on) and wipes and loads the SSAS tables.

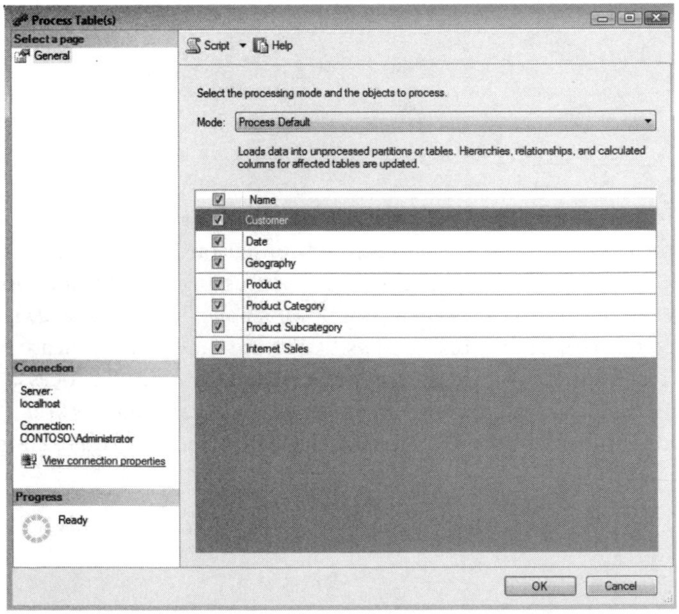

FIGURE 21-9

When you click OK, the tables begin to refresh. Figure 21-10 shows the amount of rows that were refreshed per table. If the data sources have moved (such as an Access database moving to a new directory), you can change its path in the Connections node of Management Studio.

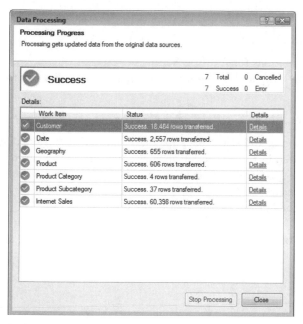

FIGURE 21-10

Backing Up and Restoring Analysis Services Databases

Without question, performing backup and restore tasks are common functions within the domain of any DBA. A backup of the Analysis Services database captures the state of the database and its objects at a particular point in time to a file on the file system (named with an .abf file extension), whereas recovery restores a particular state of the database and its objects to the server from a backup file on the file system. Backup and recovery, therefore, are useful for data recovery if problems occur with the database on the server in the future or simply to provide an audit of the state of the database. While there are ways to backup just the physical files in SSAS, using the backup steps in this section will produce one reliable file that's encrypted and compressed.

 The backups back up only the Analysis Services database contents, not the underlying data sources used to populate the database. Therefore, you must perform a backup of the data sources using a regular database or file system backup with the Analysis Services backup to capture a true state of both the Analysis Services objects and their sources at or about the same point in time.

The information that the backup includes varies depending upon the storage type configured for the database. A detailed message displayed at the bottom of the Backup Database dialog clearly communicates the various objects included in a backup based on the type of storage. Although storage options are covered a bit later, you need to know that available options to be included in the backup are the following:

➤ metadata that defines all the objects

➤ aggregations calculated

➤ source data used to populate the objects

Now let's review performing these back-up functions for Analysis Services databases. Again, you can use Management Studio to assist with the setup and configuration of these tasks and script the results to permit scheduling:

1. Open Management Studio, and connect to an Analysis Services server.

2. Right-click an Analysis Services database, and select Backup. The Backup Database dialog appears. Here you can configure the details of the backup such as applying compression, where the backup file should be located, or whether the file should be encrypted (see Figure 21-11). Storage types are covered later, but you get a clear statement of what information is part of the backup at the bottom of this dialog. Basically, the backup is backing up only the Analysis Services information (partitions, metadata, source data, and aggregations) available to a database based on the storage type.

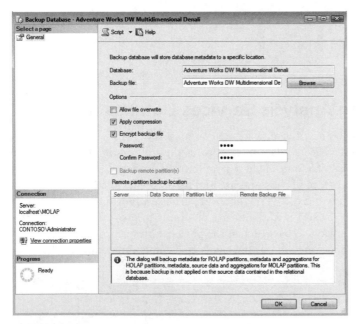

FIGURE 21-11

3. Optionally, you can script the backup by pressing the Script button along the top of the dialog. The resulting script looks like the following example (including the password not shown here):

```
<Backup xmlns="http://schemas.microsoft.com/analysisservices/2003/engine">
  <Object>
    <DatabaseID>Adventureworks DW</DatabaseID>
```

```
    </Object>
    <File>Adventureworks DW.abf</File>
    <Password>password</Password>
</Backup>
```

Now that you have a backup of an Analysis Services database, turn your attention to the recovery of Analysis Services databases. Recovery takes a previously created backup file (named with an .abf file extension) and restores it to an Analysis Services database. Several options are available during this process:

➤ Using the original database name (or specifying a new database name).

➤ Overwriting an existing database.

➤ Including existing security information (or skipping security).

➤ Changing the restoration folder for each partition.

Following are the steps needed to perform a recovery of the database:

1. Open Management Studio, and connect to an Analysis Services server.

2. Right-click an Analysis Services database, and select Restore. The Restore Database dialog appears; here you can configure the restoration details, such as including security or overwriting an existing database (see Figure 21-12).

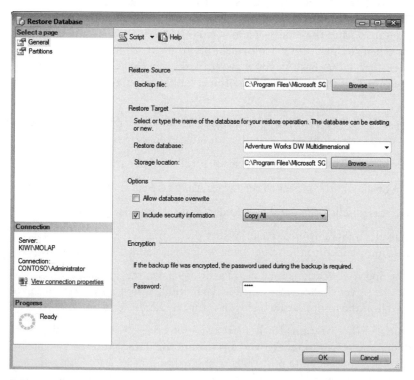

FIGURE 21-12

3. Optionally, you can script the restore by clicking the Script button along the top of the dialog. The resulting script would look like the following example (including, again, a poor practice of including the password):

```
<Restore xmlns="http://schemas.microsoft.com/analysisservices/2003/engine">
  <File>C:\Program Files\Microsoft SQL
Server\MSAS10.MSSQLSERVER\OLAP\Backup\Adventureworks DW.abf</File>
  <DatabaseName>Adventureworks DW</DatabaseName>
  <AllowOverwrite>true</AllowOverwrite>
  <Password>password</Password>
  <DbStorageLocation
xmlns="http://schemas.microsoft.com/analysisservices/2012/engine/100/100">C:\
Program Files\Microsoft SQL Server\MSAS10.MSSQLSERVER\OLAP\Data\
</DbStorageLocation>
  </Restore>
```

You can also click on the Partitions tab to change the storage location of each of the partitions.

Synchronizing Analysis Services Databases

Another important activity to perform involves synchronizing Analysis Services databases from one server to another. This is usually done as a mechanism for deploying from a test or quality-assurance server to a production server. This feature is attractive for this purpose because users can continue to browse the production cubes while the synchronization takes place. When the synchronization and processing completes, a user is automatically redirected to the newly synchronized copy of the database, and the older version is removed from the server. This differs greatly from what happens when you perform a deployment because part of the deployment usually involves processing of dimensions and cubes. As you may recall, certain types of processing of Analysis Services objects require that the cube be taken offline, making it unavailable to users until the processing completes.

As with many other database tasks, you can run the synchronization immediately from the wizard, or you can save the results of the selections to a script file for later execution or scheduling.

To synchronize an Analysis Services database between servers, follow these steps:

1. Open Management Studio, and connect to the target Analysis Services server.

2. On this target server, right-click the databases folder, and select Synchronize.

3. On the Select Databases to Synchronize page, specify the source server and database; the destination server is hard-coded to the server from which you launched the synchronization.

4. If applicable, on the Specify Locations for Local Partitions page, the source folder displays the folder name on the server that contains the local partition, whereas the destination folder can be changed to reflect the folder into which you want the database to be synchronized.

5. If applicable, on the Specify Locations for Remote Partitions page, you can modify both the destination folder and server to reflect where you want the database to be synchronized. In addition, if the location has remote partitions contained in that location that need to be included in the synchronization, you must place a check beside the Sync option.

6. On the Specify Query Criteria page, enter a value for the security definitions and indicate whether compression should be used. The security options include copying all definitions and membership information, skipping membership information but including the security definitions, and ignoring all security and membership details.

7. On the Select Synchronization Method page, you can either run the synchronization immediately or script to a file for later use in scheduling the synchronization.

Processing is one of those topics where the lines between development and production DBAs blur. The same line becomes blurred with performance tuning a cube. The developer will likely perform the base performance tuning but will rely on the DBA to create long term performance tuning through aggregations. These are covered in the next section.

ANALYSIS SERVICES PERFORMANCE MONITORING AND TUNING

Successful use of Analysis Services requires continual monitoring of how user queries and other processes perform and make the required adjustments to improve their performance. The main tools for performing these tasks include the SQL Profiler, performance counters, and the Flight Recorder.

Monitoring Analysis Services Events

There are now two ways to monitor SQL Server and Analysis Services: SQL Server Profiler and xEvents. Profiler will eventually be removed from SQL Server in a future release, making xEvents the future. The main issue holding xEvents back for now is the user interface for xEvents needs some more development before it's as easy to create as Profiler. The interface for xEvents resembles T-SQL for SQL Server or XMLA for Analysis Services. The events you trap are the same whether you use xEvents or Profiler.

Chapter 12 provides detailed coverage of how to use SQL Profiler, so here you learn what is important about using this tool for monitoring your Analysis Services events. The capabilities related to using SQL Profiler for Analysis Services were vastly improved in the 2005 release and are now quite useful for this purpose. With SQL Server Profiler, you can review what the server does during processing and query resolution. Especially important is the ability to record the data generated by profiling to either a database table or file to review or replay it later to get a better understanding of what happened. You can also now either step through the events that were recorded or replay them as they originally occurred. Last, you can place the events side by side with any machine or SSAS performance counters to spot trends affecting performance.

The main focus here is tracing the Analysis Services server activity and investigating the performance of the MDX queries submitted to the server to process user requests for information. The useful event categories include the following:

➤ Command events provide insight into the actual types of statements issued to perform actions.

➤ Discovery events detail requests for metadata about server objects, including the Discovery Server State events (such as open connections).

➤ Error and Warning events show any errors or warnings being thrown by the instance of SSAS.

➤ Query events trap queries being passed into SSAS.

Because of all the detail that a trace returns, use the Column Filter button to display only the activities sent to a specific Analysis Services database. You can also use these traces to replay against other servers to see how your server will scale. This is covered in the next section.

Creating Traces for Replay

Traces are important because they enable you to determine various elements of status information for Analysis Services through certain counters. To start a trace, you must open Performance Monitor by either selecting Performance in Administrative Tools from the Control Panel or by typing **PerfMon** at the command prompt. Two types of counters are used within Performance Monitor: predefined counters and user-defines counters. The predefined counters measure statistics for your server and process performance, whereas user-defined counters are used to analyze events that may occur. Command-line tools such as LodCtr, LogMan, ReLog, TypePerf, and UnloadCtr also capture performance metrics.

To get a better idea of how to configure these traces for replaying queries submitted to your Analysis Services server, start a trace of your own.

1. First open SQL Profiler and selecting File ➪ New Trace. When prompted, specify the Analysis Services server to connect to, and configure trace properties to resemble what is shown in Figure 21-13.

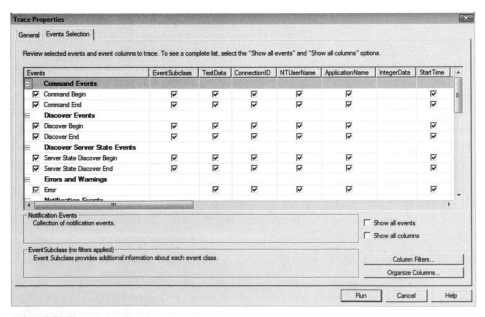

FIGURE 21-13

2. To profile user queries, ensure that the SQL Profiler captures the Audit Login event class, the Query Begin event class, and the Query End event class (see Figure 23-14). SQL server determines who was running the query and other session-specific information because you include the Audit Login event class. The Query Begin and Query End event classes simply permit understanding of which queries were submitted by reviewing the text of the query along with any parameters that would have been used during query processing.

> *Even though the instance monitored in Figure 21-14 is a Tabular model using DAX as its query language, the DAX translates to MDX behind the scenes.*

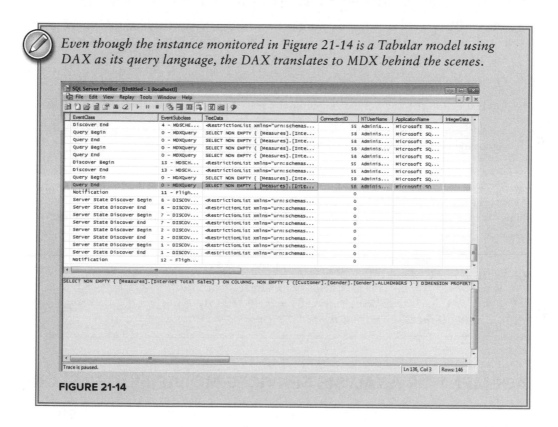

FIGURE 21-14

3. After you set up the trace, start it. Browse a cube within Management Studio to generate user activity involving the submission of queries to Analysis Services. The result in Profiler is a detailing of events along with the TextData recording the activities. For example, in Management Studio, you can add the Customer and Date dimensions while also requesting that Order Count and Average Sales Amount display. This activity is all recorded with the Profiler, with the MDX statement recorded in the TextData column (refer to Figure 21-14).

Using Flight Recorder for After-the-Fact Analysis

As an administrator, you are often disappointed when you cannot find the cause of a particular problem. Mostly, you are stymied when you cannot reproduce reported problems. These situations arise as you attempt to re-create what happened to determine how things could have been handled differently to avoid the reported problem. Using the Flight Recorder, you may be able to replay the problem conditions that led to the reported problems. This Flight Recorder operates similarly to a tape recorder: It captures the Analysis Services server activity during runtime without requiring a trace. Each time the server restarts, a new trace file automatically starts. In addition, the recorder is automatically enabled and can be configured using the Analysis Services Server Properties. To use the trace file created by the Flight Recorder to replay server activity, follow these steps:

1. Open SQL Server Profiler, and open the trace file created by the Flight Recorder, located by default at `C:\Program Files\Microsoft SQL Server\MSAS11.MSSQLSERVER\OLAP\Log` and named `FlightRecorderCurrent.trc`.

2. On the toolbar select Replay ⇨ Start.

3. On the Connect to Server dialog, enter the server name and authentication information.

4. On the Replay Configuration dialog, set up the playback features you desire, such as replaying only statements issued to the server within a given time frame.

This replay is rather useful because Analysis Services will begin to run the statements captured in the trace. Obviously, factors such as number of open connections and even the number of sessions that existed at the time of the original problem are important to consider when troubleshooting problems. When you replay the traces made by Flight Recorder, these factors are simulated on your behalf.

 You can also capture the MDX out of this trace file to run as a SQL Server Agent job. Doing so warms the SSAS cache in MOLAP model mode and brings the data off the disk and into memory (memory permitting).

MANAGEMENT OF ANALYSIS SERVICES MOLAP MODEL STORAGE

One of the main reasons for using Analysis Services centers on performance with complex data retrieval. The design of the storage within Analysis Services therefore becomes important when trying to achieve the query and processing performance expected. To understand storage design, this section first describes what modes of storage are available within Analysis Services. Next, you look at the configuration of partitions. Last, you learn how to design aggregations.

Storage Modes

Analysis Services permits configuring dimensions and measure groups using the following storage modes: Multidimensional OLAP (MOLAP), Relational OLAP (ROLAP), and Hybrid OLAP (HOLAP):

➤ **Multidimensional OLAP:** MOLAP storage mode is the most aggressive because it stores all the aggregations and a copy of the source data with the structure. In addition, the structure stores the metadata required to understand the structure. The benefit of this structure is query performance because all information needed to respond to queries is available without having to access the source data. Periodic processing is required to update the data stored within the structure, and this processing can be either incremental or full. As a result of processing the cube, data latency is introduced with this storage mode. Also as a result of this structure, storage requirements become much more important due to the volume of information that the system requires.

➤ **Relational OLAP:** Indexed views within the data source of the ROLAP structure store the aggregations, whereas a copy of the source data is not stored within Analysis Service. With this mode, any queries that the query cache cannot answer must be passed on to the data source. That makes this storage mode slower than MOLAP or HOLAP (covered in the next bullet). The benefit is that users can view data in real or near-real time, and because a copy of the source data is not being stored within the structure, the storage requirements are lower than MOLAP.

➤ **Hybrid OLAP:** As you might have guessed, the HOLAP storage mode is a combination of multidimensional OLAP and relational OLAP. This storage mode stores aggregations but does not store a copy of the source data. As a result, queries that access the aggregated values perform well, but those that do not have access perform slower. Also as a result, this storage mode requires far less storage space than MOLAP.

Partition Configuration

When you need to configure partitions for your cubes to speed up access to your data, you have two primary tasks. First, you have the configuration of the storage of the partition, and second, you have the optimization of the partition by configuring aggregations. Partitions should be created for measure groups that are either larger than 4 gigabytes in size or about 15 million rows roughly. Otherwise, the cube performance will suffer. *Aggregations* are precalculated summaries of data, primarily employed so that query response time is made faster because the cube partition has prepared and saved the data in advance of its use. These aggregations are discussed in the next section but they are involved heavily with partitions as well.

You should understand that in Analysis Services, storage is configured separately for each partition of each measure group in a cube. This enables you to optimize your cube query strategies for each partition. An example would be to keep the current year's data in one partition optimized for more detailed and narrow queries, while keeping older data in another partition optimized for broader aggregated queries.

You configure your cube storage using either SSDT or, after deployment, Management Studio. Often, developers do not need to be involved with partitioning or configuration of storage; this scenario is a better fit for using Management Studio. The downside to this situation is that the Visual Studio project will not be updated to reflect the current storage settings, and you must take care during deployment that your selections made in Management Studio are not overwritten. Specifically, you want to ensure that during deployment, when the Specify Options for Partitions and Roles page displays, you indicate that Partitions and Security should be maintained on the deployment target database and thus not overwritten by this deployment (refer to Figure 23-4).

When you deploy a cube for the first time, a measure group is set up to be entirely contained within a single partition, spanning the entire fact table used for the measures. With the BI and Enterprise Editions, you can change that to define multiple partitions by setting the `StorageMode` property for each partition. With Standard Edition, you can create up to three partitions. To set the storage options in SQL Server Management Studio for a MOLAP model, follow these steps:

1. Open Management Studio, and connect to the target Analysis Services server.

2. In Object Explorer, right-click the cube that contains the partition, and click Properties to set storage options. If you have more than one partition, right-click a partition and click Properties.

3. Select the Proactive Caching page.

4. Select the Standard Setting radio button to accept the default storage settings for the storage type specified by the slider bar. Now you may move the slider bar to change the storage type from MOLAP to HOLAP and to ROLAP (see Figure 21-15). For the purpose of this example, select Scheduled MOLAP, and then click Options.

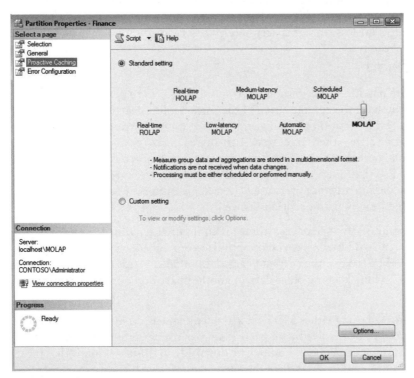

FIGURE 21-15

5. Click the Options button to display the Storage Options dialog, as shown in Figure 21-16. This screen enables you to quickly configure how the cube will be processed automatically.

If you check Enable Proactive Caching (available only in Enterprise Edition), the cube turns on the proactive caching option. For scheduled MOLAP, check Update the Cache Periodically to automatically build the cube once a day. With proactive caching, the cube remains online during the update. You can also have SSAS automatically detect changes in the underlying data warehouse and process as soon as the change is made, if you prefer to have more real-time analytics. Proactive caching is for SQL Server Enterprise Edition only in MOLAP model mode and does not scale if millions of rows are being updated every hour. Most people instead create a processing task in an SSIS package or a SQL Server Agent job to refresh their cube.

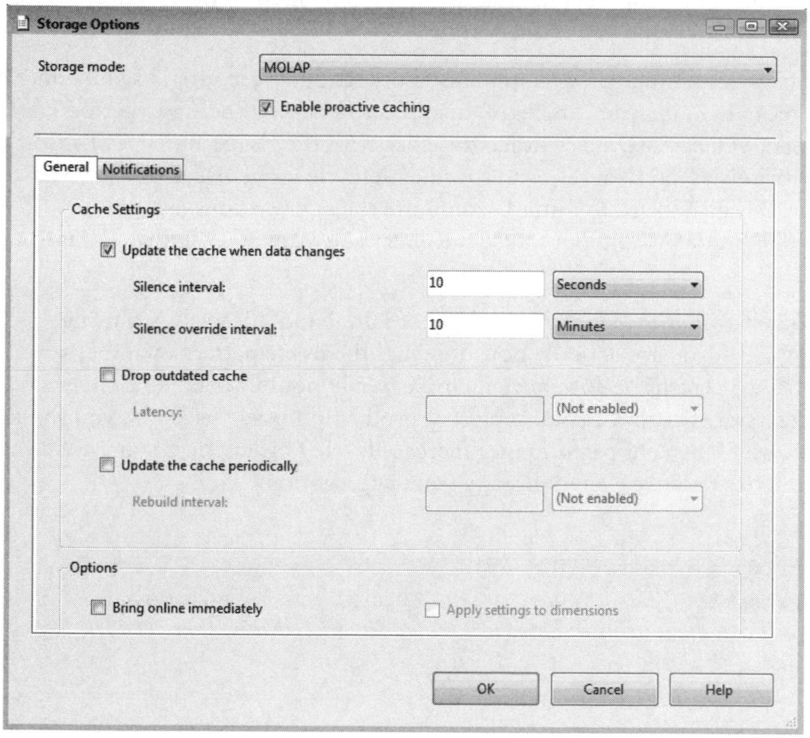

FIGURE 21-16

Designing Aggregations in the MOLAP model

Again, the primary role of aggregations is to precalculate summaries of the cube data so that user queries may be quickly answered. When a query cannot use an aggregation because it does not exist, Analysis Services must query the lowest level of details it has stored and sum the values. Aggregations are stored in a cube in cells at the intersection of the selected dimensions.

SSAS aggregations apply to MOLAP model mode only in SQL Server 2012. The Tabular model gets around this limitation by having in-memory architecture, allowing it to scan the rows much more robustly.

Designing aggregations is all about trade-offs between space and user performance. Optimizing query performance via aggregations also increases the time it takes to process the cube. When you have few aggregations, the time required to process the cube and the storage space occupied by the cube is rather small, but the query response time may be slow because the query cannot leverage a precomputed summary (aggregate) and must instead rely upon having to retrieve data from the lowest levels within the cube and summarize at query time.

You design aggregations by determining which combination of attributes are often used by queries and could benefit from precalculation. You can begin this process by using the Aggregation Design Wizard, or after deployment you can use query usage statistics with the Usage-Based Optimization Wizard. These methods obviously lend themselves to specific life-cycle usage. Developers would likely use the Aggregation Design Wizard to initially configure the aggregations prior to deployment, whereas administrators would opt to use the query statistics and the Usage-Based Optimization Wizard.

A good rule of thumb to start with is to optimize at a level of 20/80 and 80/20. When using the Aggregation Design Wizard, you are actually not sure what the usage patterns will be, so optimizing to higher than a 20 percent performance increase would not be valuable. Conversely, when you have actual query statistics that clearly represent production usage patterns, you should optimize at approximately an 80 percent performance increase level. This in effect states that you want 80 percent of user queries to be answered directly from aggregations.

Details of the Aggregation Design Wizard are not covered here because most administration of the aggregations will be performed in either Management Studio or SSDT using the Usage-Based Optimization Wizard.

Before using the Usage-Based Optimization Wizard, you need to ensure that the query log is enabled and that it has been populated. You enable this log in Management Studio via the Analysis Services Server properties. The `CreateQueryLogTable` setting enables logging to a database table when true, whereas the `QueryLogConnectionString` specifies the database in which the logging will be stored. In addition, note the setting of the `QueryLogSampling` because this determines which queries will be logged.

After the Query Log has been enabled and is populated with query statistics, you can run the Usage-Based Optimization Wizard. Following are the steps needed to use this wizard:

1. Open Management Studio, and connect to the target MOLAP model Analysis Services server.

2. Select the desired database, cube, and measure group.

3. Right-click the partitions folder, and select Usage Based Optimization.

4. On the Select Partitions to Modify dialog, specify any partitions that are to be evaluated. You can either select all partitions for the measure group, or you can select combinations of individual partitions.

5. On the Specify Query Criteria dialog, you can view query statistics for the selected measure group partition, including the total number of queries and the average response time for processing the queries. Optionally, you can set some limits to filter the queries that you would like the optimization to consider, including an interesting option for filtering the queries by users. Presumably, one notable use of this option would be to enable you to ensure that your executives' queries are delivering the best response time.

6. On the Review the Queries That Will Be Optimized dialog, you can view the specific dimension member combinations under the client request column, the occurrences of those combinations, and the average duration of those combinations. At this point, you also have a column of check boxes beside each row that enables you to indicate that you do not want some of the suggested queries optimized.

7. Under the Review Aggregation Usage page, select the default options. This screen gives you full control over how each dimension is aggregated.

8. Specify the counts of various cube objects on the Specify Object Counts dialog by clicking the Count button.

9. On the Set Aggregations Options dialog, specify how long the aggregations should be designed. Options to consider include designing aggregations until a specified amount of storage has been used, until a specified percentage of performance gain has been reached, or until you decide to stop the optimization process (see Figure 21-17). Because you base this optimization on real query statistics, you should consider optimizing until a performance gain of approximately 30 percent has been attained. This translates loosely to optimizing 30 percent of the queries to use the aggregations, which is about 52KB in this example. If you build aggregations on a system that does not have them already, 30 percent is a good starting point. For Usage Based Optimization, you probably want to see this number at 100 percent, meaning that you want to tune all the queries that you filtered on the previous screen.

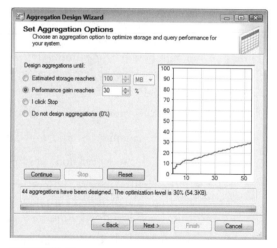

FIGURE 21-17

10. Last, the Completing the Wizard dialog displays, which you can use to review the partitions affected by the aggregation design and to indicate whether you would like the affected partitions to be processed immediately.

In Profiler, you can see whether aggregations are being used easily on a query-by-query basis. In the Progress Report End event class, you see an aggregation being read, versus a partition. There's also an event you can trap in Profiler called Get Data from Aggregation that can show when an aggregation is being read from.

You now have designed the storage of your Analysis Services cubes, set up partitions, and designed aggregations. In the next section, you learn how to apply security to Analysis Services.

APPLYING SECURITY TO ANALYSIS SERVICES IN THE MOLAP MODEL

Security within Analysis Services involves designing Active Directory user permissions to selected cubes, dimensions, cells, mining models, and data sources. Analysis Services relies on Microsoft Windows to authenticate users, and only authenticated users who have rights within Analysis Services can establish a connection to Analysis Services.

After a user connects to Analysis Services, the permissions that user has within Analysis Services are determined by the rights assigned to the Analysis Services roles to which that user belongs, either directly or through membership in a Windows role. The two roles available in Analysis Services are server roles and database roles.

Server Role

The server role permits unrestricted access to the server and all the objects contained on the server. This role also allows its members to administer security by assigning permissions to other users. By default, all members of the Administrators local group are members of the server role in Analysis Services and have serverwide permissions to perform any task. You configure this access by using Management Studio, Business Intelligence Development Studio, or an XMLA script.

To add additional Windows users or groups to this Server role, follow these steps:

1. Open Management Studio, and connect to an Analysis Services server.

2. Right-click the server node in Object Explorer, and choose Properties.

3. On the Analysis Server Properties dialog, select the Security page. Note again that no users or groups are included automatically. Although it's not shown in the dialog, only members of the local Windows Administrators group are automatically assigned this server role.

4. Click the Add button, and add users and groups with the standard Windows Select Users and Groups dialog.

5. After adding the users and groups, you can remove the local Administrators from the server role by selecting the General page and clicking the Show Advanced (ALL) Properties check box. Then set the `Security\BuiltinAdminsAreServerAdmins` property to False.

Database Role

Within Analysis Services, you can set up multiple database roles. Only the members of the server role are permitted to create these database roles within each database, grant administrative or user permissions to these database roles, and add Windows users and groups to these roles.

These database roles have no administrative capabilities unless they are granted Full Control, otherwise known as administrator rights, or a more limited set of administrator rights (such as Process the Database, Process One or More Dimensions, and Read Database Metadata).

In summary, reading Analysis Services data is only available to members of the server role and members of a database role that have Full Control unless they have specific rights to read a given dimension. Other users can get this access only if their database role expressly grants permissions to the objects in Analysis Services (dimensions, cubes, and cells).

You set up database roles using either SSDT or Management Studio. In SSDT, you use the Role Designer, whereas in Management Studio you use the Create Role dialog. When using Management Studio for setting up these roles, the changes do not require that you deploy the database because they are made in online mode.

Follow these steps to add a database role to an Analysis Services database using Management Studio:

1. Open Management Studio, and connect to an Analysis Services server.

2. Right-click the Roles folder located in one of the databases, and select New Role.

3. On the Create Role dialog (see Figure 21-18), enter **Data Admin** as the role name, and check the Full control (Administrator) check box. This automatically checks every other box. By checking this, you've given any user in the role full control of your database.

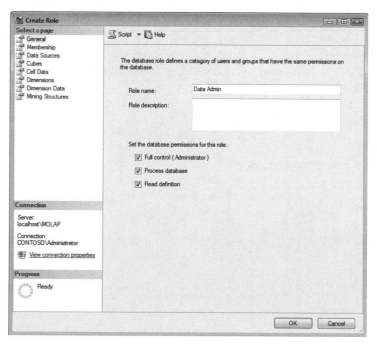

FIGURE 21-18

4. Select the Membership page, and add a Windows user account.

If a developer redeploys the cube without your knowledge, your security may be overwritten. After you change the settings, you must have the developer resynch with the live server or use the Deployment Utility going forward.

Database Role Permissions

The easiest way to understand the granularity of permissions within Analysis Services is by reviewing the Create Role dialog's pages. Previously, when you added a new role, you assigned the Full Control (Administrator) database permissions. If you did not check that check box, you would have the ability to assign granular permissions by using the various pages of the Create Role dialog.

The permissions form a sort of hierarchy in which the topmost permissions need to be assigned before any of the next lower-level permissions. This hierarchy includes Cubes, Dimensions, Dimension Data, and Cell Data (for protecting measures). Analysis Services permits a database to include more than one cube, which is why you have that as a permission set for your roles. Within the cube, you have dimensions and measures. The measures are constrained by the various dimensions. Now look at some examples of assigning these permissions.

While reviewing the role permissions available, note two in particular that are regularly used to limit access to information: Dimensions and Dimension Data. These permit you to define what the user can see when browsing the cube. For example, you can configure security such that only staff in the Marketing department can use the Promotions dimension. Access permissions to an entire dimension are configured on the Dimensions page of the Create Role dialog (see Figure 21-19). You should understand that certain permissions require that other permissions be granted. In this example, you would need to ensure that the role for the Marketing department staff has been granted permissions to access the AdventureWorks cube.

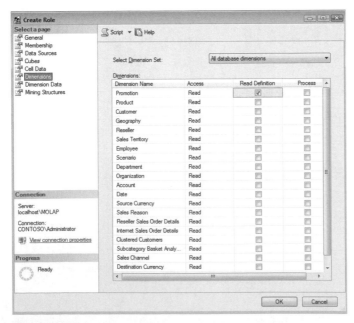

FIGURE 21-19

When access has been modified for the dimensions, you need to define the specific attribute hierarchies and members within the dimension to which role members are allowed access. If you forget to do this, the role will not have permission to view any attribute hierarchies within the dimension, nor any of their members. For example, you can permit a sales manager access to only the Customer promotions in the Dimension Data page and selecting the Promotion dimension from the Dimension combo box. Then, select the Promotion Category as the attribute hierarchy and check only the Customer member. You also need to select Deselect All Members (see Figure 21-20) so that as new members are added, the user is automatically denied rights to those members.

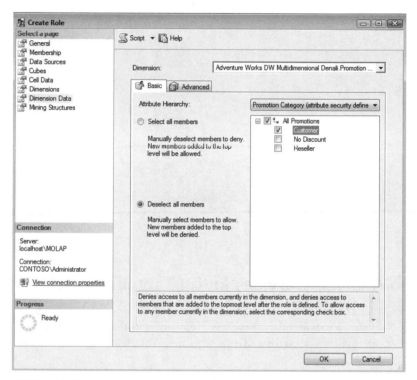

FIGURE 21-20

You may also encounter a security configuration that requires even more sophistication, and for that you have the Advanced tab on the Dimension Data page of the Create Role dialog. This tab enables the creation of complex combinations of allowed and denied listings of dimension members, along with configuration of default members for your role. Here is where administrators may need to work with developers to understand the multidimensional expression language (MDX) syntax that would be required to configure these advanced security options. If you do want there to always be a filter on the Customer promotion, select Enable Visual Totals (see Figure 21-21). By doing this, even if the promotion dimension has not been used in the query, the member is filtered out automatically. Previously you would have to use the Promotion Category attribute to see the security filter.

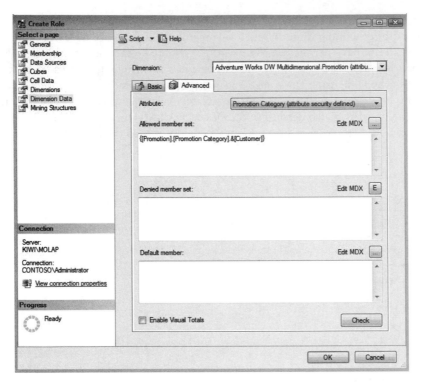

FIGURE 21-21

Applying Security to Analysis Services in the Tabular Model

The Tabular model operates much the same way as the MOLAP model for security but has fewer options and less flexibility. You can specify database-level permissions, add the users to the role, and then specify any members that you want to filter. To create a new Tabular role, follow these following steps:

1. Open Management Studio, and connect to an Analysis Services server in Tabular mode.

2. Right-click the Roles folder located in one of the databases, and select New Role.

3. In the General tab, name the role. If you want users to be administrators, check Full Control. If you want users to have selective rights, check Read.

4. In the membership tab, select the Active Directory groups or users that you want to inherit this role.

5. You can apply a filter to ensure your users of this role can see only certain rows by using a Data Analysis Expression (DAX) Filter in the Row Filters tab. A DAX filter is actually a simple language to learn and would look like Figure 21-22, which allows the user to see only U.S.-based sales.

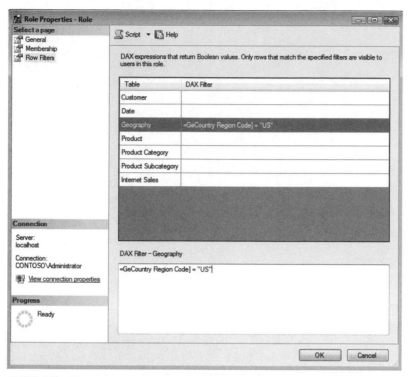

FIGURE 21-22

SUMMARY

You covered a lot of ground in understanding the various administrative functions related to Analysis Services. There are two types of models in SSAS: MOLAP and Tabular model. Administration for the new SQL Server 2012 Tabular model is similar to the MOLAP model, but the processing involves refreshing the entire table. Aggregations are used to performance tune a cube based on query patterns. Various security administration tasks include creating database roles and assigning granular permissions to the roles. Now that you've learned about administering the Business Integration services, you can move on to Chapter 22, which discusses how to administer the Reporting Services (SSRS) in SQL Server 2012.

22

SQL Server Reporting Services Administration

WHAT'S IN THIS CHAPTER?

➤ How to Use SQL Server Configuration Manager to Set Up Your Newly Installed SQL Server Reporting Services Server

➤ Navigating and Understanding the Properties Associated with an Installed Reporting Services Server

➤ Using Report Builder to Create New Reports Useful to the DBA

➤ Managing and Executing Reports with Report Manager

SQL Server Reporting Services (SSRS) is one of the simplest tools in the Microsoft stack to configure. This is because of the easy-to-use SQL Server Configuration Manager and the complete, yet understandable, properties of a Reporting Services server, accessed through SQL Server Management Studio. To understand how Reporting Services works, you need to understand how a report is built and executed. Thus a brief overview of Report Builder is in order, and you can even use it to create reports useful to DBAs. Then the real fun begins, as you see Reporting Services in action through the use of Report Manager. Report Manager is a suite of web pages that ships with SSRS. These pages enable users to easily execute their reports and give administrators methods to manage, schedule, and maximize server resources.

SQL SERVER REPORTING SERVICES CONFIGURATION MANAGER

Reporting Services is configured using its own tool, separate from the SQL Server Configuration Manager. In most cases you'll have already configured your instance of Reporting Services during the install of SQL Server. Following are reasons when you need to alter the configuration:

➤ You need to change a value, such as the service account that SSRS runs under.

➤ During install, you chose not to configure SSRS.

➤ You set up additional instances of SSRS.

➤ You need to configure a scale-out implementation of SSRS.

You can accomplish any of these tasks — and more — using the Reporting Services Configuration Manager. Complete the following steps to start using this tool:

1. To launch the configuration manager, go to Start menu ➪ Microsoft SQL Server 2012 ➪ Configuration Tools ➪ Reporting Services Configuration Manager (see Figure 22-1).

FIGURE 22-1

 The Reporting Services Configuration Manager is version-specific. The configuration tool that came with SQL Server 2012 may be used only to manage a SQL Server Reporting Services 2012 server. To manage the Reporting Services server for previous versions of SQL Server, use the configuration manager specific to that product.

2. When the tool launches, select the Reporting Services server to configure, as well as the instance of SSRS, as shown in Figure 22-2.

Typically you configure on the box the Reporting Services Connection Manager is working on, but you can manage multiple SQL Server 2012 Reporting Services servers using the same configuration manager.

FIGURE 22-2

3. After you select the server to manage, simply click Connect to open the main tool.

The opening screen in Figure 22-3 displays some basic information about the server you are configuring. You can see the specific instance name and ID, along with the specific edition and version number. The name of the database containing the reporting items is also shown. In the example shown in Figure 22-3, the default of ReportServer was taken.

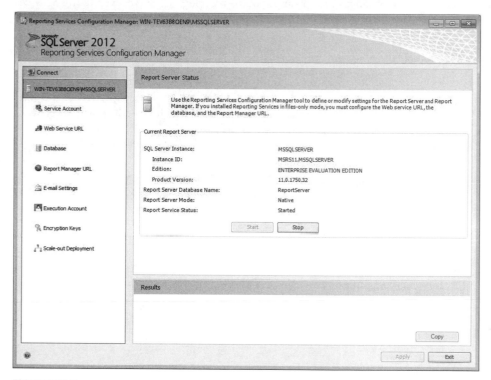

FIGURE 22-3

You can see the service runs in Native mode. SQL Server Reporting Services can also run in SharePoint Integrated mode. Starting with 2012, configuration of Reporting Services running in SharePoint Integrated mode should be done through the SharePoint console, not the SSRS configuration manager.

In SharePoint integrated mode, SharePoint manages all aspects of reporting. Reports are uploaded to and stored in SharePoint. Security is controlled within SharePoint. In addition, features of SharePoint libraries such as version control and alerts are supported with reports.

There are some disadvantages to running SSRS in integrated mode however; items such as custom security extensions, the ability to manage reports within Report Manager, and the ability to use the Reporting Services Configuration Manager are not supported when running in SharePoint integrated mode.

A discussion about how to configure with SharePoint console is outside the scope of this chapter, but you can fine more information on this topic at `http://msdn.microsoft.com/en-us/library/bb326356.aspx`.

Finally, you occasionally have changes that prompt you to recycle SQL Server Reporting Services. You can do so by starting and stopping the service, as shown in Figure 22-3.

The Service Account

The Report Server service account is the user account under which Reporting Services run. Although initially configured during the installation of SQL Server, it can be updated or modified on this screen (shown in Figure 22-4). It is under the service account that the Report Server web service, Report Manager, and background process tasks all run.

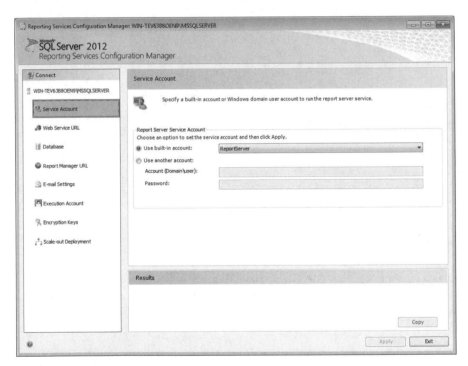

FIGURE 22-4

Should you decide to change the account, you have two options:

➤ **Built-in Account:** With Windows Server 2008 and previous versions, you may opt to use one of the built-in accounts, such as Network Service, Local System, or Local Service. Of these, Microsoft recommends the use of the Network Service account.

Beginning with Windows Server 2008 R2, SQL Server now installs all of its services, including Reporting Services, to run using virtual accounts. A virtual account is a local account on the server running under the NT Service account. SQL Server manages all this for you, and as you see in Figure 22-4, the installer has configured to run with the Report Server virtual account. When you have more than one instance of SSRS installed, their virtual accounts have the name of the instance integrated into the virtual account name.

➤ **Specific Account:** As an alternative to the built-in account, you can instead choose a specific Windows user account. This could be an account specific to a computer and entered in the format **<computer name>\<user name>**, or a domain account in the **<domain>\<user>** format. Avoid using the account of the domain administrator. This account has a greater set of permissions than are needed to run SSRS and could present a vector for a security breach. The account you select must already exist, Reporting Services Configuration Manager cannot create a new account for you. It does however handle the duty of granting the needed permissions to the account you select.

Before you set up a specific account, however, you must be aware of a few limitations.

➤ The account name cannot exceed 20 characters.

➤ If you specify a domain user account and run in a Kerberos environment, you must register a Service Principal Name for the ID you use on your Report Server.

Running SQL Server on the same server that is the domain controller is not advised. It sometimes occurs, however, especially in cases of a small development machine where a single server hosts everything. When you have that specific situation, be aware that built-in service accounts, such as Local Service or Network Service, are not supported as service accounts for SSRS.

After changing the service account, you are prompted to back up your encryption keys. You should be ready to do so because it is imperative these keys are properly backed up. Encryption keys are discussed later in this chapter, but for now be ready to back them up when prompted.

The Web Service URL

One of the great things about Reporting Services is its capability to integrate with other applications. Reports may be called as a hyperlink in a web page. They may be embedded in Report Viewer control in an ASP.Net or Windows application. All of this is possible because Reporting Services exposes its capabilities through a Web Service.

A web service is a program that uses a Uniform Resource Locator (URL) — a fancy way of saying an HTTP address — as its interface. When a formatted http command is passed to the web service address, the web service processes that request and returns data, typically formatted as an html page.

Web services can do more than just return data though. Using the SSRS web service, you can upload reports, execute them, run the report and export the data to a file, validate parameters, and more.

All these actions require you to use an application to interface to the web service. Some of the applications from Microsoft that can interact with the web service are Report Builder, SQL Server Data Tools, and Report Manager. You may also write your own application that interacts with the web service using one of the many .Net languages available.

To customize the web service URL for this instance of SSRS, use the Web Service URL page, as shown in Figure 22-5. The default URL is the name of the server, followed by the port number and then the virtual directory ReportServer, all of which are configurable.

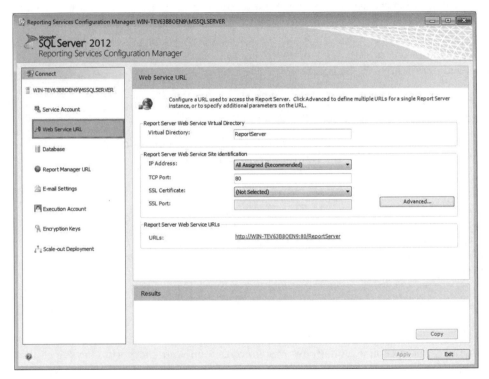

FIGURE 22-5

You can have more than one Web Service URL exposed by Reporting Services. To do so, use the Advanced button and add additional URLs to this server. Reporting Services also supports secure connections via SSL. Simply specify the SSL certificate and port number.

One of the first places you'll likely use the web service URL is within SQL Server Data Tools (SSDT, also known as Business Intelligence Developer Studio [BIDS] in former versions of SQL Server). From within SSDT you can deploy your reports to the report server. To do so you first must go to the properties page for the report project. One of the properties is the target server; it is the Web Service URL you use for this property.

Figure 22-6 shows an example of what you see if you try to navigate to the web service URL from within your web browser. It is a simple listing of the reports, with links that enable you to open or drill down into folders. This can be a good way to validate the web service URLs you use in your applications but it is a terrible interface for the average user. Fortunately, Microsoft provides a complete solution for users to interface with SSRS in the form of Report Manager, which is covered in-depth in the "Report Manager" section later in this chapter.

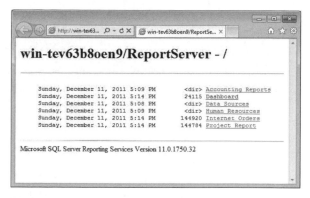

FIGURE 22-6

Reporting Services Databases

Reporting Services requires two databases to do its work. You can create these during the installation of Reporting Services or afterward using the Reporting Services Configuration Manager. By default, these databases are named ReportServer and ReportServerTempDB, although these may be renamed during their creation. Figure 22-7 shows the configuration screen for setting up these databases.

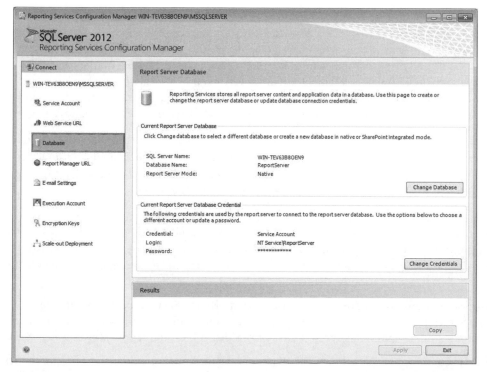

FIGURE 22-7

In Figure 22-8, you can see these databases are visible inside SQL Server Management Studio.

FIGURE 22-8

The ReportServer database stores all the reports, as well as data source information, logins, subscriptions, and more. All sensitive data is encrypted using the encryption keys, a topic covered in the "Encryption Keys" section of this chapter.

As its name implies, ReportServerTempDB holds temporary information for Reporting Services. Cached reports are one example of an entity that is stored. If you had a report that was used by many users — perhaps a morning status report — you could have that report generated and cached so that the report accesses only the source database once. Users executing the report would see the cached report, instead of having to completely regenerate it on each execution. When the cache time expires, the report is flushed from the ReportServerTempDB cache.

Important distinctions exist between the two databases you need to be aware of. It's vital that the ReportServer database be backed up because it contains all your information about the reports hosted on this instance of SQL Server Reporting Services. If a restore is needed, you can restore this database much as you would any other. After restoring it, you need to restore the encryption keys for the encrypted information to be decipherable by Reporting Services.

The ReportServerTempDB is quite the opposite. All data within the temporary database can be deleted without permanent damage to your SSRS installation. It would require, however, all reports with caching enabled to be rerun and cached because the cache would be lost if ReportServerTempDB goes away.

For disaster recovery purposes you have two options. First, you can chose to back up ReportServerTempDB along with ReportServer. However, the temporary database typically grows fairly large and can consume a lot of time and disc space in backups. For that reason many users go with the option to generate a script to create ReportServerTempDB. If a recovery occurs then the script is run, and if necessary any reports that need to be cached can be executed. To create a script, simply right-click the ReportServerTempDB database name, select Script Database As ➪ Create To ➪ File, and save the output.

The names ReportServer and ReportServerTempDB are the default names for these databases. If multiple instances of SSRS are installed on the same server, the default names are appended with an underscore and then the instance name. As a best practice, you should retain these names because that is what most SQL IT Professionals are accustomed to. You can, though, change these if the need arises.

To change the database, simply click the Change Database button. This brings up a wizard that provides two options: connect to an existing database or create a new database. After you select your option, the wizard walks you through a series of questions common to both choices. You select the server for the databases, the name of the database, the credentials to use, and so forth. When done, Reporting Services now uses the database you indicated in the wizard.

Although it's not uncommon to have the ReportServer and ReportServerTempDB databases on the same SQL Server that Reporting Services runs on, it is not required. You can elect to put the reporting databases on a separate server and have only SSRS run on the report server.

This flexibility is commonly used with a scale-out deployment. You can implement two topologies in this scenario. In the first, the ReportServer and ReportServerTempDB databases reside on a server containing a SQL Server database engine. Then, two servers are created that run only SSRS. Both point to the ReportServer and ReportServerTempDB databases on the database's first server.

The second is a slight variation that has only two servers. The first server holds both the databases and SSRS; the second runs only SSRS and points back to the first server for the ReportServer and ReportServerTempDB databases.

Although these are the most common two setups, you are not limited to only two SSRS servers in a scale-out situation. You could simply configure the additional servers to point to the central ReportServer and ReportServerTempDB databases. See the "Scale-Out Deployment" section later in this chapter for more information.

In a single server environment, if you chose to install and configure Reporting Services during the install of SQL Server, you generally won't need to alter the information in Figure 22-7. You need to understand how the reporting databases are used though, and how they can be configured within your server environment.

The Report Manager URL

SQL Server Reporting Services ships with an interface called Report Manager, which enables users to upload, configure, and run reports. Through Report Manager you can apply security to a specific user or to a group. Permissions can vary from as basic as having only the ability to run certain reports, to having full administrative control over the report server.

By default the URL is the name of the server, followed by the default port of 80, followed by the virtual directory name of Reports. This URL is configurable and may be changed on the page as seen in Figure 22-9.

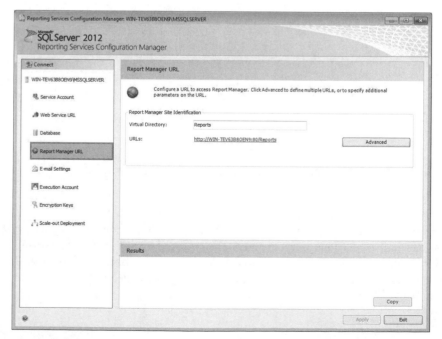

FIGURE 22-9

As with the Web Service URL, you can specify multiple URLs using the Advanced button of the Report Services Configuration Manager. For example, you may want to have one standard http style URL for internal use and a Secure Socket Layer (SSL) version of the address (https) for external use.

Report Manager is a big topic and is covered in-depth in the "Report Manager" section later in this chapter.

E-mail Settings

One of the options Reporting Services provides is the ability to set up e-mail–based subscriptions for reports. Users may elect to have reports automatically generated and e-mailed to them. To support this, Reporting Services must have access to an e-mail account. Figure 22-10 shows where to enter your e-mail information.

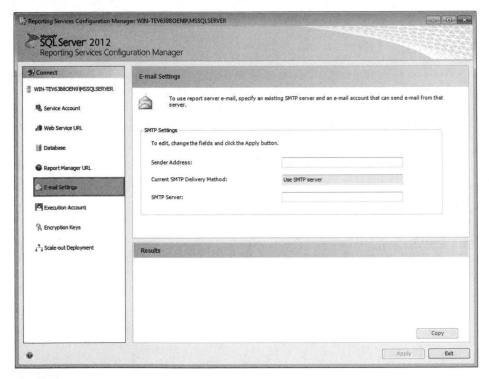

FIGURE 22-10

As with most accounts used with servers, you must ensure the account has a non-expiring password and that it has rights to e-mail the various attachment types supported by SQL Server Reporting Services. You need to take care with this ability however. Some reports can become quite large and flood your e-mail servers with attachments. Consider having reports generated and stored in a central repository and instead e-mail links to the reports.

Execution Account

There are times when a report requires data, but the credentials to get to that data haven't been stored with the report. SSRS needs a set of credentials it can use to try to retrieve the source data. Through the configuration manager (see Figure 22-11) you can select a specific domain account to use. This account then becomes the Execution Account.

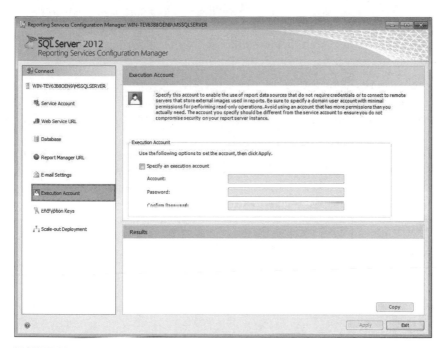

FIGURE 22-11

The domain account used for the Execution Account should have the least amount of required permissions for doing its job. For example, it should have read-only permissions to any source data used by the reports.

Reports also have the capability to display images stored external to the report. The Execution Account credentials access the location of these images.

 Don't confuse the Execution Account with the Service Account. The Service Account is the account under which all Reporting Services is actually running. The Execution Account is used strictly for accessing data or stored images when no other credentials have been supplied.

The domain account used for the Execution Account should be different from the Service Account. The Execution Account needs different and typically less permissions than the Service Account. By using different accounts you minimize your security risks.

Encryption Keys

Reporting Services requires a good deal of confidential information to do its job. Credentials, connection strings, and the like must be stored in a secure manner. This kind of sensitive data is stored in the Reporting Services report database, but before it is stored it is encrypted using an encryption key. Encryption keys are managed using the screen shown in Figure 22-12.

It is vital that this encryption key be backed up. If the Reporting Services database needs to be restored, either from a crash or moving the instance to a new server, you need to restore the encryption keys. Without doing so all the confidential information stored is unusable, and you are faced with the laborious task of re-creating all the credentials manually.

After you restore the report database, you can restore the encryption keys through the dialog, as shown in Figure 22-12. When restored Reporting Services again has the capability to properly decrypt the stored credentials, thus restoring the server to full functionality.

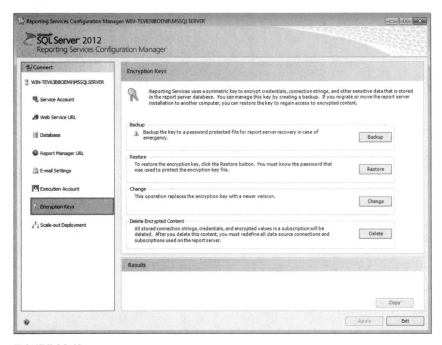

FIGURE 22-12

There may be occasions in which you want to change the security credentials. For example, you might have lost the backup of the encryption key which would present a potential security issue. Or you may have corporate rules requiring periodic refreshes of all your encryption keys. The change command in Figure 22-12 creates a new security key. Of course after changing the key, be sure to back it up.

You may also have the need to remove any sensitive data stored in the report database. You can use the Delete function to remove any confidential information stored by Reporting Services.

Scale-out Deployment

At some point the demands on your Reporting Services server may grow too large for a single server to handle effectively. Microsoft has provided for that situation through the use of Scale-out Deployment. In a Scale-out scenario, multiple servers can process reports. All the servers share a common Reporting Services database.

Before you start planning your Scale-out environment, you must be aware of some prerequisites. First, Scale-out is an Enterprise-only feature. Although you can also set it up in the Developer or Evaluation versions, this is meant strictly for learning, development, and evaluation and not a production situation. The Standard, Workgroup, and Express versions of SQL Server do not support Scale-out deployment for Reporting Services.

Next, all servers in the scale-out farm must run the same major version number and have the same updates and service packs applied. They must also be on the same domain or in a trusted domain. Finally, the servers must use the same authentication modes. If you have created any custom authorization extensions, the same extension must exist on the servers.

 Although not a strict requirement, it is best if both servers have an identical physical configuration or as close as is possible.

Now that you have met the basic requirements, it's time to configure your servers. This example uses the most common scenario; the first server has both SSRS and the ReportServer/ ReportServerTempDBs installed on it. The second server runs only SSRS.

1. Set up your first SQL Server Reporting Services server, as has been described throughout this chapter.

2. Next, install SQL Server Reporting Services on a second server. (Although you can install multiple instances of SSRS on the same server and configure them for scale-out, there is no benefit to doing so.) When you get to the installation step for SQL Server Reporting Services, select the Install but Do Not Configure Server option.

3. After installation completes, open the SQL Server Reporting Services Configuration Manager, and on the opening dialog, select your new server. Begin by going to the Database page, and point the database to the Reporting Services database on the original server.

4. Next, go to the Report Server Web Service and Report Manager pages and configure their URLs. Don't test them yet, however because they won't be available until you join this server to the Scale-out Deployment, which is the next step.

5. Close out your connection to the second Reporting Services server, re-open the configuration tool, and point it to the original server. Return to the Scale-out Deployment page; you should now see both servers listed. The original server should already show its status as Joined. Your new server should be listed; however, its status should read Waiting to Join, as shown in Figure 22-13.

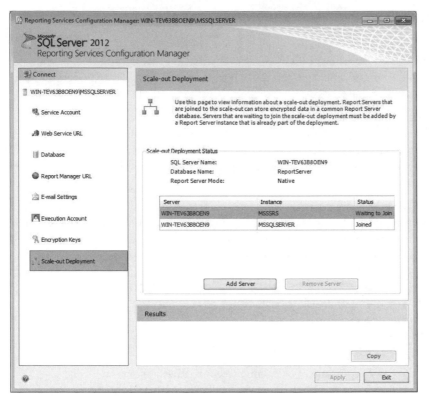

FIGURE 22-13

6. Simply select the new server, and then click the Add Server button. After it has joined, you can verify it by going to the Report Services or Report Manager URLs specified when you configured the new server.

Reporting Services also supports being installed on a network load- balanced cluster. If you do so, you must configure a few additional items. For more information, see the Books Online article "Configure a Report Server on a Network Load Balancing Cluster."

REPORT SERVER PROPERTIES

After you have SQL Server Reporting Services installed and configured, you may want to alter several properties. To do so, perform the following steps:

FIGURE 22-14

1. Start by launching SQL Server Management Studio. In the Object Explorer, click the Connect menu button; then in the list select Reporting Services, as shown in Figure 22-14.

2. In the connection dialog, ensure the server is correct as well as the authentication method; then click the Connect button.

3. When you connect, the Reporting Services server appears in Object Explorer. To access the properties, right-click the server name, and select Properties, as shown in Figure 22-15.

General Properties Page

The server properties dialog has a number of pages, listed on the left side, that enable you to explore and alter the settings within the Reporting Services server. Start by looking

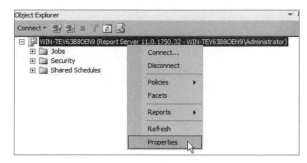

FIGURE 22-15

at the General tab, as shown in Figure 22-16. The General tab has a variety of options which are explained in the following list:

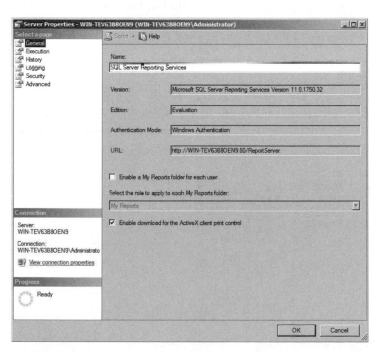

FIGURE 22-16

➤ The Name property is the name of the server displayed in Report Manager. As you'll see in the "Report Manager" section later in this chapter, the Name you enter into this property is used as the site title in Report Manager. Select a name that would be meaningful to the users, such as the name of your company or perhaps the department or application the SSRS server will be used by.

➤ The Version and Edition properties are read-only and simply display the information about the version of SQL Server Reporting Services.

➤ Authentication Mode is another read-only property, which indicates the types of authentication modes that will be accepted by this SSRS server.

➤ The URL is the http address for the web service under which SSRS can be accessed. The URL is set in the Reporting Services Configuration Manager, as shown in the previous section of this chapter.

➤ Moving down the dialog, you see a check box to enable a My Reports folder for each user. Within the Report Manager each user can have her own folder to work with. Named My Reports within Report Manager, a user can have full control to upload new reports, update existing ones, schedule them to run or execute them at will, and more.

If you choose to enable the My Reports feature, the Select the Role to Apply to Each My Reports Folder drop-down becomes enabled. This sets the permissions users have within their My Reports folder. Permissions are discussed more in the upcoming section on Report Manager.

➤ The final option on the dialog in Figure 22-16 enables or disables the ability to download a special ActiveX print control. This special control enables features such as print preview, controlling page margins, and other items common to print dialogs.

Execution Properties Page

The Execution page, as shown in Figure 22-17, controls how long a report can run before Reporting Services halts execution of the report. It has two choices; the first is Do Not Timeout Report Execution. Although this may seem like a good option, it is quite dangerous. If a report goes awry, it can remain in memory using resources until the Reporting Services server is finally restarted.

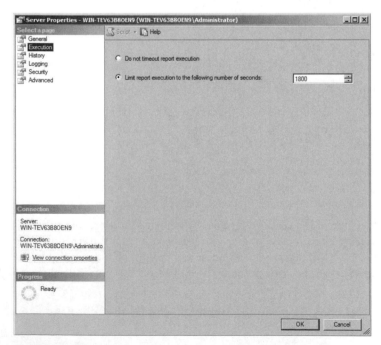

FIGURE 22-17

A better option is the default Limit Report Execution to the Following Number of Seconds. By default reports can run up to 1800 seconds (30 minutes) before SSRS halts execution of the report. In most situations this will be plenty of time, but it is not uncommon to have some reports that take longer to run. If so, you can increase the allowed run time through this setting.

History Properties Page

For any report, users can elect to have Reporting Services take a snapshot of that report and store it for historical purposes. Users can see each time a report runs, along with a copy of the report including the data associated with that particular run of the report.

Although this is a useful feature for auditing purposes, it can cause the ReportServer database to swell quickly if done on many reports. Through the History Properties Page, as shown in Figure 22-18, you can control how many historical copies of reports are maintained.

By default, SQL Server Report Services retains all snapshots of a report in history. You can instead select to limit the number of copies by choosing that option and setting a value for the number of copies to retain.

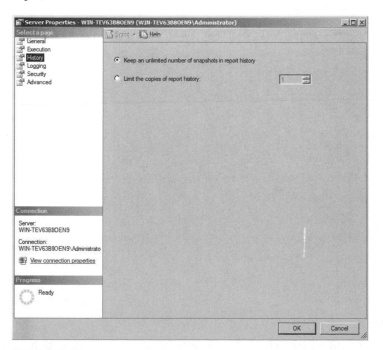

FIGURE 22-18

Logging Properties Page

Metrics are invaluable to a DBA in managing SQL Server. SSRS provides a rich set of information through its logging mechanism. Data such as the name of the report, who ran the report, how long the report took to execute, when the report ran, and more are exposed through views in the ReportServer database.

The next section examines the views in Report Builder, using them to build a useful report. For now, understand that you can control whether logging is done using the Logging Properties Page, as shown in Figure 22-19.

This dialog has two basic options. The first determines whether SQL Server Reporting Services does logging. The second option sets the number of days for which logs are retained. The default is 60 days.

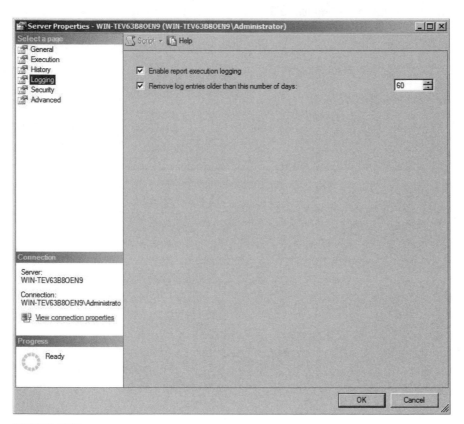

FIGURE 22-19

Security Properties Page

There are two options for working with security at the Reporting Services server level, as shown in Figure 22-20. The first specifies whether a report is allowed to connect to its data source using the security credentials of the user trying to run the report. When disabled, users can either supply credentials manually (the report must have the credentials stored with it) or no authorization needs to be given to allow access to the source data.

The second option, Enable Ad Hoc Reporting, sets whether a user can perform ad hoc queries from a Report Builder report when new reports are automatically generated when a user clicks data. Leaving this enabled can be a security risk. Turning it off mitigates denial-of-service attacks from hackers attempting to overload the report server.

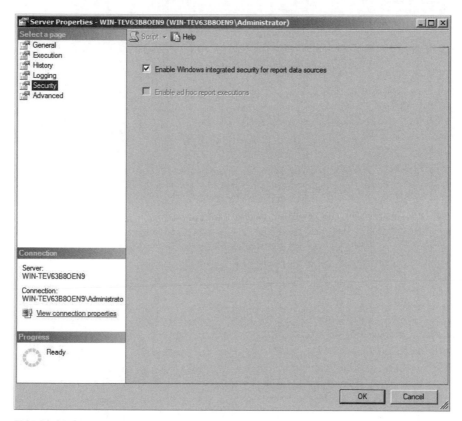

FIGURE 22-20

Advanced Properties Page

The final page of the Reporting Services server properties is the Advanced Page. As you can see in Figure 22-21, this page provides a single place to configure all the properties. Many of these may also be set on the previous pages. For example, the first line, EnableMyReports, may also be set on the General Properties Page.

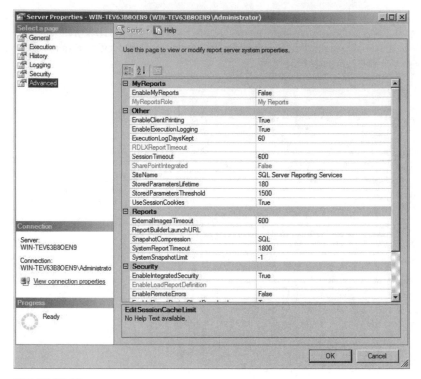

FIGURE 22-21

For details on each individual option, see Books Online at `http://technet.microsoft.com/en-us/library/bb934303(SQL.110).aspx`.

THE REPORT EXECUTION LOG

In the previous section you saw the option to turn execution logging on and off. In this section, you see what is in the report execution log. To get started, follow these steps:

1. Open SQL Server Management Studio, and connect to the Database Engine where the ReportServer database is stored. By default the database has the name ReportServer, and that's how you can refer to it here. However, if you changed the name during the install or using the Reporting Services Configuration Manager, select the database you named.

2. Within the Views branch are three views directly related to logging: ExecutionLog, ExecutionLog2, and ExecutionLog3. Each contains the same basic information — the ID of the report, the server instance the report ran on, how long it took to run the report, who ran the report, and so forth. The second and third versions of the view extend the amount of information returned. Figure 22-22 shows an example of the three views, with the first one expanded to show its columns.

FIGURE 22-22

You can create a SQL statement to extract data from the view. This statement is the basis for a report you create in the next section. The view contains most of the information you need; the only missing element is the name of the reports, which you can find in the dbo. Catalog table. Listing 22-1 shows the query that provides the information you need.

Available for
download on
Wrox.com

LISTING 22-1: SQL Script to Display Basic Error Log Information

```
SELECT [InstanceName]
    , C.[Path] AS [ReportFolder]
    , C.[Name] AS [ReportName]
    , [UserName]
    , CASE [RequestType]
        WHEN 0 THEN 'Interactive Report'
        ELSE 'Subscription Report'
        END AS [ReportType]
    , [TimeStart]
    , [TimeEnd]
    , [TimeDataRetrieval] AS [TimeDataRetrievalMilliseconds]
    , [TimeProcessing] AS [TimeProcessingMilliseconds]
    , [TimeRendering] AS [TimeRenderingMilliseconds]
    , CASE [Source]
```

continues

LISTING 22-1 *(continued)*

```
            WHEN 1 THEN 'Live'
            WHEN 2 THEN 'Cache'
            WHEN 3 THEN 'Snapshot'
            WHEN 4 THEN 'History'
            WHEN 5 THEN 'Ad Hoc'
            WHEN 6 THEN 'Session'
            WHEN 7 THEN 'RDCE'
            ELSE 'Other'
            END AS [ReportSource]
    , [Status]
    , [ByteCount]
    , [RowCount]
FROM [ReportServer].[dbo].[ExecutionLog] E
JOIN [ReportServer].[dbo].[Catalog] C ON E.ReportID = C.ItemID
```

Figure 22-23 shows the output of the query, as shown in SQL Server Management Studio.

	InstanceName	ReportFolder	ReportName	UserName	ReportT...	TimeStart	TimeEnd	TimeDataRetrievalMilliseconds	TimeProcessingMillisecon
1	WIN-TEV63B...	/Dashboard	Dashboard	WIN-TE...	Interacti...	2011-12-11 17:15:48.433	2011-12-11 17:15:50.983	1635	531
2	WIN-TEV63B...	/Product Names	Product Names	WIN-TE...	Interacti...	2012-01-06 12:23:05.297	2012-01-06 12:23:08.747	289	1347
3	WIN-TEV63B...	/Product Names	Product Names	WIN-TE...	Interacti...	2012-01-06 12:24:59.647	2012-01-06 12:24:59.683	1	10
4	WIN-TEV63B...	/Products	Products	WIN-TE...	Interacti...	2012-01-06 12:27:05.847	2012-01-06 12:27:06.127	98	86
5	WIN-TEV63B...	/Products	Products	WIN-TE...	Interacti...	2012-01-06 12:27:35.237	2012-01-06 12:27:35.307	1	37

FIGURE 22-23

This example shows a small sample of the information available within the execution logs. You can explore to see what further information is available. Keep this query because it will be the basis for the next section in this chapter.

REPORT BUILDER

To make the most of Reporting Services, you must understand how reports are created. There are two main methods: SQL Server Data Tools (formerly known as Business Intelligence Developer Studio or BIDS) and Report Builder. As SQL Server Data Tools could encompass a book of its own, in this chapter, you look at the simpler Report Builder in the following steps.

Both Report Builder and SQL Server Data Tools produce the same output: a file ending with RDL (Report Definition Language). RDL files produced in one tool can then be opened and edited in the other with no loss of formatting or information.

1. To start you first need to obtain a copy of Report Builder. It's a free download from Microsoft at `http://www.microsoft.com/download/en/details.aspx?displaylang=en&id=6116`. Alternatively, you can launch Report Builder from within Report Manager. For standard users this can be a simple way to access Report Builder. As an IT Professional, however, downloading and installing allows you to create reports and run them independent of Report Manager.

2. After downloading Report Builder, begin the install process. Most of the questions are simple, and you can take the defaults. The one screen you should be aware of is shown in Figure 22-24. It asks for the URL to the SSRS web service. This is optional, but if you fill it in now it can make deployment easier later. If you've forgotten the address, you can look it up using the Reporting Services Configuration Manager's Web Service URL, discussed in that section earlier in this chapter. After filling in the URL to use as the default, or deciding to leave it blank, you can finish the install wizard.

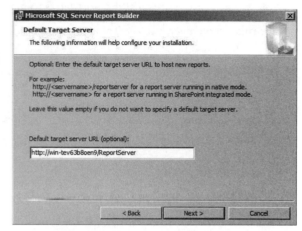

FIGURE 22-24

3. Now that you have Report Builder installed, it's time to create your first report. Before you launch the application though, there's something important you need to be aware of. If you run Report Builder on a Windows server, you get an Insufficient Rights error when you try to preview the report. To prevent this, simply run Report Builder in administrator mode. Open the Start Menu and navigate to the Report Builder menu item. Right-click Report Builder, and select Run as Administrator, as shown in Figure 22-25.

After Report Builder fires up and connects to the Reporting Services server, the opening screen displays (Figure 22-26). You can pick from quite a variety of options. In addition to creating a new report, you can also create a

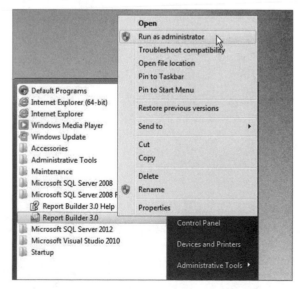

FIGURE 22-25

new dataset. A dataset is just what it sounds like; it defines a set of data that will be returned from a server. Think of it as the combination of a SQL statement along with the connection string needed to talk to the server. When you create a dataset, it can be shared across several reports. You also have the ability to open a report that already exists, and a short cut to view reports you recently edited. Now create a new report.

Within the options for creating a new report, you can create several types of reports. The Table or Matrix report creates a traditional text based report. The Chart Wizard creates a report containing one or more charts. If you need to display data geographically, the Map Wizard is for you. Should you want a blank slate to add report parts to manually, you can create a blank report.

For this simple over, use the Table or Matrix Wizard. To create a report in this manner, perform the following steps:

1. Select the **Table or Matrix Wizard,** as shown in Figure 22-26.

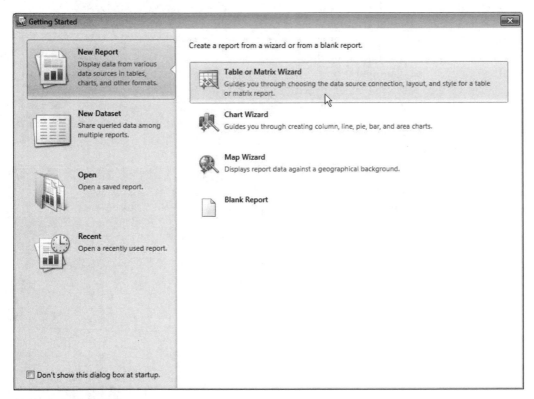

FIGURE 22-26

2. On the next screen of the wizard, shown in Figure 22-27, you are asked what dataset you want to use to populate your new report. To define where you want to get the data from, you need to define the data source, as shown in Figure 22-28.

FIGURE 22-27

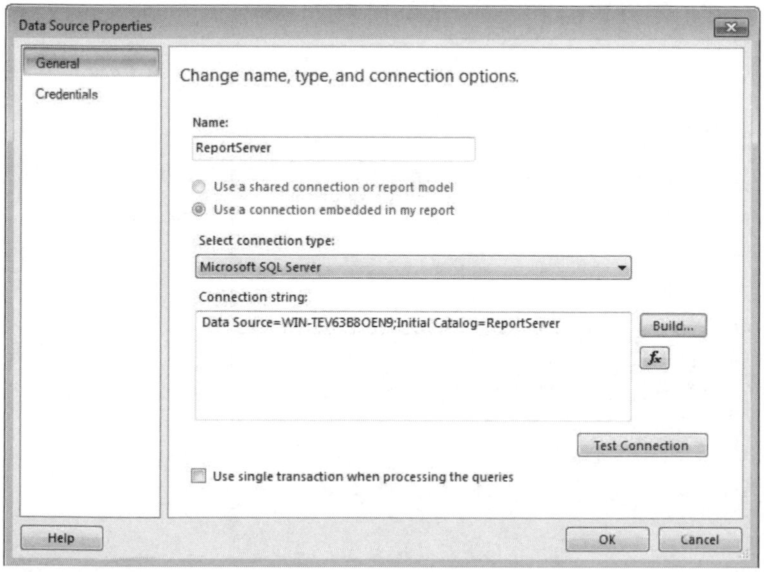

FIGURE 22-28

3. Start by giving the data source a descriptive name. Because this report gets its data from the reporting services event log, call it ReportServer. You can leave the connection type at the default of SQL Server; be aware though you can create reports from a wide variety of data sources.

4. Next define the connection string. To make it easy, you can click the Build button to bring up a dialog that lets you pick the server, username, and database name all from drop-downs.

5. For this report, pick the server where you installed the Reporting Services ReportServer database, and use the ReportServer database as the source. It's always a good idea to test the connection by clicking the Test Connection button. When complete, your dialog should resemble the one shown in Figure 22-28. Click OK to move to the next stage.

6. You are now asked what connection you want to use for the new data source. The data connection you just created should appear in the list; select it and click Next.

7. The next screen in the dialog, as shown in Figure 22-29, provides an easy way for end users to drill down into the available tables and views and select the columns they want to appear on the report. This is a great option for those unaccustomed to writing SQL. As a DBA you don't have that limitation, so instead you can use the query you created in the previous section on the execution log. If you saved the query, you may simply click the Import button and pick the .SQL file you saved the query to. If not, you can paste or type it in. (Refer to Listing 22-1 for the query).

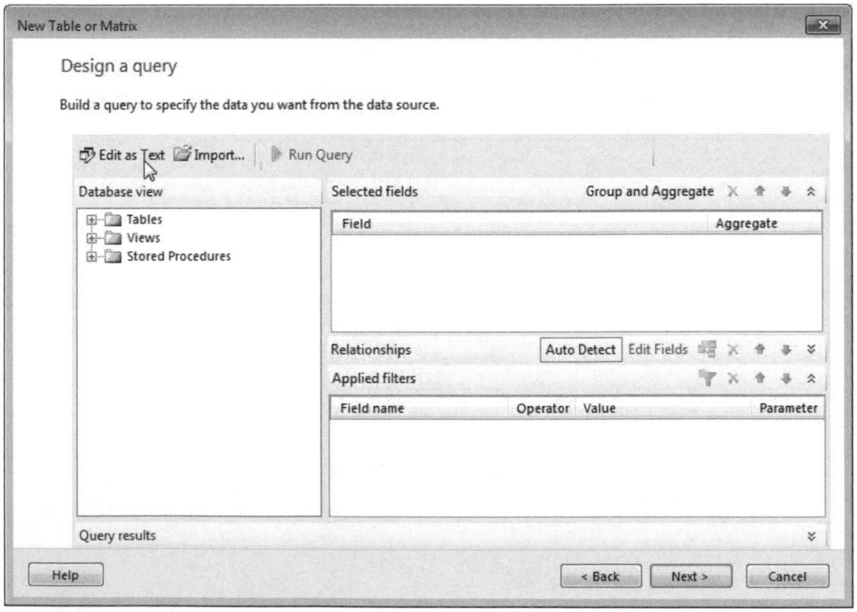

FIGURE 22-29

8. After entering the query, it is a good idea to run it, just to validate that there were no typos or other errors. To test, simply click the red exclamation mark at the top of the dialog. Figure 22-30 shows the dialog with the query entered and tested. If the results look correct, click Next to continue.

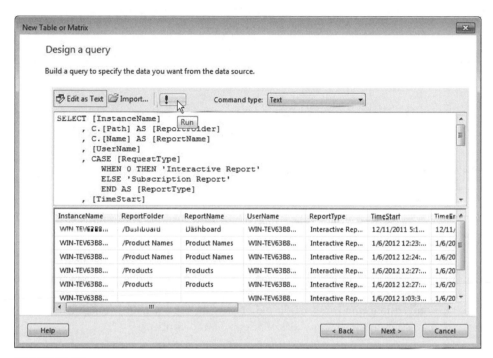

FIGURE 22-30

9. Next you are asked to arrange the fields in the order you want them. After selecting the fields to display on the report, you can group them by rows and columns. A common need for this report might be to group by instance name. Or, you may want to group by the report name, as you do in this example.

10. Drag the ReportName field into the area box Row groups. Next, drag TimeStart, TimeEnd, TimeDataRetrievalMilliseconds, TimeProcessingMilliseconds, TimeRenderingMilliseconds, ByteCount, and RowCount fields into the Values box. You are not required to use every field in your data source; for example, you can leave the other fields in the Available box. When your screen resembles the one shown in Figure 22-31, click Next.

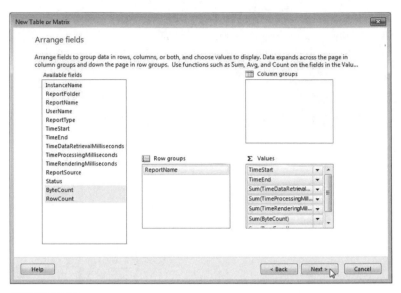

FIGURE 22-31

11. You are now asked how you want the report to be laid out (see Figure 22-32). You can choose to have totals, and if so you can indicate where you want them displayed. You can also allow the user to interact with the report by expanding and collapsing row and column groups. For this report, seeing the total execution time for a report might be useful, so leave the subtotals and grand totals displayed. There probably won't be much use in having expanding/collapsing groups, so uncheck that option and continue.

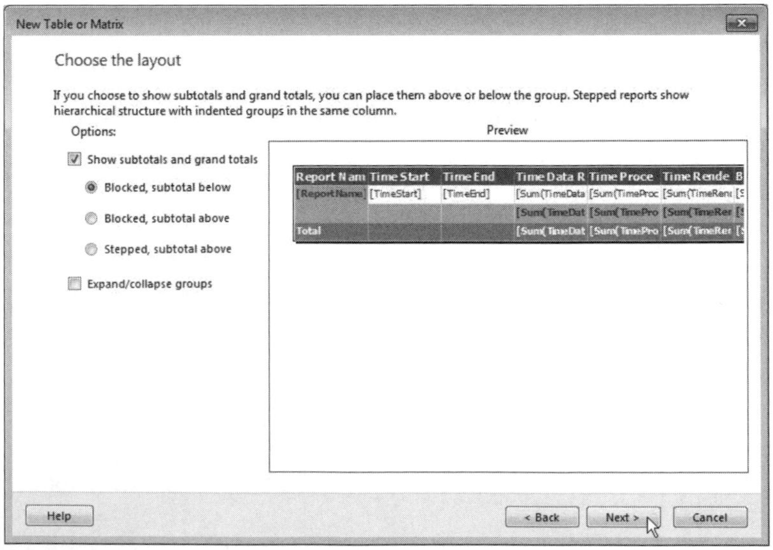

FIGURE 22-32

12. The final step in the wizard gives you the opportunity to stylize the report. The styles, shown in the left column on Figure 22-33, apply certain colorations and fonts to the report. If you don't want any special style, pick the Generic option for plain black text on a white background. For this report use the default of Ocean, but you can select one of the other colors if you want. When you have a color you like, click Finish to generate the report.

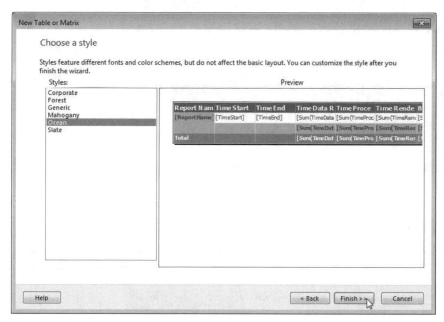

FIGURE 22-33

Now that the report has been generated, take just a moment to look around Report Builder. Figure 22-34 shows the generated report inside the Report Builder application.

Across the top is the toolbar. There are three tabs: Home, Insert, and View. The Home toolbar enables you to adjust basic things such as fonts, borders, formatting numbers, and the like. The Insert tab enables you to add additional components to the report. You can add data-driven items such as charts and graphs, tables, static items such as text boxes and lines, and subreports and report parts. The View tab is simple; it acts as a place to toggle the display of various areas of the Report Builder application. You can hide or display the ruler across the top, as well as the Row and Column groups at the bottom. You can also hide the Report Data area to the left.

In the Report Data area, you can add images, new data sources, or grab fields that you didn't originally put on the report. You can also add parameters, so users can narrow down the data they want to see, as well as access built-in fields such as the page number or report run time.

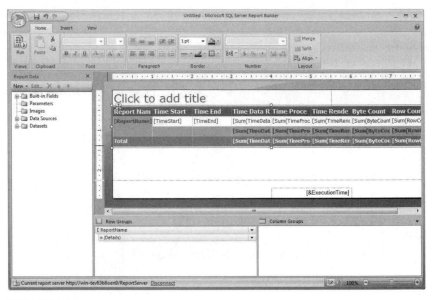

FIGURE 22-34

Now that the report is completed, you can test it before deploying it to your server. On the Home tab, click the Run button. The report executes, and you should see results similar to those in Figure 22-35. (If you didn't run Report Builder as an administrator, this is where you would see the insufficient rights error.)

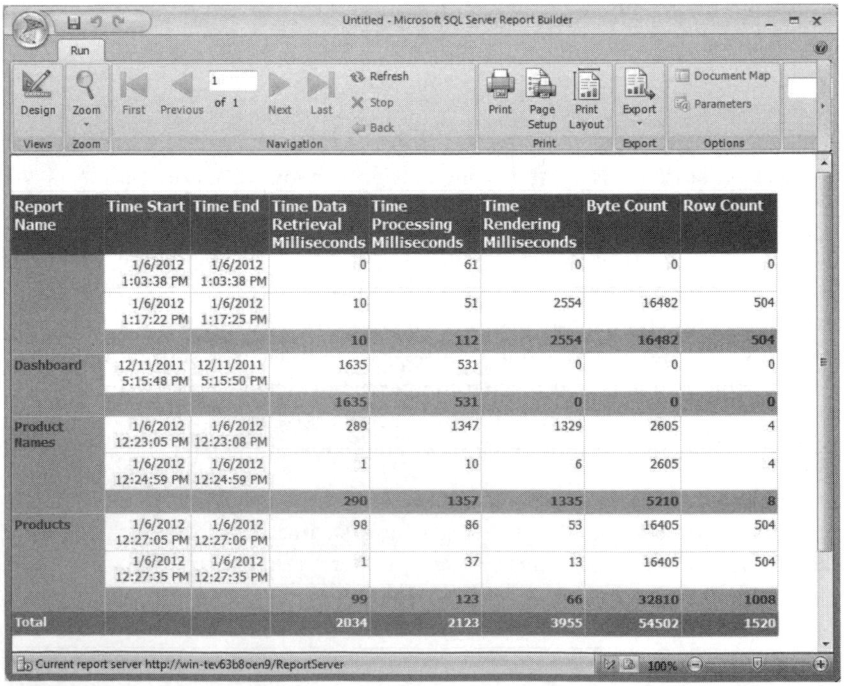

Report Name	Time Start	Time End	Time Data Retrieval Milliseconds	Time Processing Milliseconds	Time Rendering Milliseconds	Byte Count	Row Count
	1/6/2012 1:03:38 PM	1/6/2012 1:03:38 PM	0	61	0	0	0
	1/6/2012 1:17:22 PM	1/6/2012 1:17:25 PM	10	51	2554	16482	504
			10	112	2554	16482	504
Dashboard	12/11/2011 5:15:48 PM	12/11/2011 5:15:50 PM	1635	531	0	0	0
			1635	531	0	0	0
Product Names	1/6/2012 12:23:05 PM	1/6/2012 12:23:08 PM	289	1347	1329	2605	4
	1/6/2012 12:24:59 PM	1/6/2012 12:24:59 PM	1	10	6	2605	4
			290	1357	1335	5210	8
Products	1/6/2012 12:27:05 PM	1/6/2012 12:27:06 PM	98	86	53	16405	504
	1/6/2012 12:27:35 PM	1/6/2012 12:27:35 PM	1	37	13	16405	504
			99	123	66	32810	1008
Total			2034	2123	3955	54502	1520

FIGURE 22-35

Assuming everything went well, you should now save your hard work. Clicking the Save icon in the upper-left corner of Report Builder opens your save dialog. From here, you can either save to the local hard drive or to the Reporting Services server.

To save to the server, use the web services URL as described in the section, "Reporting Services Configuration Manager." Give the report a good name; for this example use `Reporting Services Execution Log.rdl`, as shown in Figure 22-36.

Report Builder is a powerful tool; you just scratched the surface of what it can do. For more information on Report Builder, see John Wiley's *Professional SQL Server 2012*

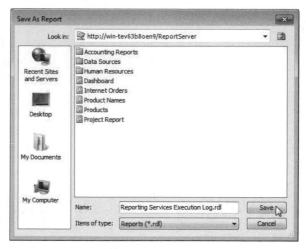

FIGURE 22-36

Reporting Services (Turley et al., 2012). Explore its capabilities; it can be a useful tool to you as a DBA. With it you can create reports to diagnose the health of the server and have those reports generated and sent to you every day, as you see in the next section on Report Manager.

REPORT MANAGER

In the previous section you learned how to use Report Builder to generate reports. After a report generates, it is ready to be passed to SQL Server Reporting Services so it can be managed. You need to use the Report Manager tool to do this.

The Report Manager is a web interface that both IT professionals and end users can use to manage and execute their collection of reports. You get to the Report Manager by opening Internet Explorer (or similar web browser) and going to the URL specified on the Report Manager URL page of the Reporting Services Configuration Manager. From here you can do a lot, but specifically you can perform three main types of tasks:

➤ From within SQL Server Data Tools you can organize reports into report projects. You can then deploy these reports from within SQL Server Data Tools to the Reporting Services server via the web services URL designated in the Reporting Services Configuration Manager.

➤ As described in the previous section, you can save reports from Report Builder directly to the Reporting Services server via the web service URL.

➤ Report Manager has the capability to upload a report to it from a disc drive.

As mentioned earlier, SQL Server Data Tools is too big a subject to cover here. In the previous section you saw how to save a report from Report Builder; in this section you take a look at uploading and managing a report within Report Manager. Before that though, you need to see how to manage Report Manager.

Managing Report Manager

Report Manager has the same quirk as Report Builder; for all the features to work correctly, you must run it in administrator mode. Just as you did with Report Builder, find the Internet Explorer icon on your Start menu, right-click it, and select Run as Administrator.

When IE is open, navigate to the Report Manager URL. Your screen should be similar to the one shown in Figure 22-37; although, don't be alarmed if it doesn't match exactly. The Figure examples in this section have a few extra reports and folders for demo purposes, in addition to the Reporting Services Execution Log you created in the previous section on Report Builder.

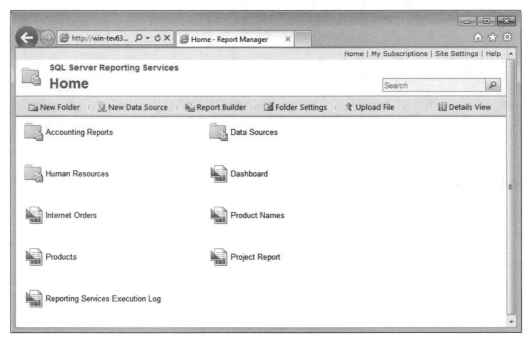

FIGURE 22-37

The Navigation Menu

In the upper-right corner of Figure 22-37 is a navigation menu. The Home option brings you back to the home page, as shown in Figure 22-37. My Subscriptions brings users to their private report storage area. If My Subscriptions is turned off, this does not appear to the users.

The Site Settings menu option is for SSRS administrators only and is not visible to anyone but designated admins. The available settings, as shown in Figure 22-38, are a subset of the properties you can set from within SQL Server Management Studio. (See the section "Report Server Properties" for more information.) The Help option provides some basic help for the Report Manager.

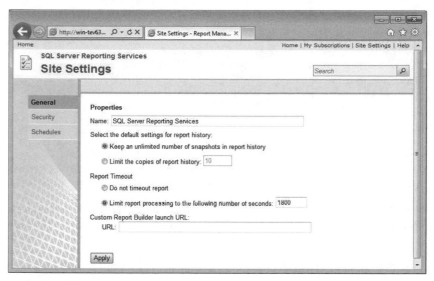

FIGURE 22-38

In the Site Settings, you should change the server name to something appropriate for your environment, if you have not done so already. Typically, this is the name of your company, but it may also be a departmental name. For test or development servers, it's a good practice to show that in the name of the server.

After you change the name of your server, or any of the other properties, you must click the Apply button, as shown in Figure 22-39. This is true not only for this page, but also for all the pages in Report Manager. Anywhere you make a change, you must click the Apply button, or your changes will be lost.

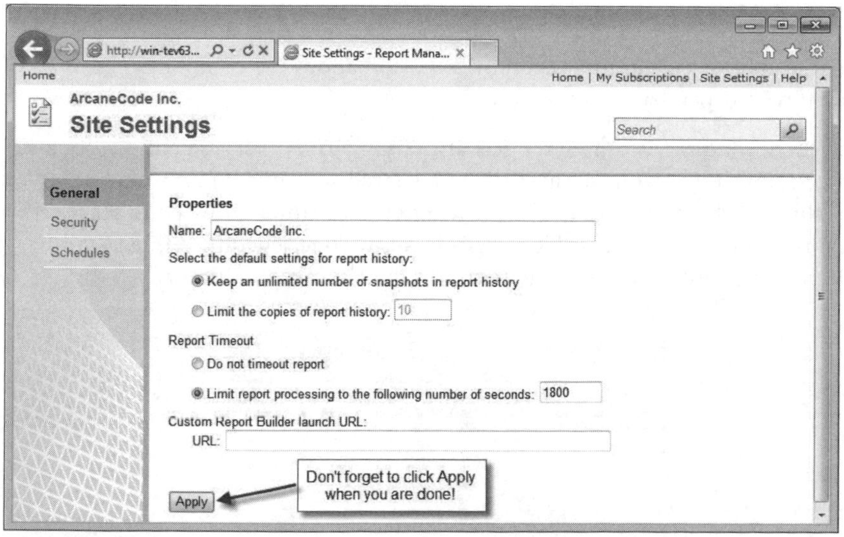

FIGURE 22-39

So far you've been looking at the General page of Site Settings, as indicated by the page menu on the left. Under it is another important page, Security. Through it you can add or edit users (or groups of users). In the screen snippet shown in Figure 22-40, you can see the two users listed for this server and the roles they have.

FIGURE 22-40

To add a new user, simply click the New Role Assignment button. A new page displays (see Figure 22-41); start by entering the Active Directory user or group name, and then check the role they should have. Choose from the two following User options:

➤ **System User role:** This is fairly straightforward. It allows the designated users to see but not alter system properties and shared schedules. They are also allowed to launch Report Builder.

➤ **System Administrator:** This should be given out only with careful thought. System Administrators can change any of the properties, add/remove users, reports, and so on. This role should be reserved for DBAs or similar IT Professionals.

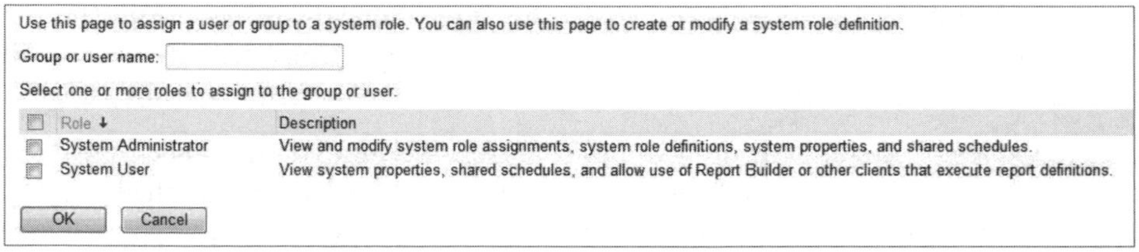

Use this page to assign a user or group to a system role. You can also use this page to create or modify a system role definition.

Group or user name: [   ]

Select one or more roles to assign to the group or user.

	Role ↓	Description
☐	System Administrator	View and modify system role assignments, system role definitions, system properties, and shared schedules.
☐	System User	View system properties, shared schedules, and allow use of Report Builder or other clients that execute report definitions.

[OK] [Cancel]

FIGURE 22-41

The Schedules page is used to establish a shared schedule for capturing snapshots of reports. Say you have three reports that have important financial information about the company. These reports may run several times a day, independent of each other.

For auditing purposes you need to run all three reports at the same time every day and store a snapshot of these. To accomplish this, you can first set up a shared schedule. Simply click the New Schedule menu option, fill out what time of day to run, what days to run, and when to start and optionally stop running the report and save it. Figure 22-42 shows one schedule named Daily Corporate Snapshot. Remember this as you see where to use this later in the chapter.

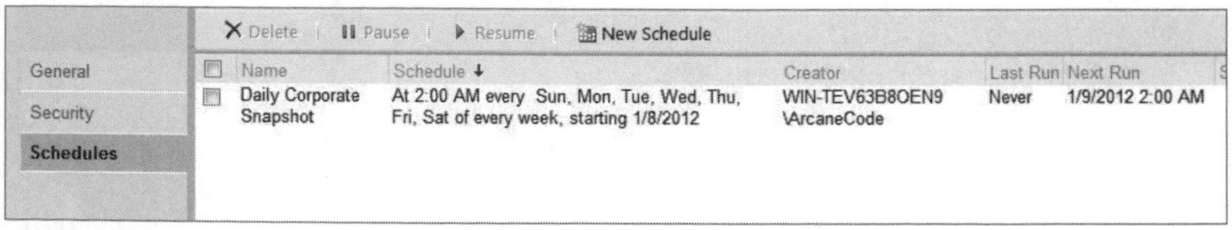

	✕ Delete	‖ Pause	▶ Resume	📑 New Schedule			
General	☐	Name	Schedule ↓		Creator	Last Run	Next Run
Security	☐	Daily Corporate Snapshot	At 2:00 AM every Sun, Mon, Tue, Wed, Thu, Fri, Sat of every week, starting 1/8/2012		WIN-TEV63B8OEN9 \ArcaneCode	Never	1/9/2012 2:00 AM
Schedules							

FIGURE 22-42

The Task Menu

Returning to the home screen (refer to Figure 22-37) there is a more prominent task menu across the screen. Starting from the left is the New Folder option. Report Manager enables reports to be organized into logical folders, similar to the way folders are used on a hard drive. When you move into a folder, the second line in the title will be updated to show the current folder name.

Figure 22-43 reflects the new name of your SSRS server and shows that you have moved into the Accounting Reports folder. This example also lets the user know there are no reports in the folder, a much better option than showing nothing and making the user wonder.

FIGURE 22-43

Next to the New Folder menu option is New Data Source. When you created your report in Report Builder, you started by building a data set. In creating that data set, the first thing you were asked was the data source. For your report you created the source and stored it within the report.

You had the option to use a shared data source. You can create a shared data source through the New Data Source option in Report Manager. Then you simply point to it from Report Builder.

Shared data sources make management much easier. If you have a group of reports that all connect to the same database, and that database is moved to a new server, the connection has to be updated only once, rather than for each report. Shared data sources also facilitate report development. You can set up a testing SSRS server, on which the data source points to a test database. When the report has passed all its tests, it can be uploaded to the production server that has a shared data source with the same name, but pointing to the production database. No update to the report would be required.

Setting up a data source, although straightforward, does require some knowledge about how SSRS works and how your reports will be used. As Figure 22-44 shows, you should start things by giving your data source a descriptive name. You can add an optional description to add clarity.

The home screen (refer to Figure 22-37), is displayed in Tile Mode. This is the mode most users use to interact with Report Manager. (There is a second mode, Details View, which is covered later.) You can suppress the display of a data source by checking Hide in Tile View, and it is common to do so. This reduces the number of items in Report Manager, therefore increasing simplicity for the users.

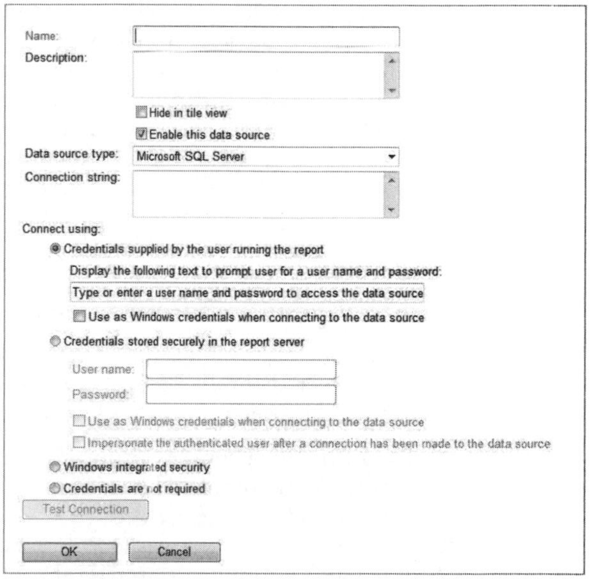

FIGURE 22-44

Moving down the page, you next see the Enable This Data Source option. As its name implies, you can disable and re-enable this data source from use.

The data source type is the next option. SSRS can access a rich set of data sources beyond SQL Server. SQL Server Analysis Services, SQL Azure, OLE DB, and Oracle are just a few of the many sources available to SSRS.

The connection string can vary by the data source type. For SQL Server, it takes the form of `Data Source=` followed by the name of the server. If the instance is not the default one, you also need to add the name of the SQL Server instance. That will be followed by a semicolon, `Initial Catalog=`, and the name of the database to get data from. Note the spaces between the words `Data Source` and `Initial Catalog`, which need to be there.

Thus, to connect to the reporting execution log for your demo test server, the connection string looks like

```
Data Source=WIN-TEV63B8OEN9;Initial Catalog=ReportServer
```

The next section, Connect Using, has four options. These have a big impact on how the report can be used on the server.

➤ **Credentials Supplied by the User Running the Report**

With this option, users are prompted each time they run the report to enter their credentials. The text of the prompt may be specified, and there is an option to use the supplied credentials as Windows credentials. Most users find having to enter their credentials each time a report is run annoying, at the very least. Thus this option is rarely used.

A good example of where it might be useful though is in a facility where large numbers of temporary works are brought in for short time periods. Setting up Active Directory accounts for all those users is not practical. This option becomes even more beneficial when the workers share a common PC, for example on a manufacturing floor production floor where maintenance is done. A handful of IDs could be created and shared among a group of workers. When maintenance people run the report, they enters a generic credential for all maintenance people, and the report displays only the data that job role is allowed to see. Likewise, a shift supervisor would see only data they are allowed, and so on.

When this method of authentication is used, the report cannot be set up for unattended execution. You see more on unattended execution in a moment.

➤ **Credentials Stored Securely in the Report Server**

With this option you must enter a specific set of credentials to run the report with. This may be SQL Server ID or an Active Directory ID. If an Active Directory ID is used you should also check the Use as Windows Credentials option.

By default the data source cannot see the Windows user as the person making the request, but rather the ID supplied here. This is good when you don't need user-specific security around the data being accessed. If, however, you do require the data source to know who the Windows user is, you can check the final option Impersonate the Authenticated User. SSRS passes the Windows user ID through to the data source, allowing it to return data based on the user's ID (or Active Directory group membership).

This is one of the two options, which enables you to run a report in unattended execution mode.

➤ **Windows Integrated Security**

With the Windows Integrated Security option, SSRS can automatically detect the Windows credentials of the user accessing SSRS and pass them along to the data source. This option cannot allow a report to be run in unattended execution mode.

➤ **Credentials Are Not Required**

There are some situations in which credentials are not required, or not even usable. A good example is a report generated from an XML file. XML has no concept of authentication. This mode enables unattended execution.

There are two basic methods for executing a report. With the first method, the report is executed on demand by a user. Commonly it is done via Report Manager, but it may also occur with reports launched from an application, such as an ASP.Net website. In this situation, Reporting Services knows who the user is and can pass their credentials to the data source. Refer to this mode as *attended execution*.

In the second method, it is SQL Server Report Services that launches the report. This occurs when a report is scheduled to be run or a snapshot is due to be created on a specific schedule. Thus the name *unattended execution* mode.

In this light the connection methods make sense. To run unattended, the credentials for the data source must be stored on the server or must not be required.

After you fill out all the information, be sure to click OK to save the shared Data Source.

You can set these same options for an individual report. You see where to do that in the next section; however, the connection options are identical for both shared and report specific data sources.

The third item in the task menu is Report Builder. This launches Report Builder for the user, and if Report Builder has not yet been installed, it installs it as well. See the "Report Builder" section earlier in this chapter for more information on how to use Report Builder.

The Folder Settings task enables you to set security for the current folder. The operation is similar to the site settings you saw in Figures 23-40 and 23-41, but specific to the current folder and by default any subfolders. The security options are slightly different though, as shown in Figure 22-45.

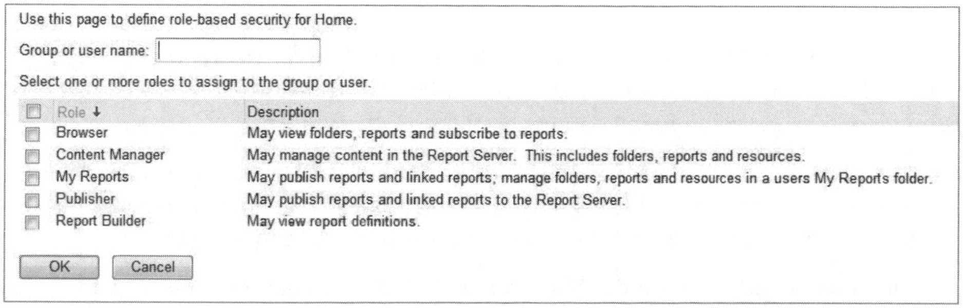

Use this page to define role-based security for Home.

Group or user name: [   ]

Select one or more roles to assign to the group or user.

	Role ↓	Description
☐	Browser	May view folders, reports and subscribe to reports.
☐	Content Manager	May manage content in the Report Server. This includes folders, reports and resources.
☐	My Reports	May publish reports and linked reports; manage folders, reports and resources in a users My Reports folder.
☐	Publisher	May publish reports and linked reports to the Report Server.
☐	Report Builder	May view report definitions.

[OK] [Cancel]

FIGURE 22-45

Microsoft did a great job on the screen shown in Figure 22-45, spelling out what rights each role has; thus they don't need much more explanation. A user may have more than one role, as needed. As with most security, it's best to start out with the most minimal right, Browser, and increase privileges as need.

In addition to saving reports directly to the server, Report Builder also enables you to save reports to a hard drive. This is a great option for reports that were built to run once and then discarded.

Some companies have tight security settings around their report servers. Users who want to develop reports must save them locally and then send the completed report (in the form of an RDL file) to IT where it can be validated.

To get the file into Report Manager, the Upload File task is used. It brings up a simple web page where a user can upload a report. When updating an existing report, the uploader must also check the Overwrite check box. This is a safety mechanism so that existing reports won't be overwritten accidentally.

In the section on defining a data source, you saw an option Hide in Tile View (refer to Figure 22-44). Although tile view is the most common way to look at reports, there is another option, Details view, which can be accessed by picking the last option in the task menu, appropriately named Details View, as shown in Figure 22-46.

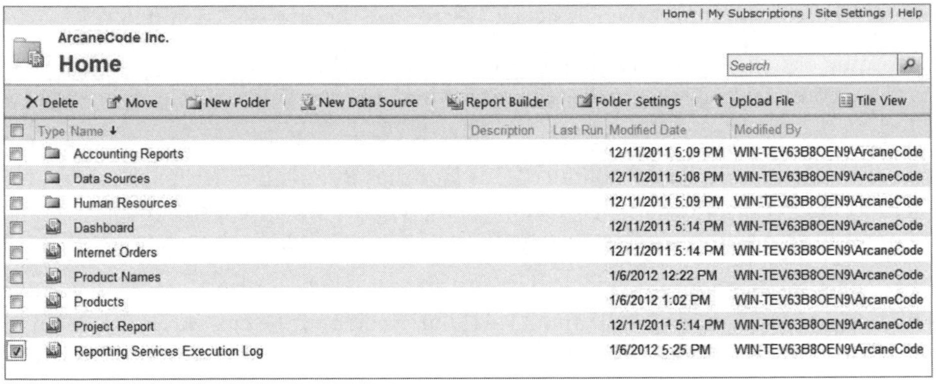

FIGURE 22-46

Details view provides additional information, such as the last run date for the report, the last modified date, and who did the modification. It also lists all objects in this folder, which might be hidden. This is how you can get to an item you may have hidden previously.

In addition, two more menu options appear in the task bar on the left: Delete and Move. When you check one or more of the objects, these buttons will be enabled, allowing you permanently delete the selected items or move them to another folder within the same Report Manager site.

So far you've seen how to manage the Report Manager, as well as manage the folders, data sources, and reports that reside in Report Manager. In the next section you see how to manage a report.

Managing Reports

Whether you are in Tile or Detail view, you begin by hovering over any report. A yellow border surrounds the report, and a yellow drop-down button appears on the right. Clicking that button opens up the report management menu, as shown in Figure 22-47.

Some of the options are self-explanatory. Move and Delete behave like they do in detail view. Download enables you to save the report or data source to your hard drive. Edit in Report Builder launches Report Builder and loads the selected report for you, ready to edit.

FIGURE 22-47

The main way to manage a report is through the Manage web pages, which you see in a moment. Subscribe, View Report History, and Security are shortcuts to pages contained in the Manage web pages; you look at those in context of the Manage pages.

The last option is Create Linked Report. This is analogous to a shortcut within Windows. It creates a clone of the entry for the report, but not the report itself. You can then change all the properties (which you'll see momentarily) in the Manage web pages. Thus you run the same report with two different sets of parameters, schedules, snapshots, and the like.

Creating a linked report is easy. After clicking the menu option, all you need to tell it is what you want the link to be named, and what folder you want to put it in. It defaults to the current folder, but you can change it if you want. From there you can alter any of the properties in the Manage area, as you see next.

Properties

When you open the Manage web page, you are greeted with the Properties page, as shown in Figure 22-48. By now you should be familiar with most of these properties and commands, having seen them in other places. The only new one here is Replace, which is just a shortcut to the Upload command. The only difference is Upload lacks the Overwrite if Exists check box. SSRS assumes if you are at this point, it's a safe assumption you want to overwrite, so it doesn't bother to ask.

With all the pages in the Manage area, be sure to click the Apply button when you finish. If you move to another page within Manage web pages without pressing Apply first, you will lose your changes.

FIGURE 22-48

Data Sources

The next page in the Manage area enables you to set the Data Sources, as shown in Figure 22-49. At the top, you can select a shared data source. (See the previous section for more information on setting up a Shared Data Source.) When you pick that option, it enables the Browse button; it is then a simple matter to navigate the folder structure and pick the data source you previously set up.

Alternatively, as shown in Figure 22-49, you can establish a data source specific to this report. When you do, the options behave identically to the shared data source.

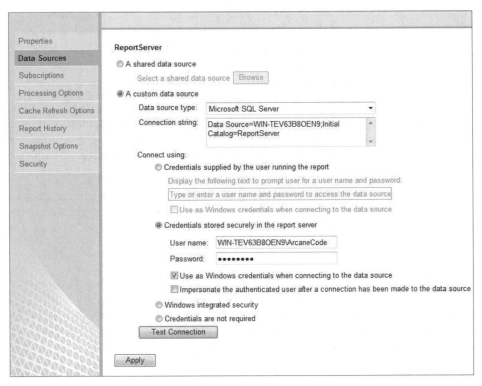

FIGURE 22-49

When the execution log report was saved from Report Builder, it used Windows integrated security as the default data source. To schedule this report, you needed to use a credential that allowed for unattended execution. Hence it was changed to store the credentials securely on the server.

 Whenever you make changes it is always a good idea to test, so be sure to take advantage of the Test Connection button.

Subscriptions

Subscriptions are a useful tool in SSRS; they enable reports to be generated and delivered to the users without their intervention. This is an ideal solution for long running reports, or when a report will be run on a regular basis, such as daily.

When entering the Subscriptions page for the first time, there won't be any subscriptions listed. You have two choices to create a subscription: New Subscription and New Data-Driven Subscription.

New Subscription

New subscriptions are run on a timed basis. When you select this option, you will be asked what delivery method you want, and when you want it to run (see Figure 22-50).

Assuming you set up an e-mail address in the Reporting Services Configuration Manager's E-mail page, you can choose between two delivery methods: E-Mail and Windows File Share. Figure 22-50 shows the E-Mail option and gives you the chance to set basic details about the mail: what format should the report be in, who should it go to, and more. The Windows File Share is similar; in it you set the path to save to, the format of the report, and the credentials used to access the file share.

On the lower half of the New Subscription page, you specify when you want the report to run. The first option enables you to set a custom schedule for this specific report. The second option enables you to use a shared schedule. Shared schedules are set up in the Site Settings area, as discussed earlier in this chapter in the "Managing the Report Manager — The Navigation Menu" section.

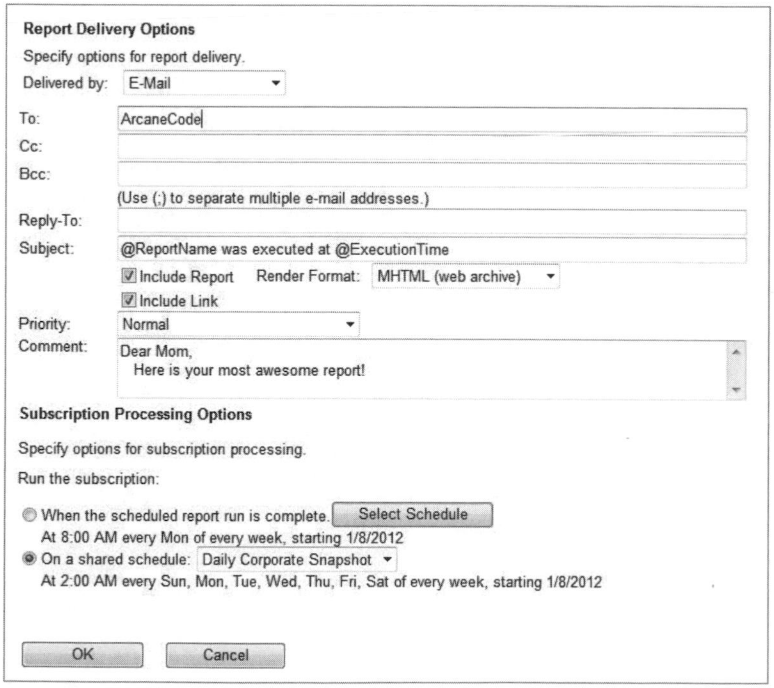

FIGURE 22-50

New Data-Driven Subscription

The second option is data-driven subscriptions. This is a bit misleading because the data referred to is not the source data. Rather it is data used to set options around the report at the time it is run. Who gets the report, how should it be delivered, and what format should it be in are examples of report execution options that can be pulled from data.

Before you can create a data-driven subscription, you must first create a table to hold the data you need. There is no set format for the table; the number of columns, column names, and sizes are all up to you.

Perform the following steps to create a table:

1. First create a simple table to hold data that could be used to drive either e-mail or output to a Windows file path. Listing 22-2 lists the T-SQL for the table. Where you store the table is up to you. In this example a new database was created called ReportSubscriptions.

Available for download on Wrox.com

LISTING 22-2: Create a Table to Hold Subscription Information

```
CREATE TABLE [dbo].[SubscriptionInfo] (
      [SubscriptionInfoID] [int] NOT NULL PRIMARY KEY
    , [SubscriberName] [nvarchar] (50) NOT NULL
    , [EmailAddress] [nvarchar] (256) NOT NULL
    , [Path] [nvarchar] (256) NOT NULL
    , [FileName] [nvarchar] (256) NOT NULL
    , [Format] [nvarchar] (20) NOT NULL
    , [Comment] [nvarchar] (256) NOT NULL
    , [ReportNameFilter] [nvarchar] (200) NOT NULL
) ON [PRIMARY]
GO
```

2. Next, put some data in the table. That's what the code in Listing 22-3 accomplishes.

Available for download on Wrox.com

LISTING 22-3: Load Subscriptions to the SubscriptionInfo Table

```
INSERT INTO [dbo].[SubscriptionInfo]
      ( [SubscriptionInfoID]
    , [SubscriberName]
    , [EmailAddress]
    , [Path]
    , [FileName]
    , [Format]
    , [Comment]
    , [ReportNameFilter]
    )
VALUES (   '1'
      , 'Brian Knight'
      , 'bogusaddress@somedomain.com'
      , '\\WIN-TEV63B8OEN9\FileShare'
```

```
                  ,   'Brians File'
                  ,   'IMAGE'
                  ,   'Hi Brian, here is your report.'
                  ,   'Reporting Services Execution Log')
           ,   (    '2'
                  ,   'Adam Jorgensen'
                  ,   'bogusaddress@somedomain.com'
                  ,   '\\WIN-TEV63B8OEN9\FileShare'
                  ,   'Adams Data'
                  ,   'MHTML'
                  ,   'Greetings Adam, here is your report'
                  ,   'Reporting Services Execution Log'
               )
           ,   (    '3'
                  ,   'Robert Cain'
                  ,   'arcanecode@gmail.com'
                  ,   '\\WIN-TEV63B8OEN9\FileShare'
                  ,   'Roberts Stuff'
                  ,   'PDF'
                  ,   'Hi Mom!'
                  ,   'Reporting Services Execution Log'
               );
```

Now that you have data to work with, you can set up a data-driven subscription. On the subscriptions page select the New Data-Driven Subscription option. Now walk through a series of steps needed to set up the subscription.

1. The first step is illustrated in Figure 22-51. After giving your subscription a name, you are asked about your delivery option; you can pick from e-mail or a Windows File Share. In the previous section on regular nondata-driven subscriptions, you used e-mail, so for this example use Windows File Share. The final option is to indicate the data source.

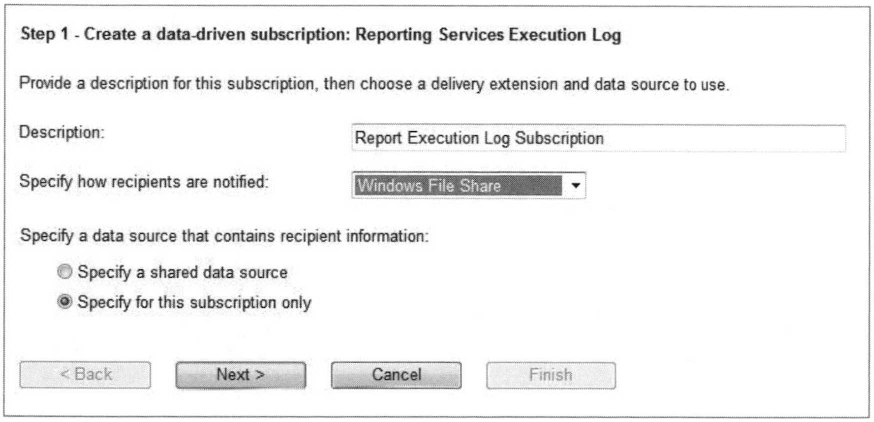

Step 1 - Create a data-driven subscription: Reporting Services Execution Log

Provide a description for this subscription, then choose a delivery extension and data source to use.

Description: Report Execution Log Subscription

Specify how recipients are notified: Windows File Share   ▼

Specify a data source that contains recipient information:

⚪ Specify a shared data source
🔘 Specify for this subscription only

[< Back]   [Next >]   [Cancel]   [Finish]

FIGURE 22-51

2. Because in the previous step the data source select was for this report only, you are now prompted for connection information, as shown in Figure 22-52. If you select a shared data source, this step would instead give you the chance to select an existing shared data source.

One annoyance: Each time performing this step, you must fill out the password. It won't retain it, so if you return to edit this subscription later, be sure to have the password.

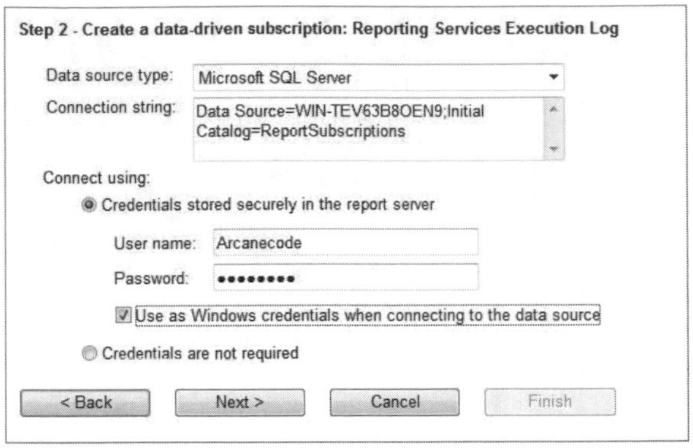

3. Now provide the appropriate SQL query to apply to the database

FIGURE 22-52

specified in the previous step (see Figure 22-53). In addition to the query, you can override the default different time-out if you have a long running query. Finally, you should always use the Validate button to ensure the SQL query you entered is valid.

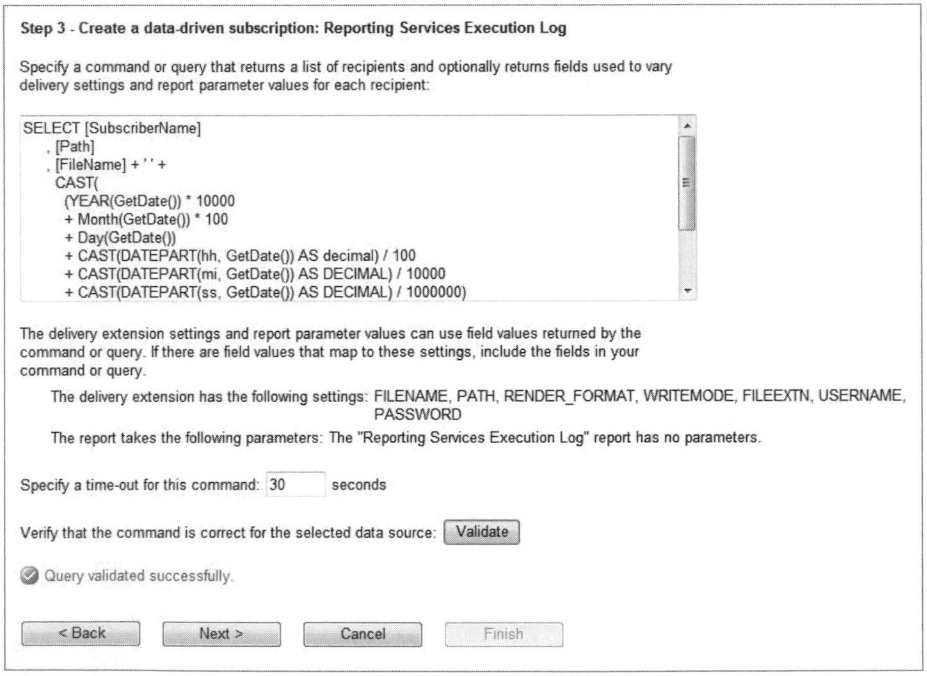

FIGURE 22-53

Because the screen is not big enough to see the full query, it is displayed here in Listing 22-4. When you run this query it returns the following information on the file share: where to put the output file, which filename to use, and what format the file should be in. Some date math is appended to the end of the filename. You typically want some mechanism to avoid duplicate files trying to be created in the target file share. The code in Listing 22-4 appends a number to the end of the filename in YYYYMMDD.HHMISS format. For example, 20121221.011221 would be 12 minutes and 21 seconds after one a.m. on the 21st of December, 2012.

LISTING 22-4: Query for a Data-Driven Subscription

```
SELECT [SubscriberName]
    , [Path]
    , [FileName] + ' ' +
      CAST(
        (YEAR(GetDate()) * 10000
        + Month(GetDate()) * 100
        + Day(GetDate())
        + CAST(DATEPART(hh, GetDate()) AS decimal) / 100
        + CAST(DATEPART(mi, GetDate()) AS DECIMAL) / 10000
        + CAST(DATEPART(ss, GetDate()) AS DECIMAL) / 1000000)
      AS nvarchar(20)) AS [FileName]
    , [Format]
    , [Comment]
  FROM [dbo].SubscriptionInfo
WHERE [ReportNameFilter] = 'Reporting Services Execution Log'
```

Incorporating the date into the file name is just one method of creating unique file names. You might also use a GUID, or have another process update the subscription table to have a new filename each time. Finally, you might have a separate process that removes all files in the share prior to the time the report is scheduled to run.

4. Next you need to supply information specific to the output method you selected. Figure 22-54 shows the screen for your selected Windows file share output. Values can be supplied from static text, as you can see with the file share ID and password. They may also be mapped from the query you ran in Step 3. The filename, path, and render format have all been mapped from the query (refer to Figure 22-54). Finally, you can decide to supply no value at all, as done with the write mode and file extension.

Step 4 - Create a data-driven subscription: Reporting Services Execution Log

Specify delivery extension settings for Report Server FileShare

File name
- Specify a static value:
- Get the value from the database: FileName

Path
- Specify a static value:
- Get the value from the database: Path

Render Format
- Specify a static value: Choose a value
- Get the value from the database: Format

Write mode
- Specify a static value: Choose a value
- Get the value from the database: Choose a field
- No value

File Extension
- Specify a static value: Choose a value
- Get the value from the database: Choose a field
- No value

User name
- Specify a static value: ArcaneCode
- Get the value from the database: Choose a field

Password
- Specify a static value: ••••••••
- Get the value from the database: Choose a field

[< Back] [Next >] [Cancel] [Finish]

FIGURE 22-54

The path must be in UNC naming format: `\\SERVERNAME\\FILESHARENAME`. In this example the UNC path to your file share (stored in the table, refer to Listing 22-3) was `\\WIN-TEV63BOEN9\FileShare`. If you had picked e-mail as your delivery option, then this step would have fields oriented toward sending e-mails. It would map the same way as you did with the file share in Figure 22-54.

5. If you had put any parameters on your report, now is the time to map values from your SQL query to the report parameters. This can be an effective manner in which to reuse reports multiple ways.

For example, a report could be created for each manager that would list the employees and total number of hours worked for the week. In the subscription table for that report, the manager's name, e-mail address, and department name could be stored. The data-driven subscription could map the department name to a parameter in the report, so only people in that department are on the instance of the report being e-mailed to the associated manager.

FIGURE 22-55

However, for the Report Execution Log report you created, there were no parameters. Figure 22-55 shows you that and allows you to move on to the next step.

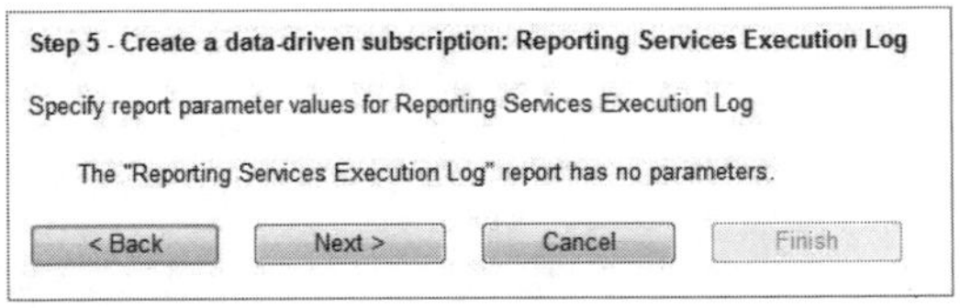

6. Next you specify when the report should execute (see Figure 22-56). The first option, When the Report Data Is Updated on the Server, is just as it implies. SSRS monitors the report data for updates and fires when it sees changes. This is useful when you have data updated on a limited, infrequent basis on an unpredictable schedule.

FIGURE 22-56

The other two options set the report to run on a time schedule. The lower option enables you to reuse an existing schedule (see the information on Site Settings in the "Navigation Menu" section earlier in this chapter). When either the first or last option is selected, the Finish button is enabled, and you are done.

If you select the middle option, you have one more step where you must set up the schedule for this subscription.

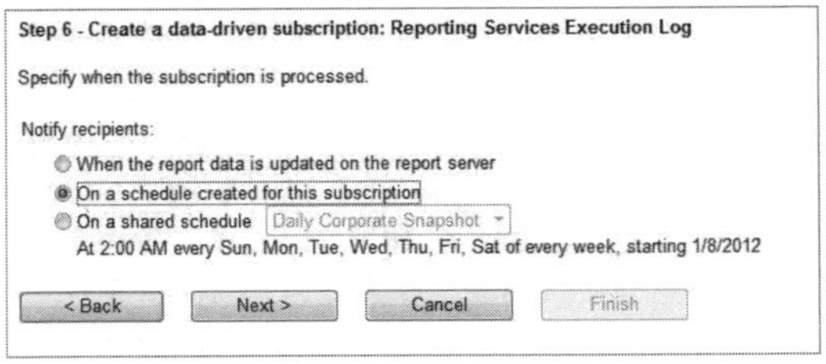

7. In the final step of setting up a data-driven subscription, you simply need to supply the information on when and how often the report should execute. Figure 22-57 shows there is a lot of flexibility when configuring the schedule.

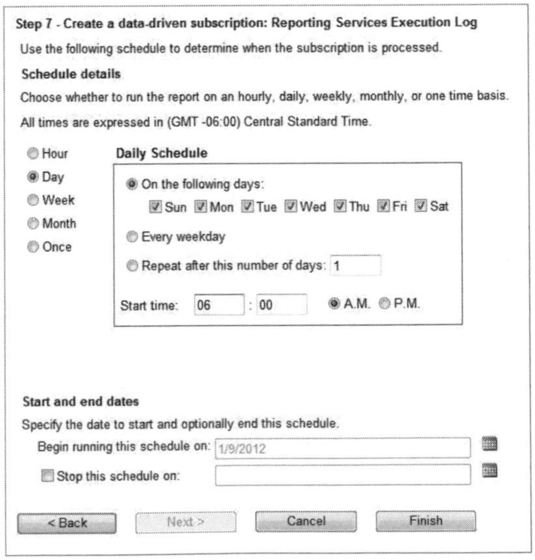

FIGURE 22-57

That was a lot of effort but well worth it. Data-driven subscriptions can be valuable when you need to run the same report many times, each time with different values for the parameters and processing options. Figure 22-58 shows the listing of existing subscriptions.

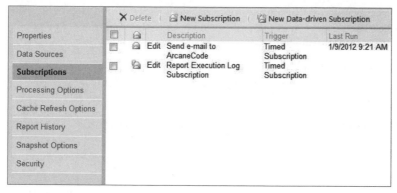

FIGURE 22-58

Processing Options

Figure 22-59 shows you a lot of different processing options, but they can be summarized as a choice between caching and snapshots. The report cache is for storing temporary copies of the report, whereas the snapshots can be retained for a specified duration. Users can see previous snapshots of reports, whereas cached reports are lost forever when they expire.

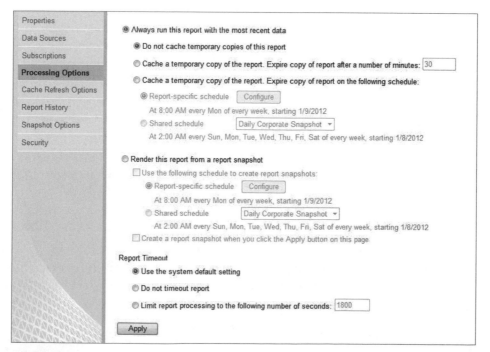

FIGURE 22-59

Of course, you can elect not to cache or snapshot reports at all, as the first option in Figure 22-59 shows. When you choose to neither cache nor snapshot the report, each time a user executes the report SSRS makes a call to the database to get the report data.

With the cache options, when a user runs a report, SSRS first checks to see if it is in the cache. If so, it returns the report from the cache instead of going to the source database. If not, it executes the report and adds it to the cache. The difference in the two options is simply when the cache expires: either after a set time or on a specific schedule.

The second option shown in Figure 22-59 enables the report to be rendered from a snapshot. As mentioned earlier, snapshots are copies of the report and its associated data that is stored long term. With this option you may also set a schedule for snapshots to be generated.

The final option enables you to override the standard settings for report timeouts for this specific report.

Cache Refresh Options

A report can get into the report cache in two ways. The first was discussed briefly in the previous section: processing options. When a report is run, if it is marked for caching but is not in the cache, it is executed and then added to the cache.

The second way is to set up a cache refresh plan, as shown in Figure 22-60. When you set up a new refresh plan, you are taken to a simple web page where you are asked if you want to create a specific schedule or reuse an existing one.

Using a cache refresh plan is a good way to ensure the reports in the cache stay fresh, while at the same time reducing the amount of time users must wait for the report.

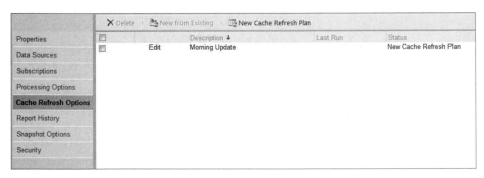

FIGURE 22-60

Report History

This section talked about snapshots and the capability of SSRS to store copies of a report as it executes. To view past snapshots of a report, use the Report History screen, as shown in Figure 22-61.

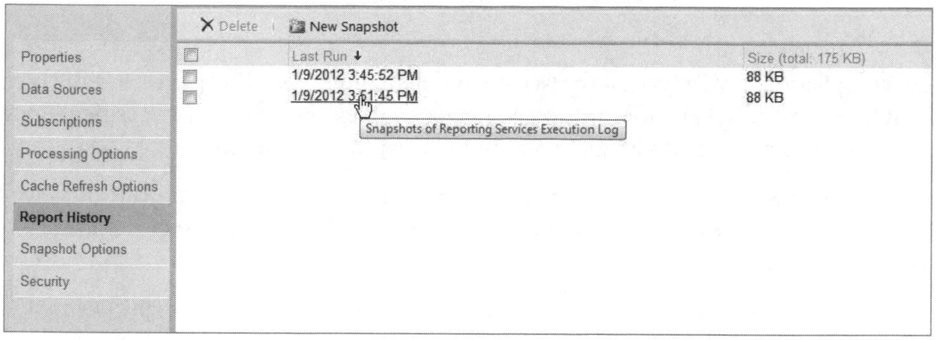

FIGURE 22-61

The Report History provides a listing of every snapshot of the report. To view one, simply click the last run date/time (refer to Figure 22-61). You also have the option to generate a new snapshot by clicking the New Snapshot button. This causes the report to execute immediately and be stored as a snapshot.

Snapshot Options

When you use snapshots you must manage them. Through the Snapshot Options, as shown in Figure 22-62, you can establish a schedule for automatically creating new snapshots. You can also determine how many snapshots should be retained.

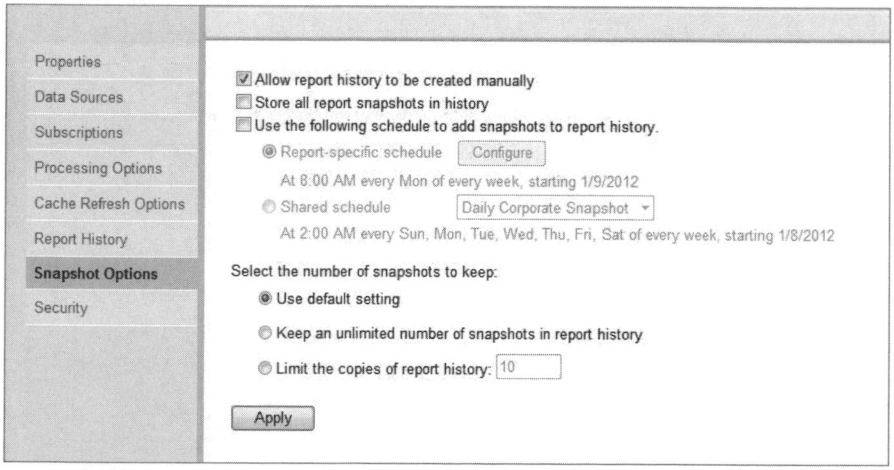

FIGURE 22-62

Security

Security is the final section of the Manage web pages. This enables you to fine-tune access for this specific report. The dialog and actions are identical to those for the folders, as seen in Figure 22-40.

SUMMARY

SQL Server Reporting Services offers a rich toolset around managing both the server and the reports it contains. The Reporting Services Configuration Manager enables you to configure critical options such as the databases SSRS needs to do its job, encryption keys, URLs, and more.

Using the properties settings in SQL Server Management Studio, you can fine-tune your instance of Reporting Services. Properties such as execution timeouts, logging, history, and security are set via SQL Server Management Studio.

Report Builder provides an easy-to-understand yet full-featured way to create the reports you'll house in SSRS. It can even be useful to you, the DBA, in creating reports from SQL Server management data, such as the SSRS execution log.

Report Manager is the tool of choice for managing and executing your reports. You can configure reports to run on schedules and be placed into a cache for reuse. You can also store and track them as snapshots.

With the understanding acquired here, the DBA will be well equipped to manage Reporting Services.

23

SQL Server 2012 SharePoint 2010 Integration

WHAT'S IN THIS CHAPTER

➤ Advanced Reporting and Self Service BI Capabilities

➤ Supporting SharePoint as a DBA

➤ Managing Data in a SharePoint Environment

With the advent of all the new features discussed in preceding chapters, Microsoft is leveraging previous improvements to SharePoint to enable increased SQL Server 2012 capabilities around business intelligence, performance, and office integration. Users demand faster access to changing data, and the business intelligence stack in SQL Server 2012 delivers that with some exciting new enhancements focused specifically at integrating with users' experience in SharePoint 2010.

SharePoint 2010 leverages the power and scalability of SQL Server to drive servicing content, configuration data, and metadata about users and security. The major area of integration for SharePoint 2010 is databases that support the service applications. This chapter dives deeper into this improvement, proving a look into the features of SQL Server that interact with and require SharePoint to experience their full functionality.

COMPONENTS OF INTEGRATION

When you think about integration in the SQL Server and SharePoint world, you are looking at service applications inside of SharePoint that interact with products or features in the SQL Server ecosystem. This integration has many components including service applications, SQL Server features, and new Reporting Services features such as Power View. The following sections cover each component in greater detail.

PowerPivot

PowerPivot is a free versatile self-service add-in for Excel. This add-in is used for working with large amounts of data within Excel and is great for BI professionals and also for DBAs working with performance data and other counters. The PowerPivot add-in in for Excel provides a lot of the capabilities of Analysis Services within Excel from a data sorting and manipulation perspective. The functionality of PowerPivot is greatly extended when used with SharePoint to provide an extension of personal BI, sometimes referred to as team BI. In either scenario use case PowerPivot provides users a simple, familiar interface for slicing data without the need for consolidating data into a data warehouse. Even with collaboration in SharePoint being the end goal, PowerPivot documents will be created inside Excel. In this PowerPivot environment, data will be imported, compressed by the VertiPaq engine, relationships built, KPIs created, and charts and graphs created.

When the initial creation of the PowerPivot document has been completed, it is saved as an Excel 2010 file just like any other Excel workbook. At this point the workbook will be uploaded to a SharePoint site for consumption by others inside the organization.

Using Excel with SharePoint

There are several requirements for setting up PowerPivot for SharePoint. This includes an Excel Services application to render the workbook in the browser for the user to consume. Additionally, you need an Analysis services instance for PowerPivot workbooks to run interactive queries. The Analysis Services instance is the main difference between the client and SharePoint versions of PowerPivot. On a client workstation analysis services runs within the context of the Excel application. In SharePoint analysis services requires their own instance.

Installation

Before installing PowerPivot, the SSAS instance name "PowerPivot" must be available. The easiest way to get PowerPivot up and running is on a new SharePoint farm installation; although you can add it after by doing the SharePoint installation and indicating you are doing the setup for an existing farm.

 PowerPivot for SharePoint is an Enterprise feature that requires the server to join to a domain. You also need to update SharePoint 2010 to Service Pack 1.

To install PowerPivot for SharePoint, follow these steps:

1. Run the SharePoint 2010 installation wizard, using either the Enterprise or Enterprise Evaluation edition.

2. At the end of the installation wizard, choose the option to configure the farm later, by unchecking the box indicating that the Product Configuration Wizard will be run after the setup finishes. This allows for PowerPivot and all the relevant database objects to be installed and then the Configuration Wizard kicks off by the SQL Server install.

3. After you install SharePoint (but before you configure it), download Service Pack 1 for SharePoint 2010.

4. Install SharePoint 2010 Service Pack 1.

5. Run the SQL Server 2012 Installation Wizard.

6. On the initial setup screen choose the SQL Server PowerPivot for SharePoint option. Optionally, you can choose the setting to include a relational database engine in the installation. When you check this option, the database engine installs under the instance name of PowerPivot. You can choose this to consolidate the databases or if you don't have an existing database engine. If a database engine is already setup, you don't need to select this option. Remember where the databases will be stored for SharePoint, another instance, or the PowerPivot instance. You need this information during the farm setup.

SharePoint Configuration

After you complete all the necessary SQL Server installation steps to create the PowerPivot instance (as described in the previous section) and after the farm configuration has been run, you need to create a new service application.

1. In Central Administration click Manage Service Applications to bring up a list of the service applications.

2. If you do not have a SQL Server PowerPivot Service Application present, you need to create one. From the New menu in the top left of the screen, select SQL Server PowerPivot Service Application.

3. Activate PowerPivot inside the site collection by browsing to it. Under the Site Collection Features section of the site settings, select Activate next to PowerPivot Feature Integration for Site Collection.

You must also set up an unattended service account to handle things such as data refresh. The security for this application account is very specific for the environment of your organization. Treat this as a regular application account that needs access to read data from your data source. The data source will likely be the SQL Server Analysis Services\PowerPivot Instance. To get started, set aside a location on the site to store the PowerPivot workbooks, which is known as a PowerPivot gallery. To create a new one, either create a site using the Business Intelligence Center or click Site Actions ⇨ More Options, and search for the PowerPivot Gallery.

From this point PowerPivot data refresh in SharePoint can be scheduled and restricted, the history retention settings can be set, workbook performance and use can be monitored all right from inside central administration.

 When first visiting a PowerPivot gallery, you may be prompted to install Silverlight. This should be acceptable as long as your corporate policies allow it.

Reporting Services

Reporting Services continues to be an integral part of the Microsoft Business Intelligence stack. With SQL Server 2012 a massive overhaul occurred on the Reporting Services SharePoint integration side. The main enhancement comes by way of a new SharePoint Service application for Reporting Services. Anyone who has configured Reporting Services for SharePoint integrated mode can appreciate this change.

Prior to SQL Server 2012

With SQL Server 2008 R2 and previous editions, Reporting Services was required to be configured as a part of the SQL Server installation and then integrated into SharePoint. This was accomplished by first creating an instance of Reporting Services, configured to run in SharePoint integrated mode instead of native mode.

One issue, although easily fixed, that would often arise is the need for the Reporting Services database to be switched from a native mode configuration to a SharePoint integrated configuration. This change had to be made through the Reporting Services Configuration Manager. Consequently, other settings would need to be managed here as well including the report server URL, the execution account, and email settings. Meanwhile all reports would be managed on the SharePoint side.

After the Windows Service was correctly configured, additional setup needed to be completed on the SharePoint Central Administration side. This final step was in place to tell SharePoint where to look for the Reporting Services instance as well as the authentication for connecting to it. At this point reports were ready to be deployed and viewed inside SharePoint.

SQL Server 2012 and Beyond

A lot has changed with SQL Server 2012; Reporting Services is now consolidated in with the rest of the SharePoint shared services. The biggest requirements for setting up Reporting Services 2012 in SharePoint integrated mode is SharePoint 2010 Service Pack 1. The first major difference in setup is now two options need to be selected on the Feature Selection page of the SQL Server installation: Reporting Services — SharePoint and Reporting Services Add-In for SharePoint Products. Following the completion of the installation, all further setup is handled within SharePoint.

Much like configuring other service applications such as Excel Services, in SharePoint 2010 Central Administration click on Manage Service Applications, click on New in the top left corner, and select SQL Server Reporting Services Service Application. All the settings that would previously have been entered in the Reporting Services Configuration manager can now be entered inside SharePoint. This includes specifying an application pool, a corresponding security account, and the location of the Reporting Services database.

While undoubtedly users can appreciate the ease provided by a consolidated installation and configuration process, this new approach provides even more benefits. As mentioned previously, the reporting databases have their location specified inside SharePoint Central Administration. This is advantageous because they can easily be placed on any server, including on the same instance as the SharePoint content databases, without the need to go outside the SharePoint environment. A Service Application is the name of an application that runs inside SharePoint. It is easy to set up multiple service applications for Reporting Services for use in the farm. When this happens each gets its own set of databases on the backend; they are not shared.

Improvements to SharePoint Integrated Mode in SQL Server 2012

Now that all the Reporting Services pieces for SharePoint integrated mode are contained inside SharePoint, the maintenance model will be simplified. Scale out can also be handled on the SharePoint side, rather than worrying about scaling Reporting Services and SharePoint.

Among the other enhancements is the dramatically improved report performance. Part of the basis for this improvement is that SharePoint no longer has to go to a separate Reporting Services server for information — it is all managed by SharePoint.

For farms with multiple servers, it is no longer required to configure the `rsreportserver.config` file on each server because this information is stored in the configuration database. Set the values once and all the machines can pick up the values. For information on how this affects licensing, visit the Microsoft Web site because the pricing model is always subject to change.

Power View

Power View is a new feature introduced with SQL Server 2012 in combination with SharePoint 2010 to provide interactive ad-hoc reporting in real time. Power View works with Developer, Enterprise, and Business Intelligence versions of SQL Server 2012 and requires an Enterprise edition of SharePoint 2010 and the Reporting Services add-in for SharePoint to be enabled.

What Is Power View

Power View provides a new innovative way to interact with your data by way of Silverlight renderings. These reports are developed and fed from PowerPivot workbooks deployed to a SharePoint PowerPivot gallery or the new tabular model deployed to an Analysis Services (SSAS) 2012 instance.

This is not meant to be a replacement for traditional Reporting Services reports or report builder. Power View is meant for ad-hoc data exploration, which is to say moving through your data and looking at how it relates across your business. The traditional file created by the current Reporting Services tools is a report definition file (RDL) and cannot be edited or viewed in Power View. Because Power View is also used only inside SharePoint, it is not applicable for use in every situation depending on the reporting needs. Each of these technologies has its place in the reporting environment.

Presentation Layer

Unlike a traditional Reporting Services report, Power View is an "always on" presentation type that doesn't require you to preview reports. The data is always live. There is also the added advantage of exporting Power View reports to PowerPoint where each individual report becomes its own slide. The full-screen viewing and PowerPoint slides work in the same way. Both enable interaction with data such as applying filters that the builder added or using visualizations. However, neither enables further development. In this state, the data is interactive, but you cannot add new filters or visualizations.

Some of the visualizations available in Power View follow:

- ➤ Table/Matrix
- ➤ Chart
- ➤ Bubble Chart
- ➤ Scatter Chart

➤ Cards

➤ Tiles

Creation

You initiate all Power View report creation from tabular model elements, xlsx files, or connection files pointing to BISM models, within SharePoint 2010 document libraries or PowerPivot Galleries. Clicking the arrow next to an applicable element can reveal an option for Create Power View Report. Selecting this option opens the Power View Designer. You can edit existing reports by clicking the drop-down arrow next to a report and selecting Edit in Power View.

When saving Power View reports, they are in RDLX format. The option to save corresponding images is also available. When exporting to PowerPoint, if you do not use the option to save images, only placeholders appear.

Service Application Architecture

Service applications refer to the new service application architecture in SharePoint 2010. Deep SharePoint architecture discussions are beyond the scope of this book. For more details see `http://technet.microsoft.com/en-us/library/cc560988.aspx`.

DATA REFRESH

As a SQL professional your job focuses on the ability to get data in and out quickly and efficiently. This is important for the performance of your data environment and the applications serviced by it. You've already seen a significant amount of DBA related items such as PowerPivot and Power View implementations in the previous section, but more is added here. This section focuses on managing and controlling data refresh with your reports and data in SharePoint. There are many possible data sources, so it is best to focus on those that typically come out of SQL Server, such as the following.

➤ Excel Services

➤ PerformancePoint Services

➤ Visio Services

➤ PowerPivot

Using Data Connections in Excel

Every Excel workbook that uses external data contains a connection to a data source. Connections consist of everything required to establish communications with and retrieve data from an external data source. These requirements include the following:

➤ Connection string, which specifies which server to connect to and how to connect to it

➤ Query, which is a string that specifies what data to retrieve

➤ Any other specifics required to get the data such as impersonation, proxy mode etc.

➤ Embedded and linked connections

Excel workbooks can contain embedded connections and can link to external connections. Embedded connections are stored internally as part of the workbook. External connections are stored in the form of Office Data Connection (ODC) files that can be referenced by a workbook.

Excel embedded and external connections function the same way. Both correctly specify all the required parameters to connect to data successfully. External connection files can be centrally stored, secured, managed, and reused. They are a good choice when planning an overall approach to getting a large group of users connected to external data. For more information, see http:// technet.microsoft.com/en-us/library/ff604007.aspx#section4.

For a single connection, a workbook can have both an embedded copy of the connection information and a link to an external connection file. The connection can be configured to always use an external connection file to refresh data from an external data source. In this case, if the external connection file cannot be retrieved, or if it does not establish a connection to the data source, the workbook cannot retrieve data to refresh what is there. The results of this vary based on the data connection settings. If the connection is not configured to use only an external connection file, Excel attempts to use the embedded copy of a connection. If that fails, Excel attempts to use the connection file to connect to the external data source.

For security purposes, Excel Services can be configured to enable only connections from connection files. In this configuration, all embedded connections are ignored for workbooks loaded on the SharePoint server, and connections are tried only when there is a link to a valid connection file that is trusted by the server administrator. For more information, see http://technet.microsoft.com/en-us/library/ff604007.aspx#section4.

 Excel Services is not available in SharePoint by default. You must turn it on and configure it.

Data Providers

Data providers are drivers that applications (such as Excel and Excel Services) use to connect to specific data sources. For example, a special MSOLAP data provider can connect to Microsoft SQL Server 2008 Analysis Services (SSAS). The data provider is specified as part of the connection string when you connect to a data source.

Data providers handle queries, parsing connection strings, and other connection-specific logic. This functionality is not part of Excel Services. Excel Services cannot control how data providers behave.

Any data provider used by Excel Services must be explicitly trusted by Excel Services. For information about how to add a new data provider to the trusted providers list, see http:// technet.microsoft.com/en-us/library/ff191200.aspx.

By default, Excel Services trusts many well-known data providers. In most cases, you do not have to add a new data provider. Data providers are typically added for custom solutions.

Authentication to External Data

Database servers require a user to be authenticated, that is, identify oneself to the server. The next step is authorization, communicating to the server the permitted actions associated with the user.

Authentication is required for the data server to perform authorization, or to enforce security restrictions that prevent data from being exposed to anyone other than authorized users.

Excel Services must communicate to the data source which user is requesting the data. In most scenarios, this is the user viewing an Excel report in a browser. This section explains authentication between Excel Services and an external data source. Authentication at this level is shown in Figure 23-1. The arrow on the right side shows the authentication link from an application server that runs Excel Calculation Services to an external data source.

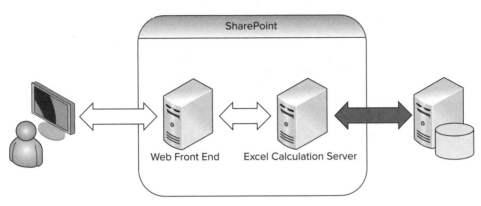

FIGURE 23-1

Excel Services supports the following authentication options:

➤ **Windows authentication:** Excel Services uses Integrated Windows authentication and attempts to connect to the data source by using the Windows identity of the user who displays the workbook.

➤ **Secure Store Service (SSS):** Excel Services uses the credentials associated with the specified Secure Store target application.

➤ **None:** Excel Services impersonates the unattended service account and passes the connection string to the data source.

The authentication option is configured in Microsoft Excel and is a property of the external data connection. The default value is Windows Authentication.

Integrated Windows Authentication

If you choose the Windows Authentication option, Excel Services attempts to pass the Windows identity of the user viewing the Excel workbook to the external data source. Kerberos delegation is required for any data source located on a different server than the server where Excel Calculation Services runs, if that data source uses Integrated Windows authentication.

In most enterprise environments, Excel Calculation Services runs on a different computer from the data source. This means that Kerberos delegation (constrained delegation is recommended) is required to enable data connections that use Windows authentication. For more information about how to configure Kerberos constrained delegation for Excel Services, see `http://technet` `.microsoft.com/en-us/library/ff829837.aspx`.

Secure Store Service

Secure Store is a SharePoint Server 2010 service application used to store encrypted credentials in a database for use by applications to authenticate to other applications. In this case, Excel Services uses Secure Store to store and retrieve credentials for use in authenticating to external data sources.

If you choose the SSS option, you must then specify the application ID of a Secure Store target application. The specified target application serves as a lookup used to retrieve the appropriate set of credentials. Each target application can have permissions set so that only specific users or groups can use the stored credentials.

When provided with an application ID, Excel Services retrieves the credentials from the Secure Store database for the user who accesses the workbook (either through the browser, or using Excel Web Services). Excel Services then uses those credentials to authenticate to the data source and retrieve data.

For information about how to use Secure Store with Excel Services, see `http://technet .microsoft.com/en-us/library/ff191191.aspx`.

None

When you select the None option, no credential retrieval occurs, and no special action is taken for authentication for the connection. Excel Services does not try to delegate credentials and does not try to retrieve credentials stored for the user from the Secure Store database. Instead, Excel Services impersonates the unattended service account and passes the connection string to the data provider that handles authentication.

The connection string may specify a username and password to connect to the data source or may specify that the Windows identity of the user or computer issuing the request be used to connect to the data source. In either case, the unattended account is impersonated first, and then the data source connection is made. The connection string and the provider determine the authorization method. Additionally, authorization can be based on either the credentials found in the connection string or the impersonated unattended account's Windows identity.

Excel Services Security and External Data

Excel Services manages workbooks and external data connections by using the following:

> **Trusted file locations:** Locations designated by an administrator from which Excel Services can load workbooks

> **Trusted data connection libraries:** SharePoint Server 2010 data connection libraries that have been explicitly trusted by an administrator from which Excel Services can load data connection files

> **Trusted data providers:** Data providers that have been explicitly trusted by an administrator

> **Unattended service account:** A low-privileged account that Excel Services can impersonate when it makes data connections

Trusted File Locations

Excel Services loads workbooks only from trusted file locations. A trusted file location is a SharePoint Server location, network file share, or Web folder address that the administrator has explicitly enabled workbooks to be loaded from. These directories are added to a list that is internal to Excel Services. This list is known as the trusted file locations list.

Trusted locations can specify a set of restrictions for workbooks loaded from them. All workbooks loaded from a trusted location adhere to the settings for that trusted location. Following is a short list of the trusted location settings that affect external data:

➤ **Allow External Data:** Defines how external data can be accessed.

➤ **No Data Access Allowed (Default):** Only connection files in a trusted SharePoint Server 2010 data connection library are allowed.

➤ **Warn on Refresh:** Defines whether to show the query refresh warnings.

➤ **Stop When Refresh on Open Fails:** Defines whether to fail the workbook load if external data does not refresh when the workbook opens. This is used in scenarios in which the workbook has cached data results that will change depending on the identity of the user viewing the workbook. The objective is to hide these cached results and make sure that any user who views the workbook can see only the data specific to that user. In this case, if the workbook is set to refresh on open and the refresh fails, the workbook does not display.

➤ **External Data Cache Lifetime:** Defines external data cache expiration times. Data is shared among many users on the server to improve scale and performance, and these cache life-times are adjustable. This accommodates scenarios in which query execution should be kept to a minimum because the query might take a long time to execute. In these scenarios, the data often changes only daily, weekly, or monthly instead of by the minute or every hour.

Trusted Data Connection Libraries and Managed Connections

A data connection library is a SharePoint Server 2010 library designed to store connection files, which can then be referenced by Office 2010 applications, such as Excel and Microsoft Visio. Excel Services loads only connection files from trusted SharePoint Server 2010 data connection libraries. A trusted data connection library is a library that the server administrator has explicitly added to an internal trusted list. Data connection libraries enable you to centrally manage, secure, store, and reuse data connections.

Managing Connections

Because workbooks contain a link to the file in a data connection library, if something about the connection changes (such as a server name or a Secure Store application ID), only a single connection file must be updated instead of potentially many workbooks. The workbooks can obtain the connection changes automatically the next time that they use that connection file to refresh data from Excel or Excel Services.

Securing Connections

The data connection library in a SharePoint library supports all the permissions that SharePoint Server 2010 does, including per-folder and per-item permissions. The advantage that this provides on the server is that a data connection library can become a locked-down data connection store that is highly controlled. Many users may have read-only access to it. This enables them to use the data connections, but they can be prevented from adding new connections. By using access control lists

(ACLs) with the data connection library, and letting only trusted authors upload connections, the data connection library becomes a store of trusted connections.

You can configure Excel Services to load connection files only from data connection libraries explicitly trusted by the server administrator and block loading of any embedded connections. In this configuration, Excel Services uses the data connection library to apply another layer of security around data connections.

You can use data connection libraries together with the new Viewer role in SharePoint Server 2010 that enables those connections to refresh workbooks rendered in a browser by Excel Services. If the Viewer role is applied, users cannot access the connection file contents from a client application, such as Excel. Therefore, the connection file contents are protected but still can be used for workbooks refreshed on the server.

Storing Connections

Storing data connections is another important role for document libraries. These data connections are stored as objects like documents or images in a library and can be accesses by services and reports throughout the farm depending on permissions.

Reusing Connections

Users can reuse connections created by other users and create different reports that use the same data source. You can have the IT department or a business intelligence expert create connections, and other users can reuse them without understanding the details about data providers, server names, or authentication. The location of the data connection library can even be published to Office clients so that the data connections display in Excel or in any other client application that uses the data connection library.

Trusted Data Providers

Excel Services uses only external data providers on the Excel Services trusted data providers list. This is a security mechanism that prevents the server from using providers that the administrator does not trust.

Unattended Service Account

Excel Services runs under a highly privileged account. Because Excel Services has no control over the data provider and does not directly parse provider-specific connection strings, using this account for the purposes of data access would be a security risk. To lessen this risk, Excel Services uses an *unattended service account*. This is a low-privileged account that is impersonated by Excel Services if any of the following conditions are true:

➤ Any time that it tries a connection where the None authentication option is selected.

➤ Whenever the Secure Store Service (SSS) option is selected and the stored credentials are not Windows credentials.

➤ If the None option is selected and the unattended account does not have access to the data source, Excel Services impersonates the unattended service account and uses information stored in the connection string to connect to the data source.

➤ If the None option is selected and the unattended account has access to the data source, a connection is successfully established using the credentials of the unattended service account. Use caution when you design solutions that intentionally use this account to connect to data. This is a single account that potentially can be used by every workbook on the server. Any user can open a workbook with an authentication setting of None using Excel Services to view that data by using the server. In some scenarios, this might be needed. However, Secure Store is the preferred solution for managing passwords on a per-user or per-group basis.

➤ If the SSS option is selected and the stored credentials are not Windows credentials, Excel Services impersonates the unattended service account and then attempts to connect to the data source by using the stored credentials.

➤ If the Windows Authentication option is selected, or if the SSS option is selected and the stored credentials are Windows credentials, then the unattended service account is not used. Instead, Excel Services impersonates the Windows identity and attempts to connect to the data source.

PerformancePoint Data Refresh

In PerformancePoint Services you must create a connection to the data source or sources you want to use in your dashboard. All data used in PerformancePoint Services is external data, living in data repositories outside of PerformancePoint. After you establish a data connection, you can use the data in the various PerformancePoint feature areas.

PerformancePoint supports both tabular data sources including SharePoint Lists, Excel Services, SQL Server tables and Excel workbooks; as well as multidimensional (Analysis Services) data sources; and also supports PowerPivot for Excel.

Tabular Data Sources

A user can create a data connection to SharePoint Lists, Excel Services, SQL Server tables, or Excel workbooks. For these kinds of data sources, you can view a sample of the data from the Dashboard Designer tool and set specific properties for the data depending how you want the data to be interpreted within PerformancePoint. For example, you can indicate which datasets should be treated as a dimension; you can specify if a dataset is to be treated as a dimension or a fact; or if you do not want the data to be included, you can select Ignore. If you decide to set the value as a fact, you can indicate how those numbers should be aggregated in PerformancePoint Services. You can also use datasets that have time values within PerformancePoint Services and use the PerformancePoint Services time intelligence features to set time parameters and create dashboard filters.

SharePoint Lists

You can use data contained in a SharePoint List on a SharePoint Site in PerformancePoint Services by creating a SharePoint List data source in Dashboard Designer. Data from SharePoint Lists can only be read but not modified. Modification to SharePoint List data must be done from SharePoint. Users may connect to any kind of SharePoint List.

Excel Services

Data in Excel files published to Excel Services on a SharePoint Site can be used in PerformancePoint Services by creating an Excel Services data source. Supported published data can be read only in PerformancePoint Services. Published parameter values can be modified from the Dashboard Designer. If you use an Excel Services parameter in calculating a KPI, it is easy to make additional changes. PerformancePoint Services supports the following Excel Services components: Named Ranges, Tables, and Parameters.

SQL Server Tables

You can create a data source connection to a SQL Server database and use the data within PerformancePoint Services. Tables and views are supported data sources within PerformancePoint Services.

Excel Workbooks

You may use the content of an actual Excel file stored in PerformancePoint as a data source in PerformancePoint Services by creating an Excel Workbook data source connection and selecting only the data to be used. The original Excel file will be independent from the PerformancePoint copy. PerformancePoint Services 2010 supports Excel 2007 and Excel 2010 workbooks as data sources.

Multidimensional Data Sources

Use data residing in a SQL Server Analysis Services multidimensional cube in PerformancePoint Services by creating a data connection to the source. PerformancePoint Services enables you to map the wanted time dimension and the required level of detail for its hierarchies to the internal PerformancePoint Services Time Intelligence.

PowerPivot for Excel

In PerformancePoint Services you can use a PowerPivot model as a data source to build your PerformancePoint Services dashboards. To use PowerPivot as a data source within a PerformancePoint Services dashboard, you must have PerformancePoint Services activated on a SharePoint Server 2010 farm and have PowerPivot for SharePoint installed. After a PowerPivot model has been created by using the PowerPivot add-in for Excel, this Excel file must be uploaded or published to a SharePoint site that has PowerPivot services enabled. Create the data source connection in Dashboard Designer using the Analysis Services data source template.

Visio Services Data Refresh

The Visio Graphics Service can connect to data sources. These include SharePoint lists, Excel workbooks hosted on the farm, databases such as Microsoft SQL Server, and custom data sources. You can control access to specific data sources by explicitly defining the data providers trusted and configuring them in the list of trusted data providers.

When Visio Services loads a data connected Web drawing, the service checks the connection information that is stored in the Web drawing to determine whether the specified data provider is a trusted data provider. If the provider is specified on the Visio Services trusted data provider list, a connection is tried; otherwise, the connection request is ignored.

After an administrator configures Visio Services to enable connections to a particular data source, additional security configurations must be made, depending on the kind of the data source. The following data sources are supported by Visio Services:

➤ Excel workbooks stored on SharePoint Server with Excel Services enabled

➤ SharePoint lists

➤ Databases such as SQL Server databases

➤ Custom data providers

➤ Visio Web drawings connected to SharePoint lists

> *Published Visio Drawings can be connected to SharePoint lists on the same farm that the drawing is hosted on. The user viewing the Web drawing must have access to both the drawing and the SharePoint list that the drawing connects to. SharePoint Server 2010 manages these permissions and credentials.*

There are a number of ways Visio content in SharePoint can be refreshed. Two of the most common ways are discussed in the following sections. They include Excel Services and SQL Server data.

Visio Web Drawings Connected to Excel Services

Published Visio drawings can connect to Excel workbooks hosted on the same farm as the Web drawing with Excel Services running and configured correctly. To view the Web drawing, the user must have access to both the drawing and the Excel workbook that the drawing connects to. These permissions and credentials are managed by SharePoint Server 2010.

Visio Web drawings Connected to SQL Server Databases

When a published Visio Web drawing is connected to a SQL Server database, Visio Services uses additional security configuration options to establish a connection between the Visio Graphics Service and the database.

Visio Services Authentication Methods

Visio supports several authentication types. These are listed here:

➤ **Integrated Windows authentication:** In this security model the Visio Graphics Service uses the drawing viewer's identity to authenticate with the database. Integrated Windows authentication with constrained Kerberos delegation is more helpful for increasing security than the other authentication methods shown in this list. This configuration requires constrained Kerberos delegation to be enabled between the application server running the Visio Graphics Service and the database server. The database might require additional configuration to enable Kerberos-based authentication.

➤ **Secure Store Service:** In this security model the Visio Graphics Service uses the Secure Store Service to map the user's credentials to a different credential that has access to the database. The Secure Store Service supports individual and group mappings for both Integrated Windows authentication and other forms of authentication such as SQL Server Authentication. This gives administrators more flexibility in defining one-to-one, many-to-one, or many-to-many relationships. This authentication model can be used only by drawings that use an Office Data Connection (ODC) file to specify the connection. The ODC file specifies the Secure Store target application that can be used for credential mapping. The ODC files must be created by using Microsoft Excel.

➤ **Unattended Service Account:** For ease of configuration the Visio Graphics Service provides a special configuration where an administrator can create a unique mapping associating all users to a single account by using a Secure Store Target Application. This mapped account, known as the unattended service account, must be a low-privilege Windows domain account that is given access to databases. The Visio Graphics Service impersonates this account when it connects to the database if no other authentication method is specified. This approach does not enable personalized queries against a database and does not provide auditing of database calls. This authentication method is the default authentication method used when you connect to SQL Server databases: If no ODC file is used in the Visio Web drawing that specifies a different authentication method, then Visio Services uses the credentials specified by the unattended account to connect to the SQL Server database.

In a larger server farm, it is likely that Visio drawings use a mix of the authentication methods described here. Consider the following:

➤ Visio Services supports usage of both the Secure Store Service and the unattended service account in the same farm. In Web drawings connected to SQL Server data that do not use ODC files, the unattended account is required and always used.

➤ If Integrated Windows authentication is selected, and authentication to the data source fails, Visio Services does not attempt to render the drawing using the unattended service account.

➤ Integrated Windows authentication can be used together with the Secure Store by configuring drawings to use an ODC file that specifies a Secure Store target application for those drawings that require specific credentials.

PowerPivot Data Refresh

PowerPivot data refresh is a scheduled server-side operation that queries external data sources to update embedded PowerPivot data in an Excel workbook stored in a content library.

Data refresh is a built-in feature of PowerPivot for SharePoint, but using it requires that you run specific services and timer jobs in your SharePoint farm. Additional administrative steps, such as installing data providers and checking database permissions, are often required for data refresh to succeed.

After you ensure that the server environment and permissions are configured, data refresh is ready to use. To use data refresh, a SharePoint user creates a schedule on a PowerPivot workbook that specifies how often data refresh occurs. Creating the schedule is typically done by the workbook owner or author who published the file to SharePoint. This person creates and manages the data refresh schedules for the workbooks that he or she owns. The following sections provide a list of steps you should follow in order to perform a successful PowerPivot data refresh.

Step 1: Enable Secure Store Service and Generate a Master Key

PowerPivot data refresh depends on Secure Store Service to provide credentials used to run data refresh jobs and to connect to external data sources that use stored credentials.

If you installed PowerPivot for SharePoint using the New Server option, the Secure Store Service is configured for you. For all other installation scenarios, you must manually create and configure a service application and generate a master encryption key for Secure Store Service. This is completed by performing the following steps:

1. In Central Administration, in Application Management, click Manage service applications.

2. In the Service Applications Ribbon, in Create, click New.

3. Select Secure Store Service.

4. In the Create Secure Store Application page, enter a name for the application.

5. In Database, specify the SQL Server instance that will host the database for this service application. The default value is the SQL Server Database Engine instance that hosts the farm configuration databases.

6. In Database Name, enter the name of the service application database. The default value is `Secure_Store_Service_DB_<guid>`. The default name corresponds to the default name of the service application. If you entered a unique service application name, follow a similar naming convention for your database name so that you can manage them together.

7. In Database Authentication, the default is Windows Authentication. If you choose SQL Authentication, refer to the SharePoint administrator guide for guidance on how to use the authentication type in your farm.

8. In Application Pool, select Create new application pool. Specify a descriptive name that can help other server administrators identify how the application pool is used.

9. Select a security account for the application pool. Specify a managed account to use. This should be a domain user account.

10. Accept the remaining default values, and then click OK. The service application appears alongside other managed services in the farm's service application list.

11. Click the Secure Store Service application from the list.

12. In the Service Applications Ribbon, click Manage.

13. In Key Management, click Generate New Key.

14. Enter and then confirm a pass phrase. The pass phrase will be used to add additional secure store shared service applications.

15. Click OK.

Audit logging of Store Service operations, which is useful for troubleshooting purposes, must be enabled before it is available.

Step 2: Turn Off Credential Options That You Do Not Want to Support

PowerPivot data refresh provides three credential options in a data refresh schedule. When workbook owners schedule data refresh, they choose one of these options, thereby determining the account under which the data refresh job runs. As an administrator, you can determine which of the following credential options are available to schedule owners.

➤ **Option 1:** Use the data refresh account configured by the administrator, which always appears on the schedule definition page but works only if you configure the unattended data refresh account.

➤ **Option 2:** Connect using the credentials show in Figure 23-2, which always appear on the page but work only when you enable the Allow Users to Enter the Custom Windows Credentials option in the service application configuration page. This option is enabled by default, but you can disable it if the disadvantages of using it outweigh the advantages. (See option 3.)

➤ **Option 3:** Connect using the credentials saved in Secure Store Service, which always appear on the page but work only when a schedule owner provides a valid target application. An administrator must create these target applications in advance and then provide the application name to those who create the data refresh schedules. This option only works if this service is configured and prevents other credentials such as option 2.

PowerPivot service application includes a credential option that allows schedule owners to enter an arbitrary Windows username and password to run a data refresh job. This is the credential option is shown in Figure 23-2 (and also referred to previously in Option 2).

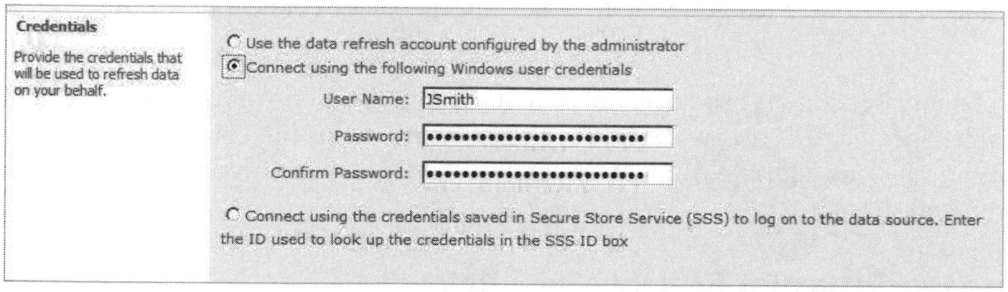

Credentials

Provide the credentials that will be used to refresh data on your behalf.

○ Use the data refresh account configured by the administrator
◉ Connect using the following Windows user credentials

User Name: JSmith

Password: •••••••••••••••••••••••••••

Confirm Password: •••••••••••••••••••••••••••

○ Connect using the credentials saved in Secure Store Service (SSS) to log on to the data source. Enter the ID used to look up the credentials in the SSS ID box

FIGURE 23-2

This credential option shown in Figure 23-2 is enabled by default. When this credential option is enabled, PowerPivot System Service generates a target application in Secure Store Service to store the username and password entered by the schedule owner. A generated target application is created using this naming convention: `PowerPivot DataRefresh_<guid>`. One target application is created for each set of Windows credentials. If a target application already exists that is owned by the

PowerPivot System Service and stores the username and password entered by the person defining the schedule, PowerPivot System Service uses that target application rather than creating a new one.

The primary advantage to use this credential option is ease of use and simplicity. Advance work is minimal because target applications are created for you. Also, running data refresh under the credentials of the schedule owner (who is most likely the person who created the workbook) simplifies permission requirements downstream. Most likely, this user already has permissions on the target database. When data refresh runs under this person's Windows user identity, any data connections that specify "current user" work automatically.

The disadvantage is limited management capability. Although target applications are created automatically, they are not deleted automatically or updated as account information changes. Password expiration policies might cause these target applications to become out of date. Data refresh jobs that use expired credentials will start to fail. If alerting is configured, DBA's can get an email or test alert. When this occurs, schedule owners need to update their credentials by providing current username and password values in a data refresh schedule. A new target application is created at that point. Over time, as users add and revise credential information in their data refresh schedules, you might have a large number of auto-generated target applications on your system.

Currently, there is no way to determine which of these target applications are active or inactive, nor is there a way to trace a specific target application back to the data refresh schedules that use it. In general, you should leave the target applications alone because deleting them might break existing data refresh schedules. Deleting a target application still in use causes data refresh to fail with the message Target Application Not Found appearing in the data refresh history page of the workbook.

If you choose to disable this credential option, you can safely delete all of the target applications that were generated for PowerPivot data refresh.

Step 3: Create Target Applications to Store Credentials Used in Data Refresh

When Secure Store Service is configured, SharePoint administrators can create target applications to make stored credentials available for data refresh purposes, including the PowerPivot unattended data refresh account or any other account used to either run the job or connect to external data sources.

Recall from the previous section that you need to create target applications for certain credential options to be usable. Specifically, you must create target applications for the PowerPivot unattended data refresh account, plus any additional stored credentials that you expect would be used in data refresh operations.

Step 4: Configure the Server for Scalable Data Refresh

By default, each PowerPivot for SharePoint installation supports both on-demand queries and scheduled data refresh.

For each installation, you can specify whether the Analysis Services server instance supports both query and scheduled data refresh, or is dedicated to a specific type of operation. If you have multiple installations of PowerPivot for SharePoint in your farm, consider dedicating a server for just data refresh operations if you find that jobs are delayed or failing.

Additionally, if the underlying hardware supports it, you can increase the number of data refresh jobs that run in parallel. By default, the number of jobs that can run in parallel is calculated based on system memory, but you can increase that number if you have additional CPU capacity to support the workload.

Step 5: Install Data Providers Used to Import PowerPivot Data

A data refresh operation is essentially a repeat of an import operation that retrieved the original data. This means that the same data providers used to import the data in the PowerPivot client application must also be installed on the PowerPivot server.

You must be a local administrator to install data providers on a Windows server. If you install additional drivers, be sure to install them on each computer in the SharePoint farm that has an installation of PowerPivot for SharePoint. If you have multiple PowerPivot servers in the farm, you must install the providers on each server.

 Remember that SharePoint servers are 64-bit applications. Be sure to install the 64-bit version of the data providers you use to support data refresh operations.

Step 6: Grant Permissions to Create Schedules and Access External Data Sources

Workbook owners or authors must have Contribute permission to schedule data refresh on a workbook. Given this permission level, they can open and edit the workbook's data refresh configuration page to specify the credentials and schedule information used to refresh the data.

In addition to SharePoint permissions, database permissions on external data sources must also be reviewed to ensure that accounts used during data refresh have sufficient access rights to the data. Determining permission requirements requires careful evaluation on your part because the permissions that you need to grant can vary depending on the connection string in the workbook and the user identity under which the data refresh job runs. When making this determination, it is important to consider the following questions:

➤ **Why do Existing Connection Strings in a PowerPivot Workbook Matter to PowerPivot Data Refresh Operations?** When data refresh runs, the server sends a connection request to the external data source using the connection string created when the data was originally imported. The server location, database name, and authentication parameters specified in that connection string are now reused during data refresh to access the same data sources. The connection string and its overall construction cannot be modified for data refresh purposes. It is simply reused as-is during data refresh. In some cases, if you use non-Windows authentication to connect to a data source, you can override the username and password in the connection string.

For most workbooks, the default authentication option on the connection is to use trusted connections or Windows integrated security, resulting in connection strings that include `SSPI=IntegratedSecurity` or `SSPI=TrustedConnection`. When this connection string is used during data refresh, the account used to run the data refresh job becomes the current user. As such, this account needs read permissions on any external data source accessed via a trusted connection.

➤ **Did You Enable the PowerPivot Unattended Data Refresh Account?** If yes, then you should grant that account read permissions on data sources accessed during data refresh. The reason why this account needs read permissions is because in a workbook that uses the default authentication options, the unattended account will be the current user during data refresh. Unless the schedule owner overrides the credentials in the connection string, this account needs read permissions on any number of data sources actively used in your organization.

➤ **Are You Using Credential Option 2: Allowing the Schedule Owner to Enter a Windows Username and Password?** Typically, users who create PowerPivot workbooks already have sufficient permissions because they have already imported the data. If these users subsequently configure data refresh to run under their own Windows user identity, their Windows user account, which already has rights on the database, will be used to retrieve data during data refresh. Existing permissions should be sufficient.

➤ **Are You Using Credential Option 3: Using a Secure Store Service Target Application to Provide a User Identity for Running Data Refresh Jobs?** Any account used to run a data refresh job needs read permissions, for the same reasons as those described for the PowerPivot unattended data refresh account.

Step 7: Enable Workbook Upgrade for Data Refresh

By default, workbooks created using the SQL Server 2008 R2 version of PowerPivot for Excel cannot be configured for scheduled data refresh on a Microsoft SQL Server 2012 version of PowerPivot for SharePoint. If you host newer and older versions of PowerPivot workbooks in your SharePoint environment, you must upgrade SQL Server 2008 R2 workbooks first before they can be scheduled for automatic data refresh on the server.

Step 8: Verify Data Refresh Configuration

To verify data refresh, you must have a PowerPivot workbook published to a SharePoint site. You must have Contribute permissions on the workbook and permissions to access any data sources included in the data refresh schedule.

When you create the schedule, select the Also Refresh as Soon as Possible check box to run data refresh immediately. You can then check the data refresh history page of that workbook to verify that it ran successfully. Recall that the PowerPivot Data Refresh timer job runs every minute. It can take at least that long to get confirmation that data refresh succeeded.

Be sure to try all the credential options you plan to support. For example, if you configured the PowerPivot unattended data refresh account, verify that data refresh succeeds using that option.

If data refresh fails, refer to the Troubleshooting PowerPivot Data Refresh page on the TechNet wiki for possible solutions. This can be found at http://technet.microsoft.com.

Modify Configuration Settings for Data Refresh

Each PowerPivot service application has configuration settings that affect data refresh operations. This section explains the two major ways to modify those settings.

Reschedule the PowerPivot Data Refresh Timer Job

Scheduled data refresh is triggered by a PowerPivot Data Refresh timer job that scans schedule information in the PowerPivot service application database at 1-minute intervals. When data refresh is scheduled to begin, the timer job adds the request to a processing queue on an available PowerPivot server.

You can increase the length of time between scans as a performance tuning technique. You can also disable the timer job to temporarily stop data refresh operations while you troubleshoot problems.

The default setting is 1 minute, which is the lowest value you can specify. This value is recommended because it provides the most predictable outcome for schedules that run at arbitrary times throughout the day. For example, if a user schedules data refresh for 4:15 P.M., and the timer job scans for schedules every minute, the scheduled data refresh request will be detected at 4:15 P.M. and processing will occur within a few minutes of 4:15 P.M.

If you raise the scan interval so that it runs infrequently (for example, once a day at midnight), all the data refresh operations scheduled to run during that interval are added to the processing queue all at once, potentially overwhelming the server and starving other applications of system resources. Depending on the number of scheduled refreshes, the processing queue for data refresh operations might build up to such an extent that not all jobs can complete. Data refresh requests at the end of the queue might be dropped if they run into the next processing interval.

To adjust the timer job schedule you can perform the following steps:

1. In Central Administration, click Monitoring.
2. Click Review Job Definitions.
3. Select the PowerPivot Data Refresh Timer Job.
4. Modify the schedule frequency to change how often the timer job scans for data refresh schedule information.

Disable the Data Refresh Timer Job

The PowerPivot data refresh timer job is a farm-level timer job that is either enabled or disabled for all PowerPivot server instances in the farm. It is not tied to a specific Web application or PowerPivot service application. You cannot disable it on some servers to force data refresh processing to other servers in the farm.

If you disable the PowerPivot data refresh timer job, requests that were already in the queue will be processed, but no new requests will be added until you reenable the job. Requests that were scheduled to occur in the past are not processed.

Disabling the timer job has no effect on feature availability in application pages. There is no way to remove or hide the data refresh feature in web applications. Users who have Contribute permissions or above can still create new schedules for data refresh operations, even if the timer job is permanently disabled.

Summary

SharePoint 2010 will continue to be an integral part of business intelligence within SQL Server 2012. Many enhancements make setup and maintenance much easier. The setup and configuration of PowerPivot along with Reporting Services being consolidated to a shared service lead the way in helping to make SharePoint a better tool. The addition of new features such as Power View will undoubtedly enhance the SharePoint experience for everyone who will begin using the new BISM analysis service format and continue using PowerPivot. In the end SharePoint 2010 together with SQL Server 2012 is getting better, more user-friendly, and more intelligent.

24

SQL Azure Administration and Configuration

WHAT'S IN THIS CHAPTER

➤ SQL Azure Configuration

➤ Server and Database Management

➤ Administration Tasks

This chapter provides a look at administering and configuring SQL Azure, assuming that you already have an Azure account and that you have some familiarity with the Azure platform. Microsoft SQL Azure is a database service provided as part of the Windows Azure Platform. Based on Microsoft SQL Server, it is a transactional database that includes many of the same SQL Server features that you know and love. Unlike SQL Server though, you don't need to worry about installing and maintaining the hardware and software in which SQL Azure runs. SQL Azure is provided as a service, hosted in a Microsoft datacenter. As such, Microsoft takes care of the physical maintenance of the hardware and software layer, enabling you to focus on the important aspects such as database design and development.

INTRODUCTION TO SQL AZURE

SQL Azure is Microsoft's transactional and relational database offering for cloud computing based on Microsoft SQL Server 2012. It supports many of the features of SQL Server including tables, primary keys, stored procedures, views, and much more.

SQL Azure exposes the tabular data stream interface for T-SQL just like SQL Server. Therefore, your database applications can use SQL Azure databases in the same way they use SQL Server. The only difference is that SQL Azure is a database delivered as a service, meaning administration is slightly different.

SQL Azure abstracts the logical administration from the physical administration. For example, you continue to administer databases, logins, and users, but Microsoft handles the administration of the physical aspects such as drives and storage and the physical server.

Even with the separation of logical and physical administration, the SQL functionality has not changed. SQL Azure is not a no-SQL database; it is a relational and transactional database that contains most of the objects and functionality found in SQL Server, such as tables, primary keys and foreign keys, indexes, stored procedures, and schemas. Yet SQL Azure offers more great features than its on-premises cousin, SQL Server. SQL Azure provides built-in High Availability (HA) and Disaster Recover (DR) without any additional cost; features that would be fairly expensive to add in an on-premises architecture.

SQL AZURE ARCHITECTURE

The SQL Azure architecture consists of four distinct layers of abstraction that work together to provide a cloud-based relational database. These four layers include:

- ➤ Client
- ➤ Services
- ➤ Platform
- ➤ Infrastructure

These four layers of architecture, as shown in Figure 24-1, enable SQL Azure to work with open source, third-party applications, as well as many of the familiar Microsoft technologies.

This layered architecture is quite similar to an on-premises architecture, except for the Services layer. The Services layer is a special SQL Azure layer that provides much of the SQL Azure-specific database platform functionality as described in the following sections.

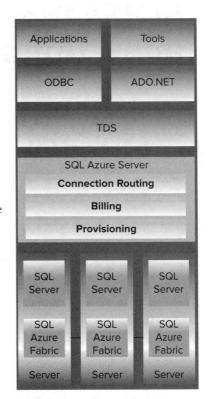

FIGURE 24-1

Client Layer

The Client layer is the layer that exists and resides closest to your application. Your application uses this layer to communicate with SQL Azure. This layer can reside on-premises or be hosted in Windows Azure. SQL Azure uses the same tabular data stream (TDS) interface as SQL Server, which enables developers to use familiar tools and libraries to develop cloud-based client applications. This layer provides data access through ADO.NET and other providers, giving you the flexibility to manipulate the data using standard T-SQL statements and familiar technologies.

Services Layer

The Services layer is the gateway between the Client layer and the Platform Layer and is responsible for the following functions:

➤ **Provisioning:** Creates and provisions the databases you specify either through the Azure platform portal or SQL Server Management Studio

➤ **Billing and Metering:** Handles the usage-based metering and billing on individual Azure platform accounts.

➤ **Connection Routing:** Handles all the connections routed between applications and the physical servers where the data resides

Again, this layer is specific to SQL Azure simply due to the need to route connections, meter and track usage, and provide billing around database usage. Additionally, this layer provides the database creation and provisioning functionality.

Platform Layer

This layer includes the physical servers and services that support the Services layer. It is the Platform layer that contains the many SQL instances of SQL Server with each instance managed by the SQL Azure Fabric.

The key part of this layer is the SQL Azure Fabric, a distributed computing system that is installed on each physical SQL Server and is made up of tightly integrated networks, servers, and storage. The SQL Azure Fabric provides the automatic failover, load balancing, and automatic replication between servers.

Infrastructure Layer

The Infrastructure layer represents the physical IT administration of the actual hardware and operating systems that support the Services layer.

The key to understanding the SQL Azure architecture is to remember the responsibilities of the Service layer; connections aren't connecting directly to the physical SQL Server. When connecting to SQL Server, connections are made to a physical server. In SQL Azure, connections are made through a TDS endpoint via the Services layer, which routes the connection to the physical server behind the Services layer. Figure 24-2 shows the differences between on-premises and SQL Azure connections.

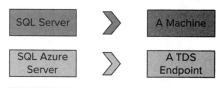

FIGURE 24-2

You can see an example of this in the differences between server names of an on-premises SQL Server and SQL Azure. For example, when connecting to an on-premises SQL Server, the server name typically is the name of the physical server. In SQL Azure, the servername is a Fully Qualified DNS Name (FQDN), which follows the format of `server.database.windows.net`.

The server portion of the FQDN is a unique 10-digit, randomly generated set of characters. The entire string must be used when making a connection to SQL Azure.

CONFIGURING SQL AZURE

After you create your Azure account, you are ready to start working with SQL Azure. First, you need to create your SQL Azure server and database and learn the different ways to work with SQL Azure. One of these is the Azure Management Portal, a web-based Azure management tool that enables you to manage all aspects of the Azure platform, including your hosted services (web roles and worker roles), storage accounts, and the Azure AppFabric (Service Bus and Access Control). The following sections walk you through these processes.

Server and Database Provisioning

The only way to provision (create) a new server is through the Azure Management Portal. You can access Azure Management Portal, shown in Figure 24-3, at `http://Windows.Azure.Com`.

Within the Azure Management Portal, you have the ability to manage all aspects of your SQL Azure subscription. Notice also (see Figure 24-3) that each account can have multiple subscriptions, each subscription can have multiple servers, and each server can contain multiple databases.

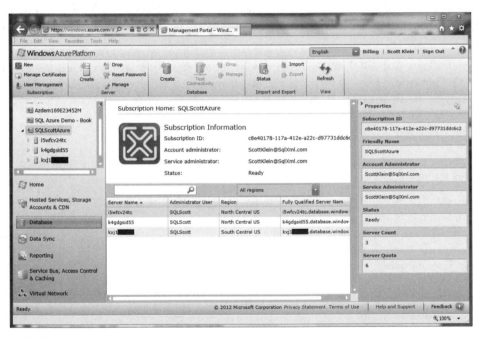

FIGURE 24-3

Creating a new SQL Azure server is as simple as selecting the appropriate subscription and clicking the Create button on the toolbar, which opens the Create Server Wizard. The Create Server Wizard guides you through a few steps necessary to create your SQL Azure server.

1. The first step in the wizard is to select a region where you would like to host your SQL Azure server (see Figure 24-4). Picking the appropriate region in which to host your SQL Azure is crucial. There are six regions to choose from: Microsoft currently has two datacenters in the United States, two in Europe, and two in Asia. Technically, you should pick the datacenter closest to where you live.

However, there are cases where that might not be true. For example, a company in Australia picked an Asia datacenter thinking that it would get better performance by selecting a datacenter closest to it. It soon discovered that it actually got better performance by selecting the South Central U.S. datacenter because the pipe between Australia and the United States was much bigger than the pipe between Australia and Asia. While it is important to take those things into consideration, most of the times the best way to choose is to start with the datacenter closest to you and test it thoroughly.

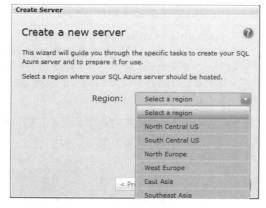

FIGURE 24-4

2. After you choose the appropriate region, select Next. The next page of the wizard asks you to create a login and password for the SQL Azure server, as shown in Figure 24-5. The login and password entered here is the server-level principle for the SQL Azure server you are creating. This login is equivalent to the SQL Server Administrator account (SA) for your on-premises server.

3. After you enter your login and password, click Next. The next page of the wizard asks you to specify firewall rules on your SQL Azure server (see Figure 24-6). The firewall rules can be specified at any time, and will be discussed in the next section. Go ahead and click Finish on the Create Server wizard.

FIGURE 24-5

FIGURE 24-6

You have now successfully created your SQL Azure server. But before you begin learning how to work with it, you must take note of some important information.

Server Name and Databases

After your server has been created, in the center section of the portal the Items List section displays the list of all the SQL Azure servers in your Azure subscription, including the one you just created. In the Navigation pane the name of the new server appears in the list of servers beneath your selected subscription, as shown in Figure 24-7.

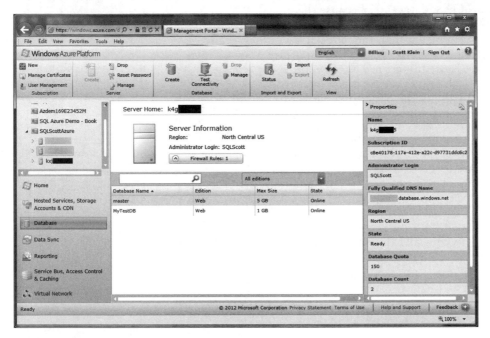

FIGURE 24-7

Just in case there is any confusion, click the subscription name in the Navigation pane. The center of the portal window, the Items List section, lists all the SQL Azure servers that pertain to your selected subscription. The list contains four columns:

➤ Server Name

➤ Administrator User

➤ Region

➤ Fully Qualified Server Name

Notice that the first part of the Fully Qualified Server Name is the same as the Server Name. When you hear people refer to the SQL Azure server, they are referring to the value in the first column; although, using the last column (Fully Qualified Server Name) as the server name reference isn't harmful. In fact, when specifying the "server name" for an application connection string, it is the value of the Fully Qualified Server Name that needs to be used, like so:

```
servername.database.windows.net
```

You need to know this server name (Fully Qualified Server Name) when the topic of connecting to SQL Azure is discussed later in the chapter, so highlight and copy to the clipboard the entire SQL Azure server. The Fully Qualified Server Name is found in the Fully Qualified DNS Name (FQDN) area of the Properties pane. The Properties pane appears when you select the server in the Navigation pane. Even though you are not connecting to a physical computer, your SQL Azure server still behaves similarly to that of an on-premises SQL Server, meaning that a SQL Azure server contains a logical group of databases and acts as the central administrative point for multiple databases. As such, you can create many of the same objects that you can with on-premises databases such as tables, views, stored procedures, and indexes. Again, in the Properties pane of the portal, use the mouse to highlight the complete server name and copy that to the clipboard (Ctrl+C) as this will be used shortly.

With your server name still selected in the Navigation pane, a couple pieces of information need to be highlighted. When the SQL Azure server is created, the master database is automatically provisioned. This database is read-only and contains configuration and security information for your databases. You can see the master database in the list of databases shown previously in Figure 24-7.

On the Server Information page, you also have the ability to manage your firewall rules by selecting the Firewall Rules button. Here you can create, modify, or delete the rules necessary to allow access to your SQL Azure server. Firewall Rules is the first level of security for SQL Azure and are critical in protecting your data. Configuring SQL Azure Firewall Rules are discussed later in this chapter.

Creating a New Database

As of this writing, SQL Azure supports two database "editions" and several database sizes based on the edition. SQL Azure includes the *Web* and *Business* database editions. The *Web* database edition includes database sizes of 1GB and 5GB. With the *Business* database edition, you can select from a 10GB, 20GB, 30GB, 40GB, 50GB, and 150GB database. There really is no difference in the databases between editions, except for size. Meaning, the functionality of the database is the same regardless of the edition you choose. To create a new database, follow these steps:

1. Select your server and click the blue Create button on the toolbar that opens the Create Database dialog, shown in Figure 24-8. In this dialog, specify the name of the database and then select the database Edition and the associated Maximum size.

2. Click OK on the Create Database dialog to first create your new database. You are then returned to the Azure Management Portal with your new database selected and the Database Information displayed, which contains information and links on how to develop and deploy applications with SQL Azure and connection information. Figure 24-9 displays the Database Information for this example.

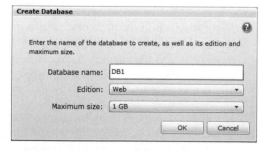

FIGURE 24-8

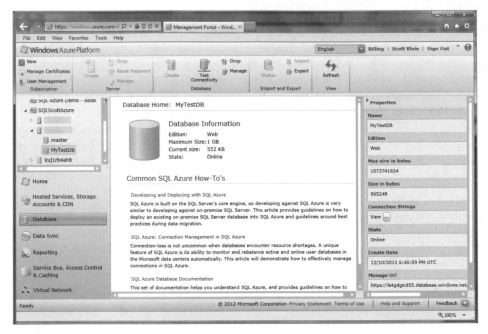

FIGURE 24-9

3. Figure 24-9 also displays a connections strings section on the right side of the page in the Properties pane. Click the ellipse button next to View here and you see a dialog in which connection strings for ADO.NET, ODBC, and PHP are already defined. Copy the appropriate connection string for your development environment and paste it into your application. Change the password when you paste the connection string into your application and you are all set.

Throttling and Load Balancing

Throttling is SQL Azure's mechanism for ensuring that one subscriber's application or code (stored procedure or T-SQL) does not seize all the resources. Since SQL Azure works behind the scenes to provide a high-performing database, it uses a *load balancer* mechanism to help ensure that a server is not in a continuous state of throttling. To fully understand throttling and load balancing, let's first take a step back and look at how, and where, SQL Azure creates new databases.

The goal for Microsoft SQL Azure is to maintain, currently, 99.9 percent availability for the subscriber's database. This high availability is achieved through several methods. First, Microsoft uses commodity hardware that can be quickly and easily replaced in the case of hardware failure. Second, and more importantly, Microsoft implements the automatic management of database replicas. When you create a database, you actually get three databases; one primary and two secondary. These databases are always in sync, automatically, without any interaction from the end user.

You, your application, or anyone else cannot access the secondary databases directly, but they are there and for an important purpose: if for any reason your primary database should become unavailable, SQL Azure will take it offline, select one of the secondary databases, promote it to primary, and then spin up another secondary database and bring that up to date. All this happens behind the scenes automatically. Any connections to the database that is now unavailable still need to be taken care of though. In this scenario, best practice states that you add to your application a connection and statement execution retry functionality. This way, if the primary database goes down, your application can pick it up, and by the time your application retries, a new primary should be ready to accept the incoming request.

> *In reality, you should be implementing a connection and statement execution retry functionality in your applications anyway. The last thing end users need to see is an error that the work they just did can't be completed. Every application should have logic that can automatically retry based on certain errors returned from SQL Server. The same applies to SQL Azure.*

The Azure platform is a *shared environment* platform, meaning that you share server resources with other Azure subscribers. On top of that, other processes running on each server along with your databases are crucial to the steady and fluent running and execution of SQL Azure, such as the SQL Azure fabric.

To ensure that one database doesn't consume critical resources from another database or from the SQL Azure server itself, Microsoft has implemented the Engine Throttling component whose job it is to ensure that the health of the machine is not jeopardized. The Engine Throttling component has the task to make sure all the appropriate process have all the resources they need to operate smoothly and efficiently, that no one uses more resources than needed, and that resource limits are not exceeded.

If limits are exceeded, such as CPU usage or log size, the Engine Throttling component steps in and applies the necessary measure to correct the situation. These measures could include dropping connections, rejecting reads or writes for a period of time (10 seconds or so), or even permanently rejecting reads and writes if the source of the problem is deemed to continue to cause problems.

As new databases are added, the load balancer determines the locations of the new primary and secondary replica databases based on the current load of the machines in the datacenter.

The location of these databases may be fine for a while, but it is impossible to foresee the workload of other subscribers. Therefore, the Load Balancer has the responsibility to ensure proper performance of the databases. If one machine becomes too loaded, the Load Balancer may automatically move a database to a server that is less loaded. This move is seamless and has no impact on the application.

Configuring SQL Azure Firewalls

You now know how to create your server and databases and what happens behind the scenes of SQL Azure to ensure high availability and great database performance. Yet, it won't do any good if you can't connect to the databases. This is where the SQL Azure Firewall comes in.

You could have developed a great application, designed a great database, set the proper connection string, and so on; but unless you define the appropriate firewall rules, it will have been all for naught. The SQL Azure Firewall is the first level of security to help protect your data and prevent unwanted access to your SQL Azure server. All access to your SQL Azure server is rejected and blocked until you specify which computers have permission. Connection attempts coming from the Internet, and even within Azure itself, cannot reach your SQL Azure server until you specify who has access.

Firewall rules are IP address-based, and only acceptable addresses or ranges can be defined. Firewall rules are defined via the Azure Management Portal (refer to Figure 24-7) in the Server Information section.

To configure a firewall rule, click the Firewall Rules button in the Management Portal in the Server Information section, which displays any defined firewall rules. Underneath the firewall rules you see three buttons: Add, Update, and Delete, as shown in Figure 24-10.

To add a new firewall rule, simply click the Add button, which displays the Add Firewall Rule dialog, as shown in Figure 24-11. In this dialog, simply give the new rule a unique name and provide the IP Address you would like to give access to SQL Azure. Alternatively, you can provide an IP Address range to allow multiple IP Addresses access.

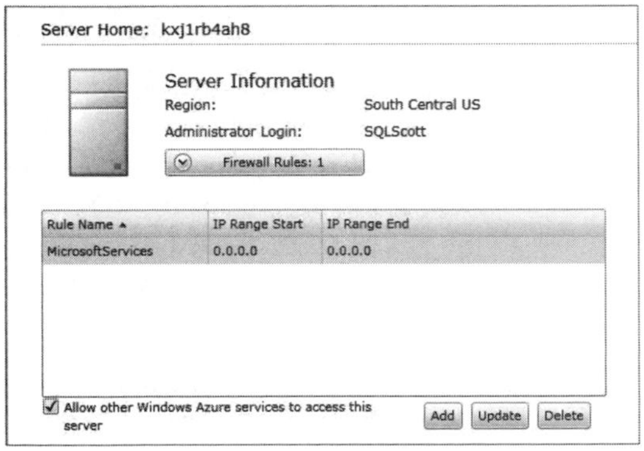

FIGURE 24-10

FIGURE 24-11

Notice also (refer to Figure 24-11), that you can easily add your IP Address because the bottom of the dialog displays it. You can simply highlight, copy, and paste the IP Address into the Start and End Range boxes (if you have added only your single IP address). After you add your IP address, click OK. You then see your firewall rule added to the management portal, as shown in Figure 24-12. At this point, you can connect to your SQL Azure via your applications and SQL Server Management Studio.

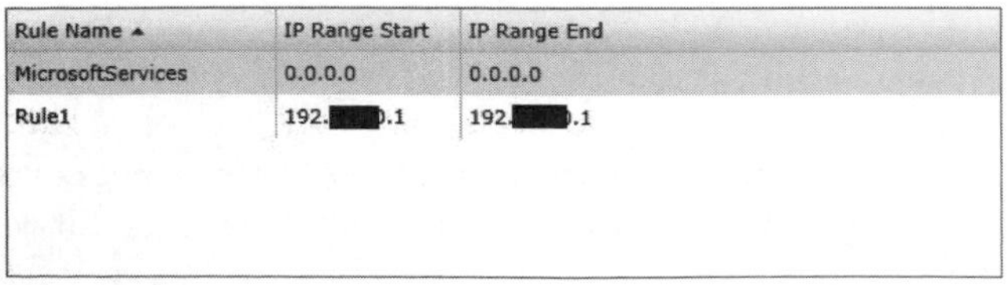

Rule Name ▲	IP Range Start	IP Range End
MicrosoftServices	0.0.0.0	0.0.0.0
Rule1	192.███.0.1	192.███.0.1

FIGURE 24-12

Finally, refer back to check box at the bottom of Figure 24-8 called Allow Other Windows Azure Services to Access This Server. Remember that all connection attempts, including those from within Azure itself, cannot reach your SQL Azure server unless you specify so. Therefore, to allow Azure services access to your SQL Azure server, you need to check this box. When you do so, you notice that a rule is added to the list of firewall rules called Microsoft Services. This allows any of your Windows Azure components, such as Worker Roles or Web Roles, access to your database. Components from other accounts cannot see your databases.

Connecting to SQL Azure

Now that you have created your databases and defined the firewall rules, you are ready to connect to your SQL Azure server. To start your SQL Azure connection journey, follow these steps:

 The examples in this section show how to connect via SQL Server Management Studio, not via an application, because the connection strings were briefly covered earlier.

1. Fire up SQL Server Management Studio. Connecting to SQL Azure requires either SQL Server 2008, SQL Server 2008 R2, or SQL Server 2012. When the Connect to Server dialog opens, as shown in Figure 24-13, you need to enter the FQDN server name. This should still be on your clipboard; otherwise, go back to the Azure Management portal and recopy it; then paste it into the Server Name box.

FIGURE 24-13

2. SQL Azure only supports SQL Authentication, so select SQL Server Authentication and then enter the user name and password you created in Figure 24-5. If you have configured your SQL Azure Firewall with the appropriate IP Address, you should successfully connect. If for some reason the firewall rules are not configured correctly, you see an error message stating so.

3. As a quick exercise, open a new query window and make sure you connect to the master database. In the query window, execute the following command:

```
SELECT @@VERSION
```

Figure 24-14 shows the Results window displaying the SQL Azure version currently running at the time of this writing.

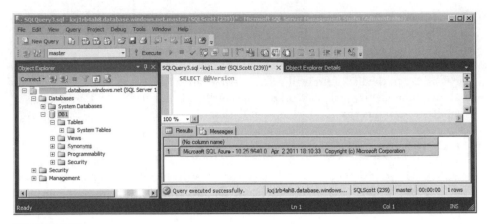

FIGURE 24-14

Now you are connected to your SQL Azure server via SSMS. Next the logical administration aspect of working with SQL Azure, including creating logins and users, is discussed.

ADMINISTERING SQL AZURE

One of the big misconceptions about SQL Azure is that it is nothing like SQL Server. The truth is that both SQL Server and SQL Azure use the same authorization model, with users and roles created in each database and associated to the user logins. SQL Server has fixed serverwide roles such as `serveradmin`, `securityadmin`, and `dbcreated`, which do not exist in SQL Azure. They don't need to though because of the logical administration aspect of SQL Azure. Instead, SQL Azure has a `loginmanager` role to create logins and a `dbmanager` role to create and manage databases. These roles can be assigned to users only in the master database.

Creating Logins and Users

SQL Azure provides the same set of security principles available in SQL Server authentication, which you can use to authorize and secure your data. In SQL Azure, logins are used to authenticate access to SQL Azure at the server level. Database users are used to grant access to SQL Azure at the database level, and database roles are used to group users and grant access to AQL Azure at the database level.

Creating a New Login

Creating a login is nearly identical to SQL Server except that you cannot create a login based on Windows credentials. Thus, all logins are SQL logins for SQL Authentication. The following steps outline how to do this.

1. In SQL Server Management Studio, open a new query window and connect to the master database using the administrator account created earlier. In the query window, type and run the following command:

```
CREATE LOGIN AzureTest WITH PASSWORD = 'T3stPwd001'
```

2. This creates a new login called AzureTest as shown in Figure 24-15.

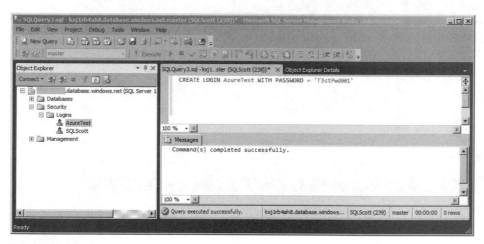

FIGURE 24-15

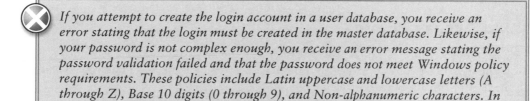

If you attempt to create the login account in a user database, you receive an error stating that the login must be created in the master database. Likewise, if your password is not complex enough, you receive an error message stating the password validation failed and that the password does not meet Windows policy requirements. These policies include Latin uppercase and lowercase letters (A through Z), Base 10 digits (0 through 9), and Non-alphanumeric characters. In SQL Azure, the password policy cannot be disabled.

3. Although Figure 24-13 shows the login created in SQL Server Management Studio, you can also query the sys.sql_logins table to view all logins for the server like so:

```
SELECT * FROM sys.sql_logins
```

Although your logins are created, you cannot log in until a user has been created, which the next section discusses.

Creating a New User

After your login is created, you need to create a user account for it. To create the user account, connect to the specific user database using the administrator account and run the following command:

```
CREATE USER AzureTest FROM LOGIN AzureTest
```

Figure 24-16 shows the command executed and the corresponding results. You can see that the user was indeed created in the DB1 database.

FIGURE 24-16

If you attempt to create a user without first creating the login account, you receive a message stating that the user is not a valid login. Loginless users are not allowed in SQL Azure.

Assigning Access Rights

The next step in the Administration process is to assign the newly created user account access rights. To allow the AzureTest account to have unlimited access to the selected user database, you need to assign the user to the db_owner group:

```
EXEC sp_addrolemember 'db_owner', 'AzureTest'
```

At this point, the AzureTest user can create tables, views, stored procedures, and more. But just like SQL Server, you can get granular with your permissions. You can grant and revoke permissions and grant insert, update, delete, create, and delete privileges just like you can with SQL Server. In SQL Server, user accounts are automatically assigned to the public role. This is not the case in SQL Azure because the public role cannot be assigned to user accounts for enhanced security. As a result, specific access rights must be granted to use a user account.

WORKING WITH SQL AZURE

Working in SQL Server Management Studio has provided a nice and easy way to create databases and tables and do a lot of the management and maintenance of SQL Server through a great user interface. However, some of the better user interface features aren't automatically available. There is still a way to enjoy them, though, if you are up for writing some code. To do so, perform the following steps:

1. Right click the database node in Object Explorer and select New Database from the Context menu. A query window appears. Figure 24-17 shows this query window with the syntax required to create a SQL Azure database in SQL Server Management Studio.

2. You don't get the Create Database dialog next, but instead, you get to write the Create Database statement yourself. As you can see in Figure 24-17, the syntax isn't all that difficult. Specify the name of the database, the edition, and the size. If you leave out the edition and size, you simply get a 1GB Web edition database.

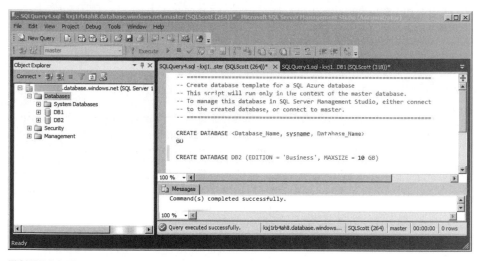

FIGURE 24-17

Similarly, you can write code to create tables and views, and when working with permissions. Figure 24-18 shows the result of right-mouse-clicking the Tables node in Object Explorer and selecting New Table from the Context menu.

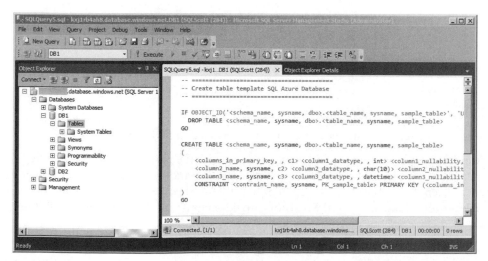

FIGURE 24-18

Even though the user-interface features aren't quite there yet, that doesn't mean that the functionality isn't there. You just need to write code (same T-SQL syntax you are used to) to accomplish most of the things you need to do.

Backups with SQL Azure

One of the biggest questions potential Azure customers have is that of backups. Currently, backups with the on-premises SQL Server do not exist in SQL Azure. Instead, a feature called Database Copy enables you to make a transactionally consistent copy of your primary SQL Azure database into another SQL Azure database. The syntax for this is simple:

```
CREATE DATABASE DB2 AS COPY OF DB1
```

You can also copy databases between servers using the same syntax; you just need to be admins on both servers. However, administering two servers does entail paying for two databases, and more important, this makes it difficult to do daily backups and keep a history.

The other backup option is to use SQL Azure Data Sync Services. SQL Azure Data Sync Services is currently available via the SQL Azure Labs site (`https://datasync.azure.com/SADataSync .aspx`) but does require you to sign up. SQL Azure Data Sync Services is a beautiful interim solution and is quite easy to set up and configure. Microsoft understands that there is a need for a better and more efficient backup solution and is working hard at providing this functionality.

Object Explorer for SQL Azure

When you connect to SQL Azure in SQL Server Management Studio, you notice that a few nodes are missing — specifically the Server Objects, Replication, and SQL Server Agent nodes. The following sections explain why these aren't there (yet) and what you might expect down the road.

Server Objects

Looking at the subnodes in Server Objects, you see the following:

➤ Backup Devices

➤ SOAP Endpoints

➤ Linked Servers

➤ Triggers

There are a few specific reasons why these items are not included in SQL Azure.

➤ **Backup Devices:** First, because you don't have access to the physical hardware that SQL Azure runs on, you don't need to create a backup device and won't have access to it anyway. Second, except for the current backup solutions discussed earlier, there isn't any other way to back up your databases. Until Microsoft provides more functional backup capabilities, the Backup Devices node doesn't need to be there.

➤ **SOAP Endpoints:** SOAP endpoints go back to SQL Server 2005 and enable you to essentially create web services that expose database access over HTTP. Microsoft has let it be known that this feature will be deprecated in future releases of SQL Server. SQL Azure has a better solution for SOAP Endpoints: OData. With just a few clicks you can expose your SQL Azure data via the OData protocol. The OData Service for SQL Azure provides a simple, no-code solution for providing an OData endpoint through an open HTTP protocol.

➤ **Linked Servers:** These are typically used to handle distributed queries. Distributed queries aren't supported in SQL Azure, but something even better will appear that makes the distributed queries a thing of the past. Microsoft announced in late 2010 a technology called SQL Azure Federation; the ability to partition, or shard, your data to improve the scalability and throughput of your database.

Sharding is the process of breaking an application's logical database into smaller chunks of data and then distributing those chunks of data across multiple physical databases to achieve application scalability. In sharding, one or more tables within a database are split by row and portioned out across multiple databases. This partitioning can be done with no downtime, and client applications can continue accessing data during sharding operations with no interruption in service.

There are quite a few blog posts and articles available on MSDN that drill into detail about this, but with SQL Azure Federation, Linked Servers aren't needed.

➤ **Triggers:** Enabling these in a shared environment creates a whole new level of complexity, such as potential security risks and possible performance issues.

Replication

Due to SQL Azure Data Sync Services, replication just isn't needed in SQL Azure. As mentioned earlier, there are three copies of every database you create: the primary and two replicas. SQL Azure keeps these in sync for you and automatically provides the high availability and redundancy you need.

If you need to "replicate" data from one database to another database, SQL Azure Data Sync Services provides an easy-to-use, wizard-driven interface that provides multi-direction data synchronization between two SQL Azure databases (primary to primary) or between SQL Azure and an on-premise SQL Server database. Therefore, replication just isn't necessary in SQL Azure.

SQL Server Agent

SQL Server agent doesn't exist for SQL Azure, but there are many articles on the web that explain how to use a Windows Azure Worker Role to mimic the functionality of the SQL Server Agent.

The SQL Server agent is a Microsoft Windows Service that executes scheduled admin tasks called jobs and provides alerting capabilities. A good look at a Windows Azure Worker Role reveals that a Windows Azure Worker Role is basically a Windows Service in the cloud. Worker Roles are roles used to perform background tasks and long running/intermittent tasks.

What makes Worker Roles great is that their structure is close to that of a Windows Service, including the starting, stopping, and configuration concepts that you see in a Windows Service. You can find a great blog post about this here: `http://blogs.msdn.com/b/sqlazure/archive/2010/0 7/30/10044271.aspx`.

WHAT'S MISSING IN SQL AZURE

As you start working with SQL Azure, or, if you are already familiar with SQL Azure, you will at some point wonder why SQL Azure doesn't have a specific feature or functionality you are looking for, such as Full-Text Search. For example, if you were to do a feature-to-feature comparison you would quickly see that at least the following features are not present in SQL Azure:

➤ SQLCLR

➤ Full-Text Search

➤ Replication

➤ SQL Agent

➤ Encryption (TDE)

This is not a complete list, but the complete list is not a long one either. It is not publicly known the reason for the lack of certain features and functionality in SQL Azure. However, this section can at least provide information on some of the items in the above list.

The SQLCLR is in fact "partially" supported. For example, the XML and Spatial data types are actually CLR data types, and you will certainly find these data types in SQL Azure. What SQL Azure doesn't support for SQLCLR is the ability to create assemblies in managed code (see Chapter 7, "SQL Server CLR Integration") and deploy those to SQL Azure. It is unknown if and when that will be supported.

Replication really isn't needed, because of the existence of SQL Azure Data Sync Services, mentioned earlier in the chapter. SQL Azure Data Sync Services works far better and is far easier to configure and use than Replication. Data Sync Services is built entirely on top of the Sync Framework and therefore includes a much richer data synchronization platform for moving data, including conflict handling and status reporting.

Microsoft is working hard at including encryption but there are certain problems they need to solve before you will see it included. The big issue really is how to support multiple levels of encryption in a shared environment. Remember that SQL Azure is a shared environment, and as such, databases are spread out over multiple instances. For example, my database and your database could potentially be located on the same server. In this scenario, the problem arises when I use one level of encryption and you use another.

These are several examples of missing features and depending on the feature, it will elicit a different response. For example, SQL Azure has SQL Azure Reporting Services, but where is the rest of the Business Intelligent (BI) stack of Analysis Services and Integration Services? Microsoft is working on them, but when and how they will be included is yet to be seen.

The moral of this story is that some features you just won't see because it doesn't make sense to include them, as is the case in Replication. With other features you just need to be patient.

SUMMARY

The goal of this chapter was to provide a solid overview of how to configure and administer SQL Azure, including creating your SQL Azure server, creating databases, and discussing what happens behind the scenes to provide the great high-availability and failover needed in a cloud-based solution.

The logical administration of SQL Azure plays an important role in understanding topics such as creating a SQL Azure Server and associated databases. While difference between on-premise SQL Server and SQL Azure do exist, SQL Azure still maintains power and flexibility as SQL Server "in the cloud."

25

AlwaysOn Availability Groups

An Availability Group is a new feature part of AlwaysOn in SQL Server 2012 that delivers robust high-availability enhancements that greatly improve the data mirroring capabilities that shipped starting with SQL Server 2005. With AlwaysOn, SQL Server 2012 implements Availability Groups that deliver similar capabilities to database mirroring. In addition to these key enhancements, it can support up to five replica partners, multiple databases in a single group, and readable replica secondary servers. The primary and replica servers can be mixed in asynchronous/synchronous modes and do not require shared disks; as a result they can deploy across different geographical locations. When these databases have dependencies, they can be grouped in a single Availability Group to failover together as a single failover unit. By supporting readable replica servers, for example, reporting or read-only workload can be offloaded to a secondary replica, reducing the load onto the primary replica where it can scale and support its production workload better and respond to requests faster. You can also perform database backups on a secondary replica to reduce the backup load on the primary server. It supports built-in transport compression/encryption; Automatic, Manual, and Forced Failover; flexible failover policy; and automatic application redirection using the Availability Group Listener network name.

AlwaysOn Availability Groups support the following features or components of SQL Server:

➤ Change data capture

➤ Change tracking

➤ Contained databases

➤ Database encryption

➤ Database snapshots

➤ FileStream and FileTable

➤ Full-text search

➤ Remote Blob Storage (RBS)

➤ Replication

➤ Service Broker

➤ SQL Server Agent

ARCHITECTURE

An Availability Group is a set of up to five configured SQL servers into an Availability Group failover for a discrete set of user databases, known as *availability databases*. Each set of availability database(s) is hosted by an *availability replica*. Every availability replica is assigned a role. Each availability replica also has associated with it an availability mode. Figure 25-1 shows an Availability Group architecture in detail and the following sections elaborate on these various components.

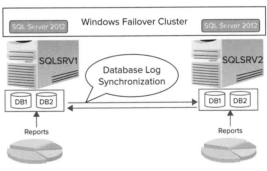

FIGURE 25-1

Availability Group Replicas and Roles

As stated previously, an availability database is hosted by an availability replica. Two types of availability replicas exist:

➤ A single *primary replica* makes the primary databases available for read-write connections from clients and also sends transaction log records for each primary database to every secondary replica.

➤ One to four *secondary replicas* maintain a set of secondary databases. Every secondary replica applies transaction log records to its own set of secondary databases and serves as a potential failover target for the Availability Group.

Optionally, you can configure one or more secondary replicas to support read-only access to secondary databases, and you can configure any secondary replica to permit backups on secondary databases.

Every availability replica is assigned an initial role — either the *primary role* or the *secondary role*, which is inherited by the availability databases of that replica. The role of a given replica determines whether it hosts read-write databases or read-only databases. The primary replica is assigned the primary role and hosts read-write databases, which are known as *primary databases*. At least one secondary replica is assigned the secondary role. A secondary replica hosts read-only databases, known as *secondary databases*.

For the replicas to participate in Availability Groups they must be deployed as a Windows Failover Cluster (WFC); therefore, to implement an Availability Group, you must first enable Windows Failover Cluster in each server participating in the Availability Group. Inside of a WFC, an Availability Group is a cluster resource with its own network name and cluster IP address used for application clients to connect to the Availability Group. However, the major difference from a SQL Server cluster installation is that an Availability Group does not require a shared disk; that is, in this configuration, each server does not share its disks with the other server.

Availability Modes

Each availability replica contains a property that determines its availability mode in relationship to the transaction record data movement that it receives, which determines how current its data is in relationship to the primary replica that is moving the data to all the other replicas. Two modes of availability are supported:

➤ **Asynchronous-commit mode:** The primary replica commits transactions without waiting for acknowledgment that an asynchronous-commit secondary replica has hardened the transaction log. Asynchronous-commit mode minimizes transaction latency on the secondary replica databases but enables them to lag behind the primary replica databases, increasing the probably in case of a failure or possible data loss.

➤ **Synchronous-commit mode:** The primary replica waits for a synchronous-commit from the secondary replicas to acknowledge that it has finished hardening the log. Synchronous-commit mode ensures that when a given secondary replica database is synchronized with the primary replica database, committed transactions are fully protected. This protection comes at the cost of increased request latency and increases the user transaction times because the latency is included in the overall database response time.

Types of Failover Supported

During failover, the primary and secondary replicas are interchangeable where one of the secondary replicas becomes the primary, and the former primary becomes the secondary replica. The new primary brings its Availability Group databases online and makes its databases available for read/write operations. The former primary that is now the secondary replica then begins to receive transactional data from the new primary replicate after the failover. If the failover is caused by a failure to the former primary such that it became unavailable for a time, when the former primary returns online it automatically joins in its Availability Group and takes a secondary replica role.

There are three modes of failover: automatic, manual, and forced (with possible data loss). Support is based on the availability mode configured, as shown in Table 25-1.

TABLE 25-1: Supported Failover Modes

AVAILABILITY MODE	FAILOVER MODE SETTING	SECONDARY REPLICA FAILOVER SUPPORTED
Synchronous	Manual	Manual (without data loss)
Synchronous	Automatic	Automatic/Manual (without data loss)
Asynchronous	Manual	Manual (Possible data loss)

The following list explains each supported failover mode from Table 25-1 in greater detail.

➤ **Manual failover (without data loss):** A manual failover occurs after a database administrator issues a manual-failover command and causes a synchronized secondary replica to transition to be the primary replica role (with guaranteed data protection) and the primary replica to transition as the secondary replica role. The database administrator can specify which secondary replica to failover to. A manual failover requires that both the primary replica and the target secondary replica run under synchronous-commit mode, and the secondary replica must already be synchronized.

➤ **Automatic failover (without data loss):** An automatic failover occurs in response to a failure that causes a synchronized secondary replica to transition to the primary role (with guaranteed data protection). When the former primary replica becomes available, it transitions to the secondary role. Automatic failover requires that both the primary replica and the target secondary replica run under synchronous-commit mode with the failover mode set to Automatic. In addition, the secondary replica must already be synchronized.

➤ **Manual (possible data loss):** Under asynchronous-commit mode, the only form of failover is manual forced failover (with possible data loss). A forced failover should only be used for disaster recovery as there is a good risk of data loss. Manual is the only form of failover possible when the target secondary replica is not synchronized with the primary replica, even for synchronous-commit mode.

Allowing Read-Only Access to Secondary Replicas

The main purpose of the Availability Group is to deliver high availability and disaster recovery, but in addition, a secondary replica can be configured for read-only database access. In such a scenario, read-only workloads are offloaded on the secondary replica databases, optimizing the primary replica to support read/write mission critical workloads. For example, if you want to run reports, rather than running them on the primary replica and overburdening it, you can select one of the secondary replicas to run the reports. You can also execute database backups from the secondary replica; full database, file, and filegroup backups are supported but differential backup is not supported. Transaction log backup is supported in the secondary replica. Consider the following capabilities of read-only secondary replicas:

➤ The secondary replica's data is maintained to near real time with the primary replica. Real time depends on the network latency between the primary and secondary, the redo operation, locking on the secondary databases, and activities running on the secondary server.

➤ Read-only on the secondary replica applies to all the Availability Group databases.

➤ To greatly reduce locking in the secondary read-only replica, the secondary replica databases are configured by default in snapshot isolation to avoid read activities blocking the redo log updating the data. Snapshot isolation adds a 14-byte row identifier to maintain row version and maintains last committed row(s) in tempdb as the redo operation updates the replica databases.

➤ For optimizing the read-only workload, any index required by the secondary replica or database statistics needs to be created in the primary replica database and transferred to all replicas by the transactional log data movement because the secondary is read-only. However, to support read-only workload, SQL Server 2012 does have the capability to create temporary database statistics that are stored in tempdb. These temporary statistics will be lost when the SQL Server instance is restarted or when the secondary replica is promoted to the primary during a failover.

➤ Similar to data mirroring, Availability Groups support automatic page repair. Each availability replica tries to automatically recover from corrupted pages on a local database by resolving certain types of errors that prevent reading a data page. If a secondary replica cannot read a page, the replica requests a fresh copy of the page from the primary replica. If the primary replica cannot read a page, the replica broadcasts a request for a fresh copy to all the secondary replicas and gets the page from the first to respond. If this request succeeds, the unreadable page is replaced by the copy, which usually resolves the error.

➤ A client application can connect to a read-only replica. You can connect to a secondary replica that supports read-only access in one of two ways: either directly by specifying the SQL Server instance name in the connection string, or by using the Availability Group Listener name and leveraging read-only routing to reconnect to the next available secondary read-only replica. For more detailed information, see the "Secondary Replica Client Connectivity" section in this chapter. Access to the secondary replica is based on the Availability Group property, as shown in Table 25-2.

TABLE 25-2: Setting for the Secondary Replicas to Support Read Operations

READABLE SECONDARY	DESCRIPTION
No	The secondary replica does not allow read operations; any connections to the secondary replica will be denied.
Read-intent only	The secondary replica allows read operations but it accepts only connections with application Intent READONLY. This READONLY intent is a new connection property available as part of new TDS protocol. Older client applications or client applications that do not specify READONLY property for application intent cannot connect to the read-only secondary replica. To connect to the secondary replica, in the connection string, you must provide the following: **ApplicationIntent = ReadOnly**.

continues

TABLE 25-2 *(continued)*

Yes	The secondary replica enables read operations. It accepts all connections including the ones that don't specify `READONLY` application intent property in the connection string. This option enables legacy client applications to connect to the secondary replica for read workload because only read-only commands succeed. Commands that try to create or modify data will fail with this error message:
	
	`Msg 3906, Level 16, State 1, Server SQLAG02, Line 1 Failed`
	`to update database "AdventureWorks" because the database is`
	`read-only.`

> *You cannot include* `master`, `msdb`, `tempdb`, *or* `model` *databases in an Availability Group; only user databases are supported.*

AVAILABILITY GROUP EXAMPLE

To learn about Availability Groups, it is beneficial to go through a step-by-step example that shows how to setup and configure them. First you will configure a new Availability Group, then add a new replica, next create a new availability database, and finally connect to the Availability Group. Once your Availability Group has been deployed, you can perform failover testing.

> *You can find all the example scripts for this chapter on this book's website at* www
> .wrox.com, *but you need to make a few modifications before running the scripts.*

Configure a New Availability Group

As stated previously, a prerequisite to deploy an Availability Group is a Windows Failover Cluster. The following steps begin with creating a Windows 2008 R2 Failover Cluster and continue through the whole process of configuring a new Availability Group:

1. Start with installing Windows 2008 R2 Failover Cluster on each server that will participate in the Availability Group. To install, see Chapter 16, "Clustering SQL Server 2012."

2. Then install SQL Server 2012 as a standalone instance on each server that will participate in the Availability Group. To install see Chapter 2, "Installing SQL Server 2012 Best Practices."

3. Next on each SQL Server that will be participating in the Availability Group, open SQL Server Configuration Manager, choose SQL Server Services, and then select the SQL Server

properties. Under AlwaysOn High Availability, check the Enable AlwaysOn Availability Groups check box, as shown in Figure 25-2.

Now you are ready to create the Availability Group.

1. Choose one of the SQL Servers as the primary replica; this SQL Server must have the database(s) that will be included in the Availability Group. In this example, it is SQLAG01 and the AdventureWorks database.

2. In the Microsoft SQL Server Management Studio, click on to the SQL Server, in this example SQLAG01, then right-click and choose New Availability Group Wizard, as shown in Figure 25-3.

3. In the Introduction, click Next and in the Specify Name, choose a name, for cxample AG1, as shown in Figure 25-4.

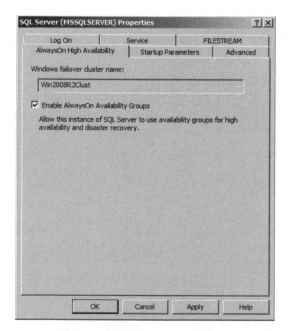

FIGURE 25-2

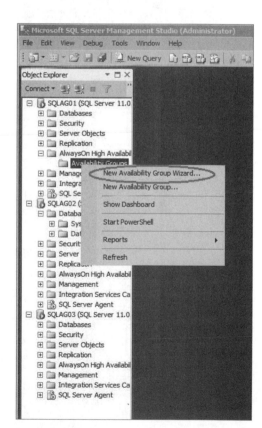

FIGURE 25-3

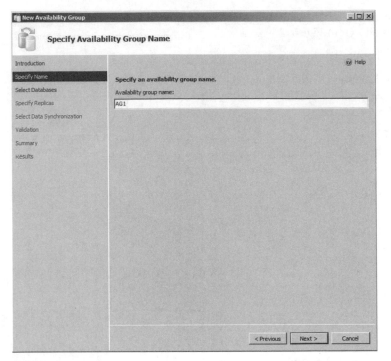

FIGURE 25-4

4. Click Next. Here on the Select Databases, click the check box for the databases, for example, AdventureWorks. If more than one database meets prerequisites, it will appear in the list for you to choose, as shown in Figure 25-5. For a database to be eligible to meet prerequisites, a database must:

➤ Be a user database. System databases cannot belong to an Availability Group.

➤ Be a read-write database. Read-only databases cannot be added to an Availability Group.

➤ Be a multiuser database.

➤ Not use AUTO_CLOSE.

➤ Use the full recovery model.

➤ Possess a full database backup.

➤ Reside on the SQL Server instance where you are creating the Availability Group and be accessible to the server instance.

➤ Not belong to another Availability Group.

➤ Not be configured for Database Mirroring.

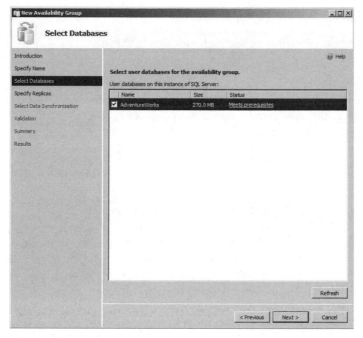

FIGURE 25-5

5. Click Next. On the Specify Replicas, under the Replicas tab, choose any secondary replica that you want to participate in the Availability Group, as shown in Figure 25-6. Table 25-3 also provides a description for each option available in this step. Click Next again.

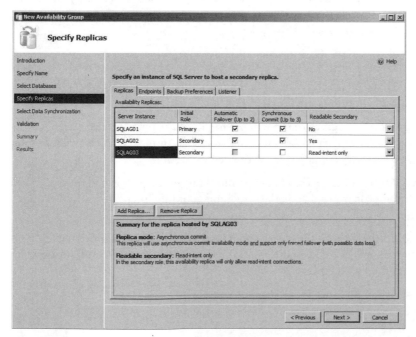

FIGURE 25-6

TABLE 25-3: Specify Replicas Option Descriptions for Step 5.

INITIAL ROLE	IDENTIFY THE INITIAL PRIMARY OR SECONDARY REPLICAS.
Automatic Failover (Up to 2)	If you want to configure automatic failover, choose up to two availability replica to be automatic failover partners where one of the partners chosen must be the initial primary replica. Both of these replicas use the synchronous-commit availability mode and only two replicas are supported in automatic failover.
Synchronous Commit (Up to 3)	If you selected Automatic Failover (Up to 2) for the two replica partners, Synchronous Commit (Up to 3) is automatically selected for them.
	Here you have the option to choose additional replicas to use synchronous-commit mode with only planned manual failover. Only three replicas are supported in synchronous-commit mode. Leave the checkbox blank if you want the replica to use asynchronous-commit availability mode. Then this replica will support only forced manual failover (with possible data loss).
Readable Secondary	**No:** No direct connections are allowed to the secondary databases of this replica. They are not available for read access. This is the default setting.
	Read-intent only: Only direct read-only connections are allowed to secondary databases of this replica. The secondary database(s) are all available for read access.
	Yes: All connections are allowed to secondary databases of this replica, but only for read access. The secondary database(s) are all available for read access.

6. On the Specify Replicas, under the Backup Preferences tab, specify where backups should occur from the following options as shown in Figure 25-7:

➤ **Prefer Secondary:** Specifies that backups should occur on a secondary replica except when the primary replica is the only replica online. In that case, the backup should occur on the primary replica. This is the default option.

➤ **Secondary Only:** Specifies that backups should never be performed on the primary replica. If the primary replica is the only replica online, then the backup should not occur.

➤ **Primary:** Specifies that the backups should always occur on the primary replica. This option supports creating differential backups, which are not supported when backup is run on a secondary replica.

➤ **Any Replica:** Specifies that you prefer for backup jobs to ignore the role of the availability replicas when choosing the replica to perform backups. Backup jobs might evaluate other factors such as backup priority of each availability replica in combination with its operational state and connected state.

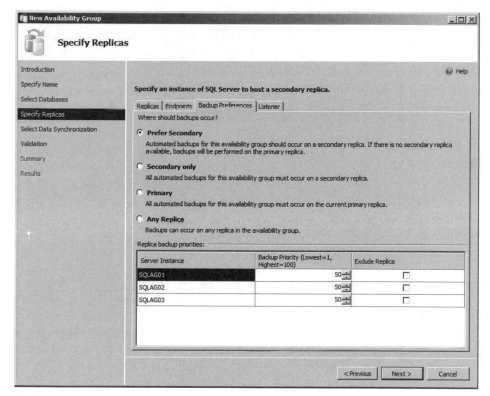

FIGURE 25-7

7. On Specify Replicas, under the Listener tab, choose Create An Availability Group Listener. Provide a Listener DNS Name, which is the network name that client applications use to connect to this Availability Group.

8. By default SQL Server listens on port 1433. If you changed the port number to a non-default value, provide that port number value.

9. Then choose either a DHCP or Static IP for the Availability Group Listener. In this example, a Static IP was given to the Availability Group Listener.

10. If you want, you can skip and create the Availability Group Listener later. For this example, the Listener is AG1_Listener with port number 1433, as shown in Figure 25-8. Click Next.

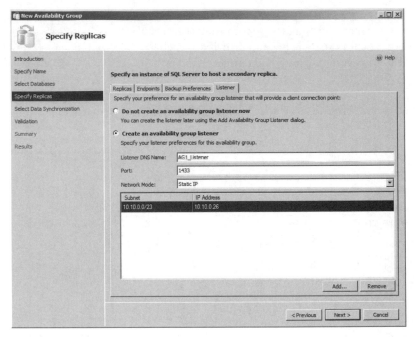

FIGURE 25-8

11. On the Select Initial Data Synchronization, choose Full. For Specify a Shared Network Location accessible by all replicas, choose a shared folder accessible by all participating replicas, for example \\SQLAG01\SQLBackups, as shown in Figure 25-9. Also, you can choose Skip Initial Data Synchronization and manually restore to each secondary replica.

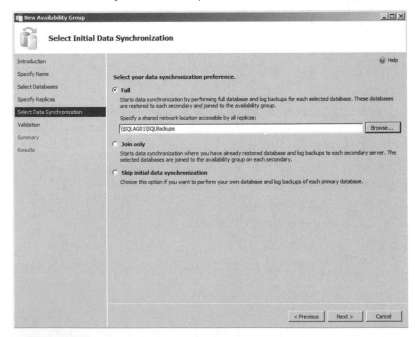

FIGURE 25-9

12. Click Next to run the validation, as shown in Figure 25-10. Then click Next on the Summary. Click Finish to create the AG1 Availability Group.

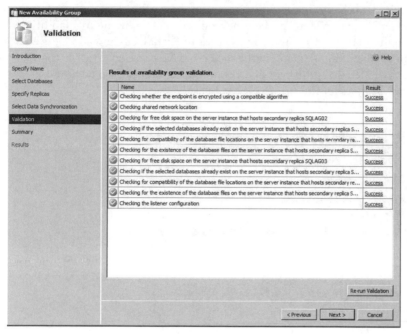

FIGURE 25-10

13. When you finish, you should be able to go to the Windows Failover Cluster Manager to see that the Availability Group has been created, as shown in Figure 25-11.

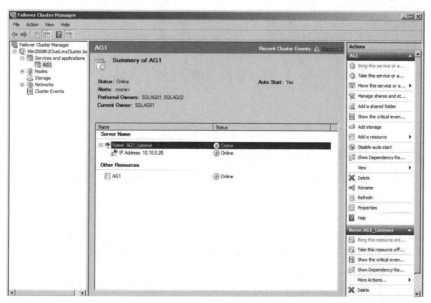

FIGURE 25-11

When a SQL Server login is added to the primary replica, the same login must be synchronized to exist on each secondary replica so that in a failover, that login will be available to authenticate. An Availability Group is not supported for System databases where the logins exists. However, new with SQL Server 2012, login data can be stored in the user database with the Contained Database feature, which means that any logins created will be synchronized as data by the Availability Group. If the database has been configured with Containment Type set to Partial, as shown in Figure 25-12, the user-login relationship can be configured and authenticated at database level rather than on the SQL Server's System database. Detailed information on contained databases can be found in Chapter 4, "Managing and Troubleshooting the Database Engine."

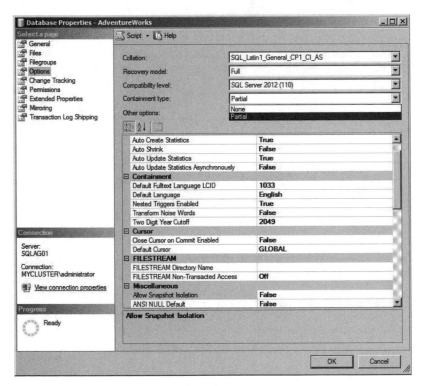

FIGURE 25-12

Configure an Existing Availability Group

Now you have an Availability Group deployed and are relying on it for your high availability, disaster recovery, and reporting needs. At some point, a new requirement may arise if one of the following situations occurs:

➤ The application is upgraded and an additional, new database is created that has dependencies to the other availability databases inside the Availability Group.

➤ The company has increased reporting requirements and needs to deploy another read-only database to offload the work on the primary replica.

➤ A disaster recovery site is identified and you are asked to deploy a replica there.

➤ Backups are running on the primary replica and are impacting its performance and you have been asked to deploy a replica to perform backups.

➤ You have consolidated several databases from the Availability Group and need to remove one of them.

➤ You want to remove a replica as it is no longer needed, or it has been replaced with another replica running on faster hardware.

For situations like those in the preceding list, Availability Groups deliver the flexibility to start with at least a two-replica Availability Group, then deploy additional replicas and availability databases as your needs change. This section covers how to deploy additional replicas with a maximum of five or additional availability databases. You can remove replicas and availability databases when they are no longer needed as part of the Availability Group. When performing these operations in a production environment, consider doing so during your maintenance window and not during normal production time.

Add/remove replica

Anytime you want to add a replica, follow these steps:

1. Join the new replica to the Windows Cluster group from Windows Failover Cluster Manager; see Chapter 16, "Clustering SQL Server 2012," for help on doing so.

2. Enable AlwaysOn Availability Group for that SQL Server instance; refer to Figure 25-2.

3. In SQL Server Management Studio, on the Availability Groups folder, right-click the Availability Group for example AG1, and choose Add Replica as shown in Figure 25-13. Then follow the wizard to add a new replica.

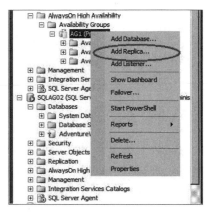

FIGURE 25-13

To remove a replica, simply choose the replica, right-click, and Delete.

To remove an Availability Group, choose the Availability Group; then right-click and choose Delete.

Add/remove a Database

Anytime you want to add an availability database, follow these steps:

1. In SQL Server Management Studio, on the Availability Groups folder, right-click the Availability Group, for example AG1, and choose Add Database as shown in Figure 25-14.

2. Then, follow the wizard to add a new database.

Doing a large database backup and file copy can adversely impact the production environment, so you may want to perform it during a maintenance window.

To remove a database from the Availability Group, simply choose the database; then right-click and choose Delete.

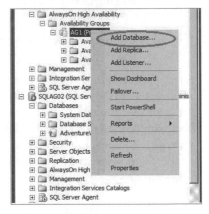

Availability Group Failover Operation

There are two failover modes available: automatic and manual. Failover of the Availability Group depends on which of these two modes the replica is configured with.

In automatic failover mode (synchronous mode), when the primary replica goes down, the secondary replica takes over without any user intervention. The client applications that are connected using the Availability Group Listener, for example `AG1_Listener`, automatically reconnect to the new primary replica.

FIGURE 25-14

In manual failover mode (synchronous mode), in a failover, the secondary replica failover requires manual failover action. From within SQL Server Management Studio, perform the following operations to manually failover:

1. Connect to a SQL Server instance that hosts a secondary replica of the Availability Group that needs to be failed over, and expand the server tree.

2. Expand the AlwaysOn High Availability, and the Availability Groups folders.

3. Right-click the Availability Group to be failed over, and select Failover.

Moreover, failover can also be performed by Transact SQL. The following code snippet forces the AG1 Availability Group to fail over to the local secondary replica.

```
ALTER AVAILABILITY GROUP AG1 FAILOVER;
```

To force a failover with data loss, use this Transact SQL command.

```
ALTER AVAILABILITY GROUP AG1 FORCE_FAILOVER_ALLOW_DATA_LOSS;
```

Additionally, failover can be performed using PowerShell. The following example performs a forced failover (with possible data loss) of the Availability Group AG1 to the secondary replica on the server instance named.

```
Switch-SqlAvailabilityGroup `-Path SQLSERVER:\Sql\SecondaryServer\InstanceName\
AvailabilityGroups\AG1 `-AllowDataLoss
```

After a forced failover, the secondary replica to which you failed over becomes the new primary replica, and all secondary databases are suspended. Before you resume any of the suspended databases however, you might need to reconfigure the Windows Failover Cluster's quorum and adjust the availability-mode configuration of the Availability Group. Consider these two scenarios:

> ➤ If you failed over outside of the automatic failover set of the Availability Group, adjust the quorum votes of the Windows Failover Cluster nodes to reflect your new Availability Group configuration (see "Chapter 16 "Clustering SQL Server 2012" for quorum settings).

> ➤ If you failed over outside of the synchronous-commit failover set, consider adjusting the availability mode and failover mode on the new primary replica and on remaining secondary replicas, to reflect your desired synchronous-commit and automatic failover configuration.

For each scenario, you must manually resume each suspended database individually. On resuming, a secondary database initiates data synchronization with the corresponding primary database. When the former primary replica becomes available, it switches to the secondary replica role, becoming a secondary replica, and immediately suspends its now-secondary databases. Under the asynchronous-commit mode, the accumulated unsent log is a possibility on any of the new secondary databases. Resuming a new secondary database causes it to discard unsent log records and to roll back any changes that were never received by the now-primary replica.

If an availability replica that failed will not be returning to the availability replica or will return too late for you to delay transaction log truncation on the new primary database, consider removing the failed replica from the Availability Group.

Suspend an Availability Database

During a performance bottleneck, you may decide to suspend a secondary availability database. An availability database that is suspended means no transaction record data movement occurs and the transaction log on the primary replica keeps growing and cannot be truncated. If you suspend a secondary database on a secondary availability replica, only the local secondary database is suspended. If the suspend database is on the primary replica, transaction record data movement is suspended to all secondary databases on every secondary replica. When a secondary database is suspended, its database state is changed to SUSPENDED and it begins to fall behind the primary database. The primary database remains available, and if you have only one secondary replica, the primary database runs exposed.

To suspend a database using SQL Server Management Studio, follow these steps:

1. In SQL Server Management Studio, connect to the SQL Server instance that hosts the availability replica on which you want to suspend a database.

2. Expand the AlwaysOn High Availability, and then the Availability Groups folders.

3. Expand the Availability Databases folder, right-click the database, and click Suspend Data Movement, as shown in Figure 25-15.

4. In the Suspend Data Movement dialog box, click OK.

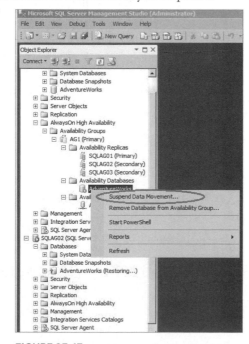

FIGURE 25-15

To suspend a database using Transact-SQL, follow these steps:

1. Connect to the SQL Server instance that hosts the replica whose database you want to suspend.

2. Suspend the secondary database by using the following ALTER DATABASE statement:

```
ALTER DATABASE database_name SET HADR SUSPEND;
```

Additionally, an availability database can be suspended by using the following PowerShell commands.

1. Change directory (cd) to the server instance that hosts the replica whose database you want to suspend.

2. Use the `Suspend-SqlAvailabilityDatabase` cmdlet to suspend the Availability Group.

Resume an Availability Database

After a database has been suspended, when the replica is resumed, the initial state is SYNCHRONIZING until it catches up. The primary database eventually resumes all its secondary databases that were suspended as the result of suspending the primary database. To resume a database using SQL Server Management Studio, follow these steps:

1. In SQL Server Management Studio, connect to the server instance that hosts the availability replica on which you want to resume a database.

2. Expand the AlwaysOn High Availability, and then the Availability Groups folders.

3. Expand the Availability Databases folder, right-click the database, and click Resume Data Movement.

4. In the Resume Data Movement dialog box, click OK.

To resume a database using Transact-SQL, follow these steps:

1. Connect to the server instance that hosts the database you want to resume.

2. Resume the secondary database by using the following ALTER DATABASE statement like so:

```
ALTER DATABASE database_name SET HADR RESUME;
```

Additionally, an availability database can be resumed by using the following PowerShell commands:

1. Change directory (cd) to the server instance that hosts the replica whose database you want to resume.

2. Use the `Resume-SqlAvailabilityDatabase` cmdlet to resume the Availability Group.

Client Application Connections

To support failover, two options are available for client applications to connect to the primary replica: using the network name assigned to the Availability Group Listener or using the database-mirroring connection strings. When you create and configure an Availability Group, you create the Availability Group Listener, which creates a network name and IP address in the Windows Server Failover Cluster (refer to Figure 25-8). Then when a failure occurs and the primary replica becomes unavailable, the secondary replica becomes the new primary replica with the network name in connection strings; the network name automatically redirects client applications to the new primary replica. You can provide client connectivity to the primary replica of a given Availability Group by using one of the two aforementioned methods, described in greater detail in the following two sections:

Availability Group Listener Network Name

When the Availability Group fails over and the client applications have the network name in the connection strings, the network name directs connections to the new primary replica. You must create a network name that is unique in the domain for each Availability Group. As you create a network name, the IP address is assigned to the network name. Only the TCP protocol is supported for using a network name and, optionally, an IP to connect to an Availability Group. In the connection strings that your client applications use to connect to the databases in the Availability Group, specify the Availability Group network name rather than the server name; then applications can connect directly to the current primary replica. Following are examples of client application connection strings:

```
Server=tcp:MynetworkName;Database=AdventureWorks;IntegratedSecurity=SSPI

Server=tcp:MynetworkName,1433;Database=AdventureWorks;IntegratedSecurity=SSPI
```

Database-Mirroring Connection Strings

While performing a migration from database mirroring to an Availability Group, if an Availability Group contains only two availability replicas and is not configured to allow read-access to the secondary replica, client applications can connect to the primary replica by using database mirroring connection strings. This approach can be useful while migrating an existing client application from database mirroring to Availability Group, as long as you limit the Availability Group to two availability replicas. However, before you add additional availability replicas, you need to create an Availability Group Listener network name for the Availability Group and update your client application to use it. When using database mirroring connection strings, the client can use either SQL Server Native Client or .NET Framework Data Provider for SQL Server. The connection string provided by a client application must minimally supply the name of one server instance, the *initial partner name*, to identify the server instance that initially hosts the availability primary replica to which you intend to connect. Optionally, the connection string can also supply the name of the secondary replica, which is the failover partner name, to identify the server instance that initially hosts the secondary replica as the failover partner name.

ACTIVE SECONDARY FOR SECONDARY READ-ONLY

This section covers the secondary replica capabilities offered by Availability Groups in relation to running reports and read-only queries on the secondary replicas. Availability Groups enable read-only secondary replicas. The primary purpose of secondary replicas is for high-availability and disaster recovery, but secondary replicas can be configured to offload read-only queries for running reports from the primary replica. Then, the primary replica can better deliver the mission critical data activity while read-only reporting is executed on a secondary replica. When configured in read-only, the secondary replica is in near real time, just seconds behind data changes from the primary replica because the latency of transaction log synchronization impacts data freshness and the redo thread to update the data in each secondary replica before it is available to a query.

Read-Only Access Behavior

When you configure read-only access for a secondary replica, all databases in the Availability Group allow read-only. The behavior that determines the type of access allowed when a replica is in a secondary role is shown in Figure 25-6 under Readable Secondary column. Read-only access does not mean that the secondary databases are set to read-only. It means that user connections to the secondary databases have read-only access to the data. Even though you cannot write any data to the secondary databases, you can write to individual databases that do not belong to the Availability Group, including system databases such as `tempdb`. An instance of SQL Server can concurrently host multiple availability replicas along with databases that do not belong to an Availability Group.

 For an explanation of the descriptive option settings for the Readable Secondary for the replica when it is configured as a secondary replica, refer to Table 25-3.

As shown in Table 25-4, the initial primary replica, SQLAG01, enables read-write connections, and the secondary replica, SQLAG02, enables all direct connections, including connections that do not include the Application Intent property. When a failover occurs the replicas switch roles; SQLAG02, which now runs under the primary role, enables read-write connections, whereas SQLAG01, which now runs under the secondary role, disallows all direct connections.

TABLE 25.4: Readable Secondary Behavior

REPLICA NAME	INITIAL ROLE	READABLE SECONDARY
SQLAG01	Primary	No
SQLAG02	Secondary	Yes

Secondary Replica Client Connectivity

When an Availability Group failover occurs, existing persistent connections to the Availability Group are terminated and the client applications must reestablish a new connection. On failover, the replicas switch roles, where the secondary replica becomes the primary. When this occurs, you want another secondary replica to take over the read-only reporting. To do so, the client applications executing read-only reporting need to know how to connect to the next available read-only secondary replicas. You can connect to a secondary replica that supports read-only access in one of two ways: either directly by specifying the SQL Server instance name in the connection string, or by using the Availability Group Listener name and leveraging read-only routing to reconnect to the next available secondary read-only replica.

Read-only routing route connections that come into an Availability Group Listener change over to a secondary replica that is configured to enable read-only workloads. Read-only routing works only if the connection string references an Availability Group Listener. An incoming connection referencing an Availability Group Listener name can automatically be routed to a read-only replica if the following are true:

➤ The application intent of the incoming connection is set to read-only.

➤ The connection access supported on the secondary replica is set to read-only.

➤ The READ_ONLY_ROUTING_URL for each replica is set by the CREATE or ALTER AVAILABILILTY GROUP Transact-SQL command, as part of the SECONDARY_ROLE replica options. You must set this option before configuring the read-only routing list.

➤ The READ_ONLY_ROUTING_LIST is set for each replica in the CREATE AVAILABILITY GROUP or ALTER AVAILABILITY GROUP Transact-SQL command, as part of the PRIMARY_ROLE replica options.

➤ The READ_ONLY_ROUTING_LIST can contain one or more routing targets. You can configure multiple routing targets, and routing will take place in the order targets are specified in the routing list.

The following example demonstrates modifying an existing Availability Group for read-only routing support:

```
ALTER AVAILABILITY GROUP [AG1]
  MODIFY REPLICA ON
N'SQLAG01' WITH
(SECONDARY_ROLE (READ_ONLY_ROUTING_URL = N'TCP://SQLAG01. contoso.com:1433'));

ALTER AVAILABILITY GROUP [AG1]
  MODIFY REPLICA ON
N'SQLAG02' WITH
(SECONDARY_ROLE (READ_ONLY_ROUTING_URL = N'TCP://SQLAG02. contoso.com:1433'));

ALTER AVAILABILITY GROUP [AG1]
MODIFY REPLICA ON
N'SQLAG01' WITH
(PRIMARY_ROLE (READ_ONLY_ROUTING_LIST=('SQLAG02','SQLAG01')));
```

Then, based on the application intent specified in the connection string, (read-write or read-only property), the client application will be directed to either the read-write or read-only replica. In this example, the application intent connection string property is read-only and the connection will be routed to the read-only secondary replica.

```
Server=tcp:AGListener,1433;Database=AdventureWorks;IntegratedSecurity=SSPI;Applicati
onIntent=ReadOnly
```

Performance

To support concurrency and avoid blocking to prevent readers and writers from blocking each other, snapshot isolation is enabled by default on the secondary replicas' databases. When read-only secondary replicas are enabled, the primary databases add 14 bytes of overhead on deleted, modified, or inserted data rows to store pointers to row versions on the secondary replica database(s). The row versioning structure is copied to the secondary databases, which generate row versions as needed by read-only workloads. Row versioning increases data storage in both the primary and secondary replicas. Also, as the 14-byte overhead is added to data rows, page splits may occur.

For running read-only workload, often indexes may need to be created to support these read-only queries. As the read-only secondary databases cannot create a new index, any indexes must be created in the primary replica and have the data movement apply them to the secondary replicas.

Statistics on columns of tables and index views are transferred from the primary replica to the secondary replicas through the transaction record data movement, but the read-only workload in the secondary replica may require additional statistics. This is addressed where temporary statistics are allowed to be created by SQL Server on the tempdb of each secondary replica. If you need to create statistics yourself, they must be created in the primary replica. There are a few actions to keep in mind when creating these statistics:

➤ To delete temporary statistics, use the DROP STATISTICS Transact-SQL statement.

➤ Monitor statistics using the sys.stats and sys.stats_columns catalog views where sys.stats contains a column, which is_temporary, to indicate which statistics are permanent and which are temporary.

➤ Temporary statistics will be automatically dropped if the secondary replica is restarted as tempdb is re-created or a failover event occurs and the replicas roles are switched.

The read-only secondary replicas are usually behind the primary replica, in most cases by seconds, as secondary replicas are impacted by the following:

➤ The length of the database transaction

➤ The workload on the secondary replica; the timely transaction record data movement processing may be reduced if the replica is busy running read-only workload.

➤ The network latency between the primary and secondary replicas

➤ When the workload is IO-intensive, that is, when data is transferred to the secondary replicas as an example of IO-intensive workloads, it can create index or bulk copy operations.

In addition, a query in the secondary replica will see data from the primary replica after the redo thread in the secondary replica has applied that data. The steps for data to arrive to a query on the secondary replica require the following operations (see Figure 25-16):

1. Data arrives to the secondary replica, and it is applied and hardened to the transaction log.

2. An acknowledgment is sent to the primary replica.

3. The redo thread applies the transaction log changes to the data page.

4. Then the query in the secondary replica can see the new data.

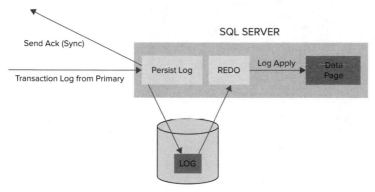

FIGURE 25-16

BACKUP ON THE SECONDARY REPLICA

One of the features of AlwaysOn in SQL Server 2012 is that you can run backups from any availability primary or secondary replicas; therefore, you can offload backup that is high IO and CPU operation from the primary replica to a secondary replica. See the "Allowing Read-Only Access to Secondary Replicas" section for more information. By offloading the backup operations to a secondary replica, you can use the primary replica to run uninterrupted, mission-critical workloads that run the business. In addition, backups can be performed on either synchronous or asynchronous replicas, and transaction log backups across the replicas can be combined to form a single transaction log chain.

A copy-only full backup, as shown in Figure 25-17, is supported on the secondary replicas for full database, files, and filegroups backups and has the following characteristics:

➤ A *copy-only full backup* is a SQL Server backup that is independent of the sequence of conventional SQL Server backups. It doesn't affect the overall backup nor restore procedures for the database.

➤ Copy-only full backups are supported in all recovery models.

➤ A copy-only full backup cannot serve as a differential base or differential backup and does not affect the differential base. Differential backups are not supported on the secondary replicas.

➤ The secondary replica backup can be performed only when that secondary replica can communicate with the primary replica, and it is in synchronized or in the process of synchronizing.

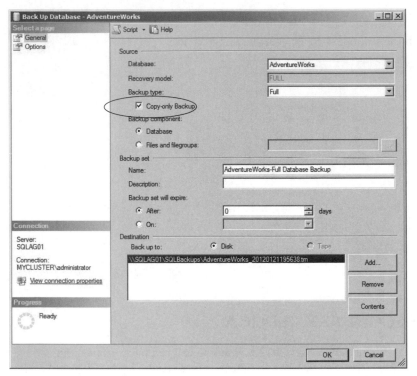

FIGURE 25-17

You can configure which primary or secondary replicas the database backup jobs will be permitted to run by using the following settings during the CREATE AVAILABILITY GROUP and ALTER AVAILABILITY GROUP Transact-SQL statements:

➤ Configure the AUTOMATED_BACKUP_PREFERENCE option to determine whether the backups run as described in Figure 25-7.

➤ AUTOMATED_BACKUP_PREFERENCE is not enforced by SQL Server. You need to evaluate the AUTOMATED_BACKUP_PREFERENCE returned value and take it into account in your backup job logic to enforce it.

➤ If you don't want one of the availability replicas to run the backups, you can set the BACKUP_PRIORITY = 0 which means no backup will run on it.

➤ At the replica level, you can specify an ordered preference among secondary replicas for running database backup jobs using the BACKUP_PRIORITY to a value from 1 to 100 where 100 is the highest priority.

Evaluate Backup Replicas Metadata

You may want to know where the database backups are running to ensure that there is free storage available, and that the secondary replica has the performance capacity to execute it. If you want to identify the preferred location of where your database backup would run, you can easily determine by running this query:

```
SELECT automated_backup_preference, automated_backup_preference_desc
FROM sys.availability_groups;
```

To interpret the returned values from the query, see Table-26-5 for a description of the `automated_backup_preference` and `automated_backup_preference_desc` columns.

TABLE 25-5: Values for the automated_backup_preference and automated_backup_preference_desc

`automated_backup_preference`	0 = Performing backups on the primary replica is preferable.
	1 = Performing backups on a secondary replica is preferable.
	2 = Performing backups on a secondary replica is preferable, but performing backups on the primary replica is acceptable if no secondary replica is available for backup operations.
	3 = No preference about whether backups are performed on the primary replica or on a secondary replica.
`automated_backup_preference_desc`	PRIMARY SECONDARY_ONLY SECONDARY NONE

To determine the priority of a given availability replica to run the database backup relative to the other replicas, it can easily be determined by running this query, where `backup_priority` represents the priority for performing backups on this replica relative to the other replicas in the same Availability Group. The value is an integer in the range of 0–100.

```
SELECT backup_priority FROM sys.availability_replicas;
```

ALWAYSON GROUP DASHBOARD

To monitor AlwaysOn Availability Groups, availability replicas, and availability databases in Microsoft SQL Server 2012, you can use the dashboard or data management views. From the dashboard, you can determine the health and performance of each Availability Group. To access the Availability Group Dashboard, follow these steps:

1. In SQL Server Management Studio, connect to the instance of SQL Server on which you want to run Availability Group Dashboard, which is either the primary or a secondary replica.

2. Expand the AlwaysOn High Availability, and the Availability Groups folders.

3. Right-click on your Availability Group name, in this example AG1, and then click Show Dashboard as shown in Figure 25-18.

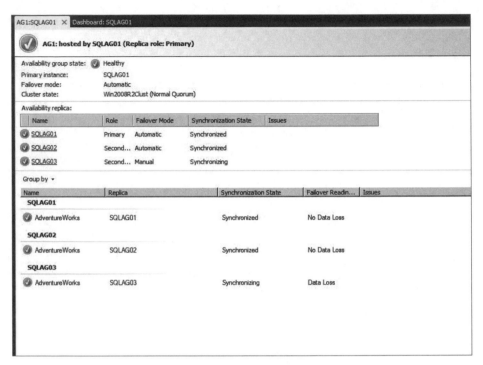

FIGURE 25-18

Table 25-6 gives an explanation of the key parameters that the dashboard displays.

TABLE 25-6: Dashboard important values

Availability Group State	Displays the state of health for the Availability Group.
Role	The current role of the availability replica values is Primary or Secondary.
Primary Instance	Name of the server instance that is hosting the primary replica of the Availability Group.
Failover Mode	Displays the failover mode for which the replica is configured. The possible failover mode values are: **Automatic**: indicates that one or more replicas is in automatic-failover mode **Manual**: indicates that no replica is in automatic-failover mode

Synchronization State	Indicates whether a secondary replica is currently synchronized with primary replica; values are: **Not Synchronized**: database is not synchronized or has not yet been joined to the Availability Group **Synchronized**: the database is synchronized with the primary database on the current primary replica, if any, or on the last primary replica. **NULL (Unknown):** This value occurs when the local server instance cannot communicate with the WSFC failover cluster (that is the local node is not part of WSFC quorum).

Additionally, instead of using the AlwaysOn Group Dashboard, you can choose to use the `sys.dm_hadr_availability_replica_states` dynamic management view to query for the preceding information.

MONITORING AND TROUBLESHOOTING

Like any solution, you need to monitor an Availability Group as part of regular operations to identify any issues with the Availability Group that may prevent the data from been synchronized with the secondary replicas or if failover to a secondary replica fails. To monitor Availability Groups, availability replicas, and availability databases using SQL Server Management Studio, follow these steps:

1. In SQL Server Management Studio, connect to the instance of SQL Server on which you want to monitor an Availability Group and click the server name.

2. Expand AlwaysOn High Availability, and the Availability Groups folders.

3. The Object Explorer Details pane displays every Availability Group for which the connected server instance hosts a replica. For each Availability Group, the Server Instance (Primary) column displays the name of the server instance currently hosting the primary replica. To display more information about a given Availability Group, select it in Object Explorer. The Object Explorer Details pane then displays the Availability Replicas and Availability Databases for the Availability Group.

To perform detail monitoring and troubleshooting, use the DMVs provided in Table 25-7 to identify, verify, and to then troubleshoot an Availability Group.

TABLE 25-7: Monitoring and Troubleshooting for Availability Groups

`sys.availability_groups`	Returns a row for each Availability Group for which the local instance of SQL Server hosts an availability replica.
`sys.dm_hadr_availability_group_states`	Returns a row for each Availability Group that possesses an availability replica on the local instance of SQL Server.

continues

TABLE 25-7 *(continued)*

`sys.availability_replicas`	Returns a row for every availability replica in each availability group for which the local instance of SQL Server hosts an availability replica.
`sys.dm_hadr_availability_replica_states`	Returns a row showing the state of each local availability replica and a row for each remote availability replica in the same availability group.
`sys.dm_hadr_database_replica_states`	Returns a row for each database that is participating in any Availability Group for which the local instance of SQL Server is hosting an availability replica.
`sys.dm_hadr_database_replica_cluster_states`	Returns a row containing information to provide detail into the health of the availability databases in each Availability Group on the Windows Server Failover Clustering (WSFC) cluster.
`sys.availability_group_listener_ip_addresses`	Returns a row for every IP address that is currently online for an Availability Group listener.
`sys.availability_group_listeners`	For a given Availability Group, returns either zero rows indicating that no network name is associated with the Availability Group, or returns a row for each availability-group listener configuration in the WSFC cluster.
`sys.dm_tcp_listener_states`	Returns a row containing dynamic-state information for each TCP listener.

SUMMARY

AlwaysOn Availability Groups provide a robust high-availability solution that supports up to five partners. This solution can be configured for synchronization and asynchronization modes with no shared disk infrastructure using a network name to seamlessly failover client applications across the replicas. In addition, you can use the secondary replicas to perform backup and to run read-only operations, therefore offloading the primary replica. The Availability Group functionality leverages the best of breed between Windows Failover Clustering and SQL Server Data Mirroring and more to deliver a feature set to support mission critical applications throughout the enterprise.

INDEX

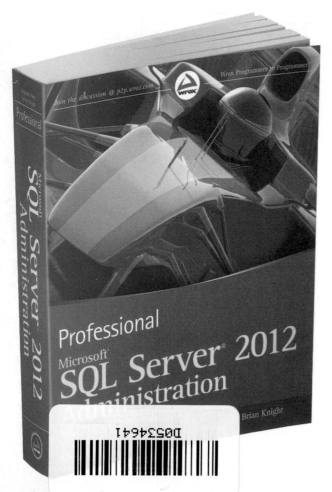